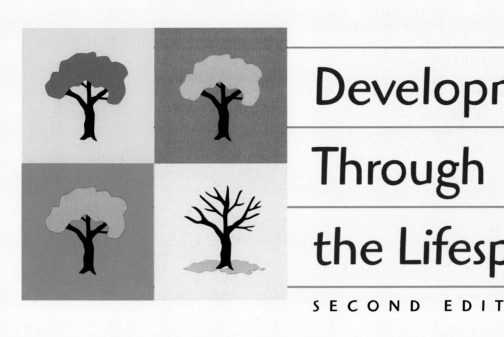

Development Through the Lifespan

SECOND EDITION

Laura E. Berk
ILLINOIS STATE UNIVERSITY

ALLYN AND BACON
Boston · London · Toronto · Sydney · Tokyo · Singapore

IN LOVING MEMORY OF MY GRANDPARENTS,
OLGA AND MARTIN LENTSCHNER
TILLIE AND MEYER EISENBERG

Executive Editor: Carolyn O. Merrill
Senior Development Editor: Sue Gleason
Senior Marketing Manager: Caroline Croley
Editorial Assistant: Lara Zeises
Editorial-Production Service: Thomas E. Dorsaneo
Text Design and Composition: Seventeenth Street Studios
Cover Coordinator: Linda Knowles
Cover Designer: Studio Nine
Composition and Prepress Buyer: Linda Cox
Manufacturing Buyer: Megan Cochran

Copyright © 2001, 1998 by Allyn & Bacon
160 Gould Street
Needham Heights, MA 02494-2310

Internet: www.abacon.com

Between the time website information is gathered and
then published, it is not unusual for some sites to have
closed. Also, the transcription of URLs can result in
unintended typographical errors. The publisher would
appreciate being notified of any problems with the URLs
so that they may be corrected in subsequent editions.

Library of Congress Cataloging-in-Publication Data
Berk, Laura E.
        Development through the lifespan / Laura E. Berk. — 2nd ed.
             p.   cm.
        Includes bibliographical references and index.
        ISBN 0-205-31602-6
        1. Developmental psychology. I. Title
BF713.B465   2000
155—dc21   00-035547

Printed in the United States of America
10 9 8 7 6 5 4 3 2 1   VHP   03 02 01 00

Laura E. Berk is a distinguished professor of psychology at Illinois State University, where she teaches human development to both undergraduate and graduate students. She received her bachelor's degree in psychology from the University of California, Berkeley, and her master's and doctoral degrees in educational psychology from the University of Chicago. She has been a visiting scholar at Cornell University, UCLA, Stanford University, and the University of South Australia. Berk has published widely on the effects of school environments on children's development and, more recently, on the development of private speech. Her research has been funded by the U.S. Office of Education and the National Institute of Child Health and Human Development. It has appeared in many prominent journals, including *Child Development*, *Developmental Psychology*, *Merrill-Palmer Quarterly*, *Journal of Abnormal Child Psychology*, and *Development and Psychopathology*. Her empirical studies have attracted the attention of the general public, leading to contributions to *Psychology Today* and *Scientific American*. Berk has served as research editor for *Young Children* and consulting editor for *Early Childhood Research Quarterly*. She is author of the chapter on the extra-curriculum for the *Handbook of Research on Curriculum* (American Educational Research Association) and of the chapter on development for *The Many Faces of Psychological Research in the Twenty-First Century* (American Psychological Association). Her books include *Private Speech: From Social Interaction to Self-Regulation*, *Scaffolding Children's Learning: Vygotsky and Early Childhood Education*, and *Landscapes of Development: An Anthology of Readings*. In addition to *Development Through the Lifespan*, she is author of the two best-selling texts *Child Development* and *Infants, Children, and Adolescents*, published by Allyn and Bacon.

■ *Laura Berk with sons Peter and David.*

BRIEF CONTENTS

8 EMOTIONAL AND SOCIAL DEVELOPMENT IN EARLY CHILDHOOD 246

9 PHYSICAL AND COGNITIVE DEVELOPMENT IN MIDDLE CHILDHOOD 278

10 EMOTIONAL AND SOCIAL DEVELOPMENT IN MIDDLE CHILDHOOD 318

18 EMOTIONAL AND SOCIAL DEVELOPMENT IN LATE ADULTHOOD   590

19 DEATH, DYING, AND BEREAVEMENT   626

M y decision to write *Development Through the Lifespan* was inspired by a wealth of professional and personal experiences. First and foremost were the interests and concerns of hundreds of students of human development with whom I have worked in three decades of college teaching. Each semester, their insights and questions have revealed how an understanding of any single period of development is enriched by an appreciation of the entire lifespan. Second, as I moved through phases of adult development myself, I began to think more intensely about factors that have shaped and reshaped my own life course—family, friends, mentors, coworkers, community, and larger society. My career well established, my marriage having stood the test of time, and my children launched into their adult lives, I felt that a deeper grasp of these multiple, interacting influences would help me better appreciate where I had been and where I would be going in the years ahead. I was also convinced that such knowledge could contribute to my becoming a better teacher, scholar, family member, and citizen. And because teaching has been so central and gratifying a part of my work life, I wanted to bring to others a personally meaningful understanding of lifespan development.

The years since *Development Through the Lifespan* first appeared have been a period of considerable expansion in theory and research. This second edition greets the new millennium with a wealth of new content that reflects five contemporary trends in the field:

■ *Diverse pathways of change are highlighted.* Investigators have reached broad consensus that variations in biological makeup and everyday tasks lead to wide individual differences in paths of change and resulting competencies. This edition pays more attention to variability in development and to recent theories that attempt to explain it. A new series of Variations boxes, with subtypes "Culture" and "Individuality," grants special attention to this emphasis in contemporary research.

■ *The lifespan perspective has been emphasized further.* A major theme in the first edition, the lifespan perspective—development as lifelong, multidimensional, multi-

directional, plastic, and embedded in multiple contexts —continues to serve as a unifying approach to understanding human change. In this edition, special "tree" icons appear beside text sections, Lifespan Vista boxes, and "Ask Yourself" questions that discuss lifespan-perspective assumptions and consider development across a wide age span. Consequently, I call even more attention to the lifespan perspective, weaving it more thoroughly into the text and its features than previously.

■ *The interconnected roles of biology and environment are given greater emphasis.* Accumulating evidence on development of the brain, motor skills, cognitive competencies, temperament and personality, and developmental problems underscores the way biological factors emerge in, are modified by, and share power with experience. The interconnection between biology and environment is integral to the lifespan perspective and is revisited throughout the text narrative.

■ *Inclusion of interdisciplinary research is expanded.* The move toward viewing thoughts, feelings, and behavior as an integrated whole, affected by a wide array of influences in biology, social context, and culture, has motivated developmental researchers to strengthen their links with other fields of psychology and other disciplines. Topics and findings included in this edition increasingly reflect the contributions of educational psychology, social psychology, health psychology, clinical psychology, neuropsychology, biology, pediatrics, geriatrics, sociology, anthropology, social welfare, and other fields.

■ *The links between theory, research, and applications are strengthened.* As researchers intensify their efforts to generate findings that can be applied to real-life situations, I have placed greater weight on social policy issues and sound theory- and research-based applications.

T EXT PHILOSOPHY

The basic approach of this book has been shaped by my own professional and personal history as a teacher, researcher, and parent. It consists of seven philosophical ingredients that I regard as essential for students to emerge from a course with a thorough understanding of lifespan development. Each theme is woven into every chapter:

1. An understanding of the diverse array of theories in the field and the strengths and shortcomings of each. The first chapter begins by emphasizing that only knowledge of multiple theories can do justice to the richness of human development. As I take up each age sector and domain of development, I present a variety of theoretical perspectives, indicate how each highlights previously overlooked aspects of development, and discuss research that has been used to evaluate it. Consideration of contrasting theories also serves as the context for an evenhanded analysis of many controversial issues.

2. A grasp of the lifespan perspective as an integrative approach to development. I introduce the lifespan perspective as an organizing framework in the first chapter and continually refer to and illustrate its assumptions throughout the text, in an effort to help students construct an overall vision of development from conception to death.

3. Knowledge of both the sequence of human development and the processes that underlie it. Students are provided a description of the organized sequence of development along with a discussion of processes of change. An understanding of process—how complex combinations of biological and environmental events produce development—has been the focus of most recent research. Accordingly, the text reflects this emphasis. But new information about the timetable of change has also emerged. In many ways, the very young and the old have proved to be far more competent than they were believed to be in the past. In addition, many milestones of adult development, such as finishing formal education, entering a career, getting married, having children, and retiring, have become less predictable. Current evidence on the sequence and timing of development, along with its implications for process, is presented for all periods of the lifespan.

4. An appreciation of the impact of context and culture on human development. A wealth of research indicates that people live in rich physical and social contexts that affect all domains of development. Throughout the book, students travel to distant parts of the world as I review a growing body of cross-cultural evidence. The text narrative also discusses many findings on socioeconomically and ethnically diverse people within the United States. Furthermore, the impact of historical time period and cohort membership receives continuous attention. In this vein, gender issues—the distinctive but continually evolving experiences, roles, and life paths of males and females—are granted substantial emphasis. Besides highlighting the effects of immediate settings, such as family, neighborhood, and school, I make a concerted effort to underscore the influence of larger social structures—societal values, laws, and government programs—on lifelong well-being.

5. An understanding of the joint contributions of biology and environment to development. The field recognizes more powerfully than ever before the joint roles of hereditary/constitutional and environmental factors—that these contributions to development combine in complex ways and cannot be separated in a simple manner. Numerous examples of how biological dispositions can be maintained as well as transformed by social contexts are presented throughout the book.

6. A sense of the interdependency of all domains of development—physical, cognitive, emotional, and social. Every chapter emphasizes an integrated approach to human development. I show how physical, cognitive, emotional, and social development are interwoven. Within the text narrative, students are often referred to other sections of the book to deepen their grasp of relationships among various aspects of change.

7. An appreciation of the interrelatedness of theory, research, and applications. Throughout this book, I emphasize that theories of human development and the research stimulated by them provide the foundation for sound, effective practices with children, adolescents, and adults. The link between theory, research, and applications is reinforced by an organizational format in which theory and research are presented first, followed by practical implications. In addition, a current focus in the field—harnessing knowledge of human development to shape social policies that support human needs throughout the lifespan—is reflected in every chapter. The text addresses the current condition of children, adolescents, and adults in the United States and around the world and shows how theory and research have combined with public interest to spark successful interventions. Many important applied topics are considered, such as family planning, infant mortality, maternal employment and child care, teenage pregnancy and parenthood, domestic violence, exercise and adult health, lifelong learning, grandparents rearing grandchildren, adjustment to retirement, and adapting to widowhood.

TEXT ORGANIZATION

I have chosen a chronological organization for *Development Through the Lifespan*. The book begins with an introductory chapter that describes the history of the field, modern theories, and research strategies. It is followed by two chapters on the foundations of development. Chapter 2 combines an overview of biological and environmental contexts into a single, integrated discussion of these multifaceted influences on development. Chapter 3 is devoted to prenatal development, birth, and the newborn baby. With this foundation, students are ready to look closely at seven major age periods: infancy and toddlerhood (Chapters 4, 5, and 6), early childhood (Chapters 7 and 8), middle childhood (Chapters 9 and 10), adolescence (Chapters 11 and 12), early adulthood (Chapters 13 and 14), middle adulthood

(Chapters 15 and 16), and late adulthood (Chapters 17 and 18). Topical chapters within each chronological division cover physical development, cognitive development, and emotional and social development. The book concludes with a chapter on death, dying, and bereavement (Chapter 19).

The chronological approach has the advantage of enabling students to get to know individuals of a given age period very well. It also eases the task of integrating the various domains of development, since each is discussed in close proximity. At the same time, a chronologically organized book requires that theories covering several age periods be presented piecemeal. This creates a challenge for students, who must link the various parts together. To assist with this task, I frequently remind students of important earlier achievements before discussing new developments, referring back to related sections with page references to encourage students to review. Also, chapters or sections devoted to the same topic (for example, cognitive development) are similarly organized, making it easier for students to draw connections across age periods and construct an overall view of developmental change.

NEW COVERAGE IN THE SECOND EDITION

Lifespan development is a fascinating and ever-changing field of study, with constantly emerging new discoveries and refinements in existing knowledge. The second edition represents this burgeoning contemporary literature, with over 1,500 new citations. Cutting-edge topics throughout the text underscore the book's major themes. Here is a sampling:

■ **Chapter 1:** Revised section on basic issues on which major theories take a stand; new Variations/Individuality box on resiliency; new Variations/Culture box on immigrant youths; new section on methods for studying culture, including ethnography; all research strategies richly illustrated with real studies.

■ **Chapter 2:** New Lifespan Vista box on the Human Genome Project; updated information on prenatal diagnosis, fetal medicine, and reproductive technologies; enhanced discussion of the development of adopted children; updated section on environmental contexts for development, with increased attention to ecological systems theory; revised discussion of the influence of socioeconomic status on family functioning; enhanced treatment of how heredity and environment combine to influence complex traits, including updated discussion of the limitations of heritability estimates and concordance rates.

■ **Chapter 3:** Expanded attention to fetal sensory and behavioral capacities; new Variations/Individuality box on fetal activity as a predictor of infant temperament; updated research on teratogens; new Lifespan Vista box

on the prenatal environment and health in later life; new Social Issues box on a cross-national perspective on health care and other policies for parents and newborn babies; new section on understanding birth complications; new evidence on the functions of REM sleep; updated research on newborn sensory capacities, with special emphasis on smell and hearing.

■ **Chapter 4:** Enhanced discussion of brain development, including synaptic pruning, lateralization, and plasticity of the cerebral cortex; enhanced coverage of sensitive periods in brain development; expanded discussion of dynamic systems research on early motor development; updated evidence on development of voluntary reaching and grasping; expanded coverage of development of hearing; new research on infants' perception of complex, meaningful patterns; new Variations/Individuality box on development of infants with severe visual impairments.

■ **Chapter 5:** Revised and updated research evaluating Piaget's theory—including (1) a new section on physical reasoning, with findings on infants' sensitivity to object solidity, gravity, object support, and physical causality, and (2) a new section on infant problem solving; expanded and updated section on early development of attention; new research on development of categorization; revised section on the impact of infant and toddler child care on mental development; new evidence on the role of emotion in early word learning; new Variations/Individuality box on parent–child interaction and cognitive development of deaf children.

■ **Chapter 6:** Expanded treatment of the functions of emotions in energizing all aspects of psychological development; new Lifespan Vista box on maternal depression and children's development; enhanced consideration of the development of emotional self-regulation; a new perspective on the structure of temperament and updated treatment of physiological measures of temperament; new Variations/Individuality box on the biological basis of shyness and sociability; expanded discussion of stability and cultural variations in temperament; updated consideration of the contributions of caregiving and infant temperament to attachment security and of attachment quality to later development; enhanced treatment of self-development, including emergence of the I-self and the me-self and the importance of self-awareness for early emotional development.

■ **Chapter 7:** New Social Issues box on treating short children with growth hormone; updated research on brain development in early childhood, with implications for lateralization; expanded discussion of factors that contribute to unintentional injuries, applying an ecological systems perspective; new research on preschoolers' problem solving and categorization; new section evaluating Vygotsky's theory; enhanced discussion of the young child's theory of mind; new Variations/Individuality box on "mindblindness" and infantile autism; new evidence on developmental outcomes associated with child-centered versus academic preschools; updated consideration of language development, including recent research on strategies young children use to acquire vocabulary.

■ **Chapter 8:** Enhanced discussion of the contributions of temperament, cognitive development, and social experience to preschoolers' understanding of emotions and emotional self-regulation; updated section on development of empathy; new sections on cultural variations in peer sociability and parental influences on early peer relations; new Variations/Individuality box on the influence of temperament on early conscience development; new research on the distinction between overt and relational aggression, including sex differences; new section on television as a source of gender stereotypes; expanded discussion of cultural variations in child-rearing styles.

■ **Chapter 9:** New Lifespan Vista box on growth stunting due to malnutrition and obesity risk; expanded discussion of the impact of culture and schooling on concrete operational thought; new evidence on the contribution of brain development to gains in information processing and cognitive inhibition in middle childhood; new findings on the impact of ethnic minority language customs on intelligence test performance; expanded treatment of bilingualism; new sections on the impact of class size and grouping practices on academic achievement; enhanced discussion of Vygotsky-inspired philosophical directions in elementary education; discussion of both mainstreaming and full inclusion in teaching children with special needs.

■ **Chapter 10:** Enhanced attention to social and cultural influences on self-concept and self-esteem; new Caregiving Concerns table on fostering a mastery-oriented approach to learning and preventing learned helplessness; expanded discussion of emotional development, including self-conscious emotions and emotional self-regulation, with implications for prosocial behavior and peer acceptance; new section on the impact of children's grasp of a domain of personal matters for moral understanding; updated consideration of friendship, with special attention to friendship qualities of prosocial and aggressive children; new research on the implications of relational aggression for girls' friendships, peer acceptance, and adjustment; new Variations/Individuality box on peer victimization; new evidence on factors promoting positive adjustment following divorce; updated research on the impact of maternal employment and dual earner families on children's development, including recent findings on

after-school care; updated research on child sexual abuse and prevention strategies, including New Zealand's national school-based program.

■ **Chapter 11:** Updated evidence on the impact of maturational timing on emotional and social development, with special attention to the role of school contexts; new section on adolescents' sleep needs; expanded discussion of adolescent motor development, sports involvement, and physical activity; updated research on eating disorders and on adolescent sexual activity; new research on biological contributions to homosexuality; new Social Issues box on homosexuality and coming out to oneself and others; enhanced consideration of adolescent fatherhood; new Lifespan Vista box on intergenerational continuity in adolescent parenthood; new research on teenage pregnancy prevention; thoroughly revised section on information processing, including research on the development of scientific reasoning and the role of metacognition in the development of formal operational thought; updated section on sex differences in mental abilities, including a new Variations/Individuality box on sex differences in spatial abilities; enhanced discussion of peer influences on academic achievement.

■ **Chapter 12:** Expanded discussion of factors affecting the development of self-concept and self-esteem; enhanced attention to parent–child relationships at adolescence, including the impact of parent and adolescent life transitions and family circumstances; expanded consideration of sex differences in adolescent friendships and their implications for development; updated research on parental influences on adolescent peer relationships; enhanced consideration of dating, including both heterosexual and homosexual relationships; extensively updated section on depression in adolescence, including biological and environment contributions and sex differences; new Lifespan Vista box on two routes to adolescent delinquency.

■ **Chapter 13:** New evidence on the role of telomeres, a special form of DNA located at the ends of chromosomes, in biological aging; new findings on the relationship of health indicators for heart disease (smoking, blood pressure, and blood cholesterol) to mortality; updated research on obesity in adulthood; updated Social Issues box on sex differences in sexual attitudes and behavior; new research on factors linked to sexual satisfaction; updated evidence on cultural influences on sexual coercion; expanded attention to factors influencing vocational choice, including a new section on access to vocational information during high school and college.

■ **Chapter 14:** New research on generational change in the social clock; inclusion of both ethological and social learning perspectives on mate selection; updated research on the role of communication in enduring intimate relationships, with special attention to sex differences in conflict resolution strategies; expanded discussion of other-sex friendships; updated research on sex differences in marital satisfaction and consequences for mental health; revised and updated Social Issues box on spouse abuse, with attention to both husband-to-wife and wife-to-husband violence; expanded attention to interventions that ease the transition to parenthood; discussion of the importance of mutual support between parents for satisfaction with and competence at child rearing; new longitudinal evidence on marital problems that predict divorce; updated research on never-married parents and gay and lesbian parents; new Variations/Culture box on vocational development of highly successful African-American women.

■ **Chapter 15:** Updated research on vision, including changes in structures of the eye and neural pathways; new findings on the health benefits and risks of hormone replacement therapy (HRT); expanded attention to cultural variations in symptoms of menopause; updated evidence on genetic contributions to cancer and socioeconomic variations; new research on gender-racial bias in diagnosis of heart disease and referral for follow-up tests; expanded discussion of stress management, including problem-centered and emotion-centered coping strategies; new evidence on matching exercise formats (group versus home based) with beginning exercisers' characteristics; enhanced treatment of age-related change in mental abilities, with special attention to gender and cohort effects; updated evidence on changes in attention.

■ **Chapter 16:** Updated research on the effects of midlife generativity on psychological adjustment; new evidence on stability and change in personality; new Variations/Individuality box on factors that promote psychological well-being in midlife; current findings on early child-rearing styles and parents' relations with adult children; expanded discussion of factors influencing grandparent–grandchild relations; new Social Issues box on grandparents rearing grandchildren: the skipped generation family; updated evidence on the impact of parental caregiving on adult children's psychological well-being; enhanced treatment of vocational development, including the glass ceiling.

■ **Chapter 17:** Updated research on nervous system and sensory changes in late adulthood; new evidence on the relationship of self-rated health to mortality; updated treatment of the interconnection between physical disability and mental health; enhanced discussion of the relationship of physical decline to cognitive performance and quality and length of life; revised and updated section on Alzheimer's disease, including familial and sporadic forms, genetic influences, prevention, and treatment; revised and updated sections on remote memory, prospective memory, comprehension of oral and written language, and everyday problem solving in late adulthood; new research on the contribution of overcoming personal hardships to late-life wisdom; enhanced discussion of factors related to cognitive change in late adulthood, including a mentally active life; updated findings on terminal decline.

■ **Chapter 18:** New research on reminiscence and life review, countering the stereotype that elders wish to be young again; enhanced evidence on development of a secure, multifaceted self-concept in late adulthood; updated research on the relation of religious involvement to physical and psychological functioning in old age; expanded discussion of control versus dependency, including conditions that induce positive and negative reactions to caregiving; new Variations/Individuality box on the impact of time perspective on social goals; updated research on designing congregate housing and nursing homes to foster elders' well-being; enhanced consideration of elder friendships; new evidence on aging parent–adult child relationships; new research on changing grandparent–grandchild relationships over time and grandchildren as sources of emotional meaning; updated evidence on elder maltreatment, including ethnic variations; expanded consideration of factors that affect the decision to retire.

■ **Chapter 19:** Enhanced discussion of development of understanding of death, with special attention to cultural variations; updated research on death anxiety, addressing symbolic immortality; revised and updated section on contextual influences on adaptations to dying, including the nature of the disease, personality and coping style, family members' and health professionals' behavior, and spirituality, religion, and culture; updated information on the legal status of euthanasia and assisted suicide, with special attention to Australia, the Netherlands, and the United States; expanded treatment of personal and situational variations in grieving, including new sections on sudden, anticipated versus prolonged, expected deaths, grieving the death of an intimate partner, and bereavement overload among children and adolescents exposed to deaths resulting from school violence; new research on the importance for long-term adjustment of finding personal benefit in the grieving experience.

INSTRUCTOR'S SUPPLEMENTS

■ A variety of teaching tools are available to assist instructors in organizing lectures, planning demonstrations and examinations, and ensuring student comprehension.

- **Instructor's Resource Manual (IRM)** Prepared by Gabrielle Principe of Cornell University, Elizabeth Kenny, and myself, this thoroughly revised IRM contains additional material to enrich your class presentations. For each chapter, the IRM provides a Chapter-at-a-Glance grid, Brief Chapter Summary, Learning Objectives, detailed Lecture Outline, Lecture Extensions, Learning Activities, Web Activities, answers to "Ask Yourself" questions, Suggested Readings, Transparencies listing, and Media Materials.

- **Test Bank** Prepared by Gabrielle Principe of Cornell University and Naomi Tyler of Vanderbilt University, the Test Bank contains over 2,000 multiple-choice questions, each of which is cross-referenced to a Learning Objective, page-referenced to chapter content, and classified by type (factual, applied, or conceptual); essay questions; and premade tests.

- **Computerized Test Bank** This computerized version of the Test Bank is available in Windows and Macintosh formats using Test Manager, the best-selling test-generation software.

- **Transparencies** Over 200 full-color transparencies taken from the text and other sources are referenced in the IRM for the most appropriate use in your classroom presentations.

- **Seasons of Life Video Series** Illustrating the text's interdisciplinary focus, this five-video series explores a multitude of biological, psychological, and social influences on development. Nearly 75 psychologists, biologists, sociologists, and anthropologists present theory, methods, and research. Student Activities are provided in the IRM to help you integrate *Seasons of Life* into your course. Your publisher's representative can provide you with details on class enrollment restrictions.

- **Films for the Humanities & Sciences: Human Development Videotape** Complementing the text's linkage of theory and research to applications, this revised two-videotape set features high-interest segments on topics such as genetic counseling, fetal alcohol syndrome, the child's theory of mind, teen depression, domestic violence, coping with menopause, and hospice and palliative care. The IRM provides synopses and Discussion Questions for each videotape.

- **"Development Through the Lifespan in Action" Observation Program** In conjunction with the Illinois State University Television Production Studio, I have revised and expanded this real-life videotape, containing a wealth of observation segments that illustrate theories, concepts, and milestones of human development. An Observation Guide helps students use the video in conjunction with the textbook, deepening their understanding of the material and applying what

they have learned to everyday life. The videotape and Observation Guide are free to instructors who adopt the text and are available to students at a discount when packaged with the text.

- **Website** http://www.abacon.com/berk Designed for students and faculty of human development classes, this comprehensive website encourages online and interactive learning and also offers current links and information about development. It includes Online Practice Tests, a Teaching Aids section, Websketches (extensions of the stories illustrating development in the text), and a variety of additional features.

- **PowerPoint CD-ROM** A PowerPoint CD-ROM offers lecture outlines and illustrations from the textbook.

- **WebCT** This unique course management system allows you to construct your own course website to enhance your teaching and your students' learning experiences.

For a complete list of study aids available to your students, see page xxvi.

ACKNOWLEDGMENTS

The dedicated contributions of many individuals helped make this book a reality and contributed to refinements and improvements in this second edition. An impressive cast of reviewers provided many helpful suggestions, constructive criticisms, and enthusiasm for the organization and content of the text. I am grateful to each one of them.

REVIEWERS OF THE FIRST EDITION

Joyce Bishop, Golden West College
Ed Brady, Belleville Area College
Michele Y. Breault, Truman State University
Joan B. Cannon, University of Massachusetts, Lowell
Gary Creasey, Illinois State University
Rhoda Cummings, University of Nevada, Reno
Carol Lynn Davis, University of Maine
Clifford Gray, Pueblo Community College
Traci Haynes, Columbus State Community College
Vernon Haynes, Youngstown State University
Paula Hillman, University of Wisconsin, Whitewater
Janet Kalinowski, Ithaca College
Kevin Keating, Broward Community College
Wendy Kliewer, Virginia Commonwealth University
Randy Mergler, California State University
Karla K. Miley, Black Hawk College
Karen Nelson, Austin College
Bob Newby, Tarleton State University

Peter Oliver, University of Hartford
Ellen Pastorino, Gainesville College
Leslee K. Polina, Southeast Missouri State University
Leon Rappaport, Kansas State University
Randall Russac, University of North Florida
Marie Saracino, Stephen F. Austin State University
Bonnie Seegmiller, City University of New York,
    Hunter College
Richard Selby, Southeast Missouri State University
Paul S. Silverman, University of Montana
Glenda Smith, North Harris College
Jeanne Spaulding, Houston Community College
Thomas Spencer, San Francisco State University
Vince Sullivan, Pensacola Junior College
Mojisola F. Tiamiyu, University of Toledo
Joe Tinnin, Richland College
Ursula M. White, El Paso Community College
Lois J. Willoughby, Miami-Dade Community College
Deborah R. Winters, New Mexico State University

R EVIEWERS OF THE SECOND EDITION

Paul C. Amrhein, University of New Mexico
Doreen Arcus, University of Massachusetts, Lowell
René L. Babcock, Central Michigan University
W. Keith Berg, University of Florida
James A. Bird, Weber State University
Michael Caruso, University of Toledo
Rita M. Curl, Minot State University
Maria P. Fracasso, Towson University
Elizabeth E. Garner, University of North Florida
Laura Hanish, Arizona State University
Lera Joyce Johnson, Centenary College of Louisiana
Robert B. McLaren, California State University, Fullerton
Karla K. Miley, Black Hawk College
Teri Miller, Milwaukee Area Technical College
Gary T. Montgomery, University of Texas, Pan American
Feleccia Moore-Davis, Houston Community College
Jill Norvilitis, Buffalo State College
Patricia O'Brien, University of Illinois at Chicago
Stephanie J. Rowley, University of North Carolina
Bruce Stam, Chemeketa Community College
Mojisola F. Tiamiyu, University of Toledo
L. Monique Ward, University of Michigan
Rob Weisskirch, California State University, Fullerton

In addition, I thank the following individuals for responding to a survey that provided vital feedback for the new
edition:

Daniel R. Bellack, Trident Technical College
Yiwei Chen, Bowling Green State University
Nancy A. Dash, Michigan Community College

Sandra Foster, Point Loma Nazerene University
Gary Gillund, College of Wooster
Karen Hambright, Coastal Georgia Community College
William Hampes, Black Hawk College
Lera Joyce Johnson, Centenary College of Louisiana
Velton Lacefield, Prairie State College
Phil Lau, DeAnza College
Linda Miller-Dunleavy, Old Dominion University
Gary T. Montgomery, University of Texas—Pan American
Patricia O'Brien, University of Illinois at Chicago
Kit Payne, Central Michigan University
Michelle Poris, University of Michigan
Anila R. Ragade, Jefferson Community College
Kathie Reid, California State University, Fresno
Karen P. Saenz, Houston Community College
Mellis Schmidt, Northern New Mexico Community College
Edythe H. Schwartz, California State University, Sacramento.

I am also indebted to several colleagues for much encouragement and interest in this project. Richard Payne, Department of Political Science, Illinois State University, is a
kind and devoted friend with whom I have shared many prof-
itable discussions about the writing process, the condition
of children and the elderly, and other topics that significantly
influenced my perspective on lifespan development. Gary
Creasey and Steven Landau, colleagues in the Department
of Psychology, provided helpful consultation in their areas
of expertise. Jeff Payne, Illinois State University Television
Production Studio, guided revision of the *Observation Video*
with great artistry and sensitivity. Freda Briggs, University
of South Australia, offered many thought-provoking insights
as the adulthood chapters took shape.

Current and former graduate students in psychology at
Illinois State University aided my research and contributed
significantly to the text's supplements. Kathy Martensen, Cory
Baxter, Carolyn Clawson, and Amy Petersen helped conduct
literature searches, secure library materials, and obtain permission for use of copyrighted material. Dorothy Welty-
Rodriguez participated in many hours of planning for the
revised *Observation Video*, collaborated with me on its accompanying *Observation Guide*, and assisted with preparation of website materials and other media supports. Dorothy's
organizational skills, expertise in human development, and
dedication have been invaluable throughout this project.

The supplement package benefited from the talents and
diligence of several other individuals. Gabrielle Principe of
Cornell University made outstanding contributions to the *Instructor's Resource Manual* and, along with Naomi Tyler of
Vanderbilt University, revised the *Test Bank* with meticulous
concern for clarity and accuracy. I am pleased to have collaborated with Amy Petersen, Illinois State University, on the
Study Guide.

I have been fortunate to work with an exceptionally capable editorial team at Allyn and Bacon. It has been a privilege

to author this book under the sponsorship of Executive Editor Carolyn Merrill. When I first met Carolyn, she told me that she was a "woman of action," and she has been true to her word! Her enthusiasm, inspiration, superb organizational skills, day-to-day communication, and prompt fielding of potential difficulties made the revision process uniquely smooth and pleasurable. Her genuine interest in human development sparked many fruitful discussions that influenced my approach to preparing sections of the book as well as its pedagogical features. As an added bonus, I'm pleased to have found in Carolyn such a warm and rewarding friendship. Many thanks, also, to Sean Wakely, editor of the first edition, for his keen sense of vision, diplomatic problem solving, and commitment to forging a true editor–author partnership, which made the creation and publication of this text possible. The rich tree images that grace the covers of both editions, radiant metaphors of lifespan development, were Sean's inspiration.

I would like to express a heartfelt thank you to Joyce Nilsen, Director of Marketing, and Caroline Croley, Marketing Manager of Psychology, for the outstanding work they have done in marketing my texts. Joyce was in command of marketing activities for *Development Through the Lifespan* during its first edition, making sure that accurate and clear information about my books and their ancillaries reached Allyn and Bacon's sales force and that the needs of prospective and current adopters were met. Each time I have watched Joyce teach others about my texts, I have been impressed with both her knowledge of their content and the vitality with which she conveys her message. After Joyce assumed the position of marketing director, Caroline took over direct marketing responsibilities for my books, and they could not be in better hands. Marci Melia, Field Marketing Specialist, has also devoted much time and energy to marketing activities, and I greatly appreciate the kind greetings she sends from time to time, despite her very busy schedule.

Sue Gleason, Senior Developmental Editor, offered astute advice and prompt and patient responses to my concerns as I prepared the revision. Her assistance over the years is very much appreciated. Many thanks, also, to Elizabeth Kenny, development editor, for the superb job she has done in coordinating the preparation of a first-rate set of text supplements.

Tom Dorsaneo managed the complex production tasks that resulted in a beautiful second edition. His competence, flexibility, efficiency, and courtesy have made working with him a great delight. Every so often, a message from Tom rolls through my FAX machine containing the latest news release on research breakthroughs in child and adult development. These thought-provoking communications have often caused me to reconsider and revise portions of the book, bringing it right to the cutting edge at publication. I am very grateful for Tom's thoughtfulness, and I look forward to a continuing partnership with him in the years to come. I thank Sarah Evertson for obtaining the exceptional photographs that so aptly illustrate the text narrative. Lara Zeises, Editorial Assistant, graciously arranged for manuscript reviews and attended to a wide variety of pressing, last-minute details.

A final word of gratitude goes to my family, whose love, patience, and understanding have enabled me to be wife, mother, teacher, researcher, and text author at the same time. My sons, David and Peter, have taken a special interest in this project. Their reflections on events and progress in their own lives, conveyed over telephone and e-mail and during holiday visits, helped mold the early adulthood chapters. My husband, Ken, willingly made room for yet another time-consuming endeavor in our life together and communicated his belief in its importance in a great many unspoken, caring ways.

—*Laura E. Berk*

A PERSONAL NOTE TO STUDENTS

My goal in preparing this second edition of *Development Through the Lifespan* is to provide a textbook that meets the instructional goals of your course as well as your own personal needs. I aimed for a text that is intellectually stimulating, that provides depth as well as breadth of coverage, and that portrays the complexities of human development in a way that will capture your interest while helping you learn.

To achieve these objectives, I have grounded this book in a carefully selected body of classic and current theory and research, brought to life with stories and vignettes of children, adolescents, and adults, many of whom I have known personally. In addition, the text discussion highlights the joint contributions of biology and environment to development throughout the lifespan, emphasizes how the research process helps solve real-world problems, and pays special attention to policy issues that are crucial to safeguarding children's and adults' well-being in today's world. I have also provided a unique pedagogical program that will assist you in mastering information, integrating the various aspects of development, critically examining controversial issues, and applying what you have learned.

PEDAGOGICAL FEATURES

Maintaining a highly accessible writing style—one that is lucid and engaging without being simplistic—continues to be one of the text's goals. I will frequently converse with you and encourage you to relate what you read to your own life. In doing so, I hope to make the study of human development involving and pleasurable.

STORIES AND VIGNETTES ABOUT REAL PEOPLE. To help you construct a clear image of development and to enliven the text narrative, each chronological age division is unified by case examples woven throughout that set of chapters. For example, within the middle childhood section, you'll share the experiences and concerns of 10-year-old Joey; 8-year-old Lizzie; their divorced parents, Rena and Drake; and their classmates Mona, Terry, and Jermaine. In the chapters on late adulthood, you'll get to know Walt and Ruth, a vibrant retired couple, along with

Walt's older brother Dick and his wife Goldie and Ruth's sister Ida, a victim of Alzheimer's disease. Besides a set of main characters who bring unity to each age period, many additional vignettes offer vivid examples of development and diversity among children, adolescents, and adults.

CHAPTER INTRODUCTIONS AND END-OF-CHAPTER SUMMARIES. To provide a helpful preview of what you are about to read, an outline and overview of chapter content appears in each chapter introduction. Especially comprehensive end-of-chapter summaries, organized according to the major headings in each chapter and including review questions and boldfaced terms, will remind you of key points in the text discussion.

ASK YOURSELF . . . Active engagement with the subject matter is also supported by critical thinking questions, which can be found at the end of major sections. The focus of these questions is divided between theory and applications. Many describe problematic situations and ask you to resolve these in light of what you have learned. In this way, the questions inspire high-level thinking and new insights.

LIFESPAN PERSPECTIVES ICON. A tree-of-life icon highlights text sections, Lifespan Vista boxes, and "Ask Yourself" questions that contain material especially relevant to the text's lifespan-perspective theme. By marking text and critical thinking questions that illustrate assumptions of the lifespan perspective and that consider constancy and change across a wide age span, the icon encourages you to deepen your understanding of lifespan development.

BOXES. Four types of boxes accentuate the philosophical themes of this book:

LIFESPAN VISTA BOXES. A special set of boxes is devoted to topics that have long-term implications for development or involve intergenerational issues. Examples include: The Human Genome Project; The Prenatal Environment and Health in Later Life; Maternal Depression and Children's Development; Like Mother, Like Child: Intergenerational Continuity in Adolescent Parenthood; Two Routes to Adolescent Delinquency; Childhood Attachment Patterns and Adult Romantic Relationships; and What Can We Learn About Aging from Centenarians?

SOCIAL ISSUES BOXES. These boxes discuss the impact of social conditions on children, adolescents, and adults and emphasize the need for sensitive social policies to ensure their well-being—for example, A Cross-National Perspective on Health Care and Other Policies for Newborn Babies; Treating Short Children with Growth Hormone; Homosexuality: Coming out to Oneself and Others; Sex Differences in Attitudes Toward Sexuality; Grandparents Rearing Grandchildren: The Skipped-Generation Family; and Voluntary Active Euthanasia: Lessons from Australia and the Netherlands.

VARIATIONS/CULTURE BOXES. This subtype of the Variations boxes highlights cross-cultural and multicultural variations in human development—for example, Immigrant Youths: Amazing Adaptation; Identity Development Among Ethnic Minority Adolescents; Work-Study Apprenticeships in Germany; Persistence, Passion, and Connection: Vocational Development of Highly Successful African-American Women; Menopause as a Biocultural Event; and Cultural Variations in Mourning Behavior.

VARIATIONS/INDIVIDUALITY BOXES. These Variations boxes focus on biological, psychological, and social factors that underlie wide individual differences in developmental pathways, traits, and capacities. Examples include Resiliency; Temperament in the Womb; Development of Infants with Severe Visual Impairments; Parent– Child Interaction and Cognitive Development of Deaf Children; "Mindblindness" and Infantile Autism; Peer Victimization; and What Factors Influence Psychological Well-Being at Midlife?

CAREGIVING CONCERNS TABLES. The relationship of theory and research to practice is woven throughout the text narrative. To accentuate this linkage, Caregiving Concerns tables provide easily accessible practical advice on the importance of caring for oneself and others throughout the lifespan. They include: Do and Don'ts for a Healthy Pregnancy; Building a Foundation for Good Eating Habits; Signs of Developmentally Appropriate Practice in Early Childhood Programs; Ways to Foster a Mastery-Oriented Approach to Learning and Prevent Learned Helplessness; Helping Children Adjust to Their Parents' Divorce; Keeping Love Alive in a Romantic Partnership; Ways Middle-Aged Parents Can Promote Positive Ties with Their Adult Children; Communicating Effectively with Alzheimer's Victims; and Resolving Grief After a Loved One Dies.

MILESTONES TABLES. A Milestones table appears at the end of each age division of the text. These tables summarize major physical, cognitive, language, and emotional and social developments, providing a convenient device for reviewing the chronology of development across the lifespan.

FYI—FOR FURTHER INFORMATION AND HELP. Students frequently ask where they can go to find out more about high-interest topics or to seek help in areas related to their own lives. To meet this need, an annotated section appears at the end of each chapter that provides the names and websites of organizations that disseminate information about human development and offer special services.

ADDITIONAL TABLES, ILLUSTRATIONS, AND PHOTOGRAPHS. Tables are liberally included to help students grasp essential points in the text narrative and extend information on a topic. The many full-color figures and illustrations depict important theories, methods, and research findings. Photos have been carefully selected to portray human development and to represent the diversity of people in the United States and around the world.

MARGINAL GLOSSARY, END-OF-CHAPTER TERM LIST, AND END-OF-BOOK GLOSSARY. Mastery of terms that make up the central vocabulary of the field is promoted through a marginal glossary, an end-of-chapter term list, and an end-of-book glossary. Important terms and concepts also appear in boldface type in the text narrative.

STUDY AIDS

Beyond the study aids found in the textbook, Allyn and Bacon offers a number of supplements for students. The website is open to all visitors to the Internet.

- *Study Guide.* Prepared by Amy Petersen and myself, this helpful guide offers Chapter Summaries, Learning Objectives, Study Questions organized according to major headings in the text, "Ask Yourself …" questions that also appear in the text, crossword puzzles for mastering important terms, and multiple-choice self-tests.

- *Practice Tests.* Twenty multiple-choice items per chapter plus an answer key with justifications are drawn in part from the Test Bank to assist you in preparing for course exams.

- *Portraits.* A booklet of expanded stories and critical thinking questions about the many characters featured in the text helps you make knowledge of human development personally meaningful, apply it to real-life situations, and get to know the characters better.

- *Website* http://www.abacon.com/berk Designed for students and faculty of human development classes, this comprehensive website encourages online and interactive learning and also offers current links and information about development. It includes Online Practice Tests, a Teaching Aids section, Websketches (extensions of the stories in the text), and a variety of additional features.

I hope that learning about human development will be as rewarding for you as I have found it over the years. I would like to know what you think about both the field of human development and this book. I welcome your comments; please feel free to send them to me at Department of Psychology, Box 4620, Illinois State University, Normal, IL 61790, or care of the publisher, who will forward them to me.

—Laura E. Berk

LEGEND FOR PHOTOS ACCOMPANYING SOFIE'S STORY

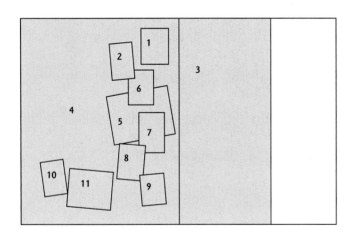

- SOFIE'S STORY is told in Chapters 1 and 19, from her birth to her death. The photos that appear at the beginning of Chapter 1 follow her through her lifespan. They are:

  1. Sofie as a baby, with her mother in 1908.

  2. Sofie at age 6, with her brother, age 8, in 1914.

  3. Sofie at age 10, before a birthday party in 1919.

  4. Sofie at age 18, high school graduation in 1926.

  5. Sofie's German passport.

  6. Sofie and Phil in their mid–thirties, during World War II, when they became engaged.

  7. Sofie, age 60, and daughter Laura on Laura's wedding day in 1968.

  8. Sofie and Phil in 1968, less than 2 years before Sofie died.

  9. Sofie, age 61, and her first grandchild, Ellen, October 1969, less than 3 months before Sofie died.

  10. Sofie's grandsons, David and Peter, ages 5 and 2, children of Laura and Ken.

  11. Laura, Ken, and sons Peter and David, ages 10 and 13, on the occasion of David's Bar Mitzvah in 1985.

Development
Through
the Lifespan

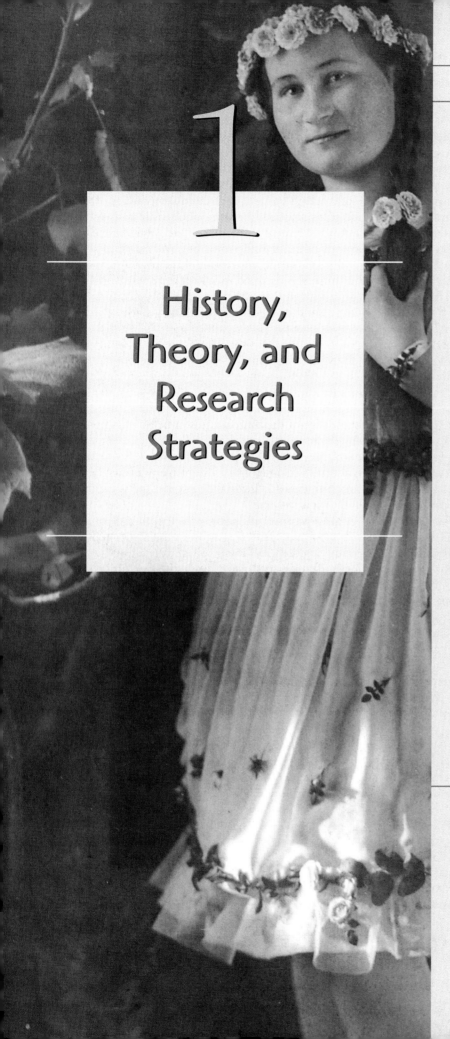

1

History, Theory, and Research Strategies

Human Development as a Scientific, Interdisciplinary, and Applied Field

Basic Issues
*Continuous or Discontinuous Development? ·
One Course of Development or Many? ·
Nature or Nurture as More Important?*

**The Lifespan Perspective:
A Balanced Point of View**
*Development as Lifelong · Development as
Multidimensional and Multidirectional ·
Development as Highly Plastic · Development
as Embedded in Multiple Contexts*
■ *Variations/Individuality: Resiliency*

Historical Foundations
*Philosophies of Childhood · Philosophies of
Adulthood and Aging · Scientific Beginnings*

Mid-Twentieth-Century Theories
*The Psychoanalytic Perspective · Behaviorism
and Social Learning Theory · Piaget's Cognitive-
Developmental Theory*

Recent Theoretical Perspectives
*Information Processing · Ethology · Vygotsky's
Sociocultural Theory · Ecological Systems Theory*

Comparing and Evaluating Theories

Studying Development
*Common Research Methods · General Research
Designs · Designs for Studying Development*
■ *Variations/Culture: Immigrant Youths:
Amazing Adaptation*
■ *A Lifespan Vista: Impact of Historical
Times on the Life Course: The Great
Depression and World War II*

Ethics in Lifespan Research

■ *This photo essay chronicles the lifespan and family
legacy of Sofie Lentschner. It begins in 1908 with
Sofie's infancy and concludes with the Bar Mitzvah
of her grandson, David, celebrated in 1985, 15 years
after Sofie's death. For a description of each photo,
see the legend on page xxviii.*

Sofie Lentschner was born in 1908, the second child of Jewish parents who made their home in Leipzig, Germany, a city of thriving commerce and cultural vitality. Her father was a successful businessman and community leader. Her mother was a socialite well known for her charm, beauty, and hospitality. As a baby, Sofie displayed the determination and persistence that would be sustained throughout her life. She sat for long periods inspecting small objects with her eyes and hands. The single event that consistently broke her gaze was the sound of the piano in the parlor. As soon as Sofie could crawl, she steadfastly pulled herself up to finger its keys and marveled at the tinkling sound.

By the time Sofie entered elementary school, she was an introspective child, often ill at ease at the festive parties that girls of her family's social standing were expected to attend. She immersed herself in her schoolwork, especially in mastering the foreign languages that were a regular part of German elementary and secondary education. Twice a week, she took piano lessons from the finest teacher in Leipzig. By the time Sofie graduated from high school, she spoke English and French fluently and had become an accomplished pianist. Whereas most German girls of her time married by age 20, Sofie postponed serious courtship in favor of entering the university. Her parents began to wonder whether their intense, studious daughter would ever settle into family life.

Sofie wanted marriage as well as education, but her plans were thwarted by the political turbulence of her times. When Hitler rose to power in the early 1930s, Sofie's father feared for the safety of his wife and children and moved the family to Belgium. Conditions for Jews in Europe quickly worsened. The Nazis plundered Sofie's family home and confiscated her father's business. By the end of the 1930s, Sofie had lost contact with all but a handful of her aunts, uncles, cousins, and childhood friends, many of whom (she later learned) were herded into cattle cars and transported to the slave labor and death camps at Auschwitz-Birkenau. In 1939, as anti-Jewish laws and atrocities intensified, Sofie's family fled to the United States.

As Sofie turned 30, her parents concluded she would never marry and would need a career for financial security. They agreed to support her return to school. Over the next 3 years, Sofie earned two master's degrees, one in music and the other in librarianship. Then, on a blind date, she met Philip, a U.S. army officer. Philip's calm, gentle nature complemented Sofie's intensity and worldliness. Within 6 months, they married. Over the next 4 years, two daughters and a son were born. Soon Sofie's father became ill. The strain of uprooting his family and losing his home and business had shattered his health. After months of being bedridden, he died of heart failure.

When World War II ended, Philip left the army and opened a small men's clothing store. Sofie divided her time between caring for the children and helping Philip in the store. Now in her forties, she was a devoted mother, but few women her age were still rearing young children. As Philip struggled with the business, he spent longer hours at work, and Sofie often felt lonely. She rarely touched the piano, which brought back painful memories of youthful life plans shattered by war. Sofie's sense of isolation and lack of fulfillment frequently left her short-tempered. Late at night, she and Philip could be heard arguing.

As Sofie's children grew older and parenting took less of her time, she returned to school once more, this time to earn a teaching credential. At age 50, she finally launched a career. For the next decade, Sofie taught German and French to high school students and English to newly arrived immigrants. Besides easing her family's financial difficulties, she felt a gratifying sense of accomplishment and creativity. These years were among the most energetic and satisfying of Sofie's life. She had an unending enthusiasm for teaching —for transmitting her facility with language, her firsthand knowledge of the consequences of hatred and oppression, and her practical understanding of how to adapt to life in a new land. She watched her children, whose young lives were free of the trauma of war, adopt many of her values and commitments and begin their marital and vocational lives at the expected time.

Sofie approached age 60 with an optimistic outlook. As she and Philip were released from the financial burden of paying for their children's college education, they looked forward to greater leisure. Their affection and respect for one another deepened. Once again, Sofie began to play the piano. But this period of contentment was short-lived.

One morning, Sofie awoke and felt a hard lump under her arm. Several days later, her doctor diagnosed cancer. Sofie's spirited disposition and capacity to adapt to radical life changes helped her meet the illness head on. She defined it as an enemy—to be fought and overcome. As a result, she lived 5 more years. Despite the exhaustion of chemotherapy, Sofie maintained a full schedule of teaching duties and continued to visit and run errands for her elderly mother. But as she weakened physically, she no longer had the stamina to meet her classes. Gradually, she gave in to the ravaging illness. Bedridden for the last few weeks, she slipped quietly into death with Philip at her side. The funeral chapel overflowed with hundreds of Sofie's students. She had granted each a memorable image of a woman of courage and caring.

One of Sophie's three children, Laura, is the author of this book. Married a year before Sofie died, Laura and her husband, Ken, often think of Sofie's message, spoken privately to them on the eve of their wedding day: "I learned from my own life and marriage that you must build a life together but also a life apart. You must grant each other the time, space, and support to forge your own identities, your own ways of expressing yourselves and giving to others.

The most important ingredient of your relationship, above all else, must be respect."

Laura and Ken settled in a small midwestern city, near Illinois State University, where they continue to teach today—Laura in the Department of Psychology, Ken in the Department of Mathematics. They have two sons, David and Peter, to whom Laura has related many stories about Sofie's life and who carry her legacy forward. David shares his grandmother's penchant for teaching; he is a first-grade teacher in California. Peter is a law student in Chicago; he shares his grandmother's love of music, playing violin, viola, and guitar in his spare time.

Sofie's story raises a wealth of fascinating issues about human life histories. For example:

■ What determines the features that Sofie shares with others and those that make her unique—in physical characteristics, mental capacities, interests, and behaviors?

■ What led Sofie to retain the same persistent, determined disposition throughout her life but to change in other essential ways?

■ How do historical and cultural conditions—for Sofie, the persecution that led to the destruction of her childhood home, the loss of family members and friends, and her flight to the United States—affect well-being throughout life?

■ In what way is the timing of events—for example, Sofie's early exposure to foreign languages but her delayed entry into marriage, parenthood, and career—important in development?

■ What factors, both intrinsic to the person and present in the environment, led Sofie to die sooner than expected?

These are central questions addressed by **human development,** a field of study devoted to understanding constancy and change throughout the lifespan. Great diversity characterizes the interests and concerns of the thousands of investigators who study human development. But all have a single goal in common: the desire to describe and identify those factors that influence the consistencies and transformations in human beings from conception until death.

HUMAN DEVELOPMENT AS A SCIENTIFIC, INTERDISCIPLINARY, AND APPLIED FIELD

Look again at the questions just listed, and you will see that they are not just of scientific interest. Each is of *applied,* or practical, importance as well. In fact, scientific curiosity about changes that take place from

infancy through old age is just one factor that has led human development to become the exciting field of study it is today. Research about development has also been stimulated by social pressures to better people's lives. For example, the beginning of public education in the early part of this century led to a demand for knowledge about what and how to teach children of different ages. The interest of the medical profession in improving people's health required an understanding of physical development, nutrition, and disease. The social service profession's desire to treat anxieties and behavior problems and to help people adjust to major life events, such as divorce, job loss, or the death of a loved one, required information about personality and social development. And parents have continually asked for expert advice about child-rearing practices and experiences that would foster happy and successful lives for their children.

Our large storehouse of information about human development is *interdisciplinary.* It grew through the combined efforts of people from many fields of study. Because of the need for solutions to everyday problems at all ages, academic scientists from psychology, sociology, anthropology, and biology joined forces in research with professionals from a variety of applied fields, including education, family studies, medicine, public health, and social service, to name just a few. Today, the field of human development is a melting pot of contributions. Its body of knowledge is not just scientifically important, but relevant and useful.

BASIC ISSUES

Research on human development is a relatively recent activity. Studies of children did not begin until the early part of the twentieth century. Investigations into adult development, aging, and change over the life course emerged only in the 1960s and 1970s (Elder, 1998). Nevertheless, ideas about how people grow and change have existed for centuries. As these speculations combined with research, they inspired the construction of *theories* of development. Although a great many definitions exist, for our purposes we can think of a **theory** as an orderly, integrated set of statements that describes, explains, and predicts behavior. For example, a good theory of infant–caregiver attachment would (1) *describe* the behaviors that lead up to babies' strong desire at around 6 to 8 months of age to seek the affection and comfort of a familiar adult, (2) *explain* why infants have such a strong desire, and (3) *predict* the consequences of this emotional bond for relationships throughout life.

Theories are vital tools in human development (and any other scientific endeavor) for two reasons. First, they provide organizing frameworks for our observations of people. In other words, they *guide and give meaning to* what we see. Second, theories that are verified by research provide a sound basis for practical action. Once a theory helps us *understand* development, we are in a much better position to know *what to do* in our efforts to improve the welfare and treatment of children and adults.

As we will see later, theories are influenced by the cultural values and belief systems of their times. But theories differ in one important way from mere opinion and belief: A theory's continued existence depends on *scientific verification* (Scarr, 1985). This means that the theory must be tested with a fair set of research procedures agreed on by the scientific community and that its findings must endure, or be replicated, over time.

In the field of human development, there are many theories with very different ideas about what people are like and how they change. The study of development provides no ultimate truth, since investigators do not always agree on the meaning of what they see. In addition, humans are complex beings; they change physically, mentally, emotionally, and socially. As yet, no single theory has been able to explain all these aspects. Finally, the existence of many theories helps advance knowledge, since researchers are continually trying to support, contradict, and integrate these different points of view.

This chapter introduces you to major theories of human development and research strategies that have been used to test them. We will return to each theory in greater detail, as well as introduce a variety of important but less grand theories, in later parts of this book. Although there are many theories, we can easily organize them, since almost all take a stance on three basic issues about human development: (1) Is the course of development continuous or discontinuous? (2) Is there one course of development that characterizes all people, or are there many possible courses? (3) Are genetic or environmental factors more important in determining development? Let's look closely at each of these issues in the following sections.

CONTINUOUS OR DISCONTINUOUS DEVELOPMENT?

How can we best describe the differences in capacities between small infants, young children, adolescents, and adults? As Figure 1.1 illustrates, major theories recognize two possibilities.

One view holds that infants and preschoolers respond to the world in much the same way as adults do. The difference between the immature and mature being is simply one of *amount or complexity* of behavior. For example, when Sofie was a baby, her perception of a piano melody, memory for past events, and ability to sort objects into categories may have been much like our own. Perhaps her only limitation was that she could not perform these skills with as much information and precision as we can. If this is true, then change in her thinking must be **continuous**—a process that consists of gradually adding on more to the same types of skills that were there to begin with.

Another view sees infants and children as having *unique ways of thinking, feeling, and behaving*—ones quite different from adults'—that must be understood on their own terms. If so, then development is a **discontinuous** process in which new understandings emerge at particular time periods. From this perspective, infant Sofie was not yet able to perceive and organize events and objects as a mature person could. Instead, she moved through a series of developmental steps, each with unique features, until she reached the highest level of functioning.

Theories that accept the discontinuous perspective include a special developmental concept: the concept of **stage.** Stages are *qualitative changes* in thinking, feeling,

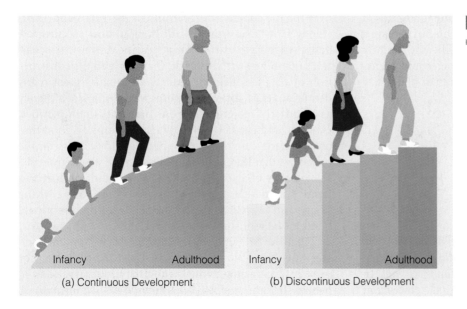

Infancy   Adulthood   Infancy   Adulthood
(a) Continuous Development   (b) Discontinuous Development

FIGURE 1.1

■ **Is development continuous or discontinuous?** (a) Some theorists believe that development is a smooth, continuous process. Individuals gradually add more of the same types of skills. (b) Other theorists think that development takes place in discontinuous stages. People change rapidly as they step up to a new level and then change very little for a while. With each new step, the person interprets and responds to the world in a qualitatively different way.

and behaving that characterize particular time periods of development. In stage theories, development is much like climbing a staircase, with each step corresponding to a more advanced, reorganized way of functioning than the one that came before. The stage concept also assumes that people undergo periods of rapid transformation as they step up from one stage to the next; in other words, change is fairly sudden rather than gradual and ongoing.

Does development actually take place in a neat, orderly sequence of stages? For now, let's note that this is a very ambitious assumption that has not gone unchallenged. We will review some very influential stage theories later in this chapter.

ONE COURSE OF DEVELOPMENT OR MANY?

Stages are always assumed to be universal across individuals and cultures; that is, stage theorists assume that people everywhere follow the same sequence of development. Yet the field of human development is becoming increasingly aware that children and adults live in distinct **contexts;** that is, they experience unique combinations of personal and environmental circumstances. For example, a shy individual, who is genetically prone to be socially fearful, develops in very different contexts from those of a sociable agemate who readily seeks out other people (Rubin & Coplan, 1998). Children and adults in non-Western village societies encounter experiences in their families and communities that differ sharply from those encountered by people in large Western cities. These different circumstances can result in markedly different intellectual capacities, social skills, and feelings about the self and others (Shweder et al., 1998).

As we will see later, contemporary theorists regard the contexts that shape development as many-layered and complex. On the personal side, they include heredity and biological makeup. On the environmental side, they include immediate settings (such as home, school, and neighborhood) as well as conditions more remote from people's everyday lives (such as community resources, societal values, and historical time period). And a special interest in culture has made researchers more conscious of diversity in development than ever before.

NATURE OR NURTURE AS MORE IMPORTANT?

In addition to describing the course of human development, each theory takes a stance on a major question about its underlying causes: Are genetic or environmental factors more important? This is the age-old **nature–nurture controversy.** By *nature,* we mean inborn biological givens—the hereditary information we receive from our parents at the moment of conception that signals the body to grow and affects all our characteristics and skills. By *nurture,* we mean the complex forces of the physical and social world that influence our biological makeup and psychological experiences before and after birth.

Although all theories grant at least some role to both nature and nurture, they vary in the emphasis placed on each. For example, consider the following questions: Is the developing person's ability to think in more complex ways largely the result of an inborn timetable of growth? Or is it primarily influenced by stimulation and encouragement from parents and teachers? Do children acquire language rapidly because they are genetically predisposed to do so or because parents tutor them from an early age? And what accounts for the vast individual differences among people—in height, weight, physical coordination, intelligence, personality, and social skills? Is nature or nurture largely responsible?

The stances theories take on nature versus nurture affect their explanations of individual differences. Some emphasize *stability*—that individuals who are high or low in a characteristic (such as verbal ability, anxiety, or sociability) will remain so at later ages. These theories typically stress the importance of *heredity.* If they regard environment as important, they usually point to *early experiences* as establishing lifelong patterns of behavior. Powerful negative events in the first few years, they argue, cannot be fully overcome by later, more positive ones (Bowlby, 1980; Sroufe, Egeland, & Kreutzer, 1990). Other theories take a more optimistic view (Chess & Thomas, 1984; Sampson & Laub, 1993; Werner & Smith, 1992). They emphasize *plasticity*—that change is possible and likely if new experiences support it.

Throughout this chapter and the remainder of this book, we will see that investigators disagree, at times sharply, on the question of **stability versus change.** Their answers often vary across *domains,* or aspects, of development. Think back to Sofie's story, and you will see that her linguistic ability and persistent approach to challenges were stable over the lifespan. In contrast, her psychological well-being and life satisfaction fluctuated considerably.

THE LIFESPAN PERSPECTIVE: A BALANCED POINT OF VIEW

So far, we have discussed basic issues of human development in terms of extremes—solutions on one side or the other. As we trace the unfolding of the field in the rest of this chapter, you will see that the positions of many theories have softened. Modern ones, especially, recognize the merits of both sides. Some theorists believe that both continuous and discontinuous changes characterize development and alternate with one another. And some acknowledge that development can have both

■ *Today, older adults are healthier and more active than in previous generations. These women, who are in their seventies, easily hike for miles while enjoying a day of bird-watching. (Photo courtesy: David Young-Wolff/PhotoEdit)*

These balanced visions owe much to the expansion of research from a nearly exclusive focus on the first two decades to include adult life. In the first half of this century, it was widely assumed that development stopped at adolescence. Infancy and childhood were viewed as periods of rapid transformation, adulthood as a plateau, and aging as a period of decline. The changing character of the American population awakened researchers to the idea that development is lifelong. Due to improvements in nutrition, sanitation, and medical knowledge, the *average life expectancy* (number of years an individual born in a particular year can expect to live) gained more in the twentieth century than in the preceding five thousand years. In 1900, it was just under age 50; today, it is around age 76½. As a result, there are more older adults, a trend that has occurred in most of the world but is especially striking in industrialized nations. People age 65 and older accounted for 4 percent of the U.S. population in 1900, 7 percent in 1950, and 13 percent in 1998. Growth in sheer number of older Americans during the twentieth century has been even more dramatic, increasing more than eleven-fold, from 3 million to 34 million (U.S. Bureau of the Census, 1960, 1999).

Older adults are not just more numerous; they are also healthier and more active. They challenge the stereotype of the withering person of earlier years. These observations required a fundamental shift in our conception of human development. Compared with other approaches, the **life-span perspective** offers a more complex vision of change

universal features and features unique to the individual and his or her contexts. Finally, recent investigators have moved away from asking which is more important, heredity or environment. Instead, they want to know precisely how nature and nurture work together to influence the individual's traits and capacities.

TABLE 1.1

Major Periods of Human Development

PERIOD	APPROXIMATE AGE RANGE	BRIEF DESCRIPTION
Prenatal	Conception to birth	The one-celled organism transforms into a human baby with remarkable capacities to adjust to life outside the womb.
Infancy and Toddlerhood	Birth to 2 years	Dramatic changes in the body and brain support emergence of a wide array of motor, perceptual, and intellectual capacities and first intimate ties to others.
Early Childhood	2 to 6 years	The play years, in which motor skills are refined, thought and language expand at an astounding pace, a sense of morality is evident, and children begin to establish ties to peers.
Middle Childhood	6 to 11 years	The school years, marked by advances in athletic abilities; logical thought processes; basic literacy skills; understanding of self, morality, and friendship; and peer-group membership.
Adolescence	11 to 20 years	Puberty leads to an adult-sized body and sexual maturity. Thought becomes abstract and idealistic and school achievement more serious. Adolescents focus on defining personal values and goals and establishing autonomy from the family.
Early Adulthood	20 to 40 years	Most young people leave home, complete their education, and begin full-time work. Major concerns are developing a career; forming an intimate partnership; and marrying, rearing children, or establishing other lifestyles.
Middle Adulthood	40 to 60 years	Many people are at the height of their careers and attain leadership positions. They must also help their children begin independent lives and their parents adapt to aging. They become more aware of their own mortality.
Late Adulthood	60 years to death	People adjust to retirement, to decreased physical strength and health, and often to the death of a spouse. They reflect on the meaning of their lives.

Physical Development
Changes in body size, proportions, appearance,
functioning of body systems, perceptual and
motor capacities, and physical health

Cognitive Development
Changes in intellectual abilities, including
attention, memory, academic and everyday
knowledge, problem solving, imagination,
creativity, and language

Emotional and Social Development
Changes in emotional communication, self-understanding,
knowledge about other people, interpersonal
skills, friendships, intimate relationships, and
moral reasoning and behavior

FIGURE 1.2

■ **Major domains of development.** The three domains are not really distinct; they overlap and interact.

and the factors that underlie it. Four assumptions make up this broader view: (1) development as lifelong; (2) development as multidimensional and multidirectional; (3) development as highly plastic; and (4) development as embedded in multiple contexts (Baltes, Lindenberger, & Staudinger, 1998; Smith & Baltes, 1999).

DEVELOPMENT AS LIFELONG

According to the lifespan perspective, no age period is supreme in its impact on the life course. Instead, events occurring during each major period, summarized in Table 1.1, can have equally powerful effects on the future path of change. Within each period, change occurs within three broad domains: *physical, cognitive,* and *social,* which we separate for convenience of discussion (refer to Figure 1.2 for a description of each). Yet, as you are already aware from reading the first part of this chapter, the domains are not really distinct; they overlap and interact a great deal.

Every age period has its own agenda, bringing with it unique demands and opportunities that yield some similarities in development across many individuals. Nevertheless, throughout life, the challenges people face and the adjustments they make are highly diverse in timing and pattern, as the remaining assumptions make clear.

DEVELOPMENT AS MULTIDIMENSIONAL AND MULTIDIRECTIONAL

Think back to Sofie's life, and notice how she was continually faced with new demands and opportunities. The lifespan perspective regards the challenges and adjustments of development as *multidimensional*—affected by an intricate blend of biological, psychological, and social forces.

Lifespan development is also *multidirectional*—in at least two ways. First, development is not limited to improved performance. Instead, at all periods, it is a joint expression of growth and decline. When Sofie directed her energies toward mastering languages and music as a school-age child, she gave up refining other skills to their full potential. When she chose to become a teacher in adulthood, she let go of other career options. Although gains are especially evident early in life and losses during the final years, people of all ages can improve current skills and develop new skills, including ones that compensate for reduced functioning (Baltes, 1998). One highly accomplished, elderly psychologist who noticed his difficulty remembering people's names devised graceful ways of explaining his memory failure. Sometimes he appealed to his age; at other times, he flattered his listener by remark-

RESILIENCY

John and his best friend Gary grew up in a run-down, crime-ridden inner-city neighborhood. By age 10, each had experienced years of family conflict followed by parental divorce. Reared for the rest of childhood and adolescence in mother-headed households, John and Gary rarely saw their fathers. Both achieved poorly, dropped out of high school, and were in and out of trouble with the police.

Then John and Gary's paths of development diverged. By age 30, John had fathered two children with women he never married, had spent time in prison, was unemployed, and drank alcohol heavily. In contrast, Gary had returned to finish high school, had studied auto mechanics at a community college, and became manager of a gas station and repair shop. Married with two children, he had saved his earnings and bought a home. He was happy, healthy, and well adapted to life.

A wealth of evidence shows that environmental risks—poverty, negative family interactions and parental divorce, job loss, mental illness, and drug abuse—predispose children to future problems (Masten & Coats-

worth, 1998). On the basis of these findings, we would have expected both John and Gary to develop serious psychological difficulties. Why did Gary "beat the odds" and come through unscathed?

New evidence on **resiliency**—the ability to adapt effectively in the face of adversity—is receiving increasing attention because investigators want to find ways to protect young people from the damaging effects of stressful life conditions (Cicchetti & Garmezy, 1993). Resiliency research was inspired by several long-term studies on the relationship of life stressors in childhood to competence and adjustment in adolescence and adulthood (Garmezy, 1993; Rutter, 1987; Werner & Smith, 1992). In each study, some individuals were shielded from negative outcomes, whereas others had lasting problems. Three broad factors seemed to offer protection from the damaging effects of stressful life events:

PERSONAL CHARACTERISTICS.
A child's biologically endowed characteristics can reduce exposure to risk or lead to experiences that compensate for early stressful events. Tem-

perament is particularly powerful. Children with calm, easygoing, sociable dispositions who are willing to take initiative have a special capacity to adapt to change and elicit positive responses from others. Children who are emotionally reactive and irritable often strain the patience of people around them (Milgram & Palti, 1993; Smith & Prior, 1995). For example, both John and Gary moved several times during their childhoods. Each time, John became anxious and angry, picking arguments with his parents, siblings, and peers. In contrast, Gary was sad to leave his home but soon looked forward to making new friends and exploring new parts of the neighborhood. Intellectual ability is another protective factor (Masten et al., 1999). It increases the chances of rewarding experiences in school that may offset the impact of a stressful home life.

A WARM PARENTAL RELATIONSHIP.
A close relationship with at least one parent who provides affection and assistance and introduces order and organization into the child's life fosters resiliency. But note that this factor (as well as the next one) is not

---

ing that he tended to forget only the names of important people! Under these conditions, he reflected, "forgetting may even be a pleasure" (Skinner, 1983, p. 240).

Second, besides being multidirectional over time, change is multidirectional within the same domain of development. Although some qualities of Sofie's cognitive functioning (such as memory) probably declined in her mature years, her knowledge of English and French undoubtedly grew throughout her life. And she also developed new forms of thinking. For example, Sofie's wealth of experience and ability to cope with diverse problems led her to become expert in practical matters—a quality of reasoning called wisdom. Recall the wise advice that Sofie gave Laura and Ken on the eve of their wedding day. We will consider the development of wisdom in Chapter 17. Notice, in these examples, how the lifespan perspective incorporates both continuous and discontinuous change.

DEVELOPMENT AS HIGHLY PLASTIC

Lifespan researchers emphasize that development is *highly plastic* at all ages. For example, consider Sofie's social reserve in childhood and her decision to study rather than marry as a young adult. As new opportunities arose, Sofie (much to her parents' surprise) moved easily into marriage and childbearing in her thirties. And although parenthood and financial difficulties posed challenges to Sofie and Philip's happiness, their relationship gradually became richer and more fulfilling. In Chapter 17, we will see that intellectual performance also remains flexible with advancing age. Elderly people respond to special training with substantial (but not unlimited) gains in a wide variety of mental abilities (Schaie, 1996).

Evidence on plasticity makes clear that aging is not an eventual "shipwreck," as has often been assumed. Instead, independent of children's personal characteristics. Children who are relaxed, socially responsive, and able to deal with change are easier to rear and more likely to enjoy positive relationships with parents and other people. At the same time, some children may develop more attractive dispositions as a result of parental warmth and attention (Smith & Prior, 1995; Wyman et al., 1999).

SOCIAL SUPPORT OUTSIDE THE IM-MEDIATE FAMILY. A person outside the immediate family—perhaps a grandparent, teacher, or close friend—who forms a special relationship with the child can promote resilience. Gary may have overcome the effects of a stressful home life because of the support he received in adolescence from his grandfather, who listened to Gary's concerns and helped him solve problems constructively. In addition, Gary's grandfather had a stable marriage and work life and handled stressors skillfully. Consequently, he served as a model of effective coping (Zimmerman & Arunkumar, 1994).

Research on resiliency highlights the complex connections between heredity and environment. Armed with positive characteristics, which

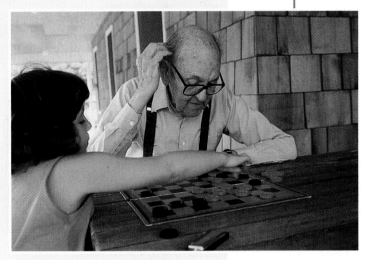

may stem from innate endowment, favorable rearing experiences, or both, children take action to reduce stressful situations. Nevertheless, when many risks pile up, they become increasingly difficult to overcome (Sameroff et al., 1993). Therefore, effective interventions need to reduce risks and enhance relationships at home, in school, and in the community that protect children against the negative effects of risk. This means attending to both the person and the environment—building the child's capacity as well as reducing problems.

■ *This child's special relationship with her grandfather provides the social support she needs to cope with stress and solve problems constructively. A warm tie with a person outside the immediate family can promote resiliency. (Photo courtesy: Alan Hicks/Stone)*

the metaphor of a "butterfly"—of metamorphosis and continued potential—provides a far more accurate picture of lifespan change (Lemme, 1999). Still, development gradually becomes less plastic, as both capacity and opportunity for change are reduced. And plasticity varies greatly across individuals. Some children and adults experience more diverse life circumstances. And as the Variations box above reveals, some adapt more easily to changing conditions than do others.

DEVELOPMENT AS EMBEDDED IN MULTIPLE CONTEXTS

According to the lifespan perspective, pathways of change are highly diverse because development is *embedded in multiple contexts.* Although these wide-ranging influences can be organized into three categories, they work together,

combining in unique ways to fashion each life course (Baltes, 1987).

■ **AGE-GRADED INFLUENCES** Events that are strongly related to age and therefore fairly predictable in when they occur and how long they last are called **age-graded influences.** For example, most individuals walk shortly after their first birthday, acquire their native language during the preschool years, reach puberty around ages 12 to 14, and (for women) experience menopause in their late forties or early fifties. These milestones are influenced by biology, but social customs can create age-graded influences as well. Starting school around age 6, getting a driver's license at age 16, and entering college around age 18 are events of this kind. Age-graded influences are especially prevalent during childhood and adolescence. During those times, biological changes are rapid, and cultures im-

■ *Starting kindergarten marks a major transition in the lives of these 5- and 6-year-olds. Because the first day of school occurs at about the same age for most children in industrialized nations, it is an age-graded influence. (Photo courtesy: Tony Freeman/PhotoEdit)*

pose many age-related experiences to ensure that young people acquire the skills needed to become competent, participating members of their society.

■ HISTORY-GRADED INFLUENCES. Development is also profoundly affected by forces unique to a particular historical era. Epidemics, wars, and periods of economic prosperity or depression; technological advances, such as the introduction of television and computers; and changing cultural values—for example, revised attitudes toward women and ethnic minorities—are examples of **history-graded influences.** These events explain why people born around the same time—called a *cohort*—tend to be alike in ways that set them apart from people born at other times.

■ NONNORMATIVE INFLUENCES. The term *normative* means typical, or average. Age-graded and history-graded influences are normative, since each affects large numbers of people in a similar way. **Nonnormative influences** are events that are irregular, in that they happen to just one or a few people and do not follow a predictable timetable. Consequently, they enhance the multidirectionality of development. Piano lessons in childhood with an inspiring teacher; a blind date with Philip; delayed marriage, parenthood, and career entry; and a battle with cancer are nonnormative influences that had a major impact on the direction of Sofie's life. Because they occur haphazardly, nonnormative events are among the most difficult for researchers to capture and study. Yet, as each of us can attest from our own experiences, they can affect us in powerful ways.

Lifespan investigators point out that nonnormative influences have become more powerful and age-graded influences less so in modern adult development. Compared with Sofie's era, the ages at which people now finish their education, enter careers, get married, have children, and retire are much more diverse (Schroots & Birren, 1990). Indeed, Sofie's "off-time" accomplishments would have been less unusual had she been born a generation or two later! Age remains a powerful organizer of everyday experiences, and age-related expectations have certainly not disappeared. But age markers have blurred, and they vary across ethnic groups and cultures. The increasing role of nonnormative events in the modern life course adds to the fluid nature of lifespan development.

Notice that instead of a single line of development, the lifespan perspective emphasizes many potential pathways and outcomes—an image more like tree branches extending in diverse directions, each of which may undergo continuous and stagewise transformations (see Figure 1.3). Throughout this book, I will remind you of the lifespan perspective with a special icon, placed in the margin next to relevant text discussion: ♠ Now let's turn to the historical foundations of the field as a prelude to discussing major theories that address various aspects of change.

■ **ASK YOURSELF** . . .

♠ *What stance does the lifespan perspective take on the issue of one course of development or many? How about nature or nurture and stability versus change? Explain.*

♠ *List as many examples as you can find of age-graded, history-graded, and nonnormative influences in Sofie's story at the beginning of this chapter.*

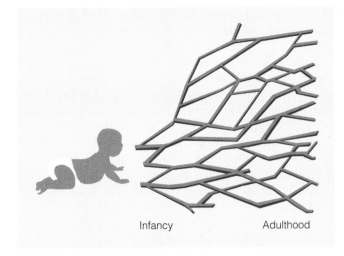

FIGURE 1.3

■ **The lifespan view of development.** Rather than envisioning a single line of stagewise or continuous change (see Figure 1.1 on page 6), lifespan theorists conceive of development as more like tree branches extending in diverse directions. Many potential pathways are possible, depending on the contexts that influence the individual's life course. Each branch in this treelike image represents a possible skill within one of the major domains of development. The crossing of the branches signifies that the domains—physical, cognitive, emotional, and social—are interrelated.

Infancy   Adulthood

HISTORICAL FOUNDATIONS

M odern theories of human development are the result of centuries of change in Western cultural values, philosophical thinking, and scientific progress. To understand the field as it exists today, we must return to its early beginnings—to influences that long preceded scientific study. We will see that many early ideas linger on as important forces in current theory and research.

PHILOSOPHIES OF CHILDHOOD

In medieval times (the sixth through the fifteenth centuries), little importance was placed on childhood as a separate phase of the life course. Instead, once children emerged from infancy, they were regarded as miniature, already-formed adults, a view called **preformationism** (Ariès, 1962). Some laws recognized that children needed protection from people who might mistreat them, and medical works provided special instructions for their care. However, even though in a practical sense there was some awareness of the vulnerability of children, there were no philosophies of the uniqueness of childhood or separate developmental periods (Borstelmann, 1983).

By the sixteenth century, a revised image of children sprang from the religious movement that gave birth to Protestantism—in particular, from the Puritan belief in original sin. Harsh, restrictive parenting practices were recommended as the most efficient means for taming the depraved child. Although punitiveness was the prevailing child-rearing philosophy of the times, love and affection for their children prevented most Puritan parents from using extremely repressive measures. Instead, they tried to promote reason in their sons and daughters so they would be able to separate right from wrong and resist temptation (Moran & Vinovskis, 1986; L. Pollock, 1987).

■ JOHN LOCKE. The seventeenth-century Enlightenment brought philosophies that emphasized ideals of human dignity and respect. The writings of John Locke (1632–1704), a leading British philosopher, served as the forerunner of an important twentieth-century perspective that we will discuss shortly: behaviorism. Locke viewed the child as a **tabula rasa.** Translated from Latin, this means "blank slate" or "white piece of paper." According to this idea, children were not basically evil. They were, to begin with, nothing at all, and their characters could be shaped by all kinds of experiences. Locke (1690/1892) described parents as rational tutors who could mold the child in any way they wished, through careful instruction,

■ *In this medieval painting, young children are depicted as miniature adults. Their dress and expressions resemble those of their elders. Through the fifteenth century, little emphasis was placed on childhood as a unique phase of the life cycle. (Eric Lessing/Art Resource, NY)*

effective example, and rewards for good behavior. His philosophy led to a change from harshness toward children to kindness and compassion.

Look carefully at Locke's ideas, and you will see that he took a firm stand on basic issues discussed earlier in this chapter. Lock regarded development as *continuous;* adult-like behaviors are gradually built up through the warm, consistent teachings of parents. Furthermore, Locke's view of the child as tabula rasa led him to champion *nurture*—the power of the environment to determine whether children become good or bad, bright or dull, kind or selfish. And his faith in nurture suggests the possibility of *many courses of development* and *change at later ages* due to new experiences. Finally, Locke's philosophy characterizes children as passive—as doing little to shape their own destinies, which are written on blank slates by others. This vision has been discarded. Instead, all contemporary theories view the developing person as an active, purposeful being who contributes substantially to his or her own development.

■ JEAN JACQUES ROUSSEAU. In the eighteenth century, a new theory of childhood was introduced by French philosopher Jean Jacques Rousseau (1712–1778). Children, Rousseau (1762/1955) thought, were not blank slates to be filled by adult instruction. Instead, they were **noble savages,** naturally endowed with a sense of right and wrong and with an innate plan for orderly, healthy growth. Unlike Locke, Rousseau thought children's built-in moral sense and unique ways of thinking and feeling would only be harmed by adult training. His was a child-centered philosophy in which the adult should be receptive to the child's needs at each of four stages of development: infancy, childhood, late childhood, and adolescence.

Rousseau's philosophy includes two vitally important concepts that are found in modern theories. The first is the concept of stage, which we discussed earlier in this chapter. The second is the concept of **maturation,** which refers to a genetically determined, naturally unfolding course of growth. If you accept the notion that children mature through a sequence of stages, then they are unique and different from adults, and their development is determined by their own inner promptings. Rousseau took a stance very different from Locke's on basic developmental issues. He saw development as a discontinuous, stagewise process that follows a single, unified course mapped out by nature.

PHILOSOPHIES OF ADULTHOOD AND AGING

Shortly after Rousseau devised his conception of childhood, the first lifespan views began to appear. In the eighteenth and early nineteenth centuries, two German philosophers—John Nicolaus Tetens (1736–1807) and

Friedrich August Carus (1770–1808)—urged that attention to development be extended through adulthood. Each asked important questions about aging.

Tetens (1777) addressed the origins and extent of individual differences, the degree to which behavior can be changed in adulthood, and the impact of historical eras on the life course. He was ahead of his time in recognizing that intellectual declines in old age can be compensated for and, at times, may reflect hidden gains. For example, Tetens suggested that some memory difficulties might be the result of trying to search for a word or name among a lifetime of accumulated information—a possibility acknowledged by modern researchers (Maylor & Valentine, 1992).

Carus (1808) moved beyond Rousseau's stages by identifying four periods that span the life course: childhood, youth, adulthood, and senescence. Like Tetens, Carus viewed aging not only as decline, but also as progression. His writings reflect a remarkable awareness of the assumptions of multidirectionality and plasticity that are at the heart of the contemporary lifespan perspective.

SCIENTIFIC BEGINNINGS

The study of development evolved quickly during the late nineteenth and early twentieth centuries. Early observations of human change were soon followed by improved methods and theories. Each advance contributed to the firm foundation on which the field rests today.

■ DARWIN: FOREFATHER OF SCIENTIFIC CHILD STUDY. Charles Darwin (1809–1882), a British naturalist, is often considered to be the forefather of scientific child study. Darwin (1859/1936) observed the infinite variation among plant and animal species. He also saw that within a species, no two individuals are exactly alike. From these observations, he constructed his famous theory of evolution.

The theory emphasized two related principles: *natural selection* and *survival of the fittest.* Darwin explained that certain species are *selected by nature* to survive in particular environments because they have characteristics that *fit with,* or are adapted to, their surroundings. Other species die off because they are not well suited to their environments. Individuals within a species who best meet the survival requirements of the environment live long enough to reproduce and pass their more favorable characteristics to future generations. We will see that Darwin's emphasis on the adaptive value of physical characteristics and behavior found its way into important developmental theories.

During his explorations, Darwin discovered that the early prenatal growth of many species is strikingly similar. This suggested that all species, including humans, were descended from a few common ancestors. Other scientists concluded from Darwin's observation that the development of the human child followed the same general plan as the evolution of the human species. Although this belief eventually proved to be inaccurate, efforts to chart parallels between child growth and human evolution prompted researchers to make careful observations of all aspects of children's behavior. Out of these first attempts to document an idea about development, scientific child study was born.

■ THE NORMATIVE PERIOD. G. Stanley Hall (1846–1924), one of the most influential American psychologists of the early twentieth century, is generally regarded as the founder of the child study movement (Dixon & Lerner, 1999). He also foreshadowed lifespan research by writing one of the few books of his time on aging. Inspired by Darwin's work, Hall and his well-known student Arnold Gesell (1880–1961) devised theories of childhood and adolescence based on evolutionary ideas. These early leaders regarded development as a genetically determined process that unfolds automatically, much like a flower (Gesell, 1933; Hall, 1904).

Hall and Gesell are remembered less for their one-sided theories than for their intensive efforts to describe all aspects of development. They launched the **normative approach** to child study. In a normative investigation, measures of behavior are taken on large numbers of individuals. Then age-related averages are computed to represent typical development. Using this method, Hall constructed elaborate questionnaires asking children of different ages almost everything they could tell about themselves—interests, fears, imaginary playmates, dreams, friendships, everyday knowledge, and more (White, 1992). In the same fashion, Gesell collected detailed normative information on the motor achievements, social behaviors, and personality characteristics of infants and children (Gesell & Ilg, 1946/1949a, 1943/1949b).

Gesell was also among the first to make knowledge about child development meaningful to parents. If, as he believed, the timetable of development is the product of millions of years of evolution, then children are naturally knowledgeable about their needs. His child-rearing advice, in the tradition of Rousseau, recommended sensitivity to children's cues (Thelen & Adolph, 1992). Along with Benjamin Spock's *Baby and Child Care*, Gesell's books became a central part of a rapidly expanding popular literature for parents.

■ THE MENTAL TESTING MOVEMENT. While Hall and Gesell were developing their theories and methods in the United States, French psychologist Alfred Binet (1857–1911) also took a normative approach to child development, but for a different reason. In the early 1900s, Binet and his colleague Theodore Simon were asked to find a way to identify retarded children in the Paris school system

■ *Darwin's theory of evolution emphasizes the adaptive value of physical characteristics and behavior. Affection and care in families is adaptive throughout the lifespan, promoting survival and psychological well-being. Here a daughter helps her elderly mother with medication. (Photo courtesy: Penny Tweedie/Stone)*

who needed to be placed in special classes. The first successful intelligence test, which they constructed for this purpose, grew out of practical educational concerns.

In 1916, at Stanford University, Binet's test was translated into English and adapted for use with American children. It became known as the Stanford-Binet Intelligence Scale. Besides providing a score that could successfully predict school achievement, the Binet test sparked tremendous interest in individual differences in development. Soon many additional tests were devised for both children and adults. Comparisons of the scores of people who vary in gender, ethnicity, birth order, family background, and other characteristics became a major focus of research. Intelligence tests also rose quickly to the forefront of the controversy over nature versus nurture that has continued to this day.

■ ASK YOURSELF . . .

■ *Suppose we could arrange a debate between John Locke and Jean Jacques Rousseau on the nature–nurture controversy. Summarize the argument that each of these historical figures is likely to present.*

Explain how central assumptions of the lifespan perspective are reflected in Tetens's and Carus's philosophies of adulthood and aging.

MID-TWENTIETH-CENTURY THEORIES

In the mid-twentieth century, human development expanded into a legitimate discipline. As it attracted increasing interest, a variety of mid-twentieth-century theories emerged, each of which continues to have followers today.

THE PSYCHOANALYTIC PERSPECTIVE

Recall that the normative and testing movements had begun to answer the question: What are human beings like at different ages? In the 1930s and 1940s, as more people sought help from professionals in dealing with emotional difficulties, a new question had to be addressed: How and why did people become the way they are? To treat psychological problems, psychiatrists and social workers turned to the **psychoanalytic perspective** on personality development because of its emphasis on understanding the unique life history of each person.

According to the psychoanalytic approach, people move through a series of stages in which they confront conflicts between biological drives and social expectations. The way these conflicts are resolved determines the individual's ability to learn, to get along with others, and to cope with anxiety. Although many individuals contributed to the psychoanalytic perspective, two have been especially influential: Sigmund Freud, founder of the psychoanalytic movement, and Erik Erikson.

■ FREUD'S THEORY. Freud (1856–1939), a Viennese physician, saw patients in his practice with a variety of nervous symptoms, such as hallucinations, fears, and paralyses, that appeared to have no physical basis. Seeking a cure for these troubled adults, Freud found that their symptoms could be relieved by having them talk freely about painful events of their childhoods. On the basis of adult remembrances, he examined the unconscious motivations of his patients and constructed his **psychosexual theory** of development. It emphasized that how parents manage their child's sexual and aggressive drives in the first few years is crucial for healthy personality development.

■ THREE PARTS OF THE PERSONALITY. In Freud's theory, three parts of the personality—id, ego, and superego—become integrated during a sequence of five stages of development summarized in Table 1.2. The *id*, the largest portion of the mind, is the source of basic biological needs and desires. The *ego*—the conscious, rational part of personality—emerges in early infancy to redirect the id's impulses so they are discharged on appropriate objects at acceptable times and places. For example, aided by the ego, the hungry baby of a few months of age stops crying when he sees his mother unfasten her clothing for breast-feeding or warm a bottle. And the more competent preschooler goes into the kitchen and gets a snack on her own.

Between 3 and 6 years of age, the *superego*, or conscience, develops from interactions with parents, who eventually insist that children conform to the values of society. Now the ego faces the increasingly complex task of reconciling the demands of the id, the external world, and

TABLE 1.2

Freud's Psychosexual Stages

PSYCHOSEXUAL STAGE	PERIOD OF DEVELOPMENT	DESCRIPTION
Oral	Birth–1 year	The new ego directs the baby's sucking activities toward breast or bottle. If oral needs are not met appropriately, the individual may develop such habits as thumb sucking, fingernail biting, and pencil chewing in childhood and overeating and smoking in later life.
Anal	1–3 years	Young toddlers and preschoolers enjoy holding and releasing urine and feces. Toilet training becomes a major issue between parent and child. If parents insist that children be trained before they are ready or make too few demands, conflicts about anal control may appear in the form of extreme orderliness and cleanliness or messiness and disorder.
Phallic	3–6 years	Id impulses transfer to the genitals, and the child finds pleasure in genital stimulation. Freud's *Oedipus conflict* for boys and *Electra conflict* for girls take place. Young children feel a sexual desire for the other-sex parent. To avoid punishment, they give up this desire and, instead, adopt the same-sex parent's characteristics and values. As a result, the superego is formed, and children feel guilty each time they violate its standards. The relations between id, ego, and superego established at this time determine the individual's basic personality orientation.
Latency	6–11 years	Sexual instincts die down, and the superego develops further. The child acquires new social values from adults outside the family and from play with same-sex peers.
Genital	Adolescence	Puberty causes the sexual impulses of the phallic stage to reappear. If development has been successful during earlier stages, it leads to marriage, mature sexuality, and the birth and rearing of children.

conscience (Freud, 1923/1974). For example, when the ego is tempted to gratify an id impulse by hitting a playmate to get an attractive toy, the superego may warn that such behavior is wrong. The ego must decide which of the two forces (id or superego) will win this inner struggle or work out a reasonable compromise, such as asking for a turn with the toy. According to Freud, the relations established between id, ego, and superego during the preschool years determine the individual's basic personality.

■ PSYCHOSEXUAL DEVELOPMENT. Freud (1938/1973) believed that over the course of childhood, sexual impulses shift their focus from the oral to the anal to the genital regions of the body. In each stage of development, parents walk a fine line between permitting too much or too little gratification of their child's basic needs. If parents strike an appropriate balance, then children grow into well-adjusted adults with the capacity for mature sexual behavior, investment in family life, and rearing of the next generation.

Freud's psychosexual theory highlighted the importance of family relationships for children's development. It was the first theory to stress the importance of early experience for later development. But Freud's perspective was eventually criticized. First, the theory overemphasized the influence of sexual feelings in development. Second, because it was based on the problems of sexually repressed, well-to-do adults, some aspects of Freud's theory did not apply in cultures differing from nineteenth-century Victorian society. Finally, Freud's ideas were called into question because he did not study children directly.

■ ERIKSON'S THEORY. Several of Freud's followers stretched and rearranged his theory in ways that improved on his vision. The most important of these neo-Freudians for the field of human development is Erik Erikson (1902–1994).

Although Erikson (1950) accepted Freud's basic psychosexual framework, he expanded the picture of development at each stage. In his **psychosocial theory,** Erikson emphasized that the ego does not just mediate between id impulses and superego demands. It is also a positive force in development. At each stage, it acquires attitudes and skills that make the individual an active, contributing member of society. A basic psychological conflict, which is resolved along a continuum from positive to negative, determines healthy or maladaptive outcomes at each stage. As Table 1.3 on page 18 shows, Erikson's first five stages parallel Freud's stages, but Erikson added three adult stages to Freud's model.

Finally, unlike Freud, Erikson pointed out that normal development must be understood in relation to each culture's life situation. For example, among the Yurok Indians (a tribe of fishermen and acorn gatherers on the Northwest coast of the United States), babies are deprived of breastfeeding for the first 10 days after birth and instead are fed a thin soup from a small shell. At age 6 months, infants are abruptly weaned, an event enforced, if necessary, by having the mother leave for a few days. These experiences, from our cultural vantage point, might seem cruel. But Erikson explained that the Yurok live in a world in which salmon fill the river just once a year, a circumstance that requires the development of considerable self-restraint for survival. In this way, he showed that child-rearing experiences can only be understood by making reference to the competencies valued and needed by the individual's society.

■ CONTRIBUTIONS AND LIMITATIONS OF PSYCHOANALYTIC THEORY. A special strength of the psychoanalytic perspective is its emphasis on the individual's unique life history as worthy of study and understanding (Emde, 1992). Consistent with this view, psychoanalytic theorists accept the *clinical method,* which synthesizes information from a variety of sources into a detailed picture of the personality functioning of a single person. (We will discuss the clinical method further at the end of this chapter.) Psychoanalytic theory has also inspired a wealth of research on many aspects of emotional and social development, including infant–caregiver attachment, aggression, sibling relationships, child-rearing practices, morality, gender roles, and adolescent identity.

Despite its extensive contributions, the psychoanalytic perspective is no longer in the mainstream of human development research (Cairns, 1998). Psychoanalytic theorists

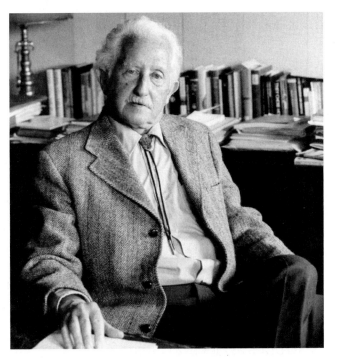

■ *Erik Erikson expanded Freud's theory, emphasizing the psychosocial outcomes of development. At each stage, a major psychological conflict is resolved. If the outcome is positive, individuals acquire attitudes and skills that permit them to contribute constructively to society. (Photo courtesy: Ted Storeshinsky/Corbis)*

TABLE 1.3

Erikson's Psychosocial Stages, with Corresponding Psychosexual Stages Indicated

PSYCHOSOCIAL STAGE	PERIOD OF DEVELOPMENT	DESCRIPTION
Basic trust versus mistrust (Oral)	Birth–1 year	From warm, responsive care, infants gain a sense of trust, or confidence, that the world is good. Mistrust occurs when infants have to wait too long for comfort and are handled harshly.
Autonomy versus shame and doubt (Anal)	1–3 years	Using new mental and motor skills, children want to choose and decide for themselves. Autonomy is fostered when parents permit reasonable free choice and do not force or shame the child.
Initiative versus guilt (Phallic)	3–6 years	Through make-believe play, children experiment with the kind of person they can become. Initiative—a sense of ambition and responsibility—develops when parents support their child's new sense of purpose and direction. The danger is that parents will demand too much self-control, which leads to overcontrol, or too much guilt.
Industry versus inferiority diffusion (Latency)	6–11 years	At school, children develop the capacity to work and cooperate with others. Inferiority develops when negative experiences at home, at school, or with peers lead to feelings of incompetence and inferiority.
Identity versus identity confusion (Genital)	Adolescence	The adolescent tries to answer the question, Who am I, and what is my place in society? Self-chosen values and vocational goals lead to a lasting personal identity. The negative outcome is confusion about future adult roles.
Intimacy versus isolation	Young adulthood	Young people work on establishing intimate ties to others. Because of earlier disappointments, some individuals cannot form close relationships and remain isolated from others.
Generativity versus stagnation	Middle adulthood	Generativity means giving to the next generation through child rearing, caring for other people, or productive work. The person who fails in these ways feels an absence of meaningful accomplishment.
Ego integrity versus despair	Old age	In this final stage, individuals reflect on the kind of person they have been. Integrity results from feeling that life was worth living as it happened. Older people who are dissatisfied with their lives fear death.

may have become isolated from the rest of the field because they were so strongly committed to the clinical approach that they failed to consider other methods. In addition, many psychoanalytic ideas, such as Freud's Oedipus conflict, the psychosexual stages, and certain outcomes of Erikson's stages (for example, generativity and ego integrity), are so vague that they were difficult or impossible to test empirically (Miller, 1993).

Nevertheless, Erikson's broad outline of lifespan change captures the essence of personality development during each major period of the life course, so we will return to it in later chapters. We will also encounter additional perspectives that clarify the attainments of early, middle, and late adulthood and that are within the tradition of stage models of psychosocial development (Levinson, 1978, 1996; Vaillant, 1977).

BEHAVIORISM AND SOCIAL LEARNING THEORY

As psychoanalytic theory gained in prominence, human development was also influenced by a very different perspective: **behaviorism,** a tradition consistent with Locke's tabula rasa. American behaviorism began with the work of psychologist John Watson (1878–1958) in the early part of the twentieth century. Watson wanted to create an objective science of psychology. Unlike psychoanalytic theorists, he believed in studying directly observable events —stimuli and responses—rather than the unseen workings of the mind (Horowitz, 1992).

■ TRADITIONAL BEHAVIORISM. Watson was inspired by some studies of animal learning carried out by famous Russian physiologist Ivan Pavlov. Pavlov knew that dogs release saliva as an innate reflex when they are given food. But he noticed that his dogs were salivating before they tasted any food—when they saw the trainer who usually fed them. The dogs, Pavlov reasoned, must have learned to associate a neutral stimulus (the trainer) with another stimulus (food) that produces a reflexive response (salivation). As a result of this association, the neutral stimulus could bring about the response. Anxious to test this idea, Pavlov successfully taught dogs to salivate at the sound of a bell by pairing it with the presentation of food. He had discovered *classical conditioning.*

Watson wanted to find out if classical conditioning could be applied to children's behavior. In a historic experiment, he taught Albert, an 11-month-old infant, to fear a neutral stimulus—a soft white rat—by presenting it several times with a sharp, loud sound, which naturally scared the baby. Little Albert, who at first had reached out eagerly to touch the furry rat, cried and turned his head away when he caught sight of it (Watson & Raynor, 1920). In fact, Albert's fear was so intense that researchers eventually questioned the ethics of studies like this one (an issue we will take up later in this chapter). On the basis of findings like these, Watson concluded that environment is the supreme force in child development. Adults could mold children's behavior in any way they wished, he thought, by carefully controlling stimulus–response associations. And development is a continuous process, consisting of a gradual increase in the number and strength of these associations.

Another form of behaviorism was B. F. Skinner's (1904–1990) *operant conditioning theory.* According to Skinner, behavior can be increased by following it with a wide variety of *reinforcers,* such as food, praise, or a friendly smile. It can also be decreased through *punishment,* such as disapproval or withdrawal of privileges. As a result of Skinner's work, operant conditioning became a broadly applied learning principle. We will consider these conditioning techniques further in Chapter 4.

■ SOCIAL LEARNING THEORY. Psychologists quickly became interested in whether behaviorism might offer a more direct and effective explanation of the development of social behavior than the less precise concepts of psychoanalytic theory. This concern sparked the emergence of **social learning theory.** Social learning theorists built on the principles of conditioning that came before them, offering expanded views of how children and adults acquire new responses.

Several kinds of social learning theory emerged. The most influential was devised by Albert Bandura (1977), who recognized that children acquire many favorable and unfavorable responses simply by watching and listening to others around them. *Modeling,* otherwise known as *imitation* or *observational learning,* became a widely recognized basis for development. The baby who claps her hands after her mother does so, the child who angrily hits a playmate in the same way that he has been punished at home, and the teenager who wears the same clothes and hairstyle as her friends at school are all displaying observational learning.

Bandura's work continues to influence much research on social development. However, like the field of human development as a whole, today his theory stresses the importance of cognition, or thinking. In fact, the most recent revision of Bandura's (1989, 1992) theory places such strong emphasis on how we think about ourselves and other people that he calls it a *social-cognitive* rather than a social learning approach.

According to this view, children gradually become more selective in what they imitate. From watching others engage in self-praise and self-blame and through feedback about the worth of their own actions, children develop *personal*

■ *Albert Bandura has made major contributions to social learning theory, conducting a wealth of research on modeling as a vital basis for learning and development. Today, his approach stresses the role of cognition, or thinking, in the actions and skills people choose to acquire. His concept of self-efficacy has had a profound impact on lifespan research. We will encounter it many times in later chapters. (Photo courtesy: Stanford University, Department of Psychology)*

standards for behavior and a *sense of self-efficacy*—the belief that their own abilities and characteristics will help them succeed. These cognitions guide responses in particular situations (Bandura, 1997). For example, imagine a parent who often remarks, "I'm glad I kept working on that challenging task," who explains the value of persistence to her child, and who encourages it by saying, "I know you can do that homework very well!" As a result, the child starts to view himself as hardworking and high achieving and, from the many people available in the environment, selects models with these characteristics to copy. In this way, as individuals acquire attitudes, values, and convictions about themselves, they control their own learning and behavior.

■ CONTRIBUTIONS AND LIMITATIONS OF BEHAVIORISM AND SOCIAL LEARNING THEORY. Like psychoanalytic theory, behaviorism and social learning theory have been helpful in treating emotional and behavior problems. Yet the techniques are decidedly different. **Applied behavior analysis** refers to procedures that combine conditioning and modeling to eliminate undesirable behaviors and increase socially acceptable responses. It has been used to relieve a wide range of difficulties in children and adults, such as persistent aggression, language delays, and extreme fears (Pierce & Epling, 1995; Wolpe & Plaud, 1997).

Nevertheless, modeling and reinforcement do not provide a complete account of development. We will see in later sections that many theorists believe that behaviorism and social learning theory offer too narrow a view of important environmental influences. These extend beyond immediate reinforcements and modeled behaviors to the richness of the physical and social worlds. Finally, in emphasizing cognition and granting individuals an active role in their own learning, Bandura is unique among theorists whose work grew out of the behaviorist tradition. Behaviorism and social learning theory have been criticized for underestimating people's contributions to their own development.

PIAGET'S COGNITIVE-DEVELOPMENTAL THEORY

If one individual has influenced research on child development more than any other, it is Swiss cognitive theorist Jean Piaget (1896–1980). North American investigators had been aware of Piaget's work since 1930. However, they did not grant it much attention until 1960, mainly because his ideas were very much at odds with behaviorism, which dominated American psychology during the middle of the twentieth century (Beilin, 1992). Piaget did not believe that knowledge was imposed on a passive, reinforced child. According to his **cognitive-developmental theory**, children actively construct knowledge as they manipulate and explore their world, and their cognitive development takes place in stages.

■ *Through careful observations of and clinical interviews with children, Jean Piaget developed his comprehensive theory of cognitive development. His work has inspired more research on children than any other theory. (Photo courtesy: Yves de Braine/Black Star)*

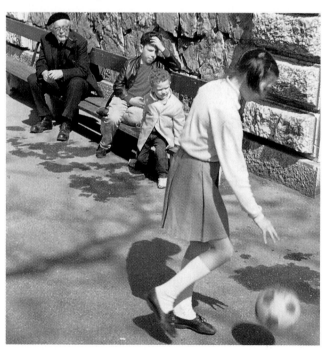

■ **PIAGET'S STAGES.** Piaget's view of development was greatly influenced by his early training in biology. Central to his theory is the biological concept of *adaptation* (Piaget, 1971). Just as the structures of the body are adapted to fit with the environment, so the structures of the mind develop during childhood to better fit with, or represent, the external world. In infancy and early childhood, children's understanding is very different from adults'. For example, Piaget believed that young babies do not realize that an object hidden from view—a favorite toy or even the mother—continues to exist. He also concluded that preschoolers' thinking is full of faulty logic. For example, children younger than age 7 commonly say that the amount of milk or lemonade changes when it is poured into a differently shaped container. According to Piaget, children eventually revise these incorrect ideas in their ongoing efforts to achieve an *equilibrium,* or balance, between internal structures and information they encounter in their everyday worlds (Beilin, 1992; Kuhn, 1992).

In Piaget's theory, children move through four broad stages of development, each of which is characterized by qualitatively distinct ways of thinking. Table 1.4 provides a brief description of Piaget's stages. In the *sensorimotor stage,* cognitive development begins with the baby's use of the senses and movements to explore the world. These action patterns evolve into the symbolic but illogical thinking of the preschooler in the *preoperational stage.* Then cognition is transformed into the more organized reasoning of the school-age child in the *concrete operational stage.* Finally, in the *formal operational stage,* thought becomes the complex, abstract reasoning system of the adolescent and adult.

■ **PIAGET'S METHODS OF STUDY.** Piaget devised special methods for investigating how children think. In the early part of his career, he carefully observed his three infant children and also presented them with everyday problems, such as an attractive object that could be grasped, mouthed, kicked, or searched for when hidden from view. From their reactions, Piaget derived his ideas about cognitive changes during the first 2 years.

In studying childhood and adolescent thought, Piaget took advantage of children's ability to describe their thinking. He adapted the clinical method of psychoanalysis, conducting open-ended *clinical interviews* in which a child's initial response to a task served as the basis for the next question he would ask. We will look at an example of a Piagetian clinical interview when we discuss research methods later in this chapter.

■ **CONTRIBUTIONS AND LIMITATIONS OF PIAGET'S THEORY.** Piaget's cognitive-developmental perspective convinced the field that children are active learners whose minds contain rich structures of knowledge. Besides in-

TABLE 1.4

Piaget's Stages of Cognitive Development

STAGE	PERIOD OF DEVELOPMENT	DESCRIPTION
Sensorimotor	Birth–2 years	Infants "think" by acting on the world with their eyes, ears, and hands. As a result, they invent ways of solving sensorimotor problems, such as pulling a lever to hear the sound of a music box, finding hidden toys, and putting objects in and taking them out of containers.
Preoperational	2–7 years	Preschool children use symbols to represent their earlier sensorimotor discoveries. Development of language and make-believe play takes place. However, thinking lacks the logical qualities of the two remaining stages.
Concrete operational	7–11 years	Children's reasoning becomes logical. School-age children understand that a certain amount of lemonade or play dough remains the same even after its appearance changes. They also organize objects into hierarchies of classes and subclasses. However, thinking falls short of adult intelligence. It is not yet abstract.
Formal operational	11 years on	The capacity for abstraction permits adolescents to reason with symbols that do not refer to objects in the real world, as in advanced mathematics. They can also think of all possible outcomes in a scientific problem, not just the the most obvious ones.

vestigating children's understanding of the physical world, Piaget explored their reasoning about the social world. As we will see in later chapters, his stages have sparked a wealth of research on children's conceptions of themselves, other people, and human relationships. Practically speaking, Piaget's theory encouraged the development of educational philosophies and programs that emphasize discovery learning and direct contact with the environment.

Despite Piaget's overwhelming contribution, in recent years his theory has been challenged. Research indicates that Piaget underestimated the competencies of infants and preschoolers. When young children are given tasks scaled down in difficulty, their understanding appears closer to that of the older child and adult than Piaget believed. Furthermore, many studies show that children's performance on Piagetian problems can be improved with training. This finding raises questions about his assumption that discovery learning rather than adult teaching is the best way to foster development. Finally, some lifespan investigators take issue with Piaget's conclusion that no major cognitive changes occur after adolescence. Several have proposed accounts of postformal thought that stress important transformations in adulthood (Arlin, 1984, 1989; Labouvie-Vief, 1985).

Today, the field of human development is divided over its loyalty to Piaget's ideas. Those who continue to find merit in the stage approach accept a modified view—one in which changes in thinking are not sudden and abrupt, but take place gradually (Case, 1992, 1998; Fischer & Bidell, 1998; Fischer & Pipp, 1984). Others have given up the idea

of cognitive stages in favor of a continuous approach to development—information processing, which we will take up in the next section.

 ASK YOURSELF . . .

■ *A 4-year-old becomes frightened of the dark and refuses to go to sleep at night. How would a psychoanalyst and a behaviorist differ in their views of how this problem developed?*

■ *What biological concept is emphasized in Piaget's cognitive-developmental approach? From which nineteenth-century theory did Piaget borrow this idea?*

Refer to Erikson's psychosocial stage of middle adulthood, generativity versus stagnation, described in Table 1.3 on page 18. Did Sofie, in the story at the beginning of this chapter, resolve this psychological conflict positively or negatively? Explain.

RECENT
THEORETICAL PERSPECTIVES

New ways of understanding the developing person are constantly emerging—questioning, building on, and enhancing the discoveries of earlier theories. Today, a burst of fresh approaches and research emphases is broadening our understanding of the lifespan.

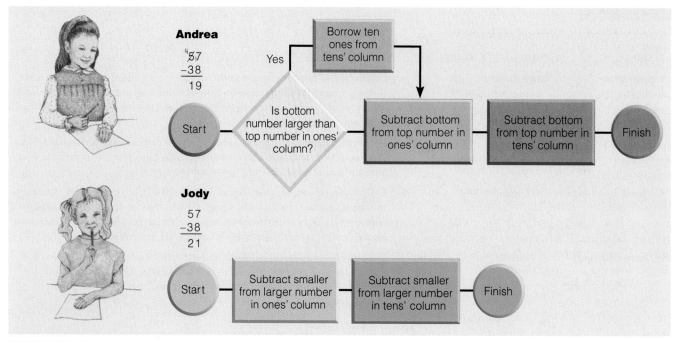

FIGURE 1.4

■ **Information-processing flowcharts showing the steps that two 8-year-olds used to solve a math problem.** In this two-digit subtraction problem with a borrowing operation, you can see that Andrea's procedure is correct, whereas Jody's results in a wrong answer.

INFORMATION PROCESSING

During the 1970s, researchers became disenchanted with behaviorism and disappointed in their efforts to verify Piaget's ideas completely. They turned to new trends in the field of cognitive psychology for ways to understand the development of thinking. Today, a leading perspective is **information processing,** a general approach that emerged with the design of complex computers that use mathematically specified steps to solve problems. These systems suggested to psychologists that the human mind might also be viewed as a symbol-manipulating system through which information flows (Klahr & MacWhinney, 1998). From presentation to the senses at *input* to behavioral responses at *output,* information is actively coded, transformed, and organized.

Information-processing researchers often use flowcharts to map the precise series of steps individuals use to solve problems and complete tasks, much like the plans devised by programmers to get computers to perform a series of "mental operations." Let's look at an example to clarify the usefulness of this approach. Figure 1.4 shows the steps that Andrea, an academically successful 8-year-old, used to complete a two-digit subtraction problem. It also shows the faulty procedure of Jody, who arrived at the wrong answer. The flowchart approach ensures that models of child and adult thinking will be very clear. By comparing the two procedures shown in Figure 1.4, we know exactly what is

necessary for effective problem solving and where Jody went wrong in searching for a solution. As a result, we can design an intervention to improve her reasoning.

A wide variety of information-processing models exist. Some (like the one in Figure 1.4) are fairly narrow in that they track the individual's mastery of one or a few tasks. Others describe the human cognitive system as a whole (Atkinson & Shiffrin, 1968; Lockhart & Craik, 1990). These general models are used as guides for asking questions about age changes in thinking. For example, does a child's ability to search the environment for information needed to solve a problem become more organized and planful with age? How much new information can preschoolers hold in memory compared to school-age children and adults? Why is speed of information processing slower among older than younger adults? Are declines in memory during old age evident on only some or all types of tasks?

Like Piaget's cognitive-developmental theory, information processing regards people as active, sense-making beings who modify their own thinking in response to environmental demands (Lutz & Sternberg, 1999). But unlike Piaget's theory, there are no stages of development. Rather, the thought processes studied—perception, attention, memory, planning strategies, categorization of information, and comprehension of written and spoken prose—are assumed to be similar at all ages but present to a lesser or greater extent. Therefore the view of development is one of continuous rather than stagewise change.

A great strength of the information-processing approach is its commitment to using careful, rigorous research methods to investigate cognition. Because it has provided precise accounts of how children and adults of different ages engage in many aspects of thinking, its findings have important implications for education (Geary, 1994; Siegler, 1998). But information processing has fallen short in some respects. Aspects of cognition that are not linear and logical, such as imagination and creativity, are all but ignored by this approach (Greeno, 1989). In addition, information-processing research has largely been conducted in artificial laboratory situations. Critics complain that it isolates thinking from important features of real-life learning situations. Recently, investigators have addressed this concern by focusing on more realistic activities. Today, they can be found studying conversations, stories, memory for everyday events, and strategies for performing academic tasks.

An advantage of having many theories is that they encourage one another to attend to previously neglected dimensions of people's lives. A unique feature of the final three perspectives we will discuss is the emphasis they place on *contexts for development.* The first of these views, ethology, emphasizes that human capacities have been shaped by a long evolutionary history in which our brains and bodies adapted to their surroundings.

ETHOLOGY

Ethology is concerned with the adaptive, or survival, value of behavior and its evolutionary history (Dewsbury, 1992; Hinde, 1989). Its origins can be traced to the work of Darwin. Two European zoologists, Konrad Lorenz and Niko Tinbergen, laid its modern foundations.

Watching diverse animal species in their natural habitats, Lorenz and Tinbergen observed behavior patterns that promote survival. The most well known of these is *imprinting,* the early following behavior of certain baby birds

that ensures that the young will stay close to the mother and be fed and protected from danger. Imprinting takes place during an early, restricted time period of development. If the mother goose is not present during this time but an object resembling her in important features is, young goslings may imprint on it instead (Lorenz, 1952).

Observations of imprinting led to a major concept in human development: the *critical period.* It refers to a limited time span during which the individual is biologically prepared to acquire certain adaptive behaviors but needs the support of an appropriately stimulating environment. Many researchers have conducted studies to find out whether complex cognitive and social behaviors must be learned during certain time periods. For example, if children are deprived of adequate food or physical and social stimulation during their early years, will their intelligence be impaired? If language is not mastered during early childhood, is the capacity to acquire it reduced?

As we address these and other similar questions in later chapters, we will discover that the term *sensitive period* offers a better account of human development than does the strict notion of a critical period (Bornstein, 1989). A **sensitive period** is a time that is optimal for certain capacities to emerge and in which the individual is especially responsive to environmental influences. However, its boundaries are less well defined than are those of a critical period. Development may occur later, but it is harder to induce at that time.

Inspired by observations of imprinting, British psychoanalyst John Bowlby (1969) applied ethological theory to the understanding of the human infant–caregiver relationship. He argued that attachment behaviors of babies, such as smiling, babbling, grasping, and crying, are built-in social signals that encourage the parent to approach, care for, and interact with the baby. By keeping the mother near, these behaviors help ensure that the infant will be fed, protected from danger, and provided with stimulation and affection necessary for healthy growth.

■ *Konrad Lorenz was one of the founders of ethology and a keen observer of animal behavior. He developed the concept of imprinting. Here, young geese who were separated from their mother and placed in the company of Lorenz during an early, sensitive period show that they have imprinted on him. They follow him about as he swims through the water, a response that promotes survival. (Photo courtesy: Nina Leen/Life Magazine/© Time Warner)*

■ *According to Lev Semenovich Vygotsky, many cognitive processes and skills are socially transferred from more knowledgeable members of society to children. Vygotsky's sociocultural theory helps us understand the wide variation in cognitive competencies from culture to culture. Vygotsky is pictured here with his daughter. (Photo courtesy: James V. Wertsch, Washington University)*

The development of attachment in humans is a lengthy process involving changes in psychological structures that lead the baby to form a deep affectional tie with the caregiver. Bowlby (1979) believed that this bond has lifelong consequences, affecting relationships "from cradle to grave" (p. 129). In later chapters, we will consider research that evaluates this assumption.

Observations by ethologists have shown that many aspects of social behavior, including emotional expressions, aggression, cooperation, and social play, resemble those of our primate ancestors. Today, efforts are also under way to apply an evolutionary perspective to cognitive development (Bjorklund, 1997; Siegler, 1996). Researchers are returning to the central question posed by Piaget: How must children and adults think to adapt to the environments in which they find themselves? We will explore some new answers in later chapters.

Although ethology emphasizes the genetic and biological roots of development, learning is also considered important because it lends flexibility and greater adaptiveness to behavior. Consequently, the interests of ethologists are broad. They want to understand the entire organism–environment system (Hinde, 1989; Miller, 1993). The evolutionary selection benefits of behavior are believed to be strongest in the first half of life—to ensure survival, reproduction, and effective parenting. As people age, social and cultural factors become increasingly important in generating and maintaining high levels of functioning (Smith & Baltes, 1999). The next contextual perspective we will discuss, Vygotsky's sociocultural theory, serves as an excellent complement to ethology, since it highlights social and cultural contexts for development.

VYGOTSKY'S SOCIOCULTURAL THEORY

The field of human development has recently seen a dramatic increase in studies addressing the cultural context of people's lives. Investigations that make comparisons across cultures, and among ethnic groups within cultures, provide insight into commonalities and individual differences in development. As a result, cross-cultural and multicultural research helps us untangle the contributions of biological and environmental factors to the timing, order of appearance, and diversity of children's and adults' behaviors (Greenfield, 1994).

In the past, cross-cultural studies focused on broad cultural differences in development—for example, whether children in one culture are more advanced in motor development or do better on intellectual tasks than children in another. However, this approach can lead us to conclude incorrectly that one culture is superior in enhancing development, whereas another is deficient. In addition, it does not help us understand the precise experiences that contribute to cultural differences in behavior.

Today, more research is examining the relationship of *culturally specific practices* to development. The contributions of Russian psychologist Lev Semenovich Vygotsky (1896–1934) have played a major role in this trend. Vygotsky's (1934/1987) perspective is called **sociocultural theory.** It focuses on how *culture*—the values, beliefs, customs, and skills of a social group—is transmitted to the next generation. According to Vygotsky, *social interaction*—in particular, cooperative dialogues with more knowledgeable members of society—is necessary for children to acquire the ways of thinking and behaving that make up a community's culture (Wertsch & Tulviste, 1992). Vygotsky believed that as adults and more expert peers help children master culturally meaningful activities, the communication between them becomes part of children's thinking. Once children internalize the essential features of these dialogues, they can use the language within them to guide their own thought and actions and acquire new skills (Berk, 2000).

Vygotsky's theory has been especially influential in the study of cognitive development. But Vygotsky's approach is quite different from Piaget's. Recall that Piaget did not regard direct teaching by adults as important. Instead, he emphasized children's active, independent efforts to make sense of their world. Vygotsky agreed with Piaget that children are active, constructive beings. But unlike Piaget, he viewed cognitive development as a *socially mediated process*—as dependent on the support that adults and more mature peers provide as children try new tasks. Finally, Vygotsky did not regard all children as moving through the same sequence of stages. Instead, as soon as children acquire language, their enhanced ability to communicate with others leads to continuous changes in thought and behavior that can vary greatly from culture to culture.

Although most research inspired by Vygotsky's theory focuses on children, his ideas apply to people of any age. A central theme is that cultures select tasks for their members, and social interaction surrounding those tasks leads to competencies essential for success in a particular culture. For example, in industrialized nations, teachers can be seen helping people learn to read, drive a car, or use a computer (Schwebel, Maher, & Fagley, 1990). Among the Zinacanteco Indians of southern Mexico, adult experts guide young girls as they master complicated weaving techniques (Childs & Greenfield, 1982). In Brazil, child candy sellers with little or no schooling develop sophisticated mathematical abilities as the result of buying candy from wholesalers, pricing it in collaboration with adults and experienced peers, and bargaining with customers on city streets (Saxe, 1988).

Findings like these reveal that children and adults develop unique strengths in every culture that are not present in others. A cultural perspective reminds us that research on development is based on only a small minority of humankind. We cannot assume that the developmental sequences we observe are "natural" or that the experiences fostering them are "ideal" without looking around the world.

At the same time, Vygotsky's emphasis on culture and social experience led him to neglect the biological side of development. Although he recognized the importance of biology, he said little about the role of heredity and brain growth in cognitive change. Furthermore, Vygotsky's emphasis on social transmission of knowledge meant that he placed less emphasis than did other theorists on children's capacity to shape their own development. Contemporary followers of Vygotsky grant the individual and society more balanced roles (Gauvain, 1999; Rogoff, 1998).

ECOLOGICAL SYSTEMS THEORY

Urie Bronfenbrenner, an American psychologist, is responsible for an approach to human development that has risen to the forefront of the field over the past two decades because it offers the most differentiated and complete account of contextual influences on development. **Ecological systems theory** views the person as developing within a complex *system* of relationships affected by multiple levels of the surrounding environment. Since the child's biological dispositions join with environmental forces to mold development, Bronfenbrenner recently characterized his perspective as a *bioecological model* (Bronfenbrenner & Morris, 1998).

Before Bronfenbrenner's (1979, 1989, 1993) theory, most researchers viewed the environment fairly narrowly —as limited to events and conditions immediately surrounding the individual. As Figure 1.5 shows, Bronfenbrenner expanded this view by envisioning the environment as a series of nested structures that includes but extends

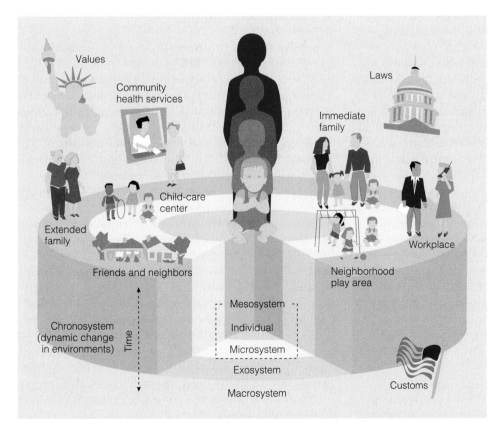

FIGURE 1.5

■ **Structure of the environment in ecological systems theory.** The *microsystem* concerns relations between the developing person and the immediate environment; the *mesosystem*, connections among immediate settings; the *exosystem*, social settings that affect but do not contain the developing person; and the *macrosystem*, the values, laws, customs, and resources of the culture that affect activities and interactions at all inner layers. The *chronosystem* is not a specific context. Instead, it refers to the dynamic, ever-changing nature of the person's environment.

■ *Urie Bronfenbrenner is the originator of ecological systems theory. He views the child as developing within a complex system of relationships affected by multiple levels of the surrounding environment, from immediate settings to broad cultural values, laws, and customs. (Photo courtesy: Urie Bronfenbrenner, Cornell University)*

beyond the home, school, neighborhood, and workplace settings in which people spend their everyday lives. Each layer of the environment is viewed as having a powerful impact on development.

■ THE MICROSYSTEM. The innermost level of the environment is the **microsystem,** which refers to activities and interaction patterns in the person's immediate surroundings. Bronfenbrenner emphasizes that to understand development at this level, we must keep in mind that all relationships are *bidirectional.* For example, adults affect children's behavior, but children's biologically and socially influenced characteristics—their physical attributes, personalities, and capacities—also influence the behavior of adults. For example, a friendly, attentive child is likely to evoke positive and patient reactions from parents, whereas an active, distractible youngster is more likely to be responded to with restriction and punishment (Danforth, Barkley, & Stokes, 1990). But whether either of these children experiences child-rearing practices that enhance or undermine development depends on environmental systems that surround and influence parent–child relationships.

■ THE MESOSYSTEM. The second level of Bronfenbrenner's model is the **mesosystem.** It refers to connections between microsystems that foster development. For example, a child's academic progress depends not just on activities that take place in classrooms. It is also promoted by parent involvement in school life and the extent to which academic learning is carried over into the home (Grolnick & Slowiaczek, 1994). Among adults, how well a person functions as spouse and parent at home is affected by experiences in the workplace, and vice versa (McLoyd, 1998).

■ THE EXOSYSTEM. The **exosystem** refers to social settings that do not contain the developing person but nevertheless affect experiences in immediate settings. These can be formal organizations, such as the board of directors in the individual's workplace or health and welfare services in the community. For example, flexible work schedules, paid maternity and paternity leave, and sick leave for parents whose children are ill are ways that work settings can help parents rear children and, indirectly, enhance the development of both adult and child. Exosystem supports can also be informal, such as social networks—friends and extended-family members who provide advice, companionship, and even financial assistance. Research confirms the negative impact of a breakdown in exosystem activities. Families who are socially isolated because they have few personal or community-based ties or who are affected by unemployment show increased rates of marital conflict and child abuse (Emery & Laumann-Billings, 1998).

■ THE MACROSYSTEM. The outermost level of Bronfenbrenner's model, the **macrosystem,** is not a specific context. Instead, it consists of the values, laws, customs, and resources of a particular culture. The priority that the macrosystem gives to the needs of children and adults affects the support they receive at inner levels of the environment. For example, in countries that require high-quality standards for child care and workplace benefits for employed parents, children are more likely to have favorable experiences in their immediate settings. And when the government provides a generous pension plan for retirees, it supports the well-being of the elderly.

■ A DYNAMIC, EVER-CHANGING SYSTEM. According to Bronfenbrenner (1995, 1997), the environment is not a static force that affects people in a uniform way. Instead, it is dynamic and ever-changing. Whenever individuals add or let go of roles or settings in their lives, the breadth of their microsystems changes. These shifts in contexts, or ecological transitions, as Bronfenbrenner calls them, take place throughout life and are often important turning points in development. Starting school, entering the workforce, marrying, becoming a parent, getting divorced, moving, and retiring are examples.

Bronfenbrenner refers to the temporal dimension of his model as the **chronosystem** (the prefix *chrono* means time). Changes in life events can be imposed externally. Alternatively, they can arise from within the person since individuals select, modify, and create many of their own settings and experiences. How they do so depends on their age; their physical, intellectual, and personality characteristics; and the environmental opportunities available to them. Therefore, in ecological systems theory, development is neither controlled by environmental circumstances nor driven by inner dispositions. Instead, people are products and producers of their environments, and therefore both people and their environments form a network of interdependent effects. We will see many more examples of these principles in later chapters.

ASK YOURSELF . . .

■ *What shortcoming of the information-processing approach is a strength of ethology, ecological systems theory, and Vygotsky's sociocultural theory?*

■ *What features of Vygotsky's sociocultural theory make it very different from Piaget's theory?*

🌳 *Is Bronfenbrenner's ecological systems theory compatible with assumptions of the lifespan perspective: development as lifelong, as multidirectional, as highly plastic, and as embedded in multiple contexts? Explain.*

COMPARING AND EVALUATING THEORIES

In the preceding sections, we reviewed theoretical perspectives that are major forces in modern human development research. They differ in many respects. First, they focus on different domains of development. Some, such as the psychoanalytic perspective and ethology, emphasize emotional and social development. Others, such as Piaget's cognitive-developmental theory, information processing, and Vygotsky's sociocultural theory, stress changes in cognition. The remaining approaches—behaviorism, social learning theory, ecological systems theory, and the lifespan perspective—discuss factors assumed to affect all aspects of development.

Second, every theory contains a point of view about what development is like. As we conclude our review of theoretical perspectives, take a moment to identify the stance that each takes on the three controversial issues presented at the beginning of this chapter. Then check your own analysis against the information given in Table 1.5 on page 28. If you had difficulty classifying any theory, return to the relevant section of this chapter and reread the description of that theory.

Finally, we have seen that theories have strengths and limitations. This may remind you of an important point we made earlier in this chapter—that no theory provides a complete account of development. As you read more about the lifespan in later chapters of this book, you may find it useful to keep a notebook in which you test your own theoretical likes and dislikes against the evidence. Don't be surprised if you revise your ideas many times, just as theorists have done throughout this century. By the end of the course, you will have built your own personal perspective. It might

turn out to be a blend of several theories, since each viewpoint we have discussed has contributed to what we know about the life course. And like the field as a whole, you will be left with some unanswered questions. I hope they will motivate you to continue your quest to understand human development in the years to come.

STUDYING DEVELOPMENT

In every science, theories, like those we've just reviewed, guide the collection of information, its interpretation, and its application to real-life situations. In fact, research usually begins with a prediction about behavior drawn from a theory, or what we call a *hypothesis*. But theories and hypotheses are only the beginning of the many activities that result in sound evidence on human development. Conducting research according to scientifically accepted procedures involves many steps and choices. Investigators must decide which participants, and how many, to include. Then they must figure out what the participants will be asked to do and when, where, and how many times each will need to be seen. Finally, they must examine relationships and draw conclusions from their data.

In the following sections, we examine research strategies commonly used in the field of human development. We begin with *research methods*—the specific activities of participants, such as taking tests, answering questionnaires, responding to interviews, or being observed. Then we turn to *research designs*—overall plans for research studies that permit the best possible test of the investigator's hypothesis. Finally, we discuss ethical issues involved in doing research with human participants.

At this point, you may be wondering, Why learn about research strategies? Why not leave these matters to research specialists and concentrate on what is already known about the developing person and how this knowledge can be applied? There are two reasons. First, each of us must be a wise and critical consumer of knowledge, not a naive sponge who soaks up facts about development. A basic appreciation of the strengths and limitations of research strategies becomes important in separating dependable information from misleading results. Second, individuals who work directly with children or adults are sometimes in a unique position to build bridges between research and practice by carrying out research studies on their own or in partnership with experienced investigators (Denner et al., 1999). At other times, they may have to provide information on how well their goals are being realized to justify continued financial support for their programs and activities. Under these circumstances, an understanding of research becomes essential practical knowledge.

TABLE 1.5

Stances of Major Theories on Basic Issues in Human Development

THEORY	CONTINUOUS OR DISCONTINUOUS DEVELOPMENT?	ONE COURSE OF DEVELOPMENT OR MANY?	NATURE OR NURTURE AS MORE IMPORTANT?
Psychoanalytic perspective	*Discontinuous:* Stages of psycho-sexual and psychosocial develop-ment are emphasized.	*One course:* Stages are assumed to be universal.	*Both nature and nurture:* Innate impulses channeled and controlled through child-rearing experiences. *The individual as stable:* Early experiences set the course of later development.
Behaviorism and social learning theory	*Continuous:* Development involves an increase in learned behaviors.	*Many possible courses:* Behaviors reinforced and modeled may vary from person to person.	*Emphasis on nurture:* Development is the result of conditioning and modeling. *The individual as open to change:* Early and later experiences are important.
Piaget's cognitive-developmental theory	*Discontinuous:* Stages of cognitive development are emphasized.	*One course:* Stages are assumed to be universal.	*Both nature and nurture:* Development occurs as the brain matures and children exercise their innate drive to discover reality in a gener-ally stimulating environment. *The individual as open to change:* Early and later experiences are important.
Information processing	*Continuous:* Children and adults show gradual changes in perception, attention, memory, and problem-solving skills.	*One course:* Typically addresses changes common to most or all children and adults.	*Both nature and nurture:* Children and adults are active, sense-making beings who modify their thinking as the brain develops and they confront new environmental demands. *The individual as open to change:* Early and later experiences are important.
Ethology	*Both continuous and discontinuous:* Children and adults gradually develop a wider range of adaptive behaviors. In addition, sensitive periods, in which qualitatively distinct capacities emerge fairly suddenly, are emphasized.	*One course:* Focuses on species-wide adaptive behaviors and sensitive periods.	*Both nature and nurture:* Evolved behavior patterns are stressed, but a stimulating envi-ronment must elicit them. *The individual as stable:* Biologically based behaviors combine with early experience to set the course of later development.
Vygotsky's sociocultural theory	*Continuous:* Through interaction with more expert members of society, children gradually acquire culturally adaptive skills.	*Many possible courses:* Socially mediated changes in thought and behavior vary from culture to culture.	*Both nature and nurture:* Brain development and dialogues with more knowledgeable members of society jointly contribute to new competencies. *The individual as open to change:* Early and later experiences are important.
Ecological systems theory	*Not specified.*	*Many possible courses:* Biological dispositions join with environmental forces at multiple levels to mold development in unique ways.	*Both nature and nurture:* Children's characteristics and the reactions of others affect each other in a bidirectional fashion. *The individual as open to change:* Early and later experiences are important.
Lifespan perspective	*Continuous and discontinuous:* Continuous gains and declines as well as discontinuous, stagewise emergence of new skills occur during all age periods.	*Many possible courses:* Develop-ment is embedded in multiple contexts that vary from person to person, leading to diverse pathways of change.	*Both nature and nurture:* Development is multidimensional, affected by an intricate blend of biological and social forces. *The individual as open to change:* Emphasizes high plasticity at all ages.

COMMON RESEARCH METHODS

How does a researcher choose a basic approach to gathering information? Common methods include sys-tematic observation, self-reports (such as questionnaires and interviews), clinical or case studies of a single individ-ual, and ethnographies of the life circumstances of a spe-cific group of people.

■ SYSTEMATIC OBSERVATION. To find out how people actually behave, a researcher may choose systematic obser-vation. Observations can be made in different ways. One approach is to go into the field, or natural environment, and observe the behavior of interest, a method called **natu-ralistic observation.**

A study of preschoolers' responses to their peers' distress provides a good example of this technique (Farver & Branstetter, 1994). Observing 3- and 4-year-olds in child-care centers, the researchers recorded each instance of crying and the reactions of nearby children—whether they ignored; watched curiously; commented on the child's unhappiness; scolded or teased; or shared, helped, or expressed sympathy. Caregiver behaviors, such as explaining why a child was crying, mediating conflict, or offering comfort, were noted to see if adult sensitivity was related to children's caring responses. A strong relationship emerged. The great strength of naturalistic observation is that investigators can see directly the everyday behaviors they hope to explain.

Naturalistic observation also has limitations. First, the presence of a watchful, unfamiliar individual may cause children and adults to react in unnatural ways. Second, not all individuals have the same opportunity to display a particular behavior in everyday life. In the study just described, some children might have witnessed a child crying more often than did others. For this reason, they might have displayed more compassion.

Researchers commonly deal with this difficulty by making **structured observations** in a laboratory. In this approach, the investigator sets up a situation that evokes the behavior of interest so that every participant has an equal opportunity to display the response. In one study, children's comforting behavior was observed by playing a tape recording of a baby crying in the next room. Using an intercom, children could either talk to the baby or push a button so they did not have to listen (Eisenberg et al., 1993). Notice how structured observation permits more control over the research situation. But its great disadvantage is that people do not necessarily behave in the laboratory as they do in everyday life.

The procedures used to collect systematic observations vary, depending on the nature of the research problem. Some investigators need to describe the entire stream of behavior—everything said and done over a certain time period. In one of my own studies, I wanted to find out how sensitive, responsive, and verbally stimulating caregivers were when they interacted with children in child-care centers (Berk, 1985). In this case, everything each caregiver said and did—even the amount of time she spent away from the children, taking coffee breaks and talking on the phone— was important. In other studies, only one or a few kinds of behavior are needed, and it is not necessary to preserve the entire behavior stream. In these instances, researchers use more efficient observation procedures in which they record only certain events or mark off behaviors on checklists.

Systematic observation provides invaluable information on how children and adults actually behave, but it tells us little about the reasoning that lies behind their responses. For this kind of information, researchers must turn to another type of method: self-reports.

■ SELF-REPORTS. Self-reports are instruments that ask participants to answer questions about their perceptions,

thoughts, abilities, feelings, attitudes, beliefs, and past experiences. They range from relatively unstructured clinical interviews, the method used by Piaget to study children's thinking, to highly structured interviews, questionnaires, and tests.

Let's look at an example of a **clinical interview,** in which Piaget questioned a 5-year-old child about his understanding of dreams:

> *Where does the dream come from?*—I think you sleep so well that you dream.—*Does it come from us or from outside?*—From outside.—*What do we dream with?* —I don't know.—*With the hands?. . . With nothing?* —Yes, with nothing.—*When you are in bed and you dream, where is the dream?*—In my bed, under the blanket. I don't really know. If it was in my stomach, the bones would be in the way and I shouldn't see it. —*Is the dream there when you sleep?*—Yes, it is in the bed beside me . . . —*You see the dream when you are in the room, but if I were in the room, too, should I see it?*—No, grownups don't ever dream.—*Can two people ever have the same dream?*—No, never.—*When the dream is in the room, is it near you?*—Yes, there! (pointing to 30 cm. in front of his eyes). (Piaget, 1926/1930, pp. 97–98)

Notice how Piaget used a flexible, conversational style to encourage the child to expand his ideas. Although a researcher interviewing more than one participant would typically ask the same first question to ensure a common task, individualized prompts are used to obtain a fuller picture of each person's reasoning (Ginsburg, 1997).

The clinical interview has two major strengths. First, it permits people to display their thoughts in terms that are as close as possible to the way they think in everyday life. Second, the clinical interview can provide a large amount of information in a fairly brief time period. For example, in an hour-long session, we can obtain a wide range of child-rearing information from a parent or extensive information on past and present life circumstances from an elder—much more than we could capture by observing for the same amount of time.

A major limitation of the clinical interview has to do with the accuracy with which people report their thoughts, feelings, and experiences. Some participants, desiring to please the interviewer, may make up answers that do not represent their actual thinking. When asked about past events, they may have trouble recalling exactly what happened. And because the clinical interview depends on verbal ability and expressiveness, it may underestimate the capacities of individuals who have difficulty putting their thoughts into words.

The clinical interview has also been criticized because of its flexibility. When questions are phrased differently for each participant, responses may be due to the manner of interviewing rather than to real differences in the way people think about a certain topic. **Structured interviews,** in which each participant is asked the same set of questions in the same way, can eliminate this problem. In addition, these instruments are much more efficient. Answers are briefer, and researchers can obtain written responses from an entire group of children or adults at the same time. Also, when structured interviews use multiple-choice, yes/no, and true/false formats, as is done on many tests and questionnaires, responses can be tabulated by machine. However, we must keep in mind that these approaches do not yield the same depth of information as a clinical interview. And they can still be affected by the problem of inaccurate reporting.

■ THE CLINICAL, OR CASE STUDY, METHOD. Earlier in this chapter, we discussed the **clinical, or case study, method** as an outgrowth of psychoanalytic theory, which stressed the importance of understanding a single life history. The clinical method brings together a wide range of information on one person, including interviews, observations, and sometimes test scores. The aim is to obtain as complete a picture as possible of that individual's psychological functioning and the experiences that led up to it.

Although clinical studies are usually carried out on children and adults who have serious emotional problems, they sometimes focus on exceptional, well-adjusted individuals. For example, the method has been used to find out what contributes to the accomplishments of *prodigies*—extremely gifted children who attain adult competence in a field before age 10 (Gardner, 1998). Consider Adam, a boy who read, wrote, and composed musical pieces before he was out of diapers. By age 4, Adam was deeply involved in mastering human symbol systems—BASIC for the computer, French, German, Russian, Sanskrit, Greek, ancient hieroglyphs, music, and mathematics. Adam's parents provided a home rich in stimulation and reared him with affection, firmness, and humor. They searched for schools in which he could both develop his abilities and form rewarding social relationships. Would Adam have realized his abilities without the chance combination of his special gift with nurturing, committed parents? Probably not, researchers concluded (Feldman & Goldsmith, 1991).

The clinical method yields case narratives that are rich in descriptive detail and that offer valuable insights into the multiplicity of factors that affect development. Nevertheless, like all other methods, it has drawbacks. Information is often collected unsystematically and subjectively, permitting too much leeway for researchers' theoretical preferences to bias their observations and interpretations. In addition, investigators cannot assume that their conclusions apply to anyone other than the person being studied. Even when patterns emerge across several cases, it is wise to try to confirm them with other research strategies.

■ METHODS FOR STUDYING CULTURE. A growing interest in the impact of culture has led researchers to adjust the methods we have just considered as well as tap procedures specially devised for cross-cultural and multicultural research. Which approach investigators choose depends on their research goals (Triandis, 1995, 1998).

Sometimes researchers are interested in characteristics believed to be universal but that vary in degree from one society to the next. These investigators might ask, Do parents make greater maturity demands of children in some cultures than in others? How strong are gender stereotypes in different nations? In each instance, several cultural groups will be compared, and all participants must be questioned or observed with equivalent measures. Therefore, researchers draw on the self-report and observational procedures we have already considered, adapting them through translation so they can be understood in each cultural context. For example, to study cultural variation in parenting attitudes, the same questionnaire, asking for ratings on such items as "If my child gets into trouble, I expect him or her to handle the problem mostly by himself or herself," is given to all participants (Chen et al., 1998).

At other times, researchers are far less certain that they can draw on their own cultural perspective to interpret another culture's practices. They want to uncover the *cultural meanings* of children's and adults' behaviors by becoming as familiar as possible with their way of life (Shweder et al., 1998). To achieve this goal, researchers rely on a method borrowed from the field of anthropology—**ethnography.** Like the clinical method, ethnographic research is largely a descriptive, qualitative technique. But instead of aiming to understand a single individual, it is directed toward understanding a culture or a distinct social group (Jessor, 1996; Shweder, 1996).

The ethnographic method achieves its goals through *participant observation.* Typically, the researcher lives with the cultural community for a period of months or years, participating in all aspects of its daily life. Extensive field notes, which consist of a mix of observations and self-reports from members of the culture and careful interpretations by the investigator, are gathered. Later, these notes are put together into a description of the community that tries to capture its unique values and social processes.

The ethnographic approach assumes that by entering into close contact with a social group, researchers can understand the beliefs and behavior of its members more accurately, in a way not possible with an observational visit, interview, or questionnaire. In some ethnographies, investigators focus on many aspects of experience, as one team of researchers did in describing what it is like to grow up in a small American town (Peshkin, 1978). In other instances, the research is limited to one or a few settings, such as home, school, or neighborhood life (LeVine et al., 1994; Peshkin, 1997; Valdés, 1998). Researchers interested in cultural comparisons may supplement traditional self-report and observational methods with ethnography if they suspect that unique meanings underlie cultural differences, as the Variations box on pages 32–33 reveals.

TABLE 1.6

Strengths and Limitations of Common Research Methods

METHOD	DESCRIPTION	STRENGTHS	LIMITATIONS
SYSTEMATIC OBSERVATION			
Naturalistic observation	Observation of behavior in natural contexts	Observations reflect participants' everyday lives.	Conditions under which participants are observed cannot be controlled.
Structured observation	Observation of behavior in a laboratory	Conditions of observation are the same for all participants.	Observations may not be typical of the way participants behave in everyday life.
SELF-REPORTS			
Clinical interview	Flexible interviewing procedure in which the investigator obtains a complete account of the participant's thoughts	Comes as close as possible to the way participants think in everyday life; great breath and depth of information can be obtained in a short time.	Participants may not report information accurately; flexible procedure makes comparing individuals' responses difficult.
Structured interviews, questionnaires, and tests	Self-report instruments in which each participant is asked the same questions in the same way	Standardized method of asking questions permits comparisons of participants' responses and efficient data collection and scoring.	Does not yield the same depth of information as a clinical interview; responses are still subject to inaccurate reporting.
CLINICAL METHOD (Case Study)	A full picture of a single individual's psychological functioning, obtained by combining interviews, observations, and test scores	Provides rich, descriptive insights into processes of development.	May be biased by researcher's theoretical preferences; findings cannot be applied to individuals other than the participant.
ETHNOGRAPHY	Understanding a culture or distinct social group through participant observation; by making extensive field notes, the researcher tries to capture the culture's unique values and social processes	Provides a more complete and accurate description than can be derived from a single observational visit, interview, or questionnaire.	May be biased by researcher's values and theoretical preferences; findings cannot be applied to individuals and settings other than the ones studied.

Ethnographers strive to minimize their influence on the culture being studied by becoming part of it. Nevertheless, at times their presence does alter the situation. And as with clinical research, investigators' cultural values and theoretical commitments sometimes lead them to observe selectively or misinterpret what they see. In addition, the findings of ethnographic studies cannot be assumed to generalize beyond the people and settings in which the research was conducted (Hammersley, 1992).

Before moving on to research designs, you may find it helpful to refer to Table 1.6, which summarizes the strengths and limitations of each research method we have just considered.

ASK YOURSELF . . .

The lifespan perspective points out that nonnormative events can affect development in powerful ways. Reread the description of nonnormative influences on page 12. Which method would be most likely to tap them?

■ *A researcher is interested in how elders experience daily life in different cultures. Which method should she use? Explain.*

GENERAL RESEARCH DESIGNS

In deciding on a research design, investigators choose a way of setting up a study that permits them to test their hypotheses with the greatest certainty possible. Two main types of designs are used in all research on human behavior: correlational and experimental.

■ CORRELATIONAL DESIGN. In a **correlational design,** researchers gather information on already-existing groups of individuals without altering their experiences in any way. Suppose we want to answer such questions as, Do parents' styles of interacting with children have any bearing on children's intelligence? Does the arrival of a baby influence a couple's marital satisfaction? Does the death of a spouse in old age affect the surviving partner's physical

IMMIGRANT YOUTHS: AMAZING ADAPTATION

During the past quarter century, a rising tide of immigrants has come to the United States, fleeing war and persecution in their homelands or otherwise seeking better life chances. Today, nearly 20 percent of the U.S. youth population has foreign-born parents; almost 30 percent of these youths are foreign born themselves (Fuligni, 1998). They are ethnically diverse; most are from Asian and Latin American countries, such as Korea, the Philippines, Vietnam, Cuba, El Salvador, and Mexico.

ACADEMIC ACHIEVEMENT AND ADJUSTMENT. Although educators and laypeople often assume that the transition to a new country has a negative impact on psychological well-being, recent evidence reveals that children of immigrant parents adapt amazingly well. Students who are first-generation (foreign-born) or second-generation (American-born with immigrant parents) achieve in school as well as or better than students of native-born parents. Their success is evident in many academic subjects, including English, even though they are likely to come from non-English-speaking homes (Fuligni, 1997; Rumbaut, 1997).

Findings on psychological adjustment resemble those on achievement. Compared with their agemates, adolescents from immigrant families are less likely to commit delinquent and violent acts, to use drugs and alcohol, and to have early sex. They are also in better health—less likely to be obese and to have missed school because of illness. And in terms of self-esteem, they feel as positively about themselves as do young people with native-born parents and report less emotional distress. These successes do not depend on having extensive time to adjust to a new way of life. The school performance and psychological well-being of immigrant high school students who recently arrived in the United States is as high—and sometimes higher—than that of students who come at younger ages (Fuligni, 1997, 1998; Rumbaut, 1997).

The outcomes just described are strongest for Asian youths, less dramatic for Hispanic adolescents (Fuligni, 1997; Kao & Tienda, 1995). Variations in parental education and income account for these ethnic differences. Still, even first- and second-generation youths from ethnic groups that face considerable economic hardship (such as Mexican and Southeast Asian) are remarkably successful (Harris, 2000; Kao, 2000). Factors other than income are responsible.

FAMILY AND COMMUNITY INFLUENCES. Ethnographies of immigrant populations reveal that uniformly, parents express the belief that education is the surest way to improve life chances. Consequently, they place a high value on their children's academic achievement (Suarez-Orozco & Suarez-Orozco, 1995; Zhou & Bankston, 1998). Aware of the challenges their children face, immigrant parents underscore the importance of trying hard. They remind their children that educational opportunities were not available in their native countries and that as a result, they themselves are often limited to menial jobs.

Adolescents from immigrant families internalize their parents' valuing of education, endorsing it more strongly than do agemates with American-born parents (Fuligni, 1997). Because minority ethnicities usually stress allegiance to family and community over individual goals, first- and second-generation young people feel a strong sense of obligation to their

health and psychological well-being? In these and many other instances, the conditions of interest are very difficult to arrange and control.

The correlational design offers a way of looking at relationships between participants' experiences or characteristics and their behavior or development. But correlational studies have one major limitation: we cannot infer cause and effect. For example, if we find that parental interaction does relate to children's intelligence, we would not know whether parents' behavior actually causes intellectual differences among children. In fact, the opposite is certainly possible. The behaviors of highly intelligent children may be so attractive that they cause parents to interact more favorably. Or a third variable that we did not even think about studying, such as amount of noise and distraction in the home, may be causing both maternal interaction and children's intelligence to change together in the same direction.

In correlational studies, and in other types of research designs, investigators often examine relationships by using a **correlation coefficient.** It is a number that describes how two measures, or variables, are associated with one another. We will encounter the correlation coefficient in discussing research findings throughout this book. So let's look at what it is and how it is interpreted. A correlation coefficient can range in value from +1.00 to −1.00. The *magnitude, or size, of the number* shows the *strength of the relationship.* A zero correlation indicates no relationship, but the closer the value is to +1.00 or −1.00, the stronger parents (Fuligni et al., 1999). They view school success as one of the most important ways they can repay their parents for the hardships they endured in coming to a new land. Both family relationships and school achievement protect these youths from risky behaviors, such as delinquency, early pregnancy, and drug use (refer to the Variations box on Resiliency on page 10).

Immigrant parents typically develop close ties to an ethnic community. It exerts additional control through a high consensus on values and constant monitoring of young people's whereabouts and activities. Consider Versailles Village, a low-income Vietnamese neighborhood in New Orleans, where the overwhelming majority of high school students say that obedience to parents and working hard are very important (Zhou & Bankston, 1998). A local education association focuses on promoting achievement by offering after-school homework tutoring sessions and English- and Vietnamese-language classes. Almost 70 percent of Vietnamese adolescents enroll, and attendance is positively related to school performance.

The comments of Vietnamese teenagers capture the power of these family and community forces:

Thuy Trang, age 14, middle-school Student of the Year: "When my

parents first immigrated from Vietnam, they spent every waking hour working hard to support a family. They have sacrificed for me, and I am willing to do anything for them."

Elizabeth, age 16, straight-A student, like her two older sisters: "My parents know pretty much all the kids in the neighborhood. . . . Everybody here knows everybody else. It's hard to get away with much." (Zhou & Bankston, 1998, pp. 93, 130)

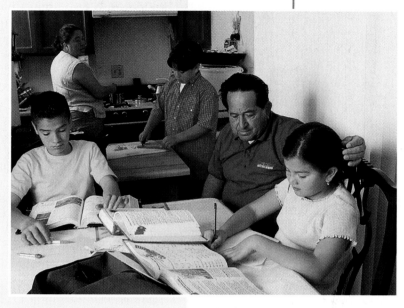

■ *This family recently immigrated from Ecuador to the United States. Ethnographic research reveals that parents in immigrant families typically place a high value on academic achievement and emphasize family and community over individual goals. Consequently, their adolescent children are likely to feel a strong sense of obligation to meeting their parents' expectations. They perform as well or better than students of native-born parents in school and are less likely to commit antisocial acts. (Photo courtesy: Michael Newman/PhotoEdit)*

the relationship that exists. For instance, a correlation of −.78 is high, −.52 is moderate, and −.18 is low. Note, however, that correlations of +.52 and −.52 are equally strong. The *sign of the number* (+ or −) refers to the *direction of the relationship*. A positive sign (+) means that as one variable increases, the other also increases. A negative sign (−) indicates that as one variable increases, the other decreases.

Let's take some examples to illustrate how a correlation coefficient works. In one study, a researcher found that a measure of maternal language stimulation at 13 months was positively correlated with the size of children's vocabularies at 20 months, at +.50 (Tamis-LeMonda & Bornstein, 1994). This is a moderately high correlation, which indicates that the more mothers talked to their infants, the more advanced

their children were in spoken language. In another study, a researcher reported that the extent to which mothers ignored their 10-month-olds' bids for attention was negatively correlated with children's willingness to comply with parental demands one year later—at −.46 for boys and −.36 for girls (Martin, 1981). These moderate correlations reveal that the more mothers ignored their babies, the less cooperative their children were during the second year of life.

Both of these investigations found a relationship between maternal behavior and children's early development. Although the researchers suspected that maternal behavior affected the children's responses, in neither study could they really be sure about cause and effect. However, finding a relationship in a correlational study suggests that track-

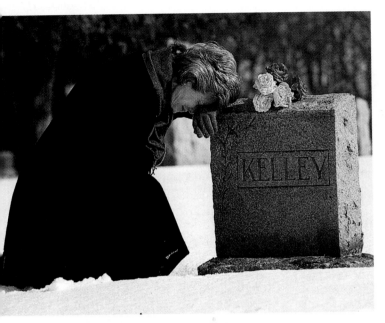

■ *Does the death of a spouse in old age affect the surviving part-ner's physical health and psychological well-being? A correla-tional design can be used to answer this question, but it does not permit researchers to determine the precise cause of their find-ings. (Photo courtesy: Murray/Monkmeyer Press)*

ing down its cause—with a more powerful experimental strategy, if possible—would be worthwhile.

■ EXPERIMENTAL DESIGN. Unlike correlational studies, **experimental design** permits inferences about cause and effect. In an experiment, the events and behaviors of inter-est are divided into two types: independent and dependent variables. The **independent variable** is the one anticipated by the investigator to cause changes in another variable. The **dependent variable** is the one the investigator expects to be influenced by the independent variable. Inferences about cause-and-effect relationships are possible because the researcher directly *controls or manipulates* changes in the independent variable. This is done by exposing partici-pants to two or more treatment conditions and comparing their performance on measures of the dependent variable.

In one *laboratory experiment,* researchers wanted to know if quality of interaction between adults (independent variable) affects young children's emotional reactions while playing with a familiar peer (dependent variable). Pairs of 2-year-olds were brought into a laboratory set up to look much like a family home. One group was exposed to a warm treatment in which two adults in the kitchen spoke in a friendly way while the children played in the living room. A second group received an angry treatment in which posi-tive communication between the adults was interrupted by an argument in which they shouted, complained, and slammed the door. The researchers *controlled* the treat-ments by carefully scripting the adults' behavior in each.

They kept other situational factors—such as the number and type of toys in the living room—constant, or identical, between the two treatments so they would not affect the re-sults. Children in the angry condition displayed much more distress (such as freezing in place, anxious facial expres-sions, and crying). They also showed more aggression to-ward their playmates than did children in the warm treatment (Cummings, Iannotti, & Zahn-Waxler, 1985). The experiment revealed that exposure to even short episodes of intense adult anger can trigger negative emo-tion and antisocial behavior in very young children.

In experimental studies, investigators must exert an-other form of control: reducing the chances that character-istics of participants will interfere with the accuracy of their findings. For example, in the study just described, if a greater number of children who had already learned to be-have in hostile and aggressive ways happened to end up in the angry treatment, we could not tell whether the indepen-dent variable or the children's background characteristics produced the results. **Random assignment** of participants to treatment conditions offers protection against this prob-lem. By using an evenhanded procedure, such as drawing numbers out of a hat or flipping a coin, the experimenter increases the likelihood that participants' characteristics will be equally distributed across treatment groups.

■ MODIFIED EXPERIMENTAL DESIGNS: FIELD AND NATURAL EXPERIMENTS. Most experiments are con-ducted in laboratories where researchers can achieve the maximum possible control over treatment conditions. But, as we have already indicated, findings obtained in lab-oratories may not always apply to everyday situations. The ideal solution to this problem is to do experiments in the field as a complement to laboratory investigations. In *field experiments,* investigators capitalize on rare opportunities to assign people randomly to different treatments in nat-ural settings. In the laboratory experiment that we just considered, we can conclude that the emotional climate es-tablished by adults affects children's behavior in the labo-ratory, but does it also do so in daily life?

Another study helps answer this question (Yarrow, Scott, & Waxler, 1973). This time, the research was carried out in a child-care center. A caregiver deliberately inter-acted differently with two groups of preschoolers. In one condition (the *nurturant treatment*), she modeled many instances of warmth and helpfulness. In the second condi-tion (the *control,* since it involved no treatment), she be-haved as usual, with no special emphasis on concern for others. Two weeks later, the researchers created several situ-ations that called for helpfulness. For example, a visiting mother asked each child to watch her baby for a few mo-ments, but the baby's toys had fallen out of the playpen. The investigators found that children exposed to the nur-turant treatment were much more likely to return toys to the baby than were those in the control condition.

Often researchers cannot randomly assign participants and manipulate conditions in the real world. Sometimes they can compromise by conducting *natural experiments.* Treatments that already exist, such as different child-care centers, schools, workplaces, or retirement villages, are compared. These studies differ from correlational research only in that groups of participants are carefully chosen to ensure that their characteristics are as much alike as possible. In this way, investigators rule out as best they can alternative explanations for their treatment effects. But despite these efforts, natural experiments are unable to achieve the precision and rigor of true experimental research.

To help you compare correlational and experimental designs, Table 1.7 summarizes their strengths and limitations. It also includes an overview of designs for studying development, to which we now turn.

DESIGNS FOR STUDYING DEVELOPMENT

Scientists interested in human development require information about the way research participants change over time. To answer questions about development, they must extend correlational and experimental approaches to include measurements at different ages. Longitudinal and cross-sectional designs are special *developmental* research strategies. In each, age comparisons form the basis of the research plan.

■ THE LONGITUDINAL DESIGN. In a **longitudinal design,** a group of participants is studied repeatedly at different ages, and changes are noted as the participants mature. The time spanned may be relatively short (a few months to several years) or very long (a decade or even a lifetime). The longitudinal approach has two major strengths. First, since it tracks the performance of each person over time, researchers can identify common patterns of development as well as individual differences. Second, longitudinal studies permit investigators to examine relationships between early and later events and behaviors. Let's take an example to illustrate these ideas.

A group of researchers wondered whether children who display extreme personality styles—either angry and explosive or shy and withdrawn—retain the same dispositions when they become adults. In addition, they wanted to know what kinds of experiences promote stability or change in personality and what consequences explosiveness and shyness have for long-term adjustment. To answer these questions, the researchers delved into the archives of the Guidance Study, a well-known longitudinal investigation initiated in 1928 at the University of California, Berkeley, and continued over several decades (Caspi, Elder, & Bem, 1987, 1988).

Results revealed that the two personality styles were only moderately stable. Between ages 8 and 30, a good

TABLE 1.7
Strengths and Limitations of Research Designs

DESIGN	DESCRIPTION	STRENGTHS	LIMITATIONS
GENERAL			
Correlational	The investigator obtains information on already existing groups, without altering participants' experiences.	Permits study of relationships between variables.	Does not permit inferences about cause-and-effect relationships.
Experimental	The investigator manipulates an independent variable and looks at its effect on a dependent variable; can be conducted in the laboratory or natural environment.	Permits inferences about cause-and-effect relationships.	When conducted in the laboratory, findings may not apply to the real world; when conducted in the field, control over the treatment is usually weaker than in the laboratory.
DEVELOPMENTAL			
Longitudinal	The investigator studies the same group of participants repeatedly at different ages.	Permits study of common patterns and individual differences in development and relationships between early and later events and behaviors.	Age-related changes may be distorted because of participant dropout, practice effects, and cohort effects.
Cross-sectional	The investigator studies groups of participants differing in age at the same point in time.	More efficient than the longitudinal design. Not plagued by such problems as participant dropout and practice effects.	Does not permit study of individual developmental trends. Age differences may be distorted because of cohort effects.
Longitudinal-sequential	The investigator studies two or more groups of participants born in different years, following each group longitudinally.	Permits both longitudinal and cross-sectional comparisons. Reveals existence of cohort effects.	May have the same problems as longitudinal and cross-sectional strategies, but the design itself helps identify difficulties.

IMPACT OF HISTORICAL TIMES ON THE LIFE COURSE: THE GREAT DEPRESSION AND WORLD WAR II

Economic disaster, wars, and periods of rapid social change can profoundly affect people's lives. Yet their impact depends on when they strike during the life course. Glen Elder (1974) capitalized on the extent to which families experienced economic hardship during the Great Depression of the 1930s to study its impact on lifespan development. He delved into the vast archives of two major longitudinal studies: (1) the Oakland Growth Study, an investigation of individuals born in the early 1920s who were adolescents when the Depression took its toll; and (2) the Guidance Study, whose participants were born in the late 1920s and were young children when their families faced severe economic losses.

In both cohorts, relationships changed when economic deprivation struck. As unemployed fathers lost status, mothers were granted greater control over family affairs. This reversal of traditional gender roles often sparked conflict. Fathers sometimes became explosive and punitive toward their children. At other times, they withdrew from family interaction into passivity and depression. Mothers often became frantic with worry over the well-being of their husbands and chil-

dren, and many entered the labor force to make ends meet (Elder, Liker, & Cross, 1984).

OUTCOMES FOR THE ADOLESCENT COHORT. Although unusual burdens were placed on them as family lives changed, the Oakland Growth Study cohort—especially the boys—weathered economic hardship quite well. As adolescents, they were too old to be wholly dependent on their highly stressed parents, and their energies were often channeled into productive activities. Boys spent less time at home as they searched for part-time jobs, and many turned toward adults and peers outside the family for emotional support. Girls took over the responsibility of household chores and caring for younger siblings. Their greater involvement in family affairs led them to be exposed to more parental conflict and unhappiness. Consequently, adjustment of adolescent girls in economically deprived homes was somewhat less favorable than that of adolescent boys (Elder, Van Nguyen, & Caspi, 1985).

These changes in adolescents' lives had major consequences for their future aspirations. Girls' interests focused on home and family even more than was typical for that time period, and they were less

likely to think about college and careers. Boys learned that economic resources could not be taken for granted, and they tended to make a very early commitment to an occupational choice.

The impact of the Depression continued to be apparent as adolescents entered adulthood. Girls from economically deprived homes remained committed to domestic life, and many married at an early age. Men had a strong desire for economic security, and they changed jobs less often than those from nondeprived backgrounds. The chance to become a parent was especially important to men whose lives had been disrupted by the Depression. Perhaps because they felt a rewarding career could not be guaranteed, these men viewed children as the most enduring benefit of their adult lives.

OUTCOMES FOR THE CHILD COHORT. Unlike the Oakland Growth Study cohort, the Guidance Study participants were within the years of intense family dependency when the Depression struck. For young boys (who, as we will see in later chapters, are especially prone to adjustment problems in the face of family stress), the impact of economic strain was severe. They showed emotional diffi-

number of individuals remained the same, whereas others changed substantially. When stability did occur, it appeared to be due to a "snowballing effect," in which children evoked responses from adults and peers that acted to maintain their dispositions (Caspi, 1998). In other words, explosive youngsters were likely to be treated with anger and hostility (to which they reacted with even greater unruliness), whereas shy children were apt to be ignored.

Persistence of extreme personality styles affected many areas of adult adjustment. For men, the results of early explosiveness were most apparent in their work lives, in the form of conflicts with supervisors, frequent job changes, and unemployment. Since few women in this sample of an

earlier generation worked after marriage, their family lives were most affected. Explosive girls grew up to be hotheaded wives and parents who were especially prone to divorce. Sex differences in the long-term consequences of shyness were even greater. Men who had been withdrawn in childhood were delayed in marrying, becoming fathers, and developing stable careers. Because a withdrawn, unassertive style was socially acceptable for females, women who had shy personalities showed no special adjustment problems.

■ PROBLEMS IN CONDUCTING LONGITUDINAL RESEARCH. Despite their strengths, longitudinal investigations pose a number of problems. For example, particiculties and poor attitudes toward school and work that persisted through the teenage years (Elder & Caspi, 1988; Elder, Caspi, & Van Nguyen, 1986).

But as the Guidance Study sample became adolescents, another major historical event occurred: in 1941, the United States entered World War II. Thousands of men left their communities for military bases—conditions that sparked dramatic life changes. For most young soldiers, war mobilization broke the hold of family hardship and vanishing opportunity. It broadened their range of knowledge and experience. It also granted time out from civilian responsibilities, giving many soldiers a chance to consider where their lives were going. And the GI Bill of Rights enabled them to expand their education and acquire new skills after the war. By middle adulthood, the Guidance Study war veterans had reversed the early negative impact of the Great Depression. They were more successful educationally and occupationally than their counterparts who had not entered the service (Elder & Hareven, 1993).

Clearly, cultural-historical change does not have a uniform impact on development. Outcomes can vary considerably, depending on the pattern of historical events and the age at which they take place.

■ *The Great Depression of the 1930s left this farm family without a steady income. The adolescent girl (in the back row on the far right) may have been more negatively affected by economic hardship than her brother (second from left). And overall, younger children probably suffered more than older children. (Culver Pictures)*

pants may move away or drop out of the research for other reasons. This changes the original sample so it no longer represents the population to whom researchers would like to generalize their findings. Also, from repeated study, people may become "test-wise." Their performance may improve as a result of *practice effects*—better test-taking skills and increased familiarity with the test—not because of factors commonly associated with development.

But the most widely discussed threat to longitudinal findings is **cohort effects,** another term that researchers use for *history-graded influences* (see page 12). Recall that cohorts are individuals born in the same time period who are influenced by a particular set of historical and cultural

conditions. Results based on one cohort may not apply to people developing in other times. For example, in the study of personality styles described in the preceding section, we might ask whether the sex differences obtained are still true, in view of recent changes in gender roles in our society. And a longitudinal study of the lifespan would probably result in quite different findings if it were carried out in the first decade of the twenty-first century, around the time of World War II, or during the Great Depression of the 1930s. (See the Lifespan Vista box above.)

■ THE CROSS-SECTIONAL DESIGN. The length of time it takes for many behaviors to change, even in limited longitudinal studies, has led researchers to turn toward a more convenient strategy for studying development. In the **cross-sectional design,** groups of people differing in age are studied at the same point in time. Because participants are measured only once, researchers do not need to be concerned about such difficulties as participant dropout or practice effects, which plague the longitudinal design.

An investigation in which students in grades 3, 6, 9, and 12 filled out a questionnaire about their sibling relationships provides a good illustration (Buhrmester & Furman, 1990). Findings revealed that sibling interaction was characterized by greater equality and less power assertion with age. Also, feelings of sibling companionship declined during adolescence. The researchers thought that these age changes were due to several factors. As later-born children become more competent and independent, they no longer need and are probably less willing to accept direction from older siblings. In addition, as adolescents move from psychological dependence on the family to greater involvement with peers, they may have less time and emotional need to invest in siblings. These intriguing ideas about the development of sibling relationships, as we will see in Chapter 12, have been confirmed in subsequent research.

■ PROBLEMS IN CONDUCTING CROSS-SECTIONAL RESEARCH. The cross-sectional design is a very efficient strategy for describing age-related trends. But when researchers choose it, they are short-changed in the kind of information they can obtain about development. Evidence about change at the level at which it actually occurs—the individual—is not available. For example, in the cross-sectional study of sibling relationships just discussed, comparisons are limited to age-group averages. We cannot tell if important individual differences exist in the development of sibling ties. Indeed, recent longitudinal findings reveal that children vary considerably in the changing quality of their sibling relationships, some becoming more supportive and intimate and others becoming increasingly distant with age (Dunn, Slomkowski, & Beardsall, 1994).

Cross-sectional studies—especially those that cover a wide age span—have another problem. Like longitudinal research, they can be threatened by cohort effects. For example, comparisons of 10-year-old cohorts, 20-year-old cohorts, and 30-year-old cohorts—groups born and reared in different years—may not really represent age-related changes. Instead, they may reflect unique experiences associated with the historical periods in which the age groups were growing up.

■ IMPROVING DEVELOPMENTAL DESIGNS. To overcome some of the limitations of longitudinal and cross-sectional research, investigators sometimes combine the two approaches. One way of doing so is the **longitudinal-sequential design.** It is called a sequential design because it is composed of a sequence of samples (two or more different age groups), each of which is followed longitudinally for a number of years.

The design has two advantages. First, it permits us to find out whether cohort effects are operating by comparing people of the same age who were born in different years. Using the example shown in Figure 1.6, we can compare the behaviors of the three samples at ages 20, 30, and 40. If they do not differ, we can rule out cohort effects. Second, we can make longitudinal and cross-sectional comparisons. If outcomes are similar in both, then we can be especially confident about our findings.

In a study that used the design in Figure 1.6, researchers wanted to find out whether adult personality development progresses as Erikson's psychosocial theory predicts (Whitbourne et al., 1992). Questionnaires measuring Erikson's stages were given to three cohorts of 20-year-olds, each born a decade apart. The cohorts have been, and will continue to be, reassessed every 10 years. Consistent with Erikson's theory, longitudinal and cross-sectional gains in identity and intimacy occurred between ages 20 and 30—a trend unaffected by historical time period. But a powerful cohort effect emerged for consolidation of the sense of industry: At age 20, Cohort 1 scored substantially below Cohorts 2 and 3. Look at Figure 1.6 again, and notice that members of Cohort 1 reached age 20 in the mid-1960s. As college students, they were part of a political protest movement that reflected disenchantment with the work ethic. Once out of college, they caught up with the other cohorts, perhaps as a result of experiencing the pressures of the work world.

To date, only a handful of longitudinal-sequential studies have been conducted. Yet the design permits researchers to profit from the strengths of both longitudinal and cross-sectional strategies. And in uncovering cohort effects, it also helps explain diversity in development (Magnusson & Stattin, 1998).

■ **ASK YOURSELF . . .**

 A researcher compares older adults with chronic heart disease to those who are free of major health problems and finds that the first group scores much lower on mental tests. Should the researcher conclude that heart disease causes declines in intellectual functioning in late adulthood? Are other interpretations possible? Explain.

■ *A researcher wants to find out if children enrolled in child-care centers during the first few years of life achieve as well in elementary school as those reared fully at home by parents. Which developmental design, longitudinal or cross-sectional, is appropriate for answering this question? Why?*

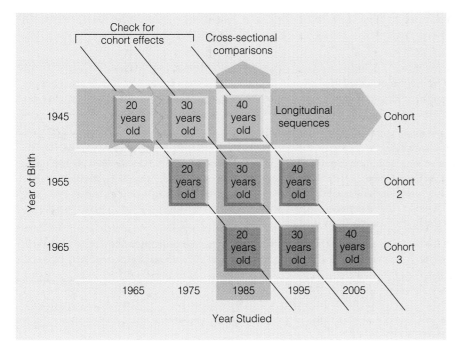

FIGURE 1.6

■ **Example of a longitudinal-sequential design.** Three cohorts, born in 1945 (blue), 1955 (pink), and 1965 (green), are followed longitudinally from 20 to 40 years of age. The design permits the researcher to check for cohort effects by comparing people of the same age who were born in different years. In a study that used this design, the Cohort 1 20-year-olds differed substantially from the 20-year-olds in Cohorts 2 and 3, indicating powerful history-graded influences. The longitudinal-sequential design also permits longitudinal and cross-sectional comparisons. Similar outcomes lend additional confidence in the results.

ETHICS IN LIFESPAN RESEARCH

Research into human behavior creates ethical issues because, unfortunately, the quest for scientific knowledge can sometimes exploit people. For this reason, special guidelines for research have been developed by the federal government, funding agencies, and research-oriented associations, such as the American Psychological Association (1994). Table 1.8 on page 40 presents a summary of basic research rights drawn from these guidelines. Once you have examined them, read the following research situations, each of which poses a serious ethical dilemma. What precautions do you think should be taken in each instance?

■ In a study of moral development, an investigator wants to assess children's ability to resist temptation by videotaping their behavior without their knowledge. Seven-year-olds are promised an attractive prize for solving some very difficult puzzles. They are also told not to look at a classmate's correct solutions, which are deliberately placed at the back of the room. If the researcher has to tell children ahead of time that cheating is being studied or that their behavior is being closely monitored, he will destroy the purpose of his study.

■ A researcher wants to study the impact of mild daily exercise on the physical and mental health of elderly patients in nursing homes. He consults each resident's doctor to make sure that the exercise routine will not be harmful. But when he seeks the consent of the residents themselves, he finds that many do not comprehend the purpose of the research. And some appear to agree simply to relieve feelings of isolation and loneliness.

As these examples indicate, when children or the aged take part in research, the ethical concerns are especially complex. Immaturity makes it difficult or impossible for children to evaluate for themselves what participation in research will mean. And since mental impairment rises with very advanced age, some older adults cannot make voluntary and informed choices. The life circumstances of others make them unusually vulnerable to pressure for participation (Kimmel & Moody, 1990; Society for Research in Child Development, 1993).

Virtually every committee that has worked on developing ethical principles for research has concluded that conflicts arising in research situations often cannot be resolved with simple right or wrong answers (Stanley & Seiber, 1992). The ultimate responsibility for the ethical integrity of research lies with the investigator. However, researchers are advised or, in the case of federally funded research, required to seek advice from others. Special committees exist in colleges, universities, and other institutions for this purpose. These committees weigh the costs of the research to participants in terms of inconvenience and possible psychological or physical injury against the study's value for advancing knowledge and improving conditions of life. If there are any negative implications for the safety and welfare of participants that the worth of the research does not justify, then preference is always given to the interests of the research participant.

TABLE 1.8

Rights of Research Participants

RESEARCH RIGHT	DESCRIPTION
Protection from harm	Participants have the right to be protected from physical or psychological harm in research. If in doubt about the harmful effects of research, investigators should seek the opinion of others. When harm seems possible, investigators should find other means for obtaining the desired information or abandon the research.
Informed consent	Participants, including children and the elderly, have the right to have explained to them, in language appropriate to their level of understanding, all aspects of the research that may affect their willingness to participate. When children are participants, informed consent of parents as well as others who act on the child's behalf (such as school officials) should be obtained, preferably in writing. Elderly people who are cognitively impaired should be asked to appoint a surrogate decision maker. If they cannot do so, then someone should be named by an ethics committee that includes relatives and professionals who know the person well. All participants have the right to discontinue participation in the research at any time.
Privacy	Participants have the right to concealment of their identity on all information collected in the course of research. They also have this right with respect to written reports and any informal discussions about the research.
Knowledge of results	Participants have the right to be informed of the results of research in language that is appropriate to their level of understanding.
Beneficial treatments	If experimental treatments believed to be beneficial are under investigation, participants in control groups have the right to alternative beneficial treatments if they are available.

Sources: American Psychological Association, 1994; Cassel, 1987, 1988; Society for Research in Child Development, 1993.

The ethical principle of *informed consent* requires special interpretation when participants cannot fully appreciate the research goals and activities. Parental consent is meant to protect the safety of children whose ability to decide is not yet mature. For children 7 years and older, their own informed consent should be obtained in addition to parental consent. Around age 7, changes in children's thinking permit them to better understand simple scientific principles and the needs of others. Researchers should respect and enhance these new capacities by providing school-age children with a full explanation of research activities in language that children can understand (Fisher, 1993; Thompson, 1990b). Extra care must be taken when telling children that the information they provide will be kept confidential and that they can end their participation at any time. Children may not understand, and sometimes do not believe, these promises (Abramovitch et al., 1991, 1995).

Most older adults require no more than the usual informed consent procedures. Researchers should not stereotype the elderly as incompetent to decide for themselves about participation (Schaie, 1988). Nevertheless, extra measures must be taken for those who are cognitively impaired or in settings for care of the chronically ill. Sometimes these individuals may agree to participate simply to obtain rewarding social interaction. Yet participation should not be automatically withheld, since it can result in personal as well as

scientific benefits (Cassel, 1987). In these instances, potential participants should be asked to appoint a surrogate decision maker. If they cannot do so, then someone should be named by an ethics committee that includes relatives and professionals who know the person well. As an added precaution, if the elderly person is incapable of consenting and the risks of the research are more than minimal, then the study should not be done unless it is likely to result in direct benefits to the participant (Cassel, 1988).

Finally, all ethical guidelines advise that special precautions be taken in the use of deception and concealment, as occurs when researchers observe people from behind one-way mirrors, give them false feedback about their performance, or do not tell them the truth regarding what the research is about. When these kinds of procedures are used, *debriefing*, in which the investigator provides a full account and justification of the activities, occurs after the research session is over. Debriefing should also take place with children, but it does not always work as well. Despite explanations, children may come away from the situation with their belief in the honesty of adults undermined. Ethical standards permit deception if investigators satisfy institutional committees that such practices are necessary. Nevertheless, since deception may have serious emotional consequences for some youngsters, researchers should try to come up with other procedures when children are involved (Cooke, 1982).

HUMAN DEVELOPMENT AS A SCIENTIFIC, INTERDISCIPLINARY, AND APPLIED FIELD

What is human development, and what factors stimulated expansion of the field?

- **Human development** is an inter-disciplinary field devoted to understanding human constancy and change throughout the lifespan. Research on human development has been stimulated by both scientific curiosity and social pressures to better people's lives.

BASIC ISSUES

Discuss three basic issues on which theories of human development take a stance.

- **Theories** of human development take a stance on three basic issues: (1) Is development a **continuous** process, or does it follow a series of **discontinuous stages?** (2) Is there one general course of development that characterizes all individuals, or are there many possible courses depending on the **contexts** in which children grow up? (3) Is development determined primarily by nature or nurture? The position that theories take on the **nature–nurture controversy** is related to their stance on the issue of **stability versus change** over the life course.

THE LIFESPAN PERSPECTIVE: A BALANCED POINT OF VIEW

Describe the lifespan perspective on development.

- The **lifespan perspective** is a bal-anced view that recognizes great complexity in human change and the factors that underlie it. According to this view, development is lifelong; no age period is supreme

in its impact on the future path of change. The lifespan perspective also assumes that development is multidirectional (affected by a blend of biological, psychological, and social forces), multidirectional (a joint expression of growth and decline), and highly plastic (open to changed with the support of new experiences).

- Furthermore, the lifespan perspec-tive regards the life course as embed-ded in multiple contexts. Although these contexts operate in an inter-connected fashion, they can be organized into three categories: (1) **age-graded influences** that are predictable in timing and duration; (2) **history-graded influences,** forces unique to a particular histori-cal era; and (3) **nonnormative in-fluences,** events unique to one or a few individuals.

HISTORICAL FOUNDATIONS

Describe major historical influences on modern theories of development.

- Modern theories of human develop-ment have roots extending far into the past. In medieval times, children were regarded as miniature adults, a view called **preformationism.** By the sixteenth century, childhood had become a distinct phase of the life course. However, the Puritan belief in original sin led to a harsh philoso-phy of child rearing. The Enlighten-ment brought new ideas favoring more humane child treatment. Locke's **tabula rasa** furnished the basis for twentieth-century behaviorism. Rous-seau's **noble savage** foreshadowed the concepts of stage and **maturation.**

- In the eighteenth and early nineteenth centuries, two German philosophers extended conceptions of development through adulthood. Tetens and Carus anticipated many aspects of the con-temporary lifespan perspective.

- Darwin's theory of evolution influ-enced important twentieth-century theories and inspired scientific child study. In the early twentieth century, Hall and Gesell introduced the **normative approach,** which produced a large body of descriptive facts about children. Binet and Simon constructed the first success-ful intelligence test, initiating the mental testing movement.

MID-TWENTIETH-CENTURY THEORIES

What theories influenced human development research in the mid-twentieth century?

- In the 1930s and 1940s, psychiatrists and social workers turned to the **psychoanalytic perspective** for help in treating people's psychological problems. In Freud's **psychosexual theory,** the individual moves through five stages, during which three portions of the personality—id, ego, and superego—become integrated. Erikson's **psychosocial theory** builds on Freud's theory by emphasizing the development of culturally relevant attitudes and skills and the lifespan nature of development.

- Academic psychology also influ-enced the study of human develop-ment. From **behaviorism** and **social learning theory** came the principles of conditioning and modeling and practical procedures of **applied behavior analysis** to eliminate undesirable behaviors and increase socially acceptable responses.

- In contrast to behaviorism, Piaget's **cognitive-developmental theory** emphasizes an active individual with a mind inhabited by rich struc-tures of knowledge. According to Piaget, children move through four stages, beginning with the baby's sensorimotor action patterns and ending with the elaborate, abstract reasoning system of the adolescent. Piaget's work has stimulated a wealth of research on children's thinking and encouraged educational programs that emphasize discovery learning.

RECENT THEORETICAL PERSPECTIVES

Describe recent theoretical perspectives on human development.

■ **Information processing** views the mind as a complex, symbol-manipulating system, operating much like a computer. This approach helps investigators achieve a detailed understanding of what individuals of different ages do when faced with tasks and problems. Information processing regards the thought processes of children and adults as similar and development as a matter of continuous change. Its findings have important implications for education.

■ Three contemporary theories place special emphasis on contexts for development. **Ethology** stresses the evolutionary origins and adaptive value of behavior and inspired the **sensitive period** concept.

■ Vygotsky's **sociocultural theory** has enhanced our understanding of cultural influences, especially on cognitive development. Through cooperative dialogues with more expert members of society, children and adults acquire culturally relevant knowledge and skills.

■ In **ecological systems theory,** nested layers of the environment—**microsystem, mesosystem, exosystem,** and **macrosystem**—are seen as major influences on the developing person. The **chronosystem** represents the dynamic, ever-changing nature of environmental influences.

COMPARING AND EVALUATING THEORIES

Identify the stance taken by each major theory on the three basic issues of human development.

■ Theoretical perspectives that are major forces in human development research vary in their focus on different domains of development, in their view of the nature of development, and in their strengths and weaknesses. (For a full summary, see Table 1.4 on page 28.)

STUDYING DEVELOPMENT

Describe commonly used methods in research on human development.

■ **Naturalistic observations,** gathered in children's and adults' everyday environments, permit researchers to see directly the everyday behaviors they hope to explain. In contrast, **structured observations** take place in laboratories, where every participant has an equal opportunity to display the behaviors of interest.

■ Self-report methods can be flexible and open-ended like the **clinical interview.** Alternatively, **structured interviews,** tests, and questionnaires, which permit efficient administration and scoring, can be given. Investigators use the **clinical, or case study, method** when they desire an in-depth understanding of a single individual.

■ A growing interest in the impact of culture has prompted researchers to adapt observational and self-report methods to permit direct comparisons of cultures. To uncover the cultural meanings of children's and adults' behaviors, researchers rely on a method borrowed from the field of anthropology—**ethnography.** It uses participant observation to understand the unique values and social processes of a culture or distinct social group.

Distinguish between correlational and experimental research designs, noting the strengths and limitations of each.

■ Two main types of design are used in all research on human behavior. The **correlational design** examines relationships between variables as they happen to occur, without any intervention. The **correlation coefficient** is often used to measure the association between variables. Correlational studies do not permit inferences about cause and effect. However, their use is justified when it is difficult or impossible to control the variables of interest.

■ An **experimental design** permits inferences about cause and effect. Researchers manipulate an **independent variable** by exposing participants to two or more treatment conditions. Then they determine what effect this has on a **dependent variable. Random assignment** increases the chances that characteristics of participants do not interfere with the accuracy of experimental findings.

■ To achieve high degrees of control, most experiments are conducted in laboratories, but their findings may not apply to everyday life. Field and natural experiments are strategies used to compare treatments in natural environments. These approaches, however, are less rigorous than laboratory experiments.

Describe designs for studying development, noting the strengths and limitations of each.

■ Longitudinal and cross-sectional designs are uniquely suited for studying development. The **longitudinal design** permits study of common patterns as well as individual differences in development and the relationship between early and later events and behaviors. Researchers face a variety of problems in conducting longitudinal research, such as participant dropout and practice effects. The most widely discussed threat to longitudinal findings is **cohort effects**—difficulty generalizing to people developing in other historical times.

■ The **cross-sectional design,** in which groups of participants differing in age are studied at the same time, offers an efficient approach to studying development. However, it is limited to comparisons of age-group averages. Like longitudinal research, cross-sectional studies can be threatened by cohort effects, especially when they cover a wide age span.

■ To overcome some of the limitations of these designs, investigators sometimes combine the two approaches, as in the **longitudinal-sequential** design. It permits them to test for cohort effects and to compare longitudinal and cross-sectional findings.

ETHICS IN LIFESPAN RESEARCH

What special ethical concerns arise in research on human development?

■ Research creates ethical issues, since the quest for scientific knowledge can sometimes exploit people. The ethical principle of informed consent requires special safeguards for children and for elderly people who are cognitively impaired or in settings for the care of the chronically ill. The use of deception in research with children is especially risky, since it may undermine their basic faith in the trustworthiness of adults.

IMPORTANT TERMS AND CONCEPTS

age-graded influences (p. 11)

applied behavior analysis (p. 19)

behaviorism (p. 18)

chronosystem (p. 26)

clinical interview (p. 29)

clinical, or case study, method (p. 30)

cognitive-developmental theory (p. 20)

cohort effects (p. 37)

contexts (p. 7)

continuous development (p. 6)

correlation coefficient (p. 32)

correlational design (p. 31)

cross-sectional design (p. 38)

dependent variable (p. 34)

discontinuous development (p. 6)

ecological systems theory (p. 25)

ethnography (p. 31)

ethology (p. 23)

exosystem (p. 26)

experimental design (p. 34)

history-graded influences (p. 12)

human development (p. 5)

independent variable (p. 34)

information processing (p. 22)

lifespan perspective (p. 8)

longitudinal design (p. 35)

longitudinal-sequential design (p. 38)

macrosystem (p. 26)

maturation (p. 14)

mesosystem (p. 26)

microsystem (p. 26)

naturalistic observation (p. 28)

nature–nurture controversy (p. 7)

noble savage (p. 14)

nonnormative influences (p. 12)

normative approach (p. 15)

preformationism (p. 13)

psychoanalytic perspective (p. 16)

psychosexual theory (p. 16)

psychosocial theory (p. 17)

random assignment (p. 34)

resiliency (p. 10)

sensitive period (p. 23)

social learning theory (p. 19)

sociocultural theory (p. 24)

stability versus change (p. 7)

stage (p. 6)

structured interview (p. 29)

structured observation (p. 29)

tabula rasa (p. 13)

theory (p. 5)

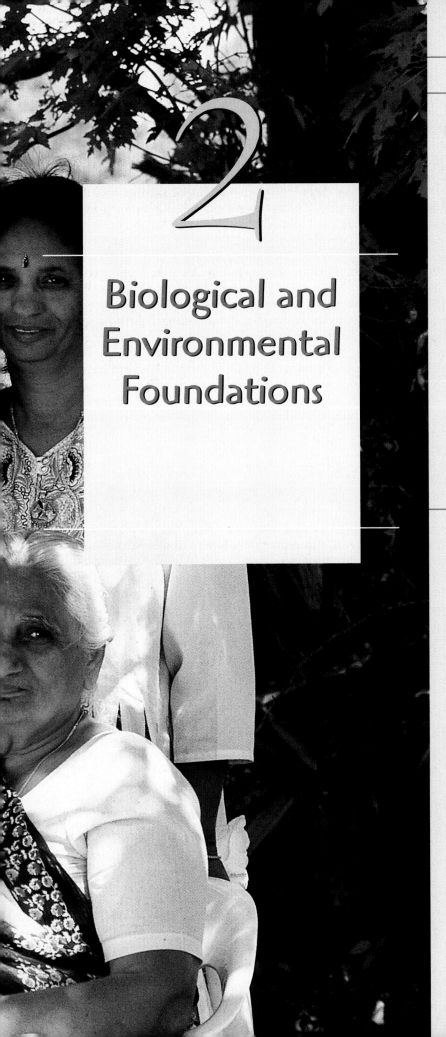

2

Biological and Environmental Foundations

■ *A complex blend of genetic and environmental influences leads members of this East Asian family, who span four generations, to be both alike and different in physical characteristics and behavior. (Photo courtesy: Susan Oristaglio/Liaison Agency)*

t's a girl," announces the doctor, who holds up the squalling little creature while her new parents gaze with amazement at their miraculous creation.

"A girl! We've named her Sarah!" exclaims the proud father to eager relatives waiting by the telephone for word about their new family member.

As we join these parents in thinking about how this wondrous being came into existence and imagining her future, we are struck by many questions. How could this well-formed baby, equipped with everything necessary for life outside the womb, have developed from the union of two tiny cells? What ensures that Sarah will, in due time, roll over, reach for objects, walk, talk, make friends, learn, imagine, and create—just like every other normal child born before her? Why is she a girl and not a boy, dark-haired rather than blond, calm and cuddly instead of wiry and energetic? What difference will it make that Sarah is given a name and place in one family, community, nation, and culture rather than another?

To answer these questions, this chapter takes a close look at the foundations of development: heredity and environment. Because nature has prepared us for survival, all humans have many features in common. Yet a brief period of time spent in the company of any person and his or her family reveals that each human being is unique. Take a moment to jot down the most obvious similarities and differences in physical characteristics and behavior for several of your friends and their parents. Did you find that one person shows combined features of both parents, another resembles just one parent, whereas a third is not like either parent? These directly observable characteristics are called **phenotypes.** They depend in part on the individual's **genotype**— the complex blend of genetic information that determines our species and influences all our unique characteristics. Yet

throughout life, phenotypes are also affected by the person's history of experiences in the environment.

We begin our discussion of development at the moment of conception, an event that establishes the hereditary makeup of the new individual. In the first section of this chapter, we review basic genetic principles that help explain similarities and differences between us in appearance and behavior. Next, we turn to aspects of the environment that play powerful roles throughout the lifespan.

As our discussion proceeds, you will quickly see that both nature and nurture are involved in all aspects of development. In fact, some findings and conclusions may surprise you. For example, many people believe that when individuals inherit unfavorable characteristics, not much can be done to help them. Others are convinced that when environments are harmful, the damage done to the developing person can easily be corrected. We will see that neither of these assumptions is true. In the final section of this chapter, we take up the question of how nature and nurture *work together* to shape the course of development.

GENETIC FOUNDATIONS

ach of us is made up of trillions of separate units called *cells.* Inside every cell is a control center, or *nucleus,* that contains rodlike structures called **chromosomes,** which store and transmit genetic information. Human chromosomes come in 23 matching pairs (an exception is the XY pair in males, which we will discuss shortly). Each pair member corresponds to the other in size, shape, and genetic functions. One is inherited from the mother and one from the father (see Figure 2.1).

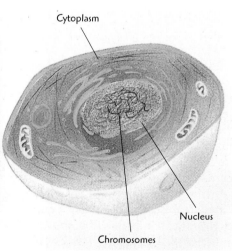

Cytoplasm

Nucleus

Chromosomes

FIGURE 2.1

■ **A karyotype, or photograph, of human chromosomes.**
The 46 chromosomes on the left were isolated from a body cell (shown on the right), stained, greatly magnified, and arranged in pairs according to decreasing size of the upper arm of each chromosome. Note the twenty-third pair, XY. The cell donor is a male. In a female, the twenty-third pair would be XX. (Photo courtesy: CNRI/Science Photo Library/ Photo Researchers, Inc.)

THE GENETIC CODE

Chromosomes are made up of a chemical substance called **deoxyribonucleic acid,** or **DNA.** As Figure 2.2 shows, DNA is a long, double-stranded molecule that looks like a twisted ladder. Each rung of the ladder consists of a specific pair of chemical substances called *bases,* joined together between the two sides. It is this sequence of bases that provides genetic instructions. A **gene** is a segment of DNA along the length of the chromosome. Genes can be of different lengths—perhaps 100 to several thousand ladder rungs long. Altogether, about 50,000 to 100,000 genes lie along the human chromosomes.

Genes accomplish their task by sending instructions for making a rich assortment of proteins to the *cytoplasm,* the area surrounding the cell nucleus. Proteins, which trigger chemical reactions throughout the body, are the biological foundation on which our characteristics are built.

A unique feature of DNA is that it can duplicate itself through a process called **mitosis.** This special ability permits the one-celled fertilized ovum to develop into a complex human being composed of a great many cells. Refer again to Figure 2.2, and you will see that during mitosis, the chromosomes copy themselves. As a result, each new body cell contains the same number of chromosomes and the identical genetic information.

THE SEX CELLS

New individuals are created when two special cells called **gametes,** or sex cells—the sperm and ovum—combine. A gamete contains only 23 chromosomes, half as many as a regular body cell. Gametes are formed through a cell-division process called **meiosis,** which ensures that a constant quantity of genetic material is transmitted from one generation to the next. When sperm and ovum unite at conception, the cell that results, called a **zygote,** will again have 46 chromosomes.

In *meiosis,* the chromosomes pair up and exchange segments, so that genes from one are replaced by genes from another. Then chance determines which member of each pair will gather with others and end up in the same gamete. These events make the chances of nontwin offspring of the same two parents being genetically the same extremely slim—about 1 in 700 trillion (Gould & Keeton, 1996). Therefore, meiosis helps us understand why siblings differ from each other, even though they have features in common, since their genotypes come from the same pool of parental genes.

In the male, four sperm are produced each time meiosis occurs. Also, the cells from which sperm arise are produced continuously throughout life. For this reason, a healthy man can father a child at any age after sexual maturity. In the female, gamete production is much more limited. Each cell division produces just one ovum. In addition, the female is born with all her ova already present in her ovaries, and she can bear children for only three to four decades. Still, there are plenty of female sex cells. About 1 to 2 million are present at birth, 40,000 remain at adolescence, and approximately 350 to 450 will mature during a woman's childbearing years (Moore & Persaud, 1998).

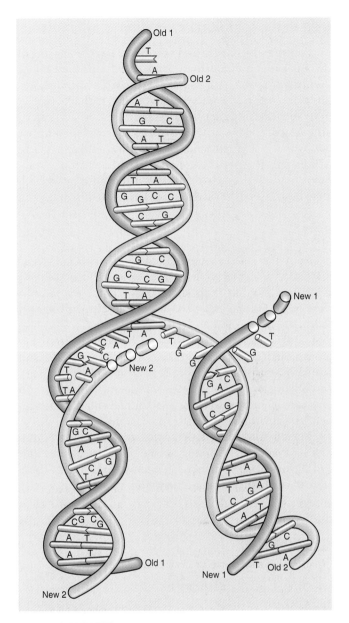

FIGURE 2.2

■ **DNA's ladderlike structure.** This figure shows that the pairings of bases across the rungs of the ladder are very specific: adenine (A) always appears with thymine (T), and cytosine (C) always appears with guanine (G). Here, the DNA ladder duplicates by splitting down the middle of its ladder rungs. Each free base picks up a new complementary partner from the area surrounding the cell nucleus.

MALE OR FEMALE?

Return to Figure 2.1, and note that 22 of the 23 pairs of chromosomes are matching pairs, called **autosomes.** The twenty-third pair consists of **sex chromosomes.** In females, this pair is called XX; in males, it is called XY. The X is a relatively long chromosome, whereas the Y is short and carries little genetic material. When gametes are formed in males, the X and Y chromosomes separate into different sperm cells. In females, all gametes carry an X chromosome. Therefore, the sex of the new organism is determined by whether an X-bearing or a Y-bearing sperm fertilizes the ovum.

MULTIPLE BIRTHS

Ruth and Peter, a couple I know well, tried for several years to have a child, without success. Ruth's doctor finally prescribed a fertility drug, and twins—Jeannie and Jason—were born. Jeannie and Jason are **fraternal,** or **dizygotic, twins,** the most common type of multiple birth. The drug that Ruth took caused two ova to be released from her ovaries, and both were fertilized. Therefore, Jeannie and Jason are genetically no more alike than ordinary siblings. Fertility drugs are only one cause of fraternal twinning (and occasionally more offspring). As Table 2.1 shows, other genetic and environmental factors are also involved.

There is another way that twins can be created. Sometimes a zygote that has started to duplicate separates into two clusters of cells that develop into two individuals. These are called **identical,** or **monozygotic, twins** because they

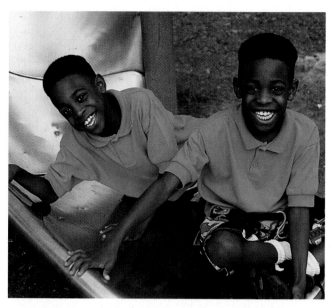

■ *These identical, or monozygotic, twins were created when a duplicating zygote separated into two clusters of cells, and two individuals with the same genetic makeup developed. Identical twins look alike, and as we will see later in this chapter, tend to resemble each other in a variety of psychological characteristics. (Photo courtesy: Reg Parker/FPG International)*

have the same genetic makeup. The frequency of identical twins is unrelated to the factors listed in Table 2.1. It is about the same around the world—about 3 of every 1,000 births (Tong, Caddy, & Short, 1997). Animal research has uncovered a variety of environmental influences that prompt this type of twinning, including temperature changes, variation in oxygen levels, and late fertilization of the ovum.

During their early years, children of single births are often healthier and develop more rapidly than twins (Moilanen, 1989). Jeannie and Jason were born early (as most twins are)—3 weeks before Ruth's due date. Like other premature infants (as we will see in Chapter 3), they required special care after birth. When the twins came home from the hospital, Ruth and Peter had to divide time between them. Perhaps because neither baby got quite as much attention as the average single infant, Jeannie and Jason walked and talked several months later than other children their age, although both caught up in development by middle childhood.

PATTERNS OF GENETIC INHERITANCE

Jeannie has her parents' dark, straight hair, whereas Jason is curly-haired and blond. Patterns of genetic inheritance—the way genes from each parent interact—explain these outcomes. Recall that except for the XY pair in males, all chromosomes come in matching pairs. Two forms of

TABLE 2.1

Maternal Factors Linked to Fraternal Twinning

FACTOR	DESCRIPTION
Ethnicity	About 8 per 1,000 births among whites, 12 to 16 per 1,000 among blacks, and 4 per 1,000 among Asians.[a]
Age	Rises with maternal age, peaking at 35 years, and then rapidly falls.
Nutrition	Occurs less often among women with poor diets, occurs more often among women who are tall and overweight or of normal weight as opposed to slight body build.
Number of births	Chances increase with each additional birth.
Fertility drugs and in vitro fertilization	Treatment of infertility with hormones and through in vitro fertilization (see page 56) increases the likelihood of multiple fraternal births, from twins to quintuplets.

[a] Worldwide rates, with the effects of fertility drugs removed.
Sources: Collins, 1994; Mange & Mange, 1998.

each gene occur at the same place on the autosomes, one inherited from the mother and one from the father. If the genes from both parents are alike, the child is **homozygous** and will display the inherited trait. If they are different, then the child is **heterozygous,** and relationships between the genes determine the trait that will appear.

■ DOMINANT–RECESSIVE INHERITANCE. In many heterozygous pairings, only one gene affects the child's characteristics. It is called *dominant;* the second gene, which has no effect, is called *recessive.* Hair color is an example of **dominant–recessive inheritance.** The gene for dark hair is dominant (we can represent it with a capital *D),* whereas the one for blond hair is recessive (symbolized by a lowercase *b).* A child who inherits a homozygous pair of dominant genes *(DD)* and a child who inherits a heterozygous pair *(Db)* will both be dark-haired, even though their genotypes are different. Blond hair (like Jason's) can result only from having two recessive genes *(bb).* Still, heterozygous individuals with just one recessive gene *(Db)* can pass that trait to their offspring. Therefore, they are called **carriers** of the trait.

Some human characteristics that follow the rules of dominant–recessive inheritance are given in Table 2.2. If we know the genetic makeup of the parents, we can predict the

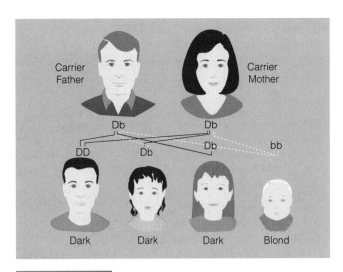

FIGURE 2.3

■ **Dominant–recessive mode of inheritance as illustrated by hair color.** By looking at the possible combinations of the parents' genes, we can predict that 25 percent of their children are likely to inherit two dominant genes for dark hair; 50 percent are likely to receive one dominant and one recessive gene, resulting in dark hair; and 25 percent are likely to receive two recessive genes for blond hair.

percentage of children in a family who are likely to display a trait or be carriers of it. Figure 2.3 shows the pattern of inheritance for hair color. Note that for Jason to be blond, both Peter and Ruth must be carriers of a recessive gene *(b).* The figure also indicates that if Peter and Ruth decide to have more children, most are likely to be dark-haired like Jeannie.

Many disabilities and diseases are also the product of recessive genes (see Table 2.3 on pages 50–51). One of the most frequently occurring recessive disorders is *phenylketonuria,* or *PKU.* PKU is an especially good example, since it shows that inheriting unfavorable genes does not always mean that the condition is untreatable.

PKU affects the way the body breaks down proteins contained in many foods. Infants born with two recessive genes lack an enzyme that converts one of the basic amino acids that make up proteins (phenylalanine) into a byproduct essential for body functioning (tyrosine). Without this enzyme, phenylalanine quickly builds to toxic levels that damage the central nervous system. By 1 year, infants with PKU are permanently retarded. All U.S. states and Canadian provinces require that each newborn be given a blood test for PKU. If the disease is found, doctors place the baby on a diet low in phenylalanine. Children who receive this treatment usually attain an average level of intelligence and have a normal lifespan. However, because even small amounts of phenylalynine interfere with brain functioning, some cognitive and motor deficits may appear in childhood and persist into adulthood (Diamond et al., 1997; Pietz et al., 1998).

TABLE 2.2

Examples of Dominant and Recessive Characteristics

DOMINANT	RECESSIVE
Dark hair	Blond hair
Normal hair	Pattern baldness
Curly hair	Straight hair
Nonred hair	Red hair
Facial dimples	No dimples
Normal hearing	Some forms of deafness
Normal vision	Nearsightedness
Farsightedness	Normal vision
Normal vision	Congenital eye cataracts
Normally pigmented skin	Albinism
Double-jointedness	Normal joints
Type A blood	Type O blood
Type B blood	Type O blood
Rh-positive blood	Rh-negative blood

Note: Many normal characteristics that were previously thought to be due to dominant–recessive inheritance, such as eye color, are now regarded as due to multiple genes. For the characteristics listed here, there still seems to be fairly common agreement that the simple dominant–recessive relationship holds.
Source: McKusick, 1998.

Examples of Dominant and Recessive Diseases

DISEASE	DESCRIPTION	MODE OF INHERITANCE	INCIDENCE	TREATMENT	PRENATAL DIAGNOSIS	CARRIER IDENTIFICATION[a]
AUTOSOMAL DISEASES						
Cooley's anemia	Pale appearance, retarded physical growth, and lethargic behavior begin in infancy.	Recessive	1 in 500 births to parents of Mediterranean descent	Frequent blood transfusion; death from complications usually occurs by adolescence.	Yes	Yes
Cystic fibrosis	Lungs, liver, and pancreas secrete large amounts of thick mucus, leading to breathing and digestive difficulties.	Recessive	1 in 2,000 to 2,500 Caucasian births; 1 in 16,000 African-American births.	Bronchial drainage, prompt treatment of respiratory infection, dietary management. Advances in medical care allow survival with good life quality into adulthood.	Yes	Yes
Phenylke-tonuria (PKU)	Inability to metabolize the amino acid phenylalanine, contained in many proteins, causes severe central nervous system damage in the first year of life.	Recessive	1 in 8,000 births	Placing the child on a special diet results in average intelligence and normal lifespan. Subtle difficulties with planning and problem-solving are often present.	Yes	Yes
Sickle cell anemia	Abnormal sickling of red blood cells causes oxygen deprivation, pain, swelling and tissue damage. Anemia and susceptibility to infections, especially pneumonia, occur.	Recessive	1 in 500 African-American births	Blood transformations, painkillers, prompt treatment of infection. No known cure; 50 percent die by age 20.	Yes	Yes
Tay-Sachs disease	Central nervous system degeneration, with onset at about 6 months, leads to poor muscle tone, blindness, deafness, and convulsions.	Recessive	1 in 3,600 births to Jews of European descent	None. Death by 3 to 4 years of age.	Yes	Yes

As Table 2.3 suggests, only rarely are serious diseases due to dominant genes. Think about why this is so. Children who inherit the dominant gene would always develop the disorder. They would seldom live long enough to reproduce, and the harmful dominant gene would be eliminated from the family's heredity in a single generation. Some dominant disorders, however, do persist. One of them is *Huntington disease,* a condition in which the central nervous system degenerates. Why has this disorder endured in some families? The reason is that its symptoms usually do not appear until age 35 or later, after the person has passed the dominant gene to his or her children.

■ C O D O M I N A N C E . In some heterozygous circumstances, the dominant–recessive relationship does not hold completely. Instead, we see **codominance,** a pattern of inheritance in which both genes influence the person's characteristics.

The *sickle cell trait,* a heterozygous condition present in many black Africans, provides an example. *Sickle cell anemia* (see Table 2.3) occurs in full form when a child inherits two recessive genes. They cause the usually round red blood cells to become sickle shaped, especially under low oxygen conditions. The sickled cells clog the blood vessels and block the flow of blood. Individuals who have the dis-

TABLE 2.3 CONTINUED

Examples of Dominant and Recessive Diseases

DISEASE	DESCRIPTION	MODE OF INHERITANCE	INCIDENCE	TREATMENT	PRENATAL DIAGNOSIS	CARRIER IDENTIFICATION[a]
AUTOSOMAL DISEASES (continued)						
Huntington disease	Central nervous system degeneration leads to muscular coordination difficulties, mental deterioration, and personality changes. Symptoms usually do not appear until age 35 or later.	Dominant	1 in 18,000 to 25,000 American births	None. Death occurs 10 to 20 years after symptom onset.	Yes	Not applicable
Marfan syndrome	Tall, slender build; thin, elongated arms and legs. Heart defects and eye abnormalities, especially of the lens. Excessive lengthening of the body results in a variety of skeletal defects.	Dominant	1 in 20,000 births	Correction of heart and eye defects sometimes possible. Death from heart failure in young adulthood common.	Yes	Not applicable
X-LINKED DISEASES						
Duchenne muscular dystrophy	Degenerative muscle disease. Abnormal gait, loss of ability to walk between 7 and 13 years of age.	Recessive	1 in 3,000 to 5,000 male births	None. Death from respiratory infection or weakening of the heart muscle usually occurs in adolescence.	Yes	Yes
Hemophilia	Blood fails to clot normally. Can lead to severe internal bleeding and tissue damage.	Recessive	1 in 4,000 to 7,000 male births	Blood transfusions. Safety precautions to prevent injury.	Yes	Yes
Diabetes insipidus	A form of diabetes present at birth caused by insufficient production of the hormone vasopressin. Results in excessive thirst and urination. Dehydration can cause central nervous system damage.	Recessive	1 in 2,500 male births	Hormone replacement.	Yes	Yes

[a] Carrier status detectable in prospective parents through blood test or genetic analyses.

Sources: Behrman, Kliegman, & Arvin, 1996; Child, 1997; Gilfillan et al., 1992; Knoers et al., 1993; McKusick, 1998; Simpson & Harding, 1993.

order suffer severe attacks involving intense pain, swelling, and tissue damage. They generally die in the first 20 years of life; few live past age 40. Heterozygous individuals are protected from the disease under most circumstances. However, when they experience oxygen deprivation—for example, at high altitudes or after intense physical exercise—the single recessive gene asserts itself, and a temporary, mild form of the illness occurs.

The sickle cell gene is common among black Africans for a special reason. Carriers of it are more resistant to malaria than are individuals with two genes for normal red blood cells. In Africa, where malaria is common, these carriers survived and reproduced more frequently than others, leading the gene to be maintained in the black population.

■ X-LINKED INHERITANCE. Males and females have an equal chance of inheriting recessive disorders carried on the autosomes, such as PKU and sickle cell anemia. But when a harmful gene is carried on the X chromosome, **X-linked inheritance** applies. Males are more likely to be affected because

FIGURE 2.4

■ **X-linked inheritance.** In the example shown here, the gene on the father's X chromosome is normal. The mother has one normal and one abnormal recessive gene on her X chromosomes. By looking at the possible combinations of the parents' genes, we can predict that 50 percent of male children will have the disorder and 50 percent of female children will be carriers of it.

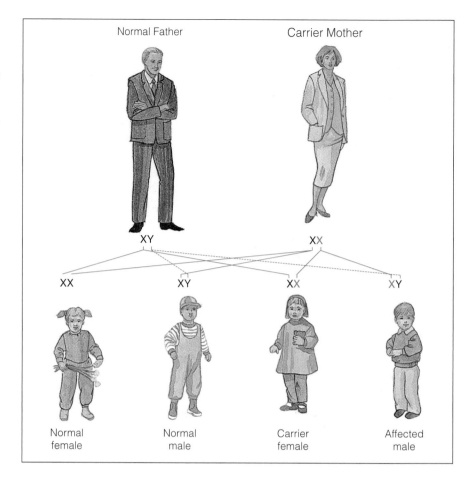

Normal Father Carrier Mother

XY XX

XX XY XX XY

Normal female Normal male Carrier female Affected male

their sex chromosomes do not match. In females, any recessive gene on one X has a good chance of being suppressed by a dominant gene on the other X. But the Y chromosome is only about one-third as long and therefore lacks many corresponding genes to override those on the X.

Return to Table 2.3 and review the disorders that are X-linked. A well-known example is *hemophilia,* a disease in which the blood fails to clot normally. Figure 2.4 shows its greater likelihood of inheritance by male children whose mothers carry the abnormal gene.

Besides X-linked disorders, many sex differences reveal the male to be at a disadvantage. Rates of miscarriage and infant and childhood deaths are greater for males. Learning disabilities, behavior disorders, and mental retardation are also more common among boys (Halpern, 1997). It is possible that these sex differences can be traced to the genetic code. The female, with two X chromosomes, benefits from a greater variety of genes. Nature, however, seems to have adjusted for the male's disadvantage. Worldwide, about 106 boys are born for every 100 girls, and judging from miscarriage and abortion statistics, an even greater number of males are conceived (Pyeritz, 1998).

Nevertheless, in recent decades the proportion of male births has declined in many industrialized countries, including Canada, Denmark, Germany, Finland, the Netherlands, Norway, and the United States (Davis, Gottlieb, & Stampnitzky, 1998). Some researchers blame increased occupational and community exposure to pesticides, which is believed to have prompted a reduction in sperm counts overall, but especially of Y-bearing sperm. In addition, many surviving Y-bearing sperm are damaged, which accounts for a greater rise in birth defects and infant deaths among males than among females.

■ GENETIC IMPRINTING. Over 1,000 human characteristics follow the rules of dominant–recessive and codominant inheritance (McKusick, 1998). In these cases, regardless of which parent contributes a gene to the new individual, the gene responds in the same way. Geneticists, however, have identified some exceptions governed by a recently discovered mode of inheritance. In **genetic imprinting,** genes are *imprinted,* or chemically marked, in such a way that one pair member (either the mother's or the father's) is activated, regardless of its makeup. The imprint is often temporary: it may be erased in the next generation, and it may not occur in all individuals (Niikawa, 1997).

Genetic imprinting helps us understand the confusion in inheritance of some disorders. For example, children are more likely to develop diabetes if their father, rather than their mother, suffers from it. And people with asthma or hay fever tend to have mothers, not fathers, with the illness. Imprinting may also explain why Huntington disease, when inherited from the father, tends to emerge at an earlier age and progress more rapidly (Day, 1993).

In these examples, genetic imprinting affects traits carried on the autosomes. It can also operate on the sex chromosomes, as *fragile X syndrome* reveals. In this disorder, an abnormal sequence of DNA bases occurs in a special spot on the X chromosome, damaging a particular gene. Fragile X syndrome is a common inherited cause of moderate mental retardation. It has also been linked to 2 to 3 percent of cases of infantile autism, a serious emotional disorder of early childhood involving bizarre, self-stimulating behavior and delayed or absent language and communication. Recent evidence indicates that the defective gene at the fragile site is expressed only when it is passed from mother to child (Fischer, 1996; Rose, 1995).

■ MUTATION AND UNFAVORABLE GENES. At this point, you may be wondering, How are harmful genes created in the first place? The answer is **mutation,** a sudden but permanent change in a segment of DNA. A mutation may affect only one or two genes, or it may involve many genes, as is the case for the chromosomal disorders we will discuss shortly. Some mutations occur spontaneously, simply by chance. Others are caused by a wide variety of hazardous environmental agents that enter our food supply or are present in the air we breathe.

For many years, ionizing radiation has been known to cause mutations. Women who receive repeated doses of radiation before conception are more likely to miscarry and give birth to children with hereditary defects. Genetic abnormalities, such as childhood cancer, are also higher when fathers are exposed to radiation in their occupations (Gardner et al., 1990; Sankaranarayanan, 1998). Does this mean that routine chest and dental X-rays are dangerous to future generations? Research indicates that infrequent and mild exposure to radiation does not cause genetic damage. Instead, moderate to high doses over a long period of time appear to be required.

■ POLYGENIC INHERITANCE. So far, we have discussed patterns of inheritance in which people either display a particular trait or do not. These cut-and-dried individual differences are much easier to trace to their genetic origins than are characteristics that vary continuously among people, such as height, weight, intelligence, and personality. These traits are due to **polygenic inheritance,** in which many genes determine the characteristic in question. Polygenic inheritance is complex, and much about it is still unknown. In the final section of this chapter, we will discuss ways that researchers infer the influence of heredity on human attributes when knowledge of precise patterns of inheritance is unavailable.

CHROMOSOMAL ABNORMALITIES

Besides harmful recessive genes, abnormalities of the chromosomes are a major cause of serious developmental problems. Most chromosomal defects are the result of mistakes during meiosis, when the ovum and sperm are formed. A chromosome pair does not separate properly, or part of a chromosome breaks off. Since these errors involve more DNA than do problems due to single genes, they usually produce disorders with many physical and mental symptoms.

■ DOWN SYNDROME. The most common chromosomal disorder, occurring in 1 out of every 800 live births, is *Down syndrome.* In 95 percent of cases, it results from a failure of the twenty-first pair of chromosomes to separate during meiosis, so the new individual inherits three of these chromosomes rather than the normal two. In other less frequent forms, an extra broken piece of a twenty-first chromosome is present. Or an error occurs during the early stages of mitosis, causing some but not all body cells to have the defective chromosomal makeup (called a *mosaic* pattern). In these instances, since less genetic material is involved, symptoms of the disorder are less extreme (Hodapp, 1996).

The behavioral consequences of Down syndrome include mental retardation, speech problems, limited vocabulary, and slow motor development. Affected individuals also have distinct physical features—a short, stocky build; a flattened face; a protruding tongue; almond-shaped eyes; and an unusual crease running across the palm of the hand. In addition, infants with Down syndrome are often born with eye cataracts and heart and intestinal defects. Because of medical advances, fewer individuals with Down syndrome die early than was the case in the past. Today, many survive into their sixties and beyond (Selikowitz, 1997).

The risk of a Down syndrome baby rises dramatically with maternal age, from 1 in 1,900 births at age 20, to 1 in 300 at age 35, to 1 in 30 at age 45 (Halliday et al., 1995; Meyers et al., 1997). Why is this so? Geneticists believe that the ova, present in the woman's body since her own prenatal period, weaken over time because of the aging process or increased exposure to harmful environmental agents. As a result, chromosomes do not separate properly as they complete the process of meiosis at conception. The mother's

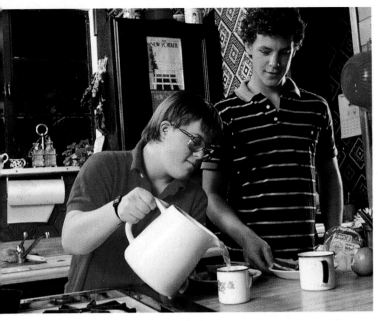

■ *The facial features and short, stocky build of the boy on the left are typical of Down syndrome. Although his intellectual development is impaired, he is doing well because he is growing up in a stimulating home where his special needs are met and he is loved and accepted. (Photo courtesy: Stephen Frisch/Stock Boston).*

gamete, however, is not always the cause of a Down syndrome child. In about 20 to 30 percent of cases, the extra genetic material originates with the father. However, Down syndrome and other chromosomal abnormalities are not related to advanced paternal age. In these instances, the mutation occurs for other unknown reasons (Blanco et al., 1998; Phillips & Elias, 1993).

■ ABNORMALITIES OF THE SEX CHROMOSOMES. Disorders of the autosomes other than Down syndrome usually disrupt development so severely that miscarriage occurs. When such babies are born, they rarely survive beyond early childhood. In contrast, abnormalities of the sex chromosomes usually lead to fewer problems. In fact, sex chromosome disorders often are not recognized until adolescence when, in some of the deviations, puberty is delayed. The most common problems involve the presence of an extra chromosome (either X or Y) or the absence of one X chromosome in females.

A variety of myths about individuals with sex chromosome disorders exist. For example, males with *XYY syndrome* are not necessarily more aggressive and antisocial than XY males, as was once assumed. Also, it is widely believed that children with sex chromosome disorders suffer from mental retardation. Yet most do not. The intelligence of XYY syndrome boys is similar to that of normal chil-

dren (Netley, 1986; Stewart, 1982). And the intellectual problems of people with other sex chromosome abnormalities are usually very specific. Verbal difficulties (for example, with reading and vocabulary) are common among girls with *triple X syndrome (XXX)* and boys with *Klinefelter syndrome (XXY)*, both of whom inherit an extra X chromosome. In contrast, girls with *Turner syndrome (XO)*, who are missing an X, have trouble with spatial relationships—for example, drawing pictures, telling right from left, following travel directions, and noticing changes in facial expressions (Money, 1993; Romans et al., 1997; Temple & Carney, 1995). These findings tell us that adding to or subtracting from the usual number of X chromosomes results in particular intellectual deficits. At present, geneticists do not know why.

■ ASK YOURSELF . . .

■ *Gilbert and Jan are planning to have children. Gilbert's genetic makeup is homozygous for dark hair; Jan's is homozygous for blond hair. What color is Gilbert's hair? How about Jan's? What proportion of their children are likely to be dark-haired?*

■ *Ashley and Harold both carry the defective gene for fragile X syndrome. Explain why Ashley's child inherited the disorder but Harold's did not.*

🌳 *Cite a recessive disorder that leads to profound disability but for which early environmental intervention can change the life course. Explain how heredity and environment work together in this example.*

REPRODUCTIVE CHOICES

T wo years after they were married, Ted and Marianne gave birth to their first child. Kendra appeared to be a healthy and lively infant, but by 4 months her growth slowed. Diagnosed as having Tay-Sachs disease (see Table 2.3), Kendra died at 2 years of age. Ted and Marianne were devastated by Kendra's death. Although they did not want to bring another infant into the world who would endure such suffering, they badly wanted to have a child. They began to avoid family get-togethers where little nieces and nephews were constant reminders of the void in their lives.

In the past, many couples with genetic disorders in their families chose not to bear a child at all rather than risk having an abnormal baby. Today, genetic counseling and prenatal diagnosis help people make informed decisions about conceiving, carrying a pregnancy to term, or adopting a child.

TABLE 2.4

Prenatal Diagnostic Methods

METHOD	DESCRIPTION
Amniocentesis	The most widely used technique. A hollow needle is inserted through the abdominal wall to obtain a sample of fluid in the uterus. Cells are examined for genetic defects. Can be performed by 11 to 14 weeks after conception but safest after 15 weeks; 1 to 2 more weeks are required for test results. Small risk of miscarriage.
Chorionic villus sampling	A procedure that can be used if results are desired or needed very early in pregnancy. A thin tube is inserted into the uterus through the vagina or a hollow needle is inserted through the abdominal wall. A small plug of tissue is removed from the end of one or more chorionic villi, the hairlike projections on the membrane surrounding the developing organism. Cells are examined for genetic defects. Can be performed at 6 to 8 weeks after conception, and results are available within 24 hours. Entails a slightly greater risk of miscarriage than does amniocentesis. Also associated with a small risk of limb deformities, which increases the earlier the procedure is performed.
Fetoscopy	A small tube with a light source at one end is inserted into the uterus to inspect the fetus for defects of the limbs and face. Also allows a sample of fetal blood to be obtained, permitting diagnosis of such disorders as hemophilia and sickle cell anemia as well as neural defects (see below). Usually performed between 15 and 18 weeks after conception, although can be done as early as 5 weeks. Entails some risk of miscarriage, which increases the earlier the procedure is performed.
Ultrasound	High-frequency sound waves are beamed at the uterus; their reflection is translated into a picture on a videoscreen that reveals the size, shape, and placement of the fetus. By itself, permits assessment of fetal age, detection of multiple pregnancies, and identification of gross physical defects. Also used to guide amniocentesis, chorionic villus sampling, and fetoscopy. When used five or more times, may increase the chances of low birth weight.
Maternal blood analysis	By the second month of pregnancy, some of the developing organism's cells enter the maternal bloodstream. An elevated level of alphafetoprotein may indicate kidney disease, abnormal closure of the esophagus, or neural tube defects, such as anencephaly (absence of most of the brain) and spina bifida (bulging of the spinal cord from the spinal column). Isolated cells can be examined for genetic defects, such as Down syndrome.
Preimplantation genetic diagnosis	After in vitro fertilization and duplication of the zygote into a cluster of about eight cells, one cell is removed and examined for hereditary defects. Only if that cell is free of detectable genetic disorders is the fertilized ovum implanted in the woman's uterus.

Sources: Canick & Saller, 1993; Eiben et al., 1997; Lissens & Sermon, 1997; Moore & Persaud, 1998; Newnham et al., 1993; Quintero, Puder, & Cotton, 1993; Shurtleff & Lemire, 1995; Steele et al., 1996; Wapner, 1997.

GENETIC COUNSELING

Genetic counseling is a communication process designed to help couples assess their chances of giving birth to a baby with a hereditary disorder and choose the best course of action in view of risks and family goals (Shiloh, 1996). Individuals likely to seek counseling are those who have had difficulties bearing children, such as repeated miscarriages, or who know that genetic problems exist in their families. In addition, women who delay childbearing past age 35 are candidates for genetic counseling. After this time, the overall rate of chromosomal abnormalities rises sharply, from 1 in every 190 to as many as 1 in every 10 pregnancies at age 48 (Meyers et al., 1997).

If a family history of mental retardation, physical defects, or inherited diseases exists, the genetic counselor interviews the couple and prepares a *pedigree*, a picture of the family tree in which affected relatives are identified. The pedigree is used to estimate the likelihood that parents will have an abnormal child, using the same genetic principles we discussed earlier in this chapter. In the case of many disorders, blood tests or genetic analyses can reveal whether the parent is a carrier of the harmful gene. Turn back to pages 50–51, and you will see that carrier detection is possible for all of the diseases listed in Table 2.3. A carrier test has been developed for fragile X syndrome as well (Ryynänen et al., 1995).

When all the relevant information is in, the genetic counselor helps people consider appropriate options. These include "taking a chance" and conceiving, choosing from among a variety of reproductive technologies (see the Social Issues box on pages 56–57), or adopting a child.

PRENATAL DIAGNOSIS AND FETAL MEDICINE

If couples who might bear an abnormal child decide to conceive, several **prenatal diagnostic methods**—medical procedures that permit detection of problems before birth—are available (see Table 2.4). Women of advanced maternal age are prime candidates for *amniocentesis* or *chorionic villus*

THE PROS AND CONS OF REPRODUCTIVE TECHNOLOGIES

Some couples decide not to risk pregnancy because of a history of genetic disease. And many others—in fact, one-sixth of all couples who try to conceive—discover that they are sterile. Today, increasing numbers of individuals are turning to alternative methods of conception—technologies that, although fulfilling the wish of parenthood, have become the subject of heated debate.

DONOR INSEMINATION AND IN VITRO FERTILIZATION. For several decades, *donor insemination*—injection of sperm from an anonymous man into a woman—has been used to overcome male reproductive difficulties. In recent years, it has also permitted women without heterosexual partners to bear children. In the United States alone, thirty thousand children are conceived through donor insemination each year (Nachtigall et al., 1997).

In vitro fertilization is another reproductive technology that has become increasingly common. Since the first "test tube" baby was born in England in 1978, many thousands of infants have been created as a result of this technique. With in vitro fertilization, hormones are given to a woman, stimulating ripening of several ova. These are removed surgically and placed in a dish of nutrients, to which sperm are added. Once an ovum is fertilized and begins to duplicate into several cells, it is injected into the mother's uterus, where, the parents hope, it will implant and develop.

In vitro fertilization is usually used to treat women whose fallopian tubes are permanently damaged, and it is successful for 20 percent of those who try it. These results have been encouraging enough that the technique has been expanded. By mixing

and matching gametes, pregnancies can be brought about when either or both partners have a reproductive problem. Fertilized ova and sperm can even be frozen and stored in embryo banks for use at some future time, thereby guaranteeing healthy zygotes should age or illness lead to fertility problems. For example, a childless widow conceived after in vitro fertilization with sperm donated by her husband before he received radiation treatment for testicular cancer, which left him sterile (Ahaja et al., 1997).

Children conceived through these methods may be genetically unrelated to one or both of their parents. In addition, most parents who have used in vitro fertilization do not tell their children about their origins, although health professionals now encourage them to do so (Cook et al., 1995). Does lack of genetic ties or secrecy surrounding these techniques interfere with parent–child relationships? Apparently not. Parenting is actually somewhat warmer for young children conceived through in vitro fertilization or donor insemination than for children who were easily conceived. A strong desire for parenthood among couples who have experienced reproductive problems seems to enhance family functioning (Golombok et al., 1995; van Balen, 1996).

Donor insemination and in vitro fertilization clearly have many benefits. Nevertheless, serious questions have arisen about their use. Many states have no legal guidelines for these procedures. As a result, donors are not always screened for genetic or sexually transmitted diseases. In addition, few American doctors keep records of donor characteristics. Yet the resulting children may someday want to know their genetic background or need to for medical reasons (Nachtigall, 1993).

SURROGATE MOTHERHOOD. A more controversial form of medically assisted conception is *surrogate motherhood*. Typically in this procedure, sperm from a man whose wife is infertile are used to inseminate a woman, called a surrogate, who is paid a fee for her childbearing services. In return, the surrogate agrees to turn the baby over to the man (who is the natural father). The child is then adopted by his wife.

Although most of these arrangements proceed smoothly, those that end up in court highlight serious risks for all concerned. In one case, both parties rejected the infant with severe disabilities that resulted from the pregnancy. In several others, the surrogate mother changed her mind and wanted to keep the baby. These children came into the world in midst of family conflict that threatened to last for years to come.

Since surrogacy favors the wealthy as contractors for infants and the less economically advantaged as surrogates, it may promote exploitation of financially needy women (Sureau, 1997). In addition, most surrogates already have children of their own, who may be deeply affected by the pregnancy. Knowledge that their mother would give away a baby for profit may cause these youngsters to worry about the security of their own family circumstances.

NEW REPRODUCTIVE FRONTIERS. Reproductive technologies are evolving faster than societies can weigh the ethics of these procedures. Doctors have used donor ova from younger women in combination with in vitro fertilization to help post-menopausal women become pregnant. Most recipients are in their forties, but a 62-year-old has given birth in Italy and a 63-year-old in the United States (Beck, 1994; Kalb,

1997). Even though candidates for postmenopausal-assisted childbirth are selected on the basis of good health, serious questions arise about bringing children into the world whose parents may not live to see them reach adulthood. Based on U.S. life expectancy data, 1 in 3 mothers and 1 in 2 fathers having a baby at age 55 will die before their children enter college (Bowman & Saunders, 1994).

Currently, experts are debating other reproductive options. At donor banks, customers can select ova or sperm on the basis of physical characteristics and even the IQ of potential donors. Some worry that this practice is a dangerous step toward selective breeding of the human species. In another controversial project, researchers delivered baby mice using the transplanted ovaries of aborted fetuses (Hashimoto, Noguchi, & Nakatsuji, 1992). If the same procedure were eventually applied to humans, it would create babies whose genetic mothers had never been born.

Finally, scientists have successfully cloned (made multiple copies of) fertilized ova in sheep, cattle, and monkeys, and they are working on effective ways to do so in humans (Haworth & Strosnider, 1997). By providing extra ova for injection, cloning might improve the success rate of in vitro fertilization. But it also opens the possibility of mass producing genetically identical people. Consequently, no federal grants are available for research on human cloning.

Although new reproductive technologies permit many barren couples to rear healthy newborn babies, laws are needed to regulate them. In Australia, New Zealand, and Sweden, individuals conceived with donated gametes have a right to information about their genetic origins (Daniels & Lewis, 1996). Pressures from those

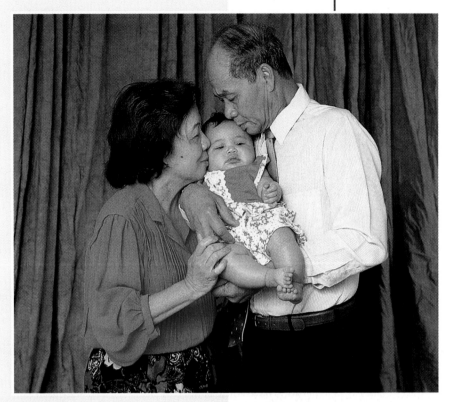

■ *Fourteen years after menopause, 63-year-old Arceli Keh gave birth to a baby using a donor ovum that was fertilized in vitro with her 61-year-old husband's sperm and injected into her uterus. Will baby Cynthia's parents live to see her reach adulthood? Postmenopausal childbearing is highly controversial. (Photo courtesy: National Enquirer)*

working in the field of assisted reproduction may soon lead to a similar policy in the United States.

In the case of surrogate motherhood, the ethical problems are so complex that 18 U.S. states have sharply restricted the practice, and Australia, Canada, and many European nations have banned it, arguing that the status of a baby should not be a matter of commercial arrangement, nor should a part of the body be rented or sold (McGee, 1997). England, France, and Italy have prohibited in vitro fertilization for women past menopause (Beck, 1994). At present nothing is known about the psychological consequences of being a product of these procedures. Research on how such children grow up, including what they know and how they feel about their origins, is important for weighing the pros and cons of these techniques.

FIGURE 2.5

■ **Amniocentesis and chorionic villus sampling.** Today, more than 250 defects and diseases can be detected before birth using these two procedures. (a) In amniocentesis, a hollow needle is inserted through the abdominal wall into the uterus. Fluid is withdrawn and fetal cells are cultured, a process that takes about 3 weeks. (b) Chorionic villus sampling can be performed much earlier in pregnancy, at 6 to 8 weeks after conception, and results are available within 24 hours. Two approaches to obtaining a sample of chorionic villus are shown: inserting a thin tube through the vagina into the uterus and inserting a needle through the abdominal wall. In both amniocentesis and chorionic villus sampling, an ultrasound scanner is used for guidance. (From K. L. Moore & T. V. N. Persaud, 1998, *Before We Are Born*, 5th ed., Philadelphia: Saunders, p. 115. Adapted by permission of the publisher and author.)

sampling (see Figure 2.5). Except for *ultrasound* and *maternal blood analysis,* prenatal diagnosis should not be used routinely, since other methods have some chance of injuring the developing organism (Steele et al., 1996).

Improvements in prenatal diagnosis have led to advances in fetal medicine. Today, some medical problems are being treated before birth. For example, by inserting a needle into the uterus, doctors can administer drugs to the fetus. Surgery has been performed to repair such problems as heart and lung malformations, urinary tract obstructions, and neural defects. Recently, a fetus with a hereditary immune deficiency received a bone marrow transplant from his father that succeeded in creating a normally functioning immune system (Flake et al., 1996).

Nevertheless, these practices remain controversial. Although some babies are saved, the techniques frequently result in complications or miscarriage (Quinn & Adzick, 1997). Yet parents may be willing to try almost any option, even if there is only a slim chance of success. Currently, the medical profession is struggling with how to help parents make informed decisions about fetal surgery. One suggestion is that the advice of an independent counselor be provided—a doctor or nurse who understands the risks but is not involved in doing research on or performing the procedure.

Fortunately, over 90 percent of pregnancies in the United States result in normal infants. The Caregiving Concerns table on the following page summarizes steps that prospective parents can take before conception to increase their chances of having a healthy baby.

Advances in *genetic engineering* also offer hope for correcting hereditary defects. Genetic repair of the prenatal organism is one goal of today's genetic engineers. As part of the Human Genome Project, researchers are mapping human chromosomes, finding the precise location of genes for specific traits and devising new, gene-based treatments to extend and improve the life course for affected individuals (see the Lifespan Vista box on pages 60–61).

ADOPTION

Adults who cannot have children, who are likely to pass along a genetic disorder, or who are older and single but want a family are turning to adoption in increasing numbers. Adoption agencies usually try to find parents of the same ethnic and religious background as the child. Where possible, they also try to choose parents who are the same age as most natural parents. Because the availability of healthy babies has declined (since fewer young unwed mothers give up their babies than in the past), more people are adopting from foreign countries or taking children who are older or who have developmental problems.

Selection of adoptive parents is important, since sometimes adoptive relationships do not work out. The risk of adoption failure is greatest for children adopted at older ages and children with disabilities, but it is not high. Over

Steps Before Conception to Increase the Chances of Having a Healthy Baby

SUGGESTION	RATIONALE
Arrange for a physical exam.	A physical exam before conception permits detection of diseases and other medical problems that might reduce fertility, be difficult to treat after the onset of pregnancy, or affect the developing organism.
Reduce or eliminate toxins under your control.	Since the developing organism is highly sensitive to damaging environmental agents during the early weeks of pregnancy (see Chapter 3), drugs, alcohol, cigarette smoke, radiation, pollution, chemical substances in the home and workplace, and infectious diseases should be avoided while trying to conceive. Furthermore, ionizing radiation and some industrial chemicals are known to cause mutations.
Consider your genetic makeup.	Find out if anyone in your family has had a child with a genetic disease or disability. If so, seek genetic counseling before conception.
Consult your physician after 12 months of unsuccessful efforts at conception.	Long periods of infertility may be due to undiagnosed spontaneous abortions, which can be caused by genetic defects in either partner. If a physical exam reveals a healthy reproductive system, seek genetic counseling.

85 percent do well in their adoptive homes. Of those who do not, 9 out of 10 are successfully placed with new parents, most of whom report high satisfaction with the adoptive experience (Glidden & Pursley, 1989; Rosenthal, 1992).

Still, adopted children and adolescents—whether born in a foreign country or the country of their adoptive parents—have more learning and emotional difficulties than occur in the general child population (Verhulst & Versluis-Den Bieman, 1995). There are many reasons for this trend. The biological mother may have been unable to care for the child because of emotional problems believed to be partly genetic, such as alcoholism or severe depression. She may have passed this tendency to her offspring. Or perhaps she experienced stress, poor diet, or inadequate medical care during pregnancy—factors that can affect the child (as we will see in Chapter 3). Furthermore, children adopted after infancy often have a history of conflict-ridden family relationships and lack of parental affection. Finally, adoptive parents and children, who are genetically unrelated, are less alike in intelligence and personality than are biological relatives—differences that may threaten family harmony.

But despite these risks, most adopted children fare surprisingly well. In a Swedish longitudinal study, researchers followed over 600 infant candidates for adoption into adolescence. Some were adopted shortly after birth; some were reared in foster homes; and some were reared by their biological mothers, who changed their minds about giving them up. As Figure 2.6 shows, adoptees developed much more favorably than did children reared in foster families or returned to their birth mothers (Bohman & Sigvardsson, 1990).

By adolescence, adoptees' lives are often complicated by unresolved curiosity about their roots. Some have difficulty accepting the possibility that they may never know their birth parents. Others worry about what they would do if

their birth parents suddenly reappeared. Nevertheless, the decision to search for birth parents is usually postponed until early adulthood, when marriage and childbirth may trigger it (Schaffer & Kral, 1988). Despite concerns about their origins, most adoptees appear well adjusted as adults.

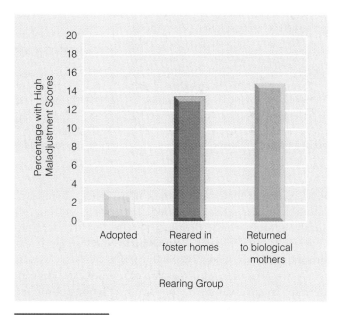

FIGURE 2.6

■ **Percentage of 15-year-olds with high maladjustment scores who were adopted, placed in foster homes, or returned to their biological mothers shortly after birth, in a Swedish longitudinal study.** All adolescents had been candidates for adoption when they were born. Compared with the other two groups, adopted young people were rated by teachers as having far fewer problems, including anxiety, withdrawal, aggression, inability to concentrate, peer difficulties, and poor school motivation. (Adapted from Bohman & Sigvardsson, 1990b.)

THE HUMAN GENOME PROJECT

Begun in 1990, the Human Genome Project is an ambitious, international research program aimed at deciphering the chemical makeup of human genetic material (genome) and identifying all 50,000 to 100,000 human genes. Its main goals are to provide powerful new approaches for understanding human evolution and the development of genetic disorders so they can be prevented and treated. An additional goal is to examine the ethical, legal, and social implications of new genetic technologies and to educate the public about them.

The research is an enormous undertaking. The human genome contains 3 billion chemical building blocks, or base pairs, enough to fill a thousand 1,000-page telephone books if each base pair were represented by a single letter. Given the size of the project, researchers have had to develop methods for DNA analysis that can process large amounts of information relatively quickly and accurately. Even with these procedures, scientists will have worked for over a decade before they attain their goal, at a cost of billions of dollars.

MAPPING AND SEQUENCING DNA. The Human Genome Project yields three main research tools, which enable scientists to identify specific genes (Lander, 1996). Each tool is a major phase of the research:

1. *Genetic map.* A genetic map consists of thousands of *markers*, or short, distinctive pieces of DNA, spaced along the chromosomes. Just as finding a landmark in your city is easier if you can narrow down its location to between two nearby points, so researchers first try to limit their search for a particular gene to a small segment of a chromosome. Genetic mapping begins with collection of blood or tissue samples from families in which a trait or disorder is common. After extracting DNA from these samples, researchers look for sequences of bases shared among affected family members, which mark the location of the gene.

2. *Physical map.* To further pinpoint the gene, researchers create a physical map, made up of overlapping DNA fragments that span the marked regions of a chromo-

some. Using various methods, the chromosome is snipped into pieces. These are cloned, stored in the order in which they originally occurred along the chromosome, and used for further studies aimed at finding the specific gene. The fragments can then be analyzed to discover the base-by-base sequence of DNA.

3. *Sequence map.* The most challenging task is the creation of a sequence map of all 3 billion DNA bases of the human genome. Now that the genetic and physical maps are largely complete, the sequence map has been constructed, which allows scientists to find specific genes. Sequencing was recently accomplished in June 2000. To make all the information available to researchers worldwide, computer methods for easy storage, retrieval, and analysis of data are being devised.

APPLICATIONS. The detailed genetic, physical, and sequence maps produced by the Human Genome Project are vital for understanding both disorders

---

And as long as their parents took steps to help them learn about their heritage in childhood, transracially or transculturally adopted young people generally develop identities that are healthy blends of their birth and rearing backgrounds (Simon, Alstein, & Melli, 1994).

As we conclude our discussion of reproductive choices, perhaps you are wondering how things turned out for Ted and Marianne. Through genetic counseling, Marianne discovered a history of Tay-Sachs disease on her mother's side of the family. Ted had a distant cousin who died of the disorder. The genetic counselor explained that the chances of giving birth to another affected baby were 1 in 4. Ted and Marianne took the risk. Their son Douglas is now 12 years old. Although Douglas is a carrier of the recessive allele, he is a normal, healthy boy. In a few years, Ted and Marianne will tell Douglas about his genetic history and explain the importance of genetic counseling and testing before he has children of his own.

ASK YOURSELF . . .

■ *A woman over 35 has just learned that she is pregnant. Although she would like to find out as soon as possible whether her child has a chromosomal disorder, she wants to minimize the risk of injury to the developing organism. Which prenatal diagnostic method is she likely to choose?*

■ *Describe the ethical pros and cons of fetal surgery, surrogate motherhood, and postmenopausal-assisted childbearing.*

How does research on adoption reveal resiliency at several periods of the life course: childhood, adolescence, and early adulthood? Of factors related to resiliency (see Chapter 1, page 10), which appears to be central in positive outcomes for adoptees?

■ *The Human Genome Project is leading to new gene-based treatments for hereditary disorders such as Alzheimer's disease. When the daughter and granddaughter of this Alzheimer's victim reach late adulthood, they may be spared this devastating illness. (Photo courtesy: © Laura Dwight)*

due to single genes and those that result from a complex interplay of multiple genes and environmental factors, including heart disease, many forms of cancer, and mental illnesses, such as depression and alcoholism. As of 1999, more than 40,000 human genes had been mapped or identified, including those for hundreds of inherited disorders, including cystic fibrosis, Huntington disease, Duchenne muscular dystrophy, and some forms of cancer (Human Genome Program, 2000).

Discovery of disease-associated genes is leading to rapid advances in genetic counseling and prenatal diagnosis as additional tests for detecting abnormal genes become available. The Human Genome Project is also providing the basis for a new, molecular medicine. Gene-based treatments are being developed for hereditary disorders, cancer, AIDS, and Alzheimer's disease. Among these procedures is *gene splicing*—delivering DNA carrying a functional gene to defective cells, thereby correcting a genetic abnormality. For example, in recent experiments, gene therapy reversed age-related withering of key brain cells in elderly rhesus monkeys. Researchers hope to adapt the technique for treatment of Alzheimer's disease in humans (Tuszynski & Kordower, 1999).

ETHICAL, LEGAL, AND SOCIAL CONCERNS. As the Human Genome Project transforms biological research and medical practice, it has sparked concerns about how its tools will be applied. A major controversy involves testing children and adults who are at risk for genetic diseases but who do not yet show symptoms. Delay between the availability of diagnostic tests and effective intervention means that affected people must live with the anxiety of a future illness they cannot prevent, such as Huntington or Alzheimer's disease. And some have encountered discrimination because of their heredity; they have lost their health insurance and even their jobs.

As a result, guidelines for responsible use of genetic technologies are being drawn up, and ethical principles have been devised to ensure the privacy of genetic information (Marshall, 1996).

The Human Genome Project is making invaluable contributions to our knowledge of the hereditary basis of human biology and disease—information that offers great promise for improving human health and longevity. As its maps and sequences become broadly available to the scientific community, investigators continue to debate the best ways to protect the public interest while reaping the project's monumental rewards.

ENVIRONMENTAL CONTEXTS FOR DEVELOPMENT

Just as complex as the genetic inheritance that sets the stage for development is the surrounding environment—a many-layered set of influences that combine to help or hinder physical and psychological well-being. Take a moment to reflect on your own childhood, and jot down a brief description of events and people that you regard as having a significant impact on your development. Next, do the same for your adult life. When I ask my students to do this, the largest number of items they list involve their families. This emphasis is not surprising, since the family is the first and longest-lasting context for development. But other settings turn out to be important as well. Friends, neighbors, school, workplace, community organizations, and church, synagogue, or mosque generally make the top 10.

Think back to Bronfenbrenner's ecological systems theory, discussed in Chapter 1. It emphasizes that the environments extending beyond the microsystem, or the immediate settings just illustrated, powerfully affect development. Indeed, there is one very important context my students rarely mention. Its impact is so pervasive that we seldom stop to think about it in our daily lives. This is the broad social climate of society—its values and programs that support and protect human development. All people need help with the demands of each phase of the lifespan—through well-designed housing, safe neighborhoods, good schools, well-equipped recreational facilities, affordable health services, and high-quality child care and other services that permit them to meet both work and family responsibilities. And some people, because of poverty or special tragedies, need considerably more help than others.

In the following sections, we take up these contexts for development. Since they affect every age period and aspect of change, we will return to them in later chapters. For now, our discussion emphasizes that besides heredity, environments can enhance or create risks for development. And when a vulnerable child or adult—an individual with physical or psychological problems—is exposed to unfavorable contexts, then development is seriously threatened.

THE FAMILY

In power and breadth of influence, no context equals the family. The family creates bonds between people that are unique. Attachments to parents and siblings usually last a lifetime and serve as models for relationships in the wider world of neighborhood, school, and community. Within the family, children learn the language, skills, and social and moral values of their culture. And at all ages, people turn to family members for information, assistance, and interesting and pleasurable interaction. Warm, gratifying family ties predict physical and psychological health throughout development. In contrast, isolation or alienation from the family is often associated with developmental problems (Parke & Buriel, 1998).

Modern investigators view the family as a set of interdependent relationships. Recall from ecological systems theory that *bidirectional influences* exist in which the behaviors of each family member affect those of others (Bronfenbrenner, 1989, 1995). Indeed, the very term *system* implies that the responses of all family members are related. These system influences operate in both direct and indirect ways.

■ *The family is a complex social system in which each person's behavior influences the behavior of others, in both direct and indirect ways. The positive mealtime atmosphere in this family is probably a product of many forces, including parents who respond to children with warmth and patience, aunts and uncles who support parents in their child-rearing roles, and children who have developed cooperative dispositions. (Photo courtesy: Michael Heron/Woodfin Camp & Associates)*

■ DIRECT INFLUENCES. The next time you have a chance to observe family members interacting, watch carefully. You are likely to see that kind, patient communication evokes cooperative, harmonious responses, whereas harshness and impatience engender angry, resistive behavior. Each of these reactions, in turn, prompts a new link in the interactive chain. In the first instance, a positive message tends to follow; in the second, a negative or avoidant one tends to occur.

These observations fit with a wealth of research on the family system. For example, many studies show that when parents' requests are accompanied by warmth and affection, children tend to cooperate. And when children willingly comply, their parents are likely to be warm and gentle in the future. In contrast, parents who discipline with hostility usually have children who refuse and rebel. And because children's misbehavior is stressful for parents, they may increase their use of punishment, leading to more unruliness by the child (Dodge, Pettit, & Bates, 1994; Patterson, Reid, & Dishion, 1992). This principle applies to other two-person family relationships, such as brother and sister, husband and wife, and parent and adult child. In each case, the behavior of one person helps sustain a form of interaction in the other that either promotes or undermines psychological well-being.

■ INDIRECT INFLUENCES. The impact of family relationships on development becomes even more complicated when we consider that interaction between any two members is affected by others present in the setting. Bronfenbrenner calls these indirect influences the effect of *third parties.*

Third parties can serve as effective supports for development. For example, when their marital relationship is warm and considerate, mothers and fathers praise and stimulate their children more and nag and scold them less. In contrast, when a marriage is tense and hostile, parents are likely to express anger, criticize, and punish (Erel & Burman, 1995; Harold & Conger, 1997). Similarly, children can affect their parents' relationship in powerful ways. For example, as we will see in Chapter 10, some children show lasting emotional problems when their parents divorce. But longitudinal research reveals that children of divorcing couples are more likely to be impulsive and undercontrolled long before the marital breakup. These behaviors may have contributed to as well as been caused by their parents' marital problems (Amato & Booth, 1996; Block, Block, & Gjerde, 1988; Cherlin et al., 1991).

Yet even when family relationships are strained by third parties, other members can help restore effective interaction. Grandparents are a case in point. They can promote children's development in many ways—both directly, by responding warmly to the child, and indirectly, by providing parents with child-rearing advice, models of child-rearing skill, and even financial assistance. Of course, like any indirect influence, grandparents can sometimes be harmful. When quarrelsome relations exist between grandparents and parents, parent–child communication may suffer.

■ ADAPTING TO CHANGE. Think back to the *chronosystem* in Bronfenbrenner's theory (see page 26). The interplay of forces within the family is dynamic and ever changing. Important events, such as the birth of a baby, a change of jobs, or an elderly parent joining the household due to declining health, create challenges that modify existing relationships. The way such events affect family interaction depends on the support provided by other family members as well as the developmental status of each participant. For example, the arrival of a new baby prompts very different reactions in a toddler than in a school-age child. And caring for an ill elderly parent is more stressful for a middle-aged adult still rearing young children than for an adult of the same age without child-rearing responsibilities.

Historical time period also contributes to a dynamic family system. In recent decades, a declining birth rate, a high divorce rate, and expansion of women's roles have led to a smaller family size. This, combined with a longer lifespan, means that more generations are alive with fewer members in the youngest ones, leading to a "top-heavy" family structure. Consequently, young people today are more likely to have older relatives than at any time in history—a circumstance that can be enriching as well as a source of tension. In sum, as this complex intergenerational system moves through time, relationships are constantly revised as members adjust to their own and others' development as well as to external pressures.

Despite these variations, some general patterns in family functioning do exist. In the United States and other Western nations, one important source of these consistencies is socioeconomic status.

SOCIOECONOMIC STATUS AND FAMILY FUNCTIONING

People in industrialized nations are stratified on the basis of what they do at work and how much they earn for doing it—factors that determine their social position and economic well-being. Researchers assess a family's standing on this continuum through an index called **socioeconomic status (SES).** It combines three interrelated, but not completely overlapping, variables: (1) years of education and (2) the prestige of and skill required by one's job, both of which measure social status; and (3) income, which measures economic status. As socioeconomic status rises and falls, people face changing circumstances that profoundly affect family functioning.

Socioeconomic status affects the timing and duration of phases of the family life cycle. People who work in skilled and semiskilled manual occupations (for example, machin-

ists, truck drivers, and custodians) tend to marry and have children earlier as well as give birth to more children than do people in white-collar and professional occupations. The two groups also differ in values and expectations. For example, when asked about personal qualities they desire for their children, lower-SES parents tend to place greater emphasis on external characteristics, such as obedience, neatness, and cleanliness. In contrast, higher-SES parents emphasize psychological traits, such as curiosity, happiness, and self-direction. In addition, higher-SES adults expect to occupy a wider range of roles, both within the family and without, than do their lower-SES counterparts.

These differences are reflected in family interaction. Lower-SES fathers focus on their provider role and devote less time to parenting, whereas higher-SES fathers often share in housework and child-rearing responsibilities (although their commitment rarely equals that of mothers). Furthermore, higher-SES parents talk to and stimulate their infants more and grant them greater freedom to explore. When their children are older, they use more explanations and verbal praise. In contrast, commands, such as "You do that because I told you to," as well as criticism and physical punishment occur more often in lower-SES households (Dodge, Pettit, & Bates, 1994; Hoff-Ginsberg & Tardiff, 1995).

The life conditions of families help explain these findings. Lower-SES adults often feel a sense of powerlessness and lack of influence in their relationships beyond the home. For example, at work, they must obey the rules of others in positions of power and authority. When they get home, their parent–child interaction seems to duplicate these experiences, only with them in the authority roles. Higher-SES parents have a greater sense of control over their own lives. At work, they are used to making independent decisions and convincing others of their point of view. At home, they teach these skills to their children (Greenberger, O'Neil, & Nagel, 1994).

Education also contributes to SES differences in family interaction. Higher-SES parents' interest in verbal stimulation and in nurturing inner traits is supported by years of schooling, during which they learned to think about abstract, subjective ideas (Uribe, LeVine, & LeVine, 1994). Furthermore, the greater economic security of higher-SES families frees them from the burden of having to worry about making ends meet on a daily basis. They can devote more time, energy, and material resources to furthering their own and their children's psychological characteristics.

As early as the second year of life, SES is positively correlated with cognitive and language development. Throughout childhood and adolescence, higher-SES youngsters do better in school (Brody, 1997; Walker et al., 1994). And by early adulthood, they attain higher levels of education, which greatly enhances opportunities for a prosperous adult life. Researchers believe that differences in family functioning have much to do with these outcomes.

THE IMPACT OF POVERTY

When families slip into poverty, development is seriously threatened. Shirley Brice Heath (1990), an anthropologist who has spent many years studying families of poverty, describes the case of Zinnia Mae, who grew up in Trackton, a close-knit black community located in a small southeastern American city. As unemployment struck Trackton in the 1980s and citizens moved away, 16-year-old Zinnia Mae caught a ride to Atlanta. Two years later, Heath visited her there. By then, Zinnia Mae was the mother of three children—a 16-month-old daughter named Donna and 2-month-old twin boys. She had moved into high-rise public housing.

Each of Zinnia Mae's days was much the same. She watched TV and talked with girlfriends on the phone. The children had only one set meal (breakfast) and otherwise ate whenever they were hungry or bored. Their play space was limited to the living room sofa and a mattress on the floor. Toys consisted of scraps of a blanket, spoons, food cartons, a small rubber ball, a few plastic cars, and a roller skate abandoned in the building. Zinnia Mae's most frequent words were, "I'm so tired." She worried about how to get papers to the welfare office, where to find a baby-sitter so she could go to the laundry or grocery, and what she would do if she located the twins' father, who had stopped sending money. She rarely had enough energy to spend time with her children.

■ *Homeless in the United States has risen over the past two decades. Families like this one travel from place to place in search of employment and a safe and secure place to live. Because of constant stress and few social supports, homeless children are usually behind in development, have frequent health problems, and show poor psychological adjustment. (Photo courtesy: Tony Freeman/PhotoEdit)*

Over the past 30 years, economic changes in the United States have caused the poverty rate to climb substantially. Today, 36 million people—14 percent of the population—are affected. Those hit hardest are parents under age 25 with young children and elderly people who live alone. Poverty is also magnified among ethnic minorities and women. For example, nearly 20 percent of American children are poor, a rate that climbs to 32 percent for Hispanic children, 40 percent for African-American children, and 32 percent for Native-American children. For single mothers with preschool children and black elderly women on their own, the poverty rate is over 60 percent (U.S. Bureau of the Census, 1999). Joblessness, a high divorce rate, a lower remarriage rate among women than men, widowhood, and (as we will see later) inadequate government programs to meet family needs are responsible for these disheartening statistics. The condition of children is particularly worrisome because the earlier poverty begins and the longer it lasts, the more devastating its effects on physical and mental health and school achievement (Children's Defense Fund, 1999; McLeod & Shanahan, 1996). Since the 1970s, the child poverty rate has been higher than that of any other age group.

The constant stresses that accompany poverty gradually weaken the family system. Poor families have many daily hassles—bills to pay, the car breaking down, loss of welfare and unemployment payments, something stolen from the house, to name just a few. When daily crises arise, family members become depressed, irritable, and distracted, and hostile interactions increase (Conger et al., 1992; McLoyd, 1998). These outcomes are especially severe in families that must live in poor housing and dangerous neighborhoods—conditions that make everyday existence even more difficult while reducing social supports that assist in coping with economic hardship (Duncan, Brooks-Gunn, & Klebanov, 1994; McLoyd et al., 1994).

Besides poverty, another problem—one that was quite uncommon 20 years ago—has reduced the life chances of many children and adults in the United States. On any given night, approximately 735,000 people have no place to live (Wright, 1999). The majority are adults on their own, some of whom have serious emotional and substance abuse problems. But nearly 40 percent of America's homeless population is made up of families, and it is believed that 1 in every 4 homeless individuals is a child. The rise in family homelessness is due to a number of factors, the most important of which is a decline in the availability of government-supported low-cost housing (Children's Defense Fund, 1999).

Most homeless families consist of women with children under age 5. Besides health problems (which affect most homeless people), homeless children suffer from developmental delays and serious emotional stress (Oberg, Bryant, & Bach, 1995). An estimated 25 to 30 percent who are old enough do not attend school. Those who do attend achieve less well than other poverty-stricken children due to poor attendance and health and emotional difficulties (Rafferty, 1995; Vostanis, Grattan, & Cumella, 1997). A common factor among the homeless is loss of supportive ties to relatives and friends.

BEYOND THE FAMILY: NEIGHBORHOODS, TOWNS, AND CITIES

In ecological systems theory, the mesosystem and exosystem underscore that ties between family and community are vital for psychological well-being throughout the lifespan. From our discussion of poverty and homelessness, perhaps you can see why. In poverty-stricken urban areas, community life is usually disrupted. Families move often, parks and playgrounds are in disarray, and community centers providing organized leisure time activities do not exist. Family violence and child abuse and neglect are greatest in neighborhoods where residents are dissatisfied with their community, describing it as a socially isolated place to live. In contrast, when family ties to the community are strong—as indicated by regular church attendance and frequent contact with friends and relatives—family stress and adjustment problems are reduced (Garbarino & Kostelny, 1993).

■ NEIGHBORHOODS. Let's take a closer look at the functions that communities serve in the lives of children and adults by beginning with the neighborhood. What were your childhood experiences like in the yards, streets, and parks surrounding your home? How did you spend your time, whom did you get to know, and how important were these moments to you?

The resources offered by neighborhoods play an important part in children's development. One study found that the more varied children's neighborhood experiences—membership in organizations (such as scouting and 4-H), contact with adults of their grandparents' generation, and places to go off by themselves or with friends (a treehouse, a fort, or a neighbor's garage)—the better their emotional and social adjustment (Bryant, 1985).

Neighborhood resources have a greater impact on the development of young people in economically disadvantaged than well-to-do neighborhoods (McLeod & Shanahan, 1996). Affluent families are not as dependent on their immediate surroundings for social support, education, and leisure pursuits. They can afford to reach beyond the streets near their homes, transporting their children to lessons and entertainment and, if necessary, to better-quality schools in distant parts of the community (Elliott et al., 1996). After-school programs that substitute for lack of resources in low-income neighborhoods by providing enrichment activities are associated with improved school performance and psychological adjustment in middle childhood (Posner & Vandell, 1994; Vandell & Posner, 1999).

Neighborhoods also influence well-being in adulthood. For example, an employed parent who can rely on a neigh-bor to assist her school-age child in her absence and who lives in an area safe for walking to and from school is granted the peace of mind essential for productive work. During late adulthood, neighborhoods become increasingly important, since the elderly spend more time in their own homes than they did in earlier years. Despite the availability of planned housing for older people, about 88 percent remain in regular housing, usually in the same neighborhood in which they lived during their working lives (Parmelee & Lawton, 1990; U.S. Bureau of the Census, 1999). Proximity to relatives and friends is a significant factor in the decision to move or stay put late in life. In the absence of nearby family members, the elderly mention neighbors and nearby friends as resources they rely on most for physical and social support (Hooyman & Kiyak, 1998).

■ TOWNS AND CITIES. Neighborhoods are embedded in towns and cities, which also mold children's and adults' daily lives. A well-known study examined the kinds of community settings children entered and the roles they played in a Midwestern town with a population of 700 (Barker, 1955). Many settings existed, and children were granted important responsibilities in them. For example, they helped

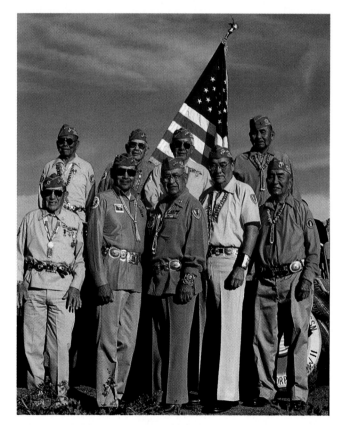

■ *Neighborhood quality is especially important during late adulthood when leisure time increases. These Native–American veterans of World War II gather in their neighborhood to prepare for a Veteran's Day parade. (Photo courtesy: Anthony Cassidy/Stone)*

stock shelves at Kane's Grocery Store, played in the town band, and operated the snow plow when help was short. As children joined in these activities, they did so alongside adults, who taught them the skills they needed to become responsible members of the community. Compared with large urban areas, small towns offer stronger connections between settings that influence children's lives. For example, since most citizens know each other and schools serve as centers of community life, contact between teachers and parents occurs often—an important factor in promoting children's academic achievement (Connell, Spencer, & Aber, 1994; Eccles & Harold, 1996).

Like children, adults in small towns penetrate more settings and are more likely to occupy positions of leadership, since a greater proportion of residents are needed to meet community needs—for example, by serving on the town council, on the school board, or in other civic roles. In late adulthood, people residing in small towns and suburbs find that their neighbors are more willing to provide assistance. As a result, they develop a greater number of warm relationships with nonrelatives (Lawton, 1980). As one 99-year-old resident of a small midwestern community, living alone and leading an active life, commented, "I don't think I could get along if I didn't have good neighbors." The family next door helps him with grocery shopping, checks each night to make sure his basement light is off (the signal that he is out of the shower and into bed), and looks out in the morning to see that his garage door is raised (the signal that he is up and okay) (Fergus, 1995).

Of course, children and adults in small towns cannot visit museums, go to professional baseball games, or attend orchestra concerts on a regular basis. The variety of settings is somewhat reduced compared to large cities. In small towns, however, active involvement in the community is likely to be greater throughout the lifespan. Also, public places in small towns are relatively safe and secure. Responsible adults are present in almost all settings to keep an eye on children. And the elderly feel a greater sense of personal safety—a strong contributor to how satisfied they are with their place of residence (Parmelee & Lawton, 1990). These conditions are hard to match in today's urban environments.

Think back to the case of Zinnia Mae and her three young children described on page 64. It reveals that community life is especially undermined in high-rise urban housing projects. In these dwellings, social contact is particularly important, since many residents have been uprooted from neighborhoods where they felt a strong sense of cultural identity and belonging. Typically, high rises are heavily populated with young single mothers, who are separated from family and friends by the cost and inconvenience of cross-town transportation. They report intense feelings of loneliness in the small, cramped apartments.

At Heath's (1990) request, Zinnia Mae agreed to tape record her family interactions over a 2-year period. In 500 hours of tape, (other than simple directions or questions about what her children were doing) Zinnia Mae started a conversation with Donna and the boys only 18 times. Cut off from community ties, she found it difficult to join in activities with her children. The result was a barren, understimulating environment—one very different from the home and community in which Zinnia Mae herself had grown up.

THE CULTURAL CONTEXT

Our discussion in Chapter 1 emphasized that human development can be fully understood only when viewed in its larger cultural context. In the following sections, we expand on this important theme. First, we illustrate ways in which cultural values and practices affect environmental contexts for development. Second, we consider how healthy development throughout the lifespan depends on laws and government programs that shield people from harm and foster their well-being.

■ CULTURAL VALUES AND PRACTICES. Cultures shape family interaction and community settings beyond the home—in short, all aspects of daily life. Many of us remain blind to aspects of our own cultural heritage until we see them in relation to the practices of others.

Each semester, I ask my students to think about the question: Who should be responsible for rearing young children? Here are some typical answers: "If parents decide to have a baby, then they should be ready to care for it." "Most people are not happy about others intruding into family life." These statements reflect a widely held opinion in the United States—that the care and rearing of children, and paying for that care, are the duty of parents, and only parents (Rickel & Becker, 1997; Scarr, 1996). This view has a long history—one in which independence, self-reliance, and the privacy of family life emerged as central American values. It is one reason, among others, that the American public has been slow to accept the idea of publicly supported health insurance and child care for children of employed parents. The strong emphasis on individualism has also contributed to the large number of American families that remain poor, despite the fact that their members are gainfully employed (Chase-Lansdale & Vinovskis, 1995).

Although many Americans value independence and privacy, cooperative family structures can be found in the United States. In large industrialized nations like ours, not all citizens share the same values. **Subcultures** exist—groups of people with beliefs and customs that differ from those of the larger culture. The values and practices of some ethnic minority groups help protect their members from the harmful effects of poverty. A case in point is the African-American family. As the Variations box on the following page indicates, the black cultural tradition of **extended family households,** in which three or more generations live together, is a vital feature of black family life that has enabled its members to survive, despite a long history of prejudice and economic deprivation.

THE AFRICAN-AMERICAN EXTENDED FAMILY

The African-American extended family can be traced to the African heritage of most black Americans. In many African societies, newly married couples do not start their own households. Instead, they marry into a large extended family that assists its members with all aspects of daily life. This tradition of a broad network of kin ties traveled to the United States during the period of slavery. Since then, it has served as a protective shield against the destructive impact of poverty and racial prejudice on African-American family life (McAdoo, 1993). Today, more black than white adults have relatives other than their own children living in the same household. African-American parents also see more kin during the week and perceive them as more important figures in their lives, respecting the advice of relatives and caring deeply about what they think is important (Wilson et al., 1995).

By providing emotional support and sharing income and essential resources, the African-American extended family helps reduce the stress of poverty and single parenthood. In addition, extended-family members often help with the rearing of children (Pearson et al., 1990). The presence of grandmothers in the households of many African-American teenagers and their infants protects babies from the negative influence of an overwhelmed and inexperienced mother. Furthermore, black adolescent mothers living in extended families are more likely to complete high school and get a job and less likely to be on welfare than are mothers living on their own—factors that return to benefit children's well-being (Trent & Harlan, 1994).

For single mothers who were very young at the time of their child's birth, extended family living is associated with more positive adult–child interaction during infancy and the preschool years. Otherwise, establishing an independent household with the help of nearby relatives is related to improved child rearing. Perhaps this arrangement permits the more mature mother who has developed effective parenting skills to implement them (Chase-Lansdale, Brooks-Gunn, & Zamsky, 1994). In families rearing adolescents, kinship support increases the likelihood of effective parenting, which is related to adolescents' self-reliance, emotional well-being, and reduced delinquency (Taylor & Roberts, 1995).

Finally, African-American elderly report a very high degree of satisfaction from family life. Compared with their white counterparts, black grandmothers are more likely to provide child-rearing assistance and financial help to their children and grandchildren. Relatives hold them in high esteem, describing them as sources of love, strength, and stability. And grandmothers play a central role in transmitting African-American culture by teaching moral and religious values, encouraging cooperation and mutual support, and teaching children about their African heritage (Tolson & Wilson, 1990). These influences strengthen family bonds, protect children's development, and increase the chances that the extended-family lifestyle will carry over to the next generation.

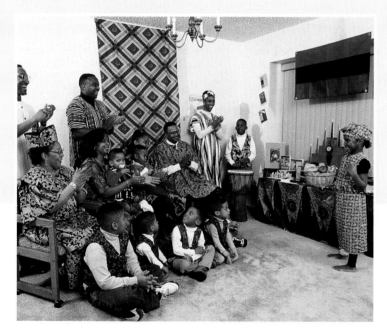

■ *Strong bonds with extended-family members have helped protect the development of many African-American children growing up under conditions of poverty and single parenthood. This extended family gathers for Kwanzaa, a cultural holiday celebrated between December 26 and January 1 by Africans and African descendants throughout the world. In Swahili, "matunda ya kwanzaa" means first fruits. Kwanzaa rituals are derived from African harvest celebrations. (Photo courtesy: Lawrence Migdale/Stone)*

Within the extended family, grandparents play meaningful roles in guiding younger generations; adults with employment, marital, or child-rearing difficulties receive assistance and emotional support; and caregiving is enhanced for children and the elderly. Active and involved extended families also characterize other American minorities, such as Asian-American, Native-American, and Hispanic subcultures (Harrison et al., 1994).

Consider our discussion so far, and you will see that it reflects a broad dimension on which cultures and subcultures differ: the extent to which *collectivism* versus *individualism* is emphasized. In **collectivist societies,** people define themselves as part of a group and stress group over individual goals. In **individualistic societies,** people think of themselves as separate entities and are largely concerned with their own personal needs (Triandis, 1995). Although individualism tends to increase as cultures become more complex, cross-national differences remain. The United States is more individualistic than most other industrialized nations. As we will see in the next section, collectivist versus individualistic values have a powerful impact on a nation's approach to protecting human development and well-being.

■ PUBLIC POLICIES AND LIFESPAN DEVELOPMENT. When widespread social problems arise, such as poverty, homelessness, hunger, and disease, nations attempt to solve them by developing **public policies**—laws and government programs designed to improve current conditions. For example, when poverty increases and families become homeless, a country might decide to build more low-cost housing, raise the minimum wage, and increase welfare benefits. When reports indicate that many children are not achieving well in school, federal and state governments might grant more tax money to school districts and make sure that help reaches pupils who need it most. And when senior citizens have difficulty making ends meet because of inflation, a nation might increase its social security benefits.

The United States is among the wealthiest of nations and has the broadest knowledge base for intervening effectively in people's lives. Still, American public policies safeguarding children and youths have lagged behind policies for the elderly. And both sets of policies have been slower to emerge in the United States than in other Western industrialized nations.

Policies for Children, Youths, and Families. We have already seen in previous sections that although many American children fare well, a large number grow up in environments that threaten their development. As Table 2.5 reveals, the United States does not rank among the top countries on any key measure of children's health and well-being.

The problems of American children and youths extend beyond the indicators in the table. For example, approximately 15 percent have no health insurance, making them the largest segment of the uninsured population (Children's Defense Fund, 1999). Furthermore, the United States has been slow to move toward national standards and funding for child care. According to recent evidence, much child care is substandard in quality (Cost, Quality, and Outcomes Study Team, 1995). In American families

TABLE 2.5

How Does the United States Compare to Other Nations on Indicators of Child Health and Well-Being?

INDICATOR	U.S. RANK	SOME COUNTRIES THE UNITED STATES TRAILS
Childhood poverty[a]	8th (among 8 industrial nations considered)	Australia, Canada, Germany, Great Britain, Norway, Sweden, Switzerland
Infant deaths in the first year of life	21st (worldwide)	Hong Kong, Ireland, Singapore, Spain
Low-birth-weight newborns	20th (worldwide)	Bulgaria, Egypt, Greece, Iran, Jordan, Kuwait, Paraguay, Romania, Saudi Arabia
Teenage pregnancy rate	11th (among 11 industrialized nations considered)	Australia, Canada, Czech Republic, France, New Zealand, Sweden
Percentage of young children immunized against measles	43rd (worldwide)	Chile, Czechoslovakia, Jordan, Poland, Romania
Expenditures on education as percentage of gross domestic product[b]	14th (among 16 industrialized nations considered)	Canada, France, Great Britain, the Netherlands, Sweden

[a]The U.S. child poverty rate of nearly 20 percent is more than twice that of any of these nations. For example, the rate is 9 percent in Australia, 9.3 percent in Canada, 4.6 percent in France, and 1.6 percent in Sweden.

[b]Gross domestic product is the value of all goods and services produced by a nation during a specified time period. It serves as an overall measure of a nation's wealth.

Sources: Bellamy, 1999; Central Intelligence Agency, 1999; Children's Defense Fund, 1999; Harris, 1996; Sivard, 1996.

affected by divorce, child support payments are inadequately enforced. Three-fourths of custodial mothers do not receive the full court-ordered allowance from their children's fathers. By the time American young people finish high school, many do not have the educational preparation they need to contribute fully to society. From 30 to 60 percent of 17-year-olds have difficulty with moderately complex reasoning in reading, writing, mathematics, and science (Campbell, Voelkl, & Donahue, 1997). Those who graduate but do not go to college generally lack vocational skills required for well-paid jobs. And about 13 percent of adolescents leave high school without a diploma. If they do not return to finish their education, they are at risk for lifelong poverty (Children's Defense Fund, 1999).

Why have attempts to help children and youths been more difficult to realize in the United States than in other industrialized nations? A complex set of political and economic forces is involved. The American ideals of self-reliance and privacy have made government hesitant to become involved in family matters. In addition, there is less consensus among American than European citizens on issues of child and family policy, such as public support for child care and health services. Finally, good social programs are expensive, and they must compete for a fair share of a country's economic resources. Children can easily remain unrecognized in this process, since they cannot vote or speak out to protect their own interests, as adult citizens do (Zigler & Finn-Stevenson, 1999). Instead, they must rely on the goodwill of others to become an important government priority.

Policies for the Elderly. Until the mid-twentieth century, the United States had few policies in place to protect its aging population. For example, social security benefits, which address the income needs of retired citizens who contributed to society through prior employment, were not awarded until the 1940s. Yet most western European nations had social security systems in place by the late nineteenth or early twentieth century (DiNitto, 1999). In the 1960s, U.S. federal spending on programs for the elderly rapidly expanded. Medicare, a national health insurance program for older people that pays partial health-care costs, was initiated. Today, spending for the aged accounts for 30 percent of all federal expenditures—5 times what was spent 30 years ago (Hooyman & Kiyak, 1998; Koff & Park, 1999).

Social Security and Medicare consume 96 percent of the U.S. federal budget for the elderly; only 4 percent is devoted to other programs. Consequently, American programs for the elderly have been criticized for neglecting social services (Hooyman & Kiyak, 1998). To meet this need, a national network for planning, coordinating, and delivering assistance to the aged has been established. Approximately 700 Area Agencies on Aging operate at regional and local levels, assessing community needs and offering communal and home-delivered meals, self-care education, elder abuse prevention, and a wide range of other social services. However, limited funding means that the Area Agencies help far too few people in need.

As we noted earlier, many senior citizens—especially women, ethnic minorities, and those living alone—remain in dire economic straits. Those who had interrupted employment histories, held jobs without benefits, or suffered lifelong poverty are not eligible for social security. Although all people age 65 and older are guaranteed a minimum income, it is less than the poverty line—the amount judged necessary for bare subsistence by the federal government. Furthermore, social security benefits are rarely enough to serve as a sole source of retirement income; they must be supplemented through other pensions and family savings. But a substantial percentage of aging citizens do not have access to these resources. Therefore, they are more likely to be among the "near poor" than are other age groups (Koff & Park, 1999).

Nevertheless, America's aging population is financially much better off than in the past. Today, the elderly are a large, powerful, well-organized constituency, far more likely than children or low-income and homeless families to attract the support of politicians. As a result, although poverty has risen in the general population, the number of aging poor has declined from 1 out of 3 people in 1960 to 1 out of 10 in the late 1990s (U.S. Bureau of the Census, 1999). And modern senior citizens are healthier and more independent

■ *Overall, senior citizens in the United States are better off economically than are children. Nevertheless, many older adults—especially women, ethnic minorities, and those living alone—are poverty stricken, and American elders are more likely to be among the "near poor" than are other age groups. (Photo courtesy: Andy Levin/Photo Researchers, Inc.)*

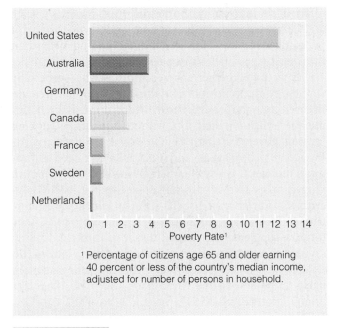

¹ Percentage of citizens age 65 and older earning 40 percent or less of the country's median income, adjusted for number of persons in household.

FIGURE 2.7

■ **Percentage of citizens age 65 and older living in poverty in seven industrialized nations, based on the most recent available data.** Among countries listed, public expenditures on social security and other income guarantees for senior citizens are highest in the Netherlands, lowest in the United States (United Nations, 1996). Consequently, poverty among the elderly is virtually nonexistent in the Netherlands but greatly exceeds that of other nations in the United States.

than ever before. Still, as Figure 2.7 shows, the elderly in the United States are not as well off as those in Australia, Canada, and Western Europe. Many are inadequately served by current policies.

■ LOOKING TOWARD THE FUTURE. Despite the worrisome state of many children, families, and aging citizens, progress is being made in improving their condition. Throughout this book, we will discuss many successful programs that could be expanded. Another positive sign is that researchers are more involved than ever before in seeking answers to policy-relevant questions about human development and communicating their findings to the country as a whole (Huston, 1994; Koff & Park, 1999).

Finally, growing awareness of the gap between what we know and what we do to better people's lives has led experts in human development to join with concerned citizens as advocates for more effective policies. Over the past few decades, several influential interest groups with the well-being of children or the elderly as their central purpose have emerged. Among the most vigorous are the Children's Defense Fund and the American Association of Retired Persons.

A private, nonprofit organization founded by Marion Wright Edelman in 1973, the *Children's Defense Fund* engages in research, public education, legal action, drafting of legislation, congressional testimony, and community organizing. Each year, it publishes *The State of America's Children,* which provides a comprehensive analysis of the current condition of children, government-sponsored programs serving them, and proposals for improving child and family programs.

Nearly half of Americans over age 50 (both retired and employed)—more than 32 million people—are members of the *American Association of Retired Persons (AARP).* Founded by Ethel Percy Andrus in 1958, AARP has a large and energetic lobbying staff that works for increased government benefits of all kinds for the aged. Each year, it releases the *AARP Public Policy Agenda,* which forms the basis for advocacy activities in diverse areas, including income, health care, social services, housing, and personal and legal rights. Among AARP's programs is an effort to mobilize elderly voters, an initiative that keeps lawmakers highly sensitive to policy proposals favoring older Americans.

Besides strong advocacy, the design and implementation of public policies that enhance human development depend on policy-relevant research that documents needs and evaluates programs to spark improvements. Today, researchers are doing a better job of establishing partnerships with government and community agencies to enhance the social relevance of their investigations. They are also making progress in communicating their findings to the public in easily understandable ways, through television documentaries, newspaper stories, and magazine articles as well as direct reports to government officials (Denner et al., 1999). As a result, they are helping to create a sense of immediacy about the condition of children, families, and the aged that is necessary to spur a society into action.

■ **ASK YOURSELF . . .**

■ *On one of your trips to the local shopping center, you see a father getting very angry at his young son. Using ecological systems theory, list as many factors as you can that might account for the father's behavior.*

🌳 *Links between family and community foster development throughout the lifespan. Provide examples and research findings from our discussion that support this idea.*

🌳 *Check your local newspaper and one or two national news magazines to see how often articles appear on the condition of children, families, and the aged. Why is it important for researchers to communicate with the general public about the well-being of these sectors of the population?*

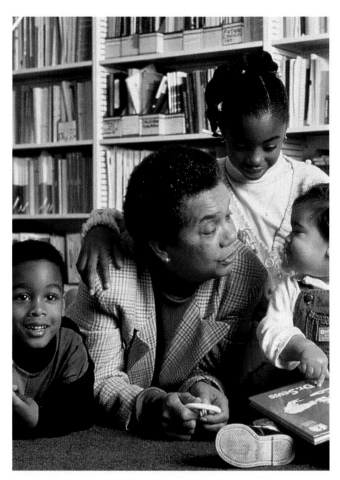

■ *In 1973, Marion Wright Edelman founded the Children' Defense Fund, a private, nonprofit organization that provides a strong, effective voice for American children, who cannot vote, lobby, or speak for themselves. Edelman continues to serve as president of the Children's Defense Fund today. (Photo courtesy: Westen-berger/Liaison Agency)*

UNDERSTANDING THE RELATIONSHIP BETWEEN HEREDITY AND ENVIRONMENT

So far in this chapter, we have discussed a wide variety of hereditary and environmental influences, each of which has the power to alter the course of development. Yet people born into the same family (and who therefore share genes and environments) are often quite different in characteristics. We also know that some individuals are affected more than others by their homes, neighborhoods, and communities. Cases exist in which a person provided with all the advantages in life does poorly, whereas another exposed to the worst of rearing conditions does well. How do scientists explain the impact of heredity and environment when they seem to work in so many different ways?

All contemporary researchers agree that both heredity and environment are involved in every aspect of development. There is no real controversy on this point because an environment is always needed for genetic information to be expressed (Plomin, 1994a). But for polygenic traits (due to many genes) such as intelligence and personality, scientists are a long way from knowing the precise hereditary influences involved. They must study the impact of genes on these characteristics indirectly, and the nature–nurture controversy remains unresolved because researchers do not agree on how heredity and environment influence these complex characteristics.

Some believe that it is useful and possible to answer the question of *how much* each factor contributes to individual differences. These researchers use special methods to find out which factor plays the major role. A second group of investigators regards the question of which factor is more important as unanswerable. They believe that heredity and environment do not make separate contributions to behavior. Instead, they are always related, and the real question we need to explore is *how* they work together. Let's consider each of these two positions in turn.

THE QUESTION, "HOW MUCH?"

Two methods—heritability and concordance rates—are used to infer the importance of heredity in complex human characteristics. Let's look closely at the information these procedures yield, along with their limitations.

■ HERITABILITY. **Heritability estimates** measure the extent to which individual differences in complex traits, such as intelligence and personality, in a specific population are due to genetic factors. Researchers have obtained heritabilities for intelligence and a variety of personality characteristics. We will take a brief, introductory look at their findings here, returning to them in later chapters devoted to these topics. Heritability estimates are obtained from **kinship studies,** which compare the characteristics of family members. The most common type of kinship study compares identical twins, who share all their genes, with fraternal twins, who share only some. If people who are genetically more alike are also more similar in intelligence and personality, then the researcher assumes that heredity plays an important role.

Kinship studies of intelligence provide some of the most controversial findings in the field of human development. Some experts claim a strong role for heredity, whereas others believe that genetic factors are barely involved (Gould, 1996; Herrnstein & Murray, 1994; Jensen, 1969, 1998). When many twin studies are examined, correlations between the scores of identical twins are consistently higher than those of fraternal twins. In a summary of more than 13,000 twin pairs, the correlation for intelligence was .86 for identical twins and .55 for fraternal twins (Scarr, 1997).

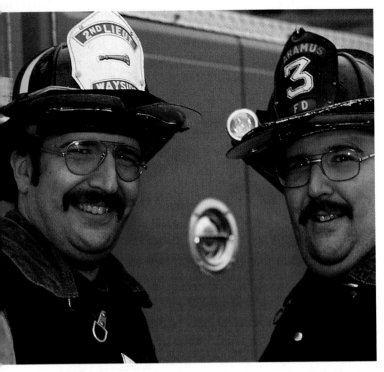

■ *Identical twins Bob and Bob were separated by adoption shortly after birth and not reunited until adulthood. The two Bobs discovered they were alike in many ways. Both hold bachelor's degrees in engineering, are married to teachers named Brenda, wear glasses, have mustaches, smoke pipes, and are volunteer firemen. The study of identical twins reared apart reveals that heredity contributes to many psychological characteristics. Nevertheless, not all separated twins match up as well as this pair, and generalizing from twin evidence to the population is controversial. (Photo courtesy: T. K. Wanstall/The Image Works)*

Researchers use a complex statistical procedure to compare these correlations, arriving at a heritability estimate ranging from 0 to 1.00. The value for intelligence is about .50 for child and adolescent twin samples in Western industrialized nations. This indicates that half the variation in intelligence can be explained by individual differences in genetic makeup (Plomin, 1994). However, heritability increases in adulthood, with some estimates as high as .80. As we will see in the final section of this chapter, one explanation is that adults exert much greater control over their intellectual experiences than do children (McGue et al., 1993). The fact that the intelligence of adopted children is more strongly correlated with the scores of their biological parents than with those of their adoptive parents offers further support for the role of heredity (Horn, 1983; Scarr & Weinberg, 1983).

Heritability research reveals that genetic factors are important in temperament and personality. For traits that have been studied a great deal (such as sociability, emotional expressiveness, and activity level), heritability esti-

mates obtained on child, adolescent, and early adult twins are moderate, at about .40 or .50 (Bouchard, 1994; Rothbart & Bates, 1998). Unlike intelligence, however, there is no evidence for an increase in heritability of personality over the lifespan (Brody, 1994).

■ CONCORDANCE. A second measure that has been used to infer the contribution of heredity to complex characteristics is the **concordance rate.** It refers to the percentage of instances in which both twins show a trait when it is present in one twin. Researchers typically use concordance to study the contribution of heredity to emotional and behavior disorders, which can be judged as either present or absent.

A concordance rate ranges from 0 to 100 percent. A score of 0 indicates that if one twin has the trait, the other one never has it. A score of 100 means that if one twin has the trait, the other one always has it. When a concordance rate is much higher for identical twins than for fraternal twins, then heredity is believed to play a major role. Twin studies of schizophrenia[1] and severe depression show this pattern of findings. In the case of schizophrenia, the concordance rate for identical twins is 50 percent, that for fraternal twins only 18 percent. The figures are 69 percent and 25 percent for severe depression (Gottesman, 1991; McGuffin & Sargeant, 1991). Once again, adoption studies lend support to these results. Biological relatives of schizophrenic and depressed adoptees are more likely to share the same disorder than are adoptive relatives (Loehlin, Willerman, & Horn, 1988).

Taken together, concordance and adoption research suggest that the tendency for schizophrenia and depression to run in families is partly due to genetic factors. However, we also know that environment is involved, since the concordance rate for identical twins would have to be 100 percent if heredity were the only influence operating. In later chapters, we will see that environmental stresses, such as poverty, family conflict, and a disorganized home life, are often associated with emotional and behavior disorders.

■ LIMITATIONS OF HERITABILITY AND CONCORDANCE. Although heritability estimates and concordance rates provide evidence that genetic factors contribute to complex human characteristics, questions have been raised about their accuracy. First, we must keep in mind that each value refers only to the particular population studied and its unique range of genetic and environmental influences. If the range of either heredity or environment changes, then heritability and concordance values will change. For example, imagine a country in which people's home, school, and community experiences are very similar. Under these conditions, individual differences in intelligence and personality

---

[1] Schizophrenia is a disorder involving serious difficulty distinguishing fantasy from reality, frequent delusions and hallucinations, and irrational and inappropriate behaviors.

would be largely due to heredity, and heritability estimates would be close to 1.00. Conversely, the more environments vary, the greater their opportunity to account for individual differences, and the lower heritability estimates are likely to be (Plomin, 1994a).

Second, the accuracy of heritability estimates and concordance rates depends on the extent to which the twin pairs on which they are computed reflect genetic and environmental variation in the population. Yet consider these findings: Identical twins reared together under highly similar conditions have more strongly correlated intelligence test scores than do those reared apart. When the former are used in research, the higher correlation causes the importance of heredity to be overestimated. To overcome this difficulty, researchers try to find twins who have been reared apart in adoptive families. But few separated twin pairs are available, and when they are, social service agencies often place them in advantaged homes that are similar in many ways (Eisenberg, 1998). Because the environments of most twin pairs do not represent the broad range of environments found in the general population, it is often difficult to generalize heritability and concordance findings to the population as a whole.

Heritability estimates are controversial measures because they can easily be misapplied. For example, high heritabilities have been used to suggest that ethnic differences in intelligence, such as the poorer performance of black children compared to white children, have a genetic basis (Jensen, 1969, 1985b). Yet this line of reasoning is widely regarded as incorrect. Heritabilities computed on mostly white twin samples do not tell us what is responsible for test score differences between ethnic groups. We have already seen that large economic and cultural differences are involved. In Chapter 9, we will discuss research indicating that when black children are adopted into economically advantaged homes at an early age, their scores are well above average and substantially higher than those of children growing up in impoverished families.

Perhaps the most serious criticism of heritability estimates and concordance rates has to do with their usefulness. Although they are interesting statistics that tell us heredity is undoubtedly involved in complex traits such as intelligence and personality, they give us no precise information about how these traits develop or how individuals might respond to environments designed to help them develop as far as possible (Bronfenbrenner & Ceci, 1994). Indeed, research shows that the heritability of intelligence is higher in advantaged homes and communities, which permit children to actualize their genetic endowment. In disadvantaged environments, children are prevented from realizing their potential. Consequently, enhancing their experiences through interventions (such as parent education and high-quality preschool or child care) has a greater impact on development (Bronfenbrenner & Morris, 1998; Scarr, 1998).

THE QUESTION, "HOW?"

According to a second perspective, heredity and environment cannot be divided into separate influences. Instead, behavior is the result of a dynamic interplay between these two forces. How do heredity and environment work together to affect development? Several important concepts shed light on this question.

■ REACTION RANGE. The first of these ideas is **range of reaction** (Gottesman, 1963). It emphasizes that each person responds to the environment in a unique way because of his or her genetic makeup. Let's explore this idea in Figure 2.8. Reaction range can apply to any characteristic; here it is illustrated for intelligence. Notice that when environments vary from extremely unstimulating to highly enriched, Ben's intelligence increases steadily, Linda's rises sharply and then falls off, and Ron's begins to increase only after the environment becomes modestly stimulating.

Reaction range highlights two important points about the relationship between heredity and environment. First, it shows that because each of us has a unique genetic makeup, we respond differently to the same environment. In Figure 2.8, notice how a poor environment results in similarly low scores for all three individuals. When environments provide an intermediate level of stimulation, Linda's score is by far

FIGURE 2.8

■ **Intellectual ranges of reaction (RR) for three children in environments that vary from extremely unstimulating to highly enriched.** *Each child, due to his or her genetic makeup, responds differently as quality of the environment changes. Ben's intelligence increases steadily, Linda's rises sharply and then falls off, and Ron's begins to increase only after the environment becomes modestly stimulating. (Adapted from Wahlsten, 1994.)*

the highest. And when environments are highly enriched, Ben does best, followed by Ron, both of whom now exceed Linda. Second, sometimes different genetic–environmental combinations can make two people look the same! For example, if Linda is reared in an unstimulating environment, her score will be about 100—average for people in general. Ben and Ron can also obtain this score, but to do so, they must grow up in a fairly enriched home.

The concept of range of reaction tells us that individuals differ in their range of possible responses to the environment. And it illustrates the meaning of the statement "Heredity and environment interact," since it shows that unique blends of heredity and environment lead to both similarities and differences in behavior (Wahlsten, 1994).

■ CANALIZATION. The concept of canalization provides another way of understanding how heredity and environment combine. **Canalization** is the tendency of heredity to restrict the development of some characteristics to just one or a few outcomes. A behavior that is strongly canalized follows a genetically set growth plan, and only powerful environmental forces can change it (Waddington, 1957). For example, infant perceptual and motor development seems to be strongly canalized, since all normal human babies eventually roll over, reach for objects, sit up, crawl, and walk. It takes extreme conditions to modify these behaviors or cause them not to appear. In contrast, intelligence and personality are less strongly canalized, since they respond easily to changes in the environment. When we look at the kinds of behaviors that are constrained by heredity, we can see that canalization is highly adaptive. Through it, nature ensures that children will develop certain species-typical skills under a wide range of rearing conditions, thereby promoting survival.

Recently, scientists expanded the notion of canalization to include environmental influences. We now know that environments can also limit development (Gottlieb, 1991). For example, when children experience harmful environments early in life, there may be little that later experiences can do to change characteristics (such as intelligence) that were quite flexible to begin with (Turkheimer & Gottesman, 1991).

Using the concept of canalization, we learn that genes restrict the development of some characteristics more than others. And over time, even very flexible behaviors can become fixed and canalized, depending on the environments to which individuals were exposed.

■ GENETIC–ENVIRONMENTAL CORRELATION. Nature and nurture work together in still another way. Several investigators point out that a major problem in trying to separate heredity and environment is that they are often correlated (Plomin, 1994; Scarr & McCartney, 1983). According to the concept of **genetic–environmental correlation,** our genes influence the environments to which we are exposed.

In support of this idea, a recent study showed that the greater the genetic similarity between pairs of adolescents, the more alike they were on many aspects of child rearing, including parental discipline, affection, conflict, and monitoring of the young person's activities (Plomin et al., 1994).

These findings indicate that heredity plays a role in molding experience. The way this happens changes with development.

Passive and Evocative Correlation. At younger ages, two types of genetic–environmental correlation are common. The first is called *passive* correlation because the child has no control over it. Early on, parents provide environments that are influenced by their own heredity. For example, parents who are good athletes are likely to enroll their children in swimming and gymnastics lessons. Besides getting exposed to an "athletic environment," the children may have inherited their parents' athletic ability. As a result, they are likely to become good athletes for both genetic and environmental reasons.

The second type of genetic–environmental correlation is *evocative.* Children evoke responses from others that are influenced by the child's heredity, and these responses strengthen the child's original style of responding. For example, an active, friendly baby is likely to receive more social stimulation from those around her than is a passive, quiet infant. And a cooperative, attentive child will probably receive more patient and sensitive interactions from parents than will an inattentive, distractible child.

Active Correlation. At older ages, *active* genetic–environmental correlation becomes common. As children ex-

■ *This mother is an accomplished musician who exposes her son to a stimulating musical environment. In addition, the boy may have inherited his mother's talent for music. When heredity and environment are correlated, they jointly foster the same capacities, and the influence of one cannot be separated from the influence of the other. (Photo courtesy: D. Smith/Monkmeyer Press)*

tend their experiences beyond the immediate family to school, neighborhood, and community and are given the freedom to make more of their own choices, they play an increasingly active role in seeking out environments that fit their genetic tendencies. The well-coordinated, muscular child spends more time at after-school sports, the musically talented youngster joins the school orchestra and practices his violin, and the intellectually curious child is a familiar patron at her local library.

This tendency to actively choose environments that complement our heredity is called **niche-picking** (Scarr & McCartney, 1983). Infants and young children cannot do much niche-picking, since adults select environments for them. In contrast, older children, adolescents, and adults are much more in charge of their own environments. The niche-picking idea explains why pairs of identical twins reared apart during childhood and later reunited may find, to their great surprise, that they have similar hobbies, food preferences, friendship choices, and vocations—a trend that is especially marked when twins' environmental opportunities are similar (Bouchard et al., 1990; Plomin, 1994b). Niche-picking also helps us understand longitudinal findings indicating that identical twins become somewhat more alike and fraternal twins and adopted siblings less alike in intelligence with age (McGue et al., 1993; Loehlin, Horn, & Willerman, 1997). The influence of heredity and environment is not constant but changes over time. With age, genetic factors may become more important in determining the environments we experience and choose for ourselves.

A major reason that researchers are interested in the nature–nurture issue is that they want to find ways to improve environments in order to help people develop as far as possible. The concepts of range of reaction, canalization, and genetic–environmental correlation remind us that development is best understood as a series of complex exchanges between nature and nurture. When a characteristic is strongly influenced by heredity, it can still be modified. However, people cannot be changed in any way we might desire. The success of any attempt to improve development depends on the characteristics we want to change, the genetic makeup of the individual, and the type and timing of our intervention.

ASK YOURSELF . . .

■ *A researcher wants to know whether alcoholism is influenced by genetic factors. Which method of inferring the importance of heredity in complex human characteristics could help answer this question?*

■ *One possible reason for the increase in heritability of intelligence in adulthood is that adults exert more control over their intellectual experiences than do children (see page 72). What type of genetic–environmental correlation is involved in this explanation? What light does it shed on the question of whether heritability estimates yield "pure" measures of genetic influences on human traits?*

SUMMARY

GENETIC FOUNDATIONS

What are genes, and how are they transmitted from one generation to the next?

■ Each individual's **phenotype,** or directly observable characteristics, is a product of both **genotype** and environment.

■ **Chromosomes,** rodlike structures within the cell nucleus, contain our hereditary endowment. Along their length are **genes,** segments of **DNA** that make us distinctly human and influence our development and characteristics.

■ **Gametes,** or sex cells, are produced by the process of cell division known as **meiosis.** Since each individual receives a unique set of genes from each parent, meiosis ensures that children will be genetically different from one another. Once sperm and ovum unite, the resulting **zygote** starts to develop into a complex human being through cell duplication, or **mitosis.**

■ If the fertilizing sperm carries an X chromosome, the child will be a girl; if it contains a Y chromosome, a boy will be born. **Fraternal,** or **dizygotic, twins** result when two ova are released from the mother's ovaries and

each is fertilized. In contrast, **identical,** or **monozygotic,** twins develop when a zygote divides in two during the early stages of cell duplication.

Describe various patterns of genetic inheritance.

■ **Dominant–recessive** and **codominant** relationships are patterns of inheritance that apply to many traits controlled by single genes. In dominant–recessive inheritance, **heterozygous** individuals with one recessive gene are **carriers** of their trait.

■ When recessive disorders are **X-linked** (carried on the X chromosome), males are more likely to be affected. **Genetic imprinting** is a newly discovered pattern of inheritance in which one parent's gene is activated, regardless of its makeup.

■ Unfavorable genes arise from **mutations,** which can occur spontaneously or be induced by hazardous environmental agents.

■ Human traits that vary continuously, such as intelligence and personality, are **polygenic,** or influenced by many genes. Since the genetic principles involved are unknown, scientists must study the influence of heredity on these characteristics indirectly.

Describe major chromosomal abnormalities, and explain how they occur.

■ Most chromosomal abnormalities are due to errors in meiosis. The most common chromosomal disorder is **Down syndrome,** which results in physical defects and mental retardation.

■ Disorders of the **sex chromosomes** are milder than defects of the **autosomes.** Contrary to popular belief, males with XYY syndrome are not prone to aggression. Studies of children with triple X, Klinefelter, and Turner syndromes reveal that adding to or subtracting from the usual number of X chromosomes leads to specific intellectual problems.

REPRODUCTIVE CHOICES

What procedures are available to assist prospective parents in having healthy, wanted children?

■ **Genetic counseling** helps couples at risk for giving birth to children with genetic abnormalities decide whether or not to conceive. **Prenatal diagnostic methods** make early detection of genetic problems possible. Although reproductive technologies, such as donor insemination, in vitro fertilization, and surrogate motherhood, permit many individuals to become parents who otherwise

would not, they raise serious legal and ethical concerns.

■ Many parents who cannot conceive or who have a high likelihood of transmitting a genetic disorder decide to adopt. Although adopted children have more learning and emotional problems than children in general, in the long run most fare quite well.

ENVIRONMENTAL CONTEXTS FOR DEVELOPMENT

Describe the social systems perspective on family functioning, along with aspects of the environment that support family well-being and development.

■ Just as complex as genetic inheritance is the surrounding environment in which human development takes place. The family is the first and foremost context for development. Ecological systems theory emphasizes that the behaviors of each family member affect those of others. The family system is also dynamic, constantly adjusting to new events, to developmental changes in its members, and to societal change.

■ Despite these variations, one source of consistency in family functioning is **socioeconomic status (SES).** Higher-SES families tend to be smaller, to place greater emphasis on nurturing psychological traits, and to promote warm, verbally stimulating interaction with children. Lower-SES families often stress external characteristics and engage in more restrictive child rearing. Development is seriously undermined by poverty and homelessness.

■ Supportive ties to the surrounding environment foster well-being throughout the lifespan. Communities that encourage constructive leisure time activities, warm interaction among residents, connections between settings, and children

and adults' active participation enhance development.

■ The values and practices of cultures and **subcultures** influence all aspects of daily life. **Extended family households,** in which three or more generations live together, are common among ethnic minorities. They protect development under conditions of high life stress.

■ In the complex world in which we live, favorable development depends on **public policies.** Effective social programs are influenced by many factors, including cultural values that stress **collectivism** over **individualism,** a nation's economic resources, and organizations and individuals that work for an improved quality of life. American policies safeguarding children and their families are not as well developed as those for the elderly. The needs of many people of all ages are inadequately served.

UNDERSTANDING THE RELATIONSHIP BETWEEN HEREDITY AND ENVIRONMENT

Explain the various ways heredity and environment may combine to influence complex traits.

■ Scientists do not agree on how heredity and environment influence complex characteristics, such as intelligence and personality. Some believe that it is useful and possible to determine "how much" each factor contributes to individual differences. These investigators compute **heritability estimates** and **concordance rates** from **kinship studies.**

■ Other scientists believe that the most important question is "how" heredity and environment work together. The concepts of **range of reaction, canalization,** and **genetic–environmental correlation** remind us that development is best understood as a series of complex exchanges between nature and nurture that change over the lifespan.

IMPORTANT TERMS AND CONCEPTS

autosomes (p. 48)

canalization (p. 74)

carrier (p. 49)

chromosomes (p. 46)

codominance (p. 50)

collectivist societies (p. 68)

concordance rate (p. 72)

deoxyribonucleic acid (DNA) (p. 47)

dominant–recessive inheritance (p. 49)

extended family household (p. 66)

fraternal, or dizygotic, twins (p. 48)

gametes (p. 47)

gene (p. 47)

genetic counseling (p. 55)

genetic–environmental correlation (p. 74)

genetic imprinting (p. 52)

genotype (p. 46)

heritability estimate (p. 71)

heterozygous (p. 49)

homozygous (p. 49)

identical, or monozygotic, twins (p. 48)

individualistic societies (p. 68)

kinship studies (p. 71)

meiosis (p. 47)

mitosis (p. 47)

mutation (p. 53)

niche-picking (p. 75)

phenotype (p. 46)

polygenic inheritance (p. 53)

prenatal diagnostic methods (p. 55)

public policies (p. 68)

range of reaction (p. 73)

sex chromosomes (p. 48)

socioeconomic status (SES) (p. 63)

subculture (p. 66)

X-linked inheritance (p. 51)

zygote (p. 47)

FYI FOR FURTHER INFORMATION AND HELP

Consult the companion website for this book, where you will find additional weblinks and associated learning activities: www.abacon.com/berk

GENETICS AND GENETIC DISORDERS

Human Genome Project
www.ornl.gov/TechResources/ Human_Genome/home.html
Provides comprehensive information about the international Human Genome Project, including project goals and current status.

March of Dimes
Birth Defects Foundation
www.modimes.org
Works to prevent genetic disorders and other birth defects through public education and community service programs.

National PKU News Organization
www.pknews.org
Provides up-to-date, accurate news and information to families and professionals dealing with phenylketonuria (PKU).

Sickle Cell Association
www.sicklecell-texas.org
Provides information to individuals affected by sickle cell disease and related blood disorders.

National Down Syndrome Congress
Web site: members.carol.net/ ~ndsc/index_fr.html
Assists parents in finding solutions to the needs of children with Down syndrome.

INFERTILITY

Resolve, Inc.
www.resolve.org
Developed by the National Infertility Association; offers counseling, referral, and support to persons with fertility problems.

ADOPTION

Adopt: Assistance Information Support
www.adopting.org
Provides assistance, information, and support on diverse aspects of adoption, including children from other countries and children with special needs.

PUBLIC POLICY AND STATUS OF AMERICAN CHILDREN, FAMILIES, AND THE ELDERLY

Children's Defense Fund
www.childrensdefense.org
An active child advocacy organization. Provides information on the condition of children and government-sponsored programs serving them.

National Center for Children in Poverty
cpmcnet.columbia.edu/dept/nccp
Aims to reduce the number of young children living in poverty by disseminating information about early education and maternal and child health and by proposing new initiatives to lawmakers.

American Association of Retired Persons
www.aarp.org
An active advocacy organization for older people. Aims to enhance quality of life, independence, and dignity.

U.S. Bureau of the Census
www.census.gov
Provides information about the people of the United States, including statistics on children, families, and the elderly related to income, housing, health, and education.

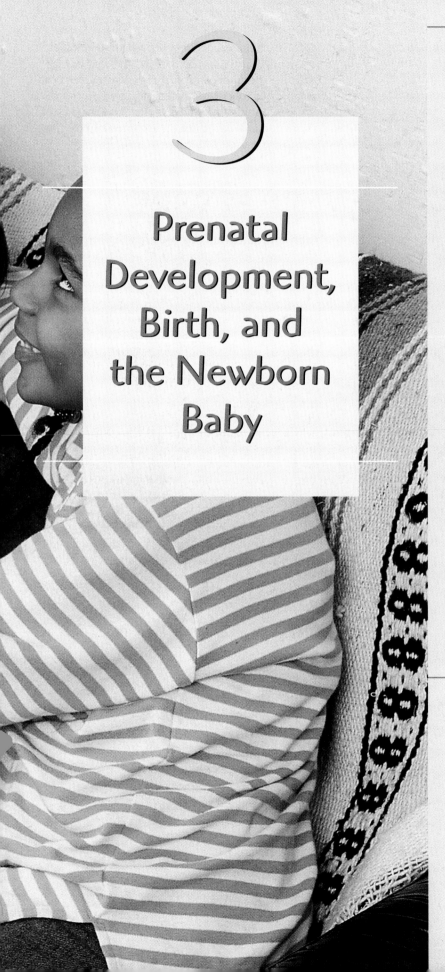

3

Prenatal Development, Birth, and the Newborn Baby

■ *As these parents teach their daughters, ages 2 and 6, about prenatal development and birth, they convey a sense of wonder and help the children welcome their new sibling. (Photo courtesy: © Laura Dwight)*

After months of wondering if the time in their own lives was right, Yolanda and Jay decided to have a baby. I met them one fall in my child development class, when Yolanda was just 2 months pregnant. Both were full of questions: "How does the baby grow before birth? When are different organs formed? Has its heart begun to beat? Can it hear, feel, or sense our presence in other ways?"

Most of all, Yolanda and Jay wanted to do everything possible to make sure their baby would be born healthy. At one time, they believed that the developing organism was completely shielded by the uterus from any dangers in the environment. All babies born with problems, they thought, had unfavorable genes. After browsing through several pregnancy books, Yolanda and Jay realized they were wrong. Yolanda started to wonder about her diet. And she asked me whether an aspirin for a headache, a glass of wine at dinnertime, or a few cups of coffee during study hours might be harmful.

In this chapter, we answer Yolanda and Jay's questions, along with a great many more that scientists have asked about the events before birth. First, we trace prenatal development, paying special attention to environmental factors that can damage the fetus or support healthy growth. Next, we turn to the events of childbirth. Today, women in industrialized nations have many more choices about where and how they give birth than ever before, and modern hospitals often go to great lengths to make the arrival of a new baby a rewarding, family-centered event.

Yolanda and Jay's son Joshua reaped the benefits of their careful attention to his needs during pregnancy. He was strong, alert, and healthy at birth. Nevertheless, the birth process does not always go smoothly. We will pay special attention to the problems of infants who are born under-weight or too early, before the prenatal period is complete. Our discussion will also examine the pros and cons of medical interventions, such as pain-relieving drugs and surgical deliveries, designed to ease a difficult birth and protect the health of mother and baby. We conclude by taking a close look at the remarkable capacities of newborns and parents' adjustment to the realities of life with a new baby.

PRENATAL DEVELOPMENT

The sperm and ovum that will unite to form the new individual are uniquely suited for the task of reproduction. The ovum is a tiny sphere, measuring $\frac{1}{175}$ inch in diameter, that is barely visible to the naked eye as a dot the size of a period at the end of this sentence. But in its microscopic world, it is a giant—the largest cell in the human body. The ovum's size makes it a perfect target for the much smaller sperm, which measure only $\frac{1}{500}$ inch.

CONCEPTION

About once every 28 days, in the middle of a woman's menstrual cycle, an ovum bursts from one of her *ovaries*, two walnut-sized organs located deep inside her abdomen, and is drawn into one of two *fallopian tubes*—long, thin structures that lead to the hollow, soft-lined uterus (see Figure 3.1). While the ovum is traveling, the spot on the ovary from which it was released, now called the *corpus luteum*, begins to secrete hormones that prepare the lining of the uterus to receive a fertilized ovum. If pregnancy does not occur, the corpus luteum shrinks, and the lining of the uterus is discarded 2 weeks later with menstruation.

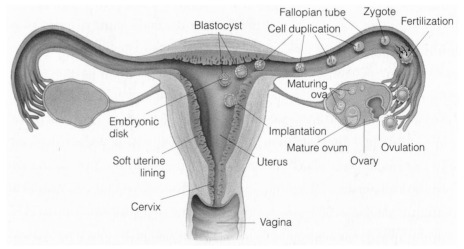

The male produces sperm in vast numbers—an average of 300 million a day—in the *testes,* two glands located in the *scrotum,* a sac that lies just behind the penis. In the final process of maturation, each sperm develops a tail that permits it to swim long distances. During sexual intercourse, about 360 million sperm move through the *vas deferens,* a thin tube in which they are bathed in a protective fluid called *semen.* After semen is ejaculated from the penis into the woman's vagina, the sperm begin to swim upstream in the female reproductive tract, through the *cervix* (opening of the uterus) and into the *fallopian tube,* where fertilization usually takes place. The journey is difficult, and many sperm die. Only 300 to 500 reach the ovum, if one happens to be present. Sperm live for up to 6 days and can lie in wait for the ovum, which survives for only 1 day after being released into the fallopian tube. However, most conceptions result from intercourse occurring during a 3-day period—on the day of or during the 2 days preceding ovulation (Wilcox, Weinberg, & Baird, 1995).

With conception, the story of prenatal development begins to unfold. The vast changes that take place during the 38 weeks of pregnancy are usually divided into three phases: (1) the period of the zygote, (2) the period of the embryo, and (3) the period of the fetus. As we look at what happens in each, you may find it useful to refer to Table 3.1, which summarizes the milestones of prenatal development.

TABLE 3.1

Major Milestones of Prenatal Development

TRIMESTER	PERIOD	WEEKS	LENGTH AND WEIGHT	MAJOR EVENTS
First	Zygote	1		The one-celled zygote multiplies and forms a blastocyst.
		2		The blastocyst burrows into the uterine lining. Structures that feed and protect the developing organism begin to form—amnion, chorion, yolk sac, placenta, and umbilical cord.
	Embryo	3–4	¼ inch	A primitive brain and spinal cord appear. Heart, muscles, backbone, ribs, and digestive tract begin to develop.
		5–8	1 inch; ⅐ ounce	Many external body structures (for example, face, arms, legs, toes, fingers) and internal organs form. The sense of touch begins to develop, and the embryo can move.
	Fetus	9–12	3 inches; less than 1 ounce	Rapid increase in size begins. Nervous system, organs, and muscles become organized and connected, and new behavioral capacities (kicking, thumb sucking, mouth opening, and rehearsal of breathing) appear. External genitals are well formed, and the fetus's sex is evident.
Second		13–24	12 inches; 1.8 pounds	The fetus continues to enlarge rapidly. In the middle of this period, fetal movements can be felt by the mother. Vernix and lanugo keep the fetus's skin from chapping in the amniotic fluid. All of the neurons that will ever be produced in the brain are present by 24 weeks. Eyes are sensitive to light, and the fetus reacts to sound.
Third		25–38	20 inches; 7.5 pounds	The fetus has a chance of survival if born around this time. Size continues to increase. Lungs gradually mature. Rapid brain development causes sensory and behavioral capacities to expand. In the middle of this period, a layer of fat is added under the skin. Antibodies are transmitted from mother to fetus to protect against disease. Most fetuses rotate into an upside-down position in preparation for birth.

Sources: Moore & Persaud, 1998; Nilsson & Hamberger, 1990.

PERIOD OF THE ZYGOTE

The period of the zygote lasts about 2 weeks, from fertilization until the tiny mass of cells drifts down and out of the fallopian tube and attaches itself to the wall of the uterus. The zygote's first cell duplication is long and drawn out; it is not complete until about 30 hours after conception. Gradually new cells are added at a faster rate. By the fourth day, 60 to 70 cells form a hollow, fluid-filled ball called a *blastocyst*. The cells on the inside, called the *embryonic disk*, will become the new organism; the outer ring will provide protective covering.

❚ IMPLANTATION. Sometime between the seventh and ninth day, **implantation** occurs: the blastocyst burrows deep into the uterine lining. Surrounded by the woman's nourishing blood, now it starts to grow in earnest. The protective outer layer quickly develops into a membrane called the **amnion.** It encloses the developing organism in *amniotic fluid*, which helps regulate temperature and acts as a cushion against jolts caused by the woman's movements. A *yolk sac* emerges that produces blood cells until the liver, spleen, and bone marrow are mature enough to take over this function (Moore & Persaud, 1998).

The events of these first 2 weeks are delicate and uncertain. As many as 30 percent of zygotes do not make it through this phase. In some, the sperm and ovum do not join properly. In others, cell duplication never begins. By preventing implantation in these cases, nature quickly eliminates most prenatal abnormalities (Sadler, 1995).

❚ *In this photo taken with the aid of a powerful microscope, sperm have completed their journey up the female reproductive tract and are beginning to penetrate the surface of the enormous-looking ovum, the largest cell in the human body. When one of the sperm is successful at fertilizing the ovum, the resulting zygote will begin to duplicate. (Photo courtesy: Jack Burns/Ace/Phototake)*

❚ *During the period of the zygote, the fertilized ovum begins to duplicate at an increasingly rapid rate, forming a hollow ball of cells, or blastocyst, by the fourth day of fertilization. Here the blastocyst, magnified thousands of times, burrows into the uterine lining between the seventh and ninth day. (Photo courtesy: © Lennart Nilsson,* A Child Is Born/*Bonniers)*

❚ THE PLACENTA AND UMBILICAL CORD. By the end of the second week, another protective membrane, called the **chorion,** surrounds the amnion. From the chorion, tiny fingerlike *villi*, or blood vessels, begin to emerge.[1] As these villi burrow into the uterine wall, the **placenta** starts to develop. By bringing the mother's and embryo's blood close together, the placenta permits food and oxygen to reach the developing organism and waste products to be carried away. A special membrane forms that allows these substances to be exchanged but prevents the mother's and embryo's blood from mixing directly.

The placenta is connected to the developing organism by the **umbilical cord,** which first appears as a tiny stalk and eventually grows to a length of 1 to 3 feet. The umbilical cord contains one large vein that delivers blood loaded with nutrients and two arteries that remove waste products. The force of blood flowing through the cord keeps it firm, so it seldom tangles while the embryo, like a spacewalking astronaut, floats freely in its fluid-filled chamber (Moore & Persaud, 1998).

By the end of the period of the zygote, the developing organism has found food and shelter. These dramatic beginnings take place before all but the most sensitive mother knows she is pregnant.

---

[1] Recall from Chapter 2 that *chorionic villus sampling* is the prenatal diagnostic method that can be performed earliest, by 6 to 8 weeks after conception. In this procedure, tissues from the ends of the villi are removed and examined for genetic abnormalities.

PERIOD OF THE EMBRYO

The period of the **embryo** lasts from the second through the eighth week of pregnancy. During these brief 6 weeks, the most rapid prenatal changes take place as the groundwork is laid for all body structures and internal organs.

■ LAST HALF OF THE FIRST MONTH. In the first week of this period, the embryonic disk forms three layers of cells: (1) the *ectoderm*, which will become the nervous system and skin; (2) the *mesoderm*, from which will develop the muscles, skeleton, circulatory system, and other internal organs; and (3) the *endoderm*, which will become the digestive system, lungs, urinary tract, and glands. These three layers give rise to all parts of the body.

At first, the nervous system develops fastest. The ectoderm folds over to form a **neural tube,** which will become the spinal cord and brain. While the nervous system is developing, the heart begins to pump blood around the embryo's circulatory system, and muscles, backbone, ribs, and digestive tract start to appear. At the end of the first month, the curled embryo consists of millions of organized groups of cells with specific functions, although it is only ¼ inch long.

■ THE SECOND MONTH. In the second month, growth continues rapidly. The eyes, ears, nose, jaw, and neck form. Tiny buds become arms, legs, fingers, and toes. Internal organs are more distinct: the intestines grow, the heart develops separate chambers, and the liver and spleen take over

■ *By 7 weeks, the embryo's posture is more upright. Body structures —eyes, nose, arms, legs, and internal organs—are more distinct. An embryo of this age responds to touch. It can also move, although at less than an inch long and an ounce in weight, it is still too tiny to be felt by the mother. (Photo courtesy: © Lennart Nilsson,* A Child Is Born/*Bonniers)*

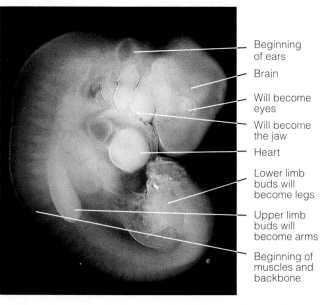

- Beginning of ears
- Brain
- Will become eyes
- Will become the jaw
- Heart
- Lower limb buds will become legs
- Upper limb buds will become arms
- Beginning of muscles and backbone

■ *This curled embryo is about 4 weeks old. In actual size, it is only ¼-inch long, but many body structures have begun to form. The primitive tail will disappear by the end of the embryonic period. (Photo courtesy: © Lennart Nilsson,* A Child Is Born/*Bonniers)*

production of blood cells so that the yolk sac is no longer needed. Changing body proportions cause the embryo's posture to become more upright. Now 1 inch long and ½ of an ounce in weight, the embryo can already sense its world. It responds to touch, particularly in the mouth area and on the soles of the feet. And it can move, although its tiny flutters are still too light to be felt by the mother (Nilsson & Hamberger, 1990).

PERIOD OF THE FETUS

Lasting from the ninth week to the end of pregnancy, the period of the **fetus** is the "growth and finishing" phase. During this longest prenatal period, the developing organism increases rapidly in size.

■ THE THIRD MONTH. In the third month, the organs, muscles, and nervous system start to become organized and connected. The fetus kicks, bends its arms, forms a fist, curls its toes, opens its mouth, and even sucks its thumb. The tiny lungs begin to expand and contract in an early rehearsal of breathing movements. By the twelfth week, the external genitals are well formed, and the sex of the fetus can be detected with ultrasound. Other finishing touches appear, such as fingernails, toenails, tooth buds, and eyelids. The heartbeat can now be heard through a stethoscope.

Prenatal development is sometimes divided into **trimesters,** or three equal time periods. At the end of the third month, the *first trimester* is complete. Two more must

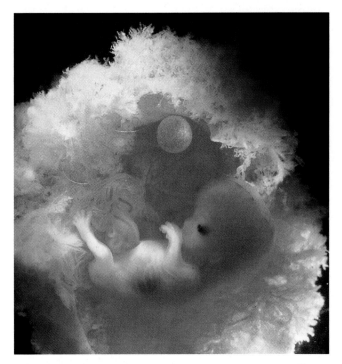

■ *During the period of the fetus, the organism increases rapidly in size, and body structures are completed. At 11 weeks, the brain and muscles are better connected. The fetus can kick, bend its arms, open and close its hands and mouth, and suck its thumb. Notice the yolk sac, which shrinks as pregnancy advances. The internal organs have taken over its function of producing blood cells. (Photo courtesy: © Lennart Nilsson,* A Child Is Born/ Bonniers)*

pass before the fetus is fully prepared to survive outside the womb.

■ THE SECOND TRIMESTER. By the middle of the second trimester, between 17 and 20 weeks, the new being has grown large enough that its movements can be felt by the mother. A white, cheeselike substance called **vernix** now protects its skin from chapping during the long months spent bathing in the amniotic fluid. White, downy hair called **lanugo** also appears over the entire body, helping the vernix stick to the skin.

At the end of the second trimester, most of the brain's *neurons* (nerve cells that store and transmit information) are in place; few will be produced after this time. However, *glial cells*, which support and feed the neurons, continue to increase at a rapid rate throughout pregnancy, as well as after birth.

Brain growth means new behavioral capacities. The 20-week-old fetus can be stimulated as well as irritated by sound. And if a doctor looks inside the uterus with fetoscopy (see Chapter 2, page 55), fetuses try to shield their eyes from the light with the hands, indicating that the sense of sight has begun to emerge (Nilsson & Hamberger, 1990). Still, a fetus born at this time cannot survive. Its

lungs are immature, and the brain cannot yet control breathing movements and body temperature.

■ THE THIRD TRIMESTER. During the final trimester, a fetus born early has a chance for survival outside the womb. The point at which it can first survive, called the **age of viability,** occurs sometime between 22 and 26 weeks (Moore & Persaud, 1998). If born between the seventh and eighth month, however, the baby usually needs help breathing. Although the brain's respiratory center is mature, tiny air sacs in the lungs are not yet ready to inflate and exchange carbon dioxide for oxygen.

The brain continues to make great strides. The *cerebral cortex*, the seat of human intelligence, enlarges. As neurological organization improves, the fetus spends more time awake. At 20 weeks, heart rate variability reveals no periods of alertness. But by 28 weeks, fetuses are awake about 11 percent of the time, a figure that rises to 16 percent just before birth (DiPietro et al., 1996a). And the vigor of the fetus's movements and its daily cycles of activity and rest reveal the beginnings of a personality (see the Variations box on the following page).

The third trimester also brings greater responsiveness to external stimulation. Around 24 weeks, fetuses can first feel pain, so after this time painkillers should be used in

■ *At 22 weeks, this fetus is almost a foot long and slightly over a pound in weight. Its movements can be clearly felt by the mother and by other family members who place a hand on her abdomen. If born at this time, a baby has a slim chance of surviving. (Photo courtesy: © Lennart Nilsson,* A Child Is Born/*Bonniers)*

TEMPERAMENT IN THE WOMB

As Yolanda, in her seventh month of pregnancy, rested one afternoon, she felt several bursts of fetal activity, interspersed with quiet periods. "Hey, little one," she whispered, looking down at her large abdomen as it bulged after a foot kick, "you're on the move again. You always do this when I try to take a nap!" Then Yolanda wondered, "Can the fetus's behavior tell us anything about what he or she will be like after birth?"

Yolanda's question is at the heart of current efforts to determine whether individual differences in temperament have genetic origins. The earlier in development that predictors of temperamental traits can be identified, the greater the likelihood that heredity contributes to those traits.

Until recently, limited access to the fetus made it hard to study the relationship between fetal measures and temperament after birth. Today, sophisticated equipment for moni-toring fetal responses permits researchers to address this issue.

In the most extensive study to date, 31 volunteer women, whose newborns were delivered healthy and full-term, were monitored periodically during the prenatal period, from 20 weeks to just before birth (DiPietro et al., 1996b). During each session, the mothers lay quietly while a variety of fetal measures, including heart rate and activity level, were recorded. Then, at 3 and 6 months after birth, the mothers were asked to rate various aspects of their baby's temperament, including fussiness, adaptability to new persons and situations, activity level, and regularity of eating and sleeping.

Findings revealed that the pattern of fetal activity in the last few weeks of pregnancy was the best predictor of infant temperament. Fetuses (like Yolanda's) who cycled between quiet and active periods tended to become calm babies with predictable sleep–waking schedules. In contrast, fetuses who were highly active for long stretches were more likely to become difficult, unpredictable babies— fussy, especially when confronted with new people and situations; irregular in eating and sleeping habits; constantly wriggling and squirming; and waking often during the night (see Figure 3.2).

But we must keep in mind that these links between prenatal measures and infant characteristics are only modest. In Chapter 6, we will see that sensitive care can modify a difficult baby's temperamental style. Furthermore, researchers have yet to determine whether fetal activity predicts *actual* infant behavior, not just *maternal judgments* of that behavior.

But if the relationships just described hold up, then parents whose fetuses are very active can prepare for extra caregiving challenges. Recognizing that their baby-to-be may have a fussy, difficult disposition, they can take extra steps to provide a sympathetic environment as soon as the baby is born.

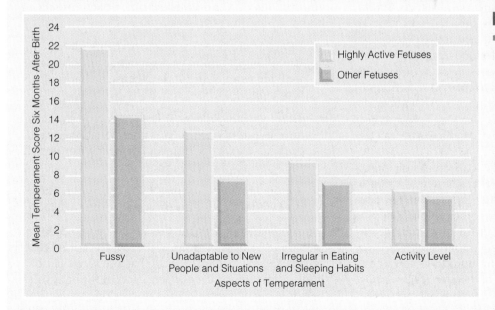

FIGURE 3.2

■ **Temperament score 6 months after birth of highly active fetuses versus other fetuses.** Fetuses who were very active in the last weeks of pregnancy developed into 6-month-old babies who were fussier, more unadaptable to new people and situations, more irregular in eating and sleeping habits, and more active, as judged by their mothers. They also woke more often at night (not shown in the graph). (Adapted from DiPietro et al., 1996b.)

■ *This 36-week-old fetus fills the uterus. To support its need for nourishment, the umbilical cord and placenta have grown very large. Notice the vernix (cheeselike substance), which protects the skin from chapping. The fetus has accumulated a layer of fat to assist with temperature regulation after birth. In another 2 weeks, it will be full term. (Photo courtesy: © Lennart Nilsson, A Child Is Born/Bonniers)*

any surgical procedures (Royal College of Obstetricians and Gynecologists, 1997). By 25 weeks, fetuses react to nearby sounds with body movements (Kisilevsky & Low, 1998). And in the last weeks of pregnancy, they learn to prefer the tone and rhythm of their mothers' voices. In one clever study, mothers read aloud Dr. Seuss's lively book *The Cat in the Hat* for the last 6 weeks of pregnancy. After birth, their infants learned to turn on recordings of the mother's voice by sucking on nipples. They showed a preference for the familiar poem by sucking harder to hear *The Cat in the Hat* than for other rhyming stories (De-Casper & Spence, 1986).

During the final 3 months, the fetus gains more than 5 pounds and grows 7 inches. In the eighth month, a layer of fat is added to assist with temperature regulation. The fetus also receives antibodies from the mother's blood that protect against illnesses, since the newborn's own immune system will not work well until several months after birth. In the last weeks, most fetuses assume an upside-down position, partly because of the shape of the uterus and because the head is heavier than the feet. Growth slows, and birth is about to take place.

ASK YOURSELF . . .

■ *Amy, who is 2 months pregnant, wonders how the embryo is being fed and what parts of the body have formed. Amy imagines that very little development has yet taken place. How would you answer Amy's questions? Will she be surprised at your response?*

■ *How does brain development relate to fetal behavior during the third trimester?*

PRENATAL ENVIRONMENTAL INFLUENCES

Although the prenatal environment is far more constant than the world outside the womb, many factors can affect the developing embryo and fetus. Yolanda and Jay learned that there was much they could do to create a safe environment for development before birth.

TERATOGENS

The term **teratogen** refers to any environmental agent that causes damage during the prenatal period. It comes from the Greek word *teras*, meaning "malformation" or "monstrosity." This label was selected because medical science first learned about harmful prenatal influences from cases in which babies had been profoundly damaged.

Yet the harm done by teratogens is not always simple and straightforward. It depends on several factors:

■ *Dose.* We will see as we discuss particular teratogens that larger doses over longer time periods usually have more negative effects.

■ *Heredity.* The genetic makeup of the mother and the developing organism plays an important role. Some individuals are better able to withstand harmful environments.

■ *Other negative influences.* The presence of several negative factors at once, such as poor nutrition, lack of medical care, and additional teratogens, can worsen the impact of a single harmful agent.

■ *Age of the prenatal organism.* The effects of teratogens vary with the age of the organism at time of exposure.

We can best understand this last idea if we think of prenatal development in terms of the *sensitive period* concept introduced in Chapter 1. Recall that a sensitive period is a limited time span during which a part of the body or a behavior is biologically prepared to develop rapidly. During that time, it is especially sensitive to its surroundings. If the environment happens to be harmful, then damage occurs, and recovery is difficult and sometimes impossible.

Figure 3.3 summarizes sensitive periods during prenatal development. In the period of the zygote, before implantation, teratogens rarely have any impact. If they do, the tiny mass of cells is usually so completely damaged that it dies. The embryonic period is the time when serious defects are most likely to occur, since the foundations for all body parts are laid down. During the fetal period, damage by teratogens is usually minor. However, some organs, such as the brain, eyes, and genitals, can still be strongly affected.

The effects of teratogens are not limited to immediate physical damage. Although deformities of the body are easy to notice, some health effects may not show up for decades (see the Lifespan Vista box on pages 88–89). Psychological consequences also may be delayed and result, indirectly, from physical damage. For example, a defect caused by drugs the mother took during pregnancy can

change reactions of others to the child as well as the child's ability to move about the environment. Over time, parent–child interaction, peer relations, and opportunities to explore may suffer. These experiences, in turn, can have far-reaching consequences for cognitive, emotional, and social development (Friedman, 1996).

Notice how an important idea about development discussed in earlier chapters is at work here—that of *bidirectional influences* between child and environment. Now let's take a look at what scientists have discovered about a variety of teratogens.

■ PRESCRIPTION AND NONPRESCRIPTION DRUGS. In the early 1960s, the world learned a tragic lesson about drugs and prenatal development. At that time, a sedative called thalidomide was widely available in Europe, Canada, and South America. When taken by mothers 4 to 6 weeks after conception, thalidomide produced gross

FIGURE 3.3

■ **Sensitive periods in prenatal development.** Each organ or structure has a sensitive period, during which its development may be disturbed. Gray horizontal lines indicate highly sensitive periods. Pink horizontal lines indicate periods that are somewhat less sensitive to teratogens, although damage can occur. (From K. L. Moore & T. V. N. Persaud, 1998, *Before We Are Born,* 5th ed., Philadelphia: Saunders, p. 166. Adapted by permission of the publisher and authors.)

THE PRENATAL ENVIRONMENT AND HEALTH IN LATER LIFE

When Michael entered the world 55 years ago, 6 weeks premature and weighing only 4 pounds, the doctor delivering him wasn't sure he would make it. Michael not only survived but enjoyed good health until his mid-forties when, during a routine medical checkup, he was diagnosed with high blood pressure and adult-onset diabetes. Michael wasn't overweight, didn't smoke, and didn't eat high-fat foods —risk factors for these conditions. Nor did the illnesses run in his family. Could the roots of Michael's health problems date back to his prenatal development? Increasing evidence suggests that prenatal environmental factors —ones not toxic (like tobacco or alcohol) but rather fairly subtle, such as the flow of nutrients and hormones across the placenta—can affect health decades later (Wheeler, Barker, & O'Brien, 1999).

LOW BIRTH WEIGHT AND HEART DISEASE, STROKE, AND DIABETES. Carefully controlled animal experiments reveal that a poorly nourished, underweight fetus experiences changes in body structure and function that result in cardiovascular dis-

ease in adulthood (Dennison et al., 1997). To explore this relationship in humans, researchers tapped public records, gathering the birth weights of every male baby born in two areas of England between 1907 and 1930—over 13,000 cases. Then, for those who had died, the cause of death was obtained. Men weighing less than 5 pounds at birth had a 50 percent greater chance of dying of heart disease and stroke, after SES and a variety of other health risks were controlled. The birth weight–cardiovascular disease connection was strongest for men whose weight-to-length ratio at birth was very low— a sign of prenatal growth stunting (Martyn, Barker, & Osmond, 1996).

In other large-scale studies, a consistent link between low birth weight and heart disease, stroke, and diabetes in middle adulthood has emerged— for both sexes and in several countries, including India, Jamaica, and the United States (Fall et al., 1998; Law et al., 1995; Rich-Edwards et al., 1997, 1999). Smallness itself does not cause later health problems; rather, researchers believe complex factors associated with it are involved.

Some speculate that a poorly nourished fetus diverts large amounts

of blood to the brain, causing organs in the abdomen to be undersized, such as the liver and kidney, involved in controlling cholesterol and blood pressure (Barker, 1999). The result is heightened later risk for heart disease and stroke. In the case of diabetes, inadequate prenatal nutrition may permanently impair functioning of the pancreas, leading glucose intolerance to rise as the person ages (Rich-Edwards et al., 1999). Yet another hypothesis, supported by both animal and human research, is that the malfunctioning placentas of some expectant mothers permit high levels of stress hormones to reach the fetus, which retards fetal growth, increases fetal blood pressure, and promotes hyperglycemia (excess blood sugar). These outcomes predispose the developing person to later disease (Benediktsson et al., 1997).

HIGH BIRTH WEIGHT AND BREAST CANCER. The other prenatal growth extreme—high birth weight—is related to breast cancer, the most common malignancy in adult women. In one study, the mothers of 589 nurses with invasive breast cancer and 1,569 nurses who did not have breast cancer were asked to provide their

deformities of the arms and legs and, less frequently, damage to the ears, heart, kidneys, and genitals. About 7,000 infants worldwide were affected (Moore & Persaud, 1998). As children exposed to thalidomide grew older, many scored below average in intelligence. Perhaps the drug damaged the central nervous system directly. Or the child-rearing conditions of these severely deformed youngsters may have impaired their intellectual development (Vorhees & Mollnow, 1987).

Another medication, a synthetic hormone called *diethylstilbestrol (DES),* was widely prescribed between 1945 and 1970 to prevent miscarriages. As daughters of these mothers reached adolescence and young adulthood, they showed unusually high rates of cancer of the vagina and malformations of the uterus. When they tried to have children, their preg-

nancies more often resulted in prematurity, low birth weight, and miscarriage than those of non-DES-exposed women. Young men showed an increased risk of genital abnormalities and cancer of the testes (Giusti, Iwamoto, & Hatch, 1995; Palmlund, 1996).

Any drug taken by the mother that has a molecule small enough to penetrate the placental barrier can enter the embryonic or fetal bloodstream. Yet many pregnant women continue to take over-the-counter drugs without consulting their doctors. Aspirin is one of the most common. Several studies suggest that regular aspirin use is linked to low birth weight, infant death around the time of birth, poorer motor development, and lower intelligence scores in early childhood, although other evidence fails to confirm these findings (Barr et al., 1990; Hauth et al., 1995;

daughters' birth weights, family health histories (such as relatives diagnosed with breast cancer), and prenatal and early life exposures (for example, smoking during pregnancy). The nurses themselves provided information on adult health. After other risk factors were controlled, high birth weight—especially more than 8.7 pounds—emerged as a clear predictor of breast cancer (see Figure 3.4). Researchers think the culprit is excessive maternal estrogen during pregnancy, which promotes large fetal size and also alters beginning breast tissue so that it may respond to estrogen in adulthood by becoming malignant (Michels et al., 1996).

PREVENTION. The prenatal development–later-life illness relationships emerging in research are not inevitable. Rather, prenatal environmental conditions *influence* adult health, and the steps we take to protect our health can prevent prenatal risks from becoming reality. Researchers advise individuals who were low birth weight to get regular medical checkups and to be attentive to diet, weight, fitness, and stress—controllable factors that contribute to heart disease and adult-onset diabetes. And high-birth-weight women should be conscientious about breast self-exams and mammograms, which permit breast cancer to be detected early and, in many instances, cured.

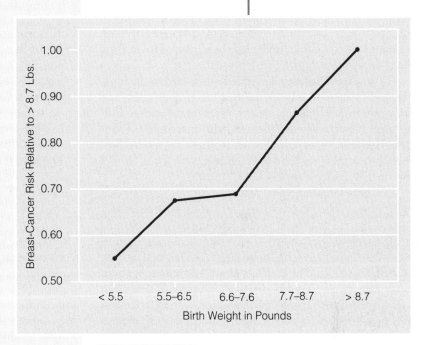

FIGURE 3.4

■ **Relationship of birth weight to breast-cancer risk in adulthood.** In a study of 589 nurses with invasive breast cancer and 1,569 nurses who did not have breast cancer, birth weight predicted breast cancer incidence after many other prenatal and postnatal health risks were controlled. The breast-cancer risk was especially high for women whose birth weights were greater than 8.7 pounds. (Adapted from Michels et al., 1996.)

Streissguth et al., 1987). Coffee, tea, cola, and cocoa contain another frequently consumed drug, caffeine. Heavy caffeine intake (more than 3 cups of coffee per day) is associated with low birth weight, miscarriage, and newborn withdrawal symptoms, such as irritability and vomiting (Dlugosz & Bracken, 1992; Eskenazi, 1993).

Because children's lives are involved, we must take findings like these quite seriously. At the same time, we cannot be sure that commonly used drugs actually cause the problems just mentioned. Often mothers take more than one kind of drug. If the prenatal organism is injured, it is hard to tell which drug might be responsible or if other factors correlated with drug taking are really at fault. Until we have more information, the safest course of action is one that Yolanda took: cut down or avoid these drugs entirely.

■ ILLEGAL DRUGS. Use of highly addictive mood-altering drugs, such as cocaine and heroin, has become more widespread, especially in poverty-stricken inner cities where drugs provide a temporary escape from a daily life of hopelessness. The number of "cocaine babies" born in the United States has reached crisis levels in recent years. About 100,000 to 375,000 infants are affected annually, a figure that is rising (Cornelius et al., 1999; Landry & Whitney, 1996).

Babies born to users of cocaine, heroin, or methadone (a less addictive drug used to wean people away from heroin) are at risk for a wide variety of problems, including prematurity, low birth weight, physical defects, breathing difficulties, and death around the time of birth. In addition, these infants arrive drug addicted. They are often feverish and irritable at birth and have trouble sleeping, and their cries are abnormally shrill and piercing—a common symptom among stressed newborns (Burkett et al., 1994; Miller, Boudreaux, & Regan, 1995; Ostrea, Ostrea, & Simpson, 1997). When mothers with many problems of their own must take care of these babies, who are difficult to calm down, cuddle, and feed, behavior problems are likely to persist.

Throughout the first year of life, heroin- and methadone-exposed infants are less attentive to the environment, and their motor development is slow. After infancy, some children get better, whereas others remain jittery and inattentive. The kind of parenting these youngsters receive may explain why there are long-term problems for some but not for others (Cosden, Peerson, & Elliott, 1997).

Growing longitudinal evidence on cocaine suggests that many prenatally exposed babies have lasting difficulties. Cocaine constricts the blood vessels, causing oxygen delivered to the developing organism to fall dramatically for 15 minutes following a high dose. It also alters the chemical balance in the fetus's brain. These effects may contribute to inattention, sensory and motor deficits, lower intelligence test scores, and behavior problems in infancy and childhood and to a specific set of cocaine-linked physical defects, including eye, bone, genital, urinary tract, kidney, and heart deformities as well as brain hemorrhages and seizures (Arendt et al., 1998; Espy, Kaufmann, & Glisky, 1999; Mayes, 1999; Richardson, 1998).

Babies born to mothers who smoke crack (a cheap form of cocaine that delivers high doses quickly through the lungs) seem worst off in terms of low birth weight and damage to the central nervous system (Bender et al., 1995; Richardson et al., 1996). Fathers may contribute to these out-

▮ *This baby, whose mother took crack during pregnancy, was born many weeks premature. He breathes with the aid of a respirator. His central nervous system may be seriously damaged. Researchers do not yet know if these outcomes are actually caused by crack or by the many other high-risk behaviors of drug users. (Photo courtesy: Chuck Nacke/Woodfin Camp & Associates)*

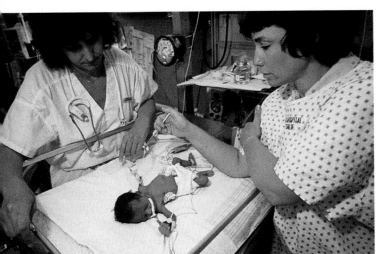

comes. Research suggests that cocaine can attach itself to sperm and "hitchhike" its way into the zygote (Yazigi, Odem, & Polakoski, 1991). Still, it is difficult to isolate the precise damage caused by cocaine, since users often take several drugs and engage in other high-risk behaviors. The joint impact of these factors along with poor caregiving may be responsible for negative outcomes and lead the development of many cocaine-exposed infants to worsen over time (Alessandri, Bendersky, & Lewis, 1998; Chasnoff et al., 1998).

Another illegal drug, marijuana, is used more widely than heroin and cocaine. Studies examining its relationship to low birth weight and prematurity reveal mixed findings (Fried, 1993). Nevertheless, prenatal marijuana exposure is related to newborn startle reactions, disturbed sleep, and inattention in infancy and childhood (Dahl et al., 1995; Fried & Makin, 1987; Fried, Watkinson, & Gray, 1998).

▮ TOBACCO. Although smoking has declined in Western nations, an estimated 25 percent of American adults are regular cigarette users. Although many women quit around the time they become pregnant, 14 percent of expectant mothers smoke regularly (U.S. Bureau of the Census, 1999). The most well-known effect of smoking during the prenatal period is low birth weight. But the likelihood of other serious consequences, such as miscarriage, prematurity, impaired breathing during sleep, infant death, and cancer later in childhood is also increased. The more cigarettes a mother smokes, the greater the likelihood that her baby will be affected. But if a pregnant woman decides to stop smoking at any time, even during the last trimester, she can help her baby. She immediately reduces the chances that the infant will be born underweight and suffer from future problems (Ahlsten, Cnattingius, & Lindmark, 1993; Groff et al., 1997).

Even when a baby of a smoking mother appears to be born in good physical condition, slight behavioral abnormalities may threaten the child's development. Newborns of smoking mothers are less attentive to sounds and display more muscle tension (Fried & Makin, 1987). An unresponsive, restless baby may not evoke the kind of interaction from adults that promotes healthy psychological development. Some studies report that prenatally exposed children have shorter attention spans and poorer mental test scores in childhood, even after many other factors have been controlled (Fergusson, Horwood, & Lynskey, 1993; Millberger et al., 1998). But other researchers have not been able to confirm these findings, so lasting effects remain uncertain (Barr et al., 1990; Streissguth et al., 1989).

Exactly how can smoking harm the fetus? Nicotine, the addictive substance in tobacco, causes the placenta to grow abnormally. This reduces transfer of nutrients, so the fetus gains weight poorly. Also, smoking raises the concentration of carbon monoxide in the bloodstreams of both mother and fetus. Carbon monoxide displaces oxygen from red blood cells. It damages the central nervous system and reduces birth weight in the fetuses of laboratory animals. Similar effects may occur in humans (Cotton, 1994; Friedman, 1996).

Finally, from one-third to one-half of nonsmoking pregnant women are "passive smokers" because their husbands, relatives, and co-workers use cigarettes. Passive smoking is also related to low birth weight, infant death, and possible long-term impairments in attention and learning (Dejin-Karlsson et al., 1998; Makin, Fried, & Watkinson, 1991). Consequently, Jay gave up cigarettes when Yolanda became pregnant.

■ ALCOHOL. In *The Broken Cord*, Michael Dorris (1989), a Dartmouth University anthropology professor, described what it was like to raise his adopted son, Adam. The boy's biological mother drank heavily throughout pregnancy and died of alcohol poisoning shortly after his birth. A Sioux Indian, Adam was born with **fetal alcohol syndrome (FAS).** Mental retardation; impaired motor coordination, attention, memory, and language; and overactivity are typical of children with the disorder. Distinct physical symptoms also accompany it. These include slow physical growth and a particular pattern of facial abnormalities: widely spaced eyes, short eyelid openings, a small upturned nose, a thin upper lip, and a small head, indicating that the brain has not developed fully. In a related condition, known as **fetal alcohol effects (FAE),** individuals display only some of these abnormalities. Usually, their mothers drank alcohol in smaller quantities (Streissguth, 1997; Mattson et al., 1998).

Even when provided with enriched diets, FAS babies fail to catch up in physical size during infancy or childhood. Mental impairment is also permanent: In his teens and twenties, Adam's intelligence remained below average, and he had trouble concentrating and keeping a routine job. He also suffered from poor judgment. He might buy something and not wait for change or wander off in the middle of a task. The more alcohol consumed by a woman during pregnancy, the poorer the child's motor coordination, speed of information processing, reasoning, and intelligence and achievement test scores during the preschool and school years (Aronson, Hagberg, & Gillberg, 1997; Hunt et al., 1995; Jacobson et al., 1993). In adolescence, prenatal alcohol exposure is associated with disrupted school experiences, trouble with the law, inappropriate sexual behavior, alcohol and drug abuse, and lasting mental health problems (Streissguth, Bookstein, & Barr, 1996).

How does alcohol produce its devastating effects? First, it interferes with brain development during the early months of pregnancy, resulting in structural damage and abnormalities in brain functioning, including transfer of messages from one part of the brain to another (Guerri, 1998; Roebuck, Mattson, & Riley, 1999). Second, the body uses large quantities of oxygen to metabolize alcohol. A pregnant woman's heavy drinking draws away oxygen that the developing organism needs for cell growth.

■ *The mother of this severely retarded boy drank heavily during pregnancy. His widely spaced eyes, thin upper lip, and short eyelid openings are typical of fetal alcohol syndrome. (Photo courtesy: George Steinmetz)*

Like heroin and cocaine, alcohol abuse is higher in poverty-stricken sectors of the population (Streissguth, 1997). On the reservation where Adam was born, many children show symptoms of prenatal alcohol exposure. Unfortunately, when girls with FAS or FAE later become pregnant, the poor judgment caused by the syndrome often prevents them from understanding why they should avoid alcohol themselves. Thus, the tragic cycle is likely to be repeated in the next generation.

How much alcohol is safe during pregnancy? One study linked as little as 2 ounces of alcohol a day, taken very early in pregnancy, to FAS-like facial features (Astley et al., 1992). But recall that other factors—both genetic and environmental—can make some fetuses more vulnerable to teratogenic effects. Therefore, a precise dividing line between safe and dangerous drinking levels cannot be established, and it is best for pregnant women to avoid alcohol entirely.

■ RADIATION. Defects due to radiation were tragically apparent in the children born to pregnant women who survived the bombing of Hiroshima and Nagasaki during World War II. Similar abnormalities surfaced in the 9 months following the 1986 Chernobyl, Ukraine, nuclear power plant accident. After each disaster, the incidence of miscarriage and babies born with underdeveloped brains, physical deformities, and slow physical growth rose dramatically (Michel, 1989; Terestchenko, Lyaginskaya, & Burtzeva, 1991).

Even when a radiation-exposed baby appears normal, problems may appear later. In middle childhood, prenatally exposed Chernobyl children had lower intelligence test scores and rates of language and emotional disorders two to three times greater than those of nonexposed Russian children. Furthermore, Chernobyl children's parents were highly anxious, due to forced evacuation from their homes and worries about living in irradiated areas. The more tension parents reported, the poorer their children's emotional functioning (Kolominsky, Igumnov, & Drozdovitch, 1999). Stressful rearing conditions seemed to combine with the damaging effects of prenatal radiation to impair children's development.

■ ENVIRONMENTAL POLLUTION. An astounding number of potentially dangerous chemicals are released into the environment in industrialized nations. In the United States, over 100,000 are in common use, and many new ones are introduced each year.

Mercury is an established teratogen. In the 1950s, an industrial plant released waste containing high levels of mercury into a bay providing food and water for the town of Minamata, Japan. Many children born at the time displayed physical deformities, mental retardation, abnormal

■ *This child's mother was just a few weeks pregnant during the Chernobyl nuclear power plant disaster. Radiation exposure is probably responsible for his limb deformities. He is also at risk for low intelligence and language and emotional disorders. (Photo courtesy: Charlton-Bourdillon/Liaison Agency)*

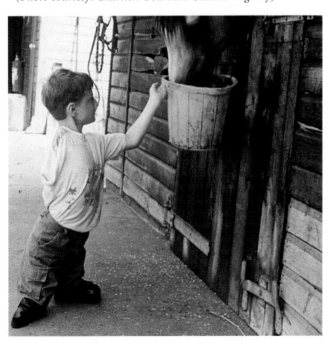

speech, difficulty in chewing and swallowing, and uncoordinated movements. Autopsies of those who died revealed widespread brain damage (Vorhees & Mollnow, 1987).

Another teratogen, *lead*, is present in paint flaking off the walls of old buildings and in certain materials used in industrial occupations. High levels of lead exposure are consistently related to prematurity, low birth weight, brain damage, and a wide variety of physical defects (Dye-White, 1986). Even low levels of prenatal lead exposure seem to be dangerous. Affected babies show slightly poorer mental development during the first 2 years (Bellinger et al., 1987).

For many years, *polychlorinated biphenyls (PCBs)* were used to insulate electrical equipment until research showed that (like mercury) they found their way into waterways and entered the food supply. In Taiwan, prenatal exposure to very high levels of PCBs in rice oil resulted in low birth weight, discolored skin, deformities of the gums and nails, brain-wave abnormalities, and delayed cognitive development (Chen & Hsu, 1994; Chen et al., 1994). Steady, low-level PCB exposure is also harmful. Newborn babies of women who frequently ate PCB-contaminated Lake Michigan fish had slightly lower than average birth weights, smaller heads (suggesting brain damage), and less interest in their surroundings than did infants whose mothers ate little or no fish (Jacobson et al., 1984). Follow-ups later in the first year and in early childhood revealed persisting memory difficulties and lower verbal intelligence test scores (Jacobson, 1998; Jacobson et al., 1992).

■ INFECTIOUS DISEASE. On her first prenatal visit, Yolanda's doctor asked if she and Jay had already had measles, mumps, and chicken pox, as well as other illnesses. In addition, Yolanda was checked for the presence of several infections, and for good reason. Certain diseases during pregnancy are major causes of miscarriage and birth defects.

Although most viruses, such as the common cold or flu, appear to have little or no impact on the developing fetus, a few can cause extensive damage. In the mid-1960s, a worldwide epidemic of *rubella* (German, or 3-day, measles) led to the birth of over 20,000 American babies with serious physical defects. Consistent with the sensitive period concept, the greatest damage occurs when rubella strikes during the embryonic period. Over 50 percent of infants whose mothers become ill during that time show heart defects; eye cataracts; deafness; genital, urinary, and intestinal abnormalities; and mental retardation. Infection during the fetal period is less harmful, but low birth weight, hearing loss, and bone defects may still occur (Eberhart-Phillips, Frederick, & Baron, 1993). Since 1966, infants and young children have been routinely vaccinated against rubella, so the number of prenatal cases today is much lower than it was a generation ago. Still, 10 to 20 percent of American women of childbearing age lack the rubella antibody, so new outbreaks are still possible (Lee et al., 1992).

The human *immunodeficiency virus (HIV),* which leads to *acquired immune deficiency syndrome (AIDS),* a disease that destroys the immune system, has infected increasing numbers of women over the past decade. When they become pregnant, they pass the deadly virus to the developing organism about 20 to 30 percent of the time (Nourse & Butler, 1998). In older children and adults, AIDS symptoms take years to emerge; in infants, the disease progresses rapidly. By 6 months, weight loss, diarrhea, and repeated respiratory illnesses are common. The virus also causes brain damage, as indicated by seizures, a gradual loss in brain weight, and delayed mental and motor development. Most prenatal AIDS babies survive for only 5 to 8 months after the appearance of these symptoms (Parks, 1996). The antiviral drug zidovudine (ZDV) reduces prenatal AIDS transmission by 60 to 70 percent, but it can also cause birth defects (Dattel, 1997).

The developing organism is especially sensitive to the family of herpes viruses, for which there is no vaccine or treatment. Among these, *cytomegalovirus* (the most frequent prenatal infection, transmitted through respiratory or sexual contact) and *herpes simplex 2* (which is sexually transmitted) are especially dangerous. In both, the virus invades the mother's genital tract, infecting babies either during pregnancy or at birth and resulting in miscarriage, low birth weight, physical malformations, and mental retardation (Behrman, Kliegman, & Arvin, 1996).

Several bacterial and parasitic diseases are also teratogens. Among the most common is *toxoplasmosis,* caused by a parasite found in many animals. Pregnant women may become infected from eating raw or undercooked meat or from contact with the feces of infected cats. About 40 percent of women who have the disease transmit it to the developing organism. If it strikes during the first trimester, it is likely to cause eye and brain damage. Later infection is linked to mild visual and cognitive impairments (Peckham & Logan, 1993). Expectant mothers can avoid toxoplasmosis by making sure the meat they eat is well cooked, having pet cats checked for the disease, and turning over the care of litter boxes to other family members.

OTHER MATERNAL FACTORS

Besides avoiding teratogens, expectant parents can support the development of the embryo or fetus in other ways. In healthy, physically fit women, regular moderate exercise, such as walking, swimming, hiking, and aerobics, is related to increased birth weight (Hatch et al., 1993). However, very frequent, vigorous exercise predicts the opposite—lower birth weight than in healthy, nonexercising controls (Bell, Palma, & Lumley, 1995). (Note, also, that pregnant women with health problems, such as circulatory difficulties or previous miscarriages, should consult their doctors about a physical fitness routine.) We exam-

ine other maternal factors—nutrition, emotional stress, blood type, and age and previous births—in the following sections.

■ NUTRITION. Children grow more rapidly during the prenatal period than at any other phase of development. During this time, they depend totally on their mothers for nutrients to support their growth.

Prenatal malnutrition can damage the central nervous system and other parts of the body. Autopsies of malnourished babies who died at or shortly after birth reveal fewer brain cells, a brain weight as much as 36 percent below average, and abnormal brain organization. The poorer the mother's diet, the greater the loss in brain weight, especially if malnutrition occurred during the last trimester. During that time, the brain is growing rapidly in size, and a maternal diet high in all the basic nutrients is necessary for it to reach its full potential (Morgane et al., 1993). An inadequate diet during pregnancy can also distort the structure of other organs, including the pancreas, liver, and blood vessels, thereby increasing the risk of heart disease and diabetes in adulthood (Barker et al., 1993).

Prenatally malnourished babies enter the world with serious problems. They frequently catch respiratory illnesses, since poor nutrition suppresses development of the immune system (Chandra, 1991). In addition, these infants are irritable and unresponsive to stimulation. Like drug-addicted newborns, they have a high-pitched cry that is particularly distressing to their caregivers. In poverty-stricken families, these effects quickly combine with a stressful home life. With age, low intelligence and serious learning problems become more apparent (Pollitt, 1996).

Many studies show that providing pregnant women with adequate food has a substantial impact on the health of their newborn babies. Yet the growth demands of the prenatal period require more than just increasing the quantity of a typical diet. Finding ways to optimize maternal nutrition through vitamin–mineral enrichment as early as possible is also crucial.

For example, the power of folic acid to prevent abnormalities of the neural tube, such as anencephaly and spina bifida (see Table 2.4 on page 55), has captured the attention of medical and public health experts. Folic acid supplementation around the time of conception reduces neural tube defects by as much as 72 percent (MCR Vitamin Study Research Group, 1991). In addition, adequate folate intake during the last 10 weeks of pregnancy cuts the risk of premature delivery and low birth weight in half (Scholl, Heidiger, & Belsky, 1996). Because of these findings, the U.S. Public Health Service recommends that all women of childbearing age consume at least 0.4 but not more than 1 milligram of folic acid per day (since excessive intake can be harmful). Currently, bread, flour, rice, pasta, and other grain products are being fortified with folic acid (McBride, 1997).

■ *This government clinic in Kenya prevents early malnutrition by promoting a proper diet for pregnant women and young children, including breast-feeding in infancy (see Chapter 4, page 127). (Photo courtesy: Betty Press/ Woodfin Camp & Associates)*

When poor nutrition persists throughout the prenatal period, successful intervention in the months after birth must not only provide much-needed nutrients, but also break the cycle of strained and apathetic mother–baby interactions. Some programs do so by teaching parents how to interact effectively with their infants, whereas others focus on stimulating infants to promote active engagement with their physical and social surroundings. In either case, the difference in intellectual development between prenatally malnourished babies and their well-nourished counterparts is greatly reduced (Grantham-McGregor et al., 1994; Grantham-McGregor, Schofield, & Powell, 1987).

Although prenatal malnutrition is highest in poverty-stricken regions of the world, it is not limited to developing countries. Each year, 80,000 to 120,000 American infants are born seriously undernourished. Although the federal government provides food packages to low-income pregnant women through its Special Supplemental Food Program for Women, Infants, and Children, funding is limited, and only 70 percent of those eligible are served (Children's Defense Fund, 1999). Finally, the diets of some economically advantaged expectant mothers are inadequate. In the United States, where thinness is the feminine ideal, women often feel uneasy about adding 25 to 30 pounds—the recommended weight gain for ensuring the health of both mother and baby.

■ EMOTIONAL STRESS. When women experience severe emotional stress during pregnancy, their babies are at risk for a wide variety of difficulties. Intense anxiety is associated with higher rates of miscarriage, prematurity,

low birth weight, and newborn respiratory illness. It is also related to certain physical defects, such as cleft palate and pyloric stenosis—tightening of the infant's stomach outlet, which must be treated surgically (Hoffman & Hatch, 1996; Omer & Everly, 1988).

To understand how the developing organism is affected, think back to the way your own body felt the last time you were under considerable stress. Fear and anxiety cause us to be "poised for action." Extra blood flows to parts of the body involved in the defensive response—the brain, the heart, and muscles in the arms, legs, and trunk. Blood flow to other organs, including the uterus, is reduced. As a result, the fetus receives less oxygen and nutrients. Stress hormones also cross the placenta, leading the fetus's heart rate and activity level to rise dramatically. Long-term exposure to these hormones may be responsible for the irritability and digestive disturbances often present in newborns of highly stressed mothers. Finally, stress weakens the immune system, making pregnant women more susceptible to infectious disease (Cohen & Williamson, 1991).

The risks of emotional stress are greatly reduced when mothers have husbands, other family members, and friends who offer social support (McLean et al., 1993; Nuckolls, Cassel, & Kaplan, 1972). The link between social support and positive pregnancy outcomes is particularly strong for low-income women (Hoffman & Hatch, 1996). These findings suggest that finding ways to provide supportive social ties to isolated expectant mothers can help prevent prenatal complications.

■ RH BLOOD INCOMPATIBILITY. When inherited blood types of mother and fetus differ, the incompatibility can sometimes cause serious problems. The most common cause of these difficulties is a blood protein called the **Rh factor.** When the mother is Rh-negative (lacks the protein) and the father is Rh-positive (has the protein), the baby may inherit the father's Rh-positive blood type. (Recall from Table 2.2 in Chapter 2 that Rh-positive blood is dominant and Rh-negative blood is recessive, so the chances are good that a baby will be Rh-positive.) If even a little of a fetus's Rh-positive blood crosses the placenta into the Rh-negative mother's bloodstream, she begins to form antibodies to the foreign Rh protein. If these enter the fetus's system, they destroy red blood cells, reducing the oxygen supply. Mental retardation, miscarriage, heart damage, and infant death can occur.

Since it takes time for the mother to produce Rh antibodies, first-born children are rarely affected. The danger increases with each additional pregnancy. Fortunately, the harmful effects of Rh incompatibility can be prevented in most cases. After the birth of each Rh-positive baby, Rh-negative mothers are routinely given a vaccine to prevent the buildup of antibodies. In emergency cases, blood transfusions can be performed immediately after delivery or even before birth.

■ MATERNAL AGE AND PREVIOUS BIRTHS. In Chapter 2, we indicated that women who delay childbearing until their thirties or forties face increased risk of infertility, miscarriage, and babies born with chromosomal defects. Are other pregnancy problems more common for older mothers?

For many years, scientists thought that aging and repeated use of the mother's reproductive organs increased the likelihood of a wide variety of pregnancy complications. Recently, these ideas have been questioned. When women without serious health difficulties are considered, even those in their forties do not experience more prenatal problems than do women in their twenties (Ales, Druzin, & Santini, 1990; Dildy et al., 1996). And a large study of over 50,000 pregnancies found no relationship between the number of previous births and prenatal problems (Heinonen, Slone, & Shapiro, 1977).

In the case of teenage mothers, does physical immaturity cause prenatal difficulties? Again, research shows that it does not. As we will see in Chapter 11, nature tries to ensure that once a girl can conceive, she is physically ready to carry and give birth to a baby. Infants of teenagers are born with a higher rate of problems for quite different reasons. Many pregnant adolescents do not have access to medical care or are afraid to seek it. In addition, most come from low-income backgrounds where stress, poor nutrition, and health problems are common (Coley & Chase-Lansdale, 1998).

THE IMPORTANCE OF PRENATAL HEALTH CARE

Yolanda had her first prenatal appointment 3 weeks after missing her menstrual period. After that, she visited the doctor's office once a month until she was 7 months pregnant, then twice during the eighth month. As the due date grew near, Yolanda's appointments increased to once a week. The doctor kept track of her general health, weight gain, and the capacity of her uterus and cervix to support the fetus. The fetus's growth was also carefully monitored.

Yolanda's pregnancy, like most, was uneventful. But unexpected difficulties can arise, especially if mothers have health problems to begin with. For example, women with diabetes need careful monitoring. Extra sugar in the mother's bloodstream causes the fetus to grow larger than average, making pregnancy and birth problems more common. Another complication, *toxemia* (sometimes called *eclampsia*), in which blood pressure increases sharply and the face, hands, and feet swell in the last half of pregnancy, is experienced by 5 to 10 percent of pregnant women. If untreated, toxemia can cause convulsions in the mother and fetal death. Usually, hospitalization, bed rest, and drugs can lower blood pressure to a safe level. If not, the baby must be delivered at once (Carlson, Eisenstat, & Ziporyn, 1996).

Unfortunately, 18 percent of pregnant women in the United States wait until after the first trimester to seek prenatal care, and 4 percent delay until the end of pregnancy or never get any at all. Most of these mothers are adolescents, unmarried, or poverty stricken. Their infants are far more likely to be born underweight and to die before birth or during the first year of life than are babies of mothers who receive early medical attention (Children's Defense Fund, 1999).

Why do these mothers delay going to the doctor? One frequent reason is a lack of health insurance. Although the very poorest of these mothers are eligible for government-sponsored health services, many low-income women do not qualify. As we will see when we take up birth complications later in this chapter, in nations where affordable medical care is universally available, late-care pregnancies and maternal and infant health problems are greatly reduced.

Besides financial hardship, there are other reasons that some mothers do not seek prenatal care. When researchers asked women who first went to the doctor late in pregnancy why they waited so long, they mentioned a wide variety of personal problems, including psychological stress, the demands of taking care of other young children, lack of transportation, ambivalence about the pregnancy, and family crises. Many were also engaging in high-risk behaviors, such as smoking and drug abuse (Melnikow & Alemagno, 1993). These women, who had no medical attention for most of their pregnancies, were among those who need it most!

■ *During a routine prenatal visit, this doctor uses ultrasound to show an expectant mother an image of her fetus and to evaluate its development. All pregnant women should receive early and regular prenatal care—to protect their own health and the health of their babies. (Photo courtesy: Deep Light Productions/Science Photo Library/Photo Researchers, Inc.)*

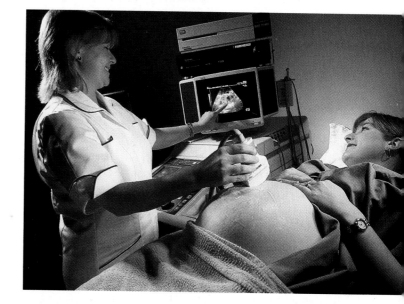

Clearly, public education about the importance of early and sustained prenatal care for all pregnant women is badly needed in the United States. The Caregiving Concerns table below summarizes "dos and don'ts" for a healthy pregnancy, based on our discussion of the prenatal environment.

ASK YOURSELF . . .

■ *Why is it difficult to determine the effects of some environmental agents, such as over-the-counter drugs and pollution, on the embryo and fetus?*

■ *Trixie has just learned that she is pregnant. Since she has always been healthy and feels good right now, she cannot understand why the doctor wants her to come in for checkups so often. Why is early and regular prenatal care important for Trixie?*

🌳 *Cite examples of prenatal environmental influences that appear to have little or no negative impact on health in infancy and childhood but that may contribute to serious health problems in adulthood.*

CHILDBIRTH

Although Yolanda and Jay completed my course 3 months before their baby was born, both agreed to return the following spring to share their experiences with my next class. When the long-awaited day arrived, they brought little Joshua, who was 2 weeks old at the time. Yolanda and Jay's story revealed that the birth of a baby is one of the most dramatic and emotional events in human experience. Jay was present throughout Yolanda's labor and delivery. Yolanda explained,

By morning, we knew that I was in labor. It was Thursday, so we went in for my usual weekly appointment. The doctor said, yes, the baby was on the way, but it would be a while. He told us to go home and relax or take a leisurely walk and come to the hospital in 3 or 4 hours. We checked in at 3 in the afternoon; Joshua arrived at 2 o'clock the next morning. When, finally, I was ready to deliver, it went quickly; a half-hour or so and some good hard pushes, and there he was! His body had stuff all over it, his face was red and puffy, and his head was misshapen, but I thought, "Oh! he's beautiful. I can't believe he's really here!"

CAREGIVING CONCERNS
Dos and Don'ts for a Healthy Pregnancy

DO	DON'T
Do make sure that you have been vaccinated against infectious diseases dangerous to the embryo and fetus, such as rubella, before you get pregnant. Most vaccinations are not safe during pregnancy.	Don't take any drugs without consulting your doctor.
Do see a doctor as soon as you suspect that you are pregnant—within a few weeks after a missed menstrual period.	Don't smoke. If you have already smoked during part of your pregnancy, you can protect your baby by cutting down or (better yet) quitting at any time. If other members of your family are smokers, ask them to quit or smoke outside.
Do continue to get regular medical checkups throughout pregnancy.	Don't drink alcohol from the time you decide to get pregnant. If you find it difficult to give up alcohol, ask for help from your doctor, local family service agency, or nearest chapter of Alcoholics Anonymous.
Do obtain literature from your doctor, local library, and bookstore about prenatal development and care. Ask questions about anything you do not understand.	
Do eat a well-balanced diet and take vitamin–mineral supplements as prescribed by your doctor. On the average, a woman should increase her intake by 300 calories a day over her usual needs—less at the beginning and more at the end of pregnancy. Gain 25 to 30 pounds gradually.	Don't engage in activities that might expose your baby to environmental hazards, such as chemical pollutants or radiation. If you work in an occupation that involves these agents, ask for a safer assignment or a leave of absence.
Do keep physically fit through mild exercise. If possible, join a special exercise class for expectant mothers.	Don't engage in activities that might expose your baby to harmful infectious diseases, such as childhood illnesses and toxoplasmosis.
Do avoid emotional stress. If you are a single parent, find a relative or friend on whom you can count for emotional support.	Don't choose pregnancy as a time to go on a diet.
Do get plenty of rest. An overtired mother is at risk for pregnancy complications.	Don't overeat and gain too much weight during pregnancy. A very large weight gain is associated with complications.
Do enroll in a prenatal and childbirth education class along with your partner. When parents know what to expect, the 9 months before birth can be one of the most joyful times of life.	

Jay was also elated by Joshua's birth. "I wanted to support Yolanda and to experience as much as I could. It was awesome, indescribable," he said, holding Joshua over his shoulder and patting and kissing him gently. In the following sections, we explore the experience of childbirth, from both the parents' and the baby's point of view.

THE STAGES OF CHILDBIRTH

It is not surprising that childbirth is often referred to as *labor.* It is the hardest physical work a woman may ever do. A complex series of hormonal changes initiates the process, which naturally divides into three stages (see Figure 3.5):

1. *Dilation and effacement of the cervix.* This is the longest stage of labor, lasting, on the average, 12 to 14 hours in a first birth and 4 to 6 hours in later births. Contractions of the uterus gradually become more frequent and powerful, causing the cervix, or uterine opening, to widen (dilate) and thin (efface) to nothing. When the cervix opens completely, contractions reach a peak called *transition.* As a result, a clear channel from the uterus into the vagina, or birth canal, is formed.

2. *Birth of the baby.* Once the cervix is fully open, the baby is ready to be born. This second stage is much shorter than the first, lasting about 50 minutes in a first birth and 20 minutes in later births. Strong contractions of the uterus continue, but the mother also feels a natural urge to squeeze and push with her abdominal muscles. As she does so with each contraction, she forces the baby down and out.

3. *Delivery of the placenta.* Labor comes to an end with a few final contractions and pushes. These cause the placenta to separate from the wall of the uterus and be delivered, in about 5 to 10 minutes.

Stage 1

(a) Dilation and Effacement of the Cervix

(b) Transition

Stage 2

(c) Pushing

(d) Birth of the Baby

Stage 3

(e) Delivery of the Placenta

FIGURE 3.5

■ **The three stages of labor.** Stage 1: (a) contractions of the uterus cause dilation and effacement of the cervix. (b) Transition is reached when the frequency and strength of the contractions are at their peak and the cervix opens completely. Stage 2: (c) The mother pushes with each contraction, forcing the baby down the birth canal, and the head appears. (d) Near the end of Stage 2, the shoulders emerge and are followed quickly by the rest of the baby's body. Stage 3: (e) With a few final pushes, the placenta is delivered.

■ *This newborn baby is held by his mother's birthing coach (on the left) and midwife (on the right) just after delivery. The umbilical cord has not yet been cut. Notice how the infant's head is molded from being squeezed through the birth canal for many hours. It is also very large in relation to his body. As the infant takes his first few breaths, his body turns from blue to pink. He is wide awake and ready to get to know his new surroundings. (Photo courtesy: Dakoda Brandon Dorsaneo)*

THE BABY'S ADAPTATION TO LABOR AND DELIVERY

At first glance, labor and delivery seem like a dangerous ordeal for the baby. The strong contractions of Yolanda's uterus exposed Joshua's head to a great deal of pressure, and they squeezed the placenta and the umbilical cord repeatedly. Each time, Joshua's supply of oxygen was temporarily reduced.

Fortunately, healthy babies are well equipped to deal with the trauma of childbirth. The force of the contractions causes the infant to produce high levels of stress hormones. Recall that during pregnancy, the effects of maternal stress can endanger the baby. In contrast, during childbirth the infant's production of stress hormones is adaptive. It helps the baby withstand oxygen deprivation by sending a rich supply of blood to the brain and heart. In addition, it prepares the baby to breathe effectively by causing the lungs to absorb excess liquid and by expanding the bronchial tubes (passages leading to the lungs). Finally, stress hormones arouse the infant into alertness. Joshua was born wide awake, ready to interact with the surrounding world (Emory & Toomey, 1988; Lagercrantz & Slotkin, 1986).

THE NEWBORN BABY'S APPEARANCE

What do babies look like after birth? My students asked Yolanda and Jay this question. "Come to think of it," Jay smiled, "Yolanda and I are probably the only people in the world who thought Joshua was beautiful!" The average newborn is 20 inches long and 7½ pounds in weight; boys tend to be slightly longer and heavier than girls. The head is very large in comparison to the trunk and legs, which are short and bowed. As we will see in later chapters, the combination of a big head (with its well-developed brain) and a small body means that human infants learn quickly in the first few months of life. But unlike most other mammals, they cannot get around on their own until much later.

Even though newborn babies may look strange, some features do make them attractive. Their round faces, chubby cheeks, large foreheads, and big eyes are just those characteristics that make adults feel like picking them up and cuddling them (Berman, 1980; Lorenz, 1943).

ASSESSING THE NEWBORN'S PHYSICAL CONDITION: THE APGAR SCALE

Infants who have difficulty making the transition to life outside the uterus must be given special help at once. To assess the infant's physical condition quickly, doctors and nurses use the **Apgar Scale**. As Table 3.2 shows, a rating of 0,

TABLE 3.2

The Apgar Scale

SIGN[a]	SCORE		
	0	1	2
Heart rate	No heartbeat	Under 100 beats per minute	100 to 140 beats per minute
Respiratory effort	No breathing for 60 seconds	Irregular, shallow breathing	Strong breathing and crying
Reflex irritability (sneezing, coughing, and grimacing)	No response	Weak reflexive response	Strong reflexive response
Muscle tone	Completely limp	Weak movements of arms and legs	Strong movements of arms and legs
Color[b]	Blue body, arms, and legs	Body pink with blue arms and legs	Body, arms, and legs completely pink

[a] To remember these signs, you may find it helpful to use a technique in which the original labels are reordered and renamed as follows: color = **A**ppearance, heart rate = **P**ulse, reflex irritability = **G**rimace, muscle tone = **A**ctivity, and respiratory effort = **R**espiration. Together, the first letters of the new labels spell **Apgar.**
[b] Color is the least reliable of the Apgar signs. The skin tone of nonwhite babies makes it difficult to apply the "pink" criterion. However, newborns of all races can be rated for pinkish glow resulting from the flow of oxygen through body tissues.
Source: Apgar, 1953.

1, or 2 on each of five characteristics is made at 1 and 5 minutes after birth. An Apgar score of 7 or better indicates that the infant is in good physical condition. If the score is between 4 and 6, the baby requires assistance in establishing breathing and other vital signs. If the score is 3 or below, the infant is in serious danger and requires emergency medical attention. Two Apgar ratings are given, since some babies have trouble adjusting at first but do quite well after a few minutes (Apgar, 1953).

APPROACHES TO CHILDBIRTH

Childbirth practices, like other aspects of family life, are molded by the society of which mother and baby are a part. In many village and tribal cultures, expectant mothers are well acquainted with the childbirth process. For example, the Jarara of South America and the Pukapukans of the Pacific Islands treat birth as a vital part of daily life. The Jarara mother gives birth in full view of the entire community, including small children. The Pukapukan girl is so familiar with the events of labor and delivery that she can frequently be seen playing at it. Using a coconut to represent the baby, she stuffs it inside her dress, imitates the mother's pushing, and lets the nut fall at the proper moment. In most nonindustrialized cultures, women are assisted during the birth process. Among the Mayans of the Yucatán, the mother leans against the body of a woman called the "head helper," who supports her weight and breathes with her during each contraction (Jordan, 1993; Mead & Newton, 1967).

In large Western nations, childbirth has changed dramatically over the centuries. Before the late 1800s, birth usually took place at home and was a family-centered event. The industrial revolution brought greater crowding to cities along with new health problems. Childbirth moved from home to the hospital, where the health of mothers and babies could be protected. Once doctors assumed responsibility for childbirth, women's knowledge of it declined, and relatives and friends were no longer welcome to participate (Borst, 1995).

By the 1950s and 1960s, women started to question the medical procedures that had come to be used routinely during labor and delivery. Many felt that frequent use of strong drugs and delivery instruments had robbed them of a precious experience and were often not necessary or safe for the baby. Gradually, a natural childbirth movement arose in Europe and spread to the United States. Its purpose was to make hospital birth as comfortable and rewarding for mothers as possible. Today, most hospitals carry this theme further by offering birth centers that are family centered in approach and homelike in appearance. *Freestanding birth centers*, which operate independently of hospitals and encourage early contact between parents and baby but offer less backup medical care, also exist. And a small but growing number of American women are rejecting institutional birth entirely and choosing to have their babies at home.

Let's take a closer look at two childbirth approaches that have grown in popularity in recent years: natural childbirth and home delivery.

NATURAL, OR PREPARED, CHILDBIRTH

Yolanda and Jay chose **natural**, or **prepared, childbirth**. Although many natural childbirth techniques exist, all try to overcome the idea that birth is a painful ordeal requiring extensive medical intervention. Most programs draw on methods developed by Grantly Dick-Read (1959) in England and Ferdinand Lamaze (1958) in France. These physicians emphasized that cultural attitudes had taught women to fear the birth experience. An anxious, frightened woman in labor tenses her muscles, turning the mild pain that sometimes accompanies strong contractions into a great deal of pain.

In a typical natural childbirth program, the expectant mother and a companion (the father, a relative, or a friend) participate in three activities:

■ *Classes.* Yolanda and Jay attended a series of classes in which they learned about the anatomy and physiology of labor and delivery. Knowledge about the birth process reduces a mother's fear.

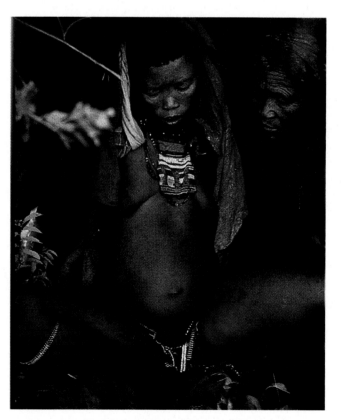

■ *Among the !Kung of Botswana, Africa, a mother gives birth in a sitting position, and she is surrounded by women who encourage and help her. (Photo courtesy: Shostak/Anthro-Photo)*

- *Relaxation and breathing techniques.* During each class, Yolanda was taught relaxation and breathing exercises aimed at counteracting the pain of uterine contractions.

- *Labor coach.* Jay was taught to be a "labor coach." He learned how to help Yolanda during childbirth—by reminding her to relax and breathe, massaging her back, supporting her body, and offering words of encouragement and affection.

Studies comparing mothers who experience natural childbirth with those who do not reveal many benefits. Because mothers feel more in control of labor and delivery, their attitudes toward the childbirth experience are more positive, and they feel less pain. As a result, they require less medication—usually very little or none at all (Hetherington, 1990; Mackey, 1995).

Social support is an important part of the success of natural childbirth techniques. In Guatemalan and American hospitals that routinely isolate patients during childbirth, some mothers were randomly assigned a companion who stayed with them throughout labor. These mothers had fewer complications, and their labors were several hours shorter than those of women who did not have companionship. Guatemalan mothers who received support also interacted more positively with their babies during the first hour after delivery (Kennell et al., 1991; Sosa et al., 1980). Social support is particularly helpful during a first childbirth, when mothers are more anxious (DiMateo & Kahn, 1997). And this aspect of natural childbirth makes Western hospital-birth customs more acceptable to women from parts of the world where assistance from family and community members is the norm (Granot et al., 1996).

HOME DELIVERY

Home birth has always been popular in certain industrialized nations, such as England, the Netherlands, and Sweden. The number of American women choosing to have their babies at home has grown in recent years, although it remains small, at about 1 percent. Some home births are attended by doctors, but most are handled by certified *nurse-midwives* who have degrees in nursing and additional training in childbirth management (Bastian, 1993; Declercq, 1992).

The joys and perils of home delivery are well illustrated by the story that Don, who painted my house as I worked on this book, related to me. "Our first child was delivered in the hospital," he said. "Even though I was present, Kathy and I found the atmosphere to be rigid and insensitive. We wanted a warmer, more personal birth environment." With the coaching of a nurse-midwife, Don delivered their second child, Cindy, at their farmhouse, three miles out of town. Three years later, when Kathy went into labor with

About to give birth at home, this mother discusses the progress of her labor with the midwife while her husband and their older child look on. Mothers who choose home birth want to make the experience an important part of family life, avoid unnecessary medical procedures, and exercise greater control over their own care and that of their babies. *(Photo courtesy: © Susan Ames)*

Marnie, a heavy snowstorm prevented the midwife from reaching the house on time. Don delivered the baby alone, but the birth was difficult. Marnie failed to breathe for several minutes; with great effort, Don revived her. The frightening memory of Marnie's limp, blue body convinced Don and Kathy to return to the hospital to have their last child. By then, hospital practices had changed, and the event was a rewarding one for both parents.

Don and Kathy's experience raises the question: Is it just as safe to give birth at home as in a hospital? For healthy women who are assisted by a well-trained doctor or midwife, it seems so, since complications rarely occur (Olsen, 1997). However, if attendants are not carefully trained and prepared to handle emergencies, the rate of infant death is high (Mehlmadrona & Madrona, 1997). When mothers are at risk for any kind of complication, the appropriate place for labor and delivery is the hospital, where life-saving treatment is available.

MEDICAL INTERVENTIONS

Two-year-old Melinda walks with a halting, lumbering gait and has difficulty keeping her balance. She has *cerebral palsy,* a general term for a variety of impairments in muscle coordination that result from brain damage before, during, or just after birth.

Like 22 percent of youngsters with cerebral palsy, Melinda's brain damage was caused by **anoxia,** or inadequate oxygen supply, during labor and delivery (Mecham, 1996). Her mother got pregnant accidentally, was frightened and alone, and arrived at the hospital at the last minute. Melinda was in **breech position** (turned so that the buttocks or feet would be delivered first), and the cord was wrapped around her neck. Had her mother come to the hospital earlier, doctors could have monitored Melinda's condition and delivered her surgically as soon as squeezing of the umbilical cord led to distress, reducing the damage or preventing it entirely.

More than anywhere in the world, childbirth in the United States is a medically monitored and controlled event (Jordan, 1993). In cases like Melinda's, medical interventions are clearly justified. But in others, they can interfere with delivery and even pose new risks. In the following sections, we examine some commonly used medical techniques.

FETAL MONITORING

Fetal monitors are electronic instruments that track the baby's heart rate during labor. An abnormal heartbeat may indicate that the baby is in distress due to anoxia and needs to be delivered immediately. Fetal monitors are required in almost all American hospitals. The most popular kind is strapped across the mother's abdomen throughout labor. A second, more accurate method involves threading a recording device through the cervix and placing it directly under the baby's scalp.

Fetal monitoring is a safe medical procedure that has saved the lives of many babies in high-risk situations. Nevertheless, the practice is controversial. In healthy pregnancies, it does not reduce the rate of infant brain damage or death. Critics also worry that fetal monitors identify many babies as in danger who, in fact, are not (Samuels & Samuels, 1996; Sheth & Malpani, 1997). Monitoring is linked to an increased rate of cesarean (surgical) deliveries, which we will discuss shortly. In addition, some women complain that the devices are uncomfortable, prevent them from moving easily, and interfere with the normal course of labor.

Still, it is likely that fetal monitors will continue to be used routinely, even though they might not be necessary in most cases. Today, doctors can be sued for malpractice if an infant dies or is born with problems and they cannot show that they did everything possible to protect the baby (Chez, 1997).

LABOR AND DELIVERY MEDICATION

Some form of medication is used in 80 to 95 percent of births in the United States (Glosten, 1998). *Analgesics*, drugs used to relieve pain, may be given in mild doses during labor to help a mother relax. *Anesthetics* are a stronger type of painkiller that blocks sensation. A regional anesthetic may be injected into the spinal column to numb the lower half of the body.

Although pain-relieving drugs enable doctors to perform essential life-saving medical interventions, they can cause problems when used routinely. Anesthesia weakens uterine contractions during the first stage of labor and interferes with the mother's ability to feel contractions and push during the second stage. As a result, labor is prolonged (Alexander et al., 1998). In addition, since labor and delivery medication rapidly crosses the placenta, the newborn baby may be sleepy and withdrawn, suck poorly during feedings, and be irritable when awake (Emory, Schlackman, & Fiano, 1996).

Does use of medication during childbirth have a lasting impact on physical and mental development? Some researchers claim so (Brackbill, McManus, & Woodward, 1985), but their findings have been challenged (Golub, 1996). Anesthesia may be related to other risk factors that could account for long-term consequences in some studies, and more research is needed to sort out these effects.

CESAREAN DELIVERY

A **cesarean delivery** is a surgical birth; the doctor makes an incision in the mother's abdomen and lifts the baby out of the uterus. Thirty years ago, cesarean delivery was rare in the United States, performed in only 3 percent of births. Since then, the cesarean rate has climbed, reaching 24 percent in 1993 and dropping slightly to 21 percent in 1998. Still, it is the highest rate in the world (U.S. Bureau of the Census, 1999).

Cesareans have always been warranted by medical emergencies, such as Rh incompatibility, premature separation of the placenta from the uterus, or serious maternal illness or infection (for example, the herpes simplex 2 virus, which can infect the baby during a vaginal delivery). However, surgical delivery is not always needed in other instances. For example, although the most common reason for a cesarean is a previous cesarean, the technique used today—a small horizontal cut in the lower part of the uterus—makes a vaginal birth safe in later pregnancies (Korte, 1997). Furthermore, in breech births, in which the baby risks head injury or anoxia (as in Melinda's case), cesareans are often justified (Cheng & Hannah, 1993). But the infant's position makes a difference. Certain breech babies fare just as well with a normal delivery as a cesarean. Sometimes the doctor can gently turn the baby into a head-down position during the early part of labor (Flamm & Quilligan, 1995).

When a cesarean delivery does occur, both mother and baby need extra support. Although the operation is quite safe, it requires more time for recovery. Since anesthetic may have crossed the placenta, newborns are more likely to be sleepy and unresponsive and to have breathing difficulties (Cox & Schwartz, 1990). These factors can negatively affect the early mother–infant relationship.

■ *What factors help the newborn baby withstand the trauma of labor and delivery?*

■ *Use of any single medical intervention during childbirth increases the likelihood that others will also be used. Provide as many examples as you can to illustrate this idea.*

🌳 *How have history-graded influences (see Chapter 1, page 12) affected approaches to childbirth in Western nations? What effects have these changes had on the health and adjustment of mothers and newborn babies?*

PRETERM AND LOW-BIRTH-WEIGHT INFANTS

B abies born 3 weeks or more before the end of a full 38-week pregnancy or who weigh less than 5½ pounds (2,500 grams) have, for many years, been referred to as "premature"—the most common birth complication. A wealth of research indicates that premature babies are at risk for many problems. Birth weight is the best available predictor of infant survival and healthy development. Many newborns who weigh less than 3⅓ pounds (1,500 grams) experience brain hemorrhages and other severe biological traumas, an effect that becomes stronger as birth weight decreases (Fletcher et al., 1997; Novy, McGregor, & Iams, 1995). Frequent illness, inattention, overactiv-

■ *This baby was born 13 weeks before her due date and weighs little more than 2 pounds. Since her lungs are too immature to function independently, she breathes with the aid of a respirator. Her survival and development are seriously at risk. (Photo courtesy: Simon Frazer/Princess Mary Hospital/Photo Researchers, Inc.)*

ity, language delays, low intelligence test scores, and deficits in motor coordination and school learning are some of the difficulties that extend into the childhood years (Hack et al., 1994, 1995; Mayes & Bornstein, 1997).

About 1 in 14 infants is born underweight in the United States. Although the problem can strike unexpectedly, it is highest among poverty-stricken women, especially ethnic minorities (Children's Defense Fund, 1999). These mothers, as we indicated earlier, are more likely to be undernourished and to be exposed to other harmful environmental influences. In addition, they often do not receive the prenatal care necessary to protect their vulnerable babies.

Recall from Chapter 2 that prematurity is also common among twins. Because space inside the uterus is restricted, twins gain less weight after the twentieth week of pregnancy than do singletons.

PRETERM VERSUS SMALL FOR DATE

Although low-birth-weight infants face many obstacles to healthy development, more than half go on to lead normal lives, including some who weighed only a few pounds at birth (Vohr & Garcia-Coll, 1988). To better understand why some of these babies do better than others, researchers have divided them into two groups. The first is called **preterm.** These infants are born several weeks or more before their due date. Although small in size, their weight may still be appropriate for the amount of time they spent in the uterus. The second group is called **small for date.** These babies are below their expected weight when length of the pregnancy is taken into account. Some small-for-date infants are actually full term. Others are preterm infants who are especially underweight.

Of the two types of babies, small-for-date infants usually have more serious problems. During the first year, they are more likely to die, catch infections, and show evidence of brain damage. By middle childhood, they have lower intelligence test scores, are less attentive, and achieve more poorly in school (Copper et al., 1993; Schothorst & van Engeland, 1996). Small-for-date infants probably experienced inadequate nutrition before birth. Perhaps their mothers did not eat properly, the placenta did not function normally, or the babies themselves had defects that prevented them from growing as they should.

CONSEQUENCES FOR CAREGIVING

Imagine a scrawny, thin-skinned infant whose body is only a little larger than the size of your hand. You try to play with the baby by stroking and talking softly, but he is sleepy and unresponsive. When you feed him, he sucks poorly. He is usually irritable during the short, unpredictable periods in which he is awake.

The appearance and behavior of preterm babies can lead parents to be less sensitive and responsive in caring for them. Compared with full-term infants, preterm babies—especially those who are very ill at birth—are less often held close, touched, and talked to gently. At times, mothers of these infants engage in interfering pokes and verbal commands in an effort to obtain a higher level of response from a baby who is a passive, unrewarding social partner (Barratt, Roach, & Leavitt, 1996). Some parents may step up these intrusive acts when ungratifying infant behavior continues. This may explain why preterm babies as a group are at risk for child abuse. When these infants are born to isolated, poverty-stricken mothers who have difficulty managing their own lives, the chances for unfavorable outcomes are increased. In contrast, parents with stable life circumstances and social supports can usually overcome the stresses of caring for a preterm infant. Under these circumstances, even sick preterm babies have a good chance of catching up in development by middle childhood (Liaw & Brooks-Gunn, 1993).

These findings suggest that how well preterm babies develop has a great deal to do with the parent–child relationship. Consequently, interventions directed at supporting both sides of this tie should help these infants recover.

INTERVENTIONS FOR PRETERM INFANTS

A preterm baby is cared for in a special plexiglass-enclosed bed called an *isolette*. Temperature is carefully controlled, since these babies cannot yet regulate their own body temperature effectively. Air is filtered before it enters the isolette to help protect the baby from infection. Infants born more than 6 weeks early commonly have a disorder called **respiratory distress syndrome** (otherwise known as *hyaline membrane disease*). Their tiny lungs are so poorly developed that the air sacs collapse, causing serious breathing difficulties. When a preterm infant breathes with the aid of a respirator, is fed through a stomach tube, and receives medication through an intravenous needle, the isolette can be very isolating indeed! Physical needs that otherwise would lead to close contact and other human stimulation are met mechanically.

■ SPECIAL INFANT STIMULATION. At one time, doctors believed that stimulating such a fragile baby could be harmful. Now we know that in proper doses, certain kinds of stimulation can help preterm infants develop. In some intensive care nurseries, preterm babies can be seen rocking in suspended hammocks or lying on waterbeds designed to replace the gentle motion they would have received while still in the mother's uterus. Other forms of stimulation have also been used—for example, an attractive mobile or a tape recording of a heartbeat, soft music, or the mother's voice. These experiences promote faster weight gain, more predictable sleep patterns, and increased alertness during the weeks after birth (Beckwith & Sigman, 1995).

Touch is an especially important form of stimulation. In baby animals, touching the skin releases certain brain chemicals that support physical growth—effects believed to occur in humans as well (Field, 1998). When preterm infants were massaged several times each day in the hospital, they gained weight faster and, at the end of the first year, were advanced in mental and motor development over preterm babies not given this stimulation (Field et al., 1986). In developing countries where hospitalization is not always possible, skin-to-skin "kangaroo baby care," in which the preterm infant is tucked between the mother's breasts, is being encouraged. It fosters oxygenation of the baby's body, temperature regulation, improved feeding, and infant survival (Hamelin & Ramachandran, 1993).

■ TRAINING PARENTS IN INFANT CAREGIVING SKILLS. When preterm infants develop more quickly, parents are likely to feel encouraged and to interact with the baby more effectively. Interventions that support the parenting side of this relationship generally teach parents about the infant's characteristics and promote caregiving skills. For parents with the economic and personal resources to care for a low-birth-weight infant, just a few sessions of coaching in recognizing and responding to the baby's needs lead to steady gains in mental test performance, until scores are similar to those of full-term children (Achenbach et al., 1990). Parenting that helps preterm infants sustain attention (for example, gently commenting on and showing the baby features of a toy) is especially helpful in promoting favorable early cognitive and language development (Smith et al., 1996).

When preterm infants live in stressed, low-income households, long-term, intensive intervention is necessary. In one study, preterm babies born into poverty received a comprehensive intervention that combined medical follow-up, weekly parent training sessions, and enrollment in cognitively stimulating child care from 1 to 3 years of age. More than four times as many intervention children as controls (39 versus 9 percent) were within normal range at age 3 in intelligence, psychological adjustment, and physical growth (Bradley et al., 1994). Yet by age 5, the intervention children had lost ground. And by age 8, group differences were no longer present for children who had been very low-birth-weight (Brooks-Gunn et al., 1994; McCarton et al., 1997). To sustain developmental gains in these vulnerable children, high-quality intervention is needed well beyond age 3 —even into the school years.

Finally, the high rate of low birth weight and infant death in the United States—one of the worst in the industrialized world—could be greatly reduced by improving the health and social conditions described in the Social Issues box on pages 104–105. Fortunately, today we can save many preterm infants. But an even better course of action would be to prevent this serious threat to infant survival and development before it happens.

A CROSS-NATIONAL PERSPECTIVE ON HEALTH CARE AND OTHER POLICIES FOR PARENTS AND NEWBORN BABIES

Infant mortality is an index used around the world to assess the overall health of a nation's children. It refers to the number of deaths in the first year of life per 1,000 live births. Although the United States has the most up-to-date health care technology in the world, it has made less progress than many other countries in reducing infant deaths. Over the past three decades, it has slipped down in the international rankings, from seventh in the 1950s to twenty-first at the end of the 1990s. Members of America's poor ethnic minorities, African-American babies especially, are at greatest risk. Black infants are more than twice as likely as white infants to die in the first year of life. Their infant mortality rate is about the same as in developing nations with poor economies, such as Trinidad and Tobago (Bellamy, 1999; Children's Defense Fund, 1999).

Neonatal mortality, the rate of death within the first month of life, accounts for 67 percent of the high infant death rate in the United States. Two factors are largely responsible for neonatal mortality. The first is serious physical defects, most of which cannot be pre-

vented. The percentage of babies born with physical defects is about the same in all ethnic and income groups. The second leading cause of neonatal mortality is low birth weight, which is largely preventable. Black babies are more than four times more likely to die because they are born early and underweight than are white infants. On an international scale, the percentage of underweight newborns born in the United States is alarmingly high. It is greater than that in 22 other countries (Bellamy, 1999).

Experts agree that widespread poverty and weak health care programs for mothers and young children are largely responsible for these trends. Each country in Figure 3.6 that outranks the United States in infant survival provides all its citizens with government-sponsored health-care benefits. And each takes extra steps to make sure that pregnant mothers and babies have access to good nutrition, high-quality medical care, and social and economic supports that promote effective parenting.

For example, all European nations guarantee women a certain number of prenatal visits at very low or no cost.

Some even offer special incentives, such as a monetary allowance, for taking advantage of health benefits! After a baby is born, a health professional routinely visits the home to provide counseling about infant care and to arrange continuing medical services. Home assistance is especially extensive in the Netherlands. For a token fee, each mother is granted a specially trained maternity helper, who assists with infant care, shopping, housekeeping, meal preparation, and the care of other children during the days after delivery (Buekens et al., 1993; Kamerman, 1993).

Paid employment leave is another vital societal intervention for new parents. It is widely available in Western Europe, where it typically ranges from 2 to 12 months. In Sweden, a couple has the right to 15 months of paid leave to share between them. Even less-developed nations provide this benefit. For example, in the People's Republic of China, a new mother is granted 3 months leave at regular pay (Hyde, 1995). Yet in the United States, the federal government mandates only 12 weeks of *unpaid* leave for employees in businesses with at least 50 workers.

UNDERSTANDING BIRTH COMPLICATIONS

In the preceding sections, we discussed a variety of birth complications that threaten children's well-being. Are there any general principles that might help us understand how infants who survive a traumatic birth are likely to develop? A landmark longitudinal study carried out in Hawaii provides answers to this question.

In 1955, Emmy Werner began to track the development of nearly 700 infants on the island of Kauai who experienced either mild, moderate, or severe birth complications. Each was matched, on the basis of social class and ethnicity, with a healthy newborn (Werner & Smith, 1982). Findings revealed that the likelihood of long-term difficulties in-

creased if birth trauma was severe. But among mildly to moderately stressed children, the best predictor of how well they did in later years was the quality of their home environments. Children growing up in stable families did almost as well on measures of intelligence and psychological adjustment as did those with no birth problems. Those exposed to poverty, family disorganization, and mentally ill parents often developed serious learning difficulties, behavior problems, and emotional disturbance during childhood and adolescence.

The Kauai study tells us that as long as birth injuries are not overwhelming, a supportive home environment can restore children's growth. But the most intriguing cases in this study were the handful of exceptions to this rule. A few children with fairly serious birth complications and troubled family environments grew into competent adults

FIGURE 3.6

■ Infant mortality in 28 nations. Despite its advanced health care technology, the United States ranks poorly. It is twenty-second in the world, with a death rate of 8 infants per 1,000 births. (Adapted from March of Dimes, 1999.)

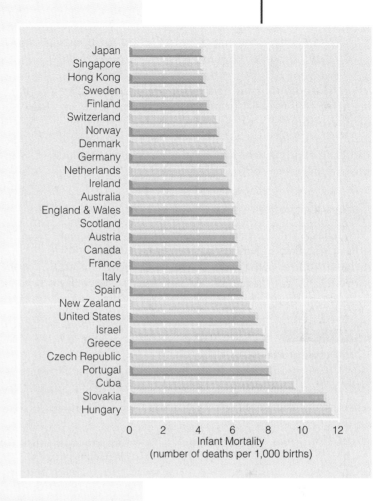

When a family is stressed by a baby's arrival, short employment leaves of 6 weeks or less (the norm in the United States) are linked to maternal anxiety and depression and negative interactions with the baby. Longer leaves of 12 weeks or more predict favorable maternal mental health and sensitive, responsive caregiving (Clark et al., 1997; Hyde et al., 1995). Single women and their babies are most hurt by the absence of a national paid leave policy. These mothers are usually the sole source of support for their families and can least afford to take time from their jobs.

In countries with low rates of infant mortality and low birth weight, expectant parents need not wonder how they will get health care and other resources to support their baby's development. The powerful impact of universal, high-quality medical and social services on maternal and infant well-being provides strong justification for implementing such programs in the United States.

who fared as well as controls in career attainment and psychological adjustment. Werner found that these children relied on factors outside the family and within themselves to overcome stress. Some had especially attractive personalities that caused them to receive positive responses from relatives, neighbors, and peers. In other instances, a grandparent, aunt, uncle, or baby-sitter established a warm relationship with the child and provided the needed emotional support (Werner, 1989, 1993; Werner & Smith, 1992).

Do these outcomes remind you of the characteristics of resilient children, discussed in Chapter 1? The Kauai study—and other similar investigations—reveal that the impact of early biological risks often wanes as children's personal characteristics and social experiences contribute increasingly to their functioning (Laucht, Esser, & Schmidt, 1997; Thompson et al., 1997). In sum, when the overall bal-

ance of life events tips toward the favorable side, children with serious birth problems can develop successfully.

  ASK YOURSELF . . .

■ *Sensitive care can help preterm infants recover, but unfortunately they are less likely to receive this kind of care than are full-term newborns. Explain why.*

■ *List all the factors discussed in this chapter that increase the chances that an infant will be born underweight. How many of these factors could be prevented by better health care for mothers and babies?*

🌳 *How do long-term outcomes reported for preterm and low-birth-weight newborns fit with findings of the Kauai study?*

THE NEWBORN BABY'S CAPACITIES

As recently as the mid-twentieth century, scientists considered the newborn baby to be a passive, disorganized being who could see, hear, feel, and do very little. Today we know that this image of an incompetent newborn is wrong. Newborn babies have a remarkable set of capacities that are crucial for survival and for evoking attention and care from parents. In relating to the physical world and building their first social relationships, they are active from the very start.

NEWBORN REFLEXES

A **reflex** is an inborn, automatic response to a particular form of stimulation. Reflexes are the newborn baby's most obvious organized patterns of behavior. As Jay placed Joshua on a table in my classroom, we saw several. When Jay bumped the side of the table, Joshua reacted by flinging his arms wide and bringing them back toward his body. As Yolanda stroked Joshua's cheek, he turned his head in her direction. When she put her finger in Joshua's palm, he grabbed on tightly. Look at Table 3.3 and see if you can name the newborn reflexes that Joshua displayed.

Some reflexes have survival value. For example, the rooting reflex helps the infant locate the mother's nipple. And if sucking were not automatic, our species probably would not have survived for a single generation!

A few reflexes form the basis for complex motor skills that will develop later. The stepping reflex looks like a primitive walking response. In infants who gain weight quickly in the weeks after birth, the stepping reflex drops out because thigh and calf muscles are not strong enough to lift the baby's chubby legs. But if the infant's lower body is dipped in water, the reflex reappears, since the buoyancy of the water lightens the load on the baby's muscles (Thelen, Fisher, & Ridley-Johnson, 1984). When the stepping reflex is exercised regularly, babies are likely to walk several weeks earlier than if it is not practiced (Zelazo, 1983; Zelazo et al., 1993). However, there is no special need for in-

TABLE 3.3

Some Newborn Reflexes

REFLEX	STIMULATION	RESPONSE	AGE OF DISAPPEARANCE	FUNCTION
Eye blink	Shine bright light at eyes or clap hand near head	Infant quickly closes eyelids	Permanent	Protects infant from strong stimulation
Withdrawal	Prick sole of foot with pin	Foot withdraws, with flexion of knee and hip	Weakens after 10 days	Protects infant from unpleasant tactile stimulation
Rooting	Stroke cheek near corner of mouth	Head turns toward source of stimulation	3 weeks (becomes voluntary head turning at this time)	Helps infant find the nipple
Sucking	Place finger in infant's mouth	Infant sucks finger rhythmically	Permanent	Permits feeding
Swimming	Place infant face down in pool of water	Baby paddles and kicks in swimming motion	4–6 months	Helps infant survive if dropped into water
Moro	Hold infant horizontally on back and let head drop slightly, or produce a sudden loud sound against surface supporting infant	Infant makes an "embracing" motion by arching back, extending legs, throwing arms outward, and then bringing arms in toward the body	6 months	In human evolutionary past, may have helped infant cling to mother
Palmar grasp	Place finger in infant's hand and press against palm	Spontaneous grasp of finger	3–4 months	Prepares infant for voluntary grasping
Tonic neck	Turn baby's head to one side while lying awake on back	Infant lies in a "fencing position." One arm is extended in front of eyes on side to which head is turned, other arm is flexed	4 months	May prepare infant for voluntary reaching
Stepping	Hold infant under arms and permit bare feet to touch a flat surface	Infant lifts one foot after another in stepping response	2 months	Prepares infant for voluntary walking
Babinski	Stroke sole of foot from toe toward heel	Toes fan out and curl as foot twists in	8–12 months	Unknown

Sources: Knobloch & Pasamanich, 1974; Prechtl & Beintema, 1965.

fants to practice the stepping reflex, since all normal babies walk in due time.

Some reflexes contribute powerfully to the infant's early social relationships. A baby who searches for and successfully finds the nipple, sucks easily during feedings, and grasps when the hand is touched encourages parents to respond lovingly and strengthens their sense of competence. Reflexes can also assist caregivers in comforting the baby. For example, on short trips with Joshua to the grocery store, Yolanda brought along a pacifier. If he became fussy, sucking helped quiet him until she could feed, change, or hold and rock him.

Look again at Table 3.3, and note that most newborn reflexes disappear during the first 6 months. Researchers believe that this is due to a gradual increase in voluntary control over behavior as the cerebral cortex matures. Pediatricians test reflexes carefully, especially if a newborn has experienced birth trauma, since reflexes provide one way of assessing the health of the baby's nervous system. Weak or absent reflexes, reflexes that are overly rigid or exaggerated, and reflexes that persist beyond the point in development when they should normally disappear can signal brain damage (Touwen, 1984).

NEWBORN STATES

Throughout the day and night, newborn infants move in and out of five different **states of arousal**, or degrees of sleep and wakefulness, described in Table 3.4 on page 108. During the first month, these states alternate frequently. Quiet alertness is the most fleeting. It usually moves quickly toward fussing and crying. Much to the relief of their fatigued parents, newborns spend the greatest amount of time asleep—on the average, 16 to 18 hours a day.

However, striking individual differences in daily rhythms exist that affect parents' attitudes toward and interaction with the baby. A few newborns sleep for long periods, increasing the energy their well-rested parents have for sensitive, responsive care. Other babies cry a great deal, and their parents must exert great effort to soothe them. If they do not succeed, parents may feel less competent and positive toward their infant. Of the five states listed in Table 3.4, the two extremes of sleep and crying have been of greatest interest to researchers. Each tells us something about normal and abnormal early development.

■ SLEEP. One day, Yolanda and Jay watched Joshua while he slept and wondered why his eyelids and body twitched and his rate of breathing varied. Sleep is made up of at least two states. Yolanda and Jay happened to observe irregular, or **rapid-eye-movement (REM), sleep.** The expression "sleeping like a baby" was probably not meant to describe this state! During REM sleep, electrical brain wave activity is remarkably similar to that of the waking

■ *In the Moro reflex, loss of support or a sudden loud sound causes this baby to arch her back, extend her arms outward, and then bring them in toward her body. (Photo courtesy: Mimi Forsyth/Monkmeyer Press)*

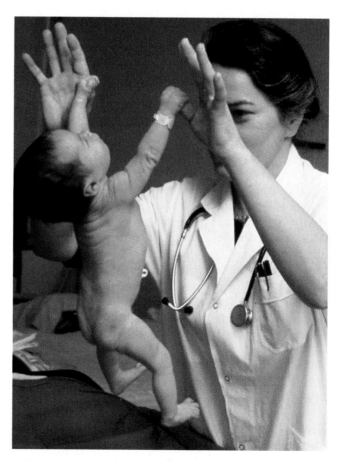

■ *The palmar grasp reflex is so strong during the first week after birth that many infants can use it to support their entire weight. (Photo courtesy: J. da Cunha/Petit Format/Photo Researchers, Inc.)*

TABLE 3.4

Infant States of Arousal

STATE	DESCRIPTION	DAILY DURATION IN NEWBORN
Regular sleep	The infant is at full rest and shows little or no body activity. The eyelids are closed, no eye movements occur, the face is relaxed, and breathing is slow and regular.	8–9 hours
Irregular sleep	Gentle limb movements, occasional stirring, and facial grimacing occur. Although the eyelids are closed, occasional rapid eye movements can be seen beneath them. Breathing is irregular.	8–9 hours
Drowsiness	The infant is either falling asleep or waking up. Body is less active than in irregular sleep but more active than in regular sleep. The eyes open and close; when open, they have a glazed look. Breathing is even but somewhat faster than in regular sleep.	Varies
Quiet alertness	The infant's body is relatively inactive, with eyes open and attentive. Breathing is even.	2–3 hours
Waking activity and crying	The infant shows frequent bursts of uncoordinated body activity. Breathing is very irregular. Face may be relaxed or tense and wrinkled. Crying may occur.	1–4 hours

Source: Wolff, 1966.

state. The eyes dart beneath the lids; heart rate, blood pressure, and breathing are uneven; and slight body movements occur. In contrast, during **non-rapid-eye-movement (NREM) sleep,** the body is almost motionless, and heart rate, breathing, and brain-wave activity are slow and regular.

Like children and adults, newborns alternate between REM and NREM sleep. However, they spend far more time in the REM state than they ever will again. REM sleep accounts for 50 percent of a newborn baby's sleep time. By 3 to 5 years, it has declined to an adultlike level of 20 percent (Roffwarg, Muzio, & Dement, 1966).

Why do young infants spend so much time in REM sleep? In older children and adults, the REM state is associated with dreaming. Babies probably do not dream, at least not in the same way we do. Young infants are believed to have a special need for the stimulation of REM sleep because they spend little time in an alert state, when they can get input from the environment. REM sleep seems to be a way in which the brain stimulates itself. Sleep researchers believe that this stimulation is vital for growth of the central nervous system. In support of this idea, the percentage of REM sleep is especially great in fetuses and in preterm babies, who are even less able to take advantage of external stimulation than are full-term newborns (DiPietro et al., 1996a; Sahni et al., 1995).

Whereas the brain-wave activity of REM sleep safeguards the central nervous system, rapid eye movements protect the health of the eye. Eye movements cause the vitreous (gelatin-like substance within the eye) to circulate, thereby delivering oxygen to parts of the eye that do not have their own blood supply. During sleep, when the eyes and the vitreous are still, visual structures are at risk for

anoxia. As the brain cycles through REM-sleep periods, rapid eye movements stir up the vitreous, ensuring that the eye is fully oxygenated (Blumberg & Lucas, 1996).

Because the normal sleep behavior of a newborn baby is organized and patterned, observations of sleep states can help identify central nervous system abnormalities. In infants who are brain damaged or have experienced serious birth trauma, disturbed REM–NREM sleep cycles are often present. Babies with poor sleep organization are likely to be behaviorally disorganized and, therefore, to have difficulty learning while awake and eliciting caregiver interactions that enhance their development (Groome et al., 1997; Halpern, MacLean, & Baumeister, 1995).

■ CRYING. Crying is the first way that babies communicate, letting parents know that they need food, comfort, and stimulation. During the weeks after birth, all infants have some fussy periods when they are difficult to console. But most of the time, the nature of the cry, combined with the experiences that led up to it, helps guide parents toward its cause. The baby's cry is a complex stimulus that varies in intensity, from a whimper to a message of all-out distress (Gustafson & Harris, 1990). As early as the first few weeks of life, infants can be identified by the unique vocal "signature" of their cry, which helps parents locate their baby from a distance (Gustafson, Green, & Cleland, 1994).

Newborn infants usually cry because of physical needs. Hunger is the most common cause, but babies may also cry in response to temperature change when undressed, a sudden noise, or a painful stimulus. Newborn crying can also be caused by the sound of another crying baby (Dondi, Simion, & Caltran, 1999). Some researchers believe this response reflects an inborn capacity to react to the suffering of others.

The next time you hear an infant cry, note your own mental and physical reaction. The sound stimulates strong feelings of arousal and discomfort in just about anyone (Boukydis & Burgess, 1982; Murray, 1985). This powerful response is probably innately programmed in humans to make sure that babies receive the care and protection they need to survive.

Although parents do not always interpret their baby's cry correctly, experience quickly improves their accuracy (Thompson & Leger, 1998). Fortunately, there are many ways to soothe a crying baby when feeding and diaper changing do not work. The technique parents usually try first, lifting the baby to the shoulder, is most effective. Being held upright against the parent's gently moving body not only encourages infants to stop crying, but also causes them to become quietly alert and attentive to the environment (Reisman, 1987). The Caregiving Concerns table below lists other common soothing methods.

Like reflexes and sleep patterns, an infant's cry offers a clue to central nervous system distress. The cries of brain-damaged babies and those who have experienced prenatal and birth complications are often shrill and piercing (Huntington, Hans, & Zeskind, 1990). Most parents try to respond with extra care and attention, but sometimes the cry is so unpleasant and the infant so difficult to soothe that parents become frustrated, resentful, and angry. Preterm and ill babies are more likely to be abused by their parents, who frequently mention a high-pitched, grating cry as one factor that caused them to lose control and harm the baby (Frodi, 1985).

■ *To soothe her crying infant, this mother holds her baby upright against her gently moving body. Besides encouraging infants to stop crying, this technique causes them to become quietly alert and attentive to the environment. (Photo courtesy: Rosanne Olson/Stone)*

CAREGIVING CONCERNS

Ways to Soothe a Crying Newborn

METHOD	EXPLANATION
Lift the baby to the shoulder and rock or walk.	This provides a combination of physical contact, upright posture, and motion. It is the most effective soothing technique.
Swaddle the baby.	Restricting movement and increasing warmth often soothe a young infant.
Offer a pacifier.	Sucking helps babies control their own level of arousal.
Talk softly or play rhythmic sounds.	Continuous, monotonous, rhythmic sounds, such as a clock ticking, a fan whirring, or peaceful music, are more effective than intermittent sounds.
Take the baby for a short car ride or walk in a baby carriage; swing the baby in a cradle.	Gentle, rhythmic motion of any kind helps lull the baby to sleep.
Massage the baby's body.	Stroke the baby's torso and limbs with continuous, gentle motions. This technique is used in some non-Western cultures to relax the baby's muscles.
Combine several of the methods listed above.	Stimulating several of the baby's senses at once is often more effective than stimulating only one.
If these methods do not work, permit the baby to cry for a short period of time.	Occasionally, a baby responds well to just being put down and will, after a few minutes, fall asleep.

Sources: Campos, 1989; Heinl, 1983; Lester, 1985; Reisman, 1987.

SENSORY CAPACITIES

On his visit to my class, Joshua looked wide-eyed at my bright pink blouse and turned to the sound of his mother's voice. During feedings, he lets Yolanda know by the way he sucks that he prefers the taste of breast milk to a bottle of plain water. Clearly, Joshua has some well-developed sensory capacities. In the following sections, we explore the newborn baby's responsiveness to touch, taste, smell, sound, and visual stimulation.

■ TOUCH. In our discussion of preterm infants, we saw that touch helps stimulate early physical growth. And as we will see in Chapter 6, it is important for emotional development as well. Therefore, it is not surprising that sensitivity to touch is well developed at birth. The reflexes listed in Table 3.3 reveal that the newborn baby responds to touch, especially around the mouth, palms, and soles of the feet. During the prenatal period, these areas, along with the genitals, are the first to become sensitive to touch (Humphrey, 1978).

Newborn babies also react to temperature change, especially to stimuli that are colder than body temperature (Humphrey, 1978). When Yolanda and Jay undress Joshua, he often expresses his discomfort by crying and becoming more active.

At birth, infants are highly sensitive to pain. If male newborns are circumcised, anesthetic is sometimes not used because of the risk of giving drugs to a very young infant. Babies typically respond with a high-pitched, stressful cry and a dramatic rise in heart rate and blood pressure (Lander et al., 1997). Recent research establishing the safety of certain local anesthetics for newborns promises to ease the pain of these procedures. Offering a nipple that delivers a sugar solution is also helpful; it quickly reduces crying and discomfort in young babies (Smith & Blass, 1996). Permitting a newborn to endure severe pain can affect later behavior. For example, compared with their anesthetized counterparts, newborns not given a local anesthetic during circumcision show a more intense pain response to routine vaccination at 4 to 6 months of age (Taddio et al., 1997).

■ TASTE AND SMELL. All babies come into the world with the ability to communicate their taste preferences to caregivers. When given a sweet liquid instead of water, Joshua uses longer sucks with fewer pauses to savor the taste of his favorite food (Crook & Lipsitt, 1976). In contrast, he is either indifferent to or rejects salty water (Beauchamp et al., 1994). Newborns also reveal their taste preferences through facial expressions. Like adults, they relax their facial muscles in response to sweetness, purse their lips when the taste is sour, and show a distinct arch-like mouth opening when it is bitter (Steiner, 1979).

These reactions are important for survival, since (as we will see in Chapter 4) the food that is ideally suited to support the infant's early growth is the sweet-tasting milk of the mother's breast. Nevertheless, newborns can readily learn to like a taste that at first evoked either a neutral or negative response. For example, babies allergic to cow's-milk formula who are given a soy or other vegetable-based substitute (typically very strong and bitter-tasting) soon prefer it to regular formula. A taste previously disliked can come to be preferred when it is paired with relief of hunger (Harris, 1997). By 4 months, babies react positively to the salty taste, a change that helps prepare them to accept solid foods (Beauchamp et al., 1994).

Like taste, certain odor preferences are innate. For example, the smell of bananas or chocolate causes a relaxed, pleasant facial expression, whereas the odor of rotten eggs makes the infant frown (Steiner, 1979). Newborns can also identify the location of an odor and, if it is unpleasant, defend themselves by turning their heads in the other direction (Reiser, Yonas, & Wikner, 1976).

In many mammals, the sense of smell plays an important role in eating and protecting the young from predators by helping mothers and babies recognize each other. Although smell is less well developed in humans, traces of its survival value remain. Three-day-old babies given a choice between the smell of their own mother's amniotic fluid and that of another mother spend more time oriented toward the familiar fluid (Marlier, Schaal, & Soussignan, 1998). By 4 days of age, breast-fed babies prefer the smell of their own mother's breast to that of an unfamiliar lactating woman (Cernoch & Porter, 1985). Bottle-fed babies remain attracted to the odor of their mother's amniotic fluid, preferring it to that of their familiar formula. At the same time, they orient to the smell of any lactating woman over the smells of formula or a nonlactating woman (Marlier & Schaal, 1997; Porter et al., 1992). Newborn infants' dual attraction to the odors of their mother and of breast milk helps them locate an appropriate food source and, in the process, distinguish their caregiver from other people.

■ HEARING. Newborn infants can hear a wide variety of sounds, but they prefer complex sounds, such as noises and voices, to pure tones (Bench et al., 1976). In the first few days after birth, infants can already tell the difference between a few sound patterns, such as a series of tones arranged in ascending versus descending order, utterances with two as opposed to three syllables, and the stress patterns of words, such as *ma*-ma versus ma-*ma* (Bijeljac-Babic, Bertoncini, & Mehler, 1993; Sansavini, Bertoncini, & Giovanelli, 1997).

Newborn babies are especially sensitive to sounds within the frequency range of the human voice, and they are biologically prepared to respond to the sounds of any language. Young infants can make fine-grained distinctions among a wide variety of speech sounds. For example, when given a nipple that turns on a recording of the "ba" sound, babies suck vigorously and then slow down as the novelty wears off. When the sound switches to "ga," sucking picks up, indicating that infants detect this subtle difference. Using this method, researchers have found only a few speech sounds that infants cannot discriminate (Jusczyk, 1995). These capacities reveal that the baby is marvelously prepared for the awesome task of acquiring language.

Listen carefully to yourself the next time you talk to a young baby. You will probably speak in a high-pitched, expressive voice and use a rising tone at the ends of phrases and sentences. Adults probably communicate with infants in this way because babies are more attentive when they do so. Indeed, newborns prefer speech with these characteristics. And they are especially attentive when the voice is their mother's and speaks their native language rather than a foreign language (Moon, Cooper, & Fifer, 1993; Spence & DeCasper, 1987). These preferences probably developed from hearing the muffled sounds of the mother's voice before birth.

■ VISION. Vision is the least developed of the senses at birth. Visual centers in the brain are not yet fully formed, nor are structures in the eye. For example, cells in the retina, a membrane lining the inside of the eye that captures light and transforms it into messages that are sent to the brain, are not as mature or densely packed as they will be in several months. Also, muscles of the lens, which permits us to adjust our visual focus to varying distances, are weak at birth (Banks & Bennett, 1988).

As a result, newborn babies cannot focus their eyes as well as an adult can, and **visual acuity,** or fineness of discrimination, is limited. At birth, infants perceive objects at a distance of 20 feet about as clearly as adults do at 600 feet (Courage & Adams, 1990). In addition, unlike adults (who see nearby objects most clearly), newborn babies see equally unclearly across a wide range of distances (Banks, 1980). As a result, images such as the parent's face, even from close up, look quite blurred.

Although newborn babies cannot see well, they actively explore their environment by scanning it for interesting sights and tracking moving objects. However, their eye movements are slow and inaccurate (Aslin, 1993). Joshua's captivation with my pink blouse reveals that he is attracted to bright objects. Although newborns prefer to look at colored rather than gray stimuli, they are not yet good at discriminating colors. It will take a month or two for color vision to improve (Adams, 1987; Adams, Courage, & Mercer, 1994).

NEONATAL BEHAVIORAL ASSESSMENT

Measures of the many capacities we have just described have been put together into tests that permit doctors, nurses, and researchers to assess a newborn infant's behavior during the first month of life. The most widely used of these tests, T. Berry Brazelton's **Neonatal Behavioral Assessment Scale** (**NBAS**), evaluates the baby's reflexes, state changes, respon-

siveness to physical and social stimuli, and other reactions (Brazelton & Nugent, 1995).

The NBAS has been given to many infants around the world. As a result, researchers have learned about individual and cultural differences in newborn behavior and how child-rearing practices can maintain or change a baby's reactions. For example, NBAS scores of Asian and Native-American babies reveal that they are less irritable than Caucasian infants. Mothers in these cultures often encourage their babies' calm dispositions through swaddling, close physical contact, and nursing at the first signs of discomfort (Chisholm, 1989; Muret-Wagstaff & Moore, 1989). In contrast, the poor NBAS scores of undernourished infants in Zambia, Africa, are quickly improved by the way their mothers care for them. The Zambian mother carries her baby about on her hip all day, providing a rich variety of sensory stimulation. By 1 week of age, a once unresponsive newborn has been transformed into an alert, contented baby (Brazelton, Koslowski, & Tronick, 1976).

Can you tell from these examples why a single NBAS score is not a good predictor of later development? Since newborn behavior and parenting styles combine to shape development, *changes in NBAS scores* over the first week or two of life (rather than a single score) provide the best estimate of the baby's ability to recover from the stress of birth. NBAS "recovery curves" predict intelligence with moderate success well into the preschool years (Brazelton, Nugent, & Lester, 1987).

The NBAS has also been used to help parents get to know their infants. In some hospitals, the examination is given in the presence of parents to teach them about their

■ *Similar to women in the Zambian culture, this mother of Bhutan—a small country in the Himalaya Mountains—carries her baby about all day, providing close physical contact and a rich variety of stimulation. (Photo courtesy: Jeffrey Aaronson/Network Aspen)*

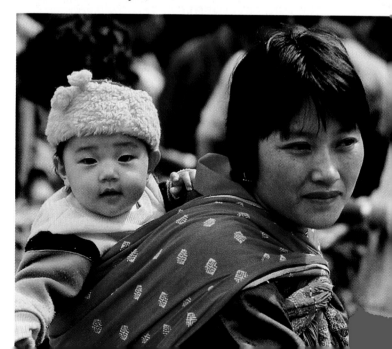

newborn baby's capacities. Parents of both preterm and full-term newborns who participate in these programs interact more confidently and effectively with their babies (Eiden & Reifman, 1996; Tedder, 1991). Although lasting effects on development have not been demonstrated, NBAS-based interventions are clearly useful in helping the parent–infant relationship get off to a good start.

ASK YOURSELF . . .

 Cite examples of how infant reflexes, state changes, and sensory capacities promote survival and provide a foundation for human motor, cognitive, and social capacities that will develop later.

■ *Jackie, who had a difficult delivery, observes her 2-day-old daughter Kelly being given the NBAS. Kelly scores poorly on many items. Jackie wonders if this means that Kelly will not develop normally. How would you respond to Jackie's concern?*

ADJUSTING TO THE NEW FAMILY UNIT

The early weeks after a new baby enters the family are full of profound changes. The mother needs to recover from childbirth and adjust to massive hormone shifts in her body. If she is breast-feeding, energies must be devoted to working out this intimate relationship. The father also needs to become a part of this new threesome while supporting the mother in her recovery. At times, he may feel ambivalent about the baby, who constantly demands and gets his

wife's attention (Jordan, 1990). And as we will see in Chapter 6, siblings—especially those who are young and previously had their parents all to themselves—understandably feel displaced and often react with jealousy and anger.

While all this is going on, the tiny infant is very assertive about his urgent physical needs, demanding to be fed, changed, and comforted at odd times of the day and night. A family schedule that was once routine and predictable is now irregular and uncertain. Yolanda spoke candidly about the changes that she and Jay experienced:

> When we brought Joshua home, we had to deal with the realities of our new responsibility. Joshua seemed so small and helpless, and we worried about whether we would be able to take proper care of him. It took us 20 minutes to change the first diaper. I rarely feel well rested because I'm up two to four times every night, and I spend a good part of my waking hours trying to anticipate Joshua's rhythms and needs. If Jay weren't so willing to help by holding and walking Joshua, I think I'd find it much harder.

How long does this time of adjustment to parenthood last? In Chapter 14, we will see that when husband and wife set aside time to listen to one another and try to support each other's needs, family relationships and routine care of the baby are worked out after a few months. Nevertheless, as one pair of counselors who have worked with many new parents point out, "As long as children are dependent on their parents, those parents find themselves preoccupied with thoughts of their children. This does not keep them from enjoying other aspects of their lives, but it does mean that they never return to being quite the same people they were before they became parents" (Colman & Colman, 1991, p. 198).

SUMMARY

PRENATAL DEVELOPMENT

List the three phases of prenatal development, and describe the major milestones of each.

■ Prenatal development is usually divided into three phases. The period of the zygote lasts about 2 weeks, from fertilization until the blastocyst becomes deeply **implanted** in the uterine lining. During this time, structures that will support prenatal growth begin to form. The embryonic disk is surrounded by the **amnion,** which is filled with amniotic fluid. From the **chorion,** villi emerge that burrow into the uterine wall,

and the **placenta** starts to develop. The developing organism is connected to the placenta by the **umbilical cord.**

■ In the period of the **embryo,** which lasts from 2 to 8 weeks, the foundations for all body structures are laid down. In the first week of this period, the **neural tube** forms, and the nervous system starts to develop. Other organs follow and grow rapidly.

■ The period of the **fetus,** lasting from the ninth week until the end of pregnancy, involves a dramatic increase in body size and completion of physical structures. By the middle of

the second **trimester,** the mother can feel movement. The fetus becomes covered with **vernix,** which protects the skin from chapping. White, downy hair called **lanugo** helps the vernix stick to the skin. At the end of the second trimester, production of neurons in the brain is complete.

■ The **age of viability** occurs at the beginning of the third trimester, sometime between 22 and 26 weeks. The brain continues to develop, and new sensory and behavioral capacities emerge. Gradually the lungs mature, the fetus fills the uterus, and birth is near.

PRENATAL ENVIRONMENTAL INFLUENCES

What factors influence the impact of teratogens on the developing organism?

■ **Teratogens** are environmental agents that cause damage during the prenatal period. Their effects conform to the sensitive period concept. The developing organism is especially vulnerable during the embryonic period. The impact of teratogens differs from one case to the next, due to amount and length of exposure, the genetic makeup of mother and fetus, and the presence or absence of other harmful agents. Although immediate physical damage is easy to notice, serious health and psychological consequences may not show up until later in development.

List agents known to be or suspected of being teratogens, and discuss evidence on the harmful impact of each.

■ The prenatal impact of many commonly used medications, such as aspirin and caffeine, is hard to separate from other factors correlated with drug taking. Babies whose mothers took heroin, methadone, or cocaine during pregnancy have withdrawal symptoms after birth and are jittery and inattentive. Cocaine is especially risky, since it is associated with physical defects and central nervous system damage.

■ Infants of parents who smoke cigarettes are often born underweight and may display inattention and learning problems in childhood. When mothers consume alcohol in large quantities, **fetal alcohol syndrome** (**FAS**), a disorder involving mental retardation, poor attention, overactivity, slow physical growth, and facial abnormalities, often results. Smaller amounts of alcohol may lead to some of these problems—a condition known as **fetal alcohol effects** (**FAE**).

■ High levels of radiation, mercury, lead, and PCBs lead to physical malformations and severe brain damage. Low-level exposure has also been linked to diverse impairments, including lower intelligence test scores and, in the case of radiation, language and emotional disorders.

■ Among infectious diseases, rubella (German, or 3 day, measles) causes a wide variety of abnormalities, which vary with the time the disease strikes during pregnancy. The human immunodeficiency virus (HIV), which leads to AIDS, is linked to brain damage, delayed mental and motor development, and early death. In the first trimester, toxoplasmosis (caused by a parasite found in many animals) may lead to eye and brain damage.

Describe the impact of additional maternal factors on prenatal development.

■ In healthy, physically fit women, regular moderate exercise is related to increased birth weight. However, very frequent, vigorous exercise results in lower birth weight. When the mother's diet is inadequate, low birth weight and damage to the brain and other organs are major concerns. Folic-acid supplementation beginning around the time of conception and extending through pregnancy can prevent neural tube defects, premature delivery, and low birth weight.

■ Severe emotional stress is linked to many pregnancy complications, although its impact can be reduced by providing the mother with emotional support. When the mother's blood is Rh-negative, or lacks the **Rh factor,** and the fetus's blood is Rh-positive, special precautions must be taken to ensure that antibodies to the Rh protein do not pass from mother to fetus.

■ Aside from the risk of chromosomal abnormalities in older women, maternal age and number of previous births are not major causes of prenatal problems. Instead, poor health and environmental risks associated with poverty are the strongest predictors of pregnancy complications.

Why is early and regular health care vital during the prenatal period?

■ Early and regular prenatal health care is important for all pregnant women. It is especially critical for women unlikely to seek it—in particular, those who are young, single, and poor.

CHILDBIRTH

Describe the three stages of childbirth, the baby's adaptation to labor and delivery, and the newborn baby's appearance.

■ Childbirth takes place in three stages, beginning with contractions that open the cervix so the mother can push the baby through the birth canal and ending with delivery of the placenta. During labor, infants produce high levels of stress hormones, which help them withstand oxygen deprivation and arouse them into alertness at birth.

■ Newborn infants have large heads, small bodies, and facial features that make adults feel like cuddling them. The **Apgar Scale** assesses the baby's physical condition at birth.

APPROACHES TO CHILDBIRTH

Describe natural childbirth and home delivery, noting any benefits and concerns associated with each.

■ **Natural,** or **prepared, childbirth** involves classes in which prospective parents learn about labor and delivery, instruction of the mother in relaxation and breathing techniques, and a companion who serves as a coach during childbirth. The method helps reduce the stress and pain of contractions. As long as mothers are healthy and assisted by a well-trained doctor or midwife, it is just as safe to give birth at home as in a hospital.

MEDICAL INTERVENTIONS

List common medical interventions during childbirth, circumstances that justify their use, and any dangers associated with each.

- Medical interventions during childbirth are more common in the United States than anywhere in the world. When pregnancy and birth complications make **anoxia** likely, **fetal monitors** help save the lives of many babies. However, when used routinely, they may identify infants as in danger who, in fact, are not.

- Medication to relieve pain is necessary in complicated deliveries. When given in large doses, it produces a depressed state in the newborn that affects the early mother–infant relationship.

- **Cesarean deliveries** are justified in cases of medical emergency and serious maternal illness and sometimes when babies are in **breech position**. Many unnecessary cesareans are performed in the United States.

PRETERM AND LOW-BIRTH-WEIGHT INFANTS

What are the risks of preterm birth and low birth weight, and what factors can help infants who survive a traumatic birth develop?

- **Preterm** and low-birth-weight babies are especially likely to be born to poverty-stricken, ethnic minority mothers. Compared with preterm babies whose weight is appropriate for time spent in the uterus, **small-for-date** infants are more likely to develop poorly. **Respiratory distress syndrome,** common in babies born more than 6 weeks early, causes serious breathing difficulties.

- The fragile appearance and unresponsive, irritable behavior of preterm infants affect the care they receive. Some interventions provide special stimulation in the intensive care nursery. Others teach parents how to care for and interact with their fragile babies. When preterm infants live in stressed, low-income households, long-term, intensive intervention is necessary to reduce developmental problems. A major cause of **infant mortality** is low birth weight.

UNDERSTANDING BIRTH COMPLICATIONS

- When infants experience birth trauma, a supportive home environment can help restore their growth. Even children with fairly serious birth complications can recover with the help of favorable life events.

THE NEWBORN BABY'S CAPACITIES

Describe the newborn baby's reflexes and states of arousal, including sleep characteristics and ways to soothe a crying baby.

- Infants begin life with remarkable skills for relating to their physical and social worlds. **Reflexes** are the newborn baby's most obvious organized patterns of behavior. Some have survival value, others provide the foundation for voluntary motor skills, and still others contribute to early social relationships.

- Although newborns move in and out of five different **states of arousal,** they spend most of their time asleep. Sleep consists of at least two states: **rapid-eye-movement (REM) sleep** and **non-rapid-eye-movement (NREM) sleep.** REM sleep provides young infants with stimulation essential for central nervous system development. Rapid eye movements ensure that structures of the eye remain oxygenated during sleep.

- A crying baby stimulates strong feelings of discomfort in nearby adults. The intensity of the cry and the experiences that led up to it help parents tell what is wrong. Once feeding and diaper changing have been tried, lifting the baby to the shoulder is the most effective soothing technique.

Describe the newborn baby's sensory capacities.

- The senses of touch, taste, smell, and sound are well developed at birth. Newborns are especially responsive to high-pitched, expressive voices, and they prefer the sound of their mothers' voices. They can distinguish almost all speech sounds in human languages.

- Vision is the least mature of the newborn's senses. At birth, focusing ability and **visual acuity** are limited. In exploring the visual field, newborn babies are attracted to bright objects but have difficulty discriminating colors.

Why is neonatal behavioral assessment useful?

- The most widely used instrument for assessing the behavior of the newborn infant is Brazelton's **Neonatal Behavioral Assessment Scale (NBAS).** The NBAS has helped researchers understand individual and cultural differences in newborn behavior. Sometimes it is used to teach parents about their baby's capacities.

ADJUSTING TO THE NEW FAMILY UNIT

Describe typical changes in the family after the birth of a new baby.

- The new baby's arrival is exciting but stressful. The demands of new parenthood often lead to a slight drop in marital happiness, and family roles become more traditional. When husband and wife are sensitive to each other's needs, adjustment problems are usually temporary, and the transition to parenthood goes well.

IMPORTANT TERMS AND CONCEPTS

age of viability (p. 84)

amnion (p. 82)

anoxia (p. 100)

Apgar Scale (p. 98)

breech position (p. 101)

cesarean delivery (p. 101)

chorion (p. 82)

embryo (p. 83)

fetal alcohol effects (FAE) (p. 91)

fetal alcohol syndrome (FAS) (p. 91)

fetal monitors (p. 101)

fetus (p. 83)

implantation (p. 82)

infant mortality (p. 104)

lanugo (p. 84)

natural, or prepared, childbirth (p. 99)

Neonatal Behavioral Assessment Scale (NBAS) (p. 111)

neural tube (p. 83)

non-rapid-eye-movement (NREM) sleep (p. 108)

placenta (p. 82)

preterm (p. 102)

rapid-eye-movement (REM) sleep (p. 107)

reflex (p. 106)

respiratory distress syndrome (p. 103)

Rh factor (p. 94)

small for date (p. 102)

states of arousal (p. 107)

teratogen (p. 86)

trimesters (p. 83)

umbilical cord (p. 82)

vernix (p. 84)

visual acuity (p. 111)

FYI FOR FURTHER INFORMATION AND HELP

Consult the companion website for this book, where you will find additional weblinks and associated learning activities: www.abacon.com/berk

GENERAL CHILDBIRTH INFORMATION

Childbirth.Org
www.childbirth.org
Through an informative website, offers a wealth of information on all aspects of childbirth.

PRENATAL HEALTH

National Center for Education in Maternal and Child Health
www.ncemch.georgetown.edu
Government-sponsored agency that provides information on all aspects of maternal and child health.

National Organization on Fetal Alcohol Syndrome
www.nofas.org
Seeks to raise public awareness of fetal alcohol syndrome, stimulate prevention efforts, and provide information on intervention.

NATURAL CHILDBIRTH

Lamaze International
www.lamaze-childbirth.com
Trains and certifies instructors in the Lamaze method of natural childbirth. Provides information to expectant parents.

American Academy of Husband-Coached Childbirth
www.bradleybirth.com
Certifies instructors in the Bradley method of natural childbirth, which emphasizes coaching by the husband.

HOME BIRTH

American College of Nurse-Midwives
www.acnm.org
Certifies nurse-midwives and provides referrals to expectant parents.

BIRTH DEFECTS

National Easter Seal Society for Crippled Children and Adults
www.easter-seals.org
Provides information on birth defects. Works with other agencies to help the disabled.

March of Dimes Birth Defects Foundation
www.modimes.org
Works to prevent birth defects through public education and community service programs.

National Information Center for Children and Youth with Disabilities
www.nichcy.org
Provides information to parents and educators on services for children with disabilities.

Parents Helping Parents
www.pacer.org/parent/parent.html
Offers a wide variety of services and educational programs to help parents rear children with special needs, including those with birth defects.

United Cerebral Palsy Association
www.ucpa.org
Seeks to better the lives of individuals with cerebral palsy and other disabilities.

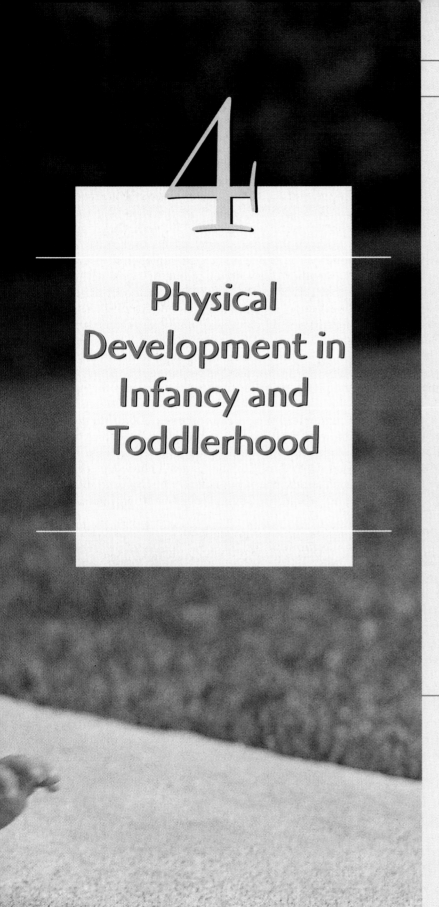

4

Physical Development in Infancy and Toddlerhood

■ *This 8-month old is exuberantly on the move! As she masters crawling, she makes dramatic strides in exploration and understanding of her surroundings. (Photo courtesy: Michael Newman/PhotoEdit*

Within a 2-day period, Lisa, Beth, and Felicia each gave birth to her first child at the same hospital. During the next 2 years, the mothers permitted me to sit in as they met once a month to talk over questions and concerns about their infants—Byron, Rachel, and April. I watched and listened as the three lap babies changed into cruising 1-year-olds and then into walking, talking toddlers.

As the infants grew, the mothers' conversations changed. At first, they worried about physical care—breast-feeding, when to introduce solid foods, and the babies' erratic sleep–waking schedules. Then, between 2 and 3 months, all three youngsters became more alert. Each mother noticed that her baby's daily rhythms were more organized and patterned. "April's much more interested in the world around her," commented Felicia. "Life is easier now that I can anticipate April's feedings and naptimes."

As the infants' motor skills developed, the home setting in which the mothers gathered changed as well. By the second half of the first year, the floor was covered with toys, and all three infants crawled about while their mothers kept a watchful eye for coffee table corners, lamp cords, and electric sockets. Soon crawling became walking. This marked the beginning of *toddlerhood*—a period that spans the second year of life. At first, the children did, indeed, "toddle" with an awkward gait, rocking from side to side and tipping over frequently. But their faces showed the thrill of being upright as they explored enthusiastically. As their 2-year-old birthdays approached, Lisa reflected, "Byron is nearly twice as tall and four times as heavy as when he was born. He's starting to look more like a little boy than a baby."

This chapter traces physical growth during the first 2 years—one of the most remarkable and busiest times of development. We will see how rapid changes in the infant's body and brain support new motor skills, ways of learning, and perceptual capacities. Byron, Rachel, and April will join us along the way, to illustrate individual differences and environmental influences on physical development.

BODY GROWTH

The next time you have a chance, briefly observe several infants and toddlers while walking in your neighborhood or at a shopping center. You will see that their capabilities are vastly different. One reason for the change in what children can do over the first 2 years is that their bodies change enormously—faster than at any other time after birth.

CHANGES IN BODY SIZE AND MUSCLE–FAT MAKEUP

As Figure 4.1 shows, by the end of the first year a typical infant's height is 50 percent greater than it was at birth, and by 2 years of age it is 75 percent greater. Weight shows similar dramatic gains. By 5 months of age, birth weight has doubled, at 1 year it has tripled, and at 2 years it has quadrupled.

Rather than steady gains, infants and toddlers grow in little spurts. In one study, children followed over the first 21 months of life went for periods of 7 to 63 days with no growth. Then they added as much as a half-inch in a 24-hour period! Almost always, parents described their babies as irritable and unusually hungry on the day before the spurt (Lampl, 1993; Lampl, Veldhuis, & Johnson, 1992).

One of the most obvious changes in Byron, Rachel, and April was their transformation into round, plump babies by the middle of the first year. The early rise in "baby fat," which peaks around 9 months, helps the small infant keep a constant body temperature (Tanner, 1990). During the second year, most toddlers slim down, a trend that continues into middle childhood. In contrast, muscle tissue increases very slowly during infancy and will not reach a peak until adolescence. Babies are not very muscular creatures, and their strength and physical coordination are limited.

■ *Rapid body growth supports new motor skills, which have a dramatic impact on the baby's approach to the world. As infants sit up and begin to crawl, their whole view of the environment and capacity to explore it changes. (Photo courtesy: Caitlin Merrill)*

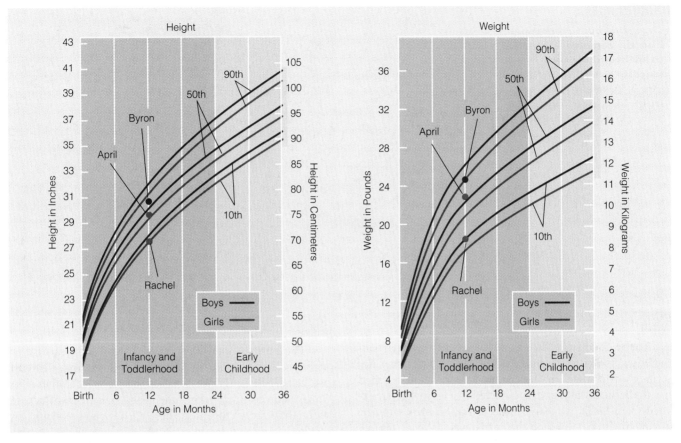

■ **Gains in height and weight during infancy and toddlerhood among North American children.** The steep rise in these growth curves shows that children grow rapidly from birth to 2 years. At the same time, wide individual differences in body size exist. Infants and toddlers who fall at the 50th percentile are average in height and weight. Those who fall at the 90th percentile are taller and heavier than 90 percent of their agemates. Those who fall at the 10th percentile are taller and heavier than only 10 percent of their peers. Notice that girls are slightly shorter and lighter than boys. As children move into early childhood, rate of growth slows.

INDIVIDUAL AND GROUP DIFFERENCES

As in all aspects of development, differences among children in body size and muscle–fat makeup exist. In infancy, girls are slightly shorter and lighter and have a higher ratio of fat to muscle than do boys. These small sex differences remain throughout early and middle childhood and will be greatly magnified at adolescence. Ethnic differences in body size are apparent as well. Look again at Figure 4.1, and you will see that Rachel, a Japanese-American child, is below the growth norms (height and weight averages) for North-American children her age. Yet she would be closer to average size if compared with agemates of Japanese ancestry. In contrast, April is slightly above North-American growth norms, as African-American children tend to be (Tanner, 1990).

Children of the same age also differ in *rate* of physical growth. In other words, some make faster progress toward a mature body size than do others. We cannot tell how quickly a child's physical growth is moving along just by looking at current body size, since children grow to different heights and weights in adulthood. For example, Byron is larger and heavier than Rachel and April, but he is not physically more mature. In a moment, you will see why.

The best way of estimating a child's physical maturity is to use *skeletal age*, a measure of bone development. It is determined by X-raying the long bones of the body to see the extent to which soft, pliable cartilage has hardened into bone. When the skeletal ages of infants and children are examined, African-American children tend to be slightly ahead of Caucasian children at all ages. And girls are considerably ahead of boys. At birth, this sex difference amounts to about 4 to 6 weeks, a gap that widens over infancy and childhood, with girls reaching their full body size several years before boys. Girls' greater physical maturity may contribute to the fact that they are more resistant to harmful environmental influences, show fewer developmental problems, and have a lower infant and childhood mortality rate.

■ **Changes in body proportions from the early prenatal period to adulthood.** This figure illustrates the cephalocaudal trend of physical growth. The head gradually becomes smaller and the legs longer in proportion to the rest of the body.

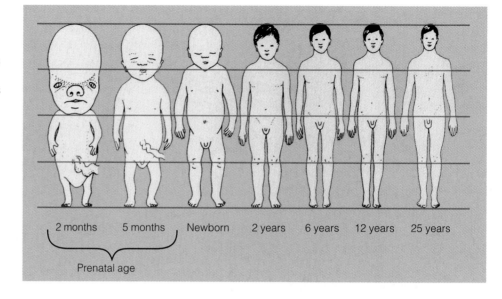

2 months   5 months   Newborn   2 years   6 years   12 years   25 years

Prenatal age

CHANGES IN BODY PROPORTIONS

As the child's overall size increases, different parts of the body grow at different rates. Two growth patterns describe these changes in body proportions. The first, called the **cephalocaudal trend,** is depicted in Figure 4.2. Translated from Latin, it means "head to tail." As you can see, during the prenatal period the head develops more rapidly than the lower part of the body. At birth, the head takes up one-fourth of total body length, the legs only one-third. Notice how the lower portion of the body gradually catches up. By age 2, the head accounts for only one-fifth and the legs for nearly one-half of body length. Perhaps this is one reason Lisa thought 2-year-old Byron was starting to look more like a little boy than a baby.

The second pattern is the **proximodistal trend,** meaning growth proceeds, literally, from "near to far," or from the center of the body outward. In the prenatal period, the head, chest, and trunk grew first, followed by the arms and legs, and finally by the hands and feet. During infancy and childhood, the arms and legs continue to grow somewhat ahead of the hands and feet. As we will see later, motor development follows these same developmental trends.

BRAIN DEVELOPMENT

At birth, the brain is nearer than any other physical structure to its adult size, and it continues to develop at an astounding pace throughout infancy and toddlerhood. To best understand brain growth, we need to look at it from two vantage points: (1) the microscopic level of individual brain cells and (2) the larger structural level of the cerebral cortex, responsible for the highly developed intelligence of our species.

DEVELOPMENT OF NEURONS

The human brain has 100 to 200 billion **neurons,** or nerve cells, that store and transmit information, many of which have thousands of direct connections with other neurons. Neurons differ from other body cells in that they are not tightly packed together. There are tiny gaps, or **synapses,** between them, where fibers from different neurons come close together but do not touch. Neurons release chemicals that cross the synapse, sending messages to one another.

The basic story of brain growth concerns how neurons develop and form this elaborate communication system. Recall from Chapter 3 that by the end of the second trimester of pregnancy, production of neurons is largely complete. After birth, the neurons form complex networks of synaptic connections. As Figure 4.3 shows, during infancy and toddlerhood growth of neural fibers and synapses increases at an astounding pace (Huttenlocher, 1994; Moore & Persaud, 1998). Because developing neurons require space for these connective structures, a surprising aspect of brain growth is that many surrounding neurons die during the peak period of synaptic growth in any brain area. Fortunately, during the prenatal period, an excess of neurons is produced—far more than the brain will ever need (Diamond & Hopson, 1999).

As neurons form connections, *stimulation* becomes important in their survival. Neurons that are stimulated by input from the surrounding environment continue to establish new synapses, forming increasingly elaborate systems of communication that lead to more complex abilities. At first, stimulation results in an overabundance of synapses, many of which serve identical functions, thereby helping to ensure that the child will acquire certain skills. Neurons seldom stimulated soon lose their synapses, a process called **synaptic pruning.** It returns neurons not needed at the moment to an uncommitted state so they can support future development (Johnson, 1998). Notice how, for this process

Birth   6 months   2 years

FIGURE 4.3

■ **Development of neurons.** Growth of neural fibers takes place rapidly from birth to 2 years. During this time, new synapses form at an astounding pace, supporting the emergence of many new capacities. Stimulation is vitally important for maintaining and increasing this complex communication network. (From J. L. Conel, *The postnatal development of the human cerebral cortex.* Cambridge, MA: Harvard University Press. Copyright © 1959 by the President and Fellows of Harvard College. All rights reserved.)

to go forward, appropriate stimulation of the child's brain is vital during periods in which the formation of synapses is at its peak (Greenough et al., 1993).

Perhaps you are wondering: If no more neurons are produced after the prenatal period, what causes the dramatic increase in brain size during the first 2 years? About half the brain's volume is made up of **glial cells,** which do not carry messages. Instead, they are responsible for **myelinization,** the coating of neural fibers with an insulating fatty sheath (called *myelin*) that improves the efficiency of message transfer. Glial cells multiply dramatically from the fourth month of pregnancy through the second year of life (Casaer, 1993). Dramatic increase in neural fibers and myelinization are responsible for the rapid gain in overall size of the brain. At birth, the brain is nearly 30 percent of its adult weight; by age 2, it reaches 70 percent (Thatcher et al., 1996).

DEVELOPMENT OF THE CEREBRAL CORTEX

The **cerebral cortex** surrounds the rest of the brain, much like a half-shelled walnut. It is the largest, most complex brain structure, accounting for 85 percent of the brain's weight and containing the greatest number of neurons and synapses. The cerebral cortex is the last part of the brain to stop growing. For this reason, it is believed to be much more sensitive to environmental influences than is any other part of the brain.

■ REGIONS OF THE CORTEX. As Figure 4.4 shows, different regions of the cerebral cortex have specific functions, such as receiving information from the senses, instructing

the body to move, and thinking. The order in which cortical regions develop corresponds to the order in which various capacities emerge in the infant and growing child. For example, a burst of synaptic growth in the auditory and visual cortexes (refer to Figure 4.4) occurs from 3 to 4 months until the end of the first year—a period of dramatic gains in auditory and visual perception. Among areas responsible for body

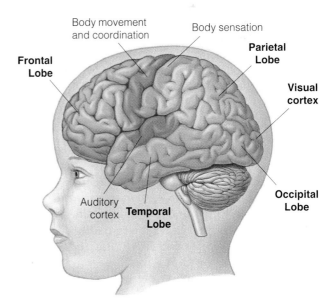

FIGURE 4.4

■ **The left side of the human brain, showing the cerebral cortex.** The cortex is divided into different lobes, each of which contains a variety of regions with specific functions. Some major ones are labeled here.

movement, neurons that control the head, arms, and chest form connections ahead of those that control the trunk and legs. (Can you name this growth trend?) As the Social Issues box on the following page indicates, problems in early cortical functioning, which prevent some babies from learning certain life-saving responses, may lead to sudden infant death syndrome, a major cause of infant mortality.

One of the last regions of the cortex to develop and myelinate is the *frontal lobes,* responsible for thought—in particular, consciousness, inhibition of impulses, and regulation of behavior through planning. From age 2 months onward, this area functions more effectively, and it continues to grow well into the second and third decades of life (Fischer & Rose, 1995; Johnson, 1998).

■ LATERALIZATION AND PLASTICITY OF THE CORTEX. The cortex has two *hemispheres,* or sides: left and right. The hemispheres do not have precisely the same functions. Some tasks are done mostly by one and some by the other. For example, each hemisphere receives sensory information from and controls only one side of the body—the one opposite to it.[1] For most of us, the left hemisphere is responsible for verbal abilities (such as spoken and written language) and positive emotion (for example, joy). The right hemisphere handles spatial abilities (judging distances, reading maps, and recognizing geometric shapes) and negative emotion (such as distress) (Banish & Heller, 1998). This pattern may be reversed in left-handed people, but, more often, the cortex of left-handers is less clearly specialized than that of right-handers.

Specialization of the two hemispheres is called **lateralization.** Researchers are interested in when brain lateralization occurs because they want to know more about **brain plasticity.** A highly *plastic* cortex is still adaptable because many areas are not yet committed to specific functions. If a part of the brain is damaged, other parts can take over tasks that would have been handled by the damaged region. But once the hemispheres lateralize, damage to a particular region means that the abilities controlled by it will be lost forever.

At birth, the hemispheres have already begun to specialize. Most newborns show greater electrical brain-wave activity in the left hemisphere while listening to speech sounds. In contrast, the right hemisphere reacts more strongly to nonspeech sounds as well as to stimuli (such as a sour-tasting fluid) that cause infants to display negative emotion (Davidson, 1994; Fox & Davidson, 1986).

Nevertheless, dramatic evidence for early plasticity comes from research on brain-damaged children. In a large sample of preschoolers with a wide variety of brain injuries sustained in the first year of life, language and spatial deficits were milder than those observed in brain-injured adults. And by age 5, cognitive impairments had largely disappeared (Stiles et al., 2000). As brain-injured children gained perceptual, cognitive, and motor experiences, other stimulated cortical structures compensated for the damaged areas, regardless of the site of injury.

Another illustration of how early experience can mold brain organization comes from studies of deaf adults who, as infants and children, learned to communicate through sign language. EEG recordings reveal that compared with hearing adults, these individuals depend more on the right hemisphere for language processing (Mills, Coffey-Corina, & Neville, 1994). Also, toddlers advanced in language development show greater left-hemispheric specialization for language than do their more slowly developing agemates. Apparently, the very process of acquiring language promotes lateralization (Mills, Coffey-Corina, & Neville, 1993, 1997).

During the first few years, the brain is more plastic than at any later time of life, perhaps because many of its synapses have not yet been established. Although the cortex is programmed from the start for hemispheric specialization, the rate and success of this genetic program are

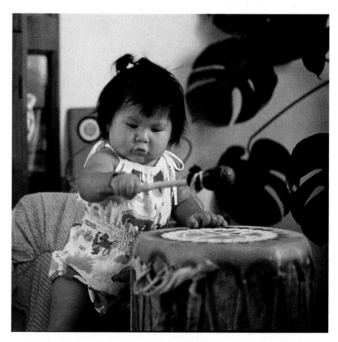

■ *This 12-month-old, growing up in the Santa Clara pueblo community of New Mexico, has climbed on a chair to beat the ceremonial drum she has seen her father play during festival dances. Her more advanced actions on objects suggest that she might be in the midst of a brain growth spurt. How brain development can best be supported through stimulation during such periods is a challenging question for future research. (Photo courtesy: Nita Winter/The Image Works)*

---

[1] The eyes are an exception. Messages from the right half of each retina go to the right hemisphere; messages from the left half of each retina go to the left hemisphere. Thus, visual information from both eyes is received by both hemispheres.

THE MYSTERIOUS TRAGEDY OF SUDDEN INFANT DEATH SYNDROME

Millie awoke with a start one morning and looked at the clock. It was 7:30, and 3-month-old Sasha had missed her night waking and early morning feeding. Wondering if she was all right, Millie and her husband Stuart tiptoed into the room. Sasha lay still, curled up under her blanket. She had died silently during her sleep.

Sasha was a victim of **sudden infant death syndrome (SIDS),** the unexpected death, usually during the night, of an infant under 1 year of age that remains unexplained after thorough investigation. In industrialized nations, SIDS is the leading cause of infant mortality between 1 week and 12 months of age. It accounts for over one-third of these deaths in the United States (Cadoff, 1995).

Although the precise cause of SIDS is not known, its victims usually show physical problems from the very beginning. Early medical records of SIDS babies reveal higher rates of prematurity and low birth weight, poor Apgar scores, and limp muscle tone (Buck et al., 1989; Malloy & Hoffman, 1995). Abnormal heart rate and respiration and disturbances in sleep–waking activity are also involved (Corwin et al., 1995; Malloy & Hoffman, 1995). At the time of death, over half of SIDS babies have a mild respiratory infection. This seems to increase the chances of respiratory failure in an already vulnerable baby (Cotton, 1990).

One hypothesis about the cause of SIDS is that problems in brain functioning prevent these infants from learning how to respond when their survival is threatened—as it is when respiration is suddenly interrupted (Lipsitt, 1990). Between 2 and 4 months of age, when SIDS is most likely, reflexes decline and are replaced by voluntary, learned responses. Respiratory and muscular weaknesses may stop SIDS babies from acquiring behaviors that replace defensive reflexes. As a result, when breathing difficulties occur during sleep, they do not wake up, shift their position, or cry out for help. Instead, they simply give in to oxygen deprivation and death.

In an effort to reduce the occurrence of SIDS, researchers are studying environmental factors related to it. Maternal cigarette smoking, both during and after pregnancy, as well as smoking by other caregivers, is strongly predictive of the disorder. Babies exposed to cigarette smoke have more respiratory infections and are 2 to 3 times more likely to die of SIDS than are nonexposed infants (Dwyer, Ponsonby, & Couper, 1999; Dybing & Sanner, 1999). Prenatal abuse of drugs that depress central nervous system functioning (opiates and barbiturates) increases the risk of SIDS tenfold (Kandall & Gaines, 1991).

SIDS babies are also more likely to sleep on their stomachs than on their backs and often are wrapped very warmly in clothing and blankets (Kleeman et al., 1999). Scientists think that smoke, depressant drugs, and excessive body warmth place a strain on the respiratory control system in the brain. In an at-risk baby, the respiratory center may stop functioning. In other cases, healthy babies sleeping face down in soft bedding may simply die from continually breathing their own exhaled breath.

Research confirms that quitting smoking, changing an infant's sleeping position, and removing a few bedclothes can reduce the incidence of SIDS. For example, if women refrained from smoking while pregnant, an estimated 30 percent of SIDS would be prevented. Public education campaigns that discourage parents from putting babies down on their stomachs have led to dramatic reductions in SIDS in many countries, including Australia, Denmark, Germany, Great Britain, New Zealand, Sweden, and the United States (American Academy of Family Physicians, 1997; Schlaud et al., 1999).

When SIDS does occur, surviving family members require a great deal of help to overcome a sudden and unexpected death. As Millie and Stuart commented 6 months after Sasha's death, "It's the worst crisis we've ever been through. What's helped us most are the comforting words of parents in our support group who've experienced the same tragedy."

---

greatly influenced by experience (Stiles, 1998). Around age 8 to 10, lateralization is largely complete. Older children and adults have only a limited capacity to recover functions following brain injury (Chugani, 1994; Johnson, 1998). A lateralized brain is certainly adaptive. It permits a far greater variety of talents than if both sides of the cortex served exactly the same functions.

BRAIN GROWTH SPURTS AND SENSITIVE PERIODS OF DEVELOPMENT

Earlier we suggested that stimulation of the brain may be vital during periods in which it is growing most rapidly—when formation of synapses is at a peak. The existence of sensitive periods in development of the cerebral cortex has been amply demonstrated in studies of animals exposed to extreme forms of sensory deprivation. For example, there seems to be a time when rich and varied visual experiences must occur for the visual centers of the brain to develop normally. If a month-old kitten is deprived of light for as brief a time as 3 or 4 days, these areas of the brain degenerate. If the kitten is kept in the dark for as long as 2 months, the damage is permanent. Severe stimulus deprivation also affects overall brain growth. When animals reared as pets are compared with animals reared in isolation, the brains of the pets are heavier and thicker (Greenough & Black, 1992).

Because we cannot ethically expose children to such experiments, researchers interested in identifying sensitive periods for human brain development must rely on less direct evidence. They have found some close parallels with the animal evidence just described. For example, without early corrective surgery, babies born with *strabismus* (a condition in which one eye does not focus because of muscle weakness) show permanent impairments in depth perception, which depends on blending visual images from both eyes (Birch, 1993).

Focusing on the cortex as a whole, several investigators have identified intermittent brain growth spurts from infancy to early adulthood, based on gains in brain weight and skull size as well as changes in electrical brain-wave activity of the cortex. For example, several surges in frontal-lobe activity, which gradually spread to other cortical regions, occur during the first year of life: at 3 to 4 months, when infants typically engage in voluntary reaching; around 8 months, when they begin to crawl and search for hidden objects; around 12 months, when they walk and display more advanced object-search behaviors; and between 1½ and 2 years, when language flourishes (Bell & Fox, 1994; Fischer & Bidell, 1998). Later electrical activity spurts, at ages 9, 12, 15, and 18 to 20, may reflect the emergence and refinement of abstract thought (Fischer & Rose, 1995; Kitchener et al., 1993).

Massive production of synapses may underlie brain growth spurts in the first 2 years. Development of more complex and efficient neural networks, due to synaptic pruning, myelinization, and longer-distance connections between the frontal lobes and other cortical regions, may account for the later ones. Researchers are convinced that what "wires" a child's brain during each of these periods is experience. But they still have many questions to answer about just how brain and behavioral development might best be supported during each growth spurt.

The evidence we do have confirms that the first few years of life are a time when the brain is particularly sponge-like, in that learning new skills is rapid and dramatic. As we will see later in this chapter and in chapters to come, understimulating infants and young children by depriving them of rich and varied experiences available in caring family environments the world over impairs their development. The more extreme and the longer-lasting the early deprivation, the harder it is to overcome with later enrichment (Rutter et al., 1998).

Besides impoverished environments, ones that overwhelm children with expectations beyond their current capacities fail to capitalize on the brain's potential. In recent years, expensive early learning centers have sprung up in which infants are trained with letter and number flash cards and slightly older toddlers are given a full curriculum of reading, math, science, art, gym, and more. Yet no sensitive periods for acquiring culturally specific knowledge and skills have been identified (Bruer, 1999). For example, although most children learn to read and write readily after they start school, adults who have not had a chance to become literate can still reach a high level of mastery.

Trying to prime infants and preschoolers with stimulation for which they are not ready can cause them to withdraw, thereby threatening their interest in learning and creating conditions much like stimulus deprivation! In addition, when such programs do not produce young geniuses, they lead to disappointed parents who may view their children as failures at a very tender age (White, 1990). Thus, they rob infants of a psychologically healthy start on the road to maturity and parents of relaxed, pleasurable participation in their children's early growth.

CHANGING STATES OF AROUSAL

Rapid brain growth means that the organization of sleep and wakefulness changes substantially between birth and 2 years, and fussiness and crying also decline. Recall from Chapter 3 that the newborn baby takes round-the-clock naps that total about 16 hours. The decline in total sleep time over the first 2 years is not great; the average 2-year-old still needs 12 to 13 hours. The greatest change is that short periods of sleep and wakefulness are put together (Whitney & Thoman, 1994). Although from birth babies sleep more at night than during the day, this pattern increases steadily with age. By the second year, children generally need only one or two naps a day (Blum & Carey, 1996).

Although these changing arousal patterns are due to brain development, they are affected by the social environment as well. In the United States and most Western nations, parents usually succeed in getting their babies to sleep through the night around 4 months of age by offering an evening feeding before putting them down in a separate, quiet room. In this way, they push young infants to the limits of their neurological capacities. Not until the middle of the first year is the secretion of *melatonin*, a hormone within the brain that promotes drowsiness, much greater at night than during the day (Sadeh, 1997).

As the Variations box on the following page shows, isolating infants to promote sleep is rare elsewhere in the world. Influenced by Japanese child-rearing customs, Beth held

CULTURAL VARIATION IN INFANT SLEEPING ARRANGEMENTS

While awaiting the birth of a new baby, American middle-SES parents typically furnish a special room as the infant's sleeping quarters. Many adults in the United States regard this nighttime separation of baby from parent as perfectly natural, and child-rearing advice from experts has strongly encouraged it. In the most recent edition of *Baby and Child Care*, Benjamin Spock continues to recommend that infants be moved out of their parents' rooms early in the first year, explaining, "Otherwise, there is a chance that they may become dependent on this arrangement" (Spock & Parker, 1998, p. 102).

Yet parent–infant "cosleeping" is common around the globe, in industrialized and nonindustrialized countries alike. Japanese children usually lie next to their mothers throughout infancy and early childhood and continue to sleep with a parent or other family member until adolescence (Takahashi, 1990). Cosleeping is also frequent in some American subcultures. African-American children are more likely than Caucasian-American children to fall asleep with parents and to remain with them for part or all of the night (Lozoff et al., 1995). Appalachian children of eastern Kentucky typically sleep with their parents for the first 2 years of life (Abbott, 1992). Among the Maya of rural Guatemala, mother–infant cosleeping is inter-rupted only by the birth of a new baby, at which time the older child is moved beside the father or to another bed in the same room (Morelli et al., 1992).

Available household space plays a minor role in infant sleeping arrangements. Dominant child-rearing beliefs are much more important. In one study, researchers interviewed American middle-SES mothers and Guatemalan Mayan mothers about their sleeping practices. American mothers frequently mentioned the importance of early independence training, preventing bad habits, and protecting their own privacy. In contrast, Mayan mothers explained that cosleeping helps build a close parent–child bond, which is necessary for children to learn the ways of people around them. When told that American infants sleep by themselves, Mayan mothers reacted with shock and disbelief, stating that it would be painful for them to leave their babies alone at night (Morelli et al., 1992).

Infant sleeping practices affect other aspects of family life. Sleep problems are not an issue for Mayan parents. Babies doze off in the midst of ongoing social activities and are carried to bed by their mothers. In the United States, getting young children ready for bed often requires an elaborate ritual that takes a good part of the evening. Perhaps bedtime struggles, so common in American homes but rare elsewhere in the world, are related to the stress young children feel when they are required to fall asleep without assistance (Kawasaki et al., 1994). The few Caucasian-American parents who permit cosleeping tend to regard their child's sleep behavior as very problematic—a sign of ambivalence about the practice (Lozoff, Askew, & Wolf, 1996).

Infant sleeping arrangements, like other parenting practices, are meant to foster culturally valued characteristics in the young. American middle-SES parents view babies as dependent beings who must be urged toward independence, and so they usually require them to sleep alone. In contrast, Japanese, Mayan, and Appalachian parents regard young infants as separate beings who need to establish an interdependent relationship with the community to survive.

Perhaps because cosleeping is rare in the United States, American parents who practice it sometimes fail to take appropriate safety precautions. Suffocation due to entrapment in soft covers, wedging between the mattress and other components of the bed, and overlying by a cosleeping adult are responsible for about 500 deaths of children under age 2 annually (Nakamura, Wind, & Danello, 1999). In countries where cosleeping is widespread, parents and infants often sleep on hard surfaces, such as floor mats and wooden planks, which minimize these dangers.

■ *This Cambodian father and child sleep together—a practice common in their culture and around the globe. When children fall asleep with their parents, sleep problems are rare during the early years. And many parents who practice cosleeping believe that it helps build a close parent–child bond. Notice that the family sleeps on hard wooden surfaces, which protect cosleeping children from suffocation due to entrapment in soft bedding. (Photo courtesy: Stephen L. Raymer/National Geographic Image Collection)*

Rachel close for much of the day. At night, Rachel slept in her mother's bed, waking to nurse at will. For infants experiencing this type of care, the average sleep period remains constant at 3 hours from 1 to 8 months of age. Only at the end of the first year do these babies move in the direction of an adultlike sleep–waking schedule (Super & Harkness, 1982).

ASK YOURSELF . . .

■ *Felicia commented that at 2 months, April's daily schedule seemed more predictable and she was much more alert. What aspects of brain development might be responsible for this change?*

🌳 *We are used to thinking of brain development as following a strict, genetically determined course, but research shows that this is not so. List examples that reveal the effects of experience on brain growth and lateralization of the cerebral cortex.*

🌳 *Why is lateralization of the cerebral cortex adaptive for lifelong learning?*

INFLUENCES ON EARLY PHYSICAL GROWTH

Physical growth, like other aspects of development, results from the continuous and complex interplay between genetic and environmental factors. Heredity, nutrition, and emotional well-being all affect early physical growth.

HEREDITY

Since identical twins are much more alike in body size than are fraternal twins, we know that heredity is important in physical growth. When diet and health are adequate, height and rate of physical growth are largely determined by heredity. In fact, as long as negative environmental influences such as poor nutrition or illness are not severe, children and adolescents typically show *catch-up growth*—a return to a genetically determined growth path.

Genetic makeup also affects body weight, since the weights of adopted children correlate more strongly with those of their biological than adoptive parents (Stunkard et al., 1986). However, as far as weight is concerned, environment—in particular, nutrition—plays an especially important role.

NUTRITION

Good nutrition is important at any time of development, but it is especially critical in infancy because the baby's brain

■ *Breast-feeding is especially important in developing countries, where infants are at risk for malnutrition and early death due to widespread poverty. This baby of Rajasthan, India, is likely to grow normally during the first year because his mother decided to breast-feed. (Photo courtesy: Jane Schreirman/ Photo Researchers, Inc.)*

and body are growing so rapidly. Pound for pound, a young baby's energy needs are twice those of an adult. Twenty-five percent of the infant's total caloric intake is devoted to growth, and extra calories are needed to keep rapidly developing organs functioning properly (Pipes, 1996).

Babies not only need enough food, they need the right kind of food. In early infancy, breast milk is especially suited to their needs, and bottled formulas try to imitate it. Later, infants require well-balanced solid foods. If a baby's diet is deficient in either quantity or quality, growth can be permanently stunted.

■ BREAST- VERSUS BOTTLE-FEEDING. For thousands of years, all babies were fed the ultimate human health food: breast milk. Only within the last hundred years has bottle-feeding been available. As formulas became easier to prepare, breast-feeding declined from the 1940s into the 1970s, when over 75 percent of American infants were bottle-fed. Partly as a result of the natural childbirth movement (see Chapter 3), breast-feeding gradually became more common, especially among well-educated, middle-SES women. Today, nearly two-thirds of American mothers breast-feed, although most do so for only a few months (U.S. Department of Health and Human Services, 1999a).

The Caregiving Concerns table summarizes the major nutritional and health advantages of breast-feeding. Because of these benefits, breast-fed babies in poverty-stricken regions of the world are much less likely to be malnourished and 6 to 14 times more likely to survive the first year of life. Too often, bottle-fed infants in developing countries get low-grade nutrients, such as rice water, highly dilute cow's and goat's milk, or commercial formula. These foods often lead to illness because they are contaminated due to poor sanitation. Also, because a mother is less likely to get pregnant while she is nursing, breast-feeding helps increase spacing among siblings, a major factor in reducing infant and childhood deaths in economically depressed populations (Grant, 1995). (Note, however, that breast-feeding is not a reliable method of birth control.)

In industrialized nations, most women who choose breast-feeding find it emotionally satisfying, but it is not for everyone. Some mothers simply do not like it or are embarrassed by it. A few others, for physiological reasons, do not produce enough milk. Occasionally, medical reasons—such as treatment with certain drugs or a viral or bacterial disease that could infect the baby—prevent a mother from nursing (Kuhn & Stein, 1997).

Breast milk is so digestible that an infant becomes hungry quite often—every 1½ to 2 hours in comparison to every 3 or 4 hours for a bottle-fed baby. This makes breast-feeding inconvenient for many employed women. A mother who is not always with her baby can still breast-feed or combine it with bottle-feeding. For example, Lisa returned to her job part-time when Byron was 2 months old. Before she left for work, she pumped her milk into a bottle for later feeding by his caregiver (Hills-Banczyk et al., 1993).

Some women who cannot or do not want to breast-feed worry that they are depriving their baby of an experience essential for healthy psychological development. Yet breast- and bottle-fed youngsters in industrialized nations do not differ in intelligence or emotional adjustment (Fergusson & Woodward, 1999; Innis et al., 1996; Malloy & Berendes, 1998). Regardless of feeding method, a mother can respond promptly to her hungry baby and hold and stroke the infant gently—aspects of feeding that foster psychological well-being.

■ ARE CHUBBY BABIES AT RISK FOR LATER OVER-WEIGHT AND OBESITY? Byron was an enthusiastic eater from early infancy. He nursed vigorously and gained weight quickly. By 5 months, he began reaching for food from his parents' plates. Lisa wondered: Was she overfeeding Byron and increasing his chances of being permanently overweight?

Only a slight correlation exists between fatness in infancy and obesity at older ages (Shapiro et al., 1984). Most

CAREGIVING CONCERNS

Nutritional and Health Advantages of Breast-Feeding

ADVANTAGE	DESCRIPTION
Correct balance of fat and protein	Compared with the milk of other mammals, human milk is higher in fat and lower in protein. This balance, as well as the unique proteins and fats contained in human milk, is ideal for a rapidly myelinating nervous system.
Nutritional completeness	A mother who breast-feeds need not add other foods to her infant's diet until the baby is 6 months old. The milks of all mammals are low in iron, but the iron contained in breast milk is much more easily absorbed by the baby's system. Consequently, bottle-fed infants need iron-fortified formula.
Protection against disease	Through breast-feeding, antibodies and other infection-fighting agents are transferred from mother to child. As a result, breast-fed babies have far fewer respiratory and intestinal illnesses and allergic reactions than do bottle-fed infants. Components of human milk that protect against disease can be added to formula, but breast-feeding provides superior immunity.
Protection against faulty jaw development and tooth decay	Breast-feeding helps avoid malocclusion, a condition in which the upper and lower jaws do not meet properly. It also protects against tooth decay due to sweet liquid remaining in the mouths of infants who fall asleep while sucking on a bottle.
Digestibility	Since breast-fed babies have a different kind of bacteria growing in their intestines than do bottle-fed infants, they rarely become constipated or have diarrhea.
Smoother transition to solid foods	Breast-fed infants accept new solid foods more easily than do bottle-fed infants, perhaps because of their greater experience with a variety of flavors, which pass from the maternal diet into the mother's milk.

Sources: Brуerd & Jones, 1996; Pickering et al., 1998; Räihä & Axelsson, 1995; Sullivan & Birch, 1994.

chubby babies thin out during toddlerhood and the preschool years, as weight gain slows and they become more active. Infants and toddlers can eat nutritious foods freely, without risk of becoming too fat.

How can concerned parents prevent their infants from becoming overweight children and adults? As the Caregiving Concerns table below indicates, one way is to encourage good eating habits. Candy, soft drinks, french fries, and other high-calorie foods loaded with sugar, salt, and saturated fats should be avoided. When given such foods regularly, young children start to prefer them (Birch & Fisher, 1995). Physical exercise also guards against excessive weight gain. Once toddlers learn to walk, climb, and run, parents should encourage their natural delight at being able to control their bodies by providing opportunities for energetic play.

MALNUTRITION

Osita is an Ethiopian 2-year-old whose mother has never had to worry about his gaining too much weight. When she weaned him at 1 year, there was little for him to eat besides starchy rice flour cakes. Soon his belly enlarged, his feet swelled, his hair began to fall out, and a rash appeared on his skin. His bright-eyed, curious behavior vanished, and he became irritable and listless.

In developing countries and war-torn areas where food resources are limited, malnutrition is widespread. Recent evidence indicates that 40 to 60 percent of the world's children do not get enough to eat (Bellamy, 1998). Among the 4 to 7 percent severely affected, malnutrition leads to two dietary diseases: marasmus and kwashiorkor.

Marasmus is a wasted condition of the body caused by a diet low in all essential nutrients. It usually appears in the first year of life when a baby's mother is too malnourished to produce enough breast milk and bottle-feeding is also inadequate. Her starving baby becomes painfully thin and is in danger of dying.

Osita has **kwashiorkor,** caused by an unbalanced diet very low in protein. Kwashiorkor usually strikes after weaning, between 1 and 3 years of age. It is common in areas of the world where children get just enough calories from starchy foods, but protein resources are scarce. The child's body responds by breaking down its own protein reserves, causing the swelling and other symptoms that Osita experienced.

Children who manage to survive these extreme forms of malnutrition grow to be smaller in all body dimensions (Galler, Ramsey, & Solimano, 1985a). In addition, the brain is seriously affected. One long-term study of marasmic children revealed that an improved diet led to some catch-up growth in height, but little improvement in head size (Stoch et al., 1982). The malnutrition probably interfered with growth of neural fibers and myelinization, causing a permanent loss in brain weight. By middle childhood, these youngsters score low on intelligence tests, show poor fine motor coordination, and have difficulty paying attention in school (Galler et al., 1984, 1990; Galler, Ramsey, & Solimano, 1985b).

Malnutrition is not confined to developing countries. More than 12 percent of American children go to bed hungry at night. Although few of these children have maras-

---

CAREGIVING CONCERNS

Building a Foundation for Good Eating Habits

SUGGESTION	DESCRIPTION
Introduce solid foods patiently and gradually.	At first, use a small spoon that permits the baby to suck off pureed food, gradually helping the infant to adapt to a solid diet. Patiently offer foods the infant rejects, gradually adding new ones. Food preferences are heavily influenced by experience.
Offer a varied, healthy diet.	Ensure that the older infant and toddler's diet is healthy by offering a wide range of nutritious foods. Limit sweets and avoid "junk" foods, since toddlers will learn to prefer them.
Permit the toddler to choose among healthy foods.	Support the early desire for independence by allowing the toddler to engage in self-feeding (even if messy) and to select from available foods. Over several meals, nutritional needs will be met, and mealtimes will also be emotionally satisfying.
Accept a toddler's idiosyncratic diet.	Relax when a toddler refuses meat and vegetables in favor of peanuts, apples, and cheese slices. These "good foods" may be suited to the child's momentary growth needs. When a varied diet is available, many selections fulfill nutritional requirements, and children eventually modify food jags on their own.
Avoid turning mealtime into an early battleground.	Do not force an infant or toddler to eat. When a young child is consistently unhappy at mealtimes, parents are probably unduly anxious about the child's eating behaviors—a circumstance that can create feeding problems.

■ *The swollen abdomen and listless behavior of this Honduran child are classic symptoms of kwashiorkor, a nutritional illness that results from a diet very low in protein. (Photo courtesy: Bob Daemmrich/ The Image Works)*

mus or kwashiorkor, their physical growth and ability to learn are still affected (Children's Defense Fund, 1999; Wachs, 1995). Recall that poverty and stressful living conditions make the impact of poor diet even worse. Malnutrition is clearly a national and international crisis—one of the most serious problems confronting us today.

EMOTIONAL WELL-BEING

We are not used to thinking of affection and stimulation as necessary for healthy physical growth, but they are just as vital as food. **Nonorganic failure to thrive** is a growth disorder resulting from lack of parental love that is usually present by 18 months of age. Infants who have it show all the signs of marasmus: their bodies look wasted, and they are withdrawn and apathetic. But no organic (or biological) cause for the baby's failure to grow can be found. Enough food is offered, and the infant does not have a serious illness.

Lana, an observant nurse at a public health clinic, became concerned about 8-month-old Melanie, who was 3 pounds lighter than she had been at her last checkup. Her mother claimed to feed her often and could not understand

why she did not grow. Lana noted Melanie's behavior. Unlike most infants her age, she did not mind separating from her mother. Lana tried offering Melanie a toy, but she showed little interest. Instead, she anxiously kept her eyes on adults in the room. When Lana smiled and tried to look into Melanie's eyes, she turned her head away (Black et al., 1994; Leonard, Rhymes, & Solnit, 1986).

Family circumstances surrounding failure to thrive help explain these typical reactions. During feeding, diaper changing, and play, Melanie's mother sometimes acted cold and distant, at other times impatient and hostile (Hagekull, Bohlin, & Rydell, 1997). Melanie tried to protect herself by keeping track of her mother's whereabouts and, when her mother approached, avoiding her gaze. Often an unhappy marriage and parental psychological disturbance contribute to these serious caregiving problems (Drotar, Pallotta, & Eckerle, 1994; Duniz et al., 1996). Melanie's alcoholic father was out of work, and her parents argued constantly. Melanie's mother had little energy to meet the psychological needs of Melanie and her other three children. Without early treatment, by helping parents or arranging for a caring foster home, failure-to-thrive infants remain small and show lasting cognitive and emotional difficulties (Heffner & Kelley, 1994).

ASK YOURSELF . . .

🌳 *Explain why breast-feeding can have lifelong consequences for the development of babies born in poverty-stricken regions of the world.*

■ *Ten-month-old Shaun is below average in height and painfully thin. He has one of two serious growth disorders. Name them, and indicate what clues you would look for to tell which one Shaun has.*

LEARNING CAPACITIES

Learning refers to changes in behavior as the result of experience. Healthy, well-nourished babies come into the world with built-in learning capacities that permit them to profit from experience immediately. Infants are capable of two basic forms of learning, which were introduced in Chapter 1: classical and operant conditioning. They also learn through their natural preference for novel stimulation. Finally, newborn babies have a remarkable ability to imitate the facial expressions and gestures of adults.

CLASSICAL CONDITIONING

In Chapter 3, we discussed a variety of newborn reflexes. These make **classical conditioning** possible. In this form of learning, a new stimulus is paired with a stimulus that leads to a reflexive response. Once the baby's nervous system makes the connection between the two stimuli, then the new stimulus by itself produces the behavior.

Classical conditioning is of great value to infants because it helps them recognize which events usually occur together in the everyday world. As a result, they can anticipate what is about to happen next, and the environment becomes more orderly and predictable (Rovee-Collier, 1987). Let's take a closer look at the steps of classical conditioning.

As Beth settled down in the rocking chair to nurse Rachel, she often stroked Rachel's forehead. Soon Beth noticed that each time Rachel's forehead was stroked, she made active sucking movements. Rachel had been classically conditioned. Here is how it happened (see Figure 4.5):

1. Before learning takes place, an **unconditioned stimulus (UCS)** must consistently produce a reflexive, or **unconditioned, response (UCR)**. In Rachel's case, sweet breast milk (UCS) resulted in sucking (UCR).

2. Next, a *neutral stimulus* that does not lead to the reflex is presented just before, or at about the same time as, the UCS. Beth stroked Rachel's forehead as each nursing period began. The stroking (neutral stimulus) was paired with the taste of milk (UCS).

3. If learning has occurred, the neutral stimulus by itself produces the reflexive response. The neutral stimulus is then called a **conditioned stimulus (CS),** and the response it elicits is called a **conditioned response (CR).**

We know that Rachel has been classically conditioned because stroking her forehead outside the feeding situation (CS) results in sucking (CR).

If the CS is presented alone enough times, without being paired with the UCS, the CR will no longer occur. In other words, if Beth strokes Rachel's forehead again and again without feeding her, Rachel will gradually stop sucking in response to stroking. This is referred to as *extinction.* The occurrence of responses to the CS during the extinction phase of classical conditioning shows that learning has taken place.

Young infants can be classically conditioned most easily when the association between two stimuli has survival value. Rachel learned quickly in the feeding situation, since learning the stimuli that accompany feeding improves the infant's ability to get food and survive (Blass, Ganchrow, & Steiner, 1984). In contrast, some responses are very difficult to condition in young babies. Fear is one of them. Until infants develop the motor skills to escape from unpleasant events, they do not have a biological need to form these associations. But between 8 and 12 months, fear is easy to condition. In Chapter 6, we will discuss the development of fear, as well as other emotional reactions.

OPERANT CONDITIONING

In classical conditioning, babies build expectations about stimulus events in the environment, but they do not

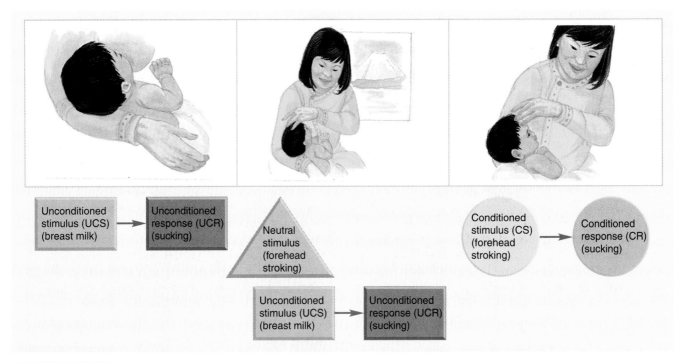

| Unconditioned stimulus (UCS) (breast milk) | → | Unconditioned response (UCR) (sucking) |

Neutral stimulus (forehead stroking)

| Unconditioned stimulus (UCS) (breast milk) | → | Unconditioned response (UCR) (sucking) |

| Conditioned stimulus (CS) (forehead stroking) | → | Conditioned response (CR) (sucking) |

FIGURE 4.5

■ **The steps of classical conditioning.** The example here shows how Rachel was classically conditioned to make sucking movements by stroking her forehead at the beginning of feedings.

influence the stimuli that occur. **Operant conditioning** is quite different. In this form of learning, infants act (or operate) on the environment, and stimuli that follow their behavior change the probability that the behavior will occur again. A stimulus that increases the occurrence of a response is called a **reinforcer.** For example, sweet liquid *reinforces* the sucking response in newborn babies. Removing a desirable stimulus or presenting an unpleasant one to decrease the occurrence of a response is called **punishment.** A sour-tasting fluid *punishes* newborn babies' sucking response. It causes them to purse their lips and stop sucking entirely.

Because the young infant can control only a few behaviors, successful operant conditioning in the early weeks of life is limited to sucking and head-turning responses. However, many stimuli besides food can serve as reinforcers. For example, researchers have created special laboratory conditions in which the baby's rate of sucking on a nipple produces a variety of interesting sights and sounds. Newborns will suck faster to see visual designs or hear music and human voices (Floccia, Christophe, & Bertoncini, 1997). As these findings suggest, operant conditioning has become a powerful tool for finding out what stimuli babies can perceive and which ones they prefer.

As infants get older, operant conditioning includes a wider range of responses and stimuli. For example, special mobiles have been hung over the cribs of 2- to 6-month-olds. When the baby's foot is attached to the mobile with a long cord, the infant can, by kicking, make the mobile turn. Under these conditions, it takes only a few minutes for infants to start kicking vigorously (Rovee-Collier, 1987; Shields & Rovee-Collier, 1992).

Operant conditioning soon modifies parents' and babies' reactions to each other. As the infant gazes into the adult's eyes, the adult looks and smiles back, and then the infant looks and smiles again. The behavior of each partner reinforces the other, and as a result, both parent and baby continue their pleasurable interaction. In Chapter 6, we will see

that this kind of contingent responsiveness plays an important role in the development of infant–caregiver attachment.

Look carefully at the findings just described, and you will see that young babies are active learners; they use any means they can to explore and control their surroundings in an effort to meet their needs for nutrition, stimulation, and social contact (Rovee-Collier, 1996). In fact, when infants' environments are so disorganized that their behavior does not lead to predictable outcomes, serious difficulties ranging from intellectual retardation to apathy and depression can result (Cicchetti & Aber, 1986; Seligman, 1975).

HABITUATION AND DISHABITUATION

Take a moment to walk through the rooms of the library, your home, or wherever you happen to be reading this book. What did you notice? Probably those things that are new and different, such as a recently purchased picture on the wall or a piece of furniture that has been moved. At birth, the human brain is set up to be attracted to novelty. **Habituation** refers to a gradual reduction in the strength of a response due to repetitive stimulation. Looking, heart rate, and respiration may all decline, indicating a loss of interest. Once this has occurred, a new stimulus—some kind of change in the environment—causes responsiveness to return to a high level. This recovery is called **dishabituation.**

Habituation and dishabituation enable us to focus our attention on those aspects of the environment we know least about. As a result, learning is more efficient. By studying the stimuli that infants of different ages habituate and dishabituate to, scientists can tell much about the infant's understanding of the world. For example, a baby who first habituates to a visual pattern (a photo of a baby) and then dishabituates to a new one (a photo of a bald man) clearly remembers the first stimulus and perceives the second one as new and different from it. This general method of studying infant perception and cognition, illustrated in Figure 4.6, can be used with

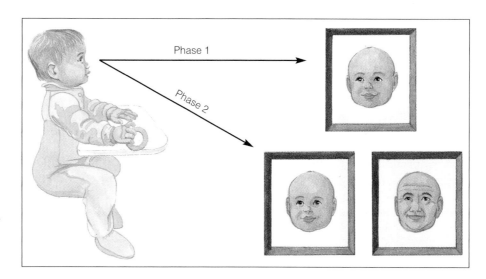

FIGURE 4.6

■ **Example of how the habituation–dishabituation sequence can be used to study infant perception and memory.** In Phase 1, infants are shown (habituated to) a photo of a baby. In Phase 2, infants are again shown the baby photo, but this time it appears alongside a photo of a bald-headed man. If infants dishabituate to (spend more time looking at) the photo of the man, then we know they remembered the baby and perceive the man's face as different from it. (Adapted from Fagan & Singer, 1979.)

FIGURE 4.7

■ **Photographs from two of the first studies of newborn imitation.** Those on the left show 2- to 3-week-old infants imitating tongue protrusion (a), and mouth opening (b). The one on the right shows a 2-day-old infant imitating a sad (c) adult facial expression. (From A. N. Meltzoff & M. K. Moore, 1977, "Imitation of Facial and Manual Gestures by Human Neonates," *Science, 198,* p. 75; and T. M. Field et al., 1982, "Discrimination and Imitation of Facial Expressions by Neonates," *Science, 218,* p. 180. Copyright 1977 and 1982, respectively, by the AAAS. Reprinted by permission.)

(a)   **(b)**   **(c)**

newborn babies, even those who are preterm. The capacity to habituate and dishabituate is evident as early as the third trimester of pregnancy (Sandman et al., 1997).

IMITATION

Newborn babies come into the world with a primitive ability to learn through **imitation**—by copying the behavior of another person. For example, Figure 4.7 above shows infants from 2 days to several weeks old imitating a variety of adult facial expressions (Field et al., 1982; Meltzoff & Moore, 1977). The newborn's capacity to imitate extends to certain gestures, such as head movements, and has been demonstrated in many ethnic groups and cultures (Meltzoff & Kuhl, 1994).

Explanations of newborn imitation are more controversial. Some researchers regard the capacity as little more than an automatic response to particular stimuli, much like a reflex. But newborns imitate many facial expressions, and they do so even after short delays—when the adult is no longer demonstrating the behavior. These observations suggest that the capacity is flexible and voluntary (Meltzoff & Moore, 1992).

As we will see in Chapter 5, infants' capacity to imitate changes greatly over the first 2 years. But however limited it is at birth, imitation provides the young baby with a powerful means of learning. Using imitation, newborns begin to get to know people by sharing behavioral states with them. In the process, babies notice similarities between their own actions and those of others, and they start to find out about themselves. Furthermore, through imitation, adults can get babies to express desirable behaviors, and once they do, adults can encourage these further. Finally, caregivers take great pleasure in a baby who imitates their facial gestures and actions. Clearly, imitation is one of those capacities that helps get the infant's relationship with parents off to a good start.

 ASK YOURSELF . . .

■ *Nine-month-old Byron has a toy with large, colored push buttons on it. Each time he pushes a button, he hears a nursery tune. Which learning capacity is the manufacturer of this toy taking advantage of? What can Byron's play with the toy reveal about his perception—specifically, his ability to distinguish sound patterns?*

■ *Earlier in this chapter, we indicated that infants with nonorganic failure to thrive are unlikely to smile at a friendly adult. Also, they keep track of nearby adults in an anxious and fearful way. Explain these reactions using the learning capacities discussed in the preceding sections.*

MOTOR DEVELOPMENT

Lisa, Beth, and Felicia each kept baby books, proudly noting when their three children held up their heads, reached for objects, sat by themselves, and walked alone. Parents' enthusiasm for these achievements makes perfect sense. With each new motor skill, babies master their bodies and the environment in a new way.

For example, sitting alone grants infants an entirely different perspective on the world. Voluntary reaching permits babies to find out about objects by acting on them. And when infants can move on their own, their opportunities for exploration are multiplied.

Babies' motor achievements have a powerful effect on their social relationships. April was the first of the three babies to master crawling. Suddenly, Felicia had to "child-proof" the household and restrict April's movements in ways that were unnecessary when, placed on a blanket, she would stay there! When April started walking, first "testing of wills" occurred (Biringen et al., 1995). Despite her mother's warnings, she sometimes continued to pull items off shelves that were "off limits."

At the same time, expressions of affection and playful activities expanded as April sought her parents out for greetings, hugs, and a gleeful game of hide-and-seek (Campos, Kermoian, & Zumbahlen, 1992). Soon after,

April turned the pages of a book while Felicia named the pictures. April's delight as she worked on new motor competencies triggered pleasurable reactions in others, which encouraged her efforts further (Mayes & Zigler, 1992). Motor skills, social competencies, cognition, and language were developing together and supporting one another.

THE SEQUENCE OF MOTOR DEVELOPMENT

Gross motor development refers to control over actions that help infants get around in the environment, such as crawling, standing, and walking. In contrast, *fine motor development* has to do with smaller movements, such as reaching and grasping. Table 4.1 below shows the average age at which infants and toddlers achieve a variety of gross and fine motor skills. Most (but not all) children follow this sequence.

TABLE 4.1

Gross and Fine Motor Development in the First Two Years

MOTOR SKILL	AVERAGE AGE ACHIEVED	AGE RANGE IN WHICH 90 PERCENT OF INFANTS ACHIEVE THE SKILL
When held upright, holds head erect and steady	6 weeks	3 weeks–4 months
When prone, lifts self by arms	2 months	3 weeks–4 months
Rolls from side to back	2 months	3 weeks–5 months
Grasps cube	3 months, 3 weeks	2–7 months
Rolls from back to side	4½ months	2–7 months
Sits alone	7 months	5–9 months
Crawls	7 months	5–11 months
Pulls to stand	8 months	5–12 months
Plays pat-a-cake	9 months, 3 weeks	7–15 months
Stands alone	11 months	9–16 months
Walks alone	11 months, 3 weeks	9–17 months
Builds tower of two cubes	13 months, 3 weeks	10–19 months
Scribbles vigorously	14 months	10–21 months
Walks up stairs with help	16 months	12–23 months
Jumps in place	23 months, 2 weeks	17–30 months
Walks on tiptoe	25 months	16–30 months

Note: These milestones represent overall age trends. Individual differences exist in the precise age at which each milestone is attained.
Sources: Bayley, 1969, 1993.

Notice that the table also presents the age ranges during which the majority of babies accomplish each skill. These indicate that although the *sequence* of motor development is fairly uniform across children, there are large individual differences in *rate* of motor progress. We would be concerned about a child's development only if many motor skills were seriously delayed.

Look at Table 4.1 once more, and you will see that there is organization and direction to the infant's motor achievements. The *cephalocaudal trend* is evident. Motor control of the head comes before control of the arms and trunk, and control of the arms and trunk before control of the legs. You can also see the *proximodistal trend:* head, trunk, and arm control is advanced over coordination of the hands and fingers. These similarities between physical and motor development suggest a genetic contribution to motor progress. But we must be careful not to think of motor skills as following a fixed, maturational timetable. As we will see in the next section, many influences—both internal and external to the child—join together to support the vast transformations in motor competencies of the first 2 years.

MOTOR SKILLS AS DYNAMIC SYSTEMS

According to a new approach to motor development, mastery of motor skills involves acquiring increasingly complex, **dynamic systems of action.** When motor skills work as a system, separate abilities blend together, each cooperating with others to produce more effective ways of exploring and controlling the environment. For example, control of the head and upper chest are combined into sitting with support. Kicking, rocking on all fours, and reaching are gradually put together into crawling. Then crawling, standing, and stepping are united into walking alone (Thelen, 1989).

Each new skill is a joint product of the following factors: (1) central nervous system development; (2) movement possibilities of the body; (3) environmental supports for the skill; and (4) the goal the child has in mind, such as getting a toy or crossing the room. Change in any one of these elements leads to loss of stability in the system, and the child explores and selects new, more effective motor patterns. The broader physical environment also has a profound impact on motor skills. For example, if children were reared in the moon's reduced gravity, they would find it more efficient to jump than to walk or run!

Once a new skill is discovered, the child tries hard to perfect it. For example, one baby who was just starting to crawl often collapsed on her tummy and moved backward instead of forward. Gradually she figured out how to propel herself along by alternately pulling with her arms and pushing with her feet. As she experimented with muscle patterns and observed the consequences of her movements, crawling gradually became smooth and accurate (Adolph, Vereijken, & Denny, 1998).

Because motor development is motivated by exploration and the desire to master new tasks, it can only be mapped out by heredity at a very general level (Hopkins & Butterworth, 1997; Thelen & Smith, 1998). And since each skill is learned by revising and combining earlier accomplishments to fit a new goal, infants achieve motor milestones in unique ways.

CULTURAL VARIATIONS IN MOTOR DEVELOPMENT

Cross-cultural research shows how early movement opportunities and a stimulating environment contribute to motor development. Several decades ago, Wayne Dennis (1960) observed infants in Iranian orphanages who were deprived of the tantalizing surroundings that induce infants to acquire motor skills. The Iranian babies spent their days lying on their backs in cribs, without toys to play with. As a result, most did not move on their own until after 2 years of age. When they finally did move, the constant experience of lying on their backs led them to scoot in a sitting position rather than crawl on their hands and knees. Since babies who scoot come up against furniture with their feet, not their hands, they are far less likely to pull themselves to a standing position in preparation for walking. Therefore, walking was delayed.

Cultural variations in infant-rearing practices also affect motor development. Take a quick survey of several parents you know, asking these questions: Can babies profit from training? Should sitting, crawling, and walking be deliberately encouraged? Answers vary widely from culture to culture. Japanese mothers believe such efforts are unnecessary and unimportant. Among the Zinacanteco Indians of Southern Mexico, rapid motor progress is actively discouraged. Babies who walk before they know enough to keep away from cooking fires and weaving looms are viewed as dangerous to themselves and disruptive to others (Greenfield, 1992).

In contrast, among the Kipsigis of Kenya and the West Indians of Jamaica, babies hold their heads up, sit alone, and walk considerably earlier than North American infants. Kipsigi parents deliberately teach these motor skills. In the first few months, babies are seated in holes dug in the ground, and rolled blankets are used to keep them upright. Walking is promoted by frequently bouncing babies on their feet (Super, 1981). As Figure 4.8 shows, the West Indian mothers use a highly stimulating formal handling routine with their babies, explaining that exercise helps infants grow up strong, healthy, and physically attractive (Hopkins & Westra, 1988).

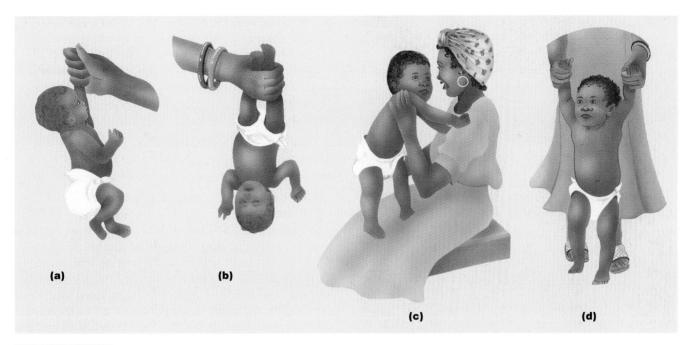

FIGURE 4.8

■ **West Indians of Jamaica use a formal handling routine with their babies.** *Exercises practiced in the first few months include* (a) *stretching each arm while suspending the baby and* (b) *holding the infant upside-down by the ankles. Later in the first year, the baby is* (c) *"walked" up the mother's body and* (d) *encouraged to take steps on the floor while supported. (Adapted from B. Hopkins & T. Westra, 1988, "Maternal Handling and Motor Development: An Intracultural Study,"* Genetic, Social and General Psychology Monographs, 14, *pp. 385, 388, 389. Reprinted by permission of the Helen Dwight Reid Educational Foundation. Published by Heldref Publications, 1319 Eighteenth St., N.W., Washington, DC 20036-1802.)*

FINE MOTOR DEVELOPMENT: VOLUNTARY REACHING AND GRASPING

Of all motor skills, voluntary reaching is believed to play the greatest role in infant cognitive development, since it opens up a whole new way of exploring the environment. By grasping things, turning them over, and seeing what happens when they are released, infants learn a great deal about the sights, sounds, and feel of objects.

Reaching and grasping, like many other motor skills, start out as gross, diffuse activity and move toward mastery of fine movements. Newborns make poorly coordinated swipes or swings, called *prereaching*, toward an object in front of them. Since they cannot control their arms and hands, they rarely succeed in contacting the object. Like newborn reflexes, prereaching eventually drops out, around 7 weeks of age.

At about 3 months, voluntary reaching appears and gradually improves in accuracy (Bushnell, 1985). Infants of this age reach just as effectively for a sounding object in the dark as for an object in the light (Clifton et al., 1993). From the start, vision is freed from the basic act of reaching so it can focus on more complex adjustments. By 5 months, babies successfully reach for moving objects and reduce their reaching when an object is moved just beyond their reach (Robin, Berthier, & Clifton, 1996; Yonas & Hartman, 1993). By 7 months, the arms become more independent; infants can reach for objects with one arm, rather than by extending both (Fagard & Pezé, 1997). And at 9 months, they can obtain a moving object that changes direction (Ashmead et al., 1993).

Once infants can reach, they modify their grasp. The newborn's grasp reflex is replaced by the *ulnar grasp*, a clumsy motion in which the fingers close against the palm. Around 4 to 5 months, when infants begin to sit up, both hands become coordinated in exploring objects. Babies of this age can hold an object in one hand and scan it with the fingertips of the other. They frequently transfer objects from hand to hand (Rochat & Goubet, 1995). By the end of the first year, infants use the thumb and index finger in a well-coordinated *pincer grasp*. Then the ability to manipulate objects greatly expands. The 1-year-old can pick up raisins and blades of grass, turn knobs, and open and close small boxes.

Between 8 and 11 months, reaching and grasping are so well practiced that attention is released from the motor skill itself to events that occur before and after attaining the object. Around this time, infants begin to solve simple

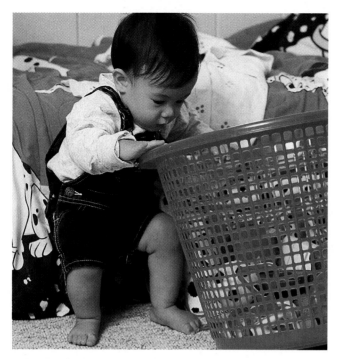

■ *Of all motor skills, voluntary reaching is believed to play the greatest role in infant cognitive development. This 8-month old can tip the basket with one hand while reaching in with the other. By exploring its contents, he adds to his knowledge of the sights, sounds, and feel of objects. (Photo courtesy: Joe Carini/ The Image Works)*

problems involving reaching, such as searching for and finding a hidden toy.

Like other motor milestones, voluntary reaching is affected by early experience. In a well-known study, institutionalized babies given a moderate amount of visual stimulation—at first, simple designs and later, a mobile hung over their cribs—reached for objects 6 weeks earlier than did infants given nothing to look at. A third group given massive stimulation—patterned crib bumpers and mobiles at an early age—also reached sooner than unstimulated babies. But this heavy enrichment took its toll. These infants looked away and cried a great deal, and they were not as advanced in reaching as the moderately stimulated group (White & Held, 1966). Recall from our discussion of brain development that more stimulation is not necessarily better. Trying to push infants beyond their readiness to handle stimulation can undermine the development of important motor skills.

ASK YOURSELF . . .

 Review the new approach to motor development, which regards motor skills as complex systems of action. Is motor development multidimensional? Explain. (Return to Chapter 1, page 9, if you need to review this assumption of the lifespan perspective.)

■ *Rosanne read in a magazine that infant motor development could be accelerated through exercise and visual stimulation. She hung mobiles and pictures all over her newborn baby's crib, and she massages and manipulates his body daily. Is Rosanne doing the right thing? Why or why not?*

PERCEPTUAL DEVELOPMENT

In Chapter 3, you learned that touch, taste, smell, and hearing—but not vision—are remarkably well developed at birth. Now let's turn to a related question: How does perception change over the first year of life?

Our discussion will focus on hearing and vision because almost all research addresses these two aspects of perceptual development. Unfortunately, we know little about how touch, taste, and smell develop after birth. Also, in Chapter 3, we used the word *sensation* to talk about these capacities. Now we are using the word *perception*. The reason is that sensation suggests a fairly passive process—what the baby's receptors detect when they are exposed to stimulation. In contrast, perception is much more active. When we perceive, we organize and interpret what we see. As we look at the perceptual achievements of infancy, you will probably find it hard to tell where perception leaves off and thinking begins. Thus, the research we are about to discuss provides an excellent bridge to the topic of Chapter 5—cognitive development during the first 2 years.

HEARING

On Byron's first birthday, Lisa bought several tapes of nursery songs, and she turned one on each afternoon at naptime. Soon Byron let her know his favorite tune. If she put on "Twinkle, Twinkle," he stood up in his crib and whimpered until she replaced it with "Jack and Jill." Byron's behavior illustrates the greatest change in hearing over the first year of life: babies start to organize sounds into complex patterns. If two slightly different melodies are played, 1-year-olds can tell that they are not the same (Morrongiello, 1986).

Responsiveness to sound provides support for the young baby's visual and tactile exploration of the environment. Infants as young as 3 days old turn their eyes and head in the general direction of a sound. The ability to identify the precise location of a sound with a look or a reach improves greatly over the first 6 months (Clifton et al., 1994; Litovsky & Ashmead, 1997). By this time, infants start to make judgments about how far away a sound is. They are less likely to try to retrieve a sounding object in the dark if it is beyond their reach (Clifton, Perris, & Bullinger, 1991).

As we will see in the next chapter, throughout the first year babies are preparing to acquire language. Recall from Chapter 3 that newborns can detect almost all sounds in human languages. As infants continue to listen actively to the talk of people around them, they learn to focus on meaningful sound variations in their own language. By 6 months of age, they "screen out" sounds that are not useful in their language community (Kuhl et al., 1992; Polka & Werker, 1994).

In the second half of the first year, infants focus on larger speech units that are critical to figuring out the meaning of what they hear. They recognize familiar words in spoken passages (Jusczyk & Hohne, 1997). Older infants can also detect phrases and clauses in sentences. For example, in one study, 7- to 10-month-olds clearly preferred speech with natural breaks to speech with pauses in unnatural places (Hirsh-Pasek et al., 1987). By 9 months, this rhythmic sensitivity is extended to individual words. Babies of this age listen much longer to speech with stress patterns common in their own language, and they perceive it in wordlike segments (Jusczyk, 1997; Morgan & Saffran, 1995).

VISION

If you had to choose between hearing and vision, which would you select? Most people pick vision, for good reason. More than any other sense, humans depend on vision for exploring their environment. Although at first a baby's visual world is fragmented, it undergoes extraordinary changes during the first 7 to 8 months of life.

Visual development is supported by rapid maturation of the eye and visual centers in the cerebral cortex. Recall from Chapter 3 that the newborn baby focuses and perceives color poorly. By 2 months, infants can focus on objects and discriminate colors about as well as adults can (Banks, 1980; Burr, Morrone, & Fiorentini, 1996). Visual acuity (fineness of discrimination) improves steadily throughout the first year. In the first 6 months, it changes from around 20/600 to 20/100. At 11 months, it reaches a near-adult level (Courage & Adams, 1990). The ability to fixate on a moving object and track it improves steadily over the first half-year (Hainline, 1993).

As babies see more clearly and explore their visual field more adeptly, they work on sorting out features of the environment and how they are arranged in space. We can best understand how they do so by examining the development of two aspects of vision: depth and pattern perception.

■ DEPTH PERCEPTION. *Depth perception* is the ability to judge the distance of objects from one another and from ourselves. It is important for understanding the layout of the environment and for guiding motor activity. To reach for objects, babies must have some sense of depth. Later, when infants crawl, depth perception helps prevent them from bumping into furniture and falling down stairs.

Figure 4.9 shows the well-known *visual cliff*, designed by Eleanor Gibson and Richard Walk (1960) and used in the earliest studies of depth perception. It consists of a glass-covered table with a platform at the center, a "shallow" side with a checkerboard pattern just under the glass, and a "deep" side with a checkerboard several feet below the glass. The researchers found that crawling babies readily crossed the shallow side, but most reacted with fear to the deep side. They concluded that around the time that infants crawl, most distinguish deep and shallow surfaces and avoid dropoffs that look dangerous.

Gibson and Walk's research shows that crawling and avoidance of dropoffs are linked, but it does not tell us how they are related or when sensitivity to depth first appears. To better understand the development of depth perception, recent research has looked at babies' ability to detect particular depth cues, using methods that do not require that they crawl.

Motion provides a great deal of information about depth, and it is the first depth cue to which infants are sensitive. Babies 3 to 4 weeks of age blink their eyes defensively when an object is moved toward their faces and its image enlarges, signaling that it is going to hit (Nánez & Yonas, 1994). *Binocular* depth cues arise because our two eyes have slightly different views of the visual field. The brain registers both images and combines them. Research in which infants wear special goggles, like those for 3-D movies, reveals that sensitivity to binocular cues emerges between 2 and 3 months and improves rapidly over the first half-year (Birch, 1993). Finally, around 6 months, babies develop sensitivity to *pictorial* depth cues—the same ones that artists use to make a painting look three-dimensional. Examples are lines that create the illusion of perspective, changes in texture (nearby textures are more detailed than faraway ones), and overlapping objects (an

FIGURE 4.9

■ **The visual cliff.** By refusing to cross the deep side and showing a preference for the shallow surface, this infant demonstrates the ability to perceive depth. (Photo courtesy: Birnbach/Monkmeyer Press)

VARIATIONS/INDIVIDUALITY

DEVELOPMENT OF INFANTS WITH SEVERE VISUAL IMPAIRMENTS

Research on infants who can see little or nothing at all dramatically illustrates the interdependence of vision, motor exploration, social interaction, and understanding of the world. In a recent longitudinal study, infants with a visual acuity of 20/800 or worse (they had only dim light perception or were blind) were followed through the preschool years. Compared with agemates who have less severe visual impairments, they showed serious delays in all aspects of development—motor, cognitive, language, and personal/social. Their motor and cognitive functioning suffered the most; with age, performance in both domains became increasingly distant from that of other children (Hatton et al., 1997).

What explains these profound developmental delays? Minimal or absent vision seems to alter the child's experiences in at least two crucial, interrelated ways.

IMPACT ON MOTOR EXPLORATION AND SPATIAL UNDERSTANDING.

Infants with severe visual impairments attain gross and fine motor milestones many months later than their sighted counterparts (Fraiberg, 1977; Tröster & Brambring, 1993). For example, on the average, blind

infants do not reach for and manipulate objects until 12 months, crawl until 13 months, and walk until 19 months (compare these averages to the norms given in Table 4.1 on page 133). Why is this so?

Infants with severe visual impairments must rely entirely on sound to identify the whereabouts of objects. But sound does not function as a precise clue to object location until much later than vision—around the middle of the first year. And because infants who cannot see have difficulty engaging their caregivers, adults may not provide them with rich, early exposure to sounding objects. As a result, the baby comes to understand relatively late that there is a world of tantalizing objects out there to explore.

Until "reaching on sound" is achieved, infants with severe visual impairments are not motivated to move on their own (Fraiberg, 1977; Tröster & Brambring, 1993). Even after they do move, their coordination is poor due to many months of inactivity. Because of their own uncertainty and parental fear of injury and resulting restriction, blind infants are typically tentative in their movements. These factors delay motor development further.

Motor and cognitive development are closely linked for infants with lit-

tle or no vision, even more than for their sighted counterparts. These babies build an understanding of the location and arrangement of objects in space only after reaching and crawling (Bigelow, 1992). Inability to imitate the motor actions of others presents additional challenges as these children get older, contributing to declines in motor and cognitive progress relative to peers with better vision (Hatton et al., 1997).

IMPACT ON THE CAREGIVER-INFANT RELATIONSHIP.

Compared to sighted babies, infants who see very poorly are less likely to elicit stimulating caregiver interaction. They cannot make eye contact, imitate, or pick up nonverbal social cues. Their emotional expressions are muted; for example, their smile is fleeting and unpredictable. Consequently, the infant may receive little adult attention, play, and other stimulation vital for all aspects of development (Tröster & Brambring, 1992).

When a visually impaired child does not learn how to participate in social interaction during infancy, communication is compromised in early childhood. In an observational study of blind children enrolled in preschools with sighted agemates, the blind children seldom

---

object partially hidden by another object is perceived to be more distant) (Yonas et al., 1986).

Why does perception of depth cues emerge in the order just described? Researchers speculate that motor development is involved. For example, control of the head during the early weeks of life may help babies notice motion cues. Improved focusing ability at 3 months may permit detection of binocular cues. Around 5 to 6 months, the ability to turn, poke, and feel the surface of objects may promote perception of pictorial cues (Bushnell & Boudreau, 1993). Indeed, as we will see next, one aspect of motor progress —independent movement—plays a vital role in refinement of depth perception.

INDEPENDENT MOVEMENT AND DEPTH PERCEPTION. At 6 months, April started crawling. "She's like a fearless daredevil," exclaimed Felicia. "If I put her down in the middle of our bed, she crawls right over the edge. The same thing's happened by the stairs."

Will April become more wary of the side of the bed and the staircase as she becomes a more experienced crawler? Research suggests that she will. In one study, infants with more crawling experience (regardless of when they started to crawl) were far more likely to refuse to cross the deep side of the visual cliff (Bertenthal, Campos, & Barrett, 1984). Avoidance of heights, the investigators concluded, is "made possible by independent locomotion" (Bertenthal & Campos, 1987, p. 563).

initiated contact with peers and teachers. When they did interact, they had trouble interpreting the meaning of others' reactions and responding appropriately (Preisler, 1991, 1993).

INTERVENTIONS. Although many infants and preschoolers with severe visual impairments are substantially behind in development, considerable variation exists. Once language emerges and the child can rely on it for learning, some children with limited or no vision show impressive rebounds, eventually acquiring a unique capacity for abstract thinking and social and practical skills that permit them to lead productive, independent lives (Warren, 1994).

Parents, teachers, and professional caregivers can help infants with minimal vision overcome early developmental delays. Especially important is stimulating, responsive interaction. Until a close emotional bond with an adult is forged, visually impaired babies cannot establish vital links with their environments. Techniques that help infants become aware of their physical and social surroundings include heightened sensory input through combining sound and touch (holding, touching, or bringing the baby's hands to the adult's face while talking or singing), many repetitions, and consistently reinforcing the infant's efforts to make contact. Mani-

pulative play with objects that make sounds is also vital (Rogow, 1988). These experiences facilitate "reaching on sound," which motivates independent movement. Finally, rich language stimulation can compensate for visual loss by granting young children a ready means of finding out about objects, events, and behaviors they cannot see.

■ *This 20-month-old, who has no vision, reacts with glee as her father guides her exploration of a novel object through touch and sound. Adults who encourage and reinforce children's efforts to make contact with their physical and social surroundings prevent developmental delays typically associated with severely impaired vision. (Photo courtesy: Byron/Monkmeyer Press)*

Independent movement contributes to other aspects of three-dimensional understanding. For example, crawling infants are better at remembering object locations and finding hidden objects than are their noncrawling agemates. The more crawling experience, the better they perform on these tasks (Bai & Bertenthal, 1992; Campos & Bertenthal, 1989).

Why does crawling make such a difference? Compare your own experience of the environment when you are driven from one place to another as opposed to when you walk or drive yourself. When you move on your own, you are much more aware of landmarks, routes of travel, and what things

look like from different points of view. The same is true for infants. In fact, crawling is so important in structuring babies' experience of the world that it seems to promote a new level of brain organization. During the weeks in which babies master crawling, electrical brainwave activity in the cerebral cortex becomes more organized. Researchers speculate that crawling leads to strengthening of certain neural connections, especially those involved in vision and understanding of space (Bell & Fox, 1996). As the Variations box above reveals, the link between independent movement and spatial knowledge is also evident in a population with a very different perceptual experience: infants with severe visual impairments.

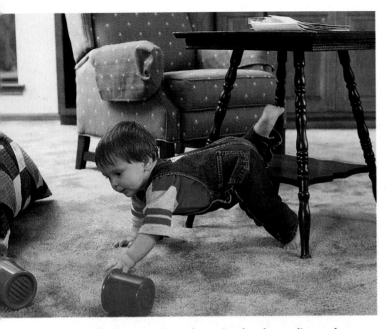

■ *Crawling promotes three-dimensional understanding, such as wariness of drop-offs and memory for object locations. As this baby moves about, he takes note of how to get from place to place, where objects are in relation to himself and to other objects, and what they look like from different points of view. (Photo courtesy: Bob Daemmrich/ The Image Works)*

■ PATTERN AND FACE PERCEPTION. Even newborns prefer to look at patterned rather than plain stimuli—for example, a drawing of the human face or one with scrambled facial features rather than a black-and-white oval (Fantz, 1961). As infants get older, they prefer more complex patterns. For example, 3-week-old infants look longest at black-and-white checkerboards with a few large squares, whereas 8- and 14-week-olds prefer those with many squares (Brennan, Ames, & Moore, 1966).

A general principle called **contrast sensitivity** explains these early pattern preferences (Banks & Ginsburg, 1985). *Contrast* refers to the difference in the amount of light between adjacent regions in a pattern. If babies *are sensitive to* (can detect) the contrast in two or more patterns, they prefer the one with more contrast. To understand this idea, look at the checkerboards in the top row of Figure 4.10. To us, the one with many small squares has more contrasting elements. Now look at the bottom row, which shows how these checkerboards appear to infants in the first few weeks of life. Because of their poor vision, very young babies cannot resolve the features in more complex patterns, so they prefer to look at the large, bold checkerboard. By 2 months of age, when detection of fine-grained detail has improved considerably, infants become sensitive to the contrast in complex patterns and spend more time looking at them (Dodwell, Humphrey, & Muir, 1987).

In the early weeks of life, infants respond to the separate parts of a pattern. For example, when shown drawings of human faces, 1-month-olds limit their visual exploration to the border of the stimulus and stare at single, high-contrast features, such as the hairline or chin (see Figure 4.11). At about 2 months, when scanning ability and contrast sensitivity have improved, infants thoroughly explore a pattern's internal features, pausing briefly to look at each part (Bronson, 1991).

Once babies can detect all parts of a stimulus, they begin to combine pattern elements. By 4 months, they are so good at detecting pattern organization that they even perceive subjective boundaries that are not really present. For example, they perceive a square in the center of Figure 4.12(a), just as you do (Ghim, 1990). Older infants apply their growing knowledge of the world to pattern perception. For example, 9-month-olds show a special preference for an organized series of moving lights that resembles a human being walking, in that they look much longer at this display

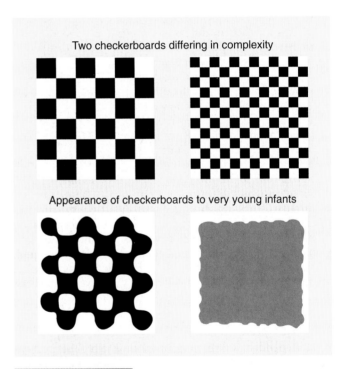

Two checkerboards differing in complexity

Appearance of checkerboards to very young infants

FIGURE 4.10

■ **The way two checkerboards differing in complexity look to infants in the first few weeks of life.** Because of their poor vision, very young infants cannot resolve the fine detail in the complex checkerboard. It appears blurred, like a gray field. The large, bold checkerboard appears to have more contrast, so babies prefer to look at it. (Adapted from M. S. Banks & P. Salapatek, 1983, "Infant Visual Perception," in M. M. Haith & J. J. Campos [Eds.], *Handbook of Child Psychology: Vol. 2. Infancy and Developmental Psychobiology* [4th ed.], New York: Wiley, p. 504. Copyright © 1983 by John Wiley & Sons. Reprinted by permission.)

FIGURE 4.11

■ **Visual scanning of the pattern of the human face by 1- and 2-month-old infants.** One-month-olds limit their scanning to single features on the border of the stimulus, whereas 2-month-olds explore internal features. (From P. Salapatek, 1975, "Pattern Perception in Early Infancy," in L. B. Cohen & P. Salapatek (Eds.), *Infant Perception: From Sensation to Cognition,* New York: Academic Press, p. 201. Reprinted by permission.)

than at upside-down or scrambled versions (Bertenthal, 1993). By 12 months, infants can detect objects represented by incomplete figures, even when as much as two-thirds of the image is missing (see Figure 4.12(b)) (Rose, Jankowski, & Senior, 1997).

The baby's tendency to search for structure in a patterned stimulus applies to face perception. Infants under 2 months show no special preference for a facial pattern. At 2 to 3 months, they do prefer a face over other, similar configurations (Dannemiller & Stephens, 1988). Perhaps you are wondering how newborns can display the remarkable imitative capacities described earlier in this chapter if they do not scan the internal features of faces and perceive the facial pattern. Recall that the facial expressions in newborn imitation research were not static poses but live demon-strations. Their dynamic quality probably caused infants to notice them.

By 3 months, infants make fine-grained distinctions among the features of different faces. For example, they can tell the difference between the photos of two strangers, even when the faces are moderately similar. Around this time, babies also recognize their mother's face in a photo, since they look longer at it than the face of a stranger (Morton, 1993). Between 7 and 10 months, infants start to perceive emotional expressions as organized wholes. They consis-tently treat positive faces (happy and surprised) as differ-ent from negative ones (sad and fearful) (Ludemann, 1991). As infants recognize and respond to the expressive behavior of others, face perception supports their earliest social relationships.

(a)   **(b)**

FIGURE 4.12

■ **Subjective boundaries in visual patterns.** (a) Do you perceive a square in the middle of the figure on the left? By 4 months of age, infants do, too. (b) What does the image on the right, missing two-thirds of its outline, look like to you? By 12 months, infants detect that it is a bicycle. After habituating to the incomplete bicycle image, they were shown an intact bicycle figure paired with a novel form. Twelve-month-olds dishabituated to (looked longer at) the novel figure, indicating that they recognized the bicycle pattern above on the basis of very little visual information. (Adapted from Ghim, 1990; Rose, Jankowski, & Senior, 1997.)

TABLE 4.2

Development of Visual Perception

	BIRTH–1 MONTH	2–4 MONTHS	5–12 MONTHS
Depth perception	Sensitivity to motion cues	Sensitivity to binocular cues	Sensitivity to pictorial cues; wariness of heights
Pattern perception	Preference for patterns with large elements	Visual exploration of entire stimulus, including internal features	Detection of increasingly complex, meaningful patterns
	Visual exploration limited to the border of a stimulus and single features	Combining pattern elements into an organized whole	
Face perception	Absence of preference for the human facial pattern	Preference for a facial pattern over other, equally complex patterns	More fine-grained discrimination of faces, including the ability to perceive emotional expressions as organized wholes
		Recognition of the mother's face in a photo	

INTERMODAL PERCEPTION

So far, we have discussed the infant's perceptual abilities one by one. When we take in information from the environment, we often use **intermodal perception.** That is, we combine stimulation from more than one *modality,* or sensory system. Recent evidence indicates that from the start, babies perceive the world in an intermodal fashion (Meltzoff, 1990; Spelke, 1987).

Recall that newborns turn in the general direction of a sound, and they reach for objects in a primitive way. These behaviors suggest that infants expect sight, sound, and touch to go together. In one study, 1-month-olds were given a pacifier with either a smooth surface or a surface with nubs on it. After exploring it in their mouths, the infants were shown two pacifiers—one smooth and one nubbed. They preferred to look at the shape they had sucked, indicating that they could match touch and visual stimulation without much experience seeing and feeling objects (Meltzoff & Borton, 1979). Within a few months, infants make impressive intermodal matches. Three- and 4-month-olds can relate a child's or adult's moving lips to the corresponding sounds in speech. And 7-month-olds can link a happy or angry voice with the appropriate face of a speaking person (Bahrick, Netto, & Hernandez-Reif, 1998; Soken & Pick, 1992).

Of course, a great many intermodal associations—the way a train sounds or a teddy bear feels—must be based on experience. Infants acquire these relationships remarkably quickly, often after just one exposure to a new situation (Spelke, 1987). In addition, when researchers try to teach intermodal matches by pairing sights and sounds that do not naturally go together, babies will not learn them (Bahrick, 1992). Intermodal perception is yet another capacity that helps infants build an orderly, predictable perceptual world.

ASK YOURSELF . . .

■ *Five-month-old Tyrone sat in his infant seat, passing a teething biscuit from hand to hand, moving it up close to his face and far away, and finally dropping it overboard onto the floor below. What aspect of visual development is Tyrone probably learning about? Explain your answer.*

■ *Diane put up bright wallpaper with detailed pictures of animals in Jana's room before she was born. During the first 2 months of life, Jana hardly noticed the wallpaper. Then, around 2 months, she showed keen interest. What new visual abilities probably account for this change?*

UNDERSTANDING PERCEPTUAL DEVELOPMENT

Now that we have reviewed the development of infant perceptual capacities, how can we put together this diverse array of amazing achievements? Eleanor and James Gibson's **differentiation theory** provides widely accepted answers. According to the Gibsons, infants actively search for **invariant features** of the environment—those that remain stable—in a constantly changing perceptual world. For example, in pattern perception, at first babies are confronted with a confusing mass of stimulation. But very quickly, they search for features that stand out along the border of a stimulus. Then they explore its internal features, noticing *stable relationships* between those features. As a result, they detect patterns, such as squares and faces. The development of intermodal perception also reflects this principle. Babies seek out invariant relationships, such as a similar tempo in an object's motion and sound, that unite information across modalities.

The Gibsons use the word *differentiation* (which means "analyze" or "break down") to describe their theory because over time, babies make finer and finer distinctions among stimuli. In addition to pattern perception, differentiation applies to depth perception; recall how sensitivity to overall motion and binocular cues precedes detection of fine-grained pictorial features. So one way of understanding perceptual development is to think of it as a built-in tendency to search for order and consistency, a capacity that becomes more fine-tuned with age (Gibson, 1970; Gibson, 1979).

Acting on the environment plays a major role in perceptual differentiation. Think back to the links between motor milestones and perceptual development discussed in this chapter. Infants constantly look for ways in which the environment *affords* opportunities for action (Gibson, 1988). By moving about and exploring the environment, they figure out which objects can be grasped, squeezed, bounced, or stroked and when a surface is safe to cross or affords the possibility of falling. As a result, they differentiate the world in new ways and act more competently when confronted with diverse perceptual experiences (Adolph, 1997).

As we conclude this chapter, it is only fair to note that some researchers believe that babies do not make sense of their world just by detecting invariant features. Instead, they *impose meaning* on what they perceive, constructing categories of objects and events in the surrounding environment. We have seen the glimmerings of this cognitive point of view in this chapter. For example, older babies *interpret* a familiar face as a source of pleasure and affection and a pattern of blinking lights as a moving human being. This cognitive perspective also has merit in understanding the achievements of infancy. In fact, many researchers combine these two viewpoints, regarding infant development as proceeding from a perceptual to a cognitive emphasis over the first year of life (Haith & Benson, 1998; Mandler, 1998).

SUMMARY

BODY GROWTH

Describe major changes in body growth over the first 2 years.

- Changes in height and weight are rapid during the first 2 years. Body fat is laid down quickly in the first 9 months, whereas muscle development is slow and gradual. Skeletal age is the best way to estimate the child's physical maturity; girls are advanced over boys. Growth of parts of the body follows **cephalocaudal** and **proximodistal trends,** resulting in changing body proportions.

BRAIN DEVELOPMENT

What changes in brain development occur during infancy and toddlerhood, at the level of individual brain cells and the level of the cerebral cortex?

- Early in development, the brain grows faster than any other organ of the body. During infancy, **neurons** form **synapses,** or connections, at a rapid rate. During the peak period of synaptic growth in any brain area, many surrounding neurons die. Stimulation determines which neurons will survive and continue to establish new synapses and which will lose their connective fibers through **synaptic pruning. Glial cells,** which are responsible for **myelinization,** multiply rapidly into the second year and contribute to large gains in brain weight.

- Different regions of the **cerebral cortex** develop in the same order in which various capacities emerge in the growing child. **Lateralization** refers to specialization of the hemispheres of the cortex. Although some brain specialization exists at birth, in the first few years of life there is high **brain plasticity.** Both heredity and early experience contribute to brain organization.

- Changes in the electrical brain-wave activity of the cortex, along with gains in brain weight and skull size, indicate that brain growth spurts occur intermittently from infancy to early adulthood. These may be sensitive periods in which appropriate stimulation is necessary for full development.

How does the organization of sleep and wakefulness change over the first 2 years?

- The infant's changing arousal patterns are primarily affected by brain growth, but the social environment also plays a role. Short periods of sleep and wakefulness are put together and better coincide with a night-and-day schedule. Infants in Western nations sleep through the night much earlier than those in many other cultures.

INFLUENCES ON EARLY PHYSICAL GROWTH

Cite evidence that heredity, nutrition, and affection and stimulation contribute to early physical growth.

- Physical growth results from a continuous and complex interplay between heredity and environment. Heredity contributes to body size and rate of physical growth.

- Breast milk is especially suited to infants' growth needs and offers protection against disease. Breast-feeding prevents malnutrition and infant death in poverty-stricken areas of the world. Breast-fed and bottle-fed babies do not differ in intelligence or emotional adjustment.

- Most chubby babies thin out during toddlerhood and early childhood. Infants and toddlers can eat nutritious foods freely, without risk of becoming overweight.

- **Marasmus** and **kwashiorkor** are dietary diseases caused by malnutrition that affect many children in developing countries. If allowed to continue, body growth and brain development can be permanently stunted. **Nonorganic failure to thrive** illustrates the importance of stimulation and affection for normal physical growth.

LEARNING CAPACITIES

Describe four infant learning capacities, the conditions under which they occur, and the unique value of each.

- Infants can be **classically conditioned** when the pairing of an **unconditioned stimulus (UCS)** and **conditioned stimulus (CS)** has survival value. Young babies are easily conditioned in the feeding situation. Classical conditioning of fear is difficult before 8 to 12 months.

- **Operant conditioning** enables infants to explore and control their surroundings. In addition to food, interesting sights and sounds serve as effective **reinforcers,** increasing the occurrence of a response. **Punishment** involves removing a desirable stimulus or presenting an unpleasant one to decrease the occurrence of a response.

- **Habituation** and **dishabituation** reveal that at birth, babies are attracted to novelty. Newborn infants also have a primitive ability to **imitate** the facial expressions and gestures of adults.

MOTOR DEVELOPMENT

Describe the general course of motor development during the first 2 years, along with factors that influence it.

- Like physical development, motor development follows the cephalocaudal and proximodistal trends. New motor skills are a matter of combining existing skills into increasingly complex **dynamic systems of action.** Each new skill is a joint product of central nervous system development, movement possibilities of the body, environmental supports for the skill, and the child's motivation to accomplish a task.

- Movement opportunities and a stimulating environment profoundly affect motor development, as shown by research on infants raised in deprived institutions. Cultural values and child-rearing customs contribute to the emergence and refinement of early motor skills.

- During the first year, infants perfect their reaching and grasping. The poorly coordinated prereaching of the newborn period drops out. Voluntary reaching gradually becomes more flexible and accurate, and the clumsy ulnar grasp is transformed into a refined pincer grasp.

PERCEPTUAL DEVELOPMENT

What changes in hearing, depth and pattern perception, and intermodal perception take place during infancy?

- Over the first year, infants organize sounds into more complex patterns and can identify their precise location. Infants also become more sensitive to the sounds and meaningful speech units of their own language.

- Rapid development of the eye and visual centers in the brain supports the development of focusing, color discrimination, and visual acuity during the first half-year. The ability to track a moving object also improves.

- Research on depth perception reveals that responsiveness to motion cues develops first, followed by sensitivity to binocular and then pictorial cues. Experience in moving about independently enhances babies' three-dimensional understanding.

- **Contrast sensitivity** accounts for babies' early pattern preferences. At first, infants look at the border of a stimulus and at single features. Around 2 months, they explore the internal features of a pattern and start to detect pattern organization. Over time, they discriminate increasingly complex, meaningful patterns. Perception of the human face follows the same sequence of development as sensitivity to other patterned stimuli.

- From the start, infants are capable of **intermodal perception.** During the first year, they quickly combine information across sensory modalities, often after just one exposure to a new situation.

UNDERSTANDING PERCEPTUAL DEVELOPMENT

Explain differentiation theory of perceptual development.

- According to **differentiation theory,** perceptual development is a matter of detecting **invariant features** in a constantly changing perceptual world. Acting on the world plays a major role in perceptual differentiation. Other researchers take a more cognitive view, suggesting that at an early age, infants impose meaning on what they perceive. Many researchers combine these two ideas.

IMPORTANT TERMS AND CONCEPTS

brain plasticity (p. 122)

cephalocaudal trend (p. 120)

cerebral cortex (p. 121)

classical conditioning (p. 129)

conditioned response (CR) (p. 130)

conditioned stimulus (CS) (p. 130)

contrast sensitivity (p. 140)

differentiation theory (p. 142)

dishabituation (p. 131)

dynamic systems of action (p. 134)

glial cells (p. 121)

habituation (p. 131)

imitation (p. 132)

intermodal perception (p. 142)

invariant features (p. 142)

kwashiorkor (p. 128)

lateralization (p. 122)

marasmus (p. 128)

myelinization (p. 121)

neurons (p. 120)

nonorganic failure to thrive (p. 129)

operant conditioning (p. 131)

proximodistal trend (p. 120)

punishment (p. 131)

reinforcer (p. 131)

sudden infant death syndrome (SIDS) (p. 123)

synapses (p. 120)

synaptic pruning (p. 120)

unconditioned response (UCR) (p. 130)

unconditioned stimulus (UCS) (p. 130)

FOR FURTHER INFORMATION AND HELP

Consult the companion website for this book, where you will find additional weblinks and associated learning activities: www.abacon.com/berk

PHYSICAL GROWTH AND HEALTH

Healthy Mothers, Healthy Babies
www.hmhb.org
A coalition of national and state organizations concerned with maternal and child health. Serves as a network through which information on nutrition, injury prevention, and infant mortality is shared.

United Nations Children's Fund (UNICEF)
www.unicef.org
International organization dedicated to addressing the problems of children around the world. Develops and implements health and nutrition programs, campaigns to have children vaccinated against disease, and coordinates delivery of food and other aid to disaster-stricken areas.

World Health Organization (WHO)
www.who.org
International health agency of the United Nations that seeks to obtain the highest level of health care for all people. Promotes prevention and treatment of disease and strives to eliminate poverty. Places special emphasis on the health needs of developing countries.

Zero to Three
www.zerotothree.org
An organization that promotes the healthy development of infants and children from birth to 3 years of age. Provides information on many aspects of early development.

BREAST-FEEDING

La Leche League International
www.lalecheleague.org
International organization that provides information and support to breast-feeding mothers. Local chapters exist in many cities.

MALNUTRITION

Food Research and Action Center
www.afj.org/mem/frac/html
Provides assistance to community organizations trying to make federal food programs more responsive to the needs of millions of hungry Americans. Seeks to enhance public awareness of the problems of hunger and poverty in the United States.

SUDDEN INFANT DEATH SYNDROME (SIDS)

National Sudden Infant Death Syndrome Foundation (NSIDSF)
www.sids-network.org
Provides assistance to parents who have lost a child to SIDS. Works with families and health professionals in caring for infants at risk due to heart and respiratory problems.

National Sudden Infant Death Syndrome (SIDS) Resource Center
www.circsol.com/sids
Provides information on SIDS and related topics, including referral services.

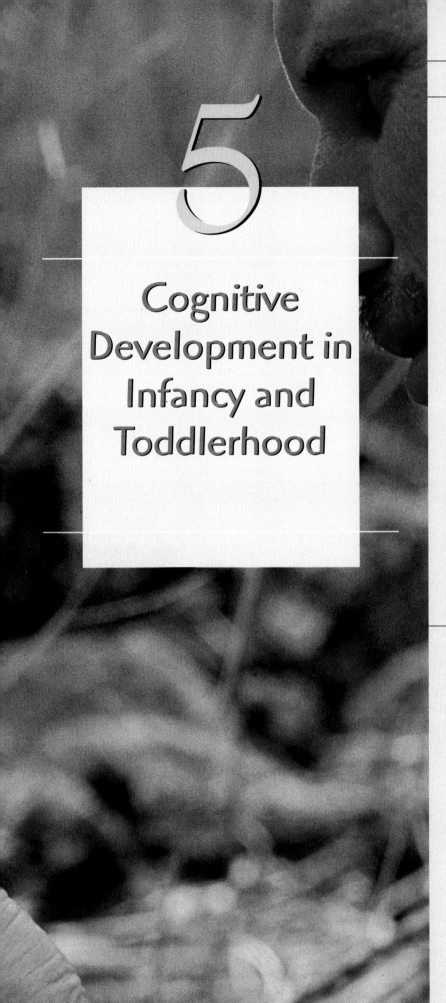

5

Cognitive Development in Infancy and Toddlerhood

■ *Infants' and toddlers' cognition develops rapidly through seeing, hearing, and touching and the sensitive support of caring adults. On an excursion to the seaside, this father and 1-year-old daughter of the Galapagos Islands examine a tortoise's textured shell. (Photo courtesy: Robert W. Madden/National Geographic Image Collection)*

When Byron, Rachel, and April were brought together by their mothers at age 18 months, the room was alive with activity. The three spirited explorers were bent on discovery. Rachel dropped shapes through holes in a plastic box that Beth held and adjusted so the harder ones would fall smoothly into the container. Once a few shapes were inside, Rachel grabbed and shook the box, squealing with delight as the lid fell open and the shapes scattered around her. The clatter attracted Byron, who picked up a shape, carried it to the railing at the top of the basement steps, and dropped it overboard, then followed with a teddy bear, a ball, his shoe, and a spoon. In the meantime, April pulled open a drawer, unloaded a set of wooden bowls, stacked them in a pile, knocked it over, then banged two bowls together.

As the toddlers experimented, I could see the beginnings of language—a whole new way of influencing the world. April was the most vocal of the three youngsters. "All gone baw!" she exclaimed as Byron tossed the bright red ball down the basement steps. "Bye-bye, baw," Rachel chimed in, waving as the ball disappeared from sight. A close look at Rachel revealed that the capacity to represent experience through words and gestures had opened up a new realm of play possibilities. Rachel could pretend. "Night-night," she said as she put her head down and closed her eyes, ever so pleased that in make-believe, she could decide for herself when and where to go to bed.

Over the first 2 years, the small, reflexive newborn baby becomes a self-assertive, purposeful being who solves simple problems and has started to master the most amazing of human abilities—language. "How does all this happen so quickly?" asked Felicia, turning to me. In this chapter, we take up three perspectives on early cognitive development: *Piaget's cognitive-developmental theory, information processing,* and *Vygotsky's sociocultural theory.* We will also consider the usefulness of tests that measure intellectual progress during this earliest phase of development.

Our discussion concludes with the beginnings of language. We will see how toddlers' first words build on early cognitive achievements. Very soon, new words and expressions greatly increase the speed and flexibility of human thinking. Throughout development, cognition and language mutually support one another.

PIAGET'S COGNITIVE-DEVELOPMENTAL THEORY

Swiss theorist Jean Piaget inspired a vision of children as busy, motivated explorers whose thinking develops as they act directly on the environment. According to Piaget, children move through four stages of de-

velopment between infancy and adolescence. The first is the **sensorimotor stage,** which spans the first 2 years of life.

KEY PIAGETIAN CONCEPTS

As the name of this stage implies, Piaget believed that infants and toddlers "think" with their eyes, ears, hands, and other sensorimotor equipment. They cannot yet carry out many activities inside their heads. But by the end of toddlerhood, children can solve practical, everyday problems and represent their experiences in speech, gesture, and play. To understand Piaget's view of how these vast changes take place, let's look at Piaget's ideas about *what changes with development,* and *how cognitive change takes place.*

■ WHAT CHANGES WITH DEVELOPMENT. Piaget believed that *psychological structures*—the child's organized ways of making sense of experience—change with age. He referred to specific structures as **schemes.** At first, schemes are motor action patterns. For example, at 6 months, Byron dropped objects in a fairly rigid way, simply by letting go of a rattle or teething ring and watching with interest. By age 18 months, his "dropping scheme" had become much more deliberate and creative. Byron tossed all sorts of objects down the basement stairs, throwing some up in the air, bouncing others off walls, releasing some gently and others forcefully. Soon Byron's schemes will move from an *action-based level* to a *mental level.* Instead of just acting on objects, he will show evidence of thinking before he acts. This change, as we will see later, marks the transition from sensorimotor to preoperational thought.

■ HOW COGNITIVE CHANGE TAKES PLACE. In Piaget's theory, two processes account for changes in schemes: *adaptation* and *organization.*

Adaptation. The next time you have a chance, notice how infants and toddlers tirelessly repeat actions that lead to interesting effects. **Adaptation** involves building schemes through direct interaction with the environment. It consists of two complementary activities: *assimilation* and *accommodation.* During **assimilation,** we use our current schemes to interpret the external world. For example, when Byron dropped objects, he was assimilating them all into his sensorimotor "dropping scheme." In **accommodation,** we create new schemes or adjust old ones after noticing that our current ways of thinking do not fit the environment completely. When Byron dropped objects in different ways, he modified his dropping scheme to take account of the varied properties of objects.

According to Piaget, the balance between assimilation and accommodation varies over time. When children are not changing very much, they assimilate more than they accommodate. Piaget called this a state of cognitive *equi-*

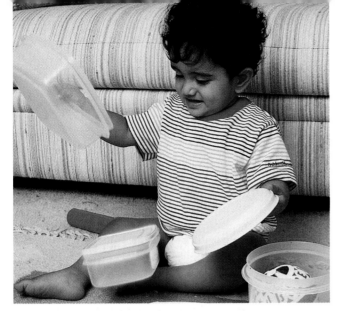

■ *According to Piaget's theory, at first schemes are motor action patterns. As this 1-year-old takes apart, bangs, and drops these containers, he discovers that his movements have predictable effects on objects and that objects influence one another in regular ways. (Photo courtesy: Laura Dwight)*

librium, implying a steady, comfortable condition. During rapid cognitive change, however, children are in a state of *disequilibrium,* or cognitive discomfort. They realize that new information does not match their current schemes, so they shift away from assimilation toward accommodation. Once they have modified their schemes, they move back toward assimilation, exercising their newly changed structures until they are ready to be modified again.

Each time this back-and-forth movement between equilibrium and disequilibrium occurs, more effective schemes are produced (Piaget, 1985). Because the times of greatest accommodation are the earliest ones, the sensorimotor stage is Piaget's most complex period of development.

Organization. Schemes change through a second process called **organization**. It takes place internally, apart from direct contact with the environment. Once children form new schemes, they start to rearrange them, linking them with other schemes to create a strongly interconnected cognitive system. For example, eventually Byron will relate "dropping" to "throwing" and to his developing understanding of "nearness" and "farness." According to Piaget, schemes reach a true state of equilibrium when they become part of a broad network of structures that can be jointly applied to the surrounding world (Piaget, 1936/1952).

THE SENSORIMOTOR STAGE

The difference between the newborn baby and the 2-year-old child is so vast that the sensorimotor stage is divided into six substages. Piaget's observations of his own three children served as the basis for this sequence of development. Although this is a very small sample, Piaget watched carefully and also presented his son and two daughters with everyday problems (such as hidden ob-

jects) that helped reveal their understanding of the world. In the following sections, we will first describe infant development as Piaget saw it. Then we will consider evidence indicating that the cognitive competence of babies is more advanced than Piaget believed it to be.

■ **THE CIRCULAR REACTION.** At the beginning of the sensorimotor stage, infants know so little about the world that they cannot purposefully explore it. The **circular reaction** provides them with a special means for adapting their first schemes. It involves stumbling onto a new experience caused by the baby's own motor activity. The reaction is "circular" because the infant tries to repeat the event again and again. As a result, a sensorimotor response that first occurred by chance becomes strengthened into a new scheme. For example, at age 2 months, Rachel accidentally made a smacking sound after a feeding. The sound was new and intriguing, so she tried to repeat it until, after a few days, she became quite expert at smacking her lips.

During the first 2 years, the circular reaction changes in several ways. At first, it centers around the infant's own body. Later, it turns outward, toward manipulation of objects. Finally, it becomes experimental and creative, aimed at producing novel effects in the environment. Piaget considered these changes in the circular reaction so important that he named the sensorimotor substages after them. As you read about each substage, you may find it helpful to refer to the summary in Table 5.1 on page 150.

■ **SUBSTAGE 1: REFLEXIVE SCHEMES (BIRTH TO 1 MONTH).** Piaget regarded newborn reflexes as the building blocks of sensorimotor intelligence. At first, babies suck, grasp, and look in much the same way, no matter what experiences they encounter (see Figure 5.1). Beth reported an amusing example of Rachel's indiscriminate sucking at age 2 weeks. She lay next to her father while he took a nap. Suddenly, he awoke with a start. Rachel had latched on and begun to suck on his back!

FIGURE 5.1

■ The newborn baby's schemes consist of reflexes, which will gradually be modified as they are applied to the surrounding environment.

TABLE 5.1

Summary of Cognitive Development During the Sensorimotor Stage

SENSORIMOTOR SUBSTAGE	TYPICAL ADAPTIVE BEHAVIORS
1. Reflexive schemes (birth to 1 month)	Newborn reflexes (see Chapter 3, page 106)
2. Primary circular reactions (1–4 months)	Simple motor habits centered around the infant's own body; limited anticipation of events
3. Secondary circular reactions (4–8 months)	Actions aimed at repeating interesting effects in the surrounding world; imitation of familiar behaviors
4. Coordination of secondary circular reactions (8–12 months)	Intentional, or goal-directed, behavior; improved anticipation of events; imitation of behaviors slightly different from those the infant usually performs; ability to find a hidden object in the first location in which it is hidden (object permanence)
5. Tertiary circular reactions (12–18 months)	Exploration of the properties of objects by acting on them in novel ways; imitation of unfamiliar behaviors; ability to search in several locations for a hidden object (AB search)
6. Mental representation (18 months–2 years)	Internal representation of objects and events, as indicated by sudden solutions to sensorimotor problems, ability to find an object that has been moved while out of sight, deferred imitation, and make-believe play

■ SUBSTAGE 2: PRIMARY CIRCULAR REACTIONS—THE FIRST LEARNED ADAPTATIONS (1 TO 4 MONTHS). Infants start to gain voluntary control over their actions by repeating chance behaviors that lead to satisfying results. This leads to some simple motor habits, such as sucking their fists or thumbs and opening and closing their hands (see Figure 5.2). Babies at this substage also start to vary their behavior in response to environmental demands. For example, they open their mouths differently for a nipple than for a spoon. They also begin to anticipate events. For example, at 3 months, when Byron awoke from his nap, he cried out with hunger. But as soon as Lisa entered the room, Byron's crying stopped. He knew that feeding time was near.

Piaget called the first circular reactions *primary*, and he regarded them as quite limited. Notice how, in the examples just given, infants' adaptations are oriented toward their own bodies and motivated by basic needs. According to Piaget, babies are not yet very concerned with the effects of their actions on the external world.

■ SUBSTAGE 3: SECONDARY CIRCULAR REACTIONS—MAKING INTERESTING SIGHTS LAST (4 TO 8 MONTHS). Between 4 and 8 months, infants sit up and become skilled at reaching for, grasping, and manipulating objects. These motor achievements play a major role in turning their attention outward toward the environment. Using the *secondary* circular reaction, infants try to repeat interesting events caused by their own actions. For example, Piaget (1936/1952) tried dangling several dolls in front of his 4-month-old son, Laurent. After accidentally knocking them and producing a fascinating swinging motion, Laurent gradually built the sensorimotor scheme of "hitting" (see Figure 5.3).

Improved control over their own behavior permits infants at this substage to imitate the behavior of others more effectively. However, babies under 8 months imitate only actions they have practiced many times. They cannot adapt flexibly and quickly, copying novel behaviors (Kaye & Marcus, 1981).

FIGURE 5.2

■ At 2 months, Byron sees his hand open and close and tries to repeat this action, in a primary circular reaction.

FIGURE 5.3

■ At 4 months, Piaget's son Laurent accidentally hits a doll hung in front of him. He tries to recapture the interesting effect of the swinging doll. In doing so, he builds a new "hitting scheme" through the secondary circular reaction.

■ SUBSTAGE 4: COORDINATION OF SECONDARY CIR-CULAR REACTIONS (8 TO 12 MONTHS). Now infants start to organize schemes, combining secondary circular reactions into new, more complex action sequences. Two landmark cognitive changes result.

First, babies can engage in **intentional,** or **goal-directed, behavior.** By 8 months, infants have had enough practice with a variety of schemes that they combine them deliberately in solving sensorimotor problems. The clearest example is provided by Piaget's famous object-hiding tasks, in which he shows the baby an attractive toy and then hides it behind his hand or under a cover. Infants at this substage can find the object. In doing so, they coordinate two schemes — "pushing" aside the obstacle and "grasping" the toy. Piaget regarded these action sequences as the first sign that babies appreciate **physical causality** (the causal action one object exerts on another through contact) and as the foundation for all problem solving.

Second, the fact that infants can retrieve hidden objects reveals that they have begun to attain **object permanence,** the understanding that objects continue to exist when out of sight (see Figure 5.4). But awareness of object permanence is not yet complete. If an object is moved from one hiding place (A) to another (B), 8- to 12-month-olds will search for it only in the first hiding place (A). Because babies make this *AB search error,* Piaget concluded that they do not have a clear image of the object as persisting when not in view.

Substage 4 brings additional advances. First, infants are better at anticipating events, so they sometimes use their new capacity for intentional behavior to try to change those events. At 10 months, Byron crawled after Lisa when she put on her coat, whimpering to keep her from leaving. Second, babies can imitate behaviors slightly different from those they usually perform. After watching someone else, they try to stir with a spoon, push a toy car, or drop raisins in a cup. Once again, they draw on their capacity for intentional behavior, purposefully modifying schemes to fit an observed action (Piaget, 1945/1951).

■ SUBSTAGE 5: TERTIARY CIRCULAR REACTIONS—DISCOVERING NEW MEANS THROUGH ACTIVE EXPERIMENTATION (12 TO 18 MONTHS). At this substage, the circular reaction—now called *tertiary*—becomes experimental and creative. Toddlers repeat behaviors *with variation,* provoking new effects. Recall how Byron dropped objects over the basement steps, trying this, then that, and then another action (see Figure 5.5). Because they approach the world in this deliberately exploratory way, 12- to 18-month-olds are far better sensorimotor problem solvers than they were before. For example, Rachel figured out how to fit a shape through a hole in a container by turning and twisting it until it fell through, and she discovered how to use a stick to get toys that were out of reach.

According to Piaget, this new capacity to experiment leads to a more advanced understanding of object permanence. Now toddlers look in several locations to find a hidden toy; they no longer make the AB search error. Their more flexible action patterns also permit them to imitate many more behaviors, such as stacking blocks, scribbling on paper, and making funny faces.

FIGURE 5.5

■ At 18 months, Byron dropped a variety of objects down the basement stairs, throwing some up in the air, bouncing others off the wall, releasing some gently and others forcefully, in a deliberately experimental approach. Byron displayed a tertiary circular reaction.

FIGURE 5.4

■ Around 8 months, infants combine schemes deliberately in the solution of sensorimotor problems. They show the beginnings of object permanence, since they can find an object in the first place in which it is hidden.

■ SUBSTAGE 6: MENTAL REPRESENTATION—INVENTING NEW MEANS THROUGH MENTAL COMBINATIONS (18 MONTHS TO 2 YEARS). Substage 5 is the last truly *sensorimotor* stage, since Substage 6 brings with it the ability to create **mental representations** of reality—internal images of absent objects and past events. As a result, the older toddler can solve problems symbolically instead of by trial-and-error behavior. One sign of this new capacity is that children arrive at solutions to sensorimotor problems suddenly, suggesting that they experiment with actions inside their heads. For example, at 19 months April played with a toy shopping cart for the first time, rolling it over the carpet and into the sofa. She paused for a moment, as if to "think," and then immediately turned the toy in a new direction. Had she been in Substage 5, she would have pushed, pulled, and bumped it in a random fashion until it was free to move again.

With the capacity to represent, toddlers arrive at a more advanced understanding of object permanence—that objects can move or be moved when out of sight. Try this object-hiding task with an 18- to 24-month-old as well as a younger child: Put a small toy inside a box and the box under a cover. Then, while the box is out of sight, dump the toy out and show the toddler the empty box. The Substage 6 child finds the hidden toy easily. Younger toddlers are baffled by this situation.

Mental representation also brings with it the capacity for **deferred imitation**—the ability to remember and copy the behavior of models who are not immediately present. A famous and amusing example is Piaget's daughter Jacqueline's imitation of another child's temper tantrum:

> Jacqueline had a visit from a little boy . . . who, in the course of the afternoon, got into a terrible temper. He screamed as he tried to get out of a playpen and pushed it backwards, stamping his feet. Jacqueline stood watching him in amazement. . . . The next day, she herself screamed in her playpen and tried to move it, stamping her foot lightly several times in succession. (Piaget, 1936/1952, p. 63)

Finally, the emergence of representation leads to a major change in the nature of play. At the end of the sensorimotor stage, children engage in **make-believe play,** in which they act out familiar activities. Like Rachel's pretending to go to sleep at the beginning of this chapter, the toddler's make-believe is very simple (see Figure 5.6). Make-believe expands greatly in early childhood and is so important for psychological development that we will return to it again.

■ RECENT RESEARCH ON SENSORIMOTOR DEVELOPMENT

Many studies show that infants display a wide array of cognitive capacities earlier than Piaget believed. You have already read about some conflicting evidence. Recall the

FIGURE 5.6

■ When Rachel engaged in make-believe by pretending to go to sleep, she created a mental representation of reality. With the capacity for mental representation, the sensorimotor stage draws to a close.

operant conditioning research reviewed in Chapter 4, in which newborns sucked vigorously on a nipple to gain access to interesting sights and sounds. This behavior, which closely resembles Piaget's secondary circular reactions, shows that babies try to explore and control the external world long before 4 to 8 months. In fact, they do so as soon as they are born.

Piaget may have underestimated infant capacities because he did not have the sophisticated experimental techniques that are available today. As we consider recent research on sensorimotor development as well as information processing (covered in a later section), we will see that operant conditioning and the habituation–dishabituation response have been used ingeniously to find out what the young baby knows.

■ REASONING ABOUT THE PHYSICAL WORLD. Piaget concluded that not until 8 to 12 months of age do infants appreciate important regularities of their physical world—that objects continue to exist when out of sight and influence one another in predictable ways. Yet as the following findings reveal, even very young babies are aware of these object characteristics.

Object Permanence. Before 8 months, do infants really believe that an object spirited out of sight no longer exists? In a series of studies in which babies did not have to engage in active search, Renée Baillargeon (1987; Baillargeon & DeVos, 1991) found evidence for object permanence as early as 3½ months of age! One of these studies is illustrated in Figure 5.7.

If 3½-month-olds grasp the idea of object permanence, then what explains Piaget's finding that much older infants (who are quite capable of voluntary reaching) do not try to search for hidden objects? One explanation is that, just as Piaget's theory suggests, young babies cannot yet put together the separate schemes to retrieve a hidden

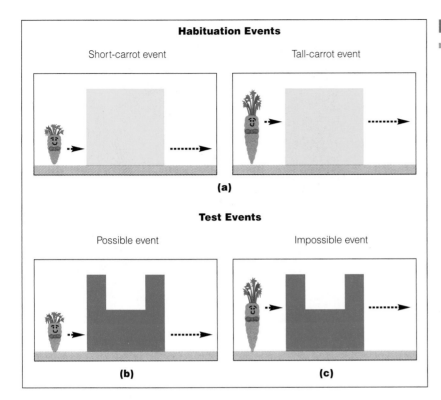

Habituation Events

Short-carrot event   Tall-carrot event

(a)

Test Events

Possible event   Impossible event

(b)   **(c)**

FIGURE 5.7

■ **Testing infants for object permanence using the habituation–dishabituation response.** (a) First, infants were habituated to two events: a short carrot and a tall carrot moving behind a yellow screen, on alternate trials. Next the researchers presented two test events. The color of the screen was changed to help infants notice its window. (b) In the *possible event,* the carrot shorter than the window's lower edge moved behind the blue screen and reappeared on the other side. (c) In the *impossible event,* the carrot taller than the window's lower edge moved behind the screen, did not appear in the window, but then emerged intact on the other side. Infants as young as 3 ½ months dishabituated to (looked longer at) the impossible event, suggesting that they understood object permanence. (Adapted from R. Baillargeon & J. DeVos, 1991, "Object Permanence in Young Infants: Further Evidence," *Child Development,* 62, p. 1230. © The Society for Research in Child Development. Reprinted by permission.)

toy, such as pushing aside the obstacle and grasping the object. In other words, what they *know* about object permanence is not yet *evident* in their searching behavior (Baillargeon et al., 1990). In support of this idea, when researchers simplify the search part of the task by reducing it to one action—permitting babies to reach directly for an object in the dark after a sound signals its location—even 6½-month-olds easily retrieve the object (Goubet & Clifton, 1998).

Once 8- to 12-month-olds actively search for hidden objects, they make the AB search error. Research suggests that one reason they search at A (where they first found the object) instead of B (its most recent location) is that they have trouble inhibiting a previously rewarded response (Diamond, Cruttenden, & Neiderman, 1994). Once again, before 12 months, infants have difficulty integrating object-location knowledge with action. The ability to integrate knowledge with action coincides with rapid development of the frontal lobes of the cerebral cortex at the end of the first year (Bell & Fox, 1992; Nelson, 1995).

Other Aspects of Physical Reasoning. Habituation–dishabituation research reveals that very young infants are aware of many object properties and the rules governing their behavior. For example, 3- to 4-month-olds realize that one solid object cannot move through another solid object. By 6 months, babies are sensitive to the effects of gravity. They look intently when a moving object stops in midair without support (Spelke et al., 1992).

In the next few months, infants extend these understandings to a wider range of circumstances. Between 6 and 7 months, they appreciate the regularities of object support. They realize that an object placed on top of another object will fall unless a large part of its bottom surface contacts the lower object (Baillargeon, 1994a). Babies of this age also know that an object on a sloping surface will roll down, not up (Kim & Spelke, 1992).

A beginning grasp of physical causality is also present quite early. When a moving object (such as a rolling ball) collides with a stationary object, 2½-month-old infants expect the stationary object to be displaced. By age 6 months, infants figure out that a larger moving object can cause the stationary object to travel farther (Baillargeon, 1994b; Kotovsky & Baillargeon, 1998).

In sum, a grasp of basic regularities of the physical world—that objects continue to exist when out of sight, cannot move through the space occupied by other objects, fall without support, and can act with force on one another—is present within the first few months, long before infants have the motor coordination to discover these properties through their own actions. These understandings are gradually refined as infants gain more experience with objects.

■ MENTAL REPRESENTATION. In Piaget's theory, infants lead purely sensorimotor lives; they cannot represent experience until about 18 months of age. Yet new studies of deferred imitation and problem solving reveal that the transition to mental representation takes place earlier.

Deferred Imitation. Piaget studied imitation by noting when his own three children demonstrated it in their everyday behavior. Under these conditions, a great deal must be known about the infant's daily life to be sure that deferred imitation has occurred.

Recent research reveals that deferred imitation, a form of representation, is present at 6 weeks of age! Infants who watched an unfamiliar adult's facial expression imitated the facial gesture when exposed to the passive face of the same adult the next day (Meltzoff & Moore, 1994). Perhaps young babies use this way of imitating to identify and communicate with people they have seen before.

As motor capacities improve, infants start to copy actions with objects. In one study, 6- to 18-month-olds were shown a puppet wearing a mitten with a jingle bell inside it. An adult removed the mitten, shook it, and replaced it on the puppet's hand. As long as these novel behaviors were repeated many times, even 6-month-olds reproduced them a day later (Barr, Dowden, & Hayne, 1996). By 14 months, toddlers use deferred imitation skillfully to enrich their range of sensorimotor schemes. They retain highly unusual modeled behaviors for several months and can imitate across a change in context—for example, by enacting in the home a behavior learned at child care (Hanna & Meltzoff, 1993; Meltzoff, 1994).

At the end of the second year, toddlers can imitate actions an adult *tries* to produce, even if these are not fully realized (Meltzoff, 1995). For example, on one occasion, a mother attempted to pour some raisins into a small bag but missed, spilling them. A moment later, her 18-month-old son began dropping the raisins into the bag, indicating that he had begun to infer others' intentions and perspectives. This advance permits young children to better understand and predict others' activities.

Problem Solving. Infants' representational skills permit more effective problem solving than Piaget's substages sug-

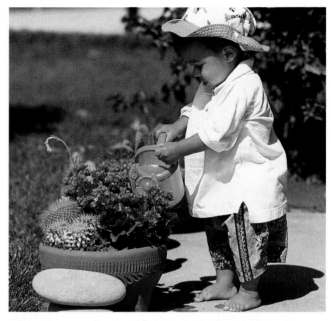

■ *Deferred imitation greatly enriches young children's adaptations to their surrounding world. This toddler probably watched an adult watering flowers. Later, he imitates the behavior, having learned through observation what the sprinkling can is for. (Photo courtesy: © Esiban/Anderson/The Image Works)*

gest. By 10 to 12 months, they can *solve problems by analogy*—take a strategy from one problem and apply it to other relevant problems. In one study, babies were given three similar problems, each requiring them to overcome a barrier, grasp a string, and pull it to get an attractive toy. The

(a)   (b)   (c)

FIGURE 5.8

■ **Analogical problem solving by 10- to 12-month-olds.** After the parent demonstrated the solution to problem (a), infants solved (b) and (c) more readily, even though those problems differed in all aspects of their specific features. (From Z. Chen, R. P. Sanchez, & T. Campbell, 1997, "From Beyond to Within Their Grasp: The Rudiments of Analogical Problem Solving in 10- to 13-month-olds." *Developmental Psychology*, 33, p. 792. Copyright © 1997 by the American Psychological Association. Reprinted by permission of the publisher and author.)

problems differed in all aspects of their specific features (see Figure 5.8). On the first problem, the parent demonstrated the solution and encouraged the infant to imitate. Babies obtained the toy more readily on each additional problem, indicating that they had formed a flexible representation of the solution that they applied in appropriate situations (Chen, Sanchez, & Campbell, 1997).

With age, children become better at reasoning by analogy, applying relevant strategies across increasingly dissimilar situations (Goswami, 1996). But even in the first year, infants have some ability to move beyond trial-and-error experimentation, represent a solution mentally, and use it in new contexts.

EVALUATION OF THE SENSORIMOTOR STAGE

Table 5.2 summarizes the remarkable cognitive attainments we have just considered. Compare this table with the description of Piaget's sensorimotor substages on page 150. On the one hand, infants anticipate events, actively search for hidden objects, flexibly vary their sensorimotor schemes, and engage in make-believe play within Piaget's time frame. Yet on the other hand, many other capacities—among them, secondary circular reactions, understanding of object properties (including permanence and physical causality), deferred imitation, and problem solving using mental representation (analogy)—emerge much earlier than Piaget expected.

Disagreements between Piaget's observations and those of recent research raise controversial questions about how early development takes place. Consistent with Piaget's ideas, infants construct some aspects of experience through motor activity. For example, in Chapter 4, we saw that babies who are experienced crawlers are better at find-

ing hidden objects and perceiving depth on the visual cliff. But infants also comprehend a great deal before they are capable of the motor behaviors Piaget assumed led to those understandings. Perhaps the beginnings of some schemes (such as imitation and a basic appreciation of the properties of objects) are wired into the brain from the start, enabling babies to acquire certain types of knowledge quickly (Haith & Benson, 1998; Spelke & Newport, 1998). And many schemes may be constructed through perceptual learning—by looking and listening—rather than through acting directly on the world (Baillargeon, 1995, 1998).

Finally, infants do not develop in the neat, stepwise fashion implied by Piaget's theory, in which a variety of skills change together and abruptly at each new substage. Instead, a baby is likely to be at one level of progress on imitation and quite another on object permanence, depending on the complexity of the task and the child's rate of biological maturation and specific experiences (Rast & Meltzoff, 1995). These ideas—that adultlike capacities are present during infancy in primitive form, that cognitive development is gradual and continuous, and that it is uneven because of the challenges of different types of tasks and children's varying exposure to them—serve as the basis for a major competing approach to cognitive development: information processing, which we take up next.

But before we turn to this alternative point of view, let's conclude our discussion of the sensorimotor stage by recognizing Piaget's enormous contributions. His work inspired a wealth of new research on infant cognition, including studies that eventually challenged his ideas. In addition, his observations have been of great practical value. Teachers and caregivers continue to look to the sensorimotor stage for guidelines on how to create developmentally appropriate environments for infants and toddlers, an issue we take up later in this chapter.

TABLE 5.2

Some Cognitive Attainments of Infancy and Toddlerhood

AGE	COGNITIVE ATTAINMENTS
Birth–1 month	Secondary circular reactions using limited motor skills, such as sucking a nipple to gain access to interesting sights and sounds
1–4 months	Awareness of many object properties and the rules governing their behavior, including object permanence, object solidity, gravity, and physical causality; deferred imitation of an adult's facial expression over a short delay
4–8 months	Improved understanding of object solidity, gravity, object support, and physical causality; deferred imitation of an adult's novel actions on objects over a short delay
8–12 months	Ability to solve sensorimotor problems by analogy to a previous similar problem
12–18 months	Deferred imitation of an adult's novel actions on objects over a long delay (several months) and across a change in context (from child care to home)
18 months–2 years	Deferred imitation of actions an adult tries to produce, even if these are not fully realized, indicating a beginning capacity to infer others' intentions and perspectives

Note: Which of the capacities listed in the table indicate that mental representation emerges earlier than predicted by Piaget's sensorimotor substages?

ASK YOURSELF . . .

■ *At 14 months, Tony pushed his toy bunny through the slats of his crib onto a nearby table. Using his "pulling scheme," he tried to retrieve it, but it would not fit back through the slats. Next Tony tried jerking, turning, and throwing the bunny. What kind of circular reaction is Tony demonstrating? How would Tony have approached this problem a few months earlier?*

■ *Mimi banged her rattle again and again on the tray of her high chair. Then she dropped the rattle, which fell out of sight on her lap, but Mimi did not try to retrieve it. Which sensorimotor substage is Mimi in? Why do you think so?*

🌳 *Three-year-old Katie solved an "animal" puzzle by matching the shape of each animal to the shape of the empty space on the puzzle board. Next, she tried a "vehicle" puzzle. "I know! Just match the shapes," she exclaimed and quickly solved the new puzzle. Does Katie's problem-solving strategy have roots in infancy? Explain.*

INFORMATION PROCESSING

Information-processing theorists agree with Piaget that children are active, inquiring beings, but they do not provide a single, unified theory of cognitive development. Instead, they investigate different aspects of thinking, from attention, memory, and categorization skills to complex problem solving.

Recall that the information-processing approach relies on computerlike flowcharts to describe the human cognitive system. The computer model of human thinking is very attractive because it is explicit and precise. Information-processing researchers find it useful because they are not satisfied with global concepts, such as assimilation and accommodation, to describe how children think. Instead, they want to know exactly what individuals of different ages do when faced with a task or problem (Klahr & MacWhinney, 1998; Siegler, 1998).

THE STRUCTURE OF THE INFORMATION-PROCESSING SYSTEM

Most general models of the human information-processing system divide the mind into three basic parts: *the sensory register; working, or short-term, memory; and long-term memory* (see Figure 5.9). As information flows through each, we can operate on and transform it using **mental strategies,** increasing the efficiency of thinking and the chances that we will retain information for later use. To understand this more clearly, let's take a brief look at each aspect of the mental system.

First, information enters the **sensory register,** where it is represented directly and very briefly. However, by using mental strategies, we can preserve selected sights and sounds. For example, you can *attend to* some information more carefully than others, increasing the chances that it will transfer to the next step of the information-processing system.

The second part of the mind is **working,** or **short-term, memory.** This is the conscious part of our mental system, where we actively "work" on a limited amount of information. For example, if you are studying this book effectively, you are constantly applying mental strategies. Perhaps you

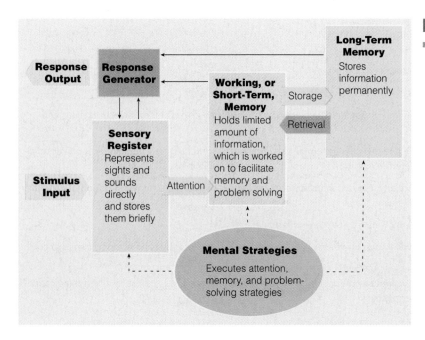

FIGURE 5.9

■ **Structure of the human information processing system.** Information flows through three parts of the mental system: the sensory register; working, or short-term, memory; and long-term memory. In each, mental strategies can be used to manipulate information, increasing the efficiency of thinking and the chances that information will be retained. Strategies also permit us to think flexibly, adapting information to changing circumstances.

are taking notes, repeating information to yourself, or grouping pieces of information together—a strategy much like Piaget's notion of organization. Organization is an especially effective way to remember the many new concepts flowing into your working memory at the moment. If you permit information to remain disconnected, you can hold very little in working memory at once, since you must focus on each item separately. But organize it, and you will not just improve your memory. You will increase the chances that information will be transferred to the third, and largest, storage area.

Long-term memory is our permanent knowledge base. Its capacity is limitless. In fact, we store so much in long-term memory that we sometimes have problems with *retrieval,* or getting information back from the system. To aid retrieval, we apply strategies, just as we do in working memory. Think about how information in your long-term memory is arranged. It is *categorized* according to a master plan based on contents, much like a library shelving system based on the contents of books. As a result, it can be retrieved quite easily by following the same network of associations used to store it in the first place.

Information-processing researchers believe that the basic structure of the mental system is similar throughout life. However, the *capacity* of the system—the amount of information that can be retained and processed at once and the speed with which it can be processed—increases, making possible more complex forms of thinking with age (Case, 1992; Miller & Vernon, 1997). Although gains in information-processing capacity are partly due to brain development, they are largely the result of improvements in strategies, such as attending to information and categorizing it effectively. The development of these strategies is already under way in the first 2 years of life.

ATTENTION

How does attention develop in early infancy? Recall from our discussion of perceptual development in Chapter 4 that between 1 and 2 months of age, infants shift from attending to a single high-contrast feature of their visual world to exploring objects and patterns more thoroughly. Besides attending to more aspects of the environment, infants gradually become more efficient at managing their attention, taking in information more quickly with age. Habituation–dishabituation research reveals that preterm and newborn babies require a long time to habituate and dishabituate to novel visual stimuli—about 3 or 4 minutes. But by 4 or 5 months, infants require as little as 5 to 10 seconds to take in a complex visual stimulus and recognize that it is different from a previous one (Slater et al., 1996).

Throughout the first year, infants attend to novel and eye-catching events. With the transition to toddlerhood, children become more capable of intentional behavior (refer back to Piaget's Substage 4). Consequently, attraction to novelty declines (but does not disappear) and *sustained attention* improves, especially when children play with toys. When a toddler can plan a play activity in even a limited way, such as stacking blocks or putting them in a container, attention must be maintained to reach the goal. As plans and activities become more complex, so does the duration of attention (Ruff & Lawson, 1990; Ruff & Rothbart, 1996).

MEMORY

Habituation also provides a window into infant memory. For example, infants can be exposed to a stimulus until they habituate. Then they can be shown the same stimulus at a later time. If they habituate more rapidly on the second occasion, this indicates that they recognize they have seen the stimulus before. Using this method, studies show that by 3 months infants remember a visual stimulus for 24 hours. By the end of the first year, they remember it for several days and, in the case of some stimuli (such as a photo of the human face), a few weeks (Fagan, 1973; Martin, 1975).

At this point, let's note that the habituation response tells us about infants' memory in the strange context of the laboratory, but it underestimates their ability to remember real-world events they can actively control. Using operant conditioning, Carolyn Rovee-Collier studied infant memory in a familiar setting—at home while babies lay in their cribs. First, 2- to 3-month-olds were taught how to move a mobile by kicking a foot tied to it with a long cord. When the infants were reattached to the mobile after a week's delay, they kicked vigorously, showing that indeed they remembered. And as long as they were reminded of the mobile's dancing motion (the experimenter briefly rotated it for the baby), infants started kicking again up to 4 weeks after they were first trained (Rovee-Collier & Bhatt, 1993; Rovee-Collier, 1999). Much like older children and adults, babies seem to remember best when experiences take place in familiar contexts and when they participate actively.

So far, we have discussed only **recognition,** the simplest form of memory because all babies have to do is indicate (by looking or kicking) whether a new stimulus is identical or similar to one previously experienced. **Recall** is more challenging, since it involves remembering something not present. Can infants engage in recall? By the middle of the first year, they can. Felicia reported that one day when her husband telephoned, 7-month-old April listened to him speak through the receiver and immediately crawled to the front door. April seemed to be *recalling* times when she had heard her father's muffled voice as he was about to arrive home from work (Ashmead & Perlmutter, 1980).

By toddlerhood, recall for people, places, and objects is excellent (Bauer, 1996). Think back to findings on deferred imitation, which show that 14-month-olds recall and reproduce highly unusual behaviors several months after having observed them. Yet a puzzling finding is that as adults, we no longer recall our earliest experiences. The Lifespan Vista box on the following page helps explain why.

CATEGORIZATION

As infants gradually remember more information, they seem to store it in a remarkably orderly fashion. Some creative variations of the operant conditioning research described earlier have been used to find out about infant categorization (see Figure 5.10). In fact, young babies categorize stimuli on the basis of shape, size, number (up to three elements), and other physical properties at such an early age that categorization is among the strongest evidence that babies' brains are set up from the start to structure experience in adultlike ways (Mandler, 1998).

The habituation–dishabituation response has also been used to study infant categorization. Researchers show babies a series of stimuli belonging to one category and then see whether they dishabituate to a picture that is not a member of the category. Findings reveal that 7- to 12-month-olds structure objects into an impressive array of adultlike categories—food items, furniture, birds, animals, vehicles, kitchen utensils, and more (Mandler & McDonough, 1993, 1996, 1998; Oakes, Coppage, & Dingel, 1997). Besides organizing the physical world, infants of this age categorize their emotional and social worlds. They sort people and their voices by gender and age (Bahrick, Netto, & Hernandez-Reif, 1998; Poulin-DuBois et al., 1994), have begun to distinguish emotional expressions, and can separate the natural movements of people from other motions (see Chapter 4, pages 140–141).

The earliest categories are *perceptual*—based on similar overall appearance or prominent object part, such as legs for animals and wheels for vehicles (Rakison & Butterworth, 1998). But by the end of the first year, categories are becoming *conceptual*—based on common function and behavior. For example, 1-year-olds group together kitchen utensils because each is used to prepare food for eating.

In the second year, children become active categorizers during their play. Try giving a toddler a set of objects that differ in shape and color (such as small blocks). See if the child spontaneously categorizes them. Research shows that around 12 months, toddlers merely touch objects that belong together, without grouping them. A little later, they form single categories. For example, when given four balls and four boxes, a 16-month-old will put all the balls together but not the boxes. And finally, around 18 months, toddlers can sort objects into two classes (Gopnik & Meltzoff, 1987).

Compared with looking behaviors studied in habituation–dishabituation research, touching, sorting, and other play behaviors are better at revealing the meaning infants attach to categories, since they are applying those meanings in their everyday activities. For example, after having

FIGURE 5.10

■ **Investigating infant categorization using operant conditioning.** Three-month-olds were taught to kick to move a mobile that was made of small blocks, all with the letter A on them. After a delay, kicking returned to a high level only if the babies were shown a mobile whose elements were labeled with the same form (the letter A). If the form was changed (from As to 2s), infants no longer kicked vigorously. While making the mobile move, the babies had grouped together its features. They associated the kicking response with the category A and, at later testing, distinguished it from the category 2 (Bhatt, Rovee-Collier, & Weiner, 1994; Hayne, Rovee-Collier, & Perris, 1987).

watched an adult give a toy dog a drink from a cup, 14-month-olds shown a rabbit and a motorcycle usually offer the drink only to the rabbit (Mandler & McDonough, 1998). Their behavior reveals a clear understanding that certain actions are more appropriate for some categories of items (animals) than for others (vehicles).

EVALUATION OF INFORMATION-PROCESSING FINDINGS

Information-processing research underscores the *continuity* of human thinking from infancy into adult life. In attending to the environment, remembering everyday events, and categorizing objects, Byron, Rachel, and April think in ways that are remarkably similar to our own, even though they are far from being the proficient mental processors we are. Findings on infant memory and categorization join with other research in challenging Piaget's view of early cognitive development. If 3-month-olds can remember events for as long as 4 weeks and categorize stimuli, then they must have some ability to represent their experiences mentally.

Information processing has contributed greatly to our view of young babies as sophisticated cognitive beings. Still,

A LIFESPAN VISTA

INFANTILE AMNESIA

If toddlers remember many aspects of their everyday lives, then what explains infantile amnesia—the fact that practically none of us can retrieve events that happened to us before age 3? Forgetting cannot be due to the passage of time, since we can recall many events that happened long ago. At present, there are several explanations of infantile amnesia.

One possibility is that brain development during early childhood accounts for it. Growth of the frontal lobes of the cortex along with other structures may be necessary before experiences can be stored in ways that permit them to be retrieved many years later (Boyer & Diamond, 1992). Consistent with this view, some researchers believe that two levels of memory exist: one operates unconsciously and automatically, whereas the other is conscious, intentional, and verbal (Newcombe & Fox, 1994).

Yet the idea of vastly different approaches to remembering in younger and older individuals has been questioned, since even toddlers can describe memories verbally and retain them for extensive periods. A growing number of researchers believe that rather than a radical change in the way experience is represented, the offset of infantile amnesia requires the emergence of a special form of recall—**autobiographical memory,** or memories of special, one-time events that are long lasting because they are imbued with personal meaning. For example, perhaps you recall the day a sibling was born, the first time you took an airplane, or a move to a new house.

For memories to become autobiographical, two developments are necessary. First, the child must have a well-developed image of the self. In the first few years, the sense of self is not yet mature enough to serve as an anchor for one-time events (Howe & Courage, 1997). Second, autobiographical memory requires that children integrate personal experiences into a meaningful life story. Recent evidence reveals that preschoolers learn to structure memories in narrative form by talking about them with adults, who expand on their recollections by explaining what happened when, where, and with whom (Nelson, 1993).

The complexity of parents' conversations about the past increases as their preschoolers' conversational skills improve. Parents who ask many, varied questions; add information to children's statements; and volunteer their own thoughts and feelings about events have children who recall past experiences in a more organized, detailed fashion (Haden, Hayne, & Fivush, 1997; Harley & Reese, 1999).

Interestingly, girls are more advanced than boys in the development of autobiographical memory. And Western children produce more elaborate autobiographical narratives than do Asian children. These differences fit with variations in parent–child conversation. Parents talk about the past in more detail with daughters (Reese, Haden & Fivush, 1996). And collectivist cultural values lead Asian parents to discourage children from talking about themselves (Han, Leichtman, & Wang, 1998). Perhaps because their early experiences were integrated into more coherent narratives, women report an earlier age of first memory and more vivid early memories than do men. Similarly, first memories of Caucasian-American adults are, on the average, 6 months earlier than those of Asians (Mullen, 1994).

■ When he gets older, this toddler won't recall the exciting party that took place on his second birthday. According to recent evidence, the offset of infantile amnesia after age 3 is due to the emergence of autobiographical memory. For this special form of recall to develop, young children must have the language skills to talk about personal experiences and, with the assistance of adults, integrate those memories into a meaningful life story. (Photo courtesy: Jeff Greenberg/Index Stock)

its greatest drawback stems from its central strength: By analyzing cognition into its components (such as perception, attention, and memory), information processing has had difficulty putting all these pieces back together into a broad, comprehensive theory. For this reason, many experts resist abandoning Piaget's ideas in favor of it (Case, 1998; Halford, 1993). But by drawing on the strengths of both perspectives, the field of human development may be moving closer to new, more powerful views of how the mind develops.

THE SOCIAL CONTEXT OF EARLY COGNITIVE DEVELOPMENT

Take a moment to review the short episode at the beginning of this chapter in which Rachel dropped shapes into a container. Notice how Rachel actively explored the toy, but she learned about it with her mother's help. With Beth's support, Rachel will gradually become better at matching shapes to openings and dropping them into the container. Then she will be able to do the activity (and others like it) on her own.

Vygotsky's sociocultural theory has brought researchers to the realization that children live in rich social contexts that affect the way their cognitive world is structured (Rogoff, 1998; Wertsch & Tulviste, 1992). Vygotsky (1930–1935/ 1978) believed that complex mental activities, such as voluntary attention, deliberate memory, and problem solving, have their origins in social interaction. Through joint activities with more mature members of their society, children come to master activities and think in ways that have meaning in their culture.

A special Vygotskian concept, the **zone of proximal** (or potential) **development,** explains how this happens. It refers to a range of tasks that the child cannot yet handle alone but can do with the help of more skilled partners. To understand this idea, think of a sensitive teacher or parent (such as Beth) who introduces a child to a new activity. The adult picks a task that the child can master but one challenging enough that the child cannot do it by herself. Or the adult capitalizes on an activity that the child has chosen. Such a task is especially suited for fostering development. Then the adult guides and supports, breaking the task into manageable units and calling the child's attention to specific features. By joining in the interaction, the child picks up mental strategies, and her competence increases. As this happens, the adult steps back, permitting the child to take over more responsibility for the task.

As we will see in Chapters 7 and 9, Vygotsky's ideas have been applied mostly at older ages, when children are more skilled in language and social communication. But recently, Vygotsky's theory has been extended to infancy and toddlerhood. Recall that babies are equipped with capacities that ensure that caregivers will interact with them.

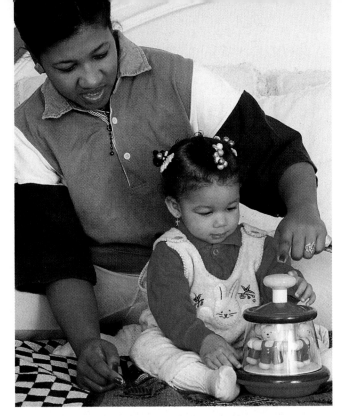

■ *This mother assists her toddler in making a musical top work through gestures and simple words. By presenting a task within the child's zone of proximal development and fine-tuning her support to the child's needs, the mother promotes her daughter's cognitive development. (Photo courtesy: © 2000 Laura Dwight)*

Then adults adjust the environment and their communication in ways that promote learning.

A study by Barbara Rogoff and her collaborators (1984) illustrates this process. The researchers watched how several adults played with Rogoff's son and daughter over the first 2 years, while a jack-in-the-box toy was nearby. In the early months, adults tried to focus the baby's attention by showing the toy and, as the bunny popped out, saying something like "My, what happened?" By the end of the first year (when the baby's cognitive and motor skills had improved), interaction centered on how to use the jack-in-the-box. When the infant reached for the toy, adults guided the baby's hand in turning the crank and putting the bunny back in the box. During the second year, adults helped from a distance. They used verbal instructions and gestures, such as rotating a hand in a turning motion near the crank. Research suggests that this fine-tuned support is related to advanced play, language, and problem solving during the second year (Bornstein et al., 1992; Tamis-LeMonda & Bornstein, 1989).

By emphasizing that many aspects of cognitive development are socially mediated, Vygotsky adds a new dimension to theories discussed earlier in this chapter. In the Variations box on the following page, you will find further evidence for this idea. And we will see even more in the next section, as we look at individual differences in mental development during the first 2 years.

VARIATIONS/CULTURE

CAREGIVER–TODDLER INTERACTION AND EARLY MAKE-BELIEVE PLAY

One of my husband Ken's activities with our two sons when they were young was to bake pineapple upside-down cake, a favorite treat. One Sunday afternoon when a cake was in the making, 21-month-old Peter stood on a chair at the kitchen sink, busily pouring water from one cup to another.

"He's in the way, Dad!" complained 4-year-old David, trying to pull Peter away from the sink.

"Maybe if we let him help, he'll give us room," Ken suggested. As David stirred the batter, Ken poured some into a small bowl for Peter, moved his chair to the side of the sink, and handed him a spoon.

"Here's how you do it, Petey," instructed David, with an air of superiority. Peter watched as David stirred, then tried to copy his motion. When it was time to pour the batter, Ken helped Peter hold and tip the small bowl.

"Time to bake it," said Ken.

"Bake it, bake it," repeated Peter, as he watched Ken slip the pan into the oven.

Several hours later, we observed one of Peter's earliest instances of make-believe play. He got his pail from the sandbox, filled it with sand, carried it into the kitchen, and put it down on the floor in front of the oven. "Bake it, bake it," Peter called to Ken. Together, father and son lifted the pretend cake inside the oven.

Until recently, most researchers studied make-believe play apart from the social environment in which it occurs, while children played alone. Probably for this reason, Piaget and his followers concluded that toddlers discover make-believe independently, as soon as they are capable of representational schemes. Vygotsky's theory has challenged this view. He believed that

society provides children with opportunities to represent culturally meaningful activities in play. Make-believe, like other complex mental activities, is first learned under the guidance of experts (Berk, 1994). In the example just described, Peter's capacity to represent daily events was extended when Ken drew him into the baking task and helped him act it out in play.

New evidence supports the idea that early make-believe is the combined result of children's readiness to engage in it and social experiences that promote it. In one observational study of middle-SES American toddlers, 75 to 80 percent of make-believe involved mother–child interaction (Haight & Miller, 1993). At 12 months, make-believe was fairly one-sided; almost all play episodes were initiated by mothers. By the end of the second year, mothers and children displayed mutual interest in getting make-believe started; half of pretend episodes were initiated by each.

When adults participate, toddlers' make-believe is more elaborate and advanced (O'Reilly & Bornstein, 1993). For example, play themes are more varied. And toddlers are more likely to combine schemes into complex sequences, as Peter did when he put sand in the bucket ("making the batter"), carried it into the kitchen, and (with Ken's help) put it in the oven ("baking the cake"). The more mothers pretend with their toddlers, the more time their children devote to make-believe. And in certain collectivist societies, such as Argentina and Japan, mother–toddler other-directed pretending, as in feeding or putting a doll to sleep, is particularly frequent and rich in maternal expressions of affection and praise (Bornstein et al., 1999a).

In some cultures, adults do not spend much time playing with young

■ *In Mexico, where sibling caregiving is common, make-believe play is more frequent as well as complex with older siblings than with mothers. This 5-year-old provides rich, challenging stimulation to her younger sister within a pretend-play scene. (Photo courtesy: Karen Halverson/Omni-Photo Communications)*

children. Instead, older siblings take over this function. For example, in Indonesia and Mexico, where extended family households and sibling caregiving are common, make-believe is more frequent as well as complex with older siblings than with mothers. As early as 3 to 4 years of age, children provide rich, challenging stimulation to their younger brothers and sisters. The fantasy play of these toddlers is just as well developed as that of their middle-SES American counterparts (Farver, 1993; Farver & Wimbarti, 1995).

As we will see in Chapter 7, make-believe is a major means through which children extend their cognitive skills and learn about important activities in their culture. Vygotsky's theory, and the findings that support it, tell us that providing a stimulating physical environment is not enough to promote early cognitive development. In addition, toddlers must be invited and encouraged by more skilled members of their culture to participate actively in the social world around them.

■ *Rachel played with toys in a more intentional, goal-directed way as a toddler than as an infant. What impact is Rachel's more advanced toy play likely to have on the development of attention?*

■ *At age 18 months, Byron's father stood behind him, helping him throw a large rubber ball into a box. When Byron showed he could throw the ball, his father stepped back and let him try on his own. Using Vygotsky's ideas, explain how Byron's father is supporting his cognitive development.*

🌳 *Which theory of cognitive development can best explain how culturally relevant skills are passed from one generation to the next? Explain.*

INDIVIDUAL DIFFERENCES IN EARLY MENTAL DEVELOPMENT

As he neared age 2, Byron had only a handful of words in his vocabulary, played in a less mature way than Rachel and April, and seemed restless and overactive. Worried about Byron's progress, Lisa decided to take him to a psychological clinic, where he was given one of many tests available for assessing the mental development of infants and toddlers.

The testing approach is very different from the cognitive theories we have just discussed, which try to explain the *process* of development—how children's thinking changes over time. In contrast, designers of mental tests are much more concerned with cognitive *products*. They seek to measure behaviors that reflect mental development and arrive at scores that *predict* future performance, such as later intelligence, school achievement, and adult vocational success. This concern with prediction arose nearly a century ago, when French psychologist Alfred Binet designed the first successful intelligence test, which predicted school achievement. It inspired the design of many new tests, including ones that measure intelligence at very early ages.

INFANT INTELLIGENCE TESTS

Accurately measuring the intelligence of infants is a challenge. Babies cannot answer questions or follow directions. All we can do is present them with stimuli, coax them to respond, and observe their behavior. As a result, most infant tests consist of perceptual and motor responses along with some tasks that tap early language and problem solving. One commonly used test is the *Bayley Scales of Infant Development,* for children between 1 month

and 3½ years. It is made up of two scales: (1) the Mental Scale, which includes such items as turning to a sound, looking for a fallen object, building a tower of cubes, and naming pictures; and (2) the Motor Scale, which assesses gross and fine motor skills, such as grasping, sitting, drinking from a cup, and jumping (Bayley, 1993).

■ COMPUTING INTELLIGENCE TEST SCORES. Intelligence tests for infants, children, and adults are scored in much the same way. When a test is constructed, it is given to a large, representative sample of individuals. Performances of people at each age level form a *normal* or *bell-shaped curve* in which most scores fall near the center (the mean or average) and progressively fewer fall out toward the extremes. On the basis of this distribution, the test designer computes *norms,* or standards against which future test takers can be compared. For example, if Byron does better than 50 percent of his agemates, his score will be 100, an average test score. If he exceeds most children his age, his score will be much higher. If he does better than only a small percentage of 2-year-olds, his score will be much lower.

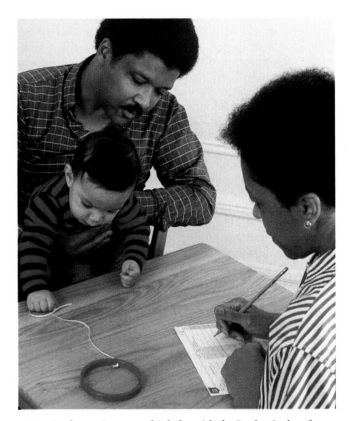

■ *A trained examiner tests this baby with the Bayley Scales of Infant Development while his father holds him and looks on. The perceptual and motor items on most infant tests are quite different from the tasks given to older children, which emphasize verbal, conceptual, and problem-solving skills. For normally developing children, infant tests predict later intelligence poorly. (Photo courtesy: Laura Dwight/PhotoEdit)*

TABLE 5.3

Meaning of Different IQ Scores

SCORE	PERCENTILE RANK CHILD DOES BETTER THAN . . . PERCENT OF SAME-AGE CHILDREN	
70	2	
85	16	
100 (average IQ)	50	
115	84	
130	98	

Scores computed in this way are called **intelligence quotients,** or **IQs,** a term you have undoubtedly heard before. Table 5.3 describes the meaning of a range of IQ scores. Notice how the IQ offers a way of finding out whether an individual is ahead, behind, or on time (average) in mental development in relation to others of the same age. The great majority of individuals (96 percent) have IQs between 70 and 130. Only a very few achieve higher or lower scores.

■ PREDICTING LATER PERFORMANCE FROM INFANT TESTS. Many people assume, incorrectly, that IQ is a measure of inborn ability that does not change with age. Despite careful construction, many infant tests predict later intelligence poorly. Longitudinal research reveals that the majority of children show substantial IQ fluctuations between toddlerhood and adolescence—in most cases, 10 to 20 points and sometimes much more (McCall, 1993).

Because infants and toddlers are especially likely to become distracted, fatigued, or bored during testing, their scores often do not reflect their true abilities. In addition, the perceptual and motor items on infant tests are quite different from the tasks given to older children, which emphasize verbal, conceptual, and problem-solving skills. Because of concerns that infant test scores do not tap the same dimensions of intelligence measured at older ages, they are conservatively labeled **developmental quotients,** or **DQs,** rather than IQs.

It is important to note that infant tests do show somewhat better long-term prediction for extremely low-scoring babies. Today, infant tests are largely used for *screening*—helping to identify babies whose very low scores mean that they are likely to have developmental problems in the future (Kopp, 1994).

Because infant tests do not predict later IQ for most children, researchers have turned to information processing for new ways to assess early mental functioning. Their findings show that speed of habituation and dishabituation to visual stimuli are the best available infant predictors of intelligence from early childhood into adolescence (McCall & Carriger, 1993; Sigman, Cohen, & Beckwith, 1997). The habituation–dishabituation response may be a more effective predictor of later IQ than traditional infant tests because it assesses quickness of thinking, a characteristic of bright individuals. It also taps basic cognitive processes—attention, memory, and response to novelty—that underlie intelligent behavior at all ages (Colombo, 1995; Rose & Feldman, 1997).

Piagetian object permanence tasks also predict later IQ more effectively than traditional infant measures, perhaps because they, too, reflect a basic intellectual process—problem solving (Wachs, 1975). The consistency of these findings prompted designers of the most recent edition of the Bayley test to include several items that tap higher-order skills, such as preference for novel stimuli, ability to find hidden objects, and categorization.

EARLY ENVIRONMENT AND MENTAL DEVELOPMENT

In Chapter 2, we indicated that intelligence is a complex blend of hereditary and environmental influences. Many studies have examined the relationship of environmental factors to infant and toddler mental test scores. As we consider this evidence, you will encounter findings that highlight the role of genetic factors as well.

■ HOME ENVIRONMENT. From what you have learned so far, what aspects of young children's home experiences would you expect to influence early mental development? The **Home Observation for Measurement of the Environment (HOME)** is a checklist for gathering information about the quality of children's home lives through observation and parental interview (Caldwell & Bradley, 1994). The Caregiving Concerns table on page 164 lists factors measured by HOME during the first 3 years. Each is positively related to toddlers' mental test performance. Also, high HOME scores are associated with IQ gains between 1 and 3 years of age, whereas low HOME scores predict declines as large as 15 to 20 points (Bradley et al., 1989).

An organized, stimulating physical setting and parental encouragement, involvement, and affection repeatedly predict infant and early childhood IQ, regardless of SES and ethnicity (Bradley et al., 1989; Klebanov et al., 1998). The extent to which parents talk to infants and toddlers is particularly important. As the final section of this chapter will reveal, it contributes strongly to early language progress. Language progress, in turn, predicts intelligence and academic achievement in elementary school (Hart & Risley, 1995).

Home Observation for Measurement of the Environment (HOME): Infancy and Toddler Subscales

SUBSCALE	SAMPLE ITEM
Emotional and verbal responsiveness of the parent	Parent caresses or kisses child at least once during observer's visit.
Acceptance of the child	Parent does not interfere with child's actions or restrict child's movements more than three times during observer's visit.
Organization of the physical environment	Child's play environment appears safe and free of hazards.
Provision of appropriate play materials	Parent provides toys or interesting activities for child during observer's visit.
Parental involvement with the child	Parent tends to keep child within visual range and to look at child often during observer's visit.
Variety in daily stimulation	Child eats at least one meal per day with mother or father, according to parental report.

Source: Elardo & Bradley, 1981.

In the research just mentioned all the children were reared by their biological parents, with whom they share not just a common environment but also a common heredity. Parents who are genetically more intelligent might provide better experiences as well as give birth to genetically brighter children, who also evoke more stimulation from their parents. Note that this hypothesis refers to *genetic–environmental correlation* (see Chapter 2, page 74), and there is evidence to support it (Cherney, 1994). Yet heredity does not account for all of the association between home environment and mental test scores. Family living conditions continue to predict children's IQ beyond the contribution of parental IQ (Luster & Dubow, 1992; Sameroff et al., 1993). In one study, infants and children growing up in less crowded homes had parents who were far more verbally responsive to them—a major contributor (as noted earlier) to language, intellectual, and academic progress (Evans, Maxwell, & Hart, 1999).

Can the research summarized so far help us understand Lisa's concern about Byron's development? Indeed, it can. Andrew, the psychologist who tested Byron, found that he scored only slightly below average. In watching Lisa play with Byron, Andrew noticed that she was anxious about his progress and therefore constantly bombarded him with questions and instructions. Andrew explained that when parents are intrusive in these ways, infants and toddlers are

likely to be distractible, show less mature forms of play, and do poorly on mental tests (Bradley et al., 1989; Fiese, 1990). He coached Lisa in how to interact sensitively with Byron. At the same time, he assured her that Byron's current performance need not forecast his future development. Warm, responsive parenting that builds on toddlers' current capacities is a much better indicator of how they will do later than is an early mental test score.

▌ INFANT AND TODDLER CHILD CARE. Home environments are not the only influential settings in which young children spend their days. Today, more than 60 percent of American mothers with a child under age 2 are employed (U.S. Bureau of the Census, 1999). Child care for infants and toddlers has become common, and its quality has a major impact on mental development. Research consistently shows that infants and young children exposed to poor-quality child care, regardless of whether they come from middle- or low-SES homes, score lower on measures of cognitive and social skills. In one American study, children who entered poor-quality child care during the first year of life and remained there over the preschool years were rated by teachers as distractible, low in task involvement, and inconsiderate of others when they reached kindergarten (Howes, 1990).

In contrast, good child care can reduce the negative impact of a stressed, poverty-stricken home life, and it sustains the benefits of growing up in an economically advantaged family (Burchinal et al., 1996; Lamb, 1998). In Swedish longitudinal research, entering high-quality child care in infancy and toddlerhood was associated with cognitive, emotional, and social competence in middle childhood and adolescence (Andersson, 1989, 1992; Broberg et al., 1997).

Visit some child-care settings, and take notes on what you see. In contrast to most European countries and to Australia and New Zealand, where child care is nationally regulated and funded to ensure its quality, reports on American child care are cause for deep concern. Standards are set by the states and vary greatly across the nation. In some places, caregivers need no special training in child development, and one adult is permitted to care for 6 to 12 babies at once (Children's Defense Fund, 1999). In a study of several hundred randomly selected child-care centers in California, Colorado, Connecticut, and North Carolina, researchers judged that only 1 in 7 provided a level of care sufficient to promote healthy psychological development (Helburn, 1995). Similar conclusions have been reached about child-care homes (Galinsky et al., 1994).

The Caregiving Concerns table on the following page lists signs of high-quality care that can be used in choosing a child-care setting for an infant or toddler, based on standards for **developmentally appropriate practice** devised by the National Association for the Education of Young Children (Bredekamp & Copple, 1997). These standards specify

Signs of Developmentally Appropriate Infant and Toddler Child Care

PROGRAM CHARACTERISTIC	SIGNS OF QUALITY
Physical setting	Indoor environment is clean, in good repair, well lighted, and well ventilated. Fenced outdoor play space is available. Setting does not appear overcrowded when children are present.
Toys and equipment	Play materials are appropriate for infants and toddlers and stored on low shelves within easy reach. Cribs, high chairs, infant seats, and child-sized tables and chairs are available. Outdoor equipment includes small riding toys, swings, slide, and sandbox.
Caregiver–child ratio	In child-care centers, caregiver–child ratio is no greater than 1 to 3 for infants and 1 to 6 for toddlers. Group size (number of children in one room) is no greater than 6 infants with 2 caregivers and 12 toddlers with 2 caregivers. In child-care homes, caregiver is responsible for no more than 6 children; within this group, no more than 2 are infants and toddlers. Staffing is consistent, so infants and toddlers can form relationships with particular caregivers.
Daily activities	Daily schedule includes times for active play, quiet play, naps, snacks, and meals. It is flexible rather than rigid, to meet the needs of individual children. Atmosphere is warm and supportive, and children are never left unsupervised.
Interactions among adults and children	Caregivers respond promptly to infants' and toddlers' distress; hold, talk to, sing, and read to them; and interact with them in a contingent manner that respects the individual child's interests and tolerance for stimulation.
Caregiver qualifications	Caregiver has at least some training in child development, first aid, and safety.
Relationships with parents	Parents are welcome anytime. Caregivers talk frequently with parents about children's behavior and development.
Licensing and accreditation	Child-care setting, whether a center or a home, is licensed by the state. Accreditation by the National Academy of Early Childhood Programs or the National Association for Family Child Care is evidence of an especially high-quality program.

Source: Bredekamp & Copple, 1997; National Association for the Education of Young Children, 1998.

program characteristics that meet the developmental and individual needs of young children, based on current research and the consensus of experts.

Of course, for parents to make this choice, enough high-quality child care must be available. Unfortunately, children most likely to have inadequate child care come from low-income and poverty-stricken families (Phillips et al., 1994). Recognizing that American child care is in crisis, in recent years Congress allocated additional funds to upgrade its quality and assist parents—especially those with low incomes—in paying for it. This is a hopeful sign, since good child care can serve as effective early intervention for children whose development is at risk, much like the programs we are about to consider in the next section.

EARLY INTERVENTION FOR AT-RISK INFANTS AND TODDLERS

Many studies indicate that children of poverty are likely to show gradual declines in intelligence test scores and to achieve poorly when they reach school age (Brody, 1992). These problems are largely due to stressful home environments that undermine children's ability to learn and increase the chances

that they will remain poor throughout their lives. A variety of intervention programs have been developed to break this tragic cycle of poverty. Although most begin during the preschool years (we will discuss these in Chapter 7), a few start during infancy and continue through early childhood.

Some interventions are center based; children attend an organized child-care or preschool program where they receive educational, nutritional, and health services, and child-rearing and other social-service supports are provided to parents as well. Other interventions are home based. A skilled adult visits the home and works with parents, teaching them how to stimulate a very young child's development. In most programs, participating youngsters score higher on mental tests than untreated controls by age 2. These gains persist as long as the program lasts and occasionally longer. The more intense the intervention (for example, full-day, year-round high-quality child care plus support services for parents), the greater children's cognitive and academic performance when they reach school age (Barnett, 1995; Campbell & Ramey, 1995).

The Carolina Abecedarian Project illustrates these positive outcomes. In the 1970s, over a hundred 3-week- to 3-month-old infants from poverty-stricken families were randomly assigned to either a treatment or a control group. Treatment infants were enrolled in full-time, year-round child care, where they remained until they entered school. There they received stimulation aimed at promoting motor, cognitive, language, and social skills and, after age 3, prereading and math concepts. At all ages, special emphasis was placed on rich, responsive adult–child verbal communication. All children received nutrition and health services; the primary difference between treatment and controls was the child-care experience.

As Figure 5.11 shows, by 12 months of age, IQs of the two groups diverged, and treatment children maintained their advantage well into adolescence. In addition, at 12 and 15 years of age, treatment youngsters were achieving considerably better, especially in reading and mathematics (Campbell & Ramey, 1991, 1994, 1995). While the children were in elementary school, the researchers conducted a second experiment to compare the impact of early and later intervention. From kindergarten through second grade, half the treatment and half the control group were provided with a resource teacher, who introduced educational activities addressing the child's specific learning needs into the home. School-age intervention had no impact on IQ (refer again to Figure 5.11). And although it enhanced children's academic achievement, the effects were much weaker than the impact of very early intervention (Campbell & Ramey, 1995).

Without some form of early intervention, many children born into economically disadvantaged families will not reach their potential. Recently, the United States Congress provided limited funding for intervention services directed at infants and toddlers who already have serious developmental problems or who are at risk for them because of poverty. At present, available programs are not nearly enough to meet the need (Children's Defense Fund, 1999). Nevertheless, those that exist are a promising beginning in a new effort to prevent serious learning difficulties by starting to help children at a very early age.

ASK YOURSELF . . .

Fifteen-month-old Joey's DQ is 100. His mother wants to know what this means and what she should do at home to support his mental development. How would you respond to her questions?

Using what you learned about brain growth in Chapter 4, explain why intensive intervention for poverty-stricken children starting in the first 2 years has a greater long-term impact on IQ than intervention beginning at a later age.

LANGUAGE DEVELOPMENT

As perception and cognition improve during infancy, they pave the way for an extraordinary human achievement—language. On the average, children say their first word at 12 months of age, with a range of about 8 to 18 months. Once words appear, language develops rapidly. Sometime between 1½ and 2 years, toddlers combine two words (Bloom, 1998). By age 6, they have a vocabulary of about 10,000 words, speak in elaborate sentences, and are skilled conversationalists.

How do children acquire language? Let's begin to address this question by examining and evaluating several prominent theories, based on what we know about language development in the first 2 years.

THREE THEORIES OF LANGUAGE DEVELOPMENT

In the 1950s, researchers did not take seriously the idea that very young children might be able to figure out important properties of the language they hear. As a result, the first two theories of how children acquire language were ex-

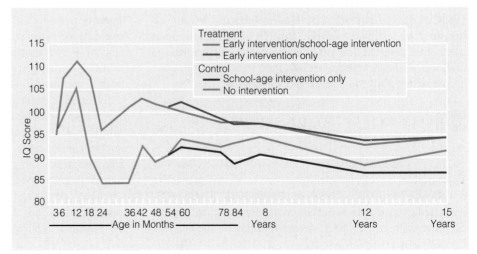

FIGURE 5.11

■ **IQ scores of treatment and control children from 6 months to 15 years in the Carolina Abecedarian Project.** School-age intervention had little impact on age-related changes in IQ; the effects of early intervention were far more powerful. (From F. A. Campbell & C. T. Ramey, 1995, "Cognitive and School Outcomes for High-Risk African-American Students at Middle Adolescence: Positive Effects of Early Intervention," *American Educational Research Journal, 32,* p. 757. Reprinted by permission of the American Educational Research Association.)

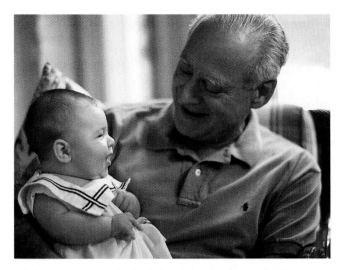

■ *Infants are communicative beings from the start, as this interchange between a 3-month-old and her grandfather indicates. How will this child accomplish the awesome task of becoming a fluent speaker of her native tongue during the first few years of life? Theorists disagree sharply on answers to this question. (Photo courtesy: Sotographs/Liaison Agency)*

treme views. One, *behaviorism,* regards language development as entirely due to environmental influences. The second, *nativism* (meaning inborn), assumes that children are prewired to master the intricate rules of their language.

■ THE BEHAVIORIST PERSPECTIVE. Well-known behaviorist B. F. Skinner (1957) proposed that language, like any other behavior, is acquired through *operant conditioning* (see Chapter 4, page 131). As the baby makes sounds, parents reinforce those that are most like words with smiles, hugs, and speech in return. For example, at 12 months, my older son, David, could often be heard babbling something like this: "book-a-book-a-dook-a-dook-a-book-a-nook-a-book-aaa." One day, I held up his picture book while he babbled away and said, "Book!" Very soon, David was saying "book-aaa" in the presence of books.

Some behaviorists rely on imitation to explain how children rapidly acquire complex utterances, such as whole phrases and sentences (Whitehurst & Vasta, 1975). And imitation can combine with reinforcement to promote language, as when a parent coaxes, "Say, 'I want a cookie,'" and delivers praise and a treat after the toddler responds, "Wanna cookie!"

Although reinforcement and imitation contribute to early language development, they are best viewed as supporting rather than fully explaining it. As Felicia remarked one day, "It's amazing how creative April is with language. She combines words in ways she's never heard before, such as 'needle it' when she wants me to sew up her teddy bear and 'allgone outside' when she has to come in." Felicia's observations reveal that children say many things that are not directly taught.

■ THE NATIVIST PERSPECTIVE. Linguist Noam Chomsky (1957) proposed a nativist theory that regards the young child's amazing language skill as etched into the structure of the human brain. Focusing on grammar, Chomsky reasoned that the rules of sentence organization are much too complex to be directly taught to or independently discovered by a young child. Instead, he argued, all children are born with a **language acquisition device (LAD),** a biologically based innate system that contains a set of rules common to all languages. It permits children, no matter which language they hear, to understand and speak in a rule-oriented fashion as soon as they have picked up enough words.

Are children biologically primed to acquire language? There is evidence that they are. Recall from Chapter 4 that newborn babies are remarkably sensitive to speech sounds and prefer to listen to the human voice. In addition, children the world over reach major language milestones in a similar sequence. This regularity of development certainly fits with Chomsky's idea of a biologically determined language program (Gleitman & Newport, 1996).

At the same time, challenges to Chomsky's theory suggest that it, too, provides only a partial account of language development. First, researchers have had great difficulty identifying a single underlying system of grammar for all languages (Maratsos, 1998; Tomasello, 1995). Second, careful study of first word combinations reveals that toddlers do not yet have a general understanding of grammatical rules (Tomasello et al., 1997). Finally, children do not acquire language quite as quickly as nativist theory suggests. Their progress in mastering many sentence constructions is not immediate, but steady and gradual. This suggests that more learning and discovery are involved than Chomsky assumed.

■ THE INTERACTIONIST PERSPECTIVE. In recent years, new ideas about language development have emerged, emphasizing that innate abilities and environmental influences *interact* to produce children's extraordinary language achievements. Although several interactionist theories exist, all stress the social context of language learning. An active child, well endowed for acquiring language, observes and participates in social exchanges. From these experiences, children gradually discover the functions and regularities of language. According to the interactionist position, native capacity, a strong desire to interact with others, and a rich linguistic and social environment combine to assist children in building a communicative system (Bohannon & Bonvillian, 1997).

Although all interactionists regard children as active, communicative beings, debate continues over the precise nature of their innate language abilities. Some theorists accept a modified view of Chomsky's position. They believe that children are primed to acquire language but form and refine hypotheses about its structure based on language experience (Slobin, 1985). Others are impressed by the remarkable cognitive capacities of infants and toddlers. They believe children make sense of language by applying pow-

Milestones of Language Development During the First Two Years

APPROXIMATE AGE	MILESTONE
2 months	Infants coo, making pleasurable vowel sounds.
4 months on	Infants and parents establish joint attention, and parents often verbally label what the baby is looking at.
	Infants babble, adding consonants to the sounds of the cooing period and repeating syllables. By 7 months, babbling of hearing infants starts to include sounds of mature spoken languages.
6–14 months	Interaction between parents and baby includes simple games, such as pat-a-cake and peekaboo. By 12 months, babies participate actively. These games provide practice in conversational turn taking and also highlight the meaning and function of spoken words.
8–12 months	Babbling contains sounds and intonation patterns of the infant's language community. Infants begin using preverbal gestures, such as showing and pointing, to influence the behavior of others. Word comprehension first appears.
12 months	Infants say their first recognizable word.
18–24 months	Vocabulary expands from about 50 to 200 words.
20–26 months	Toddlers combine two words.

erful strategies of a general cognitive kind rather than ones specifically tuned to language (Bates, 1995; MacWhinney, 1996; Tomasello & Brooks, 1999).

As we chart the course of early language growth, we will see a great deal of evidence that supports the interactionist position. But we must keep in mind that none of these theories has yet been fully tested. In reality, biology, cognition, and social experience may operate in different balances with respect to various aspects of language—vocabulary, grammar, and communication skills. Table 5.4 provides an overview of early language milestones that we will take up in the next few sections.

GETTING READY TO TALK

Before babies say their first word, they are preparing for language in many ways. They listen attentively to human speech and make speechlike sounds. And as adults, we can hardly help but respond.

■ COOING AND BABBLING. Around 2 months, babies begin to make vowel-like noises, called **cooing** because of their pleasant "oo" quality. Gradually, consonants are added, and around 4 months **babbling** appears, in which infants repeat consonant–vowel combinations in long strings, such as "bababababa" or "nananananana."

The timing of early babbling seems to be due to maturation, since babies everywhere start babbling at about the same age and produce a similar range of early sounds (Stoel-Gammon & Otomo, 1986). But for babbling to develop further, infants must be able to hear human speech. Around 7 months, babbling starts to include the sounds of mature spoken languages. If a baby's hearing is impaired, these speechlike sounds are greatly delayed, and in the case of deaf infants, they are totally absent (Eilers & Oller, 1994).

When a baby coos or babbles and gazes at you, what are you likely to do? One day, as I stood in line at the post office behind a mother and her 7-month-old daughter, the baby babbled, and three adults—myself and two people beside me—started to talk to the infant. We cooed and babbled ourselves, imitating the baby, and also said such things as "My, you're a big girl, aren't you? Out to help Mommy mail letters today?" Then the baby smiled and babbled all the more. As adults interact with infants and they listen to spoken language, babbling increases. By the end of the first year, it contains the consonant–vowel and intonation patterns of the infant's language community (Levitt & Utmann, 1992). Through babbling, babies seem to experiment with a great many sounds that can be blended into their first words.

■ BECOMING A COMMUNICATOR. Besides responding to cooing and babbling, adults interact with infants in many other situations. By age 4 months, infants start to gaze in the same direction adults are looking, a skill that becomes more accurate between 12 and 15 months of age (Tomasello, 1999). When this happens, parents often comment on what the infant sees, labeling the environment for the baby. Infants who experience this kind of *joint attention* are likely to talk earlier and show faster vocabulary development (Carpenter, Nagel, & Tomasello, 1998; Dunham, Dunham, & Curwin, 1993).

Between 3 and 4 months, the beginnings of conversation can be seen in a turn-taking pattern in which the baby vocalizes, the caregiver vocalizes in return, waits for a response, and vocalizes again. Similarly, around 6 months, interaction between parent and baby begins to include *turn-taking games*, such as pat-a-cake and peekaboo. At first, the adult is largely responsible for sustaining these playful exchanges. By 12 months, babies participate actively, trading roles with the

■ *This 15-month-old delights in playing peekaboo with her mother. As she participates, she practices the turn-taking pattern of human conversation. (Photo courtesy: Tony Freeman/PhotoEdit)*

parent. As they do so, they practice the turn-taking pattern of human conversation (Ratner & Bruner, 1978).

At the end of the first year, as infants become capable of intentional behavior, they use *preverbal gestures* to influence the behavior of others (Carpenter, Nagel, & Tomasello, 1998; Fenson et al., 1994). For example, Byron held up a toy to show it and pointed to the cupboard when he wanted a cookie. Lisa responded to his gestures and also labeled them ("Oh, you want a cookie!"). In this way, toddlers learn that using language leads to desired results. Soon they utter words along with their reaching and pointing gestures, the gestures recede, and spoken language is under way (Iverson, Capirci, & Caselli, 1994; Namy & Waxman, 1998).

FIRST WORDS

Ask several parents to list their toddlers' first words. Note how the words build on the sensorimotor foundations Piaget described and on categories children form during the first 2 years. Earliest words usually refer to important people ("Mama," "Dada"), objects that move ("car," "ball," "cat"), familiar actions ("bye-bye," "up," "more"), or outcomes of familiar actions ("dirty," "wet," "hot"). In their first 50 words, toddlers rarely name things that just *sit there*, like table or vase (Nelson, 1973).

Some early words are linked to specific cognitive achievements. For example, toddlers begin to use disappearance words, like "all gone," at about the same time they master advanced object permanence problems. And success and failure expressions, such as "There!" and "Uh-oh!", appear when toddlers can solve sensorimotor problems suddenly, in Piaget's Substage 6. According to one pair of researchers, "Children seem to be motivated to acquire words that are relevant to the particular cognitive problems they are working on at the moment" (Gopnik & Meltzoff, 1986, p. 1052).

Besides cognition, emotion influences early word learning. At first, when acquiring a new word for an object, per-

son, or event, 1½-year-olds say it neutrally; they need to listen carefully to learn, and strong emotion diverts their attention. As words become better learned, toddlers integrate talking and expressing feelings (Bloom, 1993, 1998). "Shoe!" said one enthusiastic 22-month-old as her mother tied her shoelaces before an outing. At the end of the second year, children begin to label their emotions with words like "happy," "mad," and "sad"—a development we will consider further in Chapter 6.

When young children first learn a new word, they sometimes apply it too narrowly, an error called **underextension.** For example, at 16 months, April used "doll" to refer only to the worn and tattered doll that she carried around with her much of the day. A more common error is **overextension**— applying a word to a wider collection of objects and events than is appropriate. For example, Rachel used "car" for buses, trains, trucks, and fire engines. Toddlers' overextensions reflect their sensitivity to categories. They apply a new word to a group of similar experiences, such as "car" to wheeled objects and "open" to opening a door, peeling fruit,

■ *Using a preverbal gesture, this Japanese infant points to show something to his parents. Soon words will be uttered along with these gestures and the gestures will recede as the child makes the transition to spoken language. (Photo courtesy: Fuji Fotos/The Image Works)*

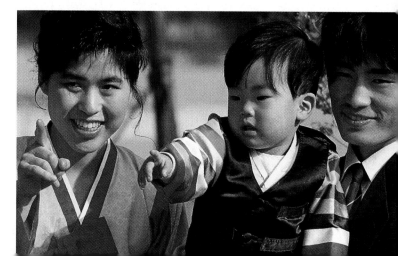

and undoing shoelaces (Behrend, 1988). This suggests that children sometimes overextend deliberately because they have difficulty recalling or have not acquired a suitable word. As their vocabularies enlarge, children make finer distinctions, and overextensions disappear.

Overextensions illustrate another important feature of language development: the distinction between language *production* (the words children use) and language *comprehension* (the words children understand). Children overextend many more words in production than they do in comprehension. That is, a 2-year-old may refer to trucks, trains, and bikes as "car" but look at or point to these objects correctly when given their names (Naigles & Gelman, 1995). At all ages, comprehension develops ahead of production. This tells us that failure to say a word does not mean that toddlers do not understand it. If we rely only on what children say, we will underestimate their knowledge of language.

THE TWO-WORD UTTERANCE PHASE

At first, toddlers add to their vocabularies slowly, at a rate of 1 to 3 words a month. Between 18 and 24 months, a spurt in vocabulary growth usually takes place. As memory, categorization, and representation improve, many children add 10 to 20 new words a week (Fenson et al., 1994; Reznick & Goldfield, 1992). When vocabulary approaches 200 words, toddlers start to combine two words, such as "Mommy shoe," "go car," and "more cookie." These two-word utterances are called **telegraphic speech** because, like a telegram, they leave out smaller and less important words. Children the world over use them to express an impressive variety of meanings.

Two-word speech is largely made up of simple formulas, such as "want + X" and "more + X" (with many different words inserted in the X position). Although toddlers rarely make gross grammatical errors (saying "chair my" instead of "my chair"), they can be heard violating the rules. For example, at 20 months, Rachel said "more hot" and "more read," combinations that are not acceptable in English grammar. The word-order regularities in toddlers' two-word utterances are usually copies of adult word pairings, as when the parent says, "That's *my book*," or "How about *more sandwich?*" (Tomasello & Brooks, 1999). But it does not take long for children to figure out grammatical rules. As we will see in Chapter 7, the beginnings of grammar are in place by age 2½.

INDIVIDUAL AND CULTURAL DIFFERENCES

Each child's progress in acquiring language results from a complex blend of biological and environmental influences. For example, earlier we saw that Byron's spoken language was delayed, in part because Lisa pressured him a great deal. But Byron is also a boy, and many studies show that girls are slightly ahead of boys in early vocabulary growth (Fenson et al., 1994). The most common biological

explanation is girls' faster rate of physical maturation, believed to promote earlier development of the left cerebral hemisphere, where language is housed. But mothers also talk much more to toddler-age girls than to boys (Leaper, Anderson, & Sanders, 1998). Besides the child's sex, personality makes a difference. Reserved, cautious toddlers often wait until they understand a great deal before trying to speak. When, finally, they do speak, their vocabularies grow rapidly (Nelson, 1973).

Young children have unique styles of early language learning. April, like most toddlers, used a **referential style.** Her vocabulary consisted mainly of words that referred to objects. In contrast, Rachel used an **expressive style.** She produced many more pronouns and social formulas, such as "stop it," "thank you," and "I want it," uttered as compressed phrases, much like single words (as in "Iwannit"). These styles reflect early ideas about the functions of language. April had an especially active interest in exploring objects, and her parents eagerly labeled them. Consequently, she thought words were for naming things. In contrast, Rachel believed words were for talking about people's feelings and needs. Beth often engaged Rachel in social routines, perhaps because Japanese culture stresses the importance of membership in the social group (Fernald & Morikawa, 1993). April's vocabulary grew faster, since all languages contain many more object labels than social phrases (Bates et al., 1994).

Sheer amount of parental speech is related to variations in early word learning. The more words caregivers use, the more toddlers pick up. And words parents say very often tend to be acquired earliest (Hart, 1991). Whereas object words (nouns) are particularly common in the vocabularies of English-speaking toddlers, action words (verbs) are more numerous among Korean and Mandarin Chinese toddlers. When caregivers' speech is examined in each culture, it reflects this difference (Choi & Gopnik, 1995; Tardif, Gelman, & Xu, 1999).

At what point should parents be concerned if their child does not talk or says very little? If a toddler's language is greatly delayed when compared with the norms in Table 5.4, then parents should consult the child's doctor or a speech and language therapist. Some toddlers who do not follow simple directions could have a hearing problem. A child over age 2 who has great difficulty putting thoughts into words may have a serious language disorder that requires immediate treatment.

SUPPORTING EARLY LANGUAGE DEVELOPMENT

There is little doubt that children are specially prepared for acquiring language, since no other species can develop as flexible and creative a capacity for communication as we can. At the same time, a great deal of evidence fits with the interactionist view that a rich social environment builds on young children's natural readiness to speak their native tongue. The Caregiving Concerns table below summarizes ways that caregivers can consciously support early language learning. They also do so unconsciously—through a special style of speech.

Adults in many countries speak to young children in **child-directed speech (CDS),** a form of language made up of short sentences with high-pitched, exaggerated expression and very clear pronunciation (Fernald et al., 1989). CDS also contains many simplified words, such as "night-night," "bye-bye," and "tummy," that are easy for toddlers to pronounce. Speakers of CDS often repeat phrases, ask questions, and give directions, perhaps as a way of checking to see if their message has been properly received. Deaf parents use a similar style of communication when signing to their deaf babies (Masataka, 1996). CDS builds on several communicative strategies we have already considered—joint attention, turn taking, and caregivers' sensitivity to children's preverbal gestures. Here is an example of Felicia using CDS with 18-month-old April:

April: "Go car."

Felicia: "Yes, time to go in the car. Where's your jacket?"

April: (looks around, walks to the closet) "Dacket!" (pointing to her jacket)

Felicia: "There's that jacket! Let's put it on. (She helps April into the jacket.) On it goes! Let's zip up. (Zips up the jacket.) Now, say bye-bye to Byron and Rachel."

April: "Bye-bye, By-on."

Felicia: "What about Rachel? Bye to Rachel?"

April: "Bye-bye, Ta-tel (Rachel)."

Felicia: "Where's your doll? Don't forget your doll."

April: (looks around)

■ *This Chinese mother speaks to her baby daughter in short, clearly pronounced sentences with high-pitched, exaggerated intonation. Adults in many countries use this form of language, called child-directed speech, with infants and toddlers. It eases the task of early language learning. (Photo courtesy: Myrleen Ferguson Cate/PhotoEdit)*

Felicia: "Look by the sofa. See? Go get the doll. By the sofa." (April gets the doll.)

From birth on, children prefer to listen to CDS over other kinds of adult talk (Cooper & Aslin, 1994). And parents constantly fine-tune it to fit their children's needs. Notice how Felicia used an utterance length just ahead of April's, creating a sensitive match between her own speech and what April was capable of understanding and producing (Murray, Johnson, & Peters, 1990).

CAREGIVING CONCERNS

Supporting Early Language Learning

SUGGESTION	CONSEQUENCE
Respond to coos and babbles with speech sounds and words.	Encourages experimentation with sounds that can later be blended into first words. Provides experience with turn-taking pattern of human conversation.
Establish joint attention and comment on what child sees.	Predicts earlier onset of language and faster vocabulary development.
Play social games, such as pat-a-cake and peekaboo.	Provides experience with turn-taking pattern of human conversation. Permits pairing of words with actions they represent.
Engage toddlers in joint make-believe play.	Promotes all aspects of conversational dialogue.
Engage toddlers in frequent conversations.	Predicts faster early language development and academic competence during the school years.
Read to toddlers often, engaging them in dialogues about picture books.	Provides exposure to many aspects of language, including vocabulary, grammar, communicative conventions, and information about print and story structures.

PARENT–CHILD INTERACTION AND COGNITIVE DEVELOPMENT OF DEAF CHILDREN

About 1 in every 1,000 American infants is born deaf (U.S. Department of Health and Human Services, 1999a). When a deaf child cannot participate fully in communication with parents and other caregivers, development is severely compromised. Yet the consequences of deafness for children's language and cognition vary with social context, as comparisons of deaf children of hearing parents with deaf children of deaf parents reveal.

Over 90 percent of deaf children have hearing parents. During toddlerhood and early childhood, these children are often delayed in language progress and in complex make-believe play. In middle childhood, many achieve poorly in school and are deficient in social skills. Yet deaf children of deaf parents escape these difficulties! Their language (use of sign) and play maturity are on a par with hearing children's. After school entry, deaf children of deaf parents learn easily and get along well with adults and peers (Bornstein et al., 1999b; Jamieson, 1995b; Spencer & Lederberg, 1997).

These differences can be traced to early parent–child communication. Beginning in infancy, hearing parents of deaf children are less positive, less effective at achieving joint attention and turn taking, and more directive

and intrusive (Meadow-Orlans & Steinberg, 1993; Spencer & Meadow-Orlans, 1996). While helping their deaf preschoolers solve a challenging puzzle, hearing parents have trouble adjusting their verbal and nonverbal assistance to the child's needs (Jamieson, 1994, 1995a). In contrast, the quality of interaction between deaf children and deaf parents is similar to that between hearing children and hearing parents.

Children with limited and less sensitive parental communication are behind their agemates in achieving verbal control over their behavior—in thinking before they act and in planning. Deaf children of hearing parents frequently display impulse-control problems (Harris, 1978).

Hearing parents are not at fault for their deaf children's problems. Instead, they lack experience with visual communication, which enables deaf parents to respond readily to a deaf child's needs. Deaf parents know they must wait for the child to turn toward them before interacting (Spencer, Bodner-Johnson, & Gutfreund, 1992). Hearing parents tend to speak or gesture while the child's attention is directed elsewhere—a strategy that works with a hearing but not with a deaf partner. When their child is confused or unresponsive, hearing parents often feel overwhelmed and become

■ *A teacher fluent in sign language interacts with this deaf toddler, born to hearing parents. Through early access to rich, natural language-learning experiences, he will be protected from serious developmental problems—delayed language, impulse-control difficulties, poor school achievement, and deficits in social skills. (Photo courtesy: David Young-Wolff/PhotoEdit)*

more controlling (Jamieson, 1994, 1995a). Furthermore, learning sign language is an immense task that requires years of effort, and few hearing parents become fluent.

The impact of deafness on language and cognitive development can best be understood by considering its effects on parents and other significant people in the child's life. Deaf children need access to language models—deaf adults and peers—to create a natural language-learning situation. And their hearing parents benefit from social support along with training in how to interact sensitively with a nonhearing partner.

Many features of CDS support early language development. For example, parents who frequently repeat part of their own or the child's previous utterance and use simple questions have 2-year-olds who make faster language progress (Hoff-Ginsburg, 1986). As the Variations box above makes clear, when a child's disability makes it difficult for parents to engage in the sensitive linguistic communication of CDS, language and cognitive development are drastically delayed. This does not mean that we should deliberately load our speech with repetitions, questions, and other characteristics of CDS! These qualities occur naturally as adults draw

young children into dialogues, accepting their attempts to talk as meaningful and worthwhile.

Conversational give-and-take between parent and toddler is one of the best predictors of early language development and academic competence during the school years. It provides many examples of speech just ahead of the child's current level as well as a sympathetic environment in which children can try out new skills (Hart & Risley, 1995; Walker et al., 1994). Dialogues about picture books are an especially effective way of conversing with young children. They expose toddlers to great breadth of language and literacy knowledge, from vocabulary, grammar, and communicative conventions to information about print and story structures (Whitehurst & Lonigan, 1998).

Do social experiences that promote language development remind you of ones discussed earlier in this chapter that strengthen cognitive development in general? Notice how CDS and parent–child conversation create a *zone of proximal development* in which children's language expands. In contrast, impatience with and rejection of children's efforts to talk lead them to stop trying and result in immature language skills (Baumwell, Tamis-LeMonda, & Bornstein, 1997). In the next chapter, we will see that sensitivity to children's needs and capacities supports their emotional and social development as well.

ASK YOURSELF . . .

■ *Erin's first words included* see, give, *and* thank you, *and her vocabulary grew slowly during the second year. What style of early language learning did she display, and what factors might explain it?*

 Eighteen-month-old Toby lives in a poverty-stricken, overcrowded household. His parents seldom have time to converse with or to read to him. Summarize evidence indicating that Toby's limited early language stimulation may result in lasting deficits in development.

SUMMARY

PIAGET'S COGNITIVE-DEVELOPMENTAL THEORY

According to Piaget, how do schemes change over the course of development?

■ In Piaget's theory, by acting directly on the environment, children move through four stages in which psychological structures, or **schemes,** achieve a better fit with external reality.

■ Schemes change in two ways. The first is through **adaptation,** which is made up of two complementary activities—**assimilation** and **accommodation.** The second is through **organization,** the internal rearrangement of schemes into a strongly interconnected cognitive system.

Describe the major cognitive achievements of the sensorimotor stage.

■ Piaget's **sensorimotor stage** is divided into six substages. Through the **circular reaction,** the newborn baby's reflexes are gradually transformed into the more flexible action patterns of the older infant and finally into the representational schemes of the 2-year-old child. During Substage 4, infants develop **intentional,** or **goal-directed, behavior** and begin to understand **object permanence** and **physical causality.** By Substage 6,

toddlers are capable of **mental representation,** as shown by **deferred imitation** and **make-believe play.**

What does recent research say about the accuracy of Piaget's sensorimotor stage?

■ Important capacities, such as secondary circular reactions, physical reasoning (including object permanence and physical causality), and mental representation (for example, deferred imitation and analogical problem solving), emerge earlier than Piaget believed. Infants do not have to construct all aspects of experience through motor activity. Some may be wired into the brain from the start, and others may be constructed through purely perceptual learning.

INFORMATION PROCESSING

Describe the information-processing view of cognitive development and the general structure of the information-processing system.

■ Unlike Piaget's stage theory, information processing views development as a continuous process; the cognitive approach of children and adults is assumed to be much the same. Information-processing researchers study many aspects of thinking. They want to know exactly

what individuals of different ages do when faced with a task or problem.

■ Most general models of the information-processing system divide the mind into three parts: the **sensory register; working,** or **short-term, memory;** and **long-term memory.** As information flows through each, **mental strategies** operate on it to increase the chances that information will be retained.

What changes in attention, memory, and categorization take place during the first 2 years?

■ With age, infants attend to more aspects of the environment and take information in more quickly. In the second year, attention to novelty declines and sustained attention improves, especially during play with toys.

■ As infants get older, they remember experiences longer. Young infants are capable of **recognition** memory, and by the middle of the first year, they can **recall** past events. By the end of toddlerhood, recall for people, places, and objects is excellent. By conversing about the past, adults help children develop an **autobiographical memory.**

■ Infants remember information in a remarkably orderly fashion. During the first year, they group stimuli into increasingly complex categories, and categorization shifts from a perceptual to a conceptual basis. By the second year, children become active categorizers, spontaneously sorting objects during play.

Describe contributions of the information-processing approach to our understanding of cognitive development, and note its limitations.

■ Information processing has contributed greatly to our appreciation of infants' cognitive capacities. Its findings challenge Piaget's view of babies as purely sensorimotor beings. However, information processing has not yet provided a broad, comprehensive theory of children's thinking.

THE SOCIAL CONTEXT OF EARLY COGNITIVE DEVELOPMENT

How does Vygotsky's concept of the zone of proximal development expand our understanding of early cognitive development?

■ According to Vygotsky's sociocultural theory, complex mental activities originate in social interaction. Through the support and guidance of more skilled partners, infants master tasks within the **zone of proximal development**—ones just ahead of their current capacities.

INDIVIDUAL DIFFERENCES IN EARLY MENTAL DEVELOPMENT

Describe the mental testing approach, the meaning of intelligence test scores, and the extent to which infant tests predict later performance.

■ The mental testing approach measures intellectual development in an effort to predict future performance. **Intelligence quotients, or IQs,** are scores on mental tests that compare a child's performance with that of same-age children.

■ Infant tests consist largely of perceptual and motor responses; they predict later intelligence poorly. As a result, scores on infant tests are called **developmental quotients, or DQs,** rather than IQs. Speed of habituation and dishabituation to visual stimuli and object permanence, which tap basic cognitive processes, are better predictors of future performance.

Discuss environmental influences on early mental development, including home, child care, and early intervention for at-risk infants and toddlers.

■ Research with the **Home Observation for Measurement of the Environment (HOME)** shows that a stimulating home environment and parental encouragement, involvement, and affection repeatedly predict early mental test scores, no matter what the child's SES and ethnic background. Although the HOME–IQ relationship is partly due to heredity, family living conditions do affect mental development.

■ The quality of infant and toddler child care also has a major impact on mental development. Standards for **developmentally appropriate practice** specify program characteristics that meet the developmental needs of young children. Intensive early intervention can prevent the gradual declines in intelligence during early childhood and the poor academic performance of many poverty-stricken children.

LANGUAGE DEVELOPMENT

Describe three theories of language development, and indicate the emphasis each places on innate abilities and environmental influences.

■ Three theories provide different accounts of how young children develop language. According to the behaviorist perspective, parents train children in language skills through operant conditioning and imitation. In contrast, Chomsky's nativist view regards children as naturally endowed with a **language acquisition device (LAD).** New interactionist theories suggest that innate abilities and a rich linguistic and social environment combine to promote language development.

Describe major milestones of language development in the first 2 years, individual differences, and ways adults can support infants' and toddlers' emerging capacities.

■ During the first year, a great deal of preparation for language takes place. Infants begin **cooing** at 2 months and **babbling** around 4 months. Adults encourage language progress by responding to infants' coos and babbles, playing turn-taking games with them, establishing joint attention and labeling what babies see, and acknowledging their preverbal gestures.

■ Around 12 months, toddlers say their first word. Young children often make errors of **underextension** and **overextension.** Between 18 and 24 months, a spurt in vocabulary growth often occurs, and two-word utterances called **telegraphic speech** appear. At all ages, language comprehension is ahead of production.

■ Individual differences in early language development exist. Girls show faster progress than boys, and reserved, cautious toddlers may wait for a period of time before trying to speak. Most toddlers use a **referential style** of language learning, in which early words are largely names for objects. A few use an **expressive style,** in which pronouns and social formulas are common and vocabulary grows more slowly.

■ Adults the world over speak to young children in **child-directed speech (CDS),** a simplified form of language that is well suited to their learning needs. CDS occurs naturally when parents engage toddlers in conversations that accept and encourage their early efforts to talk.

IMPORTANT TERMS AND CONCEPTS

accommodation (p. 148)

adaptation (p. 148)

assimilation (p. 148)

autobiographical memory (p. 159)

babbling (p. 168)

child-directed speech (CDS) (p. 171)

circular reaction (p. 149)

cooing (p. 168)

deferred imitation (p. 152)

developmental quotient, or DQ (p. 163)

developmentally appropriate practice (p. 164)

expressive style (p. 170)

Home Observation for Measurement of the Environment (HOME) (p. 163)

intelligence quotient, or IQ (p. 163)

intentional, or goal-directed, behavior (p. 151)

language acquisition device (LAD) (p. 167)

long-term memory (p. 157)

make-believe play (p. 152)

mental representation (p. 152)

mental strategies (p. 156)

object permanence (p. 151)

organization (p. 149)

overextension (p. 169)

physical causality (p. 151)

recall (p. 157)

recognition (p. 157)

referential style (p. 170)

scheme (p. 148)

sensorimotor stage (p. 148)

sensory register (p. 156)

telegraphic speech (p. 170)

underextension (p. 169)

working, or short-term, memory (p. 156)

zone of proximal development (p. 160)

FYI FOR FURTHER INFORMATION AND HELP

Consult the companion website for this book, where you will find additional weblinks and associated learning activities: www.abacon.com/berk

COGNITIVE DEVELOPMENT

Jean Piaget Society
www.piaget.org
An international organization of researchers and teachers interested in cognitive development. Contains an informative biography on Jean Piaget.

INFANT AND TODDLER DEVELOPMENT AND EDUCATION

Association for Childhood Education International (ACEI)
www.udel.edu/bateman/acei
Organization interested in promoting sound educational practice from infancy through early adolescence. Student

membership is available and includes a subscription to Childhood Education, *a bimonthly journal covering research, practice, and public policy issues.*

National Association for the Education of Young Children (NAEYC)
www.naeyc.org
Organization open to all individuals interested in acting on behalf of young children's needs, with primary focus on educational services. Student membership is available and includes a subscription to Young Children, *a bimonthly journal covering theory, research, and practice in infant and early childhood development and education.*

National Association for Family Child Care
www.nafcc.org
Organization open to caregivers, parents, and other individuals involved or interested in family child care. Serves as a national voice that promotes high-quality child care.

EARLY INTERVENTION

High/Scope Educational Research Foundation
www.highscope.org
Devoted to improving development and education from infancy through the high school years. Has designed a parent–infant education program. Conducts longitudinal research to determine the effects of early intervention on development.

LANGUAGE DEVELOPMENT

American Speech-Language-Hearing Association
www.asha.org
Provides information on early identification of speech and language delays and disorders, including signs that a child should be evaluated by a speech and language therapist.

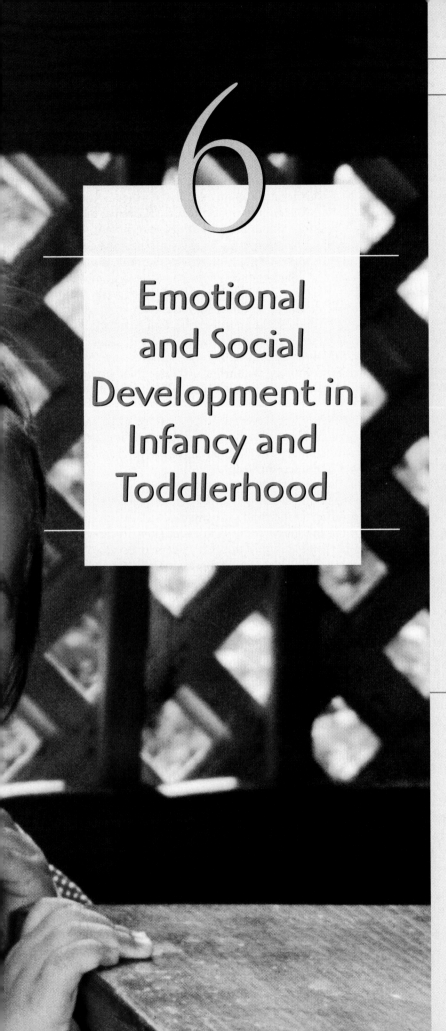

6

Emotional and Social Development in Infancy and Toddlerhood

■ *Building cultural bridges from an early age, this Cambodian-American 2-year-old and Irish-American 18-month-old have become fast friends. A warm parent–infant attachment bond lays the foundation for friendship. (Photo courtesy: Carolyn Merrill)*

isa, Beth, and Felicia's monthly conversations often focused on the emotional and social sides of their infants' development. As the babies reached 8 months of age, Beth noticed some important changes. "For some reason, Rachel's become more fearful in the last few weeks. I took her to the airport to meet my parents, who recently arrived from Japan. When they tried to hug her, she didn't return their enthusiasm, as she would have a month or two ago. Instead, she turned away and buried her head against my shoulder. Several days later, I left Rachel with my parents for several hours—the first time I'd been away from her since she was born. She wailed as soon as she saw me head for the door. And when I returned, Rachel seemed angry. She insisted on being held but also pushed me away and continued to cry. It took 10 minutes to calm her."

Lisa and Felicia also reported that Byron and April showed greater wariness of strangers and a strong desire to remain close to familiar adults. At the same time, each baby seemed more willful. An object removed from the hand at 5 months produced little response, but at 8 months Byron actively resisted when Lisa took away a table knife he had managed to reach. And he could no longer be consoled by the toys she offered in its place. Taken together, these reactions reflect two related aspects of personality that begin to develop during the first 2 years: *close ties to others* and a *sense of self*—an awareness of one's own separateness and uniqueness.

Our discussion begins with Erik Erikson's psychosocial theory, which provides an overall picture of personality development during infancy and toddlerhood. Then we take a look at factors that contribute to these changes. First, we chart the general course of emotional development. As we do so, we will discover why fear and anger became more apparent in Byron, Rachel, and April by the end of the first year. Second, our attention turns to individual differences in temperament and personality. We will examine biological and environmental contributions to these differences and their consequences for future development.

Next, we take up attachment to the caregiver, the child's first affectional tie. We will see how the feelings of security that grow out of this important bond provide a vital source of support for the child's exploration, sense of independence, and expanding social relationships.

Finally, we focus on early self-development. By the end of toddlerhood, April recognized herself in mirrors and photographs, labeled herself as a girl, and showed the beginnings of self-control. "Don't touch!" she instructed herself one day as she resisted the desire to pull a lamp cord out of its socket. Cognitive advances combine with social experiences to produce these changes during the second year.

ERIKSON'S THEORY OF INFANT AND TODDLER PERSONALITY

In Chapter 1, we pointed out that psychoanalytic theory is no longer in the mainstream of human development research. But one of its lasting contributions has been its ability to capture the essence of personality development during each phase of life. Recall from Chapter 1 that Sigmund Freud, founder of the psychoanalytic movement, believed that psychological health and maladjustment could be traced to the early years—in particular, to the quality of the child's relationships with parents.

Return to page 16 of Chapter 1 and reread the brief description of Freud's *psychosexual stages.* Freud's limited concern with the channeling of instincts and his neglect of important experiences beyond infancy and early childhood came to be heavily criticized. But the basic outlines of his theory were accepted and elaborated by several noted psychoanalysts who came after him. The leader of these neo-Freudians is Erik Erikson, whose *psychosocial theory* was introduced in Chapter 1.

Erikson (1950) characterized each Freudian stage as an inner conflict that is resolved positively or negatively, depending on the child's experiences with caregivers. When parenting supports the child's needs, the first year leads to feelings of trust and the next 2 years to a sense of autonomy—early attitudes that provide the foundation for healthy psychological development throughout life.

BASIC TRUST VERSUS MISTRUST

Freud called the first year the *oral stage* and regarded gratification of the baby's need for food and oral stimulation as vital. Erikson accepted Freud's emphasis on feeding, but he expanded and enriched Freud's view. A healthy outcome during infancy, Erikson believed, does not depend on the *amount* of food or oral stimulation offered, but rather on the *quality* of the caregiver's behavior. A mother who supports her baby's development relieves discomfort promptly and sensitively. For example, she holds the infant gently during feedings, patiently waits until the baby has had enough milk, and weans when the infant shows less interest in the breast or bottle.

Erikson recognized that no mother can be perfectly in tune with her baby's needs. Many factors affect her responsiveness—feelings of personal happiness, current life conditions (for example, whether she has one or several small children to care for), and culturally valued child-rearing practices. But when the *balance of care* is sympathetic and loving, then the psychological conflict of the first year—**basic trust versus mistrust**—is resolved on the positive

■ *According to Erikson, basic trust grows out of the quality of the early caregiving relationship. A parent who relieves the baby's discomfort promptly and holds the baby tenderly, during feeding and at other times, promotes basic trust— the feeling that the world is good and gratifying. Although Erikson emphasized maternal caregiving, fathers help infants build trust as well!* (Photo courtesy: Collins/Monkmeyer Press)

side. The trusting infant expects the world to be good and gratifying, so she feels confident about venturing out and exploring it. The mistrustful baby cannot count on the kindness and compassion of others, so she protects herself by withdrawing from people and things around her.

AUTONOMY VERSUS SHAME AND DOUBT

In the second year, during Freud's *anal stage*, instinctual energies shift to the anal region of the body. Toddlers take pleasure in retaining and releasing urine and feces at will. At the same time, society requires that elimination occur at appropriate times and places. As a result, Freud viewed toilet training, in which children must bring their anal impulses in line with social requirements, as crucial for personality development. If parents insist on training children before they are physically ready or wait too long before expecting self-control, an unresolved battle of wills between parent and child begins.

Erikson agreed that the parent's manner of toilet training is essential for psychological health. But he viewed it as only one of many important experiences for newly walking, talking toddlers. Their familiar refrains—"No!" and "Do it myself!"—reveal that they have entered a period of budding selfhood. Toddlers want to decide for themselves, not just in toileting, but in other situations as well. The great conflict of this stage, **autonomy versus shame and doubt,** is resolved favorably when parents provide young children with suitable guidance and reasonable choices. A self-confident, secure 2-year-old has been encouraged not just to use the toilet, but to eat with a spoon and to help pick up his toys. His parents do not criticize or attack him when he fails at these new skills. And they meet his assertions of independence with tolerance and understanding.

For example, they grant him an extra 5 minutes to finish his play before leaving for the grocery store and wait patiently while he tries to zip his jacket.

According to Erikson, the parent who is over- or undercontrolling in toileting is likely to be so in other aspects of the toddler's life. The outcome is a child who feels forced and shamed and doubts his ability to control his impulses and act competently on his own.

In sum, basic trust and autonomy grow out of warm, sensitive parenting and reasonable expectations for impulse control starting in the second year. If children emerge from the first few years without sufficient trust in caregivers and a healthy sense of individuality, the seeds are sown for adjustment problems. Adults who have difficulty establishing intimate ties to others, who are overly dependent on a loved one, or who continually doubt their own ability to meet new challenges may not have fully mastered the tasks of trust and autonomy during infancy and toddlerhood.

ASK YOURSELF . . .

■ *Derek's mother fed him in a warm and loving manner during the first year, but when he became a toddler, she kept him in a playpen for many hours because he got into so much mischief while exploring freely. Use Erikson's theory to evaluate Derek's early experiences.*

 Return to Chapter 1, page 18, and review Erikson's stages of psychosocial development. Select two stages beyond infancy and toddlerhood. Explain how trust and autonomy help the developing person resolve these later psychological conflicts positively.

EMOTIONAL DEVELOPMENT

In the previous chapter, I suggested that you observe babies' increasingly effective schemes for controlling the environment and ways that adults support cognitive and language development. Now focus on another aspect of infant and caregiver behavior: the exchange of emotions. While you observe, note the various emotions the infant displays, the cues you rely on to interpret the baby's emotional state, and how the caregiver responds. Researchers have conducted many such observations to find out how babies communicate their emotions and interpret those of others. They have discovered that emotions play a powerful role in organizing the attainments that Erikson regarded as so important—social relationships, exploration of the environment, and discovery of the self (Izard, 1991; Lazarus, 1991; Saarni, Mumme, & Campos, 1998).

Since infants cannot describe their feelings, determining exactly which emotions they are experiencing is a challenge. Although vocalizations and body movements provide some information, facial expressions offer the most reliable cues.

A LIFESPAN VISTA

MATERNAL DEPRESSION AND CHILDREN'S DEVELOPMENT

Approximately 8 to 10 percent of women experience chronic depression —mild to severe feelings of sadness and withdrawal that continue for months or years. Often the beginnings of this gloomy, distressed emotional state cannot be pinpointed; it has become part of the person's daily life. In other instances, it emerges or strengthens after childbirth but fails to subside as the new mother adjusts to hormonal changes in her body and gains confidence in caring for her baby. Stella experienced this type— called *postpartum depression*. Although genetic makeup increases the risk of depressive illness, Stella's case shows that social and cultural factors are also involved.

During Stella's pregnancy, her husband Kyle's lack of interest in parenthood caused her to worry that having a baby might be a mistake. Shortly after Lucy was born, Stella's mood plunged. She was anxious and weepy, overwhelmed by Lucy's needs, and angry that she no longer had control

over her own schedule. When Stella approached Kyle about her fatigue and his unwillingness to help with the baby, he snapped that she overreacted to every move he made. Stella's friends, who did not have children, stopped by once to see Lucy and did not call again.

Children of depressed parents are 2 to 5 times more likely to develop behavior problems than are children of nondepressed parents (Cummings & Davies, 1994b). Although heredity may be partly responsible, quality of parenting—in particular, less sensitive interaction—plays a major role. The more extreme the depression and the greater the number of stressors in a mother's life (such as marital discord, little or no social support, and poverty), the more the parent–child relationship suffers (Goodman et al., 1993). Stella, for example, rarely smiled and talked to Lucy, who responded to her mother's sad, vacant gaze by turning away, crying, and often looking sad or angry herself (Campbell, Cohn, & Meyers, 1995; Murray & Cooper,

1997). Each time this happened, Stella felt inadequate as a mother, and her depression deepened. By 6 months of age, Lucy showed emotional symptoms common in babies of depressed mothers—a negative, irritable mood and attachment difficulties (Teti et al., 1995).

When maternal depression persists, the parent–child relationship worsens. Depressed parents use inconsistent discipline—sometimes lax, at other times too forceful—a pattern that reflects their disengaged as well as hostile behavior (Zahn-Waxler et al., 1990). As we will see in later chapters, children who experience these maladaptive parenting practices often have serious adjustment problems. To avoid their parents' insensitivity, they sometimes withdraw into a depressive mood themselves. Or they mimic their parents' anger and become impulsive and antisocial (Conger, Patterson, & Ge, 1995).

Over time, the parenting behaviors just described lead children to develop a negative world view—one

---

Cross-cultural evidence reveals that people around the world associate photographs of different facial expressions with emotions in the same way (Ekman & Friesen, 1972). These findings, which suggest that emotional expressions are built-in social signals, inspired researchers to analyze infants' facial patterns carefully to determine the range of emotions they display at different ages.

DEVELOPMENT OF SOME BASIC EMOTIONS

Do infants come into the world with the ability to express **basic emotions**—those that can be directly inferred from facial expressions, such as happiness, interest, surprise, fear, anger, sadness, and disgust? Most researchers agree that signs of almost all these emotions are present in early infancy (Izard et al., 1995; Malatesta-Magai, Izard, & Camras, 1991). Over time, they become well-organized signals.

Around 6 months, face, voice, and posture form distinct patterns that are clearly related to social events. For example, April typically responded to her mother's playful interaction with a joyful face, pleasant cooing, and a relaxed posture, as if to say, "This is fun!" In contrast, a withdrawn, unresponsive mother is likely to evoke either a sad face, fussy sounds, and a tense body (sending the message "I'm overwhelmed") or an angry face, crying, and "pick-me-up" gestures (stating, "Change this unpleasant event!") (Weinberg & Tronick, 1994, 1996; Yale et al., 1999). If these maternal depressive signals continue, they can profoundly disrupt emotional and social development (see the Lifespan Vista box above). In sum, by the middle of the first year, emotional expressions are well organized and specific—and therefore able to tell us a great deal about the infant's internal state.

Three basic emotions—happiness, anger, and fear—have received the most research attention. Refer to Table 6.1 for an overview of changes in these emotions as well as others we will take up in this chapter.

in which they perceive their parents and other people as a threat to their well-being. Children who constantly feel in danger and whose parents have not helped them learn how to manage negative feelings are likely to lose control in the face of cognitive and social challenges (Cummings & Cicchetti, 1990). Depressed parents are also more likely to have unhappy marriages. Repeated exposure to parental arguments sensitizes children to conflict, increasing their distress and aggression (Cummings & Zahn-Waxler, 1992). Impairments in regulating emotion compound these children's difficulties.

To prevent maternal depression from having lasting consequences, early treatment is vital. Stella described her tearfulness, fatigue, and inability to comfort Lucy to her doctor. He referred her to a program for depressed mothers and their babies, where a counselor worked with the family, helping Stella and Kyle with their marital problems and encouraging them to be more sensitive and patient with Lucy. In most cases of postpartum depression, treatment is successful •

(Cooper & Murray, 1997). When a depressed mother does not respond easily to treatment, a warm relationship with the father or another caregiver and efforts to reduce the many stressors that typically accompany depression can safeguard a child's development.

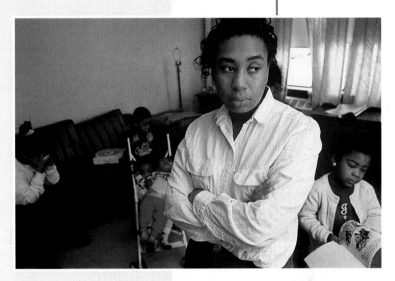

■ Depression combined with the stresses of poverty disrupts this mother's capacity to engage in positive, responsive interaction with her children. They respond in kind to her sad, vacant expression and are at risk for serious adjustment problems. (Photo courtesy: Kevin Horan/Stone)

TABLE 6.1	

Milestones of Emotional Development During the First Two Years

APPROXIMATE AGE	MILESTONES
Birth	Infants show signs of almost all the basic emotions.
2–3 months	Infants engage in social smiling and respond in kind to adults' facial expressions.
3–4 months	Infants begin to laugh at very active stimuli.
6–8 months	Emotional expressions are well organized and clearly related to social events. Infants start to become angry more often and in a wide range of situations.
	Fear, especially stranger anxiety, begins to arise. Attachment to the familiar caregiver is clearly evident, and separation anxiety appears. Infants use caregivers as a secure base for exploration.
7–12 months	Infants perceive facial expressions as organized patterns, and meaningful understanding of them improves. Social referencing appears. Infants laugh at subtle elements of surprise.
18–24 months	Self-conscious emotions of shame, embarrassment, and pride appear. A vocabulary for talking about feelings develops rapidly. Toddlers begin to appreciate that others' emotional reactions may differ from their own. Emotional self-regulation improves. First signs of empathy appear.

■ H A P P I N E S S . Happiness—first in terms of blissful smiles and later through exuberant laughter—contributes to many aspects of development. Infants smile and laugh when they achieve new skills, expressing their delight in physical and cognitive mastery. The smile also encourages caregivers to be affectionate and stimulating, so the baby will smile even more. Happiness binds parent and baby into a warm, supportive relationship and fosters the infant's developing competence.

During the early weeks, newborn babies smile when full, during sleep, and in response to gentle touches and sounds, such as stroking the skin, rocking, and the mother's soft, high-pitched voice. By the end of the first month, infants start to smile at interesting sights, but these must be dynamic and eye-catching, such as a bright object jumping suddenly across the baby's field of vision. Between 6 and 10 weeks, the human face evokes a broad grin called the **social smile** (Sroufe & Waters, 1976). Not surprisingly, these changes in smiling parallel the development of infant perceptual capacities—in particular, babies' increasing sensitivity to visual patterns, including the human face (see Chapter 4).

Laughter, which appears around 3 to 4 months, reflects faster processing of information than does smiling. But like smiling, the first laughs occur in response to very active stimuli, such as the mother saying playfully, "I'm gonna get you!" and kissing the baby's tummy. As infants understand more about their world, they laugh at events with subtler elements of surprise. At 10 months, Byron chuckled as Lisa played a silent game of peekaboo. At 1 year, he laughed heartily as she crawled on all fours and then walked like a penguin (Sroufe & Wunsch, 1972).

By the middle of the first year, infants smile and laugh more often when interacting with familiar people, a preference that strengthens the parent–child bond. During the second year, the smile becomes a deliberate social signal. Toddlers break their play with an interesting toy to communicate their delight to an attentive adult (Jones & Raag, 1989).

■ A N G E R A N D F E A R . Newborn babies respond with generalized distress to a variety of unpleasant experiences, including hunger, painful medical procedures, changes in body temperature, and too much or too little stimulation. During the first 2 months, fleeting expressions of anger appear as babies cry. These gradually increase in frequency and intensity from 4 to 6 months into the second year. Older babies also show anger in a wider range of situations—for example, when an object is taken away, the caregiver leaves for a brief time, or they are put down for a nap (Camras et al., 1992; Stenberg & Campos, 1990).

Like anger, fear rises during the second half of the first year. Older infants often hesitate before playing with a new toy, and research with the visual cliff reveals that newly crawling infants soon show fear of heights (see Chapter 4). But the most frequent expression of fear is to unfamiliar adults, a response called **stranger anxiety.** Many infants

■ As this Israeli family ventures from their kibbutz home to spend time with relatives in Jerusalem, their toddler cries in response to new people and places. Frequent terrorist attacks have led to widespread wariness of strangers—emotional reactions that are communicated to young children. Stranger anxiety is especially high among kibbutz babies. (Photo courtesy: Alan Oddie/ PhotoEdit)

and toddlers are quite wary of strangers, although the reaction does not always occur. It depends on several factors: the infant's temperament (some babies are generally more fearful), past experiences with strangers, and the situation in which baby and stranger meet (Thompson & Limber, 1991).

To understand these influences, let's return to Rachel's fearful withdrawal from her grandparents, described at the beginning of this chapter. From birth, Rachel's mother cared for her continuously. She had little opportunity to get to know strange adults. Also, she met her grandparents in an unfamiliar environment (a crowded airport), and they rushed over and tried to hold her. Under these conditions, babies are most likely to display fearful reactions. Later, at home, Rachel watched with interest and approached as her grandmother sat quietly on the sofa, smiled, and held out a teddy bear. A familiar setting, the opportunity to become acquainted from a distance, and warmth and friendliness on the part of the stranger reduced Rachel's fear (Horner, 1980).

What is the significance of this rise in anger and fear after 6 months of age? Researchers believe that these emotions have survival value as babies begin to move on their own. Older infants can use the energy mobilized by anger to defend themselves or overcome obstacles. And fear keeps babies' enthusiasm for exploration in check, increasing the likelihood that they will remain close to the mother and be careful about approaching unfamiliar people and objects. Anger and fear are also strong social signals that motivate caregivers to comfort a suffering infant.

Cognitive development plays an important role in infants' angry and fearful reactions, just as it does in their expressions of happiness. Between 8 and 12 months, when (as Piaget pointed out) babies grasp the notion of intentional behavior, they have a better understanding of the cause of their frustrations. Therefore, they know whom or what to get angry at. In the case of fear, improved memories permit older infants to distinguish familiar from unfamiliar events better than before.

Finally, culture can modify these emotions through infant rearing practices. Maternal mortality is very high among the Efe hunters and gatherers of the Congo, Africa. To ensure infant survival, a collective caregiving system exists in which Efe babies are passed from one adult to another—relatives and nonrelatives alike. Consequently, Efe infants show little stranger anxiety (Tronick, Morelli, & Ivey, 1992). In contrast, in Israeli kibbutzim (cooperative agricultural settlements), frequent terrorist attacks have led to widespread wariness of strangers. By the end of the first year, when (as we will see later) infants look to others for cues about how to respond emotionally, kibbutz babies display far greater stranger anxiety than do their city-reared counterparts (Saarni, Mumme, & Campos, 1998).

UNDERSTANDING AND RESPONDING TO THE EMOTIONS OF OTHERS

Infants' emotional expressions are closely tied to their ability to interpret the emotional cues of others. Already we have seen that within the first few months, babies match the feeling tone of the caregiver in face-to-face communication. Early on, infants detect others' emotions through a fairly automatic process of *emotional contagion,* just as we tend to smile, laugh, or feel sad when we sense these emotions in others.

Between 7 and 10 months, infants perceive facial expressions as organized patterns, and they can match the emotion in a voice with the appropriate face of a speaking person (see Chapter 4). Responding to emotional expressions as organized wholes indicates that these signals have become meaningful to babies. Soon they realize that an emotional expression not only has meaning, but is a meaningful reaction to a specific object or event (Bornstein & Lamb, 1992; Walker-Andrews, 1997).

Once these understandings are in place, infants engage in **social referencing,** in which they actively seek emotional information from a trusted person in an uncertain situation. Many studies show that the caregiver's emotional expression (happy, angry, or fearful) influences whether a 1-year-old will be wary of strangers, play with an unfamiliar toy, or cross the deep side of the visual cliff (Mumme, Fernald, & Herrera, 1996; Rosen, Adamson, & Bakeman, 1992; Sorce et al., 1985).

Social referencing grants infants and toddlers a powerful means for learning. By responding to caregivers' emotional messages, they can avoid harmful situations, such as a shock from an electric outlet or a fall down a steep staircase, without first experiencing their unpleasant consequences. Social referencing also permits toddlers to compare their own assessments of events with those of others. By the middle of the second year, they begin to appreciate that others' emo-

tional reactions may differ from their own (Repacholi & Gopnik, 1997). Furthermore, parents can capitalize on social referencing to teach their young children, whose capacity to explore is rapidly expanding, how to react to a great many novel events.

In sum, with the transition from infancy to toddlerhood, children move beyond simply reacting to others' emotional messages. They use those signals to find out about others' internal states and preferences and to guide their own actions.

EMERGENCE OF SELF-CONSCIOUS EMOTIONS

Besides basic emotions, humans are capable of a second, higher-order set of feelings, including shame, embarrassment, guilt, envy, and pride. These are called **self-conscious emotions** because each involves injury to or enhancement of our sense of self. For example, when we are ashamed or embarrassed, we feel negatively about our behavior, and we want to retreat so others will no longer notice our failings. In contrast, pride reflects delight in the self's achievements, and we are inclined to tell others what we have accomplished (Saarni, Mumme, & Campos, 1998).

Self-conscious emotions appear at the end of the second year, as the sense of self emerges. Between 18 and 24 months, children can be seen feeling ashamed and embarrassed as they lower their eyes, hang their heads, and hide their faces with their hands. Pride also emerges at this time, and envy and guilt are present by age 3 (Lewis et al., 1989; Sroufe, 1979). Besides self-awareness, self-conscious emotions require an additional ingredient: adult instruction in *when* to feel proud, ashamed, or guilty. Parents begin this tutoring early when they say, "My, look at how far you can throw that ball!" or, "You should feel ashamed for grabbing that toy from Billy!"

■ *Self-conscious emotions appear at the end of the second year. This Guatemalan 2-year-old undoubtedly feels a sense of pride as she helps care for her elderly grandmother—an activity highly valued in her culture. (Photo courtesy: Celia Roberts/Earth Images)*

Self-conscious emotions help children acquire socially and culturally valued behaviors and goals. For example, in most of the United States, children are taught from an early age to feel pride about personal achievement—throwing a ball the farthest, winning a game, and (later on) getting good grades. Around age 2, American children are likely to call a parent's attention to an achievement, such as a completed puzzle, by pointing and saying, "Look, Mom!" (Stipek, Recchia, & McClintic, 1992). Among the Zuni Indians, shame and embarrassment are responses to purely personal success, whereas pride is evoked by helpfulness and generosity (Benedict, 1934). In Japan, violating cultural standards of concern for others—a parent, a teacher, or an employer—is cause for intense shame (Lewis, 1992).

BEGINNINGS OF EMOTIONAL SELF-REGULATION

Besides expanding their range of emotional reactions, infants and toddlers begin to find ways to manage their emotional experiences. **Emotional self-regulation** refers to the strategies we use to adjust our emotional state to a comfortable level of intensity so we can accomplish our goals (Eisenberg et al., 1995; Thompson, 1994). If you drank a cup of coffee to wake up this morning, reminded yourself that an anxiety-provoking event would be over soon, or decided not to see a scary horror film, you were engaging in emotional self-regulation.

In the early months of life, infants have only a limited capacity to regulate their emotional states. Although they can turn away from unpleasant stimulation and mouth and suck when their feelings get too intense, they are easily overwhelmed. They depend for help on the soothing interventions of caregivers—lifting the distressed baby to the shoulder, rocking, and talking softly.

Rapid development of the cortex gradually increases the baby's tolerance for stimulation. Between 2 and 4 months, caregivers start to build on this capacity through engaging in face-to-face play and encouraging attention to objects. In these interactions, parents arouse pleasure in the baby while adjusting the pace of their own behavior so the infant does not become overwhelmed and distressed. As a result, the baby's tolerance for stimulation increases further (Field, 1994). By the end of the first year, infants' ability to move about permits them to regulate feelings more effectively by approaching or retreating from various situations.

As caregivers help infants regulate their emotional states, they also provide lessons in socially approved ways of expressing feelings. Beginning in the first few months, American middle-SES mothers match their baby's positive feelings far more often than the negative ones. Boys get more of this training in controlling unhappiness than do girls, in part because infant boys find it harder to regulate negative emotion. As a result, the well-known sex differ-

ence—females as emotionally expressive and males as emotionally controlled—is promoted at a very tender age (Malatesta et al., 1986; Weinberg et al., 1999). Furthermore, cultures that stress collectivism over individualism usually place greater emphasis on socially appropriate emotional behavior. Compared with Americans, Japanese and Chinese adults value emotional restraint and discourage strong emotional expression in babies (Fogel, 1993; Kuchner, 1989). By the end of the first year, Chinese and, to a lesser extent, Japanese infants smile and cry less than do American babies (Camras et al., 1998).

By the second year, growth in representation and language leads to new ways of regulating emotions. A vocabulary for talking about feelings, such as *happy, love, surprised, scary, yucky,* and *mad,* develops rapidly after 18 months (Bretherton et al., 1986). Children of this age are not yet good at using language to comfort themselves (Grolnick, Bridges, & Connell, 1996). But by describing their emotions, toddlers can guide caregivers in helping them feel better. For example, while listening to a story about monsters, Rachel whimpered, "Mommy, scary." Beth put the book down and gave Rachel a comforting hug.

ASK YOURSELF . . .

■ *Dana is planning to meet her 10-month-old niece Laureen for the first time. How should Dana expect Laureen to react? How would you advise Dana to go about establishing a positive relationship with Laureen?*

■ *One of Byron's favorite games was dancing with his mother while she sang "Old MacDonald," clapping his hands and stepping from side to side. At 14 months, Byron danced joyfully as Beth and Felicia watched. At 20 months, he began to show signs of embarrassment—smiling, looking away, and covering his eyes with his hands. What explains this change in Byron's emotional reaction?*

 Compare findings on the development of emotional self-regulation with the consequences of maternal depression for children's development (see pages 180 and 181). Do children of depressed mothers have lasting difficulties with emotional self-regulation? Explain.

TEMPERAMENT AND DEVELOPMENT

Beginning in early infancy, Byron, Rachel, and April showed distinct patterns of emotional responding. Byron was intense, active, and distractible—qualities that often made parenting quite trying for Lisa. In contrast, Rachel seemed calm, patient, and easily soothed (except on the occasion of her mother's brief absence). And April was an especially joyous baby whose friendliness consistently evoked positive responses from others.

When we describe one person as cheerful and "upbeat," another as active and energetic, and still others as calm, cautious, or prone to angry outbursts, we are referring to **temperament**—stable individual differences in quality and intensity of emotional reaction, activity level, attention, and emotional self-regulation (Rothbart & Bates, 1998). Researchers have become increasingly interested in temperamental differences among infants and children, since the psychological traits that make up temperament are believed to form the cornerstone of the adult personality.

The New York Longitudinal Study, initiated in 1956 by Alexander Thomas and Stella Chess, is the longest and most comprehensive study of temperament to date. A total of 141 children were followed from early infancy well into adulthood. Results showed that temperament is a major factor in increasing the chances that a child will experience psychological problems or, alternatively, be protected from the effects of a highly stressful home life. However, Thomas and Chess (1977) also found that temperament is not fixed and unchangeable. Parenting practices can modify children's emotional styles considerably.

These findings inspired a growing body of research on temperament, including its stability, its biological roots, and its interaction with child-rearing experiences. Let's begin to explore these issues by looking at the structure, or makeup, of temperament and how it is measured.

THE STRUCTURE OF TEMPERAMENT

Thomas and Chess's nine dimensions, listed in Table 6.2, served as the first influential model of temperament, inspiring all others that followed. When detailed descriptions of infants' and children's behavior obtained from parental interviews were rated on these dimensions, certain characteristics clustered together, yielding three types of children:

- The **easy child** (40 percent of the sample): This child quickly establishes regular routines in infancy, is generally cheerful, and adapts easily to new experiences.

- The **difficult child** (10 percent of the sample): This child is irregular in daily routines, is slow to accept new experiences, and tends to react negatively and intensely.

- The **slow-to-warm-up child** (15 percent of the sample): This child is inactive, shows mild, low-key reactions to environmental stimuli, is negative in mood, and adjusts slowly to new experiences.

Note that 35 percent of the children did not fit any of these categories. Instead, they showed unique blends of temperamental characteristics.

TABLE 6.2

Two Models of Temperament

THOMAS AND CHESS		ROTHBART AND MAURO	
DIMENSION	**DESCRIPTION**	**DIMENSION**	**DESCRIPTION**
Activity level	Proportion of active periods to inactive ones	Activity level	Level of gross motor activity
Rhythmicity	Regularity of body functions, such as sleep, wakefulness, hunger, and excretion	Rhythmicity	Regularity of body functions
Distractibility	Degree to which stimulation from the environment alters behavior—for example, whether crying stops when a toy is offered	Attention span/persistence	Duration of orienting or interest
Approach/withdrawal	Response to a new object, food, or person.	Fearful distress	Wariness and distress in response to intense or novel stimuli, including time to adjust to new situations
Adaptability	Ease with which child adapts to changes in the environment, such as sleeping or eating in a new place	Irritable distress	Fussing and crying when desires are frustrated
Attention span and persistence	Amount of time devoted to an activity, such as watching a mobile or playing with a toy	Positive affect	Frequency of expression of happiness or pleasure
Intensity of reaction	Energy level of response, such as laughing, crying, talking, or gross motor activity		
Threshold of responsiveness	Intensity of stimulation required to evoke a response		
Quality of mood	Amount of friendly, joyful behavior as opposed to unpleasant, unfriendly behavior		

Sources: Rothbart & Mauro, 1990; Thomas & Chess, 1977.

At age 4 months, Larry and Mitch were brought by their mothers to the laboratory of Jerome Kagan, who observed their reactions to a variety of unfamiliar experiences. When exposed to new sights and sounds, such as a moving mobile decorated with colorful toys, Larry tensed his muscles, moved his arms and legs with agitation, and began to cry. Mitch's body remained relaxed and quiet, and he smiled and cooed pleasurably at the excitement around him.

Larry and Mitch returned to the laboratory as toddlers. This time, each experienced a variety of procedures designed to induce uncertainty. For example, electrodes were placed on their bodies and blood pressure cuffs on their arms to measure heart rate; highly stimulating toy robots, animals, and puppets moved before their eyes; and unfamiliar people entered and behaved in atypical ways or wore unusual costumes. Larry whimpered and quickly withdrew, seeking his mother's protection. Mitch watched with interest, laughed at the strange sights, and approached the toys and strangers when invited to do so.

On a third visit, at age 4½ years, Larry barely talked or smiled during an interview with an unfamiliar adult. In contrast, Mitch spontaneously

asked questions, commented on the procedures, and communicated his pleasure at each intriguing activity. In a playroom with two unfamiliar peers, Larry pulled back, keeping an anxious eye on the other children. Mitch made friends quickly.

In longitudinal research on several hundred Caucasian children, Kagan (1998) found that about 20 percent of 4-month-old babies were easily upset by novelty (like Larry), whereas 40 percent were comfortable, even delighted, with new experiences (like Mitch). About 25 percent of these extreme groups retained their temperamental styles as they grew older. Those resembling Larry tended to become fearful, inhibited toddlers and preschoolers; those resembling Mitch developed into outgoing, uninhibited youngsters (Kagan, Snidman, & Arcus, 1998).

PHYSIOLOGICAL CORRELATES OF SHYNESS AND SOCIABILITY. Kagan believes that individual differences in arousal of the *amygdala,* an inner brain structure that controls avoidance reactions, contribute to these contrasting temperamental styles. In shy, inhibited children, novel stimuli easily excite the amygdala and its connections to the cerebral cortex and sympathetic nervous system, which prepares the body to act in the face of

threat. The same level of stimulation evokes minimal neural excitation in highly sociable, uninhibited children. In support of this theory, several physiological responses of shy infants and children resemble those of highly timid animals and are known to be mediated by the amygdala:

- *Heart rate.* As early as the first few weeks of life, the heart rates of shy children are consistently higher than those of sociable youngsters, and they speed up further in response to unfamiliar events (Snidman et al., 1995).

- *Cortisol.* Saliva concentration of cortisol, a hormone that regulates blood pressure and is involved in resistance to stress, tends to be higher in shy than in sociable children (Gunnar & Nelson, 1994; Kagan & Snidman, 1991).

- *Pupil dilation and blood pressure.* Compared with sociable children, shy children show greater pupil dilation and rise in blood pressure when faced with novelty and challenge (Kagan, 1994).

Yet another physiological correlate of approach–withdrawal to people and objects is the pattern of EEG waves in the frontal region of the cerebral cortex. Recall from Chapter 4 that the

---

Of the three temperamental types, the difficult pattern has sparked the most interest, since it places children at high risk for adjustment problems—both anxious withdrawal and aggressive behavior in early and middle childhood (Bates, Wachs, & Emde, 1994; Thomas, Chess, & Birch, 1968). Unlike difficult children, slow-to-warm-up children do not present many problems in the early years. They tend to show excessive fearfulness and slow, constricted behavior in middle childhood, after they enter school and peer groups in which they are expected to respond actively and quickly (Chess & Thomas, 1984).

A second model of temperament, devised by Mary Rothbart and Jennifer Mauro (1990), is also shown in Table 6.2. It combines dimensions of Thomas and Chess and other researchers that overlap. For example, "distractibility" and "attention span and persistence" are considered opposite ends of the same continuum and simply called "attention span/persistence." Rothbart and Mauro also include a dimension not identified by Thomas and Chess—"irritable distress"—that emphasizes emotional self-regulation. Overall, the temperamental characteristics shown in Table 6.2 provide a fairly complete picture of the traits most often studied.

left cortical hemisphere is specialized to respond with positive emotion, the right hemisphere with negative emotion. Shy infants and preschoolers show greater right than left frontal brain wave activity; their sociable counterparts show the opposite pattern (Calkins, Fox, & Marshall, 1996; Fox, Calkins & Bell, 1994). Neural activity in the amygdala is transmitted to the frontal lobe and may influence these patterns.

LONG-TERM CONSEQUENCES.
According to Kagan (1998), children who are extremely shy or sociable inherit a physiology that biases them toward a particular temperamental style. Among Caucasians, shy children are more likely to have certain physical traits—blue eyes and thin faces—known to be affected by heredity (Arcus & Kagan, 1995). The genes controlling these characteristics may also influence the excitability of the amygdala.

Yet heritability research indicates that genes make only a modest contribution to shyness and sociability. They share power with experience. When early inhibition persists into middle childhood, adolescence, and adulthood, it can lead to adjustment difficulties, such as excessive cautiousness, social withdrawal, and loneliness (Caspi & Silva, 1995). At the same time, most inhibited infants and young children cope with novelty more effectively as they get older.

Child-rearing practices affect the chances that an emotionally reactive baby will become a fearful child. Warm, supportive parenting reduces the physiological reactivity of shy babies, whereas cold, intrusive parenting heightens it (Gunnar, 1998). In addition, when parents protect infants who dislike novelty from minor stresses, they make it harder for the child to overcome an urge to retreat from unfamiliar events. In contrast, parents who make appropriate demands for their baby to approach new experiences help the child overcome fear (Rubin et al., 1997). In sum, for children to develop at their best, parenting must be tailored to their temperaments—a theme we will encounter again in this and later chapters.

■ *This shy 2-year-old retreats as an adult friend of her parents bends down to chat with her, despite her mother's reassurances and encouragement. A strong physiological response to uncertain situations prompts her social withdrawal. (Photo courtesy: Robert Brenner/PhotoEdit)*

MEASURING TEMPERAMENT

Temperament is usually assessed in one of three ways: through interviews and questionnaires given to parents; through behavior ratings by doctors, nurses, or caregivers who know the child well; or through direct observation by researchers. Parental reports have been emphasized because of their convenience and parents' depth of knowledge about the child. At the same time, they have been criticized for being biased and subjective. Nevertheless, parent ratings are moderately related to observations of children's behavior (Rothbart & Bates, 1998). And parent perceptions are useful for understanding the way parents view and respond to their child.

Recently, physiological measures have been used to supplement these techniques, in hopes of identifying biological processes at the heart of temperamental styles. Most of these efforts have focused on **inhibited, or shy, children,** who react negatively to and withdraw from novel stimuli (much like Thomas and Chess's slow-to-warm-up children), and **uninhibited,** or **sociable children,** who display positive emotion to and approach novel objects and people. As the Variations box above reveals, heart rate, hormone levels, and EEG waves in the frontal region of the cerebral cortex differentiate children with inhibited and uninhibited temperaments.

STABILITY OF TEMPERAMENT

It would be difficult to claim that temperament really exists if children's emotional styles were not stable over time. Indeed, the findings of many studies provide support for the stability of temperament. Infants and young children who score low or high on attention span, activity level, irritability, sociability, or shyness are likely to respond similarly when assessed again several months to a few years later and, occasionally, even into the adult years (Caspi & Silva, 1995; Kochanska & Radke-Yarrow, 1992; Pedlow et al., 1993; Rothbart, Derryberry, & Posner, 1994; Ruff et al., 1990).

When the evidence as a whole is examined carefully, however, temperamental stability from one age period to the next is generally low to moderate (Rothbart & Bates, 1998). Although quite a few children remain the same, a good number have changed when assessed again. In fact, some characteristics, such as shyness and sociability, are stable over the long term only in children at the extremes—those who are very inhibited or very outgoing to begin with (Kerr et al., 1994; Sanson et al., 1996).

Temperament is least stable during infancy because early behaviors change quickly with brain development and sensitive caregiving. For example, recall from Chapter 3 that the early months are a period of fussing and crying for most babies. As infants become better at regulating their emotions, many who initially seemed irritable become calm and content. Consequently, long-term prediction of temperament is best achieved from the second year of life and after, when styles of responding are better established (Caspi, 1998; Lemery et al., 1999).

At the same time, the changes shown by many youngsters in childhood suggest that biologically based temperamental traits can be modified by experience (although children rarely change from one extreme to another—that is, a shy toddler practically never becomes highly sociable). With these ideas in mind, let's turn to genetic and environmental contributions to temperament and personality.

GENETIC INFLUENCES

The word *temperament* implies a genetic foundation for individual differences in emotional style. Research shows that identical twins are more similar than fraternal twins across a wide range of temperamental and personality traits (DiLalla, Kagan, & Reznick, 1994; Emde et al., 1992; Goldsmith, Buss, & Lemery, 1997). In Chapter 2, we noted that heritability estimates suggest a moderate role for heredity in temperament and personality: About half of the individual differences among us can be traced to differences in our genetic makeup.

Consistent ethnic and sex differences in early temperament exist, again implying a role for heredity. Like Rachel, Chinese and Japanese babies tend to be less active, irritable, and vocal; more easily soothed; and better at quieting themselves than are Caucasian infants (Kagan et al., 1994; Lewis, Ramsay, & Kawakami, 1993). And Byron's high activity level is consistent with a tendency for boys to be more active and daring and girls more anxious and timid—a difference reflected in boys' higher injury rates throughout childhood and adolescence (Richardson, Koller, & Katz, 1986).

ENVIRONMENTAL INFLUENCES

Although genetic influences on temperament are clear, no study has shown that infants maintain their emotional styles in the absence of environmental supports. Instead, heredity and environment often combine to strengthen the stability of temperament, since a child's approach to the world affects the experiences to which she is exposed. To see how this works, let's take a second look at ethnic and sex differences in temperament.

As I watched Beth care for Rachel as a 3-month-old baby, her calm, soothing manner and use of gentle rocking and touching contrasted with Lisa's and Felicia's tendency to stimulate Byron and April through lively facial expressions and talking. These differences in early caregiving appear repeatedly in studies comparing Caucasian with Asian infant–mother pairs (Fogel, Toda, & Kawai, 1988). They suggest that some differences in early temperament are encouraged by cultural beliefs and practices. When asked about their approach to child rearing, Japanese mothers say that babies come into the world as independent beings who must learn to rely on their mothers through close physical contact. American mothers are likely to believe just the opposite—that they must wean babies away from dependence into autonomy (Kojima, 1986). As a result, Japanese mothers do more comforting and American mothers more stimulating—behaviors that enhance early temperamental differences between their infants.

A similar process seems to contribute to sex differences in temperament. Within the first 24 hours after birth (before they have had much experience with the baby), parents already perceive boys and girls differently. Sons are rated as larger, better coordinated, more alert, and stronger. Daughters are viewed as softer, more awkward, weaker, and more delicate (Stern & Karraker, 1989; Vogel et al., 1991). Gender-stereotyped beliefs carry over into the way parents treat their infants and toddlers. For example, parents more often encourage sons to be physically active and daughters to seek help and physical closeness (Ruble & Martin, 1998). These practices promote temperamental differences between boys and girls.

In families with several children, an additional influence on temperament is at work. Parents often look for and emphasize each child's unique characteristics (Plomin,

■ *Beginning at birth, Chinese infants are calmer, more easily soothed when upset, and better at quieting themselves than are Caucasian infants. These differences are probably hereditary, but cultural variations in child rearing support them. (Photo courtesy: Alan Oddie/Photoedit)*

1994c).You can see this in the comments they make after the birth of a second baby: "He's so much calmer," "She's a lot more active," or "He's more sociable." When one child in a family is perceived as easy, another is likely to be regarded as difficult, even though the second child might not be very difficult when compared to children in general (Schachter & Stone, 1985). Each child, in turn, evokes responses from caregivers that are consistent with parental views and with the child's actual temperamental style. In sum, temperament and personality can be understood only in terms of complex interdependencies between genetic and environmental factors.

TEMPERAMENT AND CHILD REARING: THE GOODNESS-OF-FIT MODEL

Children with different temperaments have unique child-rearing needs. If a child's disposition interferes with learning or getting along with others, it is important for adults to counteract the child's maladaptive behavior gently but consistently.

Thomas and Chess (1977) proposed a **goodness-of-fit model** to explain how temperament and environment can work together to produce favorable outcomes. Goodness of fit involves creating child-rearing environments that recognize each child's temperament while helping the youngster achieve more adaptive functioning. In short, children with different temperaments have unique child-rearing needs.

Goodness of fit helps explain why children with difficult temperaments are at high risk for later adjustment prob-

lems. These children, at least in Western middle-SES families, frequently experience parenting that fits poorly with their dispositions. As infants, they are far less likely to receive sensitive caregiving (van den Boom & Hoeksma, 1994). By the second year, parents of difficult children often resort to angry, punitive discipline, and the child reacts with defiance and disobedience. Then parents often behave inconsistently, rewarding the child's noncompliance by giving in to it, although they initially resisted (Lee & Bates, 1985). These practices maintain and even increase the child's irritable, conflict-ridden style.

Both difficult and shy children benefit from warm, accepting parenting that makes firm but reasonable demands for mastering new experiences. Yet goodness of fit depends in part on cultural values. For example, difficult children in low-SES Puerto Rican families are treated with sensitivity and patience; they are not at risk for adjustment problems (Gannon & Korn, 1983). In Western nations, shy children are regarded as socially incompetent—an attitude that discourages parents from helping them approach new situations. Yet in Chinese culture, adults evaluate shy children positively—as advanced in social maturity and understanding. Parental warmth and encouragement of new skills predict outgoingness in Western toddlers, inhibited behavior in Chinese toddlers. And in line with cultural values, Chinese toddlers are more likely to be inhibited than are their Western agemates (Chen, Rubin, & Li, 1995; Chen et al., 1998).

In cultures in which particular temperamental styles are linked to adjustment problems, a good match between rearing conditions and child temperament is best accomplished early, before unfavorable temperament–environment relationships have had a chance to produce maladjustment that is hard to undo. In the following sections, we will see that goodness of fit is also at the heart of infant–caregiver attachment. This first intimate relationship grows out of interaction between parent and baby, to which the emotional styles of both partners contribute.

ASK YOURSELF . . .

■ *Rachel, like many other Asian infants, is calm and easily soothed when upset. What factors contribute to her temperamental style?*

■ *At 18 months, highly active Byron climbed out of his high chair long before his meal was finished. Exasperated with Byron's behavior, his father made him sit at the table until he had eaten all his food. Soon Byron's behavior escalated into a full-blown tantrum. Using the concept of goodness of fit, suggest another way of handling Byron.*

Citing evidence on inhibited, or shy, children and uninhibited, or sociable, children, show how biology, parenting practices, and culture jointly influence the development of temperament.

DEVELOPMENT OF ATTACHMENT

Attachment is the strong, affectional tie we feel for special people in our lives that leads us to experience pleasure and joy when we interact with them and to be comforted by their nearness during times of stress. By the end of the first year, infants have become attached to familiar people who have responded to their needs for physical care and stimulation. Watch babies of this age, and notice how parents are singled out for special attention. A whole range of responses are reserved just for them. For example, when the mother enters the room, the baby breaks into a broad, friendly smile. When she picks him up, he pats her face, explores her hair, and snuggles against her. When he feels anxious or afraid, he crawls into her lap and clings closely.

Freud first suggested that the infant's emotional tie to the mother is the foundation for all later relationships. We will see shortly that research on the consequences of attachment is consistent with Freud's idea. But attachment has also been the subject of intense theoretical debate. Turn back to the description of Freud's and Erikson's theories at the beginning of this chapter, and notice how *psychoanalytic theory* regards feeding as the primary context in which caregivers and babies build this close emotional bond. *Behaviorism*, too, emphasizes the importance of feeding, but for different reasons. According to a well-known behaviorist account, as the mother satisfies the baby's hunger, infants learn to prefer her soft caresses, warm smiles, and tender words of comfort because these events have been paired with tension relief (Sears, Maccoby, & Levin, 1957).

Although feeding is an important context for building a close relationship, attachment does not depend on hunger satisfaction. In the 1950s, a famous experiment showed that rhesus monkeys reared with terry-cloth and wire-mesh "surrogate mothers" clung to the soft terry-cloth substitute, even though the wire-mesh "mother" held the bottle and infants had to climb on it to be fed (Harlow & Zimmerman, 1959). Observations of human infants also reveal that they become attached to family members who seldom if ever feed them, including fathers, siblings, and grandparents. And perhaps you have noticed that toddlers in Western cultures who sleep alone and experience frequent daytime separations from their parents sometimes develop strong emotional ties to cuddly objects, such as blankets and teddy bears (Passman, 1987). Yet such objects have never played a role in infant feeding!

■ *Baby monkeys reared with "surrogate mothers" from birth preferred to cling to a soft terry-cloth "mother" instead of a wire-mesh "mother" that held a bottle. These findings reveal that the drive-reduction explanation of attachment, which assumes that the mother–infant relationship is based on feeding, is incorrect. (Photo courtesy: Martin Rogers/Stock Boston)*

ETHOLOGICAL THEORY OF ATTACHMENT

Today, **ethological theory of attachment** is the most widely accepted view of the infant's emotional tie to the caregiver. According to ethology, many human behaviors have evolved over the history of our species because they promote survival. John Bowlby (1969), who first applied this idea to the infant–caregiver bond, was inspired by Konrad Lorenz's studies of imprinting in baby geese (see Chapter 1). He believed that the human infant, like the young of other animal species, is endowed with a set of built-in behaviors that help keep the parent nearby, increasing the chances that the infant will be protected from danger. Contact with the parent also ensures that the baby will be fed, but Bowlby was careful to point out that feeding is not the basis for attachment. Instead, the attachment bond itself has strong biological roots. It can best be understood in an evolutionary context in which survival of the species is of utmost importance.

According to Bowlby, the infant's relationship with the parent begins as a set of innate signals that call the adult to the baby's side. Over time, a true affectional bond develops, which is supported by new cognitive and emotional capacities as well as a history of warm, responsive care. Attachment develops in four phases:

1. *The preattachment phase* (birth to 6 weeks). A variety of built-in signals—grasping, smiling, crying, and gazing into the adult's eyes—help bring newborn babies into close contact with other humans. Once an adult responds, infants encourage her to remain nearby, since they are comforted when picked up, stroked, and talked to softly. Babies of this age can recognize their own mother's smell and voice (see Chapter 3). But they are not yet attached to her, since they do not mind being left with an unfamiliar adult.

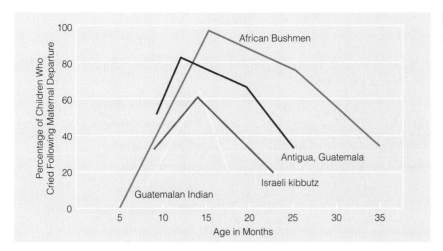

2. *The "attachment-in-the-making" phase* (6 weeks to 6–8 months). During this phase, infants start to respond differently to a familiar caregiver than to a stranger. For example, at 4 months, Byron smiled, laughed, and babbled more freely when interacting with his mother and quieted more quickly when she picked him up. But even though they can recognize the parent, babies do not yet protest when separated from her. Therefore, attachment is under way but not yet established.

3. *The phase of "clearcut" attachment* (6–8 months to 18 months–2 years). Now attachment to the familiar caregiver is clearly evident. Babies display **separation anxiety,** becoming upset when the adult whom they have come to rely on leaves. (Recall Rachel's behavior when her mother left her with her grandparents.) Separation anxiety appears universally around the world after 6 months of age, increasing until about 15 months (see Figure 6.1).

Besides protesting the parent's departure, older infants and toddlers try hard to maintain her presence. Crawling and walking babies approach, follow, and climb on her in preference to others. And they use her as a **secure base** from which to explore, venturing into the environment and then returning for emotional support.

4. *Formation of a reciprocal relationship* (18 months–2 years and on). By the end of the second year, rapid growth in representation and language permits toddlers to begin to understand the parent's coming and going and to predict her return. As a result, separation protest declines. Now children start to negotiate with the caregiver, using requests and persuasion rather than crawling after and clinging to her. For example, at age 2, April asked Felicia to read a story before leaving her with a baby-sitter. The extra time with her mother, along with a better understanding of where Felicia was going ("to a movie with Daddy") and when she would be back ("right after you go to sleep"), helped April tolerate her mother's absence.

According to Bowlby (1980), out of their experiences during these four phases, children construct an enduring affectional tie to the caregiver that they can use as a secure base in the parent's absence. This inner representation becomes a vital part of personality. It serves as an **internal working model,** or set of expectations about the availability of attachment figures and their likelihood of providing support during times of stress. This image becomes the model, or guide, for all future close relationships—through childhood and adolescence and into adult life (Bretherton, 1992).

■ **MEASURING THE SECURITY OF ATTACHMENT**

Although virtually all family-reared babies become attached to a familiar caregiver by the second year, the quality of this relationship differs from child to child. A widely used technique for assessing the quality of attachment between 1 and 2 years of age is the **Strange Situation.** In designing it, Mary Ainsworth and her colleagues reasoned that securely attached infants and toddlers should use the parent as a secure base from which to explore an unfamiliar playroom. In addition, when the parent leaves for a brief time, the child should show separation anxiety and find a strange adult less comforting than the parent. As summarized in Table 6.3 on page 192, the Strange Situation takes the baby through eight short episodes in which brief separations from and reunions with the parent occur.

Observing the responses of infants to these episodes, researchers have identified a secure attachment pattern and three patterns of insecurity (Ainsworth et al., 1978; Main & Solomon, 1990). Which of the following patterns do you think Rachel displayed in the incident described at the beginning of this chapter?

■ **Secure attachment.** These infants use the parent as a secure base from which to explore. When separated, they may or may not cry, but if they do, it is due to the parent's absence, since they prefer her to the stranger.

TABLE 6.3

Episodes in the Strange Situation

EPISODE	EVENTS	ATTACHMENT BEHAVIOR OBSERVED
1	Experimenter introduces parent and baby to playroom and then leaves.	
2	Parent is seated while baby plays with toys.	Parent as a secure base
3	Stranger enters, is seated, and talks to parent.	Reaction to unfamiliar adult
4	Parent leaves room. Stranger responds to baby and offers comfort if upset.	Separation anxiety
5	Parent returns, greets baby, and offers comfort if necessary. Stranger leaves room.	Reaction to reunion
6	Parent leaves room.	Separation anxiety
7	Stranger enters room and offers comfort.	Ability to be soothed by stranger
8	Parent returns, greets baby, offers comfort if necessary, and tries to reinterest baby in toys.	Reaction to reunion

Note: Episode 1 lasts about 30 seconds; the remaining episodes each last about 3 minutes. Separation episodes are cut short if the baby becomes very upset. Reunion episodes are extended if the baby needs more time to calm down and return to play.
Source: Ainsworth et al., 1978.

When the parent returns, they actively seek contact, and their crying is reduced immediately. About 65 percent of American babies show this pattern.

- **Avoidant attachment.** These infants seem unresponsive to the parent when she is present. When she leaves, they are usually not distressed, and they react to the stranger in much the same way as the parent. During reunion, they avoid or are slow to greet the parent, and when picked up, they often fail to cling. About 20 percent of American babies show this pattern.

- **Resistant attachment.** Before separation, these infants seek closeness to the parent and often fail to explore. When she returns, they display angry, resistive behavior, sometimes hitting and pushing. Many continue to cry after being picked up and cannot be comforted easily. About 10 to 15 percent of American infants show this pattern.

- **Disorganized–disoriented attachment.** This pattern reflects the greatest insecurity. At reunion, these infants show a variety of confused, contradictory behaviors. For example, they might look away while being held by the parent or approach her with a flat, depressed gaze. A few cry out unexpectedly after having calmed down or display odd, frozen postures.

Infants' reactions in the Strange Situation resemble their use of the parent as a secure base and their response to separation at home (Pederson & Moran, 1996; Pederson et al., 1998). For this reason, the procedure is a powerful tool for assessing attachment security.

STABILITY OF ATTACHMENT AND CULTURAL VARIATIONS

Securely attached babies more often maintain their attachment status than do insecure babies, whose relationship with the caregiver is, by definition, fragile and unreliable. In addition, for middle-SES families with stable life conditions, attachment quality is usually secure and fairly stable into the childhood years (Wartner et al., 1994). But for low-SES families with many daily stresses, attachment status is more unstable (Owen et al., 1984). And for families undergoing major life changes, such as a shift in employment or marital status, quality of attachment is also likely to change, sometimes positively and sometimes negatively (Belsky et al., 1996; Thompson, Lamb, & Estes, 1982).

Furthermore, attachment patterns must be interpreted cautiously in different cultures. For example, as Figure 6.2 reveals, German infants show considerably more avoidant attachment than American babies do. But German parents encourage their infants to be nonclingy and independent, so the baby's behavior may be an intended outcome of cultural beliefs and practices (Grossmann et al., 1985). Did you classify Rachel's attachment behavior as resistant? An unusually high number of Japanese infants display a resistant response, but the reaction may not represent true insecurity. Japanese mothers rarely leave their babies in the care of unfamiliar people, so the Strange Situation probably creates far greater stress for them than it does for infants who frequently experience maternal separations (Takahashi, 1990). Despite these cultural variations, the secure pattern is still the most common pattern of attachment in all societies studied to date (van Ijzendoorn & Kroonenberg, 1988; Thompson, 1998).

FACTORS THAT AFFECT ATTACHMENT SECURITY

What factors might affect attachment security? Researchers have looked closely at four important influences: (1) opportunity to establish a close relationship; (2) quality of caregiving; (3) the baby's characteristics; and (4) the family context in which infant and parent live.

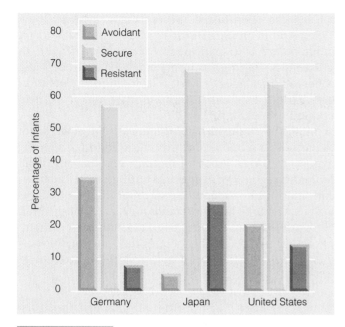

FIGURE 6.2

■ **A cross-cultural comparison of infants' reactions in the Strange Situation.** A high percentage of German babies seem avoidantly attached, whereas a substantial number of Japanese infants appear resistantly attached. Note that these responses may not reflect true insecurity. Instead, they are probably due to cultural differences in rearing practices. (Adapted from Thompson, 1998.)

■ OPPORTUNITY FOR ATTACHMENT. What happens when a baby does not have the opportunity to establish an affectional tie to a caregiver? In a series of landmark studies, René Spitz (1945, 1946) observed institutionalized babies who had been given up by their mothers between 3 and 12 months of age. The infants were placed on a large ward where they shared a nurse with at least seven other babies. In contrast to the happy, outgoing behavior they had shown before separation, they wept and withdrew from their surroundings, lost weight, and had difficulty sleeping. If a caregiver whom the baby could get to know did not replace the mother, the depression deepened rapidly.

These institutionalized babies had emotional difficulties because they were prevented from forming a bond with one or a few adults (Rutter, 1996). A more recent study supports this conclusion. Researchers followed the development of infants in an institution with a good caregiver–child ratio and a rich selection of books and toys. However, staff turnover was so rapid that the average child had 50 different caregivers by age 4½! Many of these children became "late adoptees" who were placed in homes after age 4. Most developed deep ties with their adoptive parents, indicating that a first attachment bond can develop as late as 4 to 6 years of age (Tizard & Rees, 1975).

But throughout childhood and adolescence, these youngsters were more likely to display emotional and social problems, including an excessive desire for adult attention, "over friendliness" to unfamiliar adults and peers, and few friend-

ships (Hodges & Tizard, 1989; Tizard & Hodges, 1978). Although follow-ups into adulthood are necessary to be sure, these findings leave open the possibility that fully normal development may depend on establishing close bonds with caregivers during the first few years of life.

■ QUALITY OF CAREGIVING. What kind of parental behavior promotes secure attachment? Research reveals that *sensitive caregiving* distinguishes securely from insecurely attached infants. In many studies, the extent to which mothers responded promptly, consistently, and appropriately to infant signals and held their babies tenderly and carefully was moderately related to attachment security (De Wolff & van Ijzendoorn, 1997). In contrast, insecurely attached infants tend to have mothers who dislike physical contact, handle them awkwardly, behave in a "routine" manner, and are sometimes negative, resentful, and rejecting (Ainsworth et al., 1978; Isabella, 1993; Pederson & Moran, 1996).

Are there additional caregiver behaviors that support babies' feelings of trust? In several studies, a special form of communication called **interactional synchrony** distinguished the experiences of secure and insecure babies (Isabella & Belsky, 1991; Kochanska, 1998). It is best described as a sensitively tuned "emotional dance," in which the caregiver responds to infant signals in a well-timed, appropriate fashion. In addition, both partners match emotional states, especially the positive ones.

But more evidence is needed to document the importance of interactional synchrony. Other research reveals that only 30 percent of the time are exchanges between mothers and their babies so perfectly in tune with one another. The remaining 70 percent of the time, interactive errors occur (Tronick, 1989). Perhaps warm, sensitive caregivers and their infants become especially skilled at repairing these errors and returning to a synchronous state. Also, finely tuned, coordinated interaction does not characterize mother–infant

■ *This mother and baby engage in a sensitively tuned form of communication called interactional synchrony in which they match emotional states, especially the positive ones. Interactional synchrony may support the development of secure attachment, but it does not characterize mother–infant interaction in all cultures. (Photo courtesy: Julie O'Neil/Index Stock)*

interaction everywhere. Among the Gusii people of Kenya, mothers rarely cuddle, hug, or interact playfully with their babies, although they are very responsive to their infants' needs (LeVine et al., 1994). This suggests that secure attachment depends on attentive caregiving, but its association with moment-by-moment contingent interaction is probably limited to certain cultures.

Compared with securely attached infants, avoidant babies tend to receive overstimulating, intrusive care. Their mothers might, for example, talk energetically to a baby who is looking away or falling asleep. By avoiding the mother, these infants appear to be escaping from overwhelming interaction. Resistant infants often experience inconsistent care. Their mothers are unresponsive to infant signals. Yet when the baby begins to explore, they interfere, shifting the infant's attention back to themselves. As a result, the baby is overly dependent as well as angry at the mother's lack of involvement (Cassidy & Berlin, 1994; Isabella & Belsky, 1991).

When caregiving is extremely inadequate, it is a powerful predictor of disruptions in attachment. Child abuse and neglect (topics we will consider in Chapter 8) are associated with all three forms of attachment insecurity. Among maltreated infants, the most worrisome classification—disorganized–disoriented attachment—is especially high (Carlson, 1998; Lyons-Ruth & Block, 1996). Infants of depressed mothers also show the uncertain behaviors of this pattern, mixing closeness, resistance, and avoidance while looking very sad and depressed themselves (Lyons-Ruth et al., 1990; Teti et al., 1995).

■ INFANT CHARACTERISTICS. Since attachment is the result of a *relationship* that builds between two partners, infant characteristics should affect how easily it is established. In Chapter 3, we saw that prematurity, birth complications, and newborn illness make caregiving more taxing for parents. In poverty-stricken, stressed families, these difficulties are linked to attachment insecurity (Wille, 1991). But when parents have the time and patience to care for a baby with special needs and the infant is not very sick, at-risk newborns fare quite well in the development of attachment (Pederson & Moran, 1995).

Infants also vary in temperament, but its role in attachment security has been intensely debated. Some researchers believe that babies who are irritable and fearful may simply react to brief separations with intense anxiety, regardless of the parent's sensitivity to the baby (Kagan, 1989, 1998). Consistent with this view, proneness to distress in early infancy is moderately related to later insecure attachment (Seifer et al., 1996; Vaughn et al., 1992).

But other evidence suggests that caregiving may account for this correlation. In one study, distress-prone infants who became insecurely attached tended to have rigid, controlling mothers who probably had trouble comforting a baby who often fussed and cried (Mangelsdorf et al., 1990). And in another study, an intervention that taught mothers how to respond sensitively to their irritable 6-month-olds led to gains in maternal responsiveness and children's attachment security, exploration, cooperativeness, and sociability that were still present at 3½ years of age (van den Boom, 1995).

A major reason that temperament and other infant characteristics are not strongly related to attachment quality may be that their influence depends on goodness of fit. From this perspective, *many* child attributes can lead to secure attachment as long as the caregiver sensitively adjusts her behavior to fit the baby's needs (Seifer & Schiller, 1995). But when a parent's capacity to do so is strained—for example, by her own personality or stressful living conditions—then difficult babies are at greater risk for attachment problems.

■ FAMILY CIRCUMSTANCES. Around April's first birthday, Felicia's husband, Lonnie, lost his job, and constant arguments with Felicia over monthly bills caused him to leave the family for a time. Although Felicia tried not to let these worries affect her caregiving, April sensed the tension. Several times, Felicia left April at Beth's house while she looked for employment. April, who had previously taken separations like these quite well, cried desperately on her mother's departure and clung for a long time after she returned.

April's behavior reflects a repeated finding: In families in which there is stress and instability, the rate of insecure attachment is especially high. Job loss, a failing marriage, financial difficulties, and other stressors can undermine attachment by interfering with the sensitivity of parental care. Or they can affect babies' sense of security directly, by exposing them to angry adult interactions or unfavorable child-care arrangements (Owen & Cox, 1997; Thompson, 1998). The availability of social supports, especially assistance in caregiving, reduces stress and fosters attachment security. As Felicia and Lonnie resolved their difficulties, April's clinginess declined.

Parents bring to the family context a long history of attachment experiences, out of which they construct internal working models that they apply to the bonds established with their babies. Lisa remembered her mother as tense and preoccupied and expressed regret at not having had a closer relationship. Felicia recalled her mother as deeply affectionate and caring but much too controlling. Her mother's strictness, she explained, was probably influenced by the dangerous inner-city neighborhood in which the family lived. Do these images of parenthood affect the quality of Byron's and April's attachments to their mothers?

To answer this question, researchers have assessed parents' internal working models by having them evaluate childhood memories of attachment experiences (George,

Kaplan, & Main, 1985). Mothers who show objectivity and balance in discussing their childhoods, regardless of whether they were positive or negative, tend to have securely attached infants and also behave more warmly and sensitively toward them. In contrast, mothers who dismiss the importance of early relationships or describe them in angry, confused ways usually have insecurely attached babies and engage in less sensitive caregiving (van Ijzendoorn, 1995a; Slade et al., 1999).

But we must be careful not to assume any direct transfer of parents' childhood experiences to quality of attachment with their own children. Internal working models are *reconstructed memories* affected by many factors, including relationship experiences over the life course, personality, and current life satisfaction. Consequently, adults with unhappy upbringings are not destined to become insensitive parents. Rather, the way parents *view* their childhoods—their ability to include new information in their working models, to come to terms with negative life events, and to look back on their own parents in an understanding, forgiving way—is much more influential in how they rear their children than the actual history of care they received (van Ijzendoorn, 1995b).

Felicia eventually took a job; Lisa had returned to work many months before. When mothers divide their time between work and parenting and place their infants in child care, is the quality of attachment affected? The Social Issues box on pages 196–197 reviews the controversy over whether child care in infancy threatens attachment security.

MULTIPLE ATTACHMENTS

We have already indicated that babies develop attachments to a variety of familiar people—not just mothers, but fathers, siblings, grandparents, and professional caregivers. Although Bowlby (1969) made room for multiple attachments in his theory, he believed that infants are predisposed to direct their attachment behaviors to a single special person, especially when they are distressed. For example, when an anxious, unhappy 1-year-old is permitted to choose between the mother and father for comfort and security, the infant generally chooses the mother (Lamb, 1997). This preference typically declines over the second year of life. An expanding world of attachments enriches the emotional and social lives of many babies.

FATHERS. Like mothers', fathers' sensitive caregiving predicts secure attachment—an effect that becomes stronger the more time they spend with babies (van Ijzendoorn & De Wolff, 1997). But as infancy progresses, mothers and fathers in many cultures—Australia, India, Israel, Italy, Japan, and the United States—relate to babies in different ways. Mothers devote more time to physical care and expressing affection. Fathers spend more time in playful interaction (Lamb,

1987; Roopnarine et al., 1990). Mothers and fathers also play differently with babies. Mothers more often provide toys, talk to infants, and engage in conventional games like pat-a-cake and peekaboo. In contrast, fathers tend to engage in more exciting, highly physical bouncing and lifting games, especially with their infant sons (Yogman, 1981).

However, this picture of "mother as caregiver" and "father as playmate" has changed in some families due to the revised work status of women. Employed mothers engage in more playful stimulation of their babies than do unemployed mothers, and their husbands are somewhat more involved in caregiving (Cox et al., 1992). When fathers are the primary caregivers, they often retain their highly arousing play style (Lamb & Oppenheim, 1989). Such highly involved fathers are less gender stereotyped in their beliefs; have sympathetic, friendly personalities; and regard parenthood as an especially enriching experience (Lamb, 1987; Levy-Shiff & Israelashvili, 1988).

A warm, gratifying marital relationship supports both parents' pleasurable involvement with babies and satisfaction derived from parenthood, but it is particularly important for fathers (Belsky, 1996; Grych & Clark, 1999). Striking support for this conclusion comes from the Aka hunters and gatherers of Central Africa, where fathers devote more time to infants than in any other known society. Aka fathers are within arm's reach of their babies most of the day and pick up and cuddle them at least five times more often than do fathers in other African hunting-and-gathering societies. Aka husbands and wives have unusually cooperative and intimate relationships, sharing hunting, food preparation, and leisure activities. The more Aka parents are together, the greater the father's interaction with his baby (Hewlett, 1992).

◾ *This Aka father spends much time in close contact with his baby. In Aka society, husband and wife share many tasks of daily living and have an unusually cooperative and intimate relationship. Infants are usually within arm's reach of their fathers, who devote many hours to caregiving. (Photo courtesy: Barry Hewlett)*

SOCIAL ISSUES

IS CHILD CARE IN INFANCY A THREAT TO ATTACHMENT SECURITY?

Research suggests that American infants placed in full-time child care before 12 months of age are more likely than infants who remain at home to display insecure attachment—especially avoidance—in the Strange Situation. Does this mean that infants who experience daily separations from their employed parents and early placement in child care are at risk for developmental problems? Some researchers think so (Belsky, 1989, 1992; Sroufe, 1988), whereas others disagree (Clarke-Stewart, 1992; Scarr, Phillips, & McCartney, 1990). Yet a close look at the evidence reveals that we should be cautious about concluding that child care is harmful to infants.

First, in studies reporting a child care–attachment association, the rate of insecurity is somewhat higher among child-care than non-child-care infants (36 versus 29 percent), but it resembles the overall rate of insecurity reported for children in industrialized countries (Lamb, Sternberg, & Prodromidis, 1992). In fact, most infants of employed mothers

are securely attached! Furthermore, not all investigations report a difference in attachment quality between child-care and home-reared infants (NICHD Early Child Care Research Network, 1997; Roggman et al., 1994).

Second, we have seen that family conditions affect attachment security. Many employed women find the pressures of handling two full-time jobs (work and motherhood) stressful. Some respond less sensitively to their babies because they are fatigued and harried, thereby risking the infant's security (Stifter, Coulehan, & Fish, 1993). Other employed mothers probably value and encourage their infants' independence. Or their babies are unfazed by the Strange Situation because they are used to separating from their parents. In these cases, the avoidant attachment pattern may represent healthy autonomy rather than insecurity (Lamb, 1998).

Third, poor-quality child care may contribute to a higher rate of insecure attachment among infants of employed mothers. In the NICHD Study of Early Child Care—the largest longitudinal study to date,

including 1,000 infants and their mothers in 10 areas of the country—child care alone did not contribute to attachment insecurity. But when babies were exposed to combined home and child-care risk factors—insensitive caregiving at home with insensitive caregiving in child care, long hours in child care, or more than one child-care arrangement—the rate of insecurity increased (NICHD Early Childhood Research Network, 1997).

Fourth, assessing attachment security while infants adapt to child care may not provide an accurate picture. On entering child care, infants must adjust to new routines and daily separations from the parent. Under these conditions, signs of distress are expected. But after a few months, infants enrolled in high-quality programs become more comfortable. They smile, play actively, seek comfort from sensitive caregivers they have come to know well, and begin to interact with agemates (Barnas & Cummings, 1994; Fein, Gariboldi, & Boni, 1993).

Finally, results of the NICHD Study indicate that parenting has a

■ SIBLINGS. Despite a declining family size, 80 percent of American children still grow up with at least one sibling. The arrival of a baby brother or sister is a difficult experience for most preschoolers, who quickly realize that now they must share their parents' attention and affection. They often become demanding and clingy for a time and engage in deliberate naughtiness. And their security of attachment typically declines, more so if they are over age 2 (old enough to feel threatened and displaced) and the mother is under stress due to marital or psychological problems (Teti et al., 1996).

■ *Although the arrival of a baby brother or sister is a difficult experience for most preschoolers, a rich emotional relationship quickly builds between siblings. This toddler is already actively involved in play with his 4-year-old-brother, and both derive great pleasure from the interaction. (Photo courtesy: Erika Stone/Photo Researchers, Inc.)*

far stronger impact on preschoolers' problem behavior than does early, extensive child care (NICHD Early Child Care Research Network, 1998). Indeed, having the opportunity to form a warm bond with a stable professional caregiver is particularly helpful to infants whose relationship with one or both parents is insecure. When followed into the preschool and early school years, such children show higher self-esteem and socially skilled behavior than their insecurely attached agemates who did not attend child care (Egeland & Hiester, 1995).

Taken together, research suggests that some infants may be at risk for attachment insecurity due to inadequate child care and the joint pressures of full-time employment and parenthood experienced by their mothers. However, using this as evidence to justify a reduction in infant child-care services is inappropriate. When family incomes are limited or mothers who want to work are forced to stay at home, children's emotional security is not promoted.

Instead, it makes sense to increase the availability of high-quality child care and to educate parents about the

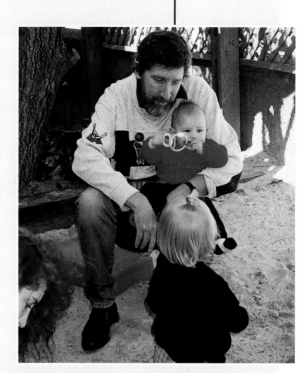

■ *This caregiver works in a child-care center that meets rigorous, professionally established standards of quality. A generous caregiver–child ratio, a limited number of children in each room, and training in child development enable him to respond to infants' and toddlers' needs to be held, comforted, and stimulated. (Photo courtesy: Laura Berk)*

vital role of sensitive caregiving in early emotional development. Return to Chapter 5, page 165, to review signs of developmentally appropriate child care for infants and toddlers. For child care to foster attachment security, the professional caregiver's relationship with the baby is vital. When caregiver–child ratios are generous, group sizes are small, and

caregivers are educated about child development and child rearing, caregivers' interactions are more positive (NICHD Early Child Care Research Network, 1996). Child care with these characteristics can become part of an ecological system that relieves rather than intensifies parental and child stress, thereby promoting healthy attachment and development.

However, resentment about being displaced is only one dimension of a rich emotional relationship that starts to build between siblings after a baby's birth. An older child can also be seen kissing, patting, and calling out, "Mom, he needs you," when the baby cries—signs of growing caring and affection. By the time the baby is about 8 months old, siblings typically spend much time together. Infants of this age are comforted by the presence of their preschool-age brother or sister during short absences of the mother (Stewart, 1983). And in the second year, they often imitate and actively join in play with the older child (Dunn, 1989).

Nevertheless, individual differences in sibling relationships appear shortly after a baby's birth that persist into early childhood (Dunn, 1992). Temperament plays an important role. For example, conflict increases when one sibling is emotionally intense or highly active (Brody, Stoneman, & McCoy, 1994; Dunn, 1994). Parenting also makes a difference. Typi-

cally, mothers are more positive and playful with second-borns than first-borns and discipline the older preschooler more—behaviors that can spark feelings of rivalry and behavior problems in the older child (Moore, Cohn, & Campbell, 1997; Volling & Elins, 1998). Secure infant–mother attachment and parental warmth toward both children are related to positive sibling ties, whereas coldness is associated with sibling friction (MacKinnon-Lewis et al., 1997; Volling & Belsky, 1992).

How can parents support harmony between babies and their preschool siblings? As the Caregiving Concerns table on page 198 suggests, setting aside special times to devote to the older child is helpful. In addition, mothers who discuss a baby's feelings and intentions have preschoolers who are more likely to comment on the infant as a person with special wants and needs. Such children behave in an especially considerate and friendly manner toward the baby (Howe & Ross, 1990).

CAREGIVING CONCERNS

Encouraging Affectional Ties Between Infants and Their Preschool Siblings

SUGGESTION	DESCRIPTION
Spend extra time with the older child.	To minimize feelings of being deprived of affection and attention, set aside time to spend with the older child. Fathers can be especially helpful in this regard, planning time with younger siblings so the mother can be with the older child.
Handle sibling misbehavior with patience.	Respond patiently to the older sibling's misbehavior and demands for attention, recognizing that these reactions are temporary. Give the preschooler opportunities to feel proud of being more grown-up than the baby. For example, encourage the older child to assist with feeding, bathing, dressing, and offering toys.
Discuss the baby's wants and needs.	Discuss the baby's feelings and intentions with the preschooler, such as, "He's so little that he just can't wait to be fed." By helping the older sibling understand the baby's point of view, parents can promote friendly, considerate behavior.

Sources: Dunn & Kendrick, 1982; Howe & Ross, 1990.

ATTACHMENT AND LATER DEVELOPMENT

According to psychoanalytic and ethological theories, the inner feelings of affection and security that result from a healthy attachment relationship support all aspects of psychological development. Consistent with this view, an extensive longitudinal study found that children who were securely attached as babies were rated by their preschool teachers as high in self-esteem, socially competent, cooperative, and popular. In contrast, their avoidantly attached agemates were viewed as isolated and disconnected, and those who were resistantly attached were regarded as disruptive and difficult. Studied again at age 11 in summer camp, children who were secure as infants had more favorable relationships with peers and better social skills, as judged by camp counselors (Elicker, Englund, & Sroufe, 1992; Matas, Arend, & Sroufe, 1978; Shulman, Elicker, & Sroufe, 1994).

These findings have been taken by some researchers to mean that secure attachment in infancy causes improved cognitive, emotional, and social competence in later years. Yet more evidence is needed before we can be certain of this conclusion. In short-term longitudinal studies, secure infants did not always show more favorable development than did their insecure counterparts (Belsky & Cassidy, 1994). And other long-term studies are inconclusive, some reporting that maternal caregiving and attachment quality in infancy predict adolescent and early-adult adjustment and others finding no consistent relationships (Beckwith, Cohen, & Hamilton, 1999; Carlson, 1998; Lewis, 1997).

Why is research on the long-term consequences of attachment quality as yet unclear? Perhaps *continuity of caregiving* determines whether attachment security is linked to later development (Lamb et al., 1985). When parents respond sensitively not just in infancy but during later years, children are likely to develop favorably. In contrast, children of parents who react insensitively for a long time and who therefore establish patterns of avoidant, resistive, or disor-

ganized behavior are at greater risk for academic, emotional, and social difficulties.

At the same time, infants and young children are resilient beings. A child who has compensating, affectional ties outside the family or whose parental caregiving improves is likely to fare well. This suggests that efforts to create warm, responsive environments are important not just in infancy and toddlerhood; they are also worthwhile at later ages, as we will see in subsequent chapters.

ASK YOURSELF . . .

■ *Recall from Chapter 5 that Lisa tended to overwhelm Byron with questions and instructions. How would you expect Byron to respond in the Strange Situation? Explain your answer.*

 As a child, Suzanne had a conflict-ridden relationship with her parents and felt angry and displaced when her sister was born. Will Suzanne's negative childhood experiences necessarily undermine her capacity to build a secure attachment with her infant daughter? Explain.

■ *Maggy works full time and leaves her 14-month-old son Vincent at a child-care center. When she arrives to pick him up at the end of the day, Vincent keeps on playing and hardly notices her. Maggy wonders whether Vincent is securely attached. Is Maggy's concern warranted?*

SELF-DEVELOPMENT DURING THE FIRST TWO YEARS

Infancy is a rich, formative period for the development of physical and social understanding. In Chapter 5, you learned that infants develop an appreciation of the permanence of objects. And in this chapter, we have seen that over the first year, infants recognize and respond appropriately to others' emotions and distinguish familiar people from strangers. The fact that both objects and people achieve an independent, stable existence in infancy implies that knowledge of the self as a separate, permanent entity emerges around this time.

SELF-AWARENESS

Felicia hung a large plastic mirror on the side of April's crib. As early as the first few months, April smiled and returned friendly behaviors to her own image. At what age did she realize that the charming baby gazing and grinning back was really herself?

■ EMERGENCE OF THE I-SELF AND ME-SELF. To answer this question, researchers have exposed infants and toddlers to images of themselves in mirrors, on videotapes, and in photos. When shown a videotaped image of themselves next to that of a peer, 3-month-olds look longer at the peer's image. This suggests that at least for babies with access to mirrors, discrimination of the self from others is under way in the first few months of life (Bahrick, Moss, & Fadil, 1996).

Researchers agree that the earliest aspect of the self to emerge is the **I-self**—a sense of self as *subject*, or *agent*, who is separate from but attends to and acts on objects and other people. According to many theorists, the beginnings of the I-self lie in infants' recognition that their own actions cause objects and people to react in predictable ways (Harter, 1998). Parents who encourage babies to explore and who respond to their signals consistently and sensitively help them construct a sense of self as agent (Pipp, Easterbrooks, & Brown, 1993).

Then, as infants act on the environment, they notice different effects that may help them sort out self from other people and objects. For example, batting a mobile and seeing it swing in a pattern different from the infant's own actions informs the baby about the relation between self and physical world. Smiling and vocalizing at a caregiver who smiles and vocalizes back helps specify the relation between self and social world. And watching the movements of one's own hand provides still another kind of feedback—one under much more direct control than other people or objects (Case, 1991; Lewis, 1994).

During the second year, toddlers start to construct a second aspect of self: the **me-self,** a reflective observer who treats the self as an object of knowledge and evaluation. Consequently, they become consciously aware of the self's features. In one study, 9- to 24-month-olds were placed in front of a mirror. Then, under the pretext of wiping the baby's face, each mother rubbed red dye on her infant's nose. Younger infants touched the mirror as if the red mark had nothing to do with themselves. But by 15 months, toddlers began to rub their strange-looking little red noses. They were keenly aware of their unique visual appearance

■ *This infant notices the correspondence between his own movements and the movements of the image in the mirror, a cue that helps him figure out that the grinning baby is really himself. (Photo courtesy: Paul Damien/Stone)*

(Lewis & Brooks-Gunn, 1979). By age 2, almost all children use their name or a personal pronoun (*I* or *me*) to label their image or refer to themselves.

Like the I-self, the me-self seems to be fostered by sensitive caregiving. Securely attached toddlers display more complex knowledge of their own and their parents' features (for example, by labeling body parts) than do their insecurely attached agemates (Pipp, Easterbrooks, & Brown, 1993).

■ SELF-AWARENESS AND EARLY EMOTIONAL AND SOCIAL DEVELOPMENT. Self-awareness quickly becomes a central part of children's emotional and social lives. Recall that self-conscious emotions depend on toddlers' emerging sense of self. Self-awareness also leads to the child's first efforts to appreciate another's perspective. For example, it is associated with the beginnings of self-conscious behavior—bashfulness and embarrassment. It is also accompanied by the first signs of **empathy**—the ability to understand another's emotional state and *feel with* that person, or respond emotionally in a similar way. For example, toddlers start to give to others what they themselves find comforting—a hug, a reassuring comment, or a favorite doll or blanket (Bischof-Köhler, 1991; Zahn-Waxler et al., 1992). At the same time, they demonstrate clearer awareness of how to upset other people. One 18-month-old heard her mother comment to another adult, "Anny (sibling) is really frightened of spiders. In fact, there's a particular toy spider that we've got that she just hates" (Dunn, 1989, p. 107). The innocent-looking toddler ran to get the spider out of the toy box, returned, and pushed it in front of Anny's face!

CATEGORIZING THE SELF

Self-awareness permits toddlers to compare themselves to other people, in much the same way that they group together physical objects (see Chapter 5). Between 18 and 30 months, children categorize themselves and others on the basis of age ("baby," "boy," or "man"), sex ("boy" or "girl"), physical characteristics ("big," "strong"), and even goodness and badness ("I a good girl" and "Tommy mean!") (Stipek, Gralinski, & Kopp, 1990). Toddlers' understanding of these social categories is quite limited, but they use this knowledge to organize their own behavior. For example, children's ability to label their own gender is associated with a sharp rise in gender-stereotyped responses (Fagot & Leinbach, 1989). As early as 18 months, toddlers select and play in a more involved way with toys that are stereotyped for their own gender—dolls and tea sets for girls, trucks and cars for boys. Then parents encourage these preferences by responding positively when toddlers display them (Fagot, Leinbach, & O'Boyle, 1992). As we will see in Chapter 8, gender-typed behavior increases dramatically in early childhood.

EMERGENCE OF SELF-CONTROL

Self-awareness also provides the foundation for **self-control,** the capacity to resist an impulse to engage in socially disapproved behavior. Self-control is essential for morality, another dimension of the self that will flourish during childhood and adolescence. To behave in a self-controlled fashion, children must have some ability to think of themselves as separate, autonomous beings who can direct their own actions. And they must also have the representational and memory capacities to recall a caregiver's directive (such as "April, don't touch that light socket!") and apply it to their own behavior (Kopp, 1987).

The first glimmerings of self-control appear as **compliance.** Between 12 and 18 months, children show clear awareness of caregivers' wishes and expectations and can obey simple requests and commands (Kaler & Kopp, 1990). And as every parent knows, they can also decide to do just the opposite! One way toddlers assert their autonomy is by resisting adult directives. But among toddlers who experience warm, sensitive caregiving and reasonable expectations for mature behavior, opposition is far less common than compliance with an eager, willing spirit, which suggests that the child is beginning to adopt the adult's directive as his or her own (Kochanska, 1997b; Kochanska, Tjebkes, & Forman, 1998). Compliance quickly leads to toddlers' first conscience-like verbalizations, as when April said, "No, can't" as she reached out for a light socket (Kochanska, 1993).

Around 18 months, the capacity for self-control appears, and it improves steadily into early childhood. In one study, toddlers were given three tasks that required them to resist temptation. In the first, they were asked not to touch a toy telephone that was within arm's reach. In the second, raisins were hidden under cups, and they were instructed to wait until the experimenter said it was all right to pick up a cup and eat a raisin. In the third, they were told not to open a gift until the experimenter had finished her work. On all three problems, the ability to wait increased steadily between 18 and 30 months. Toddlers who were especially self-controlled were advanced in language development. In fact, some sang and talked to themselves to keep from touching the desired objects (Vaughn, Kopp, & Krakow, 1984).

As self-control improves, mothers require toddlers to follow more rules, from safety and respect for property and people to family routines, manners, and simple chores (Gralinski & Kopp, 1993). Still, toddlers' control over their own actions is fragile. It depends on constant oversight and reminders by parents. To get April to stop playing to go on an errand, Felicia found that several prompts ("Remember, we're going to go in just a minute") and gentle insistence were usually necessary. The Caregiving Concerns table on the following page summarizes effective ways of helping toddlers develop compliance and self-control. As the second year of life drew to a close, Lisa, Beth, and Felicia were delighted at their youngsters' readiness to learn the rules of social life. As we will see in Chapter 8, advances in cognition and language, along with parental warmth and reasonable maturity demands, lead children to make tremendous strides in this area during early childhood.

■ *Encouraging this toddler to help wipe up spilled milk fosters compliance and the beginnings of self-control. He joins in the clean-up task with an eager, willing spirit, which suggests he is beginning to adopt the adult's directive as his own. (Photo courtesy: Laura Dwight)*

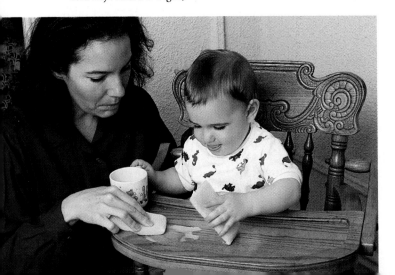

ASK YOURSELF . . .

■ *Nine-month-old Harry turned his cup upside down and spilled juice all over the tray of his high chair. His mother said sharply, "Harry, put your cup back the right way!" Can Harry comply with his mother's request? Why or why not?*

🌳 *Why is the development of compliance and self-control crucial for later cognitive and social development?*

Helping Toddlers Develop Compliance and Self-Control

SUGGESTION	RATIONALE
Respond to the toddler warmly and sensitively.	Toddlers who experience warmth and sensitivity are far more compliant and cooperative than negative and resistant.
Provide advance notice when the toddler must stop an enjoyable activity.	Toddlers find it more difficult to stop a pleasant activity already under way than to wait before engaging in a desired action.
Offer many prompts and reminders.	Toddlers' ability to remember and comply with rules is limited; they need continuous adult oversight.
Respond to self-controlled behavior with verbal and physical approval.	Praise and hugs reinforce appropriate behavior, increasing its likelihood of occurring again.
Support language development.	Early language development is related to self-control. During the second year, children begin to use language to remind themselves about adult expectations.
Gradually increase rules in accord with the toddler's developing capacities.	As cognition and language improve, toddlers can follow more rules related to safety, respect for people and property, family routine, and simple chores.

 UMMARY

ERIKSON'S THEORY OF INFANT AND TODDLER PERSONALITY

What personality changes take place during Erikson's stages of basic trust versus mistrust and autonomy versus shame and doubt?

■ According to Erikson, warm, responsive caregiving leads infants to resolve the psychological conflict of **basic trust versus mistrust** on the positive side. During toddlerhood, the conflict of **autonomy versus shame and doubt** is resolved favorably when parents provide appropriate guidance and reasonable choices. If children emerge from the first few years without sufficient trust and autonomy, the seeds are sown for adjustment problems.

EMOTIONAL DEVELOPMENT

Describe changes in happiness, anger, and fear over the first year, noting the adaptive function of each.

■ Signs of almost all the **basic emotions** are present in infancy. The **social smile** appears between 6 and 10 weeks, laughter around 3 to 4 months. Happiness strengthens the parent–child bond and reflects as well as supports physical and cognitive mastery. Anger and fear, especially in the form of **stranger anxiety,** increase in the second half of the first year. These reactions have survival value as infants' motor capacities improve.

Summarize changes in understanding others' emotions, expression of self-conscious emotions, and emotional self-regulation during the first 2 years.

■ The ability to understand the feelings of others expands over the first year. Between 7 and 10 months, babies perceive facial expressions as organized patterns. Soon after, **social referencing** appears; infants actively seek emotional information from caregivers in uncertain situations. By the middle of the second year, infants begin to appreciate that others' emotional reactions may differ from their own.

■ During toddlerhood, self-awareness and adult instruction provide the foundation for **self-conscious emotions,** such as shame, embarrassment, and pride. Caregivers help infants with **emotional self-regulation** by relieving distress, engaging in stimulating play, and discouraging negative emotion. During the second year, growth in representation and language leads to more effective ways of regulating emotion.

TEMPERAMENT AND DEVELOPMENT

What is temperament, and how is it measured?

■ Infants differ greatly in **temperament,** or quality and intensity of emotion, activity level, attention, and emotional self-regulation. On the basis of parental descriptions of children's behavior, three patterns of temperament—the **easy child,** the **difficult child,** and the **slow-to-warm-up child**—were identified in the New York Longitudinal Study. Difficult children, especially, are likely to display adjustment problems.

- Physiological measures of temperament have supplemented parent reports, behavior ratings, and direct observations of children. They distinguish **inhibited, or shy, children** from **uninhibited, or sociable, children.** These youngsters may inherit a physiology that biases them toward a particular temperamental style.

Discuss the role of heredity and environment in the stability of temperament, including the goodness-of-fit model.

- Stability of temperament from one age period to the next is generally low to moderate. Temperament has biological roots, but child rearing and cultural beliefs and practices have much to do with maintaining or changing it. The **goodness-of-fit model** describes how temperament and a child's environment work together to affect later development. Parenting practices that have a good fit with the child's temperament are important for all children, but especially for those who are difficult or shy and withdrawn.

DEVELOPMENT OF ATTACHMENT

Describe ethological theory of attachment and the development of attachment during the first 2 years.

- The development of **attachment,** infants' strong affectional tie to familiar caregivers, has been the subject of intense theoretical debate. The most widely accepted perspective is **ethological theory of attachment,** which views babies as biologically prepared to contribute actively to ties established with their caregivers, which promote survival.

- In early infancy, a set of built-in behaviors encourages the parent to remain close to the baby. Around 6 to 8 months, **separation anxiety** and use of the parent as a **secure base** indicate that a true attachment bond has formed. As representation and language develop, toddlers will try to alter the parent's coming and going through requests and persuasion rather than following and clinging. Out of early caregiving experiences, children construct an **internal working model** that serves as a guide for all future close relationships.

Describe the Strange Situation, the four attachment patterns assessed by it, and factors that affect attachment security.

- The **Strange Situation** is a widely used technique for measuring the security of attachment between 1 and 2 years of age. Four attachment patterns have been identified: **secure attachment, avoidant attachment, resistant attachment,** and **disorganized–disoriented attachment.** Cultural conditions must be considered in interpreting reactions in the Strange Situation.

- Attachment quality is influenced by the infant's opportunity to develop a close affectional tie with one or a few adults, the caregiver's sensitivity, the fit between the baby's temperament and parenting practices, and family circumstances. In some (but not all) cultures, **interactional synchrony** characterizes communication between mothers and securely attached babies. Mothers' internal working models are good predictors of infant attachment patterns.

Discuss infants' attachments to fathers and siblings.

- Besides attachments to mothers, infants develop strong affectional ties to fathers, usually through stimulating, playful interaction. Early in the first year, infants begin to build rich emotional relationships with siblings that mix affection and caring with rivalry and resentment. Individual differences in the quality of sibling relationships are influenced by temperament and parenting practices.

Describe and interpret the relationship between secure attachment in infancy and cognitive, emotional, and social competence in childhood.

- Evidence for the impact of early attachment quality on cognitive, emotional, and social competence in later years is mixed. Continuity of caregiving may be the crucial factor that determines whether attachment security is linked to later development.

SELF-DEVELOPMENT DURING THE FIRST TWO YEARS

Describe the development of self-awareness in infancy and toddlerhood, along with the emotional and social capacities it supports.

- The earliest aspect of the self to emerge is the **I-self,** a sense of self as subject or agent. Its beginnings lie in infants' recognition that their own actions cause objects and people to react in predictable ways. During the second year, toddlers start to construct the **me-self,** a reflective observer that treats the self as an object of knowledge and evaluation. They become keenly aware of the self's visual appearance and, by age 2, use their name or a personal pronoun to refer to themselves.

- Self-awareness leads to toddlers' first efforts to appreciate another's perspective and to compare themselves to others. Social categories based on age, sex, physical characteristics, and goodness and badness are evident in toddlers' language. Self-awareness also provides the foundation for self-conscious emotions, **empathy, compliance,** and **self-control.**

IMPORTANT TERMS AND CONCEPTS

attachment (p. 190)

autonomy versus shame and doubt (p. 179)

avoidant attachment (p. 192)

basic emotions (p. 180)

basic trust versus mistrust (p. 178)

compliance (p. 200)

difficult child (p. 185)

disorganized–disoriented attachment (p. 192)

easy child (p. 185)

emotional self-regulation (p. 184)

empathy (p. 199)

ethological theory of attachment (p. 190)

goodness-of-fit model (p. 189)

I-self (p. 199)

inhibited, or shy, child (p. 187)

interactional synchrony (p. 193)

internal working model (p. 191)

me-self (p. 199)

resistant attachment (p. 192)

secure attachment (p. 191)

secure base (p. 191)

self-conscious emotions (p. 183)

self-control (p. 200)

separation anxiety (p. 191)

slow-to-warm-up child (p. 185)

social referencing (p. 183)

social smile (p. 182)

Strange Situation (p. 191)

stranger anxiety (p. 182)

temperament (p. 185)

uninhibited, or sociable, child (p. 187)

FOR FURTHER INFORMATION AND HELP

Consult the companion website for this book, where you will find additional weblinks and associated learning activities: www.abacon.com/berk

MENTAL HEALTH

American Academy of Child and Adolescent Psychiatry
www.aacap.org

An organization of medical professionals dedicated to treating and improving quality of life for infants, children, and adolescents with emotional or behavior disorders. Distributes Facts for Families, *an information sheet on childhood mental health that can be accessed through its website. Also disseminates scholarly research through its journal.*

American Academy of Pediatrics
www.aap.org
An organization of over 50,000 pediatricians dedicated to the physical and mental health of infants, children, and adolescents. Disseminates a wide variety of health-related information to professionals and parents through its publications, which include Pediatrics, *a scholarly journal;* Healthy Kids *magazine; and child-care books and brochures.*

AGE	PHYSICAL	COGNITIVE	LANGUAGE	EMOTIONAL/SOCIAL
Birth–6 months	■ Rapid height and weight gain. (118) ■ Reflexes decline. (106–107) ■ Sleep organized into a day-night schedule. (124) ■ Holds head up, rolls over, and reaches for objects. (133, 135) ■ Can be classically and operantly conditioned. (130–131) ■ Habituates to unchanging stimuli; dishabituates to novel stimuli. (131–132) ■ Hearing well developed; by the end of this period, displays greater sensitivity to speech sounds of own language. (137) ■ Depth and pattern perception emerge and improve. (137–140)	■ Engages in immediate imitation and deferred imitation of adults' facial expressions. (132, 154) ■ Repeats chance behaviors leading to pleasurable and interesting results. (150) ■ Aware of object permanence and other object properties in habituation –dishabituation tasks. (152–153) ■ Attention becomes more efficient. (157) ■ Recognition memory for people, places, and objects improves. (157) ■ Forms perceptual categories based on objects' similar features. (158)	■ Engages in cooing and babbling. (168) ■ Establishes joint attention with caregiver, who labels objects and events. (168) 	■ Shows signs of almost all basic emotions (happiness, interest, surprise, fear, anger, sadness, disgust). (180) ■ Social smile and laughter emerge. (182) ■ Matches adults' emotional expressions during face-to-face interaction. (180, 183) ■ Emotional expressions become better organized and clearly tied to social events. (180) ■ I-self emerges. (199)
7–12 months	■ Sits alone, crawls, and walks. (133) ■ Shows refined pincer grasp. (133) ■ Perceives larger speech units crucial to understanding meaning. (137) ■ Depth and pattern perception improve further. (137–140) 	■ Combines sensorimotor schemes. (151) ■ Engages in intentional, or goal-directed, behavior. (151) ■ Finds object hidden in one place. (151) ■ Understanding of object properties and physical causality expands. (153) ■ Engages in deferred imitation of adults' actions with objects. (154) ■ Recall memory for people, places, and objects improves. (157) ■ Groups stimuli into wide range of meaningful categories. (158)	■ Babbling expands to include sounds of spoken languages and, by the end of this period, sounds of the child's language community. (168) ■ Uses preverbal gestures (showing, pointing) to communicate. (169) 	■ Anger and fear increase in frequency and intensity. (182) ■ Stranger anxiety and separation anxiety appear. (182) ■ Uses caregiver as a secure base for exploration. (191) ■ Shows "clear-cut" attachment to familiar caregivers. (191) ■ Ability to detect the meaning of others' emotional expressions improves. (183) ■ Engages in social referencing. (183)

AGE	PHYSICAL	COGNITIVE	LANGUAGE	EMOTIONAL/SOCIAL
13–18 months	■ Height and weight gain rapid, but not as great as in first year. (118) ■ Walking better coordinated. (133) ■ Manipulates small objects with improved coordination. (133, 135)	■ Experiments with objects in a trial-and-error fashion. (151) ■ Finds object hidden in more than one place. (151) ■ Sorts objects into categories. (158) ■ Imitates actions across a change in context—for example, from child care to home. (152, 154)	■ Joins in turn-taking games, such as pat-a-cake and peekaboo. (168) ■ Says first word. (166) ■ Makes errors of underextension and overextension. (169)	■ Joins in play with familiar adults and siblings. (197) ■ Me-self emerges; recognizes image of self in mirror and on videotape. (199) ■ Shows signs of empathy. (199) ■ Complies with simple directives. (200)

AGE	PHYSICAL	COGNITIVE	LANGUAGE	EMOTIONAL/SOCIAL
19–24 months	■ Jumps, runs, and climbs. (133) ■ Manipulates objects with good coordination. (133, 135)	■ Solves sensorimotor problems suddenly. (152) ■ Finds object moved while out of sight. (152) ■ Engages in deferred imitation of actions an adult *tries* to produce, even if not fully realized. (154) ■ Engages in make-believe play. (161) ■ Sorts objects into categories more effectively. (158) ■ Recall memory for people, places, and objects improves further. (157)	■ Vocabulary increases to 200 words. (170) ■ Combines two words. (170)	■ Displays self-conscious emotions (shame, embarrassment, and pride). (183) ■ Acquires a vocabulary of emotional terms. (184) ■ Starts to use language to assist with emotional self-regulation. (184) ■ Begins to tolerate caregiver absences more easily. (191) ■ Uses own name or personal pronoun to label self. (199) ■ Categorizes self and others on the basis of age, sex, physical characteristics, and goodness and badness. (200) ■ Shows gender-stereotyped toy choices. (200) ■ Self-control appears. (200)

Note: Numbers in parentheses indicate the page on which each milestone is discussed.

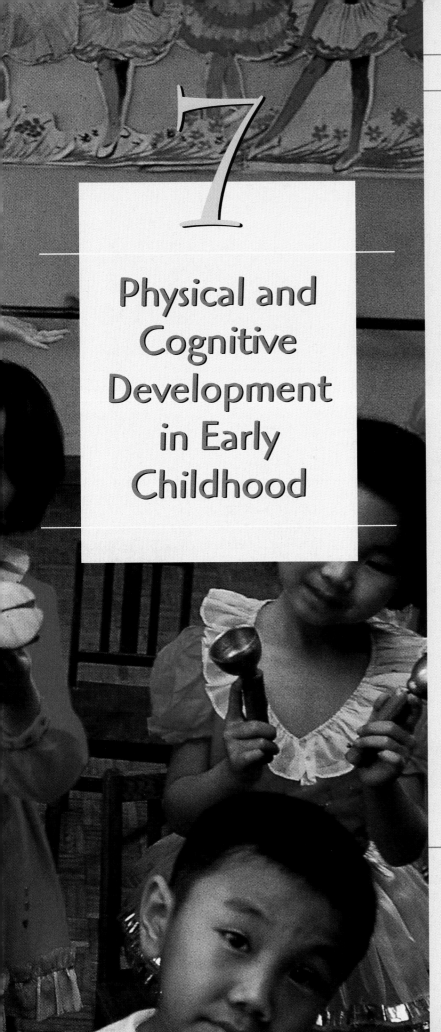

7

Physical and Cognitive Development in Early Childhood

■ *A transformed body and explosion of new motor and cognitive skills contribute to an expanding sense of competence in early childhood. These kindergarteners in Beijing, China, proudly perform on tambourines, drums, and other musical instruments for admiring family members. (Photo courtesy: Dean Conger/National Geographic Image Collection)*

For more than a decade, my fourth-floor office window overlooked the preschool and kindergarten play yard of our university laboratory school. On mild fall and spring mornings, the doors of the classrooms swung open, and sand table, woodworking bench, easels, and large blocks spilled out into a small, fenced courtyard. Around the side of the building was a grassy area with jungle gyms, swings, a small playhouse, and a flower garden planted by the children. Beyond it, I could see a circular path lined with tricycles and wagons. Each day, the setting was alive with activity.

The years from 2 to 6 are often called "the play years," and aptly so, since play blossoms during this time and supports every aspect of development. Our discussion of early childhood opens with the physical achievements of this period—growth in body size, improvements in motor coordination, and refinements in perception. We pay special attention to biological and environmental factors that support these changes, as well as to their intimate connection with other aspects of development.

Then we explore the many facets of early childhood cognition, drawing from three theories with which you are already familiar. We begin with Piaget's preoperational stage, which, for the most part, emphasizes young children's deficits rather than strengths. Recent research on preoperational thought, along with Vygotsky's sociocultural theory and information processing, extends our understanding of preschoolers' cognitive competencies. Next, we turn to a variety of factors that contribute to early childhood mental development—the home environment, the quality of preschool and child care, and the many hours children spend watching television. Our chapter concludes with language development, the most awesome achievement of the preschool years.

The children whom I came to know well, first by watching from my office window and later by observing at close range in their classrooms, will join us as we trace the changes of early childhood. They will provide us with many examples of developmental trends and individual differences.

PHYSICAL DEVELOPMENT

BODY GROWTH

Look at Figure 7.1, and you will see that the rapid increase in body size that took place in infancy tapers off into a slower pattern of growth during early childhood. On the average, children add 2 to 3 inches in height and about 5 pounds in weight each year. Boys continue to be slightly larger than girls. At the same time, the "baby fat" that

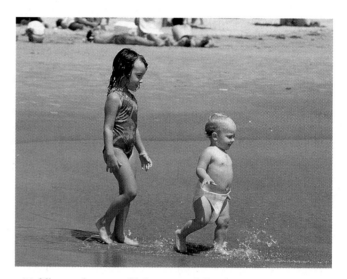

■ *Toddlers and 5-year-olds have very different body shapes. During early childhood, body fat declines, the torso enlarges to better accommodate the internal organs, and the spine straightens. Compared to her younger brother, this girl looks more streamlined. Her body proportions resemble those of an adult. (Photo courtesy: Bob Daemmrich/Stock Boston)*

began to decline in toddlerhood drops off further. The child gradually becomes thinner, although girls retain somewhat more body fat, and boys are slightly more muscular. As the torso lengthens and widens, internal organs tuck neatly inside, and the spine straightens. By age 5, the top-heavy, bowlegged, potbellied toddler has become a more streamlined, flat-tummied, longer-legged child with body proportions similar to those of adults (Tanner, 1990). Consequently, posture and balance improve—changes that support the gains in motor coordination that we will take up later.

Individual differences in body size are even more apparent during early childhood than in infancy and toddlerhood. Looking down at the play yard one day, I watched 5-year-old Darryl speed around the bike path. At 48 inches tall and 55 pounds, he towered over his kindergarten classmates and was, as his mother put it, "off the growth charts" at the doctor's office. (The average American 5-year-old boy is 43 inches tall and weighs 42 pounds.) Priti, an Asian-Indian child, was unusually small because of genetic factors linked to her cultural ancestry. Lynette and Hallie, two Caucasian children with impoverished home lives, were well below average for reasons we will discuss shortly.

SKELETAL GROWTH

Skeletal changes under way in infancy continue throughout early childhood. Between ages 2 and 6, approximately 45 new *epiphyses*, or growth centers in which cartilage hardens into bone, emerge in various parts of the skeleton. Other

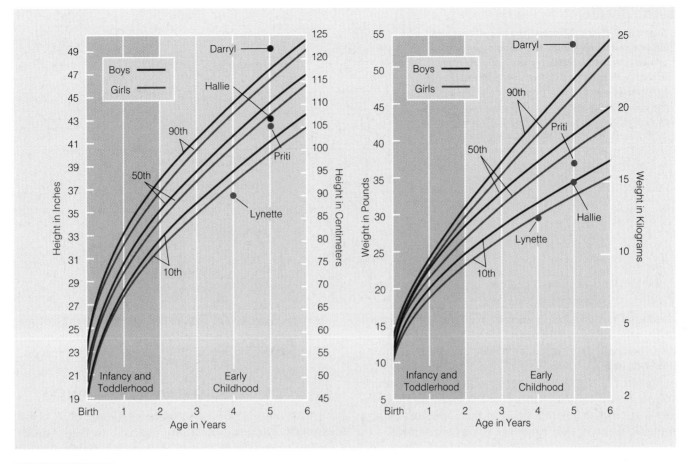

FIGURE 7.1

■ **Gains in height and weight during early childhood among North American children.** Compared with the first 2 years of life, growth is slower. Girls continue to be slightly shorter and lighter than boys. Wide individual differences in body size exist, as the percentiles on these charts reveal. Darryl, Priti, Lynette, and Hallie's heights and weights differ greatly.

epiphyses will appear in middle childhood. X-rays of these growth centers permit doctors to estimate children's *skeletal age,* or progress toward physical maturity (see Chapter 4, page 119). During early and middle childhood, information about skeletal age can help diagnose growth disorders.

Parents and children are especially aware of another aspect of skeletal growth: By the end of the preschool years, children start to lose their primary, or "baby," teeth. The age at which they do so is heavily influenced by genetic factors. For example, girls, who are ahead of boys in physical development, lose their primary teeth sooner. Environmental influences, especially prolonged malnutrition, can delay the appearance of permanent teeth.

Even though primary teeth are temporary, care of them is important. Diseased baby teeth can affect the health of permanent teeth. Consistent brushing, avoiding sugary foods, drinking fluoridated water, and getting topical fluoride treatments during regular dental visits prevent tooth cavities. Unfortunately, childhood tooth decay remains high, especially among low-SES children. Poor diet, lack of

fluoridation in some communities, and inadequate health care are responsible (Edelstein & Douglass, 1995).

ASYNCHRONIES IN PHYSICAL GROWTH

From what you have learned so far in this chapter and in Chapter 4, can you come up with a single overall description of physical growth? If you answered no, you are correct. As Figure 7.2 on the following page shows, physical growth is *asynchronous:* different body systems have unique, carefully timed patterns of maturation. Body size (as measured by height and weight) and a variety of internal organs follow the **general growth curve.** It involves rapid growth during infancy, slower gains in early and middle childhood, and rapid growth again during adolescence. Yet there are exceptions to this trend. The genitals develop slowly from birth to age 4, change little throughout middle childhood, and then grow rapidly during adolescence. In contrast, the lymph tissue (small clusters of glands found throughout the body) grows at an astounding pace in infancy and

FIGURE 7.2

■ **Growth of three different organ systems and tissues contrasted with the body's general growth.** Growth is plotted in terms of percentage of change from birth to 20 years. Notice how the lymph tissue rises to nearly twice its adult level by the end of childhood. Then it declines. (Reprinted by permission of the publisher from J. M. Tanner, 1990, *Foetus into Man*, 2nd ed., Cambridge, MA: Harvard University Press, p. 16. Copyright © 1990 by J. M. Tanner. All rights reserved.)

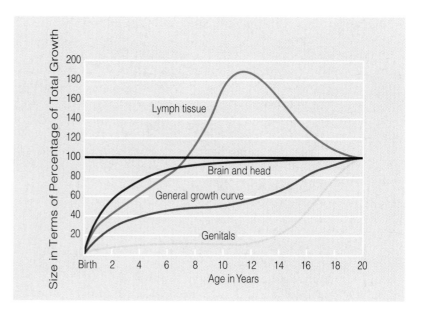

childhood but declines in adolescence. The lymph system helps fight infection and assists with absorption of nutrients, thereby supporting children's health and survival (Malina & Bouchard, 1991).

Figure 7.2 displays another growth trend with which you are already familiar: During the first few years, the brain grows faster than any other part of the body. Let's look at some highlights of early childhood brain development.

BRAIN DEVELOPMENT

Between 2 and 6 years, the brain increases from 70 to 90 percent of its adult weight (Tanner, 1990). As *myelinization* and *synaptic pruning* of neural fibers continue (see Chapter 4), preschoolers improve in a wide variety of skills—physical coordination, perception, attention, memory, language, logical thinking, and imagination.

Recall that the cortex is made up of two *hemispheres*. Measures of brain electrical activity reveal that the hemispheres develop at different rates. For most children, the left hemisphere shows a dramatic growth spurt between 3 and 6 years and then levels off. In contrast, activity in the right hemisphere increases slowly throughout early and middle childhood, with a slight spurt between ages 8 and 10 (Thatcher, Walker, & Giudice, 1987).

These findings fit nicely with what we know about several aspects of cognitive development. Language skills (typically housed in the left hemisphere) increase at an astonishing pace in early childhood. In contrast, spatial skills (such as finding one's way from place to place, drawing pictures, and recognizing geometric shapes) develop gradually over childhood and adolescence. Differences between the two hemispheres in rate of development suggest that they

are continuing to *lateralize*, or specialize, in cognitive functions. Let's take a closer look at brain lateralization in early childhood by focusing on the development of handedness.

LATERALIZATION AND HANDEDNESS

One morning on a visit to the preschool, I watched 3-year-old Moira as she drew pictures, worked puzzles, joined in snacktime, and played outside. Unlike most of her classmates, Moira does most things—drawing, eating, and zipping her jacket—with her left hand. But she uses her right hand for a few activities, such as throwing a ball. By age 2, hand preference is fairly stable, and it strengthens during early and middle childhood.

■ *Twins typically lie in the uterus in opposite orientations during the prenatal period, which may explain why they are more often opposite-handed than are ordinary siblings. Although left-handedness is associated with developmental problems, the large majority of left-handed children are completely normal. (Photo courtesy: © Laura Dwight)*

A strong hand preference reflects the greater capacity of one side of the brain—the individual's **dominant cerebral hemisphere**—to carry out skilled motor action. Other abilities located on the dominant side may also be superior. In support of this idea, for right-handed people, who make up 90 percent of the population, language is housed with hand control in the left hemisphere. For the remaining 10 percent who are left-handed, language is often shared between the hemispheres rather than located in only one. This indicates that the brains of left-handers tend to be less strongly lateralized than those of right-handers (Dean & Anderson, 1997). Consistent with this idea, many left-handed individuals (like Moira) are also *ambidextrous.* Although they prefer their left hand, they sometimes use their right hand skillfully as well (McManus et al., 1988).

Is handedness and, along with it, specialization of brain functions hereditary? Although researchers disagree on this issue, certain findings argue against a genetic explanation. Twins—whether identical or fraternal—are more likely than ordinary siblings to differ in handedness. The hand preference of each twin is related to body position during the prenatal period (twins usually lie in opposite orientations) (Derom et al., 1996). According to one theory, the way most fetuses lie—turned toward the left—may promote greater postural control by the right side of the body (Previc, 1991).

What about children like Moira whose hand use suggests an unusual organization of brain functions? Do these youngsters develop normally? Perhaps you have heard that left- or mixed-handedness is more frequent among severely retarded and mentally ill people than it is in the general population. Although this is true, recall that when two variables are correlated, one does not necessarily cause the other. Atypical lateralization is probably not responsible for the problems of these individuals. Instead, they may have suffered early damage to the left hemisphere, which caused their disabilities and also led to a shift in handedness. In support of this idea, left-handedness is associated with prenatal and birth difficulties that can result in brain damage, including prolonged labor, prematurity, Rh incompatibility, and breech delivery (O'Callaghan et al., 1993; Powls et al., 1996). In the case of mixed-handedness, individuals with severe mental disabilities may have been less able to profit from early experiences that foster lateralization of motor, language, and other skills (Provins, 1997).

Keep in mind, however, that only a small number of left-handers show developmental problems of any kind. The great majority, like Moira, are normal in every respect. In fact, unusual lateralization may have certain advantages. Although we do not yet know why, left- and mixed-handed youngsters are more likely than their right-handed agemates to develop outstanding verbal and mathematical talents by adolescence (Flannery & Liederman, 1995).

OTHER ADVANCES IN BRAIN DEVELOPMENT

Besides the cortex, other parts of the brain make strides during early childhood (see Figure 7.3). As we look at these changes, you will see that all involve establishing links between different parts of the brain, increasing the coordinated functioning of the central nervous system.

At the rear and base of the brain is the **cerebellum,** a structure that aids in balance and control of body movement. Fibers linking the cerebellum to the cerebral cortex begin to myelinate after birth, but they do not complete this process until about age 4 (Tanner, 1990). This change undoubtedly contributes to dramatic gains in motor control, so that by the end of the preschool years children can play a simple game of hopscotch, pump a swing, and throw a ball with a well-organized set of movements.

The **reticular formation,** a structure of the brain that maintains alertness and consciousness, myelinates throughout early childhood and into adolescence. Neurons in the

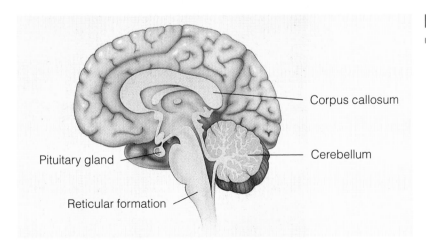

Pituitary gland

Reticular formation

Corpus callosum

Cerebellum

FIGURE 7.3

■ **Cross-section of the human brain, showing the location of the cerebellum, the reticular formation, and the corpus callosum.** These structures undergo considerable development during early childhood. Also shown is the pituitary gland, which secretes hormones that control body growth (see page 212).

reticular formation send out fibers to the frontal lobes of the cortex, contributing to improvements in sustained, controlled attention.

The **corpus callosum** is a large bundle of fibers that connects the two cortical hemispheres so they can communicate directly. Myelinization of the corpus callosum does not begin until the end of the first year of life. By age 4 to 5, its development is fairly advanced, supporting gains in the efficiency of thinking (Banish, 1998).

ASK YOURSELF . . .

■ *After graduating from dental school, Norm entered the Peace Corps and was assigned to rural India. He found that many Indian children had extensive tooth decay. In contrast, the young patients of his dental school friends in the United States had much less. What factors probably account for this difference?*

■ *Crystal has a left-handed cousin who is mentally retarded. Recently, she noticed that her 2-year-old daughter Shana is also left-handed. Crystal has heard that left-handedness is a sign of developmental problems, so she is worried about Shana. How would you respond to Crystal's concern?*

🌳 *Explain why brain growth in early childhood involves not only an increase in neural connections, but also a loss of synapses and cell death. Which assumption of the lifespan perspective do these processes illustrate? (If you need to review, see Chapter 1, page 9, and Chapter 4, page 120.)*

INFLUENCES ON PHYSICAL GROWTH AND HEALTH

In earlier chapters, we considered a wide variety of influences on physical growth during the prenatal period and infancy. As we discuss growth and health in early childhood, you will encounter some familiar themes. Although heredity remains important, environmental factors continue to play crucial roles. Emotional well-being, good nutrition, relative freedom from disease, and physical safety are essential.

HEREDITY AND HORMONES

The impact of heredity on physical growth is evident throughout childhood. Children's physical size and rate of growth are related to their parents' (Malina & Bouchard, 1991). Genes influence growth by controlling the body's

production of hormones, especially two that are released by the **pituitary gland,** located at the base of the brain.

The first is **growth hormone (GH),** which is necessary for physical development from birth on. Children who lack it reach an average mature height of only 4 feet, 4 inches. When treated with injections of GH starting at an early age, such children show catch-up growth and then grow at a normal rate. Consult the Social Issues box on the following page for a current controversy surrounding GH treatment—whether it should be used for short children who are not GH deficient.

The second pituitary hormone affecting children's growth is **thyroid-stimulating hormone (TSH).** It stimulates the thyroid gland (located in the neck) to release *thyroxine*, which is necessary for normal development of the nerve cells of the brain and for GH to have its full impact on body size. Infants born with a deficiency of thyroxine must receive it at once or they will be mentally retarded. At later ages, children with too little thyroxine grow at a below-average rate. By then, the central nervous system is no longer affected, since the most rapid period of brain development is complete. With prompt treatment, such children catch up in body growth and eventually reach normal adult size (Tanner, 1990).

■ *The very short, GH-deficient boy on the left in this class of kindergarteners has been given GH to speed his growth, increase his height, and protect him from social stigma. Should short children who are not GH deficient also be treated with injections of GH? As research reviewed in the Social Issues box reveals, the cost of doing so is staggering and the outcome uncertain. (Photo courtesy: © Laura Dwight)*

SOCIAL ISSUES

TREATING SHORT CHILDREN WITH GROWTH HORMONE

Through childhood and adolescence, Stephen was among the shortest 3 percent of his age group. He recalls being teased and tormented by insensitive peers and being called shrimp, pea, midget, squirt, and a dozen other insults. He looks back on these experiences calmly, perhaps because a late growth spurt led him to reach a final height of 5 feet 6 inches (Hall, 1996). But now, as he awaits the birth of his first child, he wonders, "Would treatment with GH have relieved the pain I experienced? Would it have added to or merely accelerated my growth? If my child is short, should I have him or her treated with a powerful drug for psychological pain induced by society's prejudices?"

Genetically engineered GH has been available since 1985, permitting successful treatment of short stature for children with GH deficiency. But since the GH gene was cloned, research has been conducted on unusually short, normal-GH children to see if they might benefit from hormone injections. Thousands of concerned parents have sought GH therapy for their children.

ARE SHORT, NORMAL-GH CHIL-DREN MALADJUSTED? A major justification for treating short, non-GH-deficient children is to improve their psychological functioning. Frequently reported problems include social stigma due to deviant appearance, poor social skills, social isolation, low self-esteem, and poor academic achievement. But most studies include only GH-deficient

children (Meyer-Bahlburg, 1990). Do these negative outcomes apply to short, normal-GH children as well?

Recent findings are mixed. In a British investigation comparing very short with average-stature children on self-esteem, social behavior, and academic achievement, differences between the two groups were minimal on some measures and nonexistent on others (Vance, 1994). An American study found very short 4- to 18-year-old boys, but not girls, to have an above-average incidence of parent-reported emotional and behavior problems. But when boys themselves—not their parents— were asked, they reported good self-esteem as well as athletic competence. They seemed to find their niche in certain sports in which height was not essential (Sandberg, Brook, & Campos, 1994).

In sum, research suggests that a biological height deficit by itself does not lead to poor psychological adjustment. Family attitudes and social experiences that sensitize children to their short stature appear to be very powerful.

DOES GH TREATMENT LEAD TO HEIGHT GAINS? Many studies show that GH-deficient children benefit from GH therapy; their final height is considerably greater than it would have been without treatment. But the verdict is not yet in for short, normal-GH children. Several follow-ups of American and Canadian boys who began treatment in late childhood or early adolescence reveal faster initial growth—an outcome that may be emotionally beneficial for some

youngsters. But most did not exceed the adult height they had been predicted to achieve naturally (Kaplowitz, 1995; Loche et al., 1994). Furthermore, withdrawal of GH treatment seems to have a rebound effect, causing growth to slow for as long as 18 months (Lampit et al., 1998).

Both biological and social forces influence a doctor's decision to prescribe GH for a short but otherwise normal child. On the biological side, doctors are more likely to treat an extremely short child who is growing very slowly but has a normal skeletal age—a combination of factors that increases the chances of becoming a very short adult. On the social side, when the child's parents strongly desire treatment, the child is more likely to get it (Cuttler et al., 1996).

Yet until more evidence is in, great caution should be exercised in prescribing GH for short, GH-normal children (Bercu, 1996; Diller, 1996). The estimated cost is staggering— $15,000 to $30,000 annually for a regimen that must continue until the child reaches near-adult height. Potential side effects include allergy, diabetes-like symptoms, fluid retention, and—for genetically susceptible individuals—curvature of the spine and leukemia.

Because "heightism" exists in society, treatment of short children may be warranted in some instances. But doctors and parents should recognize the unjust social values that lead them to consider intervening in a condition that results from biologically normal human diversity.

EMOTIONAL WELL-BEING

As in infancy, mind and body continue to be closely linked during childhood. Preschoolers with very stressful home lives (due to divorce, financial difficulties, or a change in their parents' employment status) suffer more respiratory and intestinal illnesses and unintentional injuries (Beautrais, Fergusson, & Shannon, 1982; Cohen & Herbert, 1996).

When emotional deprivation is extreme, it can interfere with the production of growth hormone and lead to **deprivation dwarfism,** a growth disorder that appears between 2 and 15 years of age. Lynette, the very small 4-year-old mentioned earlier in this chapter, was diagnosed with this condition. She had been placed in foster care after child welfare authorities discovered that she spent most of the day at home alone, unsupervised. She may also have been physically abused. To help her recover, Lynette was enrolled in our laboratory preschool. She showed the typical characteristics of deprivation dwarfism—very short stature, light weight in proportion to her height, immature skeletal age, and decreased GH secretion. When such children are removed from their emotionally inadequate environments, their GH levels quickly return to normal, and they grow rapidly. But if treatment is delayed, the dwarfism can be permanent (Oates, Peacock, & Forrest, 1985).

NUTRITION

With the transition to early childhood, many children become unpredictable and picky eaters. One father I know wistfully recalled his son's eager sampling of the cuisine at a Chinese restaurant during toddlerhood. "He ate rice, chicken chow mein, egg rolls, and more. Now, at age 3, the only thing he'll try is the ice cream!"

This decline in appetite is normal. It occurs because growth has slowed. And preschoolers' wariness of new foods is adaptive, since they are still learning which items are safe to eat and which are not. By sticking to familiar foods, they are less likely to swallow dangerous substances when adults are not around to protect them (Birch & Fisher, 1995).

Even though they eat less, preschoolers need a high-quality diet. They require the same foods adults do—only smaller amounts. Fats, oils, and salt should be kept to a minimum because of their link to high blood pressure and heart disease in adulthood (Fisher, Van Horn, & McGill, 1997). Foods high in sugar should also be avoided. In addition to causing tooth decay, sugary cereals, cookies, cakes, soft drinks, and candy reduce young children's appetite for healthy foods.

How can preschoolers be encouraged to eat a variety of foods? Repeated exposure to a new food (without any di-

rect pressure to eat it) increases children's acceptance. In one study, preschoolers were given one of three versions of a food they had never eaten (sweet, salty, or plain tofu). After 8 to 15 exposures, they readily ate the food. But they preferred the version they had already tasted. For example, children in the "sweet" condition liked sweet tofu best, and those in the "plain" condition liked plain tofu best (Sullivan & Birch, 1990). These findings reveal that children's tastes are trained by foods served often in their culture. Adding sugar or salt in hopes of increasing a young child's willingness to eat a healthy food simply teaches the child to like a sugary or salty taste.

The emotional climate at mealtimes has a powerful impact on children's eating habits. Many parents worry about how well their preschoolers eat, so meals become unpleasant and stressful. Sometimes parents bribe their children, saying, "Finish your vegetables, and you can have an extra cookie." Unfortunately, this practice only causes children to like the healthy food less and the treat more (Birch, Johnson, & Fisher, 1995). The Caregiving Concerns table on the following page offers some suggestions for promoting healthy, varied eating in young children.

Finally, as indicated in earlier chapters, many children in the United States and in developing countries are deprived of diets that support healthy growth. Five-year-old Hallie was bused to our laboratory preschool from a poor neighborhood. His mother's welfare check barely covered her rent, let alone food. Hallie's diet was deficient in protein as well as essential vitamins and minerals—iron (to prevent anemia), calcium (to support development of bones and teeth), vitamin A (to help maintain eyes, skin, and a variety of

■ *Children's food tastes are trained by foods served often in their culture. Many Western children would refuse the spicy noodle dish these Japanese preschoolers are eating with enthusiasm. (Photo courtesy: Tom McCarthy/PhotoEdit)*

Encouraging Good Nutrition in Early Childhood

SUGGESTION	DESCRIPTION
Offer a varied, healthy diet.	Provide a well-balanced variety of nutritious foods that are colorful and attractively served. Avoid serving sweets and "junk" foods as a regular part of meals and snacks.
Offer predictable meals as well as several snacks each day.	Preschoolers' stomachs are small, and they may not be able to eat enough in three meals to satisfy energy requirements. They benefit from extra opportunities to eat.
Offer small portions, and permit the child to ask for seconds.	When too much food is put on the plate, preschoolers may be overwhelmed and not even try to eat.
Offer new foods early in the meal and over several meals, and respond with patience if the child rejects the food.	Introduce new foods before the child's appetite is satisfied. Let children see you eating and enjoying the new food. If the child rejects it, accept the refusal and serve it again at another meal. As foods become more familiar, they are more readily accepted.
Keep mealtimes pleasant, and include the child in mealtime conversations.	A pleasant, relaxed eating environment helps children develop positive attitudes about food. Avoid confrontations over disliked foods and table manners.
Avoid using food as a reward.	Saying "No dessert until you clean your plate" tells children that they must eat regardless of how hungry they are and that dessert is the best part of the meal.

Sources: Birch, Johnson, & Fisher, 1995; Kendrick, Kaufman, & Messenger, 1991.

internal organs), and vitamin C (to facilitate iron absorption and wound healing). These are the most common dietary deficiencies of the preschool years. Not surprisingly, Hallie was small for his age, and he often seemed tired. By age 7, American low-SES children are, on the average, about 1 inch shorter than their economically advantaged counterparts (Yip, Scanlon, & Trowbridge, 1993).

INFECTIOUS DISEASE

Two weeks into the school year, I looked out my window and noticed that Hallie was absent from the play yard. Several weeks passed; still, I did not see him. When I asked Leslie, his preschool teacher, what had happened, she explained, "Hallie's been hospitalized with the measles. He's had a difficult time recovering—lost weight when there wasn't much to lose in the first place." In well-nourished children, ordinary childhood illnesses have no effect on physical growth. But when children are undernourished, disease interacts with malnutrition in a vicious spiral, and the consequences for physical growth can be severe.

INFECTIOUS DISEASE AND MALNUTRITION.
Hallie's reaction to the measles is commonplace among children in developing nations, where a large proportion of the population lives in poverty. In these countries, many children do not receive a program of immunizations. Illnesses such as measles and chicken pox, which typically do not appear until after age 3 in industrialized nations, occur much earlier. Poor diet depresses the body's immune system, making children far more susceptible to disease. Disease, in turn, is a major cause of malnutrition and, through it, hinders physical growth. Illness reduces appetite and limits the body's ability to absorb foods. These outcomes are especially severe in children with intestinal infections. In developing countries, diarrhea is widespread and increases in early childhood due to unsafe water and contaminated foods, leading to growth stunting and several million childhood deaths each year (Grant, 1995).

Most growth retardation and deaths due to diarrhea can be prevented with nearly cost-free **oral rehydration therapy (ORT)**, in which sick children are given a glucose, salt, and water solution that quickly replaces fluids the body loses. Since 1990, public health workers have taught nearly half of families in the developing world how to administer ORT. As a result, the lives of more than 1 million children are being saved annually (Bellamy, 1998).

IMMUNIZATION.
In industrialized nations, childhood diseases have declined dramatically during the past half century, largely due to widespread immunization of infants and young children. Hallie got the measles because, unlike his classmates from more advantaged homes, he did not receive a full program of immunizations during his first 2 years of life. Although the majority of preschoolers in the United States are immunized, some do not receive full protection until 5 or 6 years of age, when it is required for school entry (Children's Defense Fund, 1999).

To remedy this problem, in 1994 all medically uninsured American children were guaranteed free immunizations. As a result, immunization rates in the United States improved, but they continue to lag behind those of Canada and Western European nations. For example, 29 percent of American preschoolers are not fully immunized, a rate that rises to 40 percent for poverty-stricken children (U.S. Department of Health and Human Services, 1999g). In contrast, fewer than 10 percent of preschoolers lack immunizations in Canada, Denmark, and Norway; fewer than 7 percent in the Netherlands and Sweden (Bellamy, 1999; de Winter, Balleduz, & de Mare, 1997).

How is it that these countries have managed to achieve high rates of immunization, whereas the United States' record is so poor? In earlier chapters, we noted that many children in the United States do not have access to the medical care they need. Because American health insurance is an optional, employment-related fringe benefit rather than government sponsored and universally available, 11.6 million children from low- and moderate-income families are uninsured and, therefore, without affordable health care (Children's Defense Fund, 1999).

Inability to pay for vaccines, however, is only one cause of lower immunization rates in the United States. Misconceptions about safe medical practices also contribute. American parents often report that they delay taking their child in for a vaccination because they believe the child might have an adverse reaction (Abbots & Osborn, 1993). Public education programs that increase parental knowledge about the importance and safety of timely immunizations are badly needed.

■ *Widespread, government-sponsored immunization of infants and young children is a cost-effective means of supporting healthy growth by dramatically reducing the incidence of childhood diseases. Although this boy finds a routine inoculation painful, it will offer him lifelong protection. (Photo courtesy: Bruce Ayres/Stone)*

CHILDHOOD INJURIES

Three-year-old Tory caught my eye as I visited the preschool classroom one day. More than any other child, he had trouble sitting still and paying attention at storytime. Outside, he darted from one place to another, spending little time at a single activity. On a field trip to our campus museum, Tory ignored Leslie's directions and ran across the street without holding his partner's hand. Later in the year, I read in our local newspaper that Tory had narrowly escaped serious injury when he put his mother's car into gear while she was outside scraping its windows. The vehicle rolled through a guardrail and over the side of a 10-foot concrete underpass. There it hung until rescue workers arrived. Tory's mother was charged with failing to use a restraint seat for children under age 5.

Unintentional injuries—auto collisions, pedestrian accidents, drownings, poisonings, firearm wounds, burns, falls, and swallowing foreign objects—are the leading cause of childhood mortality. These largely preventable events account for 40 to 50 percent of deaths in early and middle childhood and as many as 75 percent during adolescence. Approximately 22,000 American youngsters die from these incidents each year. And for each death, thousands of other injured children survive but suffer pain, brain damage, and permanent physical disabilities (Kronenfeld & Glik, 1995).

As Figure 7.4 shows, auto and traffic accidents, drownings, and burns are the most common injuries during the preschool years. Motor vehicle collisions are by far the most frequent source of injury from 1 year of age through early adulthood.

■ FACTORS RELATED TO CHILDHOOD INJURIES. We are used to thinking of childhood injuries as "accidental." But a close look reveals that meaningful causes underlie them, and we can, indeed, do something about them.

As Tory's case suggests, individual differences exist in the safety of children's behaviors. Because of their higher activity level and greater willingness to take risks during play, boys are more likely to be injured than girls. (Look again at Figure 7.4.) Temperamental characteristics—irritability, inattentiveness, and negative mood—are also related to childhood injuries. As we saw in Chapter 6, children with these traits present special child-rearing challenges. They are likely to protest when placed in auto seat restraints, refuse to take a companion's hand when crossing the street, and disobey after repeated adult instruction and discipline (Matheny, 1991).

At the same time, families whose preschoolers get injured tend to have characteristics that increase the likelihood of exposure to danger. Poverty and low parental education are strongly associated with injury deaths. Parents who must cope with many daily stresses often have little time and energy to monitor the safety of their youngsters. And their

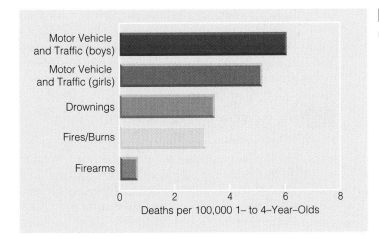

FIGURE 7.4

■ **Rate of injury mortality in the United States for children between 1 and 4 years of age by type of injury.** Between 1 and 4 years of age, motor vehicle and traffic fatalities are greater for boys than girls. For other injuries depicted here, death rates for boys and girls are similar until age 5, when boys begin to outdistance girls in all categories. (From U. S. Department of Health and Human Services, 1999g.)

homes and neighborhoods pose further risks. Noise, crowding, and confusion characterize these environments, and they tend to be located in run-down, inner-city neighborhoods with few safe places to play (Peterson & Brown, 1994).

Broad societal conditions also affect childhood injury. Among Western industrialized nations, the United States ranks among the highest in childhood injury mortality. Although injury deaths have steadily declined in nearly all developed countries during the past 30 years, they have dropped only minimally in the United States (U.S. Department of Health and Human Services, 1999d). Widespread poverty, a shortage of high-quality child care (to supervise children in their parents' absence), and a high rate of births to teenagers (who are neither psychologically nor financially ready to be parents) account for this trend. But children from advantaged families are also at somewhat greater risk for injury in the United States than they are in European nations (Williams & Kotch, 1990). This indicates that besides reducing poverty and teenage pregnancy and upgrading the status of child care, additional steps must be taken to ensure children's safety.

■ PREVENTING CHILDHOOD INJURIES. Childhood injuries have many causes, so a variety of approaches are needed to control them. Laws prevent a great many injuries by requiring car safety seats, child-resistant caps on medicine bottles, flameproof clothing, and fenced-in backyard swimming pools (the site of 90 percent of early childhood drownings).

Communities can help by modifying their physical environments. Inexpensive and widely available public transportation can reduce the time that children spend in cars. Playgrounds, a common site of injury, can be covered with protective surfaces, such as rubber matting, sand, and wood chips. Free, easily installed window guards can be given to families in high-rise apartment buildings to prevent falls. And widespread media campaigns and information distributed in doctors' offices, schools, and child-care centers help inform parents and children about safety issues.

Nevertheless, many dangers cannot be eliminated from the environment. And even though they know better, many parents and children behave in ways that compromise safety. How can we change human behavior? A variety of programs based on *applied behavior analysis* (modeling and reinforcement) have improved safety practices. In one, counselors helped parents identify dangers in the home—fire hazards, objects that young children might swallow, poisons, firearms, and others. Then they demonstrated specific ways to eliminate the dangers (Tertinger, Greene, & Lutzker, 1984). Several interventions reward parents and children with prizes if the children arrive at child care or school each morning in car seats (Roberts, Alexander, & Knapp, 1990).

Efforts like these have been remarkably successful, yet their focus is fairly narrow—on decreasing specific environmental risks and risky behaviors (Peterson & Brown, 1994). Attention must also be paid to family conditions that can prevent childhood injury—relieving crowding in the home, providing social supports to ease parental stress, and teaching parents to use effective discipline, a topic we will take up in Chapter 8.

 ASK YOURSELF . . .

■ *One day, Leslie prepared a new snack to serve at preschool: celery stuffed with ricotta cheese and pineapple. The first time she served it, few of the children touched it. How can Leslie encourage her pupils to accept the snack? What should she avoid doing?*

■ *Using ecological systems theory (see Chapter 1), suggest ways to reduce childhood injuries by intervening in the microsystem, the mesosystem, and the macrosystem.*

🌳 *Using research on malnutrition or unintentional injuries, show how physical growth and health in early childhood result from the continuous and complex interplay between heredity and environment.*

MOTOR DEVELOPMENT

Visit a playground at a neighborhood park, pre-school, or child-care center, and observe several 2- to 6-year-olds. You will see that an explosion of new motor skills occurs in early childhood, each of which builds on the simpler movement patterns of toddlerhood.

The same principle that governs motor development during the first 2 years of life continues to operate during the preschool years. Children integrate previously acquired skills into more complex *dynamic systems of action.* (Return to Chapter 4, page 134, if you need to review this concept.) Then they revise each new skill as their bodies grow larger and stronger, their central nervous systems develop, and their environments present new challenges.

GROSS MOTOR DEVELOPMENT

As children's bodies become more streamlined and less top-heavy, their center of gravity shifts downward, toward the trunk. As a result, balance improves greatly, paving the way for new motor skills involving large muscles of the body (Ulrich & Ulrich, 1985). By age 2, preschoolers' gaits become smooth and rhythmic—secure enough that soon they leave the ground, at first by running and later by jumping, hopping, galloping, and skipping.

As children become steadier on their feet, their arms and torsos are freed to experiment with new skills—throwing and catching balls, steering tricycles, and swinging on horizontal bars and rings. Then upper and lower body skills combine into more refined actions. Five- and 6-year-olds steer and pedal a tricycle at the same time and flexibly move their whole body when throwing, catching, hopping, and jumping. By the end of the preschool years, all skills are performed with greater speed and endurance. Table 7.1 provides a closer look at gross motor development in early childhood.

FINE MOTOR DEVELOPMENT

Like gross motor development, fine motor skills take a giant leap forward during the preschool years. Because control of the hands and fingers improves, young children put puzzles together, build with small blocks, cut and paste, and string beads. To parents, fine motor progress is most apparent in two areas: (1) children's care of their own bodies, and (2) the drawings and paintings that fill the walls at home, child care, and preschool.

■ SELF-HELP SKILLS. As Table 7.1 shows, young children gradually become self-sufficient at dressing and feeding, although parents need to be patient about these abilities. When tired and in a hurry, young children often revert to eating with their fingers. And the 3-year-old who dresses himself sometimes ends up with his shirt on inside out, his pants on backward, and his left snow boot on his right foot!

Perhaps the most complex self-help skill of early childhood is shoe tying, mastered around age 6. Success requires a longer attention span, memory for an intricate series of hand movements, and the dexterity to perform them. Shoe tying illustrates the close connection between motor and cognitive development. Drawing and writing offer additional examples.

TABLE 7.1

Changes in Gross and Fine Motor Skills During Early Childhood

AGE	GROSS MOTOR SKILLS	FINE MOTOR SKILLS
2–3 years	Walks more rhythmically; hurried walk changes to run. Jumps, hops, throws, and catches with rigid upper body. Pushes riding toy with feet; little steering.	Puts on and removes simple items of clothing. Zips and unzips large zippers. Uses spoon effectively.
3–4 years	Walks up stairs, alternating feet, and downstairs, leading with one foot. Jumps and hops, flexing upper body. Throws and catches with slight involvement of upper body; still catches by trapping ball against chest. Pedals and steers tricycle.	Fastens and unfastens large buttons. Serves self food without assistance. Uses scissors. Copies vertical line and circle. Draws first picture of person, using tadpole image.
4–5 years	Walks downstairs, alternating feet. Runs more smoothly. Gallops and skips with one foot. Throws ball with increased body rotation and transfer of weight on feet; catches ball with hands. Rides tricycle rapidly, steers smoothly.	Uses fork effectively. Cuts with scissors following line. Copies triangle, cross, and some letters.
5–6 years	Increases running speed. Gallops more smoothly; engages in true skipping. Displays mature throwing and catching pattern. Rides bicycle with training wheels.	Uses knife to cut soft food. Ties shoes. Draws person with six parts. Copies some numbers and simple words.

Sources: Furuno et al., 1987; Newborg, Stock, & Wnek, 1984.

■ **Examples of young children's drawings.** The universal tadpolelike shape that children use to draw their first picture of a person is shown on the left. The tadpole soon becomes an anchor for greater detail as arms, fingers, toes, and facial features sprout from the basic shape. By the end of the preschool years, children produce more complex, differentiated pictures like the one on the right drawn by a 6-year-old child. (Tadpole drawings from H. Gardner, 1980, *Artful Scribbles: The Significance of Children's Drawings,* New York: Basic Books, p. 64. Reprinted with permission of Basic Books, a division of HarperCollins Publishers, Inc. Six-year-old's picture from E. Winner, August 1986, "Where Pelicans Kiss Seals," *Psychology Today, 20*[8], p. 35. Reprinted by permission of the author.)

■ DRAWING AND WRITING. When given crayon and paper, even toddlers scribble in imitation of others. As young children's ability to represent the world expands, marks on the page take on meaning. A variety of factors combine with fine motor control in the development of children's artful representations. These include cognitive advances, such as gains in planning skills and spatial understanding (a move from a focus on separate objects to a broader visual perspective), and exposure to pictorial images in their environment (Golomb, 1992).

■ FROM SCRIBBLES TO PICTURES. At first, children's artful representation occurs through gestures. For example, one 18-month-old hopped her crayon around the page, explaining as she made a series of dots, "Rabbit goes hop-hop." Around age 2, children realize that pictures can depict pretend objects—a basic feature of artistic expression (Kavanaugh & Harris, 1994). By age 3, children's scribbles become pictures. Often this happens after they make a gesture with the crayon, notice that they have drawn a recognizable shape, and then decide to label it (Winner, 1986).

A major milestone in children's drawing occurs when they use lines to represent the boundaries of objects. This permits them to draw their first picture of a person by age 3 or 4. Look at the tadpole image on the left in Figure 7.5. It is a universal one in which the limits of the preschooler's fine motor skills reduce the figure to the simplest form that still looks human.

■ *When young children experiment with crayons and paint, they not only develop fine motor skills but acquire the artistic traditions of their culture. This Australian Aboriginal 4-year-old creates a dot painting. To Westerners, it looks abstract. To the child, it expresses a "dreamtime" story about the life and land of his ancestors. If asked about the painting, he might respond, "Here are the boulders on the creek line, the hills with kangaroos and emus, and the campsites." (Photo courtesy: Laura Berk)*

Unlike many adults, young children do not demand that a drawing be realistic. But as they get older and their fine motor control improves, they learn to desire greater realism. As a result, they create more complex drawings, like the one on the right in Figure 7.5 by a 6-year-old child. Still, there are perceptual distortions, since only at the end of the preschool years do children start to represent depth in their drawings (Braine et al., 1993).

■ CULTURAL VARIATIONS IN DEVELOPMENT OF DRAWING. In cultures that emphasize artistic expression, children's drawings reflect the conventions of their culture and are more sophisticated. In cultures with little interest in art, children produce simpler drawings.

Schooling provides opportunities to draw and write, see pictures, and grasp the notion that artistic forms have socially shared meanings (Cox, 1993). The Jimi Valley is a remote region of Papua New Guinea with no indigenous pictorial art, and many Jimi children do not go to school. When a Western researcher asked nonschooled Jimi 10- to 15-year-olds to draw a human figure for the first time, most produced nonrepresentational scribbles or simple "stick" or "contour" images (see Figure 7.6). Compared with the Western tadpole image, Jimi figures emphasize the body, hands, and feet over the head and face—a different view of the human form (Martlew & Connolly, 1996).

That older Jimi children with no schooling often produce nonrepresentational forms suggests that this is a universal beginning stage in drawing. When they realize lines

(a)   (b)   (c)

■ **Drawings produced by nonschooled 10- to 15-year-old children of the Jimi Valley of Papua New Guinea when asked to draw a human figure for the first time.** Many produced nonrepresentational scribbles and shapes (a), "stick" figures (b), or "contour" figures (c). Compared with the Western tadpole form, the Jimi "stick" and "contour" figures emphasize the hands and feet. Otherwise, the drawings of these older children resemble those of young preschoolers. (From M. Martlew & K. J. Connolly, 1996, "Human Figure Drawings by Schooled and Unschooled Children in Papua New Guinea," *Child Development*, 67, pp. 2750–2751. © The Society for Research in Child Development, Inc. Adapted by permission.)

must evoke human features, they find solutions to figure drawing that vary somewhat from culture to culture but, overall, follow the sequence described earlier.

■ EARLY PRINTING. As young children experiment with lines and shapes, notice print in storybooks, and observe people writing, they try to print letters and, later on, words. Often the first word printed is the child's name. Initially, it may be represented by a single letter. "How do you make a *D*?" my older son, David, asked at age 3. When I printed a large uppercase *D*, he tried to copy. "*D* for David," he said as he wrote, quite satisfied with his backward, imperfect creation. A year later, David added several letters, and around age 5, he wrote his name clearly enough that others could read it. Like many children, David continued to reverse some letters in his printing until well into second grade. Not until they learn to read do children find it useful to distinguish between mirror-image forms, such as *b* and *d* and *p* and *q* (Bornstein, 1999; Casey, 1986).

INDIVIDUAL AND SEX DIFFERENCES IN MOTOR SKILLS

We have largely discussed motor milestones in terms of the average age at which children reach them, but, of course, there are wide individual differences. Body build influences gross motor abilities. A child with a tall, muscular body tends to move more quickly and acquire certain skills earlier than a short, stocky youngster. Researchers believe that body build contributes to the superior performance of African-American over Caucasian-American children in running and jumping. African-American youngsters tend to have longer limbs, so they have better leverage (Lee, 1980; Wakat, 1978).

Sex differences in motor skills are evident in early childhood. Boys are slightly ahead of girls in skills that emphasize force and power. By age 5, they can jump slightly farther, run slightly faster, and throw a ball much farther (about 5 feet beyond the distance covered by girls). Girls have an edge in fine motor skills and in certain gross motor skills that require a combination of good balance and foot movement, such as hopping and skipping. Boys' greater muscle mass and (in the case of throwing) slightly longer forearms may contribute to their skill advantages. And girls' greater overall physical maturity may be partly responsible for their better balance and precision of movement.

From an early age, boys and girls are usually encouraged into different physical activities. For example, fathers often play catch with their sons but seldom do so with their daughters. Baseballs and footballs are purchased for boys, jump ropes, hula hoops, and skates for girls. As children get older, sex differences in motor skills get larger, yet differences in physical capacity remain small until adolescence. These trends suggest that social pressures for boys to be active and physically skilled and for girls to play quietly at fine motor activities may exaggerate small, genetically based sex differences (Coakley, 1990; Greendorfer, Lewko, & Rosengren, 1996).

Children master the motor skills of early childhood as part of their everyday play. Aside from throwing (where direct instruction seems to make some difference), there is no evidence that preschoolers exposed to formal lessons are ahead in motor development (Roberton, 1984). When children have play spaces appropriate for running, climbing, jumping, and throwing and puzzles, construction sets, and art materials that promote manipulation, drawing, and writing, they respond eagerly to these challenges.

Finally, the social climate created by adults can enhance or dampen preschoolers' motor progress. When parents and teachers criticize a child's performance or push specific motor skills, they risk undermining young children's self-confidence, and, in turn, their motor progress (Kutner, 1993). Adult involvement in young children's motor activities should focus on "fun" rather than learning the "correct" technique.

■ ASK YOURSELF . . .

 Mabel and Chad want to do everything they can to support their 3-year-old daughter's motor progress and to foster an early, positive attitude toward athletics that will persist into middle childhood and adolescence. What advice would you give them?

■ *Five-year-old Heather draws elaborate pictures at preschool, whereas Michael's drawings are limited to tadpole shapes with little detail. What factors might contribute to the gap in drawing competence between Heather and Michael?*

COGNITIVE DEVELOPMENT

One rainy morning, as I observed in our laboratory preschool, Leslie, the children's teacher, joined me at the back of the room to watch for a moment herself. "Preschoolers' minds are such a blend of logic, fantasy, and faulty reasoning," Leslie reflected. "Every day, I'm startled by the maturity and originality of what they say and do. Yet at other times, their thinking seems limited and inflexible."

Leslie's comments sum up the puzzling contradictions of early childhood cognition. Over the previous week, I had seen many examples as I followed the activities of 3-year-old Sammy. That day, I found him at the puzzle table, moments after a loud clash of thunder outside. Sammy looked up, startled, then turned to Leslie and pronounced, "The man turned on the thunder!" Leslie patiently explained that people can't turn thunder on or off. "Then a lady did it," Sammy stated with certainty.

In other respects, Sammy's cognitive skills seemed surprisingly advanced. At snack time, he accurately counted, "One, two, three, four!" and then got four cartons of milk, giving one to each child at his table. But when more than four children joined his snack group, Sammy's counting broke down. And some of his notions about quantity seemed as fantastic as his understanding of thunder. Across the snack table, Priti dumped out her raisins, and they scattered in front of her. "How come you got lots, and I only got this little bit?" asked Sammy, failing to realize that he had just as many; they were simply all bunched up in a tiny red box. Piaget's theory helps us understand Sammy's curious reasoning.

PIAGET'S THEORY: THE PREOPERATIONAL STAGE

As children move from the sensorimotor to the **preoperational stage,** the most obvious change is an extraordinary increase in representational, or symbolic, activity. Recall that infants and toddlers have some ability to represent the world mentally. During early childhood, this capacity blossoms.

■ ADVANCES IN MENTAL REPRESENTATION

Piaget acknowledged that language is our most flexible means of mental representation. By detaching thought from action, it permits cognition to be far more efficient than it was during the sensorimotor stage. When we think in words, we overcome the limits of our momentary perceptions. We can deal with the past, present, and future all at once, creating larger, interconnected images of reality (Miller, 1993).

Despite the power of language, Piaget did not believe that it plays a major role in cognitive development. According to Piaget, language does not give rise to representational thought. Instead, sensorimotor activity provides the foundation for language, just as it underlies deferred imitation and make-believe play. Can you think of evidence that supports Piaget's view? Recall from Chapter 5 that the first words toddlers use have a strong sensory basis. In addition, toddlers acquire an impressive range of cognitive categories long before they use words to label them (see page 158). Still, other theorists regard Piaget's account of the link between language and thought as incomplete, as we will see later in this chapter.

■ MAKE-BELIEVE PLAY

Make-believe play is another example of representation. Like language, it increases dramatically during early childhood. Piaget believed that through pretending, young children practice and strengthen newly acquired representational schemes. Drawing on his ideas, several investigators have traced the development of make-believe during the preschool years.

■ DEVELOPMENT OF MAKE-BELIEVE. One day, Sammy's 18-month-old brother, Dwayne, came to visit the classroom. Dwayne wandered around, picked up the receiver of a toy telephone, said, "Hi, Mommy," and then dropped it. In the housekeeping area, he found a cup, pretended to drink, and then toddled off again.

In the meantime, Sammy joined a group of children in the block area for a space shuttle launch. "That can be our control tower," he suggested to Vance and Lynette, pointing to a corner by a bookshelf. "Countdown!" Sammy announced, speaking into a small wooden block, his pretend walkie-talkie. "Five, six, two, four, one, blastoff!" Lynette made a doll push a pretend button, and the rocket was off!

A comparison of Dwayne's pretend with that of Sammy illustrates three important changes in make-believe. Each reflects the preschool child's growing symbolic mastery.

1. *Over time, play becomes increasingly detached from the real-life conditions associated with it.* In early pretending, toddlers use only realistic objects—for example,

■ *These 4-year-olds coordinate several make-believe roles with the assistance of a very cooperative family pet. Their enjoyment of sociodramatic play contributes to cognitive, emotional, and social development. (Photo courtesy: Tom McCarthy/Uniphoto)*

a toy telephone to talk into or a cup to drink from. Around age 2, they use less realistic toys, such as a block for a telephone receiver, more frequently. Sometime during the third year, children can imagine objects and events without support from the real world, as when Sammy invented the control tower in a corner of the room. We can see that children's representations are becoming more flexible, since a play symbol no longer must resemble the object for which it stands (Corrigan, 1987; O'Reilly, 1995).

2. *The way the "child as self" participates in play changes with age.* At first, make-believe is directed toward the self—for example, Dwayne pretends to feed only himself. A short time later, children direct pretend actions toward other objects, as when the child feeds a doll. And early in the third year, they use objects as active agents. The child becomes a detached participant who makes a doll feed itself or (in Lynette's case) push a button to launch a rocket. Make-believe gradually becomes less self-centered as children realize that agents and recipients of pretend actions can be independent of themselves (Corrigan, 1987; McCune, 1993).

3. *Make-believe gradually includes more complex scheme combinations.* For example, Dwayne can pretend to drink from a cup but he does not yet combine pouring and drinking. Later, children combine schemes, especially in **sociodramatic play,** the make-believe with others that is under way by age 2½ and increases rapidly during the next few years (Haight & Miller, 1993; Howes & Matheson, 1992). Already, Sammy and his classmates create and coordinate several roles in an elaborate plot. By the end of early childhood, children have a sophisticated understanding of role relationships and story lines (Göncü, 1993).

The appearance of complex sociodramatic play indicates that children do not just represent their world; they are *aware* that make-believe is a representational activity—an understanding that increases between ages 4 and 8 (Lillard, 1998). Listen closely to preschoolers as they assign roles and negotiate make-believe plans: "You *pretend to be* the astronaut, I'll *act like* I'm operating the control tower!" In communicating about pretend, children think about their own and others' fanciful representations. This indicates they have started to reason about people's mental activities, a topic we will return to later in this chapter.

■ ADVANTAGES OF MAKE-BELIEVE. Today, Piaget's view of make-believe as mere practice of representational schemes is regarded as too limited. Research indicates that make-believe play not only reflects, but contributes to children's cognitive and social skills (Nicolopoulou, 1993; Singer & Singer, 1990). Compared with social nonpretend activities (such as drawing or putting puzzles together), during sociodramatic play preschoolers' interactions last longer, show more involvement, draw larger numbers of children into the activity, and are more cooperative (Creasey, Jarvis, & Berk, 1998).

When we consider these findings, it is not surprising that preschoolers who spend more time at sociodramatic play are advanced in general intellectual development and seen as more socially competent by their teachers (Burns & Brainerd, 1979; Connolly & Doyle, 1984). And many studies reveal that make-believe strengthens a wide variety of mental abilities, including memory, logical reasoning, language and literacy, imagination, creativity, and the ability to reflect on one's own thinking and take another's perspective (Berk, 1994; Kavanaugh & Engel, 1998). We will return to the topic of early childhood play in Chapter 8.

LIMITATIONS OF PREOPERATIONAL THOUGHT

Aside from gains in representation, Piaget described preschoolers in terms of what they *cannot*, rather than *can*, understand (Beilin, 1992). He compared them to older, more competent children in the concrete operational stage, as the term "*preoperational*" suggests. According to Piaget, young children are not capable of *operations*—mental actions that obey logical rules. Instead, their thinking is rigid, limited to one aspect of a situation at a time, and strongly influenced by the way things appear at the moment.

■ EGOCENTRISM. For Piaget, the most serious deficiency of preoperational thinking, the one that underlies all others, is **egocentrism.** He believed that when children begin to represent the world mentally, they are unaware of any perspectives other than their own, and they believe everyone else perceives, thinks, and feels the same way they do (Piaget, 1950).

Piaget's most convincing demonstration of egocentrism involves a task called the *three-mountains problem*, described in Figure 7.7. Egocentrism, Piaget pointed out, shows up in other aspects of children's reasoning. Recall Sammy's firm insistence that someone must have turned on the thunder, in much the same way that he uses a switch to turn on a light or radio. Similarly, Piaget regarded egocentrism as responsible for preoperational children's **animistic thinking**—the belief that inanimate objects have lifelike qualities, such as thoughts, wishes, feelings, and intentions, just like themselves. The 3-year-old who charmingly explains that the sun is angry at the clouds and has chased them away is demonstrating this kind of reasoning. According to Piaget, because young children egocentrically

FIGURE 7.7

■ **Piaget's three-mountains problem.** Each mountain is distinguished by its color and by its summit. One has a red cross, another a small house, and the third a snow-capped peak. Children at the preoperational stage are egocentric. They cannot select a picture that shows the mountains from the doll's perspective. Instead, they simply choose the photo that reflects their own vantage point.

assign human purposes to physical events, magical thinking is especially common during the preschool years.

Piaget argued that egocentrism leads to the rigidity and illogical nature of young children's thinking. Thought proceeds so strongly from a single point of view that children do not *accommodate*, or revise their faulty reasoning, in response to their physical and social worlds. But to appreciate this shortcoming fully, let's consider some additional tasks that Piaget gave to children.

■ INABILITY TO CONSERVE. Piaget's famous conservation tasks reveal a variety of deficiencies of preoperational thinking. **Conservation** refers to the idea that certain physical characteristics of objects remain the same, even when their outward appearance changes. At snack time, Priti and Sammy each had identical boxes of raisins, but after Priti spread hers out on the table, Sammy was convinced that she had more.

Another type of conservation task involves liquid. The child is shown two identical tall glasses of water and asked if they contain equal amounts. Once the child agrees, the water in one glass is poured into a short, wide container, changing the appearance of the water but not its amount. Then the child is asked whether the amount of water is still

Conservation Task	Original Presentation	Transformation
Number	Are there the same number of pennies in each row?	Now are there the same number of pennies in each row, or does one row have more?
Length	Is each of these sticks just as long as the other?	Now are the two sticks each equally as long, or is one longer?
Liquid	Is there the same amount of water in each glass?	Now is there the same amount of water in each glass, or does one have more?
Mass	Is there the same amount of clay in each ball?	Now does each piece have the same amount of clay, or does one have more?

FIGURE 7.8

■ **Some Piagetian conservation tasks.** Children at the preoperational stage cannot yet conserve.

the same or whether it has changed. Preoperational children think the quantity of water is no longer the same. They explain, "There is less now because the water is way down here" (that is, its level is so low in the short, wide container) or, "There is more now because it is all spread out." In Figure 7.8, you will find other conservation tasks that you can try with children.

Preoperational children's inability to conserve highlights several related aspects of their thinking. First, their understanding is *centered,* or characterized by **centration.** They focus on only one aspect of a situation, neglecting other important features. In conservation of liquid, the child centers on the height of the water, failing to realize that all changes in height are compensated by changes in width. Second, their thinking is **perception-bound.** They are easily distracted by the appearance of objects. It *looks like* there is less water in the short, wide container, so there *must be* less water. Third, children focus on **states rather than transformations.** In the conservation-of-liquid problem, they treat the initial and final *states* of the water as completely unrelated events, ignoring the *dynamic transformation* (pouring of water) between them.

The most important illogical feature of preoperational thought is its **irreversibility.** Children of this stage cannot mentally go through a series of steps in a problem and then reverse direction, returning to the starting point. *Reversibility* is part of every logical operation. After Priti spills her box of raisins, Sammy cannot reverse by thinking to himself, "I know that Priti doesn't have more raisins than I do. She just poured them out of that little red box, and if we put them back in again, her raisins and my raisins would look just the same."

■ LACK OF HIERARCHICAL CLASSIFICATION. Lack of logical operations leads preschoolers to have difficulty with **hierarchical classification.** That is, they cannot yet organize objects into classes and subclasses on the basis of similarities and differences. Piaget's famous *class inclusion problem,* illustrated in Figure 7.9, demonstrates this limitation. Preoperational children center on the overriding perceptual feature of yellow. They do not think reversibly by moving from the whole class (flowers) to the parts (yellow and blue) and back again.

Flowers

Blue flowers

Yellow flowers

FIGURE 7.9

■ **A Piagetian class inclusion problem.** Children are shown 16 flowers, 4 of which are blue and 12 of which are yellow. Asked whether there are more yellow flowers or more flowers, the preoperational child responds, "More yellow flowers," failing to realize that both yellow and blue flowers are included in the category of "flowers."

RECENT RESEARCH ON PREOPERATIONAL THOUGHT

Over the past two decades, researchers have challenged Piaget's notion of the preschool child as cognitively deficient. Their findings indicate that many Piagetian problems contain confusing or unfamiliar elements or too many pieces of information for young children to handle at once. As a result, preschoolers' responses do not reflect their true abilities. Piaget also missed many naturally occurring instances of preschoolers' effective reasoning.

■ EGOCENTRIC, ANIMISTIC, AND MAGICAL THINKING. Are young children really so egocentric that they believe a person standing elsewhere in a room sees the same thing they see? When researchers change the nature of the three-mountains problem to include familiar objects and use methods other than picture selection (which is difficult even for 10-year-olds), 4-year-olds show clear awareness of others' vantage points (Borke, 1975; Newcombe & Hutten-locher, 1992).

Nonegocentric responses also appear in young children's conversations. For example, preschoolers adapt their speech to fit the needs of their listeners. Sammy uses shorter, simpler expressions when talking to his little brother, Dwayne, than to agemates or adults (Gelman & Shatz, 1978). Also, in describing objects, children do not use such words as *big* and *little* in a rigid, egocentric fashion. Instead, they *adjust* their descriptions, taking account of context. By age 3, children judge a 2-inch shoe as small when seen by itself (because it is much smaller than most shoes) but as big for a very tiny, 5-inch doll (Ebeling & Gelman, 1994).

Recent studies also indicate that Piaget overestimated children's animistic beliefs because he asked children about objects with which they have little direct experience, such as the clouds, sun, and moon. Children as young as 3 rarely think that very familiar inanimate objects, such as rocks and crayons, are alive. They do make errors about certain

vehicles, such as trains and airplanes, that have some lifelike features—for example, headlights that look like eyes and animate-like movements (Massey & Gelman, 1988; Poulin-Dubois & Héroux, 1994). Preschoolers' responses result from incomplete knowledge about some objects, not from a rigid belief that inanimate objects are alive.

The same is true for other fantastic beliefs of the preschool years. Most 3- and 4-year-olds believe in the supernatural powers of fairies, goblins, and other enchanted creatures that appear in storybooks and movies. But they deny that magic can alter their everyday experiences—for example, turn a picture into a real object (Subbotsky, 1994).

■ *Which of the children in this audience realize that a magician's powers depend on trickery? The younger children look surprised and bewildered. The older children think the magician's antics are funny. Between 4 and 8 years, as familiarity with physical events and principles increases, children's magical beliefs decline. (Photo courtesy: J. Sohm/The Image Works)*

Between 4 and 8 years, as familiarity with physical events and principles increases, children's magical beliefs decline (Phelps & Wooley, 1994; Wooley et al., 1999). Most figure out who is really behind the activities of Santa Claus and the Tooth Fairy and know that wishes often do not come true. How quickly children give up certain fantastic ideas varies with religion and culture. For example, Jewish children express greater disbelief in Santa Claus and the Tooth Fairy than do their Christian agemates. Having been taught at home about the unreality of Santa, they seem to generalize this attitude to other mythical figures (Woolley, 1997).

■ ILLOGICAL THOUGHT. Many studies have reexamined the illogical characteristics of the preoperational stage. Results show that when preschoolers are given simplified tasks made relevant to their everyday lives, they do better than Piaget might have expected.

For example, when a conservation-of-number task is scaled down to include only three items instead of six or seven, preschoolers respond correctly (Gelman, 1972). And when preschoolers are asked carefully worded questions about what happens to substances (such as sugar) after they are dissolved in water, they give accurate explanations. Most 3- to 5-year-olds know that the substance is conserved—that it continues to exist, can be tasted, and makes the liquid heavier, even though it is invisible in the water (Au, Sidle, & Rollins, 1993; Rosen & Rozin, 1993).

Preschoolers' ability to notice and reason about transformations is evident on other problems. For example, they can engage in impressive *reasoning by analogy* (taking an idea from one situation and applying it to another) about physical changes. Presented with the picture-matching problem, *play dough is to cut-up play dough as apple is to ?,* even 3-year-olds choose the correct answer (a cut-up apple) from a set of alternatives, several of which share physical features with the right choice (a bitten apple, a cut-up loaf of bread) (Goswami, 1996).

Indeed, 3- and 4-year-olds' descriptions of their world reveal that they use causal terms, such as *if–then* and *because,* with the same degree of accuracy as adults do (McCabe & Peterson, 1988). Illogical reasoning seems to occur only when preschoolers grapple with topics they know little about or are given contradictory facts, which they have trouble reconciling (Ruffman, 1999). Although young children cannot consider the complex interplay of forces that adolescents and adults can, they often analyze their everyday experiences accurately in terms of basic cause-and-effect relations.

■ CATEGORIZATION. Even though preschoolers have difficulty with Piagetian class inclusion tasks, their everyday knowledge is organized into nested categories at an early age. Recall that by the second half of the first year, children have begun to form a variety of global categories, such as furniture, animals, vehicles, plants, and kitchen utensils (Mandler, 1998). Notice that each of these categories includes objects that differ widely in appearance. This challenges Piaget's assumption that preschoolers' thinking is always perception-bound.

Over the preschool years, these global categories differentiate. Children form many *basic-level categories*—ones at an intermediate level of generality, such as "chairs," "tables," and "beds." By the third year, children easily move back and forth between basic-level categories and *general categories,* such as "furniture." Soon after, they break down basic-level categories into *subcategories,* such as "rocking chairs" and "desk chairs," clarify the features that distinguish subcategories, and perfect their understanding of hierarchical relations (Johnson, Scott, & Mervis, 1997).

How do young children become such skilled categorizers? Their rapidly growing vocabularies and general knowledge contribute. As they label and learn more about their world, preschoolers devise theories about underlying characteristics that category members share. For example, they realize that animals have internal organs and certain physical features and behaviors that determine their identity (Hirshfeld, 1995; Krascum & Andrews, 1998). Also, adults frequently label and explain the basis of categories, and picture-book reading seems to be an especially rich context for doing so. While looking at books with their preschoolers, parents make statements like this: "Penguins live at the South Pole, swim, and catch fish" (Gelman et al., 1998). Such information helps guide children's inferences about categories.

In sum, preschoolers' category systems are not yet very complex. But the capacity to classify hierarchically is present in early childhood.

■ APPEARANCE VERSUS REALITY. So far, we have seen that when presented with familiar situations and simplified problems, young children show some remarkably advanced reasoning. Yet in certain situations, they are easily tricked by the outward appearance of things.

In a series of studies, John Flavell and his colleagues presented children with objects that were disguised in various ways and asked what the items were, "really and truly." Preschoolers were easily tricked by sights and sounds. When asked whether a white piece of paper placed behind a blue filter is "really and truly blue" or whether a can that sounds like a baby crying when turned over is "really and truly a baby," they often responded, "Yes!" Not until age 6 to 7 did children do well on these tasks (Flavell, 1993; Flavell, Green, & Flavell, 1987).

Preschoolers have difficulty with these problems because they must recall the real image of an object in the face of a second, contradictory representation. How do they master distinctions between appearance and reality? Make-believe play may be important. Preschoolers can tell the difference between pretend play and real experiences long before they answer many appearance–reality tasks correctly (Golomb & Galasso, 1995). Experiencing the contrast between everyday and playful use of objects may help children refine their understanding of what is real and what is unreal in the surrounding world.

EVALUATION OF THE PREOPERATIONAL STAGE

The evidence as a whole indicates that Piaget was partly wrong and partly right about young children's cognitive capacities. When given scaled-down tasks based on familiar experiences, preschoolers show the beginnings of logical operations. But their reasoning is not as well developed as that of school-age children, since they fail Piaget's three-mountains, conservation, and class inclusion problems and have difficulty separating appearance from reality.

That preschoolers have some logical understanding suggests that they attain logical operations gradually. Over time, they rely on increasingly effective mental as opposed to perceptual approaches to solving problems. Evidence that preschool children can be trained to perform well on Piagetian problems, such as conservation and class inclusion, also supports the idea that operational thought is not absent during one age period and suddenly present at the next (Roazzi & Bryant, 1997; Siegler, 1995). It makes sense that children who possess part of a capacity will benefit from training, unlike those who have no understanding at all.

The gradual development of logical operations poses a serious challenge to Piaget's stage concept, which assumes sudden and abrupt change toward logical reasoning around 6 or 7 years of age. Does a preoperational stage of development really exist? Some researchers no longer think so. They believe that children work out their understanding of each type of task separately. Their thought processes are regarded as basically the same at all ages—just present to a greater or lesser extent. Recall from earlier chapters that this view of cognitive development as continuous forms the basis for an alternative approach: *information processing,* which we take up shortly.

Other experts think the stage concept is still valid but must be modified. For example, some theorists combine Piaget's stage approach with the information-processing emphasis on task-specific change (Case, 1998; Fischer & Farrar, 1987; Halford, 1992). They believe that Piaget's strict stage definition needs to be transformed into a less tightly knit concept, one in which a related set of competencies develops over an extended time period, depending on brain development and experience. This flexible stage notion recognizes the unique qualities of early childhood thinking. At the same time, it provides a better account of why, to use Leslie's words, "preschoolers' minds are such a blend of logic, fantasy, and faulty reasoning."

PIAGET AND EDUCATION

Piaget's theory has had a major impact on education, especially during early childhood. Leslie was greatly influenced by Piaget's work, which she studied in college. Three educational principles derived from his theory have become realities in her classroom:

- *An emphasis on discovery learning.* In a Piagetian classroom, children are encouraged to discover for themselves through spontaneous interaction with the environment. Leslie's classroom has a rich variety of materials and play areas designed to promote exploration and discovery—art, puzzles, table games, dress-up clothing, building blocks, reading corner, woodworking, and more.

- *Sensitivity to children's readiness to learn.* A Piagetian classroom does not try to speed up development. Instead, Piaget believed that appropriate learning experiences build on children's current thinking. Leslie watches and listens to her pupils, introducing experiences that permit them to practice newly discovered cognitive schemes and that are likely to challenge their incorrect ways of viewing the world. But she does not impose new skills before children indicate they are interested and ready (Johnson & Hooper, 1982).

- *Acceptance of individual differences.* Piaget's theory assumes that all children go through the same sequence of development, but at different rates. Leslie plans activities for individual children and small groups rather than for the total class. In addition, she evaluates educational progress by comparing each child to his or her own previous development. She is less interested in how children measure up to normative standards, or the average performance of same-age peers.

Educational applications of Piaget's theory, like his stages, have met with criticism. Perhaps the greatest challenge has to do with his insistence that young children learn mainly through acting on the environment. In the next section, we will see that they also use language-based routes to knowledge, which Piaget de-emphasized.

ASK YOURSELF . . .

- *Recently, 2-year-old Brooke's father shaved off his thick beard and mustache. When Brooke saw him, she was very upset. Using Piaget's theory, explain why Brooke was distressed by her father's new appearance.*

- *One weekend, 4-year-old Will went fishing with his family. When his father asked, "Why do you think the river is flowing along?" Will responded, "Because it's alive and wants to." Yet at home, Will understands very well that his tricycle isn't alive and can't move by itself. What explains this contradiction in Will's reasoning?*

VYGOTSKY'S SOCIOCULTURAL THEORY

Piaget's de-emphasis on language brought on yet another challenge, this time from Vygotsky's sociocultural theory, which stresses the social context of cognitive development. During early childhood, rapid growth in language broadens preschoolers' ability to participate in social dialogues while engaged in culturally meaningful tasks. Soon children start to talk to themselves in much the same way they converse with others. This greatly enhances the complexity of their thinking and their ability to control their own behavior. Let's see how this happens.

PRIVATE SPEECH

Watch preschoolers as they go about their daily activities, and you will see that they frequently talk out loud to themselves. For example, as Sammy worked a puzzle, he said, "Where's the red piece? Now, a blue one. No, it doesn't fit. Try it here."

Piaget (1923/1926) called these utterances *egocentric speech,* reflecting his belief that young children are unable to take the perspectives of others. For this reason, he said, their talk is often "talk for self" in which they run off thoughts in whatever form they happen to occur, regardless of whether a listener can understand. According to Piaget, cognitive maturity and certain social experiences—namely, disagreements with peers—eventually bring an end to egocentric speech. Through arguments with agemates, children repeatedly see that others hold viewpoints different from their own. As a result, egocentric speech declines.

Vygotsky (1934/1987) voiced a powerful objection to Piaget's conclusion that young children's language is egocentric and nonsocial. He reasoned that children speak to themselves for self-guidance and self-direction. Because language helps children think about their own behavior and plan courses of action, Vygotsky viewed it as the foundation for all higher cognitive processes, including controlled attention, deliberate memory, planning, problem solving, and self-reflection. As children get older and find tasks easier, their self-directed speech is internalized as silent, *inner speech*—the verbal dialogues we carry on with ourselves while thinking and acting in everyday situations.

Over the past two decades, almost all studies have supported Vygotsky's perspective. As a result, children's "speech-to-self" is now referred to as **private speech** instead of egocentric speech. Research shows that children use more of it when tasks are difficult and they are confused about how to proceed (Berk, 1992a; 1994b). Also, just as Vygotsky predicted, private speech goes underground with age, changing into whispers and silent lip movements (Berk & Landau, 1993). Finally, children who use private speech

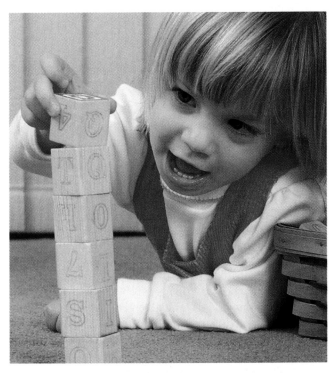

■ *During the preschool years, children frequently talk to themselves as they play and explore the environment. Research supports Vygotsky's theory that children use private speech to guide their behavior when faced with challenging tasks. With age, private speech is transformed into silent, inner speech, or verbal thought. (Photo courtesy: Kopstein/Monkmeyer Press)*

freely during a challenging activity are more attentive and involved and do better than their less talkative agemates (Berk & Spuhl, 1995; Bivens & Berk, 1990).

SOCIAL ORIGINS OF EARLY CHILDHOOD COGNITION

Where does private speech come from? Recall from Chapter 5 that Vygotsky believed children's learning takes place within a *zone of proximal development*—a range of tasks too difficult for the child to do alone but that can be accomplished with the help of others. During infancy, communication in the zone of proximal development is largely nonverbal. In early childhood, verbal dialogues are added as adults and more skilled peers help children master challenging activities. Consider the way Sammy's mother helped him put a difficult puzzle together:

Sammy: "I can't get this one in." (tries to insert a piece in the wrong place)

Mother: "Which piece might go down here?" (points to the bottom of the puzzle)

Sammy: "His shoes." (looks for a piece resembling the clown's shoes but tries the wrong one)

Mother: "Well, what piece looks like this shape?" (pointing again to the bottom of the puzzle)

Sammy: "The brown one." (tries it and it fits, then attempts another piece and looks at his mother)

Mother: "Try turning it just a little." (gestures to show him)

Sammy: "There!" (puts in several more pieces while his mother watches)

Eventually, children take the language of these dialogues, make it part of their private speech, and use this speech to organize their own thinking and behavior.

To be effective, the adult's communication must be carefully coordinated with the child's current abilities (Wood, 1989). Notice how Sammy's mother offers help at just the right moment and in the right amount. As Sammy becomes better at handling the task himself, his mother permits him to take over her guiding role and apply it to his own activity.

Is there evidence to support Vygotsky's ideas on the social origins of private speech and cognitive development? In several studies, mothers who provided more support when the child had difficulty and less when the child could work alone had children who used more private speech and were more successful at the task (Behrend, Rosengren, & Perlmutter, 1992; Berk & Spuhl, 1995; Conner, Knight, & Cross, 1997). Other research shows that although children benefit from working on tasks with same-age peers, their planning and problem solving show more improvement when their partner is either an "expert" peer (especially capable at the task) or an adult (Azmitia, 1988; Radziszewska & Rogoff, 1988). And peer conflict and disagreement (emphasized by Piaget) does not seem to be as important in fostering cognitive development as the extent to which children resolve differences of opinion and cooperate (Cannella, 1993; Tudge, 1992).

▌VYGOTSKY AND EDUCATION

Today, educators are eager to use Vygotsky's ideas. Piagetian and Vygotskian classrooms clearly have features in common. Both emphasize active participation and acceptance of individual differences. But a Vygotskian classroom goes beyond independent discovery learning. It promotes *assisted discovery.* Teachers guide children's learning with explanations, demonstrations, and verbal prompts, carefully tailoring their efforts to each child's zone of proximal development. Assisted discovery is also helped along by peer collaboration. Teachers arrange *cooperative learning* experiences, grouping together classmates of differing abilities and encouraging them to teach and help one another.

Vygotsky (1935/1978) saw make-believe play as the ideal social context for fostering cognitive development in early childhood. In make-believe, he explained, children learn to follow internal ideas and social rules rather than their immediate impulses. For example, a child pretending

■ *A Vygotskian classroom promotes assisted discovery. Teachers guide children's learning, carefully tailoring their efforts to each child's zone of proximal development. They also arrange cooperative learning experiences, grouping together classmates of differing abilities and encouraging them to guide and help one another. (Photo courtesy: Will Faller)*

to go to sleep follows the rules of bedtime behavior. Another child imagining himself to be a father and a doll to be a child conforms to the rules of parental behavior. According to Vygotsky, make-believe play is a unique, broadly influential zone of proximal development in which children try out a wide variety of challenging activities and acquire many new competencies (Smolucha & Smolucha, 1998). Turn back to page 223 to review findings that make-believe play enhances a diverse array of cognitive and social skills.

▌EVALUATION OF VYGOTSKY'S THEORY

Some of Vygotsky's ideas, like Piaget's, have been challenged. Verbal communication may not be the only means through which children's thinking develops, or even the most important means, in some cultures. For example, the young child learning to sail a canoe in Micronesia or weave a garment on a foot loom in Guatemala may gain more from direct observation and practice than from joint participation with and verbal guidance by adults (Rogoff, 1998; Rogoff & Chavajay, 1995).

In one study, researchers asked caregivers to help young children with challenging tasks (getting dressed and operating novel toys) in four communities—two middle-SES urban areas, one in Turkey and one in the United States; a Mayan town in Guatemala; and a tribal village in India (Rogoff et al., 1993). In the middle-SES communities, parents verbally instructed and conversed—communication resembling the teaching that takes place in school. In contrast, in the Mayan and Indian communities, adults expected children to take greater responsibility for acquiring new skills through keen observation. As the child showed interest, caregivers often demonstrated with gestures, a style of interaction suited to conditions in which children learn by participating in daily activities with adults.

In cultures everywhere, caregivers guide children's mastery of the practices of their community. Yet the type of assistance offered varies, depending on the tasks that must be mastered. Thus, we are reminded once again that children learn in a great many ways, and as yet, no single theory provides a complete account of cognitive development.

ASK YOURSELF . . .

■ *Tanisha sees her 5-year-old son Toby talking out loud to himself while he plays. She wonders whether she should discourage this behavior. Use Vygotsky's theory to explain why Toby talks to himself. How would you advise Tanisha?*

🌳 *According to Vygotsky, what ingredients are necessary at any age to promote learning and development?*

INFORMATION PROCESSING

Return for a moment to the model of information processing discussed on page 156 of Chapter 5. Recall that information processing focuses on *mental strategies* that children use to transform stimuli flowing into their mental systems. During early childhood, advances in representation and children's ability to guide their own behavior lead to more efficient ways of attending, manipulating information, and solving problems. Preschoolers also become more aware of their own mental life and begin to acquire academically relevant knowledge important for school success.

ATTENTION

Parents and teachers are quick to notice that compared with school-age children, preschoolers spend only short times involved in tasks, have difficulty focusing on details, and are easily distracted. But recall from Chapter 5 that sustained attention improves in toddlerhood, a trend that continues over the preschool years, and fortunately so, since children will rely on this capacity greatly once they enter school.

By the end of early childhood, attention also becomes more *planful*. When looking for a lost object, older preschoolers searched more systematically and exhaustively than 3-year-olds (Wellman, Somerville, & Haake, 1979). Still, planful attention has a long way to go. When asked to judge detailed pictures as the same or different, pre-

schoolers fail to scan them thoroughly. And on complex tasks with many steps, they rarely make decisions about what to do first and what to do next in an orderly fashion (Friedman & Scholnick, 1997; Ruff & Rothbart, 1996). Clearly, planning places heavy demands on the information-processing system.

MEMORY

Unlike infants and toddlers, preschoolers have the language skills to describe what they remember, and they can follow directions on simple memory tasks. As a result, memory development becomes easier to study in early childhood.

■ RECOGNITION AND RECALL. Try showing a young child a set of 10 pictures or toys. Then mix them up with some unfamiliar items and ask the child to point to the ones in the original set. You will find that preschoolers' *recognition* memory (ability to tell whether a stimulus is the same as or similar to one they have seen before) is remarkably good. In fact, 4- and 5-year-olds perform nearly perfectly.

Now give the child a more demanding task. Keep the items out of view and ask the child to name the ones she saw. This requires *recall*—that the child generate a mental image of an absent stimulus. Young children's recall is much poorer than their recognition. At age 2, they can recall no more than 1 or 2 of the items, at age 4 only about 3 or 4 (Perlmutter, 1984).

Of course, recognition is much easier than recall for adults as well, but compared with adults', children's recall is quite deficient. The reason is that young children are less effective at using **memory strategies,** deliberate mental activities that improve our chances of remembering. For example, when you want to retain information, you might *rehearse*, or repeat the items over and over again. Or you might *organize*, grouping together items that are alike so you can easily retrieve them by thinking of their similar characteristics.

Preschoolers do show the beginnings of memory strategies. For example, when circumstances permit, they arrange items in space to aid their memories. In a study of 2- to 5-year-olds, an adult placed either an M&M or a wooden peg in each of 12 identical containers and handed them one by one to the child, who was asked to remember where the candy was hidden. By age 4, children put the candy containers in one place on the table and the peg containers in another. This strategy almost always led to perfect recall (DeLoache & Todd, 1988). But preschoolers do not yet rehearse or organize items into categories (for example, all the vehicles together, all the animals together) when asked to remember. Even when trained to do so, their memory performance may not improve, and they rarely apply these strategies in new situations (Gathercole, Adams, & Hitch, 1994; Miller & Seier, 1994).

Perhaps young children are not very strategic memorizers because they see little need to remember information for its own sake. Yet another reason that memory strategies are rarely used in early childhood is that they tax young children's limited working memories (Bjorklund & Coyle, 1995). Preschoolers have difficulty holding on to the to-be-learned information and applying a strategy at the same time.

■ MEMORY FOR EVERYDAY EXPERIENCES. Think about the difference in your recall of the listlike information discussed in the previous section and your memory for common, everyday experiences. In remembering lists, you recall isolated pieces of information, reproducing them exactly as you originally learned them. In remembering everyday experiences, you recall complex, meaningful events.

In Chapter 5 we considered one type of memory for everyday experiences—*autobiographical memory,* or representations of one-time events that are particularly meaningful in terms of the life story each of us creates about ourselves. A second type of everyday memory involves recall of familiar, repeated events. Like adults, preschoolers remember these in terms of **scripts,** general descriptions of what occurs and when it occurs in a particular situation.

Young children's scripts begin as a structure of main acts. For example, when asked to tell what happens when you go to a restaurant, a 3-year-old might say, "You go in, get the food, eat, and then pay." Although children's first scripts contain only a few acts, they are almost always recalled in correct sequence (Fivush, Kuebli, & Clubb, 1992). With age, scripts become more elaborate, as in the following restaurant account given by a 5-year-old child: "You go in. You can sit in the booths or at a table. Then you tell the waitress what you want. You eat. If you want dessert, you can have some. Then you pay and go home" (Hudson, Fivush, & Kuebli, 1992).

Once formed, a script can be used to predict what will happen on similar occasions in the future. In this way, scripts are a basic means through which children organize and interpret repeated events. For example, children rely on scripts when listening to and telling stories. They also use script structures for planning and acting out scenes in make-believe play. Listen carefully to preschoolers, and you will hear everyday scripts reflected in their dialogues as they pretend to go on a trip or play school.

THE YOUNG CHILD'S THEORY OF MIND

As representation of the world, memory, and problem solving improve, children start to reflect on their own thought processes. They begin to construct a *theory of mind,* or set of beliefs about mental activities. This understanding is often called **metacognition.** The prefix *meta-,* meaning beyond or higher, is included in the term because *metacognition* means "thinking about thought."

As adults, we have a complex appreciation of our inner mental worlds. For example, you can tell the difference between believing, knowing, remembering, guessing, forgetting, and imagining, and you are aware of a great many factors that influence these cognitions. We rely on these understandings to interpret our own and others' behavior and to improve our performance on various tasks. How early are preschoolers aware of their mental lives, and how complete and accurate is their knowledge?

■ AWARENESS OF AN INNER MENTAL LIFE. Children's conversations reveal that awareness of mental activity emerges remarkably early. *Think, remember,* and *pretend* are among the first verbs in children's vocabularies, and after age 2½, they use them appropriately to refer to internal states (Wellman, 1990). Despite their use of mental terms, 2- to 3-year-olds have only a beginning grasp of the distinction between mental life and behavior. They think that people always behave in ways consistent with their desires and do not understand that beliefs affect their actions.

Between ages 3 and 4, children figure out that both *beliefs* and *desires* determine behavior. Dramatic evidence for this new understanding comes from games that involve tricking another person about the location of an object by moving it, laying false tracks, or giving incorrect information. By age 4, children realize that belief and reality can differ—in other words, that people can hold *false beliefs* (Robinson & Mitchell, 1994; Sodian et al., 1991). Children's grasp of false belief strengthens over the preschool years, becoming more secure between ages 4 and 6 (Flavell & Miller, 1998). During that time, it becomes a powerful tool for understanding the self and others and a good predictor of peer social-interaction skills (Watson et al., 1999).

How do children manage to develop a theory of mind at such a young age? Language and cognitive development, permitting children to reflect on thinking, is crucial. Language ability of an average 4-year-old or higher as well as planning and cognitive flexibility predict mastery of false belief (Jenkins & Astington, 1996; Hughes, 1998). And a rich, mental-state vocabulary is helpful. Among the Quechua of the Peruvian highlands, adults refer to such states as "think" and "believe" indirectly, since their language lacks mental-state terms. Quechua children have difficulty with false-belief tasks for years after Western children have mastered them (Vinden, 1996).

Social experience also promotes understanding of the mind. Preschoolers with older siblings are advanced in awareness of false belief, perhaps because relating to older siblings highlights the influence of beliefs on behavior—through teasing, trickery, and discussing feelings (Ruffman et al., 1998). Peer interaction also contributes. Three- and 4-year-olds who often engage in mental state talk with friends and in make-believe play are ahead in their understanding of false belief and other aspects of the mind (Hughes & Dunn,

1998; Taylor & Carlson, 1997). Furthermore, interacting with more mature members of society is helpful. In a study of Greek preschoolers, daily contact with many adults and older children predicted mastery of false belief (Lewis et al., 1996). These encounters offer extra opportunities to observe different viewpoints and talk about inner states.

Many researchers believe that to profit from the social experiences just described, children must be biologically prepared to develop a theory of mind. Consistent with this assumption, children with infantile autism, who are indifferent to other people and display poor knowledge of social rules, seem to be impaired in mental understanding. See the Variations box on the following page to find out more about the biological basis of reasoning about the mind.

■ LIMITATIONS OF THE YOUNG CHILD'S THEORY OF MIND. Although surprisingly advanced, preschoolers' awareness of mental activities is far from complete. When questioned about subtle distinctions between mental states, such as "know" and "forget," children below age 5 often express confusion (Lyon & Flavell, 1994). Furthermore, young children believe that all events must be directly observed to be known. They do not understand that *mental inferences* can be a source of knowledge (Carpendale & Chandler, 1996). Finally, preschoolers are unaware that people continue to think while they are waiting or otherwise not doing something. They conclude that mental activity stops when there are no obvious external cues to indicate a person is thinking (Flavell, Green, & Flavell, 1995; Flavell et al., 1997).

These findings suggest that young children view the mind as a passive container of information. They believe that physical experience with the environment determines mental experience. Although they have begun to master false belief, they greatly underestimate the amount of mental activity that goes on in people and are poor at inferring what people know or are thinking about. In contrast, older children view the mind as an active, constructive agent, capable of selecting and transforming information (Chandler & Carpendale, 1998; Pillow, 1995). We will consider this change further in Chapter 9 when we take up metacognition in middle childhood.

■ EARLY CHILDHOOD LITERACY

One week, Leslie's pupils brought empty food boxes from home to place on special shelves in the classroom. Soon a make-believe grocery store opened. Children labeled items with prices, made shopping lists, and wrote checks at the cash register. A sign at the entrance announced the daily specials: *APLS BNS 5¢* ("apples bananas 5¢").

As their grocery store play reveals, preschoolers understand a great deal about written language long before they learn to read or write in conventional ways. This is not surprising when we consider that children in industrialized nations live in a world filled with written symbols. Each day, they observe and participate in activities involving storybooks, calendars, lists, and signs. As part of these experiences, they try to figure out how written symbols convey meaning.

Young preschoolers search for units of written language as they "read" memorized versions of stories and recognize familiar signs, such as PIZZA at their favorite fast-food counter. But their early ideas about how written language is related to meaning are quite different from our own. For example, many preschoolers think that a single letter stands for a whole word or that each letter in a person's signature represents a separate name. Gradually, children revise these ideas as their perceptual and cognitive capacities improve, as they encounter writing in many different contexts, and as adults help them with written communication (Sulzby, 1985).

Soon, preschoolers become aware of some general characteristics of written language and create their own print-like symbols, as in the "story" and "grocery list" written by a 4-year-old in Figure 7.10. Eventually, children figure out that letters are parts of words and are linked to sounds in systematic ways, as you can see in the invented spellings that are typical between ages 5 and 7. At first, children rely heavily on the names of letters, as in *ADE LAFWTS KRMD NTU A LAVATR* ("eighty elephants crammed into a[n] elevator"). Over time, they will switch to conventional spelling (Gentry, 1981; McGee & Richgels, 2000).

Literacy development builds on a broad foundation of spoken language and knowledge about the world. The more literacy-related experiences young children have in their everyday lives, the better prepared they are to tackle the complex tasks involved in reading and writing. Adults

(a)   (b)

FIGURE 7.10

■ **A story (a) and a grocery list (b) written by a 4-year-old child.** This child's writing has many features of real print. It also reveals an awareness of different kinds of written expression. (From L. M. McGee & D. J. Richgels, 2000, *Literacy's Beginnings*, Third Edition, Boston: Allyn and Bacon, p. 69. Reprinted by permission.)

"MINDBLINDNESS" AND INFANTILE AUTISM

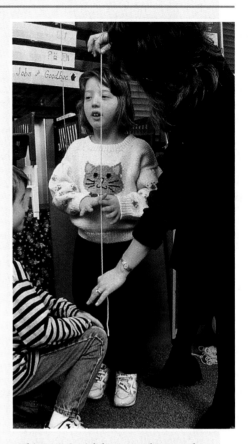

Sidney stood at the water table in his preschool classroom, repeatedly filling a plastic cup and dumping out its contents. Dip–splash, dip–splash, dip–splash he went, until his teacher came over and redirected his actions. Without looking at his teacher's face, Sidney moved to a new repetitive pursuit: pouring water from one cup into another and back again. As other children entered the play space and conversed, Sidney hardly noticed. He rarely spoke, and when he did, he usually used words to get things he wanted, not to exchange ideas.

Sidney has *infantile autism,* the most severe behavior disorder of childhood. The term *autism* means "absorbed in the self," an apt description of Sidney. Like other children with the disorder, Sidney is impaired in emotional and gestural (nonverbal) behaviors required for successful social interaction. In addition, his language is delayed and stereotyped; some autistic children do not speak at all. Sidney's interests, which focus on the physical world, are narrow and overly intense. For example, one day he sat for more than an hour making a toy ferris wheel go round and round.

Autism is highly heritable; its concordance is much greater for identical than fraternal twins. Growing evidence suggests that one psychological factor involved is a severely deficient or absent theory of mind. Long after they reach the intellectual level of an average 4-year-old, autistic children have great difficulty with false-belief tasks. Most cannot attribute mental states to others or themselves. Such words as *believe, think, know,* and *pretend* are rarely part of their vocabularies (Happé, 1995; Tager-Flusberg & Sullivan, 1994; Yirmiya, Solomonica-Levi, & Shulman, 1996).

As early as the second year, autistic children show deficits in capacities believed to contribute to an understanding of mentality. For example, they less often establish joint attention, engage in social referencing, or imitate an adult's novel behaviors than do normal children (Charman et al., 1997; Sigman et al., 1992). Furthermore, they are relatively insensitive to a speaker's gaze as a cue to what he or she is talking about. Instead, autistic children often assume that an adult's verbal label refers to what they themselves are attending to—a possible reason that they use many nonsensical expressions (Baron-Cohen, Baldwin, & Crowson, 1997). Finally, autistic children engage in much less make-believe play than do age- and mental-ability matched comparison groups—both normal children and children with other developmental problems (Hughes, 1998).

Do these findings indicate that autism is due to an impairment in an innate social-cognitive brain module, which leaves the child "mindblind" and therefore unable to engage in human sociability? Some researchers think so (Baron-Cohen, 1993). A second, related speculation is that infantile autism results from a deficit in comprehending emotion, which is essential for understanding others. In support of this view, autistic children have trouble interpreting emotional stimuli, such as facial expressions (Hobson, 1993).

Yet a third conjecture is that autism is due to a general memory deficit, which makes it hard to retain the parts of complex tasks (Bennetto, Pennington, & Rogers, 1996). Perhaps this explains autistic children's preoccupation with simple, repetitive acts. It may also account for their difficulty with problems, such as conservation, that require them to integrate

▪ *This autistic girl does not take note of a speaker's gaze as a cue to what he or she is talking about. For this reason, the girl's teacher takes extra steps to capture her attention in a science lesson. Researchers disagree on whether autistic children's "mindblindness" is due to an impairment in an innate social-cognitive brain module or to a general memory deficit. (Photo courtesy: Will Hart)*

several contexts at once (before, during, and after the transformation of a substance) (Yirmiya & Shulman, 1996). A memory deficit would also interfere with understanding the social world, since social interaction takes place quickly and requires integration of information from various sources.

At present, it is not clear which of these hypotheses is correct. Perhaps several biologically based deficits underlie the tragic social isolation of children like Sidney.

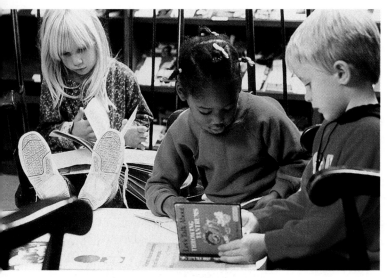

■ *Preschoolers acquire a great deal of literacy knowledge informally as they participate in everyday activities involving written symbols. They try to figure out how print conveys meaningful information, just as they strive to make sense of other aspects of their world. (Photo courtesy: Jim Pickerell)*

can provide literacy-rich physical environments and encourage literacy-related play (Roskos & Neuman, 1998; Neuman, Copple, & Bredekamp, 2000). Storybook reading with caregivers, especially, is related to preschoolers' language and reading readiness scores, which predict success in school. And adult-supported writing activities focusing on connected discourse (preparing a letter or a story) also foster literacy progress (Purcell-Gates, 1996; Whitehurst & Lonigan, 1998).

In early childhood, adults need not be overly concerned about the correctness of children's interpretations of written language. Instead, they can help most by accepting preschoolers' ideas and supporting their active efforts to revise and extend their knowledge.

YOUNG CHILDREN'S MATHEMATICAL REASONING

Mathematical reasoning, like literacy, builds on a foundation of informally acquired knowledge. In the second year, children have a beginning grasp of **ordinality,** or order relationships between quantities, such as three is more than two and two is more than one. Soon they attach verbal labels (such as "lots," "little," "big," "small") to different

■ *Counting on fingers is an early, spontaneous approach that children use to experiment with strategies for solving basic math facts. As they try out various routes to solution and select those that are efficient and accurate, answers become more strongly associated with problems. Soon children give up counting on fingers in favor of retrieving the right answer. (Photo courtesy: Myrleen Ferguson Cate/PhotoEdit)*

amounts and sizes. And between ages 2 and 3, they begin to count. At first, counting is little more than a memorized routine, as in "Onetwothreefourfivesix!" Or children repeat a few number words while vaguely pointing in the direction of objects (Fuson, 1992).

Very soon counting becomes more precise. Most 3- to 4-year-olds have established an accurate one-to-one correspondence between a short sequence of number words and the items they represent. Sometime between ages 4 and 5, they grasp the vital principle of **cardinality.** They understand that the last number in a counting sequence indicates the quantity of items in a set (Bermejo, 1996). By the late preschool years, children no longer need to start a counting sequence with the number "one." Instead, knowing that there are six items in one pile and some additional ones in another, they begin with the number "six" and *count on* to determine the total quantity. Eventually, they generalize this strategy and *count down* to find out how many items remain after some are taken away. Once they master these procedures, children start to manipulate numbers without countable objects (Fuson, 1988). At this point, counting on fingers becomes an intermediate step on the way to automatically doing simple addition and subtraction.

Cross-cultural research suggests this basic arithmetic knowledge emerges universally around the world. However, children acquire it at different rates, depending on the availability of informal counting experiences in their everyday lives. In homes and preschools where adults provide many occasions for counting, children master these basic understandings sooner (Geary, 1995). Then they are solidly available as supports for the mathematical skills they will be taught in school.

ASK YOURSELF . . .

■ *Piaget believed that preschoolers' egocentrism prevents them from reflecting on their own mental activities. What evidence in the preceding sections contradicts this assumption?*

🌳 *Lena wonders why Gregor's preschool teacher permits him to spend so much time playing instead of teaching him academic skills. Gregor's teacher responds, "I am teaching him academics—through play. It's the best way to ensure that he will become a competent, self-confident reader and writer." Explain what she means.*

INDIVIDUAL DIFFERENCES IN MENTAL DEVELOPMENT

Five-year-old Hallie sat in a testing room while Sarah gave him an intelligence test. Some of the questions Sarah asked were *verbal*. For example, she held out a picture of a shovel and said, "Tell me what this shows"—an item measuring vocabulary. Then she tested his memory by asking him to repeat sentences and lists of numbers back to her. Other *nonverbal* tasks largely assessed spatial reasoning. Hallie copied designs with special blocks, figured out the pattern in a series of shapes, and indicated what a piece of paper folded and cut would look like when unfolded (Thorndike, Hagen, & Sattler, 1986).

Preschoolers differ markedly in cognitive progress, just as they vary in physical growth and motor skills. Psychologists and educators typically measure these differences with intelligence tests, such as the one Hallie took. Scores are computed in the same way as they are for infants and toddlers. But instead of emphasizing perceptual and motor responses, tests for preschoolers sample a wide range of verbal and nonverbal cognitive abilities. By age 5 to 6, intelligence tests become good predictors of later intelligence and academic achievement (Hayslip, 1994).

Note that the questions Sarah asked Hallie tap knowledge and skills that not all children have had equal opportunity to learn. The issue of *cultural bias* in mental testing is a hotly debated topic that we will take up in Chapter 9. For now, keep in mind that intelligence tests do not sample all human abilities, and performance is affected by cultural and situational factors (Sternberg, 1997). At the same time, test scores remain important because they predict school achievement, which, in turn, is related to vocational success in industrialized societies. Let's see how the environments in which young children spend their days—home, preschool, and child care—affect mental test performance.

HOME ENVIRONMENT AND MENTAL DEVELOPMENT

A special version of the *Home Observation for Measurement of the Environment (HOME)*, covered in Chapter 5, assesses aspects of 3- to 6-year-olds' home lives that support intellectual growth (see the Caregiving Concerns table below). As Piaget's and Vygotsky's theories suggest, physical surroundings and child-rearing practices play important roles. Preschoolers who develop well intellectually have homes rich in toys and books. Their parents are warm and affectionate, stimulate language and academic knowledge, and arrange outings to places with interesting things to see and do. They also make reasonable demands for socially mature behavior—for example, that the child do simple chores and behave courteously toward others. And when conflicts arise, these parents use reason to resolve them instead of physical force and punishment (Bradley & Caldwell, 1979, 1982).

As we saw in Chapter 2, these characteristics are less likely to be found in poverty-stricken families in which parents lead highly stressful lives (Garrett, Ng'andu, & Ferron, 1994). When low-SES parents manage, despite daily pressures, to obtain high HOME scores, their preschoolers do substantially better on intelligence tests (Bradley & Caldwell,

CAREGIVING CONCERNS

Home Observation for Measurement of the Environment (HOME): Early Childhood Subscales

SUBSCALE	SAMPLE ITEM
Stimulation through toys, games, and reading material	Home includes toys that teach colors, sizes, and shapes.
Language stimulation	Parent teaches child about animals through books, games, and puzzles.
Organization of the physical environment	All visible rooms are reasonably clean and minimally cluttered.
Pride, affection, and warmth	Parent spontaneously praises child's qualities once or twice during observer's visit.
Stimulation of academic behavior	Child is encouraged to learn colors.
Modeling and encouragement of social maturity	Parent introduces interviewer to child.
Variety in daily stimulation	Family member takes child on one outing at least every other week (picnic, shopping).
Avoidance of physical punishment	Parent neither slaps nor spanks child during observer's visit.

Source: Bradley & Caldwell, 1979.

1981; Klebanov et al., 1998). These findings (as well as others we will discuss in Chapter 9) suggest that the home plays a major role in the generally poorer intellectual performance of low-SES children in comparison to their higher-SES peers.

PRESCHOOL AND CHILD CARE

Children between 2 and 6 spend even more time away from their homes and parents than infants and toddlers do. Over the last 30 years, the number of young children enrolled in preschool or child care has steadily increased. This trend is largely due to the dramatic rise in women's participation in the paid labor force. Currently, 64 percent of American preschool-age children have mothers who are employed (U.S. Bureau of the Census, 1999). Figure 7.11 shows where preschoolers spend their days while their parents are at work.

A *preschool* is a program with planned educational experiences aimed at enhancing the development of 2- to 5-year-olds. In contrast, *child care* identifies a variety of arrangements for supervising children of employed parents, ranging from care in someone else's or the child's own home to some type of center-based program. The line between preschool and child care is a fuzzy one. As Figure 7.11 indicates, parents often select a preschool as a child care option. Many preschools (and public school kindergartens as well) have increased their hours from half to full days in response to the needs of employed parents (U.S. Department of Education, 1999). At the same time, today we know that good child care is not simply a matter of keeping children safe and adequately fed in their parents' absence. Child care should provide the same high-quality educational experiences that an effective preschool does, the only difference being that children attend for an extended day.

■ TYPES OF PRESCHOOL. Preschool programs come in great variety, ranging along a continuum from child-centered to teacher-directed. In **child-centered preschools,** teachers provide a wide variety of activities from which children select, and most of the day is devoted to free play. In contrast, in **academic preschools,** teachers structure the program. Children are taught letters, numbers, colors, shapes, and other academic skills through repetition and drill, and play is de-emphasized.

Despite grave concern about the appropriateness of the approach, preschool teachers have felt increased pressure to stress formal academic training. The trend is motivated by a widespread belief that academic instruction at earlier ages will improve the ultimate achievement of American youths. Yet emphasizing formal academic training in early childhood undermines motivation and other aspects of emotional well-being. A recent study revealed that compared with children in teacher-directed classrooms, 3- to 6-year-olds in child-centered classrooms perceived their abilities to be higher, more often preferred challenging problems, and were less likely to seek adult approval or worry about school (Stipek et al., 1995). In yet another study, 4-year-olds in child-centered preschools actually scored better on assessments of academic, language, motor, and social skills than did those in academic or philosophically unclear preschools (Marcon, 1999).

■ EARLY INTERVENTION FOR AT-RISK PRESCHOOLERS. For low-SES children, the intellectual benefits of preschool are considerable—much more than for middle-SES children, whose home lives already provide many advantages. In the 1960s, when the United States launched a "War on Poverty," a wide variety of preschool intervention programs for disadvantaged children were initiated. Their underlying assumption was that learning problems are best treated early, before formal schooling begins. **Project Head Start,** begun by the federal government in 1965, is the most extensive of these experiments.

A typical Head Start program provides children with a year or two of preschool, along with nutritional and medical services. Parent involvement is central to the Head Start philosophy. Parents serve on policy councils and contribute to program planning. They also work directly with children in classrooms, attend special programs on parenting and child development, and receive services directed at their own emotional, social, and vocational needs. Currently, over 1,300 Head Start centers serve about 720,000 children each year (Currie & Thomas, 1997).

Over two decades of research establishing the long-term benefits of preschool intervention have helped Head

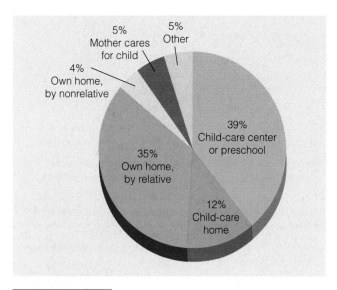

FIGURE 7.11

■ **Who's minding America's preschoolers?** The chart refers to settings in which 3- and 4-year-olds spend most of their time while their parents are at work. Over one-fourth of 3- and 4-year-olds experience more than one type of child care, a fact not reflected in the chart. (U.S. Bureau of the Census, 1997.)

Start survive. The most important of these studies combined data from seven university-based interventions. Results showed that children who attended programs scored higher in IQ and school achievement than did controls during the first 2 to 3 years of elementary school. After that time, differences in test scores declined. Nevertheless, children who received intervention remained ahead on measures of real-life school adjustment into adolescence. They were less likely to be placed in special education or retained in grade, and a greater number graduated from high school. There were also lasting benefits in attitudes and motivation. Children who attended programs were more likely to give achievement-related reasons (such as school or job accomplishments) for being proud of themselves, and their mothers held higher vocational aspirations for them (Lazar & Darlington, 1982).

Do these findings on the impact of outstanding university-based programs generalize to Head Start centers located in American communities? As long as programs are of high quality, the outcomes are much the same (Zigler & Styfco, 1994a). In fact, as the Lifespan Vista box on page 238 indicates, the Head Start model, which combines early childhood education with support for parents in improving their own lives, may be especially likely to induce lasting changes in both generations.

CHILD CARE. We have seen that high-quality early intervention can enhance the development of economically disadvantaged children. However, as we noted in Chapter 5, much child care in the United States is not of this high quality. Regardless of whether they come from middle- or low-income homes, preschoolers exposed to inadequate child care score lower on measures of cognitive and social skills (Hausfather et al., 1997; Howes, 1988, 1990; Lamb, 1998).

What are the ingredients of high-quality child care during the preschool years? Large-scale studies of center- and home-based settings reveal that the following factors are important: group size (number of children in a single space), caregiver–child ratio, caregiver's educational preparation, and caregiver's personal commitment to learning about and caring for children. When these characteristics are favorable, adults are more verbally stimulating and sensitive to children's needs, and children do especially well on measures of intelligence, language, and social development (Galinsky et al., 1994; Helburn, 1995; Howes, Phillips, & Whitebook, 1992). Other research shows that spacious, well-equipped environments and activities that meet the needs and interests of preschool-age children also contribute to positive outcomes (Scarr, 1998).

The Caregiving Concerns table summarizes characteristics of high-quality early childhood programs, based on

CAREGIVING CONCERNS

Signs of Developmentally Appropriate Early Childhood Programs

PROGRAM CHARACTERISTICS	SIGNS OF QUALITY
Physical setting	Indoor environment is clean, in good repair, and well ventilated. Classroom space is divided into richly equipped activity areas, including make-believe play, blocks, science, math, games, puzzles, books, art, and music. Fenced outdoor play space is equipped with swings, climbing equipment, tricycles, and sandbox.
Group size	In preschools and child-care centers, group size is no greater than 18 to 20 children with 2 teachers.
Caregiver–child ratio	In preschools and child-care centers, teacher is responsible for no more than 8 to 10 children. In family child-care homes, caregiver is responsible for no more than 6 children.
Daily activities	Most of the time, children work individually or in small groups. Children select many of their own activities and learn through experiences relevant to their own lives. Teachers facilitate children's involvement, accept individual differences, and adjust expectations to children's developing capacities.
Interactions among adults and children	Teachers move among groups and individuals, asking questions, offering suggestions, and adding more complex ideas. They use positive guidance techniques, such as modeling and encouraging expected behavior and redirecting children to more acceptable activities.
Teacher qualifications	Teachers have college-level specialized preparation in early childhood development, early childhood education, or a related field.
Relationships with parents	Parents are encouraged to observe and participate. Teachers talk frequently with parents about children's behavior and development.
Licensing and accreditation	Program is licensed by the state. If a preschool or child-care center, accreditation by the National Academy of Early Childhood Programs is evidence of an especially high-quality program. If a child-care home, accreditation by the National Association for Family Child Care is evidence of high-quality experiences for children.

Sources: Bredekamp & Copple, 1997; National Association for the Education of Young Children, 1998.

THE FUTURE OF EARLY INTERVENTION

The impact of preschool intervention may be considerably greater than previous evidence suggests. For example, studies reporting only minimal benefits of Head Start are often biased by one very important factor: Because not all poor children can be served, Head Start typically enrolls the most economically disadvantaged. Controls to whom they are compared often do not come from such extremely impoverished families. In a series of studies that took this into account, Head Start children showed *greater gains* on mental tests than did "other preschool" and "no preschool" comparison groups. Two years later, this advantage remained, although it was no longer as great as it had been immediately after Head Start (Lee, Brooks-Gunn, & Schnur, 1988; Lee et al. 1990). However, Head Start graduates entered poorer quality public schools, which explains, at least in part, why test score effects often fade out (Currie & Thomas, 1997). When intervention begun at age 4 is extended until third grade, gains in reading and math achievement persist at least until junior high (Reynolds & Temple, 1998).

Even with declining test performance, Head Start graduates (like those of university-based programs)

show an improved ability to meet basic educational requirements during elementary and secondary school. And in one experimental program, high-quality preschool education plus parent involvement was associated with a reduction in delinquency and teenage pregnancy and a greater likelihood of employment in early adulthood (Schweinhart, Barnes, & Weikart, 1993).

Although researchers are not sure how these lasting effects are achieved, one possibility is that they are the result of changes in the attitudes, behaviors, and life circumstances of parents, who create better environments for both themselves and their children. Consequently, new interventions are being conceived as *two-generation models.* A typical parent component of early intervention emphasizes teaching child-rearing skills and providing other supports that encourage parents to act as supplementary interveners for their children. Researchers believe these efforts may not be enough. By expanding intervention to include developmental goals for both parents and children, program benefits might be extended (Smith, 1995). A parent helped to move out of poverty with education, vocational training, and other social services is likely to show

improved psychological well-being and greater interest in planning for the future. When combined with child-centered intervention, these gains may translate into lasting changes in parents' lives and exceptionally strong benefits for children (Ramey & Ramey, 1998).

At present, the two-generation approach is too new to have yielded much research (McLoyd, 1998). But one pioneering effort, New Chance, is cause for optimism. In it, teenage mothers received services for themselves as well as their babies, including education, employment, family planning, life management, parent training, and child health care. In addition, each teenager was paired with a community woman, who served as mentor, role model, and friend. A follow-up when children were 5 years old revealed that parent participants were less likely to be on welfare and had higher family earnings than did controls receiving less intensive intervention. In addition, program children experienced warmer and more stimulating home environments, were more likely to have enrolled in Head Start, and had higher verbal IQs (Quint, Box, & Polit, 1997).

Head Start and other programs like it are highly cost-effective. Program expenses are far less than the funds required to provide special education, treat delinquency, and support welfare (Zigler & Styfco, 1994b). More intensive, longer-lasting efforts that focus on the development of both parents and children offer hope of increasing its positive outcomes.

■ *These economically disadvantaged 4-year-olds benefit from the comprehensive early intervention services of Project Head Start. A rich, stimulating preschool experience is an essential part of the program. As parents like this classroom volunteer participate, they improve their own life circumstances as well as their children's development. (Photo courtesy: N. Rowan/The Image Works)*

standards for developmentally appropriate practice devised by the National Association for the Education of Young Children. Together, they offer a set of worthy goals as we strive to expand and upgrade child care and educational services for young children.

EDUCATIONAL TELEVISION

Besides home and preschool, young children spend much time in another learning environment: television. The average 2- to 6-year-old watches TV from 1½ to 3 hours a day—a very long time in the life of a young child (Comstock, 1993). Each afternoon, Sammy looked forward to certain educational programs, including "Sesame Street"—his favorite.

Find a time to watch an episode of "Sesame Street" yourself. The program was originally designed for the same population served by Head Start—low-SES children who enter school academically behind their more economically advantaged peers. It uses lively visual and sound effects to stress basic literacy and number concepts and engaging puppet and human characters to teach general knowledge, emotional and social understanding, and prosocial skills. Today, more than 75 percent of American preschoolers and 60 percent of kindergartners watch "Sesame Street," and it is broadcast in more than 40 countries (Zill, Davies, & Daly, 1994).

"Sesame Street" works well as an academic tutor. The more children watch, the higher they score on tests and observations that measure the program's learning goals (Fisch, Truglio, & Cole, 1999). One study reported gains in academic achievement lasting into high school (Anderson et al., 1998). In recent years, "Sesame Street" has reduced its rapid-paced, adlike format in favor of leisurely episodes with a clear story line (Truglio, 2000). When different types of programs are compared, ones with slow-paced action and easy-to-follow narratives, such as "Mr. Rogers' Neighborhood" and "Barney and Friends," lead to more elaborate make-believe play. Those presenting quick, disconnected bits of information do not (Singer & Singer, 1998; Tower et al., 1979).

Some experts argue that because television presents such complete data to the senses, in heavy doses it encourages passive thinking. Too much television also takes time away from reading, playing, and interacting with others (Singer & Singer, 1990). But television can support cognitive development as long as children's viewing is not excessive and programs meet their developmental needs. We will look at the impact of television on young children's emotional and social development in the next chapter.

ASK YOURSELF . . .

Senator Smith heard that IQ gains resulting from Head Start do not last, so he plans to vote against funding for the program. Write a letter to Senator Smith explaining why he should support Head Start and what aspects of intervention foster lasting benefits.

LANGUAGE DEVELOPMENT

Language is intimately related to virtually all the cognitive changes discussed in this chapter. Between ages 2 and 6, children make awesome and momentous advances in language. Preschoolers' remarkable achievements, as well as their mistakes along the way, indicate that they master their native tongue in an active, rule-oriented fashion.

VOCABULARY

At age 2, Sammy had a vocabulary of 200 words. By age 6, he will have acquired around 10,000 words. To accomplish this feat, Sammy will learn about 5 new words each day (Anglin, 1993). How do children build their vocabularies so quickly? Researchers have discovered that they can connect a new word with an underlying concept after only a brief encounter, a process called **fast-mapping.**

Young preschoolers fast-map some words more accurately and easily than others. For example, they learn labels for objects especially rapidly because these refer to concrete items they already know much about, and caregivers' speech often emphasizes names for things (Bloom, 1998; Menyuk, Liebergott, & Schultz, 1995). Soon action words *(go, run, broke)* as well as modifiers referring to noticeable features of objects and people *(red, round, sad)* increase in frequency. If modifiers are related to one another in meaning, they take somewhat longer to learn. For example, 2-year-olds grasp the general distinction between *big* and *small*, but not until age 3 to 5 are more refined differences between *tall* and *short, high* and *low,* and *long* and *short* understood. Similarly, children acquire *now–then* before *yesterday–today–tomorrow* (Clark, 1983; Stevenson & Pollitt, 1987).

Preschoolers figure out the meanings of new words by contrasting them with ones they already know. But exactly how they discover which concept each word picks out is not yet fully understood. Ellen Markman (1989, 1992) believes that in the early phases of vocabulary growth, children adopt a **principle of mutual exclusivity.** They assume that words refer to entirely separate (nonoverlapping) categories. Consistent with this idea, when 2-year-olds are told the names of two very different novel objects (a clip and a horn), they assign each label correctly, to the whole object and not a part of it (Waxman & Senghas, 1992).

However, sometimes adults call a single object by more than one name. Under these conditions, preschoolers look for cues in the adult's behavior to determine whether the new word refers either to a higher- or lower-order category or to particular features, such as a part of the object, its shape, its color, or its proper name (Hall, 1996; Tomasello & Barton, 1994). When no such cues are available, children as young as 2 demonstrate remarkable flexibility in their word learning strategies. They abandon the mutual exclusivity principle and treat the new word as a second name for the object (Deák & Maratsos, 1998; Waxman & Hatch, 1992).

These findings tell us something about how children master labels for objects, but far less is known about the principles they use for other types of words. Preschoolers seem to draw on other aspects of language to help in these instances. By observing how words are used in the structure of sentences, they can figure out many word meanings. Consider an adult who says, "This is a *citron* one," while showing the child a yellow car. Two- and 3-year-olds interpret a new word used as an adjective as referring to a property of the object (Hall & Graham, 1999; Waxman & Markow, 1998). Children also rely on social cues. For example, when an adult uses a new label while looking back and forth between the child and an object in an inviting way, the label probably refers to an action *(come, help,* or *play),* not the object (Tomasello & Akhtar, 1995).

Once preschoolers have a sufficient vocabulary, they use words creatively to fill in for ones they have not learned. As early as age 2, children coin new words in systematic ways. For example, Sammy said *plant-man* for a gardener (created a compound word) and *crayoner* for a child using crayons (added the ending *-er*) (Clark, 1995). Preschoolers also extend language meanings through metaphor. For example, one 3-year-old used the expression "fire engine in my tummy" to describe a stomachache (Winner, 1988). Not surprisingly, the metaphors of young preschoolers involve concrete, sensory comparisons, such as "clouds are pillows" and "leaves are dancers." Once vocabulary and general knowledge expand, they appreciate nonsensory comparisons as well, such as, "Friends are like magnets" (Karadsheh, 1991; Keil, 1986). Metaphors permit young children to communicate in especially vivid and memorable ways.

GRAMMAR

Grammar refers to the way we combine words into meaningful phrases and sentences. Between ages 2 and 3, English-speaking children use simple sentences that follow a subject–verb–object word order. Children learning other languages adopt the word orders of the adult speech to which they are exposed (Maratsos, 1998). This shows that they have a beginning grasp of the grammar of their language.

As young children conform to rules about word order, they also begin to make the small additions and changes in words that enable us to express meanings flexibly and efficiently. For example, they add -s for plural (*cats*), use prepositions (*in* and *on*), and form various tenses from the verb to be (*is, are, were, has been, will*). All English-speaking children master these grammatical markers in a regular sequence, starting with the ones that involve the simplest meanings and structures (Brown, 1973; de Villiers & de Villiers, 1973).

By age 3½, children have acquired a great many of these rules, and they apply them so consistently that once in a while they overextend the rules to words that are exceptions, a type of error called **overregularization.** "My toy car breaked," "I *runned* faster than you," and "We each have two *feets*" are expressions that start to appear between 2 and 3 years of age (Marcus et al., 1992; Marcus, 1995).

Between 3 and 6, children master even more complex grammatical forms, although they make predictable errors along the way. In asking questions, preschoolers are reluctant to let go of the subject–verb–object structure of the English language. At first, they use only a rising intonation and fail to invert the subject and verb, as in "Mommy baking cookies?" and "What you are doing, Daddy?" Because they cling to a consistent word order, they also have trouble with some passive sentences. When told, "The car was pushed by the truck," young preschoolers often make a toy car push a truck. By age 5, they understand expressions like these, but full mastery of the passive form is not complete until the end of middle childhood (Horgan, 1978; Lempert, 1989).

Even though they make errors, preschoolers' grasp of grammar is impressive. By age 4 to 5, children use embedded sentences ("I think *he will come*"), tag questions ("Dad's going to be home soon, *isn't he?*"), and indirect objects ("He showed *his friend* the present"). As the preschool years draw to a close, children use most of the grammatical constructions of their language competently (Tager-Flusberg, 1997).

CONVERSATION

Besides acquiring vocabulary and grammar, children must learn to engage in effective and appropriate communication with others. This practical side of language is called **pragmatics,** and preschoolers make considerable headway in mastering it.

At the beginning of early childhood, children are already skilled conversationalists. In face-to-face interaction with peers, they take turns, respond appropriately to their partners' remarks, and maintain a topic over time (Garvey, 1975; Podrouzek & Furrow, 1988). The number of turns over which children can sustain interaction increases with age. These surprisingly advanced abilities grow out of early interactive experiences with adults and siblings. When adults respond to children's utterances in a timely manner and continue the child's topic of conversation, 2-year-olds are more likely to reply in kind (Dunham & Dunham, 1996).

By age 4, children already know a great deal about culturally accepted ways of adjusting their speech to fit the age, sex, and social status of their listeners. For example, in acting out different roles with hand puppets, 4- to 7-year-olds use more commands when playing both high status and "masculine" roles, such as doctor, teacher, and father. In contrast, they speak more politely and use more indirect requests when acting out lower status and "feminine" roles, such as patient, pupil, and mother (Anderson, 1984). Older preschoolers also adjust their speech on the basis of how well they know their conversational partner. They give fuller explanations to a stranger than to someone with whom they share common experiences, such as a family member or friend (Sonnenschein, 1986).

■ *In highly demanding situations, such as conversing on the phone, preschoolers often do not communicate clearly. They lack the supports available in face-to-face interaction, such as visual access to a partner's reaction and to objects that are topics of conversation. (Photo courtesy: Oscar Burriel/Science Photo Laboratory/Photo Researchers, Inc.)*

Preschoolers' conversational skills occasionally do break down. For example, have you tried talking on the telephone with a preschooler? Here is an excerpt of one 4-year-old's phone conversation with his grandfather:

Grandfather: "How old will you be?"

John: "Dis many." (Holding up four fingers)

Grandfather: "Huh?"

John: "Dis many." (Again holding up four fingers) (Warren & Tate, 1992, pp. 259–260)

Young children's conversations appear less mature in highly demanding situations in which they cannot see their listeners' reactions or rely on typical conversational aids, such as gestures and objects to talk about. However, when asked to tell a listener how to solve a simple puzzle, 3- to 6-year-olds' directions are more specific over the phone than in person, indicating that they realize more verbal description is necessary in the phone context (Cameron & Lee, 1997). Between ages 4 and 8, both conversing and giving directions over the phone improve greatly. Telephone talk provides yet another example of how preschoolers' competencies depend on the demands of the situation.

SUPPORTING LANGUAGE LEARNING IN EARLY CHILDHOOD

How can adults foster preschoolers' language development? Interaction with more skilled speakers, which is so important in toddlerhood, remains vital during early childhood. Conversational give-and-take with adults, ei-

ther at home or in preschool, is consistently related to general measures of language progress (Hart & Risley, 1995; Helburn, 1995).

Sensitive, caring adults use additional techniques that promote early language skills. When children use words incorrectly or communicate unclearly, they give helpful, explicit feedback, as in "There are several balls over there, and I can't tell exactly which one you want. Do you mean a large or small one or a red or green one?" At the same time, such adults do not overcorrect, especially when children make grammatical mistakes. Criticism discourages children from actively experimenting with language rules in ways that lead to new skills.

Instead, adults provide subtle, indirect feedback about grammar by using two strategies, often in combination: **expansions** and **recasts** (Bohannon & Stanowicz, 1988). For example, if a child says, "I gotted new red shoes," the parent might respond, "Yes, you got a pair of new red shoes," *expanding* the complexity of the child's statement and *recasting* it into appropriate form. Nevertheless, some researchers question whether expansions and recasts are as important in children's mastery of grammar as mere exposure to a rich language environment containing abundant examples of correct forms. Adults do not use these techniques often, and they are not provided to children in all cultures (Marcus, 1993; Valian, 1996).

Do the findings just described remind you once again of Vygotsky's theory? In language as in other aspects of intellectual growth, effective parents and teachers seem to interact with young children in ways that gently prompt them to take the next developmental step forward. Children strive to master language because they want to attain social connectedness to other people. Adults, in turn, respond to children's natural desire to become competent speakers by listening attentively, elaborating on what children say, modeling correct usage, and stimulating children to talk further. In the next chapter, we will see that this special combination of warmth and encouragement of mature behavior is at the heart of early childhood emotional and social development as well.

ASK YOURSELF . . .

■ *One day, Sammy's mother explained to him that the family would take a vacation in Miami. The next morning, Sammy emerged from his room with belongings spilling out of a suitcase and remarked, "I gotted my bag packed. When are we going to Your-ami?" What do Sammy's errors reveal about his approach to mastering language?*

🌳 *What can adults do to support children's language development? Provide a list of research-based recommendations. Are those strategies likely to promote academic achievement once the child enters school? Explain.*

UMMARY

PHYSICAL DEVELOPMENT

BODY GROWTH

Describe major trends in body growth during early childhood.

■ Children grow more slowly in early childhood than they did in infancy. Body fat declines, and children become longer and leaner. New growth centers appear in the skeleton, and by the end of early childhood, children start to lose their primary teeth.

■ Different parts of the body grow at different rates. Overall body size (as measured by height and weight) increases rapidly in infancy, more slowly in early and middle childhood, and rapidly again in adolescence—a pattern represented by the **general growth curve.**

BRAIN DEVELOPMENT

Describe brain development during early childhood, including lateralization (as reflected in handedness) and myelinization of specific structures.

■ During early childhood, the left cerebral hemisphere grows more rapidly than the right, supporting young children's rapidly expanding language skills.

■ Hand preference is stable by age 2 and increases during early and middle childhood, indicating that lateralization strengthens during this time. Handedness indicates an individual's **dominant cerebral hemisphere.** Although left-handedness is associated with developmental problems, the great majority of left-handed children show no abnormalities of any kind.

■ During early childhood, connections are established among different brain structures. Fibers linking the

cerebellum to the cerebral cortex myelinate, enhancing balance and motor control. The **reticular formation,** responsible for alertness and consciousness, and the **corpus callosum,** which connects the two cerebral hemispheres, also myelinate rapidly.

INFLUENCES ON PHYSICAL GROWTH AND HEALTH

Explain how heredity influences physical growth.

■ Heredity influences physical growth by controlling the release of hormones from the **pituitary gland.** Two hormones are especially influential: **growth hormone (GH)** and **thyroid-stimulating hormone (TSH).**

Describe the effects of emotional well-being, nutrition, and infectious disease on physical growth in early childhood.

■ Emotional well-being continues to influence body growth in middle childhood. An emotionally inadequate home life can lead to **deprivation dwarfism.**

■ Preschoolers' slower growth rate causes their appetites to decline, and often they become picky eaters. Repeated exposure to new foods and a positive emotional climate at mealtimes can promote healthy, varied eating in young children.

■ Malnutrition can combine with infectious disease to undermine healthy growth. In developing countries, diarrhea is widespread and claims millions of young lives. Teaching families how to administer **oral rehydration therapy (ORT)** can prevent most of these deaths.

■ Immunization rates are lower in the United States than in other industrialized nations because many eco-

nomically disadvantaged children do not have access to health insurance and good medical care.

What factors increase the risk of unintentional injuries, and how can childhood injuries be prevented?

■ Unintentional injuries are the leading cause of childhood mortality. Injury victims are more likely to be boys; to be temperamentally irritable, inattentive, and negative; and to be growing up in stressed, poverty-stricken inner-city families.

■ A variety of approaches are needed to prevent childhood injuries, including reducing poverty and other sources of family stress; passing laws that promote child safety; creating safer home, travel, child-care, and play environments; improving public education; and changing parent and child behaviors.

MOTOR DEVELOPMENT

Cite major milestones of gross and fine motor development in early childhood.

■ During early childhood, the child's center of gravity shifts toward the trunk, and balance improves, paving the way for many gross motor achievements. Preschoolers run, jump, hop, gallop, eventually skip, throw and catch, and generally become better coordinated.

■ Increasing control of the hands and fingers leads to dramatic improvements in fine motor skills. Preschoolers gradually become self-sufficient at dressing and using a knife and fork. By age 3, children's scribbles become pictures. Their drawings increase in complexity with age and are greatly influenced by the art of their society and by schooling. They also try to print letters of the alphabet and, later, words.

Describe individual and sex differences in motor skills.

■ Body build and opportunity for physical play affect early childhood motor development. Sex differences favoring boys in skills requiring force and power and girls in skills requiring good balance and fine movements are partly genetic, but environmental pressures exaggerate them. Children master the motor skills of early childhood through informal play experiences.

COGNITIVE DEVELOPMENT

PIAGET'S THEORY: THE PREOPERATIONAL STAGE

Describe advances in mental representation and limitations of thinking during the preoperational stage.

■ Rapid advances in mental representation, notably language and make-believe play, mark the beginning of Piaget's **preoperational stage.** With age, make-believe becomes increasingly complex, evolving into **sociodramatic play** with others.

■ Aside from representation, Piaget described the young child in terms of deficits rather than strengths. Preoperational children are **egocentric**—unable to imagine the perspectives of others and reflect on their own thinking. Egocentrism leads to a variety of illogical features of thought. Preschoolers engage in **animistic thinking,** and their cognitions are **perception-bound, centered,** focused on **states rather than transformations,** and **irreversible.** Because of these difficulties, they fail **conservation** and **hierarchical classification** tasks.

What are the implications of recent research for the accuracy of the preoperational stage?

■ When young children are given simplified problems relevant to their everyday lives, their performance appears more mature than Piaget assumed. Operational thinking develops gradually over the preschool years, a finding that challenges Piaget's concept of stage.

What educational principles can be derived from Piaget's theory?

■ Piaget's theory has had a major impact on education for young children. A Piagetian classroom promotes discovery learning, sensitivity to children's readiness to learn, and acceptance of individual differences.

VYGOTSKY'S SOCIOCULTURAL THEORY

Explain Vygotsky's perspective on the origins and significance of children's private speech, and describe applications of his theory to education.

■ In contrast to Piaget, Vygotsky regarded language as the foundation for all higher cognitive processes. According to Vygotsky, **private speech,** or language used for self-guidance, emerges out of social communication as adults and more skilled peers help children master challenging tasks. Eventually private speech is internalized as inner, verbal thought.

■ A Vygotskian classroom emphasizes assisted discovery. Verbal guidance from teachers and peer collaboration are vitally important.

INFORMATION PROCESSING

How do attention and memory change during early childhood?

■ Preschoolers spend only short times involved in tasks, have difficulty focusing on details, and are easily distracted. Attention gradually becomes more sustained and planful during early childhood.

■ Young children's recognition memory is very accurate. Their recall for listlike information is much poorer than that of older children and adults because preschoolers use **memory strategies** less effectively. Like adults, preschoolers remember recurring everyday experiences in terms of **scripts,** which become more elaborate with age.

Describe the young child's theory of mind.

■ Preschoolers begin to construct a theory of mind, indicating that they are capable of **metacognition,** or thinking about thought. Between ages 3 and 4, they understand that people can hold false beliefs. Many factors contribute to young children's understanding of mental life, including language development, having older siblings, peer interaction, and contact with more mature members of society. Preschoolers' understanding of the mind is far from complete; they regard it as a passive container of information rather than as an active, constructive agent.

Summarize children's literacy and mathematical knowledge during early childhood.

■ Children understand a great deal about literacy long before they read or write in conventional ways. Preschoolers gradually revise incorrect ideas about the meaning of written symbols as their perceptual and cognitive capacities improve, as they encounter writing in many different contexts, and as adults help them make sense of written information.

■ In the second year, children have a beginning grasp of ordinality, which serves as the basis for more complex understandings. Soon they experiment with counting strategies and discover additional mathematical principles, including **cardinality.** Both literacy and mathematical reasoning build on a foundation of informally acquired knowledge.

INDIVIDUAL DIFFERENCES IN MENTAL DEVELOPMENT

Describe early childhood intelligence tests and the impact of home, preschool and child care, and educational television on mental development in early childhood.

- Intelligence tests in early childhood sample a wide variety of verbal and nonverbal skills. By age 5 to 6, they are good predictors of later intelligence and academic achievement. Children growing up in warm, stimulating homes with parents who make reasonable demands for mature behavior score higher on mental tests.

- **Child-centered preschools** emphasize spontaneous play. In **academic preschools,** teachers train academic skills through repetition and drill. Formal academic instruction, however, is inconsistent with young children's developmental needs and undermines their emotional well-being.

- **Project Head Start** is the largest federally funded preschool program for low-income children in the United States. High-quality preschool intervention results in immediate test score gains and long-term improvements in school adjustment. The Head Start model, which combines early childhood education with parental support, is especially effective. Poor-quality child care undermines the children's cognitive and social development, regardless of SES background.

- Children pick up many cognitive skills from educational television programs like *Sesame Street.* Programs with slow-paced action and easy-to-follow story lines foster make-believe play.

LANGUAGE DEVELOPMENT

Trace the development of vocabulary, grammar, and conversational skills in early childhood.

- Supported by **fast-mapping,** children's vocabularies grow dramatically during early childhood. Preschoolers figure out the meaning of new words by contrasting them with ones they already know. The **principle of mutual exclusivity** explains their acquisition of some, but not all, early words. Children also look for cues in an adult's behavior and in how words are used in the structure of sentences. Once preschoolers have sufficient vocabulary, they extend language meanings, coining new words and creating metaphors.

- Between ages 2 and 3, children adopt the basic word order of their language. As they master grammatical rules, they occasionally **overregularize,** or apply the rules to words that are exceptions. By the end of early childhood, children have acquired complex grammatical forms.

- **Pragmatics** refers to the practical, social side of language. In face-to-face interaction with peers, young preschoolers are already skilled conversationalists. By age 4, they adapt their speech to their listeners in culturally accepted ways. Preschoolers' communicative skills appear less mature in highly demanding contexts.

Cite factors that support language learning in early childhood.

- Conversational give-and-take with more skilled speakers fosters preschoolers' language skills. Adults often provide explicit feedback on the clarity of children's language and indirect feedback about grammar through **expansions** and **recasts.** However, the impact of these strategies on grammatical development has been challenged. For this aspect of language, exposure to a rich language environment may be sufficient.

IMPORTANT TERMS AND CONCEPTS

FOR FURTHER INFORMATION AND HELP

Consult the companion website for this book, where you will find additional weblinks and associated learning activities: www.abacon.com/berk

GROWTH DISORDERS

Human Growth Foundation
www.hgfound.org
Provides information on various growth disorders, including growth hormone (GH) deficiency.

INFECTIOUS DISEASE IN CHILDHOOD

American Academy of Pediatrics
www.aap.org
Provides public education on a variety of childhood health issues. Among the many pamphlets and publications available are written guidelines for effective control of infectious disease.

Child Care Information Exchange
www.ccie.com
A bimonthly publication written especially for child-care directors that addresses the practical issues of running a center. Articles discussing health and safety are often included.

U.S. Centers for Disease Control
www.cdc.gov
Surveys national disease trends and environmental health problems. Has organized an agency network to address problems of

infectious disease in child care. Offers information to child-care staff on techniques that prevent the spread of infection.

CHILDHOOD INJURY CONTROL

U.S. Consumer Product Safety Commission
www.cpsc.gov
Establishes and enforces product safety standards. Operates a hot line providing information on safety issues and recall of dangerous consumer products.

EARLY CHILDHOOD DEVELOPMENT AND EDUCATION

Association for Childhood Education International (ACEI)
www.udel.edu/bateman/acei
Organization interested in promoting sound educational practice from infancy through early adolescence. Student membership is available and includes a subscription to Childhood Education, *a bimonthly journal covering research, practice, and public policy issues.*

National Association for the Education of Young Children (NAEYC)
www.nncc.org
Organization open to all individuals interested in acting on behalf of young children's needs, with primary focus on

educational services. Student membership is available and includes a subscription to Young Children, *a bimonthly journal covering theory, research, and practice in infant and early childhood development and education.*

PRESCHOOL INTERVENTION

National Head Start Association
www.nhsa.com
Association of Head Start directors, parents, staff, and others interested in the Head Start program. Works to upgrade the quantity and quality of Head Start services.

High/Scope Educational Research Foundation
www.highscope.org
Devoted to improving development and education from infancy through adolescence. Conducts longitudinal research to determine the effects of early intervention on development.

CHILD CARE

National Association for Family Child Care
www.nncc.org
Organization open to caregivers, parents, and other individuals involved or interested in family child care. Serves as a national voice that promotes high-quality child care.

Emotional and Social Development in Early Childhood

■ *Initiative—a spirited, enterprising, purposeful approach to new tasks—is a landmark attainment of early childhood. This 4-year-old radiates a sense of initiative as he collaborates with his father in building a birdhouse. (Photo courtesy: Rosanne Olson/Stone)*

As the children in Leslie's classroom moved through the preschool years, their personalities took on clearer definition. By age 3, they voiced firm likes and dislikes as well as new ideas about themselves. "Stop bothering me," 3-year-old Sammy said to his classmate Mark as he aimed a beanbag toward the mouth of a large clown face. "See, I'm great at this game," Sammy announced with confidence, an attitude that kept him trying, even though he missed most of the throws.

The children's conversations also revealed their first notions about morality. Often they combined statements about right and wrong they had heard from adults with forceful attempts to defend their own desires. "You're 'posed to share," stated Mark, grabbing a beanbag out of Sammy's hand.

"I was here first! Gimme it back," demanded Sammy, who pushed Mark while reaching for the beanbag. The two boys struggled until Leslie intervened, provided an extra set of beanbags, and showed them how they could both play at once.

As Sammy and Mark's interaction reveals, preschoolers are quickly becoming complex social beings. Although arguments and aggression take place among all young children, cooperative exchanges are far more frequent. Between the years of 2 and 6, first friendships emerge in which children converse, act out complementary roles, and learn that their own desires for companionship and toys are best met when they consider the needs and interests of others.

Children's developing understanding of their social world was especially evident in the attention they gave to the dividing line between male and female. While Lynette and Karen cared for a sick baby doll in the housekeeping area, Sammy, Vance, and Mark transformed the block corner into a busy intersection. "Green light, go!" shouted police officer Sammy as Vance and Mark pushed large wooden cars and trucks across the floor. Already, the children preferred to interact with same-sex peers, and their play themes mirrored the gender stereotypes of their cultural community.

This chapter is devoted to the many facets of emotional and social development in early childhood. We begin with Erik Erikson's overview of personality change during the preschool years. Then we consider children's concepts of themselves, their insights into their social and moral worlds, and their increasing ability to manage their emotional and social behaviors. In the final sections of this chapter, we answer the question, What is effective child rearing? We also consider the complex conditions that support good parenting or lead it to break down. Today, child abuse and neglect rank among America's most serious national problems.

ERIKSON'S THEORY: INITIATIVE VERSUS GUILT

Erikson (1950) described early childhood as a period of "vigorous unfolding" (p. 255). Once children have a sense of autonomy and feel secure about separating from parents, they become more relaxed and less contrary than they were as toddlers. Their energies are freed for tackling the critical psychological conflict of the preschool years: **initiative versus guilt.** The word *initiative* means spirited, enterprising, and ambitious. It suggests that young children have a new sense of purposefulness. They are eager to tackle new tasks, join in activities with peers, and discover what they can do with the help of adults.

Erikson regarded play as a central means through which young children find out about themselves and their social world. Play permits preschoolers to try out new skills with little risk of criticism and failure. It also creates a small social organization of children who must cooperate to achieve common goals. Make-believe, especially, offers unique opportunities for developing initiative. In cultures around the world, children act out family scenes and highly visible occupations—police officer, doctor, and nurse in Western societies, rabbit hunter and potter among the Hopi Indians, and hut builder and spear maker among the Baka of West Africa (Garvey, 1990; Roopnarine et al., 1998). In this way,

■ *As this Mexican Indian folk healer administers herbal remedies to a patient, the healer's grandchildren watch and play at the art of healing. By acting out highly visible occupations in their culture during play, children acquire insight into what they can do and develop a sense of initiative. (Photo courtesy: Mark Godfrey/The Image Works)*

make-believe provides children with important insights into the link between self and wider society.

Recall that Erikson's theory builds on Freud's psychosexual stages. Freud's *phallic stage* of early childhood is a time when sexual impulses transfer to the genitals, and the well-known *Oedipus and Electra conflicts* arise. The young child wishes to possess the parent of the other sex—feelings that lead to intense anxiety, since children fear punishment and loss of parental love for their unacceptable wishes. To master the anxiety, avoid punishment, and maintain the affection of parents, children form a *superego*, or conscience, through **identification** with the same-sex parent. They take the parent's characteristics into their personality and, as a result, adopt the moral and gender-role standards of their society. Each time the child disobeys standards of conscience, painful feelings of guilt occur.

For Erikson, the negative outcome of early childhood is an overly strict superego, one that causes children to feel too much guilt because they have been threatened, criticized, and punished excessively by adults. When this happens, preschoolers' exuberant play and bold efforts to master new tasks break down. Their self-confidence is shattered, and they approach the world timidly and fearfully.

Although Freud's Oedipus and Electra conflicts are no longer regarded as satisfactory explanations of children's emotional, moral, and gender-role development, Erikson's image of initiative captures the diverse changes in young children's emotional and social lives. The preschool years are, indeed, a time when children develop a confident self-image, more effective control over emotions, new social skills, the foundations of morality, and a clear sense of themselves as boy or girl. Now let's look closely at each of these aspects of development.

SELF-DEVELOPMENT

During early childhood, new powers of representation permit children to reflect on themselves. Language enables them to talk about the *I-self*— their own subjective experience of being (Harter, 1998). In Chapter 7, we noted that preschoolers quickly acquire a vocabulary for talking about their inner mental lives and begin to refine their understanding of mental states. As the I-self becomes more firmly established, children focus more intently on the *me-self*—knowledge and evaluation of the self's characteristics. They start to develop a **self-concept,** the set of attributes, abilities, attitudes, and values that an individual believes defines who he or she is.

FOUNDATIONS OF SELF-CONCEPT

Ask a 3- to 5-year-old to tell you about him- or herself, and you will probably hear something like this:

"I'm Tommy. See, I got this new red T-shirt. I'm 4 years old. I can brush my teeth, and I can wash my hair all by myself. I have a new Tinkertoy set, and I made this big, big tower." As these statements indicate, preschoolers' self-concepts are very concrete. Usually, they mention observable characteristics, such as their name, physical appearance, possessions, and everyday behaviors (Harter, 1996; Watson, 1990).

By age 3½, preschoolers also describe themselves in terms of typical emotions and attitudes, as in "I'm happy when I play with my friends" or "I don't like being with grown-ups" (Eder, 1989). This suggests that they have some awareness of their unique psychological characteristics. As further support for this budding grasp of personality, when given a trait label, such as "shy" or "mean," 4-year-olds use it to make appropriate inferences about motives and feelings. For example, they know that a shy person doesn't like to be with unfamiliar people (Heyman & Gelman, 1999). But preschoolers do not refer directly to traits when describing themselves. This capacity must wait for the greater cognitive maturity of middle childhood.

In fact, very young preschoolers' concepts of themselves are so bound up with specific possessions and actions that they spend much time asserting their rights to objects, as Sammy did in the beanbag incident at the beginning of this chapter. The stronger the child's self-definition, the more possessive he or she tends to be about objects, claiming them as "Mine!" (Levine, 1983). These findings indicate that rather than a sign of selfishness, early struggles over objects seem to be a sign of developing selfhood, an effort to clarify boundaries between self and others.

A firmer sense of self also permits children to cooperate for the first time in playing games, solving simple problems, and resolving disputes over objects (Brownell & Carriger, 1990; Caplan et al., 1991). Adults might take both of these capacities into account when trying to promote friendly peer interaction. For example, teachers and parents can accept the young child's possessiveness as a sign of self-assertion ("Yes, that's your toy") and then encourage compromise ("but in a little while, can you give someone else a turn?"), rather than simply insisting on sharing.

EMERGENCE OF SELF-ESTEEM

Another aspect of self-concept emerges in early childhood: **self-esteem,** the judgments we make about our own worth and the feelings associated with those judgments. Self-esteem ranks among the most important aspects of self-development, since evaluations of our own competencies affect emotional experiences, future behavior, and long-term psychological adjustment. Take a moment to think about your own self-esteem. Besides a global appraisal of your worth as a person, you have a variety of separate self-judgments. For example, you may regard yourself as well liked by others, very good at schoolwork, but only so-so at sports.

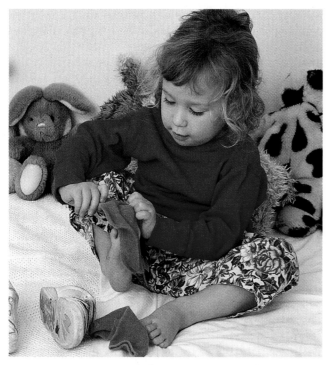

■ *In their early self-descriptions, children usually emphasize observable characteristics, including physical appearance, possessions, and everyday behaviors. When asked to tell about herself, this 4-year-old might say proudly, "I can put my socks and shoes on all by myself!" (Photo courtesy: © 2000 Laura Dwight)*

Preschoolers' self-esteem is not as well defined as that of older children and adults. And usually they rate their own ability as extremely high and underestimate the difficulty of tasks (Harter, 1990, 1998). Sammy's announcement that he was great at beanbag throwing despite his many misses is a typical self-evaluation during early childhood. High self-esteem contributes greatly to preschoolers' initiative during a period in which they must master many new skills. Most young children know they are growing bigger and stronger, and they see that failure on one occasion often translates into success on another. Their belief in their own capacities is supported by the patience and encouragement of adults, who realize that a child who has trouble riding a tricycle or cutting with scissors will be able to do so a short time later.

Nevertheless, by age 4, some children give up easily when faced with a challenge, such as working a hard puzzle or building a tall block tower. They conclude that they cannot do the task and are discouraged after failure (Cain & Dweck, 1995; Smiley & Dweck, 1994). When these young nonpersisters are asked to act out with dolls an adult's reaction to failure, they often respond, "He's punished because he can't do the puzzle," or, "Daddy's mad and is going to spank her" (Burhans & Dweck, 1995). They are also likely to report that their parents would berate them for making small mistakes (Heyman, Dweck, & Cain, 1992). The Caregiving Concerns table below suggests ways to avoid these self-defeating reactions and foster a healthy self-image in young children.

CAREGIVING CONCERNS

Fostering a Healthy Self-Image in Young Children

SUGGESTION	DESCRIPTION
Build a positive relationship.	Indicate that you want to be with the child by arranging times to be fully available. Listen without being judgmental, and express some of your own thoughts and feelings. Mutual sharing helps children feel valued.
Nurture success.	Adjust expectations appropriately, and provide assistance when asking the child to do something beyond his or her current limits. Accentuate the positive in the child's work or behavior. Promote self-motivation by emphasizing praise over concrete rewards. Instead of simply saying, "That's good," mention effort and specific accomplishments. Display the child's artwork and other products, pointing out increasing skill.
Foster the freedom to choose.	Choosing gives children a sense of responsibility and control over their own lives. Where children are not yet capable of deciding on their own, involve them in some aspect of the choice, such as when and in what order a task will be done.
Acknowledge the child's emotions.	Accept the child's strong feelings, and suggest constructive ways to handle them. When a child's negative emotion results from an affront to his or her self-esteem, offer sympathy and comfort along with a realistic appraisal of the situation so that child feels supported and secure.
Use a warm, rational approach to child rearing.	The strategies discussed on pages 256–257 and 269 (induction and authoritative child rearing) promote self-confidence and self-control.

Source: Berne & Savary, 1993.

EMOTIONAL DEVELOPMENT

Gains in representation, language, and self-concept support emotional development in early childhood. Between ages 2 and 6, children achieve a better understanding of their own and others' feelings, and their ability to regulate the expression of emotion improves. Self-development also contributes to a rise in *self-conscious emotions*, such as shame, embarrassment, guilt, envy, and pride.

UNDERSTANDING EMOTION

Preschoolers' vocabulary for talking about emotion expands rapidly. Early in the preschool years, they refer to causes, consequences, and behavioral signs of emotion. Over time, their understanding becomes more accurate and complex. By age 4 to 5, children correctly judge the causes of many basic emotions, as in "He's happy because he's swinging very high" or "He's sad because he misses his mother." However, they are likely to emphasize external factors over internal states as explanations—a balance that changes with age (Levine, 1995).

Nevertheless, 4- and 5-year-olds realize that thinking and feeling are interconnected—that a person reminded of a previous sad experience is likely to feel sad (Lagattuta, Wellman, & Flavell, 1997). And they are good at predicting what a playmate expressing a certain emotion might do next. For example, they say that an angry child might hit someone and that a happy child is more likely to share (Russell, 1990). They are even aware that a lingering mood can affect a person's behavior for an extended time period (Bretherton et al., 1986).

As these examples suggest, young children use emotional language not only to comment on and explain the reactions of others, but also to guide and influence a companion's behavior. Furthermore, preschoolers suggest effective ways to relieve others' negative feelings. For example, they suggest physical comfort to reduce sadness and giving a desired object to a playmate to reduce anger (Fabes et al., 1988). Overall, preschoolers have an impressive ability to interpret, predict, and change others' feelings.

At the same time, there are limits to young children's emotional understanding. In situations in which there are conflicting cues about how a person is feeling, preschoolers have difficulty making sense of what is going on. For example, when asked what might be happening in a picture showing a happy-faced child with a broken bicycle, 4- and 5-year-olds tended to rely on the emotional expression: "He's happy because he likes to ride his bike." Older children more often reconciled the two cues: "He's happy because his father promised to help fix his broken bike"

(Gnepp, 1983; Hoffner & Badzinski, 1989). As in their approach to Piagetian tasks, preschoolers focus on the most obvious aspect of a complex emotional situation to the neglect of other relevant information.

EMOTIONAL SELF-REGULATION

Language contributes to preschoolers' improved *emotional self-regulation,* or ability to control the expression of emotion. By age 3 to 4, children verbalize a variety of strategies for adjusting their emotional arousal to a more comfortable level. For example, they know that emotions can be blunted by restricting sensory input (covering your eyes or ears to block out a scary sight or sound), talking to yourself ("Mommy said she'll be back soon"), or changing your goals (deciding that you don't want to play anyway after being excluded from a game) (Thompson,   Children's awareness and use of these strategies means that intense emotional outbursts become less frequent over the preschool years.

Temperament affects the development of emotional self-regulation. Children who experience negative emotion very intensely have greater difficulty inhibiting their feelings and shifting their attention away from disturbing events. As early as the preschool years, they are likely to respond with irritation to others' distress and get along poorly with adults and peers (Eisenberg et al., 1996, 1997a, 1997b).

At the same time, the social environment powerfully affects children's capacity to cope with stress. By watching adults handle their own feelings, children pick up strategies for regulating emotion. When parents have difficulty controlling anger and hostility, children have problems as well (Cummings & Davies, 1994a). Adult–child conversations also provide techniques for regulating feelings. When parents prepare children for difficult experiences by describing what to expect and ways to handle anxiety, they offer coping strategies that children can use on their own. Preschoolers' vivid imaginations combined with their difficulty in separating appearance from reality make fears common in early childhood. The Caregiving Concerns table on page 252 lists ways that parents can help young children manage them.

SELF-CONSCIOUS EMOTIONS

One morning in Leslie's classroom, a group of children crowded around for a bread-baking activity. Leslie asked them to wait patiently while she got a baking pan. In the meantime, Sammy reached to feel the dough, but the bowl tumbled over the side of the table. When Leslie returned, Sammy looked at her for a moment, covered his eyes with his hands, and said, "I did something bad." He was feeling ashamed and guilty.

Helping Children Manage Common Fears of Childhood

FEAR	SUGGESTION
Monsters, ghosts, and darkness	Reduce exposure to frightening stories in books and on TV until the child is better able to sort out appearance from reality. Make a thorough "search" of the child's room for monsters, showing him or her that none are there. Leave a night-light burning, sit by the child's bed until he or she falls asleep, and tuck in a favorite toy for protection.
Preschool or child care	If the child resists going to preschool but seems content once there, then the fear is probably separation. Under these circumstances, provide a sense of warmth and caring while gently encouraging independence. If the child fears being at preschool, try to find out what is frightening—the teacher, the children, or perhaps a crowded, noisy environment. Provide extra support by accompanying the child at the beginning and lessening the amount of time you are present.
Animals	Do not force the child to approach a dog, cat, or other animal that arouses fear. Let the child move at his or her own pace. Demonstrate how to hold and pet the animal, showing the child that when treated gently, the animal reacts in a friendly way. If the child is bigger than the animal, emphasize this: "You're so big. That kitty is probably afraid of *you!*"
Very intense fears	If a child's fear is very intense, persists for a long time, interferes with daily activities, and cannot be reduced in any of the ways just suggested, it has reached the level of a *phobia.* Sometimes phobias are linked to family problems, and special counseling is needed to reduce them. At other times, phobias diminish without treatment.

As children's self-concepts become better developed, they experience *self-conscious emotions* more often—feelings that involve injury to or enhancement of their sense of self (see Chapter 6). By age 3, self-conscious emotions are clearly linked to self-evaluation (Lewis, 1995). Yet as Sammy's reaction indicates, preschoolers do not yet label these emotions precisely. And they experience them under somewhat different conditions than do older children and adults. For example, young children are likely to feel guilty for any act that can be described as wrongdoing, even if it was accidental (Graham, Doubleday, & Guarino, 1984). Also, the presence of an audience seems to be necessary for preschoolers to experience self-conscious emotions. In the case of pride, children depend on external recognition, such as a parent or teacher saying, "That's a great picture you drew." And they are likely to experience guilt and shame only if their misdeeds are observed or detected by others (Harter & Whitesell, 1989).

Self-conscious emotions play an important role in children's achievement-related and moral behavior. Since preschoolers are still developing standards of excellence and conduct, they depend on instruction, feedback, and examples from adults to know when to feel pride, guilt, and shame. As children develop guidelines for good behavior, the presence of others will no longer be necessary to evoke these emotions. In addition, pride and guilt will be limited to situations in which children feel personally responsible

for an outcome, whereas shame will more often be experienced when violating a standard is unintentional—accidentally dropping spaghetti on one's shirt or forgetting an appointment (Mascolo & Fischer, 1995; Stipek, 1995).

EMPATHY

Another emotional capacity—*empathy*—becomes more common in early childhood. In the preschool years, empathy becomes an important motivator of **prosocial,** or **altruistic, behavior**—actions that benefit another person without any expected reward for the self (Eisenberg & Fabes, 1998). Compared with toddlers, preschoolers rely more on words to communicate their empathic feelings, a change that indicates a more reflective level of empathy. And as the ability to take another's perspective improves, empathic responding increases.

Yet empathy, or *feeling with* another person and responding emotionally in a similar way, does not always yield acts of kindness and helpfulness. In some children, empathizing with an upset adult or peer escalates into personal distress. In trying to reduce these feelings, the child focuses on himself rather than the person in need. As a result, empathy does not give way to **sympathy**—feelings of concern or sorrow for another's plight.

Whether empathy prompts a personally distressed, self-focused response or sympathetic, prosocial behavior is re-

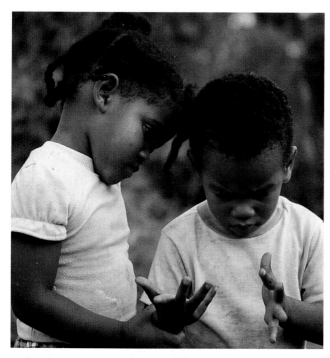

■ *A 5-year-old empathizes with and comforts her 3-year-old brother, who has injured his finger. As young children's language skills expand and their ability to take the perspective of others improves, empathic responding increases and becomes an important motivator of prosocial, or altruistic, behavior. (Photo courtesy: Eastcott/Momatiuk/The Image Works)*

PEER RELATIONS

s children become increasingly self-aware, more effective at communicating, and better at understanding the thoughts and feelings of others, their skill at interacting with peers improves rapidly. Peers provide young children with learning experiences they can get in no other way. Because peers relate to one another on an equal footing, they must assume greater responsibility for keeping a conversation going, cooperating, and setting goals in play than when they associate with adults or older siblings. With peers, children form friendships—special relationships marked by attachment and common interests.

ADVANCES IN PEER SOCIABILITY

Mildred Parten (1932), one of the first to observe peer sociability among 2- to 5-year-olds, noticed a dramatic rise with age in the ability to engage in joint, interactive play. She concluded that social development proceeds in a three-step sequence. It begins with **nonsocial activity**—unoccupied, onlooker behavior and solitary play. Then it shifts to a limited form of social participation called **parallel play,** in which a child plays near other children with similar materials but does not try to influence their behavior. At the highest level, preschoolers engage in two forms of true social interaction. One is **associative play,** in which children en-

lated to both temperament and early experience. Children who are sociable, assertive, and good at regulating emotion are more likely to help, share, and comfort others in distress. In contrast, children who are poor emotion regulators less often display sympathetic concern and prosocial behavior (Eisenberg et al., 1992, 1996, 1998). And parents who are warm and encouraging and show a sensitive, empathic concern for their children have preschoolers who are likely to react in a concerned way to the distress of others—relationships that persist into adolescence and young adulthood (Eisenberg & McNally, 1993; Koestner, Franz, & Weinberger, 1990).

In contrast, angry, punitive parenting is related to disruptions in empathy and sympathy at an early age. In one study, researchers observed physically abused preschoolers at a child-care center. Compared with nonabused agemates, they rarely showed signs of empathy. Instead, they responded to a peer's unhappiness with fear, anger, and physical attacks (Klimes-Dougan & Kistner, 1990). The children's reactions resembled the behavior of their parents, since both responded insensitively to the suffering of others.

■ *These children are engaged in parallel play. Although they sit side by side and use similar materials, they do not try to influence one another's behavior. Parallel play remains frequent and stable over the preschool years, accounting for about one-fifth of children's play time. (Photo courtesy: George Doedwin/ Monkmeyer Press.*

■ *As these preschoolers trade toys and comment on each other's activities at the sand table, they engage in a form of true social interaction called associative play. (Photo courtesy: Mary Kate Denny/PhotoEdit)*

gage in separate activities, but they interact by exchanging toys and commenting on one another's behavior. The other is **cooperative play**—a more advanced type of interaction in which children orient toward a common goal, such as acting out a make-believe theme or working on the same product, for example, a sand castle or a painting.

■ RECENT EVIDENCE ON PEER SOCIABILITY. Longitudinal evidence indicates that these play forms emerge in the order suggested by Parten, but they do not form a neat developmental sequence in which later-appearing ones replace earlier ones (Howes & Matheson, 1992). Instead, all types coexist during the preschool years. Furthermore, although nonsocial activity declines with age, it is still the most frequent form of behavior among 3- to 4-year-olds. Even among kindergartners it continues to take up as much as a third of children's free-play time. Also, solitary and parallel play remain fairly stable from 3 to 6 years, accounting for as much of the young child's play as highly social, cooperative interaction. Social development during the preschool years is not just a matter of eliminating nonsocial and partially social activity from the child's behavior.

We now understand that it is the *type*, rather than the amount, of solitary and parallel play that changes in early childhood. In studies of preschoolers' play in Taiwan and the United States, researchers rated the *cognitive maturity* of nonsocial, parallel, and cooperative play by applying the categories shown in Table 8.1. Within each of Parten's play types, older children displayed more cognitively mature behavior than did younger children (Pan, 1994; Rubin, Watson, & Jambor, 1978).

Often parents wonder whether a preschooler who spends large amounts of time playing alone is developing normally. Only *certain types* of nonsocial activity—aimless wandering, hovering near peers, and functional play involving immature, repetitive motor action (see Table 8.1)—are cause for concern (Rubin & Coplan, 1998). Most nonsocial play of preschoolers is positive and constructive, and teachers encourage it by setting out art materials, puzzles, and building toys during free play. Children who spend much time in these activities are not maladjusted. Instead, they tend to be very bright youngsters who, when they do play with peers, show socially skilled behavior.

As we noted in Chapter 7, *sociodramatic play* (or make-believe with peers) becomes especially common during the preschool years. It supports both cognitive and social development. In joint make-believe, preschoolers act out and respond to one another's pretend feelings. Their play is rich in references to emotional states. Young children also explore and gain control over fear-arousing experiences when they play doctor or dentist or pretend to search for monsters in a magical forest. As a result, they are better able to understand the feelings of others and regulate their own. Finally, to create and manage complex plots, preschoolers must resolve their disputes through negotiation and compromise. These experiences contribute greatly to their ability to get along with others (Howes, 1992).

■ CULTURAL VARIATIONS. In collectivist societies, peer sociability takes different forms than in individualistic cultures like the United States. For example, children in India generally play in large groups that require high levels of cooperation. Much of their behavior during sociodramatic play and early games is imitative, occurs in unison, and involves

TABLE 8.1

Developmental Sequence of Cognitive Play Categories

PLAY CATEGORY	DESCRIPTION	EXAMPLES
Functional play	Simple, repetitive motor movements with or without objects. Especially common during the first 2 years of life.	Running around a room, rolling a car back and forth, kneading clay with no intent to make something
Constructive play	Creating or constructing something. Especially common between 3 and 6 years.	Making a house out of toy blocks, drawing a picture, putting together a puzzle
Make-believe play	Acting out everyday and imaginary roles. Especially common between 2 and 6 years.	Playing house, school, or police officer; acting out fairy tales or television characters

Source: Rubin, Fein, & Vandenberg, 1983.

■ *These Chinese girls demonstrate an intricate hand-clapping game in which they must respond quickly and in unison. Preschoolers in the People's Republic of China frequently perform such games for classmates and parents. Their play reflects the value their culture places on group harmony. (Photo courtesy: Jeff Greenberg/PhotoEdit)*

close physical contact. In a game called Bhatto Bhatto, children act out a script about a trip to the market, touching each other's elbows and hands as they pretend to cut and share a tasty vegetable (Roopnarine et al., 1994).

Cultural beliefs about play also affect early peer interaction. Caregivers who view play as mere entertainment are less likely to provide props and encourage pretend than are those who value its cognitive and social benefits (Farver & Wimbarti, 1995). Korean-American parents, who emphasize task persistence as vital for learning and de-emphasize self-expression, have preschoolers who spend less time at joint make-believe and more time unoccupied and in parallel play than do their Caucasian-American counterparts (Farver, Kim, & Lee, 1995).

FIRST FRIENDSHIPS

As preschoolers interact, first friendships form that serve as important contexts for emotional and social development. Take a moment to jot down what the word *friendship* means to you. You probably thought of a mutual relationship involving companionship, sharing, understanding of thoughts and feelings, and caring for and comforting one another in times of need. In addition, mature friendships endure over time and survive occasional conflicts.

Preschoolers understand something about the uniqueness of friendship. They know that a friend is someone "who likes you" and with whom you spend a lot of time playing (Youniss, 1980). Yet their ideas about friendship are far from mature. Four- to 7-year-olds regard friendship as pleasurable play and sharing of toys. As yet, friendship does not have a long-term, enduring quality based on mutual

trust (Selman, 1980). Indeed, Sammy could be heard declaring, "Mark's my best friend," on days when the boys got along well. But he would state just the opposite—"Mark, you're not my friend!"—when a dispute arose that was not quickly settled.

Nevertheless, interactions between friends already have unique features. Preschoolers give twice as much reinforcement, in the form of greetings, praise, and compliance, to children whom they identify as friends, and they also receive more from them. Friends are also more emotionally expressive, talking, laughing, and looking at each other more often than nonfriends (Hartup, 1996). Apparently, sensitivity, spontaneity, and intimacy characterize friendships very early, although children are not able to say that these qualities are essential to a good friendship until much later.

PARENTAL INFLUENCES ON EARLY PEER RELATIONS

Outside of preschool and child care, young children are limited in their ability to find playmates. Parents who frequently arrange informal peer play activities tend to have preschoolers with larger peer networks and who are more socially skilled (Ladd, LeSieur, & Profilet, 1993). In providing play opportunities, parents show children how to initiate their own peer contacts.

Parents also influence their children's social relations by offering guidance and examples of how to act toward others. In one study, parents who phrased their directives positively and politely ("Why don't you try . . ." instead of "Don't!") had preschoolers who were more successful in influencing peers (Kochanska, 1992). And children whose parents are warm, help them regulate negative emotion, and offer skillful advice on how to solve peer problems get along especially well with agemates (Isley et al., 1999; Mize & Pettit, 1997).

As early as the preschool years, some children have great difficulty with peer relations. In Leslie's classroom, Robbie was one of them. His demanding, aggressive behavior caused other children to dislike him. Wherever he happened to be, such comments as "Robbie ruined our block tower" and "Robbie hit me for no reason" could be heard. You will learn more about how Robbie's family environment contributed to his problems as we take up moral development in the next section.

ASK YOURSELF . . .

■ *Reread the description of Sammy and Mark's argument at the beginning of this chapter. On the basis of what you know about self-development, why was it a good idea for Leslie to resolve the dispute by providing an extra set of beanbags so that both boys could play at once?*

■ *Four-year-old Tia had just gotten her face painted at a carnival. Soon the heat of the afternoon caused her balloon to pop. When Tia started to cry, her mother said, "Oh, Tia, balloons aren't such a good idea when it's hot outside. We'll get another on a cooler day. If you cry, you'll mess up your beautiful face painting." What emotional capacity is Tia's mother trying to promote, and why is her intervention likely to help Tia?*

How does emotional self-regulation contribute to the development of empathy and sympathy? Why are these emotional capacities vital for positive peer relations? What can parents do in early childhood to promote favorable peer ties?

FOUNDATIONS OF MORALITY

If you watch children's behavior and listen in on their conversations, you will find many examples of their developing moral sense. By age 2, they often react with alarm to behaviors that are aggressive or that might otherwise harm someone. Soon they comment directly on their own and others' actions: "I naughty. I wrote on wall" or (after having been hit by another child) "Connie not nice" (Kochanska, Casey, & Fukumoto, 1995).

Throughout the world, adults take note of this budding capacity to distinguish right from wrong. In some cultures, special terms are used to describe it. The Utku Indians of Hudson Bay say the child develops *ihuma* (reason). The Fijians believe that *vakayalo* (sense) appears. In response, parents hold children more responsible for their behavior (Kagan, 1998). By the end of early childhood, children can state a great many moral rules, such as "You're not supposed to take things without asking" or "Tell the truth!" In addition, they argue over matters of justice, as when they say, "You sat there last time, so it's my turn," or, "It's not fair. He got more!"

All theories of moral development recognize that conscience begins to take shape in early childhood. And most agree that at first, the child's morality is *externally controlled* by adults. Gradually it becomes regulated by *inner standards*. Truly moral individuals do not just do the right thing when authority figures are around. Instead, they have developed principles of good conduct and compassion, which they follow in a wide variety of situations.

Although there are points of agreement among major theories, each emphasizes a different aspect of morality. Psychoanalytic theory stresses the *emotional side* of conscience development—in particular, identification and guilt as motivators of good conduct. Social learning theory focuses on *moral behavior* and how it is learned through reinforcement and modeling. And the cognitive-developmental perspective emphasizes *thinking*—children's ability to reason about justice and fairness.

THE PSYCHOANALYTIC PERSPECTIVE

Recall from our discussion earlier in this chapter that according to Freud, young children form a *superego*, or conscience, by *identifying* with the same-sex parent, whose moral standards they adopt. Children obey the superego to avoid *guilt*, a painful emotion that arises each time they are tempted to misbehave. Moral development, Freud believed, is largely complete by 5 to 6 years of age, at the end of the phallic stage.

Today, most researchers disagree with Freud's account of conscience development. Notice how discipline promoting fear of punishment and loss of parental love is assumed to motivate young children to behave morally (Kochanska, 1993). Yet children whose parents frequently use threats, commands, or physical force usually feel little guilt after harming others. In the case of love withdrawal—for example, when a parent refuses to speak to or actually states a dislike for the child—children often respond with high levels of self-blame after misbehaving. They might think to themselves, "I'm no good, and nobody loves me." Eventually, these children may protect themselves from overwhelming feelings of guilt by denying the emotion when they do something wrong. So they, too, develop a weak conscience (Kochanska, 1991; Zahn-Waxler et al., 1990).

In contrast, a special type of discipline called **induction** does support conscience formation. It involves pointing out the effects of the child's misbehavior on others. For example, a parent might say, "If you keep pushing him he'll fall down and cry," or, "She feels so sad because you won't give back her doll" (Hoffman, 1988). As long as the explanation matches the child's capacity to understand, induction is effective with children as young as 2 years of age. Preschoolers whose parents use it are more likely to make up for their mis-

■ *This teacher uses inductive discipline to explain to a child the impact of her transgression on others. Induction supports conscience development by clarifying how the child should behave, encouraging empathy and sympathetic concern, and permitting the child to grasp the reasons behind parental expectations. (Photo courtesy: Nancy Sheehan)*

When her mother reprimanded her sharply for pouring water on the floor as she played in her bath, 3-year-old Katherine burst into tears. An anxious, sensitive child, Katherine was so distressed that it took her mother 10 minutes to calm her down. Outside in the front yard the next day, Katherine's mother watched as her next-door neighbor patiently asked her 3-year-old son, who was about to pick the first tulips to blossom in the garden, not to touch the flowers. Alex, an active, adventurous child, paid no attention. As he pulled at another tulip, Alex's mother grabbed him, scolded him harshly, and carried him inside. Alex responded by kicking, hitting, and screaming, "Let me down, let me down!"

What explains Katherine's and Alex's very different reactions to firm parental discipline? Grazyna Kochanska (1995) points out that children's temperaments affect the parenting practices that best promote responsibility and concern for others. She found that for temperamentally inhibited 2- and 3-year-olds, maternal gentle discipline—reasoning, polite requests, suggestions, and distractions—predicted conscience development at age 5, measured in terms of not cheating in games and completing stories about moral issues with prosocial themes (not taking someone else's toys, helping a child who is hurt). In contrast, for relatively fearless, impulsive children, mild disciplinary tactics showed no relationship to moral internalization. Instead a secure attachment bond with the mother predicted a mature conscience (Kochanska, 1997a).

According to Kochanska, inhibited children like Katherine, who are prone to anxiety, are easily overcome by intense discipline. Mild, patient tactics are sufficient to motivate them to internalize parental messages. But impulsive children, such as Alex, may not respond to gentle interventions with enough discomfort to promote internalization. Yet frequent use of power-assertive methods is not effective either, since these techniques spark anger and resentment, which interfere with the child's processing of parental messages.

Why is secure attachment predictive of conscience development in nonanxious children? Kochanska suggests that when children are so low in anxiety that typically effective disciplinary practices fail, a close bond with the caregiver provides an alternative foundation for conscience formation. It motivates children unlikely to experience negative emotion to internalize rules as a means of preserving a spirit of affection and cooperation with the parent.

To foster early moral development, parents must tailor their child-rearing strategies to their child's temperament. In Katherine's case, a soft-spoken correction would probably be effective. For Alex, taking extra steps to build a warm, caring relationship during times when he behaves well is likely to promote moral internalization. Although Alex's parents need to use firmer and more frequent discipline than Katherine's do, emphasizing power assertion is counterproductive for both children. Do these findings remind you of the notion of *goodness of fit,* discussed in Chapter 6? Return to page 189 to review this idea.

deeds, and they more often display prosocial behavior (Zahn-Waxler, Radke-Yarrow, & King, 1979).

The success of induction may lie in its power to motivate the child's active commitment to moral standards (Turiel, 1998). How does it do so? First, induction tells children how to behave so they can use this information in future situations. Second, by pointing out the impact of the child's actions on others, parents encourage empathy and sympathy, which promote prosocial behavior (Krevans & Gibbs, 1996). Third, providing children with reasons for changing their behavior encourages them to adopt moral standards because they make sense. In contrast, discipline that relies too heavily on threats of punishment or love withdrawal makes children so anxious and afraid that they cannot think clearly enough to figure out what they should do. As a result, these practices do not get children to internalize moral rules.

Furthermore, Freud's theory places a heavy burden on parents, who must ensure through their disciplinary practices that children develop an internalized conscience. Although good discipline is crucial, parent–child interaction is a two-way street. As the Variations box above illustrates, children's characteristics can affect the success of parenting techniques.

Finally, although there is little support for Freudian ideas about conscience development, Freud was correct that guilt is an important motivator of moral action. Around age 3, guilt reactions are clearly evident. But guilt is not the only force that compels us to act morally. And contrary to what Freud believed, moral development is not complete by the end of early childhood. Instead, it is a far more gradual process, beginning in the preschool years and extending into adulthood.

BEHAVIORISM AND SOCIAL LEARNING THEORY

According to the traditional behaviorist view, *operant conditioning* is an important way in which children pick up new responses. From this perspective, children start to behave in ways consistent with adult moral standards because parents and teachers follow up "good behavior" with *positive reinforcement* in the form of approval, affection, and other rewards.

THE IMPORTANCE OF MODELING.

Operant conditioning is not enough for children to acquire moral responses. Recall from Chapter 4 that for a behavior to be reinforced, it must first occur spontaneously. Yet many prosocial acts, such as sharing, helping, or comforting an unhappy playmate, do not occur often enough at first for reinforcement to explain their rapid development in early childhood. Instead, social learning theorists believe that children largely learn to act morally through *modeling*—by observing and imitating people who demonstrate appropriate behavior (Bandura, 1977; Grusec, 1988). Once children acquire a moral response, such as sharing, helping, or telling the truth, reinforcement in the form of praise, along with adult reminders of the rules for moral behavior, increases its frequency (Mills & Grusec, 1989).

Many studies show that models who behave helpfully or generously increase young children's prosocial responses. The model's characteristics affect children's willingness to imitate in the following ways:

- *Warmth and responsiveness.* Preschoolers are more likely to copy the prosocial actions of an adult who is warm and responsive than one who is cold and aloof (Yarrow, Scott, & Waxler, 1973). Warmth seems to make children more attentive and receptive to the model, and it is an example of a prosocial response.

- *Competence and power.* Children admire and therefore tend to select competent, powerful models to imitate—the reason they are especially willing to copy the behavior of older peers and adults (Bandura, 1977).

- *Consistency between assertions and behavior.* When models say one thing and do another—for example, announce that "It's important to help others" but rarely engage in helpful acts—children generally choose the most lenient standard of behavior that adults demonstrate (Mischel & Liebert, 1966).

Models are most influential during the preschool years. At the end of early childhood, children with a history of consistent exposure to caring adults tend to behave prosocially regardless of whether a model is present. By that time, they have internalized prosocial rules from repeated observations of and encouragement by others (Mussen & Eisenberg-Berg, 1977).

EFFECTS OF PUNISHMENT.

Most parents are aware of the limited usefulness of *punishment*, such as scolding, criticism, and spankings, and apply it sparingly. Using sharp reprimands or physical force to restrain or move a child is justified when immediate obedience is necessary—for example, when a 3-year-old is about to run into the street. In fact, parents are most likely to use forceful methods under these conditions. When they are interested in fostering long-term goals, such as acting kindly toward others, they tend to rely on warmth and reasoning (Kuczynski, 1984). And parents often combine power assertion with reasoning in response to very serious transgressions, such as lying and stealing (Grusec & Goodnow, 1994).

Indeed, a great deal of research shows that when used frequently, punishment promotes only momentary compliance, not lasting changes in children's behavior. For example, Robbie's parents punished often, spanking, shouting, and criticizing when he did something wrong. Robbie usually stopped misbehaving when his mother and father were around, but he engaged in the behavior again as soon as they were out of sight and he thought he could get away with it. As a result, Robbie was especially unmanageable in settings away from the home, such as preschool (Strassberg et al., 1994).

Harsh punishment has undesirable side effects. First, when parents spank, they often do so in response to children's aggression (Holden, Coleman, & Schmidt, 1995). Yet the punishment itself models aggression! Second, children who are frequently punished soon learn to avoid the punishing adult. When Robbie's parents came into the room, Robbie braced himself for something unpleasant and kept his distance. Consequently, they had little opportunity to teach Robbie desirable behaviors. Finally, as punishment "works" to stop children's misbehavior temporarily, it offers immediate relief to adults, and they are reinforced for using coercive discipline. For this reason, a punitive adult is likely to punish with greater frequency over time, a course of action that can spiral into serious abuse.

ALTERNATIVES TO HARSH PUNISHMENT.

Alternatives to criticism, slaps, and spankings can reduce the undesirable side effects of punishment. A technique called **time out** involves removing children from the immediate setting—for example, by sending them to their rooms—until they are ready to act appropriately. Time out is useful when a child is out of control and other effective methods of discipline cannot be applied at the moment (Betz, 1994). It usually requires only a few minutes to change behavior, and it also offers a "cooling off" period for angry parents. Another approach is *withdrawal of privileges,* such as playing outside or watching a favorite TV program. Removing privileges may generate some resentment in children, but parents avoid harsh techniques that could easily intensify into violence.

When parents decide to use punishment, they can increase its effectiveness in three ways. The first is *consistency.*

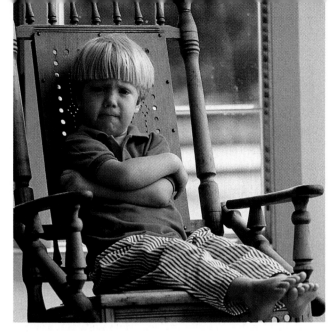

One alternative to harsh punishment is *time out*, in which children are removed from the immediate setting until they are ready to act appropriately. Time out is useful when a child is out of control and other methods of discipline cannot be applied at the moment. But the best way to motivate good conduct is to let children know ahead of time how to act, serve as good examples, and praise them when they behave well. Then time out will seldom be necessary. (Photo courtesy: Ariel Skelley/The Stock Market)

Permitting children to act inappropriately on some occasions but scolding them on others confuses children, and the unacceptable act persists. In a study in which researchers had mothers carry on a telephone conversation while their 2-year-olds played, reprimanding half of the children's inappropriate demands for attention ("Please don't interrupt") and giving in to the other half led to a dramatic increase in children's unruly behavior (see Figure 8.1) (Acker & O'Leary, 1996). Second, a *warm parent–child relationship* is vital. Children of involved, caring parents

find punishment especially unpleasant and want to regain parental warmth and approval as quickly as possible. Finally, *explanations* help children recall the misdeed and relate it to expectations for future behavior. Pairing reasons with mild punishment (such as time out) leads to a far greater reduction in misbehavior than using punishment alone (Larzelere et al., 1996).

■ POSITIVE DISCIPLINE. The most effective forms of discipline encourage good conduct—by building a positive relationship with the child, offering models of appropriate behavior, letting children know ahead of time how to act, and praising them when they behave well (Zahn-Waxler & Robinson, 1995). Warm, cooperative parent–child ties lead children to want to heed parental demands because they feel a sense of commitment to the relationship. This frees parents from restricting and punishing to focus on encouraging children's competent behavior.

Preschoolers whose parents use this proactive approach are less likely to violate parental standards and to display behavior problems at age 5 (Kochanska, 1997b; Kuczynski & Kochanska, 1995). Such parents also do much to reduce opportunities for misbehavior. For example, on a long car trip, they bring along back-seat activities that relieve restlessness and boredom. At the supermarket, they engage preschoolers in conversation and encourage them to assist with shopping (Holden & West, 1989). When adults help children acquire acceptable behaviors to replace forbidden acts, the need for coercive discipline is reduced.

THE COGNITIVE-DEVELOPMENTAL PERSPECTIVE

The psychoanalytic and behaviorist approaches to morality focus on how children acquire ready-made standards

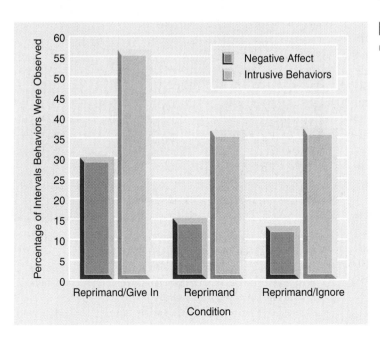

FIGURE 8.1

■ **How does inconsistent punishment affect children's behavior?** To find out, researchers had mothers talk on the telephone while their toddlers played. Mothers in the "reprimand/give in" condition (who reprimanded half of their child's inappropriate demands and gave in to the other half) had toddlers with far higher rates of negative affect and intrusive behaviors, such as climbing on the mother's lap and pulling the phone cord, than did mothers in the "reprimand" condition (who reprimanded every inappropriate demand) and mothers in the "reprimand/ignore" condition (who reprimanded half the inappropriate demands and ignored the other half). (Adapted from Acker & O'Leary, 1996).

of good conduct from adults. The cognitive-developmental perspective is different. It regards children as *active thinkers* about social rules. As early as the preschool years, children make moral judgments, deciding what is right or wrong on the basis of concepts they construct about justice and fairness (Gibbs, 1991).

Young children already have some well-developed ideas about morality. For example, 3-year-olds think that a child who intentionally knocks a playmate off a swing is worse than one who does so accidentally (Yuill & Perner, 1988). By age 4, children can tell the difference between truthfulness and lying (Cameron & Lee, 1997). They are also aware that disobeying *moral rules,* such as being kind to others and not taking someone else's possessions, is much more serious than violating *social conventions,* such as not saying "please" or "thank you" or eating messy food with fingers (Smetana & Braeges, 1990; Turiel, 1998).

How do young children come to make these distinctions? According to cognitive-developmental theorists, not through direct teaching, modeling, and reinforcement, since adults insist that children conform to social conventions just as often as they press for obedience to moral rules. Instead, children *actively make sense* of their experiences. They observe that people respond differently to violations of moral rules than to breaks with social convention. When a moral offense occurs, children react emotionally, describe their own injury or loss, tell another child to stop, or retaliate (Arsenio & Fleiss, 1996). An adult who intervenes is likely to call attention to the rights and feelings of the victim. In contrast, children are less likely to react to violations of social convention. And in these situations, adults tend to demand obedience without explanation, as when they state, "Say the magic word!" or "Don't eat with your fingers" (Turiel, Smetana, & Killen, 1991).

Young children are clearly off to a good start in appreciating that moral rules are important because they protect people's rights and welfare. Disputes with siblings and peers over rights, possessions, and property give preschoolers opportunities to work out their first ideas about justice and fairness (Killen & Nucci, 1995). The way adults handle rule violations and discuss moral issues also helps children reason about morality. Children who are advanced in moral thinking have parents who adapt their communications about fighting, honesty, and ownership to what their children can understand, respect the child's opinion, and gently stimulate the child to think further, without being hostile or critical (Janssens & Deković, 1997; Walker & Taylor, 1991a).

Preschoolers who are disliked by peers because of their aggressive approach to resolving conflict have trouble distinguishing between moral rules and social conventions, and they violate both often (Sanderson & Siegal, 1988). Without special help, such children show long-term disruptions in moral development.

THE OTHER SIDE OF MORALITY: DEVELOPMENT OF AGGRESSION

Beginning in late infancy, all children display aggression from time to time as they become better at identifying sources of anger and frustration. By the early preschool years, two forms of aggression emerge. The most common is **instrumental aggression.** In this form, children want an object, privilege, or space and, in trying to get it, they push, shout at, or otherwise attack a person who is in the way. The other type, **hostile aggression,** is meant to hurt another person.

Hostile aggression comes in two varieties. The first is **overt aggression,** which harms others through physical injury or the threat of such injury—for example, hitting, kicking, or threatening to beat up a peer. The second is **relational aggression,** which damages another's peer relationships, as in social exclusion or rumor spreading. "Go away, I'm not your friend anymore!" and "Don't play with Margie, she's a nerd" are examples of relational aggression.

For most preschoolers, instrumental aggression declines with age as they learn to compromise over possessions. In contrast, hostile aggression increases between 4 and 7, although it is rare compared with children's friendly interactions (Shantz, 1987). This rise in hostile encounters occurs as children become better at detecting others' inten-

■ *An occasional expression of aggression is normal in early childhood. This preschooler displays instrumental aggression as she grabs an attractive toy from a classmate. Instrumental aggression declines with age as children learn how to compromise and share. (Photo courtesy: © Laura Dwight)*

tions. Older preschoolers are more likely to recognize when another child is being deliberately malicious and to try to get even by attacking in return.

Although children of both sexes show this general pattern of development, on the average boys are more overtly aggressive than girls, a trend that appears in many cultures (Whiting & Edwards, 1988a). The sex difference is, in part, due to biology—in particular, to male sex hormones, or androgens. Androgens contribute to boys' greater physical activity, which may increase their opportunities for physically aggressive encounters (Collaer & Hines, 1995). At the same time, gender typing (a topic we will take up shortly) is important. As soon as 2-year-olds become dimly aware of gender stereotypes—that males and females are expected to behave differently—overt aggression drops off in girls but is maintained in boys (Fagot & Leinbach, 1989).

But preschool and school-age girls are not less aggressive than boys! Instead, they are likely to express their hostility differently—through relational aggression (Crick, Casas, & Mosher, 1997; Crick, Casas, & Ku, 1999). When trying to harm a peer, children seem to do so in ways especially likely to thwart that child's social goals. Boys more often attack physically to block the dominance goals typical of boys. Girls resort to relational aggression because it interferes with close, intimate bonds especially important to girls.

An occasional aggressive exchange between young children is normal and expected. But some preschoolers, like Robbie, show abnormally high rates of aggression. Researchers have traced their problems to strife-ridden families, poor parenting practices, and exposure to television violence—factors that often can be found together.

■ THE FAMILY AS TRAINING GROUND FOR AGGRESSIVE BEHAVIOR. "I can't control him, he's impossible," complained Nadine, Robbie's mother, at a conference with Leslie. When Leslie asked what might be going on at home that made it hard to handle Robbie, she discovered that Robbie's parents fought constantly and resorted to harsh, inconsistent discipline. The same child-rearing practices that undermine moral internalization—love withdrawal, power assertion, physical punishment, and inconsistency—are linked to aggression from early childhood through adolescence, in children of both sexes (Coie & Dodge, 1998; Nix et al., 1999).

Observations in families like Robbie's reveal that anger and punitiveness quickly spread from one family member to another, creating a conflict-ridden family atmosphere and an "out-of-control" child. The pattern begins with forceful discipline, which is made more likely by stressful life experiences, a parent's own personality, or a temperamentally difficult child. Once the parent threatens, criticizes, and punishes, then the child whines, yells, and refuses until the parent finds the child's behavior to be too much and "gives in." As these cycles become more frequent, they

generate anxiety and irritability among other family members, who soon join in the hostile interactions (Patterson, 1995, 1997). Aggressive children who are products of these family processes soon learn to view the world from a violent perspective. Because they expect others to react with anger and physical force, they see hostile intent where it does not exist (Dodge & Somberg, 1987). As a result, they make many unprovoked attacks, which contribute to aggressive cycles.

For at least two reasons, boys are more likely than girls to become involved in family interactions that promote aggressive behavior. First, parents more often use commands and physical punishment with sons, which encourage them to adopt the same tactics (Deater-Deckard & Dodge, 1997). Second, parents are less likely to interpret fighting among boys as aggressive, so they may overlook it more than they do with girls (Condry & Ross, 1985). By middle childhood, boys expect less parental disapproval and report feeling less guilty over aggression than do girls (Perry, Perry, & Weiss, 1989).

Unfortunately, highly aggressive children often develop serious adjustment problems. Because of their hostile style of responding and their poor self-control, they tend to be rejected by peers, to fail in school, and (by adolescence) to seek out deviant peer groups, which lead them toward violent delinquency and adult criminality. We will consider this life-course path of antisocial activity in Chapter 12.

■ TELEVISION AND AGGRESSION. In the United States, 57 percent of television programs between 6 A.M. and 11 P.M. contain violent scenes, often in the form of repeated aggressive acts that go unpunished. In fact, most TV violence does not show victims experiencing any serious harm, and few programs condemn violence or depict other ways of solving problems. To the contrary, over one-third of violent TV scenes are embedded in humor, a figure that rises to two-thirds for children's shows. Of all TV programs, children's cartoons are the most violent (Center for Communication and Social Policy, 1998).

Young children are especially likely to be influenced by television. One reason is that below age 8, children do not understand a great deal of what they see on TV. Because they have difficulty connecting separate scenes into a meaningful story line, they do not relate the actions of a TV character to motives or consequences (Collins et al., 1978). Young children also find it hard to separate true-to-life from fantasized television content. Not until age 7 do they fully realize that fictional characters do not retain the same roles in real life (Wright et al., 1994). These misunderstandings increase young children's willingness to accept uncritically and imitate what they see on TV.

Reviewers of thousands of studies have concluded that TV violence provides children with an extensive "how-to course in aggression" (Slaby et al., 1995, p. 163). Violent programming not only creates short-term difficulties in parent and peer relations, but has long-term effects as well. Longitudinal research reveals that highly aggressive children have a greater appetite for violent TV. As they watch more, they become increasingly likely to resort to hostile ways of solving problems. This spiraling pattern of learning contributes to serious antisocial acts by adolescence and young adulthood (Huesmann, 1986). Television violence also "hardens" children to aggression, making them more willing to tolerate it in others. Heavy TV viewers begin to see the world as a mean and scary place where aggressive acts are a normal and acceptable means for solving problems (Donnerstein, Slaby, & Eron, 1994).

The ease with which television can manipulate the beliefs and behavior of children has resulted in strong public pressures to improve its content. As the Social Issues box on the following page indicates, these efforts have not been very successful. At present, it is up to parents to regulate their children's exposure—a heavy burden, given that children find TV so attractive.

■ HELPING CHILDREN AND PARENTS CONTROL AGGRESSION. Help for aggressive children must break the cycle of hostilities between family members, replacing it with effective interaction styles. Leslie suggested that Robbie's parents see a family therapist, who observed their inept practices and coached them in alternatives. They learned not to give in to Robbie, to pair commands with reasons, and to replace verbal insults and spankings with more effective punishments, such as time out and withdrawal of privileges (Patterson, 1982).

At the same time, Leslie began teaching Robbie more successful ways of relating to peers. As opportunities arose, she encouraged Robbie to talk about a playmate's feelings and express his own. This helped Robbie take the perspective of others, empathize, and feel sympathetic concern. Soon he showed a greater willingness to share and cooperate (Feshbach & Feshbach, 1982). Robbie also participated in *social problem-solving training*. Over several months, he met with Leslie and a small group of classmates to act out common conflicts with puppets, discuss effective and ineffective ways of resolving them, and try out successful strategies. Children who receive such training show gains in social competence still present several months later (Shure, 1997). Effective social problem solving also provides children with a sense of mastery in the face of stressful life events. It reduces the risk of adjustment difficulties in children from low-income and troubled families (Goodman, Gravitt, & Kaslow, 1995).

Finally, Robbie's parents got help with their marital problems. This, in addition to their improved ability to manage Robbie's behavior, greatly reduced tension and conflict in the household.

ASK YOURSELF...

Alice and Wayne want their two young children to develop a strong, internalized conscience and to become generous, caring individuals. List as many parenting practices as you can that would foster these goals.

■ *Nanette told her 3-year-old son, Darren, not to go into the front yard without asking, since the house faces a very busy street. Darren disobeyed several times, and now Nanette thinks it's time to punish him. How would you recommend that Nanette discipline Darren, and why?*

Suzanne has a difficult temperament, and her parents respond to her angry outbursts with harsh, inconsistent discipline. Explain why Suzanne is at risk for long-term difficulties in conscience development and peer relations.

GENDER TYPING

The process of developing *gender roles*, or gender-linked preferences and behaviors valued by the larger society, is called **gender typing.** Early in the preschool years, gender typing is well under way. In Leslie's classroom, children tended to play and form friendships with peers of their own sex. Girls spent more time in the housekeeping, art, and reading corners, whereas boys gathered more often in blocks, woodworking, and active play spaces.

The same three theories that provide accounts of morality have been used to explain gender-role development. According to *psychoanalytic theory,* gender-stereotyped beliefs and behaviors are adopted in the same way as other social standards—through identification with the same-sex parent. But as in the area of morality, Freud's ideas have difficulty accounting for gender typing. Research shows that the same-sex parent is only one of many influences in gender-role development. The other-sex parent, peers, teachers, and the broader social environment are important as well.

Social learning theory, with its emphasis on modeling and reinforcement, and *cognitive-developmental theory,* with its focus on children as active thinkers about their social world, are major current approaches to understanding gender typing. We will see that neither is adequate by itself. Consequently, a third perspective that combines elements of both, called *gender schema theory,* has gained favor. In the following sections, we consider the early development of gender typing, along with genetic and environmental contributions to it.

REGULATING CHILDREN'S TELEVISION

Exposure to television is almost universal in the United States and other Western industrialized nations. Ninety-eight percent of American homes have at least one television set, and a TV is switched on in a typical household for a total of 7.1 hours a day. TV enters the lives of children at an early age, becoming a major teacher of undesirable attitudes and behavior. Yet television has as much potential for good as it does for ill. If the content of television were changed, it could promote prosocial attitudes and behavior and convey information about nonviolent aspects of the world, such as history, science, literature, fine arts, and other cultures (Graves, 1993).

Unfortunately, recent changes in the media world have increased children's exposure to harmful messages. Over 65 percent of American families are cable subscribers, and over 80 percent own VCRs—rates that are rapidly increasing (U.S. Bureau of the Census, 1999). Children with cable or VCR access can see films with far more graphic violence and sexual content than are shown on commercial TV. Although the greatest concern is violence, TV messages fostering gender and ethnic stereotyping and uncritical consumerism are also damaging to children.

Many organizations concerned with the well-being of children and families have recommended government regulation of TV. But the First Amendment right to free speech has made the federal government reluctant to place limits on television content. Consequently, professionals and committed public officials have sought ways to counteract the negative impact of television that are consistent with the First Amendment. Instead of imposing bans, the federal government now requires broadcasters to provide at least 3 hours per week of educational programming for children. In addition, broadcasters must rate television content and manufacturers must build

the V-Chip (also called the Violence-Chip) into new TV sets so viewers can use the rating system to block undesired violent and sexual material.

The V-Chip, however, is far from a complete solution. The rating system is based largely on frequency of offensive content. Yet research indicates that the context of violent acts—their realism, intensity, motivation, and consequences—affects children's emotional reactions, evaluations, and imitation. Furthermore, the ratings may make shows more appealing to young audiences—an outcome supported for boys (Cantor & Harrison, 1996). Children may go to other homes to watch programs forbidden by their parents.

Sometimes it takes a tragedy to mobilize action to protect children. In 1992, a Canadian teenager, who believed that TV violence contributed to his sister's rape and murder, organized a petition to reduce violent programs. Over 1 million people signed it (Dubow & Miller, 1996). The Canadian television industry responded with a voluntary code that bans violence that is gratuitous (unnecessary to the plot) and that requires the consequences of violence to be shown in all children's programs. Still, American programs that violate the code slip through on Canadian cable TV.

Parents face an awesome task in monitoring and controlling children's TV viewing, given the extent of harmful messages on the screen. Here are some strategies they can use:

- Avoid using TV as a baby-sitter. Provide children with clear rules that limit the amount of time they can watch—for example, an hour a day and only certain programs—and stick to the rules.

- Do not use television to reward or punish children, a practice that increases its attractiveness.

- Encourage children to watch programs that are child-appropriate, informative, and prosocial.

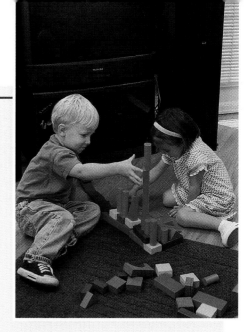

In this home, the television is turned off, and preschool children cooperate in building with blocks. Using television to promote active engagement with the surrounding world and prosocial behavior is a great challenge for parents in the United States, given the antisocial content of many TV programs. (Photo courtesy: David Young-Wolff/PhotoEdit)

- As much as possible, watch with children, helping them understand what they see. When adults express disapproval of on-screen behavior, raise questions about the realism of televised information, and encourage children to discuss it, they teach children to evaluate TV content rather than to accept it uncritically.

- Build on TV programs in constructive ways, encouraging children to move away from the set into active engagement with their surroundings. For example, a program on animals might spark a trip to the zoo or new ways of observing and caring for the family pet.

- Avoid excess television viewing, especially violent programs, yourself. Parental viewing patterns influence children's viewing patterns.

- Respond to children with warmth and reasonable demands for mature behavior. Children who experience these practices prefer programs with prosocial content and are less attracted to violent TV.

GENDER-STEREOTYPED BELIEFS AND BEHAVIOR

Recall from Chapter 6 that around age 2, children begin to label their own sex and that of other people. As soon as basic gender categories are established, children start to sort out what they mean in terms of activities and behavior. A wide variety of gender stereotypes are quickly mastered.

Preschoolers associate many toys, articles of clothing, tools, household items, games, occupations, and even colors (pink and blue) with one sex as opposed to the other (Ruble & Martin, 1998). And their actions fall in line with their beliefs—not only in play preferences, but in personality traits as well. We have already seen that boys tend to be more active, assertive, and overtly aggressive, whereas girls tend to be more fearful, dependent, compliant, emotionally sensitive, and relationally aggressive (Brody & Hall, 1993; Eisenberg & Fabes, 1998; Feingold, 1994; Saarni, 1993).

Over the preschool years, children's gender-stereotyped beliefs become stronger—so much so that they operate like blanket rules rather than flexible guidelines (Biernat, 1991; Martin, 1989). Once, when Leslie showed the children a picture of a Scottish bagpiper wearing a kilt, they insisted, "Men don't wear skirts!" During free play, they often exclaimed that girls don't drive fire engines and can't be police officers and boys don't take care of babies and can't be the teacher. These one-sided ideas are a joint product of gender stereotyping in the environment and young children's cognitive limitations. As we will see later, most preschoolers do not yet realize that characteristics *associated* with sex—activities, toys, occupations, hairstyle, and clothing—do not *determine* whether a person is male or female.

GENETIC INFLUENCES ON GENDER TYPING

The sex differences we have just described appear in many cultures around the world (Whiting & Edwards, 1988b). Certain of them—the preference for same-sex playmates as well as male activity level and overt aggression—are also widespread among animal species (Beatty, 1992). To what extent might gender typing be influenced by genetic factors?

Eleanor Maccoby (1990) argues that hormonal differences between males and females have important consequences for gender typing. Early on, hormones affect play styles, leading to rough, noisy movements among boys and calm, gentle actions among girls. Then, as children begin to interact with peers, they choose same-sex partners whose interests and behaviors are compatible with their own. Over the preschool years, girls increasingly seek out other girls and like to play in pairs because of a common preference for quieter activities. And boys come to prefer larger-group play with other boys, who share a desire to run, climb, play-fight, and build up and knock down. At age 4, children already spend three times as much time with same-sex as with other-sex playmates. By age 6, this ratio has climbed to 11 to 1 (Benenson, Apostoleris, & Parnass, 1997; Maccoby & Jacklin, 1987).

However, we must be careful not to overemphasize the role of heredity in gender typing. As we will see in the next section, a wide variety of environmental forces build on genetic influences to promote children's awareness of and conformity to gender roles.

ENVIRONMENTAL INFLUENCES ON GENDER TYPING

A wealth of evidence reveals that family influences, encouragement by teachers and peers, and examples in the broader social environment combine to promote the vigorous gender typing of early childhood.

■ THE FAMILY. Beginning at birth, parents hold different perceptions and expectations of their sons and daughters. Many parents state that they want their children to play with "gender-appropriate" toys, and they also believe that boys and girls should be reared differently. Parents are likely to describe achievement, competition, and control of emo-

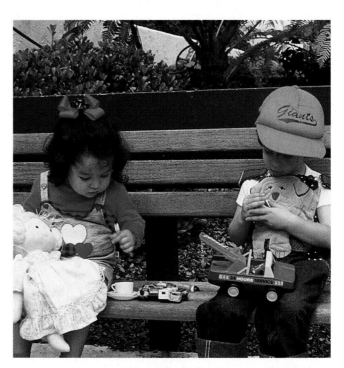

■ *Gender-stereotyped game and toy choices are present by age 2 and strengthen with age. Already, these 3-year-olds play in highly gender-stereotyped ways. (Photo courtesy: E. Zuckerman/ PhotoEdit)*

tion as important for sons and warmth, "ladylike" behavior, and close supervision of activities as important for daughters (Brooks-Gunn, 1986; Turner & Gervai, 1995).

These beliefs carry over into actual parenting practices. Mothers and fathers are far more likely to purchase guns, cars, and footballs for sons and dolls, tea sets, and jump ropes for daughters—toys that promote very different play styles. In addition, parents actively reinforce many gender-typed behaviors. For example, they react more positively when a young son plays with cars and trucks, demands attention, or tries to take toys from others (Fagot & Hagan, 1991; Leaper et al., 1995). In contrast, they more often direct play activities, provide help, and encourage participation in household tasks with a daughter (Lytton & Romney, 1991). Furthermore, parents converse differently with preschool boys and girls. Mothers more often *label emotions* when talking to girls, thereby teaching them to "tune in" to others' feelings. In contrast, they more often *explain emotions,* noting causes and consequences, to boys—an approach that emphasizes why it is important to control the expression of emotion (Cervantes & Callanan, 1998).

These factors are major influences in children's gender-role learning, since parents who consciously avoid behaving in these ways have less gender-typed children (Weisner & Wilson-Mitchell, 1990). Other family members also contribute to gender typing. For example, preschoolers with older, other-sex siblings have many more opportunities to imitate and participate in "cross-gender" play (Stoneman, Brody, & MacKinnon, 1986). In any case, of the two sexes, boys are clearly the more gender typed. One reason is that parents—particularly fathers—are far less tolerant of "cross-gender" behavior in their sons than in their daughters. They are more concerned if a boy acts like a sissy than if a girl acts like a tomboy (Gervai, Turner, & Hinde, 1995; Lytton & Romney, 1991).

■ TEACHERS. Besides parents, teachers encourage children's gender typing. Several times, Leslie caught herself promoting gender segregation and stereotyping in her classroom. One day, she called out, "Will the girls line up on one side and the boys on the other?" Then, as the class became noisy, she pleaded, "Boys, I wish you'd quiet down like the girls!"

As at home, girls get more encouragement to participate in adult-structured activities at preschool. They can frequently be seen clustered around the teacher, following directions in an activity. In contrast, boys more often choose areas of the classroom where teachers are minimally involved (Carpenter, 1983). As a result, boys and girls practice very different social behaviors. Compliance and bids for help occur more often in adult-structured contexts, whereas assertiveness, leadership, and creative use of materials appear more often in unstructured pursuits.

■ PEERS. Children's same-sex peer groups strengthen gender-stereotyped beliefs and behavior. By age 3, same-sex peers positively reinforce one another for gender-typed play by praising, imitating, or joining in the activity of an age-mate who shows a "gender-appropriate" response (Langlois & Downs, 1980). In contrast, when preschoolers engage in "gender-inappropriate" activities—for example, when boys play with dolls or girls with woodworking tools—they receive criticism from peers. Boys are especially intolerant of "cross-gender" play in their male companions (Fagot, 1984). A boy who frequently crosses gender lines is likely to be ignored by other boys even when he does engage in "masculine" activities!

Children also develop different styles of social influence in gender-segregated peer groups. To get their way with male peers, boys more often rely on commands, threats, and physical force, whereas girls emphasize polite requests, persuasion, and acceptance. These tactics succeed with other girls but not with boys, who pay little attention to girls' gentle tactics (Leaper, 1994; Leaper, Tenenbaum, & Shaffer, 1999). Consequently, an additional reason that girls may stop interacting with boys is that they do not find it very rewarding to communicate with an unresponsive social partner.

■ TELEVISION. Television is yet another powerful source of gender stereotypes. In TV programs, women appear less often than men, filling only one-fourth to one-third of character roles. Today, women are more often shown as involved in careers (Allan & Coltrane, 1996). But overall, they continue to be portrayed as young, attractive, emotional, victimized, and in romantic and family situations. In contrast men are depicted as dominant and powerful (Zillman, Bryant, & Huston, 1994). Gender stereotyping is especially strong in entertainment programs for children. For example, male cartoon characters are usually problem solvers, whereas females are sweet, childlike followers (Huston et al., 1992).

As television illustrates, children's everyday environments contain many examples of gender-typed behavior. As we will see in the next section, young children do not just imitate the many gender-linked responses they observe. They also start to view themselves and their environment in gender-biased ways, a perspective that can seriously limit their interests and skills.

GENDER IDENTITY

As adults, each of us has a **gender identity**—an image of oneself as relatively masculine or feminine in characteristics. By middle childhood, researchers can measure gender identity by asking children to rate themselves on personality traits. Individuals differ considerably in their responses. A child or adult with a "masculine" identity scores high on traditionally masculine items (such as self-sufficient, ambitious, and forceful) and low on traditionally feminine ones (such as affectionate, soft-spoken, and cheerful). Someone with a "feminine" identity does just the reverse. Although most individuals view themselves in gender-typed terms, a substantial minority (especially females) have a kind of gender identity called **androgyny.** They score high on *both* masculine and feminine characteristics (Bem, 1974; Boldizar, 1991).

Gender identity is a good predictor of psychological adjustment. Masculine and androgynous children and adults have higher self-esteem, whereas feminine individuals often think poorly of themselves, perhaps because many feminine traits are not highly valued in our society (Alpert-Gillis & Connell, 1989; Boldizar, 1991). Androgynous individuals are more adaptable in behavior—for example, able to show masculine independence or feminine sensitivity, depending on the situation (Taylor & Hall, 1982). Research on androgyny shows that it is possible for children to acquire a mixture of positive qualities traditionally associated with each gender—an orientation that may best help them realize their potential.

■ EMERGENCE OF GENDER IDENTITY. How do children develop a gender identity? Both social learning and cognitive-developmental answers exist. According to *social learning theory,* behavior comes before self-perceptions. Preschoolers first acquire gender-typed responses through modeling and reinforcement. Only then do they organize these behaviors into gender-linked ideas about themselves.

In contrast, *cognitive-developmental theory* regards the direction of development as the other way around. Over the preschool years, children first acquire a cognitive appreciation of the permanence of their sex. They develop **gender constancy,** the understanding that sex remains the same even if clothing, hairstyle, and play activities change. Then children use this idea to guide their behavior, and a preference for gender-typed activities appears (Kohlberg, 1966).

Research indicates that gender constancy is not present in most children until the end of the preschool years, when they pass Piagetian conservation tasks (De Lisi & Gallagher, 1991). Shown a doll whose hairstyle and clothing are transformed before their eyes, a child younger than age 6 is likely to insist that the doll's sex has changed as well (McConaghy, 1979). And when asked such questions as "When you (a girl) grow up, could you ever be a daddy?" or "Could you be a boy if you wanted to?" young children freely answer yes (Slaby & Frey, 1975).

Yet cognitive immaturity is not the only reason for preschoolers' poor performance on gender constancy tasks. It also results from limited social experience—in particular, lack of opportunity to learn about genital differences between the sexes. In many households in Western cultures, young children do not see members of the opposite sex

naked. Therefore, they distinguish males and females using the only information they do have—the way each gender dresses and behaves. Children as young as 3 who are aware of genital differences usually answer gender constancy questions correctly (Bem, 1989).

Is cognitive-developmental theory correct that gender constancy is responsible for children's gender-typed behavior? Evidence for this assumption is weak. "Gender-appropriate" behavior appears so early in the preschool years that modeling and reinforcement must account for its initial appearance, as social learning theory suggests. At present, researchers disagree on just how gender constancy contributes to gender-role development. But they do know that once children begin to reflect on gender roles, they form basic gender categories that strengthen gender-typed self-images and behavior. Yet another theoretical perspective shows how this happens.

■ GENDER SCHEMA THEORY. **Gender schema theory** is an information-processing approach to gender typing that combines social learning and cognitive-developmental features. It emphasizes that both environmental pressures and children's cognitions work together to shape gender-role development (Martin, 1993; Martin & Halverson, 1987). Beginning at an early age, children respond to instruction from others, picking up gender-stereotyped preferences and behaviors. At the same time, they start to organize their experiences into *gender schemas,* or masculine and feminine categories, that they use to interpret their world. A young child who says, "Only boys can be doctors," or, "Cooking is a girl's job," already has some well-formed gender schemas. As soon as preschoolers can label their own sex, they begin to select gender schemas consistent with it, applying those categories to themselves (Fagot & Leinbach, 1989; Martin & Little, 1990). As a result, their self-perceptions become gender typed and serve as additional schemas that they use to process information and guide their own behavior.

Let's look at the example in Figure 8.2 to see exactly how this network of gender schemas strengthens gender-typed preferences and behavior. Three-year-old Mandy has been taught that "dolls are for girls" and "trucks are for boys." She also knows that she is a girl. Mandy uses this information to make decisions about how to behave. Because her schemas lead her to conclude that "dolls are for me," when given a doll, she approaches it, explores it, and learns more about it. In contrast, on seeing a truck, she uses her gender schemas to conclude that "trucks are not for me" and responds by avoiding the "gender-inappropriate" toy. Gender schemas are so powerful that when children see others behaving in "gender-inconsistent" ways, they often cannot remember the information or distort it to make it "gender-consistent" (Liben & Signorella, 1993; Signorella & Liben, 1984).

FIGURE 8.2

■ **Impact of gender schemas on gender-typed preferences and behaviors.** Mandy's network of gender schemas leads her to approach and explore "feminine" toys, such as dolls, and to avoid "masculine" toys, such as trucks. (From C. L. Martin & C. F. Halverson, Jr., 1981, "A Schematic Processing Model of Sex Typing and Stereotyping in Children," *Child Development, 52,* p. 1121. © The Society for Research in Child Development, Inc. Adapted by permission.)

REDUCING GENDER STEREOTYPING IN YOUNG CHILDREN

How can we help young children avoid developing rigid gender schemas that restrict their behavior and learning opportunities? As the Lifespan Vista box on page 268 illustrates, when a nation makes a concerted effort to promote gender equality through its child and family policies, gender stereotyping is substantially reduced and life options across generations are enhanced.

In cultures in which values are slower to change, gender-linked associations are usually so pervasive that parents and teachers must work especially hard to prevent young children from absorbing them (Bem, 1998). Adults can begin by eliminating gender stereotyping from their own behavior and from the alternatives they provide for children. For example, mothers and fathers can take turns making dinner, bathing children, and driving the family car. They can provide sons and daughters with both trucks and dolls and pink and blue clothing. Teachers can make sure that all children spend some time each day in both adult-structured and unstructured activities. Also, efforts can be made to shield children from television and other media presentations that indicate males and females differ in what they can do.

Once children notice the vast array of gender stereotypes in their society, parents and teachers can point out exceptions. For example, they can arrange for children to see men and women pursuing nontraditional careers. And they can reason with children, explaining that interests and skills, not sex, should determine a person's occupation and activities. Research shows that such reasoning is very effective in reducing children's tendency to view the world in a gender-biased fashion (Bigler & Liben, 1992).

And as we will see in the next section, a rational approach to child rearing promotes healthy, adaptable functioning in many other areas as well.

ASK YOURSELF . . .

■ *Geraldine cut her 3-year-old daughter Fern's hair very short for the summer. When Fern looked in the mirror, she said, "I don't wanna be a boy," and began to cry. Why is Fern upset about her short hairstyle, and what can Geraldine do to help?*

 When 4-year-old Roger was in the hospital, he was cared for by a male nurse named Jared. After Roger recovered, he told his friends about Dr. Jared. Using gender schema theory, explain why Roger remembered Jared as a doctor, not a nurse. Why are gender schemas likely to persist, affecting children's thinking and behavior for years to come?

CHILD REARING AND EMOTIONAL AND SOCIAL DEVELOPMENT

Throughout this chapter and the previous one, we have seen how parents can foster their children's development—by serving as warm models and reinforcers of mature behavior, by using reasoning and inductive discipline, by avoiding harsh punishment, and by encouraging children to master new skills. Now let's put these elements together into an overall view of effective parenting.

A LIFESPAN VISTA

SWEDEN'S COMMITMENT TO GENDER EQUALITY: IMPACT ACROSS THE LIFESPAN

Of all nations in the world, Sweden is unique in its valuing of gender equality and its social programs that translate this commitment into action. Over a century ago, Sweden's ruling political party adopted equality as a central tenet. One social class was not to exploit another, nor one gender another. In the 1960s, Sweden's expanding economy required that women enter the labor force in large numbers. When the question arose as to who would help sustain family life, the Swedish populace called on the principle of equality and answered: fathers, just like mothers.

The Swedish "equal roles family model" maintains that husband and wife should have the same opportunity to pursue a career and be equally responsible for housework and child care. To support this goal, child-care centers had to be made available outside the home. Otherwise, a class of less privileged women might be exploited for caregiving and domestic work—an outcome that would contradict the principle of equality. And since full-time employment for both parents often strains a family with young children, Sweden mandated that mothers and fathers with chil-

dren under age 8 could reduce the length of their working day to 6 hours, with a corresponding reduction in pay but not in benefits (Sandqvist, 1992).

According to several indicators, Sweden's family model has affected the experiences, beliefs, and behaviors of both adults and young people. Maternal employment is extremely high; over 80 percent of mothers with infants or preschoolers work outside the home. Child-care centers are numerous, of high quality, and heavily subsidized by the government (Kallós & Broman, 1997). Although Swedish fathers do not yet share housework and child care equally with mothers, they are more involved than fathers in North America and other Western European nations. In one international study of 40 countries, Swedish men rated themselves lowest in "masculine" traits. On most, they fell at about the same level as Swedish women, and on some, below them (Hofstede, 1980). These findings provide further evidence that gender roles in Sweden are less differentiated than elsewhere.

Parenting of young children has also changed. In interviews with three generations of Swedish women about their childhoods, a shift toward more democratic child rearing and greater

freedom and independence appeared (Aström, 1986). Swedish parents try especially hard to be sensitive and empathic, to ensure participation in decision making, and to spend most of their free time with their children. These parenting characteristics, as we will see shortly, are consistently related to positive psychological outcomes for children.

Finally, a study of adolescent gender-related attitudes revealed that valuing the "masculine" over the "feminine" role was less pronounced in Sweden than in the United States. Swedish young people regarded each gender as a blend of instrumental and expressive traits. Furthermore, Swedish girls felt considerably better about their gender—a difference that might be due to greater equalization in men's and women's pay scales and a widespread attitude in Sweden that "feminine" work is important to society. Compared with American adolescents, Swedish young people more often viewed gender roles as a matter of learned tasks than as inborn personality traits or sets of rights and duties (Intons-Peterson, 1988).

Traditional gender typing is not completely eradicated in Sweden. But great progress has been made as a result of steadfastly pursuing a program of equal opportunity for males and females for several decades—an approach that has had a significant impact on the lives of children, adolescents, and adults.

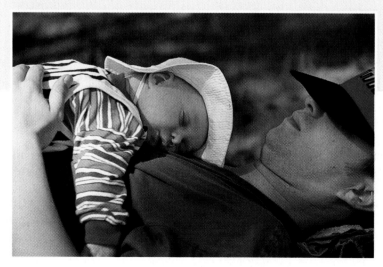

■ Sweden places a high value on gender equality. Swedish parents try especially hard to be sensitive and empathic, to ensure joint participation in decision making, and to spend most of their free time with their children. Compared with fathers in North America and other Western European nations, Swedish fathers are more involved in housework and child care. This Swedish father enjoys a paid paternity leave during the first 15 months of his child's life (see Chapter 3, page 104). (Photo courtesy: Alex Farnsworth/The Image Works)

CHILD-REARING STYLES

In a landmark series of studies, Diana Baumrind gathered information on child-rearing practices by watching parents interact with their preschoolers. Two broad dimensions of child rearing emerged. The first is *demandingness.* Some parents establish high standards for their children and insist that their youngsters meet those standards. Other parents demand very little and rarely try to influence their children's behavior. The second dimension is responsiveness. Some parents are accepting of and responsive to their children. They frequently engage in open discussion and verbal give-and-take. Others are rejecting and unresponsive. As Table 8.2 shows, the various combinations of demandingness and responsiveness yield four styles of child rearing. Baumrind's research focused on three of them: authoritative, authoritarian, and permissive.

■ AUTHORITATIVE CHILD REARING. The **authoritative style** is the most adaptive approach to child rearing. Authoritative parents make reasonable demands for maturity and enforce them by setting limits and insisting that the child obey. At the same time, they express warmth and affection, listen patiently to their child's point of view, and encourage participation in family decision making. Authoritative child rearing is a rational, democratic approach that recognizes and respects the rights of both parents and children.

Baumrind's findings revealed that children of authoritative parents were developing especially well. They were lively and happy, self-confident in their mastery of new tasks, and self-controlled (Baumrind, 1967). These children also seemed less gender typed. Girls scored particularly high in independence and desire to master new tasks and boys in friendly, cooperative behavior (Baumrind & Black, 1967).

■ AUTHORITARIAN CHILD REARING. Parents who use an **authoritarian style** are also demanding, but they place such a high value on conformity that they are unresponsive—even outright rejecting—when children are unwilling to obey. "Do it because I said so!" is the attitude of these parents. As a result, they engage in very little give-and-take with children, who are expected to accept the adult's word in an unquestioning manner. If the child does not, authoritarian parents resort to force and punishment.

Baumrind found that preschoolers with authoritarian parents were anxious, withdrawn, and unhappy. When interacting with peers, they tended to react with hostility when frustrated (Baumrind, 1967). Boys, especially, showed high rates of anger and defiance. Girls were dependent and lacking in exploration, and they retreated from challenging tasks (Baumrind, 1971).

■ PERMISSIVE CHILD REARING. The **permissive style** of child rearing is nurturant and accepting, but it

TABLE 8.2

A Two-Dimensional Classification of Parenting Styles

	RESPONSIVE	UNRESPONSIVE
DEMANDING	Authoritative parent	Authoritarian parent
UNDEMANDING	Permissive parent	Uninvolved parent

Source: Adapted from E. E. Maccoby & J. A. Martin, 1983, "Socialization in the Context of the Family: Parent–Child Interaction," in E. M. Hetherington (Ed.), *Handbook of Child Psychology: Vol. 4, Socialization, Personality, and Social Development* (4th ed., p. 39), New York: Wiley. Copyright ©1983 by John Wiley & Sons. Reprinted by permission.

avoids making demands or imposing controls of any kind. Permissive parents allow children to make many of their own decisions at an age when they are not yet capable of doing so. They can eat meals and go to bed when they feel like it and watch as much television as they want. They do not have to learn good manners or do any household chores. Although some permissive parents truly believe that this approach is best, many others lack confidence in their ability to influence their child's behavior and are disorganized and ineffective in running their households.

Baumrind found that children of permissive parents were very immature. They had difficulty controlling their impulses and were disobedient and rebellious when asked to do something that conflicted with their desires. They were also overly demanding and dependent on adults, and they showed less persistence on tasks at preschool than did children whose parents exerted more control. The link between permissive parenting and dependent, nonachieving behavior was especially strong for boys (Baumrind, 1971).

WHAT MAKES AUTHORITATIVE CHILD REARING SO EFFECTIVE?

Since Baumrind's early work, a great many studies have confirmed her findings. Throughout childhood and adolescence, authoritative parenting is associated with high self-esteem, social and moral maturity, and academic achievement (Eccles et al., 1997; Luster & McAdoo, 1996; Steinberg, Darling, & Fletcher, 1995).

Why does authoritative parenting work so well? First, control that appears fair and reasonable to the child, not abrupt and arbitrary, is far more likely to be complied with and internalized. Second, nurturant parents who are secure in the standards they hold for their children provide models of caring concern as well as confident, self-controlled behavior. Finally, authoritative parents make demands that are reasonable in terms of their child's developing capacities. By adjusting expectations to children's ability to take responsibility for their own behavior, these parents let children know that they are competent individuals who can do things successfully for themselves. As a result, high self-esteem and mature, independent behavior are fostered.

CULTURAL VARIATIONS

Despite broad agreement on the advantages of authoritative child rearing, ethnic groups often have distinct child-rearing beliefs and practices. Some involve variations in demandingness that are adaptive when viewed in light of cultural values and family living conditions.

For example, Chinese adults describe their parenting techniques as highly demanding. They are more directive in teaching and scheduling their children's time—an emphasis that reflects deeply ingrained Confucian beliefs in the importance of strict discipline, respect for elders, and teaching socially desirable behavior (Berndt et al., 1993; Chao, 1994; Huntsinger, Jose, & Larson, 1998). In Hispanic and Asian Pacific Island families, high parental control (particularly by the father) is paired with unusually high maternal warmth. This combination is believed to promote compliance and strong family commitment in children (Harrison et al., 1994).

Although wide variation among African-Americans exists, black mothers (especially those who are younger, less educated, and single) often rely on an adult-centered approach in which they expect immediate obedience from children (Kelley, Power, & Wimbush, 1992). Black parents may use very firm child rearing to promote self-reliance, self-control, and a vigilant approach to dangerous living conditions (Brody & Flor, 1998). Consistent with this view, in several studies, physical discipline in early childhood predicted aggression during the school years only for Caucasian-American children, not for African-American children (Deater-Deckard & Dodge, 1997; Deater-Deckard et al., 1996). This does not mean that slaps and spankings are effective strategies. But it

■ *Asked about their child-rearing practices, the grandparents and mother in this Chinese family would probably describe themselves as quite demanding. Yet clearly, the control they exert occurs in the context of high responsiveness—expressions of warmth and acceptance toward the child. (Photo courtesy: Ira Kirschenbaum/ Stock Boston)*

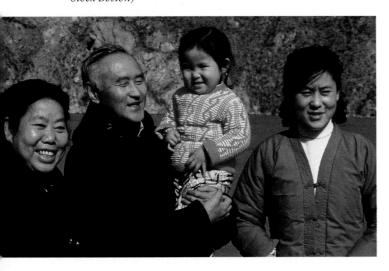

does suggest ethnic differences in how children view parental behavior that can modify its consequences. African-American parents who use "no-nonsense" discipline typically combine it with warmth and support, which predict favorable adjustment regardless of ethnicity (Petit, Bates, & Dodge, 1998).

Turn back to Table 8.2, and you will see that we have not yet considered the *uninvolved style* of parenting, which combines undemanding with indifferent, rejecting behavior. Often uninvolved parents are emotionally detached and depressed and so overwhelmed by life stress that they have little time and energy for children. At its extreme, uninvolved parenting is a form of child maltreatment called neglect. Especially when it begins early, it disrupts virtually all aspects of development, including attachment, cognition, and emotional and social skills (see Chapter 6, pages 180–181). As we turn now to the topic of child maltreatment, we will see that effective child rearing is sustained not just by the desire of mothers and fathers to be good parents. Almost all want to be. Unfortunately, when vital supports for good parenting break down, children as well as their parents can suffer terribly.

CHILD MALTREATMENT

Child maltreatment is as old as human history, but only recently has there been widespread acceptance that the problem exists and research aimed at understanding it. Perhaps the increase in public concern has occurred because child maltreatment is especially common in large industrialized nations. In the United States, 3 million cases were reported to juvenile authorities in 1997, an increase of 132 percent over the previous decade (U.S. Department of Health and Human Services, 1999c). The true figure is surely much higher, since most cases go unreported.

Child maltreatment takes the following forms:

- *Physical abuse:* assaults on children that produce pain, cuts, welts, bruises, burns, broken bones, and other injuries

- *Sexual abuse:* sexual comments, fondling, intercourse, and other forms of exploitation

- *Physical neglect:* living conditions in which children do not receive enough food, clothing, medical attention, or supervision

- *Emotional neglect:* failure of caregivers to meet children's needs for affection and emotional support

- *Psychological abuse:* actions, such as ridicule, humiliation, or terrorizing, that damage children's cognitive, emotional, or social functioning

Although all experts recognize that these five types exist, they differ on how frequent and intense an adult's actions must be to be called maltreatment. All of us can agree that broken bones, cigarette burns, and bite marks are abusive, but the decision is harder to make in instances in which an adult touches or makes degrading comments to a child (Barnett, Manly, & Cicchetti, 1993). Some investigators regard psychological and sexual abuse as the most destructive forms. The rate of psychological abuse may be the highest, since it accompanies most other types. Over 200,000 cases of child sexual abuse are reported each year (U.S. Department of Health and Human Services, 1999c). Yet this statistic greatly underestimates the actual number, since affected children feel frightened, confused, and guilty and are usually pressured into silence. Although children of all ages are targets, the largest number of sexual abuse victims are identified in middle childhood. Therefore, we will pay special attention to this form of maltreatment in Chapter 10.

■ ORIGINS OF CHILD MALTREATMENT. Early findings suggested that child maltreatment was rooted in adult psychological disturbance (Kempe et al., 1962; Spinetta & Rigler, 1972). But it soon became clear that although child maltreatment was more common among disturbed parents, a single "abusive personality type" did not exist. Sometimes even "normal" parents harmed their children! Also, parents who had been abused as children did not always repeat the cycle with their own youngsters (Buchanan, 1996; Simons et al., 1991).

For help in understanding child maltreatment, researchers turned to ecological systems theory (see Chapters 1 and 2). They discovered that many interacting variables—at the family, community, and cultural levels—promote child abuse and neglect. Table 8.3 summarizes factors associated with child maltreatment. The more of these risks that are present, the greater the likelihood that it will occur. Let's examine each set of influences in turn.

The Family. Within the family, certain children—those whose characteristics make them more of a challenge to rear—are more likely to become targets of abuse. These include premature or very sick babies and children who are temperamentally difficult, inattentive and overactive, or who have other developmental problems. But whether such children actually are maltreated depends on characteristics of parents (Belsky, 1993). In one study, temperamentally difficult youngsters who were physically abused had mothers who believed that they could do little to control the child's behavior. Instead, they attributed the child's unruliness to a stubborn or bad disposition, a perspective that led them to move quickly toward physical force when the child misbehaved (Bugental, Blue, & Cruzcosa, 1989).

Once child abuse gets started, it quickly becomes part of a self-sustaining family relationship. The small irritations to which abusive parents react—a fussy baby, a preschooler who knocks over a glass of milk, or a child who will not mind immediately—soon become bigger ones. Then the harshness of parental behavior increases. By the preschool years, abusive and neglectful parents seldom interact with their children. When they do, they rarely express pleasure and affection; the communication is almost always negative (Trickett et al., 1991).

Most parents, however, have enough self-control not to respond to their child's misbehavior with abuse, and not all children with developmental problems are mistreated. Other factors must combine with these conditions to prompt an extreme parental response. Unmanageable parental stress is strongly associated with all forms of maltreatment. Abusive parents respond to stressful situations with high emotional arousal. At the same time, low income, unemployment, marital conflict, overcrowded living conditions, frequent moves, and extreme household disorganization are common in abusive homes (Garbarino, 1997; Magura & Laudet, 1996). These personal and situational conditions increase the chances that parents will be too overwhelmed to meet basic child-rearing responsibilities or will vent their frustrations at their children (Pianta, Egeland, & Erickson, 1989).

TABLE 8.3

Factors Related to Child Maltreatment

FACTOR	DESCRIPTION
Parent characteristics	Psychological disturbance; alcohol and drug abuse; history of abuse as a child; belief in harsh, physical discipline; desire to satisfy unmet emotional needs through the child; unreasonable expectations for child behavior; young age (most under 30); low educational level
Child characteristics	Premature or very sick baby; difficult temperament; inattentiveness and overactivity; other developmental problems
Family characteristics	Low income; poverty; homelessness; marital instability; social isolation; physical abuse of mother by husband or boyfriend; frequent moves; large families with closely spaced children; overcrowded living conditions; disorganized household; lack of steady employment; other signs of high life stress
Community	Characterized by social isolation; few parks, child-care centers, preschool programs, recreation centers, and churches to serve as family supports
Culture	Approval of physical force and violence as ways to solve problems

Sources: Belsky, 1993; Cicchetti & Toth, 1998.

The Community. The majority of abusive and neglectful parents are isolated from both formal and informal social supports in their communities. There are at least two causes of this social isolation. First, because of their own life histories, many of these parents have learned to mistrust and avoid others. They do not have the skills necessary for establishing and maintaining positive relationships with friends and relatives (Polansky et al., 1985). Second, maltreating parents are more likely to live in poverty-stricken neighborhoods that provide few links between family and community, such as parks, child-care centers, preschool programs, recreation centers, and churches (Coulton et al., 1995). For these reasons, they lack "lifelines" to others and have no one to turn to for help during particularly stressful times.

The Larger Culture. Cultural values, laws, and customs profoundly affect the chances that parents who feel overburdened will maltreat their children. Societies that view violence as an appropriate way to solve problems set the stage for child abuse. These conditions exist in the United States. Although all 50 states have laws designed to protect children from maltreatment, strong support still exists for the use of physical force with children. For example, during the past 30 years, the United States Supreme Court twice upheld the right of school officials to use corporal punishment. Crime rates are high in American cities, and television sets beam graphic displays of violence into family living rooms. In view of the widespread acceptance of violent behavior in American culture, it is not surprising that over 90 percent of American parents report using slaps and spankings to discipline their children (Staub, 1996). In countries where physical punishment is not accepted, such as China, Japan, Luxembourg, and Sweden, child abuse is rare (Zigler & Hall, 1989).

■ CONSEQUENCES OF CHILD MALTREATMENT. The family circumstances of maltreated children impair the development of emotional self-regulation, empathy and sympathy, self-concept, and social skills. Over time, these youngsters show serious learning and adjustment problems, including academic failure, severe depression, difficulties with peers, substance abuse, and delinquency (Cicchetti & Toth, 1998a).

What explains these damaging consequences? Think back to our earlier discussion of hostile cycles of parent–child interaction, which are especially severe for abused children. Indeed, a family characteristic strongly associated with child abuse is domestic violence (Holden, Geffner, & Jouriles, 1998). Clearly, the home lives of abused children overflow with opportunities to learn to use aggression as a way of solving problems. The low warmth and control to which neglected children are exposed also promote aggressive, acting-out behavior (Miller et al., 1993).

Furthermore, demeaning parental messages, in which children are ridiculed, humiliated, rejected, or terrorized, result in low self-esteem, high anxiety, self-blame, and efforts to escape from extreme psychological pain—at times severe enough to lead to attempted suicide in adolescence (Sternberg et al., 1993). At school, maltreated children are serious discipline problems. Their noncompliance, poor motivation, and cognitive immaturity interfere with academic achievement—an outcome that further undermines their chances for life success (Eckenrode, Laird, & Doris, 1993).

■ PREVENTING CHILD MALTREATMENT. Since child maltreatment is embedded in families, communities, and society as a whole, efforts to prevent it must be directed at each of these levels. Many approaches have been suggested. These include interventions that teach high-risk parents effective child-rearing and disciplinary strategies, high school child development courses that include direct experience with children, and broad social programs aimed at bettering economic conditions for low-income families.

In earlier parts of this book, we saw that providing social supports to families is very effective in easing parental stress.

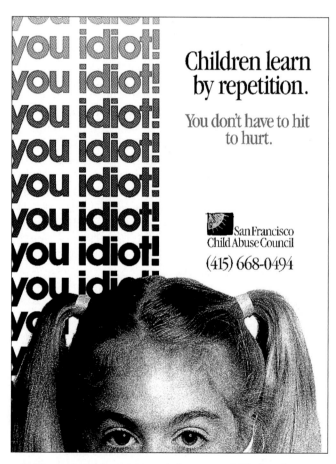

■ *Public service announcements help prevent child abuse by educating people about the problem and informing them of where to seek help. This poster reminds adults that degrading remarks can hit as hard as a fist. (Photo courtesy: San Francisco Child Abuse Council)*

It sharply reduces child maltreatment as well. Research indicates that a trusting relationship with another person is the most important factor in preventing mothers with childhood histories of abuse from repeating the cycle with their own youngsters (Caliso & Milner, 1992; Egeland, Jacobvitz, & Sroufe, 1988). Parents Anonymous, a national organization that has as its main goal helping child-abusing parents learn constructive parenting practices, does so largely through social supports. Its local chapters offer self-help group meetings, daily phone calls, and regular home visits to relieve social isolation and teach alternative child-rearing skills.

Even with intensive treatment, some adults persist in their abusive acts. An estimated 1,500 American children die from maltreatment each year (U.S. Department of Health and Human Services, 1999c). In cases in which parents are unlikely to change their behavior, taking the drastic step of separating parent from child and legally terminating parental rights is the only reasonable course of action.

Child maltreatment is a distressing and horrifying topic—a sad note on which to end our discussion of a period of childhood that is so full of excitement, awakening, and discovery. But there is reason to be optimistic. Great strides have been made over the past several decades in understanding and preventing child maltreatment.

ASK YOURSELF . . .

- *Earlier in this chapter, we discussed induction as an especially effective form of discipline. Of Baumrind's three child-rearing styles, which is most likely to be associated with use of induction, and why?*

- *Chandra heard a news report that 10 severely abused and neglected children, living in squalor in an inner-city tenement, were discovered by Chicago police. Chandra thought, "What could possibly lead parents to mistreat their children so badly?" How would you answer Chandra's question? Why are these children likely to suffer lasting impairments to development?*

SUMMARY

ERIKSON'S THEORY: INITIATIVE VERSUS GUILT

What personality changes take place during Erikson's stage of initiative versus guilt?

- According to Erikson, preschoolers develop a new sense of purposefulness as they grapple with the psychological conflict of **initiative versus guilt.** A healthy sense of initiative depends on resolving the Freudian Oedipus and Electra conflicts, in which conscience is formed through identification with the same-sex parent. Although Freud's ideas are no longer widely accepted, Erikson's image of initiative captures the emotional and social changes of early childhood.

SELF-DEVELOPMENT

Describe preschoolers' self-concepts and self-esteem.

- Preschoolers' **self-concepts** consist largely of observable characteristics and typical beliefs, emotions, and attitudes. Their increasing self-awareness underlies struggles over objects as well as first efforts to cooperate.

- Preschoolers' high **self-esteem** contributes to their mastery-oriented approach to the environment. However, even a little adult disapproval can undermine a young child's self-esteem and enthusiasm for learning.

EMOTIONAL DEVELOPMENT

Cite changes in understanding and expression of emotion during early childhood.

- Young children have an impressive understanding of the causes, consequences, and behavioral signs of basic emotions. By age 3 to 4, they are also aware of various strategies for emotional self-regulation. Temperament, modeling, and conversations about feelings influence preschoolers' capacity to handle negative emotion.

- Preschoolers experience self-conscious emotions more often as their self-concepts become better developed and they become increasingly sensitive to the praise and criticism of others. Empathy becomes more common over the preschool years. Temperament and parenting affect the extent to which empathy prompts **sympathy,** leading to **prosocial,** or **altruistic, behavior.**

PEER RELATIONS

Describe the development of peer sociability, the quality of preschoolers' friendships, and cultural and parental influences on early peer relations.

- During early childhood, interactive play with peers increases. According to Parten, it begins with **nonsocial activity,** shifts to **parallel play,** and then moves to **associative** and

cooperative play. However, preschoolers do not follow this straightforward developmental sequence. Solitary play and parallel play remain common throughout early childhood. Sociodramatic play becomes especially frequent and supports many aspects of emotional and social development. In collectivist societies, play with peers is highly cooperative.

- Preschoolers view friendship in concrete, activity-based terms. Their interactions with friends are especially positive and cooperative. Parents influence early peer relations by arranging informal peer play activities and offering guidance and examples of how to act toward others.

FOUNDATIONS OF MORALITY

What are the central features of psychoanalytic, behaviorist and social learning, and cognitive-developmental approaches to moral development?

- The psychoanalytic and behaviorist and social learning approaches to morality focus on how children acquire ready-made standards held by adults. In contrast to Freud's theory, discipline using fear of punishment and loss of parental love does not foster conscience development. Instead, **induction** is far more effective in encouraging self-control and prosocial behavior.

- Behaviorism and social learning theory regard reinforcement and modeling as the basis for moral action. Effective adult models of morality are warm, powerful, and practice what they preach. Harsh punishment does not promote moral internalization and socially desirable behavior. Alternatives, such as **time out** and withdrawal of privileges, can reduce the undesirable side effects of punishment as long as parents apply

them consistently, maintain a warm relationship with the child, and offer explanations for why the misdeed is wrong.

- The cognitive-developmental perspective views children as active thinkers about social rules. Preschoolers understand that disobeying moral rules is more serious than violating social conventions. Parents who discuss moral issues with their children help them reason about morality.

Describe the development of aggression in early childhood, including family and television as major influences.

- All children display aggression from time to time. During early childhood, **instrumental aggression** declines while **hostile aggression** increases. Two types of hostile aggression appear: **overt aggression,** more common among boys, and **relational aggression,** more common among girls.

- Ineffective discipline and a conflict-ridden family atmosphere promote and sustain aggression in children. Televised violence also promotes childhood aggression. Young children's limited understanding of TV content increases their willingness to accept uncritically and imitate what they see on TV. Teaching parents effective child-rearing practices, providing children with social problem-solving training, reducing family hostility, and shielding children from violent TV can reduce aggressive behavior.

GENDER TYPING

Discuss genetic and environmental influences on preschoolers' gender-stereotyped beliefs and behavior.

- **Gender typing** is well under way in the preschool years. Genetic factors play a role in boys' higher activity level and overt aggression and

children's preference for same-sex playmates. At the same time, parents, teachers, peers, television, and the broader social environment encourage many gender-typed responses.

Describe and evaluate the accuracy of major theories of the emergence of gender identity.

- Although most people have a traditional **gender identity,** some are **androgynous,** combining both masculine and feminine characteristics.

- According to social learning theory, preschoolers first acquire gender-typed responses through modeling and reinforcement and then organize them into gender-linked ideas about themselves. Cognitive-developmental theory suggests that **gender constancy** must be mastered before children develop gender-typed behavior. In contrast to cognitive-developmental predictions, gender-role behavior is acquired long before gender constancy.

- **Gender schema theory** is an information-processing approach to gender typing that combines social learning and cognitive-developmental features. As children acquire gender-stereotyped preferences and behaviors, they form masculine and feminine categories, or gender schemas, that they apply to themselves and use to interpret their world.

CHILD REARING AND EMOTIONAL AND SOCIAL DEVELOPMENT

Describe the impact of child-rearing styles on children's development, explain why authoritative parenting is effective, and note cultural variations in child rearing.

- Compared with the **authoritarian** and **permissive styles,** the **authoritative style** of child rearing promotes cognitive, emotional, and social competence. Warmth, explanations, and reasonable demands for mature behavior account for the effectiveness of the authoritative style. Certain ethnic groups, including Chinese, Hispanic, Asian Pacific Island, and African-American, rely on highly demanding parenting that appears adaptive in light of cultural values and family circumstances.

Discuss the multiple origins of child maltreatment, its consequences for development, and effective prevention.

- Child maltreatment is related to factors within the family, community, and larger culture. Child and parent characteristics often feed on one another to produce abusive behavior. Unmanageable parental stress and social isolation greatly increase the chances that abuse and neglect will occur. When a society approves of violence as a means of solving problems, child abuse is promoted.

- Maltreated children are impaired in emotional self-regulation, empathy and sympathy, self-concept, social skills, and learning in school. Over time, they show serious adjustment problems. Successful prevention of child maltreatment requires efforts at the family, community, and societal levels.

IMPORTANT TERMS AND CONCEPTS

androgyny (p. 266)

associative play (p. 253)

authoritarian style (p. 269)

authoritative style (p. 269)

cooperative play (p. 254)

gender constancy (p. 266)

gender identity (p. 265)

gender schema theory (p. 266)

gender typing (p. 262)

hostile aggression (p. 260)

identification (p. 249)

induction (p. 256)

initiative versus guilt (p. 248)

instrumental aggression (p. 260)

nonsocial activity (p. 253)

overt aggression (p. 260)

parallel play (p. 253)

permissive style (p. 269)

prosocial, or altruistic, behavior (p. 252)

relational aggression (p. 260)

self-concept (p. 249)

self-esteem (p. 249)

sympathy (p. 252)

time out (p. 258)

FYI FOR FURTHER INFORMATION AND HELP

Consult the companion website for this book, where you will find additional weblinks and associated learning activities: www.abacon.com/berk

CHILDREN'S TELEVISION

National Institute on Media and the Family
www.mediaandthefamily.org/home.html

An organization that provides research, education, and information on the impact of electronic media on children and families. Website features a rating system for evaluating various media, resources for parents and educators, and quizzes for evaluating family media habits.

CHILD ABUSE AND NEGLECT

Child Help USA, Inc.
www.childhelpusa.org

Promotes public awareness of child abuse through publications, media campaigns, and a speakers' bureau. Supports the National Child Abuse Hotline, (800) 4-A-CHILD. Callers may request information about child abuse or speak with a crisis counselor.

Parents Anonymous
www.parentsanon.org

Dedicated to prevention and treatment of child abuse. Local groups provide support to child-abusing parents and training in nonviolent child-rearing techniques.

National Clearinghouse on Child Abuse and Neglect Information
www.calib.com/nccanch

Provides information to states and communities wishing to develop programs and activities that identify, prevent, and treat child abuse and neglect.

M ILESTONES

OF DEVELOPMENT IN EARLY CHILDHOOD

AGE	PHYSICAL	COGNITIVE	LANGUAGE	EMOTIONAL/SOCIAL
2 years	■ Slower gains in height and weight than in toddlerhood. (208) ■ Balance improves, walking becomes better coordinated. (208) ■ Running, jumping, hopping, throwing, and catching develop. (218) ■ Puts on and removes some items of clothing. (218) ■ Uses spoon effectively. (218)	■ Make-believe becomes less dependent on realistic toys, less self-centered, and more complex. (222) ■ Can take the perspective of others in simple situations. (225) ■ Recognition memory well developed. (230) ■ Aware of the difference between inner mental and outer physical events. (231)	■ Vocabulary increases rapidly. (239) ■ Sentences follow basic word order of native language; grammatical markers are added. (240) ■ Displays effective conversational skills, such as turn taking and topic maintenance. (240) 	■ Begins to develop self-concept and self-esteem. (249) ■ Cooperation and instrumental aggression appear. (249, 260) ■ Understands causes, consequences, behavioral signs of basic emotions. (251) ■ Empathy increases. (252) ■ Gender-stereotyped beliefs and behavior increase. (264)
3–4 years	■ Running, jumping, hopping, throwing, and catching become better coordinated. (218) ■ Galloping and one-foot skipping appear. (218) ■ Rides tricycle. (218) ■ Uses scissors, draws first picture of a person. (218–219) ■ Can tell the difference between writing and nonwriting. (220) 	■ Notices transformations, reverses thinking, and has a basic understanding of causality in familiar situations. (226) ■ Classifies familiar objects hierarchically. (226) ■ Uses private speech to guide behavior in challenging tasks. (228) ■ Attention becomes more sustained and planful. (230) ■ Uses scripts to recall familiar experiences. (231) ■ Understands that both beliefs and desires can determine behavior. (231) ■ Aware of some meaningful features of written language. (232) ■ Counts small numbers of objects and grasps cardinality. (234)	■ Masters increasingly complex grammatical structures. (240) ■ Occasionally overextends grammatical rules to exceptions. (240) ■ Understands many culturally accepted ways of adjusting speech to fit the age, sex, and social status of speakers and listeners. (240) "Nose your touch!" "That's backwards!" 	■ Emotional self-regulation improves. (251) ■ Self-conscious emotions become more common. (252) ■ Nonsocial activity declines and joint, interactive play increases. (254) ■ Instrumental aggression declines and hostile aggression increases. (260) ■ Forms first friendships. (255) ■ Distinguishes moral rules from social conventions. (260) ■ Preference for same-sex playmates strengthens. (265)

AGE	PHYSICAL	COGNITIVE	LANGUAGE	EMOTIONAL/SOCIAL
5–6 years	■ Body is streamlined and longer-legged with proportions similar to those of adults. (208) ■ First permanent tooth erupts. (209) ■ Skipping appears. (218) ■ Shows mature throwing and catching patterns. (218) ■ Ties shoes, draws more elaborate pictures, writes name. (218–220)	■ Ability to distinguish appearance from reality improves. (226) ■ Attention continues to improve. (230) ■ Recall and scripted memory improve. (230–231) ■ Understands that letters and sounds are linked in systematic ways. (232) ■ Counts on and counts down, engaging in simple addition and subtraction. (234)	■ Vocabulary reaches about 10,000 words. (239) ■ Has mastered many complex grammatical forms. (240)	■ Ability to interpret, predict, and influence others' emotional reactions improves. (251) ■ Relies more on language to express empathy. (252) ■ Has acquired many morally relevant rules and behaviors. (256) ■ Gender-stereotyped beliefs and behavior continue to increase. (264) ■ Grasps the genital basis of sex differences and shows gender constancy. (266)

Note: Numbers in parentheses indicate the page on which each milestone is discussed.

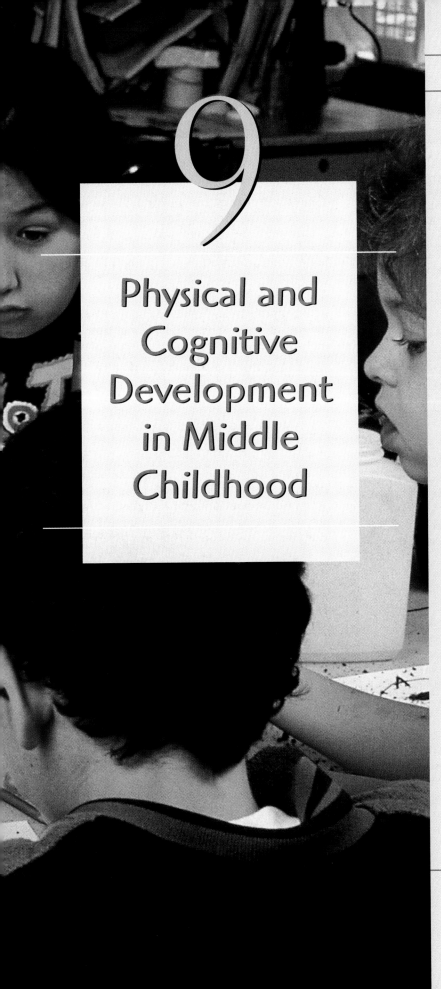

9

Physical and Cognitive Development in Middle Childhood

■ *An improved capacity to remember, reason, and reflect on one's own thinking makes middle childhood a time of dramatic advances in academic learning and problem solving. Here, fourth graders in an accelerated science class collaborate in testing soil samples for water absorbency. (Photo courtesy: Laura Dwight)*

"I'm on my way, Mom!" hollered 10-year-old Joey as he stuffed the last bite of toast into his mouth, slung his book bag over his shoulder, dashed out the door, jumped on his bike, and headed down the street for school. Joey's 8-year-old sister Lizzie followed, quickly kissing her mother good-bye and pedaling furiously until she caught up with Joey. Rena, the children's mother and one of my colleagues at the university, watched from the front porch as her son and daughter disappeared in the distance.

"They're branching out," Rena remarked to me over lunch that day as she described the children's expanding activities and relationships. Homework, household chores, soccer teams, music lessons, scouting, friends at school and in the neighborhood, and Joey's new paper route were all part of the children's routine. "It seems as if the basics are all there; I don't have to monitor Joey and Lizzie so constantly anymore. But being a parent is still very challenging. Now it's more a matter of refinements—helping them become independent, competent, and productive individuals."

Joey and Lizzie have entered middle childhood, which spans the years from 6 to 11. Around the world, children of this age are assigned new responsibilities. Joey and Lizzie, like other youngsters in industrialized nations, spend many long hours in school. Indeed, middle childhood is often called the "school years," since its onset is marked by the start of formal schooling. In village and tribal cultures, the school may be a field or a jungle. But universally, mature members of society guide children of this age period toward more realistic tasks that increasingly resemble those they will perform as adults (Rogoff, 1996).

This chapter focuses on physical and cognitive development in middle childhood—changes that are less spectacular than those of the earlier years. By age 6, the brain has reached 90 percent of its adult weight, and the body continues to grow slowly. In this way, nature grants school-age children the mental powers to master challenging tasks as well as added time to learn before reaching physical maturity.

We begin by reviewing typical growth trends, special health concerns, and gains in motor abilities. Then we return to Piaget's theory and the information-processing approach, which provide an overview of cognitive changes during the school years. Next, we examine the genetic and environmental roots of IQ scores, which often enter into important educational decisions. Our discussion continues with language, which blossoms further during middle childhood. Finally, we consider the importance of schools in children's learning and development.

BODY GROWTH

The rate of physical growth during the school years is an extension of the slow, regular pattern that characterized early childhood. At age 6, the average child weighs about 45 pounds and is 3½ feet tall. As Figure 9.1 shows, children add about 2 to 3 inches in height and 5 pounds in weight each year.

Look at Figure 9.1, and you will see that at ages 6 to 8 girls are slightly shorter and lighter than boys. By age 9, this trend reverses. Already, Rena noticed, Lizzie was starting to catch up with Joey in size. For many girls, the 10-year-old height spurt overlaps with the much more dramatic adolescent growth spurt, which takes place 2 years earlier in girls than boys.

Because the lower portion of the body is growing fastest, Joey and Lizzie appeared longer-legged than they had in early childhood. Rena discovered that they grew out of their jeans more quickly than their jackets and frequently needed larger shoes. As in early childhood, girls have slightly more body fat and boys more muscle. After age 8, girls begin accumulating fat at a faster rate, and they will add even more during adolescence (Tanner, 1990).

During middle childhood, the bones of the body lengthen and broaden. However, ligaments are not yet firmly at-

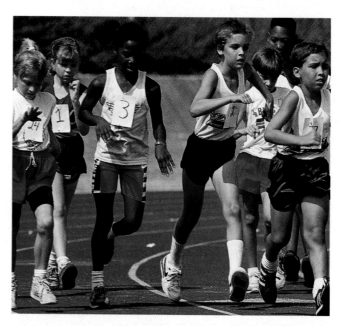

■ *During middle childhood, the lower portion of the body is growing fastest, so children appear longer-legged than they had in early childhood. They grow out of their jeans more quickly than their jackets and frequently need larger shoes. (Photo courtesy: Bob Daemmrich/The Image Works)*

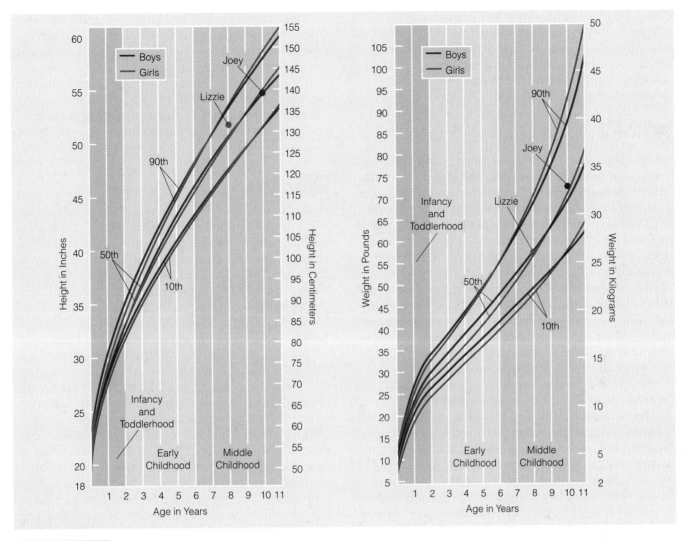

FIGURE 9.1

■ **Gains in height and weight during middle childhood among North American children.** The slow rate of growth established in early childhood extends into the school years. Girls are slightly shorter and lighter than boys until age 9, at which time this trend is reversed as girls approach the adolescent growth spurt. Eight-year-old Lizzie is beginning to catch up with 10-year-old Joey in physical size. Wide individual differences in body size continue to exist, as the percentiles on these charts reveal.

tached to bones. This, combined with increasing muscle strength, grants children unusual flexibility of movement as they turn cartwheels and perform handstands. As their bodies become stronger, many children experience a greater desire for physical exercise. Nighttime "growing pains"—stiffness and aches in the legs—are common as muscles adapt to an enlarging skeleton (Walco, 1997).

Between ages 6 and 12, all 20 primary teeth are replaced by permanent ones, with girls losing their teeth slightly earlier than boys. The first teeth to go are the lower and upper front teeth, giving many first and second graders a "toothless" smile. For a while, permanent teeth seem much too large. Growth of facial bones, especially the jaw and chin, gradually causes the child's face to lengthen and mouth to widen, accommodating the newly erupting teeth.

COMMON HEALTH PROBLEMS

Children like Joey and Lizzie, who come from economically advantaged homes, appear to be at their healthiest in middle childhood, full of energy and play. The cumulative effects of good nutrition, combined with rapid development of the body's immune system, offer greater protection against disease. At the same time, growth of the lungs permits more air to be exchanged with each breath, so children are better able to exercise vigorously without tiring.

Nevertheless, a variety of health problems do occur. We will see that many of them are more common among low-SES youngsters. Because economically disadvantaged families in the United States often lack health insurance (see Chapter 7), many youngsters do not have regular access to a doctor. And a substantial number also lack such basic necessities as a comfortable home and regular meals. Not surprisingly, poverty continues to be a powerful predictor of ill health during the school years.

VISION AND HEARING

The most common vision problem in middle childhood is *myopia,* or nearsightedness. By the end of the school years, nearly 25 percent of children are affected, a rate that rises to 60 percent by early adulthood. Heredity contributes to myopia, but the condition is also related to experience, since it has increased in recent generations (Sperduto et al., 1996). Parents often warn their children not to read in dim light or sit too close to the TV or computer screen, exclaiming, "You'll ruin your eyes." Their concern may be well founded. Myopia is one of the few health conditions that increases with family income and education. The more time people spend reading and doing other close-up work, the more likely they are to be myopic (Angle & Wissmann, 1980). Fortunately, for those youngsters who develop nearsightedness because they love reading, drawing, or model building, the condition can be corrected easily with glasses.

During middle childhood, the eustachian tube (canal that runs from the inner ear to the throat) becomes longer, narrower, and more slanted, preventing fluid and bacteria from traveling so easily from the mouth to the ear. As a result, ear infections become less frequent. Still, about 3 to 4 percent of the school-age population, and as many as 18 to 20 percent of low-income youngsters, develop permanent hearing loss from repeated ear infections (Mott, James, & Sperhac; 1990). Regular screening for both vision and hearing problems is important so that defects can be corrected before they lead to serious learning difficulties.

MALNUTRITION

School-age children need a well-balanced, plentiful diet to provide energy for successful learning in school and increased physical activity. Many youngsters are so focused on play, friendships, and new activities that they spend little time at the table. Readily available, healthy between-meal snacks—cheese, fruit, raw vegetables, and peanut butter—help meet nutritional needs in middle childhood.

As long as parents encourage healthy eating, the mild nutritional deficits that result from the child's busy daily schedule have no impact on development. But as we have seen in earlier chapters, many poverty-stricken children in developing countries and in the United States suffer from serious and prolonged malnutrition. By middle childhood, the effects are apparent in retarded physical growth, low intelligence test scores, poor motor coordination, inattention, and distractibility.

Unfortunately, when malnutrition persists for many years, permanent damage is done. Prevention through government-sponsored food programs beginning in the early years and continuing throughout childhood and adolescence is necessary. In studies carried out in Egypt, Kenya, and Mexico, quality of food (protein, vitamin, and mineral content) was far more important than quantity of food in predicting favorable cognitive development during the school years (Sigman, 1995; Wachs et al., 1995; Watkins & Pollitt, 1998).

OBESITY

Mona, a very overweight child in Lizzie's class, often stood on the sidelines and watched during recess. When she did join in the children's games, she was slow and clumsy. On a daily basis, Mona was the target of unkind comments: "Move it, Tubs!" "No fatsoes allowed!" On most afternoons, she walked home from school by herself while the other children gathered in groups, talking, laughing, and chasing. Once at home, Mona sought comfort in high-calorie snacks, which promoted further weight gain.

Mona is one of about 25 percent of American children who suffer from **obesity,** a greater-than-20-percent increase over average body weight, based on the child's age, sex, and physical build (U.S. Department of Health and Human Services, 1999c). Overweight and obesity are growing problems in affluent nations, especially the United States. Obesity is also rising in developing nations, as greater urbanization is accompanied by a shift toward sedentary lifestyles and diets high in refined foods, meats, and eggs (Popkin & Doak, 1998; Troiana & Flegal, 1998). And as the Lifespan Vista box on the following page reveals, growth stunting due to malnutrition leaves many children in developing countries vulnerable to later excessive weight gain.

Besides serious emotional and social difficulties, obese children are at risk for life-long health problems. High blood pressure and cholesterol levels along with respiratory abnormalities begin to appear in the early school years, symptoms that are powerful predictors of heart disease, adult-onset diabetes, certain forms of cancer, and early death.

■ CAUSES OF OBESITY. Not all children are equally at risk for becoming overweight. Fat children tend to have fat parents, and identical twins are more likely to share the disorder than are fraternal twins. But similarity among family members is not strong enough for genetics to account for more than a tendency to gain weight (Bouchard, 1994). One indication that environment is powerfully important is the consistent relation between SES and obesity. Low-SES youngsters in industrialized nations are not just at greater risk for malnutrition. They are also more likely to be overweight (Stunkard & Sørensen, 1993). Among factors responsible are lack of knowledge about healthy diet; a tendency to buy high-fat, low-cost foods; and family stress, which

A LIFESPAN VISTA

GROWTH STUNTING DUE TO MALNUTRITION: RISK FACTOR FOR CHILDHOOD OBESITY

In research on overweight children in four developing nations, a disheartening link between early growth stunting due to malnutrition and childhood obesity has emerged. Nationwide surveys in Brazil, China, Russia, and South Africa yielded information on height for age (a measure of poor diet and stunting) and weight for height (a measure of obesity) for thousands of children (Popkin, Richards, & Montiero, 1996). The proportion of children who were stunted (very short for their age) ranged from 15 percent in Brazil to 22 percent in China and 30 percent in South Africa. In Russia, stunting is a new problem. It has emerged only in the last 10 years, after poverty rose while government-sponsored maternal and child nutrition programs deteriorated. About 9 percent of Russian children are growth stunted.

As Figure 9.2 shows, in each country except Brazil, rate of overweight was far greater among stunted than nonstunted children. Short, growth-retarded children were twice as likely as their peers to be fat in South Africa, three times as likely in China, and seven times as likely in Russia. Family income seemed to account for the lack of association between stunting and fatness in Brazil; many overweight Brazilian children come from financially better-off homes. But in the other three countries, income had no impact on the stunting–overweight relationship.

What explains excessive weight gain among growth-stunted children? Researchers believe two physiological changes are involved:

- To protect itself, a malnourished body establishes a low basal metabolism rate, stretching its energy resources as far as possible—a

change that may endure after nutrition improves.

- Early malnutrition may cause brain structures responsible for appetite control to be reset at a higher level. Consequently, stunted children are likely to overeat when food—especially high-fat products—becomes more widely available as developing nations gain economically and modernize (Barker, 1994; Popkin, 1994).

The growth stunting–obesity link is evident among certain low-income, ethnic minorities in the United States, including Mexican-American and Hmong (Laotian) groups (Himes et al., 1992; Valdez et al., 1994). As economic conditions improve worldwide, a high-quality diet from the earliest ages may be vital for shielding children everywhere from an epidemic of obesity.

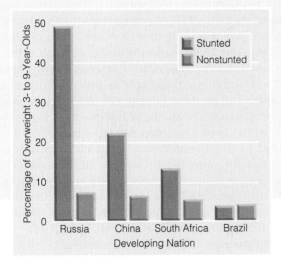

FIGURE 9.2

■ **Relationship of growth stunting to overweight among 3- to 9-year-olds in four developing nations.** Children identified as growth stunted were below the second percentile in height for their age, based on World Health Organization standards. Children identified as overweight were above the ninety-eighth percentile in weight for their height. Stunted children were twice as likely as their peers to be fat in South Africa, three times as likely in China, and seven times as likely in Russia. Family income seems to account for the lack of association between stunting and overweight in Brazil. (Adapted from Popkin, Richards, & Montiero, 1996.)

prompts overeating in some individuals. And 6 percent of American low-SES children are growth stunted due to malnutrition and therefore at increased risk for obesity (consult the Lifespan Vista box).

Parental feeding practices contribute to childhood obesity. In infancy and early childhood, some parents anx-

iously overfeed their children, interpreting almost all their discomforts as a desire for food. Others are overly controlling, constantly monitoring what their children eat. In either case, they fail to help children learn to regulate their own energy intake. Furthermore, parents of obese children often use food to reward other behaviors—a practice that leads children to attach greater value to the treat (Birch & Fisher, 1995). Gradually high-calorie snacks and desserts come to symbolize warmth, comfort, and relief of tension.

Because of these feeding experiences, obese children soon develop maladaptive eating habits (Johnson & Birch, 1994). They are more responsive to external stimuli associated with food—taste, sight, smell, and time of day—and less responsive to internal hunger cues than are normal-weight individuals (Ballard et al., 1980). They also eat faster and chew their food less thoroughly, a behavior pattern that appears as early as 18 months of age (Drabman et al., 1979).

Furthermore, fat children are less physically active than their normal-weight peers. This inactivity is both cause and consequence of their overweight condition. Recent evidence indicates that the rise in childhood obesity in the United States over the past 30 years is in part due to television viewing. Next to already existing obesity, time spent in front of the TV set is the best predictor of future obesity among school-age children (Gortmaker, Dietz, & Cheung, 1990). Television greatly reduces the time devoted to physical exercise, and TV ads encourage children to eat fattening, unhealthy snacks. When researchers gave third and fourth graders 18 lessons over 2 months in reducing TV viewing and videogame use, the children not only watched less but lost weight and body fat (Robinson, 1999).

Finally, the broader food environment affects the incidence of obesity. The Pima Indians of Arizona, who recently changed from a traditional diet of plant foods to an affluent, high-fat diet, have one of the highest rates of obesity in the world. Compared with descendants of their ancestors living in the remote Sierra Madre region of Mexico, the Arizona Pima have body weights 50 percent higher. Half the population has diabetes (8 times the national average), with many disabled by the disease in their twenties and thirties—blind, in wheelchairs, and on kidney dialysis (Gladwell, 1998; Ravussin et al., 1994). Although the Pima have a genetic susceptibility to overweight, it emerges only under Western dietary conditions.

■ PSYCHOLOGICAL CONSEQUENCES OF OBESITY. Unfortunately, physical attractiveness is a powerful predictor of social acceptance in Western societies. Both children and adults rate obese youngsters as less likable than children with a wide range of physical disabilities (Brenner & Hinsdale, 1978; Lerner & Schroeder, 1971). By middle childhood, obese children have a low sense of self-esteem, report feeling more depressed, and display more behavior problems than their peers. A vicious cycle emerges in which unhappiness and overeating contribute to one another, and the child remains overweight (Braet & Mervielde, 1997). As we will see in Chapter 13, these psychological consequences combine with continuing discrimination to result in reduced life chances in close relationships and employment.

■ TREATING OBESITY. Childhood obesity is difficult to treat because it is a family disorder. In Mona's case, the school nurse suggested that Mona and her obese mother enter a weight loss program together. But Mona's mother, unhappily married for many years, had her own reasons for overeating. She rejected this idea, claiming that Mona would eventually lose weight on her own.

When parents decide to seek treatment for an obese child, long-term changes in body weight do occur. A recent study found that the most effective intervention was family based and focused on changing behaviors. Both parent and child revised eating patterns, exercised daily, and reinforced each other with praise and points for progress, which they exchanged for special activities and times together. Follow-ups after 5 and 10 years showed that children maintained their weight loss more effectively than did adults—a finding that underscores the importance of intervening at an early age. Furthermore, weight loss was greater when treatments focused on both dietary and lifestyle changes, including regular vigorous exercise (Epstein et al., 1990, 1994).

Getting obese children to exercise, however, is challenging, since they find being sedentary so pleasurable. Rewarding them for spending less time inactive is helpful. In two studies, giving obese children tickets to the zoo or a baseball game (or similar rewards) for reducing sedentary time led to greater liking for physical activity and more weight loss than did rewarding them directly for exercising (Epstein, Saelens, & O'Brien, 1995: Epstein et al., 1997). Reinforcing children for giving up sedentary pursuits seems to increase

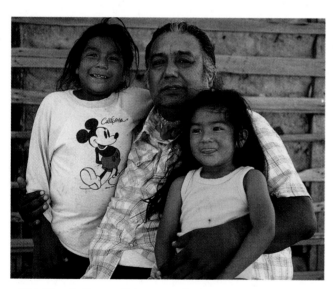

■ *This Pima Indian medicine man of Arizona is very obese. By the time his children reach adolescence, they are likely to follow in his footsteps. Because of a high-fat diet, the Pima residing in the Southwestern United States have one of the highest rates of obesity in the world. In contrast, the Pima living in the remote Sierra Madre region of Mexico are average weight. (Photo courtesy: Stephen Trimble)*

their sense of personal control over exercising—a factor linked to sustained physical activity.

BEDWETTING

One Friday afternoon, Terry called Joey to see if he could sleep over, but Joey refused. "I can't," said Joey anxiously, without giving an explanation.

"Why not? We can take our sleeping bags out in the backyard. Come on, it'll be super!"

"My mom won't let me," Joey responded, unconvincingly. "I mean, well, I think we're busy, we're doing something tonight."

"Gosh, Joey, this is the third time you've said no. See if I'll ask *you* again!" snapped Terry as he hung up the phone.

Joey is one of 8 percent of American school-age children who suffer from **nocturnal enuresis,** or bedwetting during the night (Rappaport, 1993). Enuresis evokes considerable distress in children and parents alike. In the overwhelming majority of cases, the problem has biological roots. Heredity is a major contributing factor. Parents with a history of bedwetting are far more likely to have a child with the problem, and identical twins share the problem more often than do fraternal twins (Christophersen & Edwards, 1992). Enuresis is unrelated to the depth of a child's sleep. Most often, it is caused by a failure of muscular responses that inhibit urination or a hormonal imbalance that permits too much urine to accumulate during the night (Houts, 1991). Punishing a school-age child for wetting is only likely to make matters worse.

The most effective treatment for enuresis is a urine alarm that wakes the child at the first sign of dampness and works according to conditioning principles. Success rates of about 60 to 70 percent occur after 4 to 6 months of treatment. Most children who relapse achieve dryness after trying the alarm a second time (Houts, Berman, & Abramson, 1994). Although many children outgrow enuresis without any form of intervention, it generally takes years for them to do so.

ILLNESSES

Children experience a somewhat higher rate of illness during the first 2 years of elementary school than they will later, due to exposure to sick children, an immune system that is not yet mature, and greater physical activity, which sometimes leads to physical injury. Allergies, colds, influenza, muscle sprains, and bone fractures are common reasons for missing school.

But the most frequent cause of school absence and childhood hospitalization is *asthma*, a condition in which the bronchial tubes (passages that connect the throat and lungs) are highly sensitive (Kliewer, 1997). In response to a variety of stimuli, such as cold weather, infection, exercise, or allergies, they fill with mucus and contract, leading to cough-

ing, wheezing, and serious breathing difficulties. The number of children with asthma has increased by 40 percent over the last decade. Today, 6 to 12 percent of American youngsters are affected, and asthma-related deaths have risen in recent years (Chadwick, 1996; Creer & Bender, 1995).

Although heredity contributes to asthma, researchers believe that environmental factors are necessary to spark the illness. Boys, African-American children, and children who had low birth weights, whose parents smoke, and who live in poverty are at greatest risk (Kay, Mortimer, & Jaron, 1995). Perhaps black and poverty-stricken youngsters experience a higher rate of asthma because of pollution in inner-city areas (which triggers allergic reactions), stressful home lives, and lack of access to good health care.

UNINTENTIONAL INJURIES

As we conclude our discussion of threats to children's health during the school years, let's return for a moment to the topic of unintentional injuries (discussed in detail in Chapter 7). As Figure 9.3 shows, the frequency of injury fatalities increases from middle childhood into adolescence, with the rate for boys rising considerably above that for girls.

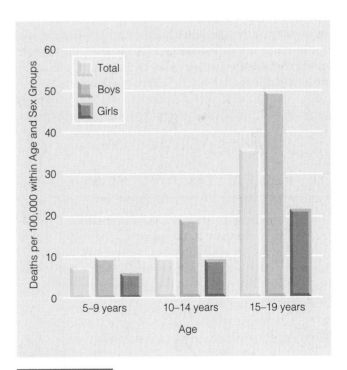

FIGURE 9.3

■ **Rate of injury mortality in the United States from middle childhood to adolescence.** Injury fatalities increase, and the gap between boys and girls expands. Motor vehicle (passenger and pedestrian) accidents are the leading cause, with bicycle injuries next in line. (From U.S. Department of Health and Human Services, 1999c.)

Motor vehicle accidents, with children as passengers or pedestrians, continue to be the leading cause of injury, with bicycle accidents next in line (U.S. Department of Health and Human Services, 1999c). Pedestrian injuries most often result from midblock dart-outs, bicycle accidents from disobeying traffic rules. Young school-age children are not yet good at thinking before they act, especially when many stimuli impinge on them at once (Tuchfarber, Zins, & Jason, 1997). They need frequent reminders, supervision, and prohibitions against venturing into busy traffic on their own.

As children range farther from home, safety education becomes especially important. School-based programs with lasting effects use extensive modeling, role playing, and rehearsal of safety practices; give children feedback about their performance along with praise and tangible rewards for acquiring safety skills; and provide occasional booster sessions (Zins et al., 1994). An important part of injury prevention is educating parents about children's age-related safety capacities, since parents often overestimate their child's safety knowledge and behavior (Rivara, 1995).

By middle childhood, the greatest risk-takers tend to be children whose parents do not act as safety-conscious models or who try to enforce rules with punitive or inconsistent discipline. These child-rearing techniques, as we saw in Chapter 8, spark defiance in children and may actually promote high-risk behavior. Highly active, impulsive boys remain particularly susceptible to injury. Although they have just as much safety knowledge as their peers, they are far less likely to implement it (Mori & Peterson, 1995). The greatest challenge for injury control programs is how to reach these "difficult to reach" youngsters, alter their family contexts, and reduce the dangers to which they are exposed.

MOTOR DEVELOPMENT AND PLAY

Gains in body size and muscle strength support improved motor coordination during middle childhood. In addition, greater cognitive and social maturity permit older children to use their new motor skills in more complex ways. A major change in children's play takes place at this time.

GROSS MOTOR DEVELOPMENT

During middle childhood, running, jumping, hopping, and ball skills become more refined. Third to sixth graders burst into sprints as they race across the playground, jump quickly over rotating ropes, engage in intricate patterns of hopscotch, kick and dribble soccer balls, bat at balls pitched by their classmates, and balance adeptly as they walk toe-to-toe across narrow ledges. These diverse skills reflect gains in four basic motor capacities:

- *Flexibility.* Compared with the movements of preschoolers, those of school-age children are more pliable and elastic, a difference that can be seen as children swing a bat, kick a ball, jump over a hurdle, and execute tumbling routines.

- *Balance.* Improved balance supports advances in many athletic skills, including running, hopping, skipping, throwing, kicking, and the rapid changes of direction required in many team sports.

- *Agility.* Greater quickness and accuracy of movement are evident in the fancy footwork of jump rope and hopscotch, as well as in the forward, backward, and sideways motions older children use as they dodge opponents in tag and soccer.

- *Force.* Older youngsters can throw and kick a ball harder and propel themselves farther off the ground when running and jumping than they could at earlier ages (Cratty, 1986).

Although body growth contributes greatly to school-age children's improved motor performance, more efficient information processing also plays an important role. Steady improvements in reaction time occur, with 14-year-olds responding almost twice as quickly as 6-year-olds (Kail, 1991; Southard, 1985). As a result, younger children often have difficulty with skills that require immediate responding, such as batting and dribbling. Since 6- and 7-year-olds are seldom successful at batting a thrown ball, T-ball is more appropriate for them than baseball. And handball, four-square, and kickball should precede instruction in tennis, basketball, and football (Seefeldt, 1996).

■ *This Chinese third grader is well along in mastering writing. She can form many Chinese characters. Here she prints the Roman alphabet during her English lesson. (Photo courtesy: Laura Berk)*

Ted's Picture with Label

RETURN OF THE ÜEDI

Ted's Space Trip Story

The rocket is blasting off! They are going through 100 galaxies! People are climbing a ladder to see them. It has a special shield all around it. In case there is an attack on the rocket. Because you never know. They are on TV also.

Ted's War of 1812 Essay

There were several reasons that Congress declared war with Britain. First, the British attacked American ships to keep France from obtaining supplies. Second, Britain kidnapped American sailors. But Britain claimed that they were deserters, and Britain forced sailors to serve the British Navy. Third, settlers feared the British in Canada because they wanted to claim land in Canada. Fourth, all peaceful solutions failed. So that's what caused the War of 1812.

FIGURE 9.4

■ **Fine motor coordination improves over middle childhood, as these writing samples reveal.** At age 5, Ted printed in large upper-case letters, asking for help in spelling the words. By age 7, he had mastered the lowercase alphabet, and his printing was small and evenly spaced. At age 9, he used cursive writing. Notice, also, how letter reversals and invented spellings decline with age. (Ted's picture with label and space trip story from L. M. McGree & D. J. Richgels, 1990, *Literacy's Beginnings: Supporting Young Readers and Writers,* Boston: Allyn and Bacon, p. 312. Reprinted by permission of the authors. Ted's War of 1812 essay from D. J. Richgels, L. M. McGee, & E. A. Slaton, 1989, "Teaching Expository Text Structure in Reading and Writing," in K. D. Muth, Ed., *Children's Comprehension of Text,* Newark, DE: International Reading Association, p. 180. Reprinted by permission.)

FINE MOTOR DEVELOPMENT

Fine motor development also improves steadily over the school years. On rainy afternoons, Joey and Lizzie could be found experimenting with yo-yos, building model airplanes, and weaving pot holders on small looms. Like many children, they took up musical instruments, which demand considerable fine motor control.

By age 6, most children can print the alphabet, their first and last names, and the numbers from 1 to 10 with rea-sonable clarity. However, as Figure 9.4 reveals, their writing tends to be quite large because they use the entire arm to make strokes rather than just the wrist and fingers. Children usually master uppercase letters first because their horizontal and vertical motions are easier to control than the small curves of the lowercase alphabet. Legibility of writing gradually increases as children produce more accurate letters with uniform height and spacing. These improvements prepare children for mastering cursive writing by third grade.

FIGURE 9.5

▪ **Increase in organization, detail, and depth cues in school-age children's drawings.** Compare both drawings to the one by a 6-year-old on page 219. In the drawing on the left, an 8-year-old depicts her family—father, mother, and three children. Notice how all parts are depicted in relation to one another, and the human figures are given much more detail. (The artist is your author, as a third grader. In the drawing, Laura can be found between her older sister and younger brother.) Integration of depth cues increases dramatically over the school years, as shown in the drawing on the right, by a 10-year-old artist from Singapore. Here, depth is indicated by overlapping objects, diagonal placement, and converging lines, as well as by making distant objects smaller than near ones. (Photos courtesy: Laura Berk and International Museum of Children's Art)

Children's drawings show dramatic gains in middle childhood. By the end of the preschool years, children can accurately copy many two-dimensional shapes, and they integrate these into their drawings. Some depth cues have also begun to appear, such as making distant objects smaller than near ones (Braine et al., 1993). Around 9 to 10 years, the third dimension is clearly evident through overlapping objects, diagonal placement, and converging lines. Furthermore, as Figure 9.5 shows, school-age children not only depict objects in considerable detail, but relate them to one another as part of an organized whole (Case, 1998; Case & Okamoto, 1996).

SEX DIFFERENCES

Sex differences in gross motor skills that appeared during the preschool years extend into middle childhood and, in some instances, become more pronounced. Girls remain ahead in the fine motor area, including handwriting and drawing. They also continue to have an edge in skipping, jumping, and hopping, which depend on balance and agility. But on all other gross motor skills, boys outperform girls, and in throwing and kicking, the gender gap is large (Cratty, 1986).

School-age boys' genetic advantage in muscle mass is not great enough to account for their superiority in so many

gross motor skills. Instead, environment plays a much larger role. In a study of over 800 elementary school pupils, children of both sexes viewed sports in a gender-stereotyped fashion—as much more important for boys. And boys more often stated that it was vital to their parents that they participate in athletics. These attitudes affected children's self-confidence and behavior. Girls saw themselves as having less talent at sports, and by sixth grade they devoted less time to athletics than did their male classmates (Eccles & Harold, 1991; Eccles, Jacobs, & Harold, 1990).

Special measures need to be taken to raise girls' confidence that they can do well at sports. Educating parents about the minimal differences in school-age boys' and girls' physical capacities and sensitizing them to unfair biases against girls' athletic ability may prove helpful. In addition, greater emphasis on skill training for girls along with increased attention to their athletic achievements in schools and communities is likely to improve their performance. Middle childhood is a crucial time to take these steps, since school-age children are starting to discover what they are good at and to make some definite skill commitments.

ORGANIZED GAMES WITH RULES

The physical activities of school-age children reflect an important advance in the quality of their play: Organized games with rules become common. In cultures around the world, the variety of children's spontaneous, rule-based games is enormous. Some are variants on popular sports, such as soccer, baseball, and basketball. Others are well-known childhood games, such as tag, jacks, and hopscotch. Children have also invented hundreds of additional games, including red rover, statues, leapfrog, kick the can, and prisoner's base (Sierra & Kaminski, 1995).

Gains in perspective taking—in particular, children's ability to understand the roles of several players in a game—permit this transition to rule-oriented games. Their contribution to development is great. Child-invented games usually involve simple physical skills and a sizable element of luck. As a result, they rarely become contests of individual ability. Instead, they permit children to try out different styles of competing, winning, and losing with little personal risk. Also, in their efforts to organize a game, children discover why rules are necessary and which ones work well. In fact, children often spend as much time working out the details of how a game should proceed as they do playing the game itself! As we will see in Chapter 10, these experiences help children form more mature concepts of fairness and justice.

Today, television, video games, and adult-organized sports (such as Little League Baseball and city soccer and hockey leagues) fill many hours that children used to devote to spontaneous play. Some researchers worry that adult-structured athletics, which mirror professional sports, are endangering their development. So far, research indicates

■ *Is this coach careful to encourage rather than criticize? To what extent does he emphasize teamwork, fair play, courtesy, and skill development over winning? These factors determine whether or not adult-organized sports are pleasurable, constructive experiences for children. (Photo courtesy: Lawrence Migdale/Photo Researchers)*

that for most children, these experiences do not result in psychological damage (Smoll & Smith, 1996). But the arguments of critics are valid in some cases. Children who join teams so early that the skills demanded are beyond their capabilities soon lose interest (Bailey & Rasmussen, 1996). And when parents and coaches are critical and do not let players forget about defeat, a few children react with intense anxiety. Eventually, they may avoid athletics entirely. The Caregiving Concerns table below summarizes the pros and cons of adult-organized athletics and suggests ways to make them positive experiences in the lives of children.

CAREGIVING CONCERNS

Pros and Cons of Adult-Organized Sports in Middle Childhood

PROS	CONS	RECOMMENDATIONS FOR COACHES AND PARENTS
Adult-structured athletics prepares children for realistic competition—the kind they may face as adults.	Adult involvement leads games to become overly competitive, placing too much pressure on children.	Permit children to select from among appropriate activities the ones that suit them best. Do not push children into sports they do not enjoy.
Regularly scheduled games and practices ensure that children get plenty of exercise and fill free time that might otherwise be devoted to less constructive pursuits.	When adults control the game, children learn little about leadership, followership, and fair play. When adults assign children to specific roles (such as catcher, first base), children lose the opportunity to experiment with rules and strategies.	For children younger than age 9, emphasize basic skills, such as kicking, throwing, and batting, and simplified games that grant all participants adequate playing time. Permit children to progress at their own pace and to play for the fun of it, whether or not they become expert athletes. Adjust practice time to children's attention spans and need for unstructured time with peers, with family, and for homework. Two practices a week, each no longer than 30 minutes for younger school-age children and 60 minutes for older school-age children, are sufficient.
Children get instruction in physical skills necessary for future success in athletics.	Highly structured, competitive sports are less fun than child-organized games; they resemble "work" more than "play."	Emphasize effort, skill gains, and teamwork rather than winning. Avoid criticism for errors and defeat, which promote anxiety and avoidance of athletics.
Parents and children share an activity that both enjoy.		Involve children in decisions about team rules. To strengthen desirable responses, reinforce compliance rather than punishing noncompliance.

Sources: Kolata, 1992; Smith & Smoll, 1997.

PHYSICAL EDUCATION

Physical activity supports many aspects of children's development—the health of their bodies, their sense of self-worth as active and capable beings, and the cognitive and social skills necessary for getting along with others. Yet only one-third of elementary school pupils have a daily physical education class. The average school-age child gets only 20 minutes of physical education a week (Steinhardt, 1992; Wurtele, 1996).

On their own, American children often do not get enough vigorous physical activity. Many ride to and from school in buses and cars, sit in classrooms most of the day, and watch TV for 3 to 4 hours after they return home. The National Children and Youth Fitness Study, which tested thousands of schoolchildren on a variety of fitness items (such as pull-ups, sit-ups, and one-mile run), found that only two-thirds of 10- to 12-year-old boys and half of 10- to 12-year-old girls met basic fitness standards for children their age (Looney & Plowman, 1990).

Besides offering more frequent physical education classes, many experts believe that schools need to change their physical education programs. Training in competitive sports is a high priority, but it is unlikely to reach the least physically fit youngsters, who draw back when an activity demands a high level of skill (Portman, 1995). Instead, programs should emphasize informal games that most children can perform well and individual exercise—walking, running, jumping, tumbling, and climbing. Furthermore, children of varying skill levels tend to sustain physical activity when teachers focus on each child's progress and contribution to team accomplishment (Whitehead & Corbin, 1997). Then physical education fosters a healthy lifestyle and a positive sense of self while satisfying school-age children's need for relatedness.

ASK YOURSELF . . .

■ *Joey complained to his mother one evening that it wasn't fair that his younger sister Lizzie was almost as tall as he was. He worried that he wasn't growing fast enough. How should Rena respond to Joey's concern?*

Joshua is a South African child whose growth is stunted due to malnutrition. Maggy is an overweight Pima Indian child who lives in Arizona. Explain why both Joshua and Maggy are at risk for obesity and lifelong health problems.

■ *On Saturdays, 8-year-old Gina gathers with friends at a city park to play kickball. Besides improved ball skills, what is she learning?*

■ *Physical activity supports many aspects of children's development—the health of their bodies, their sense of self-worth as active and capable beings, and the cognitive and social skills necessary for getting along with others. These Chinese elementary school pupils play relay races during their physical education class. (Photo courtesy: Ann & Myran Sutton/FPI International)*

COGNITIVE DEVELOPMENT

Finally!" Lizzie exclaimed the day she entered first grade. "Now I get to go to real school just like Joey!" Rena remembered how 6-year-old Lizzie had walked confidently into her classroom, pencils, crayons, and writing pad in hand, ready for a more disciplined approach to learning than she had experienced in early childhood.

Lizzie entered a whole new world of challenging mental activities. In a single morning, she and her classmates wrote in journals, met in reading groups, worked on addition and subtraction, and sorted leaves gathered on the playground for a science project. As Lizzie and Joey moved through the elementary school grades, they tackled increasingly complex tasks and became more accomplished at reading, writing, math skills, and general knowledge of the world. Cognitive development had prepared them for this new phase.

PIAGET'S THEORY: THE CONCRETE OPERATIONAL STAGE

When Lizzie visited my child development class as a 4-year-old, she was easily confused by Piaget's conservation problems. For example, in conservation of liquid, she insisted that the amount of water had changed after it had been poured from a tall, narrow container into a short, wide one. At age 8, when Lizzie returned, these tasks were easy. "Of course it's the same," she exclaimed. "The water's shorter but it's also wider. Pour it back," she instructed the college student who was interviewing her. "You'll see, it's the same amount!"

ACHIEVEMENTS OF THE CONCRETE OPERATIONAL STAGE

Lizzie has entered Piaget's **concrete operational stage,** which spans the years from 7 to 11. During this period, thought is far more logical, flexible, and organized than it was during early childhood.

■ CONSERVATION. The ability to pass *conservation tasks* provides clear evidence of *operations*—mental actions that obey logical rules. Notice how Lizzie coordinates several aspects of the task rather than *centering* on only one. She is capable of **decentration;** she recognizes that a change in one aspect of the water (its height) is compensated for by a change in another aspect (its width). Lizzie also demonstrates **reversibility,** the capacity to think through a series of steps and then mentally reverse direction, returning to the starting point. Recall from Chapter 7 that reversibility is part of every logical operation. It is solidly achieved in middle childhood.

■ HIERARCHICAL CLASSIFICATION. By the end of middle childhood, children pass Piaget's *class inclusion problem* (see page 225). This indicates that they are more aware of classification hierarchies and can focus on general and specific categories at the same time (Hodges & French, 1988). You can see this in children's play activities. Collections—stamps, coins, baseball cards, rocks, bottle caps, and more—become common in middle childhood. At age 10, Joey spent hours sorting and resorting his large box of baseball cards. At times he grouped them by league and team, at other times by playing position and batting average. He could separate the players into a variety of classes and subclasses and flexibly move back and forth between them.

■ SERIATION. The ability to order items along a quantitative dimension, such as length or weight, is called **seriation.** To test for it, Piaget asked children to arrange sticks of different lengths from shortest to longest. Older preschoolers can create the series, but they make many errors and take a long time to correct them. In contrast, 6- to 7-year-olds are guided by an orderly plan. They create the series efficiently by beginning with the smallest stick, then moving to the next smallest, and so on, until the ordering is complete.

The concrete operational child's improved grasp of quantitative arrangements is also evident in a more challenging seriation problem—one that requires children to se-

■ *An improved ability to categorize underlies children's interest in collecting objects during middle childhood. These older school-age children sort baseball cards into an elaborate structure of classes and subclasses. (Photo courtesy: Bob Daemmrich/The Image Works)*

riate mentally. This ability is called **transitive inference.** In a well-known transitive inference problem, Piaget showed children pairings of differently colored sticks. From observing that Stick A is longer than Stick B and Stick B is longer than Stick C, children must make the mental inference that A is longer than C. Not until age 9 or 10 do children perform well on this task (Chapman & Lindenberger, 1988).

■ SPATIAL REASONING. Piaget found that school-age youngsters have a more accurate understanding of space, as illustrated by their ability to give directions. When asked to name an object to the left or right of another person, 5- and 6-year-olds answer incorrectly; they simply apply their own frame of reference. Between 7 and 8 years, children start to perform *mental rotations*, in which they align the self's frame to match that of a person in a different orientation. As a result, they can identify left and right for positions they do not occupy (Roberts & Aman, 1993). Around 8 to 10 years, children can give clear, well-organized directions for how to get from one place to another by using a "mental walk" strategy in which they imagine another person's movements along a route. Without special prompting, 6-year-olds focus on the end point and do not say exactly how to get there (Gauvain & Rogoff, 1989; Plumert et al., 1994).

LIMITATIONS OF CONCRETE OPERATIONAL THOUGHT

Although school-age children are far more capable problem solvers than they were during the preschool years, concrete operational thinking suffers from one important limitation. Children think in an organized, logical fashion only when dealing with concrete information that they can perceive directly. Their mental operations work poorly with abstract ideas—ones not apparent in the real world.

Children's solutions to transitive inference problems provide a good illustration. When shown pairs of sticks of unequal length, Lizzie easily figured out that if Stick A is longer than Stick B and Stick B is longer than Stick C, then Stick A is longer than Stick C. But she had great difficulty with a hypothetical version of this task, such as "Susan is taller than Sally and Sally is taller than Mary. Who is the tallest?" Not until age 11 or 12 can children solve this problem easily.

That logical thought is at first tied to immediate situations helps account for a special feature of concrete operational reasoning. Perhaps you noticed that school-age children master Piaget's concrete operational tasks step by step, not all at once. For example, they usually grasp conservation problems in a certain order: first number, followed by length, mass, and liquid. Piaget used the term **horizontal décalage** (meaning development within a stage) to describe this gradual mastery of logical concepts. The horizontal décalage is another indication of the concrete operational child's difficulty with abstractions. School-age children do not come up with the general principle of conservation and then apply it to all relevant situations. Rather, they seem to work out the logic of each problem separately.

RECENT RESEARCH ON CONCRETE OPERATIONAL THOUGHT

According to Piaget, brain maturation combined with experience in a rich and varied external world should lead children everywhere to reach the concrete operational stage. Yet recent evidence indicates that specific cultural and school practices have a great deal to do with mastery of Piagetian tasks (Rogoff & Chavajay, 1995). Furthermore, the information-processing approach helps explain the gradual mastery of logical concepts in middle childhood.

■ THE IMPACT OF CULTURE AND SCHOOLING. In tribal and village societies, conservation is often greatly delayed. For example, among the Hausa of Nigeria, who live in small agricultural settlements and rarely send their children to school, even the most basic conservation tasks—number, length, and liquid—are not understood until age 11 or later (Fahrmeier, 1978).

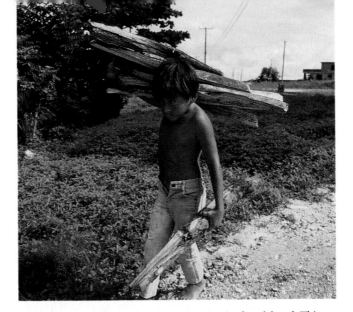

■ In tribal and village societies, conservation is often delayed. This boy, who is growing up in Belize, Central America, gathers firewood for his family. His everyday activities may not promote the kind of reasoning required to pass Piagetian conservation tasks. Compared with his agemates in Western industrialized nations, he may have fewer opportunities to see the same quantity arranged in different ways. (Photo courtesy: Jeff Lawrence/Stock Boston)

This suggests that for children to master conservation and other Piagetian concepts, they must take part in everyday activities that promote this way of thinking (Light & Perret-Clermont, 1989). Joey and Lizzie, for example, think of fairness in terms of equal distribution—a value emphasized in their culture. They frequently divide materials, such as crayons, Halloween treats, and lemonade, equally among themselves and their friends. Because they often see the same quantity arranged in different ways, they grasp conservation early. But in societies in which equal sharing of goods is not common, conservation is unlikely to appear at the expected age.

The very experience of going to school seems to promote mastery of Piagetian tasks. When children of the same age are tested, those who have been in school longer do better on transitive inference problems (Artman & Cahan, 1993). Opportunities to seriate objects, learn about order relations, and remember the parts of complex problems are probably responsible. Yet certain nonschool, informal experiences can also foster operational thought. Brazilian 6- to 9-year-old street vendors, who seldom attend school, do poorly on Piagetian class-inclusion tasks but very well on versions relevant to street vending—for example, "If you have 4 units of mint and 2 units of grape chewing gum, is it better to sell me the mint gum or [all] the gum?" (Ceci & Roazzi, 1994).

On the basis of findings like these, some investigators have concluded that the forms of logic required by Piagetian tasks do not emerge spontaneously in children but are socially generated—as outcomes of practical activities in particular cultures. Does this view remind you of Vygotsky's sociocultural theory, which we discussed in earlier chapters?

■ AN INFORMATION-PROCESSING VIEW OF CONCRETE OPERATIONAL THOUGHT. Piaget's notion of the horizontal décalage raises a familiar question about his theory: Is an abrupt stagewise transition to logical thought the best way to describe cognitive development in middle childhood?

Some theorists argue that the development of operational thinking can best be understood in terms of gains in information-processing capacity rather than a sudden shift to a new stage. For example, Robbie Case (1992, 1998) proposes that with practice, cognitive schemes demand less attention and become more automatic. This frees up space in *working memory* (see page 156) so children can focus on combining old schemes and generating new ones. For instance, the child confronted with water poured from one container to another recognizes that the height of the liquid changes. As this understanding becomes routine, the child notices that the width of the water changes as well. Soon the child coordinates these observations, and conservation of liquid is achieved. Then, as this logical idea becomes well practiced, the child transfers it to more demanding situations, such as area and weight.

Eventually, school-age children coordinate several logical ideas into a general logical structure, which permits them to think about a wide range of situations in more advanced ways (Case, 1996, 1998). At this point, thinking becomes highly efficient and abstract—the kind of change we will see when we discuss formal operational thought in Chapter 11.

■ **E**VALUATION OF THE CONCRETE OPERATIONAL STAGE

Piaget was indeed correct that school-age youngsters approach a great many problems in systematic and rational ways that were not possible just a few years before. But still at issue is whether this period is best viewed in terms of *continuous* improvement in logical skills or *discontinuous* restructuring of children's thinking as they enter a new stage. A growing number of researchers think that both types of change may be involved (Case, 1998; Elman et al., 1996; Fischer & Bidell, 1998). From early to middle childhood, children apply logical schemes to many more tasks. Yet in the process, their thought seems to undergo qualitative change—toward a comprehensive grasp of the underlying principles of logical thought. Piaget himself seems to have recognized this possibility in the very concept of the horizontal décalage. So perhaps some blend of Piagetian and information-processing ideas holds greatest promise for understanding cognitive development in middle childhood.

ASK YOURSELF . . .

■ *Nine-year-old Adrienne spends many hours helping her father build furniture in his woodworking shop. Explain how this experience may have contributed to Adrienne's advanced performance on Piagetian seriation problems.*

INFORMATION PROCESSING

In contrast to Piaget's focus on overall cognitive change, the information-processing perspective examines separate aspects of thinking. Attention and memory, which underlie every act of cognition, are central concerns in middle childhood, just as they were during infancy and the preschool years. Also, increased understanding of how school-age children process information is being applied to their academic learning—in particular, to reading and mathematics.

Researchers believe that brain development contributes to two basic changes in information processing that facilitate the diverse aspect of thinking we are about to consider:

■ *An increase in information-processing capacity.* Time needed to process information on a wide variety of cognitive tasks declines rapidly between ages 6 and 12 (Kail & Park, 1992, 1994). This suggests a biologically based gain in speed of thinking, possibly due to continued myelinization and synaptic pruning in the brain (see Chapter 4, pages 120–121) (Miller & Vernon, 1997). More efficient thinking increases information-processing capacity, since a faster thinker can hold onto and operate on more information at once.

■ *Gains in cognitive inhibition.* Although **cognitive inhibition**—the ability to resist interference from irrelevant information—improves from infancy on, great strides occur during middle childhood. Gains in cognitive inhibition are believed to be due to further development of the frontal lobes of the cerebral cortex (Dempster, 1993, 1995). By clearing unnecessary information from working memory, cognitive inhibition supports many information-processing skills.

Besides brain development, strategy use contributes to more effective information processing. As we will see, school-age children are much more strategic thinkers than are preschoolers.

■ **A**TTENTION

During middle childhood, attention changes in three ways. It becomes more selective, adaptable, and planful.

CHILDREN WITH ATTENTION-DEFICIT HYPERACTIVITY DISORDER

While the other fifth graders worked quietly at their desks, Calvin squirmed in his seat, dropped his pencil, looked out the window, fiddled with his shoelaces, and talked out. "Hey Joey," he yelled over the top of several desks, "wanna play ball after school?" Joey didn't answer. He wasn't eager to play with Calvin. Out on the playground, Calvin was a poor listener and failed to follow the rules of the game. He had trouble taking turns at bat. In the outfield, he tossed his mitt up in the air and looked elsewhere when the ball came his way. Calvin's desk at school and his room at home were a chaotic mess. He often lost pencils, books, and other materials necessary for completing assignments.

SYMPTOMS OF ADHD. Calvin is one of 3 to 5 percent of school-age children with **attention-deficit hyperactivity disorder (ADHD)** (American Psychiatric Association, 1994). Boys are diagnosed 5 to 10 times more often than girls. However, many girls with ADHD may be overlooked because their symptoms are usually not as flagrant (Gaub & Carlson, 1997).

Children with ADHD have great difficulty staying on task for more than a few minutes. They often act impulsively, ignoring social rules and lashing out with hostility when frustrated. Many (but not all) are *hyperactive.* They charge through their days with excessive motor activity, leaving parents and teachers frazzled and other children annoyed. ADHD youngsters have few friends; they are soundly rejected by their classmates.

The intelligence of children with ADHD is normal, and they show no signs of serious emotional disturbance. According to one view, their diverse symptoms are due to an impairment in inhibition, which makes it hard to delay action in favor of thought (Barkley, 1997b). Consequently, they do poorly on tasks requiring sustained attention, find it hard to ignore irrelevant information, and lag behind their agemates in many information-processing capacities (Barkley, 1997b; Denckla, 1996).

ORIGINS OF ADHD. Heredity plays a major role in ADHD, since the disorder runs in families and identical twins share it more often than do fraternal twins (Sherman, Iacono, & McGue, 1997). Children with ADHD also show abnormal brain functioning, including reduced electrical activity and blood flow in the frontal lobes and a smaller corpus callosum, which transfers information from one cerebral hemisphere to the other (Lyoo et al., 1996; Novak, Solanto, & Abikoff, 1995; Riccio et al., 1993).

At the same time, ADHD is associated with environmental factors. Prenatal teratogens (particularly those involving long-term exposure, such as illegal drugs, alcohol, and cigarettes) are linked to inattention and hyperactivity (Milberger et al., 1997). In addition, these children are more likely to come from homes in which marriages are unhappy and family stress is high (Bernier & Siegel, 1994). But a stressful home life rarely causes ADHD. Instead, the behaviors of these children can contribute to family problems, which, in turn, are

First, children become better at deliberately attending to just those aspects of a situation that are relevant to their goals, ignoring other information. Researchers study this increasing selectivity of attention by introducing irrelevant stimuli into a task and seeing how well children attend to its central elements. Performance improves sharply between 6 and 9 years of age as children apply strategies for selecting information more effectively (Miller & Seier, 1994).

Second, older children flexibly adapt their attention to momentary requirements of situations. For example, when studying for a spelling test, 10-year-old Joey devoted most attention to words he knew least well. Lizzie was much less likely do so (Masur, McIntyre, & Flavell, 1973).

Finally, *planning*—thinking out a sequence of acts ahead of time and allocating attention accordingly—improves

greatly in middle childhood (Scholnick, 1995). School-age children scan detailed pictures and written materials for similarities and differences more thoroughly than do preschoolers. And on tasks with many parts, they make decisions about what to do first and what to do next in an orderly fashion. In one study, 5- to 9-year-olds were given lists of 25 items to obtain from a play grocery store. Before starting on a shopping trip, older children more often took time to scan the store, and they also followed shorter routes through the aisles (Szepkouski, Gauvain, & Carberry, 1994).

Unfortunately, some children have great difficulty paying attention, a problem that often remains with them into adulthood. See the Variations box above for a discussion of the serious learning and behavior problems of children with attention-deficit hyperactivity disorder.

likely to intensify the child's preexisting difficulties.

TREATING ADHD. Calvin's doctor eventually prescribed stimulant medication, the most common treatment for ADHD. As long as dosage is carefully regulated, these drugs reduce activity level and improve attention, academic performance, and peer relations for 70 percent of children who take them (Barkley, 1997a). Researchers do not know precisely why stimulants are helpful. Some speculate that they change the chemical balance in brain regions that inhibit impulsivity and hyperactivity, thereby decreasing the child's need to engage in off-task and self-stimulating behavior.

Although stimulant medication is relatively safe, its impact is short term. Drugs cannot teach children ways of compensating for inattention and impulsivity. Combining medication with interventions that model and reinforce appropriate academic and social behavior seems to be the most effective treatment approach (Barkley,

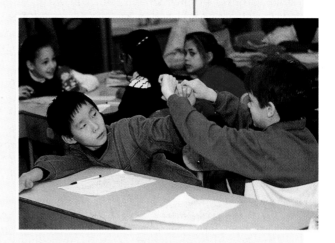

■ *The boy on the right frequently engages in disruptive behavior, disturbing his classmates while they try to work. Children with ADHD have great difficulty staying on task and often act impulsively. (Photo courtesy: Elena Rooraid/PhotoEdit)*

1997a; Pelham & Hoza, 1996). Family intervention is also important. Inattentive, overactive children strain the patience of parents, who are likely to react punitively and inconsistently in return—a child-rearing style that strengthens inappropriate behavior. Breaking this cycle is as important for ADHD children as it is for the defiant, aggressive youngsters we discussed in Chapter 8. In fact, at least 35 percent of the time, these two sets of behavior problems occur together (Lahey & Loeber, 1997).

Because ADHD can be a lifelong disorder, it often requires long-term therapy. Adults with ADHD need help structuring their environments, regulating negative emotion, selecting appropriate careers, and understanding their condition as a biological deficit rather than a character flaw. When adults with ADHD were asked what factors had helped them most, they mentioned people who had been particularly supportive (Weiss & Hechtman, 1993).

MEMORY STRATEGIES

As attention improves with age, so do *memory strategies,* the deliberate mental activities we use to store and retain information. When Lizzie had a list of things to learn, such as a phone number or the state capitals of the United States, she immediately used **rehearsal,** repeating the information to herself over and over again. This memory strategy first appears in the early grade school years. Soon after, a second strategy becomes common: **organization.** Children group related items together (for example, all state capitals in the same part of the country), an approach that improves recall dramatically (Bjorklund & Muir, 1988).

Memory strategies require time and effort to perfect. For example, 8-year-old Lizzie rehearsed in a piecemeal fashion. After being given the word *cat* in a list of items, she said, "Cat, cat, cat." In contrast, 10-year-old Joey combined previous

words with each new item, saying, "Desk, man, yard, cat, cat" (Kunzinger, 1985). Joey also organized more skillfully, grouping items into fewer categories. In addition, he used organization in a wide range of memory tasks, whereas Lizzie used it only when categorical relations among items were obvious (Bjorklund et al., 1994). And Joey often combined several strategies—for example, organizing, stating the category names, and rehearsing (Coyle & Bjorklund, 1997). For all these reasons, Joey retained much more information.

By the end of middle childhood, children start to use **elaboration.** This strategy involves creating a relationship, or shared meaning, between two or more pieces of information that are not members of the same category. For example, suppose the words *fish* and *pipe* are among those you want to learn. You might generate a mental image of a fish smoking a pipe. Once children discover this memory technique, they find it so effective that it tends to replace other strategies. Elaboration develops late because it requires considerable mental effort and working-memory capacity. It becomes increasingly common during adolescence and young adulthood (Schneider & Pressley, 1997).

Because the strategies of organization and elaboration combine items into *meaningful chunks*, they permit children to hold on to much more information at once. As a result, these strategies contribute to expansion of working memory. In addition, when children link a new item to information they already know, they can *retrieve* it easily by thinking of other items associated with it. As we will see in the next section, this is one reason that memory improves steadily during the school years.

THE KNOWLEDGE BASE AND MEMORY PERFORMANCE

During middle childhood, the long-term knowledge base grows larger and becomes organized into elaborate, hierarchically structured networks. Many researchers believe this rapid growth of knowledge helps children use strategies and remember. In other words, knowing more about a topic makes new information more meaningful and familiar so it is easier to store and retrieve (Schneider, 1993).

To test this idea, Michelene Chi (1978) looked at how well third- through eighth-grade chess experts could remember complex chessboard arrangements. The children recalled the configurations considerably better than adults, who knew how to play chess but were not especially knowledgeable. Yet the adults did better than the children at recalling lists of numbers on a standard memory test. The children showed superior memory performance only in the domain of knowledge in which they were expert.

Although knowledge clearly plays an important role in memory development, it must be quite broad and well structured before it can facilitate strategy use and recall (DeMarie-Dreblow, 1991). Furthermore, knowledge is not the only important factor in children's strategic memory processing. Children who are expert in an area, whether it be chess, math, social studies, or spelling, are usually highly motivated. As a result, they not only acquire knowledge more quickly, but they *actively use what they know* to add more. In contrast, academically unsuccessful children fail to ask how previously stored information can clarify new material. This, in turn, interferes with the development of a broad knowledge base (Schneider & Bjorklund, 1998). So at least by the end of the school years, knowledge acquisition and use of memory strategies are intimately related and support one another.

CULTURE AND MEMORY STRATEGIES

Think about situations in which the strategies of rehearsal, organization, and elaboration are useful. People usually employ these techniques when they need to remember information for its own sake. On many other occasions, they participate in daily activities that produce excellent memory as a natural by-product of the activity itself.

A repeated finding is that people in non-Western cultures who have no formal schooling do not use or benefit from instruction in memory strategies (Rogoff & Chavajay, 1995). Tasks that require children to recall isolated bits of information are common in classrooms, and they provide children with a great deal of motivation to come up with ways to memorize. In fact, Western children get so much practice with this type of learning that they do not refine other techniques for remembering that rely on spatial location and arrangement of objects, cues that are readily available in everyday life. Australian Aboriginal and Guatemalan Mayan children are considerably better at these memory skills (Kearins, 1981; Rogoff, 1986). Looked at in this way, the development of memory strategies is not just a matter of a more competent information-processing system. It is also a product of task demands and cultural circumstances.

THE SCHOOL-AGE CHILD'S THEORY OF MIND

During middle childhood, children's *theory of mind*, or beliefs about mental activities, becomes more elaborate and refined. Recall from Chapter 7 that this awareness of cognitive processes is often called *metacognition*. School-age children's improved ability to reflect on their own mental life is another reason for their advances in thinking and problem solving.

Unlike preschoolers, who view the mind as a passive container, older children regard it as an active, constructive agent capable of selecting and transforming information (Chandler & Carpendale, 1998). Consequently, they have a much better understanding of the impact of psychological factors on performance. They know, for example, that mental inferences can be a source of knowledge and that doing well on a task depends on focusing attention—concentrating on it, wanting to do it, and not being tempted by anything else (Carpendale & Chandler, 1996; Miller & Bigi, 1979). They are also aware that in studying material for later recall, it is helpful to devote most effort to items you know least well. And school-age children are far more conscious of memory strategies, including which ones are likely to work best (Justice et al., 1997).

What promotes this active, process-oriented view of the mind? Perhaps children become aware of mental activities through quiet-time reflection on their own thinking (Wellman & Hickling, 1994). Formal schooling may also contribute. Asking children to keep their minds on what they are doing and to remember mental steps calls atten-

■ *School-age children have an improved ability to reflect on their own mental life. This child is aware that external aids to memory are often necessary to ensure that information will be retained. (Photo courtesy: Laura Dwight)*

tion to thought processes. And as children read, write, and solve math problems, they often use private speech, first out loud and then silently in their heads. As they "hear themselves think," they may detect many aspects of mental life (Flavell, Green, & Flavell, 1995).

Once children are aware of the many factors that influence mental activity, they combine these into an integrated understanding. School-age children take account of *interactions* among variables—how age and motivation of the learner, effective use of strategies, and nature and difficulty of the task work together to affect cognitive performance (Wellman, 1990). In this way, metacognition truly becomes a comprehensive theory.

COGNITIVE SELF-REGULATION

Although metacognition expands, school-age youngsters often have difficulty putting what they know about thinking into action. They are not yet good at **cognitive self-regulation,** the process of continuously monitoring progress toward a goal, checking outcomes, and redirecting unsuccessful efforts. For example, Lizzie is aware that she should group items together in a memory task and read a complicated paragraph more than once to make sure she understands it. But she does not always do these things when working on an assignment.

Self-regulation develops slowly over middle childhood and adolescence. By secondary school, it is a strong predictor of academic success (Joyner & Kurtz-Costes, 1997). Students who do well in school know when they possess a skill and when they do not. If they run up against obstacles, such as poor study conditions, a confusing text passage, or an unclear class presentation, they take steps to organize

the learning environment, review the material, or seek other sources of support. This active, purposeful approach contrasts sharply with the passive orientation of students who do poorly (Zimmerman & Risemberg, 1997).

Parents and teachers can foster children's self-regulation by pointing out the special demands of tasks, encouraging the use of strategies, and emphasizing the value of self-correction. Many studies show that providing children with instructions to check and monitor their progress toward a goal has a substantial impact on how well they do (Pressley, 1995). In addition, training that emphasizes why a strategy is effective enhances children's use of it in similar situations (Schunk & Zimmerman, 1994).

Children who acquire effective self-regulatory skills develop confidence in their own ability—a belief that supports the use of self-regulation in the future (Zimmerman & Risemberg, 1997). Unfortunately, some children receive messages from parents and teachers that seriously undermine their academic self-esteem and self-regulatory skills. We will consider the special problems of these *learned-helpless* youngsters, along with ways to help them, in Chapter 10.

APPLICATIONS OF INFORMATION PROCESSING TO ACADEMIC LEARNING

Over the past decade, fundamental discoveries about the development of information processing have been applied to children's learning of reading and mathematics. Researchers have begun to identify the cognitive ingredients of high-level performance and to pinpoint ways in which poor learners are deficient. They hope, as a result, to design teaching methods that will help school-age children master these essential skills.

■ READING. While reading, we use a large number of skills at once, taxing all aspects of our information-processing systems. Joey and Lizzie must perceive single letters and letter combinations, translate them into speech sounds, hold chunks of text in working memory while interpreting their meaning, and combine the meanings of various parts of a text passage into an understandable whole. In fact, reading is so demanding that most or all of these skills must be done automatically. If one or more are poorly developed, they will compete for space in our limited working memories, and reading performance will decline (Perfetti, 1988).

Researchers do not yet know how children manage to acquire and combine all these varied skills into fluent reading. Currently, psychologists and educators are engaged in a "great debate" about how to teach beginning reading. On one side are those who take a **whole-language approach** to reading instruction. They argue that reading should be taught in a way that parallels natural language learning. From the very beginning, children should be exposed to text in its complete form—stories, poems, letters, posters, and lists—so they can appreciate the communicative function of written language. According to these experts, as long as reading is kept whole and meaningful, children will be motivated to discover the specific skills they need as they gain experience with the printed word (Goodman, 1986; Watson, 1989). On the other side of the debate are those who advocate a **basic-skills approach.** According to this view, children should be given simplified text materials. At first, they should be coached on *phonics*—the basic rules for translating written symbols into sounds. Only later, after they have mastered these skills, should they get complex reading material (Rayner & Pollatsek, 1989).

As yet, research does not show clear-cut superiority for either of these approaches (Stahl, 1999; Stahl, McKenna, & Pagnucco, 1994). In fact, a third group of experts believes that children learn best when they receive a mixture of both. Kindergartners benefit from an emphasis on whole language, with gradual introduction of phonics as reading skills improve (Sacks & Mergendoller, 1997). In the early grades, balancing the two methods seems most effective (Hatcher, Hulme, & Ellis, 1994). Learning the basics—relationships between letters and sounds—enables children to decipher words they have never seen before. As this process becomes automatic, it releases children's attention to the higher-level activities involved in comprehending the text's meaning. But if basic skills are overemphasized, children may lose sight of the goal of reading—understanding. Many teachers report cases of pupils who can read aloud fluently but who register little or no meaning. These children might have been spared serious reading problems if they had been given meaning-based instruction that included attention to basic skills.

■ M A T H E M A T I C S .   Once children enter elementary school, they apply their rich informal knowledge of number concepts and counting to more complex mathematical skills. For example, children first understand multiplication as repeated addition. When given the following problem, "Sue has 5 books. Joe has 3 times as many. How many books does Joe have?" Lizzie thought to herself, "What's 5 × 3?" When she had difficulty remembering the answer, she said, "Okay, it's got to be 5 books + 5 books + 5 books. It's 15!" Lizzie's use of addition strengthened her understanding of multiplication. It also helped her recall a multiplication fact that she had been trying to memorize.

Mathematics as taught in many classrooms, however, does not make good use of children's basic grasp of number concepts. Children are given procedures for solving problems without linking these to their informally acquired understandings. Consequently, they often apply a rule that is close to what they have been taught but that yields a wrong answer. Their mistakes indicate that they have tried to memorize a method but do not comprehend its underlying logic (Geary, 1994).

Arguments about how to teach early mathematics closely resemble those in the area of reading. Drill in computa-

tional skills is pitted against "number sense" or understanding. Yet once again, a blend of the two is probably best. In learning math facts, poor math students spend little time experimenting with strategies but, instead, move quickly toward trying to retrieve answers from memory. When asked to explain math concepts, their performance is weak (Canobi, Reeve, & Pattison, 1998). By trying out strategies (as Lizzie did when she solved 5 × 3), good students grapple with underlying concepts and develop effective solution techniques (Siegler, 1996). This suggests that encouraging children to apply strategies and making sure they understand why certain strategies work well are vital for solid mastery of basic math.

In Asian countries, pupils receive supports for learning mathematics that are not broadly available in the United States. For example, use of the metric system helps Asian children think in ways that foster a grasp of place value. The consistent structure of number words in Asian languages ("ten two" for 12, "ten three" for 13) also makes this idea clear (Miller et al., 1995). Furthermore, Asian number words are shorter and more quickly pronounced. Therefore, more digits can be held in working memory at once, increasing the speed of arithmetic computation (Geary et al., 1996). Finally, as we will see later in this chapter, in Asian classrooms, much more time is spent exploring underlying math concepts and much less on drill and repetition.

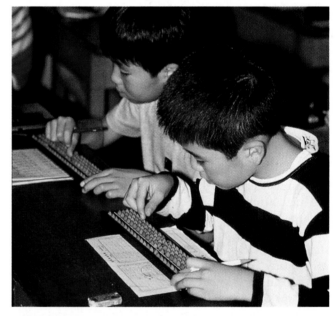

■ *Culture and language-based factors contribute to Asian children's skill at mathematics. The abacus supports these Japanese pupils' understanding of place value. Ones, tens, hundreds, and thousands are represented by a different column of beads, and calculations are performed by moving the beads to different positions. As children become skilled at using the abacus, they learn to think in ways that facilitate solving complex arithmetic problems. (Photo courtesy: Fuji Fotos/The Image Works)*

ASK YOURSELF . . .

■ *One day, the children in Lizzie and Joey's school saw a slide show about endangered species. They were asked to remember as many animal names as they could. Fifth and sixth graders recalled considerably more than second and third graders. What factors might account for this difference?*

■ *Lizzie knows that if you have difficulty learning part of a task, you should devote most of your attention to that aspect. But she plays each of her piano pieces from beginning to end instead of picking out the hard parts for extra practice. What explains Lizzie's failure to apply what she knows?*

INDIVIDUAL DIFFERENCES IN MENTAL DEVELOPMENT

During middle childhood, intelligence tests become increasingly important for assessing individual differences in mental development. Around age 6, IQ becomes more stable than it was at earlier ages, and it correlates well with academic achievement. Because IQ predicts school performance, it enters into educational decisions. Do intelligence tests provide an accurate indication of the school-age child's ability to profit from academic instruction? Let's take a close look at this controversial issue.

DEFINING AND MEASURING INTELLIGENCE

Virtually all intelligence tests provide an overall score (the IQ), which is taken to represent *general intelligence* or reasoning ability. Yet as Figure 9.6 on page 300 shows, a diverse array of tasks appears on most tests for children. Today, there is widespread agreement that intelligence is a collection of many mental capacities, not all of which are included on currently available tests.

Test designers use a complicated statistical technique called *factor analysis* to identify the various abilities assessed by intelligence tests. This procedure determines which sets of items on the test correlate strongly with one another. Those that do are assumed to measure a similar ability and, therefore, are designated as a separate factor. Most intelligence tests offer a variety of factor scores in addition to an overall IQ.

The intelligence tests that Joey and Lizzie take every so often in school are *group administered tests*. They permit large numbers of pupils to be tested at once and require very little training of teachers who give them. Group tests are useful for instructional planning and identifying children who require more extensive evaluation with *individu-*

ally administered tests. Unlike group tests, individually administered ones demand considerable training and experience to give well. The examiner not only considers the child's answers but observes the child's behavior, noting such things as attentiveness to and interest in the tasks and wariness of the adult. These reactions provide insight into whether the test score is accurate or underestimates the child's abilities. Two individual tests—the Stanford-Binet and the Wechsler—are often used to identify highly intelligent children and diagnose those with learning problems.

The *Stanford-Binet Intelligence Scale*, the modern descendent of Alfred Binet's first successful intelligence test, is appropriate for individuals between 2 years of age and adulthood. It measures general intelligence and four intellectual factors: verbal reasoning, quantitative reasoning, spatial reasoning, and short-term memory (Thorndike, Hagen, & Sattler, 1986). Within these factors are 15 subtests that permit a detailed analysis of each child's mental abilities. The verbal and quantitative factors emphasize culturally loaded, fact-oriented information, such as knowledge of vocabulary and sentence comprehension. The spatial factor is believed to be less culturally biased because it requires little in the way of specific information (see the spatial visualization item in Figure 9.6).

The *Wechsler Intelligence Scale for Children (WISC-III)* is the third edition of a widely used test for 6- through 16-year-olds (Wechsler, 1991). In addition to general intelligence, it assesses two broad intellectual factors: verbal and performance, each of which contains 6 subtests. Performance items (see examples in Figure 9.6) require the child to arrange materials rather than talk to the examiner. They provided one of the first means through which non-English-speaking children and children with speech and language disorders could demonstrate their intellectual strengths. The WISC was also the first text to be standardized on children representing the total population of the United States, including ethnic minorities.

RECENT ADVANCES IN DEFINING INTELLIGENCE

Researchers have begun to combine the factor analytic approach to defining intelligence with information processing. They believe that factors on intelligence tests are of limited use unless we can identify the cognitive processes responsible for them. Once we understand the underlying basis of IQ, we will know much more about why a particular child does well or poorly and what capacities must be worked on to improve performance. These researchers conduct *componential analyses* of children's mental test scores. This means that they look for relationships between aspects (or components) of information processing and children's IQs.

Many studies reveal that speed of processing is related to IQ (Deary, 1995; Kranzler & Jensen, 1989; Vernon, 1993). This suggests that individuals whose nervous systems

FIGURE 9.6

■ **Test items like those on common intelligence tests for children.** In contrast to verbal items, nonverbal items do not require reading or direct use of language. Performance items are also nonverbal, but they require the child to draw or construct something rather than merely give a correct answer. As a result, they appear only on individually administered intelligence tests. (Logical reasoning, picture oddities, and spatial visualization examples are adapted with permission of The Free Press, a Division of Macmillan, Inc., from A. R. Jensen, 1980, *Bias in Mental Testing,* New York: Free Press, pp. 150, 154, 157.)

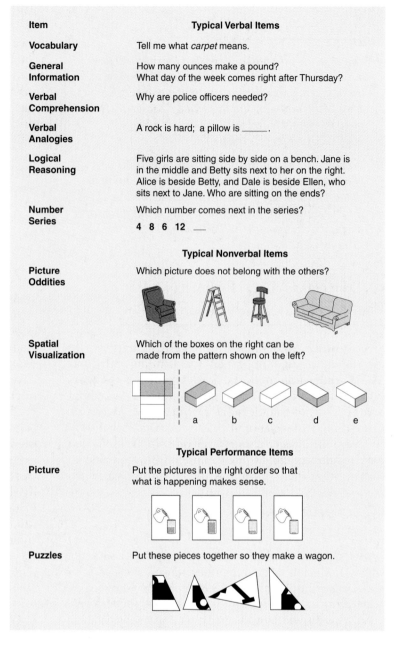

Item	Typical Verbal Items
Vocabulary	Tell me what *carpet* means.
General Information	How many ounces make a pound? What day of the week comes right after Thursday?
Verbal Comprehension	Why are police officers needed?
Verbal Analogies	A rock is hard; a pillow is _____.
Logical Reasoning	Five girls are sitting side by side on a bench. Jane is in the middle and Betty sits next to her on the right. Alice is beside Betty, and Dale is beside Ellen, who sits next to Jane. Who are sitting on the ends?
Number Series	Which number comes next in the series? **4 8 6 12** ___

Typical Nonverbal Items

Picture Oddities — Which picture does not belong with the others?

Spatial Visualization — Which of the boxes on the right can be made from the pattern shown on the left?

a   b   c   d   e

Typical Performance Items

Picture — Put the pictures in the right order so that what is happening makes sense.

Puzzles — Put these pieces together so they make a wagon.

function more efficiently, permitting them to take in and manipulate information quickly, have an edge in intellectual skills. But strategy use also predicts IQ, and it explains some of the association between response speed and intelligence (Miller & Vernon, 1992). Children who apply strategies effectively acquire more knowledge. Then they use that knowledge to engage in fast, accurate thinking, which seems to carry over to performance on intelligence tests.

The componential approach has one major shortcoming: It regards intelligence as entirely due to causes within the child. Yet throughout this book, we have seen how cultural and situational factors affect children's cognitive skills. Robert Sternberg has expanded the componential approach into a comprehensive theory that regards intelligence as a product of both inner and outer forces.

■ STERNBERG'S TRIARCHIC THEORY OF INTELLIGENCE. As Figure 9.7 shows, Sternberg's (1985, 1997) **triarchic theory of intelligence** is made up of three interacting subtheories. The first, the *componential subtheory,* spells out the information-processing skills that underlie intelligent behavior. You are already familiar with its main elements—strategy application, knowledge acquisition, metacognition, and self-regulation.

According to Sternberg, children's use of these components is not just a matter of internal capacity. It is also a function of the conditions under which intelligence is assessed. The *experiential subtheory* states that highly intelligent individuals, compared to less intelligent ones, process information more skillfully in novel situations. When given a new task, the bright person learns rapidly, making strategies

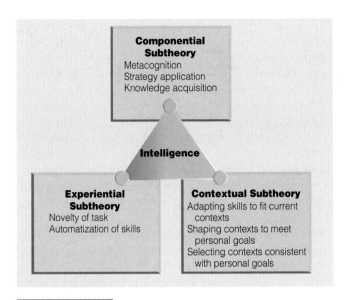

FIGURE 9.7

■ **Sternberg's triarchic theory of intelligence.**

automatic so working memory is freed for more complex aspects of the situation.

Think, for a moment, about the implications of this idea for measuring children's intelligence. To accurately compare children in brightness—in ability to deal with novelty and learn efficiently—all children would need to be presented with equally unfamiliar test items. Otherwise some children will appear more intelligent than others simply become of their past experiences, not because they are really more cognitively skilled.

This point brings us to the third part of Sternberg's model, the *contextual subtheory*. It proposes that intelligent people skillfully *adapt* their information-processing skills to fit with their personal desires and the demands of their everyday worlds. When they cannot adapt to a situation, they try to *shape*, or change, it to meet their needs. If they cannot shape it, they *select* new contexts that are consistent with their goals. The contextual subtheory emphasizes that intelligent behavior is never culture-free. Because of their backgrounds, some children come to value behaviors required for success on intelligence tests, and they easily adapt to the tasks and testing conditions. Others with different life histories misinterpret the testing context or reject it entirely because it does not suit their needs.

Sternberg's theory emphasizes the complexity of intelligent behavior. As you can already see, his ideas are relevant to the controversy surrounding cultural bias in intelligence testing, which we will address shortly.

■ GARDNER'S THEORY OF MULTIPLE INTELLIGENCES. Howard Gardner's (1983, 1993, 2000) **theory of multiple intelligences** provides yet another view of how information-processing skills underlie intelligent behavior. But unlike the componential approach, it does not begin with existing mental tests and try to isolate the processing elements required to succeed on them. Instead, Gardner believes that intelligence should be defined in terms of distinct sets of processing operations that permit individuals to engage in a wide range of culturally valued activities. Therefore, Gardner dismisses the idea of general intelligence and proposes eight independent intelligences (see Table 9.1).

TABLE 9.1

Gardner's Multiple Intelligences

INTELLIGENCE	PROCESSING OPERATIONS	END-STATE PERFORMANCE POSSIBILITIES
Linguistic	Sensitivity to the sounds, rhythms, and meanings of words and the different functions of language	Poet, journalist
Logico-mathematical	Sensitivity to, and capacity to detect, logical or numerical patterns; ability to handle long chains of logical reasoning	Mathematician
Musical	Ability to produce and appreciate pitch, rhythm (or melody), and aesthetic-sounding tones; understanding of the forms of musical expressiveness	Violinist, composer
Spatial	Ability to perceive the visual-spatial world accurately, to perform transformations on those perceptions, and to recreate aspects of visual experience in the absence of relevant stimuli	Sculptor, navigator
Bodily-kinesthetic	Ability to use the body skillfully for expressive as well as goal-directed purposes; ability to handle objects skillfully	Dancer, athlete
Naturalist	Ability to recognize and classify all varieties of animals, minerals, and plants	Biologist
Interpersonal	Ability to detect and respond appropriately to the moods, temperaments, motivations, and intentions of others	Therapist, salesperson
Intrapersonal	Ability to discriminate complex inner feelings and to use them to guide one's own behavior; knowledge of one's own strengths, weaknesses, desires, and intelligences	Person with detailed, accurate self-knowledge

Sources: Gardner, 1983, 1993, 1998a, 2000.

■ *According to Gardner, children are capable of at least eight distinct intelligences. As these children classify wildflowers they collected during a walk through a forest and meadow, they enrich their naturalist intelligence. (Photo courtesy: B. Daemmrich/ The Image Works)*

Gardner argues that each intelligence has a unique biological basis, a distinct course of development, and different expert, or "end-state," performances. At the same time, he emphasizes that a lengthy process of education is required to transform any raw potential into a mature social role. This means that cultural values and learning opportunities have a great deal to do with the extent to which a child's intellectual strengths are realized and how they are expressed.

Gardner's list of abilities has yet to be firmly grounded in research. For example, biological evidence for the independence of his abilities is weak. Furthermore, current mental tests do tap several of Gardner's intelligences (linguistic, logico-mathematical, and spatial), and research suggests that they have some common features. Nevertheless, Gardner's theory has been especially helpful in efforts to understand and nurture children's special talents, a topic we will discuss at the end of this chapter.

EXPLAINING INDIVIDUAL AND GROUP DIFFERENCES IN IQ

When we compare individuals in terms of academic achievement, years of education, and the status of their occupations, it quickly becomes clear that certain sectors of the population are advantaged over others. In trying to explain these differences, researchers have examined the intelligence test performance of children varying in ethnicity and SES. Many studies show that American black children score, on the average, 15 IQ points below American white children, although the difference has been shrinking (Suzuki

& Valencia, 1997). SES differences in IQ also exist. The gap between middle-SES and low-SES children is about 9 points (Jensen & Figueroa, 1975). These figures are, of course, averages. There is considerable variation *within* each ethnic and SES group. Still, group differences in IQ are large enough and of serious enough consequence that they cannot be ignored.

In 1969, psychologist Arthur Jensen published a controversial article entitled, "How Much Can We Boost IQ and Scholastic Achievement?" Jensen's answer to this question was "not much." He argued that heredity is largely responsible for individual, ethnic, and SES variations in intelligence, a position he continues to maintain (Jensen, 1980, 1985, 1998). Jensen's work was followed by an outpouring of responses and research studies, leading to a heated nature–nurture debate on the origins of IQ. Recently, the controversy was rekindled in Richard Herrnstein and Charles Murray's (1994) *The Bell Curve.* Like Jensen, these authors concluded that the contribution of heredity to individual and SES differences in IQ is substantial. At the same time, they stated that the relative role of heredity and environment in the black–white IQ gap remains unresolved. Let's look closely at some important evidence.

■ NATURE VERSUS NURTURE. In Chapter 2, we introduced the *heritability estimate.* Recall that heritabilities are obtained from *kinship studies,* which compare family members. The most powerful evidence on the role of heredity in IQ involves twin comparisons. The IQ scores of identical twins (who share all their genes) are more similar than those of fraternal twins (who are genetically no more alike than ordinary siblings). On the basis of this and other kinship evidence, researchers estimate that about half the differences in IQ among children can be traced to their genetic makeup (Plomin 1994a). However, in Chapter 2 we noted that heritabilities risk overestimating genetic influences and underestimating environmental influences. Although research offers convincing evidence that genes contribute to IQ, disagreement persists over just how large the role of heredity really is (Sternberg & Grigorenko, 1997).

Furthermore, a widespread misconception exists that if a characteristic is heritable, then the environment can do little to affect it. A special type of kinship study, involving adopted children, shows that this assumption is incorrect. In one investigation of this kind, children of two extreme groups of biological mothers, those with IQs below 95 and those with IQs above 120, were adopted at birth by parents well above average in income and education. During the school years, children of the low-IQ biological mothers scored above average in IQ, indicating that test performance can be greatly improved by an advantaged home life. At the same time, they did not do as well as children of high-IQ biological mothers placed in similar adoptive families (Horn, 1983; Loehlin, Horn, & Willerman, 1997). Adoption research confirms the balanced position that both heredity and environment affect IQ scores.

Some intriguing adoption evidence sheds light on the black–white IQ gap. Black children placed in well-to-do white homes during the first year of life also score high on intelligence tests. In two such studies, they attained mean IQs of 110 and 117 by middle childhood, well above average and 20 to 30 points higher than the typical scores of children growing up in low-income black communities (Moore, 1986; Scarr & Weinberg, 1983). Although the test scores of black adoptees declined by adolescence, they remained above the IQ average for low-income African Americans (Weinberg, Scarr, & Waldman, 1992).

Adoption findings do not completely resolve questions about ethnic differences in IQ. Nevertheless, the IQ gains of adopted black children "reared in the culture of the tests and schools" are consistent with a wealth of evidence indicating that poverty severely depresses the intelligence of large numbers of ethnic minority youngsters (McLoyd, 1998). And in many other cases, unique cultural values and practices do not prepare these children for the intellectual tasks sampled by intelligence tests and valued in school.

■ CULTURAL INFLUENCES. Jermaine, an African-American child in Lizzie's third-grade class, participated actively in class discussion and wrote complex, imaginative stories. Two years earlier, as a first grader, Jermaine had responded, "I don't know," to the simplest of questions, including "What's your name?" Fortunately, Jermaine's teacher understood his uneasiness. She helped him build a bridge between the learning style fostered by his cultural background and the style necessary for academic success. A growing body of evidence reveals that IQ scores are affected by specific learning experiences, including exposure to certain language customs and knowledge.

Language Customs. Ethnic minority subcultures often foster unique language skills that do not fit the expectations of most classrooms and testing situations. Shirley Brice Heath (1982, 1989), an anthropologist who spent many hours observing in low-SES black homes in a southeastern American city, found that adults asked black children very different kinds of questions than is typical in white middle-SES families. From an early age, white parents ask knowledge-training questions, such as "What color is it?" and "What's this story about?" that resemble the questioning style of tests and classrooms. In contrast, the black parents asked only "real" questions—ones that they themselves did not know the answer to. Often these were analogy questions ("What's that like?") or story-starter questions ("Didja hear Miss Sally this morning?") that called for elaborate responses about personal experiences and had no single right answer.

These experiences lead low-SES black children to develop complex verbal skills at home, such as storytelling and exchanging quick-witted remarks. But their language differs from that of white middle-SES children in emphasizing social and emotional topics rather than facts about the world (Blake, 1994). Not surprisingly, black children may be confused by the "objective" questions they encounter in classrooms and on tests.

Other minority children also develop distinct language customs. For example, children of Hispanic immigrants are taught to respect adult authority rather than express their own knowledge and opinions. Yet American teachers, who value self-assertive speaking, typically equate the silence of Hispanic children with having a negative attitude toward learning (Greenfield & Suzuki, 1998). As the child listens politely but does not answer, a culturally valued style of communicating quickly leads to unfair, negative evaluations in school and on mental tests.

When faced with the strangeness of the testing situation, the minority child may look to the adult for cues about how to respond. Yet most intelligence tests permit tasks to be presented in only one way, without any feedback. Consequently, minority children may simply give the first answer that comes to mind, not one that represents what they know.

Familiarity with Test Content. Many researchers argue that IQ scores are affected by specific information acquired as part of majority-culture upbringing. Unfortunately, attempts to change tests by eliminating fact-oriented verbal tasks and relying only on spatial reasoning and performance items (believed to be less culturally loaded) have not raised the scores of low-SES minority children very much (Reynolds & Kaiser, 1990).

Yet even these nonverbal test items depend on learning opportunities. In one study, children's performance on a spatial reasoning task was related to their experience playing a popular but expensive game that (like the test items) required them to arrange blocks to duplicate a design as quickly as possible (Dirks, 1982). Videogame play also fosters success on spatial test items (Subrahmanyam & Greenfield, 1996). Low-income minority children, who often grow up in more "people oriented" than "object oriented" homes, may lack play materials that promote certain intellectual skills. In line with this possibility, when ethnically diverse parents were asked to describe their view of an intelligent first grader, Anglo-Americans emphasized cognitive traits. In contrast, ethnic minorities (Cambodian, Filipino, Vietnamese, and Mexican immigrants) saw noncognitive characteristics—motivation, self-management, and social skills—as equally or more important (Okagaki & Sternberg, 1993).

That specific experiences affect performance on intelligence tests is also supported by evidence indicating that the amount of time a child spends in school is a strong predictor of IQ. When children of the same age but in different grades are compared, those who have been in school longer score higher on intelligence tests (Ceci, 1991; Ceci & Williams, 1997). Taken together, these findings indicate

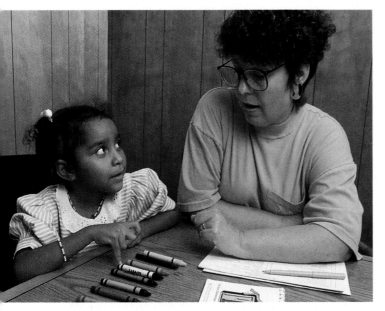

▬ *Dynamic testing introduces purposeful teaching into the testing situation to find out what the child can attain with social support. Many ethnic minority children perform more competently on test items after adult assistance. And the approach helps identify the teaching style to which the child is most responsive. (Photo courtesy: Bob Daemmrich/Stock Boston)*

that teaching children the factual knowledge and ways of thinking valued in classrooms has a sizable impact on their intelligence test performance.

▬ REDUCING CULTURAL BIAS IN INTELLIGENCE TESTS. Although not all experts agree, today there is greater acknowledgment that IQ scores can underestimate the intelligence of culturally different children. A special concern exists about incorrectly labeling minority children as slow learners and assigning them to remedial classes, which are far less stimulating than regular school experiences. Because of this danger, test scores need to be combined with assessments of adaptive behavior—children's ability to cope with the demands of their everyday environments (Landesman & Ramey, 1989). The child who does poorly on an IQ test yet plays a complex game on the playground or figures out how to rewire a broken TV is unlikely to be mentally deficient.

In addition, culturally relevant testing procedures enhance minority children's test performance. In one approach, called *dynamic testing,* the adult introduces purposeful teaching into the testing situation to see what the child can attain with social support. Many minority children perform more competently after adult assistance. And the approach helps identify forms of intervention likely to help children who are learning poorly in classrooms (Grigorenko & Sternberg, 1998; Lidz, 1997).

In sum, intelligence tests are useful when interpreted carefully by examiners who are sensitive to cultural influences on test performance. And despite their limitations, IQ scores continue to be fairly accurate measures of school learning potential for the majority of Western children.

ASK YOURSELF . . .

🌳 *Desiree, a low-SES African-American child, was quiet and withdrawn while taking an intelligence test. Later she remarked to her mother, "I can't understand why that lady asked me all those questions. She's a grownup. She* must *know what a ball and stove are for!" Using Sternberg's triarchic theory, explain Desiree's reaction to the testing situation. What interventions in the classroom and in the testing situation can enhance Desiree's academic development?*

■ *Explain how dynamic testing is consistent with Vygotsky's concept of the zone of proximal development. (See Chapter 5, page 160 and Chapter 7, page 228.)*

LANGUAGE DEVELOPMENT

Vocabulary, grammar, and pragmatics continue to develop in middle childhood, although the changes are less obvious than those of earlier ages. In addition, school-age children's attitude toward language undergoes a fundamental shift. They develop *language awareness.*

V OCABULARY

The average 6-year-old's vocabulary is already quite large (about 10,000 words). By the end of the school years, recognition vocabulary reaches about 40,000 words, a rate of growth that exceeds that of early childhood. In addition to the fast-mapping process discussed in Chapter 7, school-age children enlarge their vocabularies by analyzing the structure of complex words. From *happy* and *decide,* they quickly derive the meanings of *happiness* and *decision* (Anglin, 1993). Many more words are picked up from context, especially while reading (Miller, 1991).

As their conceptual knowledge becomes better organized, school-age children can think about and use words more precisely. Word definitions offer examples of this change. Five- and 6-year-olds give very concrete descriptions that refer to functions or appearance—for example, *knife:* "when you're cutting carrots"; *bicycle:* "it's got wheels, a chain, and handlebars." By the end of elementary school, synonyms and explanations of categorical relationships appear—for example, *knife:* "something you could cut with. A saw is like a knife. It could also be a weapon" (Wehren, De Lisi, & Arnold, 1981). This advance reflects the older child's ability to deal with word meanings on an entirely verbal plane. Older children no longer need to be shown what a word refers to in order to understand it. They can add new words to their vocabulary simply by being given a definition (Dickinson, 1984).

School-age children's more reflective and analytical approach to language permits them to appreciate the multiple meanings of words. For example, they recognize that a great many words, such as *cool* or *neat,* have psychological as well as physical meanings: "What a *cool* shirt!" or "That movie was really *neat!*" This grasp of double meanings permits 8- to 10-year-olds to comprehend subtle metaphors, such as "sharp as a tack" and "spilling the beans" (Wellman & Hickling, 1994; Winner, 1988). It also leads to a change in children's humor. In middle childhood, riddles and puns requiring children to go back and forth between different meanings of the same key word are common.

GRAMMAR

Although children have mastered most of the grammar of their language by the time they enter school, use of complex grammatical constructions improves. For example, during middle childhood, children use the passive voice more frequently, and it expands from an abbreviated structure ("It broke") into full statements ("The glass was broken by Mary") (Horgan, 1978; Lempert, 1989; Pinker, Lebeaux, & Frost, 1987).

Another grammatical achievement of middle childhood is the understanding of infinitive phrases, such as the difference between "John is eager to please" and "John is easy to please" (Chomsky, 1969). Like gains in vocabulary, appreciation of these subtle grammatical distinctions is supported by an improved ability to analyze and reflect on language.

PRAGMATICS

Improvements in *pragmatics,* the communicative side of language, also take place. Children become better at adapting to the needs of listeners in challenging communicative situations, such as describing one object among a group of very similar objects. Whereas preschoolers tend to give ambiguous descriptions, such as "the red one," school-age children are much more precise. They might say, "the round red one with stripes on it" (Deutsch & Pechmann, 1982).

Conversational strategies also become more refined. For example, older children are better at phrasing things to get their way. When faced with an adult who refuses to hand over a desired object, 9-year-olds, but not 5-year-olds, state their second requests more politely (Axia & Baroni, 1985). School-age children are also sensitive to subtle distinctions between what people say and what they really mean. Lizzie,

for example, knew that when her mother said, "The garbage is beginning to smell," she really meant, "Take that garbage out!" (Ackerman, 1978).

LEARNING TWO LANGUAGES AT A TIME

Like most American children, Joey and Lizzie speak only one language, their native tongue of English. Yet throughout the world, a great many children grow up *bilingual.* They learn two languages, and sometimes more than two, during childhood. An estimated 6 million American school-age children speak a language other than English at home, a figure expected to increase (U. S. Bureau of the Census, 1999).

BILINGUAL DEVELOPMENT. Children can become bilingual in two ways: (1) by acquiring both languages at the same time in early childhood, or (2) by learning a second language after mastering the first. Children of bilingual parents who teach them both languages in early childhood show no special problems with language development. They acquire normal native ability in the language of their surrounding community and good to native ability in the second language, depending on their exposure to it. When children acquire a second language after they already speak a first language, it generally takes them 3 to 5 years to become as fluent as native-speaking age-mates (Ramirez et al., 1991).

As with first-language development, a *sensitive period* for second-language development exists. That is, mastery of language must begin sometime in childhood for full development to occur (Mayberry, 1994). In a study of Chinese and Korean adults who had immigrated to the United States at varying ages, those who began mastering English between 3 and 7 years scored as well as native speakers on a test of grammatical knowledge. As age of arrival in the United States increased through adolescence, test scores gradually declined (Newport, 1991). The ability to pronounce a second language without accent also decreases with age—gradually during childhood and sharply at adolescence (Anderson & Graham, 1994).

Research shows that bilingualism has a positive impact on cognitive development. Children who are fluent in two languages do better than others on tests of selective attention, analytical reasoning, concept formation, and cognitive flexibility (Bialystok, 1999; Hakuta, Ferdman, & Diaz, 1987). In addition, bilingual children are advanced in ability to reflect on language. They are more aware that words are arbitrary symbols, more conscious of language structure and detail, and better at noticing errors of grammar and meaning in spoken and written prose—capacities that enhance their reading achievement (Bialystok, 1997; Campbell & Sais, 1995; Ricciardelli, 1992).

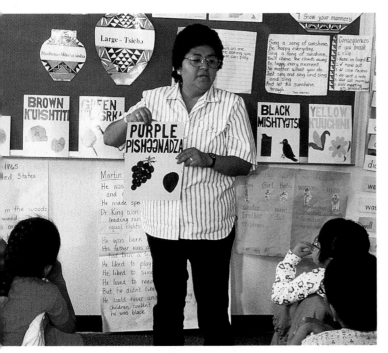

■ *These Pueblo children attend a bilingual education program in which they receive instruction in their native language and in English. In classrooms where both the first and second language are integrated into the curriculum, ethnic minority children are more involved in learning, participate more actively in class discussions, and acquire the second language more easily. (Photo courtesy: Robert E. Daemmrich/Stone)*

■ BILINGUAL EDUCATION. The advantages of bilingualism provide strong justification for bilingual education programs in schools. In Canada, where both English and French are official languages, *language immersion programs*, in which English-speaking elementary school children are taught entirely in French, are very successful in developing fully bilingual children (Piatt, 1993).

Yet the question of how American ethnic minority children with limited English proficiency should be educated is hotly debated. On one side of the controversy are those who believe that time spent communicating in the child's native tongue detracts from English language achievement, which is crucial for success in the worlds of school and work. On the other side are educators committed to truly *bilingual education*—developing minority children's native language while fostering mastery of English. Providing instruction in the native tongue lets minority children know that their heritage is respected (McGroarty, 1992). In addition, it prevents *semilingualism*, or inadequate proficiency in both languages. When minority children gradually lose their first language as a result of being taught the second, they end up limited in both languages for a time, a circumstance that leads to serious academic difficulties (August & Garcia, 1988). Semilingualism is believed to contribute to

high rates of school failure and dropout among low-SES Hispanic youngsters, who make up nearly 50 percent of the American language-minority population.

At present, public opinion sides with the first of these two viewpoints. Many states have passed laws declaring English to be their official language, creating conditions in which schools have no obligation to teach minority pupils in languages other than English. In 1998, California voters passed a law that eliminated bilingual education in favor of a one-year, English-only immersion course for non-English-speaking pupils, a move expected to spread to other states. Yet in classrooms where both languages are integrated into the curriculum, minority children are more involved in learning, participate more actively in class discussions, and acquire the second language more easily. In contrast, when teachers speak only in a language their pupils can barely understand, children display frustration, boredom, and withdrawal (Crawford, 1995, 1997).

American English-only supporters often point to the success of language immersion programs in Canada. Yet different educational strategies appear necessary for low-income minority children whose native language is not valued by the larger society (Mohanty & Perregaux, 1997). Bilingualism offers one of the best examples of how language, once learned, becomes an important tool of the mind and fosters cognitive development. From this perspective, the goals of schooling could reasonably be broadened to include helping all children become bilingual, thereby fostering the cognitive, language, and cultural enrichment of the entire nation.

 ASK YOURSELF . . .

■ *Ten-year-old Shana arrived home from school after a long day, sank into the living room sofa, and commented, "I'm totally wiped out!" Megan, her 5-year-old sister, looked puzzled and asked, "What did'ya wipe out, Shana?" Explain Shana's and Megan's different understandings of the meaning of this expression.*

🌳 *Cite ways that truly bilingual education can contribute to minority children's cognitive and academic development and later-life success.*

LEARNING IN SCHOOL

Throughout this chapter, we have touched on evidence indicating that schools are vital forces in children's cognitive development. How do schools exert such a powerful impact? Research looking at schools as complex social systems—their class size, educational philosophies, teacher–pupil interaction patterns, and the larger cultural context in which they are embedded—provides important insights into this question.

CLASS SIZE

As each school year began, Rena telephoned the principal's office and asked how large Joey's and Lizzie's classes would be. Her concern is well founded. Class size influences children's learning. In a large field experiment, over 6,000 Tennessee kindergartners were randomly assigned to three class types: small (13 to 17 pupils), regular (22 to 25 pupils), and regular with a full-time teacher's aide. These arrangements continued into third grade. Small-class pupils—especially minority children—scored higher in reading and math achievement and continued to do so after they returned to regular-size classes in fourth and fifth grades. Adding teachers' aides to regular-size classes had no consistent impact on achievement (Mosteller, 1995).

Why is small class size beneficial? Teachers of fewer children spend less time disciplining and more time giving individual attention, and children's attitudes toward school and peer interactions are more positive. The learning advantages of small classes are greatest in the early years of schooling, when children require more adult assistance (Blatchford & Mortimore, 1994).

EDUCATIONAL PHILOSOPHIES

Each teacher brings to the classroom an educational philosophy that plays a major role in children's learning. Two philosophical approaches have received the most research attention. They differ in what children are taught, the way they are believed to learn, and how their progress is evaluated.

■ TRADITIONAL VERSUS OPEN CLASSROOMS. In a **traditional classroom,** children are relatively passive in the learning process. The teacher is the sole authority and does most of the talking. Pupils spend most of their time at their desks—listening, responding when called on, and completing assigned tasks. Their progress is evaluated by how well they keep pace with normative standards for their grade.

In an **open classroom,** children are viewed as active agents in their own development. The teacher assumes a flexible authority role, sharing decision making with pupils, who learn at their own pace. Pupils are evaluated in relation to their own prior development; comparisons with same-age pupils are less important. A glance inside an open classroom reveals richly equipped learning centers, small groups of pupils working on tasks they choose themselves, and a teacher responding to individual needs.

During the past few decades, the pendulum in American education has swung back and forth between these two views. In the 1960s and early 1970s, open education gained in popularity, inspired by Piaget's vision of the child as an active, motivated learner. Then, when concern over the academic progress of American children and youths increased, a "back to basics" movement arose. Classrooms returned to traditional instruction, a style still prevalent today.

Although older children in traditional classrooms have a slight edge in academic achievement, open settings are associated with other benefits—gains in critical thinking, greater valuing of individual differences in classmates, and more positive attitudes toward school (Walberg, 1986). Furthermore, when whole-class, teacher-directed instruction is emphasized in kindergarten, children display more stress behaviors, such as wiggling, rocking, and talking out, and poorer study habits when they get to grade school (Burts et al., 1992; Hart et al., 1998). These negative outcomes are strongest for low-SES children. Yet teachers tend to prefer a traditional approach for economically disadvantaged pupils, despite its negative impact on motivation and learning (Stipek & Byler, 1997).

■ NEW PHILOSOPHICAL DIRECTIONS. The philosophies of some teachers fall in between traditional and open. They want to foster high achievement as well as critical thinking, positive social relationships, and excitement about learning. New experiments in elementary education, grounded in Vygotsky's sociocultural theory, represent this intermediate point of view (Forman, Minick, & Stone, 1993). Vygotsky's emphasis on the social origins of higher cognitive processes has inspired the following educational themes:

- *Teachers and children as partners in learning.* A classroom rich in dialogue—both teacher–child and child–child collaboration—fosters transfer of culturally valued ways of thinking to children.

- *Experiences with many types of symbolic communication in meaningful activities.* As children master reading, writing, and quantitative reasoning, they become aware of their culture's communication systems, reflect on their own thinking, and bring it under voluntary control. (Can you identify research presented earlier in this chapter that supports this theme?)

- *Teaching adapted to each child's zone of proximal development.* Providing assistance that is responsive to current understandings but that encourages children to take the next step helps ensure that each pupil makes the best progress possible.

The most extensive educational reform based on Vygotsky's theory is the *Kamehameha Elementary Education Program (KEEP).* KEEP classrooms are rich in activity settings designed to enhance teacher–child and child–child interaction. In each setting, children work on a project that ensures that their learning will be active and directed toward a meaningful goal. For example, they might read a story and discuss its meaning or draw a map of the playground to promote an understanding of geography. All children enter a focal activity setting, called Center One, at least once each morning for scaffolding of challenging literacy skills. Text content is carefully selected to relate to children's experiences, and teaching builds on children's ideas. The precise organization of each KEEP classroom is adjusted to fit the learning styles of its pupils, creating culturally responsive environments (Au, 1997; Tharp, 1993, 1994).

Thousands of low-SES minority children have attended KEEP classrooms in Hawaii and Los Angeles and on a Navajo reservation in Arizona. Research suggests that the approach is highly effective. In KEEP schools, minority pupils performed at their expected grade level in reading, much better than children of the same background enrolled in traditional schools. Furthermore, KEEP pupils more often participated in class discussion, used elaborate language structures, and more often supported one another's learning than did non-KEEP controls. As the KEEP model is more widely applied, it may prove successful with all types of children because of its comprehensive goals and effort to meet the learning needs of a wide range of pupils.

TEACHER–PUPIL INTERACTION

In all classrooms, teachers vary in their interactions with children—differences that affect academic achievement. Whereas Lizzie's teacher emphasized factual knowledge, Joey's teacher encouraged children to grapple with ideas and apply their knowledge to new situations. In a study of fifth-grade social studies and math lessons, students were far more attentive when teachers encouraged high-level thinking (Stodolsky, 1988). And in a longitudinal investigation of middle-school students, those in academically more demanding classrooms showed better attendance and larger gains in math achievement over the next 2 years (Phillips, 1997). The Caregiving Concerns table below suggests ways to encourage school-age children to think critically—to consider deeper meanings by reflecting, evaluating, and expressing their ideas in clear and useful ways.

Teachers do not interact in the same way with all children. Some get more attention and praise than others. Well-behaved, high-achieving pupils experience positive interactions with their teachers. In contrast, teachers especially dislike children who achieve poorly and are also disruptive. These unruly pupils are often criticized and are rarely called on in class discussions. When they seek special help or permission, their requests are usually denied (Good & Brophy, 1996).

CAREGIVING CONCERNS

Encouraging Critical Thinking in School-Age Children

SUGGESTION	DESCRIPTION
Promote open-ended questioning and interaction.	Engaging in open-ended questioning ("why" and "how") and discussing answers to those questions encourage children to be adventurous and inquiring and to prompt each other's thinking.
Ask children to clarify and draw inferences.	Asking "What is the main point?" "What does it mean?" or "What might happen next?" encourages children to be active, precise thinkers and to consider the implications of their ideas.
Help children view situations from multiple perspectives.	Once children give their own opinion on an issue, ask them to state and try to support opposing perspectives. Seeing things from other viewpoints makes children more aware of their own thinking patterns and encourages them to be open-minded and flexible.
Use a precise "language of thinking."	When adults use a specific "thinking vocabulary" that includes such terms as *hypothesis, reasons, conclusions, evidence,* and *opinion,* their verbal cues evoke a richer variety of thought processes in children.
Explain thinking possibilities.	Explaining thinking possibilities makes children conscious of the ingredients of critical thinking and, therefore, more likely to apply this knowledge. For example, an adult might discuss with children what the word *hypothesis* means and how a hypothesis in science differs from one in history or everyday life.
Model critical thinking.	When children observe adults engaged in critical thinking, they are more likely to adopt it as a valued activity for themselves.
Give feedback that supports critical thinking.	Positive feedback and suggestions for how to do better rather than criticism establish a safe haven for critical thinking that permits children to take risks.

Sources: Byrnes, 1993; Tishman, Perkins, & Jay, 1995.

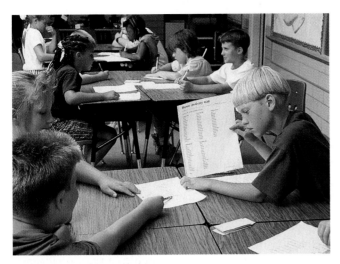

■ *In this combined third–fourth, multigrade classroom, teachers and children expect some pupils to be advanced over others. Rather than competing, children often cooperate and help one another. Research shows that academic achievement, self-esteem, and attitudes toward school are consistently more favorable in the multigrade than single-grade arrangement. (Photo courtesy: Marc Pikempner/Impact Visuals)*

Unfortunately, once teachers' attitudes toward pupils are established, they are in danger of becoming more extreme than is warranted by children's behavior. A special concern is that an **educational self-fulfilling prophecy** can be set in motion: Children may adopt teachers' positive or negative views and start to live up to them. Many studies show that school-age pupils become increasingly aware of teacher opinion, and it can influence their performance (Skinner & Belmont, 1993). This effect is especially strong in classrooms where teachers emphasize competition and frequently make public comparisons among children (Weinstein et al., 1987).

When teachers hold inaccurate views, low achievers are affected more than high achievers (Madon, Jussim, & Eccles, 1997). High-achieving pupils have less room to improve when teachers think well of them, and they can fall back on their history of success when a teacher is critical. Low-achieving pupils' sensitivity to self-fulfilling prophecies can be beneficial when teachers believe in them. But they may only rarely have the chance to reap these benefits.

GROUPING PRACTICES

In many schools, pupils are assigned to *homogeneous* groups or classes in which children of similar ability levels are taught together. In "low" groups, pupils get more drill on basic facts and skills, a slower learning pace, and less time on academic work. Gradually, they show a drop in self-esteem and are viewed by themselves and others as "not smart." Not surprisingly, ability grouping widens the

gap between high and low achievers (Dornbusch, Glasgow, & Lin, 1996).

Partly because of these findings, some schools have increased the *heterogeneity* of pupils taught together by combining two or three adjacent grades. In multigrade classrooms, academic achievement, self-esteem, and attitudes toward school are consistently more favorable than in the single-grade arrangement (Lloyd, 1999). Perhaps mixed-grade grouping decreases competition, increases classroom harmony, and promotes peer tutoring. When older or more expert pupils teach younger or less expert pupils, both tutors and tutees benefit in achievement and self-esteem (Renninger, 1998). But for peer tutoring to succeed, tutors need extensive training and guidance.

TEACHING CHILDREN WITH SPECIAL NEEDS

We have seen that effective teachers flexibly adjust their teaching strategies to accommodate pupils with a wide range of characteristics. But such adjustments are increasingly difficult at the very low and high ends of the ability distribution. How do schools serve children with special learning needs?

■ **MAINSTREAMING CHILDREN WITH LEARNING DIFFICULTIES.** The Individuals with Disabilities Education Act (Public Law 101–475) mandates that schools place children requiring special supports for learning in the "least restrictive" environments that meet their educational needs. The law led to a rapid increase in **mainstreaming** of pupils with learning difficulties in regular classrooms for part of the school day, a practice designed to prepare them better for participation in society. Largely due to parental pressures, mainstreaming has been extended to **full inclusion**—placement in regular classrooms full time.

Some mainstreamed pupils are **mildly mentally retarded**—children whose IQs fall between 55 and 70 and who also show problems in adaptive behavior, or skills of everyday living (American Psychiatric Association, 1994). But the largest number have **learning disabilities.** Learning disabled pupils, who constitute 5 to 10 percent of school-age children, have difficulties with one or more aspects of learning, usually with reading. As a result, their achievements are considerably behind what would be expected on the basis of their IQs. Their problems cannot be traced to any obvious physical or emotional difficulty or to environmental disadvantage. Instead, faulty brain functioning is believed to be responsible (Bender, 1996; Polloway et al., 1997). In most instances, the cause is unknown.

How Effective Are Mainstreaming and Full Inclusion? Does placement of these pupils in regular classes succeed in providing more appropriate academic experiences as well as integrated participation in classroom life? At pre-

■ *The pupil on the left, who has a learning disability, has been fully included in a regular classroom. Because his teacher takes special steps to encourage peer acceptance, individualizes instruction, minimizes comparisons with classmates, and promotes cooperative learning, this boy looks forward to school and is doing well. (Photo courtesy: Will Hart)*

sent, the evidence is not positive on either of these points. Achievement differences between mainstreamed pupils and those in self-contained classrooms are not great (Buysse & Bailey, 1993; MacMillan, Keogh, & Jones, 1986). Furthermore, children with disabilities in regular classrooms are often rejected by peers. Those who are mentally retarded are overwhelmed by the social skills of their classmates; they cannot interact quickly or adeptly in a conversation or game. And the processing deficits of some children with learning disabilities also lead to problems in social awareness and responsiveness (Gresham & MacMillan, 1997; Vaughn, Elbaum, & Schumm, 1996).

Does this mean that children with special needs cannot be served in regular classrooms? This extreme conclusion is not warranted. When high-quality support services are available, full inclusion can help many pupils with mild disabilities. Otherwise, children may do best when they receive instruction in a resource room for part of the day and in the regular classroom for the remainder. In the resource room, a special education teacher works with pupils on an individual and small-group basis. Then, depending on their abilities, children are mainstreamed for different subjects and amounts of time. This flexible approach helps ensure that the unique academic needs of each child will be served (Hocutt, 1996; Lerner, 1989).

Once children enter the regular classroom, special steps must to be taken to promote peer acceptance. Cooperative learning and peer-tutoring experiences in which main-

streamed children and their classmates work together lead to friendly interaction and improved social acceptance (Siegel, 1996). Teachers can also prepare children for the arrival of a special-needs pupil and enlist parents' assistance in encouraging positive attitudes—a process best begun early, before children have become less accepting of peers with disabilities (Okagaki et al., 1998).

■ GIFTED CHILDREN. In Joey and Lizzie's school, some children were **gifted.** They displayed exceptional intellectual strengths. Like mainstreamed pupils, their characteristics were diverse. In every grade were one or two pupils with IQ scores above 130, the standard definition of giftedness based on intelligence test performance (Gardner, 1998b). High-IQ children, as we have seen, are particularly quick at academic work. Yet recognition that intelligence tests do not sample the entire range of human mental skills has led to an expanded conception of giftedness in schools.

Creativity and Talent. High creativity can result in a child being designated as gifted. Tests of creativity tap **divergent thinking**—the generation of multiple and unusual possibilities when faced with a task or problem. Divergent thinking contrasts sharply with **convergent thinking,** which involves arriving at a single correct answer and is emphasized on intelligence tests (Guilford, 1985).

Recognizing that highly creative children (like high-IQ children) are often better at some tasks than others, researchers have devised verbal, figural, and "real-world-problem" tests of divergent thinking (Runco, 1992; Torrance, 1988). A verbal measure might ask children to name as many uses for common objects (such as a newspaper) as they can. A figural measure might ask them to come up with as many drawings based on a circular motif as possible (see Figure 9.8). A "real-world problem" measure either gives children everyday problems or requires them to think of such problems and then suggest solutions. Responses to all these tests can be scored for the number of ideas generated as well as for their originality.

Yet critics of these measures point out that at best, they are imperfect predictors of creative accomplishment in everyday life, since they tap only one of the complex cognitive contributions to creativity (Cramond, 1994). Also involved are the ability to define a new and important problem, to evaluate divergent ideas and choose the most promising, and to call on relevant knowledge to understand and solve the problem (Sternberg & Lubart, 1995).

Consider these additional ingredients, and you will see why both children and adults usually demonstrate creativity in only one or a few related areas. Partly for this reason, definitions of giftedness have been extended to include *specialized talent.* There is clear evidence that outstanding performances in particular fields, such as mathematics, science, music, art, athletics, and leadership, have roots in specialized skills that first appear in childhood.

FIGURE 9.8

■ **Responses of an 8-year-old who scored high on a figural measure of divergent thinking.** This child was asked to make as many pictures as she could from the circles on the page. The titles she gave her drawings, from left to right, are as follows: "Dracula," "one-eyed monster," "pumpkin," "Hula-Hoop," "poster," "wheelchair," "earth," "moon," "planet," "movie camera," "sad face," "picture," "stoplight," "beach ball," "the letter O," "car," and "glasses." Tests of divergent thinking tap only one of the complex cognitive contributions to creativity. (Test form copyright © 1980 by Scholastic Testing Service, Inc. Reprinted by permission of Scholastic Testing Service, Inc., from *The Torrance Tests of Creative Thinking* by E. P. Torrance. Child's drawings reprinted by permission of Laura Berk.)

At the same time, talent must be nurtured in a favorable environment. Studies of the backgrounds of talented children and highly accomplished adults often reveal homes rich in stimulating activities and parents who emphasize curiosity (Albert, 1994; Perleth & Heller, 1994). In addition, such parents recognize their child's creative potential and provide special lessons and (as the talent develops) apprenticeship under inspiring teachers (Feldman, 1991; Winner, 1996). Classrooms in which children can take risks, challenge the instructor, and reflect on ideas without being rushed to the next assignment are also important (Sternberg & Lubart, 1991).

Educating the Gifted. Although programs for the gifted exist in many schools, debate about their effectiveness usually focuses on factors irrelevant to giftedness—whether to offer enrichment in regular classrooms, to pull children out for special instruction (the most common practice), or to advance brighter pupils to a higher grade. Children of all ages fare well academically and socially within each of these models (Moon & Feldhusen, 1994). Yet the extent to which they foster creativity and talent depends on opportunities to acquire relevant skills.

Recently, Gardner's theory of multiple intelligences has inspired several model programs that include all pupils. Meaningful activities, each tapping a specific intelligence or set of intelligences, serve as contexts for assessing strengths and weaknesses and, on that basis, teaching new knowledge and original thinking. For example, linguistic intelligence might be fostered through storytelling or playwriting, spatial intelligence through drawing, sculpting, or taking apart and reassembling objects (Gardner, 1993, 2000).

Evidence is still needed on how effectively these programs nurture children's talents (Plucker, Callahan, & Tomchin, 1996). But so far, they have succeeded in one way—by highlighting the strengths of some pupils who previously had been considered ordinary or even at risk for school failure. Consequently, they may be especially useful in identifying talented minority children, who are underrepresented in school programs for the gifted (Suzuki & Valencia, 1997).

HOW WELL EDUCATED ARE AMERICA'S CHILDREN?

Our discussion of schooling has largely focused on what teachers can do to support the education of children. Yet a great many factors, both within and outside schools, affect children's learning. Societal values, school resources, quality of teaching, and parental encouragement all play important roles. Nowhere are these multiple influences more apparent than when schooling is examined in cross-cultural perspective.

EDUCATION IN JAPAN, TAIWAN, AND THE UNITED STATES

Why do Asian children perform so well academically? Research examining societal, school, and family conditions in Japan, Taiwan, and the United States provides some answers.

CULTURAL VALUING OF ACADEMIC ACHIEVEMENT. In Japan and Taiwan, natural resources are limited. Progress in science and technology is essential for economic well-being. Since a well-educated workforce is necessary to meet this goal, children's mastery of academic skills is vital. In the United States, attitudes toward academic achievement are far less unified. Many Americans believe it is more important to encourage children to feel good about themselves and to explore various areas of knowledge than to perform well in school.

EMPHASIS ON EFFORT. Japanese and Taiwanese parents and teachers believe that all children have the potential to master challenging academic tasks if they work hard enough. In contrast, many American

parents and teachers regard native ability as the key to academic success (Stevenson, 1992). These differences in attitude may contribute to the fact that American parents are less inclined to encourage activities at home that might enhance school performance. Japanese and Taiwanese children spend more free time studying, reading, and playing academic-related games than do children in the United States (Stevenson & Lee, 1990).

INVOLVEMENT OF PARENTS IN EDUCATION. Asian parents devote many hours to helping their children with homework. American parents spend very little and do not regard homework in elementary school as especially important. Overall, American parents are far more satisfied with the quality of their children's education, hold lower standards for their children's academic performance, and are less concerned about how well their children are doing in school (Stevenson, Chen, & Lee, 1993; Stevenson & Lee, 1990).

HIGH-QUALITY EDUCATION FOR ALL. Unlike American teachers,

Japanese and Taiwanese teachers do not make early educational decisions on the basis of achievement. There are no separate ability groups or tracks in elementary school. Instead, all pupils receive the same nationally mandated, high-quality instruction. Academic lessons are particularly well organized and presented in ways that capture children's attention. Topics in mathematics are treated in greater depth, and there is less repetition of material taught the previous year.

MORE TIME DEVOTED TO INSTRUCTION. In Japan and Taiwan, the school year is over 50 days longer than in the United States. When one American elementary school experimented by adding 30 days to its school year, extended-year pupils scored higher in reading, general-knowledge, and (especially) math achievement than did pupils in similar-quality schools with a traditional calendar (Frazier & Morrison, 1998).

Furthermore, on a day-to-day basis, Japanese and Taiwanese teachers devote much more time to academic pursuits, especially mathematics. However, Asian schools are not regimented places, as many

Perhaps you are aware from recent news reports that American students achieve poorly when compared with students in other industrialized nations. In previous international studies of mathematics and science achievement, young people from Hong Kong, Japan, Korea, and Taiwan have consistently been among the top performers, whereas Americans have scored no better than at the mean and often below it (Lapointe, Askew, & Mead, 1992; Lapointe, Mead, & Askew, 1992). The most recent assessment revealed a sharp decline in performance with increasing grade. In math, American fourth graders were even with fourth graders in many other countries; in science, they were near the top. By eighth grade, math performance dropped below the international average; by twelfth grade, U.S. math and science knowledge was near the bottom in

relation to 21 participating countries (U.S. Department of Education, 1998).

Why do American children fall behind in academic accomplishment? According to the international study, math instruction in the United States is not as challenging and focused as it is in other countries—findings consistent with in-depth research on learning environments in top-performing Asian nations. Except for the influence of language on early counting skills (see page 298), they do not start school with cognitive advantages over their American peers (Geary, 1996). Instead, as the Variations box above explains, a variety of social forces combine to foster a strong commitment to learning in Asian families and schools.

The Japanese and Taiwanese examples underscore that families, schools, and the larger society must work together

Americans believe. An 8-hour school day permits extra recesses and a longer lunch period, with plenty of time for play, social interaction, field trips, and extracurricular activities. Frequent breaks may increase children's capacity to learn (Pellegrini & Smith, 1998).

COMMUNICATION BETWEEN TEACHERS AND PARENTS. Japanese and Taiwanese teachers get to know their pupils especially well. They teach the same children for 2 or 3 years and make visits to the home once or twice a year. Teachers and parents communicate by writing messages about assignments, academic performance, and behavior in small notebooks, which children carry back and forth every day. No such formalized system of frequent teacher–parent communication exists in the United States (Stevenson & Lee, 1990).

Do Japanese and Taiwanese children pay a price for the pressure placed on them to succeed? By high school, academic work often displaces other experiences, since Asian adolescents must pass a highly competitive entrance exam to gain admission to college. Yet Asian parenting practices that encourage academic competence do not undermine children's social development. In fact, the highest performing Asian students are very well adjusted (Crystal et al., 1994; Huntsinger, Jose, & Larson, 1998). Awareness of the ingredients of Asian success has prompted Americans to rethink current educational practices.

■ *Japanese children achieve considerably better than their American counterparts for a variety of reasons. A longer school day permits frequent alternation of academic instruction with pleasurable activity, an approach that fosters learning. During a break from academic subjects, these Japanese elementary-school children enjoy a class in the art of calligraphy. (Photo courtesy: Cameramann/The Image Works)*

to upgrade education. The current educational reform movement in the United States is an encouraging sign. Throughout the country, academic standards and teacher certification requirements are being strengthened. In addition, many schools are working to increase parent involvement in children's education. Parents who create stimulating learning environments at home, monitor their child's academic progress, help with homework, and communicate often with teachers have children who consistently show superior academic progress (Connors & Epstein, 1996). The returns of these efforts can be seen in recent national assessments of educational progress (Campbell, Voelkl, & Donahue, 1997). After two decades of decline, children's overall achievement in reading, math, and science seems to be on the rise.

ASK YOURSELF . . .

🌳 *Ricardo's first-grade teacher uses teacher-directed, whole-class instruction and has placed him in a low-ability reading group. Vincente attends a mixed-grade classroom with first through third graders, and his teacher has small, heterogeneous groups of pupils work on projects in learning centers. Which child, Ricardo or Vincente, is likely to show higher achievement and to like school better? Explain.*

🌳 *Carrie is a mainstreamed first grader with a learning disability. What steps can her school and teacher take to ensure that she develops at her best, academically and socially?*

PHYSICAL DEVELOPMENT

BODY GROWTH

Describe major trends in body growth during middle childhood.

- Gains in body size during middle childhood extend the pattern of slow, regular growth established during the preschool years. Bones continue to lengthen and broaden, and all 20 primary teeth are replaced by permanent ones. By age 9, girls overtake boys in physical size.

COMMON HEALTH PROBLEMS

What vision and hearing problems are common in middle childhood?

- During middle childhood, children from economically advantaged homes are at their healthiest, due to good nutrition and rapid development of the immune system. At the same time, a variety of health problems do occur, many of which are more prevalent among low-SES children.

- The most common vision problem in middle childhood is myopia, or nearsightedness. It is influenced by heredity and the way children use their eyes. Myopia is one of the few health conditions that increase with family education and income. Because of untreated ear infections, many low-income children experience some hearing loss during the school years.

Describe the causes and consequences of serious nutritional problems in middle childhood, granting special attention to obesity.

- Poverty-stricken children in developing countries and in the United States continue to suffer from malnutrition during middle childhood.

When malnutrition is allowed to persist for many years, its negative impact on physical growth, intelligence, motor coordination, and attention is permanent.

- Overweight and **obesity** are growing problems in affluent nations like the United States. Although heredity contributes to obesity, parental feeding practices, maladaptive eating habits, and lack of exercise also play important roles. Obese children are often rejected by peers and have serious adjustment problems. Family-based interventions in which both parents and children change eating patterns and sedentary lifestyles are the most effective approaches to treatment.

What factors contribute to nocturnal enuresis and asthma, and how can these health problems be reduced?

- In the majority of cases, **nocturnal enuresis,** or bedwetting during the night, has biological roots. The most effective treatment is a urine alarm that works according to conditioning principles.

- Asthma is the most common cause of school absence and childhood hospitalization. Although heredity contributes to asthma, environmental factors—pollution, stressful home lives, and lack of access to good health care—have led the illness to increase.

Describe changes in unintentional injuries in middle childhood.

- Unintentional injuries increase over middle childhood and adolescence, especially for boys, with auto and bicycle accidents accounting for most of the rise. Safety education programs that teach safety practices and reward children for following them are especially important during the school years.

MOTOR DEVELOPMENT AND PLAY

Cite major changes in motor development and play during middle childhood.

- Gains in flexibility, balance, agility, force, and reaction time contribute to school-age children's gross motor development. Fine motor development also improves. Children's writing becomes more legible, and their drawings show increases in organization, detail, and representation of depth. Gender stereotypes, which affect parental encouragement, largely account for boys' superior performance on a wide range of gross motor skills.

- Organized games with rules become common during the school years. Children's spontaneous games support cognitive and social development. Many school-age youngsters are not physically fit. Frequent, high-quality physical education classes help ensure that all children have access to the benefits of regular exercise and play.

COGNITIVE DEVELOPMENT

PIAGET'S THEORY: THE CONCRETE OPERATIONAL STAGE

What are the major characteristics of concrete operational thought?

- During the **concrete operational stage,** children can reason logically about concrete, tangible information. Mastery of conservation indicates that children can **decenter** and **reverse** their thinking. They are also better at hierarchical classification, **seriation,** and **transitive inference.** School-age youngsters' spatial reasoning improves, as their understanding of distance and ability to give directions reveal.

- Piaget used the term **horizontal décalage** to describe the school-age child's gradual mastery of logical concepts. Concrete operational thought is limited in that children have difficulty reasoning about abstract ideas.

Discuss recent research on concrete operational thought.

- Recent evidence indicates that specific cultural practices, especially those associated with schooling, affect children's mastery of Piagetian tasks. Some researchers believe that the gradual development of operational thought can best be understood within an information-processing framework.

INFORMATION PROCESSING

Cite two basic changes in information processing, and describe the development of attention and memory in middle childhood.

- Brain development contributes to gains in information-processing capacity and cognitive inhibition. These changes facilitate many aspects of thinking.

- During the school years, attention becomes more selective, adaptable, and planful, and memory strategies also improve. **Rehearsal** appears first, followed by **organization** and then **elaboration.** The serious attentional difficulties of children with **attention-deficit hyperactivity disorder** (ADHD) may be due to an impairment in inhibition and lead to both academic and social problems.

- Development of the long-term knowledge base facilitates memory by making new information easier to store and retrieve. Children's motivation to use what they know also contributes to memory development. Memory strategies are promoted by learning activities in school.

Describe the school-age child's theory of mind and capacity to engage in self-regulation.

- Metacognition expands over middle childhood. School-age children regard the mind as an active, constructive agent, and they develop an integrated theory of mind. **Cognitive self-regulation**—putting what one knows about thinking into action—develops slowly over middle childhood and adolescence. It improves with instruction in how to check and monitor progress toward a goal.

Discuss current controversies in teaching reading and mathematics to elementary school children.

- Skilled reading draws on all aspects of the information-processing system. Experts disagree on whether a **whole-language approach** or **basic-skills approach** should be used to teach beginning reading. A mixture of both appears most effective. Teaching that blends practice in basic skills with conceptual understanding also seems best in mathematics.

INDIVIDUAL DIFFERENCES IN MENTAL DEVELOPMENT

Describe major approaches to defining and measuring intelligence.

- During the school years, IQ becomes more stable, and it correlates well with academic achievement. Most intelligence tests yield an overall score as well as scores for separate intellectual factors. The Stanford-Binet Intelligence Scale and Wechsler Intelligence Scale for Children–III (WISC–III) are widely used individually administered intelligence tests.

- Aspects of information processing related to IQ include speed of thinking and effective strategy use. Sternberg's **triarchic theory** views intelligence as a complex interaction of information-processing skills, specific experiences, and contextual (or cultural) influences. According to Gardner's **theory of multiple intelligences,** eight mental abilities exist, each of which has a unique biological basis and distinct course of development. Gardner's theory has been especially helpful in understanding and nurturing children's talents.

Describe evidence indicating that both heredity and environment contribute to intelligence.

- Heritability estimates and adoption research indicate that intelligence is a product of both heredity and environment. Studies of black children adopted into well-to-do white homes indicate that the black–white IQ gap is substantially determined by environment.

- IQ scores are affected by specific learning experiences, including exposure to certain language customs and knowledge sampled by the test. Cultural bias in intelligence testing can lead test scores to underestimate minority children's intelligence.

LANGUAGE DEVELOPMENT

Describe changes in school-age children's vocabulary, grammar, and pragmatics, along with the advantages of bilingualism for development.

- During middle childhood, vocabulary continues to grow rapidly, and children have a more precise and flexible understanding of word meanings. Grasp of complex grammatical constructions and use of conversational strategies also become more refined.

- A sensitive period for first- and second-language development exists. Mastery must begin in childhood for full development to occur. Bilingual children are advanced in cognitive development and language awareness. Nevertheless, bilingual education for American non-English-speaking minority children is hotly debated.

LEARNING IN SCHOOL

Describe the impact of class size and educational philosophies on children's motivation and academic achievement.

■ As class size in the lower grades drops to 13 to 17 pupils, academic achievement improves. Older pupils in **traditional classrooms** have a slight edge in academic achievement. Those in **open classrooms** tend to be critical thinkers who respect individual differences and have more positive attitudes toward school.

■ The Kamehameha Elementary Education Program (KEEP) uses a balanced philosophical viewpoint based on Vygotsky's theory. It is highly effective in promoting learning among children who typically achieve poorly.

Discuss the role of teacher–pupil interaction and grouping practices in academic achievement.

■ Instruction that encourages high-level thinking fosters children's interest and academic progress. **Educational self-fulfilling prophecies** are most likely to occur in classrooms that emphasize competition and public evaluation. Teachers' inaccurate views have a greater impact on low achievers than high achievers.

Under what conditions is placement of children with mild mental retardation and learning disabilities in regular classrooms successful?

■ Pupils with **mild mental retardation** and **learning disabilities** are often placed into regular classrooms, usually through **mainstreaming** but also through **full inclusion.** The success of regular class placement depends on meeting individual learning needs and positive peer relations.

■ **Giftedness** includes high IQ, high creativity, and exceptional talent. Tests of creativity tap **divergent thinking,** which contrasts with the **convergent thinking** emphasized on intelligence tests. Gifted children are best served by educational programs that build on their special strengths.

Why do American children fall behind children in other industrialized nations in academic accomplishments?

■ American children fare poorly when their achievement is compared with that of children in other industrialized nations. In contrast, children from Asian nations are consistently among the top performers. A strong commitment to learning in families and schools underlies the greater academic success of Asian pupils.

IMPORTANT TERMS AND CONCEPTS

attention-deficit hyperactivity disorder (ADHD) (p. 294)
basic skills approach (p. 298)
cognitive inhibition (p. 293)
cognitive self-regulation (p. 297)
concrete operational stage (p. 291)
convergent thinking (p. 310)
decentration (p. 291)
divergent thinking (p. 310)
educational self-fulfilling prophecy (p. 309)

elaboration (p. 295)
full inclusion (p. 309)
gifted (p. 310)
horizontal décalage (p. 292)
learning disabilities (p. 309)
mainstreaming (p. 309)
mild mental retardation (p. 309)
nocturnal enuresis (p. 285)
obesity (p. 282)
open classroom (p. 307)

organization (p. 295)
rehearsal (p. 295)
reversibility (p. 291)
seriation (p. 291)
theory of multiple intelligences (p. 301)
traditional classroom (p. 307)
transitive inference (p. 291)
triarchic theory of intelligence (p. 300)
whole language approach (p. 297)

Consult the companion website for this book, where you will find additional weblinks and associated learning activities: www.abacon.com/berk

ADULT-ORGANIZED SPORTS FOR CHILDREN

Little League Baseball
www.littleleague.org

Organizes baseball and softball programs for 6- to 18-year-olds. Operates a special division for children with disabilities and sponsors an annual world series.

U.S. Youth Soccer Association
www.usysa.org

Supports soccer programs for 6- to 18-year-olds. Seeks to encourage widespread participation and offer equal opportunity regardless of ability or sex.

ATTENTION-DEFICIT HYPERACTIVITY DISORDER (ADHD)

Children and Adults with Attention-Deficit Hyperactivity Disorder
www.chadd.org

Provides support and education to families of children and adults with attention-deficit hyperactivity disorder. Encourages schools and health care professionals to be responsive to their needs.

BILINGUAL EDUCATION

National Association for Bilingual Education
www.nabe.org

An organization of educators, public citizens, and students aimed at increasing public understanding of the importance of bilingual education.

LEARNING DISABILITIES

Learning Disabilities Association of America
www.ldanatl.org

An organization of parents of children with learning disabilities and interested professionals. Local groups provide parent support and education and sponsor recreational programs and summer camps for children.

GIFTEDNESS

Association for the Gifted of the Council for Exceptional Children
www.cec.sped.org

An organization of educators and parents aimed at stimulating interest in program development for gifted children. Publishes Journal for the Education of the Gifted.

National Association for Gifted Children
www.nagc.org

Association of scholars, educators, and librarians devoted to advancing education for gifted children. Distributes information and sponsors institutes. Publishes the journal Gifted Child Quarterly.

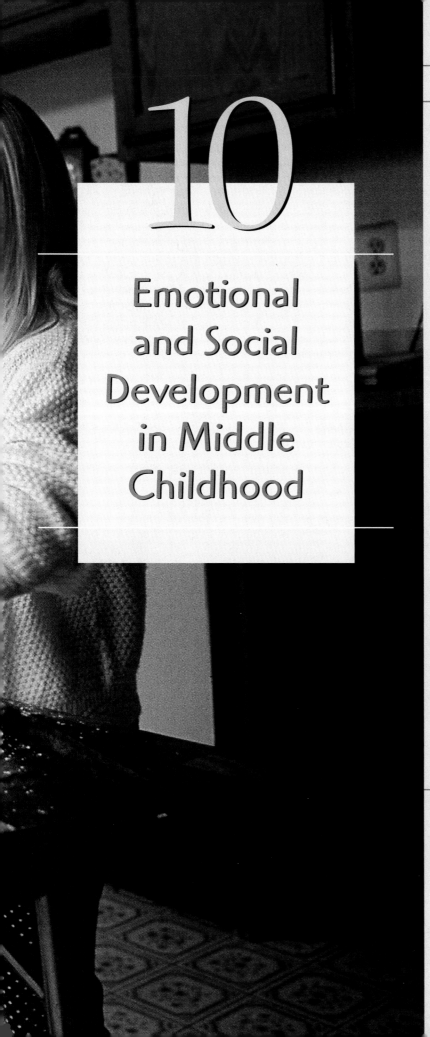

10

Emotional and Social Development in Middle Childhood

■ *The industriousness of middle childhood
involves mastery of useful skills and tasks. As
this 10-year-old boy and 6-year-old girl, who
are brother and sister, bake dinner rolls, they
become aware of each other's unique capacities,
learn the value of division of labor, and come to
view themselves as responsible, capable, and
helpful. (Photo courtesy: Brian Gordon Green/
National Geographic Image Collection)*

One late afternoon, Rena heard Joey dash through the front door, run upstairs, and call up his best friend, Terry. "Terry, gotta talk to you," pleaded Joey, out of breath from running home. "Everything was going great until that word I got—*porcupine*," remarked Joey, referring to the fifth-grade spelling bee at school that day. "Just my luck! *P-o-r-k*, that's how I spelled it! I can't believe it. Maybe I'm not so good at social studies," Joey confided, "but I *know* I'm better at spelling than that stuck-up Belinda Brown. Gosh, I knocked myself out studying those spelling lists. Then *she* got all the easy words. Did'ya see how snooty she acted after she won? If I *had* to lose, why couldn't it be to a nice person, anyhow!"

Joey's conversation reflects a whole new constellation of emotional and social capacities. First, Joey shows evidence of *industriousness*. By entering the spelling bee, he energetically pursued meaningful achievement in his culture—a major change of the middle childhood years. At the same time, Joey's social understanding has expanded. He can size himself and others up in terms of strengths, weaknesses, and personality characteristics. Furthermore, friendship means something quite different to Joey than it did at younger ages. Terry is a best friend whom Joey counts on for understanding and emotional support.

We begin this chapter by returning to Erikson's theory for an overview of the personality changes of middle childhood. Then we take a close look at emotional and social development. We will see how, as children reason more ef-

fectively and spend more time in school and with peers, their views of themselves, of others, and of social relationships become more complex.

Although school-age children spend less time with parents than they did at younger ages, the family remains a powerful context for development. Joey and Lizzie are growing up in homes profoundly affected by social change. Unlike her own mother, Rena has been employed since her children were preschoolers. In addition, Joey and Lizzie's home life has been disrupted by family discord: Rena is divorced. Although family lifestyles are more diverse than ever before, Joey's and Lizzie's experiences will help us appreciate that family functioning is far more important than family structure in ensuring children's well-being. Our chapter concludes with some common emotional problems of middle childhood.

ERIKSON'S THEORY: INDUSTRY VERSUS INFERIORITY

According to Erikson (1950), the personality changes of the school years build on Freud's *latency stage* (see Chapter 1, page 16). Although Freud's theory is no longer widely accepted, children whose experiences have been positive enter middle childhood with the calm confidence Freud intended by the term *latency*. Their energies are redirected from the make-believe of early childhood into realistic accomplishment.

Erikson believed that the combination of adult expectations and children's drive toward mastery sets the stage for the psychological conflict of middle childhood: **industry versus inferiority.** Industry means developing competence at useful skills and tasks. In cultures everywhere, improved physical and cognitive capacities mean that adults impose new demands. Children, in turn, are ready to meet these challenges and benefit from them.

In industrialized nations, the transition to middle childhood is marked by the beginning of formal schooling. With it comes literacy training, which prepares children for the vast array of specialized careers in complex societies. In school, children become aware of their own and others' unique capacities, learn the value of division of labor, and develop a sense of moral commitment and responsibility. The danger at this stage is *inferiority*, reflected in the sad pessimism of children who have little confidence in their ability to do things well. This sense of inadequacy can develop when family life has not prepared children for school life or when experiences with teachers and peers are so negative that they destroy children's feelings of competence and mastery.

■ *When Joey and Belinda Brown competed in the spelling bee, they showed evidence of industriousness by pursuing meaningful achievement in their culture. According to Erikson, developing a sense of industry is the critical psychosocial task of middle childhood. (Photo courtesy: David Lassman/The Image Works)*

Erikson's sense of industry combines several developments of middle childhood: a positive but realistic self-concept, pride in doing things well, moral responsibility, and cooperative participation with agemates. Let's see how these aspects of self and social relationships change over the school years.

SELF-DEVELOPMENT

Several transformations in self-understanding take place in middle childhood. First, children can describe themselves in terms of psychological traits. Second, they start to compare their own characteristics with those of their peers. Finally, they speculate about the causes of their strengths and weaknesses. These new ways of thinking about the self have a major impact on children's developing self-esteem.

CHANGES IN SELF-CONCEPT

During the school years, children develop a much more refined *me-self,* or self-concept, organizing their observations of behaviors and internal states into general dispositions, with a major change taking place between ages 8 and 11. The following self-description from an 11-year-old reflects this change:

> My name is A. I'm a human being. I'm a girl. I'm a truthful person. I'm not pretty. I do so-so in my studies. I'm a very good cellist. I'm a very good pianist. I'm a little bit tall for my age. I like several boys. I like several girls. I'm old-fashioned. I play tennis. I am a very good swimmer. I try to be helpful. I'm always ready to be friends with anybody. Mostly I'm good, but I lose my temper. I'm not well-liked by some girls and boys. I don't know if I'm liked by boys or not. (Montemayor & Eisen, 1977, pp. 317–318)

Notice that instead of specific behaviors, this child emphasizes competencies, as in "I'm a very good cellist" (Damon & Hart, 1988). Also, she clearly describes her personality and mentions both positive and negative attributes—"truthful" but "not pretty," "a good cellist [and] pianist" but only "so-so in my studies." Older school-age children are far less likely than younger children to describe themselves in all-or-none ways (Harter, 1996).

Another change in self-concept takes place in middle childhood: Around age 7, children begin to make **social comparisons.** They judge their appearance, abilities, and behavior in relation to those of others. In commenting on the spelling bee, Joey expressed some thoughts about how good he was compared to Belinda Brown—better at spelling but not so great at social studies (Ruble & Frey, 1991).

What factors are responsible for these revisions in self-concept? Cognitive development affects the changing *structure* of the self—children's ability to combine typical experiences and behaviors into psychological dispositions. The *content* of self-concept is due to both cognitive capacities and feedback from others. Sociologist George Herbert Mead (1934) proposed that a well-organized psychological self emerges when the child's *I-self* adopts a view of the *me-self* that resembles others' attitudes toward the child. Mead's ideas indicate that *perspective-taking skills*—in particular, an improved ability to infer what other people are thinking—are crucial for the development of a self-concept based on personality traits. As we will see later, school-age children become better at "reading" the messages they receive from others and incorporating these into their self-definitions.

During middle childhood, children look to more people for information about themselves as they enter a wider range of settings in school and community. This is reflected in children's frequent reference to social groups in their self-descriptions (Livesley & Bromley, 1973). "I'm a Boy Scout, a paper boy, and a Prairie City soccer player," Joey remarked when asked to describe himself. Gradually, as children move toward adolescence, their sources of self-definition become more selective. Although parents remain influential, between ages 8 and 15 peers become more important. And over time, self-concept becomes increasingly vested in feedback from close friends (Oosterwegel & Oppenheimer, 1993).

DEVELOPMENT OF SELF-ESTEEM

Recall that most preschoolers have very high self-esteem. As children move into middle childhood, they receive much more feedback about their performance in different activities compared with that of their peers. As a result, self-esteem differentiates, and it also adjusts to a more realistic level.

■ A HIERARCHICALLY STRUCTURED SELF-ESTEEM. Susan Harter (1982, 1990) asked children to indicate the extent to which a variety of statements, such as "I am good at homework" or "I'm usually the one chosen for games," were true of themselves. Her findings, and those of other researchers, reveal that classrooms, peer groups, and playgrounds are key contexts for self-evaluation. By age 6 to 7, children have formed at least three separate self-esteems—academic, social, and physical—that become more refined with age. For example, academic self-worth divides into performance in different school subjects, social self-worth into peer and parental relationships. School-age children also combine their separate self-evaluations into a general self-esteem (Harter, 1998; Marsh, 1990). As a result, self-esteem takes on the hierarchical structure shown in Figure 10.1 on the following page.

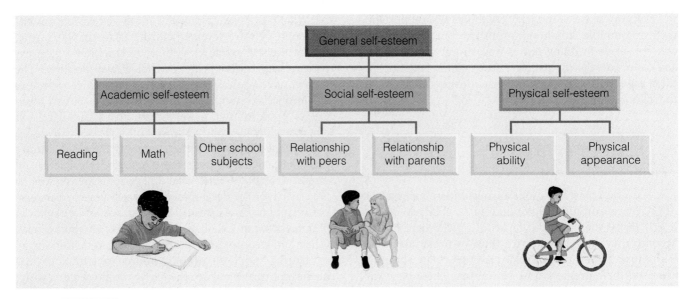

FIGURE 10.1

■ **Hierarchical structure of self-esteem in the mid-elementary school years.** From their experiences in different settings, children form at least three separate self-esteems—academic, social, and physical. These differentiate into additional self-evaluations and combine to form an overall sense of self-worth.

Separate self-esteems, however, do not contribute equally to general self-esteem. Children attach greater importance to certain self-judgments. Although individual differences exist, during childhood and adolescence, perceived physical appearance correlates more strongly with overall self-worth than does any other self-esteem factor (Harter, 1990, 1998). The emphasis that society and the media place on appearance has major implications for satisfaction with the self.

■ CHANGES IN LEVEL OF SELF-ESTEEM. As children adjust their self-judgments to fit the opinions of others and compare their attributes with those of many other peers, self-esteem drops during the first few years of elementary school (Butler, 1998; Stipek & MacIver, 1989). Typically, this decline is not great enough to be harmful. Most (but not all) children appraise their characteristics and competencies realistically while maintaining an attitude of self-acceptance and self-respect. Then, from fourth to sixth grade, self-esteem rises for the majority of youngsters, who feel especially good about their peer relationships and athletic capabilities (Nottelmann, 1987).

INFLUENCES ON SELF-ESTEEM

From middle childhood on, strong relationships exist between self-esteem and everyday behavior. Academic self-esteem predicts children's school achievement (Marsh, Smith, & Barnes, 1985). Children with high social self-esteem are better liked by peers (Harter, 1982). And as we saw in Chapter 9, boys come to believe they have more athletic talent than do girls, and they are more advanced in a variety of physical skills. What social influences might lead self-esteem to be high for some children and low for others?

■ CULTURE. Cultural forces profoundly affect self-esteem. For example, an especially strong emphasis on social comparison in school may explain why Japanese and Taiwanese children score lower in self-esteem than do American children, despite their higher academic achievement (Chiu, 1992–1993; Hawkins, 1994). In Asian classrooms, competition is tough and standards are high. At the same time, Asian children less often call on social comparisons to promote their own self-esteem. Because their culture values modesty and social harmony, they tend to be reserved about judging themselves positively but generous in their praise of others (Heine & Lehman, 1995; Falbo et al., 1997).

■ CHILD-REARING PRACTICES. Children whose parents use an *authoritative* child-rearing style (see Chapter 8) feel especially good about themselves (Deković & Meeus, 1997; Feiring & Taska, 1996). Warm, positive parenting lets children know that they are accepted as competent and worthwhile. And firm but appropriate expectations, backed up with explanations, seem to help children evaluate their own behavior against reasonable standards.

Yet note that these findings are correlational. We cannot actually tell whether child-rearing styles are causes of or reactions to children's characteristics and behavior. Research on the precise content of adults' messages to children has been far more successful at isolating factors that affect children's sense of self-worth. Let's see how these messages mold children's evaluations of themselves in achievement contexts.

■ MAKING ACHIEVEMENT-RELATED ATTRIBUTIONS. *Attributions* are our common, everyday explanations for the causes of behavior—our answers to the question, Why did I (or another person) do that? Notice how Joey, in talk-

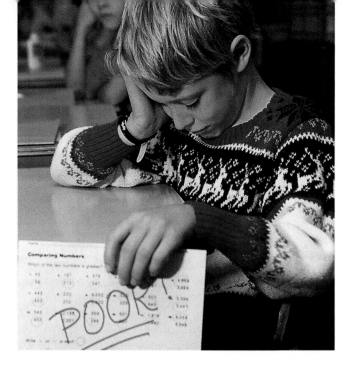

■ INFLUENCES ON ACHIEVEMENT-RELATED ATTRIBUTIONS. What accounts for the very different attributions of mastery-oriented and learned-helpless children? Adult communication plays a key role. Learned-helpless children have parents who set unusually high standards yet believe their child is not very capable and has to work harder to succeed (Parsons, Adler, & Kaczala, 1982). When these children fail, the adult might say, "You can't do that, can you? It's OK if you quit" (Hokoda & Fincham, 1995).

In a longitudinal study of over 1,600 third to eighth graders, pupils who viewed their teachers as providing positive, supportive learning conditions (for example, making expectations clear, checking to see that the child understands) worked harder and participated more in class—factors that predicted high achievement, which sustained children's willingness to try hard. In contrast, pupils with unsupportive teachers regarded their performance as externally controlled (by powerful teachers or luck), which predicted disengagement and declining achievement—outcomes that led children to doubt their ability (Skinner, Zimmer-Gembeck, & Connell, 1998).

Some children are especially likely to have their performance undermined by negative adult feedback. Despite their consistently higher achievement, girls more often than boys receive messages from teachers and parents that their ability is at fault when they do not do well. They also underestimate their academic competence and are more likely to be learned-helpless (Cole et al., 1999; Phillips & Zimmerman, 1990). And in several studies, African-American and Mexican-American children received less favorable feedback from teachers (Irvine, 1986; Losey, 1995). Furthermore, when ethnic minority children observe that adults in their own family are not rewarded by society for their achievement efforts, they may give up themselves. Many African-American children come to believe that even if they do try in school, social prejudice will prevent them from succeeding (Ogbu, 1997).

■ SUPPORTING CHILDREN'S SELF-ESTEEM. Even adults who are, on the whole, warm and supportive may send subtle messages to children that undermine their competence. *Attribution retraining* is an intervention approach that encourages learned-helpless children to believe that they can overcome failure by exerting more effort. Most often, children are given tasks hard enough so they will experience some failure. Then they get repeated feedback such as "You can do it if you try harder." Children are also taught to view their successes as due to both ability and effort

ing about the spelling bee at the beginning of this chapter, attributes his disappointing performance to *luck* (Belinda got all the easy words) and his usual success to *ability* (he *knows* he's a better speller than Belinda). Joey also appreciates that *effort* makes a difference; he "knocked himself out studying those spelling words."

Cognitive development permits school-age children to separate all these variables in explaining performance (Skinner, 1995). Yet they differ greatly in how they account for their successes and failures. Children who are high in academic self-esteem make **mastery-oriented attributions.** They believe their successes are due to ability—a characteristic they can improve through trying hard and can count on when faced with new challenges. And they attribute failure to factors that can be changed and controlled, such as insufficient effort or a very difficult task (Heyman & Dweck, 1998). So regardless of whether these children succeed or fail, they take an industrious, persistent approach to learning.

Unfortunately, children who develop **learned helplessness** give very discouraging explanations for their performance. They attribute their failures, not their successes, to ability. When they succeed, they are likely to conclude that external factors, such as luck, are responsible. Furthermore, unlike their mastery-oriented counterparts, they have come to believe that ability is fixed and cannot be changed by trying hard. So when a task is difficult, these children experience an anxious loss of control—in Erikson's terms, a pervasive sense of inferiority. They give up before they have really tried (Elliott & Dweck, 1988).

Over time, the ability of learned-helpless children no longer predicts their performance. Because they fail to make the connection between effort and success, learned-helpless children do not develop metacognitive and self-regulatory skills necessary for high achievement (see Chapter 9). Lack of effective learning strategies, reduced persistence, and a sense of being controlled by external forces sustain one another in a vicious cycle (Heyman & Dweck, 1992).

rather than chance, by giving them additional feedback after they succeed, such as "You're really good at this." Another approach is to encourage low-effort children to focus less on grades and more on mastering a task for its own sake (Ames, 1992). Finally, learned-helpless children may need instruction in metacognition and self-regulation to make up for learning lost in this area because of their attributional styles (Borkowski & Muthukrisna, 1995).

To work well, attribution retraining is best begun early, before children's views of themselves become hard to change (Eccles, Wigfield, & Schiefele, 1998). An even better approach is to prevent learned helplessness before it happens, using the strategies summarized in the Caregiving Concerns table below.

ASK YOURSELF . . .

■ *Return to page 288 of Chapter 9 and review the messages that parents send to girls about their athletic talent. On the basis of what you know about children's attributions for success and failure, why do school-age girls perform more poorly at sports than do boys, devoting less time to athletics from childhood into adulthood?*

■ *In view of Joey's attributions for his spelling bee performance, is he likely to enter the next spelling bee and try hard to do well? Why or why not?*

EMOTIONAL DEVELOPMENT

Greater self-awareness and social sensitivity support emotional development in middle childhood. Gains take place in experiencing of self-conscious emotions, awareness of emotional states, and emotional self-regulation.

SELF-CONSCIOUS EMOTIONS

In middle childhood, the self-conscious emotions of pride and guilt become clearly governed by personal responsibility. A teacher or parent no longer has to be present for a new accomplishment to spark a glowing sense of pride or for a transgression to arouse painful pangs of guilt (Harter, Wright, & Bresnick, 1987). Also, children do not report guilt for any mishap, as they did at younger ages, but only for intentional wrongdoing, such as ignoring responsibilities, cheating, or lying (Ferguson, Stegge, & Damhuis, 1991).

Pride motivates children to take on further challenges. And guilt prompts them to make amends and strive for self-improvement as well. But harsh, insensitive reprimands from adults—such as, "Everyone else can do it! Why can't you?"—can lead to excessive guilt for the act and shame at having exposed the self as bad. When these self-conscious emotions become very intense, they are particularly destructive. They involve taking one or two unworthy acts to be the whole of self-worth, setting up maladaptive responses of

CAREGIVING CONCERNS

Ways to Foster a Mastery-Oriented Approach to Learning and Prevent Learned Helplessness

TECHNIQUE	DESCRIPTION
Provision of tasks	Select tasks that are meaningful, responsive to a diversity of pupil interests, and appropriately matched to current competence so that the child is challenged but not overwhelmed.
Parent and teacher encouragement	Communicate warmth, confidence in the child's abilities, the value of achievement, and the importance of effort in success.
	Model high effort in overcoming failure.
	(For teachers) Communicate often with parents, suggesting ways to foster children's effort and progress.
	(For parents) Monitor schoolwork; provide assistance that promotes knowledge of effective strategies and self-regulation.
Performance evaluations	Make evaluations private; avoid publicizing success or failure through wall posters, stars, privileges to "smart" children, and prizes for "best" performance.
	Stress individual progress and self-improvement.
School environment	Offer small classes, which permit teachers to provide individualized support for mastery.
	Provide for cooperative learning and peer tutoring, in which children assist each other; avoid ability grouping, which makes evaluations of children's progress public.
	Accommodate individual and cultural differences in styles of learning.
	Create an atmosphere that values academics and sends a clear message to teachers, parents, and children that all pupils can learn.

Sources: Ames, 1992; Eccles, Wigfield, & Schiefele, 1998.

high self-blame and passive retreat or intense anger at others who participated in the humiliating situation (Ferguson et al., 1999; Lindsay-Hartz, de Rivera, & Mascolo, 1995).

EMOTIONAL UNDERSTANDING

School-age children's understanding of psychological dispositions means that they are more likely to explain emotion by referring to internal states than to external events (Strayer, 1993). They are also much more aware of the diversity of emotional experiences. By age 8, children recognize that they can experience more than one emotion at a time, each of which may be positive or negative and differ in intensity (Wintre & Vallance, 1994). For example, recalling the birthday present he received from his grandmother, Joey reflected, "I was very happy that I got something but a little sad that I didn't get just what I wanted."

Besides a better understanding of their own emotions, children take more information into account in detecting the emotions of others. School-age children can reconcile contradictory facial and situational cues in figuring out another's feelings, whereas preschoolers rely only on the emotional expression (see Chapter 8). Furthermore, older children can use a person's past experiences to predict how he or she will feel in a new situation—for example, that a child rejected by her best friend will probably feel sad at later meeting that friend (Gnepp, 1983).

As with self-understanding, gains in emotional understanding are supported by cognitive development and social experiences, especially adults' sensitivity to children's feelings and willingness to discuss emotions. Together, these factors lead to a rise in empathy, which continues to contribute to prosocial behavior in middle childhood (Ricard & Kamberk-Kilicci, 1995; Roberts & Strayer, 1996). As children move closer to adolescence, advances in perspective taking permit an empathic response not just to people's immediate distress, but also to their general life condition (Hoffman, 1991). As Joey and Lizzie imagined how less fortunate people feel, they gave part of their allowance to charity and joined in fundraising projects through school, church, and scouting.

EMOTIONAL SELF-REGULATION

Rapid gains in emotional self-regulation occur in middle childhood. As children engage in social comparison, they more often encounter distressing events in which they must manage negative emotion that threatens their self-esteem.

By age 10, most children have an adaptive set of strategies for managing emotion (Kliewer, Fearnow, & Miller, 1996). In situations in which they have some control over an outcome (an anxiety-provoking test at the end of the week), they view problem solving and seeking social support as the best strategies. When outcomes are beyond their control (having received a bad grade), they opt for distraction or redefining the situation ("Things could be worse. There'll be another test.") (Aldwin, 1994; Compas, Phares, & Ledoux, 1989).

Emotionally well-regulated children are generally upbeat in mood, more empathic and prosocial, and better liked by their peers. In contrast, poorly regulated children are overwhelmed by negative emotion, a response that interferes with prosocial behavior and peer acceptance (Eisenberg, Fabes, & Losoya, 1997). Recall from previous chapters that temperament and parenting influence emotional self-regulation. We will revisit these themes when we take up peer acceptance and children's ability to cope with stressful family circumstances.

UNDERSTANDING OTHERS: PERSPECTIVE TAKING

Already we have seen that middle childhood brings major advances in **perspective taking,** the capacity to imagine what other people may be thinking and feeling—changes that support self-development, understanding of others, and a wide variety of social skills. Robert Selman's five-stage sequence describes changes in perspective-taking skill, based on children's and adolescents' responses to social dilemmas in which characters have differing information and opinions about an event.

As Table 10.1 indicates, at first, children have only a limited idea of what other people might be thinking and

TABLE 10.1

Selman's Stages of Perspective Taking

STAGE	APPROXIMATE AGE RANGE	DESCRIPTION
Level 0: Undifferentiated perspective taking	3–6	Children recognize that self and other can have different thoughts and feelings, but they frequently confuse the two.
Level 1: Social-informational perspective taking	4–9	Children understand that different perspectives may result because people have access to different information.
Level 2: Self-reflective perspective taking	7–12	Children can "step in another person's shoes" and view their own thoughts, feelings, and behavior from the other person's perspective. They also recognize that others can do the same.
Level 3: Third-party perspective taking	10–15	Children can step outside a two-person situation and imagine how the self and other are viewed from the point of view of a third, impartial party.
Level 4: Societal perspective taking	14–adult	Individuals understand that third-party perspective taking can be influenced by one or more systems of larger societal values.

Sources: Selman, 1976; Selman & Byrne, 1974.

feeling. Over time, they become more aware that people can interpret the same event in quite different ways. Soon, they can "step in another person's shoes" and reflect on how that person might regard their own thoughts, feelings, and behavior, as when they make statements like this: "I *thought you would think* I was just kidding when I said that." Finally, they can evaluate two people's perspectives simultaneously, at first from the vantage point of a disinterested spectator and, finally, by making reference to societal values. The following explanation reflects this advanced level: "I know why Joey hid the stray kitten in the basement, even though his mom was against keeping it. He believes in not hurting animals. If you put the kitten outside or give it to the pound, it might die."

Perspective taking varies greatly among children of the same age. Individual differences are due to cognitive maturity as well as experiences in which adults and peers explain their viewpoints, encouraging children to notice another's perspective (Dixon & Moore, 1990). Children with very poor social skills—in particular, the angry, aggressive styles that we discussed in Chapter 8—have great difficulty imagining the thoughts and feelings of others. They often mistreat adults and peers without feeling the guilt and remorse prompted by awareness of another's point of view. Interventions that provide coaching and practice in perspective taking are helpful in reducing antisocial behavior and increasing empathy and prosocial responding (Chalmers & Townsend, 1990; Chandler, 1973).

MORAL DEVELOPMENT

Recall from Chapter 8 that preschoolers pick up a great many morally relevant behaviors through modeling and reinforcement. By middle childhood, they have had time to reflect on these experiences and internalize rules for good conduct, such as "It's good to help others in trouble" or "It's wrong to take something that doesn't belong to you." This change leads children to become considerably more independent and trustworthy. They can take on many more responsibilities, from running errands at the supermarket to watching over younger siblings (Weisner, 1996). Of course, these advances take place only when children have had much time to profit from the consistent guidance and example of caring adults.

In Chapter 8, we also saw that children do not just copy their morality from others. As the cognitive-developmental approach emphasizes, they actively think about right and wrong. Children's expanding social world and perspective-taking skill lead moral understanding to improve greatly in middle childhood.

LEARNING ABOUT JUSTICE THROUGH SHARING

In everyday life, children frequently experience situations that involve **distributive justice**—beliefs about how to divide resources fairly. Heated discussions take place over how much weekly allowance is to be given to siblings of different ages, who has to sit where in the family car on a long trip, and in what way an eight-slice pizza is to be shared by six hungry playmates. William Damon (1977, 1988) has studied children's changing concepts of distributive justice over early and middle childhood.

Even 4-year-olds recognize the importance of sharing, but their reasons for doing so often seem contradictory and self-serving: "I shared because if I didn't, she wouldn't play with me" or "I let her have some, but most are for me because I'm older." As children enter middle childhood, they express more mature notions of distributive justice. Their basis of reasoning follows an age-related, three-step sequence:

1. *Equality* (5 to 6 years). Children in the early school grades are intent on making sure that each person gets the same amount of a treasured resource, such as money, turns in a game, or a delicious treat.

2. *Merit* (6 to 7 years). A short time later, children say extra rewards should go to someone who has worked especially hard or otherwise performed in an exceptional way.

3. *Benevolence* (around 8 years). Finally, children recognize that special consideration should be given to those who are at a disadvantage—for example, that an extra amount might be given to a child who cannot produce as much or who does not get any allowance. Older children also adapt their basis of fairness to fit the situation, relying more on equality when interacting with strangers and more on benevolence when

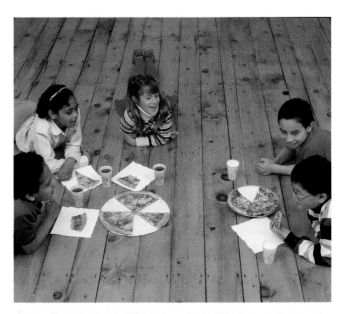

■ *These five school-age children have figured out how to divide up two pizzas fairly among themselves. Already, they have a well-developed sense of distributive justice. (Photo courtesy: Will Faller)*

interacting with friends (McGillicuddy-De Lisi, Watkins, & Vinchur, 1994).

According to Damon (1988), the give-and-take of peer interaction makes children more sensitive to others' perspectives, and this, in turn, supports their developing ideas of justice. Advanced distributive justice reasoning, in turn, is associated with more effective social problem solving and a greater willingness to help and share with others (Blotner & Bearison, 1984; McNamee & Peterson, 1986).

CHANGES IN MORAL AND SOCIAL-CONVENTIONAL UNDERSTANDING

As their ideas about justice advance, children clarify and create links between moral rules and social conventions. During middle childhood, they realize that moral rules and social conventions sometimes overlap. For example, saying "Thank you" after receiving a present is an arbitrary practice arrived at by social agreement. At the same time, not doing so can injure others by hurting their feelings (Turiel, 1998).

Children in Western as well as diverse non-Western cultures use the same criteria to distinguish moral and social-conventional concerns (Bersoff & Miller, 1993; Nucci, Camino, & Sapiro, 1996; Tisak, 1995). Certain behaviors are classified differently across cultures, but the reasoning behind them reveals that not harming or violating the rights of others is a universal basis for morality. For example, East Indian Hindu children believe that eating chicken the day after a father's death is morally wrong, whereas American children do not (Shweder, Mahapatra, & Miller, 1990). But Hindu religious teachings specify that eating chicken harms the father's soul by preventing it from receiving salvation! In India, as in many developing countries, practices that strike outsiders as arbitrary often have profound moral and religious significance.

THE PERSONAL DOMAIN AND MORAL UNDERSTANDING

In all cultures, children also identify a unique domain of personal matters. For example, they argue that hairstyle, choice of friends, and contents of a diary are up to the individual—a view that strengthens between ages 8 and 16 (Nucci, Camino, & Sapiro, 1996). When children challenge parental authority, they typically do so within the personal domain (Nucci & Weber, 1995). To Rena's question about who she was talking to on the phone, Lizzie replied indignantly, "Mom, that's none of your business!"

Children's sense of the personal domain strengthens moral understanding because it fosters concepts of personal rights and freedom (Nucci, 1996). Over time, children think more intently about conflicts between personal freedoms and social and moral obligations—for example, whether schools should be able to restrict their dress, speech, and other individual rights. These concerns will increase greatly in adolescence.

ASK YOURSELF

■ *Joey's fourth-grade class participated in a bowl-a-thon to raise money for a charity serving children with cancer. Explain how activities like this one foster emotional development, perspective taking, and moral understanding.*

🌳 *Why are the strategies for regulating emotion described on page 325 important for long-term psychological adjustment?*

PEER RELATIONS

In middle childhood, the society of peers becomes an increasingly important context for development. Peer contact, as we have seen, plays an important role in perspective taking and understanding of self and others. These developments, in turn, contribute to the quality of peer interaction, which becomes more prosocial over the school years. In line with this change, aggression declines, but the drop is greatest for physical attacks (Rubin, Bukowski, & Parker, 1998). As we will see, other types of aggression continue as children form peer groups and start to distinguish "insiders" from "outsiders."

PEER GROUPS

Watch children in the school yard or neighborhood, and notice how groups of three to a dozen or more often gather. The organization of these collectives changes greatly with age. By the end of middle childhood, children display a strong desire for group belonging. Together, they generate unique values and standards for behavior. They also create a social structure of leaders and followers that ensures group goals will be met. When these characteristics are present, a **peer group** is formed.

The practices of these informal groups lead to a "peer culture" that typically consists of a specialized vocabulary, dress code, and place to "hang out" during leisure hours. For example, Joey formed a club with three other boys. They met in the treehouse in Joey's backyard, used nicknames, and wore a "uniform" consisting of T-shirts, jeans, and tennis shoes. Calling themselves "the pack," the boys developed a secret handshake and chose Joey as their leader. Their activities included improving the clubhouse, trading baseball cards, making trips to the video arcade, and—just as important—keeping girls and adults out!

As children develop these exclusive associations, the codes of dress and behavior that grow out of them become

■ *Peer groups first form in middle childhood. These girls have probably established a social structure of leader and followers as they gather for joint activities. Their body language suggests that they feel a strong sense of group belonging. (Photo courtesy: Ellen Senisi/The Image Works)*

more broadly influential. At school, children who deviate are often rebuffed by their peers. "Kissing up" to teachers, wearing the wrong kind of shirt or shoes, and tattling on classmates are grounds for critical glances and comments.

These special customs bind peers together, creating a sense of group identity. Within the group, children acquire many valuable social skills—cooperation, leadership, followership, and loyalty to collective goals. Through these experiences, children experiment with and learn about social organizations.

The beginning of peer group ties is also a time when some of the "nicest children begin to behave in the most awful way" (Redl, 1966, p. 395). From third grade on, relational aggression—gossip, rumor spreading, and exclusion —rise among girls, who (because of gender-role expectations) express hostility in subtle, indirect ways (Crick & Grotpeter, 1995). Boys are more straightforward in their hostility toward the "outgroup." Prank playing, such as egging a house, making a funny phone call, or ringing a doorbell and running away, often occurs among small groups of boys, who provide one another with temporary social support for these mildly antisocial behaviors (Fine, 1980).

The school-age child's desire for group belonging can also be satisfied through formal group ties—Girl Scouts, Boy Scouts, 4-H, church groups, and other associations.

Adult involvement holds in check the negative behaviors associated with children's informal peer groups. In addition, children gain in social and moral understanding as they work on joint projects and help in their communities (Keasey, 1971).

FRIENDSHIPS

Whereas peer groups provide children with insight into larger social structures, one-to-one friendships contribute to the development of trust and sensitivity. During the school years, friendship becomes more complex and psychologically based. Look at the following 8-year-old's answers to questions about what makes a best friend:

> *Why is Shelly your best friend?* Because she helps me when I'm sad, and she shares. . . . *What makes Shelly so special?* I've known her longer, I sit next to her and got to know her better. . . . *How come you like Shelly better than anyone else?* She's done the most for me. She never disagrees, she never eats in front of me, she never walks away when I'm crying, and she helps me with my homework. . . . *How do you get someone to like you?* . . . If you're nice to [your friends], they'll be nice to you. (Damon, 1988, pp. 80–81)

As these responses show, friendship is no longer just a matter of engaging in the same activities. Instead, it is a mutually agreed-on relationship in which children like each other's personal qualities and respond to one another's needs and desires. And once a friendship forms, *trust* becomes its defining feature. School-age children state that a good friendship is based on acts of kindness that signify each person can be counted on to support the other. Consequently, events that break up a friendship are quite different than they were during the preschool years. Older children regard violations of trust, such as not helping when others need help, breaking promises, and gossiping behind the other's back, as serious breaches of friendship (Damon, 1977; Selman, 1980).

Because of these features, school-age children's friendships are more selective. Whereas preschoolers say they have lots of friends, by age 8 or 9, children have just a handful of people they call friends and, very often, just one best friend. Girls, especially, are likely to be exclusive in their friendships because they demand greater closeness than do boys. In addition, children tend to select friends like themselves in age, sex, race, ethnicity, and SES. Friends also resemble one another in personality (sociability, aggression), peer popularity, and academic achievement (Hartup, 1996). Note, however, that school and neighborhood characteristics affect friendship choices. For example, in integrated schools, as many as 50 percent of pupils report at least one close other-race friend (DuBois & Hirsch, 1990).

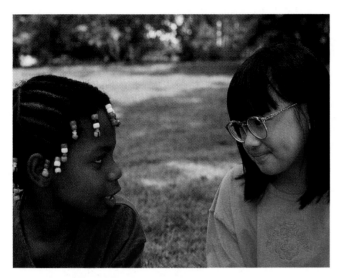

■ *During middle childhood, concepts of friendship become more psychologically based. These girls want to spend time together because they like each other's personal qualities. Mutual trust is a defining feature of their friendship. Each counts on the other to provide support and assistance. In integrated schools, many children form close other-race friendships. (Photo courtesy: Carol Palmer/The Picture Cube)*

Through friendship, children learn the importance of emotional commitment. They come to realize that close relationships can survive disagreements if friends are secure in their liking for one another and resolve conflicts in ways that meet both partners' needs (Laursen, Hartup, & Koplas, 1996; Rose & Asher, 1999). Yet the extent to which children's friendships support development depends on the company they keep. Children who bring kindness and compassion to their friendships behave more prosocially toward others in general (Hartup, 1996). In contrast, aggressive children's friendships often magnify antisocial acts. Those of relationally aggressive girls are high in exchange of private feelings but full of jealousy, conflict, and betrayal (Grotpeter & Crick, 1996). Among boys, aggressive friends' talk contains frequent coercive statements and attacks, even during videotaping in a laboratory (Dishion, Andrews, & Crosby, 1995).

As these findings reveal, the social problems of aggressive children operate within their closest peer ties. As we will see next, these children are also at risk for rejection in the wider world of peers.

PEER ACCEPTANCE

Peer acceptance refers to likability—the extent to which agemates view a child as a worthy social partner. In Chapter 9, we saw that obese children and children with serious learning problems often have difficulty with peer acceptance. Yet there are other children whose appearance and

intellectual abilities are quite normal but whose classmates still despise them.

Researchers assess peer acceptance with self-report measures that ask classmates to evaluate one another's likability. Children's responses reveal four different categories: **popular children,** who get many positive votes; **rejected children,** who are actively disliked; **controversial children,** who get a large number of positive and negative votes; and **neglected children,** who are seldom chosen, either positively or negatively. About two-thirds of pupils in a typical elementary school classroom fit one of these categories. The rest are *average* in peer acceptance; they do not receive extreme scores (Coie, Dodge, & Coppotelli, 1982).

Peer acceptance is a powerful predictor of psychological adjustment. Rejected children, especially, are unhappy, alienated, poorly achieving children with low self-esteem. Both teachers and parents rate them as having a wide range of emotional and social problems. Peer rejection in middle childhood is also strongly associated with poor school performance, dropping out, antisocial behavior, and delinquency in adolescence and criminality in young adulthood (Bagwell, Newcomb, & Bukowski, 1998; Parker et al., 1995).

■ DETERMINANTS OF PEER ACCEPTANCE. What causes one child to be liked and another to be rejected? A wealth of research reveals that social behavior plays a powerful role. Popular children communicate with peers in sensitive, friendly, and cooperative ways. When they do not understand another child's reaction, they ask for an explanation. If they disagree with a play partner in a game, they go beyond voicing their displeasure and suggest what the other child could do instead. When they want to enter an ongoing play group, they adapt their behavior to the flow of the activity (Ladd & Price, 1987; Newcomb, Bukowski, & Pattee, 1993).

Rejected children, in contrast, display a wide range of negative social behaviors. At least two subtypes exist. **Rejected-aggressive children,** the largest subgroup, show high rates of conflict, hostility, and hyperactive, inattentive, and impulsive behavior. They are also deficient in social understanding. For example, they are more likely than other children to misinterpret the innocent behaviors of peers as hostile, to blame others for their social difficulties, and to act on their angry feelings (Coie & Dodge, 1998; Dekovic & Gerris, 1994; Rubin et al., 1995). In contrast, **rejected-withdrawn children,** a smaller subgroup, are passive and socially awkward. These children, especially, feel lonely, hold negative expectations for how peers will treat them, and are very concerned about being scorned and attacked (Boivin & Hymel, 1997; Ladd & Burgess, 1999). Because of their inept, submissive style of interaction, they are at risk for abuse by bullies (see the Variations box on page 330).

Consistent with the mixed peer opinion they engender, controversial children display a blend of positive and

PEER VICTIMIZATION

Follow the activities of aggressive children over a school day, and you will see that they reserve their hostilities for certain peers. A particularly destructive form of interaction is **peer victimization,** in which certain children become frequent targets of verbal and physical attacks or other forms of abuse. What sustains these repeated assault–retreat cycles between pairs of children?

Research indicates that the majority of victims reinforce bullies by giving in to their demands, crying, assuming defensive postures, and failing to fight back. Victimized boys display passivity in situations in which active behavior is expected, hanging around chatting or wandering alone on the playground (Boulton, 1999). Biologically based traits—an inhibited, fearful temperament and a frail physical appearance—contribute to their behavior. But they also have histories of resistant attachment; overly intrusive, controlling child rearing; and (among boys) maternal overprotectiveness. These parenting behaviors prompt anxiety, low self-esteem, and dependency, resulting in a fearful demeanor that radiates vulnerability (Ladd & Ladd, 1998; Olweus, 1993).

By elementary school, 10 percent of children are harassed by aggressive agemates, and peers expect these victims to give up desirable objects, show signs of distress, and fail to retaliate. In addition, children (especially those who are aggressive) feel less discomfort at the thought of causing pain and suffering to victims than to nonvictims, thereby minimizing the possibility of harmful consequences (Perry, Williard, & Perry, 1990). Although bullies and victims are most often boys, at times they are girls who bombard a vulnerable classmate with relational hostility (Crick & Grotpeter, 1996). As early as kindergarten, victimization leads to a variety of adjustment difficulties, including sadness and depression, loneliness, and dislike and avoidance of school (Boulton & Underwood, 1992; Ladd, Kochendorfer, & Coleman, 1997).

Aggression and victimization are not polar opposites. A small number of extreme victims are also aggressive, picking arguments and fights (Boulton & Smith, 1994). Perhaps these children foolishly provoke stronger agemates, who then prevail over them. Although both aggressive and victimized children are rejected by peers, these highly aggressive–highly abused youngsters are the most despised, placing them at severe risk for maladjustment.

Interventions that change victimized children's negative opinions of themselves and that teach them to respond in nonreinforcing ways to their attackers are vital. Nevertheless, victimized children's behavior should not be taken to mean they are to blame for their abuse. Developing a school code against bullying, enlisting parents' assistance in changing both bullies' and victims' behavior, and moving aggressive children to another class or school can greatly reduce bully–victim problems, which account for a substantial portion of peer aggression in middle childhood (Olweus, 1995).

Yet another way to help victimized children is to assist them in acquiring the social skills needed to form and maintain a gratifying friendship. Anxious, withdrawn children who have a mutual best friend seem better equipped to withstand peer attacks. They show fewer adjustment problems than do victims with no close friends (Hodges et al., 1999).

■ *Children who are bullied by agemates have characteristics that make them easy targets. They are highly anxious, physically weak, rejected by peers, and afraid to defend themselves. Both temperamental traits and child-rearing experiences underlie their cowering behavior, which reinforces their attackers' abusive acts. (Photo courtesy: Aloma/Monkmeyer Press)*

negative social behaviors. Like rejected-aggressive youngsters, they are hostile and disruptive, but they also engage in positive, prosocial acts. Even though some peers dislike them, they have qualities that protect them from social exclusion. As a result, they appear to be relatively happy and comfortable with their peer relationships (Newcomb, Bukowski, & Pattee, 1993).

Finally, perhaps the most surprising finding is that neglected children, once thought to be in need of treatment, are usually well adjusted. Although these youngsters engage in low rates of interaction and are considered shy, the majority are just as socially skilled as average children. They do not report feeling especially lonely or unhappy, and when they want to, they can break away from their usual pattern of playing by themselves (Crick & Ladd, 1993; Harrist et al., 1997).

Neglected children remind us that there are other paths to emotional well-being besides the outgoing, gregarious personality style so highly valued in Western culture. Recall from Chapter 6 that in China, adults view cautious, inhibited children as advanced in social maturity. In accord with this standard, shyness is associated with peer acceptance and social competence and leadership among Chinese 8- to 10-year-olds (Chen, Rubin, & Li, 1995).

■ HELPING REJECTED CHILDREN. A variety of interventions exist to improve rejected children's peer relations and psychological adjustment. Most involve coaching, modeling, and reinforcing positive social skills, such as how to begin interacting with a peer, cooperate in games, and respond to another child with friendly emotion and approval. Sometimes, training in perspective taking and social problem solving is included. Several programs have produced lasting gains in social competence and peer acceptance (Asher & Rose, 1997).

Some researchers believe that these interventions might be even more effective when combined with other treatments. Often rejected children are poor students, and their low academic self-esteem magnifies negative reactions to teachers and classmates. Intensive academic tutoring improves both their school achievement and social acceptance (Coie & Kreihbel, 1984; O'Neil et al., 1997). Still another approach is to increase rejected children's expectations for social success. Many conclude, after repeated rebuffs from peers, that no matter how hard they try, they will never be liked (Rubin, Bukowski, & Parker, 1998; Toner & Munro, 1996). Rejected children make better use of the social skills they do have if they believe peers will accept them.

Finally, rejected children's socially incompetent behaviors often originate in a poor fit between the child's temperament and parenting practices (see Chapters 6 and 8). Therefore, interventions that focus only on the child are unlikely to be sufficient. If the quality of parent–child interaction is not changed, children may soon return to their old behavior patterns.

GENDER TYPING

C hildren's understanding of gender roles broadens in middle childhood, and their gender-role identities (views of themselves as relatively masculine or feminine) change as well. We will see that development is different for boys and girls, and it can vary considerably across cultures.

GENDER-STEREOTYPED BELIEFS

During the school years, children extend the gender-stereotyped beliefs they acquired in early childhood. As they think more about people as personalities, they label some traits as more typical of one gender than the other. For example, they regard "tough," "aggressive," "rational," and "dominant" as masculine and "gentle," "sympathetic," and "dependent" as feminine, just as adults do (Best et al., 1977; Serbin, Powlishta, & Gulko, 1993). Children derive these distinctions from observing gender differences as well as from adult treatment. Parents, for example, use more directive speech (telling the child what to do) with girls, less often encourage girls to make their own decisions, and praise girls less for accomplishment (Leaper, Anderson, & Sanders, 1998; Pomerantz & Ruble, 1998).

Shortly after entering elementary school, children figure out which academic subjects and skill areas are "masculine" and which are "feminine." Throughout the school years, they regard reading, art, and music as more for girls and mathematics, athletics, and mechanical skills as more for boys (Eccles, Jacobs, & Harold, 1990; Jacobs & Weisz, 1994). These stereotypes influence children's preferences for certain subjects and, in turn, how well they do at them. For example, boys feel more competent than girls at math, whereas girls feel more competent than boys at reading— even when children of equal skill level are compared (Eccles et al.,1993c). As we will see in Chapter 12, these beliefs become realities in adolescence.

Although school-age children are aware of many stereotypes, they have a more open-minded view of what males and females *can do*. The ability to classify flexibly underlies this change. School-age children realize that a person can belong to more than one social category—for example, be a "boy" yet "like to play house" (Bigler, 1995). But acknowledging that people *can* cross gender lines does not mean that children always *approve* of doing so. One study showed that both children and adults are fairly tolerant of girls' violations of gender roles. But they judge boys' violations ("playing with dolls" or "wearing a dress") very harshly—as just as bad as violating a moral rule! (Levy, Taylor, & Gelman, 1995).

GENDER IDENTITY AND BEHAVIOR

Boys' and girls' gender-role identities follow different paths in middle childhood. From third to sixth grade, boys strengthen their identification with masculine personality traits, whereas girls' identification with feminine traits declines. Although girls still lean toward the feminine side, they begin to describe themselves as having some "other-gender" characteristics (Serbin, Powlishta, & Gulko, 1993). This difference is also evident in children's activities. Although boys usually stick to "masculine" pursuits, girls feel free to experiment with a wider range of options. Besides cooking, sewing, and baby-sitting, they join organized sports teams, take up science projects, and build forts in the backyard.

In Chapter 8, we saw that parents are especially concerned about boys' gender-role conformity. Pressure from gender-segregated peer groups is similar. A tomboyish girl can make her way into boys' activities without losing status with her female peers, but a boy who hangs out with girls is likely to be ridiculed and rejected. Finally, perhaps school-age girls realize that society attaches greater prestige to "masculine" characteristics. As a result, they want to try some of the activities and behaviors associated with the more highly valued gender role.

CULTURAL INFLUENCES ON GENDER TYPING

Although the sex differences just described are typical in Western nations, they do not apply to children everywhere. Girls are less likely to experiment with "masculine" activities in cultures and subcultures in which the gap between male and female roles is especially wide. And when social and economic conditions make it necessary for boys to take over "feminine" tasks, their personalities and behavior are less stereotyped.

For example, in Nyansongo, a small agricultural settlement in Kenya, mothers work 4 to 5 hours a day in the gardens. They assign the care of young children, the tending of the cooking fire, and the washing of dishes to older siblings. Since school-age children of both sexes perform these duties, girls are relieved of total responsibility for "feminine" tasks and have more time to interact with agemates. Their greater freedom and independence leads them to score higher than girls of other village and tribal cultures in dominance, assertiveness, and playful roughhousing. In contrast, boys' caregiving responsibilities mean that they frequently engage in help giving and emotional support (Whiting & Edwards, 1988a, 1988b).

Should these findings be taken to suggest that boys in Western cultures be assigned more "cross-gender" tasks? The consequences of doing so are not straightforward. Recent evidence shows that when fathers hold traditional gender-role beliefs and their sons engage in "feminine" housework, boys experience strain in the father–child relationship, feel stressed by their responsibilities, and judge themselves as less competent (McHale et al., 1990). So parental values may need to be consistent with task assignments for children to benefit from those tasks.

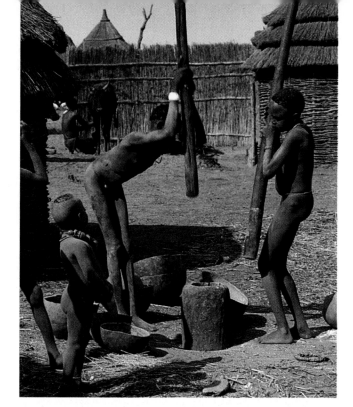

■ *These boys of the Kinka tribe in Kenya are assigned "feminine" tasks—grinding corn and looking after younger siblings. Consequently, they are less likely to be gender stereotyped in personality traits than are most boys in other cultures. (Photo courtesy: Akhtar Hussein/Woodfin Camp & Associates)*

ASK YOURSELF

Apply your understanding of attributions to rejected children's social self-esteem. How are rejected children likely to explain their failure to gain peer acceptance? What impact on future efforts to get along with others are these attributions likely to have?

■ *Return to Chapter 8, page 266 and review the concept of androgyny. Which of the two sexes is more androgynous in middle childhood, and why?*

FAMILY INFLUENCES

As children move into school, peer, and community contexts, the parent–child relationship changes. At the same time, the child's developing sense of competence continues to depend on the quality of family interaction. In the following sections, we will see that contemporary changes in the American family—high rates of divorce, remarriage, and maternal employment—can have positive as well as negative effects on children. In later chapters, we will take up other family forms, including gay and lesbian families and the increasing numbers of grandparents rearing grandchildren.

PARENT–CHILD RELATIONSHIPS

In middle childhood, the amount of time children spend with parents declines dramatically. The child's growing independence means that parents must deal with new issues. "I've struggled with how many chores to assign, how much allowance to give, and whether their friends are good influences," noted Rena. "And then there's the problem of how to keep track of them when they're out of the house or even when they're home and I'm not there to see what's going on."

Although parents face new concerns, child rearing actually becomes easier for those who established an authoritative style during the early years. Reasoning works more effectively with school-age children because of their greater capacity for logical thinking and increased respect for parents' expert knowledge (Braine et al., 1991). Of course, older children sometimes use their cognitive powers to bargain and negotiate. Perhaps because parents and children have, over time, learned how to resolve conflicts, coercive discipline declines over the school years (Collins, Harris, & Susman, 1996).

As children demonstrate that they can manage daily activities and responsibilities, effective parents gradually shift control from adult to child. This does not mean they let go entirely. Instead, they engage in **coregulation,** a transitional form of supervision in which they exercise general oversight while permitting children to be in charge of moment-by-moment decision making. Coregulation supports and protects children, who are not yet ready for total independence. At the same time, it prepares them for adolescence, when they will need to make many important decisions themselves.

Coregulation grows out of a cooperative relationship between parent and child. Here is a summary of its critical ingredients:

First, [parents] must monitor, guide, and support their children at a distance—that is, when their children are out of their presence; second, they must effectively use the times when direct contact does occur; and third, they must strengthen in their children the abilities that will allow them to monitor their own behavior, to adopt acceptable standards of good [conduct], to avoid undue risks, and to know when they need parental support and guidance. Children must be willing to inform parents of their whereabouts, activities, and problems so that parents can mediate and guide when necessary. (Maccoby, 1984, pp. 191–192)

Although school-age children often press for greater independence, they know how much they need their parents' continuing support. In one study, fifth and sixth graders described parents as the most influential people in their lives.

They often turned to mothers and fathers for affection, advice, enhancement of self-worth, and assistance with everyday problems (Furman & Buhrmester, 1992).

SIBLINGS

In addition to parents and friends, siblings are important sources of companionship, help with difficult tasks, and emotional support for school-age children. Yet sibling rivalry tends to increase in middle childhood. As children participate in a wider range of activities, parents often compare siblings' traits and accomplishments. The child who gets less parental attention, more disapproval, and fewer material resources is likely to resent a sibling who receives more favorable treatment (Brody, Stoneman, & McCoy, 1994; Dunn, 1996).

When siblings are close in age and the same sex, parental comparisons are more frequent, resulting in more quarreling and antagonism. This effect is particularly strong when fathers prefer one child. Perhaps because fathers spend less time with children, their favoritism is more noticeable, thereby triggering greater anger during sibling interactions (Brody, Stoneman, & McCoy, 1994; McHale et al., 1995).

Siblings often take steps to reduce this rivalry by striving to be different from one another (Huston, 1983). For

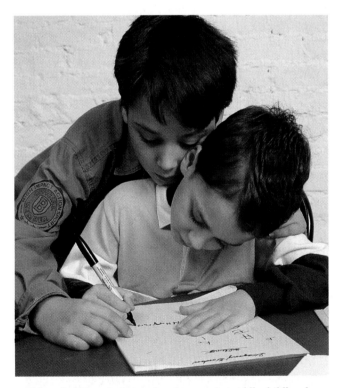

■ *Although sibling rivalry tends to increase in middle childhood, siblings also provide one another with emotional support and help with difficult tasks. (Photo courtesy: Erika Stone)*

example, two brothers I know deliberately selected different school subjects, athletic pursuits, and music lessons. If the older one did especially well at an activity, the younger one did not want to try it. Of course, parents can reduce these effects by making a special effort not to compare children. But some feedback about their competencies is inevitable, and as siblings strive to win recognition for their own uniqueness, they shape important aspects of each other's development.

Birth order plays an important role in sibling experiences. For a time, oldest children have their parents' attention all to themselves. Even after brothers and sisters are born, they receive greater parental pressure for mature behavior. For this reason, oldest children are slightly advantaged in IQ and school achievement (Zajonc & Mullally, 1997). Younger siblings, in contrast, tend to be more popular with agemates, perhaps as the result of becoming skilled at negotiating and compromising from interacting with more powerful brothers and sisters (Miller & Maruyama, 1976).

ONLY CHILDREN

Although sibling relationships bring many benefits, they are not essential for normal development. Contrary to popular belief, only children are not spoiled and selfish. In-

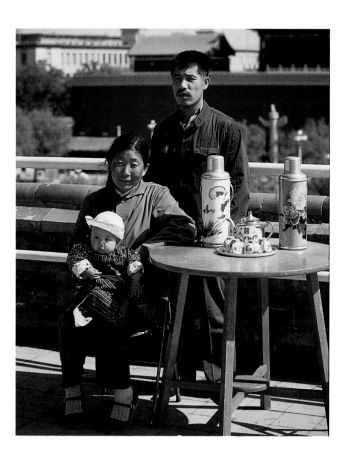

stead, they are just as well adjusted as other children and advantaged in some respects. Children growing up in one-child families score higher in self-esteem and achievement motivation. Consequently, they do better in school and attain higher levels of education (Falbo, 1992). One reason may be that only children have somewhat closer relationships with parents, who exert more pressure for mastery and accomplishment (Falbo & Polit, 1986).

Favorable development also characterizes only children in China, where a one-child family policy is strictly enforced to control overpopulation. Compared with agemates who have siblings, Chinese only children are advanced in cognitive development and in academic achievement (Falbo & Poston, 1993; Jiao, Ji, & Jing, 1996). They also feel more emotionally secure, perhaps because government disapproval promotes tension in families with more than one child (Yang et al., 1995). Although many Chinese adults are convinced that the one-child family policy breeds self-centered "little emperors," Chinese only children do not differ from children with siblings in social skills and peer acceptance (Chen, Rubin, & Li, 1994).

DIVORCE

Children's interactions with parents and siblings are affected by other aspects of family life. Joey and Lizzie's relationship, Rena told me, had been particularly negative only a few years before. Joey pushed, hit, taunted, and called Lizzie names. Although she tried to retaliate, she was little match for Joey's larger size. The arguments usually ended with Lizzie running in tears to her mother. Joey and Lizzie's fighting coincided with Rena and her husband's growing marital unhappiness. When Joey was 8 and Lizzie 5, their father, Drake, moved out.

The children were not alone in having to weather this traumatic event. Between 1960 and 1985, the divorce rate in the United States doubled and then stabilized. Currently, it is the highest in the world. About half of American marriages end in divorce; three-fourths of these involve children. At any given time, about one-fourth of American children live in single-parent households. Although the large majority reside with their mothers, father custody has increased over the past decade, from 9 to 14 percent (Hetherington & Stanley-Hagan, 1997).

Children spend an average of 5 years in a single-parent home, or almost a third of their total childhood. For many, divorce eventually leads to new family relationships. About two-thirds of divorced parents marry a second time. Half of

▬ *Limiting family size is a basic national policy in the People's Republic of China. In urban areas, the majority of couples have no more than one child. (Photo courtesy: Marc Bernheim/Woodfin Camp & Associates)*

their children eventually experience a third major change—the end of a parent's second marriage (Hetherington & Henderson, 1997).

These figures reveal that divorce is not a single event in the lives of parents and children. Instead, it is a transition that leads to a variety of new living arrangements, accompanied by changes in housing, income, and family roles and responsibilities. Since the 1960s, many studies have reported that marital breakup is quite stressful for children (Hetherington, Bridges, & Insabella, 1998). But the research also reveals great individual differences in how children respond. The custodial parent's psychological health, the child's characteristics, and social supports within the family and surrounding community contribute to children's adjustment.

■ IMMEDIATE CONSEQUENCES. "Things were worst during the period Drake and I decided to separate," Rena reflected. "We fought over everything—from custody of the children to the living room furniture, and the kids suffered. Sobbing, Lizzie told me she was 'sorry she made Daddy go away.' Joey kicked and threw things at home and didn't do his work at school. In the midst of everything, I could hardly deal with their problems. We had to sell the house; I couldn't afford it alone. And I needed a better-paying job."

Rena's description captures conditions in many newly divorced households. Family conflict often rises as parents try to settle disputes over children and personal belongings. Once one parent moves out, additional events threaten supportive interactions between parents and children. Mother-headed households typically experience a sharp drop in income. Three-fourths of divorced mothers get less than the full amount of child support from the absent father or none at all (Children's Defense Fund, 1999). They often have to move to new housing for economic reasons, reducing supportive ties to neighbors and friends.

These life circumstances often lead to a highly disorganized family situation called "minimal parenting" (Wallerstein & Kelly, 1980). "Meals and bedtimes were at all hours, the house didn't get cleaned, and I stopped taking Joey and Lizzie on weekend outings," said Rena. As children react with distress and anger to their less secure home lives, discipline may become harsh and inconsistent. Contact with noncustodial fathers decreases over time (Hetherington, Bridges, & Insabella, 1998). When fathers see their children only occasionally, they are inclined to be permissive and indulgent. This often conflicts with the mother's style of parenting and makes her task of managing the child on a day-to-day basis even more difficult.

In view of these changes, it is not surprising that children experience painful emotional reactions. But the intensity of their feelings and the way they are expressed vary with the child's age, temperament, and sex.

Children's Age. Five-year-old Lizzie's fear that she had caused her father to leave is not unusual. The cognitive im-

■ *After parents divorce, most children reside with their mothers. Those who also stay involved with their fathers fare best in development. For girls, a good father–daughter relationship appears to contribute to heterosexual development. For boys, it seems to play a crucial role in overall psychological well-being. (Photo courtesy: Will Hart)*

maturity of preschool and early school-age children makes it difficult for them to grasp the reasons behind their parents' separation. Younger children often blame themselves and take the marital breakup as a sign that they could be abandoned by both parents. They may whine and cling, displaying intense separation anxiety (Hetherington, 1989).

Older children are better able to understand the reasons behind their parents' divorce, which may reduce some of the pain they feel (Mazur, 1993). Still, many school-age and adolescent youngsters react strongly, particularly when family conflict is high and supervision of children is low (Forehand et al., 1991). Some escape into undesirable peer activities, such as running away, truancy, early sexual activity, and delinquency (Simons & Chao, 1996; Tasker & Richards, 1994).

However, not all older children react this way. For some—especially the oldest child in the family—divorce can trigger more mature behavior. These youngsters may willingly take on extra burdens, such as household tasks, care and protection of younger siblings, and emotional support of a depressed, anxious mother. But if these demands are too great, older children may eventually become resentful and withdraw into some of the destructive behavior patterns just described (Hetherington, 1995, 1999).

Children's Temperament and Sex. When temperamentally difficult children are exposed to stressful life events and inadequate parenting, their problems are magnified. In contrast, easy children are less often targets of parental anger and are also better at coping with adversity when it hits.

These findings help us understand sex differences in response to divorce. Girls sometimes respond as Lizzie did, with internalizing reactions, such as crying, self-criticism, and withdrawal. More often, they show some demanding, attention-getting behavior. But in mother-custody families, boys experience more serious adjustment problems. Recall from Chapter 8 that boys are more active and noncompliant—behaviors that increase with exposure to parental conflict and inconsistent discipline. Coercive mother–child interaction and impulsive, defiant behavior on the part of sons are common in divorcing households (Hetherington, 1991).

Perhaps because their behavior is so unruly, boys receive less emotional support from mothers, teachers, and peers. And as Joey's behavior toward Lizzie illustrates, the coercive cycles of interaction between boys and their divorced mothers soon spread to sibling relations (MacKinnon, 1989). These outcomes compound boys' difficulties. Children of both sexes show declines in school achievement during the aftermath of divorce, but school problems are greater for boys (Guidubaldi & Cleminshaw, 1985).

■ LONG-TERM CONSEQUENCES. Rena eventually found better-paying work and gained control over the daily operation of the household. Her own feelings of anger and rejection also declined. And after several meetings with a counselor, Rena and Drake realized the harmful impact of their quarreling on Joey and Lizzie. They resolved to keep the children out of future disagreements. Drake visited regularly and handled Joey's unruliness with firmness and consistency. Soon Joey's school performance improved, his behavior problems subsided, and both children seemed calmer and happier.

Most children show improved adjustment by 2 years after divorce. Yet a few continue to have serious difficulties into early adulthood (Chase-Lansdale, Cherlin, & Kiernan, 1995). Boys and children with difficult temperaments are especially likely to experience lasting emotional problems. Among girls, the major long-term effects involve heterosexual behavior—a rise in sexual activity at adolescence, in teenage childbearing, and in risk of divorce in adulthood (Cherlin, Kiernan, & Chase-Lansdale, 1995; Hetherington, 1997).

The overriding factor in positive adjustment following divorce is effective parenting—in particular, how well the custodial parent handles stress and shields the child from conflict and the extent to which each parent uses authoritative child rearing (Amato & Gilbreth, 1999; Simons & Johnson, 1996). Contact with noncustodial fathers is important for children of both sexes. For girls, a good father–child relationship appears to contribute to heterosexual development. For boys, it seems to affect overall psychological well-being. In fact, several studies indicate that outcomes for sons are better when the father is the custodial parent (Camara & Resnick, 1988; Clark-Stewart & Hayward, 1996). Fathers are more likely than mothers to praise

a boy's good behavior and less likely to ignore his disruptiveness. The father's image of greater power and authority may also help him obtain more compliance from a son.

Although divorce is painful for children, remaining in a stressed intact family is much worse than making the transition to a low-conflict, single-parent household (Amato, Loomis, & Booth, 1995). When divorcing parents put aside their disagreements and support one another in their child-rearing roles, children have the best chance of growing up competent, stable, and happy. Caring extended family members, teachers, siblings, and friends are also important in reducing the likelihood that divorce will result in long-term disruption (DeGarmo & Forgatch, 1999; Grych & Fincham, 1997).

■ DIVORCE MEDIATION, JOINT CUSTODY, AND CHILD SUPPORT. Awareness that divorce is highly stressful for children and families has led to interventions aimed at helping families through this difficult time. One is **divorce mediation.** It consists of a series of meetings between divorcing adults and a trained professional, who tries to help them settle disputes, such as property division and child custody. Its purpose is to avoid legal battles that intensify family conflict. Research reveals that it increases out-of-court settlements and positive parental communication about child-related matters for years to come (Dillon & Emery, 1996).

To encourage both parents to remain involved with children, courts today more often award **joint custody,** which grants the mother and father equal say in important decisions about the child's upbringing. Yet many experts have raised questions about the practice. Joint custody results in a variety of living arrangements. In most instances, children reside with one parent and see the other on a fixed schedule, much like the typical sole-custody situation. But in other cases, parents share physical custody, and children must move between homes and sometimes schools and peer groups. These transitions introduce a new kind of instability that is especially hard on some children. The success of joint custody requires a cooperative relationship between divorcing parents (Tamis-LeMonda & Cabrera, 1999). If they continue to quarrel, it prolongs children's exposure to a hostile family atmosphere.

Finally, many single-parent families depend on child support from the absent parent to relieve financial strain. In response to a recent federal law, all states have established procedures for withholding wages from parents who fail to make these payments. Although child support is usually not enough to lift a single-parent family out of poverty, it can ease its burdens substantially. An added benefit is that children are more likely to maintain contact with a noncustodial father if he pays child support (Garfinkel & McLanahan, 1995). The Caregiving Concerns table on the following page summarizes ways to help children adjust to their parents' divorce.

Helping Children Adjust to Their Parents' Divorce

SUGGESTION	EXPLANATION
Shield children from conflict.	Witnessing intense parental conflict is very damaging to children. If one parent insists on expressing hostility, children fare better if the other parent does not respond in kind.
Provide children with as much continuity, familiarity, and predictability as possible.	Children adjust better during the period surrounding divorce when their lives have some stability—for example, the same school, bedroom, baby-sitter, and playmates and a dependable daily schedule.
Explain the divorce and tell children what to expect.	Children are more likely to develop fears of abandonment if they are not prepared for their parents' separation. They should be told that their mother and father will not be living together any more, which parent will be moving out, and when they will be able to see that parent. If possible, mother and father should explain the divorce together. Parents should provide a reason for the divorce that the child can understand and assure the child that he or she is not to blame.
Emphasize the permanence of the divorce.	Fantasies of parents getting back together can prevent children from accepting the reality of their current life. Children should be told that the divorce is final and that there is nothing they can do to change that fact.
Respond sympathetically to children's feelings.	Children need a supportive and understanding response to their feelings of sadness, fear, and anger. For children to adjust well, their painful emotions must be acknowledged, not denied or avoided.
Promote a continuing relationship with both parents.	When parents disentangle their lingering hostility toward the former spouse from the child's need for a continuing relationship with the other parent, children adjust well. Grandparents and other extended family members can help by not taking sides.

Source: Teyber, 1992.

REMARRIAGE

"If you get married to Wendell, and Daddy gets married to Carol," Lizzie wondered aloud to Rena, "then I'll have two sisters and one more brother. And let's see, how many grandmothers and grandfathers? Gosh, a lot!" exclaimed Lizzie. "But what will I call them all?" she asked, looking worried.

Life in a single-parent family is often temporary. Many parents find a new partner within a few years. As Lizzie's comments indicate, entry into these *blended,* or *reconstituted, families* leads to a complex set of new relationships. For some children, this expanded family network is a positive turn of events that brings greater adult attention. But for most, it presents difficult adjustments. Stepparents often use different child-rearing practices than the child was used to, and having to switch to new rules and expectations can be stressful. In addition, children often regard steprelatives as "intruders" into the family. But how well children adapt is, once again, related to the overall quality of family functioning (Bray, 1999). This often depends on which parent forms a new relationship and on the child's age and sex. As we will see, older children and girls seem to have the hardest time.

■ MOTHER–STEPFATHER FAMILIES. The most frequent form of blended family is a mother–stepfather arrangement, since mothers generally retain custody of the child. Boys usually adjust quickly. They welcome a stepfa-

ther who is warm and responsive and who offers relief from the coercive cycles of interaction that tend to build with their divorced mothers. Mothers' friction with sons also declines due to greater economic security, another adult to share household tasks, and an end to loneliness (Stevenson & Black, 1995). In contrast, girls adapt less favorably when custodial mothers find new partners. Stepfathers disrupt the close ties many girls establish with their mothers in a single-parent family, and girls often react to the new arrangement with sulky, resistant behavior (Hetherington, 1993).

Note, however, that age affects these findings. Older school-age and adolescent youngsters of both sexes find it harder to adjust to blended families (Bray & Berger, 1993). Perhaps because they are more aware of the impact of remarriage on their own lives, they challenge some aspects of it that younger children simply accept, creating more relationship issues with their steprelatives.

■ FATHER–STEPMOTHER FAMILIES. Research reveals more confusion for children in father–stepmother families. Remarriage of noncustodial fathers often leads to reduced contact. They tend to withdraw from their "previous" families, more so if they have daughters rather than sons (Hetherington, 1997). When fathers have custody, children typically react negatively to remarriage. One reason is that children living with fathers often start out with more problems. Perhaps the biological mother could no longer handle the unruly child (usually a boy), so the father and his new wife are faced with a youngster who has serious behavior problems. In other instances, the father is granted custody because of a very close relationship with the child, and his remarriage disrupts this bond (Buchanan, Maccoby, & Dornbusch, 1996).

Girls, especially, have a hard time getting along with their stepmothers (Hobart & Brown, 1988). Sometimes (as just mentioned) this occurs because the girl's relationship with her father is threatened by the remarriage. In addition, girls often become entangled in loyalty conflicts between their two mother figures. But the longer girls live in father–stepmother households, the more positive their interaction with stepmothers becomes. With time and patience they do adjust, and eventually girls benefit from the support of a second mother figure (Hetherington & Jodl, 1994).

MATERNAL EMPLOYMENT AND DUAL-EARNER FAMILIES

Today, single and married mothers are in the labor market in nearly equal proportions, and over 70 percent of those with school-age children are employed (U.S. Bureau of the Census, 1999). In Chapter 6, we saw that the impact of maternal employment on infant development depends on the quality of substitute care and the continuing parent–child relationship. This same conclusion applies during later years. In addition, a host of factors—the mother's work satisfaction, the support she receives from her husband, the child's sex, and the family's SES—have a bearing on how children fare.

■ MATERNAL EMPLOYMENT AND CHILD DEVELOPMENT. Children of mothers who enjoy their work and remain committed to parenting show especially positive adjustment—higher self-esteem, more positive family and peer relations, less gender-stereotyped beliefs, and better grades in school (Hoffman, 1989; Williams & Radin, 1993). Outcomes are especially positive for girls, who profit from the image of female competence. Daughters of employed mothers have higher educational aspirations and, in college, are more likely to choose nontraditional careers, such as law, medicine, and physics (Hoffman, 1989).

These benefits undoubtedly result from parenting practices. Employed mothers who value their parenting role are more likely to use authoritative child rearing (Greenberger & Goldberg, 1989). Also, children in dual-earner households devote more daily hours to doing homework under parental guidance. And contrary to popular belief, maternal employment does not reduce the time school-age children and adolescents spend with their mothers. But it does result in more time with fathers, who take on greater child-care responsibility. More paternal contact is related to higher achievement, mature social behavior, and a more flexible view of gender roles (Coltrane, 1996; Radin, 1994).

However, when employment places heavy demands on the mother's schedule, children are at risk for ineffective parenting. Working long hours and spending little time with school-age children are associated with less favorable adjustment (Moorehouse, 1991). In contrast, part-time employment seems to have benefits for children of all ages, probably because it prevents work overload, thereby helping mothers meet children's needs (Lerner & Abrams, 1994).

■ SUPPORT FOR EMPLOYED MOTHERS AND FATHERS. When mothers have the necessary supports to engage in effective parenting, maternal employment offers children many advantages. In dual-earner families, the husband's willingness to share responsibilities is crucial. If the father helps very little or not at all, the mother carries a double load, at home and at work, leading to fatigue, distress, and reduced time and energy for children.

Besides fathers, work settings and government policies can help employed mothers. Part-time employment and liberal paid maternity and paternity leaves (including time off when children are ill) make juggling the demands of work and child rearing easier. Although these workplace supports are available in Canada and Western Europe, at present only unpaid leave is mandated by U.S. federal law. Equal pay and employment opportunities for women are also important. Because these policies enhance financial status and morale, they improve the way mothers feel and behave when they arrive home at the end of the working day.

■ CHILD CARE FOR SCHOOL-AGE CHILDREN. High-quality child care is vital for parents' peace of mind and children's well-being, even during middle childhood. In recent years, much public concern has been voiced about the estimated 2.4 million 5- to 13-year-olds in the United States who regularly look after themselves during after-school hours.

Research on these **self-care children** reveals inconsistent findings. Some studies report that they suffer from low self-esteem, antisocial behavior, poor academic achievement, and fearfulness, whereas others show no such effects (Padilla & Landreth, 1989). What explains these contradictions? The way self-care children spend their time seems to be the crucial factor. Children who have a history of authoritative child rearing, are monitored from a distance by parental telephone calls, and have regular after-school chores appear responsible and well-adjusted. In contrast, those left to their own devices are more likely to bend to peer pressures and engage in antisocial behavior (Steinberg, 1986).

Parents must consider children's maturity before deciding on self-care. Before age 9 or 10, children should not be left unsupervised because most are not yet competent to deal with emergencies (Galambos & Maggs, 1991). Unfortunately, when children are not mature enough to handle the self-care arrangement, many employed parents have few alternatives. Although after-school programs for 6- to 13-year-olds are increasing in the United States, they remain scarce. When high-quality "after-care" is available with positive caregiver–child interaction and varied activities that

■ *High-quality, after-school child-care programs can enhance school performance, social skills, and emotional adjustment. These children's "after-care" experiences regularly include conversing and playing games with senior citizens, who volunteer in the program. (Photo courtesy: Peter Hvizdak/The Image Works)*

allow for child choice, boys show better social skills and emotional adjustment (Pierce, Hamm, & Vandell, 1999). And low-SES children of both sexes who participate in "after-care" enrichment activities (scouting, music, or art lessons) show gains in school performance and adjustment from third to fifth grade (Posner & Vandell, 1994, 1999).

ASK YOURSELF . . .

■ *"How come you don't study hard and get good grades like your sister?" a mother exclaimed in exasperation after seeing her son's poor report card. What impact do remarks like this have on sibling interaction, and why?*

🌳 *What advice would you give a divorcing couple about how to promote long-term, favorable adjustment in their two school-age sons?*

■ *Nine-year-old Bobby's mother has just found employment, so Bobby takes care of himself after school. What factors are likely to affect how well Bobby fares under this arrangement? Should Bobby's mother enroll him in an "after-care" program? Explain.*

SOME COMMON PROBLEMS OF DEVELOPMENT

Throughout our discussion, we have considered a variety of stressful experiences that place children at risk for future problems. In the following sections, we touch on two more areas of concern: school-age children's fears and anxieties and the consequences of child sexual abuse. Finally, we sum up factors that help children cope effectively with stress.

FEARS AND ANXIETIES

Although fears of the dark, thunder and lightning, and supernatural beings (stimulated by movies and television) occasionally persist into middle childhood, children's anxieties are largely directed toward new concerns. As children begin to understand the realities of the wider world, the possibility of personal harm (being robbed, stabbed, or shot) and events they witness through the media (war, disasters, and school violence) often trouble them. Other common worries include academic performance, parents' health, physical injuries, and rejection by classmates (Silverman, La Greca, & Wasserstein, 1995).

Most children handle their fears constructively, by talking about them with parents, teachers, and friends and relying on the more sophisticated emotional self-regulation strategies that develop in middle childhood. Consequently fears decline with age, especially for girls, who express more fears than do boys throughout childhood and adolescence (Gullone & King, 1997).

About 20 percent of school-age children develop an intense, unmanageable anxiety of some kind (Beidel, 1991). **School phobia** is an example. Typically, children with this disorder are middle-SES youngsters whose achievement is average or above. Still, they feel severe apprehension about attending school, often accompanied by physical complaints (dizziness, nausea, stomachaches, and vomiting) that disappear once they are allowed to remain home. About one-third are 5- to 7-year-olds, most of whom do not fear school so much as separation from their mothers. The difficulty can often be traced to a troubled parent–child relationship in which the mother encourages dependency. Intensive family therapy is necessary to help these children (Pilkington & Piersel, 1991).

Most cases of school phobia appear later, around 11 to 13, during the transition from middle childhood to adolescence. These children usually find a particular aspect of school frightening—an overcritical teacher, a school bully, a threatening gang, or too much parental pressure for school success. Treating this form of school phobia may require a change in school environment or parenting practices. Firm insistence that the child return to school along with training in how to cope with difficult situations is also helpful (Blagg & Yule, 1996).

Severe childhood anxieties may arise from harsh living conditions. In inner-city ghettos and war-torn areas of the world, a great many children live in the midst of constant deprivation, chaos, and violence. They learn to drop to the floor at the sound of gunfire and witness the wounding and killing of friends and relatives. As the Lifespan Vista box on page 340 reveals, these youngsters often suffer from long-term emotional distress. Finally, as we saw in our discussion

On May 27, 1992, Zlata Filipovic, a 10-year-old Bosnian girl, recorded the following reactions to the intensifying Serb attack on the city of Sarajevo in her diary:

SLAUGHTER! MASSACRE! HORROR! CRIME! BLOOD! SCREAMS! TEARS! DESPAIR!

That's what Vaso Miskin Street looks like today. Two shells exploded in the street and one in the market. Mommy was nearby at the time. . . . Daddy and I were beside ourselves because she hadn't come home. I saw some of it on TV but I still can't believe what I actually saw. . . . I've got a lump in my throat and a knot in my tummy. HORRIBLE. They're taking the wounded to the hospital. It's a madhouse. We kept going to the window hoping to see Mommy, but she wasn't back. . . . Daddy and I were tearing our hair out. . . . I looked out the window one more time and . . . I SAW MOMMY RUNNING ACROSS THE BRIDGE. As she came into the house she started shaking and crying. Through her tears she told us how she had seen dismembered

bodies. . . . Thank God, Mommy is with us. Thank God. (Filipovic, 1994, p. 55)

Violence stemming from ethnic and political tensions is increasingly being felt around the world. Today, nearly all armed conflicts are internal civil wars in which well-established ways of life are threatened or destroyed and children are frequently victims (Mays et al., 1998).

Children's experiences under conditions of armed conflict are diverse. Some may participate in the fighting, either because they are forced or because they want to please adults. Others are kidnapped, terrorized, or tortured. Those who are bystanders often come under direct fire and may be killed or physically maimed for life. And as Zlata's diary entry illustrates, many children of war watch in horror as family members, friends, and neighbors flee, are wounded, or die (Ladd & Cairns, 1996).

When war and social crises are temporary, most children are comforted by caregivers' reassuring messages and do not show long-term emotional difficulties. But chronic danger requires children to make substantial adjustments, and their psychological functioning can be seriously impaired. Many children of war lose their sense of safety, become desensitized to violence, are haunted by terrifying memories, become suspicious of others, and build a pessimistic view of the future (Cairns, 1996).

The extent to which children are negatively affected by war depends on other factors. Closeness to wartime events increases the chances of maladjustment. For example, an estimated 50 percent of traumatized 6- to 12-year-old Cambodian war refugees continued to show intense stress reactions when they reached young adulthood (Kinzie et al., 1989). The support and affection of parents is the best safeguard against lasting problems. Unfortunately, many children of war are separated from family members. Sometimes, the child's community can offer protection. For example, Israeli children who lost a parent in battle fared best when they lived in kibbutzim, cohesive agricultural settlements where many adults knew the child well and felt responsible for his or her welfare (Lifschitz et al., 1977).

When wartime drains families and communities of resources, international organizations must step in and help children. Until we know how to prevent war, efforts to preserve children's physical, psychological, and educational well-being may be the best way to stop transmission of violence to the next generation in many parts of the world.

■ *These traumatized ethnic Albanian refugee children from Kosovo are victims of the Serbian program of "ethnic cleansing." Here they receive humanitarian aid at a refugee center. Some of the children have seen their homes burned and family members wounded or killed. Without special support from caring adults, they are likely to show lasting emotional problems. (Photo courtesy: AP/Wide World Photos)*

of child abuse in Chapter 8, too often violence and other destructive acts become part of adult–child relationships. During middle childhood, child sexual abuse increases.

CHILD SEXUAL ABUSE

Until recently, child sexual abuse was viewed as a rare occurrence. When children came forward with it, adults usually did not take their claims seriously. In the 1970s, efforts by professionals along with widespread media attention caused child sexual abuse to be recognized as a serious and widespread problem. Several hundred thousand cases are reported in the United States each year (see Chapter 8).

■ CHARACTERISTICS OF ABUSERS AND VICTIMS. Sexual abuse is committed against children of both sexes, but more often against girls. Reported cases are highest in middle childhood, but sexual abuse also occurs at younger and older ages. Few children experience only a single incident. For some, the abuse begins early in life and continues for many years (Burkhardt & Rotatori, 1995; Holmes & Slap, 1998).

Generally, the abuser is male—a parent or someone the parent knows well. Often it is a father, stepfather, or live-in boyfriend, somewhat less often an uncle or older brother. In a few instances, mothers are the offenders, more often with sons than daughters. If it is a nonrelative, it is usually someone the child has come to know and trust (Kolvin & Trowell, 1996).

In the overwhelming majority of cases, the abuse is serious—vaginal or anal intercourse, oral-genital contact, fondling, and forced stimulation of the adult. Abusers make the child comply in a variety of distasteful ways, including deception, bribery, verbal intimidation, and physical force (Gomez-Schwartz, Horowitz, & Cardarelli, 1990).

You may be wondering how any adult—especially a parent or close relative—could possibly violate a child sexually. Many offenders deny their own responsibility. They blame the abuse on the willing participation of a seductive youngster. Yet children are not capable of making a deliberate, informed decision to enter into a sexual relationship! Even at older ages, they are not free to say yes or no. Instead, abusers tend to have characteristics that predispose them toward sexual exploitation. They have great difficulty controlling their impulses, may suffer from psychological disorders, and are often addicted to alcohol and drugs. Often they pick children who are unlikely to defend themselves—those who are physically weak, emotionally deprived, and socially isolated (Faller, 1990).

Reported cases of child sexual abuse are strongly linked to poverty, marital instability, and resulting weakening of family ties. Children who live in homes with a history of constantly changing characters—repeated marriages, separations, and new partners—are especially vulnerable. But community surveys reveal that middle-SES children in relatively stable homes are also victims; they are simply more likely to escape detection (Gomez-Schwartz, Horowitz, & Cardarelli, 1990).

■ CONSEQUENCES FOR CHILDREN. The adjustment problems of child sexual abuse victims are often severe. Depression, low self-esteem, mistrust of adults, and feelings of anger and hostility can persist for years after the abusive episodes. Younger children often react with sleep difficulties, loss of appetite, and generalized fearfulness. Adolescents may run away and show suicidal reactions, substance abuse, and delinquency (Kendall-Tacket, Williams, & Finkelhor, 1993; Tebbutt et al., 1997).

Sexually abused children frequently display sexual knowledge and behavior beyond their years. They have learned from their abusers that sexual overtures are acceptable ways to get attention and rewards. As they move toward young adulthood, they tend to be promiscuous and to enter into unhealthy relationships. Women are likely to choose partners who abuse both them and their children (Faller, 1990). As mothers, they often show poor parenting skills, abusing and neglecting their youngsters (Pianta, Egeland, & Erickson, 1989). In these ways, the harmful impact of sexual abuse is transmitted to the next generation.

■ PREVENTION AND TREATMENT. Treating child sexual abuse is difficult. The reactions of family members —anxiety about harm to the child, anger toward the abuser, and sometimes hostility toward the victim for telling— can increase children's distress. Since sexual abuse typically appears in the midst of other serious family problems,

■ *This poster for Keeping Ourselves Safe, New Zealand's national, school-based child abuse prevention program described on pages 342–343, illustrates the importance of teaching children to recognize abusive adult behaviors so they can take steps to protect themselves. Parents are informed about children's classroom learning experiences and encouraged to support and extend them at home. (Photo courtesy: New Zealand Police)*

SOCIAL ISSUES

CHILDREN'S EYEWITNESS TESTIMONY

Increasingly, children are being called on to testify in court cases involving child abuse and neglect, child custody, and other matters. Having to provide such information can be difficult and traumatic. Almost always, children must report on highly stressful events. In doing so, they may have to speak against a parent or other relative to whom they feel loyal. In some family disputes, they may fear punishment for telling the truth. In addition, child witnesses are faced with an unfamiliar situation—at the very least an interview in the judge's chambers, and at most an open courtroom with judge, jury, spectators, and the possibility of unsympathetic cross-examination. Not surprisingly, there is considerable debate about the accuracy of children's recall under these conditions.

AGE DIFFERENCES. Until recently, it was rare for children under age 5 to testify, whereas those age 6 and older often did so. Children between ages 10 and 14 have historically been assumed competent to testify. Yet as a result of societal reactions to rising rates of child abuse and difficulties in prosecuting perpetrators, legal requirements for child testimony have been relaxed in Canada and the United States. Children as young as age 3 are frequently serving as witnesses (Ceci & Bruck, 1998).

Compared with preschoolers, school-age children are better able to give detailed descriptions of past experiences and make accurate inferences about others' motives and intentions. Older children are also

more resistant to misleading questions of the sort asked by attorneys when they probe for more information or, in cross-examination, try to influence the content of the child's response (Ceci & Bruck, 1993; Goodman & Tobey, 1994). Nevertheless, when properly questioned, even 3-year-olds can recall recent events accurately—including ones that were highly stressful (Baker-Ward et al., 1993; Goodman et al., 1991).

SUGGESTIBILITY. Yet court testimony often involves repeated interviews. When adults lead children by suggesting incorrect facts ("He touched you there, didn't he?"), they increase the likelihood of incorrect reporting, among preschoolers and school-age children alike. Events that children fabricate in response to leading questions can be quite fantastic. In one study, after a visit to a doctor's office, children said yes to questions about events that not only never occurred but that implied abuse—"Did the doctor lick your knee?" "Did the nurse sit on top of you?" (Ornstein et al., 1997). To ease the task of providing testimony, special interviewing methods have been devised for children. In many child sexual abuse cases, anatomically correct dolls are used to prompt children's recall. However, this method is highly suggestive; it can encourage reports of physical and sexual contact that did not happen (Ceci & Bruck, 1998).

By the time children come to court, it is weeks, months, or even years after the occurrence of the target events. When a long delay is combined with suggestions about what

happened and stereotyping of the accused ("He's in jail because he's been bad"), children can easily be misled into giving false information (Ceci, Leichtman, & Bruck, 1994; Leichtman & Ceci, 1995).

INTERVENTIONS. Child witnesses need to be prepared so they understand the courtroom process and know what to expect. In some places, "court schools" exist in which children are taken through the setting and given an opportunity to role-play court activities. As part of this process, children can be encouraged to admit not knowing an answer rather than guessing or going along with what an adult expects of them. At the same time, legal professionals must take steps to lessen the risk of suggestibility—by limiting the number of times children are interviewed and asking questions in nonleading ways.

If a child is likely to experience emotional trauma or later punishment (in a family dispute), then courtroom procedures can be adapted to protect them. For example, they can testify over closed-circuit TV so they do not have to face an abuser. When it is not wise for a child to participate directly, expert witnesses can provide testimony that reports on the child's psychological condition and includes important elements of the child's story. But for such testimony to be worthwhile, witnesses need to be impartial and trained in how to question to minimize false reporting (Bruck, Ceci, & Hembrooke, 1998).

long-term therapy with children and families is usually necessary (Doyle, 1994).

The best way to reduce the suffering of victims is to prevent child sexual abuse from continuing. Today, courts are prosecuting abusers (especially nonrelatives) more vigorously and taking children's testimony more seriously (see the Social Issues box above).

Educational programs can teach children to recognize inappropriate sexual advances and show them where to go for help. Yet because of controversies over educating children about sexual abuse, few schools offer these interventions. New Zealand is the only country in the world with a national, school-based prevention program targeting sexual abuse. In Keeping Ourselves Safe, 5- to 13-year-olds learn that abusers are usually not strangers but rather are close to their victims. Parent involvement ensures that home and school work together in teaching children self-protection skills. Evaluations reveal that virtually all New Zealand parents and children support the program and that it has helped many children avoid or report abuse (Briggs & Hawkins, 1996, 1999).

FOSTERING RESILIENCE IN MIDDLE CHILDHOOD

Throughout middle childhood—and other phases of development as well—children are confronted with challenging and sometimes threatening situations that require them to cope with psychological stress. In this and the previous chapter, we have considered such topics as learning disabilities, achievement expectations, divorce, and child sexual abuse. Each taxes children's coping resources, creating serious risks for development.

At the same time, only a modest relationship between stressful life experiences and childhood psychological disturbance exists (Garmezy, 1993). In our discussion in Chapter 3 of the long-term consequences of birth complications, we noted that some children manage to overcome the combined effects of birth trauma, poverty, and a deeply troubled family life. The same is true when we look at school difficulties, family transitions, and child maltreatment. Recall from Chapter 1 that research on resilient children indicates that three broad factors can protect against maladjustment: (1) the child's personal characteristics, including an easy temperament and a mastery-oriented approach to new situations; (2) a warm, well-organized family life; and

(3) an adult outside the immediate family who offers the child a support system and a positive coping model.

Although any one of these factors can promote resilience, we have seen many examples of how unfavorable life experiences increase the chances that parents and children will act in ways that expose them to further hardship. Children can usually handle one stressor, even if it is chronic. But when negative conditions pile up, such as marital discord, poverty, crowded living conditions, neighborhood violence, and abuse, the rate of maladjustment is multiplied (Sameroff et al., 1993; Wyman et al., 1999).

Social supports are especially important during periods of developmental transition—when children are more vulnerable because they are faced with many new tasks. One such turning point is the beginning of middle childhood, a time of new challenges in academic work and peer relations. As the next two chapters will reveal, another major turning point is the transition to adolescence. Especially at these times, families, schools, communities, and society as a whole can do much to enhance development.

ASK YOURSELF . . .

Consider the following stressful experiences encountered by some school-age children: evaluations by parents and teachers that attribute failures to low ability; wartime trauma; and child sexual abuse. For each, cite factors that can protect children from lasting adjustment problems. What do the protective factors have in common?

SUMMARY

ERIKSON'S THEORY: INDUSTRY VERSUS INFERIORITY

What personality changes take place during Erikson's stage of industry versus inferiority?

- According to Erikson, children who successfully resolve the psychological conflict of **industry versus inferiority** develop the capacity for productive work, learn the value of division of labor, and develop a sense of moral commitment and responsibility.

SELF-DEVELOPMENT

Describe school-age children's self-concept and self-esteem, and discuss factors that affect their achievement-related attributions.

- During middle childhood, children's self-concepts include personality traits and **social comparisons. Self-esteem** becomes hierarchically organized and declines over the early school years as children adjust their self-judgments to feedback from the environment.

- Children with **mastery-oriented attributions** credit their successes to high ability and failures to insufficient effort. In contrast, children who receive negative feedback about their ability develop **learned helplessness,** attributing their successes to luck and failures to low ability.

EMOTIONAL DEVELOPMENT

Cite changes in understanding and expression of emotion in middle childhood.

- In middle childhood, the self-conscious emotions of pride and guilt become clearly governed by personal responsibility. School-age children recognize that people can experience more than one emotion at a time and attend to more cues in interpreting another's feelings, and empathy increases. By the end of middle childhood, most children have an adaptive set of strategies for regulating emotion.

UNDERSTANDING OTHERS: PERSPECTIVE TAKING

How does perspective taking change in middle childhood?

■ **Perspective taking** improves greatly during the school years, as Selman's five-stage sequence indicates. Cognitive maturity and experiences in which adults and peers encourage children to take note of another's viewpoint support gains in perspective-taking skill. Good perspective takers are more socially skilled.

MORAL DEVELOPMENT

Describe changes in moral understanding during middle childhood.

■ By middle childhood, children have internalized a wide variety of moral rules. Their concepts of **distributive justice** change, from equality to merit to benevolence. School-age children also begin to grasp the linkage between moral rules and social conventions. The personal domain strengthens from middle childhood to adolescence and fosters concepts of personal rights and freedom.

PEER RELATIONS

How do peer sociability and friendship change in middle childhood?

■ In middle childhood, peer interaction becomes more prosocial, and aggression declines. By the end of the school years, children organize themselves into **peer groups.**

Friendships develop into mutual relationships based on trust.

Describe major categories of peer acceptance and ways to help rejected children.

■ On measures of peer acceptance, **popular children** are liked by many agemates; **rejected children** are actively disliked; **controversial children** are both liked and disliked; and **neglected children** are seldom chosen, either positively or negatively.

■ At least two subtypes of children rejected by peers exist: **rejected-aggressive children,** who show severe conduct problems, and **rejected-withdrawn children,** who are passive, socially awkward, and at risk for **peer victimization.** Both subgroups often experience lasting adjustment difficulties. Interventions that provide coaching in social skills, training in social understanding, academic tutoring, and increased expectations for social success have been used to help rejected youngsters.

GENDER TYPING

What changes in gender-stereotyped beliefs and gender identity take place during middle childhood?

■ School-age children extend their awareness of gender stereotypes to personality characteristics and academic subjects. They also develop a more open-minded view of what males and females can do. Boys strengthen their identification with the masculine role, whereas girls often experiment with "other-gender" activities. Cultures shape gender-typed behavior through daily activities assigned to children.

FAMILY INFLUENCES

How do parent–child communication and sibling relationships change in middle childhood?

■ Effective parents of school-age youngsters engage in **coregulation,** exerting general oversight while permitting children to be in charge of moment-by-moment decision making. Coregulation depends on a cooperative relationship between parent and child.

■ Sibling rivalry increases as children participate in a wider range of activities and parents compare their abilities. Oldest children are slightly advantaged in IQ and school achievement. Younger siblings are more popular with peers. Only children are as well adjusted as children with siblings, and they do better in school and attain higher levels of education.

What factors influence children's adjustment to divorce and remarriage?

■ Divorce is common in the lives of American children. Although most experience painful emotional reactions, children with difficult temperaments and boys in mother-custody homes are more likely to show lasting adjustment problems.

■ The overriding factor in positive adjustment following divorce is effective parenting. Contact with noncustodial fathers is important for children of both sexes, and outcomes for sons are better under father custody. Because **divorce mediation** helps parents resolve disputes, it can reduce children's exposure to conflict. **Joint custody** is a controversial practice that may create additional strains for children.

■ When divorced parents enter new relationships, girls, older children, and children in father–stepmother families display the greatest adjustment problems.

How do maternal employment and life in dual-earner families affect school-age children?

■ As long as mothers enjoy their work and remain committed to parenting, maternal employment is associated with higher self-esteem in children, more positive family and peer relations, less gender-stereotyped beliefs, and better grades in school. In dual earner families, the father's willingness to share responsibilities is vital. Workplace supports, such as part-time employment and generous parental leave, assist parents in rearing children.

■ **Self-care children** who are monitored from a distance and experience authoritative parenting appear responsible and well adjusted. Children in high-quality after-school programs show gains in school performance and emotional adjustment.

SOME COMMON PROBLEMS OF DEVELOPMENT

Cite common fears and anxieties in middle childhood.

■ School-age children's fears are directed toward new concerns having to do with physical safety, events portrayed through the media, academic performance, parents' health, and peer relations. Some children develop intense, unmanageable fears, such as **school phobia.** Severe anxiety can also result from harsh living conditions.

Discuss factors related to child sexual abuse and its consequences for children's development.

■ Child sexual abuse is generally committed by male family members, more often against girls than boys. Abusers have characteristics that predispose them toward sexual exploitation. Reported cases are strongly associated with poverty and marital instability. Abused children often have severe adjustment problems.

Cite factors that foster resiliency in middle childhood.

■ Overall, only a modest relationship exists between stressful life experiences and psychological disturbance in childhood. Personal characteristics of children; a warm, well-organized family life; and social supports outside the family are related to childhood resilience in the face of stress.

IMPORTANT TERMS AND CONCEPTS

controversial children (p. 329)
coregulation (p. 333)
distributive justice (p. 326)
divorce mediation (p. 336)
industry versus inferiority (p. 320)
joint custody (p. 336)
learned helplessness (p. 323)

mastery-oriented attributions (p. 323)
neglected children (p. 329)
peer group (p. 327)
peer victimization (p. 330)
perspective taking (p. 325)
popular children (p. 329)
rejected children (p. 329)

rejected-aggressive children (p. 329)
rejected-withdrawn children (p. 329)
school phobia (p. 339)
self-care children (p. 338)
social comparisons (p. 321)

FYI FOR FURTHER INFORMATION AND HELP

Consult the companion website for this book, where you will find additional weblinks and associated learning activities: www.abacon.com/berk

DIVORCE AND SINGLE PARENTHOOD

Parents Without Partners
www.parentswithoutpartners.org

Organization of custodial and noncustodial single parents that provides support in the upbringing of children. Many local groups exist throughout the United States.

Center for Divorce Education
www.divorce-education.com

An organization of psychologists and lawyers committed to educating the public about the effects of divorce. Has developed a comprehensive education program for divorcing families.

BLENDED FAMILIES

Stepfamily Association of America
www.stepfam.org

Association of families interested in stepfamily relationships. Organizes support

groups and offers education and children's services.

Stepfamily Foundation
www.stepfamily.org

Organization of remarried parents, interested professionals, and divorced individuals. Arranges group counseling sessions for stepfamilies and provides training for professionals.

AGE	PHYSICAL	COGNITIVE	LANGUAGE	EMOTIONAL/SOCIAL
6–8 years	■ Slow gains in height and weight continue until adolescent growth spurt. (280) ■ Gradual replacement of primary teeth by permanent teeth throughout middle childhood. (281) ■ Writing becomes smaller and more legible. Letter reversals decline. (287) ■ Drawings become more organized and detailed and include some depth cues. (288) ■ Organized games with rules become common. (289)	■ Thought becomes more logical, as shown by the ability to pass Piagetian conservation, class inclusion, and seriation problems. (291) ■ Understanding of spatial concepts improves, as illustrated by ability to give clear, well-organized directions. (291) ■ Attention becomes more selective, adaptable, and planful. (294) ■ Uses memory strategies of rehearsal and organization. (295) ■ Regards the mind as an active, constructive agent, capable of transforming information. (296) ■ Awareness of the importance of memory strategies and the impact of psychological factors (attention, motivation) in task performance improves. (296)	■ Vocabulary increases rapidly throughout middle childhood. (304) ■ Word definitions are concrete, referring to functions and appearance. (304) ■ Language awareness improves. (304)	■ Self-concept begins to include personality traits and social comparisons. (321) ■ Self-esteem differentiates, becomes heirarchically organized, and declines to a more realistic level. (321–322) ■ Self-conscious emotions of pride and guilt are governed by personal responsibility. (324) ■ Recognizes that individuals can experience more than one emotion at a time. (325) ■ Attends to more cues—facial, situational, and past experiences—in interpreting another's feelings. (325) ■ Understands that access to different information often causes people to have different perspectives. (325–326) ■ Becomes more responsible and independent. (333) ■ Distributive justice reasoning changes from equality to merit to benevolence. (326) ■ Peer interaction becomes more prosocial, and physical aggression declines. (327)

AGE	PHYSICAL	COGNITIVE	LANGUAGE	EMOTIONAL/SOCIAL
9–11 years	■ Adolescent growth spurt begins 2 years earlier in girls than boys. (280) ■ Gross motor skills of running, jumping, throwing, catching, kicking, batting, and dribbling are executed more quickly and with better coordination. (286) ■ Reaction time improves, contributing to motor skill development. (286) ■ Representation of depth in drawings expands. (288)	■ Logical thought remains tied to concrete situations. (292) ■ Piagetian tasks continue to be mastered in a step-by-step fashion. (292) ■ Memory strategies of rehearsal and organization become more effective. Begins to use elaboration. (295–296) ■ Applies several memory strategies at once. (295) ■ Long-term knowledge base grows larger and becomes better organized. (296) ■ Cognitive self-regulation improves. (297)	■ Word definitions emphasize synonyms and categorical relations. (304) ■ Grasps double meanings of words, as reflected in comprehension of metaphors and humor. (305) ■ Use of complex grammatical constructions improves. (305) ■ Adapts messages to the needs of listeners in complex communicative situations. (305) ■ Conversational strategies become more refined. (305)	■ Self-esteem tends to rise. (322) ■ Has an adaptive set of strategies for regulating emotion. (325) ■ Can "step into another's shoes" and view the self from that person's perspective. (325–326) ■ Later, can view the relationship between self and other from the perspective of a third, impartial party. (325–326) ■ Appreciates the linkage between moral rules and social conventions. (327) ■ Sense of a unique domain of personal matters strengthens (327) ■ Peer groups emerge. (327) ■ Friendships are based on mutual trust. (328) ■ Becomes aware of more gender stereotypes, including personality traits and school subjects, but has a more flexible appreciation of what males and females can do. (331) ■ Sibling rivalry tends to increase. (333)

Note: Numbers in parentheses indicate the page on which each milestone is discussed.

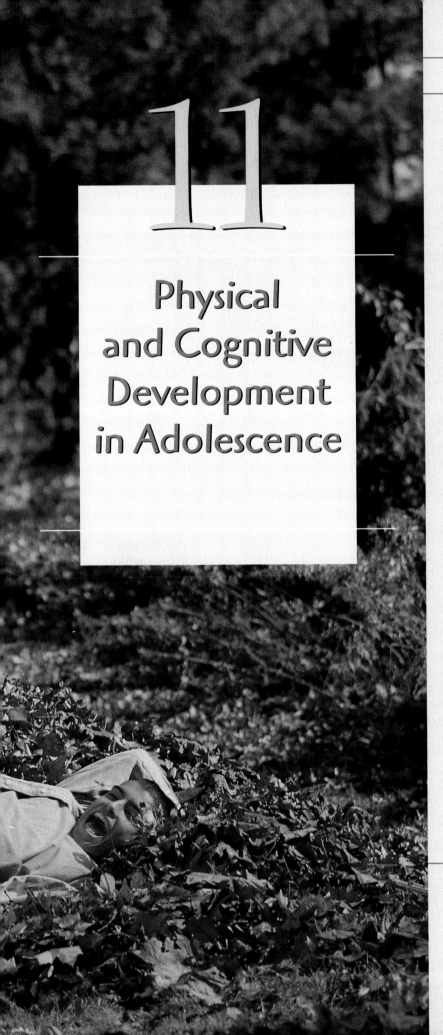

11

Physical and Cognitive Development in Adolescence

■ *The dramatic physical and cognitive changes of adolescence make puberty both an exhilarating and apprehensive phase of the lifespan. Although their bodies are full-grown and sexually mature, this boy and girl have many skills to acquire and hurdles to overcome before they are ready for full assumption of adult roles. (Photo courtesy: Richard Hutchings/PhotoEdit)*

On her eleventh birthday, Sabrina's friend Joyce gave her a surprise party, but Sabrina appeared somber during the celebration. Although Sabrina and Joyce had been close friends since third grade, their relationship was faltering. Sabrina was a head taller and some 20 pounds heavier than most of the other girls in her sixth-grade class. Her breasts were well developed, her hips and thighs had broadened, and she had begun to menstruate. In contrast, Joyce still had the short, lean, flat-chested body of a school-age child.

Ducking into the bathroom while Joyce and the other girls set the table for cake and ice cream, Sabrina looked herself over in the mirror and whispered, "Gosh, I feel so big and heavy." At church youth group on Sunday evenings, Sabrina broke away from Joyce and spent time with the eighth-grade girls, around whom she didn't feel so large and awkward.

Once every two weeks, parents gathered at Sabrina and Joyce's school for discussions about child-rearing concerns. Sabrina's Italian-American parents, Franca and Antonio, came whenever they could. "How you know they are becoming teenagers is this," Antonio volunteered one evening. "The bedroom door is closed, and they want to be alone. Also, they contradict and disagree. I tell Sabrina, 'You have to go to Aunt Gina's for dinner with the family.' The next thing I know, she is arguing with me."

Sabrina has entered **adolescence,** a period in which she will cross the dividing line between childhood and adulthood. In modern societies, the skills young people must master are so complex and the choices confronting them so diverse that adolescence lasts for nearly a decade. But around the world, the basic tasks of this phase are much the same. Sabrina must accept her full-grown body, acquire adult ways of thinking, attain emotional and economic independence, develop more mature ways of relating to peers of both sexes, and construct an identity—a secure sense of who she is, sexually, morally, politically, and vocationally.

The beginning of adolescence is marked by **puberty,** a flood of biological events leading to an adult-sized body and sexual maturity. As Sabrina's reactions suggest, entry into adolescence can be a trying time, more so for some youngsters than for others. In this chapter, we trace the events of puberty, highlighting sex differences in physical and motor development that appear at this time. Then we take up a variety of health concerns—nutrition, sexual activity, and serious health problems affecting teenagers who encounter difficulties on the path to maturity.

Adolescence brings with it the capacity for abstract thinking, which opens up new realms of learning. Teenagers can grasp complex scientific principles, grapple with social and political issues, detect the hidden meaning of a poem or story, and deal with language in increasingly flex-

ible, creative ways. The second part of this chapter traces these extraordinary changes from both Piaget's and the information-processing perspective. Then we take a close look at some findings that have attracted a great deal of public attention: sex differences in mental abilities. The final portion of this chapter is devoted to the primary setting in which adolescent thought takes shape: the school.

PHYSICAL DEVELOPMENT

CONCEPTIONS OF ADOLESCENCE

THE BIOLOGICAL PERSPECTIVE

Ask several parents of young children what they expect their sons and daughters to be like as teenagers. You will probably get answers like these: "Rebellious and uncontrollable." "Full of rages and tempers." This view, widespread in contemporary American society, dates back to the writings of eighteenth-century philosopher Jean-Jacques Rousseau, who was introduced in Chapter 1. Rousseau (1762/1955) believed that a natural outgrowth of the biological upheaval of puberty was heightened emotionality, conflict, and defiance of adults.

In the twentieth century, this storm-and-stress perspective was picked up by major theorists. The most influential was G. Stanley Hall, whose view of development was grounded in Darwin's theory of evolution. Hall (1904) described adolescence as a cascade of instinctual passions, a phase of growth so turbulent that it resembled the period in which humans evolved from savages into civilized beings. Sigmund Freud, as well, emphasized the emotional storminess of the teenage years. He called adolescence the *genital stage,* a period in which instinctual drives reawaken and shift to the genital region of the body, resulting in psychological conflict and volatile, unpredictable behavior. Gradually, as adolescents find romantic partners, inner forces achieve a new, more mature harmony, and the stage concludes with marriage, birth, and rearing of children. In this way, Freud emphasized, young people fulfill their biological destiny: sexual reproduction and survival of the species.

THE ENVIRONMENTAL PERSPECTIVE

Recent research on large numbers of teenagers suggests that the notion of adolescence as a biologically determined period of storm and stress is greatly exaggerated. A number of problems, such as eating disorders, depression, suicide, and lawbreaking, occur more often in adolescence than earlier. But the overall rate of psychological disturbance rises only slightly (by 2 percent) from childhood to adolescence, when it is the same as in the adult population—about 20 percent (Costello & Angold, 1995). Although some teenagers encounter serious difficulties, emotional turbulence is not a routine feature of adolescence.

The first researcher to point out the wide variability in adolescent adjustment was anthropologist Margaret Mead (1928). She traveled to the Pacific islands of Samoa and returned with a startling conclusion: Because of the culture's relaxed social relationships and openness toward sexuality, adolescence "is perhaps the pleasantest time the Samoan girl (or boy) will ever know" (p. 308).

Mead offered an alternative view in which the social environment is entirely responsible for the range of teenage experiences, from erratic and agitated to calm and stress-free. Yet this conclusion is just as extreme as the biological perspective it tried to replace! Later researchers found that Samoan adolescence was not as untroubled as Mead had assumed (Freeman, 1983). Still, Mead convinced researchers that greater attention must be paid to social and cultural influences for adolescent development to be understood.

A BALANCED POINT OF VIEW

Today, we know that adolescence is a product of *both* biological and social forces. Biological changes are universal—found in all primates and all cultures. These internal stresses and the social expectations accompanying them—that the young person give up childish ways, develop new interpersonal relationships, and take on greater responsibility—are likely to prompt moments of uncertainty, self-doubt, and disappointment in all teenagers.

At the same time, the length of adolescence varies greatly from one culture to the next. Although simpler societies have a shorter transition to adulthood, usually adolescence is not absent. A study of 186 tribal and village cultures revealed that almost all had an intervening phase, however brief, between childhood and full assumption of adult roles (Schlegel & Barry, 1991).

In industrialized societies, where successful participation in economic life requires many years of education, adolescence is greatly extended. Young people face extra years of dependence on parents and postponement of sexual gratification as they prepare for a productive work life. We will see that the extent to which the social environment supports young people in achieving adult responsibilities has much to do with how well they fare. For all the biological tensions and uncertainties about the future that modern teenagers feel, most are surprisingly good at negotiating this period of life. With this idea in mind, let's look closely at puberty, the dawning of adolescent development.

PUBERTY: THE PHYSICAL TRANSITION TO ADULTHOOD

The changes of puberty are dramatic and momentous. Within a few years, the body of the school-age child is transformed into that of a full-grown adult. Pubertal growth is regulated by genetically influenced hormonal processes. Girls, who have been advanced in physical maturity since the prenatal period, reach puberty, on the average, 2 years earlier than do boys.

HORMONAL CHANGES

The complex hormonal changes that underlie puberty take place gradually and are underway by age 8 or 9. Secretions of *growth hormone (GH)* and *thyroxine* (see Chapter 7, page 212) increase, leading to tremendous gains in body size and attainment of skeletal maturity.

Sexual maturation is controlled by the sex hormones. Although *estrogens* are thought of as female hormones and *androgens* as male hormones, both types are present in each sex, but in different amounts. The boy's testes release large quantities of the androgen *testosterone*, which leads to muscle growth, body and facial hair, and other male sex characteristics. Testosterone also contributes to gains in body size. Estrogens released by the girl's ovaries cause the breasts, uterus, and vagina to mature, the body to take on feminine proportions, and fat to accumulate. In addition, estrogens help regulate the menstrual cycle. *Adrenal androgens*, released from the adrenal glands on top of each kidney, influence the girl's height spurt and stimulate growth of underarm and pubic hair. They have little impact on boys, whose physical characteristics are mainly affected by androgen secretions from the testes.

■ *The pubertal growth spurt takes place, on the average, 2 years earlier for girls than for boys. Although this boy and girl are both sixth graders, the girl is far taller, heavier, and more mature-looking. (Photo courtesy: B. Daemmrich/The Image Works)*

As you can already tell, pubertal changes can be divided into two broad types: (1) overall body growth; and (2) maturation of sex characteristics. Although we will discuss these changes separately, they are interrelated. We have seen that the hormones responsible for sexual maturity also affect body growth; boys and girls differ in both aspects. In fact, puberty is the time of greatest sexual differentiation since prenatal life.

BODY GROWTH

The first outward sign of puberty is the rapid gain in height and weight known as the **growth spurt.** On the average, it is underway for North American girls shortly after age 10, for boys around age 12½ (Malina, 1990). The girl is taller and heavier during early adolescence, but this advantage is short-lived. At age 14, she is surpassed by the typical boy, whose adolescent growth spurt has started, whereas hers is almost finished. Growth in body size is complete for most girls by age 16 and for boys by age 17½, when the epiphyses at the ends of the long bones close completely (see Chapter 7, page 208). Altogether, adolescents add almost 10 inches in height and about 40 pounds in weight during puberty. Figure 11.1 provides an overview of general body growth from infancy through adolescence.

■ **BODY PROPORTIONS.** In adolescence, the cephalocaudal growth trend of infancy and childhood reverses. At first, the hands, legs, and feet accelerate, and then the torso, which accounts for most of the adolescent height gain (Wheeler, 1991). This pattern of development helps us understand why early adolescents often appear awkward and out of proportion—long-legged, with giant feet and hands.

Large sex differences in body proportions also appear, caused by the action of sex hormones on the skeleton. Boys' shoulders broaden relative to the hips, whereas girls' hips broaden relative to the shoulders and waist. Of course, boys also end up considerably larger than girls, and their legs are longer in relation to the rest of the body. The major reason is that boys have 2 extra years of preadolescent growth, when the legs are growing fastest (Graber, Petersen, & Brooks-Gunn, 1996).

■ **MUSCLE–FAT MAKEUP AND OTHER INTERNAL CHANGES.** One reason 11-year-old Sabrina became concerned about her weight is that compared to her later-developing girlfriends, her body had accumulated much more fat. Around age 8, girls start to add fat on their arms, legs, and trunk, and they continue to do so throughout puberty. In contrast, arm and leg fat of adolescent boys decreases. Although both sexes gain in muscle, this increase

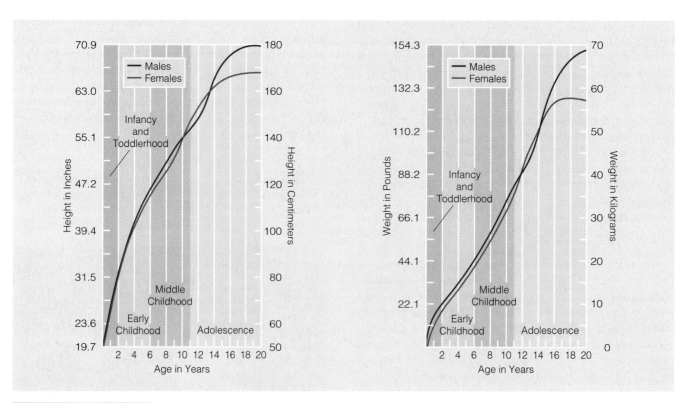

FIGURE 11.1

■ **Average height and weight from infancy through adolescence among North American young people.** Note that the adolescent growth spurt takes place earlier for girls than boys. (From R. M. Malina, 1975, *Growth and Development: The First Twenty Years in Man,* Minneapolis: Burgess Publishing Company, p. 19. Adapted by permission.)

is much greater for boys, who develop larger skeletal muscles, hearts, and lung capacity. Also, the number of red blood cells, and therefore the ability to carry oxygen from the lungs to the muscles, increases in boys but not in girls. Altogether, boys gain far more muscle strength than do girls, a difference that contributes to boys' superior athletic performance during the teenage years (Beunen & Malina, 1996).

■ CHANGING STATES OF AROUSAL. Adolescence is a time of substantial change in sleep and wakefulness. On the average, sleep declines from 10 hours in middle childhood to 7.5 to 8 hours in adolescence. Yet teenagers need almost as much sleep as they did during the school years—about 9.2 hours.

Adolescents go to bed much later than they did as children yet must get up early for school—before their sleep needs are satisfied. Biological changes may underlie this sleep "phase delay," as the tendency to stay up late strengthens with pubertal maturation (Carskadon, Viera, & Acebo, 1993). But afternoon and evening activities, part-time jobs, and social pressures also contribute. Although most teenagers say they enjoy staying up late, they also complain of daytime sleepiness (Wolfson & Carskadon, 1998). Sleep-deprived adolescents tend to achieve less well in school, more often suffer from depressed mood, and report irregular sleep schedules, which add to their daytime sleepiness and behavior problems (Link & Ancoli-Israel, 1995). Later school start times ease sleep loss but do not eliminate it (Kowalski & Allen, 1995).

MOTOR DEVELOPMENT AND PHYSICAL ACTIVITY

Puberty is accompanied by steady improvement in gross motor performance, but the pattern of change is quite different for boys and girls. Girls' gains are slow and gradual, leveling off by age 14. In contrast, boys show a dramatic spurt in strength, speed, and endurance that continues through the teenage years. The gender gap in physical skill widens over time. By midadolescence, for example, very few girls perform as well as the average boy in such skills as running speed, broad jump, and throwing distance. And practically no boys score as low as the average girl (Malina & Bouchard, 1991).

Because girls and boys are no longer well matched physically, gender-segregated physical education usually begins in junior high school. At the same time, athletic options for both sexes expand. Many new sports are added to the curriculum—track and field, wrestling, tackle football, weight lifting, floor hockey, archery, tennis, and golf, to name just a few.

In 1972, the federal government required schools receiving public funds to provide equal opportunities for males and females in all educational programs, including athletics. As Figure 11.2 shows, high school girls' sports participation quadrupled during the following decade and has continued to increase, although it still falls far short of boys'. In Chapter 9, we saw that beginning at an early age, girls get less encouragement and recognition for athletic achievement, a pattern that persists into the teenage years.

The sex differences just described also characterize physical activity rates of American adolescents. Overall, 74 percent of high school boys but only 52 percent of girls report regular vigorous physical activity (at least 20 minutes 3 days a week). The number of boys engaging in regular exercise increases from ninth to twelfth grade. In contrast, about 15 percent of girls who were physically active in ninth grade are no longer exercising regularly by twelfth grade (U.S. Department of Health and Human Services, 1999h).

Besides improving motor performance, sports and exercise influence cognitive and social development. Interschool and intramural athletics provide important lessons in com-

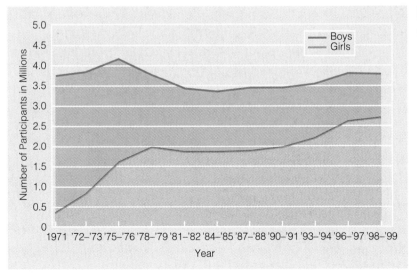

FIGURE 11.2

■ **High school sports participation trends in the United States, 1971–1997.** A legal mandate for equality of opportunity in school athletic participation led girls' involvement in sport to increase dramatically from the early 1970s to 1980. Since then, girls' participation has continued to rise gradually, although it still falls far short of boys'. (From National Federation of State High School Associations, 1999).

petition, assertiveness, problem solving, and teamwork— experiences less available to girls (Newcombe & Boyle, 1995). And regular, sustained physical activity has lifelong health benefits. Yet only 60 percent of American secondary school students are enrolled in physical education (U.S. Department of Health and Human Services, 1999h). Required daily physical education, aimed at helping all teenagers find pleasure in sports and exercise, is a vital means of promoting adolescent physical and psychological well-being.

SEXUAL MATURATION

Accompanying the rapid increase in body size are changes in physical features related to sexual functioning. Some, called **primary sexual characteristics,** involve the reproductive organs (ovaries, uterus, and vagina in females; penis, scrotum, and testes in males). Others, called **secondary sexual characteristics,** are visible on the outside of the body and serve as additional signs of sexual maturity (for example, breast development in females, underarm and pubic hair in both sexes). As Table 11.1 shows, these characteristics develop in a fairly standard sequence, although the age at which each begins and is completed varies greatly.

■ SEXUAL MATURATION IN GIRLS. Female puberty usually begins with the budding of the breasts and the growth spurt. **Menarche,** or first menstruation, typically happens around 12½ years for North American girls, 13 for Europeans. But the age range is wide, extending from 10½ to 15½ years. Following menarche, pubic hair and breast development are completed, and underarm hair appears. Most girls take 3 to 4 years to complete this sequence, although this, too, can vary greatly.

Notice in Table 11.1 how nature delays sexual maturity until the girl's body is large enough for childbearing; menarche occurs after the peak of the height spurt. As an extra measure of security, for 12 to 18 months following menarche, the girl's ovaries usually do not produce mature ova. However, this temporary period of sterility does not apply to all girls, and it cannot be counted on for protection against pregnancy (Tanner, 1990).

■ SEXUAL MATURATION IN BOYS. The first sign of puberty in boys is the enlargement of the testes (glands that manufacture sperm), accompanied by changes in the texture and color of the scrotum. Pubic hair emerges a short time later, about the same time that the penis begins to enlarge (Graber, Petersen, & Brooks-Gunn, 1996).

Refer again to Table 11.1, and you will see that the growth spurt occurs much later in the sequence of pubertal events for boys than for girls. When it reaches its peak (around age 14), enlargement of the testes and penis is nearly complete, and underarm hair appears soon after. Facial and body hair also emerge just after the peak in body growth and gradually increase for several years. Another landmark of male physical maturity is the deepening of the voice as the larynx enlarges and the vocal cords lengthen. (Girls' voices also deepen slightly.) Voice change usually takes place at the peak of the male growth spurt and is often not complete until puberty is over.

While the penis is growing, the prostate gland and seminal vesicles (which together produce semen, the fluid in which sperm are bathed) enlarge. Then, around age 13, **spermarche,** or first ejaculation, occurs (Jorgensen & Keiding, 1991). For a while, the semen contains few living sperm. So, like girls, boys have an initial period of reduced fertility.

TABLE 11.1

Average Age and Age Range of Major Pubertal Changes in North American Girls and Boys

GIRLS	AVERAGE AGE	AGE RANGE	BOYS	AVERAGE AGE	AGE RANGE
Breasts begin to "bud"	10	(8–13)	Testes begin to enlarge	11.5	(9.5–13.5)
Height spurt begins	10	(8–13)	Pubic hair appears	12	(10–15)
Pubic hair appears	10.5	(8–14)	Penis begins to enlarge	12	(10.5–14.5)
Peak of strength spurt	11.6	(9.5–14)	Height spurt begins	12.5	(10.5–16)
Peak of height spurt	11.7	(10–13.5)	Spermarche (first ejaculation) occurs	13	(12–16)
Menarche (first menstruation) occurs	12.8	(10.5–15.5)	Peak of height spurt	14	(12.5–15.5)
Adult stature reached	13	(10–16)	Facial hair begins to grow	14	(12.5–15.5)
Breast growth completed	14	(10–16)	Voice begins to deepen	14	(12.5–15.5)
Pubic hair growth completed	14.5	(14–15)	Penis growth completed	14.5	(12.5–16)
			Peak of strength spurt	15.3	(13–17)
			Adult stature reached	15.5	(13.5–17.5)
			Pubic hair growth completed	15	(14–17)

Sources: Malina & Bouchard, 1991; Tanner, 1990.

INDIVIDUAL AND GROUP DIFFERENCES

Heredity is partly responsible for the timing of pubertal maturation, since identical twins generally reach menarche within a month or two of each other, whereas fraternal twins differ by about 12 months (Tanner, 1990). Nutrition and exercise also contribute. In females, a sharp rise in body weight and fat may trigger sexual maturation. Girls who begin serious athletic training at young ages or who eat very little (both of which reduce the percentage of body fat) often show greatly delayed menstruation. In contrast, over-weight girls typically start menstruating early (Rees, 1993).

Variations in pubertal growth can also be found between regions of the world and SES groups. Heredity probably plays little role, since adolescents with very different genetic origins living under similarly advantaged conditions resemble one another in pubertal timing (Eveleth & Tanner, 1976). Instead, physical health is largely responsible. In poverty-stricken regions where malnutrition and infectious disease are widespread, menarche is greatly delayed. In many parts of Africa, it does not occur until age 14 to 17. And within countries, girls from higher-income families reach menarche 6 to 18 months earlier than those living in economically disadvantaged homes.

A **secular trend,** or generational change, in pubertal timing lends added support to the role of physical well-being in adolescent growth. In industrialized nations, age of menarche declined steadily from 1860 to 1970, by about 3 to 4 months per decade. Nutrition, health care, sanitation,

■ *Because of improved health and nutrition, a secular trend in physical growth has taken place in industrialized nations. The adolescent girl on the left is taller than her grandmother, mother, and aunt, and she probably reached menarche at an earlier age. Improved nutrition and health are responsible for gains in body size and faster physical maturation from one generation to the next. (Photo courtesy: Bob Daemmrich/The Image Works)*

and control of infectious disease improved greatly during this time. Of course, humans cannot keep maturing earlier indefinitely, since we cannot exceed the genetic limitations of our species. Secular gains have slowed or stopped in some developed countries, such as Canada, Great Britain, Sweden, Norway, Japan, and the United States (McAnarney et al., 1992; Roche, 1979). Consequently, modern young people reared under good nutritional circumstances are likely to resemble their parents in physical growth more than at any time during the previous 130 years.

THE PSYCHOLOGICAL IMPACT OF PUBERTAL EVENTS

Think back to your late elementary and junior high school days. As you reached puberty, how did your feelings about yourself and your relationships with others change? As we will see in the following sections, pubertal events affect the adolescent's self-image, mood, and interaction with parents and peers. Some of these outcomes are a response to dramatic physical change, regardless of when it occurs. Others have to do with the timing of pubertal maturation.

REACTIONS TO PUBERTAL CHANGES

A generation or two ago, menarche was often traumatic. Today, girls commonly react with "surprise," undoubtedly due to the sudden nature of the event. Otherwise, they typically report a mixture of positive and negative emotions— "excited and pleased" as well as "scared and upset." Yet wide individual differences exist that depend on prior knowledge and support from family members. Both are influenced by cultural attitudes toward puberty and sexuality.

For girls who have no advance information, menarche can be shocking and disturbing. In the 1950s, up to 50 percent were given no prior warning (Shainess, 1961). Today, no more than 10 to 15 percent are uninformed (Brooks-Gunn, 1988b). This shift is probably due to modern parents' greater willingness to discuss sexual matters with their youngsters. Currently, almost all girls get some information from their mothers. And girls whose fathers are told about pubertal changes adjust especially well. Perhaps a father's involvement reflects a family atmosphere that is highly understanding and accepting of physical and sexual matters (Brooks-Gunn & Ruble, 1980, 1983).

Like girls' reactions to menarche, boys' responses to spermarche reflect mixed feelings. Virtually all boys know about ejaculation ahead of time, but few get any information from parents. Usually they obtain it from reading material (Gaddis & Brooks-Gunn, 1985). In addition, whereas almost all girls eventually tell a friend that they are menstruating, far fewer boys tell anyone about spermarche (Brooks-Gunn et al., 1986; Downs & Fuller, 1991). Overall, boys get much less social support for the physical changes of puberty than do girls. This suggests that boys might benefit, especially, from opportunities to ask questions and discuss feelings with a sympathetic parent or health professional.

The experience of puberty is affected by the larger culture in which boys and girls live. Many tribal and village societies celebrate puberty with a *rite of passage*—a community-wide event that marks an important change in privilege and responsibility. Consequently, all young people know that pubertal changes are honored and valued in their culture. In contrast, Western societies grant little formal recognition to movement from childhood to adolescence or from adolescence to adulthood. Certain religious ceremonies, such as confirmation and the Jewish bar or bat mitzvah, do resemble a rite of passage. But they usually do not lead to any meaningful change in social status.

Instead, Western adolescents are confronted with many ages at which they are granted partial adult status—for example, an age for starting employment, for driving, for leaving high school, for voting, and for drinking. In some contexts (on the highway and at work), they may be treated like adults. In others (at school and at home), they may still be regarded as children. The absence of a widely accepted marker of physical and social maturity makes the process of becoming an adult especially confusing.

■ *In this adolescent initiation ceremony, two pipe players of the Camiura tribe of Brazil celebrate the transition to adulthood of a group of young girls, who have been secluded from society in this thatched hut for a year. Soon the men will enter the hut and, while dancing and playing the pipes, lead the girls through the village. Then they will be married and inducted into adult society. (Photo courtesy: John Moss/Photo Researchers, Inc.)*

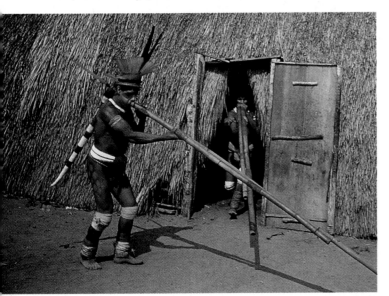

PUBERTAL CHANGE, EMOTION, AND SOCIAL BEHAVIOR

In the preceding section, we considered adolescents' reactions to their sexually maturing bodies. Puberty can also affect emotional state and social behavior. A common belief is that puberty has something to do with adolescent moodiness and the desire for greater physical and psychological separation from parents.

■ **ADOLESCENT MOODINESS.** Although research reveals that higher pubertal hormone levels are linked to greater moodiness, these relationships are not strong (Buchanan, Eccles, & Becker, 1992). And we cannot be sure that a rise in pubertal hormones actually causes adolescent moodiness.

What else might contribute to the common observation that adolescents are moody creatures? In several studies, the mood fluctuations of children, adolescents, and adults were tracked over a week by having them carry electronic pagers. At random intervals, they were beeped and asked to write down what they were doing, who they were with, and how they felt.

As expected, adolescents reported somewhat lower moods than did school-age children or adults (Csikszentmihalyi & Larson, 1984; Larson & Lampman-Petraitis, 1989). But young people whose moods were especially negative were experiencing a greater number of negative life events, such as difficulties with parents, disciplinary actions at school, and breaking up with a boyfriend or girlfriend. Negative events increased steadily from childhood to adolescence, and teenagers also seemed to react to them with greater emotion than did children (Larson & Ham, 1993).

Furthermore, compared with the moods of adults, adolescents' feelings were less stable. They often varied from cheerful to sad and back again. But teenagers also moved from one situation to another more often, and their mood swings were strongly related to these changes. High points of their days were times spent with friends and in self-chosen leisure and hobby activities. Low points tended to occur in adult-structured settings—class, job, school halls, school library, and religious services. Taken together, these findings suggest that situational factors may combine with hormonal influences to affect teenagers' moodiness—an explanation consistent with the balanced view of adolescence described earlier in this chapter.

■ **PARENT–CHILD RELATIONSHIPS.** Sabrina's father noticed that as his children entered adolescence, their bedroom doors started to close, they resisted spending time with the family, and they became more argumentative. Within a 2-day period, Sabrina and her mother squabbled over Sabrina's messy room ("Mom, it's *my* room. You don't have to live in it!") and her clothing purchases ("Sabrina, if you *buy* it, then *wear* it. Otherwise, you are wasting money!"). And

Sabrina resisted the family's regular weekend visit to Aunt Gina's ("Why do I have to go *every* week?"). Many studies show that puberty is related to a rise in parent–child conflict. Bickering and standoffs increase as adolescents move toward the peak of pubertal growth. During this time, both parents and teenagers report feeling less close to one another (Holmbeck, 1996; Holmbeck & Hill, 1991).

Why should a youngster's new, more adultlike appearance trigger these petty disputes between parent and child? Researchers believe the association may have some adaptive value. Among nonhuman primates, the young typically leave the family group around puberty. The same is true in many nonindustrialized cultures (Caine, 1986; Schlegel & Barry, 1991). Departure of young people from the family discourages sexual relations between close blood relatives. But because children in industrialized societies remain economically dependent on parents long after puberty, they cannot leave the family. Consequently, a modern substitute for physical departure seems to have emerged—psychological distancing between parents and children (Steinberg, 1987).

As we will see later, adolescents' new powers of reasoning may also contribute to a rise in family tensions. Also, the need for families to redefine relationships as children demand to be treated in adultlike ways can produce a temporary period of conflict. The greater the gap between parents' and adolescents' views of teenagers' readiness to take on new responsibilities (such as handling their own money or choosing a philosophy of life), the more quarreling there tends to be (Deković, Noom, & Meeus, 1997).

The conflict that does take place is generally mild, diminishing by age 14 or 15. In reality, parents and adolescents display both conflict and affection. Although separation from parents is adaptive, both generations benefit from warm, protective family bonds throughout the lifespan (Steinberg, 1990).

EARLY VERSUS LATE MATURATION

"All our children were early maturers," said Franca during the parents' discussion group. "The three boys were tall by age 12 or 13, but it was easier for them. They felt big and important. Sabrina was skinny as a little girl, but now she says she is too fat and wants to diet. She thinks about boys and doesn't concentrate on her schoolwork."

Findings of several studies match the experiences of Sabrina and her brothers. Early maturing boys were seen as relaxed, independent, self-confident, and physically attractive by both adults and peers. Popular with agemates, they held many leadership positions in school and tended to be athletic stars. In contrast, late maturing boys were not well liked. Adults and peers viewed them as anxious, overly talkative, and attention seeking (Brooks-Gunn, 1988a; Clausen, 1975; Jones, 1965; Jones & Bayley, 1950).

■ *These boys are all 13 years old, yet they differ sharply in timing of pubertal maturation. The two early maturing boys are probably popular, self-confident, athletic stars with a positive body image. The three late maturing boys are likely to have a low sense of self-esteem and a negative body image. (Photo courtesy: Kopstein/Monkmeyer Press)*

Among girls, the impact of maturational timing was just the reverse. Early maturing girls were below average in popularity; appeared withdrawn, lacking in self-confidence, and psychologically stressed; and held few positions of leadership (Ge, Conger, & Elder, 1996; Jones & Mussen, 1958). They were also more involved in deviant behavior (getting drunk, participating in early sexual activity) and achieved less well in school (Caspi et al., 1993). In contrast, their late maturing counterparts were especially well off. They were regarded as physically attractive, lively, sociable, and leaders at school.

Two factors seem to account for these trends: (1) how closely the adolescent's body matches cultural ideals of physical attractiveness, and (2) how well young people "fit in" physically with their peers.

■ THE ROLE OF PHYSICAL ATTRACTIVENESS. Flip through the pages of your favorite popular magazine. You will see evidence for our society's view of an attractive female as thin and long-legged and a good-looking male as tall, broad-shouldered, and muscular. The female image is a girlish shape that favors the late developer. The male image fits the early maturing boy.

A consistent finding is that early maturing girls have a less positive **body image**—conception of and attitude toward their physical appearance—than do their on-time and late maturing agemates. Among boys, the opposite is true: early maturation is linked to a positive body image, whereas late maturation predicts dissatisfaction with the physical self (Alsaker, 1995). The conclusions young people draw about their appearance strongly affect their self-esteem and psychological well-being (Mendelson, White, & Mendelson, 1996; Usmiani & Daniluk, 1997).

■ THE IMPORTANCE OF FITTING IN WITH PEERS. A second way of explaining differences in adjustment between early and late maturers is in terms of their physical status in relation to peers. From this perspective, early maturing girls and late maturing boys have difficulty because they fall at the extremes of physical development and are self-conscious about not "fitting in." Not surprisingly, adolescents feel most comfortable with peers who match their own level of biological maturity (Brooks-Gunn et al., 1986; Stattin & Magnusson, 1990).

Because few agemates of the same pubertal status are available, early maturing adolescents of both sexes seek older companions, sometimes with unfavorable consequences. Older peers often encourage them into activities that they are not yet ready to handle emotionally, including sexual activity, drug and alcohol use, and minor delinquent acts. Perhaps because of involvements like these, the academic performance of early maturers tends to suffer (Caspi et al., 1993; Stattin & Magnusson, 1990).

Interestingly, school contexts can modify these maturational timing effects. In one study, early maturing sixth-grade girls felt better about themselves when they attended kindergarten through sixth-grade (K–6) schools rather than kindergarten through eighth-grade (K–8) schools, where they could mix with older adolescents. In the K–6 settings, they were relieved of pressures to adopt behaviors for which they were not ready (Blyth, Simmons, & Zakin, 1985). Similarly, a New Zealand study found that delinquency among early maturing girls was greatly reduced in all-girl schools, which limit opportunities to associate with norm-violating peers (most of whom are older boys) (Caspi et al., 1993).

■ LONG-TERM CONSEQUENCES. Do the effects of early and late maturation persist into adulthood? Long-term follow-ups show striking turnabouts in overall well-being. Many early maturing boys and late maturing girls, who had been so admired in adolescence, became rigid, conforming, and somewhat discontented adults. In contrast, late maturing boys and early maturing girls, who were stress-ridden as teenagers, often developed into adults who were independent, flexible, cognitively competent, and satisfied with the direction of their lives (Livson & Peshkin, 1980; Macfarlane, 1971). What explains these remarkable reversals? Perhaps the confidence-inducing adolescence of

early maturing boys and late maturing girls does not promote the coping skills needed to solve life's later problems. In contrast, painful experiences associated with off-time pubertal growth may, in time, contribute to sharpened awareness, clarified goals, and greater stability.

It is important to note, however, that these outcomes may not hold completely in all cultures. In a Swedish study, achievement difficulties of early maturing girls persisted into young adulthood, in the form of lower educational attainment than their on-time and later maturing counterparts (Stattin & Magnusson, 1990). In countries with highly selective college entrance systems, perhaps early maturers have more difficulty recovering from declines in school performance. Clearly, the effects of maturational timing involve a complex blend of biological, immediate social setting, and cultural factors.

■ ASK YOURSELF . . .

■ *Millie, mother of an 11-year-old son, is convinced that the rising sexual passions of puberty cause teenage rebelliousness. Where did this belief originate? Explain why it is incorrect.*

Explain why early maturing girls, as opposed to early maturing boys, often experience adjustment problems. Cite school and cultural factors that affect the development of early maturing girls—during adolescence and adulthood.

■ *How might adolescent moodiness contribute to the psychological distancing between parents and children that accompanies puberty? (Hint: Think about bidirectional influences in parent–child relationships discussed in previous chapters.)*

HEALTH ISSUES

As young people move into adolescence, they begin to view physical health in a broader way—as more than just the absence of illness. To teenagers, being healthy means functioning physically, mentally, and socially at their best (Millstein & Litt, 1990). Consistent with this new view, the arrival of puberty is accompanied by new health concerns related to the young person's striving to meet physical and psychological needs. As adolescents are granted greater autonomy, their personal decision making becomes important, in health as well as other areas (Bearison, 1998). Yet none of the health difficulties we are about to discuss can be traced to a single cause within the individual. Throughout development, biological, psychological, family, and cultural factors jointly contribute to health and well-being.

NUTRITIONAL NEEDS

When their sons reached puberty, Franca and Antonio reported a "vacuum cleaner effect" in the kitchen as the boys routinely emptied the refrigerator. Rapid body growth leads to a dramatic rise in food intake. During the growth spurt, boys require about 2,700 calories a day and much more protein than they did earlier, girls about 2,200 calories and somewhat less protein than boys because of their smaller size and muscle mass (Larson, 1996).

This increase in nutritional requirements comes at a time when the diets of many young people are the poorest. Of all age groups, adolescents are the most likely to consume empty calories and eat on the run. These eating habits are particularly harmful if they extend a lifelong pattern of poor nutrition, less serious if they are just a temporary response to peer influences and a busy schedule.

The most common nutritional problem of adolescence is iron deficiency. A tired, irritable teenager may be suffering from anemia rather than unhappiness and should have a medical checkup. Most adolescents do not get enough calcium, and they are also deficient in riboflavin (vitamin B_2) and magnesium, both of which support metabolism. And contrary to what many parents believe, obese children rarely outgrow their weight problem when they become teenagers (Serdula et al., 1993).

Adolescents, especially girls concerned about their weight, tend to be attracted to fad diets. Unfortunately, most are too limited in nutrients and calories to be healthy for fast-growing, active teenagers (Donatelle & Davis, 2000). When a youngster insists on trying a special diet, parents should, in turn, insist that he or she first consult a doctor or dietitian.

EATING DISORDERS

Franca worried about Sabrina's desire to lose weight, explained to her that she was really quite average in build for an adolescent girl, and reminded Sabrina that her Italian ancestors thought a plump female body was more beautiful than a thin one. Girls who reach puberty early, who are very dissatisfied with their body image, and who grow up in economically advantaged homes where a cultural concern with weight and thinness is especially strong are at risk for serious eating problems.

■ ANOREXIA NERVOSA. **Anorexia nervosa** is a tragic eating disturbance in which young people starve themselves because of a compulsive fear of getting fat. About 1 in every 50 teenage girls in the United States is affected, with a peak age of onset between 14 and 18. Asian Americans, Caucasian Americans, and Hispanics are at greater risk than African Americans, who are more satisfied with their size and shape (Abood & Chandler, 1997; Halpern et al., 1999; Robinson et al., 1996). Anorexia nervosa occurs

■ *This anorexic girl's strict, self-imposed diet and obsession with strenuous exercise has led her to become painfully thin. Even so, her body image is so distorted that she probably regards herself as fat. (Photo courtesy: © Kansas City Star/The Liaison Agency)*

equally often among economically advantaged and economically disadvantaged teenagers (Rogers et al., 1997).

Anorexics have an extremely distorted body image. Even after they have become severely underweight, they conclude that they are fat. Most go on self-imposed diets so strict that they struggle to avoid eating in response to hunger. To enhance weight loss, they exercise strenuously.

In their attempt to reach "perfect" slimness, anorexics lose between 25 and 50 percent of their body weight and appear painfully thin. Because a normal menstrual cycle requires about 15 percent body fat, either menarche does not occur or menstrual periods stop. Malnutrition causes pale skin; brittle, discolored nails; fine dark hairs all over the body; and extreme sensitivity to cold. If allowed to continue, anorexia nervosa can result in shrinking of the heart muscle, kidney failure, permanent loss of bone mass, and brain damage. About 6 percent die of the disorder (Neumärker, 1997).

Forces within the individual, the family, and the larger culture give rise to anorexia nervosa. We have already seen that the societal image of "thin is beautiful" contributes to the poorer body image of early maturing girls, who are at greatest risk for anorexia (Graber et al., 1994). But though almost all adolescents go on diets at one time or another, anorexics persist in weight loss to an extreme. Many are perfectionists with high standards for their own behavior and performance. Typically, these girls are excellent students who are responsible and well behaved—ideal daughters in many respects.

Yet family interactions of parents and anorexic daughters reveal problems related to adolescent autonomy. Often these parents have high expectations for achievement and social acceptance and are overprotective and controlling. Although the daughter tries to meet these demands, inside she is angry at not being recognized as an individual in her own right. Instead of rebelling openly, the anorexic girl indirectly tells her parents, "I am a separate person from you, and I can do what I want with my own body!" At the same time, this youngster, who has been so used to having parents make decisions for her, meets the challenges of adolescence with little self-confidence. Starving herself is also a way of avoiding new expectations by returning to a much younger, preadolescent image (Halmi, 1987; Maloney & Kranz, 1991).

Because anorexic girls typically deny that any problem exists, treating the disorder is difficult. Hospitalization is often necessary to prevent life-threatening malnutrition. Family therapy, aimed at changing parent–child interaction and expectations, is the most successful treatment. Still, only about 50 percent of anorexics fully recover (Fichter & Quadflieg, 1996).

■ BULIMIA. When Sabrina's 16-year-old brother, Louis, brought his girlfriend, Cassie, to the house, Sabrina admired her good figure. "What willpower! Cassie hardly touches food," Sabrina thought to herself. "But what in the world is wrong with Cassie's teeth?"

Willpower was not the secret of Cassie's slender shape. When it came to food, she actually had great difficulty controlling herself. Cassie suffered from **bulimia,** an eating disorder in which young people (again, mainly girls, but gay adolescent boys are also vulnerable) engage in binge eating followed by deliberate vomiting, purging with laxatives, and strict dieting. When by herself, Cassie often felt lonely, unhappy, and anxious. She responded with eating rampages, consuming thousands of calories in an hour or two. The vomiting that followed eroded the enamel on Cassie's teeth. In some cases, life-threatening damage to the throat and stomach occurs.

Bulimia is much more common than anorexia nervosa. About 1 to 5 percent of teenage girls are affected; only 5 percent have previously been anorexic (Fairburn & Belgin, 1990). Bulimics share with anorexics a pathological fear of getting fat and a family background with high expectations, but they may have experienced their parents as disengaged and emotionally unavailable rather than controlling. One conjecture is that bulimics turn to food to compensate for a feeling of emptiness resulting from lack of parental involvement (Attie & Brooks-Gunn, 1996; Johnson & Connors, 1987).

Typically, bulimics are not just impulsive eaters; they also lack self-control in other areas of their lives. Many engage in petty shoplifting and alcohol abuse. Unlike anorexics, bulimics are aware of their abnormal eating habits and feel depressed and guilty about them. As a result, bulimia is usually easier to treat through individual and family therapy, support groups, and nutrition education (Thackwray et al., 1993).

SEXUAL ACTIVITY

Louis and Cassie hadn't planned to have intercourse; it "just happened." But before and after, a lot of things passed through their minds. Cassie had been dating Louis for 3 months, and she began to wonder, "Will he think I'm normal if I don't have sex with him? If he wants to and I say no, will I lose him?" Both young people knew their parents wouldn't approve. In fact, when Franca and Antonio noticed how attached Louis was to Cassie, they talked to him about the importance of waiting and the dangers of pregnancy. But that Friday evening, Louis and Cassie's feelings for each other seemed overwhelming. As things went farther and farther, Louis thought, "If I don't make a move, will she think I'm a wimp?" And Cassie had heard from one of her girlfriends that you couldn't get pregnant the first time.

With the arrival of puberty, hormonal changes—in particular, the production of androgens in young people of both sexes—lead to an increase in sex drive (Halpern, Udry, & Suchindran, 1997; Udry, 1990). As Louis and Cassie's inner thoughts reveal, adolescents become very concerned about how to manage sexuality in social relationships. New cognitive capacities involving perspective taking and self-reflection affect their efforts to do so. Yet like the eating behaviors we have just discussed, adolescent sexuality is heavily influenced by the young person's social context.

■ THE IMPACT OF CULTURE. Think, for a moment, about when you first learned the "facts of life" and how you found out about them. In your family, was sex discussed openly or treated with secrecy? Exposure to sex, education about it, and efforts to limit the sexual curiosity of children and adolescents vary widely around the world.

Despite the publicity granted to the image of a sexually free modern adolescent, sexual attitudes in the United States are relatively restrictive. Typically, American parents give children little information about sex, discourage them from engaging in sex play, and rarely talk about sex in their presence. When young people become interested in sex, they seek information from friends, books, magazines, movies, and television. On prime-time TV, which adolescents watch the most, sex between partners with little commitment to each other occurs often and is spontaneous and passionate. Characters are rarely shown taking steps to avoid pregnancy or sexually transmitted disease (Ward, 1995).

The messages delivered by these two sets of sources are contradictory and confusing. On one hand, adults emphasize that sex at a young age and outside of marriage is bad. On the other hand, adolescents encounter much in the broader social environment that extols the excitement and romanticism of sex. American teenagers are left bewildered, poorly informed about sexual facts, and with little sound advice on how to conduct their sex lives responsibly.

■ ADOLESCENT SEXUAL ATTITUDES AND BEHAVIOR. Although differences between subcultural groups exist, the sexual attitudes of American adolescents and adults have become more liberal over the past 30 years. Compared to a generation ago, more people believe that sexual intercourse before marriage is all right, as long as two people are emotionally committed to one another (Michael et al., 1994). Recently a slight swing back in the direction of conservative sexual beliefs has occurred, largely due to the risk of sexually transmitted disease, especially AIDS (Glassman, 1996).

Trends in the sexual behavior of adolescents are quite consistent with their attitudes. The rate of premarital sex among young people rose over several decades but recently declined. For example, among unmarried 15- to 19-year-olds, females claiming to have had sexual intercourse grew from 28 percent in 1971 to 55 percent in 1990 and then dropped to 49 percent in 1998 (U.S. Department of Health and Human Services, 1999h). As Table 11.2 reveals, a substantial minority of boys and girls are sexually active quite early, by ninth grade. Males tend to have their first intercourse earlier than females, and sexual activity is especially high among African-American adolescents—particularly boys.

Yet timing of first intercourse provides only a limited picture of adolescent sexual behavior. Most teenagers engage in relatively low levels of sexual activity. The typical 15- to 19-year-old sexually active male—white, black, or Hispanic — has relations with only one girl at a time and spends half the year with no partner at all (Sonenstein, Pleck, & Ku, 1991). Contrary to popular belief, a runaway sexual revolution does not characterize American young people. In fact, the rate of teenage sexual activity is about the same in the United States as in Western European nations (Creatsas et al., 1995).

■ CHARACTERISTICS OF SEXUALLY ACTIVE ADOLESCENTS. Early and frequent teenage sexual activity is linked to a wide range of personal, family, peer, and educational characteristics. These include early physical maturation,

■ *Adolescence is an especially important time for the development of sexuality. American teenagers receive contradictory and confusing messages from the social environment about the appropriateness of sex. Although the rate of premarital sex has risen among adolescents, most engage in low levels of sexual activity and have only a single partner. (Photo courtesy: Richard Hutchings/ PhotoEdit)*

parental divorce, large family size, sexually active friends and older siblings, poor school performance, lower educational aspirations, and tendency to engage in norm-violating acts, including alcohol and drug use and delinquency (Braverman & Strasburger, 1994; Cooper & Orcutt, 1997).

Since many of these factors are associated with growing up in a low-income family, it is not surprising that early sexual activity is more common among young people from economically disadvantaged homes. In fact, the high rate of premarital intercourse among black teenagers can largely be accounted for by widespread poverty in the black population (Sullivan, 1993).

■ CONTRACEPTIVE USE. Although adolescent contraceptive use has increased in recent years, one-third to one-half of sexually active American teenagers are at risk for

TABLE 11.2

Teenage Sexual Activity Rates by Sex, Ethnic Group, and Grade

SEX	ETHNIC GROUP			GRADE				TOTAL
	WHITE	BLACK	HISPANIC	9	10	11	12	
Male	43.3	80.3	57.7	41.8	41.7	49.3	60.1	48.9
Female	44.0	65.6	45.7	34.0	43.5	50.3	61.9	47.7
Total	43.6	72.7	52.2	38.0	42.5	49.7	60.9	48.5

Note: Data reflect the percentage of high school students who report ever having had sexual intercourse.
Source: U.S. Department of Health and Human Services, 1999h.

HOMOSEXUALITY: COMING OUT TO ONESELF AND OTHERS

Cultures vary as much in their acceptance of homosexuality as they do in their approval of premarital sex. In the United States, homosexuals are stigmatized, as shown by the degrading language often used to describe them. This makes forming a sexual identity a much greater challenge for gay and lesbian youths than for their heterosexual counterparts.

Wide variations in homosexual identity formation exist, depending on personal, family, and community factors. Yet interviews with homosexual adolescents and adults reveal that many move through a three-phase sequence in coming out to themselves and others:

FEELING DIFFERENT. Many gay men and some lesbians say they felt different from other children when they were young (Diamond, 1998; Savin-Williams, 1998). Typically, this first sense of their biologically determined sexual orientation appears between ages 6 and 12 and results from play interests more like those of the other gender (Mondimore, 1996). Boys may find that they

are less interested in sports, drawn to quieter activities, and more emotionally sensitive than other boys, girls that they are more athletic and active than other girls.

In Chapter 8, we saw that children who do not conform to traditional gender roles (especially boys) are often ridiculed—an early experience of many homosexuals. In addition, when children hear derogatory labels for homosexuality, they absorb a bias against their own sexual orientation at an early age.

CONFUSION. With the arrival of puberty, feeling different begins to include feeling sexually different. In research on ethnically diverse gay, lesbian, and bisexual youths, awareness of a same-sex attraction occurred, on the average, between ages 11 and 12 for boys and 14 and 15 for girls, perhaps because adolescent social pressures toward heterosexuality are particularly intense for girls (Diamond, 1998; Herdt & Boxer, 1993). Realizing that homosexuality has personal relevance generally sparks confusion, largely because most young people had

assumed they were heterosexual like everyone else.

A few adolescents resolve their discomfort by crystallizing a gay or lesbian identity quickly, with a flash of insight into their sense of being different. Most experience an inner struggle and deep sense of isolation—outcomes intensified by lack of role models and social support. Some throw themselves into activities they have come to associate with heterosexuality. Boys may go out for athletic teams, girls may drop the softball team in favor of dance. And they may try heterosexual dating. Others are so bewildered, uncomfortable, guilt-ridden, and lonely that they escape into alcohol and drug abuse and suicidal thinking (Mondimore, 1996).

ACCEPTANCE. The majority of gay and lesbian teenagers reach a point of accepting their homosexuality. Then they face another crossroad: whether to tell others. The most difficult disclosure is to parents, but many fear rejection by peers as well (Cohen & Savin-Williams, 1996). Powerful stigma against their sexual orientation at home and school lead some to decide

---

unplanned pregnancy because they do not use contraception at all or delay using it for months after they have become sexually active (Moore et al., 1998). Why do so many fail to take precautions? As we will see when we take up adolescent cognitive development, teenagers can consider many more possibilities when faced with a problem. But at first, they fail to apply this reasoning to everyday situations. When asked to explain why they did not use contraception, they often give answers like these: "I was waiting until I had a steady boyfriend." "I wasn't planning to have sex."

One reason for responses like these is that advances in perspective taking lead teenagers, for a time, to be extremely concerned about others' opinions of them. Recall how Cassie and Louis each worried about what the other would think if they did not have sex. Furthermore, in the midst of

everyday social pressures, adolescents often overlook the consequences of engaging in risky behaviors (Beyth-Marom & Fischhoff, 1997).

The social environment also contributes to teenagers' reluctance to use contraception. Adolescents who talk openly about sex with their parents are not less sexually active, but they are more likely to use birth control (Brooks-Gunn, 1988b). Unfortunately, many adolescents are too scared or embarrassed to ask parents questions. And too many leave sex education classes with incomplete or factually incorrect knowledge. Some do not know where to get birth control counseling and devices. When they do, they often worry that a doctor or family planning clinic might not keep their visits confidential (Alan Guttmacher Institute, 1994; Winn, Roker, & Coleman, 1995).

that no disclosure is possible. As a result, they self-define but otherwise "pass" as heterosexual. In one interview study of gay adolescents, 85 percent said they tried concealment for a time (Newman & Muzzonigro, 1993).

Many homosexuals eventually acknowledge their sexual orientation publicly, usually by telling trusted friends first, then family members and acquaintances. When people whose love and acceptance is strongly desired react positively, coming out strengthens the young person's view of homosexuality as a valid, meaningful, and fulfilling identity. Contact with other gays and lesbians is important for reaching this phase, and changes in society permit many adolescents in urban areas to attain it earlier than they did a decade or two ago (Anderson, 1994; Edwards, 1996). Gay and lesbian communities exist in large cities, along with specialized interest groups, social clubs, religious groups, newspapers, and periodicals. Increasing numbers of favorable media images are also helpful. Small towns and rural areas remain difficult places to meet other homosexuals and to find a supportive environment. Teenagers in these locales have a special need for caring adults and peers who can help them find self- and social acceptance.

Gay and lesbian adolescents who succeed in coming out to themselves and others integrate their sexual orientation into a broader sense of identity, a process we will address in Chapter 12. As a result, they no longer need to focus so heavily on their homosexual self, and energy is freed for other aspects of psychological growth. In sum, coming out in a sympathetic social context has the potential to foster many aspects of adolescent development, including self-esteem, psychological well-being, and relationships with family, friends, and co-workers.

■ *This gay couple enjoys an evening at a high school prom. As long as friends and family members react with acceptance, coming out strengthens the young person's view of homosexuality as a valid, meaningful, and fulfilling identity. (Photo courtesy: Donna Binder/Impact Visuals)*

■ SEXUAL ORIENTATION. Up to this point, our discussion has focused only on heterosexual behavior. About 3 to 6 percent of teenagers discover that they are lesbian or gay (see the Social Issues box above). An as yet unknown but significant number are bisexual (Michael et al., 1994; Patterson, 1995). Adolescence is an equally crucial time for the sexual development of these young people, and societal attitudes, once again, loom large in how well they fare.

New evidence indicates that heredity makes an important contribution to homosexuality. Identical twins of both sexes are much more likely than fraternal twins to share a homosexual orientation. The same is true for biological as opposed to adoptive relatives (Bailey & Pillard, 1991; Bailey et al., 1993). Furthermore, male homosexuality tends to be more common on the maternal than paternal side of

families. This suggests that it might be X-linked (see Chapter 2). Indeed, one gene-mapping study found that among 40 pairs of homosexual brothers, 33 (88 percent) had an identical segment of DNA on the X chromosome. One or several genes in that region might predispose males to become homosexual (Hamer et al., 1993).

How might heredity lead to homosexuality? According to some researchers, certain genes affect prenatal sex hormone levels, which modify brain structures in ways that induce homosexual feelings and behavior (Bailey et al., 1995; LeVay, 1993). Keep in mind, however, that both genetic and environmental factors can alter prenatal hormones. Girls exposed prenatally to very high levels of androgens or estrogens—because of either a genetic defect or drugs given to the mother to prevent miscarriage—are more likely to become homosexual or bisexual (Meyer-Bahlburg et al., 1995). Furthermore, homosexual men tend to be later in birth order and have a higher-than-average number of older brothers (Blanchard et al., 1995; Blanchard & Bogaert, 1996). One controversial speculation is that mothers with several male children sometimes produce antibodies to androgens, which reduce the prenatal impact of male sex hormones on the brains of later-born boys.

Stereotypes and misconceptions about homosexuality continue to be widespread. For example, contrary to common belief, most homosexual adolescents are not "gender deviant" in dress or behavior. Furthermore, attraction to members of the same sex is not limited to gay and lesbian teenagers. Among heterosexual adolescents, about 18 per-

cent of boys and 6 percent of girls report participating in at least one homosexual act (Braverman & Strasburger, 1993).

SEXUALLY TRANSMITTED DISEASE

Sexually active adolescents, both homosexual and heterosexual, are at risk for sexually transmitted disease (STD) (see Table 11.3). Adolescents have the highest rates of STD of any age group. Despite a recent decline in STD in the United States, one out of six sexually active teenagers contracts one of these illnesses each year. If left untreated, sterility and life-threatening complications can result. Teenagers in greatest danger of STD are the same ones who tend to engage in irresponsible sexual behavior—poverty-stricken

TABLE 11.3

Most Common Sexually Transmitted Diseases of Adolescence

DISEASE	INCIDENCE AMONG 15- TO 19-YEAR-OLDS (RATE PER 100,000)	CAUSE	SYMPTOMS AND CONSEQUENCES	TREATMENT
AIDS	20[a]	Virus	Fever, weight loss, severe fatigue, swollen glands, and diarrhea. As the immune system weakens, severe pneumonias and cancers, especially on the skin, appear. Death due to other diseases usually occurs.	No cure; experimental drugs prolong life
Chlamydia	1,132	Bacteria	Discharge from the penis in males; painful itching, burning vaginal discharge, and dull pelvic pain in females. Often no symptoms. If left untreated, can lead to inflammation of the pelvic region, infertility, and sterility.	Antibiotic drugs
Cytomegalovirus	Unknown[b]	Virus of the herpes family	No symptoms in most cases. Sometimes, a mild flu-like reaction. In a pregnant woman, can spread to the embryo or fetus and cause miscarriage or serious birth defects (see page 93).	None; usually disappears on its own
Genital warts	451	Virus	Warts that typically grow near the vaginal opening in females, on the penis or scrotum in males. Can cause severe itching. Related to cancer of the cervix.	Removal of warts, but virus persists
Gonorrhea	570	Bacteria	Discharge from the penis or vagina, painful urination. Sometimes no symptoms. If left untreated, can spread to other regions of the body, resulting in such complications as infertility, sterility, blood poisoning, arthritis, and inflammation of the heart.	Antibiotic drugs
Herpes simplex 2 (genital herpes)	167	Virus	Fluid-filled blisters on the genitals, high fever, severe headache, and muscle aches and tenderness. No symptoms in a few people. In a pregnant woman, can spread to the embryo or fetus and cause birth defects (see page 93).	No cure; can be controlled with drug treatment
Syphilis	6.4	Bacteria	Painless chancre (sore) at site of entry of germ and swollen glands, followed by rash, patchy hair loss, and sore throat within 1 week to 6 months. These symptoms disappear without treatment. Latent syphilis varies from no symptoms to damage to the brain, heart, and other organs after 5 to 20 years. In pregnant women, can spread to the embryo and fetus and cause birth defects.	Antibiotic drugs

[a]This figure includes both adolescents and young adults. For most of these cases, the virus is contracted in adolescence, and symptoms appear in early adulthood.

[b]Cytomegalovirus is the most common STD. Because there are no symptoms in most cases, its precise rate of occurrence is unknown. Half of the population or more may have had the virus sometime during their lives.

Source: U.S. Centers for Disease Control, 1999.

young people who feel a sense of hopelessness about their lives (Holmbeck, Waters, & Brookman, 1990).

By far the most serious STD is AIDS. One-fifth of cases in the United States occur between ages 20 and 29. Nearly all of these originate in adolescence, since AIDS symptoms typically take 8 to 10 years to develop. Drug-abusing and homosexual adolescents account for most cases, but heterosexual spread of the disease is increasing, especially among females. It is at least twice as easy for a male to infect a female with any STD, including AIDS, as it is for a female to infect a male (U.S. Centers for Disease Control, 1999).

As the result of school course and media campaigns, over 90 percent of high school students are aware of basic facts about AIDS. But some hold false beliefs that put them at risk—for example, that birth control pills provide some protection or that it is possible to tell whether people have AIDS by looking at them (DiClemente, 1993). Almost all parents favor AIDS education in the public schools, and most states now require it. The Caregiving Concerns table below lists strategies for preventing STD.

ADOLESCENT PREGNANCY AND PARENTHOOD

Cassie was lucky not to get pregnant after having sex with Louis, but some of her high school classmates weren't so fortunate. Over 900,000 American teenage girls—20 percent of those who have had sexual intercourse—become pregnant annually, 30,000 under age 15. Despite a steady decline since 1991, the adolescent pregnancy rate in the United States is higher than that of most other industrialized countries (see Figure 11.3 on page 366). The United States differs from these nations in three important ways: (1) effective sex education reaches fewer teenagers; (2) convenient, low-cost contraceptive services for adolescents are scarce; and (3) many more families live in poverty, which encourages young people to take risks without considering the future implications of their behavior.

About 40 percent of teenage pregnancies end in abortion, 14 percent in miscarriage (Alan Guttmacher Institute, 1998). Because the United States has one of the highest adolescent abortion rates of any developed country, the number of teenage births is actually lower than it was 30 years ago (Ventura et al., 1997). But teenage parenthood is a much greater problem today because modern adolescents are far less likely to marry before childbirth. In 1960, only 15 percent of teenage births were to unmarried females, whereas today, 75 percent are (Coley & Chase-Lansdale, 1998). Increased social acceptance of single motherhood, along with the belief that a baby might fill a void in their lives, has meant that only a small number of girls give up their infants for adoption. Each year, about 320,000 unmarried adolescent girls take on the responsibilities of parenthood before they are psychologically mature.

CAREGIVING CONCERNS

Preventing Sexually Transmitted Disease

STRATEGY	DESCRIPTION
Know your partner well.	Take time to get to know your partner. Find out whether your partner has had sex with many people or has used injectable drugs.
Maintain mutual faithfulness.	For this strategy to work, neither partner can have an STD at the start of the relationship.
Do not use drugs.	Using a needle, syringe, or drug liquid previously used by others can spread STD. Alcohol, marijuana, or other illegal substances impair judgment, reducing your capacity to think clearly about the consequences of behavior.
Always use a latex condom and vaginal contraceptive when having sex with a nonmarital partner.	Latex condoms give good (but not perfect) protection against STD by reducing the passage of bacteria and viruses. Vaginal contraceptives containing nonoxynol-9 can kill several kinds of STD microbes. They increase protection when combined with condom use.
Do not have sex with a person you know has an STD.	Even if you are protected by a condom, your risk of contracting the disease is still there. In the case of the AIDS virus, you are risking your life. If either partner has engaged in behavior that might have risked HIV infection, a blood test must be administered and repeated at least 6 months after that behavior, since it takes time for the body to develop antibodies.
If you get an STD, inform all recent sexual partners.	Notifying people you may have exposed to STD permits them to get treatment before spreading the disease to others.

Source: Daugirdas, 1992.

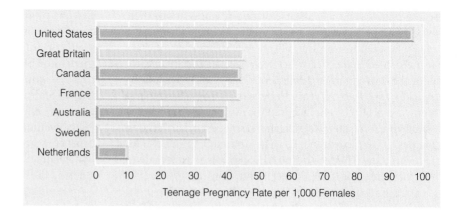

FIGURE 11.3

■ **Teenage pregnancy rate in seven industrialized nations.** (Adapted from Alan Guttmacher Institute, 1998.)

■ CORRELATES AND CONSEQUENCES OF ADOLESCENT PARENTHOOD. Becoming a parent is challenging and stressful for anyone, but it is especially difficult for adolescents. Teenage parents have not yet established a clear sense of direction for their own lives. Also, teenage mothers are many times more likely to be poor than are agemates who postpone childbearing. Their life experiences often include low parental warmth and involvement; poor school performance; alcohol and drug use; adult models of unmarried parenthood, limited education, and unemployment; and residence in neighborhoods where other adolescents also display these risks (Fagot et al., 1998; Scaramella et al., 1998). A high percentage of out-of-wedlock births are to members of low-income minorities, especially African-American, Native-American, and Hispanic teenagers. Many of these young people seem to turn to early parenthood as a way to move into adulthood when educational and career avenues are unavailable (Luker, 1996).

Early childbearing imposes lasting hardships on two generations—adolescent and newborn baby. The lives of pregnant teenagers are often troubled in many ways, and after the baby is born, their circumstances tend to worsen in at least three respects:

■ *Educational attainment.* Giving birth before age 18 reduces the likelihood of finishing high school. Only 50 percent of adolescent mothers graduate with either a diploma or general equivalency degree (GED), compared with 96 percent of girls who wait to become parents (Hotz, McElroy, & Sanders, 1997).

■ *Marital patterns.* Teenage motherhood reduces the chances of marriage. When these mothers do marry, they are more likely to divorce than are their peers who delay childbearing (Moore et al., 1993). Consequently, teenage mothers spend more of their parenting years as single parents. Often they have additional out-of-wedlock births in quick succession.

■ *Economic circumstances.* Because of low educational attainment, marital instability, and poverty, many teenage mothers are on welfare. If they are employed, their limited education restricts them to unsatisfying, low-paid jobs (Moore et al., 1993). Adolescent fathers work more hours than their nonparent agemates in the years following their child's birth. Perhaps for this reason, they obtain less education and are also economically disadvantaged (Brien & Willis, 1997).

Because many pregnant girls do not receive early prenatal care, their babies often experience prenatal and birth complications, especially low birth weight (Scholl, Heidiger, & Belsky, 1996). Children of teenagers are also at risk for poor parenting. Compared with adult mothers, adolescent mothers know less about child development, have unrealistically high expectations, perceive their infants as more difficult, and interact less effectively with them (Brooks-Gunn & Chase-Lansdale, 1995). Many of their children score low on intelligence tests, achieve poorly in school, and engage in disruptive social behavior. As the Lifespan Vista box above reveals, too often the cycle of adolescent pregnancy is repeated in the next generation (Furstenberg, Hughes, & Brooks-Gunn, 1992; Moore, Morrison, & Green, 1997).

Still, how well adolescent parents and their children fare varies a great deal. If the adolescent finishes high school, avoids additional births, and finds a stable marriage partner, long-term disruptions in her own and her child's development are less severe. The small minority of young mothers who fail in all three of these areas face a life of continuing misfortune (Furstenberg, Brooks-Gunn, & Morgan, 1987).

■ PREVENTION STRATEGIES. Preventing teenage pregnancy means addressing the many factors underlying early sexual activity and lack of contraceptive use. Informing adolescents about sex and contraception is crucial. Too often, sex education courses are given too late (after sexual activity has begun), last only a few sessions, and are limited to a cat-

A LIFESPAN VISTA

LIKE MOTHER, LIKE CHILD: INTERGENERATIONAL CONTINUITY IN ADOLESCENT PARENTHOOD

What are the long-term consequences of being the child of an adolescent parent? Does adolescent parenthood increase the chances of teenage childbearing in the next generation? To find out, Janet Hardy and her collaborators (1998) conducted a 30-year follow-up of over 1,700 inner-city mothers (first generation) and their children (second generation). The first generation became parents between 1960 and 1964—about 28 percent as teenagers. As young people in the second generation grew up, they became parents between the mid-1970s and early 1990s—25 percent as teenagers.

The researchers capitalized on extensive childhood data that had been gathered on the second generation, including IQ and achievement scores and information about family conditions. In addition, they interviewed both generations between 1992 and 1994, when the second generation reached 27 to 33 years of age, asking for recollections of the second generation's adolescent and early-adult life course.

First-generation mothers' age at first birth was strongly associated with the age at which second-generation young people became parents (see Figure 11.4). Yet becoming a second-generation teenage parent was not just a matter of having been born to an adolescent mother. Rather, adolescent parenthood was linked to a wide array of unfavorable rearing conditions, which

predicted intergenerational continuity in teenage childbearing. For example, compared with second-generation daughters who postponed parenthood, daughters who became teenage mothers were more likely to grow up in a single-parent household, have four or more siblings (reducing parental attention and resources available to each), score lower in IQ and reading skill, repeat one or more grades, and (in adolescence) have a higher frequency of police arrests for delinquency. Similar trends were found for second-generation sons who became teenage parents. And as these early child bearers moved into adulthood, they fared less well in education, physical and mental health, and financial security than did their agemates who waited to become parents.

Finally, even when children born to teenage mothers did not repeat the pattern of early childbearing, their development was compromised. Although they fared better than their counterparts who became adolescent parents, they scored lower than other second-generation members in virtually all child and adult indicators of well-being. In sum, the likelihood of graduating from high school, achieving financial independence, enjoying good physical and mental health, and avoiding adolescent parenthood with all its costly future consequences is much greater for children born to older mothers than for those born to teenagers.

FIGURE 11.4

■ **Intergenerational continuity in adolescent parenthood in a 30-year study of over 1,700 inner-city parents and their children.** The graph shows the percentage of second generation daughters and sons who became adolescent parents for each of three groups of first-generation parents: those who had a first child as a teenager, between ages 20 and 24, or at age 25 or older. First-generation adolescent parents were more likely to have children who were adolescent parents, a tendency that was stronger for second-generation girls than boys. Fewer boys in this study reported adolescent parenthood. They might not always have known about the birth of a child. And in some cases, they might have chosen not to disclose it. (Adapted from Hardy et al., 1998.)

alogue of facts about anatomy and reproduction. Sex education that goes beyond this minimum does not encourage early sex, as some opponents claim. It does improve awareness of sexual facts—knowledge that is necessary for responsible sexual behavior (Katchadourian, 1990).

Knowledge, however, is not sufficient to influence teenagers' behavior. Sex education must also help them build a bridge between what they know and what they do (Frost &

Forrest, 1995). Today, more effective sex education programs have emerged with the following key elements:

■ Teaching skills for handling sexual situations through creative discussion and role-playing techniques, which permit teenagers to confront sexual situations similar to those they will encounter in everyday life

■ *Early parenthood imposes lasting hardships on both generations —adolescent and newborn baby. Teenage fathers, like teenage mothers, suffer educationally and economically. This young father must work extra hours to pay for baby clothing and care. His new burden will probably mean less opportunity for continued education and a lower income in the years to come. (Photo courtesy: SHIA/Impact Visuals)*

■ Promoting the value of abstinence to teenagers not yet sexually active

■ Providing information about and ready access to contraceptives

The most controversial aspect of adolescent pregnancy prevention involves providing easy access to contraceptives. Some large cities have school-based health clinics that offer this service. Many Americans argue that placing birth control pills or condoms in the hands of teenagers is equivalent to saying that early sex is okay. Yet in Western Europe, where these clinics are common, teenage sexual activity is no higher than in the United States, but pregnancy, childbirth, and abortion rates are much lower (Zabin & Hayward, 1993).

Efforts to prevent adolescent pregnancy and parenthood must go beyond sex education and contraception to build social competence. In one study, researchers randomly assigned at-risk high school students either to a year-long community service class, called Teen Outreach, or to regular classroom experiences in health or social studies. In Teen Outreach, adolescents participated in at least 20 hours per week of volunteer work tailored to their interests. They returned to school for discussions that focused on enhancing their community service skills and ability to cope with everyday challenges. At the end of the school year, pregnancy, school failure, and school suspension were substantially lower in the group enrolled in Teen Outreach, which fostered social skills, connectedness to the community, and self-respect (Allen et al., 1997).

Finally, teenagers who look forward to a promising future are far less likely to engage in early and irresponsible sex. By expanding educational, vocational, and employment opportunities, society can provide young people with good reasons to postpone childbearing.

■ INTERVENING WITH ADOLESCENT PARENTS. The most difficult and costly way to deal with adolescent parenthood is to wait until after it has happened. Young single mothers need health care for themselves and their children, encouragement to stay in school, job training, instruction in parenting and life management techniques, and high-quality, affordable child care. Schools that provide these services reduce the incidence of low-birth-weight babies, increase mothers' educational success, and prevent additional childbearing (Seitz & Apfel, 1993, 1994).

Adolescent mothers also benefit from family relationships that are sensitive to their developmental needs. Our discussion of the African-American family in Chapter 2 indicated that older teenage mothers display more effective parenting when they establish their own residences with the help of relatives—an arrangement that grants the teenager a balance of autonomy and support. Similarly, adolescent mothers of other ethnic backgrounds who live apart from grandmothers but receive high levels of assistance from them have warmer extended family ties and children who are developing more favorably (East & Felice, 1996).

Programs focusing on fathers are attempting to increase their financial and emotional commitment to the baby (Coley & Chase-Lansdale, 1998). Although almost half of young fathers visit their children during the first few years after birth, contact usually diminishes. By school age, fewer than one-fourth are still involved (Lerman, 1993). But new laws that encourage mothers to help establish paternity and that enforce child support payments may lead to a turnabout in paternal responsibility and interaction. Teenage mothers who receive financial and child-care assistance from their child's father are less distressed and interact more favorably with their infants (Caldwell & Antonucci, 1997). And children of teenagers with warm ties to their fathers show better long-term adjustment (Furstenberg & Harris, 1993).

SUBSTANCE USE AND ABUSE

At age 14, Louis took some cigarettes out of his uncle's pack, waited until he was alone in the house, and smoked. At an unchaperoned party, he and Cassie drank several cans of beer, largely because everyone else was doing it. Louis got little physical charge out of these experiences. He was a good student, was well liked by peers, and got along well with his parents. He had no need for drugs as an escape valve from daily life. But he knew of others at school for whom things were different—students who started with alcohol and cigarettes, moved to harder substances, and eventually were hooked.

In the United States, teenage alcohol and drug use is pervasive—higher than in any other industrialized nation. By age 14, 56 percent of young people have already tried cigarette smoking, 81 percent drinking, and 39 percent at least one illegal drug (usually marijuana). By the end of high school, 16 percent are regular cigarette users, 30 percent have engaged in heavy drinking at least once, and over 45 percent have experimented with illegal drugs. Of these, about one-third have tried at least one highly addictive and toxic substance, such as amphetamines, cocaine, phencyclidine (PCP), or heroin (U.S. Department of Health and Human Services, 1999e).

These high figures represent a steady increase in adolescent alcohol and drug use over the past few years, after a decade of decline (see Figure 11.5). Why do so many young people subject themselves to the health risks of these substances? Part of the reason is cultural. Modern adolescents live in a drug-dependent society. They see adults using caffeine to wake up in the morning, cigarettes to cope with daily hassles, a drink to calm down in the evening, and other remedies to relieve stress, depression, and physical illness. Recent reduced parental, school, and media attention to the hazards of drugs may explain the recent upsurge in adolescent drug taking.

For most young people, substance use simply reflects their intense curiosity about "adultlike" behaviors. Research reveals that the majority of teenagers dabble in alcohol, tobacco, and marijuana. These minimal *experimenters* are not headed for a life of decadence and addiction. Instead, they are psychologically healthy, sociable, curious young people (Shedler & Block, 1990). In a society in which substance use is commonplace, some involvement with drugs is normal and to be expected.

Yet adolescent drug experimentation should not be taken lightly. Because most drugs impair perception and thought processes, a single heavy dose can lead to perma-nent injury or death. And a worrisome minority of teenagers move from substance *use* to *abuse*—taking drugs regularly, requiring increasing amounts to achieve the same effect, and finding themselves unable to stop.

■ CORRELATES AND CONSEQUENCES OF ADOLESCENT SUBSTANCE ABUSE. In contrast to experimenters, drug abusers are seriously troubled young people who express their unhappiness through antisocial acts. Their impulsive, disruptive style is often present in early childhood and is promoted by other factors, including low SES, family mental health problems, parental and older sibling drug abuse, lack of parental warmth and involvement, and poor school performance. By early adolescence, peer encouragement—friends who use and provide access to illegal substances—is a strong predictor of substance abuse (Chassin et al., 1996; Wills et al., 1996).

Adolescent substance abuse often has lifelong consequences. When adolescents depend on alcohol and hard drugs to deal with daily stresses, they fail to learn responsible decision-making skills and alternative coping techniques—crucial lessons during this time of transition to adulthood. These young people show serious adjustment problems, including depression and antisocial behavior (Luthar & Cushing, 1997). They often enter into marriage, parenthood, and the work world prematurely and fail at them—painful outcomes that encourage further addictive behavior.

■ PREVENTION AND TREATMENT. School-based programs that promote effective parenting (including monitoring of teenagers' activities), educate adolescents about the dangers of drugs, and teach them skills for resisting peer pressure help reduce experimentation to some degree (Steinberg, Fletcher, & Darling, 1994). But some drug taking seems inevitable. Weekend on-call transportation services that any young person can contact for a safe ride home, with no questions asked, can prevent teenagers from endangering themselves and others when they do experiment.

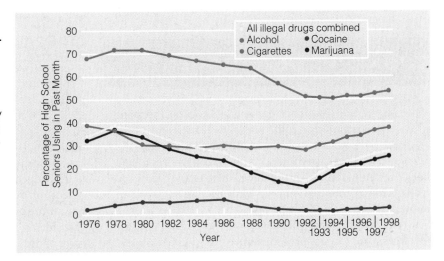

■ **Percentages of high school seniors reporting use of alcohol, cigarettes, and illegal drugs in the past month, 1976–1998.** Substance use continues to be widespread among adolescents. Although it declined from 1982 to 1992, a sharp increase in the past few years—largely accounted for by marijuana and cigarette smoking —has sounded a note of alarm. (From U.S. Department of Health and Human Services, 1999e.)

Drug abuse, as we have seen, occurs for quite different reasons than does occasional use. Therefore, different prevention strategies are required. One approach is to work with parents early, reducing family adversity and improving parenting skills, before children are old enough to become involved with drugs (Luthar, Cushing, & McMahon, 1997). Programs that teach at-risk teenagers strategies for handling life stressors and that build competence through community service have been found to reduce alcohol and drug use, just as they reduce teenage pregnancy (Richards-Colocino, McKenzie, & Newton, 1996).

When an adolescent becomes a drug abuser, hospitalization is often a necessary and even lifesaving first step. Once the young person is weaned from the drug, therapy to treat low self-esteem, anxiety, and impulsivity and academic and vocational training to improve life success and satisfaction are generally needed. Not much is known about the best way to treat adolescent drug abuse. Even the most comprehensive programs have alarmingly high relapse rates—from 35 to 70 percent (Segal & Stewart, 1996).

ASK YOURSELF . . .

■ *Fourteen-year-old Lindsay says she couldn't possibly get pregnant because her boyfriend would never do anything to "mess her up." What factors might account for Lindsay's unrealistic reasoning?*

 At age 16, Veronica gave birth to her first child. When, at age 17, she had a second, her parents told her they didn't have room for two babies. Veronica dropped out of school and moved in with her boyfriend, Todd. A few months later, Todd left because he couldn't stand being tied down by the babies. Why are Veronica and her children likely to experience long-term hardships?

■ *Explain how adolescent substance abuse follows the pattern of other teenage health problems in being the product of both psychological and social forces.*

COGNITIVE DEVELOPMENT

One mid-December evening, a knock at the front door announced the arrival of Franca and Antonio's oldest son, Jules, home for vacation after the fall semester of his sophomore year at college. Moments later, the family gathered around the kitchen table. "How did it all go, Jules?" inquired Antonio while passing out pieces of apple pie.

"Well, physics and philosophy were awesome. The last few weeks, our physics prof introduced us to Einstein's rel-

ativity theory. Boggles my mind, it's so incredibly counter-intuitive."

"Counter-what?" asked Sabrina, trying hard to follow the conversation.

"Counterintuitive. Unlike what you'd normally expect," explained Jules. "Imagine you're on a train, going unbelievably fast, like 160,000 miles a second. The faster you go approaching the speed of light, the slower time passes and the denser and heavier things get relative to on the ground. The theory revolutionized the way we think about time, space, matter—the entire universe."

Sabrina wrinkled her forehead, unable to comprehend Jules's otherworldly reasoning. "Time slows down when I'm bored, like right now, not on a train when I'm going somewhere exciting. No speeding train ever made me denser and heavier, but this apple pie will if I eat any more of it," Sabrina announced, getting up and leaving the table.

Sixteen-year-old Louis reacted differently. "Totally cool, Jules. So what'd you do in philosophy?"

"It was a course in philosophy of technology. We studied the ethics of futuristic methods in human reproduction. For example, we argued the pros and cons of a world in which all embryos develop in artificial wombs."

"What do you mean?" asked Louis. "You order your kid at the lab?"

"That's right. I wrote my paper on it. I had to evaluate it in terms of principles of justice and freedom. I can see some advantages but also lots of dangers. . . ."

As this conversation illustrates, adolescence brings with it vastly expanded powers of reasoning. At age 11, Sabrina finds it difficult to move beyond her firsthand experiences to a world of possibilities. Over the next few years, her thinking will take on the abstract qualities that characterize the cognition of her older brothers. Jules juggles variables in complex combinations and thinks about situations not easily detected in the real world or that do not exist at all. Compared with school-age children's thinking, adolescent thought is more enlightened, imaginative, and rational.

PIAGET'S THEORY: THE FORMAL OPERATIONAL STAGE

According to Piaget, the capacity for abstract thinking begins around age 11. At the **formal operational stage,** the adolescent reasons much like a scientist searching for solutions in the laboratory. Concrete operational children can only "operate on reality," but formal operational adolescents can "operate on operations." In other words, concrete things and events are no longer required as objects of thought. Instead, adolescents can come up with new, more general logical rules through internal reflection (Inhelder & Piaget, 1955/1958). Let's look at two major features of the formal operational stage.

■ *In Piaget's formal operational stage, adolescents engage in hypothetico-deductive reasoning. These high school students, who are members of a mock jury, listen to evidence presented by both the prosecution and the defense. Then they will imagine all possible factors that might have affected the outcome of the problematic situation, evaluate each in terms of the evidence, and make a reasoned decision. (Photo courtesy: Jerry Wachter/Photo Researchers, Inc.)*

HYPOTHETICO-DEDUCTIVE REASONING

At adolescence, young people become capable of **hypothetico-deductive reasoning.** When faced with a problem, they start with a *general theory* of all possible factors that might affect the outcome and *deduce* from it specific *hypotheses* (or predictions) about what might happen. Then they test these hypotheses in an orderly fashion to see which ones work in the real world. Notice how this form of problem solving begins with possibility and proceeds to reality. In contrast, concrete operational children start with reality—with the most obvious predictions about a situation. When these are not confirmed, they cannot think of alternatives and fail to solve the problem.

Adolescents' performance on Piaget's famous *pendulum problem* illustrates this new approach. Suppose we present several school-age children and adolescents with strings of different lengths, objects of different weights to attach to the strings, and a bar from which to hang the strings. Then we ask each of them to figure out what influences the speed with which a pendulum swings through its arc.

Formal operational adolescents come up with four hypotheses: (1) the length of the string, (2) the weight of the object hung on it, (3) how high the object is raised before it is released, and (4) how forcefully the object is pushed. Then, by varying one factor at a time while holding all the others constant, they try out each of these possibilities. Eventually they discover that only string length makes a difference.

In contrast, concrete operational children experiment unsystematically. They cannot separate out the effects of each variable. For example, they may test for the effect of string length without holding weight constant by compar-

ing a short, light pendulum with a long, heavy one. Also, school-age youngsters fail to notice variables that are not immediately suggested by the concrete materials of the task—the height at which and forcefulness with which the pendulum is released.

PROPOSITIONAL THOUGHT

A second important characteristic of the formal operational stage is **propositional thought.** Adolescents can evaluate the logic of propositions (verbal statements) without referring to real-world circumstances. In contrast, children can evaluate the logic of statements only by considering them against concrete evidence in the real world.

In a study of propositional reasoning, an experimenter showed children and adolescents a pile of poker chips and asked whether statements about the chips were true, false, or uncertain. In one condition, the experimenter hid a chip in her hand and presented the following propositions:

"*Either* the chip in my hand is green or it is not green."

"The chip in my hand is green *and* it is not green."

In another condition, the experimenter held either a red or a green chip in full view and made the same statements.

School-age children focused on the concrete properties of the poker chips. When the chip was hidden from view, they replied that they were uncertain about both statements. When it was visible, they judged both statements to be true if the chip was green and false if it was red. In contrast, adolescents analyzed the logic of the statements. They understood that the "either–or" statement is always true and the "and" statement is always false, regardless of the poker chip's color (Osherson & Markman, 1975).

Although Piaget believed that language does not play a central role in children's cognitive development (see Chapter 7), he acknowledged it is more important in adolescence. Abstract thought requires language-based systems of representation that do not stand for real things, such as those in higher mathematics. Secondary school students use these systems in algebra and geometry. Formal operational thought also involves verbal reasoning about abstract concepts. Jules showed that he could think in this way when he pondered the relation among time, space, and matter in physics and wondered about justice and freedom in philosophy.

RECENT RESEARCH ON FORMAL OPERATIONAL THOUGHT

Recent research on formal operational thought poses questions similar to those we discussed with respect to Piaget's earlier stages: Is there evidence that abstract thinking appears earlier than Piaget expected? Do all individuals reach formal operations during their teenage years?

■ ARE CHILDREN CAPABLE OF ABSTRACT THINKING?
Adolescents are capable of a much deeper grasp of scientific principles than they were at younger ages. For example, in simplified situations—ones involving no more than two possible causal variables—6-year-olds understand that hypotheses must be confirmed by appropriate evidence (Ruffman et al., 1993). But school-age children cannot sort out evidence that bears on three or more variables at once. And as we will see when we take up information-processing research, children have difficulty explaining why a pattern of observations supports a hypothesis, even when they recognize the connection between the two.

School-age children's capacity for propositional thought is also limited. For example, they have great difficulty reasoning from premises that contradict reality or their own beliefs. Consider the following set of statements: "If dogs are bigger than elephants and elephants are bigger than mice, then dogs are bigger than mice." Children younger than 10 judge this reasoning to be false, since all the relations specified do not occur in real life (Moshman & Franks, 1986). They fail to grasp the *logical necessity* of propositional reasoning—that the validity of conclusions drawn from premises rests on the rules of logic, not on real-world confirmation.

As Piaget's theory indicates, people in Western nations become much better at analyzing the logic of propositions, irrespective of their content, around age 11. Propositional thought improves steadily over the adolescent years (Markovits & Vachon, 1989, 1990).

■ DO ALL INDIVIDUALS REACH THE FORMAL OPERATIONAL STAGE? Try giving one or two of the formal operational tasks just described to your friends, and see how well they do. Even well-educated adults have difficulty with abstract reasoning! About 40 to 60 percent of college students fail Piaget's formal operational problems (Keating, 1979).

Why is it that so many college students, and adults in general, are not fully formal operational? The reason is that people are most likely to think abstractly in situations in which they have had extensive experience. This is supported by evidence that taking college courses leads to improvements in formal operational reasoning related to course content (Lehman & Nisbett, 1990). The physics student grasps Piaget's pendulum problem with ease. The English enthusiast excels at analyzing the themes of a Shakespeare play, whereas the history buff skillfully evaluates the causes and consequences of the Vietnam War. Because of differences in training and experience, the person who does well at one of these tasks may not be especially good at the others.

Finally, recall from Chapter 9 that the development of concrete operational thought is greatly delayed in some village and tribal societies. In many of these cultures, formal operational tasks are not mastered at all (Cole, 1990; Gellatly, 1987). Piaget acknowledged that because of lack of opportunity to solve hypothetical problems, abstract thought might not be evident in some societies. Still, these findings raise further questions about Piaget's stage sequence. Is the formal operational stage largely an outgrowth of children's and adolescent's independent efforts to make sense of their world? Or is it a culturally transmitted way of reasoning that is particularly useful in literate societies and fostered by experiences encountered in school? Just how do young people make the transition from concrete to formal operational thought? These issues have prompted many investigators to turn toward an information-processing view.

AN INFORMATION-PROCESSING VIEW OF ADOLESCENT COGNITIVE DEVELOPMENT

Information-processing theorists agree with the broad outlines of Piaget's description of adolescent cognition (Case, 1992, 1998; Demetriou et al., 1993). However, they refer to a variety of specific mechanisms of cognitive change, each of which was discussed in previous chapters. Now let's draw them together:

■ *Attention* becomes more thorough and better adapted to the demands of tasks.

■ *Strategies* become more effective, improving storage, representation, and retrieval of information.

■ *Knowledge* increases, easing strategy use.

■ *Metacognition* (awareness of thought) expands, leading to new insights into effective strategies for acquiring information and solving problems.

■ *Processing capacity* increases due to the joint effects of brain development and the factors just mentioned. Consequently, space in working memory is freed so more information can be held at once and combined into highly efficient, abstract representations.

As we look at some influential findings from an information-processing perspective, we will see some of these mechanisms of change in action. And we will discover that researchers regard one of them—*metacognition*—as central to the development of abstract thought.

SCIENTIFIC REASONING: COORDINATING THEORY WITH EVIDENCE

During a free moment in physical education class, Sabrina wondered why more of her tennis serves and returns seemed to pass the net and drop into her opponent's court when she used a particular brand of balls. "Maybe it's something about their color or size? Hmm, more likely it's their surface texture, which might affect their bounce," she thought to herself.

At the heart of scientific reasoning is coordinating theories with evidence. Deanna Kuhn has conducted extensive research into the development of scientific reasoning, giving children and adolescents problems like those used by Piaget in that several variables might affect an outcome. In one series of studies, third, sixth, and ninth graders and adults were provided evidence, sometimes consistent and sometimes conflicting with theories. Then they were questioned about the accuracy of each theory.

For example, participants were given a problem much like the one Sabrina posed. They were asked to theorize about which of several features of sports balls—size (large or small), color (light or dark), texture (rough or smooth), and presence or absence of ridges on its surface—influences the quality of a player's serve. Next, they were told about the theory of Mr. (or Ms.) S, who believes size is important, and the theory of Mr. (or Ms.) C, who thinks color makes a difference. Finally, the interviewer presented evidence by placing balls with certain characteristics in two baskets labeled "good serve" and "bad serve" (see Figure 11.6).

■ **Which features of these sports balls—size, color, surface texture, or presence or absence of ridges—influence the quality of a player's serve?** This set of evidence suggests that color might be important, since light-colored balls are largely in the good-serve basket and dark-colored balls in the bad-serve basket. But the same is true for texture! The good-serve basket has mostly smooth balls, the bad-serve basket rough balls. Since all light-colored balls are smooth and all dark-colored balls are rough, we cannot tell whether color or texture makes a difference. But we can conclude that size and presence or absence of ridges are not important, since these features are equally represented in the good-serve and bad-serve baskets. (Adapted from Kuhn, Amsel, & O'Loughlin, 1988.)

The youngest participants often ignored conflicting evidence or distorted it in ways consistent with their theories. Instead of viewing evidence as separate from and bearing on a theory, children often blended the two into a single representation of "the way things are." The ability to distinguish theory from evidence and use logical rules to examine their relationship in complex, multivariable situations improves from childhood into adolescence and adulthood (Foltz, Overton, & Ricco, 1995; Kuhn et al., 1995; Schauble, 1996).

HOW SCIENTIFIC REASONING DEVELOPS

What factors support adolescents' skill at coordinating theory with evidence? Greater information-processing capacity, permitting a theory and the effects of several variables to be compared at once, is vital. Beyond this, metacognition—thinking about thought—is especially important (Kuhn, 1989, 1993). Individuals must be able to represent the theory as an object of thought rather than a mirror image of reality. And they must also set aside their own preference for the theory and consider what the evidence says as their sole basis for judgment.

How does skill in coordinating theory with evidence increase? Performance is strongly influenced by years of schooling (Kuhn, 1993). But even at advanced levels of education, scientific reasoning is rarely taught directly. Instead, in all subject-matter areas, students receive practice in setting aside their own experiences and beliefs to infer conclusions that follow from information given. Repeated opportunities to pit theory against evidence prompt adolescents to reflect on their current strategies, revise them, and become aware of the nature of logic (Kuhn et al., 1995; Moshman, 1998; Schauble, 1996).

Research reveals that adolescents develop formal operational thinking in a similar, step-by-step fashion on different types of tasks. In a series of studies, 10- to 20-year-olds were given sets of problems graded in difficulty. For example, one set consisted of quantitative-relational tasks like the pendulum problem on page 371. Another set contained verbal propositional tasks like the poker chip problem on page 371. And still another set was causal-experimental tasks like the sports ball problem described in the previous section.

In each type of task, adolescents mastered component skills in sequential order by expanding their metacognitive awareness. For example, on causal-experimental tasks, they first became aware of the many variables that could influence an outcome. This enabled them to formulate and test hypotheses. Over time, adolescents combined separate skills into a smoothly functioning system. They constructed a general model that could be applied to many instances of a given type of problem. In the researcher's words, young people seem to form a "hypercognitive system," or supersystem, that understands, organizes, and influences other aspects of cognition (Demetriou, Efklides, & Platsidou, 1993; Demetriou et al., 1993; Demetriou et al., 1996).

Piaget also underscored the role of metacognition in formal operational thought when he spoke of "operating on operations" (see page 370). However, information-processing findings reveal that scientific reasoning is not the result of an abrupt, stagewise change, as Piaget believed. Instead, it develops gradually out of many specific experiences that require children and adolescents to match theories against evidence and reflect on and evaluate their thinking.

CONSEQUENCES OF ABSTRACT THOUGHT

The development of formal operations leads to dramatic revisions in the way adolescents see themselves, others, and the world in general. But just as adolescents are occasionally awkward in the use of their transformed bodies, they are initially faltering and clumsy in their abstract thinking. Parents and teachers must be careful not to mistake the many typical reactions of the teenage years—argumentativeness, self-concern, insensitive remarks, and indecisiveness—for anything other than inexperience with new reasoning powers. The Caregiving Concerns table below suggests ways to handle the everyday consequences of teenagers' newfound capacity for abstraction.

ARGUMENTATIVENESS

As adolescents acquire formal operations, they are motivated to use them. The once pliable school-age child becomes a feisty, argumentative teenager who can marshal facts and ideas to build a case (Elkind, 1994). "A simple, straightforward explanation used to be good enough to get Louis to obey," complained Antonio. "Now he wants a thousand reasons. And worse yet, he finds a way to contradict them all!"

As long as parent–child disagreements remain focused on principles and do not deteriorate into meaningless battles, they can promote development. Through discussions of family rules and practices, adolescents become more aware of their parents' values and the reasons behind them. Gradually, they come to see the validity of parental beliefs and adopt many as their own (Alessandri & Wozniak, 1987). Teenagers' capacity for effective argument also opens the door to intellectually stimulating pastimes, such as debate teams and endless bull-sessions with friends over moral, ethical, and political concerns. By proposing, justifying, criticizing, and defending a variety of solutions, adolescents often move to a higher level of understanding than they attain in individual reasoning (Moshman, 1999).

SELF-CONSCIOUSNESS AND SELF-FOCUSING

Adolescents' ability to reflect on their own thoughts, combined with the physical and psychological changes they are undergoing, means that they start to think more about themselves. Piaget believed that the arrival of formal operations is accompanied by a new form of egocentrism: the inability to distinguish the abstract perspectives of self and other (Inhelder & Piaget, 1955/1958). As teenagers imagine what others must be thinking, two distorted images of the relation between self and other appear.

CAREGIVING CONCERNS

Ways to Handle the Consequences of Teenagers' New Capacity for Abstraction

CONSEQUENCE	SUGGESTION
Argumentativeness	During disagreements, remain calm, rational, and focused on principles. Express your point of view and the reasons behind it. Although adolescents may continue to challenge, explanations permit them to consider the validity of your beliefs at a later time.
Sensitivity to public criticism	Refrain from finding fault with the adolescent in front of others. If the matter is important, wait until you can speak to the teenager alone.
Exaggerated sense of personal uniqueness	Acknowledge the adolescent's unique characteristics. At opportune times, point out how you felt similarly as a young teenager, encouraging a more balanced perspective.
Idealism and criticism	Respond patiently to the adolescent's grand expectations and critical remarks. Point out positive features of targets, helping them see that all worlds and people are blends of virtues and imperfections.
Difficulty making everyday decisions	Refrain from deciding for the adolescent. Offer patient reminders and diplomatic suggestions until he or she can make choices more confidently.

■ *These seventh- and eighth-grade drama students really are on stage. But the imaginary audience leads them to think that everyone is monitoring their performance at other times as well. Consequently, young teenagers are extremely self-conscious and go to great lengths to avoid embarrassment. (Photo courtesy: Will Hart)*

The first is called the **imaginary audience.** Young teenagers regard themselves as always on stage. They are convinced that they are the focus of everyone else's attention and concern (Elkind & Bowen, 1979). As a result, they become extremely self-conscious, often going to great lengths to avoid embarrassment. Sabrina, for example, woke up one Sunday morning with a large pimple on her chin. "I can't possibly go to church!" she cried. "Everyone will notice how ugly I look." The imaginary audience helps us understand the hours adolescents spend inspecting every detail of their appearance. It also accounts for their sensitivity to public criticism. To teenagers, who believe that everyone is monitoring their performance, a critical remark from a parent or teacher can be mortifying.

A second cognitive distortion is the **personal fable.** Because teenagers are so sure that others are observing and thinking about them, they develop an inflated opinion of their own importance. They start to feel that they are special and unique. Many adolescents view themselves as reaching great heights of glory as well as sinking to unusual depths of despair—experiences that others could not possibly understand (Elkind, 1994). On one occasion, for example, Sabrina had a crush on a boy who failed to return her affections. As she lay on the sofa feeling depressed, Franca tried to assure her that there would be other boys. "Mom," Sabrina snapped, "you don't know what it's like to be in love!" The personal fable may contribute to adolescent risk taking. Teenagers who have sex without contraceptives or weave in

and out of traffic at 80 miles an hour seem, at least for the moment, convinced of their uniqueness and invulnerability.

The imaginary audience and personal fable are strongest during the transition to formal operations. They gradually decline as abstract reasoning becomes better established (Enright, Lapsley, & Shukla, 1979; Lapsley et al., 1988). Yet these distorted visions of the self may not represent a return to egocentrism. Instead, they seem to be an outgrowth of gains in perspective taking, which cause young teenagers to be very concerned with what others think (Lapsley, 1993; Vartanian & Powlishta, 1996). Adolescents also have emotional reasons for clinging to the idea that others are preoccupied with their appearance and behavior. Doing so helps them maintain a hold on important relationships as they struggle to separate from parents and establish an independent sense of self (Vartanian, 1997).

IDEALISM AND CRITICISM

Because abstract thinking permits adolescents to go beyond the real to the possible, it opens up the world of the ideal and of perfection. Teenagers can imagine alternative family, religious, political, and moral systems, and they want to explore them. Doing so is part of investigating new realms of experience, developing larger social commitments, and defining their own values and preferences.

The idealism of teenagers leads them to construct grand visions of a perfect world—with no injustice, discrimination, or tasteless behavior. They do not make room for the shortcomings of everyday life. Adults, with their longer life experience, have a more realistic outlook. The disparity between adults' and teenagers' world views is often called the "generation gap," and it creates tension between parent and child. Aware of the perfect family against

■ *This teenage girl looks as if she has nothing in common with her parents. Her idealistic image of a perfect world, to which her family cannot measure up, leads to a "generation gap," creating tension between parent and adolescent child. Over time, she will forge a better balance between the ideal and the real. (Photo courtesy: John Lawlor/FPG International)*

which their real parents and siblings do not measure up, adolescents may become fault-finding critics.

Yet overall, teenage idealism and criticism are advantageous. Once adolescents learn to see others as having both strengths and weaknesses, they are better able to work constructively for social change and to form positive and lasting relationships (Elkind, 1994). Parents can help teenagers forge a better balance between the ideal and the real by being tolerant of their criticism while reminding the young person that all people, including adolescents themselves, are blends of virtues and imperfections.

PLANNING AND DECISION MAKING

Adolescents, who think more analytically, handle cognitive tasks more effectively than they did at younger ages. Given a homework assignment, they are far better at *cognitive self-regulation*—planning what to do first and what to do next, monitoring progress toward a goal, and redirecting actions that prove unsuccessful. For this reason, study skills improve from middle childhood into adolescence.

But when it comes to planning and decision making in everyday life, teenagers (especially young ones) often feel overwhelmed by the possibilities before them. Their efforts to choose among alternatives frequently break down, and they may resort to habit, act on impulse, or not make a decision at all (Elkind, 1994). On many mornings, for example, Sabrina tried on five or six outfits before leaving for school. Often she shouted from the bedroom, "Mom, what shall I wear?" Then, when Franca made a suggestion, Sabrina rejected it, opting for one of the two or three sweaters she had worn for weeks. Similarly, Louis procrastinated about registering for college entrance tests. When Franca mentioned that he was about to miss the deadline, Louis sat over the forms, unable to decide when or where he wanted to take the test.

Everyday planning and decision making are challenging for teenagers because they have many more opportunities to create options for themselves. Consequently, they ask, "What behaviors could I perform?" before choosing a course of action. When they were younger, adults usually specified their options, reducing the number of decisions that had to be made. As adolescents gather more experience, they make choices with greater confidence.

ASK YOURSELF . . .

■ *Cassie insisted that she had to have high heels to go with her prom dress. "No way I can wear those low heels, Mom. They'll make me look way too short next to Louis, and the whole evening will be ruined!" Why is Cassie so concerned about a detail of her appearance that most people would be unlikely to notice?*

 Adolescent idealism and criticism, although troublesome for parents, are beneficial in the long run, both for the developing individual and society. Explain why this is so.

SEX DIFFERENCES IN MENTAL ABILITIES

Sex differences in intellectual performance have been studied since the beginning of this century, and they have sparked almost as much controversy as the ethnic and SES differences in IQ considered in Chapter 9. Although boys and girls do not differ in general intelligence, they do vary in specific mental abilities. Throughout the school years, girls attain higher scores on reading achievement tests and account for a lower percentage of children referred for remedial reading instruction (Halpern, 1992; Mullis et al., 1994). Girls' advantage on tests of general verbal ability is still present in adolescence. However, it is so slight that it is not really meaningful (Hyde & Linn, 1988).

By adolescence, boys start to do better than girls in mathematics, especially on tests of abstract reasoning, primarily on complex word problems and geometry (Bielinski & Davison, 1998; Hedges & Nowell, 1995). The gender gap is largest among gifted youngsters. In some publicized research on bright seventh and eighth graders invited to take the Scholastic Aptitude Test (SAT), boys outscored girls on the mathematics subtest year after year. Twice as many boys as girls had scores above 500; 13 times as many scored over 700 (Benbow & Stanley, 1983; Lubinski & Benbow, 1994).

Some researchers believe that the gender gap in mathematics—especially the tendency for many more boys to be extremely talented at math—is genetic. One assumption is that it is rooted in boys' biologically based superior spatial reasoning. See the Variations box on the following page for a discussion of this issue.

Although heredity is involved, social pressures contribute to girls' underrepresentation among the mathematically talented. Long before sex differences in math achievement appear, both boys and girls view math as a "masculine" subject. In addition, girls regard math as less useful for their future lives and more often blame their errors on lack of ability. These beliefs, in turn, lead girls to be less likely to consider math- or science-related careers and to take fewer math courses in high school and college. The end result is that girls are less likely to acquire abstract mathematical concepts and reasoning skills (Byrnes & Takahira, 1993; Catsambis, 1994).

A positive sign is that sex differences in cognitive abilities of all kinds have declined steadily over the past several decades. Paralleling this change is an increase in girls'

VARIATIONS/INDIVIDUALITY

SEX DIFFERENCES IN SPATIAL ABILITIES

Spatial abilities have become a key focus of researchers' efforts to explain the male advantage in mathematical reasoning. Clear sex differences in spatial skills exist, but they occur only on certain types of tasks (see Figure 11.7). The gender gap favoring males is large for *mental rotation tasks*, in which individuals must rotate a three-dimensional figure rapidly and accurately inside their heads. In addition, males do considerably better on *spatial perception tasks*, in which people must determine spatial relationships by considering the orientation of the surrounding environment. Sex differences on *spatial visualization tasks*, involving analysis of complex visual forms, are weak or nonexistent, perhaps because many strategies can be used to solve them. Both sexes may come up with effective procedures (Linn & Petersen, 1985; Voyer, Voyer, & Bryden, 1995).

Sex differences in spatial abilities emerge by middle childhood and persist throughout the lifespan (Kerns & Berenbaum, 1991). The pattern is consistent enough to suggest a biological explanation. One hypothesis is that heredity, perhaps through prenatal exposure to androgen hormones, enhances right hemispheric functioning, granting males a spatial advantage. (Recall that for most people, spatial skills are housed in the right hemisphere of the cerebral cortex.) Consistent with this idea, girls and women

whose prenatal androgen levels were abnormally high show superior performance on spatial rotation tasks (Collaer & Hines, 1995). And people with severe prenatal deficits in either male or female hormones have difficulty with spatial reasoning (Hier & Crowley, 1982; Temple & Carney, 1995).

However, research on hormone variations within normal range is less clear. Two studies report a link between prenatal androgens and spatial abilities during the preschool years, but only for girls and in the opposite direction expected: The greater the hormone exposure, the lower the spatial score (Finegan, Niccols, & Sitarenios, 1992). Prenatal hormones seem to affect spatial skills, but not in a straightforward fashion.

Although biology is involved in males' superior spatial performance, experience also makes a difference. Children who engage in manipulative activities, such as block play, model-building, and carpentry, do better on spatial tasks (Baenninger & Newcombe, 1995). Furthermore, playing

video games that require rapid mental rotation of visual images enhances spatial scores of boys and girls alike (Okagaki & Frensch, 1996; Subrahmanyam & Greenfield, 1996). Boys spend far more time at all these pursuits than do girls.

Do superior spatial skills contribute to the greater ease with which males solve complex math problems? Research indicates that they do (Casey et al., 1995). Yet in a study of high-ability college-bound adolescents, *both* mental rotation ability and self-confidence at doing math predicted higher scores on the math subtest of the SAT (Casey, Nuttall, & Pezaris, 1997). Boys are advantaged not only in mental rotation but in math self-confidence. Even when their grades are poorer than girls', boys judge themselves to be better at math (Eccles et al., 1993c). In sum, biology and environment *jointly* determine variations in spatial and math performance—within and between the sexes.

■ **Types of spatial tasks.** Large sex differences favoring males appear on mental rotation, and males do considerably better than females on spatial perception. In contrast, sex differences on spatial visualization are weak or nonexistent. (From M. C. Linn & A. C. Petersen, 1985, "Emergence and Characterization of Sex Differences in Spatial Ability: A Meta-Analysis," *Child Development, 56*, pp. 1482, 1483, 1485. © The Society for Research in Child Development, Inc. Reprinted by permission.)

Mental Rotation
Choose the responses that show the standard in a different orientation.

Standard   Responses
                  1   2   3   4

Spatial Perception
Pick the tilted bottle that has a horizontal water line.

1   2   3   4

Spatial Visualization
Find the figure embedded in this complex shape.

enrollment in advanced high school math and science courses, although girls still take fewer of these courses than do boys (Campbell, Voelkl, & Donahue, 1997; Davenport et al., 1998).

Clearly, extra steps must be taken to promote girls' interest in and confidence at doing math and science. When parents hold nonstereotyped gender-role values, daughters are less likely to show declines in math and science achievement at adolescence (Updegraff, McHale, & Crouter, 1996). In schools, teachers need to do a better job of demonstrating the relevance of math and science to everyday life. Girls, especially, respond positively toward math and science taught from an applied, hands-on perspective (Eccles, 1994). At the same time, teachers must ensure that girls participate fully in hands-on group activities and are not reduced to a passive role by boys' more assertive style of peer interaction (Jovanovic & King, 1998). And all students benefit from encouragement and constructive feedback rather than criticism when engaged in problem solving. Finally, exposure to role models of successful women is likely to improve girls' belief in their capacity to do well at math and science.

■ ASK YOURSELF . . .

■ *Research shows that girls perform more poorly than boys on certain formal operational tasks, such as the pendulum problem. On the basis of what you know about the development of formal operational thought and sex differences in cognitive abilities, how would you account for this finding?*

 What steps can be taken to increase girls' interest in taking math and sciences? What impact are these efforts likely to have on lifelong development?

LEARNING IN SCHOOL

In complex societies, adolescence coincides with entry into secondary school. Most young people move into either a middle or a junior high school and then into a high school. With each change, academic achievement becomes more serious, affecting college choices and job opportunities. In the following sections, we take up a variety of aspects of secondary school life.

■ SCHOOL TRANSITIONS

When Sabrina started junior high, she left a small, intimate, self-contained sixth-grade classroom for a much larger, impersonal school. "I don't know most of the kids in my classes," Sabrina complained to her mother at the end

of the first week. "Besides, there's just too much homework. I get assignments in all my classes at once. I can't do all this!" she shouted, bursting into tears.

■ IMPACT OF SCHOOL TRANSITIONS.

As Sabrina's reactions suggest, school transitions can drastically alter academic and social experiences, creating new adjustment problems. With each school change—from elementary to middle or junior high and then to high school—adolescents' grades decline. The drop is partly due to tighter academic standards. At the same time, the transition to secondary school often brings with it less personal attention, more whole-class instruction, and less chance to participate in classroom decision making (Eccles, Lord, & Buchanan, 1996).

Inevitably, students must readjust their feelings of self-confidence and self-worth as environments become more impersonal and academic expectations are revised. A large-scale study showed that the earlier the school transition, the more powerful and longer-lasting its consequences, especially for girls (Simmons & Blyth, 1987). The researchers followed over 300 adolescents living in a large Midwestern city from sixth to tenth grade. Some were enrolled in schools with a 6–3–3 grade organization (a K–6 elementary school, a 3-year junior high, and a 3-year high school). These students made two school changes, one to junior high and one to high school. A comparison group attended schools with an 8–4 grade organization. They made only one school transition, from a K–8 elementary school to high school.

For the sample as a whole, grade point average dropped and feelings of anonymity increased after each transition. Participation in extracurricular activities declined more in the 6–3–3 than in the 8–4 arrangement, with the drop being greater for girls. Sex differences in self-esteem were even more striking. As Figure 11.8 shows, boys' self-esteem increased steadily, except in 6–3–3 schools, where it leveled off after entry into high school. Girls in the 6–3–3 arrangement fared especially poorly. Their self-esteem declined with each school change. In contrast, their 8–4 counterparts gained steadily in feelings of self-worth throughout secondary school.

These findings show that any school transition is likely to depress adolescents' psychological well-being temporarily, but the earlier it occurs, the more dramatic and long-lasting its impact. Girls in 6–3–3 schools fared poorest, the researchers argued, because movement to junior high tended to coincide with other life changes—namely, puberty and the beginning of dating. Adolescents who face added life stresses, such as family disruption or a shift in residence, around the time they change schools are at greatest risk for academic and emotional difficulties.

Poorly achieving and poverty-stricken young people show an especially sharp drop in school performance after

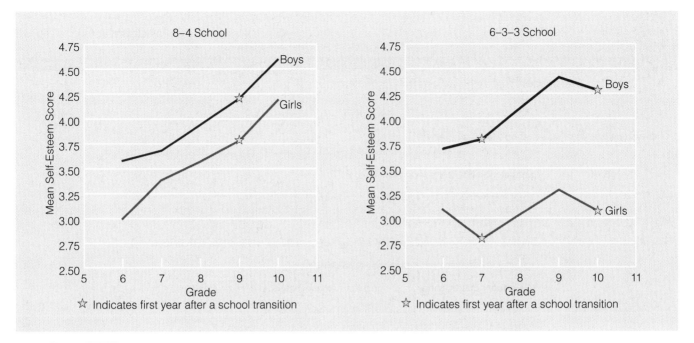

FIGURE 11.8

■ **Self-esteem from sixth to tenth grade by school type for boys and girls.** In this longitudinal study of more than 300 adolescents, self-esteem increased steadily for both sexes in the 8–4 school arrangement. Girls in 6–3–3 schools fared especially poorly. Their self-esteem dropped sharply after each school change. (Adapted from Simmons & Blyth, 1987.)

the junior high transition (Seidman et al., 1994). For some, it initiates a downward spiral in academic performance and school involvement that eventually leads to failure and dropping out (Simmons, Black, & Zhou, 1991).

■ HELPING ADOLESCENTS ADJUST TO SCHOOL TRANSITIONS. Consider the findings just reviewed, and you will see that school transitions often lead to environmental changes that fit poorly with adolescents' developmental needs. They disrupt close relationships with teachers at a time when adolescents need adult support. They emphasize competition during a period of heightened self-focusing. They reduce decision making and choice as the desire for autonomy increases.

Fortunately, there are ways to ease the strain of going from elementary to secondary school. Since most students do better in an 8–4 school arrangement, school districts considering reorganization should seriously consider this plan. When this is not possible, smaller social units can be formed within large schools, permitting closer relations with teachers and peers and greater extracurricular involvement (Seidman & French, 1997). Students can also be assigned to classes with several familiar peers or a constant group of new peers—arrangements that promote emotional security and social support. These interventions lead to better academic performance and psychological adjustment and reduce the rate of school dropout (Felner & Adan, 1988).

Finally, successful transitions are most likely to occur in schools that foster adolescents' growing capacity for autonomy, responsibility, and control over their own lives. Rigid school rules that strike young people as unfair and punitive frustrate their developmental needs, contributing to long-term dissatisfaction with school life (Eccles et al., 1993a).

A CADEMIC ACHIEVEMENT

Adolescent achievement is the result of a long history of cumulative effects. Early on, positive educational environments, both family and school, lead to personal traits that support achievement—intelligence, confidence in one's own abilities, the desire to succeed, and high educational aspirations. Nevertheless, improving an unfavorable environment can help a poorly performing young person bounce back, opening the door to a more satisfying adult life. The Caregiving Concerns table on page 380 summarizes environmental factors that enhance achievement during the teenage years.

■ CHILD-REARING PRACTICES. Authoritative parenting (which combines warmth with firm, reasonable demands for maturity) is linked to achievement in adolescence, just as it predicts mastery-oriented behavior during the childhood years. In research involving thousands of adolescents, authoritative parenting predicted higher grades, whereas

CAREGIVING CONCERNS

Factors That Support High Achievement During Adolescence

FACTOR	DESCRIPTION
Child-rearing practices	Authoritative parenting (warmth with moderate to high demandingness, in accord with the young person's ethnic background)
	Joint parent–adolescent decision making
	Parent involvement in the adolescent's education
Peer influences	Peer valuing of and support for high achievement
School characteristics	Teachers who are warm and supportive and develop personal relationships with parents
	Learning activities that encourage high-level thinking
	Active student participation in learning activities and classroom decision making
Employment schedule	Job commitment limited to less than 15 to 20 hours per week
	High-quality vocational education for non-college-bound adolescents

authoritarian and permissive styles were associated with lower grades (Dornbusch et al., 1987; Steinberg, Darling, & Fletcher, 1995). Parents who engage in joint decision making with adolescents, gradually permitting more autonomy with age, have youngsters who achieve especially well (Dornbusch et al., 1990).

The relationships just described vary somewhat with ethnicity. Recall from Chapter 8 that some Asian and African-

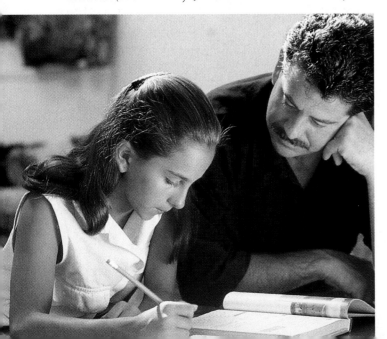

■ *This father is involved in his adolescent daughter's school career. Besides keeping tabs on her progress, he is probably in regular contact with the school. He sends a message to his daughter about the importance of education and teaches her how to solve academic problems and make wise educational decisions. (Photo courtesy: Jose L. Pelaez/The Stock Market)*

American parents are highly demanding of their children. For Asian parents, high control represents deep parental concern and commitment, stemming from Confucian values. For African-American parents, dangerous inner-city neighborhoods may require greater strictness to foster children's competence. Consistent with these trends, parenting especially high in control is linked to better grades among Asian and African-American teenagers (Florsheim, Tolan & Gorman-Smith, 1996; Glasgow et al., 1997; Steinberg et al., 1994).

Parent involvement in the adolescent's secondary school career also fosters academic success. High-achieving young people typically have parents who keep tabs on their child's progress, communicate with teachers, and make sure that their child is enrolled in challenging, well-taught classes. These efforts are just as important during junior and senior high school as they were earlier (Grolnick & Slowiaczek, 1994). Parents living in low-income, high-risk neighborhoods face daily stresses that reduce the time and energy they have for school involvement. Yet schools could relieve some of this stress by forging stronger home–school links, through personal relationships with teachers and meaningful parental roles in school planning and governance that ensure parents are invested in school goals (Eccles & Harold, 1993).

■ PEER INFLUENCES. Peers play an important role in adolescent achievement, in a way that is related to both family and school. Teenagers whose parents value achievement are likely to choose friends who share those values (Berndt & Keefe, 1995). For example, when Sabrina began to make new friends in junior high, she often studied with her girlfriends. Each wanted to do well in school and reinforced the same desire in the others.

Peer support for high achievement also depends on the overall climate of the peer culture. Sometimes low-SES African-American and other minority students react against working hard, convinced that getting good grades will have little payoff in the future and regarding it as a threat to their ethnic identity (Ogbu, 1997). Yet not all economically disadvantaged minority students respond this way. A case study of six inner-city, poverty-stricken African-American adolescents who were high-achieving and optimistic about their futures revealed that they were intensely aware of oppression but believed in striving to alter their social position (O'Connor, 1997). How did they develop this sense of agency? Parents, relatives, and teachers had convinced them through discussion and example that injustice should not be tolerated and that together, blacks could overcome it—a perspective that facilitated academic motivation in the face of peer pressures against doing well in school.

■ SCHOOL CHARACTERISTICS. Adolescents need classroom environments that are responsive to their expanding powers of reasoning and emotional and social needs. Without appropriate learning experiences, the potential for abstract thought is unlikely to be realized.

Classroom Learning Experiences. As noted earlier, the large, departmentalized school organization of most secondary schools leads many adolescents to report that their classes lack warmth and supportiveness—a circumstance that dampens their motivation (Eccles et al., 1993b). Adolescents (not just children) need to form close relationships with teachers. As they begin to develop an identity beyond the family, they seek out adult models other than their parents (Eccles & Harold, 1996).

Of course, an important reason for separate classes in each subject is that adolescents can be taught by experts, who are more likely to encourage high-level thinking—factors that promote school attendance and achievement (Phillips, 1997). But the classroom experiences of many secondary school students do not work out this way. In a study of English, social studies, and science teachers with reputations for excellence, students were not equally or consistently given assignments that stimulated abstract thought (Sanford, 1985).

Because of the uneven quality of instruction in American schools, a great many seniors graduate from high school deficient in basic academic skills. Although the achievement gap separating African-American and Hispanic students from white students has declined since the 1970s, mastery of reading, writing, mathematics, and science by low-SES ethnic minority students remains disappointing (Campbell, Voelkl, & Donahue, 1997; Ogbu, 1997). Many attend underfunded schools with run-down buildings, outdated equipment, and textbook shortages. In some, crime and discipline problems have become so overwhelming that they have stolen attention from learning and instruction. By junior high, large numbers of poverty-stricken minority students have been placed in low academic tracks, compounding their learning difficulties.

Tracking. Ability grouping, as we saw in Chapter 9, is detrimental during the elementary school years. At least into middle or junior high school, mixed-ability classes are desirable. Research shows that they do not stifle the more able students, and they have intellectual and social benefits for poorly performing youngsters (Oakes, Gamoran, & Page, 1992).

By high school, some grouping is unavoidable because certain aspects of education must dovetail with the young person's future educational and career plans. In the United States, high school students are counseled into college preparatory, vocational, or general education tracks. Unfortunately, this sorting tends to perpetuate educational inequalities of earlier years. Low-income minority students are assigned in large numbers to noncollege tracks. One study found that a good student from an economically disadvantaged family had only half as much chance of ending up in an academically oriented program as a student of equal ability from a middle-SES background (Vanfossen, Jones, & Spade, 1987).

High school students are separated into academic and vocational tracks in virtually all industrialized nations. But in China, Japan, and most Western European nations, students take a national examination to determine their placement in high school. The outcome usually fixes future possibilities for the young person. In the United States, educational decisions are more fluid. Students who are not assigned to a college preparatory track or who do poorly in high school can still get a college education. But by the adolescent years, SES differences in quality of education and academic achievement have already sorted American students more drastically than is the case in other countries. In the end, many young people do not benefit from this more open system. Compared with other developed nations, the United States has a higher percentage of high school dropouts and adolescents with very limited academic skills (McAdams, 1993).

■ PART-TIME WORK. Almost half of American high school students work part-time during the school year—a greater percentage than in any other developed country. Most are middle-SES adolescents in pursuit of spending money rather than vocational training. Low-income teenagers who need to contribute to family income find it harder to get jobs (Children's Defense Fund, 1999).

Furthermore, the jobs adolescents hold are limited to low-level repetitive tasks that provide little contact with adult supervisors. A heavy commitment to such jobs is harmful.

Students who work more than 15 hours per week have poorer school attendance, lower grades, and less time for extracurricular activities. They also report more drug and alcohol use and feel more distant from their parents. And perhaps because of the menial nature of their jobs, employed teenagers tend to be cynical about work life. Many admit to having stolen from their employers (Barling, Rogers, & Kelloway, 1995; Steinberg, Fegley, & Dornbusch, 1993).

When work experiences are specially designed to meet educational and vocational goals, outcomes are different. Work–study programs are related to positive school and work attitudes and improved achievement among teenagers whose low-income backgrounds and weak academic skills make them especially vulnerable to school dropout and unemployment (Owens, 1982; Steinberg, 1984). Yet high-quality vocational preparation for non-college-bound American adolescents is scarce. Unlike Western European nations, the United States has no widespread training system to prepare its youths for skilled business and industrial occupations and manual trades (Marshall, 1997). The federal government does support some job training programs. But most are too short to make a difference in the lives of poorly skilled adolescents, who need intensive training and academic remediation before they are ready to enter the job market. And at present, these programs serve only a small minority of young people who need assistance.

DROPPING OUT

Across the aisle from Louis in math class sat Norman, who daydreamed, crumpled his notes into his pocket after class, and rarely did his homework. On test days, he twirled a rabbit's foot for good luck but left most of the questions blank. Louis had been in school with Norman since fourth grade, but the two boys had little to do with one another. To Louis, who was quick at schoolwork, Norman seemed to live in another world. Once or twice each week, Norman cut class, and one spring day, he stopped coming altogether.

Norman is one of 11 percent of American young people who, by 18 years of age, leave high school without a diploma (U.S. Department of Education, 1999). The dropout rate is particularly high among low-income ethnic minority youths, especially Hispanic teenagers (see Figure 11.9). The decision to leave school has dire consequences. As Figure 11.10 shows, dropouts are far less likely to be employed than are high school graduates who do not go to college. And even when they are employed, they have a much greater chance of remaining in menial, low-paying jobs and of being out of work from time to time.

■ FACTORS RELATED TO DROPPING OUT. Long before he stopped coming, Norman showed signs that he would leave school early. Because of a history of poor school per-

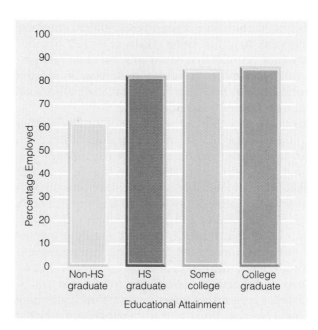

FIGURE 11.9

■ **Percentage of high school dropouts in the United States by ethnicity.** Because African-American and Hispanic teenagers are more likely to come from low-income and poverty-stricken families, their dropout rates are above the national average. The rate for Hispanic young people is especially high. (From U.S. Department of Education, 1999b.)

FIGURE 11.10

■ **Employment rates of 20- to 24-year-olds by educational attainment in the United States.** Those who do not graduate from high school are much less likely to get jobs than are their counterparts with high school diplomas. Employment rates increase with years of schooling completed. (From U.S. Department of Education, 1999b.)

formance, his perception of his own ability was extremely low. He gave up on tasks that presented the least bit of challenge and counted on luck—his rabbit's foot—to get him by. As Norman got older, he attended class less regularly, failed to pay attention when he was there, rarely did his homework, and was a discipline problem. He didn't participate in any school clubs or sports but, instead, often used drugs and engaged in lawbreaking acts. Because he was so uninvolved, few teachers or students got to know him well. The day Norman left, he felt alienated from all aspects of school life.

As with other dropouts, Norman's family background contributed to his problems. Compared to other students, even those with the same grade profile, dropouts are more likely to have parents who are less involved in their youngster's education. Many did not finish high school themselves and are unemployed, on welfare, or coping with the aftermath of divorce. When the adolescent brings home a poor report card, these parents are more likely to respond with punishment and anger—reactions that cause the young person to rebel further against academic work (Garnier, Stein, & Jacobs, 1997; Melby & Conger, 1996).

Academically marginal students who drop out often have school experiences that undermine their chances for success. Recent reports indicate that over 60 percent of adolescents in some inner-city high schools do not graduate. Students in general education and vocational tracks, where teaching tends to be the least stimulating, are three times more likely to drop out than are those in an a college preparatory track (Office of Educational Research and Improvement, 1999).

■ PREVENTION STRATEGIES. Strategies for helping teenagers at risk for dropping out are diverse, but several common themes are related to success:

- *High-quality vocational training.* For many marginal students, the real-life nature of vocational education is more comfortable and effective than purely academic work. But to work well, it must carefully integrate academic and job-related instruction so students see the relevance of what happens in the classroom to their future goals (Ianni & Orr, 1996).

- *Remedial instruction and counseling that offer personalized attention.* Most potential dropouts need intensive remedial instruction in small classes that permit warm, caring teacher–student relationships to form. To overcome the negative psychological effects of repeated school failure, good academic assistance must be combined with social support and special counseling (Rumberger, 1990).

- *Efforts to address the many factors in students' lives related to leaving school early.* Programs that strengthen parent involvement, offer flexible work–study arrangements, and provide on-site child care for teenage mothers can make staying in school easier for at-risk adolescents.

- *Participation in extracurricular activities.* Another way of helping marginal students is to draw them into the community life of the school (Mahoney & Cairns, 1997). The most powerful influence on extracurricular involvement is small school size. In smaller high schools (500 to 700 students or less), a greater proportion of the student body is needed to staff and operate activities. Potential dropouts are far more likely to participate, feel needed, gain recognition for their abilities, and remain until graduation. Note that "house" plans, which create smaller units within large schools, can have the same effect (Berk, 1992b).

As we conclude our discussion of academic achievement, let's place the school dropout problem in historical perspective. Over the last half of the twentieth century, the percentage of American adolescents completing high school rose dramatically—from 39 percent in 1940 to 89 percent in the late 1990s. During this same period, college attendance also increased. Today, nearly 40 percent of 18- to 24-year-olds are working toward college degrees—the highest rate in the world. Finally, about one-third of all high school dropouts return to finish their education within a few years, and some extend their schooling further (Children's Defense Fund, 1999). As the end of adolescence approaches, many young people realize how essential education is for a rewarding job and career.

ASK YOURSELF . . .

Tanisha is finishing sixth grade. She could either continue in her current school through eighth grade or switch to a much larger junior high school. What would you suggest she do, and why might her decision have lasting consequences for her academic development and educational attainment?

■ *In a workshop for parents of adolescents, one father asks what he might do to encourage his teenage children to do well in school. Provide a list of suggestions along with reasons each is effective.*

PHYSICAL DEVELOPMENT

CONCEPTIONS OF ADOLESCENCE

How have conceptions of adolescence changed over the twentieth century?

■ **Adolescence,** initiated by **puberty,** is the period in which young people cross the dividing line between childhood and adulthood. Early biologically oriented theories viewed adolescence as an inevitable period of storm and stress. An alternative perspective regarded the social environment as entirely responsible for the wide variability in adolescent adjustment. Modern research shows that adolescence is a product of both biological and social forces.

PUBERTY: THE PHYSICAL TRANSITION TO ADULTHOOD

Describe pubertal changes in body size, proportions, motor performance, and sexual maturity.

■ Hormonal changes beginning in middle childhood initiate puberty, on the average, 2 years earlier for girls than boys. The first outward sign of puberty is the **growth spurt.** As the body enlarges, girls' hips and boys' shoulders broaden. Girls add more fat, boys more muscle.

■ Pubertal changes lead gross motor performance to improve; boys show much larger gains than do girls. Although girls' involvement in high school sports has increased, they continue to receive less athletic encouragement than do boys. Overall, the number of American boys participating in regular physical activity increases from ninth to twelfth grade, whereas the number of physically active girls declines.

■ Sex hormones regulate changes in **primary** and **secondary sexual characteristics. Menarche** occurs late in the girl's sequence of pubertal events, following the rapid increase in body size. Among boys, as the sex organs and body enlarge and pubic and underarm hair appear, **spermarche** (first ejaculation) takes place.

What factors influence the timing of puberty?

■ In addition to heredity, nutrition and overall physical health contribute to the timing of puberty. A **secular trend** toward an earlier age of menarche has occurred in industrialized nations.

THE PSYCHOLOGICAL IMPACT OF PUBERTAL EVENTS

What factors influence adolescents' reactions to the physical changes of puberty?

■ Girls generally react to menarche with surprise and mixed emotions, but whether their feelings lean in a positive or negative direction depends on advance information and support from family members. Boys usually know ahead of time about spermarche, but they receive less support for the physical changes of puberty than do girls.

■ Besides higher hormone levels, negative life events and situational changes are associated with adolescent moodiness. Puberty is accompanied by psychological distancing between parent and child. The reaction may be a modern substitute for physical departure from the family, which typically occurs at sexual maturity in primate species.

Describe the impact of maturational timing on adolescent adjustment, noting sex differences.

■ Early maturing boys and late maturing girls, whose appearance closely matches cultural standards of physical attractiveness, have a more positive **body image** and usually adjust well in adolescence. In contrast, early maturing girls and late maturing boys, who fit in least well physically with peers, experience emotional and social difficulties.

HEALTH ISSUES

Describe nutritional needs and cite factors related to serious eating disturbances during adolescence.

■ As the body grows, nutritional requirements increase. Because of poor eating habits, many adolescents suffer from iron, vitamin, and mineral deficiencies.

■ Girls who reach puberty early, who are very dissatisfied with their body images, and who grow up in homes where thinness is idealized are at increased risk for eating disorders. **Anorexia nervosa** tends to appear in girls with perfectionist personalities and overprotective, controlling parents. The impulsive eating and purging of **bulimia** is associated with lack of self-control in other areas of life.

Discuss social and cultural influences on adolescent sexual attitudes and behavior.

■ The hormonal changes of puberty lead to an increase in sex drive, but social factors affect how teenagers manage their sexuality. Compared with most other cultures, the United States is fairly restrictive in its attitude toward adolescent sex. Young people receive contradictory messages from the social environment. Sexual attitudes and behavior of adolescents have become more liberal, with a slight swing back recently.

■ Early sexual activity is linked to a variety of factors associated with economic disadvantage. About half of sexually active American teenagers do not practice contraception regularly. Adolescent cognitive processes and a lack of social support for responsible sexual behavior underlie the failure of many young people to protect themselves against pregnancy.

Describe factors involved in the development of homosexuality.

■ About 3 to 6 percent of adolescents discover that they are lesbian or gay. Biological factors, including heredity and prenatal hormone levels, play an important role in homosexuality. Lesbian and gay teenagers face special problems in developing a positive sexual identity.

Discuss factors related to sexually transmitted disease and teenage pregnancy and parenthood.

■ A high rate of sexually transmitted disease (STD) among American adolescents is another consequence of early sexual activity and inconsistent contraceptive use. Many young adults with AIDS contracted the virus as teenagers.

■ Adolescent pregnancy, abortion, and parenthood rates are higher in the United States than in most other industrialized nations. Teenage parenthood is often associated with school dropout, reduced chances of marriage, greater likelihood of divorce, and poverty—circumstances that risk the well-being of both adolescent and newborn child.

■ Improved sex education, access to contraceptives, programs that build social competence, and expanded educational and vocational opportunities help prevent early pregnancy. Adolescent mothers benefit from family support that is sensitive to their developmental needs. When

teenage fathers stay involved, their children develop more favorably.

What personal and social factors are related to adolescent substance use and abuse?

■ Teenage alcohol and drug use is widespread in the United States. For most young people, drug experimentation reflects curiosity about these forbidden substances. The minority who move from use to abuse have serious psychological, family, and school problems. Programs that work with parents early to reduce family adversity and improve parenting skills and that build teenagers' competence help prevent substance abuse.

COGNITIVE DEVELOPMENT

PIAGET'S THEORY: THE FORMAL OPERATIONAL STAGE

What are the major characteristics of formal operational thought?

■ During Piaget's **formal operational stage,** abstract thinking appears. Adolescents engage in **hypothetico-deductive reasoning.** When faced with a problem, they think of all possibilities and test them systematically. **Propositional thought** also develops. Young people can evaluate the logic of verbal statements without considering them against real-world circumstances.

Discuss recent research on formal operational thought and its implications for the accuracy of Piaget's formal operational stage.

■ Adolescents are capable of a much deeper grasp of scientific principles than are school-age children. However, college students and adults think abstractly only in situations in which they have had extensive experience, and formal thought does not appear in many village and tribal

cultures. These findings indicate that Piaget's highest stage is affected by specific learning opportunities.

AN INFORMATION-PROCESSING VIEW OF ADOLESCENT COGNITIVE DEVELOPMENT

How do information-processing researchers account for the development of abstract reasoning?

■ Information-processing researchers believe that a variety of specific mechanisms of change foster abstract thought, including improved attention, more effective strategies, greater knowledge, gains in information-processing capacity, and, especially, advances in metacognition.

■ Research on scientific reasoning indicates that the ability to coordinate theory with evidence improves during adolescence as young people solve increasingly complex problems, reflect on and revise their strategies, and become aware of the nature of logic. Adolescents develop formal operational thinking in a similar, step-by-step fashion on different types of tasks, constructing general models that can be applied to many instances of a given type of problem.

CONSEQUENCES OF ABSTRACT THOUGHT

Describe typical reactions of adolescents that result from new abstract reasoning powers.

■ Using their new cognitive powers, teenagers become more argumentative, idealistic, and critical. As they think more about themselves, two distorted images of the relation between self and other appear—the **imaginary audience** and **personal fable.** Adolescents show gains in cognitive self-regulation, but they often have difficulty making decisions in everyday life.

SEX DIFFERENCES IN MENTAL ABILITIES

Describe sex differences in mental abilities at adolescence.

■ During adolescence, the female advantage in verbal ability is very slight. Boys do better in abstract mathematical reasoning. Biological factors common to spatial and mathematical reasoning may contribute to the gender gap. At the same time, a variety of environmental factors, including childhood play activities, self-confidence and interest in doing math, and math and science course taking, contribute to the gender gap. Girls' environmental disadvantage stems from stereotyping of math as a "masculine" subject.

LEARNING IN SCHOOL

Discuss the impact of school transitions on adolescent adjustment.

■ School transitions in adolescence can be stressful. Girls experience more adjustment difficulties, since other life changes (puberty and the beginning of dating) tend to occur at the same time. Teenagers who must cope with added stresses—especially poorly achieving and poverty-stricken young people—are at greatest risk for academic and emotional problems.

Discuss family, peer, school, and employment influences on academic achievement during adolescence.

■ Authoritative parenting and parent involvement in the adolescent's secondary school career promote high achievement. Teenagers with parents who encourage achievement are likely to choose friends who do the same. Warm, supportive learning environments with activities that emphasize high-level thinking enable adolescents to realize their academic potential. Working more than 15 hours a week undermines school performance.

■ By high school, separate educational tracks that dovetail with students' future plans are necessary. Unfortunately, high school tracking in the United States usually extends the educational inequalities of earlier years.

What factors are related to dropping out of school?

■ Eleven percent of American young people leave high school without a diploma. Many are low-income, minority youths. Dropping out is the result of a slow, cumulative process of disengagement from school. Family and school influences combine to undermine the young person's chances for success.

IMPORTANT TERMS AND CONCEPTS

adolescence (p. 350)

anorexia nervosa (p. 359)

body image (p. 357)

bulimia (p. 360)

formal operational stage (p. 370)

growth spurt (p. 352)

hypothetico-deductive reasoning (p. 371)

imaginary audience (p. 375)

menarche (p. 354)

personal fable (p. 375)

primary sexual characteristics (p. 354)

propositional thought (p. 371)

puberty (p. 350)

secondary sexual characteristics (p. 354)

secular trend (p. 355)

spermarche (p. 354)

Consult the companion website for this book, where you will find additional weblinks and associated learning activities: www.abacon.com/berk

ADOLESCENT HEALTH

AMA–Adolescent Health On-Line
www.ama-assn.org/adolhlth

A site created by the American Medical Association that provides information on adolescent health issues for professionals, adolescents, and their families.

EATING DISORDERS

Anorexia Nervosa and Related Eating Disorders, Inc.
www.anred.com

An association of anorexics and bulimics, their families and friends, and concerned professionals that provides information about the disorders.

SEXUAL BEHAVIOR

Alan Guttmacher Institute
www.agi-usa.org/home.html

Compiles statistics on sexual behavior and fertility and promotes public policy related to birth control. Publishes the journal Family Planning Perspectives, *which includes articles on teenage sexual behavior, pregnancy, and parenthood.*

SEXUALLY TRANSMITTED DISEASE (STD)

American Social Health Association
www.sunsite.unc.edu/asha

A national health agency that works to expand research, provide information to communities, and improve public health policy related to STD. Operates the Herpes Resource Center, a support program for sufferers of incurable genital herpes.

ADOLESCENT PREGNANCY AND PARENTHOOD

National Campaign to Prevent Teen Pregnancy
www.teenpregnancy.org

A nonprofit initiative aimed at reducing the adolescent pregnancy rate by one-third by the year 2005.

SUBSTANCE ABUSE

Cocaine Anonymous World Services Online
www.ca.org

An organization devoted to helping adolescents and adults recover from addiction to cocaine and other mood-altering drugs.

(See page 453 for additional organizations related to alcohol abuse.)

DROPOUT PREVENTION

National Dropout Prevention Center
www.dropoutprevention.org

A center offering information on school dropout prevention and identifying high-risk youth. Provides consultation and referral services to school systems, agencies, and associations dealing with the dropout problem.

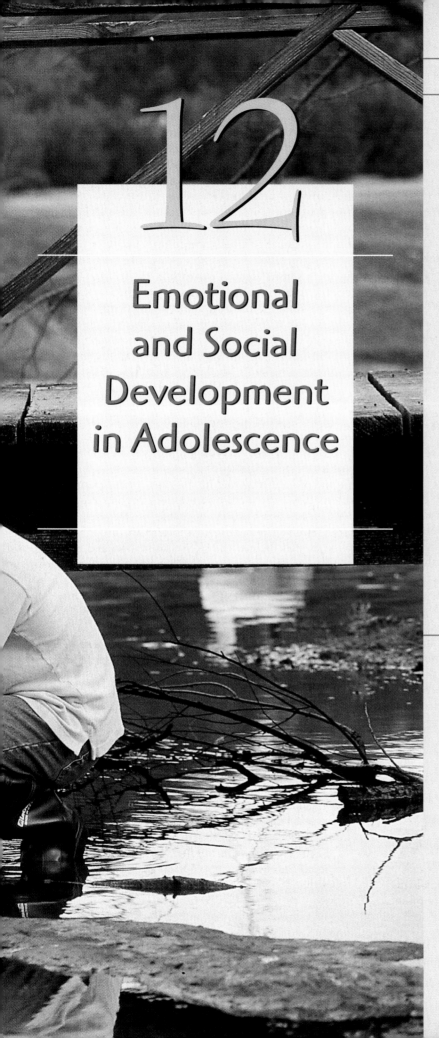

12

Emotional and Social Development in Adolescence

■ *These teenagers test a polluted Texas tributary for signs of life. At adolescence, young people develop a stronger sense of connection to their community and culture. As they search for personally meaningful values to have faith in, they bring a sense of idealism and hopefulness to society. (Photo courtesy: B. Daemmrich/The Image Works)*

Louis sat on the grassy hillside overlooking the high school, waiting for his best friend, Darryl, to arrive from his fourth-period class. The two boys often met at noontime and then crossed the street to have lunch at a nearby hamburger stand.

Watching as hundreds of students poured onto the school grounds, Louis reflected on what Mrs. Kemp had said in government class that day. "Suppose by chance I *had* been born in the People's Republic of China. I'd be sitting here, speaking a different language, being called by a different name, and thinking about the world in different ways. Gosh, I am who I am through some quirk of fate," Louis pondered.

Louis awoke from his thoughts with a start. Darryl was standing in front of him. "Hey, dreamer! I've been shouting and waving from the bottom of the hill for five minutes. How come you're so spaced out lately, Louis?" Darryl asked as they walked off.

"Oh, just wondering about stuff—like what I want, what I believe in. My older brother Jules—I envy him. He seems to know just where he's going. Most of the time, I'm up in the air about it. You ever feel that way?"

"Yeah, a lot," admitted Darryl, looking at Louis seriously as they approached the hamburger stand. "I often think—What am I really like? Who will I become?"

Louis and Darryl's introspective remarks are signs of a major reorganization of the self at adolescence: the development of identity. Both young people are attempting to formulate who they are—their personal values and the directions they will pursue in life. We begin this chapter with Erikson's account of identity development and the research it has stimulated on teenagers' thoughts and feelings about themselves. The quest for identity extends to many aspects of development. We will see how a sense of cultural belonging, moral understanding, and masculine and feminine self-images are refined during the teenage years. And as parent–child relationships are revised and young people become increasingly independent of the family, friendships and peer networks become crucial contexts for bridging the gap between childhood and adulthood. Our chapter concludes with a discussion of several serious adjustment problems of adolescence: depression, suicide, and delinquency.

ERIKSON'S THEORY: IDENTITY VERSUS IDENTITY CONFUSION

Erikson (1950, 1968) was the first to recognize **identity** as the major personality achievement of adolescence and as a crucial step toward becoming a productive, happy adult. Constructing an identity involves defining who you are, what you value, and the directions you choose to pursue in life. One expert described it as an explicit theory of oneself as a rational agent—one who acts on the basis of reason, takes responsibility for those actions, and can explain them (Moshman, 1998). This search for what is true and real about the self is the driving force behind many new commitments—to a sexual orientation; to a vocation; to interpersonal relationships and community involvement; to ethnic group membership; and to moral, political, religious, and cultural ideals.

Erikson called the psychological conflict of adolescence **identity versus identity confusion.** He believed that successful outcomes of earlier stages pave the way toward its positive resolution. For example, young people who reach adolescence with a weak sense of *trust* have trouble finding ideals to have faith in. Those with little *autonomy* or *initiative* do not engage in the active exploration required to choose among alternatives. And those who lack a sense of *industry* fail to select a vocation that matches their interests and skills.

Although the seeds of identity formation are planted early, not until adolescence do young people become absorbed in this task. According to Erikson, in complex societies, teenagers experience an *identity crisis*—a temporary period of confusion and distress as they experiment with alternatives before settling on values and goals. Adolescents who go through a process of inner soul-searching eventually arrive at a mature identity. They sift through characteristics that defined the self in childhood and combine them with new commitments. Then they mold these into a solid inner core that provides a sense of sameness as they move through different roles in daily life. Once formed, identity continues to be refined in adulthood as people reevaluate earlier commitments and choices.

Current theorists agree with Erikson that questioning of the self's values, plans, and priorities is necessary for a mature identity, but they no longer refer to this process as a "crisis" (Grotevant, 1998). For some young people, identity development is traumatic and disturbing, but for most it is not. *Exploration* better describes the typical adolescent's gradual, uneventful approach to identity formation. The many daily choices that teenagers make—"whom to date, whether or not to break up, having intercourse, taking drugs, going to college or working, which college, what major, studying or playing, being politically active"—and the reasons for them are gradually put together into an organized self-structure (Marcia, 1980, p. 161; Moshman, 1999).

The negative outcome of Erikson's fifth stage is *identity confusion.* Some adolescents appear shallow and directionless, either because earlier conflicts have been resolved negatively or because society restricts their choices to ones that do not match their abilities and desires. As a result, they are unprepared for the psychological challenges of adulthood. For example, individuals find it difficult to risk the self-

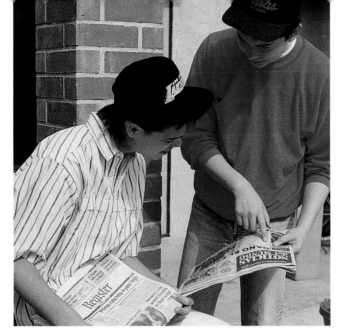

■ *As these adolescents exchange opinions about a recent news event, they become more aware of a diversity of viewpoints. Exploring competing beliefs and values is essential for mature identity development—clarifying what is real and true about the self. (Photo courtesy: Tony Freeman/PhotoEdit)*

sharing involved in Erikson's young adult stage—*intimacy*—if they do not have a firm sense of self (an identity) to which they can return.

Is there research to support Erikson's ideas about identity development? In the following sections, we will see that adolescents go about the task of defining themselves in ways that closely match Erikson's description.

SELF-DEVELOPMENT

During adolescence, cognitive advances transform the young person's vision of the self into a more complex, well-organized, and consistent picture. Changes in self-concept and self-esteem set the stage for development of a unified personal identity.

CHANGES IN SELF-CONCEPT

Recall that by the end of middle childhood, children describe themselves in terms of personality traits, such as "I'm smart," "I'm shy," or "I'm honest." This change permits young people to link their past, present, and future selves. But the self-statements of early adolescents are not interconnected, and often they include contradictory descriptions. For example, 12- to 14-year-olds might mention such opposing traits as "smart" and "dumb" or "shy" and "outgoing." These disparities result from social pressures to display different selves in different relationships—with parents, classmates, close friends, and romantic partners (Harter, 1998).

By middle to late adolescence, the capacity for abstract thinking permits teenagers to combine their various traits into an organized system. And they begin to use qualifiers ("I have a *fairly* quick temper," "I'm not *thoroughly* honest"), revealing their awareness that psychological qualities often change from one situation to the next. Older adolescents also add integrating principles, which make sense out of formerly troublesome contradictions. For example, one young person remarked, "I'm very adaptable. When I'm around my friends, who think that what I say is important, I'm very talkative; but around my family I'm quiet because they're never interested enough to really listen to me" (Damon, 1990, p. 88).

Teenagers' self-statements also reflect their concern about being liked and viewed in a positive light by others. Compared with school-age children, they place more emphasis on social virtues, such as being friendly, considerate, kind, and cooperative (Damon & Hart, 1988). In addition, personal and moral values appear as key themes in older adolescents' self-concepts. As adolescents' views of themselves start to include enduring beliefs and plans, they move toward the unity of self that is central to identity development.

CHANGES IN SELF-ESTEEM

Self-esteem, the evaluative side of self-concept, continues to differentiate during adolescence. Besides academic competence, social self-worth, and physical ability, new dimensions reflecting important concerns of this period are added: close friendship, romantic appeal, and job competence (Harter, 1990).

Level of self-esteem also changes. Turn back to Figure 11.8 on page 379, and you will see that except for a temporary decline associated with school transitions, self-esteem rises for most adolescents (Nottelmann, 1987). This steady increase is yet another reason that modern researchers question the assumption that adolescence is a time of emotional turmoil. To the contrary, for most young people, becoming an adolescent leads to feelings of pride and self-confidence (Powers, Hauser, & Kilner, 1989).

Of course, as we saw in Chapter 11, adolescents vary widely in self-esteem. Those who are off-time in pubertal development, who are heavy drug users, or who fail in school feel poorly about themselves. In addition, of those young people whose self-esteem drops in adolescence, most are girls (Block & Robins, 1994; Zimmerman et al., 1997). Recall that girls worry more about their physical appearance and feel more insecure about their abilities.

At the same time, the contexts in which young people find themselves can modify these group differences. Authoritative parenting (warmth and reasonable maturity demands) continues to predict high self-esteem in adolescence, just as it did in childhood (Steinberg, Darling, & Fletcher, 1995). In contrast, when support from adults or peers is *conditional* (withheld unless the young person meets overly

■ *These teenagers volunteered to repaint Valencia Gardens, a housing project for low-income families in San Francisco. Community service activities like this one undoubtedly contribute to the rise in self-esteem that characterizes most young people during adolescence. (Photo courtesy: Gary Wagner/Stock Boston)*

high standards), teenagers frequently engage in behaviors they consider "false"—not representative of their true self. Adolescents who often "act phony" to protect themselves from disapproval suffer from low self-esteem, depression, and pessimism about the future (Harter et al., 1996). Finally, teenagers who attend schools or live in neighborhoods where their SES or ethnic group is well represented have fewer self-esteem problems (Rosenberg, 1988). Schools and communities that are accepting of the young person's cultural heritage support a positive sense of self-worth as well as a solid and secure personal identity.

PATHS TO IDENTITY

Adolescents' well-organized self-descriptions and expanded sense of self-esteem provide the cognitive foundation for identity development. Using a clinical interviewing procedure, researchers group adolescents into four categories, which show their progress in formulating a mature identity (Marcia, 1980). Table 12.1 summarizes these *identity statuses:* **identity achievement, moratorium, identity foreclosure,** and **identity diffusion.**

Adolescents often shift from one status to another until identity is achieved. For example, in junior high school, Louis accepted his parents' religious beliefs (foreclosure) and gave only passing thought to a vocational direction (diffusion). In high school, he began to explore these identity issues. Many young people start out as identity-foreclosed and diffused, but by late adolescence they have moved toward moratorium and identity achievement (Archer, 1982; Meilman, 1979). College triggers increased exploration, exposing young people to new career options and lifestyles. Most teenagers who go to work after high school graduation settle on a self-definition earlier than do college-bound youths (Munro & Adams, 1977). But those who find it difficult to realize their occupational goals because of lack of training or vocational choices are at risk for identity diffusion (Archer, 1989).

TABLE 12.1

The Four Identity Statuses

IDENTITY STATUS	DESCRIPTION	EXAMPLE
Identity achievement	Having already explored alternatives, identity-achieved individuals are committed to a clearly formulated set of self-chosen values and goals. They feel a sense of psychological well-being, of sameness through time, and of knowing where they are going.	When asked how willing she would be to give up going into her chosen occupation if something better came along, Darla responded, "Well, I might, but I doubt it. I've thought long and hard about law as a career. I'm pretty certain it's for me."
Moratorium	The word *moratorium* means "delay or holding pattern." These individuals have not yet made definite commitments. They are in the process of exploration—gathering information and trying out activities, with the desire to find values and goals to guide their lives.	When asked if he had ever had doubts about his religious beliefs, Ramon said, "Yes, I guess I'm going through that right now. I just don't see how there can be a God and yet so much evil in the world."
Identity foreclosure	Identity-foreclosed individuals have committed themselves to values and goals without taking time to explore alternatives. Instead, they accept a ready-made identity that authority figures (usually parents but sometimes teachers, religious leaders, or romantic partners) have chosen for them.	When asked if she had ever reconsidered her political beliefs, Hillary answered, "No, not really, our family is pretty much in agreement on these things."
Identity diffusion	Identity-diffused individuals lack clear direction. They are not committed to values and goals, nor actively trying to reach them. They may have never explored alternatives or have found the task too threatening and overwhelming.	When asked about his attitude toward nontraditional gender roles, Joel responded, "Oh, I don't know. It doesn't make much difference to me. I can take it or leave it."

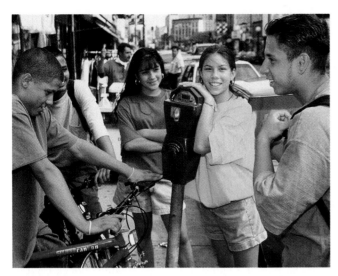

■ *These Hispanic teenagers congregate in a city neighborhood where their ethnicity is well represented. Schools and communities that are accepting of the young person's cultural heritage promote high self-esteem. (Photo courtesy: Don Smetzer/Stone)*

At one time, researchers thought that adolescent girls postponed establishing an identity and focused instead on Erikson's sixth stage, intimacy development. Girls do show more sophisticated reasoning than boys in identity areas related to intimacy, such as sexuality and family versus career priorities. Otherwise, the process and timing of identity formation are the same for both sexes (Archer & Waterman, 1994).

IDENTITY STATUS AND PSYCHOLOGICAL WELL-BEING

Identity achievement and moratorium are psychologically healthy routes to a mature self-definition, whereas foreclosure and diffusion are maladaptive. Young people who are identity achieved or actively exploring have a higher sense of self-esteem, are more likely to think abstractly and critically, report greater similarity between their ideal self (what they hoped to become) and their real self, and are advanced in moral reasoning (Josselson, 1994; Marcia et al., 1993). Also, identity-achieved individuals are less self-conscious and self-focused and more secure about revealing their true selves to others (O'Connor, 1995).

Adolescents who get stuck in either foreclosure or diffusion have adjustment difficulties. Foreclosed individuals tend to be dogmatic, inflexible, and intolerant. Some use their commitments defensively, regarding any difference of opinion as a threat (Kroger, 1995). Most are afraid of rejection by people on whom they depend for affection and self-esteem. A few foreclosed teenagers who are alienated from their families and society may join cults or other extremist groups, uncritically adopting a way of life that is different from their past.

Long-term diffused teenagers are the least mature in identity development. They typically entrust themselves to luck or fate, have an "I don't care" attitude, and tend to go along with whatever the "crowd" is doing at the moment. As a result, they are most likely to use and abuse drugs. At the heart of their apathy is often a sense of hopelessness about the future (Archer & Waterman, 1990). Ethnic and religious prejudices are typical of both foreclosed and diffused young people. The foreclosed teenager tends to pick them up from authority figures, the diffused young person from peers (Streitmatter & Pate, 1989).

FACTORS THAT AFFECT IDENTITY DEVELOPMENT

Adolescent identity is the beginning of a lifelong process of refinement in personal commitments. Whenever the individual or his or her situational context changes, the possibility for reformulating identity exists (Grotevant, 1998). A wide variety of factors influence identity development.

Personality—in particular, a flexible, open-minded approach to grappling with competing beliefs and values—fosters a mature identity. Adolescents who assume that absolute truth is always attainable tend to be foreclosed, whereas those who lack confidence about ever knowing anything with certainty are more often identity diffused or in a state of moratorium. Adolescents who appreciate that rational criteria can be used to choose among alternative visions are likely to be identity achieved (Boyes & Chandler, 1992).

Recall from Chapter 6 that toddlers with a healthy sense of self have parents who provide both emotional support and freedom to explore. Similarly, when the family serves as a "secure base" from which teenagers can confidently move out into the wider world, identity development is enhanced. Adolescents who feel attached to their parents but also free to voice their own opinions tend to be identity achieved or in a state of moratorium (Grotevant & Cooper, 1985, 1998; Lapsley, Rice, & FitzGerald, 1990). Foreclosed teenagers usually have close bonds with parents, but they lack opportunities for healthy separation. And diffused young people report the lowest levels of warm, open communication at home (Papini, 1994).

Identity development also depends on schools and communities offering rich and varied opportunities for exploration. Erikson (1968) noted that it is "the inability to settle on an occupational identity which most disturbs young people" (p. 132). Classrooms that promote high-level thinking, extracurricular and community activities that enable teenagers to take on responsible roles, teachers and counselors who encourage low-SES students to go to college, and vocational training programs that immerse young people in the real world of adult work foster identity achievement (Cooper, 1998). A chance to talk with adults and older peers who have worked through identity questions can also be helpful (Waterman, 1989).

Finally, the larger cultural context and historical time period affect identity development. Among today's adolescents, exploration and commitment take place earlier in vocational choice and gender-role preference than in religious and political values. Yet 30 years ago, when the Vietnam War divided Americans, political beliefs took shape sooner (Archer, 1989; Waterman, 1985). Societal forces are also responsible for the special problems that gay and lesbian youths (see Chapter 11) and some ethnic minority young people face in forming a secure personal identity (see the Variations box on the following page). The Caregiving Concerns table below summarizes ways that adults can support adolescents in their quest for identity.

ASK YOURSELF . . .

■ *Review the conversation between Louis and Darryl in the opening of this chapter. What identity status best characterizes the two boys? Explain your answer.*

Summarize personal characteristics associated with identity achievement, and explain how they promote favorable cognitive, emotional, and social development. Why is identity development a lifelong process?

CAREGIVING CONCERNS

Ways Adults Can Support Healthy Identity Development in Adolescence

STRATEGY	RATIONALE
Warm, open communication	Provides both emotional support and freedom to explore values and goals
Discussions at home and school that promote high-level thinking	Encourages rational and deliberate selection among competing beliefs and values
Opportunities to participate in extracurricular activities and vocational training programs	Permits young people to explore the real world of adult work
Opportunities to talk with adults and peers who have worked through identity questions	Offers models of identity achievement and advice on how to resolve identity concerns
Opportunities to explore ethnic heritage and learn about other cultures in an atmosphere of respect	Fosters identity achievement in all areas and ethnic tolerance, which supports the identity explorations of others

MORAL DEVELOPMENT

S abrina sat at the kitchen table reading the Sunday newspaper, her face wide-eyed with interest. "You gotta see this," she said to Louis, who sat munching cereal. Sabrina held up a page of large photos showing a 70-year-old woman standing in her home. The floor and furniture were piled with stacks of newspapers, cardboard boxes, tin cans, glass containers, food, and clothing. The plaster on the walls was crumbling, the pipes in the house were frozen, and the sinks, toilet, and furnace no longer worked. The headline read: "Loretta Perry: My Life Is None of Their Business."

"Look what they're trying to do to this poor lady," exclaimed Sabrina. "They wanna throw her out of her house and tear it down! Those city inspectors must not care about anyone. Here it says, 'Mrs. Perry has devoted much of her life to doing favors for people.' Why doesn't someone help *her?*"

"Sabrina, you missed the point," Louis responded. "Mrs. Perry is in violation of 30 building code standards. The law says you're supposed to keep your house clean and in good repair."

"But Louis, she's old and she needs help. She says her life will be over if they destroy her home."

"The building inspectors aren't being mean, Sabrina. Mrs. Perry is stubborn. She refuses to obey the law. By not taking care of her house, she's not just a threat to herself. She's a danger to her neighbors, too. Suppose her house caught on fire. You can't live around other people and say your life is nobody's business."

"You don't just knock someone's home down," Sabrina replied angrily. "Where're her friends and neighbors in all this? Why aren't they over there fixing up that house? You're like those building inspectors, Louis. You've got no feeling!"

Louis and Sabrina's disagreement over Mrs. Perry's plight illustrates tremendous advances in moral understanding. Changes in cognition and social experience permit adolescents to better understand larger social structures—societal institutions and lawmaking systems—that govern moral responsibilities. As their grasp of social arrangements expands, adolescents' ideas about what ought to be done when the needs and desires of people are in conflict also change, toward increasingly just, fair, and balanced solutions to moral problems (Gibbs, 1995).

PIAGET'S THEORY OF MORAL DEVELOPMENT

The most influential approach to moral development is Lawrence Kohlberg's cognitive-developmental perspective, which was inspired by Piaget's early work on the moral judgment of the child. Piaget (1932/1965) saw children as moving through two broad stages of moral understanding.

IDENTITY DEVELOPMENT AMONG ETHNIC MINORITY ADOLESCENTS

Most Caucasian-American adolescents are aware of their cultural ancestry, but it is not a matter of intense concern for them. Since the values of their home lives are consistent with those of mainstream American culture, ethnicity does not prompt intense identity exploration (Phinney, 1993).

But for teenagers who are members of minority groups, ethnicity is central to the quest for identity, and it presents difficult, sometimes overwhelming challenges. As they develop cognitively and become more sensitive to feedback from the social environment, minority youths become painfully aware that they are targets of discrimination and inequality. The discovery complicates their efforts to develop a sense of cultural belonging and a set of personally meaningful life goals. One African-American journalist, looking back on his own adolescence, remarked, "If you were black, you didn't quite measure up.... [Y]ou didn't see any black people doing certain things, and you couldn't rationalize it. I mean, you don't think it out but you say, 'Well, it must mean that white people are better than we are. Smarter, brighter—whatever'" (Monroe, Goldman, & Smith, 1988, pp. 98–99).

Minority youths often feel caught between the standards of the larger society and the traditions of their culture of origin. Some respond by rejecting aspects of their ethnic background. In one study, Asian-American 15- to 17-year-olds were more likely than blacks and Hispanics to hold negative attitudes toward their subcultural group. Perhaps the absence of a social movement stressing ethnic pride of the kind available to black and Hispanic teenagers underlies this finding (Phinney, 1989). Some parents are overly restrictive of their teenagers out of fear that assimilation into the larger society will undermine their cultural traditions, and their youngsters rebel. One Southeast-Asian refugee described his

daughter's behavior: "She complains about going to the Lao temple on the weekend and instead joined a youth group in a neighborhood Christian Church. She refused to wear traditional dress on the Lao New Year. The girl is setting a very bad example for her younger sisters and brothers" (Nidorf, 1985, pp. 422–423).

Other minority teenagers react to years of shattered self-esteem, school failure, and barriers to success in the American mainstream by defining themselves in contrast to majority values. A Mexican-American teenager who had given up on school commented, "Mexicans don't have a chance to go on to college and make something of themselves." Another, responding to the question of what it takes to be a successful adult, pointed to his uncle, leader of a local gang, as an example (Matute-Bianchi, 1986, pp. 250–251).

The challenges of blending mainstream and ethnic-group values are apparent in the experiences of academically successful African-American adolescents. To avoid being labeled white by their peers, they may reduce their academic effort or conceal their accomplishments. Because it is painful and confusing, minority high school students often dodge the task of forming an ethnic identity. Many are diffused or foreclosed on ethnic identity issues (Markstrom-Adams & Adams, 1995).

How can society help minority adolescents resolve identity conflicts constructively? A variety of efforts are relevant, including

- reducing poverty
- promoting effective parenting, in which children and adolescents benefit from family ethnic pride yet are encouraged to explore the meaning of ethnicity in their own lives
- ensuring that schools respect minority youths' native languages and unique learning styles

■ *These Native-American adolescents dress in traditional costume in preparation for demonstrating a ceremonial dance to citizens of a small Wyoming town. When minority youths encounter respect for their cultural heritage in schools and communities, they are more likely to retain ethnic values and customs as an important part of their identities. (Photo courtesy: John Eastcott/Yva Momatiuk/The Image Works)*

- fostering multicultural knowledge, contact, and respect between ethnic groups in integrated schools and neighborhoods (García Coll & Magnuson, 1997)

A secure ethnic identity is associated with better psychological adjustment. But forming a **bicultural identity**—by exploring and adopting values from *both* the adolescent's subculture and the dominant culture—offers added benefits. Biculturally identified adolescents tend to be achieved in other areas of identity as well. They also have a higher sense of self-esteem, a greater sense of mastery over the environment, and more positive relations with members of other ethnic groups (Phinney & Kohatsu, 1997). In sum, ethnic-identity achievement enhances many aspects of emotional and social development.

The first stage is **heteronomous morality,** which extends from about 5 to 10 years of age. The word *heteronomous* means "under the authority of another." As the term suggests, children of this stage view rules as handed down by authorities (God, parents, and teachers), as having a permanent existence, as unchangeable, and as requiring strict obedience. Also, in judging an act's wrongness, they focus on objective consequences rather than intent to do harm. When asked to decide which child is naughtier—John, who accidentally breaks 15 cups while on his way to dinner, or Henry, who breaks 1 cup while stealing some jam—a 6- or 7-year-old chooses John.

According to Piaget, around age 10 children make the transition to the stage of **autonomous morality.** They realize that people can have different perspectives on moral matters and that intentions, not just outcomes, should serve as the basis for judging behavior. Piaget believed that improvements in perspective taking, which result from cognitive development and opportunities to interact with peers, are responsible for this change. Autonomous individuals no longer view rules as fixed. Instead, they regard them as socially agreed-on principles that can be revised when there is a need to do so. In creating and changing rules, older children and adolescents use a standard of fairness called *reciprocity.* They express the same concern for the welfare of others as they do for themselves. Most of us are familiar with reciprocity in the form of the Golden Rule: "Do unto others as you would have others do unto you."

Take a moment to consider Piaget's theory in light of what you learned about moral development in earlier chapters (return to pages 259–260 and 326–327). You will see that his account of young children as rigid, external, and focused on physical consequences underestimates their moral capacities. Nevertheless, Piaget's theory of morality, like his cognitive theory, does describe the general direction of moral development. Although children are more sophisticated moral thinkers than Piaget made them out to be, they are not as advanced as adolescents and adults. Over the past two decades, Piaget's groundbreaking work has been replaced by Kohlberg's more comprehensive theory, which regards moral development as extending beyond childhood into adolescence and adulthood in a six-stage sequence.

KOHLBERG'S EXTENSION OF PIAGET'S THEORY

Kohlberg used a clinical interviewing procedure to study the development of moral understanding. He gave children and adolescents *moral dilemmas*—stories that present a conflict between two moral values—and asked them what the main actor should do and why. The best known of these is the "Heinz dilemma," which presents a choice between the value of obeying the law (not stealing) and the value of human life (saving a dying person):

> In Europe a woman was near death from cancer. There was one drug that the doctors thought might save her. A druggist in the same town had discovered it, but he was charging ten times what the drug cost him to make. The sick woman's husband, Heinz, went to everyone he knew to borrow the money, but he could only get together half of what it cost. The druggist refused to sell it cheaper or let Heinz pay later. So Heinz got desperate and broke into the man's store to steal the drug for his wife. Should Heinz have done that? Why? (paraphrased from Colby et al., 1983, p. 77)

Kohlberg emphasized that it is *the way an individual reasons* about the dilemma, not *the content of the response* (whether to steal or not to steal), that determines moral maturity. Individuals who believe Heinz should take the drug and those who think he should not can be found at each of Kohlberg's first four stages. Only at the two highest stages are moral reasoning and content integrated into a coherent ethical system (Kohlberg, Levine, & Hewer, 1983). Given a choice between obeying the law and preserving individual rights, the most advanced moral thinkers support individual rights (in the Heinz dilemma, stealing the drug to save a life). Does this remind you of adolescents' effort to formulate a sound, well-organized set of personal values in identity development? According to some theorists, the development of identity and moral understanding are part of the same process.

■ KOHLBERG'S STAGES OF MORAL UNDERSTANDING. Kohlberg organized his six stages into three general levels of moral development. He believed that moral understanding is promoted by the same factors Piaget thought

■ *This teenager's efforts to repair his friend's car may be motivated by his understanding of the Golden Rule: "Do unto others as you would have others do unto you." A sophisticated grasp of reciprocity—expressing the same concern for others as for oneself—contributes to advances in moral understanding in older children and adolescents. (Photo courtesy: Aaron Haupt/Photo Researchers, Inc.)*

TABLE 12.2

Relations Among Kohlberg's Moral, Piaget's Cognitive, and Selman's Perspective-Taking Stages

KOHLBERG'S MORAL STAGE	DESCRIPTION	PIAGET'S COGNITIVE STAGE	SELMAN'S PERSPECTIVE-TAKING STAGE[a]
Punishment and obedience orientation	Fear of authority and avoidance of punishment	Preoperational, early concrete operational	Social-informational
Instrumental purpose orientation	Satisfying personal needs	Concrete operational	Self-reflective
"Good boy–good girl" orientation	Maintaining the affection and approval of friends and relatives	Early formal operational	Third-party
Social-order-maintaining orientation	A duty to uphold laws and rules for their own sake	Formal operational	Societal
Social contract orientation	Fair procedures for changing laws to protect individual rights and the needs of the majority		
Universal ethical principle orientation	Abstract universal principles that are valid for all humanity		

[a] To review these stages, return to Chapter 10, page 325.

were important for cognitive growth: (1) actively grappling with moral issues and noticing weaknesses in one's current reasoning; and (2) advances in perspective taking, which permit individuals to resolve moral conflicts in more effective ways. As Table 12.2 shows, Kohlberg's moral stages are related to Piaget's cognitive and Selman's perspective-taking stages. As we examine Kohlberg's developmental sequence and illustrate it with responses to the Heinz dilemma, look for changes in perspective taking that each stage assumes.

The Preconventional Level. At the **preconventional level,** morality is externally controlled. As in Piaget's heteronomous stage, children accept the rules of authority figures and judge actions by their consequences. Behaviors that result in punishment are viewed as bad and those that lead to rewards are seen as good.

Stage 1: The punishment and obedience orientation. Children at this stage find it difficult to consider two points of view in a moral dilemma. As a result, they ignore peoples' intentions and, instead, focus on fear of authority and avoidance of punishment as reasons for behaving morally.

> *Prostealing:* "If you let your wife die, you will get in trouble. You'll be blamed for not spending the money to help her and there'll be an investigation of you and the druggist for your wife's death." (Kohlberg, 1969, p. 381)

> *Antistealing:* "You shouldn't steal the drug because you'll be caught and sent to jail if you do. If you do get away, [you'd be scared that] the police would catch up with you any minute." (Kohlberg, 1969, p. 381)

Stage 2: The instrumental purpose orientation. Children become aware that people can have different perspectives in a moral dilemma, but this understanding is, at first, very concrete. Individuals view right action as what satisfies their personal needs, and they believe others also act out of self-interest. Reciprocity is understood as equal exchange of favors—"you do this for me and I'll do that for you."

> *Prostealing:* "The druggist can do what he wants and Heinz can do what he wants to do. . . . But if Heinz decides to risk jail to save his wife, it's his life he's risking; he can do what he wants with it. And the same goes for the druggist; it's up to him to decide what he wants to do." (Rest, 1979, p. 26)

> *Antistealing:* "[Heinz] is running more risk than it's worth [to save a wife who is near death]." (Rest, 1979, p. 27)

The Conventional Level. At the **conventional level,** individuals continue to regard conformity to social rules as necessary, but not for reasons of self-interest. They believe that actively maintaining the current social system is important for ensuring positive human relationships and societal order.

Stage 3: The "good boy–good girl" orientation, or the morality of interpersonal cooperation. The desire to obey rules because they promote social harmony first appears in the context of close personal ties. Stage 3 individuals want to maintain the affection and approval of friends and relatives by being a "good person"—trustworthy, loyal, respectful, helpful, and nice. The capacity to view a two-person relationship from the vantage point of an impartial, outside observer supports this new approach to morality. At this stage, the individual understands reciprocity in terms of the Golden Rule.

> *Prostealing:* "No one will think you're bad if you steal the drug, but your family will think you're an inhuman husband if you don't. If you let your wife die, you'll never be able to look anyone in the face again." (Kohlberg, 1969, p. 381)

Antistealing: "It isn't just the druggist who will think you're a criminal, everyone else will too. After you steal it, you'll feel bad thinking how you've brought dishonor on your family and yourself; you won't be able to face anyone again." (Kohlberg, 1969, p. 381)

Stage 4: The social-order-maintaining orientation. At this stage, the individual takes into account a larger perspective—that of societal laws. Moral choices no longer depend on close ties to others. Instead, rules must be enforced in the same evenhanded fashion for everyone, and each member of society has a personal duty to uphold them. The Stage 4 individual believes that laws cannot be disobeyed under any circumstances because they are vital for ensuring societal order.

Prostealing: "He should steal it. Heinz has a duty to protect his wife's life; it's a vow he took in marriage. But it's wrong to steal, so he would have to take the drug with the idea of paying the druggist for it and accepting the penalty for breaking the law later."

Antistealing: "It's a natural thing for Heinz to want to save his wife, but . . . [y]ou have to follow the rules regardless of how you feel or regardless of the special circumstances. Even if his wife is dying, it's still his duty as a citizen to obey the law. No one else is allowed to steal, why should he be? If everyone starts breaking the law in a jam, there'd be no civilization, just crime and violence." (Rest, 1979, p. 30)

The Postconventional or Principled Level. Individuals at the **postconventional level** move beyond unquestioning support for the laws and rules of their own society. They define morality in terms of abstract principles and values that apply to all situations and societies.

Stage 5: The social contract orientation. At Stage 5, individuals regard laws and rules as flexible instruments for furthering human purposes. They can imagine alternatives to their social order, and they emphasize fair procedures for interpreting and changing the law when there is a good reason to do so. When laws are consistent with individual rights and the interests of the majority, each person follows them because of a *social contract orientation*—free and willing participation in the system because it brings about more good for people than if it did not exist.

Prostealing: "Although there is a law against stealing, the law wasn't meant to violate a person's right to life. Taking the drug does violate the law, but Heinz is justified in stealing in this instance. If Heinz is prosecuted for stealing, the law needs to be reinterpreted to take into account situations in which it goes against people's natural right to keep on living."

Stage 6: The universal ethical principle orientation. At this highest stage, right action is defined by self-chosen ethical principles of conscience that are valid for all humanity, regardless of law and social agreement. These values are abstract, not concrete moral rules like the Ten Commandments. Stage 6 individuals typically mention such principles as equal consideration of the claims of all human beings and respect for the worth and dignity of each person.

Prostealing: "If Heinz does not do everything he can to save his wife, then he is putting some value higher than the value of life. It doesn't make sense to put respect for property above respect for life itself. [People] could live together without private property at all. Respect for human life and personality is absolute and accordingly [people] have a mutual duty to save one another from dying. (Rest, 1979, p. 37)

■ RESEARCH ON KOHLBERG'S STAGE SEQUENCE. Longitudinal studies provide the most convincing evidence for Kohlberg's stage sequence. With few exceptions, individuals move through the stages in the order that Kohlberg expected (Colby et al., 1983; Walker, 1989; Walker & Taylor, 1991b). A striking finding is that moral development is very slow and gradual. Stages 1 and 2 reasoning decrease in early adolescence, whereas Stage 3 increases through mid-adolescence and then declines. Stage 4 reasoning rises over the teenage years until, by early adulthood, it is the typical response. Few people move beyond it to Stage 5. In fact, postconventional morality is so rare that there is no clear evidence that Kohlberg's Stage 6 actually follows Stage 5. The highest level of moral reasoning is still a matter of speculation and may represent a reflective, philosophical orientation that lies beyond the realm of commonplace, spontaneous moral thought (Gibbs, 1991).

As you read the Heinz dilemma, you probably came up with your own solution to it. Now, try to think of a moral dilemma you recently faced in everyday life. How did you solve it, and did your reasoning fall at the same stage as your thinking about Heinz and his dying wife? Real-life conflicts often elicit moral reasoning below a person's actual capacity because they bring out the many practical considerations involved in an actual moral conflict and mix cognition with intense emotion. In working through everyday moral challenges, people report feeling drained, confused, and torn by temptation. As one person observed, "It's a lot easier to be moral when you have nothing to lose" (Walker et al., 1995, p. 381; Walker & Hennig, 1997).

The influence of situational factors on moral judgments suggests that like Piaget's cognitive stages, Kohlberg's moral stages are best viewed in terms of a loose rather than strict concept of stage. Each individual draws on a range of moral responses, which vary with context. With age, this range shifts upward as less mature moral reasoning is gradually replaced by more advanced moral thought.

ARE THERE SEX DIFFERENCES IN MORAL REASONING?

Real-life moral dilemmas, as mentioned in the previous section, often highlight the contribution of emotion to moral judgment. Return once again to Sabrina and Louis's moral discussion at the beginning of this section. Sabrina's argument focuses on caring and commitment to others. Louis's approach is more impersonal. He looks at the dilemma of Loretta Perry in terms of competing rights and justice.

Carol Gilligan (1982) is the most well-known figure among those who have argued that Kohlberg's theory does not adequately represent the morality of girls and women. She believes that feminine morality emphasizes an "ethic of care" that is devalued in Kohlberg's system. For example, Sabrina's reasoning falls at Stage 3 (because it focuses on the importance of mutual trust and affection between people), whereas Louis's is at Stage 4 (because he emphasizes the value of obeying the law to ensure societal order). According to Gilligan a concern for others as a basis for moral judgment is *different from*, not less valid than, a focus on impersonal rights.

Many studies have tested Gilligan's claim that Kohlberg's approach underestimates the moral maturity of females, and most do not support it (Turiel, 1998). On hypothetical dilemmas as well as everyday moral problems, adolescent and adult females do not fall behind males in development. Also, themes of justice and caring appear in the responses of both sexes, and when girls do raise interpersonal concerns, they are not downscored in Kohlberg's system (Jadack et al., 1995; Kahn, 1992; Walker, 1995). These findings suggest that although Kohlberg emphasized justice rather than caring as the highest of moral ideals, his theory taps both sets of values.

Still, Gilligan's claim that the study of moral development has been limited by too much attention to rights and justice (a "masculine" ideal) and too little attention to care and responsiveness (a "feminine" ideal) is a powerful one. Some evidence shows that although the morality of males and females taps both orientations, females do tend to stress care, whereas males either stress justice or use justice and care equally (Galotti, Kozberg, & Farmer, 1991; Garmon et al., 1996; Wark & Krebs, 1996). The difference appears most often on real-life rather than hypothetical dilemmas. Consequently, it may be largely a function of women's greater involvement in daily activities involving care and concern for others.

ENVIRONMENTAL INFLUENCES ON MORAL REASONING

Many environmental factors promote moral stage change, including child-rearing practices, schooling, peer interaction, and aspects of culture. In line with Kohlberg's belief, growing evidence suggests that the way these experiences work is to present young people with cognitive challenges, which stimulate them to think about moral problems in more complex ways.

■ CHILD-REARING PRACTICES. As in childhood, moral understanding in adolescence is fostered by warm, democratic child rearing and discussions of moral concerns. Teenagers who gain most in moral development have parents who create a supportive atmosphere by listening sensitively, asking clarifying questions, and presenting higher-level reasoning. In contrast, parents who lecture, use threats, or make sarcastic remarks have youngsters who change little or not at all (Boyes & Allen, 1993; Walker & Taylor, 1991a).

■ SCHOOLING. Years of schooling completed is one of the most powerful predictors of moral development. Longitudinal research reveals that moral reasoning advances in late adolescence and early adulthood only as long as a person enters and remains in college (Rest & Narvaez, 1991; Speicher, 1994). Perhaps higher education has a strong impact on moral development because it introduces young people to social issues that extend beyond personal relationships to entire political and social groups. Consistent with this idea, college students who report more academic perspective-taking opportunities (for example, classes that emphasize open discussion of opinions) and who indicate that they have become more aware of social diversity tend to be advanced in moral reasoning (Mason & Gibbs, 1993).

■ PEER INTERACTION. Many studies confirm Piaget's belief that interaction among peers, who confront one another with differing viewpoints, promotes moral understanding. But peer interaction must have certain features to be effective. Look back at Sabrina and Louis's argument over the plight of Loretta Perry on page 394. Each teenager directly confronts and criticizes the other's statements, and emotionally intense expressions of disagreement occur. Peer discussions like this lead to much greater stage change

■ *Intense, animated discussions about moral issues in which peers confront and criticize each other's statements lead to gains in moral understanding. (Photo courtesy: Jeff Greenberg/Photo Researchers, Inc.)*

than do those in which adolescents state their opinions in a disorganized, uninvolved way (Berkowitz & Gibbs, 1983; Haan, Aerts, & Cooper, 1985).

Nevertheless, conflict resolution, rather than conflict per se, may be the feature of peer disagreements that stimulates moral development. Peers typically require one another to justify their actions, which reduces conflict. When young people engage in negotiation and compromise, they realize that social life can be based on cooperation between equals rather than authority relations (Killen & Nucci, 1995). Recall from Chapter 10 that within friendships, conflicts often arise but are worked out collaboratively. The mutuality of friendship, which fosters decisions based on consensual agreement, may contribute importantly to moral development.

■ CULTURE. Young people in industrialized nations move through Kohlberg's stages more quickly and advance to higher levels than do individuals in simpler societies, who rarely move beyond Stage 3. In tribal and village cultures, moral cooperation is based on direct relations between people (Miller, 1997). Laws and government institutions do not exist to regulate it. Yet Stage 4 to 6 reasoning depends on an understanding of the role of larger societal structures in resolving moral conflict (Snarey, 1995).

In cultures in which young people participate in the institutions of their society at early ages, moral development is advanced. For example, on *kibbutzim*, small but technologically advanced agricultural settlements in Israel, children receive training in the governance of their community in middle childhood. By third grade, they mention more concerns about societal laws and rules when discussing moral conflicts than do Israeli city-reared or American children (Fuchs et al., 1986). During adolescence and young adulthood, a greater percentage of kibbutz than American individuals reach Kohlberg's Stages 4 and 5 (Snarey, Reimer, & Kohlberg, 1985).

These cultural differences raise the question of whether Kohlberg's highest stages are culturally universal or limited to Western societies. Researchers have tried to answer this question by studying cultures just as complex as Western nations but guided by very different religious and philosophical traditions. In one investigation, adolescents and adults in India showed the same pattern of movement through Kohlberg's stages as their American agemates, and just as many or more reached the postconventional level. Still, the East Indian participants often dealt with moral conflicts in ways that did not fit neatly into Kohlberg's scheme. For example, many stated that moral problems (such as Heinz's) cannot be solved at the level of a single individual's conscience. Instead, their resolution is the responsibility of the entire society (Vasudev & Hummel, 1987). Kohlberg's theory does seem to tap an important universal dimension of morality—a focus on rights and justice. At the same time, it does not capture all aspects of moral thinking in every culture.

■ *Young people growing up on Israeli kibbutzim receive training in the governance of their community at an early age. As a result, they understand the role of societal laws in resolving moral conflict and are advanced in moral reasoning. (Photo courtesy: Louis Goldman/Photo Researchers)*

■ MORAL REASONING AND BEHAVIOR

A final question about moral development concerns the relation between moral reasoning and behavior. If people do not act in accord with their principles, then their morality must be questioned. Kohlberg believed that moral thought and action come closer together at the higher levels of moral understanding. Mature moral thinkers realize that behaving in line with their beliefs is an important part of creating a just social world (Gibbs, 1995). Consistent with this idea, higher-stage individuals more often engage in prosocial acts, such as helping, sharing, and defending victims of injustice. They are also more honest. For example, they are less likely to cheat on assignments and tests in school (Harris, Mussen, & Rutherford, 1976).

Yet even though a clear connection between advanced moral reasoning and action exists, it is only moderate. As we saw in earlier chapters, moral behavior is influenced by many factors besides cognition, including the emotions of empathy and guilt and a long history of experiences that affect moral decision making. Researchers have yet to discover how all these complex facets of morality work together (Blasi, 1990).

GENDER TYPING

As Sabrina entered adolescence, some aspects of her thinking and behavior became more gender typed. For example, she began to place more emphasis on excelling in the traditionally feminine subjects of language, art, and music than in math and science. And when with peers, Sabrina worried about how she should walk, talk, eat, dress, laugh, and compete, judged according to accepted social standards for maleness and femaleness.

Research suggests that early adolescence is a period of **gender intensification**—increased gender stereotyping of attitudes and behavior (Galambos, Almeida, & Petersen, 1990). Although it occurs in both sexes, gender intensification is stronger for girls, who feel less free to experiment with "cross-gender" activities and behavior than they did in middle childhood (Huston & Alvarez, 1990).

What accounts for gender intensification? Biological, social, and cognitive factors are involved. Puberty magnifies sex differences in appearance, causing teenagers to spend more time thinking about themselves in gender-linked ways. Pubertal changes also prompt gender-typed pressures from others. Parents (especially those with traditional gender-role beliefs) may encourage "gender-appropriate" activities and behavior to a greater extent than they did in middle childhood (Crouter, Manke, & McHale, 1995). And when adolescents start to date, they often become more gender typed as a way of increasing their attractiveness to the other sex (Crockett, 1990). Finally, cognitive changes—in particular, greater concern with what others think—make young teenagers more responsive to gender-typed expectations.

Gender intensification declines by middle to late adolescence, but not all young people move beyond it to the same degree. Teenagers who are encouraged to explore non-gender-typed options and to question the value of gender stereotypes for themselves and society are more likely to build an androgynous gender identity (see Chapter 8, page 266). Overall, androgynous adolescents tend to be psychologically healthier—more self-confident, better liked by peers, and identity achieved (Dusek, 1987; Massad, 1981; Ziegler, Dusek, & Carter, 1984).

Now let's turn to two aspects of adolescent social experience that play powerful roles in the identity, moral, and gender-role processes we have considered: family and peer relations.

THE FAMILY

Franca works as a chemist in a large drug company. Antonio owns and operates a downtown hardware store. Both parents remember Louis's freshman year of high school as a difficult time. Because of a demanding project at work, Franca was away from home many evenings and weekends. Antonio took over in her absence, but when two of his employees quit, he, too, had less time for the family. That year, Louis and two friends used their computer know-how to crack the code of a long-distance telephone service. From the family basement, they made calls around the country. Louis's grades fell, and he often left the house without saying where he was going. Franca and Antonio began to feel uncomfortable about the long hours Louis spent in the basement and their lack of contact with him. Finally, when the telephone company traced the illegal calls to the family's phone number, Franca and Antonio knew they had cause for concern.

Development at adolescence involves striving for **autonomy** on a much higher plane than during the second year of life, when independence first became a major issue for the child. Teenagers seek to establish themselves as separate, self-governing individuals. This means relying more on oneself and less on parents for guidance and decision making (Hill & Holmbeck, 1986; Steinberg & Silverberg, 1986). A major way that teenagers seek greater self-directedness is to shift away from family to peers, with whom they explore courses of action that depart from earlier, more secure and stable patterns. Nevertheless, parent–child relationships remain vital for assisting adolescents in becoming autonomous, responsible individuals.

PARENT–CHILD RELATIONSHIPS

Adolescents require freedom to experiment. Yet as Franca and Antonio's episode with Louis reveals, they also need guidance and, at times, protection from dangerous situations. Think back to what we said earlier about parent–child relationships that foster academic achievement (Chapter 11), identity formation, and moral maturity. Effective parenting of adolescents strikes a balance between connection and separation. Parental warmth and acceptance combined with firm (but not overly restrictive) monitoring of the teenagers' activities is related to many aspects of competence—in adolescents of diverse SES and ethnic backgrounds and family structures (single-parent, two-parent, and stepparent) (Eccles et al., 1997; Herman et al., 1997; Steinberg et al.,

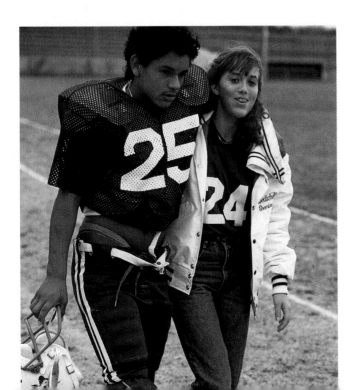

■ *Early adolescence is a period of gender intensification. Puberty magnifies gender differences in appearance, causing teenagers to begin thinking about themselves in gender-linked ways. And when adolescents start to date, they often become more gender typed as a way of increasing their attractiveness to the other sex. (Photo courtesy: Bob Daemmrich/Stock Boston)*

■ *During her first summer away from her family as a foreign exchange student, this teenager will carry with her the memory of her mother's warm, supportive send-off. Adolescent autonomy is effectively achieved in the context of warm parenting that relaxes control in accord with the young person's readiness for new responsibilities. (Photo courtesy: D. Young-Wolff/PhotoEdit)*

1994). Note that these features make up the authoritative style that was so adaptive in childhood as well.

Maintaining an authoritative style during adolescence involves special challenges and adjustments. In Chapter 11, we showed that puberty brings increased parent–child conflict, for both biological and cognitive reasons. Teenagers' improved ability to reason about social relationships adds to family tensions as well. Perhaps you can recall a time when you stopped viewing your parents as all-knowing and perfect and saw them as "just people." Once teenagers *de-idealize* their parents, they no longer bend as easily to parental authority as they did at earlier ages. They begin to regard many matters—such as cleaning their rooms, coming and going from the household, and doing their schoolwork—as their own personal business, whereas parents continue to think of these as shared concerns (Nucci, 1996; Smetana & Asquith, 1994). Disagreements are harder to settle when parents and adolescents approach situations from such different perspectives.

In Chapter 2, we described the family as a *system* that must adapt to changes in its members. Adolescents are not the only family members undergoing a major life transition. Many parents are in their forties and are reassessing their own lives. While teenagers face a boundless future and a wide array of choices, their parents must come to terms with the fact that their own possibilities are narrowing. The pressures experienced by each generation act in opposition to one another (Holmbeck, 1996). Parents often can't understand why the adolescent wants to skip family activities to be with peers. And teenagers fail to appreciate that parents want the family to be together as often as possible because an important stage

in adult life—parenthood—will soon be over. In addition, parents and adolescents—particularly early adolescents—differ sharply on the appropriate age for granting certain responsibilities and privileges, such as control over clothing, school courses, and going out with friends (Collins et al., 1997). Parents typically say the young person is not ready for these signs of independence, whereas teenagers think they should have been granted long ago!

As adolescents move closer to adulthood, the task for parents and children is not one of just separating. They must establish a blend of togetherness and independence. In healthy families, teenagers remain attached to parents and continue to seek their advice, but they do so in a context of greater freedom. By middle to late adolescence, most parents and children achieve this more mature, mutual relationship (Allen et al., 1994; Larson et al., 1996).

F AMILY CIRCUMSTANCES

As Franca and Antonio's experience with Louis reminds us, difficulties at work as well as other life stresses can interfere with nurturant, involved child rearing and (in turn) with children's adjustment at any phase of development. However, we must keep in mind that maternal employment or a dual-earner family does not by itself reduce parental time with teenagers, nor is it harmful to adolescent development (Richards & Duckett, 1994). To the contrary, parents who are financially secure, invested in their work, and content with their marriages usually find it easier to grant their teenagers an appropriate degree of autonomy (Seltzer & Ryff, 1994). When Franca and Antonio's work pressures eased and they realized Louis's need for more support and guidance, his problems subsided.

Less than 10 percent of families with adolescents have seriously troubled relationships—chronic and escalating levels of conflict and repeated arguments over serious issues. Of these, most have difficulties that began in childhood (Paikoff & Brooks-Gunn, 1991). Table 12.3 summarizes family cir-

TABLE 12.3

Family Circumstances with
Implications for Adolescent Adjustment

FAMILY CIRCUMSTANCE	TO REVIEW, TURN TO . . .
Type of family	
Adoptive	Chapter 2, pages 58–59
Divorced and single-parent	Chapter 10, pages 334–336
Blended	Chapter 10, pages 337–338
Employed mother and dual-earner	Chapter 10, page 338
Family conditions	
Child maltreatment	Chapter 8, pages 270–273
	Chapter 10, pages 341–343
Economic hardship	Chapter 2, pages 63–65
Adolescent parenthood	Chapter 11, pages 365–368

cumstances considered in earlier chapters that pose challenges for adolescents. Teenagers who develop well despite family stresses continue to benefit from personal and situational factors that fostered resiliency in earlier years: an appealing, easygoing disposition; high self-esteem; a caring parent who combines warmth with high expectations; and (especially if parental supports are lacking) a bond with an adult outside the family who cares deeply about the adolescent's well-being (Masten & Coatsworth, 1998).

SIBLINGS

Like parent–child relationships, sibling interactions adapt to change at adolescence. As younger siblings mature and become more self-sufficient, they accept less direction from their older brothers and sisters. Consequently, older siblings' influence declines. Sibling relationships also become less intense, in both positive and negative feelings. As teenagers become more involved in friendships and romantic relationships, they invest less time and energy in siblings, who are part of the family from which they are trying to establish autonomy (Furman & Buhrmester, 1992; Stocker & Dunn, 1994). An overly intrusive older sibling, much like a coercive parent, undermines self-esteem and promotes adjustment difficulties (Conger, Conger, & Scaramella, 1997).

Despite a drop in companionship, attachment between siblings, like closeness to parents, remains strong for most young people. The quality of sibling interaction is quite stable over time. Brothers and sisters who established a positive bond in early childhood continue to display greater affection and caring during the teenage years (Dunn, Slomkowski, & Beardsall, 1994).

PEER RELATIONS

As adolescents spend less time with family members, peers become increasingly important. In industrialized nations, young people spend most of each weekday with agemates in school. Teenagers also spend much out-of-class time together, especially in the United States. American teenagers average 18 nonschool hours with peers, compared with 12 hours for Japanese and 9 hours for Taiwanese adolescents (Fuligni & Stevenson, 1995). Higher rates of maternal employment and less demanding academic standards probably account for this difference.

Is the large amount of time American teenagers spend together beneficial or harmful? We will see that adolescent peer relations can be both positive and negative. At their best, peers serve as critical bridges between the family and adult social roles.

FRIENDSHIPS

Adolescents report their most favorable moods when in the company of friends (Larson & Richards, 1991). The number of "best friends" declines from about four to six in early adolescence to one or two in adulthood. At the same time, the nature of the relationship changes. When asked about the meaning of friendship, teenagers stress two characteristics. The first, and most important, is *intimacy*. Adolescents seek psychological closeness, trust, and mutual understanding from their friends—the reason that self-disclosure to friends increases steadily over the adolescent years (see Figure 12.1). Second, more than younger children, teenagers want their friends to be *loyal*—to stick up for them

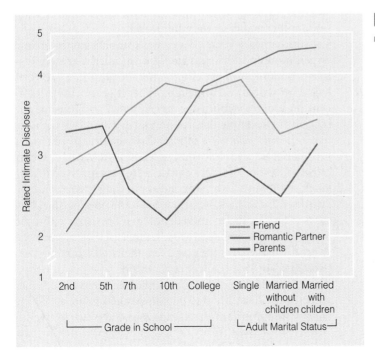

FIGURE 12.1

■ **Age changes in reported self-disclosure to parents and peers, based on data from several studies.** Self-disclosure to friends increases steadily during adolescence, reflecting intimacy as a major basis of friendship. Self-disclosure to romantic partners also rises. However, not until the college years does it surpass intimacy with friends. Self-disclosure to parents declines in early adolescence, a time of mild parent–child conflict. As family relationships readjust to the young person's increasing autonomy, self-disclosure to parents rises. (From D. Buhrmester, 1996, "Need Fulfillment, Interpersonal Competence, and the Developmental Contexts of Early Adolescent Friendship," in W. M. Bukowski, A. F. Newcomb, & W. W. Hartup, Eds., *The Company They Keep: Friendship During Childhood and Adolescence,* New York: Cambridge University Press, p. 168. Reprinted by permission.)

and not to leave them for somebody else (Berndt & Perry, 1990; Buhrmester, 1996).

As frankness and faithfulness increase in friendships, teenagers get to know each other better as personalities. In addition to the many characteristics school-age friends share (see Chapter 10, page 328), adolescent friends are alike in educational aspirations, political beliefs, and willingness to try drugs and engage in law-breaking acts. And they become more similar in these ways over time (Berndt & Keefe, 1995). Cooperation and mutual affirmation between friends also rise, and teenagers are less possessive of their friends than are children (Rubin, Bukowski, & Parker, 1998; Windle, 1994). These changes may reflect greater effort and skill at preserving the relationship as well as increased sensitivity to a friend's needs and desires.

Ask several adolescent girls and boys to describe their close friendships. You are likely to find a consistent sex difference. Emotional closeness is more common in the friendships of girls than boys (Buhrmester & Prager, 1995). Whereas girls frequently get together to "just talk," boys more often gather for an activity—usually sports and competitive games. When boys talk, they often focus on their own or others' achievements (Buhrmester, 1996). Through friendship, girls typically satisfy communal needs, boys status and mastery needs. This does not mean that boys rarely form close friendship ties. They often do, but the quality of their friendships is more variable. The intimacy of boys' friendships is related to gender identity. Androgynous boys are just as likely as girls to form intimate same-sex ties, whereas boys with a "masculine" identity are less likely to do so (Jones & Dembo, 1989).

What benefits do adolescents derive from their friendships? Although young people who are well adjusted to begin with are better able to form and sustain close peer ties, friendships further their emotional and social development. The reasons are several.

■ *During adolescence, intimacy and loyalty become defining features of friendship. Yet girls place a higher value on emotional closeness than do boys. Girls more often get together to "just talk," and they rate their friendships as higher in self-disclosure and emotional support. (Photo courtesy: Robert Harbison)*

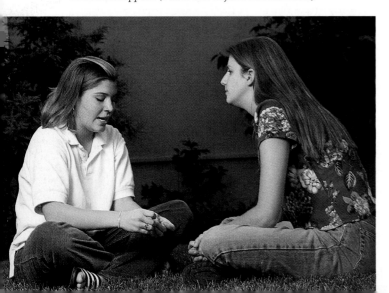

■ *Close friendships provide opportunities to explore the self and develop a deep understanding of another.* Through open, honest communication, adolescent friends become sensitive to each other's strengths and weaknesses, needs and desires. This process supports the development of self-concept, perspective taking, identity, and intimate ties beyond the family.

■ *Close friendships help young people deal with the stresses of adolescence.* Teenagers with supportive friendships report fewer daily hassles and more "uplifts" than do others (Kanner et al., 1987). As a result, anxiety and loneliness are reduced while self-esteem and sense of well-being are fostered.

■ *Close friendships can improve attitudes toward school and academic performance.* When teenagers enjoy interacting with friends at school, perhaps they begin to view all aspects of school life more positively (Berndt & Keefe, 1995).

CLIQUES AND CROWDS

Friends also gather in *peer groups* (see Chapter 10), which become increasingly common and more tightly structured and exclusive than they were in middle childhood. Adolescent peer groups are organized around **cliques,** small groups of about five to seven members who are good friends and, therefore, resemble one another in family background, attitudes, and values. In early adolescence, cliques are limited to same-sex members, but by midadolescence mixed groups become common. The cliques within a typical high school can be identified by their interests and social status, as the well-known "popular" and "unpopular" groups reveal (Cairns et al., 1995; Gillmore et al., 1997). Cliques develop dress codes, ways of speaking, and behaviors that separate them from one another and from the adult world.

Sometimes several cliques with similar values form a larger, more loosely organized group called a **crowd.** Unlike the more intimate clique, membership in a crowd is based on reputation and stereotype. It grants the adolescent an identity within the larger social structure of the school. For example, Louis and Darryl hung out with the debate team, who wore identical sweatshirts to practices, tournaments, and informal weekend gatherings. Other crowds included the "jocks," who were very involved in athletics; the "brains," who worried about their grades; and the "workers," who had part-time jobs and lots of spending money. The "druggies" used drugs on more than a one-time basis, while the "greasers" wore leather jackets, crossed the street to smoke cigarettes, and felt alienated from most aspects of school life (Urberg et al., 1995).

What influences the assortment of teenagers into cliques and crowds? In addition to personality and interests, family factors are important. In a study of 8,000 ninth to twelfth

These high school international club members form a crowd. Unlike the more intimate clique, the larger, more loosely organized crowd grants adolescents an identity within the larger social structure of the school. (Photo courtesy: Will Faller)

graders, adolescents who described their parents as authoritative were members of "brain," "jock," and "popular" groups that accepted both the adult and peer reward systems of the school. In contrast, boys whose parents were permissive valued interpersonal relationships and aligned themselves with the "fun culture," or "partyer" crowd. And teenagers who viewed their parents as uninvolved more often affiliated with "partyer" and "druggie" crowds, suggesting lack of identification with adult reward systems (Durbin et al., 1993).

Cultural variations in group norms also exist. The strong emphasis Asian parents place on academic achievement and interpersonal harmony carries over to peer affiliations. Among Chinese young people, scholastic rank, cooperation, politeness, hard work, and restrained behavior are especially salient bases of peer group membership (Leung, 1996).

These findings indicate that many peer group values are extensions of ones acquired at home. But once adolescents join a clique or crowd, it can modify their beliefs and behavior. However, the positive impact of having academically and socially skilled peers is greatest for teenagers whose own parents are authoritative. And the negative impact of having antisocial, drug-using friends is strongest for teenagers whose parents use less effective child-rearing styles (Mounts & Steinberg, 1995). In sum, family experiences affect the extent to which adolescents become like their peers over time.

In early adolescence, as interest in dating increases, boys' and girls' cliques come together. As mixed-sex cliques form and "hang out," they provide a supportive context for boys and girls to get to know each other. Cliques offer models for how to interact with the other sex and a chance to do so without having to be intimate. Gradually, the larger group divides into couples, several of whom spend time to-

gether, going to parties and movies. By late adolescence, boys and girls feel comfortable enough about approaching each other directly that the mixed-sex clique is no longer needed and disappears (Padgham & Blyth, 1990).

Crowds also decline in importance. As adolescents formulate personal values and goals, they no longer feel a need to broadcast, through dress, language, and preferred activities, who they are. Nevertheless, both cliques and crowds serve vital functions. The clique provides a context for acquiring new social skills and for experimenting with values and roles in the absence of adult monitoring. The crowd offers adolescents the security of a temporary identity as they separate from the family and begin to construct a coherent sense of self (Brown, 1990).

DATING

Although sexual interest is affected by the hormonal changes of puberty, the beginning of dating is regulated by social expectations of the peer group. In one study, adolescents were asked about their reasons for dating. Younger teenagers were more likely to date for recreation and to achieve status with agemates. By late adolescence, as young people became ready for greater psychological intimacy in a dating relationship, they looked for someone who shared their interests, had clear goals for the future, and was likely to make a good permanent partner (Roscoe, Diana, & Brooks, 1987).

The achievement of intimacy in dating relationships typically lags behind that of same-sex friendships (Buhrmester & Furman, 1987). Perhaps because communication between boys and girls remains stereotyped and shallow through mid-adolescence, early dating does not foster social maturity (Zani, 1993). It also carries with it a higher risk of premarital pregnancy. Sticking with group activities, such as parties and dances, before becoming involved with a steady boyfriend or girlfriend is best for young teenagers.

As long as dating does not begin too soon, it extends the benefits of adolescent friendships. Besides fun and enjoyment, dating promotes sensitivity, empathy, and identity development as teenagers relate to someone whose needs are different from their own. (Photo courtesy: Jeff Greenberg/Index Stock)

Homosexual youths face special challenges in initiating and maintaining visible romances. Their first dating relationships seem to be short-lived and to involve little emotional commitment for reasons different from those of heterosexuals: They fear peer harassment and rejection (Sears, 1991). Recall from Chapter 11 that because of intense prejudice, homosexual adolescents often retreat into heterosexual dating. In addition, many have difficulty finding a same-sex partner because their homosexual peers have not yet come out—a circumstance that prompts profound feelings of loneliness. Homosexuals with a high proportion of same-sex romances are usually "out" to peers. Yet a sense of isolation from the larger peer world frequently means that dating partners place unreasonable demands on each other—for fulfilling all social needs (Savin-Williams, 1996).

As long as it does not begin too soon, dating provides lessons in cooperation, etiquette, and how to deal with people in a wider range of situations. As teenagers relate to someone whose needs are different from their own, sensitivity, empathy, and identity development are enhanced (Furman & Wehner, 1994). About half of first romances do not survive high school graduation, and those that do become less satisfying (Shaver, Furman, & Buhrmester, 1985). Because young people are still forming their identities, those who like each other at one point in time often find that they do not have much in common later.

PEER PRESSURE AND CONFORMITY

When Franca and Antonio discovered Louis's lawbreaking during his freshman year of high school, they began to worry (as many parents do) about the negative side of adolescent peer networks. Although conformity to peer pressure is greater during adolescence than in childhood or early adulthood, it is a complex process that varies with the young person's age and need for social approval and with the situation.

In one study of nearly 400 junior and senior high school students, adolescents felt greatest pressure to conform to the most obvious aspects of the peer culture—dressing and grooming like everyone else and participating in social activities, such as dating and going to parties and school dances. Peer pressure to engage in proadult behavior, such as getting good grades and cooperating with parents, was also strong. Although pressure toward misconduct rose in early adolescence, compared with other areas it was low. Many teenagers said that their friends actively discouraged antisocial acts. These findings show that peers and parents often act in concert, toward desirable ends! Finally, peer pressures were only modestly related to teenagers' values and behaviors. Clearly, these young people did not always follow the dictates of peers (Brown, Lohr, & McClenahan, 1986).

Perhaps because of greater concern with what their friends think of them, early adolescents are more likely than younger or older individuals to give in to peer pressure (Brown, Clasen, & Eicher, 1986). Yet when parents and peers disagree, even young teenagers do not consistently rebel against the family. Instead, parents and peers differ in their spheres of greatest influence. Parents have more impact on teenagers' basic life values and educational plans (Sebald, 1986). Peers are more influential in short-term day-to-day matters, such as dress, music, and choice of friends. Adolescents' personal characteristics also make a difference. Young people who feel competent and worthwhile are less likely to fall in line behind peers.

Finally, authoritative child rearing is related to resistance to unfavorable peer pressure (Chassin et al., 1998; Fletcher et al., 1995). In contrast, adolescents who experience extremes of parental behavior—either too much restrictiveness or too little monitoring—tend to be highly peer oriented (Mason et al., 1996; Pettit et al., 1999). They more often rely on friends for advice about their personal lives and futures and are more willing to break their parents' rules; ignore their schoolwork; smoke, drink, and use drugs; commit delinquent acts; and engage in other problem behaviors.

ASK YOURSELF . . .

■ *How does Louis and Darryl's lunchtime conversation at the beginning of this chapter reflect the characteristics of adolescent friendship?*

 Phyllis likes her 14-year-old daughter Farrah's friends, but she wonders what Farrah gets out of hanging out at Jake's Pizza Parlor with them on Friday and Saturday evenings. Explain to Phyllis what Farrah is learning that will be of value in adulthood.

■ *How might gender intensification contribute to the shallow quality of early adolescent dating relationships?*

PROBLEMS OF DEVELOPMENT

Although most young people move through adolescence with little difficulty, we have seen that some encounter major disruptions in development, such as premature parenthood, substance abuse, and school failure. Our discussion has also shown that psychological and behavior problems cannot be explained by any single factor. Instead, biological and psychological change, families, schools, peers, communities, and culture act together to produce particular outcomes. This theme is apparent in three additional problems of the teenage years: depression, suicide, and delinquency.

DEPRESSION

Depression—feeling sad, frustrated, and hopeless about life, accompanied by loss of pleasure in most activities and disturbances in sleep, appetite, concentration, and energy—is the most common psychological problem of adolescence.

FIGURE 12.2

■ **Change in depressive symptoms from age 12 to 20 in a cross-sectional study of over 12,000 Norwegian adolescents.** *Girls showed a more rapid rise in depression around the time of puberty than did boys. Similar trends occur in other industrialized nations. (From L. Wichstrøm, 1999, "The Emergence of Gender Difference in Depressed Mood During Adolescence: The Role of Intensified Gender Socialization," Developmental Psychology, 35, p. 237. Copyright © 1999 by the American Psychological Association. Reprinted by permission of the publisher and author.)*

About 15 to 20 percent of teenagers have had one or more major depressive episodes (a rate comparable to that of adults). From 2 to 8 percent are chronically depressed—gloomy and self-critical for many months and sometimes years (Birmaher et al., 1996; Kessler et al., 1994). Depression is not absent in childhood. Yet as Figure 12.2 shows, depressive symptoms start to increase around the time of puberty. This change is understandable if we think about the many challenges adolescents face and their greater capacity for focusing on themselves. Depression occurs twice as often in adolescent girls as in adolescent boys—a difference sustained throughout the lifespan.

Depression prevents young people from mastering critical developmental tasks. Without treatment, depressed teenagers have a high likelihood of becoming depressed adults. Adolescent depression is also associated with persistent anxiety, drug abuse, lawbreaking, and auto accidents, and it predicts future problems in school performance, employment, marriage, and child rearing (Harrington, Rutter, & Fombonne, 1996; Kovacs et al., 1994).

Unfortunately, depressive symptoms tend to be overlooked by parents and teachers alike. Because of the popular stereotype of adolescence as a period of storm and stress, many adults interpret depressive reactions as "normal" and just a passing phase (Strober, McCracken, & Hanna, 1990). Depression is also hard to recognize in teenagers because they manifest it in a wide variety of ways. Some engage in excessive brooding, worries about their health, and restless, undirected behavior. Others act it out through hostility and rebellion, which often deepen depression by disrupting relations with parents, teachers, and peers. The first pattern is more typical of girls, the second more characteristic of boys (Gjerde, 1995).

■ FACTORS RELATED TO DEPRESSION. Researchers believe that diverse combinations of biological and environmental factors lead to depression; the precise blend differs from one individual to the next. Kinship studies reveal that heredity plays an important role. Genes can induce depression by affecting the chemical balance in the brain, the development of brain regions involved in inhibiting negative emotion, or the body's hormonal response to stress (Cicchetti & Toth, 1998).

But experience can also activate depression, promoting any of the biological changes just described. Parents of depressed children and adolescents have a high incidence of depression and other psychological disorders. Although a genetic risk may be passed from parent to child, in earlier chapters we saw that depressed or otherwise stressed parents often engage in maladaptive parenting. As a result, their child's emotional self-regulation, attachment, and self-esteem may be impaired, with serious consequences for many cognitive and social skills (Garber, Braafladt, & Weiss, 1995; Garber et al., 1991).

Depressed youths usually display a learned-helpless attributional style (see Chapter 10) in which they view positive outcomes in school performance and peer relations as beyond their control. Consequently, numerous events can spark depression in a vulnerable young person—for exam-

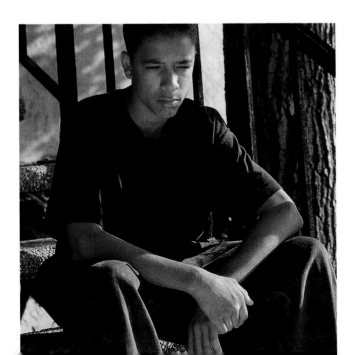

■ *Depression in teenagers should not be dismissed as a temporary side effect of puberty. Because adolescent depression can lead to long-term emotional problems, it deserves to be taken seriously. Without treatment, depressed teenagers have a high likelihood of becoming depressed adults. (Photo courtesy: Tony Freeman/PhotoEdit)*

ple, failing at something important, parental divorce, or the end of a close friendship or romantic partnership. The inability of depressed teenagers to imagine a worthwhile future for themselves seriously disrupts identity development (Chandler, 1994).

■ SEX DIFFERENCES. Why are girls more prone to depression? Biology cannot account for the gender gap, since it is limited to industrialized nations. In developing countries, rates of depression are similar for males and females and occasionally higher in males (Culbertson, 1997).

Instead, the challenges of adolescence combined with gender-typed coping styles seem to be responsible. Early maturing girls, who often have a negative body image and are less well liked by peers, are prone to depression, especially when they face other life stresses (see Chapter 11). At the same time, the gender intensification of early adolescence strengthens girls' passivity and dependency—maladaptive approaches to the tasks expected of teenagers in complex cultures and to stressful life events (Nolen-Hoeksema & Girgus, 1994; Rudolph & Hammen, 1999). Consistent with this explanation, adolescents who identify strongly with "feminine" traits are more depressed than their "masculine" and "androgynous" agemates, regardless of their sex (Wichstrøm, 1999).

SUICIDE

Profound depression can lead to suicidal thoughts, which all too often are translated into action. When a teenager tries or succeeds at taking his or her own life, depression is one of the factors that precedes it.

■ FACTORS RELATED TO ADOLESCENT SUICIDE. The suicide rate increases over the lifespan. As Figure 12.3 shows, it is lowest in childhood and highest in old age, but it jumps sharply at adolescence. Currently, suicide is the third-leading cause of death among American young people, after motor vehicle collisions and homicides. It is a

growing national problem, the rate having tripled over the past 30 years, perhaps because modern teenagers face more stresses and have fewer supports than in decades past. Adolescent suicide varies widely among industrialized nations (U.S. Department of Health and Human Services, 1999g). Japan and most of Western Europe have low rates; Australia and Canada, like the United States, have intermediate rates; and China, New Zealand, and Russia have very high rates. Although many theories exist, international differences remain unexplained (Turner, 1998).

Striking sex differences in suicidal behavior exist. The number of boys who kill themselves exceeds the number of girls by 4 or 5 to 1. This may seem surprising, since girls show a higher rate of depression. Yet the findings are not inconsistent. Girls make more unsuccessful suicide attempts and use methods with a greater likelihood of revival, such as a sleeping pill overdose. In contrast, boys tend to select more active techniques that lead to instant death, such as firearms or hanging. Once again, gender-role expectations may be responsible. There is less tolerance for feelings of helplessness and failed efforts in males than in females (Garland & Zigler, 1993).

Compared with the white majority, certain American ethnic-minority teenagers, including African Americans and Hispanics, have lower suicide rates—a difference that increases in adulthood. Higher levels of support through extended families may be responsible. In contrast, suicide among Native American and Canadian Aboriginal youths is several times the national average. It appears to be linked to high rates of profound family poverty, alcohol use, depression, and a sense of hopelessness (Strickland, 1997).

Suicide tends to occur in two types of young people. In the first group are adolescents who are highly intelligent but solitary, withdrawn, and unable to meet their own high standards or those of important people in their lives. A second, larger group shows antisocial tendencies. These young people express their despondency through bullying, fighting, stealing, and increased risk taking and drug abuse (Leh-

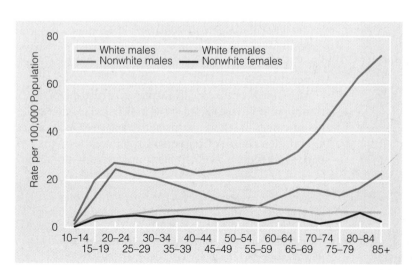

FIGURE 12.3

■ **Suicide rates over the lifespan in the United States.** Although teenagers do not commit suicide as often as adults and the aged, the suicide rate rises sharply from childhood to adolescence. Rates are greater for males than for females and for white majority than for nonwhite ethnic minority individuals. (From U.S. Bureau of the Census, 1999.)

nert, Overholser, & Spirito, 1994). Besides turning their anger and disappointment inward, they are hostile and destructive toward others.

Family turmoil, parental emotional problems, and marital breakup are common in the backgrounds of suicidal teenagers, who typically feel distant from parents and peers (Shagle & Barber, 1993). Their fragile self-esteem disintegrates in the face of stressful life events. Common circumstances just before a suicide include the breakup of an important peer relationship or the humiliation of having been caught engaging in irresponsible, antisocial acts (King, 1997).

Why is suicide on the rise in adolescence? Teenagers' improved ability to plan ahead seems to be involved. Few successful suicides are sudden and impulsive. Instead, young people at risk usually take purposeful steps toward killing themselves. Warning signs, some of which are intended as calls for help, are listed in Table 12.4. The cognitive changes of adolescence also contribute. Belief in the personal fable leads many depressed young people to conclude that no one could possibly understand the intense pain they feel. As a result, their despair, hopelessness, and isolation deepen.

■ PREVENTION AND TREATMENT. Picking up on the signals that a troubled teenager sends is a critical first step in suicide prevention. Parents and teachers need to be trained in warning signs. Schools can help by providing sympathetic counselors, peer support groups, and information about telephone hotlines. Once a teenager takes steps toward suicide, staying with the young person, listening, and expressing sympathy and concern until professional

TABLE 12.4
Warning Signs of Suicide
Efforts to put personal affairs in order—smoothing over troubled relationships, giving away treasured possessions
Verbal cues—saying goodbye to family members and friends, making direct or indirect references to suicide ("I won't have to worry about these problems much longer"; "I wish I were dead")
Feelings of sadness, despondency, "not caring" anymore
Extreme fatigue, lack of energy, boredom
No desire to socialize; withdrawal from friends
Easily frustrated
Emotional outbursts—spells of crying or laughing, bursts of energy
Inability to concentrate, distractible
Decline in grades, absence from school, discipline problems
Neglect of personal appearance
Sleep change—loss of sleep or excessive sleepiness
Appetite change—eating more or less than usual
Physical complaints—stomachaches, backaches, headaches

help can be obtained are essential. The Caregiving Concerns table below suggests specific ways to respond to a young person who might be suicidal.

Intervention with depressed and suicidal adolescents ranges from antidepressant medication to individual, family, and group therapy. Sometimes hospitalization is necessary to ensure the teenager's safety and swift entry into

CAREGIVING CONCERNS

Ways to Respond to a Young Person Who Might Be Suicidal

STRATEGY	DESCRIPTION
Be psychologically and physically available.	Grant the young person your full attention; indicate when and where you can be located, and emphasize that you are always willing to talk.
Communicate a caring, capable attitude.	Such statements as "I'm concerned. I care about you" encourage the adolescent to discuss feelings of despair. Conveying a capable attitude helps redirect the young person's world of confusion toward psychological order.
Assess the immediacy of risk.	Gently inquire into the young person's motives with such questions as "Do you want to harm yourself? Do you want to die or kill yourself?" If the answer is yes, ask about the adolescent's plan. If it is specific (involves a method and a time), the risk of suicide is very high, and you should contact school officials or a health professional as soon as possible.
Empathize with the young person's feelings.	Empathy, through such statements as "I can understand your confusion and pain," increases your persuasive power and defuses the adolescent's negative emotion.
Oppose the suicidal intent.	Communicate sensitively but firmly that suicide is not an acceptable solution and that you want to help the adolescent explore other options.
Offer a plan for help.	Offer to assist the young person in finding professional help and in telling others, such as parents and school officials, who need to know about the problem.
Obtain a commitment.	Ask the adolescent to agree to the plan. If he or she refuses, negotiate a promise to contact you or another supportive person if and when suicidal thoughts return.

Source: Kirk, 1993.

Persistent adolescent delinquency follows two paths of development, one with an onset of conduct problems in childhood, the second with an onset in adolescence. Longitudinal research reveals that the early-onset type is far more likely to lead to a life-course pattern of aggression and criminality. The late-onset type usually does not last beyond the transition to young adulthood (Loeber & Stouthamer-Loeber, 1998).

Childhood-onset and adolescent-onset youths show comparable levels of serious offenses, involvement with deviant peers, substance abuse, unsafe sex, dangerous driving, and time spent in correctional facilities. Why does antisocial activity more often continue and escalate into potentially lethal violence—including school and neighborhood knifings and shootings—in the first group than in the second? Longitudinal research extending from childhood into early adulthood sheds light on this question (Garbarino, 1999).

So far, investigations have focused largely on boys because of their greater involvement in delinquent

activity. Yet preliminary evidence suggests that girls who were aggressive in childhood are also at increased risk for adolescent and adult problems, including criminality and diverse psychiatric disorders (Wangby, Bergman, & Magnesson, 1999).

EARLY-ONSET TYPE. These boys are emotionally negative, restless, and willful as early as age 3. In addition, they show subtle deficits in cognitive functioning that seem to contribute to disruptions in the development of language, memory, and cognitive and emotional self-regulation (Moffitt et al., 1996; Moffitt, Lynam, & Silva, 1994). Some have attention-deficit hyperactivity disorder (ADHD), which compounds their learning and self-control problems (see Chapter 9, page 294) (Moffitt, 1990; White et al., 1996).

Yet these biological risks are not sufficient to sustain antisocial behavior, since about half of early-onset boys do not display serious delinquency followed by adult criminality. Among those who follow the life-course path, inept parenting—harshness, inconsistency, lack of

monitoring, and abuse—transforms their undercontrolled style into hostility and defiance. As they fail academically and are rejected by peers, they befriend other deviant youths, who provide the attitudes and motivations for violent behavior (see Figure 12.4) (Simons et al., 1994). Compared with their adolescent-onset counterparts, early-onset teenagers feel distant from their families and leave school early (Moffitt et al., 1996). Their limited cognitive and social skills result in high rates of unemployment, contributing further to their antisocial involvements.

LATE-ONSET TYPE. A larger number of youths begin to display antisocial behavior around the time of puberty, gradually increasing their involvement. Their conduct problems arise from the peer context of early adolescence, not from biological deficits and a history of unfavorable development (Moffitt, Lynam, & Silva, 1994). For some, quality of parenting may decline for a time, perhaps due to family stresses or the challenges of disciplining an unruly teenager. When age brings gratifying adult

treatment. Until the adolescent improves, parents are usually advised to remove weapons, knives, razors, scissors, and drugs from the home. On a broader scale, gun control legislation that limits adolescents' access to the most frequent and deadly suicide method would greatly reduce both the number of suicides and the high teenage homicide rate (Clark & Mokros, 1993).

After a suicide, family and peer survivors need support to assist them in coping with grief, anger, and guilt for not having been able to help the victim. Teenage suicides often take place in clusters. When one occurs, it increases the likelihood of others among peers who knew the young person or heard about the death through the media. In view of this trend, an especially watchful eye must be kept on vulnerable adolescents after a suicide happens. Restraint by

journalists in reporting teenage suicides on television or in newspapers can also aid in preventing them (Diekstra, Kienhorst, & de Wilde, 1995).

DELINQUENCY

Juvenile delinquents are children or adolescents who engage in illegal acts. Young people under age 21 account for a large proportion of police arrests in the United States—about 30 percent (U.S. Department of Justice, 1999). Yet when teenagers are asked directly and confidentially about law-breaking, almost all admit that they are guilty of an offense of one sort or another (Farrington, 1987). Most of the time, they do not commit major crimes. Instead, they engage in petty stealing, disorderly conduct, and acts that

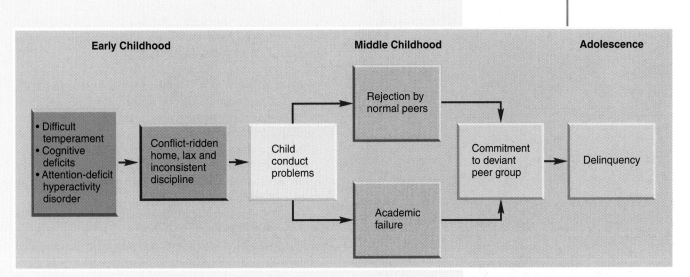

Early Childhood

• Difficult temperament
• Cognitive deficits
• Attention-deficit hyperactivity disorder

Conflict-ridden home, lax and inconsistent discipline

Child conduct problems

Middle Childhood

Rejection by normal peers

Academic failure

Adolescence

Commitment to deviant peer group

Delinquency

FIGURE 12.4

■ **Developmental path to chronic delinquency for adolescents with childhood-onset antisocial behavior.** Difficult temperament and deficits in cognitive functioning characterize many of these youths in early childhood; some have attention-deficit hyperactivity disorder. But these risks are not sufficient to sustain antisocial behavior. Instead, inept parenting transforms biologically based self-control difficulties into hostility and defiance. (Adapted from Patterson, DeBaryshe, & Ramsey, 1989.)

privileges, they draw on prosocial skills mastered before adolescence and give up their antisocial ways (Moffitt et al., 1996).

A few late-onset youths, however, continue to engage in antisocial acts. The seriousness of their adolescent offenses seems to act as a snare, trapping them in situations that rule out opportunities for responsible behavior. In one study, finding a steady, well-paying job and entering a happy marriage led to a large reduction in repeat offending. One former delinquent commented, "I worked steadily to support [my family] and take care of my responsibilities. I never had any time to get into trouble." In contrast, the longer antisocial young people spent in prison, the more likely they were to sustain a life of crime (Sampson & Laub, 1993).

These findings suggest a need for a fresh look at policies aimed at stopping youth crime. Keeping adolescent and young adult offenders locked up for many years disrupts their vocational and marital lives during a crucial period of development, committing them to a future that is bleak.

are illegal only for minors, such as underage drinking, violating curfews, and running away from home.

Both police arrests and self-reports show that delinquency rises over the early teenage years, remains high during middle adolescence, and then declines into young adulthood. What is responsible for this trend? Recall that the desire for peer approval increases antisocial behavior among young teenagers. Over time, peers become less influential, moral reasoning matures, and young people enter social contexts (such as marriage, work, and career) that are less conducive to law-breaking.

For most adolescents, a brush with the law does not forecast long-term antisocial behavior. But repeated arrests are cause for concern. Teenagers are responsible for 27 percent of violent crimes (homicide, rape, robbery, and as-sault) and 42 percent of property crimes (burglary and theft) (U.S. Department of Justice, 1999). A small percentage commit most of them, developing into recurrent offenders. Some enter a life of crime. As the Lifespan Vista box above reveals, childhood-onset conduct problems are far more likely to persist than are conduct problems that emerge during the teenage years.

■ FACTORS RELATED TO DELINQUENCY. In adolescence, the gender gap in overt aggression widens. Depending on the estimate, about 3 to 8 times as many boys as girls commit major crimes. Although SES and ethnicity are strong predictors of arrests, they are only mildly related to teenagers' self-reports of antisocial acts. This is probably due to biases in the juvenile justice system—in

■ *Most of the time, juvenile delinquency involves petty stealing, disorderly conduct, and acts that are illegal only for minors, such as underage drinking. Usually two or more peers commit these acts together. In early adolescence, the desire for peer approval increases antisocial behavior among young people. (Photo courtesy: Smith/Monkmeyer Press)*

particular, the tendency to arrest, charge, and punish low-SES African-American, Hispanic, and Native-American youths more often than their higher-SES white and Asian counterparts (Elliott, 1994).

Difficult temperament, low intelligence, poor school performance, peer rejection in childhood, and entry into antisocial peer groups are also linked to delinquency. How do these factors fit together? One of the most consistent findings about delinquent youths is that their family environments are low in warmth, high in conflict, and characterized by inconsistent discipline. Beginning in early childhood, these forms of child rearing breed antisocial behavior (Feldman & Weinberger, 1994; Miller et al., 1993).

Return to our discussion of the development of aggression on page 261 of Chapter 8. It explains how ineffective parenting can promote and sustain hostile responding in all family members. Boys are more likely than girls to be targets of angry, inconsistent discipline because they are more active and impulsive and therefore harder to control. When children extreme in these characteristics are exposed to inept parenting, aggression rises during childhood, is transformed into violent offenses by adolescence, and persists into adulthood (refer again to the Lifespan Vista box).

Factors beyond the family and peer group also contribute to delinquency. Students in schools that fail to meet their developmental needs—those with large classes, poor-quality instruction, and rigid rules—show higher rates of law-breaking, even after other influences are controlled (Hawkins & Lam, 1987). And in poverty-stricken neighborhoods with fragmented community ties and adult criminal subcultures, teenagers have few constructive alternatives to antisocial behavior (Staub, 1996). Youth gangs often originate in these environments.

■ PREVENTION AND TREATMENT. Because delinquency has roots in childhood and results from events in several contexts, prevention must start early and take place at multiple levels. Helping parents to use authoritative child rearing, schools to teach more effectively, and communities to provide the economic and social conditions necessary for healthy development would go a long way toward reducing adolescent criminality.

Treating serious offenders also requires an approach that recognizes the multiple determinants of delinquency. So far as possible, adolescents are best kept in their own homes and communities to increase the possibility that treatment changes will transfer to their daily environments. Many treatment models exist, including individual therapies and community-based interventions involving halfway houses, day treatment centers, special classrooms, work experience programs, and summer camps. Those that work best are lengthy and intensive and use problem-focused methods that teach cognitive and social skills needed to overcome family, peer, and school difficulties (Guerra, Attar, & Weissberg, 1997).

Yet even these multidimensional treatments can fall short if young people remain embedded in hostile home lives, antisocial peer groups, and violent neighborhoods. Intensive efforts, beginning early in life, to create nonaggressive environments—at the family, community, and cultural levels—are needed to support the interventions just described and to cultivate humane, nonviolent attitudes and behavior in all young people.

ASK YOURSELF . . .

🌳 *Throughout childhood, Mac had difficulty learning, was disobedient, and picked fights with peers. At age 16, he was arrested for burglary. Zeke had been a well-behaved child, but around age 13, he started spending time with the "wrong crowd." At age 16, he was arrested for property damage. Which boy is more likely to become a long-term offender, and why?*

■ *Return to Chapter 11 and reread the sections on adolescent pregnancy and parenthood. What factors do these problems have in common with suicide and delinquency? How would you explain the finding that teenagers who experience one of these difficulties are likely to display others?*

SUMMARY

ERIKSON'S THEORY: IDENTITY VERSUS IDENTITY CONFUSION

According to Erikson, what is the major personality achievement of adolescence?

■ Erikson's theory emphasizes **identity** as the major personality achievement of adolescence. Young people who successfully resolve the psychological conflict of **identity versus identity confusion** construct a solid self-definition consisting of self-chosen values and goals.

SELF-DEVELOPMENT

Describe changes in self-concept and self-esteem during adolescence.

■ Changes in self-concept and self-esteem set the stage for identity formation. Adolescents' self-descriptions become more organized and consistent, and personal and moral values appear as key themes. New dimensions of self-esteem are also added.

■ For most young people, self-esteem rises over the teenage years, although it continues to be profoundly affected by feedback from others. Parental warmth, approval, and appropriate expectations and schools and neighborhoods that respect the young person's SES and ethnic group support self-esteem.

Describe the four identity statuses, along with factors that promote identity development.

■ In complex societies, a period of exploration is necessary to form a personally meaningful identity. **Identity achievement** and **moratorium** are psychologically healthy identity statuses. Long-term **identity foreclosure** and **identity diffusion** are related to adjustment difficulties.

■ Adolescents who have a flexible, open-minded approach to grappling with competing beliefs and who feel attached to parents but free to disagree are likely to be advanced in identity development. Schools and communities that provide young people with options for exploration support the search for identity. Ethnic minority youths who construct a **bicultural identity** are advantaged in many aspects of emotional and social development.

MORAL DEVELOPMENT

Describe Piaget's theory of moral development and Kohlberg's extension of it, and evaluate the accuracy of each.

■ Piaget identified two stages of moral understanding: (1) **heteronomous morality,** in which moral rules are viewed as fixed dictates of authority figures, and (2) **autonomous morality,** in which rules are seen as flexible, socially agreed-on principles. Although Piaget's theory describes the general direction of moral development, it underestimates young children's moral capacities.

■ According to Kohlberg, moral development is a gradual process that extends into adulthood. Moral reasoning advances through three levels, each of which contains two stages: (1) the **preconventional level,** in which morality is viewed as controlled by rewards, punishments, and the power of authority figures; (2) the **conventional level,** in which conformity to laws and rules is regarded as necessary to preserve positive human relationships and societal order; and (3) the **postconventional level,** in which individuals develop abstract, universal principles of justice. Because situational factors affect moral judgments, Kohlberg's moral stages are best viewed in terms of a loose rather than a strict concept of stage.

Evaluate claims that Kohlberg's theory does not adequately represent the morality of females.

■ Kohlberg's theory does not underestimate the morality of females. Instead, justice and caring moralities coexist but vary in emphasis between males and females and across situations.

What environmental factors affect moral reasoning, and how are moral reasoning and behavior related?

■ Many experiences contribute to moral maturity, including warm, rational child-rearing practices, schooling, peer discussions of moral issues, and the complexity of society. Kohlberg's theory does not capture all aspects of moral thinking in every culture.

■ As individuals advance to higher stages, moral reasoning and behavior come closer together. Many other factors, including the individual's capacity to feel empathy and guilt and history of morally relevant experiences, affect moral action.

GENDER TYPING

Why is early adolescence a period of gender intensification?

■ **Gender intensification** occurs in early adolescence for several reasons. Physical and cognitive changes prompt young teenagers to view themselves in gender-linked ways, and gender-typed pressures from parents and peers increase. Teenagers who eventually build an androgynous gender identity show better psychological adjustment.

THE FAMILY

Discuss changes in parent–child and sibling relationships during adolescence.

- Effective parenting of adolescents requires an authoritative style that strikes a balance between connection and separation. Adapting family interaction to meet adolescents' need for **autonomy** is especially challenging. As teenagers de-idealize their parents, they often question parental authority. Because both adolescents and parents are undergoing major life transitions, they approach situations from different perspectives.

- Parents who are financially secure, invested in their work, and content with their marriages usually find it easier to grant teenagers support, guidance, and appropriate autonomy. When parents and adolescents have seriously troubled relationships, the difficulties usually began in childhood.

- Sibling relationships become less intense as adolescents separate from the family and turn toward peers. Still, attachment to siblings remains strong for most young people.

PEER RELATIONS

Describe adolescent friendships, peer groups, and dating relationships and their consequences for development.

- During adolescence, the nature of friendship changes, toward greater intimacy and loyalty. Girls' friendships place greater emphasis on intimate sharing, boys' on status and mastery. Close friendships promote perspective taking, self-concept,

identity, and the capacity for romantic involvement. They also help young people deal with stress and can foster improved academic performance.

- Adolescent peer groups are organized into **cliques,** small groups of friends with common interests, dress styles, and behavior. Sometimes several cliques form a larger, more loosely organized group called a **crowd** that grants the adolescent an identity within the larger social structure of the school. Mixed-sex cliques provide a supportive social context for boys and girls to get to know one another.

- Intimacy in dating relationships lags behind that of same-sex friendships. Because of prejudice, initiating and maintaining visible romances is especially challenging for homosexual youths. First romances serve as practice for later, more mature bonds. They generally dissolve or become less satisfying after graduation from high school.

Discuss conformity to peer pressure in adolescence.

- Peer conformity is greater during adolescence than at younger or older ages. Young teenagers are most likely to give in to peer pressure for antisocial behavior. Yet most peer pressures are not in conflict with important adult values. Peers have greatest influence on short-term, day-to-day matters. Adults have more impact on long-term values and educational plans. Authoritative parenting is related to resistance to unfavorable peer pressure.

PROBLEMS OF DEVELOPMENT

What factors are related to adolescent depression and suicide?

- Depression is the most common psychological problem of the teenage years. Adolescents who are severely depressed are likely to remain so as adults. Heredity contributes to depression, but stressful life events are necessary to trigger it. Depression is more common in girls than in boys—a difference believed to be due to identification with "feminine" traits.

- Profound depression often leads to suicidal thoughts. The suicide rate increases dramatically at adolescence. Boys account for most teenage suicides, whereas girls make more unsuccessful attempts. Teenagers at risk for suicide are sometimes solitary and withdrawn; more often, they are antisocial. Family stress is common in the backgrounds of suicidal adolescents, who react intensely to loss, failure, or humiliation.

Discuss factors related to delinquency.

- Almost all teenagers become involved in some delinquent activity, but only a few are serious repeat offenders. Most of these are boys with a childhood history of conduct problems. Although many factors are related to delinquency, one of the most consistent is a family environment low in warmth, high in conflict, and characterized by inconsistent discipline. Schools that fail to meet adolescents' developmental needs and poverty-stricken neighborhoods with high crime rates also promote adolescent law-breaking.

IMPORTANT TERMS AND CONCEPTS

autonomous morality (p. 396)

autonomy (p. 401)

bicultural identity (p. 395)

clique (p. 404)

conventional level (p. 397)

crowd (p. 404)

gender intensification (p. 401)

heteronomous morality (p. 396)

identity (p. 390)

identity achievement (p. 392)

identity diffusion (p. 392)

identity foreclosure (p. 392)

identity versus identity confusion (p. 390)

moratorium (p. 392)

postconventional level (p. 398)

preconventional level (p. 397)

FYI FOR FURTHER INFORMATION AND HELP

Consult the companion website for this book, where you will find additional weblinks and associated learning activities: www.abacon.com/berk

SUICIDE

American Association of Suicidology
www.suicidology.org

Promotes research, public awareness, education, and training for professionals and volunteers on suicide and suicide prevention. Serves as a national clearinghouse for information on suicide.

American Foundation for Suicide Prevention
www.afsp.org

Supports research and education on suicide and suicide prevention. Includes a special section on youth suicide.

DELINQUENCY

National Council on Crime and Delinquency
www.cas.comm/users/nccd

An organization of professionals and other concerned individuals interested in the development of programs that prevent and treat crime and delinquency. Publishes the journal Crime and Delinquency.

AGE	PHYSICAL	COGNITIVE	EMOTIONAL/SOCIAL
11–14 years	■ If a girl, reaches peak of growth spurt. (354) ■ If a girl, adds more body fat than muscle. (352) ■ If a girl, starts to menstruate. (354) ■ If a boy, begins growth spurt. (354) ■ If a boy, starts to ejaculate seminal fluid. (354) ■ Likely to become aware of sexual orientation. (362) ■ If a girl, motor performance gradually increases and then levels off. (353)	■ Becomes capable of formal operational reasoning. (370) ■ Becomes better at coordinating theory with evidence. (373) ■ Can argue more effectively. (374) ■ Becomes more self-conscious and self-focused. (374–375) ■ Becomes more idealistic and critical. (375–376) ■ Metacognition and cognitive self-regulation continue to improve. (373, 376)	■ Moodiness and parent–child conflict increase. (356–357) ■ Is likely to show increased gender stereotyping of attitudes and behavior. (401) ■ Spends less time with parents and siblings. (401, 403) ■ Spends more time with peers. (403) ■ Friendships are based on intimacy and loyalty. (403–404) ■ Peer groups become organized around cliques. (404) ■ Cliques with similar values come together, forming crowds. (404) ■ Conformity to peer pressure increases. (406)

AGE	PHYSICAL	COGNITIVE	EMOTIONAL/SOCIAL
15–20 years	■ If a girl, completes growth spurt. (354) ■ If a boy, reaches peak and then completes growth spurt. (354) ■ If a boy, voice deepens. (354) ■ If a boy, adds muscle while body fat declines. (352) ■ May have had sexual intercourse. (361) ■ If a boy, motor performance increases dramatically. (353)	■ Is likely to show formal operational reasoning on familiar tasks. (372) ■ Masters the components of formal operational reasoning in sequential order on different types of tasks. (373) ■ Becomes less self-conscious and self-focused. (375) ■ Becomes better at everyday planning and decision making. (376)	■ Combines features of the self into an organized self-concept. (391) ■ Self-esteem differentiates further. (391) ■ Self-esteem tends to rise. (391) ■ Is likely to be searching for an identity. (392) ■ Is likely to engage in societal perspective taking. (397) ■ Is likely to have a conventional moral orientation. (397–398) ■ Importance of cliques and crowds declines. (405) ■ Has probably started dating. (405) ■ Conformity to peer pressure may decline. (406)

Note: Numbers in parentheses indicate the page on which each milestone is discussed.

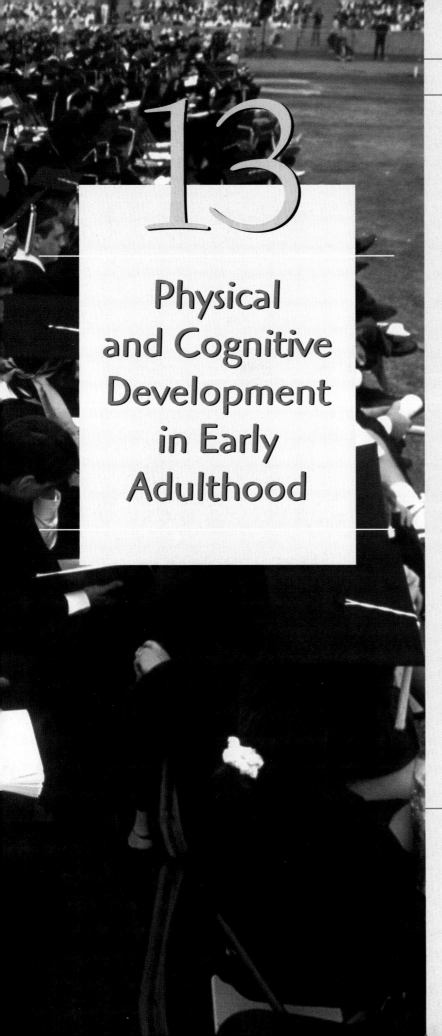

13

Physical and Cognitive Development in Early Adulthood

■ *Commencement means "new beginning." On the threshold of early adulthood, these college graduates face a succession of major life changes, including starting full-time work, attaining economic independence, and establishing a long-term sexually intimate relationship. (Photo courtesy: Joseph Sohm/ChromoSohm, Inc./Corbis)*

The back seat and trunk piled high with belongings, 22-year-old Sharese hugged her mother and brother good-bye, jumped in the car, and headed toward the interstate with a sense of newfound independence mixed with apprehension. Three months earlier, the family had watched proudly as Sharese received her bachelor's degree in chemistry from a small university 40 miles from her home. Her college years had been ones of gradual release from economic and psychological dependence on her family. She returned home on weekends as often as she desired and lived there during the summer months. Her mother supplemented Sharese's loans with a monthly allowance. But this day marked a turning point. She was moving to her own apartment in a new city 800 miles away, with plans to begin working on a master's degree the following week. In charge of all her educational and living expenses, Sharese felt more self-sufficient than at any previous time in her life.

The college years had been ones in which Sharese made important lifestyle changes and settled on a vocational direction. Overweight throughout high school, she lost twenty pounds during her freshman year, revised her diet, and began a regimen of exercise by joining the university's Ultimate Frisbee team. The sport helped her acquire healthier habits and leadership skills as team captain. A summer spent as a counselor at a camp for chronically ill children, combined with personal events we will take up later, convinced Sharese to apply her background in science to a career in public health.

Still, she wondered whether her choice was right. Two weeks before she was scheduled to leave, Sharese confided to her mother that she had doubts and might not go. Her mother advised, "Sharese, we never know ahead of time whether the things we choose are going to suit us just right, and most times they aren't perfect. It's what we make of them—how we view and mold them—that turns a choice into a success." And so Sharese embarked on her journey and found herself face to face with a multitude of exciting challenges and opportunities.

In this chapter, we take up the physical and cognitive sides of early adulthood—the period of the twenties and thirties. In Chapter 1, we emphasized that the adult years are difficult to divide into discrete periods, since the timing of important milestones varies greatly among individuals—much more so than in childhood and adolescence. But for most people, this first phase of adult life involves a common set of tasks: leaving home, completing education, beginning full-time work, attaining economic independence, establishing a long-term sexually intimate relationship, and starting a family. As Sharese's conversation with her mother reveals, the momentous decisions of early adulthood inevitably lead to second thoughts and disappointments. But with the help of family, community, and societal contexts, most young adults make the best of wrong turns and solve problems successfully. These are energetic decades that, more than any phase, offer the potential for living to the fullest.

PHYSICAL DEVELOPMENT

In earlier chapters, we saw that throughout childhood and adolescence, the body grows larger and stronger, coordination improves, and sensory systems gather information more effectively. Once body structures reach maximum capacity and efficiency in the teens and twenties, **biological aging,** or **senescence,** begins—genetically influenced declines in the functioning of organs and systems that are universal in all members of our species (Cristofalo et al., 1999). However, like physical growth, biological aging is *asynchronous* (see Chapter 7, pages 209–210). Change varies widely across parts of the body, with some structures not affected at all. In addition, individual differences are great—variation that the lifespan perspective helps us understand. Biological aging is influenced by a host of contextual factors, each of which can accelerate or slow age-related declines. These include the person's unique genetic makeup, lifestyle, living environment, and historical period (Arking, 1991). As

■ *The decades of early adulthood—the twenties and thirties—are an energetic time that, more than any other period of the lifespan, offer the potential for living to the fullest. (Photo courtesy: Strauss/ Curtis/The Stock Market)*

a result, the physical changes of the adult years are, indeed, multidimensional and multidirectional.

In the following sections, we examine the process of biological aging, first at the larger level of human life expectancy and limits of the human lifespan. Then we turn to theories of aging and physical and motor changes already under way in early adulthood. Our discussion will show that biological aging is not fixed and immutable. Instead, it can be modified substantially through behavioral and environmental interventions.

LIFE EXPECTANCY

AVERAGE LIFE EXPECTANCY

Dramatic gains in **average life expectancy**—the number of years an individual born in a particular year can expect to live—provide powerful support for the malleability of biological aging. An American baby born in 1900 had an average life expectancy of just under 50 years. In 1997, the figure reached 76.5 years. Twentieth-century gains in life expectancy were so extraordinary that they equaled those of the previous 5,000 years! Improved nutrition, medical treatment, sanitation, and safety seem to be responsible. Steady declines in infant mortality (see Chapter 3) are a major contributor to longer life expectancy. But death rates among adults have decreased as well. For example, heart disease, the leading cause of overall adult death in the United States, has dropped by nearly 50 percent in the past 30 years. If all mortality due to heart disease could be eliminated, 12 years would be added to life expectancy.

As Figure 13.1 shows, in early adulthood, unintentional injuries (two-thirds of which are due to motor vehicle collisions) continue to be the leading cause of death, followed by cancer, heart disease, suicide, and AIDS. During the past 15 years, young adult deaths from various forms of cancer have dropped between 20 and 43 percent, extending life expectancy by several years (U.S. Bureau of the Census, 1999).

Aspects of personality and a good marriage can also add to life, as the Lifespan Vista box on pages 422–423 reveals.

Consistent group differences in life expectancy underscore the joint contribution of heredity and environment to biological aging. On the average, women can look forward to 4 to 7 more years of life than can men—a sex difference found in almost all cultures (Central Intelligence Agency, 1998). The female life expectancy advantage also characterizes several animal species, including rats, mice, and dogs (Shock, 1977). The protective value of the female's extra X chromosome (see Chapter 2) is believed to be responsible. Yet since the early 1970s, some industrialized nations have experienced a narrowing of this gender gap, due to a slowing in life expectancy gains for females compared with males. The trend is believed to be due to women's increasing resemblance to men in lifestyle factors linked to health risks, such as workplace stress, cigarette smoking, and alcohol use (Trovato & Lalu, 1998).

Life expectancy varies substantially between SES and ethnic groups and nations. For example, a white child born in the United States around the year 2000 is likely to live 5 to 7 years longer than a black child—a gap accounted for by higher rates of infant mortality, unintentional injuries, violent death, life-threatening disease, and poverty-linked stress in the African-American population (McGinnis & Lee, 1995; U.S. Bureau of the Census, 1999). Length of life can be predicted by the quality of health care, housing, and social services a country provides. Among the world's nations, the United States ranks only nineteenth in life expectancy. In developing nations with widespread poverty, malnutrition, disease, and armed conflict, average life expectancy hovers around 50 years and is sometimes lower (Bellamy, 1999; Sivard, 1996).

MAXIMUM LIFESPAN AND ACTIVE LIFESPAN

Perhaps you are wondering: What is the **maximum lifespan,** or genetic limit to length of life for a person free of ex-

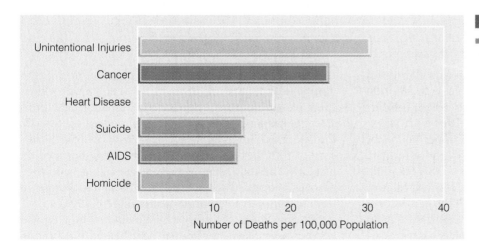

FIGURE 13.1

■ **Leading causes of death between 25 and 44 years of age in the United States.** (Adapted from U.S. Bureau of the Census, 1999.)

A LIFESPAN VISTA

AGING AND DEATH OF THE "TERMITES": PSYCHOLOGICAL PREDICTORS OF LONGEVITY

In 1921, Louis Terman, who adapted Binet's original intelligence test for use with American children (see Chapter 1), recruited 1,500 highly intelligent (IQs of at least 135) California boys and girls into one of the most comprehensive longitudinal studies ever conducted. The clever participants, who were observed, tested, and interviewed throughout their lives, nicknamed themselves the Termites. Today, an enormous data base charting all aspects of their development exists. Since half the Termites are now dead, the lifespan archives offered an unusual opportunity to examine the effects of personality, stressful life events, and health-related behaviors on length of life (Friedman et al., 1995).

Researchers have long believed that people with resilient personalities—able to withstand major disruptions in their lives—are less prone to disease and premature death. What kind of personality makes a difference, and just how do life stress and personal resources combine to affect longevity?

To find out, investigators focused on two sources of stress: parental divorce in childhood and marital instability in adulthood. Each was a powerful predictor of age of death. Average life expectancy among the Termites was 76 for men whose parents divorced, 80 for men whose parents stayed married. For women, the corresponding figures were 82 and 86 years (Schwartz et al., 1995). Marital instability in adulthood had similar effects. At age 40, Termites who were "steadily married" (had one lasting marriage) or who had never married were at lowest risk for premature death. Risk increased considerably for those who were "inconsistently married" (remarried after divorce), and it was highest for those who were separated, divorced, or widowed.

Furthermore, stressful life events tended to go together. Termites whose parents divorced were themselves more likely to divorce. And they more often reported a highly stressful early home environment and unhealthy behaviors and adjustment difficulties in adulthood (Tucker et al., 1997). Still, each stressful marital event contributed independently to a shorter lifespan. And the longer life expectancy for steadily married than for inconsistently married Termites suggests lasting negative effects of divorce that are not completely overcome by remarriage.

■ *Shelley Smith Mydans is one of the continuously married, long-lived Termites. As a child in the 1920s, she was stubborn and artistic. After three years of college at Stanford University, she became a journalist for Life magazine and married Life photographer Carl Mydans. Shortly thereafter, Shelley and Carl were sent to cover the unfolding of World War II in Europe and then in Asia, where they were interned by the Japanese. This photo was taken just after the couple's release and return to the United States in 1943. Shelly soon became a mother and, like other women of her era, turned down career opportunities to rear her children. Later she authored several best-selling historical novels. (Photo courtesy: Bettman/CORBIS)*

ternal risk factors? According to current estimates, it varies between 70 and 110 years for most people, with 85 or 90 about average (Olshansky, Carnes, & Cassel, 1990). The oldest verified age to which an individual has lived is 122 years.

Do these figures actually reflect the upper bound of human longevity, or can our lifespans be extended further? At present, scientists disagree on answers to this question. Some believe that about 85 or 90 years is as much as most humans can expect, since gains in average life expectancy are largely the result of reducing health risks in the first 20 or 30 years; expected life for persons age 65 and older has increased very little (about 5 months) over the past decade (U.S. Department of Health and Human Services, 1999c). Others think we have not yet identified the human genetic limit, since the lifespans of several species have been stretched in the laboratory. For example, biologists have doubled the lifespan of fruit flies through selective breeding, increased the lifespan of roundworms 70 percent through genetic engineering, and raised rodents that live 30 percent longer by feeding them very low-calorie diets (Langreth, 1993).

The possibility of similar achievements in humans raises another issue: *Should* the lifespan be increased as far as pos-

Finally, childhood personality characteristics contributed to length of life. In previous research, outgoing, cheerful children were found to be especially resilient in the face of stress (see Chapter 1, page 10). In this study, however, conscientiousness and dependability predicted survival; impulsive, untrustworthy, and selfish individuals tended to have shorter lives. And sociability—expected to foster longevity—did just the opposite! Cheerful, "happy-go-lucky" children (as well as children whose parents divorced) grew into adults more likely to smoke, drink, and take risks—behaviors known to shorten length of life. As the researchers explained, whereas sociability may be helpful in the midst of difficult times, it can be harmful in the long run if it leads a person to be careless and irresponsible throughout life (Friedman et al., 1995).

In view of the many variables that affect longevity, the role of psychological factors in this study, summarized in Figure 13.2, is striking. The bright participants faced unique life challenges and developed in a particular historical context, so we should be cautious about generalizing the results. Nevertheless, we will see that they fit quite well with recent evidence on the relationship of psychological stress to mortality.

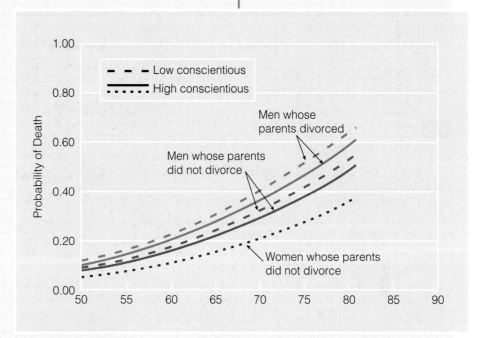

FIGURE 13.2

■ Age-related likelihood of death for a 20-year-old Termite by conscientiousness and parental divorce. The bottom curve shows the longest-lived women. The difference between this curve and the lowest curve for men highlights the well-known gender difference in longevity. But note that the difference between these two curves at age 70 is smaller than the difference between the highest and lowest men's curves. This indicates that the combined effects of personality and parental divorce on length of life are greater than the effect of gender. (Adapted from H. S. Friedman et al., 1995, "Psychosocial and Behavioral Predictors of Longevity: The Aging and Death of the 'Termites'," *American Psychologist, 50,* p. 73. Copyright © by Howard S. Friedman. Adapted by permission.)

sible? In considering this question, most people respond that *quality of life*, not just quantity, is the truly important goal. When researchers estimate **active lifespan,** they find that Americans can expect an average of 64 years of vigorous, healthy life, a level that has actually declined slightly over the past few years (U.S. Department of Health and Human Services, 1999c). This disheartening trend is largely due to continued high rates of preventable illness, death, and disability among low-income and ethnic minority sectors of the population. Many experts argue that only after reducing health risks among these groups and wiping out age-related diseases does it make sense to invest in extending the maximum lifespan.

THEORIES OF BIOLOGICAL AGING

At an intercollegiate tournament, Sharese dashed across the playing field for hours, leaping into the air to catch Frisbees sailing her way. In her early twenties, she is at her peak in strength, endurance, sensory acuteness, and immune system responsiveness. Why will she begin to age over the next two decades, gradually showing more noticeable declines in physical functioning as she moves into middle and late adulthood?

Biological aging is the combined result of many causes, some operating at the level of DNA, others at the level of cells, and still others at the level of tissues, organs, and whole organisms. Hundreds of theories exist, indicating that our understanding is still in an early stage (Cristofalo et al., 1999). One popular but inaccurate idea—the "wear-and-tear" theory—is that the body wears out from use. But unlike parts of a machine, worn-out parts of the body usually replace or repair themselves. Furthermore, no relationship exists between hard physical work and early death. To the contrary, vigorous exercise predicts a healthier and longer life (Alessio & Blasi, 1997). We now know that this "wear-and-tear" theory is an oversimplification.

AGING AT THE LEVEL OF DNA AND BODY CELLS

Current explanations of biological aging at the level of DNA and body cells are of two types: (1) those that emphasize the *programmed effects of specific genes,* and (2) those that emphasize the *cumulative effects of random events,* both internal and external, that damage genetic and cellular material. Support for both views exists, and it is likely that a combination will eventually prove to be correct.

Genetically programmed aging receives some support from kinship studies indicating that longevity is a family trait. People whose parents had long lives tend to live longer themselves, and there is greater similarity in the lifespans of identical than fraternal twins. But the heritability of longevity is quite modest—about .20 (McGue et al., 1993). Rather than inheriting longevity directly, people probably inherit one or more risk factors, which influence their chances of dying earlier or later.

One "genetic programming" theory proposes the existence of "aging genes" that control certain biological changes, such as menopause, gray hair, and deterioration of body cells. The strongest evidence for this view comes from research showing that human cells allowed to divide in the laboratory have a lifespan of 50 divisions plus or minus 10. With each duplication, the cells lose more of a special type of DNA—called *telomeres,* located at the ends of chromosomes—that is vital for cell duplication, until the cells no longer duplicate at all. When researchers replace telomere activity in cells that have lost it through genetic engineering, they can extend the lifespan of human cells in the laboratory (Vaziri & Benchimol, 1998).

According to an alternative, "random" view, DNA in body cells is gradually damaged due to spontaneous or externally caused mutations. As these accumulate, cell repair and replacement are less efficient, or abnormal cancerous cells are produced. Studies of various animal species confirm an increase in DNA breaks and deletions and damage to other cellular material with age. Among humans, similar evidence is accumulating (Gilchrest & Bohr, 1997; Wei, 1998).

One probable cause of age-related DNA and cellular abnormalities is the release of **free radicals,** naturally occurring, highly reactive chemicals that form in the presence of oxygen. (Radiation and certain pollutants and drugs can trigger sim-

ilar effects.) When oxygen molecules break down within the cell, the reaction strips away an electron, creating a free radical. As it seeks a replacement from its surroundings, it destroys nearby cellular material, including DNA, proteins, and fats essential for cell functioning (Sohal & Weindruch, 1996). Free radicals are thought to be involved in more than 60 disorders of aging, including heart disease, cancer, cataracts, and arthritis. Although our bodies produce substances that neutralize free radicals, some harm occurs and accumulates.

Some researchers believe that genes for longevity work by defending against free radicals. In this way, a programmed genetic response may limit random DNA and cellular deterioration. Foods rich in vitamins C and E and beta-carotene forestall free-radical damage as well (Diplock, 1997).

AGING AT THE LEVEL OF ORGANS AND TISSUES

What consequences might the DNA and cellular deterioration just described have for the structure and functioning of organs and tissues? There are many possibilities. Among those with clear support is the **cross-linkage theory** of aging. Over time, protein fibers that make up the body's connective tissue form bonds, or links, with one another. When these normally separate fibers cross link, tissue becomes less elastic, leading to many negative outcomes, including loss of flexibility in the skin and other organs, clouding of the lens of the eye, clogging of arteries, and damage to the kidneys. Like other aspects of aging, cross-linking can be reduced by external factors, including regular exercise and a vitamin-rich, low-fat diet (Arking, 1991; Schneider, 1992).

Gradual failure of the endocrine system, which is responsible for production and regulation of hormones, is yet another route to aging. An obvious example is decreased estrogen production in women, which culminates in menopause. Since hormones affect so many body functions, disruptions in the endocrine system can have widespread effects on health and survival. At present, scientists are studying the impact of key hormones on aging. Recent evidence indicates that a gradual drop in growth hormone (GH) is associated with loss of muscle, addition of body fat, and thinning of the skin. In adults with abnormally low levels of GH, hormone therapy can slow these symptoms, but it has serious side effects for most people (Veldhuis, Iranmanesh, & Weltman, 1997). So far, diet and physical activity are safer ways to control these outcomes.

Finally, declines in immune system functioning contribute to many conditions of aging. Among these are increased susceptibility to infectious disease, heightened risk of cancer, and changes in blood vessel walls associated with cardiovascular disease. Decreased vigor of the immune response seems to be genetically programmed, but other aging processes we have considered can intensify it (Bergeman, 1997). Indeed, combinations of theories—the ones just reviewed as well as others—are needed to explain the complexities of biological aging. With this in mind, let's look closely at physical signs and other characteristics of aging in the following sections.

PHYSICAL CHANGES

During the twenties and thirties, changes in physical appearance and declines in body functioning are so gradual that many are hardly noticeable. Later, they will accelerate. The physical changes of aging are summarized in Table 13.1 on page 426. We will examine several in detail, taking up others in later chapters. But before we begin, it is important to note that the data forming the basis for these trends are largely cross-sectional. Since younger cohorts have experienced better health care and nutrition, cross-sectional studies can exaggerate impairments associated with aging (Arking, 1991). Fortunately, longitudinal evidence is expanding, helping to correct this picture.

CARDIOVASCULAR AND RESPIRATORY SYSTEMS

During her first month in graduate school, Sharese pored over research articles on cardiovascular functioning. In her African-American extended family, her father, an uncle, and three aunts had died of heart attacks in their forties and fifties. The tragedies had prompted Sharese to worry about her own lifespan, reconsider her health-related behaviors, and enter the field of public health in hopes of finding ways to relieve the health problems of black Americans. *Hypertension*, or high blood pressure, occurs 12 percent more often in the American black than in the American white population; the rate of death from heart disease is 47 percent greater (U.S. Department of Health and Human Services, 1999c).

Sharese was surprised to learn that there are fewer age-related changes in the heart than we might expect, in view of the fact that heart disease rises with age and is a leading

cause of adult death. In healthy individuals, the heart's ability to meet the body's oxygen requirements under typical conditions (as measured by heart rate in relation to volume of blood pumped) does not change during adulthood. Only when people are stressed by exercise does performance of the heart decline with age. The change is due to a decrease in maximum heart rate and greater rigidity of the heart muscle. Consequently, the heart has difficulty delivering enough oxygen to the body during high activity and bouncing back from strain (Arking, 1991).

One of the most serious diseases of the cardiovascular system is *atherosclerosis*, in which heavy deposits of plaque containing cholesterol and fats collect on the walls of the main arteries. If it is present, it usually begins early in life, progresses during middle adulthood, and culminates in serious illness. Atherosclerosis is multiply determined, making it hard to separate the contributions of biological aging from individual genetic and environmental influences. The complexity of causes is illustrated by animal research indicating that before puberty, a high-fat diet produces only fatty streaks on the artery walls. In sexually mature adults, it leads to serious plaque deposits (Arking, 1991). These findings suggest that sex hormones may heighten the insults of a high-fat diet.

As mentioned earlier, heart disease has decreased considerably since the middle of the twentieth century. An especially large drop occurred during the last 15 years due to cultural changes in diet, exercise, cigarette smoking, and medical detection and treatment of high blood pressure and cholesterol (U.S. Department of Health and Human Services, 1999c). And as longitudinal research with several hundred thousand participants reveals, young and middle-aged adults at low risk for heart disease—defined by not smoking, low blood cholesterol, and normal blood pressure—show 40 to 60 percent reduced death rates over the next 16 to 22 years (see Figure 13.3) (Stamler et al., 1999). Later, when we consider health and fitness, we will see why heart attacks were so

FIGURE 13.3

■ **Death rates of individuals at low risk for heart disease— defined as not smoking, low blood cholesterol, and normal blood pressure—compared with other individuals.** Findings come from two longitudinal studies—the Multiple Risk Factor Intervention Trial (MRFIT) and the Chicago Heart Association Detection Project in Industry (CHA)—in which five cohorts, totaling over 350,000 adults, were followed for 16 to 22 years. Those who did not smoke, whose total blood cholesterol was under 200 mg/dL, and whose systolic/diastolic blood pressure was 120/80 or lower showed death rates that were 40 to 60 percent lower than same-sex agemates. (Adapted from Stamler et al., 1999.)

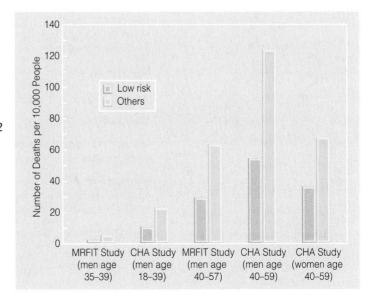

TABLE 13.1

Physical Changes of Aging

ORGAN OR SYSTEM	TIMING OF CHANGE	DESCRIPTION
Sensory		
Vision	From age 30	As the lens stiffens and thickens, ability to focus on close objects declines. Yellowing of the lens, weakening of muscles controlling the pupil, and clouding of the vitreous (gelatin-like substance that fills the eye) reduce light reaching the retina, impairing color discrimination and night vision. Visual acuity, or fineness of discrimination, decreases, with a sharp drop between ages 70 and 80.
Hearing	From age 30	Sensitivity to sound declines, especially at high frequencies but gradually extending to all frequencies. Change is more than twice as rapid for men than women.
Taste	From age 60	Sensitivity to the four basic tastes—sweet, salty, sour, and bitter—is reduced. May be due to factors other than aging, since number and distribution of taste buds do not change.
Smell	From age 60	Loss of smell receptors reduces ability to detect and identify odors.
Touch	Gradual	Loss of touch receptors reduces sensitivity on the hands, particularly the fingertips.
Cardiovascular	Gradual	As the heart muscle becomes more rigid, maximum heart rate decreases, reducing the heart's ability to meet the body's oxygen requirements when stressed by exercise. As artery walls stiffen and accumulate plaque, blood flow to body cells is reduced.
Respiratory	Gradual	Under physical exertion, respiratory capacity decreases and breathing rate increases. Stiffening of connective tissue in the lungs and chest muscles makes it more difficult for the lungs to expand to full volume.
Immune	Gradual	Shrinking of the thymus limits maturation of T cells and disease-fighting capacity of B cells, impairing the immune response.
Muscular	Gradual	As nerves stimulating them die, fast-twitch muscle fibers (responsible for speed and explosive strength) decline in number and size to a greater extent than do slow-twitch fibers (which support endurance). Tendons and ligaments (which transmit muscle action) stiffen, reducing speed and flexibility of movement.
Skeletal	Begins in the late 30s, accelerates in the 50s, slows in the 70s	Cartilage in the joints thins and cracks, leading bone ends beneath it to erode. New cells continue to be deposited on the outer layer of the bones, and mineral content of bone declines. The resulting broader but more porous bones weaken the skeleton and make it more vulnerable to fracture. Change is more rapid in women than in men.
Reproductive	In women, accelerates after age 35; in men, begins after age 40	Fertility problems (including difficulty conceiving and carrying a pregnancy to term) and risk of having a baby with a chromosomal disorder increase.
Nervous	From age 60	Brain weight declines as neurons die, mostly in the cerebral cortex, and as ventricles (spaces) within the brain enlarge. Development of new synapses can, in part, compensate for the decline in number of neurons.
Skin	Gradual	Epidermis (outer layer) is held less tightly to the dermis (middle layer); fibers in the dermis and hypodermis (inner layer) thin; fat cells in the hypodermis decline. As a result, the skin becomes looser, less elastic, and wrinkled. Change is more rapid in women than in men.
Hair	From age 35	Grays and thins.
Height	From age 50	Loss of bone strength leads to collapse of disks in the spinal column, leading to a height loss of as much as 2 inches by the seventies and eighties.
Weight	Increases to age 50; declines from age 60	Weight change reflects a rise in fat and a decline in muscle and bone mineral. Since muscle and bone are heavier than fat, the resulting pattern is weight gain followed by loss. Body fat accumulates on the torso and decreases on the extremities.

Sources: Abrass, 1990; Arking, 1991; Fabsitz, Sholinsky, & Carmelli, 1994; Pearson et al., 1995; Receputo et al., 1994; Thornbury & Mistretta, 1981; Whitbourne, 1996.

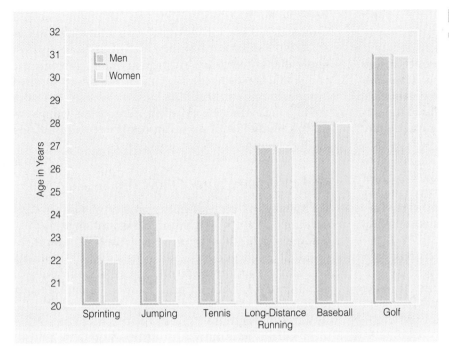

FIGURE 13.4

■ **Age of peak performance of Olympic and professional athletes by type of sport for men and women.** Sprinting, jumping, and tennis, which require speed of limb movement, explosive strength, and gross body coordination, peak in the early twenties. Long-distance running, baseball, and golf, which depend on endurance, arm–hand steadiness, and aiming, peak in the late twenties and early thirties. (Adapted from Schulz & Curnow, 1988.)

common in Sharese's family—and occur at especially high rates in the African-American population.

Like the heart, functioning of the lungs shows few age-related changes at rest, but during physical exertion, respiratory volume decreases and breathing rate increases with age. Maximum vital capacity (amount of air that can be forced in and out of the lungs) declines by 50 percent from the 20s to the 80s. Connective tissue in the lungs, chest muscles, and ribs stiffens with age, making it more difficult for the lungs to expand to full volume. Fortunately, under normal conditions, we use less than half our vital capacity; most of it is held in reserve (Arking, 1991). Nevertheless, aging of the lungs contributes to the fact that during heavy exercise, older adults find it more difficult to meet the body's oxygen needs.

MOTOR PERFORMANCE

Declines in heart and lung functioning under conditions of exertion, combined with gradual muscle loss, lead to changes in motor performance. In ordinary people, the impact of biological aging on motor skills is difficult to separate from decreases in motivation and practice. Therefore, re-searchers study outstanding athletes, who try to attain their very best performance in real life. As long as athletes continue intensive training, their attainments at each age approach the limits of what is biologically possible (Ericsson, 1990).

Many studies show that athletic skill peaks between ages 20 and 30 and then declines. In several investigations, the mean ages for best performance of Olympic and professional athletes in a variety of sports were charted over time. Absolute performance in many events improved over the past century. Athletes continually set new world records, suggesting improved training methods. Nevertheless, ages of best performance remained relatively constant. As Figure 13.4 reveals, athletic tasks that require speed of limb movement, explosive strength, and gross body coordination—sprinting, jumping, and tennis—peak in the early twenties. Those that depend on endurance, arm–hand steadiness, and aiming—long-distance running, baseball, and golf—peak in the late twenties and early thirties. Since these tasks have to do with either stamina or precise motor control, they take longer to develop (Schulz & Curnow, 1988).

■ *Athletic skill peaks between ages 20 and 30 and then declines. However, as long as practice continues, performance drops only slightly—about 2 percent per decade—into the sixties and seventies. Here John Kelley, age 78, smiles as he approaches the finish line of the Boston Marathon, his fifty-fifth completion of the race. Although his two first-place finishes occurred in his twenties and thirties, he continued to train and run for many more years. (Photo courtesy: AP/Wide World Photos)*

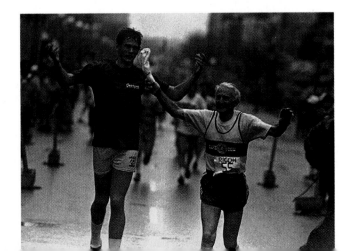

Research on outstanding athletes tells us that the upper biological limit of motor capacity is reached in the first part of early adulthood. How quickly do athletic skills weaken in later years? Longitudinal research on master runners reveals that as long as practice continues, performance drops only slightly—about 2 percent per decade—into the sixties and seventies (Hagberg et al., 1985). Indeed, sustained training leads to adaptations in body structures that minimize motor decline. For example, vital capacity is almost twice as great in older people actively participating in sports as in healthy controls without a history of exercise (Hagberg, 1987). Training also slows muscle loss and leads fast-twitch muscle fibers to be converted into slow-twitch fibers, which support excellent long-distance running performance as well as other endurance skills (Ericsson, 1990).

In sum, although athletic skill is at its best in early adulthood, only a small part of age-related decline is due to biological aging. Lower levels of performance in older healthy people largely reflect reduced capacities that result from adaptation to a less physically demanding lifestyle.

IMMUNE SYSTEM

The immune response is the combined work of specialized cells that neutralize or destroy antigens (foreign substances) in the body. Two types of white blood cells play vital roles. *T cells,* which originate in the bone marrow and mature in the thymus (a small gland located in the upper part of the chest), attack antigens directly. *B cells,* manufactured in the bone marrow, secrete antibodies into the bloodstream that multiply, capture antigens, and permit the blood system to destroy them. Since receptors on their surfaces recognize only a single antigen, T and B cells come in great variety. They join forces with additional cells to produce immunity.

The capacity of the immune system to offer protection against disease increases through adolescence and declines after age 20. The trend is partly due to changes in the thymus, which is largest during the teenage years and shrinks to being barely detectable after age 50. As a result, production of thymic hormones is reduced, and the thymus is less able to promote full maturity and differentiation of T cells. Since B cells release far more antibodies when T cells are present, the immune response is compromised further (Smith, 1993a). Research indicates that administering thymic hormones can help the aging body fight disease (Goya & Bolognani, 1999).

Withering of the thymus, however, is not the only reason that the body gradually becomes less effective in warding off illness. The immune system interacts with the nervous and endocrine systems. For example, stress can weaken the immune response. During final exams, Sharese found herself more susceptible to colds. And in the month after her father died, she had great difficulty recovering from the flu. Divorce, caring for an ill aging parent, and chronic depression can also reduce immunity (Bernston et al., 1998). The link between stress and illness makes perfect sense when we consider that stress hormones mobilize the body for action, whereas the immune response is fostered by reduced activity (Maier, Watkins, & Fleshner, 1994). But this also means that increased difficulty coping with physical and psychological stress can contribute to age-related declines in immune system functioning.

REPRODUCTIVE CAPACITY

Sharese was born when her mother was in her early twenties—an age at which Sharese was still single and entering graduate school a generation later. Many people believe that pregnancy during the twenties is ideal, not only because the risks of miscarriage and chromosomal disorders are reduced (see Chapter 2), but also because younger parents have more energy to keep up with active children. However, as Figure 13.5 reveals, first births to women in their thirties have increased greatly over the past two decades. Many people are delaying childbearing until their education is complete, their careers are well established, and they know they can support a child.

FIGURE 13.5

■ **First births to American women by age in 1970 and 1997.** The birth rate decreased over this period for women 20 to 24 years of age, whereas it increased for women 25 years and older. For women in their thirties, the birth rate more than doubled. (Adapted from U.S. Department of Health and Human Services, 1999c; Ventura, 1989.)

Nevertheless, reproductive capacity does decline with age. Fertility problems among women increase from ages 15 to 50, with a sharp rise in the mid-thirties. Between ages 25 and 34, nearly 14 percent are affected, a figure that climbs to 26 percent for 35- to 44-year-olds (U.S. Department of Health and Human Services, 1999d). Age also affects male reproductive capacity. Amount of semen and concentration of sperm in each ejaculation gradually decline after age 40 (Murray & Meacham, 1993). Although there is no best time during adulthood to begin parenthood, individuals who decide to put off childbirth until their late thirties or their forties risk having fewer children than they desired or none at all.

ASK YOURSELF . . .

🌳 *Explain why the United States ranks only nineteenth in life expectancy among the world's nations. (For help in answering this question, return to the section on public policies and lifespan development in Chapter 2, pages 68–70.)*

■ *Len noticed the term* free radicals *in an article on adult health in his local newspaper, but he doesn't understand how they contribute to biological aging. Explain the role of free radicals to Len.*

🌳 *Penny is a long-distance runner for her college's track team. She wonders what her running performance will be like 10 or 20 years from now. Describe physical changes and environmental factors that will affect Penny's long-term athletic skill.*

HEALTH AND FITNESS

Look back at Figure 13.1 on page 421, which shows the leading causes of death in early adulthood. In later chapters, we will see that the number of adults whose lives are cut short by unintentional injury or homicide declines with age, whereas the number affected by disease and physical disability rises. Biological aging clearly contributes to this trend. But we have already noted wide individual and group differences in physical changes that are linked to environmental risks and health-related behaviors.

SES variations in health over the lifespan reflect these influences. Income, education, and occupational status show a strong and continuous relationship to almost every disease and health indicator (Adler et al., 1994). Furthermore, when a representative sample of 3,600 Americans were asked about chronic illnesses and health-related limitations on their daily lives, SES differences were relatively small at 25 to 35 years, widened between ages 35 and 65, and contracted during old age (see Figure 13.6). Longitudinal findings confirm that economically advantaged and well-educated individuals tend to sustain good health over most of their adult lives, whereas the health of lower-income individuals with limited education steadily declines (House et al., 1990a, 1990b). SES differences in health-related circumstances and habits—stressful life events, crowding, pollution, health care, diet, exercise, substance use, and access to supportive social relationships—are largely responsible (Lantz et al., 1998).

These findings reveal, once again, that the living conditions that surround us and those we create for ourselves

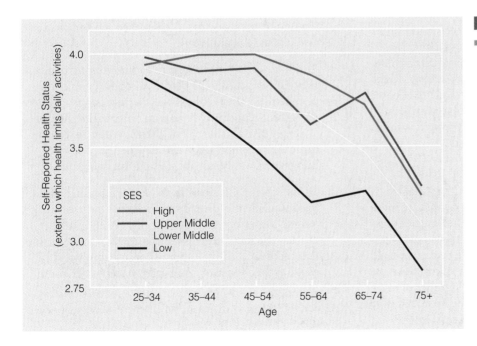

FIGURE 13.6

■ **Age differences in self-reported health status by socioeconomic status (SES).** Variations between income groups are small at 25 to 34 years, increase from 35 to 64 years, and then contract. Environmental risks and poor health habits contribute to the earlier decline in health status among low-income and poverty-stricken adults. (From J. S. House et al., 1990, "Age, Socioeconomic Status, and Health," *Milbank Quarterly, 68,* p. 396. Reprinted by permission.)

play powerful roles in how well we age. Since the incidence of health problems is much lower during the twenties and thirties than in succeeding decades, early adulthood is an excellent time to prevent later problems by adopting a healthier lifestyle. In the following sections, we take up a variety of major health concerns—nutrition, exercise, substance abuse, sexuality, and psychological stress.

NUTRITION

Bombarded with advertising claims and an extraordinary variety of food choices, adults in industrialized nations find it increasingly difficult to make wise dietary decisions. An abundance of food combined with a heavily scheduled life means that most Americans eat because they feel like it or because it is time to do so rather than to maintain the body's functions (Donatelle & Davis, 2000). As a result, many eat the wrong types and amounts of food. Overweight and obesity and a high-fat diet are widespread nutritional problems with long-term consequences for health in adulthood.

■ OVERWEIGHT AND OBESITY. Obesity (a 20 percent increase over average body weight, based on age, sex, and physical build) is increasing in the United States, having doubled since 1900. Currently, 22 percent of the population is affected. The incidence is particularly high among low-income ethnic minorities, especially females. Sharese learned that obesity rises to 60 percent among African-American women over age 40—an important reason (as we will see in a moment) that several of Sharese's family members succumbed to heart attacks in middle age. Obesity is even more prevalent among Hispanic and Native-American groups (U.S. Department of Health and Human Services, 1999c).

Overweight—a less extreme but nevertheless unhealthy condition—has increased by one-quarter during the last 30 years, from 44 percent to 54 percent of Americans (U.S. Department of Health and Human Services, 1999c). Recall from Chapter 9 that fat children are very likely to become fat adults. But a substantial number of people (4 percent of men and 8 percent of women) show large weight gains in adulthood, most often between ages 25 and 34. And young adults who were already overweight or obese (especially women) typically get heavier (Mokdad et al., 1999).

Causes and Consequences. As noted in Chapter 9, heredity plays a role in body weight; some people are more vulnerable to obesity than others. But environmental pressures underlie the rising rates of obesity in the United States and other industrialized nations. With the decline in need for physical labor in the home and workplace, our lives have become more sedentary. And the average number of calories and amount of fat Americans consume increased over most of the twentieth century (Koplan & Dietz, 1999).

Adding some weight between 25 and 50 is a normal part of aging, since **basal metabolic rate (BMR),** the amount of energy the body uses at complete rest, gradually declines as the number of active muscle cells (which create the greatest energy demand) drops off (see Table 13.1). But excess fat is strongly associated with serious health problems. These include high blood pressure, circulatory difficulties, atherosclerosis, adult-onset diabetes,[1] arthritis, sleep and digestive disorders, several forms of cancer, and early death (Allison et al., 1999; Must et al., 1999). Furthermore, fat adults suffer enormous social discrimination. They are less likely to find mates and to be rented apartments, given financial aid for college, and offered jobs (Allison & Pi-Sunyer, 1994; Gortmaker et al., 1993).

Treatment. Because obesity climbs in early adulthood, treatment for adults should begin as soon as possible—preferably in the early 20s. Even moderate weight loss reduces health problems substantially (Robison et al., 1993). But successfully intervening in obesity is difficult. At present, 95 percent of individuals who start a weight-loss program return to their original weight within 5 years (Allison & Pi-Sunyer, 1994). The high rate of failure is partly due to limited knowledge of just how obesity disrupts the complex neural, hormonal, and metabolic factors that maintain a normal body-weight setpoint. Until more information is available, researchers are examining the characteristics of treatments and participants associated with greater success. The following elements promote lasting behavior change:

■ *Low-fat diet plus exercise.* To lose weight, Sharese sharply reduced calories and fat in her diet and exercised regularly. This combination is essential for limiting the impact of a genetic tendency to overweight. In addition (as we will see shortly), exercise offers physical and psychological benefits that help prevent overeating. Yet less than half of American obese adults are advised by their doctors to control eating and to exercise (Galuska et al., 1999).

■ *Training participants to keep an accurate record of what they eat.* About 30 to 35 percent of obese people sincerely believe they eat less than they do, and from 25 to 45 percent report problems with binge eating (Bruce & Wilfley, 1996; Fairburn et al., 1998). When Sharese became aware of how often she ate when she was not hungry, she was better able to limit her food intake.

■ *Social support.* Group or individual counseling and encouragement of friends and relatives help sustain weight-loss efforts by fostering self-esteem (Prochaska, DiClemente, & Norcross, 1992). Once Sharese decided to act with the support of her family and a weight-loss counselor, she began to feel better about

---

[1]A mild form of diabetes first appearing in adulthood that is usually treated through dietary management and exercise.

herself—walking and holding herself differently—even before the first pounds were shed.

- *Teaching problem-solving skills.* Acquiring cognitive and behavioral strategies for coping with tempting situations and periods of slowed progress is associated with long-term change. Weight-loss maintainers are more likely than individuals who relapse to be conscious of their behavior, use social support, confront problems directly, and use personally developed strategies (Kayman, Bruvold, & Stern, 1990).

- *Extended intervention.* Longer treatments (from 25 to 40 weeks) that include the components just listed grant people time to develop new habits.

Finally, it is important to note that nearly 50 percent of American women and 25 percent of American men report that they are trying to lose weight (Robison et al., 1993). Although many dieters are overweight, others are within normal range. Recall from Chapter 11 that the high value placed on thinness in American society creates unrealistic expectations about desirable body weight and contributes to dangerous eating disorders of anorexia nervosa and bulimia, which remain common in early adulthood (see pages 359–360). Overweight people in weight-loss programs who set too-stringent weight goals are more likely to regain their lost pounds. And normal-weight people who diet often display "starvation syndrome" symptoms, including depression, anxiety, weakness, and preoccupation with food. A sensible body weight—neither too low nor too high—predicts physical and psychological health and longer life (Manson et al., 1995).

■ DIETARY FAT. After entering college, Sharese altered the diet of her childhood and adolescent years, sharply limiting red meat, eggs, butter, and fried foods. Public service announcements about the health risks of a high-fat diet have led the fat consumption of American adults to drop slightly —from an average of 36 to 34 percent of caloric intake— during the past 10 years (U.S. Department of Health & Human Services, 2000). The nation's health goals include reducing dietary fat to 30 percent, with no more than 10 percent made up of saturated fat. Fat consumption may play a role in breast cancer and (when it includes large amounts of red meat) is clearly linked to colon cancer (Clifford & Kramer, 1993). But the main reasons people need to watch how much fat they eat are the strong connection of total dietary fat with obesity and of saturated fat with cardiovascular disease.

Fat is a type of molecule made up of carbon atoms dotted with hydrogen atoms. *Saturated fat* has as many hydrogen atoms as it can chemically hold, generally comes from meat and dairy products, and is solid at room temperature.

Unsaturated fat has less than its full complement of hydrogen atoms and includes most vegetable oils that are liquid at room temperature.

Moderate fat consumption is essential for normal body functioning. But when we consume too much, especially of the saturated variety, some is converted to cholesterol, which accumulates as plaque on the arterial walls in atherosclerosis. Earlier in this chapter, we noted that atherosclerosis is determined by multiple biological and environmental factors. But excess fat consumption (along with other societal conditions) is largely responsible for the high incidence of heart disease in the American black population, since black Africans have among the lowest rates of heart disease in the world (Begley, 1995).

The best rule of thumb is to eat less fat of all kinds and use unsaturated instead of saturated fat whenever possible. Furthermore (as we will see next), regular exercise can reduce the harmful influence of dietary fat, since it creates chemical by-products that help eliminate cholesterol from the body.

E XERCISE

Three times a week, over the noon hour, Sharese delighted in running, making her way to a wooded trail that cut through a picturesque area of the city. Regular exercise kept her fit and slim. Compared to earlier days when she had been sedentary and overweight, it also limited the number

■ *Regular exercise, through such activities as volleyball, basketball, running, swimming, cycling, rowing, or brisk walking, can lead to a healthier, longer life. About 20 minutes, three to five times a week, of relatively vigorous use of large muscles of the body can help protect against obesity, enhance the immune response, and foster a positive outlook on life. (Photo courtesy: Ariel Skelley/The Stock Market)*

of respiratory illnesses she caught. And as Sharese explained to a friend one day, "Exercise gives me a positive outlook. It calms me down—takes the edge off. Afterward, I feel a burst of energy that gets me through the day. If I don't do it, I get tired in the afternoon." Although most Americans are aware of the health benefits of exercise, only 23 percent engage in moderate physical activity for 20 minutes or more at least five times a week (U.S. Department of Health and Human Services, 1999c).

Besides reducing body fat and building muscle, exercise fosters resistance to disease. Frequent bouts of moderate-intensity exercise enhance the immune response, thereby lowering the risk of colds or flu and, when these illnesses do strike, promoting faster recovery (Nieman, 1994). Furthermore, in several longitudinal studies extending over 10 to 20 years, physical activity was linked to reduced incidence of cancer at all body sites except the skin, with the strongest findings for cancer of the rectum and colon (Albanes, Blair, & Taylor, 1989; Wannamethee, Shaper, & Macfarlane, 1993). Exercise also helps prevent adult-onset diabetes (Kriska, Blair, & Pereira, 1994). Finally, physically active people are less likely to develop cardiovascular disease. If they do, it typically occurs at a later age and is less severe than among their inactive agemates (Bokovoy & Blair, 1994).

Just how does exercise help prevent the serious illnesses just mentioned? It may do so by reducing the incidence of obesity—a risk factor for heart disease, diabetes, and several forms of cancer. In addition, people who exercise probably adopt other healthful behaviors, thereby lowering the risk of diseases associated with high-fat diets, alcohol consumption, and smoking. Exercise can also have a direct impact on disease prevention. For example, in animal research, it inhibits growth of cancerous tumors beyond the impact of diet, body fat, and the immune response (Mackinnon, 1992). And it promotes cardiovascular functioning by strengthening the heart muscle, producing a form of "good cholesterol" (high-density lipoproteins) that helps remove "bad cholesterol" (low-density lipoproteins) from the artery walls, and decreasing blood pressure (Donatelle & Davis, 2000).

Yet another way that exercise may guard against illness is through its mental health benefits. Many studies show that physical activity reduces anxiety and depression, improves mood, and enhances alertness and energy (Kirkby & Lindner, 1998; Weyerer & Kupfer, 1994). The impact of exercise on a "positive outlook," as Sharese expressed it, is most obvious just after a workout and can last for several hours (Chollar, 1995). The stress-reducing properties of exercise undoubtedly strengthen immunity to disease. And as physical activity enhances psychological well-being, it promotes self-esteem, ability to cope with stress, on-the-job productivity, and life satisfaction.

When we consider the evidence as a whole, it is not surprising that physical activity is associated with substan-tially lower death rates from all causes (Blair et al., 1989). The contribution of exercise to longevity cannot be accounted for by preexisting illness in inactive people, since sedentary individuals who start to exercise live longer than those who remain inactive (Paffenbarger et al., 1993).

How much exercise is recommended for a healthier, happier, and longer life? The usual prescription is 20 minutes, three to five times a week, of relatively vigorous use of the large muscles of the body in which heart rate is elevated to 60 to 90 percent of its maximum—through rowing, cycling, dancing, cross-country skiing, swimming, running, or brisk walking (American College of Sports Medicine, 1998). At the same time, exercise should be pleasurable, not a chore. If the exercise program is too stressful, its health benefits will be reduced.

SUBSTANCE ABUSE

Despite an overall decrease in use of both legal and illegal substances in recent years, alcohol and drug dependency remain serious problems in early adulthood. They impair cognitive processes, intensify psychological problems that underlie addiction, and increase the risk of unintentional injury and death. Return to Chapter 11, page 369, and review the personal and situational factors that lead individuals to become substance abusers in adolescence. The same characteristics are predictive in the adult years. Cigarette smoking and alcohol consumption are the two most common substance disorders (Lowinson, Ruiz, & Millman, 1992).

■ CIGARETTE SMOKING. Dissemination of information on the harmful effects of cigarette smoking has helped reduce its prevalence from 40 percent of American adults in 1965 to 25 percent in 1997. Still, smoking has declined very slowly. Most of the drop is among college graduates; those who did not finish high school have changed very little. And smoking among young people enrolled in college is on the rise—for students of both sexes and of diverse ethnicities (Wechsler et al., 1998). More than 90 percent of men and 85 percent of women who smoke started before age 21. The average number of cigarettes smoked per day is high—about 20. And the earlier people start smoking, the greater their daily cigarette consumption, an important reason that preventive efforts with adolescents and young adults are vital (Breslau, 1993; U.S. Department of Health and Human Services, 1999c).

The ingredients of cigarette smoke—nicotine, tar, carbon monoxide, and other chemicals—leave their damaging mark throughout the body. As the person inhales, delivery of oxygen to tissues is reduced, and heart rate and blood pressure rise. Over time, insufficient oxygen results in limited night vision, more rapid wrinkling of the skin, and a lower sperm count and higher rate of male sexual impotence (Margolin, Morrison, & Hulka, 1994; Tur, Yosipovitch, & Oren-Vulfs, 1992). More deadly outcomes include increased risk of heart attack, stroke, and cancer of the mouth, throat, larynx, esophagus, lungs, pancreas, kidneys, and bladder. Cigarette smoking is the single most important preventable cause of death in industrialized nations. One of every three young people who become regular smokers will die from a smoking-related disease (Allen, Picone, & D'Amanda, 1993; U.S. Department of Health and Human Services, 1999c).

The link between smoking and mortality is dose related. The more cigarettes consumed, the greater the chance of premature death. At the same time, the benefits of quitting are great, including return of disease risks to nonsmoker levels within 3 to 8 years and a healthier living environment. Although millions of people have stopped smoking without help, those in treatment programs or using cessation aids (for example, nicotine gum, nasal spray, or patches, designed to reduce dependency gradually) often fail. After 1 year, 70 to 80 percent start smoking again (Brigham, 1998).

Unfortunately, too few treatments are long enough or teach skills for avoiding relapse. Sometimes a personal experience or the advice of a doctor is enough to energize quitting. My father, a heavy smoker in his 20s and 30s, sought treatment for chronic bronchitis (inflammation of the bronchial tubes, common among smokers). His doctor told him that if he did not stop smoking, he would not live to see his children grow up. That day marked his last cigarette. He died at age 80, having lived nearly 30 years longer than the average life expectancy for his year of birth.

■ ALCOHOL. National surveys reveal that about 13 percent of men and 3 percent of women in the United States are heavy drinkers (average two or more drinks per day). About one-third of these are *alcoholics*—people who are unable to limit their alcohol use and are often unaware that it is the cause of their problems. In men, alcoholism usually begins in the teens and early twenties and worsens over the following decade. In women, its onset is typically later, in the twenties and thirties, and its course more variable. Many alcoholics are also addicted to other drugs. About 80 percent are heavy cigarette smokers (Goodwin, 1997).

Twin and adoption studies support a genetic contribution to alcoholism (Anthenelli & Schuckit, 1992). But whether or not a person comes to deal with life's problems through drinking is greatly affected by personal characteristics and circumstances, since half of hospitalized alcoholics do not have a family history of problem drinking (Hawkins, Catalano, & Miller, 1992). Alcoholism crosses SES and ethnic lines, but it is higher in some groups than others. For example, in cultures in which alcohol is a traditional part of religious or ceremonial activities, people are less likely to abuse it. Where access to alcohol is carefully controlled and a sign of adulthood, dependency is more

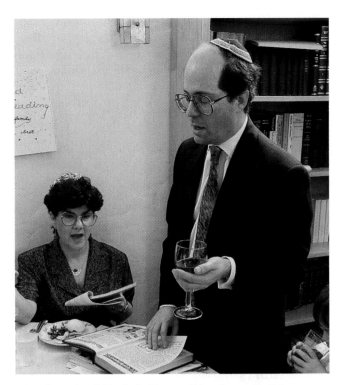

■ *In cultures in which alcohol is a traditional part of religious or ceremonial activities, people are less likely to abuse it. Here, during a Jewish Passover service, participants say the blessing over the wine. (Photo courtesy: Bill Aron/PhotoEdit)*

likely. Poverty and hopelessness also promote it (Donatelle & Davis, 2000).

Alcohol acts as a depressant, impairing the ability of the brain to control thought and action. In a heavy drinker, it relieves guilt and anxiety, then induces these states as its effects wear off, so the alcoholic drinks again. Chronic alcohol use does widespread damage to the body. Its most well-known complication is liver disease, but it is also linked to cardiovascular disease, inflammation of the pancreas, irritation of the intestinal tract, bone marrow problems, disorders of the blood and joints, and some forms of cancer. Over time, alcohol damages the central nervous system, leading to confusion, apathy, inability to learn, and impaired memory. The costs to society are enormous. About 40 percent of highway fatalities in the United States involve drivers who have been drinking. Nearly half of convicted felons are alcoholics, and about half of police activities in large cities involve alcohol-related offenses. Alcohol frequently plays a part in date rape, other forms of sexual coercion, and domestic violence (Goodwin, 1997; Murphy & O'Farrell, 1996).

The most successful treatments are comprehensive, combining personal and family counseling, group support, and aversion therapy (in which medication is used to produce a physically unpleasant reaction, such as nausea and vomiting, to alcohol). Alcoholics Anonymous, a community support approach, helps many people exert greater control over their lives through the encouragement of others with similar problems. Nevertheless, breaking an addiction that has dominated a person's life is difficult; about 60 percent of alcoholics relapse within 3 months after treatment (Goodwin, 1997).

SEXUALITY

By the time their teenage years are over, more than 80 percent of young people have had sexual intercourse; by age 22, the figure rises to 90 percent (Michael et al., 1994). Compared with earlier generations, a wider range of sexual choices and lifestyles can be observed in modern adults, including cohabitation, marriage, extramarital experiences, and orientation toward a heterosexual or homosexual partner. In this chapter, we explore the attitudes, behaviors, and health concerns related to sexual activity becoming a regular event in young people's lives. In Chapter 14, we focus on the emotional side of close relationships.

HETEROSEXUAL ATTITUDES AND BEHAVIOR.
One Friday evening, Sharese accompanied her roommate Heather to a young singles bar. Shortly after they arrived, two young men joined them. Faithful to her boyfriend Ernie (whom she met in college and who worked in another city), Sharese remained aloof for the next hour. In contrast, Heather was talkative and friendly and gave one of the men (Rich) her phone number. The next weekend, Heather went out with Rich. On the second date, they had intercourse, but the romance was short-lived. Within a few weeks, each went in search of a new partner. Aware of Heather's varied sex life, Sharese couldn't help but wonder whether her own was normal. Only after nearly a year of dating exclusively had she and Ernie slept together.

Since the 1950s, public display of sexuality in movies, newspapers, magazines, and books has steadily increased, fostering the impression that Americans are more sexually active than ever before. This escalation in sexual openness has prompted people whose sexual history falls short of popular images to question whether they might be missing something. What are modern adults' sexual attitudes and behaviors really like? Answers to this question have been difficult to obtain, until the completion of the National Health and Social Life Survey, the first in-depth study of Americans' sex lives based on a nationally representative sample. Nearly 4 out of 5 randomly chosen 18- to 59-year-olds agreed to participate—3,400 in all. Findings were remarkably similar to recent survey results in France, Great Britain, and Finland (Laumann et al., 1994; Michael et al., 1994).

Recall from Chapter 11 that the sex lives of most teenagers do not dovetail with exciting media images. A similar picture emerges for adults. Although their sexual practices are diverse, Americans are far less sexually active than we have come to believe. Couples like Sharese and Ernie are more typical (and satisfied) than are those like Heather and Rich.

Sexual partners, whether dating, cohabiting, or married, usually do not select each other arbitrarily. Instead, they tend to be alike in age (within 5 years), education, ethnicity, and (to a lesser extent) religion. In addition, most people who establish lasting relationships meet in conventional ways: They are introduced by family members or friends or get to know each other at work, school, or social events where people similar to themselves congregate. Only 10 percent of adults who marry and 14 percent who decide to live together meet at bars, through personal ads, or on vacations. The powerful influence of social networks on sexual choice is adaptive, since sustaining an intimate relationship is easier when adults share interests and values and people they know approve of the match.

Consistent with popular belief, Americans today have more sexual partners than they did a decade or two ago. For example, one-third of adults over age 50 have had five or more partners in their lives, whereas half of 30- to 50-year-olds have accumulated that many in much less time. But when adults—either younger or older—are asked how many partners they have had in the past year, the usual reply (for 71 percent) is one.

What explains this trend toward more relationships in the context of sexual commitment? In the past, dating several partners was followed by marriage. Today, dating more often gives way to cohabitation, which leads either to marriage or to breakup. In addition, people are marrying later, and the divorce rate remains high. Together, these factors create more opportunities for new sexual partners. Still, most people spend the majority of their lives with one partner. And only a small minority of Americans (3 percent), most of whom are men, report five or more partners in a single year. (See the Social Issues box on the following page for a discussion of sex differences in attitudes toward sexuality.)

How often do Americans have sex? Not nearly as frequently as the media would have us believe. Only one-third of 18- to 59-year-olds have intercourse as often as twice a week, another third have it a few times a month, and the remaining third have it a few times a year or not at all. Three factors affect frequency of sexual activity: (1) age, (2) whether people are married or cohabiting, and (3) how long the couple has been together. Younger, dating people have more partners, but this does not translate into more sex! Sexual activity increases through the twenties as people either marry or cohabit. Then, around age 30, it declines, even though hormone levels have not changed much. The demands of daily life—working, commuting, taking care of home and children—are probably responsible. Despite the common assumption that sexual practices vary greatly across social groups, the patterns just described are unaffected by education, SES, or ethnicity.

SEX DIFFERENCES IN ATTITUDES TOWARD SEXUALITY

Differences between men and women in sexual attitudes and behavior are widely assumed, and modern theories offer diverse explanations for them. For example, Nancy Chodorow, a feminist psychoanalytic theorist, and Carol Gilligan, a feminist theorist of moral development (see Chapter 12, page 399), believe that the emotional intensity of the infant–caregiver relationship is carried over into future intimate ties for girls. However, it is disrupted for boys as they form a "masculine" gender identity stressing individuation and independence (Chodorow, 1978; Gilligan, 1982). According to an alternative ethological view, sexuality is powerfully shaped by the desire to have children and ensure their survival. Since sperm are plentiful and ova far less numerous, women must be more careful than men about

selecting a partner with the commitment and resources needed to protect children's development (Buss, 1999; Bjorklund & Shackelford, 1999). Finally, social learning theory views sex differences as due to modeling and reinforcement of gender-role expectations (see Chapter 8, pages 264–265). Women receive more disapproval for having numerous partners and engaging in casual sex than do men, who are sometimes rewarded with admiration and social status.

Both small-scale studies and large-scale surveys confirm that women are more opposed to premarital and extramarital sex than are men. However, the difference, although substantial, has decreased over the past three decades (Laumann et al., 1994; Oliver & Hyde, 1993). Furthermore, when a small number of men with a great many sexual partners are excluded, modern men and women dif-

fer very little in average number of lifetime sexual partners (Chatterjee, Handcock, & Simonoff, 1995). Why is this so? From an ethological perspective, more effective contraception has permitted sexual activity without risk of reproduction. Under these circumstances, women can have as many partners as men without risking the welfare of their offspring.

Still, when women complain that the men they meet are not interested in long-term commitments, their laments have a ring of truth. Many more men than women report that they are looking for sexual play and pleasure, with marriage and love not necessarily a part of the equation. And when infidelity occurs, men are more upset at the thought of their partner having sex with another person, women at the thought of their partner feeling affection for someone else—an outcome that could mean loss of investment in their offspring (Buss, 1999). These conflicting goals and attitudes are greatest for young adults. With age, both sexes seem to become more traditional, regarding a loving relationship as more central to sexuality (Michael et al., 1994).

■ *Despite media images of exciting, varied sex lives, for most men and women satisfying sex is attained in the context of love, affection, and fidelity. People tend to seek out partners similar in age, education, and background to themselves, and partners in committed relationships have sex more often and are more satisfied. (Photo courtesy: Walter Bibikow/The Image Bank)*

Although most Americans have only modest amounts of sex, they are happy with their sex lives. For those in committed relationships, feeling "extremely physically and emotionally satisfied" exceeds 80 percent; it rises to 88 percent for married couples. As number of sex partners increases, satisfaction declines sharply. These findings challenge the stereotype of marriage as sexually dull and people with many partners as having the "hottest" sex.

Furthermore, only a minority of adults—women more often than men—report persistent sexual problems. The two most frequent difficulties for women are lack of interest in sex (33 percent) and inability to achieve orgasm (24 percent); for men, climaxing too early (29 percent) and anxiety about performance (16 percent) are most common. Sexual difficulties are linked to low SES and psychological stress. They are also more common among people who are not married, have had more than five partners, and have experienced sexual abuse during childhood or (for women) sexual coercion in adulthood (Laumann, Paik, & Rosen, 1999). As these findings suggest, unfavorable personal relationships and sexual experiences increase the risk of sexual dysfunction.

But overall, the survey findings indicated that a completely trouble-free physical experience is not essential for sexual happiness. Satisfying sex involves more than technique; it is attained in the context of love, affection, and fidelity. In the words of the researchers, "happiness with partnered sex is linked to happiness with life" (Michael et al., 1994, p. 130).

■ HOMOSEXUAL ATTITUDES AND BEHAVIOR. The tragic spread of AIDS has increased the visibility of homosexuals in the United States, reenergizing the gay liberation movement of the 1970s. Efforts at AIDS prevention, securing health care, and combating discrimination against people with AIDS have resulted in renewed attention to the civil rights of homosexuals. Attitudes toward homosexuals, although still quite negative, have begun to change, particularly in the area of equal employment opportunities. The majority of Americans support equal job opportunities for gay men, lesbians, and bisexuals, even when they disapprove of other rights, such as military service (Purcell & Hicks, 1996; Strand, 1998). Homosexuals' greater openness about their sexual orientation has contributed to slow gains in acceptance, since exposure to and interpersonal contact with gay men and lesbians reduce negative attitudes (Ellis & Vasseur, 1993). Men judge homosexuals more harshly than do women, perhaps because heterosexual men are more concerned with conforming to prescribed gender roles (Kite & Whitley, 1998).

In the National Health and Social Life Survey, 2.8 percent of men and 1.4 percent of women regarded themselves as homosexual or bisexual—figures that are similar to those of other recent national surveys conducted in the United States, France, and Great Britain (Billy et al., 1993; Spira, 1992; Wellings et al., 1994). These low numbers—and the possible unwillingness of homosexuals to answer questions about their sexual practices in a climate of persecution—have limited what researchers have been able to find out about the sex lives of gay men and lesbians. The little evidence available indicates that homosexual sex follows many of the same rules as heterosexual sex: People tend to seek out partners similar in education and background to themselves; partners in committed relationships have sex more often and are more satisfied; and the overall frequency of sex is modest (Laumann et al., 1994; Michael et al., 1994).

Although homosexuals are few in number, they tend to live in large cities where many others share their sexual orientation, rather than in small towns and rural areas. Gay pride has filtered down to some nonurban communities, but it is still rare (Michaels, 1996). Living outside of big cities, without a social network in which to find compatible homosexual partners and where prejudices are more intense, can be isolating and lonely. People who identify themselves as gay or lesbian also tend to be well educated. In the National Health and Social Life Survey, twice as many college-educated as high-school-educated men and 8 times as many college-educated as high-school-educated women stated they were homosexual. Although the reasons for these findings are not clear, they probably reflect greater social and sexual liberalism among the more highly educated and therefore greater willingness to disclose homosexuality.

■ SEXUALLY TRANSMITTED DISEASE. A large number of Americans—one in four—are likely to contract a sexually transmitted disease (STD) some time in their lives; 1.5 percent report having had one in the past year (Barringer, 1993; Laumann et al., 1994). (See Chapter 11, page 364, for a description of the most common STDs.) Although the incidence is highest in adolescence, STD continues to be prevalent in early adulthood. During the teens and twenties, people accumulate most of their sexual partners, and they often do not take appropriate precautions to prevent the spread of STD (see page 365). The overall rate of STD is higher among women than men, since it is at least twice as easy for a man to infect a woman with any STD, including AIDS, as it is for a woman to infect a man (Michael et al., 1994).

Although AIDS, the most deadly STD, remains concentrated among gay men and intravenous drug abusers, many homosexuals have responded to its spread by changing their sexual practices—limiting the number of partners with whom they have sex, choosing partners more carefully, and using latex condoms consistently and correctly. Heterosexuals who are high risk due to a history of many partners have done the same (Feinleib & Michael, 1998; Laumann et al., 1994). As a result, the number of infections is lower among gay and heterosexual men today than it was in the early 1980s. However, AIDS has not declined among drug abusers and their sexual partners. Consequently, some experts fear that it will spread most rapidly in marginal groups in which intravenous drug abuse is high and combines with poverty, inadequate education, poor health, high life stress, and hopelessness. People overwhelmed by these problems are least likely to take preventive measures (Jonsen & Stryker, 1992).

Yet AIDS can be contained and reduced—through sex education extending from childhood into adulthood and access to health services, condoms, and clean needles and syringes for high-risk individuals (Stryker et al., 1995). In view of the rise in AIDS cases among women over the past decade, a special need exists for female-controlled preventive measures. The recently developed female condom offers some promise, but its effectiveness and acceptability are not yet established (Seal & Ehrhardt, 1999).

■ SEXUAL COERCION. STD is not the only serious health threat to accompany sexual activity. After a long day of classes, Sharese flipped on the TV and caught a talk show on sex without consent. Karen, a 25-year-old woman, described her husband Mike pushing, slapping, and verbally insulting her, and forcing her to have sex. "It was a control thing," Karen explained tearfully. "He complained that I wouldn't always do what he wanted. I was confused and blamed myself. I didn't leave because I was sure he'd come after me and get more violent."

One day, as Karen was speaking long distance to her mother on the phone, Mike grabbed the receiver and shouted, "She's not the woman I married! I'll kill her if she doesn't shape up!" Karen's parents realized the seriousness of her situation, arrived by plane to rescue her the next day, and helped her start divorce proceedings and get treatment.

An estimated 14 to 25 percent of women have endured *rape,* legally defined as intercourse by force, by threat of harm, or when the victim is incapable of giving consent (due to mental illness, mental retardation, or intoxication). Nearly half have experienced other forms of sexual aggression. The majority of victims (8 out of 10) are under age 30 (Koss, 1993). Women are vulnerable in the company of partners, acquaintances, and strangers. But most of the time their abusers are men they know well (Hamberger, Saunders, & Hovey, 1992). Sexual coercion crosses SES and ethnic lines; people of all walks of life are offenders and victims. For example, in a national sample of over 6,000 American college students, 44 percent of women reported having

experienced sexual coercion, and 19 percent of men said they had obtained sex through force (Koss, 1998).

Personal characteristics of the man with whom a woman is involved are far better predictors of her chances of becoming a victim than her own characteristics. Men who engage in sexual assault tend to believe in traditional gender roles, approve of violence against women, and accept rape myths ("Women want to be raped" or "Any healthy woman can resist if she really wants to"). Many have an intense desire to dominate their victims but deny this, reasoning that "she brought it on herself" (Scully & Marolla, 1998). Perpetrators also have difficulty interpreting women's social behavior accurately. They are likely to view friendliness as seductiveness, assertiveness as hostility, resistance as desire (Allison & Wrightsman, 1993).

Cultural forces—in particular, strong gender typing—contribute to sexual coercion. When men are taught from an early age to be dominant, competitive, and aggressive and women to be submissive, cooperative, and passive, the themes of rape are reinforced. Under these conditions, men may view a date not in terms of getting to know a partner, but in terms of sexual conquest. And a husband may regard satisfaction of his sexual needs as his wife's duty, even when she is uninterested (Amaro, 1995). The widespread acceptance of violence in American society also sets the stage for rape, which typically occurs in relationships in which other forms of aggression are commonplace (Browne, 1993). Exposure to sexually aggressive pornography and other media images, which portray women desiring and enjoying the assault, also promote sexual coercion by lessening sensitivity to its harmful consequences (Donnerstein & Linz, 1998).

Consequences. Women's psychological reactions to rape resemble those of survivors of extreme trauma. Immediate responses include shock, confusion, withdrawal, and psychological numbing. These eventually give way to chronic fatigue, tension, disturbed sleep, depression, and suicidal thoughts (Resnick & Newton, 1992). When sexual coercion is ongoing, taking any action may seem dangerous (as it did to Karen), so the victim falls into a pattern of extreme passivity and fear (Goodman, Koss, & Russo, 1993). If she has a history of sexual abuse or received negative feedback after trying to tell someone, she is more likely to blame herself, which strengthens helpless reactions (Arata, 1999; Ullman, 1996).

One-third to one-half of rape victims are physically injured. Some contract sexually transmitted diseases, and

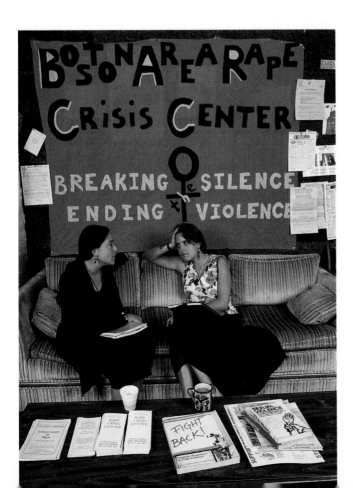

■ *Psychological reactions to rape are severe enough that therapy is vital. In this rape crisis center, a professional counselor assists a victim in recovering from trauma through social support, validation of her experience, and safety planning. (Photo courtesy: Rob Crandall/Stock Boston)*

pregnancy results in about 5 percent of cases. Furthermore, women victimized by rape (and other crimes) report more symptoms of illness across almost all body systems. And they are more likely to engage in negative health behaviors, including smoking and alcohol use (Koss, Koss, & Woodruff, 1991).

Prevention and Treatment. Many rape victims are not as fortunate as Karen, since their anxiety about provoking another attack keeps them from confiding even in trusted family members and friends. If they seek help for other problems, conflict over issues surrounding sexuality may lead a sensitive health professional to detect a possible rape. A variety of community services exist to assist women in taking refuge from abusive partners, including safe houses, crisis hotlines, support groups, and legal assistance. Most, however, are underfunded and cannot reach out to everyone in need.

The trauma induced by rape is severe enough that therapy is important. Many experts advocate group intervention, since contact with other survivors is especially helpful in countering isolation and self-blame (Koss & Harvey, 1991). Other critical features that foster recovery include

- *routine screening for victimization* when women seek health care to ensure referral to community services and protection from future harm.

- *validation of the experience,* by acknowledging that many other women have been physically and sexually assaulted by intimate partners; that such assaults lead to a wide range of persisting symptoms, are illegal and inappropriate, and should not be tolerated; and that the trauma can be overcome.

- *safety planning,* even when the abuser is no longer present, to prevent recontact and reassault. This includes how to obtain police protection, legal intervention, a safe shelter, and other aid should a rape survivor find herself at risk again.

Finally, many steps can be taken at the level of the individual, the community, and society to prevent sexual coercion. Some are listed in the Caregiving Concerns table below.

■ MENSTRUAL CYCLE. The menstrual cycle is central to women's lives, and it presents unique health concerns. Although almost all women experience some discomfort during menstruation, others have more severe difficulties. **Premenstrual syndrome (PMS)** refers to an array of physical and psychological symptoms that usually appear 6 to 10 days prior to menstruation. The most common are abdominal cramps, fluid retention, diarrhea, tender breasts, backache, headache, fatigue, tension, irritability, and depression; the precise combination varies from person to person. PMS is usually experienced for the first time after age 20. Nearly 40 percent of women have some form of it, usually mild. For 10 percent, PMS is severe enough to interfere with academic, occupational, and social functioning. PMS is a worldwide phenomenon—just as common in Italy and the Islamic nation of Bahrain as it is in the United States (Brody, 1992; Ugarriza, Klingner, & O'Brien, 1998).

The causes of PMS are not well established, but evidence for a biological basis is accumulating. Researchers believe that some women may have a genetic susceptibility (Freeman & Halbreich, 1998). PMS is related to hormonal changes that follow ovulation and precede menstruation. But since hor-

■ CAREGIVING CONCERNS

Preventing Sexual Coercion

SUGGESTION	DESCRIPTION
Reduce gender stereotyping and gender inequalities.	The roots of sexual coercion lie in the historically subordinate role of women. Restricted educational and employment opportunities keep many women economically dependent on men and therefore poorly equipped to avoid partner violence.
Mandate treatment for men who physically or sexually assault women.	Ingredients of effective intervention include inducing personal responsibility for violent behavior; teaching social awareness, social skills, and anger management; and developing a support system to prevent future attacks.
Expand interventions for children and adolescents who have witnessed violence between adult caregivers.	Although most child witnesses do not become involved in abusive relationships as adults, boys are at increased risk of assaulting their female partners and girls are at increased risk of becoming victims if they observed violence between their parents.
Teach women to take precautions that lower the risk of sexual assault.	Risk of sexual assault can be reduced by communicating sexual limits clearly to a date; developing neighborhood ties to other women; increasing the safety of the immediate environment (for example, installing deadbolt locks, checking the back seat of the car before entering); avoiding deserted areas; and not walking alone after dark. (For additional suggestions, consult *The New Our Bodies, Ourselves: A Book by and for Women.*)

Sources: Boston Women's Health Book Collective, 1992; Browne, 1993.

mone treatment is not consistently effective, sensitivity of brain centers to these hormones, rather than the hormones themselves, may be responsible (Lewis, 1992; Seippel & Backstrom, 1998). Besides hormones, current treatments include analgesics for pain, diuretics for fluid buildup, limiting caffeine intake (which often intensifies symptoms), vitamin therapy, exercise, and other strategies for reducing stress. Although each of these approaches is helpful in certain cases, as yet no method has been successful in curing PMS.

PSYCHOLOGICAL STRESS

A final health concern, threaded throughout previous sections, has such a broad impact that it merits a comment of its own. Psychological stress, measured in terms of adverse social conditions, negative life events, or daily hassles, is related to a wide variety of health outcomes (Lazarus, 1985, 1991). In addition to its association with many unhealthy behaviors, stress has clear physical consequences. For example, as it mobilizes the body for action, it elevates blood pressure. Chronic stress resulting from economic hardship and inner-city living is consistently linked to hypertension, a relationship that contributes to the high incidence of heart disease in low-income groups, especially African Americans (Calhoun, 1992). Earlier we mentioned that psychological stress also interferes with immune system functioning, a link that may underlie its relationship to several forms of cancer. And by reducing digestive activity

as blood flows to the brain, heart, and extremities, stress can cause gastrointestinal difficulties, including constipation, diarrhea, colitis, and ulcers (Donatelle & Davis, 2000).

In previous chapters, we repeatedly noted the stress-buffering effect of social support, which continues throughout adulthood (Markides & Cooper, 1989). Consequently, helping people who are isolated develop and maintain satisfying social ties is as important a health intervention as any we have mentioned. Before we turn to the cognitive side of early adulthood, you may find it helpful to examine the Caregiving Concerns table below, which summarizes the many ways we can foster a healthy adult life.

ASK YOURSELF . . .

🌳 *List as many factors as you can that may have contributed to heart attacks and early death among Sharese's relatives.*

🌳 *Tom began going to a health club three days a week after work. Soon the pressures of his job and his desire to spend more time with his girlfriend convinced him that he no longer had time for so much exercise. Explain to Tom why he should keep up his exercise regimen, and suggest ways to fit it into his busy life.*

■ *Why are people in committed relationships likely to be more sexually active and satisfied than those who are dating several partners?*

CAREGIVING CONCERNS

Fostering a Healthy Adult Life

SUGGESTION	DESCRIPTION
Engage in healthy eating behavior.	Educate yourself and those with whom you live about the makeup of a healthy diet. Eat in moderation, and learn to separate true hunger from eating due to boredom or stress.
Maintain a reasonable body weight.	If you need to lose weight, make a commitment to a lifelong change in the way you eat, not just a temporary diet. Select a sensible, well-balanced dietary plan, eat small meals spaced over the day, and exercise regularly.
Keep physically fit.	Choose a specific time to exercise, and stick with it. To help sustain physical activity and make it more enjoyable, exercise with your partner or a friend and encourage one another. Set reasonable expectations, and allow enough time to reach your fitness goals; many people become exercise dropouts because their expectations were too high.
Control alcohol intake, and do not smoke cigarettes.	Drink moderately or not at all. Do not allow yourself to feel you must drink to be accepted or to enjoy a social event. If you smoke, choose a time that is relatively stress-free to quit. Seek the support of your partner or a friend.
Engage in responsible sexual behavior.	Identify attitudes and behaviors that you need to change to develop a healthy intimate relationship. Educate yourself about sexual anatomy and functioning so you can make sound decisions about contraception and protect yourself against sexually transmitted disease.
Manage stress.	Seek a reasonable balance among work, family, and leisure. Become more aware of stressors, and identify ways of coping with them so you are better prepared when they arise. Engage in regular exercise, and find time each day for relaxation and quiet reflection.

Source: Donatelle & Davis, 2000.

COGNITIVE DEVELOPMENT

How does cognition change with the transition to adulthood? Lifespan theorists have examined this question from three familiar vantage points. First, they have proposed transformations in the structure of thought—new, qualitatively distinct ways of thinking that extend the cognitive-developmental changes of childhood and adolescence. Second, adulthood is a time of attaining advanced knowledge in a particular area, an accomplishment that has important implications for information processing and creativity. Finally, researchers have been interested in the extent to which the diverse mental abilities assessed by intelligence tests remain stable or change during the adult years. To clarify how thinking is restructured in adulthood, let's look at some influential theories.

CHANGES IN THE STRUCTURE OF THOUGHT

Sharese described her first year in graduate school as a "cognitive turning point." As part of her internship in a public health clinic, she observed firsthand the many factors that affect human health-related behaviors. For a time, she was intensely uncomfortable about the fact that clear-cut solutions to dilemmas in the everyday world were so hard to come by. "Working in this messy reality is so different from the problem solving I did in my undergraduate classes," she commented to her mother in a phone conversation one day.

Sharese's reflections agree with those of a variety of researchers who have studied **postformal thought**—cognitive development beyond Piaget's formal operational stage. Even Piaget (1967) acknowledged the possibility that important advances in thinking follow the attainment of formal operations. He observed that adolescents place excessive faith in abstract systems, preferring a logical, internally consistent but inaccurate perspective on the world to one that is vague, contradictory, and adapted to particular circumstances (see Chapter 11, page 375). To clarify how thinking is restructured in adulthood, let's look at some influential theories.

P ERRY'S THEORY

In a well-known study, William Perry (1970, 1981) interviewed students at the end of each of their four years of college, asking "what stood out" during the previous year. Responses indicated that students' cognitive perspectives changed as they were exposed to the complexities of university life and moved closer to adult roles.

Younger students regarded knowledge as made up of separate units (beliefs and propositions) whose truth could be determined by comparing them to abstract standards—ones that exist apart from the thinking person and his or her situation. As a result, they engaged in **dualistic thinking,** dividing information, values, and authority into right and wrong, good and bad, we and they. As one college freshman stated, "When I went to my first lecture, what the man said was just like God's word. I believe everything he said because he is a professor . . . and this is a respected position" (Perry, 1981, p. 81).

In contrast, older students were aware of a diversity of opinions on almost any topic. They moved toward **relativistic thinking,** viewing all knowledge as embedded in a framework of thought. Consequently, they gave up the possibility of absolute truth in favor of multiple truths, each relative to its context. Their thinking had become more flexible, tolerant, and realistic. A college senior reasoned, "Just seeing how [famous philosophers] fell short of an all-encompassing answer, [you realize] that ideas are really individualized. And you begin to have respect for how great their thought could be, without its being absolute" (p. 90). Relativistic thinking leads to the realization that commitment to one truth system is partly a matter of choice, since several frameworks may satisfy the criterion of internal logical consistency (Sinnott, 1998).

Perry's (1970, 1981) theory is based on a highly educated sample. He acknowledges that movement from dualism to relativism is probably limited to young people confronted with the multiplicity of viewpoints typical of a college education. But the underlying theme of *adaptive cognition*—thought less constrained by the need to find one answer to a question and more responsive to its context—is also evident in two additional views of the restructuring of thinking in adulthood.

S CHAIE'S THEORY

According to K. Warner Schaie (1977/1978), it would be difficult for human cognitive capacities to exceed the complexity of Piaget's formal operational stage. But with entry into adulthood, the situations in which people must reason become more diverse. As a result, the goals of mental activity shift from acquiring knowledge to using it, as the following stage sequence reveals:

1. The **acquisitive stage** (childhood and adolescence). The first two decades of life are largely devoted to *knowledge acquisition.* As young people move from concrete to formal operational thought, they develop more powerful procedures for storing information, combining it, and drawing conclusions.

2. The **achieving stage** (early adulthood). In early adulthood, people must adapt their cognitive skills to situations (such as marriage and employment) that have

■ *Compared with adolescents, young adults focus less on acquiring knowledge and more on applying it to everyday life. Problems encountered at work, unlike those posed in classrooms or on intelligence tests, often do not have a single correct solution. (Photo courtesy: Rob Lewine/The Stock Market)*

profound implications for *achieving long-term goals.* As a result, they focus less on acquiring knowledge and more on applying it to everyday life. The problems encountered in work, intimate relationships, and child rearing, unlike those posed in classrooms or on intelligence tests, often do not have single correct solutions. Yet how the individual handles them can affect the entire life course. Therefore, young adults must attend to both the problem and its context, not just the problem, to be successful.

3. The **responsibility stage** (middle adulthood). In middle adulthood, as families and work lives become well established, *expansion of responsibilities to others* takes place on the job, in the community, and at home. As a result, cognition extends to situations involving social obligations. Maintaining a gratifying relationship with an intimate partner, staying involved in children's lives, assuming greater leadership on the job, and fulfilling community roles must be juggled simultaneously and effectively. The most advanced form of this type of thinking, called the **executive stage,** characterizes individuals whose responsibilities have become highly complex. People at the helm of large organizations—businesses, academic institutions, and churches—must monitor organizational progress and the activities of many people. This demands that they understand the dynamic forces that affect an elaborate social structure and combine information from many sources to make decisions.

4. The **reintegrative stage** (late adulthood). As the future becomes shorter, the need to acquire knowledge and monitor decisions in terms of later consequences declines. In addition, executive thought becomes less important with retirement. The cognitive challenges of late adulthood move beyond "What should I know?" and "How should I use what I know?" to "Why should I know?" (Schaie & Willis, 1992, pp. 390–391). In this stage, people reexamine and *reintegrate their interests, attitudes, and values,* using them as a guide for what knowledge to acquire and apply. Consequently, the elderly are more selective about the circumstances in which they expend their cognitive energies. They are less likely than younger people to waste time on tasks that appear meaningless to them or that rarely occur in their daily lives.

LABOUVIE-VIEF'S THEORY

Gisella Labouvie-Vief's (1980, 1985) portrait of adult cognition echoes features of Schaie's theory. Adolescence, she points out, permits the individual to operate within a world of possibility. Adulthood brings a return to pragmatic concerns—thinking focused on concrete situations. But rather than a regression to less mature thinking, movement from hypothetical to **pragmatic thought** is a structural advance in which logic becomes a tool to solve real-world problems.

According to Labouvie-Vief, the need to specialize motivates this change. As adults select and pursue one path out of many alternatives, they become more aware of the constraints of everyday life. And in the course of balancing various roles, they give up their earlier need to resolve contradictions. Instead, they accept inconsistencies as part of life and develop ways of thinking that thrive on imperfection and compromise. Sharese's friend Christy, a student and mother of two young children, illustrates:

> I've always been a feminist, and I wanted to remain true to my beliefs in family and career. But this is Gary's first year of teaching high school, and he's saddled with four preparations and coaching the school's basketball team. At least for now, I've had to settle for "give-and-take feminism"— going to school part-time and shouldering most of the responsibility for the kids while he gets used to his new job. Otherwise, we'd never make it financially.

Awareness of multiple truths, integration of logic with reality, and tolerance for the gap between the ideal and real sum up qualitative transformations in thinking during the adult years (Sinnott, 1998). As we will see in the next section, adults' increasingly specialized and context-bound thought, although closing off options, also opens new cognitive doors to higher levels of competence.

INFORMATION PROCESSING: EXPERTISE AND CREATIVITY

In Chapter 9, we noted that children's expanding knowledge of the world improves their ability to remember new information related to what they already know. **Expertise**—acquisition of extensive knowledge in a field or endeavor—is supported by the specialization that begins with selecting a college major or an occupation, since it takes many years for a person to master any complex domain. Once expertise is attained, it has a profound impact on information processing.

Compared with novices, experts remember and reason more quickly and effectively. This makes sense, since the expert knows more domain-specific concepts and represents them in richer ways—at a deeper and more abstract level and as having more features that can be linked to other concepts. As a result, experts approach problems with underlying principles in mind, whereas the understanding of novices is superficial. For example, a highly trained physicist notices when several problems deal with conservation of energy and can therefore be solved similarly. In contrast, a beginning physics student focuses only on surface features—whether the problem contains a disk, a pulley, or a coiled spring (Chi, Glaser, & Farr, 1988). Experts appear more cognitively mature because they can use what they know to arrive at solutions automatically—through quick and easy remembering. And when a problem is especially challenging, they are more likely to plan ahead, analyzing and categorizing it before attempting to solve it.

Besides enhancing problem solving, expertise is necessary for creativity. The creative products of adulthood differ from those of childhood in that they are not just original, but directed at a social or aesthetic need. Consequently, mature creativity requires a unique cognitive capacity—the ability to formulate new, culturally meaningful problems, to ask significant questions that have not been posed before. According to Patricia Arlin (1984, 1989), movement from *problem solving* to *problem finding* is a core feature of postformal thought evident in highly accomplished artists and scientists.

A century of research reveals that creative accomplishment rises in early adulthood, peaks in the late thirties or early forties, and gradually declines. However, important exceptions to this trend exist. People off to an early start in creativity tend to peak and drop off sooner, whereas "late bloomers" show their full stride at older ages. This suggests that creativity is more a function of "career age" than chronological age. The course of creativity also varies across disciplines. For example, artists and musicians typically show an early rise in creativity, perhaps because they do not need to undergo extensive formal education before they begin to produce. Academic scholars and scientists usually display their achievements later and over a longer time, since they must earn a higher degree and spend years doing research to make worthwhile contributions (Simonton, 1988, 1991).

Creativity is rooted in expertise, but not all experts are creative. Other qualities are needed, including an innovative thinking style, tolerance of ambiguity, a special drive to succeed, and a willingness to experiment and try again after failure (Sternberg & Lubart, 1995). In addition, creativity requires time and energy. For women especially, it can be postponed or disrupted by child rearing, divorce, or an unsupportive partner (Vaillant & Vaillant, 1990). In sum, creativity is multiply determined. When personal and situational factors that promote it are present, it can continue for many decades, well into old age.

■ *Expertise is supported by specialization. This sculptor's knowledge of her craft permits her to move from problem to solution quickly and effectively. (Photo courtesy: Rhoda Sidney/PhotoEdit)*

CHANGES IN MENTAL ABILITIES

Intelligence tests are a convenient tool for assessing changes in a variety of mental abilities during the adult years. Factors included on tests for adults are similar to those for school-age children and adolescents (see page 300). Think back to our discussion of postformal thought. It suggests that intelligence tests, well suited to measuring skills needed for success in school, are less adequate for assessing competencies relevant to many adults' everyday lives (Schaie & Willis, 1996), Consistent with this view, in a study of bank managers ranging in age from 24 to 59, verbal and spatial IQs bore no relation to managerial skill, based on job performance ratings and salary raises. But a measure of practical knowledge, which required participants to rate the quality of solutions to work-related problems, did predict outstanding on-the-job achievement (Colonia-Willner, 1998).

Nevertheless, research with mental tests sheds light on the widely held belief that intelligence declines in adulthood as structures in the brain deteriorate. Many cross-sectional studies show this pattern—a peak in intelligence test performance at age 35 followed by a steep drop into old age. But widespread testing of young adults in college and in the armed services during the 1920s offered researchers a convenient opportunity to conduct longitudinal research, retesting people in middle adulthood. Results revealed an age-related increase! What explains this contradiction? To find out, K. Warner Schaie (1994, 1998) applied the *longitudinal-sequential design*, which combines longitudinal and cross-sectional approaches (see Chapter 1, page 38), in the Seattle Longitudinal Study.

In 1956, people ranging in age from 22 to 70 were tested cross-sectionally. Then, at regular intervals, longitudinal follow-ups were conducted and new samples added, yielding a total of 5,000 participants, five cross-sectional comparisons, and longitudinal data spanning 35 years. Findings on five mental abilities showed the typical cross-sectional drop after the mid-thirties. But longitudinal trends revealed modest gains sustained into the fifties and early sixties, after which performance decreased very gradually.

Figure 13.7 illustrates Schaie's cross-sectional and longitudinal outcomes for just one mental ability. *Cohort effects*—improvements in education and health from one generation to the next—are responsible for the difference. Since each new generation performed better than the one before it, the early cross-sectional decline is an illusion. Instead, the picture of development, accurately portrayed in longitudinal research, is one of steady improvement in diverse intellectual performances from early to middle adulthood, followed by a modest drop that is not under way until late in life. In later chapters, we will return to factors that affect this pattern as well as vast individual differences present throughout the adult years.

ASK YOURSELF . . .

■ *While taking a college human development course, Marcia wrote a paper on disciplining children. In the paper, she explained that behaviorists and psychoanalysts would view physical punishment as ineffective, but for different reasons. Both viewpoints, she concluded, could be valid. Explain how Marcia's reasoning illustrates postformal thought.*

As a college sophomore, Steven took a course in decision making but didn't find it very interesting. At age 25, newly married and employed, he realized the value of what the professor had taught him. How do changes in the structure of thought help explain Steven's revised attitude?

How does the development of creativity in adulthood illustrate assumptions of the lifespan perspective? (Return to Chapter 1, pages 7–12, if you need to review.)

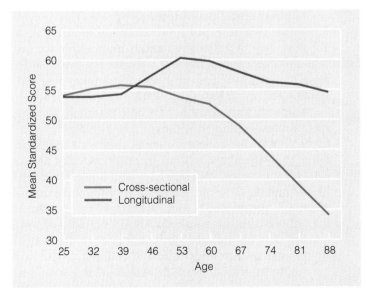

FIGURE 13.7

■ **Cross-sectional and longitudinal trends in verbal ability (ability to understand ideas expressed in words).** The cross-sectional decline is due to cohort effects—improvements in education and health in younger generations. When adults are followed longitudinally, their performance rises over early and middle adulthood and declines very gradually in the later years. A similar pattern holds for four other mental abilities: spatial orientation, inductive reasoning, numeric ability, and verbal memory. (Adapted from K. W. Schaie, 1988, "Variability in Cognitive Functioning in the Elderly." In M. A. Bender, R. C. Leonard, & A. D. Woodhead, Eds., *Phenotypic Variation in Populations,* New York: Plenum, p. 201. Reprinted by permission.)

THE COLLEGE EXPERIENCE

Looking back at the trajectory of their lives, many people view the college years as formative—more influential than any other period of adulthood. This is not surprising, since college serves as a "developmental testing ground," a time when full attention can be devoted to exploring alternative values, roles, and behaviors. To facilitate this exploration, college exposes young people to a form of "culture shock"—encounters with new ideas, new teachers and friends with varied beliefs, new freedoms and opportunities, and new academic and social demands (Pascarella & Terenzini, 1991). In the United States, 75 percent of high school graduates—more than in any other nation in the world—enroll in an institution of higher education. Besides offering a route to a high-status career and its extrinsic rewards (salary and job security), Americans expect colleges and universities to have a transforming impact on the coming generation. A wealth of evidence suggests that they do.

PSYCHOLOGICAL IMPACT OF ATTENDING COLLEGE

A comprehensive review of thousands of studies revealed broad psychological changes from the freshman to senior years of college (Pascarella & Terenzini, 1991). In addition to knowledge of their major field of study, students gain in ways less obviously tied to their academic programs. As Perry's theory of postformal thought predicts, they become better at applying reason and evidence to problems for which there is no clear answer and identifying the strengths and weaknesses of different sides of complex issues. These cognitive changes are complemented by revisions in attitudes and values—increased interest in literature, the performing arts, and philosophical and historical issues and greater tolerance for ethnic and cultural diversity. As noted in Chapter 12, college also leaves its mark on moral reasoning by fostering concern with individual rights and human welfare. Finally, gains in reflective thought combined with exposure to multiple world views encourage young people to look more closely at themselves. During the college years, students develop greater self-understanding, enhanced self-esteem, and a firmer sense of identity.

How do these interrelated changes come about? Type of college attended makes little difference, since cognitive growth is just as great for students who initially enroll in a two-year community college as for those who attend a four-year institution (Bohr et al., 1994). Instead, the impact of college is jointly determined by the person's involvement in academic and nonacademic activities and the richness and diversity of the campus setting. Residential living is one of the most consistent determinants of change because it maximizes involvement in the educational and social

■ *The impact of attending college on cognition, attitudes, and values is enhanced by residential living. When students live on campus, they are more likely to experience the richness and diversity of the campus setting. (Photo courtesy: Richard Pasley/Stock Boston)*

systems of the institution (Pascarella et al., 1993). Since over half of American college students commute, these findings underscore the importance of programs that integrate commuting students into campus life. Quality of academic experiences also affects college outcomes. Students' effort and willingness to participate in class combined with instruction that is challenging, that integrates learning in separate courses around a central theme, and that provides extensive contact with faculty are linked to a wide range of psychological benefits (Franklin, 1995; Pascarella & Terenzini, 1991).

DROPPING OUT

A college degree channels people's postcollege lives, affecting their interests and opportunities in enduring ways. Yet 40 percent of freshmen drop out, most within the first year and many within the first 6 weeks. The price paid is high, in lifelong earnings and personal development (Edwards, Cangemi, & Kowalski, 1990).

Academic factors are not the sole reason for leaving, since young people who withdraw usually have the ability to succeed in the college to which they were admitted. Other student and institutional characteristics play a larger role. Most entering freshmen have high hopes for college life but find the transition difficult. Those who have trouble adapting—due to lack of motivation, poor study skills, financial pressures, or emotional dependence on parents—quickly develop negative attitudes toward the college environment, which leads them to abandon it. Often these exit-prone students do not meet with their advisors or professors. At the same time, colleges that do little to help high-risk students through encouragement, understanding, and assistance with decision making have a higher percentage of students who do not graduate (Cangemi, 1983).

Factors involved in the decision to withdraw from college are usually not catastrophic; they are typical problems of early adulthood. Most dropouts either find it harder to deal with these difficulties or are unable to get assistance in doing so. Reaching out to students, especially during the early weeks and throughout the first year, is crucial. Young people who sense that they have entered a college community concerned about them as individuals are far more likely to persist to graduation (Billson & Terry, 1987).

VOCATIONAL CHOICE

Young adults—college- and non-college-bound alike—face a major life decision: the choice of a suitable work role. Being a productive worker calls for many of the same qualities needed to be an active citizen and nurturant family member—good judgment, responsibility, dedication, and cooperation. An individual well prepared for work can better fulfill other adult roles. How do young people make decisions about careers, and what influences their choices? What is the transition from school to work like, and what factors make it easy or difficult?

SELECTING A VOCATION

In societies with an abundance of career possibilities, occupational choice is a gradual process, beginning long before adolescence. Major theorists view the young person as moving through several phases of vocational development (Ginzberg, 1972, 1988; Super, 1980, 1984):

1. The **fantasy period** (early and middle childhood). As we saw in Chapter 7, young children gain insight into career options by fantasizing about them. However, their preferences are largely guided by familiarity, glamour, and excitement and bear little relation to the decisions they will eventually make.

2. The **tentative period** (early and middle adolescence). Between ages 11 and 17, adolescents start to think about careers in more complex ways. At first, they evaluate vocational options in terms of their interests. Later, as they become more aware of personal and educational requirements for different vocations, they take into account their *abilities and values.* "I like science and the process of discovery," Sharese thought to herself as she neared high school graduation. "But I'm also good with people, and I'd like to do something to help others. So maybe teaching or medicine would suit my needs."

3. The **realistic period** (late adolescence and early adulthood). By the early twenties, the economic and practical realities of adulthood are just around the corner, and young people start to narrow their options. At first, many do so through further *exploration*, gathering more information about a set of possibilities that blends with their personal characteristics. Then they enter a final phase of *crystallization* in which they focus on a general vocational category. Within it, they experiment for a period of time before settling on a single occupation. As a college sophomore, Sharese pursued her interest in science, but she had not yet selected a major. Once she decided on chemistry, she considered whether to pursue teaching, medicine, or public health.

FACTORS INFLUENCING VOCATIONAL CHOICE

Although most people follow this general pattern of vocational development, there are exceptions in both timing and sequence. A few know from an early age just what they want to be and follow a direct path to a career goal. Others keep their options open for an extended period. College students are granted ample time to explore and decide. In contrast, the life conditions of low-income youths prevent them from having the choices that economically advantaged young people do.

Consider for a moment how an occupational choice is made, and you will see that it is not just a rational process in which young people weigh abilities, interests, and values against career options. Like other developmental milestones, it is the result of a dynamic interaction between person and environment. A great many influences feed into the decision.

■ PERSONALITY. People are attracted to occupations that complement their personalities. John Holland (1966, 1985) has identified six personality types that affect vocational choice:

- The *investigative person,* who enjoys working with ideas and is likely to select a scientific occupation (for example, anthropologist, physicist, or engineer)

- The *social person,* who likes interacting with people and gravitates toward human services (counseling, social work, or teaching)

- The *realistic person,* who prefers real-world problems and work with objects and tends to choose a mechanical occupation (construction, plumbing, or surveying)

- The *artistic person,* who is emotional and high in need for individual expression and looks toward an artistic field (writing, music, or the visual arts)

- The *conventional person,* who likes well-structured tasks and values material possessions and social status—traits well suited to certain business fields (accounting, banking, or quality control)

- The *enterprising person,* who is adventurous, persuasive, and a strong leader and is drawn to sales and supervisory positions and politics

Research reveals a clear relationship between personality and vocational choice, but it is only moderate (Holland, 1985). Personality is not a stronger predictor because many people are blends of several personality types and can do well at more than one kind of occupation. Furthermore, career decisions are made in the context of family background, educational opportunities, and current life circumstances. For example, Sharese's friend Christy scored high on Holland's "investigative" dimension. But when she married and had children early, she postponed her dream of becoming a college professor and chose a human services career that required fewer years of educational preparation. As Christy's case illustrates, personality takes us only part way in understanding vocational choice.

■ FAMILY INFLUENCES. Young peoples' vocational aspirations are strongly correlated with the jobs of their parents. Individuals who grew up in higher-SES homes are more likely to select high-status, white-collar occupations, such as doctor, lawyer, scientist, and engineer. In contrast, those with low-income backgrounds tend to choose lower-status, blue-collar careers—for example, plumber, construction worker, food service employee, and secretary. Parent–child similarity is partly a function of educational attainment. The single best predictor of occupational status is number of years of schooling completed (Featherman, 1980).

Family resemblance in occupational choice also comes about for other reasons. Higher-SES parents are more likely to give their children important information about the world of work and to have connections with people who can help the young person obtain a high-status position (Grotevant & Cooper, 1988). Parenting practices also shape work-related values. Recall from Chapter 2 that higher-SES parents tend to promote independence and curiosity, which are required in many high-status careers. Lower-SES parents, in contrast, are more likely to emphasize conformity and obedience. At work, they are used to following the directives of others. Eventually, young people choose careers that are compatible with these values. The jobs that appeal to them tend to be like those of their parents (Mortimer & Borman, 1988).

Although consistency between parent and child occupational choice is considerable, it is far from perfect. Parental pressure to do well in school and encouragement toward high-status occupations predict vocational attainment beyond SES (Bell et al., 1996). Although parental values and goals frequently lead adolescents to seek occupations similar to their parents', parents can also foster higher aspirations.

■ TEACHERS. Teachers also play a powerful role in career decisions. In one study, college freshmen were asked who had the greatest impact on their choice of a field of study. The people most often mentioned (by 39 percent of the sample) were high school teachers (Johnson, 1967, as cited by Rice, 1999). Young people who go to college have more opportunities to develop closer relations with teachers than do their non-college-educated counterparts, whose parents are more influential. These findings provide yet another reason to promote positive teacher–student relations, especially for high school students from low-SES families. The power of teachers as role models could serve as an important source of upward mobility for these young people.

■ GENDER STEREOTYPES. Over the past two decades, young men's career preferences have remained strongly gender stereotyped, whereas young women have expressed increasing interest in occupations largely held by men (Gottfredson, 1996). Changes in gender-role attitudes along with the dramatic rise in employed mothers, who serve as career-oriented models for their daughters (see Chapter 10), are common explanations for women's growing attraction to nontraditional careers.

At the same time, women's progress in entering and excelling at male-dominated professions has been slow. As Table 13.2 shows, the percentage of women engineers, lawyers, and doctors increased between 1972 and 1998 in the United States, but it falls far short of equal representation. Women remain heavily concentrated in the less well-paid, traditionally feminine professions of literature, social work, education, and nursing (U.S. Bureau of the Census, 1999). In virtually all fields, their achievements lag behind

TABLE 13.2

Percentage of Females in Various Professions, 1972, 1983, 1998

PROFESSION	1972	1983	1998
Engineering	0.8	5.8	11.1
Law	3.8	15.8	28.5
Medicine	9.3	15.8	26.6
Business—executive and managerial	17.6	32.4	44.4[a]
Writing, art, entertainment	31.7	42.7	51.4
Social work	55.1	64.3	68.4
Elementary and secondary education	70.0	70.9	75.3
Higher education	28.0	36.3	42.3
Library, museum curatorship	81.6	84.4	80.8
Nursing	92.6	95.8	92.5

Source: U.S. Bureau of the Census, 1999.

[a] This percentage includes executives and managers at all levels. Women make up only 10 percent of senior management at big firms, although that figure represents a threefold increase in the past decade.

those of men, who write more books, make more discoveries, hold more positions of leadership, and produce more works of art.

Ability cannot account for these dramatic sex differences. Recall from Chapter 11 that the gender gap in cognitive performance of all kinds is small and is declining. Instead, gender-stereotyped messages play a key role. Although girls' grades are higher than boys', girls reach secondary school less confident of their ability and more likely to underestimate their achievement (Bornholt, Goodnow, & Cooney, 1994). Between tenth and twelfth grade, the percentage of girls in gifted programs decreases. When asked what discouraged them from continuing in gifted classes, parental and peer pressures and attitudes of teachers and counselors ranked high on girls' lists (Read, 1991; Winner, 1996).

During college, the career aspirations of academically talented females decline further. In one longitudinal study, high school valedictorians were followed over a 10-year period—through college and into the work world. By their sophomore year, young women showed a decline in estimates of their intelligence, whereas men did not. Women also shifted their expectations toward less demanding careers because of concerns about combining work with child rearing and unresolved questions about their ability. Even though female valedictorians outperformed their male counterparts in college courses, they achieved at lower levels after career entry (Arnold, 1994). Another study reported similar results. Educational aspirations of mathematically talented women declined considerably during college, as did the number majoring in the sciences (Benbow & Arjmand, 1990). The underrepresentation of women in physical-science careers is severe. They constitute only 9 percent of employed engineers and physicists (U.S. Bureau of the Census, 1999).

These findings reveal a pressing need for programs that sensitize high school and college personnel to the special problems women face in developing and maintaining high career aspirations. Research shows that the aspirations of young women rise in response to career guidance that encourages them to set goals that match their abilities, interests, and values. Those who continue to achieve usually have four experiences in common:

- A college environment that values and supports the accomplishments of women and that attends to women's experiences in its curriculum

- Frequent interaction with faculty and professionals in their chosen fields

- The opportunity to test their abilities in a nurturing environment

- Models of accomplished women who have successfully dealt with family–career role conflict (Arnold, 1994; Pascarella et al., 1997; Schroeder, Blood, & Maluso, 1993).

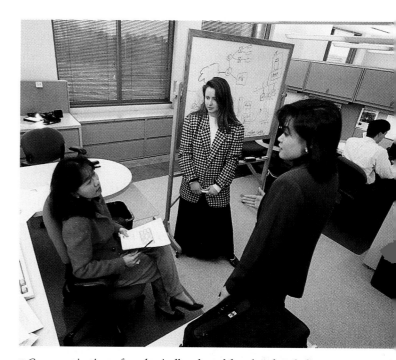

■ *Career aspirations of academically talented females often decline in adolescence and early adulthood. When college environments value and support the accomplishments of women and provide opportunities for them to test their abilities in a nurturing environment, they sustain high aspirations and usually achieve them. Each of these young women has attained her initial career goal of securing a well-paid position with high responsibility in a corporate setting. (Photo courtesy: Mark Richards/PhotoEdit)*

■ ACCESS TO VOCATIONAL INFORMATION. Finally, many young people could profit from greater access to career information. In a longitudinal study of a nationally representative sample of over 1,200 American high school students followed for 5 years, youths of all SES levels and ethnicities were highly ambitious. Compared with previous generations, many more expected to graduate from college and enter professional jobs. But about half were unaware of the steps involved in reaching their goal (Schneider & Stevenson, 1999). They had only sketchy knowledge of their chosen vocation, of the educational requirements to enter it, and of the future demand for it.

These high-ambition/low-knowledge young people were at risk for becoming "drifting dreamers," who failed to make strategic choices about how to invest their efforts wisely. Especially if they entered a community college with plans to transfer to a four-year institution, they frequently found that they did not have the high school prerequisites to take the courses they needed. And often they chose courses without checking to make sure that credit would transfer to a four-year college. Consequently, some remained in school for an unnecessarily long period of time, whereas others did not complete their educational plans—for both academic and economic reasons.

Choosing an occupation goal and knowing how to realize it do not lock young people into a vocational goal. High-ambition/high-knowledge youths often change their career interests and college majors. But when they do, they are better equipped to make meaningful choices. In contrast, high-ambition/low-knowledge students tend to make poor educational decisions from which they have difficulty recovering. Four-year institutions need to familiarize high school and community college students with the admissions process earlier, so they can develop a better understanding of the link between their current course work and educational and vocational opportunities. And at both the high school and college levels, teachers and counselors need to help young people learn about the work they are interested in—by introducing them to people in those jobs, encouraging participation in relevant extracurricular activities, and offering internships that provide firsthand experiences.

VOCATIONAL PREPARATION OF NON-COLLEGE-BOUND YOUNG ADULTS

Sharese's younger brother Leon graduated from high school in a vocational track. Like 25 percent of young people with a high school diploma, he had no plans to go to college. While in school, Leon held a part-time job selling candy at the local shopping mall. He hoped to work in data processing after graduation, but 6 months later he was still a part-time sales clerk at the candy store. Although Leon had filled out many job applications, he got no interviews or offers. He soon despaired of any relationship between his schooling and a career.

Leon's inability to find a job other than the one he held as a student is typical for American non-college-bound high school graduates. Although they are more likely to find employment than youths who drop out, they have fewer work opportunities than they did several decades ago. More than one-fifth of recent high school graduates who do not continue their education are unemployed (U.S. Department of Education, 1999a). When they do find work, most are limited to low-paid, unskilled jobs. In addition, they have few alternatives to turn to for vocational counseling and job placement as they make the transition from school to work (Bailey, 1993).

Unlike Western European nations, the United States has no widespread training system to prepare its youths for skilled business and industrial occupations and manual trades (Marshall, 1997). The federal government does support some job training programs, and funding for them has increased. But most are too short to make a difference in the lives of poorly skilled individuals, who need intensive training and academic remediation before they are ready to enter the job market. And at present, these programs serve only a small minority of young people who need assistance.

Inspired by successful programs in Western Europe, youth apprenticeship strategies that coordinate on-the-job training with classroom instruction are being considered as an important dimension of educational reform in the United States. The Variations box on the following page describes Germany's highly successful apprenticeship system. Bringing together the worlds of schooling and work offers many benefits. These include helping non-college-bound young people establish productive lives right after graduation, motivating at-risk youths to stay in school, and contributing to the nation's economic growth (Hamilton, 1993; Safyer, Leahy, & Colan, 1995).

Although vocational development is a lifelong process, the most important periods for launching a career are adolescence and early adulthood. Young people well prepared for an economically and personally satisfying work life are much more likely to become productive citizens, devoted family members, and contented adults. The support of families, schools, businesses, communities, and society as a whole can contribute greatly to a positive outcome. We will take up the challenges of establishing a career and integrating it with other life tasks in Chapter 14.

ASK YOURSELF . . .

■ *During her freshman year of college, Sharese participated in a program in which a professor and five students met once a month to talk about common themes in three courses that the students took together. Why is this program likely to increase student retention?*

 Jordan, a community college student, wants to become a teacher but has little idea of the course work needed to achieve his vocational goal. Why might the gap between Jordan's ambition and knowledge of his chosen vocation have negative consequences for his educational and occupational attainment? What steps can colleges take to prevent students like Jordan from becoming "drifting dreamers"?

WORK–STUDY APPRENTICESHIPS IN GERMANY

Rolf, an 18-year-old German vocational student, is an apprentice at Brandt, a large industrial firm known worldwide for its high-quality products. Like many German companies, Brandt has a well-developed apprenticeship program that includes a full-time professional training staff, a suite of classrooms, and a lab equipped with the latest learning aids. Apprentices move through more than 10 major divisions in the company that are carefully selected to meet their learning needs. Rolf has worked in purchasing, inventory, production, personnel, marketing, sales, and finance. Now in cost accounting, he assists Herr Stein, his supervisor, in designing a computerized inventory control system. Rolf draws a flowchart of the new system under the direction of Herr Stein, who explains that each part of the diagram will contain a set of procedures to be built into a computer program.

Rolf is involved in complex and challenging projects, guided by caring mentors who love their work and want to teach it to others. Two days a week, he attends the *Berufsschule*, a part-time vocational school. On the job, Rolf applies a wide range of academic skills, including reading, writing, problem solving, and logical thinking. His classroom learning is directly relevant to his daily life (Hamilton, 1990).

Germany has one of the most successful apprenticeship systems in the world for preparing young people to enter modern business and industry. More than 60 percent of adolescents participate in it, making it the most common form of secondary education. German adolescents who do not go to a *Gymnasium* (college preparatory high school) usually complete full-time schooling by age 15 or 16, but education remains compulsory until age 18. They fill the 2-year gap with part-time vocational schooling combined with apprenticeship. Students are trained for a wide range of occupations—more than 400, leading to over 20,000 specialized careers. Each apprenticeship is jointly planned by educators and employers. Apprentices who complete training and pass a qualifying examination are certified as skilled workers and earn union-set wages for that occupation. Businesses provide financial support for the program because they know it guarantees a competent, dedicated workforce (Hamilton, 1990, 1994).

The German apprenticeship system offers a smooth and rewarding path from school to career for young people who do not enter higher education. Many apprentices are hired by the firms that trained them. Most others find jobs in the same occupation. For those who change careers, the apprentice certificate is a powerful credential. Employers view successful apprentices as responsible and capable workers. They are willing to invest in further training to adapt the individual's skills to other occupations. As a result, German young people establish themselves in well-paid careers with security and advancement possibilities between ages 18 and 20 (Hamilton, 1990).

The success of the German system—and of several similar systems in Austria, Denmark, Switzerland, and several East European countries—suggests that some kind of national apprenticeship program would improve the transition from school to work for young people in the United States. Nevertheless, implementing an American apprenticeship system

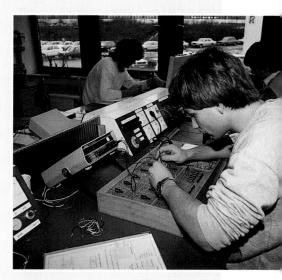

■ *High-quality vocational training combined with apprenticeship enables German youths who do not go to college to enter well-paid careers. This electronics trainee works in a hydraulics system factory. His education involves integrating academic skills with on-the-job experience to ensure that he becomes competent at both. (Photo courtesy: M. Granitsas/The Image Works)*

poses major challenges. Among these are overcoming the reluctance of employers to assume part of the responsibility for vocational training; creating institutional structures that ensure cooperation between schools and businesses; and finding ways to prevent low-income youths from being concentrated in the lowest-skilled apprenticeship placements, which would perpetuate current social inequalities (Bailey, 1993; Hamilton, 1993). Pilot apprenticeship projects are currently under way, in an effort to solve these problems and build a bridge between learning and working in the United States.

PHYSICAL DEVELOPMENT

LIFE EXPECTANCY

Discuss changes in life expectancy over the past century and the extent to which maximum lifespan and active lifespan can be improved.

■ Both heredity and environment affect **average life expectancy.** Twentieth-century gains in length of life, amounting to over 35 years in the United States, are largely due to improved nutrition, medicine, sanitation, and safety. These changes clearly indicate that **biological aging,** or **senescence,** can be modified by behavior and environmental interventions.

Discuss the extent to which maximum lifespan and active lifespan can be improved.

■ Scientists disagree about whether **maximum lifespan** can be extended beyond an average of 85 or 90 years. Reducing health problems among low-income and ethnic minority groups would most likely add to Americans' **active lifespan** of 64 years.

THEORIES OF BIOLOGICAL AGING

Describe current theories of biological aging, including those at the level of DNA and body cells and those at the level of tissues and organs.

■ The programmed effects of specific genes may control certain age-related biological changes in DNA and body cells. DNA may also be damaged as random mutations accumulate, leading to less efficient cell repair and replacement and to abnormal cancerous cells. Release of highly reactive **free radicals** is a probable cause of age-related DNA

and cellular damage. Biological aging may eventually prove to be the combined result of the programmed effects of specific genes and random events that cause cells to deteriorate.

■ Genetic and cellular deterioration affects organs and tissues. The **cross-linkage theory** of aging suggests that over time, protein fibers form links and become less elastic, producing negative changes in many organs. Declines in the endocrine and immune systems may also contribute to aging.

PHYSICAL CHANGES

Describe the physical changes of aging, paying special attention to the cardiovascular and respiratory systems, motor performance, the immune system, and reproductive capacity.

■ The physical changes of aging are gradual in early adulthood but accelerate later. Declines in heart and lung performance show up only during exercise. Heart disease is a leading cause of death in adults, although it has decreased considerably in the past 50 years due to lifestyle changes and medical advances. Atherosclerosis is a serious, multiply determined cardiovascular disease involving fatty deposits on artery walls.

■ Athletic skills requiring speed, strength, and gross body coordination peak in the early twenties; those requiring endurance, arm–hand steadiness, and aiming peak in the late twenties and early thirties. Less active lifestyles, rather than biological aging, account for most of the subsequent decline in athletic skill and motor performance.

■ The immune response strengthens in adolescence and declines after age 20. This trend is partly due to

shrinking of the thymus gland. Increased difficulty coping with physical and psychological stress also contributes.

■ Reproductive capacity declines with age, especially after age 35 in women and age 40 in men.

HEALTH AND FITNESS

Describe the impact of SES, nutrition, and exercise on health, and discuss obesity in adulthood.

■ Economically advantaged and well-educated individuals tend to sustain good health over most of their adult lives, whereas the health of lower-income individuals with limited education declines. SES differences in health-related living conditions and habits are largely responsible.

■ Many Americans eat the wrong kinds and amounts of food. Obesity has doubled in the United States since 1900, currently affecting 22 percent of the population, especially low-income ethnic minority females. Heredity, sedentary lifestyles, and high-fat diets contribute to obesity, which is associated with serious health problems, social discrimination, and early death.

■ Adding some weight between ages 25 and 50 is normal due to a decrease in **basal metabolic rate (BMR),** but many young adults show large gains. Successful treatments for obesity typically involve a low-fat diet plus exercise, accurate recording of food consumption, social support, teaching problem-solving skills, and extended intervention.

■ Regular exercise reduces body fat, builds muscle, helps prevent illness (including cardiovascular disease), and enhances psychological well-being. Nevertheless, only 23 percent of Americans engage in regular, moderate physical activity.

What are the two most common substance disorders, and what health risks do they entail?

■ Cigarette smoking and alcohol consumption, the two most common substance disorders, are problems in early adulthood and can be difficult to overcome. Most adults who smoke began before age 21. They are at increased risk for heart attack, stroke, numerous cancers, and premature death.

■ About one-third of heavy drinkers suffer from alcoholism, to which both heredity and environment contribute. Alcohol is implicated in liver and cardiovascular disease, certain cancers, numerous other physical disorders, and social problems such as highway fatalities, crime, and sexual coercion.

Describe sexual attitudes and behavior of young adults, and discuss sexually transmitted disease, sexual coercion, and premenstrual syndrome (PMS).

■ American adults are less sexually active than popular media images suggest, but compared with earlier generations, they display a wider range of sexual choices and lifestyles and have had more sexual partners. Nevertheless, most people spend the majority of their lives with one partner. Adults in committed relationships report high satisfaction with their sex lives. Only a minority of adults report persistent sexual problems—difficulties linked to low SES, stress, having many partners, and a history of childhood sexual abuse or adult sexual coercion.

■ Negative attitudes toward homosexual men and women have begun to change, particularly in the area of equal employment opportunities. Homosexual relationships share many characteristics with heterosexual relationships, including similarity between partners in education and background, greater satisfaction in committed relationships, and modest frequency of sexual activity.

■ Twenty-five percent of Americans are likely to contract a sexually transmitted disease (STD) during their lifetime; women are more vulnerable than men. AIDS remains concentrated among gay men and intravenous drug abusers, but changes in sexual practices have reduced the number of infections.

■ An estimated 14 to 25 percent of women have been raped, typically by men they know well; they suffer psychological trauma that warrants therapy. Cultural acceptance of strong gender typing and of violence contributes to sexual coercion.

■ Nearly 40 percent of women experience **premenstrual syndrome (PMS)**, usually in mild form. For some, PMS is severe enough to interfere with daily life.

How does psychological stress affect health?

■ Chronic psychological stress induces physical responses that contribute to heart disease, several types of cancer, and gastrointestinal problems. Supportive social ties can help alleviate stress.

COGNITIVE DEVELOPMENT

CHANGES IN THE STRUCTURE OF THOUGHT

What are the characteristics of adult thought, and how does thinking change in adulthood?

■ Cognitive development beyond Piaget's formal operational stage is known as **postformal thought.** Adult cognition typically reflects an awareness of multiple truths, integrates logic with reality, and tolerates the gap between the ideal and the real.

■ According to Perry's theory, college students move from **dualistic thinking,** dividing information into right and wrong, to **relativistic thinking,** or awareness of multiple truths.

■ In Schaie's theory, the emphasis shifts from acquiring to using knowledge as a person goes through the **acquisitive stage** in childhood and adolescence; the **achieving stage** in early adulthood; the **responsibility stage** and, for some, the **executive stage** in middle adulthood; and finally, the **reintegrative stage** in late adulthood.

■ According to Labouvie-Vief's theory, the need to specialize motivates adults to progress from the adolescent's ideal world of possibilities to **pragmatic thought,** which uses logic as a tool to solve real-world problems.

INFORMATION PROCESSING: EXPERTISE AND CREATIVITY

What roles do expertise and creativity play in adult thought?

■ Specialization in college and in an occupation leads to **expertise,** which enhances problem solving and is necessary for creativity. Mature creativity involves formulating meaningful new problems and questions. Although creativity tends to rise in early adulthood and peak in the late thirties or early forties, its development varies considerably and is multiply determined.

CHANGES IN MENTAL ABILITIES

What do intelligence tests reveal about changes in adults' mental abilities over the life course?

■ Cross-sectional studies show a peak in intelligence test performance around age 35 followed by a steep decline, whereas longitudinal studies reveal an age-related increase. Applying the longitudinal-sequential design in the Seattle Longitudinal Study, Schaie discovered that the cross-sectional decline is due to cohort effects. Intellectual performance improves steadily into middle adulthood and does not decline until late in life.

THE COLLEGE EXPERIENCE

Describe the impact of a college education on young people's lives, and discuss the problem of dropping out.

■ Through involvement in academic programs and campus life, college students engage in exploration that produces gains in knowledge and reasoning ability, revised attitudes and values, enhanced self-esteem and self-knowledge, and preparation for a high-status career. The 40 percent of freshmen who find the transition to college life so difficult that they drop out are usually struggling with typical problems of early adulthood. They could benefit from interventions that demonstrate concern about students as individuals.

VOCATIONAL CHOICE

Trace the development of vocational choice, and cite factors that influence it.

■ Vocational development moves through three phases: a **fantasy period** in which children explore career options through play; a **tentative period,** in which teenagers weigh different careers against their interests, abilities, and values; and a **realistic period,** in which young people settle on a vocational category and then a specific career.

■ Vocational choice is influenced by personality; parents' occupational status and provision of educational opportunities and vocational information; close relationships with teachers; gender stereotypes; and access to vocational information in high schools and colleges.

Discuss sex differences in occupational preferences and achievement.

■ Young men's career preferences have remained strongly gender stereotyped, whereas young women's interest in male-dominated occupations has increased. Yet women's progress in male-dominated professions has been slow, and their achievements lag behind those of men in virtually all fields. Gender-stereotyped messages prevent many women from reaching their career potential.

What problems do American non-college-bound young people face in preparing for a vocation?

■ American non-college-bound high school graduates have fewer work opportunities today than they did several decades ago. More than one-fifth are unemployed, and most are limited to low-paid, unskilled jobs. To address their need for vocational training, youth apprenticeships inspired by those in Western Europe are being considered as an important dimension of educational reform in the United States.

IMPORTANT TERMS AND CONCEPTS

achieving stage (p. 441)

acquisitive stage (p. 441)

active lifespan (p. 423)

average life expectancy (p. 421)

basal metabolic rate (BMR) (p. 430)

biological aging, or senescence (p. 420)

cross-linkage theory (p. 424)

dualistic thinking (p. 440)

executive stage (p. 441)

expertise (p. 442)

fantasy period (p. 445)

free radicals (p. 424)

maximum lifespan (p. 421)

postformal thought (p. 440)

pragmatic thought (p. 441)

premenstrual syndrome (PMS) (p. 438)

realistic period (p. 445)

reintegrative stage (p. 441)

relativistic thinking (p. 440)

responsibility stage (p. 441)

tentative period (p. 445)

FOR FURTHER INFORMATION AND HELP

Consult the companion website for this book, where you will find additional weblinks and associated learning activities: www.abacon.com/berk

INFERTILITY

(See page 77 for organizations related to infertility.)

CARDIOVASCULAR DISEASE

American Heart Association
www.amhrt.org

Supports research, public education, and community service programs to reduce disability and premature death from cardiovascular disease.

World Hypertension League
www.mco.edu/whl

Works in conjunction with the World Health Organization to control hypertension in countries around the world.

OVERWEIGHT AND OBESITY

Overeaters Anonymous
www.overeatersanonymous.org

An international organization aimed at helping people who have a desire to stop eating compulsively. Patterned after the treatment approach of Alcoholics Anonymous.

ALCOHOL ABUSE

Alcoholics Anonymous
www.alcoholics-anonymous.org

An international organization aimed at helping people recover from alcoholism. Local chapters exist in many countries.

Mothers Against Drunk Driving (MADD)
www.grannet.com/mad.htm

Encourages citizens to work toward reducing the drunk driving problem. Engages in public education, lobbies for more stringent laws, and provides assistance to victims and their families.

(See pages 115 and 387 for additional organizations related to substance abuse.)

GAY AND LESBIAN CIVIL RIGHTS

International Gay and Lesbian Human Rights Commission
www.iglhrc.org

Monitors and responds to human rights violations against lesbians, gays, bisexuals, and people with AIDS worldwide. Promotes AIDS education and prevention.

National Gay and Lesbian Task Force
www.ngltf.org

Dedicated to the elimination of prejudice based on sexual orientation. Lobbies Congress, engages in community organizing, and disseminates information to the public.

SEXUALLY TRANSMITTED DISEASE (STD)

U.S. Centers for Disease Control and Prevention
www.cdc.gov

Government-sponsored agency that monitors the incidence and spread of diseases in the United States and recommends preventive measures. Sponsors the National STD Hotline, (800) 227-8922, and the National AIDS Hotline, (800) 342-AIDS (English) and (800) 344-SIDA (Spanish).

(See page 387 for additional organizations related to sexually transmitted diseases.)

VOCATIONAL CHOICE

Office of Apprenticeship Training, Employer, and Labor Services
www.doleta.gov/bat/index.htm

Part of the U.S. Department of Labor, Employment, and Training Administration, provides information on government-approved school-to-apprenticeship opportunities for American young people who plan to enter the workforce immediately after high school.

14

Emotional and Social Development in Early Adulthood

■ *The warm, mutual gaze of these Russian Orthodox newlyweds shows that they are passionately in love. Still, many adjustments lie ahead. A lasting relationship with an intimate partner requires effort, compromise, sensitivity, and respect. (Photo courtesy: James B. Blair/National Geographic Image Collection)*

After completing her master's degree, Sharese returned to her hometown, where her marriage to Ernie was soon to take place. A year-long engagement had preceded the wedding, during which Sharese had vacillated about whether to follow through. At times, she looked with envy at Heather, still unattached and free to pursue the full range of career options before her.

Sharese also pondered the life circumstances of Christy and her husband, Gary—married their junior year in college and two children born within the next few years. Despite his good teaching performance, Gary's relationship with the high school principal deteriorated, and he quit his teaching position by the end of his first year. Financial pressures and the demands of parenthood had put Christy's education and career plans on hold. Sharese began to wonder if it was possible for a woman to have both family and career.

Sharese's ambivalence intensified as her wedding day approached. When Ernie asked why she was so agitated, she blurted out that she had doubts about getting married. Ernie's admiration and respect for Sharese had strengthened over their courtship, and he reassured her of his love. His career was launched, and at age 27, he felt ready to start a family. Uncertain and conflicted, Sharese felt swept toward the altar. Relatives, friends, and presents began to arrive. On the appointed day, she walked down the aisle.

In this chapter, we take up the emotional and social sides of early adulthood. Having achieved independence from the family, young people find that they still want and need close, affectionate ties. Yet like Sharese, they often fear losing their freedom. Once this struggle is resolved, the years from 20 to 40 lead to new family units and parenthood, accomplished in the context of diverse lifestyles. At the same time, young adults must learn to perform the skills and tasks of their chosen occupation. We will see that love and work are inevitably intertwined, and society expects success at both. In negotiating both arenas, young adults do more choosing, planning, and changing course than any other age group. When their decisions are in tune with themselves and their social and cultural worlds, they acquire many new competencies, and life is full and rewarding.

ERIKSON'S THEORY: INTIMACY VERSUS ISOLATION

Erikson's contributions have energized the study of adult personality development. All modern theories have been influenced by his vision (McCrae & Costa, 1990). According to Erikson (1964), adults move through three stages, each of which confronts the individual with both opportunity and risk—"a turning point for bet-

ter or worse" (p. 139). The critical psychological conflict of early adulthood is **intimacy versus isolation.** It is reflected in the young person's thoughts and feelings about making a permanent commitment to an intimate partner.

As Sharese's inner turmoil reveals, establishing a mutually gratifying close relationship is challenging. Most young adults have only recently attained economic independence from parents, and many are still involved in the quest for identity. Yet intimacy requires that they give up some of their newfound independence and redefine their identity in terms of the values and interests of two people, not just themselves. During their first year of marriage, Sharese separated from Ernie twice as she tried to reconcile her needs for independence and intimacy. Maturity involves balancing these two forces. Without a sense of independence, people define themselves only in terms of their partner and sacrifice self-respect and initiative. Without intimacy, they face the negative outcome of Erikson's stage of early adulthood: loneliness and self-absorption. Ernie's patience and stability helped Sharese realize that marriage requires generosity and compromise but not total surrender of the self.

A secure sense of intimacy is also evident in the quality of other close relationships. For example, in friendships and work ties, young people who have achieved intimacy are cooperative, tolerant, and accepting of differences in background and values. Although they enjoy being with others, they are also comfortable when alone. People who have a sense of isolation hesitate to form close ties because they fear loss of their own identity, tend to compete rather than cooperate, are not accepting of differences, and are easily

■ *Establishing a mutually gratifying close relationship is a challenging task for young adults. Intimacy demands that they give up some of their newfound independence and redefine their identity in terms of two people. This husband and wife, both police officers, share an occupation—a basis for mutual interests. But to achieve intimacy, they must also be tolerant and accepting of differences in background and values. (Photo courtesy: Dick Blume/ The Image Works)*

threatened when others get too close (Hamachek, 1990). Erikson believed that successful resolution of intimacy versus isolation prepares the individual for the middle adulthood stage, which focuses on *generativity*—caring for the next generation and helping to improve society.

Research based on self-reports confirms that intimacy is a central concern of early adulthood (Ryff & Migdall, 1984; Whitbourne et al., 1992). But it also reveals (as we have noted before) that a fixed series of tasks tied neatly to age does not describe the life course of many adults. Childbearing and child rearing (aspects of generativity) usually occur in the twenties and thirties, and contributions to society through work are also under way at this time. Furthermore, as we will see shortly, many combinations of marriage, children, and career exist, each with a unique pattern of timing and commitment (McAdams, de St. Aubin, & Logan, 1993; Weiland, 1993).

In sum, both intimacy and generativity seem to emerge in early adulthood, with shifts in emphasis that differ from one person to the next. Recognizing that Erikson's theory provides only a broad sketch of adult personality development, other theorists have expanded and modified his stage approach, adding detail and flexibility.

OTHER THEORIES OF ADULT PSYCHOSOCIAL DEVELOPMENT

In the 1970s, growing interest in adult development, sparked by people's personal experiences with change, led to the publication of several widely read books on the topic. Two of these volumes—Daniel Levinson's (1978) *The Seasons of a Man's Life* and George Vaillant's (1977) *Adaptation to Life*—present psychosocial theories in the

tradition of Erikson that have gathered considerable research support. Each is summarized in Table 14.1.

LEVINSON'S SEASONS OF LIFE

Conducting extensive biographical interviews with forty 35- to 45-year-old men from four occupational subgroups (hourly workers in industry, business executives, university biologists, and novelists), Levinson (1978) looked for an underlying order in the adult life course. Later he investigated the lives of forty-five women, also 35 to 45 years of age, from three subgroups (homemakers, business executives, and university professors). His results, and those of others, reveal a common path of change, within which men and women approach developmental tasks in somewhat different ways (Levinson, 1996; Roberts & Newton, 1987).

Like Erikson, Levinson (1978, 1996) conceives of development as a sequence of qualitatively distinct eras (stages or seasons), each of which has its own time and brings certain psychological challenges to the forefront of the person's life. Within each era, important changes occur in a predictable age-related sequence jointly determined by biological and social forces. As Table 14.1 shows, each era begins with a *transition,* lasting about 5 years, which concludes the previous era and prepares the person for the next one. Between transitions, people move into stable periods in which they concentrate on building a life structure that harmonizes the inner personal and outer societal demands of that phase.

The **life structure,** a key concept in Levinson's theory, is the underlying pattern or design of a person's life at a given time. Its components are the person's relationships with significant others—individuals, groups, and institutions. The life structure can have many components, but usually only a few (having to do with marriage/family and occupation) are central to the person's life. However, wide

---

TABLE 14.1

Stages of Adult Psychosocial Development

PERIOD OF DEVELOPMENT	ERIKSON	LEVINSON	VAILLANT
Early adulthood (20–40 years)	Intimacy versus isolation	Early adult transition: 17–22 years	Intimacy
		Entry life structure for early adulthood: 22–28 years	
		Age 30 transition: 28–33 years	Career consolidation
		Culminating life structure for early adulthood: 33–40 years	
Middle adulthood (40–65 years)	Generativity versus stagnation	Midlife transition: 40–45 years	Generativity
		Entry life structure for middle adulthood: 45–50 years	
		Age 50 transition (50–55 years)	Keeper of meanings
		Culminating life structure for middle adulthood (55–60 years)	
Late adulthood (65 years–death)	Ego integrity versus despair	Late adult transition (60–65 years)	Ego integrity
		Late adulthood (65 years–death)	

individual differences in the weight of central and peripheral components exist.

Look again at Table 14.1, and notice that each of Levinson's eras consists of alternating transitional and structure-building periods. The primary task of a structure-building period is to select and integrate components in ways that enhance one's life. A structure-building period ordinarily lasts about 5 to 7 years—at most, 10 years. Then the life structure that formed the basis for stability comes into question, and a new transition arises in preparation for modifying it. Take a moment to list the components of your own life structure. Are you in the midst of building—choosing and blending components and pursuing values and goals within that structure? Or are you in transition—terminating an existing structure to create possibilities for a new one?

Biographical reports of many individuals confirm Levinson's description of the life course. They also reveal that early adulthood is the era of "greatest energy and abundance, contradiction and stress" (Levinson, 1986, p. 5). These years can bring rich satisfactions in love, sexuality, family life, occupational advancement, and realization of major life goals. But they also carry great burdens—serious decisions about marriage, children, work, and lifestyle before many people have the life experience to choose wisely.

■ DREAMS AND MENTORS. How do young adults cope with the opportunities and hazards of this period? Levinson found that during the early adult transition (17 to 22 years), most construct a dream, an image of the self in the adult world that guides their decision making. The more specific the dream, the more purposeful the individual's structure building. For men, the dream usually emphasizes an independent achiever in an occupational role. In contrast, only a minority of women report dreams in which career dominates. Instead, most career-oriented women display "split dreams" in which both marriage and career are prominent. Also, women's dreams tend to define the self in terms of relationships with husband, children, and colleagues. Men's dreams are more individualistic: They view significant others, especially wives, as vital supporters of their goals. Less often do they see themselves as supporters of the goals of others.

Young adults also form a relationship with a mentor who facilitates the realization of their dream. The mentor is generally several years older and experienced in the world the person seeks to enter. Most of the time, a senior colleague at work fills this role, occasionally a friend, neighbor, or relative. Mentors may act as teachers who enhance the person's occupational skills; guides who acquaint the person with the values, customs, and characters of the occupational setting; and sponsors who foster the person's advancement in the workplace. As we will see when we take up vocational development, finding a supportive mentor is easier for men than for women.

■ To realize their dream, young adults form a relationship with a mentor, who fosters their occupational skills and knowledge of the values, customs, and characters of the workplace. This senior executive advises an apprentice engineer in an aircraft parts plant. Generally, finding a supportive mentor is easier for men than for women. (Photo courtesy: L. Skoogfors/Woodfin Camp & Associates)

According to Levinson, men oriented toward high-status careers (doctor, lawyer, scientist) spend their twenties acquiring the skills, values, and credentials of their profession. Although some women follow this path, for many others the process of developing a career extends well into middle age (Levinson, 1978, 1996; Roberts & Newton, 1987).

■ THE AGE 30 TRANSITION. During the age 30 transition, young people reevaluate their life structure and try to change components they find inadequate. Those who were preoccupied with their career and are still single usually become concerned with finding a life partner. However, men rarely reverse the relative priority of career and family, whereas career-oriented women sometimes do.

Women who stressed marriage and motherhood early often develop more individualistic goals at this time. Recall that Christy had dreamed of becoming a college professor. In her mid-thirties, she finally got her doctoral degree and undertook the task of making it professionally. During the age 30 transition, women become conscious of aspects of their marriage that threaten to inhibit further development of the independent side of their dream. Married women tend to demand that their husbands recognize and accommodate their interests and aspirations beyond the home.

For men and women who are satisfied with neither their relational nor occupational accomplishments, the age 30 transition can be a crisis. For many others who question whether they will be able to create a meaningful life structure, this is a period of considerable conflict and instability.

■ SETTLING DOWN FOR MEN, CONTINUED INSTA-
BILITY FOR WOMEN. Levinson (1978, 1996) describes
age 33 to 40 as a period of settling down. To create the culminating life structure of early adulthood, men emphasize
certain relationships and aspirations and make others secondary or set them aside. In doing so, they try to establish a
stable niche in society by anchoring themselves more firmly
in family, occupation, and community. At the same time,
they advance within the structure—by improving their
skills and contributing to society in ways consistent with
their values, whether those be wealth, power, prestige, artistic
or scientific achievement, or particular forms of family or
community participation. During these years, Sharese's husband Ernie expanded his knowledge of real estate accounting, became a partner in his firm, coached his son's soccer
team, and was elected treasurer of his church. He paid less
attention to golf, travel, and playing the guitar than he had in
his twenties.

"Settling down," however, does not accurately describe
women's experiences during their thirties. Many remain
highly unsettled because of the addition of an occupational
or relationship commitment that must be integrated into
their life structure. When her two children were born, Sharese felt torn between her research position in the state health
department and spending time with her family. She took 6
months off after the arrival of each baby. When she returned
to work, she did not pursue attractive administrative openings because they required travel and time away from home.
And shortly after Christy got her Ph.D., she and Gary divorced. Becoming a single parent while starting her professional life introduced new strains. Not until middle adulthood do many women attain the stability typical of men in
their thirties—reaching professional maturity and taking on
more authority in the community (Levinson, 1996).

VAILLANT'S ADAPTATION TO LIFE

Vaillant (1977) examined the development of 94 men
born in the 1920s, selected for study while they were students
at a highly competitive liberal arts college and followed over
the next 30 years. In college, the participants underwent extensive interviews. During each succeeding decade, they
answered lengthy questionnaires about their current lives.
Then Vaillant interviewed each man at age 47 about work,
family, and physical and psychological health.

Other than denying a strict age-related schedule of
change, Vaillant's theory is compatible with Levinson's.
Both agree that quality of relationships with important
people shape the life course. In examining the ways that
men altered themselves and their social world to adapt to
life, Vaillant confirmed Erikson's stages but filled in gaps between them. Following a period in their twenties devoted to
intimacy concerns, the men focused on career consolidation in their thirties—working hard and making the grade
in their occupations. During their forties, they pulled back

from individual achievement and became more generative—giving to and guiding others. In their fifties, they became "keepers of meaning," or guardians of their culture.
Many became more philosophical—concerned about the
values of the new generation and the state of their society.
They wanted to teach others what they had learned from
life experience and sought to perpetuate a capacity to care
(Vaillant & Koury, 1994).

Unlike Levinson, Vaillant (1977) did not study women.
But longitudinal research that includes women born
around the same time as his participants suggests a similar
series of changes (Block, 1971; Oden & Terman, 1968).

LIMITATIONS OF LEVINSON'S AND VAILLANT'S THEORIES

Although there is substantial consensus among psychosocial theorists about adult development, we must keep
in mind that their conclusions are largely based on interviews with people born in the 1920s to 1940s. The patterns
identified by Levinson and Vaillant fit the life paths of
Sharese, Ernie, Christy, and Gary, but it is still possible that
they do not apply as broadly to modern young people as
they do to the previous generation (Rossi, 1980).

Two other factors limit the conclusions of these theorists. First, although non-college-educated, low-income
adults were included in Levinson's sample, they were few in
number, and low-SES women remain almost entirely un-
investigated. Yet SES can profoundly affect the life course.
For example, Levinson's blue-collar workers rarely imple-
mented an occupational dream. Perhaps because career
advancement is less salient for them, lower-SES men perceive "early adulthood" to end and "maturity" to arrive at a
younger age than do their higher-SES counterparts (Neugarten, 1979). Vaillant (1993) examined longitudinal archives on a sample of men who had grown up in Boston
inner-city neighborhoods in the 1940s, half of whom remained low-income in adulthood. Although he reported
evidence for his stage sequence, he acknowledged that the
sample was highly restricted.

Finally, Levinson's participants were middle aged when
interviewed, and they might not have remembered all aspects of their early adult lives accurately. In sum, studies of
new generations—both men and women, of diverse SES
and cultural backgrounds—are needed before we can definitely conclude that the developmental sequences just described apply to most or all young people.

THE SOCIAL CLOCK

In the previous section and in earlier parts of this book,
we emphasized that changes in society from one generation to the next can affect the life course. Bernice Neugarten (1968, 1979) points out that an important cultural and
generational influence on adult development is the **social**

clock—age-graded expectations for life events, such as beginning a first job, getting married, birth of the first child, buying a home, and retiring. All societies have timetables for accomplishing major developmental tasks. Being on time or off time can profoundly affect self-esteem, since adults (like children and adolescents) make social comparisons, measuring the progress of their lives against their friends', siblings', and colleagues'. Especially when evaluating family and occupational attainments, people often ask, "How am I doing for my age?"

A major source of personality change in adulthood is conformity to or departure from the social clock. In a study of college women born in the 1930s who were followed up at ages 27 and 43, researchers determined how closely participants followed a "feminine" social clock (marriage and parenthood in the early or mid-twenties) or a "masculine" social clock (entry into a high-status career and advancement by the late twenties). Those who started families on time became more responsible, self-controlled, tolerant, and nurturant but declined in self-esteem and felt more vulnerable as their lives progressed. Those who followed an occupational timetable typical for men became more dominant, sociable, independent, and intellectually effective, a trend also found in a cohort born a decade later (Vandewater & Stewart, 1997). Women not on a social clock—who had neither married nor begun a career by age 30—were doing especially poorly. They suffered from self-doubt, feelings of incompetence, and loneliness. One stated, "My future is a giant question mark" (Helson, 1992; Helson, Mitchell, & Moane, 1984, p. 1090).

As noted in Chapter 1, expectations for appropriate behavior during early, middle, and late adulthood are no longer as definite as they once were. When Australian college students were asked for the best age at which to accomplish various milestones of development, they advocated later ages for

marriage and grandparenthood and a broader age range for retirement than people did thirty years ago (Peterson, 1996). Still, many adults experience some psychological distress when they are substantially behind in timing of life events (Antonucci & Akiyama, 1997; Rook, Catalano, & Dooley, 1989). Following a social clock of some kind seems to foster confidence during early adulthood because it guarantees that the young person will engage in the work of society, develop skills, and increase in understanding of the self and others (Helson, 1997; Helson & Moane, 1987). As Neugarten (1979) suggests, the stability of society depends on having people committed to social clock patterns. With this in mind, let's take a closer look at how young men and women traverse the major tasks of young adulthood.

ASK YOURSELF . . .

■ *Return to Chapter 1 and review commonly used methods of studying human development. Which method did Vaillant use to chart the course of adult life? What are its strengths and limitations?*

■ *In Levinson's theory, during which periods are people likely to be moving within a social clock timetable? When are they likely to be reflecting on and reconsidering this schedule?*

■ *Using the concept of the social clock, explain why Sharese was so conflicted about getting married to Ernie after she finished graduate school.*

CLOSE RELATIONSHIPS

To establish an intimate tie to another person, people must find a partner, build an emotional bond, and sustain it over time. Although young adults are especially concerned with romantic love, intimacy is also reflected in other relationships in which there is a mutual commitment—friends, siblings, and co-workers. Let's examine the multiple faces of intimacy.

ROMANTIC LOVE

During her junior year of college, Sharese glanced around the room in government class, her eyes often set-

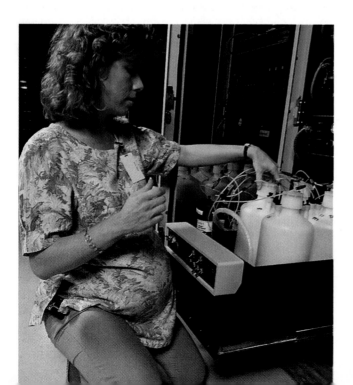

■ *All societies have social clocks, or timetables for accomplishing major developmental tasks. Yet today, expectations for appropriate behavior are not as definite as they once were. This first-time mother has taken time to establish herself as a research scientist before having children. Is she departing from the social clock or establishing a new pattern? (Photo courtesy: Bob Daemmrich/The Image Works)*

tling on Ernie, a senior and one of the top students. One weekend, Sharese and Ernie were invited to a party given by a mutual friend, and they struck up a conversation. Within a short time, Sharese discovered that Ernie was as warm and interesting as he had seemed from a distance. And Ernie found Sharese to be lively, intelligent, and attractive. By the end of the evening, the couple realized they had similar opinions on important social issues and liked the same leisure activities. They began to date steadily. Four years later, they married.

Finding a partner with whom to share one's life is a major milestone of adult development, with profound consequences for self-concept and psychological well-being. It is also a complex process that unfolds over time and is affected by a variety of events, as Sharese and Ernie's relationship reveals.

■ SELECTING A MATE. Recall from Chapter 13 that intimate partners tend to meet in places where there are people of their own age, ethnicity, SES, and religion. Once in physical proximity, people usually select partners who resemble themselves in other ways—attitudes, personality, educational plans, intelligence, physical attractiveness, and even height (Keith & Schafer, 1991; Simpson & Harris, 1994). Although romantic partners sometimes have abilities that complement one another, there is little support for the idea that "opposites attract." Instead, compatibility is the most powerful force in transforming strangers into lovers. The more similar two people are, the more satisfied they tend to be with their relationship and the more likely they are to stay together (Caspi & Herbener, 1990).

Sex differences exist in the importance placed on certain characteristics. Women assign greater weight to intelligence, ambitiousness, financial status, character, and commitment, men to physical attractiveness and domestic skills. Women prefer a same-age or slightly older partner, men a younger partner (Feingold, 1992; Kenrick & Keefe, 1992; Pines, 1998). Ethological theory helps us understand why. Recall from Chapter 13 that because their capacity to reproduce is limited, women seek a mate with traits that help ensure children's survival and well-being. In contrast, men look for a mate with characteristics that signal youth, health, and ability to provide sexual pleasure and bear offspring. Consistent with this view, men often want the relationship to move quickly toward physical intimacy. Women typically desire psychological intimacy—a longer time for partners to get to know each other—before sexual intercourse occurs.

According to an alternative, social learning perspective, societal gender roles profoundly influence criteria for mate selection. Beginning in childhood, men learn to be assertive and independent—behaviors that lead to success in the work world. Women acquire nurturant behaviors, which facilitate caregiving. Then each sex learns to value traits in the other that fit with a traditional division of labor. In support

of this theory, in cultures with greater gender equality in government and the workplace, women place less emphasis on a man's financial status and men are less concerned about a woman's domestic skills. And both sexes care less about a potential mate's age relative to their own. Nevertheless, men value physical attractiveness more than women do, irrespective of societies' level of gender equality (Eagly & Wood, 1999). Most likely, a blend of biological and social forces underlie sex differences in mate preferences.

As the Lifespan Vista box on pages 462–463 reveals, yet another influence on the partner we choose and the quality of the relationship we build is our early parent–child bonds. Finally, for romance to lead to marriage, it must happen at the right time. Two people may be right for each other, but if one or both are not ready to marry in terms of their own development or social clock, then the relationship is likely to dissolve.

■ THE COMPONENTS OF LOVE. What feelings and behaviors tell us that we are in love? According to one well-known theory, love has three components: intimacy, passion, and commitment. *Intimacy* is the emotional component. It involves warm, tender communication, expressions of concern about the other's well-being, and a desire for the partner to reciprocate. *Passion*, the desire for sexual activity and romance, is the physical and psychological arousal component. *Commitment* is the cognitive component. It leads partners to decide that they are in love and to maintain that love (Sternberg, 1987, 1988).

The balance among these components changes as romantic relationships develop. At the beginning, **passionate love**—intense sexual attraction—is strong. Gradually, passion declines in favor of intimacy and commitment, which form the basis for **companionate love**—warm, trusting affection and caregiving (Fehr, 1994; Hatfield, 1988). Each aspect of love, however, helps sustain modern relationships. Early passionate love is a strong predictor of whether partners stay together. But without the quiet intimacy, predictability, and shared attitudes and values of companionate love, most romances eventually break up (Hendrick & Hendrick, 1992).

An ongoing relationship with a mate requires effort from both partners, as a study of newlyweds' feelings and behavior over the first year of marriage reveals. Husbands and wives gradually felt less "in love" and pleased with married life. A variety of factors contributed to this change. A sharp drop in time spent talking to one another and in doing things that brought each other pleasure (for example, saying "I love you" or making the other person laugh) occurred. In addition, although couples engaged in just as many joint activities at the beginning and end of the year, leisure pursuits gave way to household tasks and chores. Less pleasurable activities may have contributed to the decline in satisfaction (Huston, McHale, & Crouter, 1986).

A LIFESPAN VISTA

CHILDHOOD ATTACHMENT PATTERNS AND ADULT ROMANTIC RELATIONSHIPS

Recall from Chapter 6 (page 198) that according to Bowlby's ethological theory, patterns of attachment originating in the infant–caregiver relationship are crucial for later emotional and social development. Early attachment bonds lead to the construction of an *internal working model*, or set of expectations about attachment figures, that serves as a guide for close relationships throughout life. In Chapter 6, we saw that adults' evaluations of their early attachment experiences are related to their parenting behaviors—specifically, to the quality of attachments they build with their own babies (see page 195). Additional evidence indicates that recollections of childhood attachment patterns are also strong predictors of romantic relationships in adulthood.

In studies carried out in Australia, Israel, and the United States, researchers asked people to describe their early parental bonds (attachment history), their attitudes toward intimate relationships (internal working model), and their actual experiences with romantic partners. Consistent with Bowlby's theory, adults' recall and interpretation of childhood attachment patterns[1] served as remarkably good indicators of current internal working models and relationship experiences:

SECURE ATTACHMENT. Adults who described their attachment history as secure (warm, loving, and supportive) had internal working models that reflected this security. They viewed themselves as likable and easy to get to know, were comfortable with intimacy, and rarely worried about abandonment or someone getting too close to them. In line with these attitudes, they characterized their most important love relationship in terms of trust, happiness, and friendship.

AVOIDANT ATTACHMENT. Adults with an avoidant attachment history (demanding, disrespectful, and critical parents) displayed internal working models that stressed independence, mistrust of love partners, and anxiety about people getting too close. They were convinced that others disliked them and that romantic love is hard to find and rarely lasts. Jealousy, emotional distance, and lack of acceptance pervaded their most important love relationship.

RESISTANT ATTACHMENT. Adults who described a resistant attachment history (parents who responded unpredictably and unfairly) presented internal working models in which they wanted to merge completely with another person and fell in love quickly. At the same time, they worried that their intense feelings would overwhelm others, who really did not love them and would not want to stay with them. Their most important love relationship was riddled with jealousy, emotional highs and lows, and desperation about whether the partner would return their affection (Bartholomew & Horowitz, 1991; Hazan & Shaver, 1987; Kirkpatrick & Davis, 1994; Mikulincer & Erev, 1991; Shaver & Brennan, 1992; Simpson, Rholes, & Nelligan, 1992).

Bowlby's predictions about the long-term consequences of early attachment are reflected not only in adults' self-reports, but also in the reports of their acquaintances and by their social behavior. Peers describe young adults who recall a secure attachment history as more competent, charming, cheerful, and likable than their insecure counterparts

But couples whose relationships endure generally report that they love each other more than they did earlier (Sprecher, 1999). In the transformation of romantic involvements from passionate to companionate, commitment may be the aspect of love that determines whether a relationship survives. Communicating that commitment—through warmth, sensitivity, caring, acceptance, and respect—can be of great benefit (Knapp & Taylor, 1994). For example, Sharese's doubts about getting married subsided largely because of Ernie's expressions of commitment. In the most dramatic of these, he painted a large sign on her birthday and placed it in their front yard. It read, "I LOVE SHARESE." Sharese returned Ernie's sentiments, and the intimacy of their bond deepened.

Intimate partners who consistently express their commitment report higher-quality relationships (Duck, 1994; Hecht, Marston, & Larkey, 1994). An important feature of their communication is constructive conflict resolution—raising issues gently and avoiding the escalation of negative interaction sparked by criticism, contempt, defensiveness, and stonewalling (Gottman et al., 1998). These negative escalation cycles are one of the strongest predictors of marital distress and future divorce. How men handle conflict is particularly important, since on the average men are more wary of dealing with it and less skilled at negotiating it than are women (Karney & Bradbury, 1997; Prado & Markman, 1998). The Caregiving Concerns table on page 464 lists ways to help keep the embers of love aglow in a romantic partnership.

(Kobak & Sceery, 1988). Perhaps because secure adults tend to choose partners who also remember a childhood history of attachment security, their conflict resolution strategies are more constructive and their dating relationships and marriages are more satisfying and enduring (Collins & Read, 1990; Feeney, 1994, 1998; Hill, Young, & Nord, 1994). Insecure attachment histories are associated with a variety of maladaptive social behaviors. For example, avoidant adults tend to deny attachment needs through excessive work and brief sexual encounters and affairs. Resistant adults are quick to express fear and anger, and they disclose information about themselves at inappropriate times. Both groups drink excessive amounts of alcohol to reduce tension and anxiety (Brennan & Shaver, 1995).

Because current psychological state might bias recall of parental behavior, we cannot know for sure whether adults' descriptions of their childhood attachment experiences are accurate (Fox, 1995). Also, we must keep in mind that quality of attachment to parents is not the only factor that influences later intimate ties. Characteristics of the partner

and current life conditions can powerfully affect relationships. When adults with unhappy love lives have opportunities to form new, more satisfying intimate ties, they may revise their internal working models, thereby weakening the continuity between early and later relationships (Feeney, 1999). Still, a wealth of evidence suggests that unfavorable childhood attachment experiences predispose people to conclude that they are undeserving of love or that their intimate partners cannot be trusted.

[1] To review patterns of infant–caregiver attachment, return to pages 191–192.

■ *Gazing at a family photo of herself as a toddler in the arms of her mother, this woman reflects back on her early attachment experiences. Research indicates that how adults interpret their childhood parental bonds is a good indicator of the quality of their current romantic relationships. (Photo courtesy: Kevin Thomas)*

■ CULTURE AND THE EXPERIENCE OF LOVE. Passion and intimacy, which form the basis for romantic love, became the dominant basis for marriage in twentieth-century Western nations as the value of individualism strengthened. From this vantage point, mature love is based on autonomy, appreciation of the partner's unique qualities, and intense emotion. Trying to satisfy dependency needs through an intimate bond is regarded as immature (Hatfield, 1993).

This Western view contrasts sharply with the perspectives of Eastern cultures, such as China and Japan. In Japanese, *amae*, or love, means "to depend on another's benevolence." Dependency throughout life is accepted and viewed positively. The traditional Chinese collectivist view defines the self in terms of role relationships. A Chinese man considers himself a son, a brother, a husband, and a father; he rarely thinks in terms of an independent self (Chu, 1985). Because feelings of affection are distributed across a broad social network, the intensity of any one relationship is reduced.

In choosing a mate, Chinese and Japanese young people are expected to consider obligations to others, especially parents. As one writer summarized, "An American asks, 'How does my heart feel?' A Chinese asks, 'What will other people say?'" (Hsu, 1981, p. 50). Consistent with this difference, college students of Asian ethnicity are less likely than those of American, Canadian, or European descent to endorse a view of love based on physical attraction and deep emotion. Instead they stress companionship and practical matters, such as similarity of background, career promise, and likelihood of being a good parent (Dion & Dion, 1993).

Keeping Love Alive in a Romantic Partnership

SUGGESTION	DESCRIPTION
Make time for your relationship.	To foster relationship satisfaction and a sense of being "in love," plan regular times to be together during enjoyable activities.
Tell your partner of your love.	Express affection and caring, including the powerful words "I love you," at appropriate times. These messages increase perceptions of commitment and encourage your partner to respond in kind.
Be available to your partner in times of need.	Provide emotional support, giving of yourself when your partner is distressed.
Communicate constructively and positively about relationship problems.	When you or your partner are dissatisfied, suggest ways of overcoming difficulties, and ask your partner to collaborate in choosing and implementing a course of action. Avoid the four enemies of a gratifying, close relationship: criticism, contempt, defensiveness, and stonewalling.
Show an interest in important aspects of your partner's life.	Ask about your partner's work, friends, family, and hobbies, and express appreciation for his or her special abilities and achievements. In doing so, you grant your partner a sense of being valued.
Confide in your partner.	Share innermost feelings, keeping intimacy alive.
Forgive minor offenses, and try to understand major offenses.	Whenever possible, overcome feelings of anger through forgiveness. In this way, you acknowledge unjust behavior but avoid becoming preoccupied with it.

Sources: Donatelle & Davis, 2000; Harvey & Pauwels, 1999; Horowitz, McLaughlin, & White, 1997.

FRIENDSHIPS

Like romantic partners and childhood friends, adult friends are usually similar in age, sex, and SES—factors that contribute to common interests, experiences, and needs and therefore to the pleasure derived from the relationship. Friends offer many of the same benefits in adulthood that they did in earlier years. They enhance self-esteem through affirmation and acceptance and provide social support during times of stress (Hartup & Stevens, 1999). Friends also make life more interesting by expanding social opportunities and access to knowledge and points of view.

Trust, intimacy, and loyalty continue to be important in adult friendships, as they were in middle childhood and adolescence. Sharing thoughts and feelings is sometimes greater in friendship than in marriage, although commitment is less strong as friends come and go over the life course. Even so, some adult friendships continue for many years. In one study of people age 60 and older, the majority reported having at least one friendship that lasted throughout life (Roberto & Kimboko, 1989). Friendship continuity is greater for women, who also see their friends more often —a factor that helps maintain the relationship (Field & Minkler, 1988).

■ SAME-SEX FRIENDSHIPS. Throughout life, women continue to have more intimate same-sex friendships than do men. When together, female friends say they prefer to "just talk," whereas male friends say they like to "do something," such as play sports, extending a pattern evident in childhood and adolescence (see Chapter 12, page 404). Men report barriers to intimacy with other men. For example, they indicate that they sometimes feel in competition with male friends and are therefore unwilling to disclose any weaknesses. And they also worry that if they tell about themselves, their friends may not reciprocate (Reid & Fine, 1992). Because a balance of power and equality in social giving and taking is basic to a good friendship, women generally evaluate their same-sex friendships more positively than men do (Veniegas & Peplau, 1997).

Of course, individual differences in friendship quality exist, to which gender identity and marital status contribute. Compared with traditionally oriented adults, androgynous men and women report disclosing more intimate information to their friends (Fischer & Narus, 1981; Lombardo & Lavine, 1981). But involvement in family roles affects reliance on friends for fulfilling emotional and social needs. For single adults, friends are the preferred companions and confidants. With marriage, young people—especially men—direct more of their disclosures toward their spouses. Still, friendships continue to be vital contexts for personal sharing throughout early adulthood (turn back to Figure 12.1 on page 403 to view these trends)(Carbery & Buhrmester, 1998).

■ OTHER-SEX FRIENDSHIPS. Other-sex friendships are also important, although they occur less often and do not last as long as same-sex friendships. These bonds are as common as romantic relationships during the college years. They decline after marriage for men but increase with age for women, who tend to form them in the workplace. Highly educated, employed women have the largest number of other-sex friends. Through these relationships, young adults learn a great deal about masculine and feminine styles of intimacy. And because males confide especially easily in their female friends, men with other-sex friends are granted a unique opportunity to broaden their expressive capacity (Swain, 1992).

In platonic, other-sex friendships, sexual attraction is not necessarily absent, but it is regulated more than in romantic ties. Consequently, both men and women generally rate sexual overtones in these relationships as minimal (Monsour et al., 1994). Men are more likely than women to feel sexually attracted to an other-sex friend. If these feelings persist and increase in intensity, the relationship is likely to change into a romantic bond or disintegrate (Kaplan & Keys, 1997). When a solid other-sex friendship does evolve into a romance, it may be more stable and enduring than a romantic relationship formed without a friendship foundation (Hendrick & Hendrick, 1993).

■ SIBLINGS AS FRIENDS. Whereas intimacy is essential to friendship, commitment—in terms of willingness to maintain a relationship and care about the other—is the defining characteristic of family ties. As young people marry and need to invest less time in developing a romantic partnership, siblings—especially sisters whose earlier bond was positive—become more frequent companions than they were in adolescence. Often there is spillover between friend and sibling roles. For example, Sharese described Heather's practical assistance—helping with moving and running errands during an illness—in kin terms: "She's like a sister to me. I can always turn to her." And sibling ties in adulthood are often like friendships, in which the main concern is keeping in contact, offering social support, and enjoying being together (O'Connor, 1992). Relationships between same-sex siblings can be especially close. Despite rivalries and differences in interests that emerged in childhood, a shared background of experiences within the family promotes similarity in values and perspectives and the possibility for deep mutual understanding.

Sibling relationships are among the longest we have in life. As we grow older, they become increasingly important sources of well-being. In Vaillant's (1977) study of well-educated men, the single best predictor of emotional health at age 65 was having had a close tie with a sibling in early adulthood. In another investigation, one-fifth of married women identified a sister as a best friend (Oliker, 1989).

LONELINESS

Because it is a time when people expect to form intimate ties, early adulthood is a vulnerable period for **loneliness**— unhappiness that results from a gap between social relationships we currently have and those we desire. Adults may feel lonely because they do not have an intimate partner or because they lack gratifying friendships. Both situations give rise to similar emotions, but they are not interchangeable (Brehm, 1992). For example, even though she had several enjoyable friendships, Heather felt lonely from time to time because she was not dating someone she cared about. And although Sharese and Ernie were happily married, they felt lonely after moving to a new town where they did not know anyone.

Loneliness is at its peak during the late teens and early twenties, after which it declines steadily into the seventies (Brehm, 1992; Liefbroer & de Jong-Gierveld, 1990). This is understandable, since young people must constantly develop new relationships as they move through school and employment settings. Also, younger adults may expect much more from their intimate ties than do older adults, who have learned to live with imperfections.

Who is most likely to experience loneliness, and under what conditions? Separated, divorced, or widowed adults are lonelier than their married, cohabiting, or single counterparts, suggesting that loneliness is intense after loss of an intimate tie (Rubenstein & Shaver, 1982; Stroebe et al., 1996). When not involved in a romantic relationship, men feel lonelier than women, perhaps because they have fewer alternatives for satisfying intimacy needs. In marriages, wives report greater loneliness than husbands, especially if they are unemployed, have recently moved, or have young children—circumstances that limit their access to a wider social network (Fischer & Phillips, 1982).

■ *Loneliness is at its peak during the late teens and early twenties. It usually stems from lack of an intimate partner or gratifying friendships. When loneliness persists, it is associated with negative self-evaluations and socially unresponsive and insensitive behavior—responses that promote further isolation. (Photo courtesy: Ron Coppock/Liaison Agency)*

Personal characteristics also contribute to the likelihood of being lonely. Temperament is involved, since shy, socially anxious people report more loneliness (Bruch et al., 1989). When loneliness persists, it is associated with a wide variety of self-defeating attitudes and behaviors. Lonely people evaluate themselves and others more negatively, tend to be socially unresponsive and insensitive, and are slow to develop intimacy because they are reluctant to tell others about themselves. The extent to which these responses are cause or consequence of loneliness is unclear, but once in place, they certainly promote further isolation (Jones, 1990).

Although loneliness is extreme for some people, most young adults encounter it from time to time as they struggle with unfulfilled relationship desires. As long as it is not overwhelming, loneliness can motivate young people to take social risks and reach out to others. It can also encourage them to find ways to be comfortably alone and use this time to deepen self-understanding. Much of healthy personality development involves striking this balance—between "[developing] satisfying relationships with other people and [creating] a secure, internal base of satisfaction within ourselves" (Brehm, 1992, p. 345).

ASK YOURSELF . . .

After dating for 2 years, Mindy and Graham reported that their love and satisfaction with their relationship were greater than during the first few months they had known each other. What features of communication probably contributed to a deepening of their bond, and why is it likely to endure?

■ *Claire and Tom, both married to other partners, got to know each other at work and occasionally have lunch together. What is each likely to gain from this other-sex friendship?*

THE FAMILY LIFE CYCLE

For the majority of young people, the quest for intimacy leads to marriage. Their life course takes shape within the **family life cycle**—a sequence of phases that characterizes the development of most families around the world (Framo, 1994). In early adulthood, people typically live on their own, marry, and bear and rear children. As they become middle-aged and their children leave home, their parenting responsibilities diminish. Late adulthood brings retirement, growing old, and (mostly for women) death of one's spouse (Duvall, 1977; McGoldrick, Heiman, & Carter, 1993).

However, we must be careful not to think of the family life cycle as a fixed progression. Recall from Chapter 2 that the family is a dynamic system of interdependent relationships embedded in community, cultural, and historical contexts. All of these factors affect the way it changes over time. Today, wide variations in sequence and timing of these phases exist. High rates of out-of-wedlock births, delayed childbearing, divorce, and remarriage are but a few illustrations. And some people—either voluntarily or involuntarily—do not experience some or all of the family life cycle.

Still, the family life cycle approach is useful. It provides us with an organized way of thinking about how the family system changes over time and the impact of these changes on both the family unit and the individuals within it. Each phase requires that roles be modified and needs be met in new ways.

LEAVING HOME

After Sharese had been away at college for 6 months, she noticed a change in the way she related to her mother. She found it more enjoyable to discuss daily experiences and life goals, sought advice and listened with greater openness, and expressed affection more freely. Over the next few years, Sharese's bedroom gradually began to seem more like a guest room. Looking around before she moved out permanently, Sharese felt some pangs of nostalgia for the warmth and security of her childhood days coupled with a sense of pride at being on her own.

Departure from the parental home is a major step in assuming adult responsibilities. The average age of leaving has decreased in recent years as more young people live independently before marriage. In 1940, over 80 percent of American 18- to 24-year-olds resided with their parents. Today, only about 50 percent do. Most industrialized nations show this trend (Kerckhoff & Macrae, 1992; White, 1994).

Timing of departure varies with the reason for leaving. Departures for education tend to be at younger ages, those for full-time work and marriage later. Since a larger percentage of young adults go to college in the United States than other nations, more Americans leave home early, around age 18. Some young people who want to get away from friction at home also tend to depart early—as soon as they can (Stattin & Magnusson, 1996). Still, studies of nationally representative samples in Australia, Great Britain, and the United States show that marriage is the most common reason for departure in all three nations (Kerckhoff & Macrae, 1992). And because women usually marry at a younger age than men, they are likely to leave home sooner.

Nearly half of young adults return home for a brief time after initial leaving. Those who departed to marry are least likely to return. But premarital independent living is a fragile arrangement. As people encounter unexpected twists and turns on the road to independence, the parental home serves as a safety net and base of operation for launching adult life. Failures in work or marriage can prompt a move back home. Also, young people who left because of family conflict usually return—largely because they were not ready for independent living. But most of the time, role transitions, such as the end of college or military service and the beginning of full-time work, bring people back. Contrary to popular belief, returning home is usually not a sign of weakness. Instead, it is a common and ordinary event among unmarried adults (Graber & Brooks-Gunn, 1996; White, 1994).

Although most high school seniors expect to live on their own before marriage, the extent to which they do so varies with SES and ethnicity. Economically well-off young people are more likely to establish their own residence. Among African Americans and Hispanics, poverty and a cultural tradition of extended family living lead to low rates of home leaving. Unmarried Asian Americans also tend to live with their parents. But the longer Asian families have been in the United States and are exposed to individualistic values, the more likely their children are to move out after finishing high school (Goldscheider & Goldscheider, 1993).

When young people are prepared for independence, departure from the home is linked to more satisfying parent–child interaction and successful transition to adult roles (Bloom, 1987). However, leaving home very early may contribute to long-term disadvantage, since it is associated with an emphasis on employment rather than education and lack of parental financial assistance, advice, and emotional support. Not surprisingly, those who depart at a young age have less successful marriages and work lives (White, 1994).

Besides timing of departure, personal characteristics make a difference. For example, young adults who perceive themselves as adaptable and in control of their environments and who find a middle ground between closeness and distance in family relationships adjust especially well to the first year of college. For men, attaining this middle ground often means developing themselves emotionally and expressively. For women, it usually means acquiring a firmer sense of autonomy (Holmbeck & Wandrei, 1993). Interventions directed at helping young people reevaluate traditional gender roles may be especially valuable at this time.

JOINING OF FAMILIES IN MARRIAGE

The United States remains a culture strongly committed to marriage. Nearly 90 percent of Americans marry at least once in their lives. Young adults wait considerably longer before marrying today than they did at midcentury. In 1950, the average age of first marriage was 20.3 for women and 22.8 for men; in 1997, it was 24.8 and 27.1, respectively (U.S. Bureau of the Census, 1999). As Figure 14.1 shows, the number of first and second marriages has declined over the last few decades as more people remain single, cohabit, or do not remarry after divorce. Still, both marriage and divorce rates remain high.

Marriage is often thought of as the joining of two individuals. In actuality, it requires that two entire systems—the husband's and wife's families—adapt and overlap to create a new subsystem. Consequently, marriage presents couples with complex challenges, especially today when husband–wife roles have only begun to move in the direction of a true partnership—educationally, occupationally, and in emotional connectedness (McGoldrick, Heiman, & Carter, 1993).

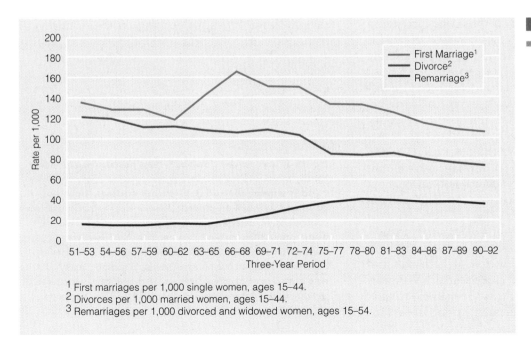

1 First marriages per 1,000 single women, ages 15–44.
2 Divorces per 1,000 married women, ages 15–44.
3 Remarriages per 1,000 divorced and widowed women, ages 15–54.

FIGURE 14.1

■ **Rates of first marriage, divorce, and remarriage for women, 1951 to 1992.** The number of first marriages has dropped steadily since mid-century. After increasing between 1960 and 1980, the divorce rate stabilized and then declined slightly. Remarriages rose sharply in the 1960s as divorce climbed. Since then, they have decreased. Still, both marriage and divorce rates are high in the United States. (From U.S. Bureau of the Census, 1999.)

■ MARITAL ROLES. Their wedding and honeymoon over, Sharese and Ernie turned to a myriad of issues that they had previously decided individually or that their families of origin had prescribed. They had to consider everyday matters—when and how to eat, sleep, talk, work, relax, have sex, and spend money. They also had to decide which family traditions and rituals to retain and which to develop for themselves. And relationships with parents, siblings, extended family, friends, and co-workers had to be renegotiated.

Recent alterations in the context of marriage, including changing gender roles and living farther away from family members, mean that modern couples must do more work to define their relationships. Although husbands and wives are usually similar in religious and ethnic background, "mixed" marriages occur more often today than they did in the past. Since 1970, other-race unions have quadrupled, affecting over 3.4 million American couples, or 6 percent of the married population (U.S. Bureau of the Census, 1999). More young people also choose a mate of a different religion. For example, between one-third and one-half of American Jews who marry today select a non-Jewish spouse (Greenstein, Carlson, & Howell, 1993). When their backgrounds are very distinct, these couples face extra challenges in achieving a successful transition to married life.

Many modern couples live together before marriage, making it less of a turning point in the family life cycle than in the past. Still, the burden of defining marital roles can be great. American women who marry before age 20 (25 percent) are twice as likely to divorce as those who marry in their twenties. Women who marry after age 30 (20 percent) are least likely to divorce, but if they do, they end the marriage sooner (McGoldrick, Heiman, & Carter, 1993).

These findings suggest that it is better to marry later than earlier. They also indicate that people who fall outside the normative age range for marriage often face stresses that make the transition more difficult. Those who marry early may be running away from their own family or seeking the family they never had. Most have not developed a secure enough identity or sufficient independence to be ready for a mature marital bond. Early marriage followed by childbirth and reversals of family life cycle events (childbirth before marriage) are more common among low-SES young people. This acceleration of family formation complicates adjustment to life as a couple (Leonard & Roberts, 1998). People who marry very late—most of whom are economically advantaged adults—are sometimes ambivalent about compromising their independence or in conflict about marriage and career.

Despite progress in the area of women's rights, **traditional marriages** still exist in Western nations. In this form of marriage, there is a clear division of husband's and wife's roles. The man is the head of household; his primary responsibility is to provide for the economic well-being of his family. The woman devotes herself to caring for her husband and children and to creating a nurturant, comfortable home. However, traditional marriages have changed in recent decades. Motherhood remains a full-time job—or at least the top priority—while children are young, but many women return to their occupations at a later date. Unlike previous generations, their role is not fixed throughout adult life.

Egalitarian marriages reflect the values of the women's movement. Husband and wife relate as equals, and power and authority are shared. Both partners try to balance the time and energy they devote to the workplace, the children, and their relationship. Well-educated, career-oriented couples tend to adopt this form of marriage—especially before they have children. But at least so far, women's employment has not had a dramatic effect on household division of labor. Men in these families participate more than do those in single-earner families. But their wives continue to do the bulk of the housework, averaging almost three times as many hours as their husbands (see Figure 14.2). True equality in marriage is still rare, and couples who strive for it more often attain a form of marriage in between traditional and egalitarian (Starrels, 1994).

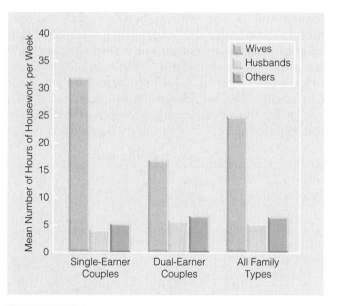

FIGURE 14.2

■ **Hours of housework done by wives, husbands, and other family members for single-earner couples (only the husband is employed) and dual-earner couples (both husband and wife are employed).** Wives in dual-earner households continue to do most of the work, averaging almost three times as many hours as their husbands. Total number of hours devoted to domestic work is lowest in these families because they have fewer children and tend to hire household help. In addition, many employed women handle work overload by reducing time devoted to housework. (Adapted from Starrels, 1994; U.S. Department of Health and Human Services, 1994.)

■ MARITAL SATISFACTION. Despite its rocky beginnings, Sharese and Ernie's marriage grew to be especially happy. In contrast, Christy and Gary became increasingly discontent. What distinguishes marriages high in satisfaction from less successful partnerships? Differences between the two couples mirror the findings of a large body of research, summarized in Table 14.2.

Christy and Gary had a brief courtship, married at a young age, had children early, and struggled financially. Gary's negative, critical personality led him to get along poorly with Christy's parents and to feel threatened when he and Christy disagreed. Christy tried her best to offer Gary encouragement and support, but her own needs for nurturance and individuality were not being met. Gary felt threatened by Christy's career aspirations. As she came closer to attaining them, the couple grew farther apart. In contrast, Sharese and Ernie married later, after their educations were complete. They postponed having children until their careers were under way and they had built a sense of togetherness that allowed each to thrive as an individual. Patience, caring, shared values, enjoyment of each other's company, and good conflict resolution skills contributed to their compatibility.

Although the factors just described differentiate troubled from gratifying marital relationships, research also reveals clear sex differences in marital satisfaction. Many more men than women report being happily married (Holahan, 1984; Kaslow, Hansson, & Lundblad, 1994; Levenson, Carstensen, & Gottman, 1993). Simply being married is associated with gains in men's mental and physical health—an outcome that stems from enhanced feelings of attachment, belonging, and social support. For women, however, *relationship quality* has a greater impact on mental health. Consequently, women suffer more than men when a marriage has problems (Horowitz, White, & Howell-White, 1996; Horowitz, McLaughlin, & White, 1997). Marriage can take a heavy toll on women's marital satisfaction when they are overwhelmed by the demands of husband, children, housework, and career (Wilkie, Ferree, & Ratcliff, 1998). And women are more willing to evaluate a relationship as unsatisfying and try to work on it. As noted earlier in our discussion of love, men often withdraw from conflict, magnifying the stress on their wives.

At their worst, marital relationships can become contexts for intense opposition, dominance–submission, and emotional and physical violence. As the Social Issues box on pages 470–471 explains, although women are more likely to be targets of severe spouse abuse, both husbands and wives are perpetrators and victims.

■ MARITAL EXPECTATIONS AND MYTHS. In a study in which 50 happily married couples were interviewed about their marriages, each participant reported good times and bad; none was happy all the time. Many admitted that there were moments when they wanted out, when they felt they had made a mistake. Clearly, marital happiness did not signify a "rose garden." Instead, it was grounded in mutual respect, pleasure and comfort in each other's company, and joint problem solving. All couples emphasized the need to reshape their relationship in response to new circumstances and each partner's changing needs and desires (Wallerstein & Blakeslee, 1995).

Yet cultural expectations work against this view of marriage as an ongoing project requiring both partners' involvement and cooperation. Historically, women had little power in marriage and society; a wife's status came from her husband. This gender gap has such deep cultural roots that it continues to influence marital expectations today. In a study of college students, more women than men said their partners should be superior to themselves, and more men than women said their partners should be inferior to themselves—in intelligence, education, voca-

TABLE 14.2

Factors Related to Marital Satisfaction

FACTOR	HAPPY MARRIAGE	UNHAPPY MARRIAGE
Family backgrounds	Similar in SES, education, religion, and ages of partners	Very different in SES, education, religion, or ages of partners
Age of marriage	After age 20	Before age 20
Length of courtship	At least 6 months	Less than 6 months
Timing of first pregnancy	After first year of marriage	Before or within first year of marriage
Relationship to extended family	Warm and positive	Negative, wish to maintain distance
Marital patterns in extended family	Stable	Unstable; frequent separations and divorces
Financial and employment status	Secure	Insecure
Personality characteristics	Emotionally positive; good conflict resolution skills	Emotionally negative and impulsive; poor conflict resolution skills

Note: The more factors present, the greater the likelihood of marital happiness or unhappiness.
Sources: Gottman et al., 1998; Levenson, Carstensen, & Gottman, 1993; Karney & Bradbury, 1997; McGoldrick, Heiman, & Carter, 1993; Russell & Wells, 1994.

Violence has reached epidemic proportions in the United States, permeating many families. In previous chapters, we discussed domestic violence several times: child maltreatment in Chapter 8, child sexual abuse in Chapter 10, and marital sexual assault in Chapter 13. Here we focus on spouse abuse.

Within families, violence in one form predicts its occurrence in another. Recall the story of Karen in Chapter 13. Her husband, Mike, not only assaulted her sexually and physically but also abused her psychologically—isolating, humiliating, and demeaning her. Property destruction can occur as well. Violent spouses may break their partners' favorite possessions, punch holes in walls, or throw things. If children are present, they may also be victims (Carden, 1994).

Spouse abuse of the kind illustrated by Mike and Karen, in which husbands are perpetrators and wives are physically injured victims, is the type most likely to be reported to police and to appear in the media. Crime studies consistently show higher rates of assaulting men and physically injured women. When family violence gets under way, women have a higher probability of sustaining wounds that require medical treatment. But most acts of family violence are not reported. In surveys that ask married couples how many fights during the previous year led to hitting, throwing things, or other acts of hostility, men and women report very similar rates of marital assault (Straus, 1999; Zlotnick et al., 1998).

Some research indicates that most wife-inflicted violence occurs in self-defense (Currie, 1999). Although self-defense is a frequent cause of domestic assaults by women, other studies document fairly equal rates of "striking first" by men and women (Stets & Straus, 1990; Carrado et al., 1996). "Getting my partner's attention," "gaining control," and "expressing anger" are other admitted reasons that wives and husbands at times abuse each other (Hamberger et al., 1997; Straus, 1999).

FACTORS RELATED TO SPOUSE ABUSE. Marital relationships in which spouse abuse occurs are diverse. Dominance–submission may proceed from husband to wife, at other times from wife to husband. About half of couples surveyed report both partners to be violent (Cook, 1997). Marvin and Pat's relationship—which resembled Mike and Karen's except that in this case the husband was the victim—helps us understand how spouse abuse may escalate. During their courtship, Pat felt suspicious of Marvin's friends, so he began to distance himself from them. Shortly after their wedding, Pat began to spew insults about Marvin's family and co-workers. Once, she walked into his law office and openly insulted his receptionist and business partners. Then, after an illness that required hospitalization, Pat started to restrict Marvin's activities, complaining about the demands of his job and insisting that he be home early to care for her. When he resisted, she hurled epithets, threw objects, and slapped him. One evening, Marvin became so angry at Pat's hostilities that he hurled a dish against the wall, threw his wedding ring at her, and left the house. The next morning, Pat apologized and promised not to attack again. But her outbursts only became more frequent and desperate.

These abuse–remorse cycles in which aggression escalates characterize many abusive situations (Walker, 1979). Why do they occur? As with other forms of domestic violence, the reasons are multiple and complex. Personality and developmental history, family circumstances, and cultural factors combine to make spouse abuse more likely.

Abusers usually have serious psychological problems. Many are overly dependent on their spouses as well as

tional success, and income (Ganong & Coleman, 1992). Under these circumstances, women are likely to play down their abilities, sacrificing part of themselves. And men tend to limit themselves to the provider role rather than participating fully in family life.

Furthermore, many young people have a mythical image of marital bliss—one that is a far cry from reality. For example, a substantial number of college students endorse the following beliefs not supported by facts:

- A couple's satisfaction increases through the first year of marriage.

- The best single predictor of marital satisfaction is the quality of a couple's sex life.

- If my spouse loves me, he or she should instinctively know what I want and need to be happy.

- No matter how I behave, my spouse should love me simply because he or she is my spouse. (Larson, 1988, p. 5)

As these myths are overturned, couples react with disappointment, and marriage becomes less satisfying and more conflictual.

jealous, possessive, and controlling. For example, the thought of Karen ever leaving him induced such high anxiety in Mike that he monitored all her activities and resorted to violence to keep her (Allen et al., 1989). Dissatisfaction with life is manifested in depression, anxiety, and low self-esteem. Trivial events, such as an unironed shirt or a late meal, can set off violent episodes, indicating great difficulty managing anger in response to frustration (Else et al., 1993; Vaselle-Augenstein & Ehrlich, 1992).

A high proportion of spouse abusers grew up in homes where parents were aggressive toward each other, used coercive discipline, and were physically and psychologically abusive toward their children (Capaldi & Clark, 1998). Perhaps this explains why conduct problems in childhood and violent delinquency in adolescence are also predictive of spouse abuse (Magdol et al., 1998). Adults with childhood exposure to domestic violence are not doomed to repeat it. But their parents provided them with expectations and behaviors to model in their future close relationships. Stressful life events, such as job loss or financial difficulties, increase the likelihood of spouse abuse, although it occurs in couples of all SES backgrounds (Emery & Laumann-Billings, 1998). Alcohol abuse is also related to it (Leonard, 1999).

At a societal level, cultural norms that endorse male dominance and female submissiveness and use of physical force to preserve this inequality promote spouse abuse (Stith & Farley, 1993). And a covert tolerance of women slapping men for being insensitive, often portrayed as acceptable by the media, promotes this behavior in families. Despite the much lower chance of serious physical injury from attacks by women, these minor assaults are still dangerous because they can provoke severe retaliation by men (Goodyear-Smith & Laidlaw, 1999).

Why don't people leave these destructive relationships before the abuse escalates? A variety of situational factors discourage them from doing so. A victimized wife may be dependent on her husband's greater earning power or fear endangering herself or her children further. And victims of both sexes, but especially men, are deterred by the embarrassment associated with going to the police. Also, they may falsely hope that their spouse, as he or she promises after each explosive episode, will change (Arias, 1999; Straus, 1999). Finally, anxiety, depression, and physical injury can prevent a victim from thinking clearly about how to get help.

INTERVENTION AND TREATMENT. Community services available to women who are victims of sexual coercion also offer shelter, protection, and advocacy for battered women (see pages 437–438). Because many return to their abusive partners several times before making their final move, community agencies usually offer treatment for male batterers. The therapies available are diverse, and no single approach has been shown to be superior. Most rely on group sessions that confront rigid gender stereotyping; teach communication, problem solving, and anger control; and use social support to foster change behavior (Harway & Hansen, 1994).

Although existing treatments are far better than no treatment, almost all are too brief to pay sufficient attention to alcohol problems and marital difficulties. Consequently, of the small number who agree to participate, at least half continue their violent behavior with either the same or a new partner (Carden, 1994). At present, very few intervention strategies acknowledge that men can also be abuse victims. Yet ignoring their needs perpetuates domestic violence. To be optimally effective, treatment requires a whole-family approach that addresses maladaptive husband–wife relationships.

In view of its long-term implications, it is surprising that most couples spend little time reflecting on the decision to marry before their wedding day (McGoldrick, Heiman, & Carter, 1993). Courses in family life education in high schools and colleges can help dispel marital myths and promote better mate selection. And premarital counseling aimed at helping couples discuss their desires openly and use positive, respectful conflict resolution strategies can ease adjustment to marriage and enhance relationship quality (Harvey & Omarzu, 1997; Markman, Stanley, & Blumberg, 1994).

PARENTHOOD

In the past, the issue of whether to have children was, for many adults, "a biological given or an unavoidable cultural demand" (Michaels, 1988, p. 23). Today, in Western industrialized nations, it is a matter of true individual choice. Effective birth control techniques enable adults who do not want to become parents to avoid having children in most instances. And changing cultural values allow people to remain childless with less fear of social criticism and rejection than was the case a generation or two ago.

In 1950, 78 percent of married couples were parents. Today, 72 percent of couples bear children, and they tend to have their first child at a later age. Consistent with this pattern of delayed childbearing, family size in industrialized nations has declined. In 1950, the average number of children per couple was 3.1. Currently, it is 1.8, a downward trend that is expected to continue (U.S. Bureau of the Census, 1999).

Nevertheless, the vast majority of married people continue to embrace parenthood as one of life's most meaningful experiences. Why do they do so, and how do the challenges of child rearing affect the adult life course?

■ THE DECISION TO HAVE CHILDREN. The choice of parenthood is affected by a complex array of factors, including financial circumstances, personal and religious values, and biological and medical conditions. Overall, women with traditional gender identities are more likely to have children. Whether a woman is employed has less impact on her decision than her occupation. Women who work in managerial positions are less likely to become parents than women in less demanding careers (White & Kim, 1987).

When American couples are asked about their desire to have children, they mention a variety of advantages and disadvantages, which are listed in Table 14.3. Take a moment to consider which ones are most important to you. Although some ethnic and regional differences exist, reasons for having children that are most important to all groups include the desire for a warm, affectionate relationship and the stimulation and fun that children provide. Also frequently mentioned are growth and learning experiences that children bring into the lives of adults, the desire to have someone carry on after one's own death, and the feelings of accomplishment and creativity that come from helping children (Cowan & Cowan, 1992).

Most young adults are also aware that having children means years of extra burdens and responsibilities. When asked about the disadvantages of parenthood, they mention "loss of freedom" most often, followed by "financial strain." Indeed, the cost of child rearing is a major factor in modern family planning. According to a conservative estimate, today's new parents will spend about $260,000 to rear a child from birth through four years of college (U.S. Department of Labor, 2000). Finally, many adults worry greatly about bringing children into a troubled world—one filled with crime, war, and pollution (Michaels, 1988).

Careful weighing of the pros and cons of having children is increasingly common today. This means that many more couples are making informed and personally meaningful choices about becoming parents—a trend that should increase the chances that they are ready to have children and that their own lives will be enriched by their decision.

■ TRANSITION TO PARENTHOOD. Childbirth profoundly alters the lives of husband and wife. Disrupted sleep schedules, less time to devote to each other and to leisure activities, and new financial responsibilities often lead to a mild decline in marital happiness. In addition, entry of children into the family usually causes the roles of husband and wife to become more traditional (Cowan & Cowan, 1997; Huston & Vangelisti, 1995). This is true even for couples like Sharese and Ernie, who were strongly committed to gender equality and used to sharing household tasks. Movement toward traditional roles is hardest on new mothers who have been involved in their careers. The larger the difference in men's and women's responsibilities, the greater the rise in conflict and decline in marital satisfaction and mental health after childbirth, especially for women (Hawkins et al., 1993; Levy-Shiff, 1994).

TABLE 14.3

Advantages and Disadvantages of Parenthood Mentioned by Modern American Couples

ADVANTAGES	DISADVANTAGES
Giving and receiving warmth and affection	Loss of freedom, being tied down
Experiencing the stimulation and fun that children add to life	Financial strain
Being accepted as a responsible and mature member of the community	Worries over children's health, safety, and well-being
Experiencing new growth and learning opportunities that add meaning to life	Interference with mother's employment opportunities
Having someone carry on after one's own death	Risks of bringing up children in a world plagued by crime, war, and pollution
Gaining a sense of accomplishment and creativity from helping children grow	Reduced time to spend with spouse
Learning to become less selfish and to sacrifice	Loss of privacy
Having offspring who help with parents' work or add their own income to the family's resources	Fear that children will turn out badly, through no fault of one's own

Source: Cowan & Cowan, 1992.

Violated expectations about jointly caring for a new baby contribute to the decline in marital happiness. Women, especially, count on far more help from their husbands than usually occurs (Hackel & Ruble, 1992). Postponing childbearing until the late twenties or thirties, as more couples are doing today (see Chapter 13, page 428), eases the transition to parenthood. Waiting permits couples to pursue occupational goals and gain life experience. Under these circumstances, men are more enthusiastic about becoming fathers and therefore more willing to participate actively. And women whose careers are under way are more likely to encourage their husbands to share housework and child care (Coltrane, 1990).

Men who view themselves as especially nurturant and caring show less decline in marital satisfaction after the birth of a baby, probably because they are better at meeting the needs of their wives and infants. The father's involvement may increase his understanding of the challenges a mother faces in coping with a new baby, reduce his feelings of being an "outsider" as the infant demands his wife's attention, and free up time for partners to spend together. Also, men's participation enhances the marital relationship because women tend to see it as a loving act toward themselves (Bird, 1999; Levy-Shiff, 1994).

In many non-Western cultures, the birth of children is less likely to threaten marital satisfaction. In these societies, parenthood is highly valued, family life is central for women, and traditional gender roles are widely accepted. Consequently, becoming a mother grants a woman considerable status, and husband–wife division of labor is not questioned. In addition, the extended family typically assists with household and child-care tasks (Levy-Shiff, 1994; Lozoff, Jordan, & Malone, 1988). In Western industrialized nations, however, the trend toward gender equality and isolation of the nuclear family unit leads marital and parenting roles to be closely linked. In a longitudinal study of over 2,000 couples diverse in age, SES, and ethnicity, marital quality was the strongest predictor of parenting satisfaction. Changes in happiness in each role were accompanied by similar changes in the other (Rogers & White, 1998).

Special interventions exist to ease the transition to parenthood. For parents who are not at high risk for problems, couples' groups led by counselors are highly effective. In one program, first-time expectant couples met once a week for 6 months to discuss their dreams for the family and changes in relationships sparked by the baby's arrival. Eighteen months after the program ended, participating fathers reported being more involved with their child than did fathers in a no-intervention condition. Perhaps because of fathers' caregiving assistance, participating mothers maintained their prebirth satisfaction with family and work roles. Three years after the birth, the marriages of all participating couples were intact and just as happy as they had been before parenthood. In contrast, 15 percent of couples receiving no intervention had divorced (Cowan & Cowan, 1997). For

▪ *The demands of new parenthood, from baby care to added financial responsibilities, often lead to a mild decline in marital satisfaction. This father's involvement can limit marital unhappiness by freeing up time for the mother to attend to her personal needs and for the couple to spend time together—factors that return to benefit the parent-infant relationship. (Photo courtesy: Nancy Durrell McKenna/Photo Researchers, Inc.)*

high-risk parents struggling with poverty or the birth of a child with disabilities, interventions must be much more intensive, focusing on enhancing social and economic support and parenting skills (Cowan & Cowan, 1995).

▪ ADDITIONAL BIRTHS. How many children a couple chooses to have is affected by the same array of factors that influenced their decision to become parents in the first place. Besides more effective birth control, a major reason that family size has declined in industrialized nations is the increased career orientation of many women. Also, the high divorce rate means that many couples do not complete their childbearing plans.

Research indicates that adults and children benefit from small family size. Because parents are less economically and emotionally stressed, they are more patient with each other and have more time to devote to each child's development. Furthermore, in smaller families, siblings are more likely to be widely spaced (born more than 2 years apart), which adds to the attention and resources husband and wife can invest in one another and in each child. Together, these findings may account for the fact that marital satisfaction tends to be greater and children tend to have higher IQs, do better in school, and attain higher levels of education in smaller families (Anderson, Russell, & Schumm, 1983; Downey, 1995; Powell & Steelman, 1993).

▪ FAMILIES WITH YOUNG CHILDREN. Before parenthood, if a spouse leaves, the family system dissolves; afterward, it continues. In this way, the arrival of children constitutes a key change in the family life cycle.

A year after the birth of their first child, Sharese and Ernie received a phone call from Heather, who asked how they liked being parents: "Is it a joy, a dilemma, a stressful experience—how would you describe it?"

Chuckling, Sharese and Ernie responded in unison, "All of the above!"

Child rearing is an enormous task, and seldom are young people fully prepared for it. In today's complex world, men and women are not as certain about how to rear children as they were in previous generations. Clarifying child-rearing values and implementing them in warm, supportive, and appropriately demanding ways are crucial for the welfare of the next generation and society. Yet cultures do not always place a high priority on parenting, as indicated by the lack of many societal supports for children and families in the United States (see Chapter 2, pages 68–69). Furthermore, changing family forms mean that the lives of modern parents differ substantially from those of past generations.

In previous chapters, we discussed a wide variety of influences on child-rearing styles—personal characteristics of children and parents, family economic conditions, SES, ethnicity, and more. The marital relationship is also important. Husbands and wives who work together as a "coparenting team," cooperating and showing respect for each other in parenting roles, are more likely to feel competent as parents and to be sensitive to their children. Support from the spouse, as noted in Chapter 6, is an especially strong predictor of fathers' involvement in child rearing (Floyd, Gilliom, & Costigan, 1998; McBride & Rane, 1998). And it can reduce the disruptive impact of stressful life events, economic strain, and parental depression on parent–child interaction (Simons et al., 1992, 1993).

For employed parents, a major struggle during this phase of family life is finding good child care. The younger

the child, the greater parents' sense of risk and difficulty finding the help they need (Lamb, 1998). When competent, convenient, affordable child care is not available, it usually leads to additional pressures on the woman. Either she must curtail or give up her career, or she must endure unhappy children, missed workdays, and constant searches for new arrangements.

Despite its many challenges, rearing young children is a powerful source of adult development. Parents report that it expands their emotional capacities and enriches their lives. For example, Ernie remarked that he was very "goal oriented" before his children were born but felt "rounded out" by sharing in their care. Other involved parents say that child rearing helped them tune into others' feelings and needs and become more tolerant, self-confident, and responsible (Coltrane, 1990).

■ FAMILIES WITH ADOLESCENTS. Adolescence brings sharp changes in parental roles. In Chapters 11 and 12, we noted that parents of adolescents must establish a new relationship with their children—blending guidance with freedom and gradually relinquishing control. As adolescents gain in autonomy and explore values and goals in their search for identity, parents often complain that their teenager is too focused on peers and no longer seem to care about their family.

Flexibility is the key to family success during this period. As adolescents move from childhood to adulthood, they alternately become dependent when they cannot handle things alone and experiment with greater independence. Their behavior seems unpredictable and ever-changing. When parents try to tighten the reins by disciplining in ways appropriate for younger children or withdraw to avoid conflict, they heighten family tensions. Although most couples handle these difficulties, others reach impasses. More people seek or are referred for family therapy during this phase of the family life cycle than during any other (Young, 1991).

■ PARENT EDUCATION. In the past, when there was greater continuity across generations in family life, adults learned what they needed to know about parenting through modeling and direct experience. Today's world confronts husbands and wives with a host of societal factors that impinge on their ability to succeed as parents. In addition, the scientific literature on child development has mushroomed, much of it offering practical implications that can help parents do a better job of rearing children.

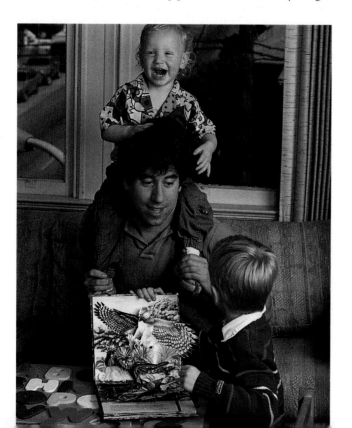

■ *Despite its many challenges, rearing young children is a powerful source of adult development. Parents report that it expands their emotional capacities and enriches their lives. Involved parents say that child rearing helped them become more sensitive, tolerant, self-confident, and responsible. (James Wilson/ Woodfin Camp & Associates)*

Parents eagerly seek information on child rearing through popular books. New mothers regard these sources as particularly valuable, second in importance only to their doctors (Deutsch et al., 1988). Special courses have also emerged, designed to help parents understand how children develop, clarify child-rearing values, explore family communication, and apply more effective parenting strategies. Child-care centers, schools, churches, community health centers, and colleges often sponsor these parent education programs. A variety of positive outcomes have been demonstrated, including improved parent–child interaction, more open and flexible parent attitudes, and heightened awareness by parents of their role as educators of their children (Powell, 1986; Shumow, 1998). Although these courses take a variety of forms, at present there is no convincing evidence that any one approach is best (Todres & Bunston, 1993). Perhaps the most effective programs adapt their goals and procedures to fit the specific needs of their participants.

ASK YOURSELF . . .

After her wedding, Sharese was convinced she had made a mistake and never should have gotten married. Cite factors that helped sustain her marriage to Ernie and that led it to become especially happy.

Suggest several ways a new mother and father can help each other make an effective adjustment to parenthood.

THE DIVERSITY OF ADULT LIFESTYLES

The modern array of adult lifestyles arose in the 1960s, a decade of rapid social change in which American young people began to question the conventional wisdom of previous generations. Many asked, How can I find happiness? What kinds of commitments should I make to live a full and rewarding life? As the public became more accepting of diverse lifestyles, choices seemed more available than in the past—among them, staying single, cohabiting, remaining childless, and divorcing.

Today, nontraditional family options have penetrated the American mainstream. Many adults experience not just one, but several. As we consider these variations in the following sections, we will see that the factors that induce people to enter them are complex. Some adults make a deliberate decision to adopt a lifestyle, whereas others drift into it. The lifestyle may be imposed by society, as is the case for cohabiting homosexual couples, who cannot marry legally. Or people may decide on a certain lifestyle because they feel pushed away from another, such as a marriage gone sour. Thus, the adoption of a lifestyle can be within or beyond the person's control.

SINGLEHOOD

On finishing her education, Heather joined the Peace Corps and spent 5 years in Africa. Although open to a long-term relationship with a man whose sense of adventure equaled her own, she had only fleeting romances. When she returned to the United States, she accepted an executive position with an insurance company. Professional challenge and travel preoccupied her. At age 35, she reflected on her life circumstances over lunch with Sharese: "I was open to marriage, but after my career took off, it would have interfered. Now I'm so used to independence that it would take a lot of adjustment to live with another person. I like being able to pick up and go where I want, when I want, without having to ask anybody or think about having to take care of anybody. But there's a trade-off: I sleep alone, eat most of my meals alone, and spend a lot of my leisure time alone."

Singlehood characterizes an individual not living with an intimate partner. It has increased in recent years, especially among young adults. For example, the number of never-married 30- to 34-year-olds has risen sixfold since 1970, to 29 percent among males and 21 percent among females. Besides more people marrying later or not at all, divorce has added to the rate of singlehood. In view of these trends, it is likely that most Americans will spend a substantial part of their adult lives single, and a growing minority—about 10 to 12 percent—will stay that way (U.S. Bureau of the Census, 1999).

Because they marry later, more men than women are single in early adulthood. But women are far more likely than men to remain single for many years or their entire life. As women get older, there are fewer men available with characteristics that most look for in a mate—the same age or older, better educated, and more professionally successful. Men—whether never married, divorced, or widowed—find partners more easily, since they can select from a large pool of younger unmarried women. Because of the tendency for women to "marry up" and men to "marry down," men in blue-collar occupations and women in highly demanding, prestigious careers are overrepresented among singles after age 30.

Ethnic differences also exist. For example, the percentage of never-married African Americans is nearly twice as great as that of Caucasian Americans in early adulthood. As we will see later, high unemployment among black men interferes with marriage. But many African Americans eventually marry in their late thirties and forties, a period in which the black and white marriage rates come closer together (Cherlin, 1992; U.S. Bureau of the Census, 1999).

Singlehood is a multifaceted experience with different meanings. At one extreme are people who choose it deliberately, at the other people who regard themselves as single because of circumstances beyond their control. Most, like Heather, are in the middle—adults who wanted to marry but made choices that took them in a different direction

(Shostak, 1987). In a study in which never-married, childless women were interviewed about their lives, some said they focused on occupational goals instead of marriage. Others reported that they found singlehood preferable to the disappointing relationships they had with men. And still others commented that they just did not meet "the right person" (Dalton, 1992).

Of the various advantages of singlehood, those mentioned most often are freedom and mobility. But singles also recognize drawbacks—loneliness, the dating grind, limited sexual and social life, reduced sense of security, and feelings of exclusion from the world of married couples (Chasteen, 1994). Single men have more physical and mental health problems than do single women, who usually come to terms with their lifestyle and fare well. The greater social support available to women through intimate same-sex friendships is partly responsible. In addition, never-married men are more likely to have problem family backgrounds and personal characteristics that contribute to both their singlehood and their adjustment difficulties (Buunk & Driel, 1989).

Many single people go through a stressful period in their late twenties, when more of their friends get married and they become an exception. The mid-thirties is another trying time for single women, due to the approaching biological deadline for bearing children. A few decide to become parents through adoption, artificial insemination, or an extramarital affair.

COHABITATION

Cohabitation refers to the lifestyle of unmarried couples who have an intimate, sexual relationship and share a residence. Until the 1960s, cohabitation in Western nations was largely limited to low-income people. Since then, it has increased in all groups, with an especially dramatic rise among well-educated and economically advantaged young adults. As Figure 14.3 shows, seven times as many American couples were cohabiting in the 1990s as did in 1970. About one-third of these households include children, since in half

of cohabiting relationships, one or both partners are separated or divorced (U.S. Bureau of the Census, 1999).

Like singlehood, cohabitation has different meanings. For some, it serves as *preparation for marriage*—a time to test the relationship and get used to the realities of living together. For others, it is an *alternative to marriage*—an arrangement that offers the rewards of sexual intimacy and companionship along with the possibility of easy departure if there is a decline in satisfaction. In view of this variation, it is not surprising that great range exists in the extent to which cohabitors share money and possessions and take responsibility for each other's children.

Americans are more open to cohabitation than they were in the past, although attitudes are not yet as positive as they are in Western Europe. In the Netherlands, Norway, and Sweden, cohabitation is thoroughly integrated into society. As a result, cohabitors are nearly as devoted to one another as are married people (Kaslow, Hansson, & Lundblad, 1994; Ramsøy, 1994). When they decide to marry, Dutch, Norwegian, and Swedish cohabitors more often do so to legalize their relationships, especially for the sake of children. American cohabitors typically marry to confirm their love and commitment—sentiments that their Western European counterparts attach to cohabitation.

Largely as a result of cultural ambivalence about cohabitation, American cohabitors differ from people who are married or living in separate residences. They are less religious, more politically liberal, more androgynous, and have had more sexual partners. Overall, they are more likely to endorse and engage in nonconventional behavior. In addition, a larger number have parents who are divorced and say they get along poorly with them (Cunningham & Antill, 1994; Thornton, 1991; Thornton, Axinn, & Hill, 1992).

These personal characteristics are responsible for outcomes associated with cohabitation. Compared with married people, American cohabitors are less likely to pool finances or jointly own a house. (This difference is much smaller in Western Europe.) Furthermore, American couples who live together before marriage—and their Canadian

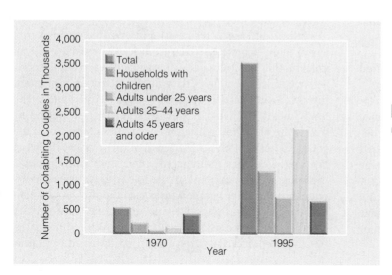

FIGURE 14.3

■ **Rates of cohabitation in 1970 and 1995 in the United States.** The figure shows total number of cohabiting couples, number of cohabiting couples with children, and number cohabiting by age. Notice the dramatic rise in cohabitation for all groups. However, postponement of marriage and the high rate of divorce (see Figure 14.1) have caused the age distribution of cohabitors to change. In 1970, the majority were middle-aged and elderly. Today, most are young adults. (From U.S. Bureau of the Census, 1999.)

counterparts as well—are more prone to divorce, an association not present in other Western countries (Cherlin, 1992; Krishnan, 1998). But we must keep in mind that American cohabitors have experienced more conflict in their own homes, and they tend to emphasize self-fulfillment over obligations to others in their relationships. As they carry this individualistic outlook into marriage, they are more likely to dissolve a union when it becomes less satisfying.

Certain couples are exceptions to the trends just described. People who cohabit after separation or divorce often test a new relationship carefully to prevent another painful failure, especially when children are involved. As a result, they cohabit longer and are less likely to move toward marriage (Cherlin, 1992). In contrast to American heterosexual cohabitors, homosexual couples report strong commitment—as intense as that of married people (Peplau, 1991). When their relationships become difficult, they end more often than marriages do only because there are fewer barriers to separating, including children in common, financial dependence on a partner, and concerns about the costs of divorce (Kurdek, 1998).

Clearly, cohabitation has advantages and drawbacks. For people not ready for marriage, it combines the rewards of a close relationship with the opportunity to remain at least partially uncommitted. Although most couples cohabit to avoid legal obligations, they can encounter difficulties because they do not have them. Bitter fights over property, money, rental contracts, and responsibility for children are the rule rather than the exception when unmarried couples split up (Buunk & Driel, 1989).

CHILDLESSNESS

At work, Sharese got to know Beatrice and Daniel. Married for 7 years and in their mid-thirties, they did not have children and were not planning to have any. To Sharese, their relationship seemed especially caring and affectionate. "At first, we were open to becoming parents," Beatrice explained, "but eventually we decided to focus on our marriage."

Our discussion of reproductive technologies in Chapter 2 revealed that about 20 percent of couples have fertility problems. Because treatment is not always successful, some remain *involuntarily* childless. Others who are childless by circumstance simply did not find a partner with whom to share parenthood. Beatrice and Daniel are in another category—men and women who are *voluntarily* childless.

How many American couples choose not to have children is a matter of dispute. Some researchers claim the rate has been low for several decades—between 3 and 6 percent (Jacobson & Heaton, 1989). Others say it rose in the 1980s and early 1990s and is currently higher than ever before—from 10 to 15 percent (Ambry, 1992; Morell, 1994). These differing reports may be due to the fact that voluntary childlessness is not always a permanent condition. A few people decide very early that they do not want to be parents and stick to these plans. But most, like Beatrice and Daniel, make their decision after they are married and have developed a lifestyle they do not want to give up. Later, some change their minds.

Besides marital satisfaction and freedom from child-care responsibilities, common reasons for not having children include the woman's career and economic security. Consistent with these motives, the voluntarily childless are usually college educated, have prestigious occupations, and are highly committed to their work. Many were only or first-born children whose parents encouraged achievement and independence. In a culture that negatively stereotypes childlessness, it is not surprising that voluntarily childless women are more self-reliant and assertive. Typically the wife is responsible for the decision not to have children (Houseknecht, 1987; Morell, 1994).

Voluntarily childless adults are just as content with their lives as are parents who have rewarding relationships with their children. In contrast, adults who cannot overcome their infertility and parents whose children have serious psychological or physical problems are likely to be dissatisfied and depressed (Connidis & McMullin, 1993). Think about these findings, and you will see that they do not support the prevailing stereotype of childless people as lonely and unfulfilled. Instead, they indicate that parenthood enhances well-being only when the parent–child relationship is warm and affectionate. And childlessness interferes with adjustment and life satisfaction only when it is beyond a person's control.

DIVORCE AND REMARRIAGE

If current rates continue (see Figure 14.1 on page 467), about half of all marriages in the United States will end in separation or divorce. Most people who divorce do so within 5 to 10 years of their marriage, so many divorces happen when children are still at home. Furthermore, 61 percent of divorced men and 54 percent of divorced women remarry (Hetherington, Law, & O'Connor, 1994). Divorce occurs at an especially high rate during the first few years of second marriages—7 percent above that for first marriages. Afterward, the divorce rate for first and second marriages is about the same (Cherlin, 1992; Ganong & Coleman, 1994).

■ FACTORS RELATED TO DIVORCE. Why do so many marriages fail? As Christy and Gary's divorce illustrates, the most obvious reason is a disrupted husband–wife relationship. Christy and Gary did not argue more often than Sharese and Ernie did. But their style of resolving conflict was markedly different. When Christy raised concerns, Gary responded with resentment, anger, and retreat—a conflict-confronting–conflict-avoiding pattern that can be found in many partners who split up. Another typical style involves little conflict, but partners increasingly lead separate lives because they have different expectations of marriage and family life and few shared interests, activities, or friends (Hetherington, Law, & O'Connor, 1994).

What problems underlie these maladaptive communication patterns? In a 9-year longitudinal study, researchers telephoned a national sample of 2,000 married people, asking about marital problems in 1980 and following up in 1983, 1988, and 1992 to find out who had divorced or separated permanently (Amato & Rogers, 1997). Wives reported more problems than husbands, with the gender difference largely involving the wife's emotions, such as anger, hurt feelings, and moodiness. Husbands seemed to have difficulty sensing their wife's distress, which contributed to her view of the marriage as unhappy. Regardless of which spouse reported the problem or was judged responsible for it, the strongest predictors of divorce during the following decade were infidelity, spending money foolishly, drinking or using drugs, jealousy, irritating habits, and moodiness.

Younger age at marriage, not attending church, being previously divorced, and having parents who had divorced increased the chances of divorce, in part because these background factors were linked to marital difficulties (Amato, 1996; Amato & Rogers, 1997). For example, couples who married at younger ages were more likely to report infidelity and jealousy. Perhaps their marriages are unstable because they are more easily drawn into extramarital affairs. Not going to religious services may raise divorce odds by subtracting an influential context for instilling positive marital behaviors. And parental divorce elevates certain problems in the next generation—especially infidelity, irritating habits, and foolish spending of money—that interfere with a mutually rewarding intimate bond.

A few decades ago, unhappy couples like Christy and Gary usually stayed together, despite the problems just mentioned. Shifting societal conditions, including widespread family poverty and the changing status of women, provide the larger context for today's high divorce rate. Economically disadvantaged couples who suffer multiple life stresses are especially likely to split up. But Christy's case represents another trend—rising marital breakup among well-educated, economically independent women. Women are twice as likely as men to initiate divorce (Rice, 1994).

■ CONSEQUENCES OF DIVORCE. When Sharese heard that Christy and Gary's marriage had dissolved, she remarked that it seemed as if "someone had died." Her description is fitting, since divorce involves the loss of a way of life and therefore part of the self sustained by that way of life. As a result, it carries with it opportunities for both positive and negative change.

Immediately after separation, both men and women are depressed and anxious and display impulsive, antisocial behavior. For most, these reactions subside within 2 years. Women who were in traditional marriages and who organized their identities around their husbands have an especially hard time. As one divorcée remarked, "I used to be Mrs. John Jones, the bank manager's wife. Now I'm Mary Jones. Who is Mary Jones?" (Hetherington, Law, & O'Connor,

1994, p. 216). Many noncustodial fathers feel disoriented and rootless as a result of decreased contact with their children. Others distract themselves through a frenzy of social activity (Cherlin, 1992).

Finding a new partner contributes most to the life satisfaction of divorced adults. But it is more crucial for men, who show more positive adjustment in the context of marriage than on their own. Despite loneliness and reduced income (see Chapter 10), most divorced women prefer their new life to an unhappy marriage. For example, Christy developed new skills and a sense of self-reliance that might not have emerged had she remained married to Gary. However, a few women—especially those who are anxious and fearful or who remain strongly attached to their ex-spouses—show a drop in self-esteem, become depressed, and tend to form repeated unsuccessful relationships (Ganong & Coleman, 1994). Job training, continued education, career advancement, and social support from family and friends play vital roles in the economic and psychological well-being of divorced women (De-Garmo & Forgatch, 1997; Hetherington, 1995).

■ REMARRIAGE. On the average, people remarry within 4 years of divorce, men somewhat faster than women. Why do many remarriages break up? There are several reasons. First, although people often remarry for love, practical matters—financial security, help in rearing children, relief from loneliness, and social acceptance—figure more heavily into a second marriage than a first. These concerns do not provide a sound footing for a lasting partnership. Second, some people transfer the negative patterns of interaction and problem solving learned in their first marriage to the second. Third, people who have already had a failed marriage are more likely to view divorce as an acceptable solution when marital difficulties resurface. And finally, remarried couples experience more stress from stepfamily situations (Bray, 1999; Ganong & Coleman, 1994). Recall from Chapter 10 that adults in blended families have few societal guidelines for how to relate to their steprelatives, including stepchildren. As we will see in the next section, stepparent–stepchildren ties are powerful predictors of marital happiness.

In divorce and remarriage, as in other adult lifestyles, there are multiple pathways leading to diverse outcomes. It generally takes about 3 to 5 years for blended families to develop the connectedness and comfort of intact biological families (Ihinger-Tallman & Pasley, 1997). Family life education and couples and group therapy can help divorced and remarried adults adapt to the complexities of their new circumstances (Forgatch, Patterson, & Ray, 1996).

VARIANT STYLES OF PARENTHOOD

Diverse family forms result in varied styles of parenthood. Among these are a growing number of remarried parents, never-married parents, and gay and lesbian parents. Each type of family presents unique challenges to parenting competence and adult psychological well-being.

■ REMARRIED PARENTS. Whether stepchildren live in the household or visit only occasionally, stepparents are in a difficult position. Since the parent–child tie predates the remarriage, the stepparent enters as an outsider. All too often, stepparents try to move into their new role too quickly. Because they do not have a warm attachment bond to build on, their discipline is usually ineffective. Stepparents frequently criticize the biological parent for being too lenient. The parent, in turn, tends to view the stepparent as too harsh. These differences can become major issues that divide the remarried couple (Ganong, Coleman, & Fine, 1995; Papernow, 1993).

Stepmothers, especially, are likely to experience conflict and poor adjustment. Expected to be in charge of family relationships, they quickly find that stepparent–stepchild ties do not develop instantly. Even when their husbands do not have custody, stepmothers feel stressed (MacDonald & DeMaris, 1996). As stepchildren go in and out of the home, stepmothers compare life with and without resistant children, and many prefer life without! No matter what a stepmother does to build a close parent–child bond, her efforts are probably doomed to failure in the short run.

Stepfathers with children of their own have an easier time. They establish positive ties with stepchildren relatively quickly, perhaps because they feel less pressure to plunge into parenting than do stepmothers. At the same time, they have had enough experience to know how to build a warm parent–child relationship. Stepfathers without biological children are new to child rearing. When they have unrealistic expectations or their wives push them into the father role, their interactions with stepchildren can be troublesome. After making several overtures that are ignored or rebuffed, they often withdraw from parenting (Bray, 1992; Hetherington & Clingempeel, 1992).

A caring husband–wife relationship, the cooperation of the absent biological parent, and the willingness of children to accept their parent's new spouse are crucial for stepparent adjustment. Because stepparent–stepchild bonds are hard to establish, the divorce rate is higher for couples with stepchildren than for those without (Bray, 1999; Ganong & Coleman, 1994).

■ NEVER-MARRIED PARENTS. About 10 percent of American children have parents who have never married. Of these, 89 percent are mothers, 11 percent fathers (U.S. Bureau of the Census, 1999). Earlier we mentioned that single adults occasionally decide to become parents and rear children on their own. Births to women in high-status occupations who have not married by their thirties have increased in recent years. However, they are still few in number, and little is known about how these mothers and their children fare.

The largest group of never-married parents are African-American young women. In 1997, over 60 percent of births to black women in their twenties were out of wedlock, compared with only 18 percent to white women. A sharp difference between blacks and whites in the timing of family life cycle events underlies these trends. African-American women postpone marriage more and childbirth less than do all other American ethnic groups (Glick, 1997; U.S. Bureau of the Census, 1999).

Job loss, persisting unemployment, and consequent inability of many black men to support a family have contributed to never-married parenthood among African Americans (Rice, 1994). African Americans have also responded to changing family values—the shift toward cohabitation, postponement of marriage, and separation of marriage from childbearing that has spread throughout American culture (Raley, 1996).

Recall from Chapter 2 that never-married black mothers tap a traditional source of strength in their culture by relying heavily on their own mothers and other extended family members for help in caring for their children. For most, marriage follows birth of the first child by several years and is not necessarily to the child's biological father. Nevertheless, these couples function much like other first-marriage parents. Their children are often unaware that the father is a stepfather, and parents do not report the relationship problems typical of blended families (Ganong & Coleman, 1994).

Still, never-married parenthood among low-income women is costly, since living in a female-headed household makes it harder to overcome poverty. Never-married mothers are much less likely to receive paternal child sup-

■ *For most never-married African-American mothers, marriage follows birth of the first child by several years and is not necessarily to the child's father. Nevertheless, these couples function much like other first-marriage parents. The children are often unaware that the father is a stepfather, and parents do not report the relationship problems typical of blended families. (Photo courtesy: Bernard Boutrit/Woodfin Camp & Associates)*

port payments than are divorced mothers (Hill, 1997). When their children lack the warmth and involvement of a father, they achieve more poorly in school and display more antisocial behavior than do children in low-income, first-marriage families. These adjustment problems make life more stressful for their mothers (Coley, 1998; Florsheim, Tolan, & Gorman-Smith, 1998). Strengthening social support, education, and employment opportunities for low-income parents would encourage marriage as well as help unmarried-mother families.

■ GAY AND LESBIAN PARENTS. Several million American gay men and lesbians are parents, most through previous heterosexual marriages, a few through adoption or reproductive technologies (Patterson, 1996). In the past, laws assuming that homosexuals could not be adequate parents led those who divorced a heterosexual partner to lose custody of their children. Today, several states hold that sexual orientation is irrelevant to custody. In others, fierce prejudice against homosexual parents still prevails.

Families headed by a homosexual parent or a gay or lesbian couple are very similar to those of heterosexuals. Gay and lesbian parents are as committed to and effective at the parental role, and sometimes more so. Indeed, some research indicates that gay fathers are more consistent in setting limits and more responsive to their children's needs than are heterosexual fathers, perhaps because gay men's less traditional gender identity fosters involvement with children (Bigner & Jacobsen, 1989). In lesbian families, quality of mother–child interaction is as positive as in heterosexual families. And children of lesbian mothers regard their mother's partner as very much a parent (Brewaeys et al., 1997). Whether born to or adopted by their parents or conceived through donor insemination, children in homosexual families are as well adjusted as other children, and the large majority are heterosexual (Bailey et al., 1995; Chan, Raboy, & Patterson, 1998; Golombok & Tasker, 1996).

■ *Homosexual parents are as committed to and effective at child rearing as are heterosexual parents. Their children are well adjusted, and the large majority develop a heterosexual orientation. (Photo courtesy: Tom McKitterick/Impact Visuals)*

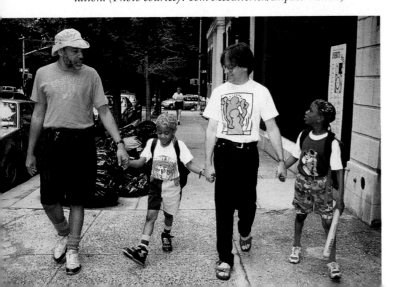

When extended family members have difficulty accepting them, homosexual mothers and fathers often build "families of choice" through friends, who assume the roles of relatives. But most of the time, parents of gays and lesbians cannot endure a permanent rift. With time, interactions of homosexual parents with their families of origin become more positive and serve as supports for child rearing (Hare, 1994).

Partners of homosexual parents usually take on some caregiving responsibilities and are attached to the children. But their involvement varies with the way children were brought into the relationship. When children were adopted or conceived through reproductive technologies, partners tend to be more involved than when children resulted from a previous heterosexual relationship (Hare & Richards, 1993). In a few instances, homosexual partners have become the joint legal parents of children, an arrangement that enhances family stability (Green & Bozett, 1991).

Overall, families headed by homosexuals can be distinguished from other families only by issues related to living in a nonsupportive society. The greatest concern of gay and lesbian parents is that their children will be stigmatized by their parents' sexual orientation (Hare, 1994).

■ **ASK YOURSELF . . .**

🌳 *Return to Chapter 10, pages 334–338 and review the impact of divorce and remarriage on children and adolescents. How do those findings resemble outcomes for adults? What might account for the similarities?*

■ *After dating for a year, Wanda and Scott decided to live together. Wanda's mother heard that couples who cohabit before marriage are more likely to get divorced. She worried that cohabitation would reduce Wanda and Scott's chances for a successful life together. Is her fear justified? Why or why not?*

VOCATIONAL DEVELOPMENT

Besides family life, vocational life is a vital domain of social development in early adulthood. After choosing an occupation, young people must learn how to perform its tasks well, get along with co-workers, respond to authority, and protect their own interests. When work experiences go well, adults develop new competencies, feel a sense of personal accomplishment, make new friends, and become financially independent and secure. And as we have already seen, for women especially but also for men who support their spouses' vocational development, aspirations and accomplishments in the workplace and the family are interwoven.

ESTABLISHING A VOCATION

Our discussion of Levinson's and Vaillant's theories earlier in this chapter highlighted diverse paths and timetables for vocational development in contemporary adulthood. Consider, once again, the wide variations among Sharese, Ernie, Christy, and Gary in establishing their careers. As is typical for men, Ernie's and Gary's vocational lives were long and *continuous,* beginning after completion of formal education and ending with retirement. Like many women, Sharese and Christy had *discontinuous* career paths —ones that were interrupted or deferred by childbearing and child rearing (Betz, 1993; Ornstein & Isabella, 1990). Furthermore, not all people embark on the vocation of their dreams. For example, although half of young people aspire to professional occupations, only 20 percent of the work force attains them (U.S. Bureau of the Census, 1999).

Even for young people who enter their chosen field, initial experiences can be discouraging. At the health department, Sharese discovered that committee meetings and paperwork consumed much of her day. Since each grant proposal and research project had a deadline, the pressure of productivity weighed heavily on her. Adjusting to unanticipated disappointments in salary, supervisors, and co-workers is difficult. As new workers become aware of the gap between their expectations and reality, resignations are common. On the average, people in their twenties move to a new job every 2 years; five or six changes are not unusual (Seligman, 1994).

After a period of evaluation and adjustment, young adults generally settle into an occupation. In careers with opportunities for promotion, high aspirations must often be revised downward, since the structure of most work settings resembles a pyramid. In businesses, there are few high-level executive positions; in factories, there are a limited number of supervisory jobs. In a longitudinal study of over 400 AT&T lower-level male managers, the importance of work in men's lives varied with career advancement and age (Howard & Bray, 1988). For men who advanced very little, "work disengagement" occurred early; family, recreation, and community service assumed greater importance by the early thirties. Men with average levels of career success emphasized nonwork roles at a later age. In contrast, men who were highly successful became more involved in their jobs over time. Although the desire for advancement tends to decline with age, most workers still seek challenges and find satisfaction in their work roles.

Besides opportunity, personal characteristics affect career progress. As we will see in the next section, a sense of *self-efficacy*—belief in one's own ability to be successful— affects career choice and development. (Return to Chapter 1, page 19 if you need to review this concept.) Young people who are very anxious about the possibility of failing or making mistakes tend to set career aspirations that are either too high or too low. When they encounter obstacles, they quickly conclude that career tasks are too hard and give

up (Farmer, 1997; Lopez, 1989). As a result, they achieve far less than their abilities would permit.

Recall from our discussion of Levinson's theory that success in a career often depends on the quality of a mentoring relationship. Access to an effective mentor—a person with advanced experience and knowledge who is emotionally invested in the junior person's development and who fosters a bond of trust and attachment—is jointly affected by the availability of willing people and the worker's capacity to select an appropriate individual (Crosby, 1998). Interestingly, the best mentors are usually not top executives, who tend to be preoccupied and therefore less helpful and sympathetic. Most of the time, it is better for a young person to choose a mentor lower on the corporate ladder (Seligman, 1994).

WOMEN AND ETHNIC MINORITIES

Although women and ethnic minorities have penetrated nearly all professions, they attain less than they otherwise would if their talents were developed to the fullest. Women in general—and African-American, Hispanic, and Native-American women in particular—remain concentrated in occupations that offer little opportunity for advancement, and they are underrepresented in executive and managerial roles (see Chapter 13, page 446). Despite the massive influx of women into the labor force, their earnings relative to men's have changed little during the past 50 years. For every dollar earned by a man, the average American woman earns only 76 cents, a gap that is larger in the United States than in Western European nations (U.S. Department of Labor, 1999).

Women seem to go through a different, often more complex process of vocational development than do men. Especially for those who pursue traditionally feminine occupations, career planning is often short-term and subject to considerable change. Low self-efficacy with respect to male-dominated fields limits not only women's occupational choices, but their progress once their vocational lives have begun. Women who pursue nontraditional careers usually have "masculine" qualities—high achievement orientation, an emphasis on individualism, and the expectation that they will have to make a life for themselves through their own efforts (Seligman, 1994).

Even when women enter high-status professions, very few move into high-level management positions. Gender-stereotyped images of women as followers rather than leaders and role conflict between work and family slow their advancement. Singlehood or late marriage and few or no children are strongly associated with career achievement in women—a relationship that does not hold for men (Betz & Fitzgerald, 1987). Furthermore, since men dominate high-status fields, few women are available to serve as mentors. (A similar situation exists for ethnic minorities.) Although amount of mentor support is similar in same-sex and cross-sex mentoring relationships, some evidence suggests that

PERSISTENCE, PASSION, AND CONNECTION: VOCATIONAL DEVELOPMENT OF HIGHLY SUCCESSFUL AFRICAN-AMERICAN WOMEN

What are the vocational experiences of ethnic minority women like, and what factors help them surmount the combined effects of gender and racial discrimination in the workplace? To answer these questions, researchers intensively interviewed 18 prominent, highly successful American women, 9 of whom were African-American, asking about their career paths, influences on success, and sources of career stress and ways of handling them (Richie et al., 1997). The women were leaders across diverse occupational fields, including business, education, athletics, science, medicine, law, politics, visual arts, literary arts, journalism, and broadcasting. They ranged in age from 34 to 72.

Three common themes emerged in the women's occupational life stories. First, all reported persistence in the face of gender and racial discrimination, low SES, and other barriers to achievement. Comments like these, by an African-American literary editor, were typical: "[Y]ou say,

why didn't you ever give up? It never occurred to me to stop. I tried different things to keep going, but it never occurred to me to stop" (Richie et al., 1997, p. 139). Second, despite the fame and wealth resulting from their accomplishments, most of the women were intensely passionate about their work, regarding its intrinsic rewards as much more personally important than the recognition and affluence it had brought. Many described feeling privileged to do work that they love. Third, the women often expressed a vision of connection to others—of how their own experiences, including workplace barriers, had the potential to benefit the world at large. They were dedicated to making work settings fairer places for women and ethnic minorities. An African-American educator commented,

Now to be a minority means you gotta be super good because you gotta keep the door open for someone else. And the other lesson you learn is you reach back and you help other people

come through. . . . [W]omen have to help women and minorities have to help minorities, because otherwise we don't get through that door very often. (p. 141)

Almost all the African-American women emphasized that the combined effects of sexism and racism heightened obstacles to career development. They mentioned instances of outright discrimination, prejudicial attitudes, and professional isolation. The most painful report came from an African-American artist and author, who described blatant exclusion from meetings and social gatherings important for advancing her work.

Mutually supportive relationships with other women appeared essential for counteracting the isolation of being pioneers in their fields. Each mentioned a variety of people who had been instrumental in her career development, including husband or partner, family members, teachers, colleagues, and friends. African-American women frequently described their mothers as inspirational role models and as having

women with female mentors are more productive (Goldstein, 1979; O'Neill, Horton, & Crosby, 1999). Perhaps female mentors are more likely to be perceived as role models and to provide guidance on the unique problems women encounter in the workplace. As the Variations box above illustrates, ethnic minority women face special challenges in finding mentors and realizing their career potential.

Despite obstacles to success, women benefit greatly from achievement in the outside world. Recall the study of the highly gifted "Termites" who were followed over their life course, described in Chapter 13 (see page 422). At age 60, women who reported the highest levels of life satisfaction had developed rewarding careers. Even though they followed a typical path for their generation, the least satisfied women had been housewives all their lives (Sears & Barbie, 1977). These findings suggest that at least some of the prob-

lems experienced by married women may not be due to marriage per se, but rather to lack of a gratifying vocation. Consistent with this idea, most young women express a preference for blending work and family in their adult lives (Barnett & Rivers, 1996). For women in financially stressed families, this is usually not a choice; it is a necessity.

COMBINING WORK AND FAMILY

Whether women work because they want to or have to (or both), the dominant family form today is the **dual-earner marriage,** in which both husband and wife are employed. Most dual-earner couples are also parents, since the majority of women with children are in the work force (see Chapter 10). In about one-third of these families, moderate to severe conflict occurs over trying to meet both work and

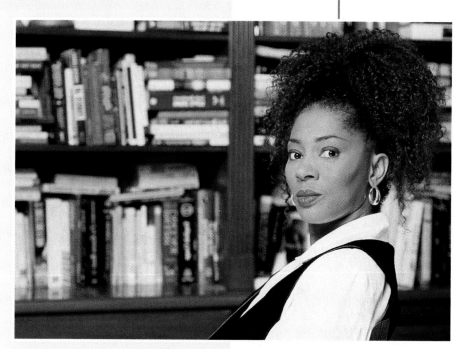

■ *Famed contemporary author Terry McMillan uses the theme of women's struggles in her best-selling books, which include* Disappearing Acts, How Stella Got Her Groove Back, Mama, *and* Waiting to Exhale. *Persistence in the face of gender and racial discrimination, a passion for writing, and a vision of connection to others, especially other African-American women, underlie her success. (Photo courtesy: Terry McMillan/Gamma)*

set high standards for them, and several noted the positive influence of their fathers. Others mentioned support they had received from their African-American communities and noted that a deep sense of connection to their people had empowered them.

In sum, the African-American women displayed an unusually strong sense of self-efficacy (Byars & Hackett, 1998). They attacked problems head-on and followed internal standards of excellence, despite repeated encounters with discrimination. In contrast to the rugged individualism often depicted in traditionally masculine images of achievement, these women combined communal traits—nurturance, sensitivity, and obligation to others —with self-reliance and determination. Their reflections suggest that passion, persistence, and connection can spur career accomplishment, even in the face of fierce gender and racial oppression. The following statement captures the bold, caring spirit of these highly successful, African-American women:

Everybody ought to have that dream of what they want to be. And even if you can't be it now, understand that it's still possible. You should understand that no does not mean never. No means not now. No, not right now, but it doesn't mean no, not tomorrow. Every dream you have— it's very possible. (Richie et al., 1997, p. 147)

family responsibilities (Gilbert & Brownson, 1998; Phillips & Imhoff, 1997).

What are the main sources of strain in dual-earner marriages? When Sharese returned to her job after her children were born, she felt a sense of *work overload*. Not only did she have a demanding career, but (like most employed women) she shouldered most of the household and child-care tasks. Furthermore, Sharese and Ernie felt torn between the desire to excel at their jobs and the desire to spend more time with each other and their children. At times, their lives became so busy that they had little energy left over for visiting or entertaining friends, relatives, and work associates (Robinson & Godbey, 1997).

Work–family role conflict is greater for women, and it negatively affects quality of life in both settings. It is especially intense for wives in low-status occupations with rigid schedules and little worker autonomy (Marshall, 1997). Couples in prestigious careers have more control over both work and family domains. For example, Sharese and Ernie devised ways to spend more time with their children. They picked them up at child care early one day a week, compensating by doing certain occupational tasks on evenings and weekends. Like other career-oriented mothers, Sharese coped with role pressures by setting priorities. She decreased the amount of time she spent on household chores, not child rearing (Duxbury & Higgins, 1994).

Having two careers in one family usually means that certain career decisions become more complex. A move to a new job can mean vocational sacrifices for one partner. Usually this is the wife, since a decision in favor of the husband's career (typically further along and better paid) is more likely to maximize family income. One solution to

Strategies That Help Dual-Earner Couples Combine Work and Family Roles

STRATEGY	DESCRIPTION
Devise a plan for sharing household tasks.	As soon as possible in the relationship, talk about division of household responsibilities. Decide who does a particular chore on the basis of who has the needed skill and time, not gender. Schedule regular times to rediscuss your plan to fit changing family circumstances.
Begin sharing child care right after the baby's arrival.	For fathers, strive to spend equal time with the baby early. For mothers, refrain from imposing your standards on your partner. Instead, share the role of "child-rearing expert" by discussing parenting values and concerns often. Attend a parent education course together.
Talk over conflicts about decision making and responsibilities.	Face conflict through communication. Clarify your feelings and needs and express them to your partner. Listen and try to understand your partner's point of view. Then be willing to negotiate and compromise.
Establish a balance between work and family.	Critically evaluate the time you devote to work in view of your values and priorities. If it is too much, cut back.
Make sure your relationship receives regular nurturance and attention.	See the Caregiving Concerns table on page 462.
Press for workplace and public policies that assist dual-earner couples.	Difficulties faced by dual-earner couples are partly due to lack of workplace and societal supports. Encourage your employer to provide benefits that help combine work and family roles, such as flexible work hours; parental leave with pay; and onsite high-quality, affordable child care. Communicate with lawmakers and other citizens about improving public policies for children and families.

the geographical limitations of the dual-earner marriage is to live apart. Although more couples are doing this, the strain of separation and risk of divorce are high.

Clearly, dual-earner marriages pose difficulties, but when couples cooperate to surmount these, they gain in many ways. Besides higher earnings and a better standard of living, the greatest advantage for college-educated couples is self-fulfillment and improved well-being of the wife (Swanson et al., 1997). Ernie took great pride in Sharese's accomplishments, and he reaped other benefits. Sharese's career orientation contributed to his view of her as an interesting, self-confident, and capable helpmate in life.

In sum, a challenging, rewarding occupation in the context of a supportive spouse can strengthen a marriage and foster adult development. Under other circumstances—for example, when a woman tries to combine a low-status, low-paying job with marriage to a disapproving man—the physical and psychological toll can be severe. The Caregiving Concerns table above lists strategies that help dual-earner couples combine work and family roles in ways that promote mastery and pleasure in both spheres of life.

ASK YOURSELF . . .

Heather climbed the career ladder of her company quickly, reaching a top-level executive position by her early thirties. In contrast, Sharese and Christy did not attain managerial roles in early adulthood. What accounts for the disparity in career progress of the three women?

■ *Work life and family life are inseparably intertwined. Explain how this is so in early adulthood.*

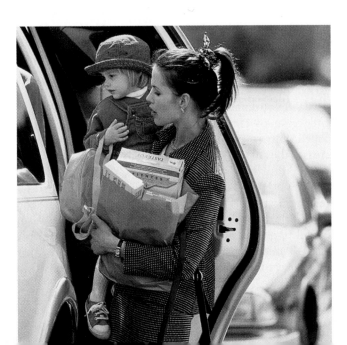

■ *After a full day at the office, this mother picks up her preschooler and runs errands, attending to her second full-time job. Like most women in dual-earner marriages, she shoulders most of the child-care and household tasks. Work–family role conflict is greater for women. (Photo courtesy: Ariel Skelley/The Stock Market)*

SUMMARY

ERIKSON'S THEORY: INTIMACY VERSUS ISOLATION

According to Erikson, what personality changes take place during early adulthood?

■ In Erikson's theory, young adults must resolve the conflict of **intimacy versus isolation,** balancing independence and intimacy as they form a close relationship with a partner. Research indicates that young people deal with intimacy concerns in the context of a variety of lifestyles. It also shows that aspects of generativity, including work and career as well as childbearing and child rearing, are prime concerns in the twenties and thirties.

OTHER THEORIES OF ADULT PSYCHOSOCIAL DEVELOPMENT

Describe Levinson's and Vaillant's psychosocial theories of adult personality development.

■ Building on Erikson's stage approach, both Levinson and Vaillant outlined patterns of change in the adult life course that have been supported by research.

■ Levinson described a predictable series of eras, each consisting of a transition and a stable period, in which the **life structure** is revised and elaborated. Young adults usually construct a dream, typically involving career for men and both marriage and career for women, and find a mentor to help them realize their career goals. In their thirties, they focus on aspects of their lives that have received less attention. Men settle down, whereas women continue in an unsettled phase into middle adulthood.

■ Vaillant refined Erikson's stages, portraying the twenties as devoted to intimacy, the thirties to career consolidation, the forties to guiding others, and the fifties to cultural and philosophical values.

What is the social clock, and how does it affect personality in adulthood?

■ Although societal expectations have become less rigid, conformity to or departure from the **social clock,** the culturally determined timetable for major life events, can be a major source of personality change in adulthood. Following a social clock grants confidence to young adults, whereas deviating can bring psychological distress.

CLOSE RELATIONSHIPS

Describe factors that affect mate selection and the role of romantic love in the young adult's quest for intimacy.

■ Finding a partner is a major milestone of adult development. Intimate partners tend to resemble one another in age, ethnicity, SES, education, and various personal and physical attributes. Sex differences exist in the importance placed on certain characteristics. According to ethological theory, women seek a mate with traits that help ensure children's survival, whereas men seek a mate with characteristics signaling sexual pleasure and ability to bear offspring. An alternative, social learning perspective emphasizes that gender roles profoundly influence criteria for mate selection.

■ The balance among passion, intimacy, and commitment changes as romantic relationships move from the intense sexual attraction of **passionate love** toward more settled **companionate love.** Effort and commitment are key in enduring relationships. The emphasis placed on romantic love as the basis for mate selection in Western nations does not characterize all cultures.

Describe adult friendships and sibling relationships and the role of loneliness in adult development.

■ Adult friendships have many of the same characteristics and benefits as earlier friendships and are based on trust, intimacy, and loyalty. Women's same-sex friendships tend to be more intimate than men's. Other-sex friendships are important in adulthood but less frequent and enduring than same-sex friendships.

■ Siblings become more frequent companions in early adulthood than they were in adolescence, often taking on the characteristics of friendship, especially between same-sex siblings.

■ Young adults are vulnerable to **loneliness,** but it declines with age as they form satisfying intimate ties. As long as it is not too intense, loneliness can encourage young people to reach out to others and learn to be comfortably alone.

THE FAMILY LIFE CYCLE

Trace phases of the family life cycle that are prominent in early adulthood, and cite factors that influence these phases today.

■ Although the majority of young people marry, wide variations exist in the sequence and timing of phases of the **family life cycle.**

■ Leaving home is a major step in assuming adult responsibilities. A large percentage of American teenagers depart relatively early when they go to college. SES and ethnicity influence the likelihood that a young person will live independently before marriage. Returning to live at home for a period of time is common among unmarried young adults.

■ Nearly 90 percent of Americans marry, although most do so later than in the past. Both **traditional marriages** and **egalitarian marriages** are affected by women's employment and changing gender roles. Husbands and wives today must work harder to define their marital roles.

- Men tend to be happier and healthier in marriage than do women, who suffer more when a relationship is difficult. Many young people enter marriage with unrealistic expectations. Even happy marriages have their ups and downs and require adaptability on the part of both partners.

- Effective birth control techniques and changing cultural values make childbearing a matter of choice in Western industrialized nations. Although most American couples bear children, they are doing so later, having fewer children, and weighing the pros and cons more carefully than in the past.

- The arrival of children is a key change in the family life cycle, making the family system permanent for the first time. New parents must adjust to increased responsibilities, less time for each other, and more traditional roles. Marital satisfaction typically declines somewhat with these adjustments. In contrast to many non-Western cultures, in Western industrialized nations marital and parenting roles are closely linked.

- Challenges facing families with young children include inadequate preparation for child rearing, lack of societal supports for parenting, the need for cooperation in the marital relationship, and difficulties in finding good child care. Husbands and wives who work together as "coparenting teams" are more likely to feel competent as parents and be sensitive to their children.

- In families with adolescents, parents must establish new relationships with their increasingly autonomous teenagers, blending guidance with freedom and gradually relinquishing

control. Although marital satisfaction is often lowest in this phase, most parents handle these difficulties. Parent education programs can help parents clarify their child-rearing values and use more effective strategies.

THE DIVERSITY OF ADULT LIFESTYLES

Discuss the diversity of adult lifestyles, focusing on singlehood, cohabitation, and childlessness.

- Diverse nontraditional family options are now part of the American mainstream. Adults may deliberately choose a lifestyle, drift into it, or be forced into it by circumstances.

- Singlehood has risen in recent years and includes both never-married and divorced individuals. Women with high-status careers and men who are unemployed or in blue-collar occupations are most likely to remain single. Single women tend to be better adjusted than single men.

- **Cohabitation** has risen dramatically, especially among well-educated, economically advantaged young adults. It serves either as preparation for marriage or as an alternative to marriage. Often it includes divorced partners and their children. Because American cohabitors tend to be less conventional in values and behavior than other people, their subsequent marriages are more likely to fail.

- Voluntarily childless adults tend to be well educated and career oriented and are just as satisfied with their lives as are parents who have good relationships with their children.

Discuss today's high rates of divorce and remarriage, and cite factors that contribute to them.

- Half of all marriages in the United States are expected to end in separation or divorce, often while children are at home. More than half of divorced people will remarry, and many will divorce again. Maladaptive

communication patterns, family poverty, and the changing status of women contribute to the divorce rate.

- Finding a new partner is important to many divorced adults, especially men. Remarriages break up for several reasons, including the prominence of practical concerns rather than love in the decision to remarry, the persistence of negative patterns of interaction, the acceptance of divorce as a solution to marital difficulties, and problems adjusting to a stepfamily.

Discuss the challenges associated with variant styles of parenthood, including remarried parents, never-married parents, and gay and lesbian parents.

- Establishing stepparent–stepchild ties is difficult, especially for stepmothers and for stepfathers without children of their own. A caring husband–wife relationship, the cooperation of the absent biological parent, and children's acceptance are crucial for stepparent adjustment.

- Never-married parenthood is especially high among low-income African-American women in their twenties. Unemployment among black men and changing American family values contribute to this trend. Although these young mothers often receive help from extended family members, they find it difficult to overcome poverty.

- Families headed by homosexuals face difficulties related to living in an unsupportive society. Gay and lesbian parents are just as loving and effective as heterosexual parents.

VOCATIONAL DEVELOPMENT

Discuss men's and women's patterns of vocational development, and cite difficulties faced by women, ethnic minorities, and couples seeking to combine work and family.

- In addition to intimacy and family concerns, vocational development is a key task for young adults. Men's career paths are usually continuous, whereas women's are often discontinuous due to childbearing and child rearing. After adjusting to the realities of the work world, young adults settle into an occupation. Their progress is affected by opportunities for promotion in their chosen occupations, personal characteristics such as self-efficacy, and access to an effective mentor.

■ Women and ethnic minorities have penetrated nearly all professions but have made limited progress in advancement and earnings. Women tend to be hampered by low self-efficacy with respect to traditionally male-dominated fields, gender stereotypes, role conflict between work and family, and difficulties in finding a suitable mentor.

■ Couples, and particularly women, in **dual-earner marriages** experience stresses from work overload, work–family role conflict, and the need of one partner to make vocational sacrifices to further the other partner's career. Benefits include higher earnings, a better standard of living, and self-fulfillment of the wife.

IMPORTANT TERMS AND CONCEPTS

cohabitation (p. 476)

companionate love (p. 461)

dual-earner marriage (p. 482)

egalitarian marriage (p. 468)

family life cycle (p. 466)

intimacy versus isolation (p. 456)

life structure (p. 457)

loneliness (p. 464)

passionate love (p. 461)

social clock (p. 459)

traditional marriage (p. 468)

FOR FURTHER INFORMATION AND HELP

Consult the companion website for this book, where you will find additional weblinks and associated learning activities: www.abacon.com/berk

PARENTHOOD AND PARENT EDUCATION

Family Resource Coalition of America
www.frca.org

Helps families develop support systems to strengthen family life and children's development. Educates public, government, and business leaders about the needs of families and how family resource programs can meet those needs.

Parenthood 2000
www.Parenthood2000.com

An organization of parents interested in altering their work life to make more time for family.

SINGLEHOOD AND CHILDLESSNESS

Single Mothers by Choice
www3.parentsplace.com/ readroom/smc

Organization of primarily single professional women in their thirties and forties who have either decided to have or are considering having children outside of marriage.

Childless by Choice
www.now2000.com/cbc

Organization dedicated to educating potential parents about the parenting choice and supporting couples who have voluntarily chosen to be childless.

DIVORCE AND REMARRIAGE

Parents Without Partners
www.parentswithoutpartners.org

Organization of custodial and noncustodial single parents that provides support in the upbringing of children. Many local groups exist throughout the United States.

Stepfamily Association of America
www.stepfam.org

Association of families interested in stepfamily relationships. Organizes support groups and offers education and children's services.

GAY AND LESBIAN PARENTS

Gay and Lesbian Parents Coalition International
www.familypride.org

Strives to educate people about the compatibility of homosexuality and parenting. Supports efforts to eliminate discrimination due to sexual orientation, coordinates support groups for parents and children, and conducts public education programs.

AGE	PHYSICAL	COGNITIVE	EMOTIONAL/SOCIAL
20–30 years	■ Athletic skills that require speed of limb movement, explosive strength, and gross body coordination peak early in this decade and then decline. (427) ■ Athletic skills that depend on endurance, arm–hand steadiness, and aiming peak at the end of this decade and then decline. (427) ■ Declines in touch sensitivity; respiratory, cardiovascular, and immune system functioning; and elasticity of the skin begin and continue throughout adulthood. (426) ■ As basal metabolic rate declines, gradual weight gain begins in the middle of this decade and continues through middle adulthood. (430) ■ Sexual activity increases. (434)	■ If college educated, dualistic thinking (dividing information, values, and authority into right and wrong) declines in favor of relativistic thinking (viewing all knowledge as embedded in a framework of thought). (440) ■ Narrows vocational options and settles on a specific career. (445) ■ With entry into marriage and employment situations, focuses less on acquiring knowledge and more on applying it to everyday life. (440) ■ Develops expertise (acquisition of extensive knowledge in a field of endeavor), which enhances problem solving. (442) ■ Creativity (generating useful original products) increases. (442) ■ Modest gains in a variety of mental abilities assessed by intelligence tests occur during this and the following decade. (443)	■ Leaves home permanently. (466) ■ Strives to make a permanent commitment to an intimate partner. (461, 467) ■ Usually constructs a dream, an image of the self in the adult world that guides decision making. (458) ■ Usually forms a relationship with a mentor, who facilitates realization of the dream. (458) ■ If in a high-status career, acquires professional skills, values, and credentials (for women, may be delayed and take a longer time). (480–482) ■ Begins to develop mutually gratifying adult friendships and work ties. (463) ■ May cohabit, marry, and bear children. (467, 472, 476) ■ Sibling relationships become more companionate. (463) ■ As people move in and out of relationships, loneliness peaks early in this decade and then declines steadily throughout adulthood. (464)

AGE	PHYSICAL	COGNITIVE	EMOTIONAL/SOCIAL
30–40 years	■ Declines in vision, hearing, and the skeletal system begin and continue throughout adulthood. (426) ■ In women, fertility problems increase sharply in the middle of this decade. (429) ■ Hair begins to gray and thin in the middle of this decade. (426) ■ Sexual activity declines, probably due to the demands of daily life. (434)	■ As family and work lives expand, the cognitive capacity to juggle many responsibilities simultaneously improves. (441) ■ Creativity (generating useful original products) often peaks. (442)	■ Reevaluates life structure and tries to change components that are inadequate. (458) ■ Establishes more stable niche within society through family, occupation, and community activities (for women, career consolidation may be delayed). (459)

Note: Numbers in parentheses indicate the page on which each milestone is discussed.

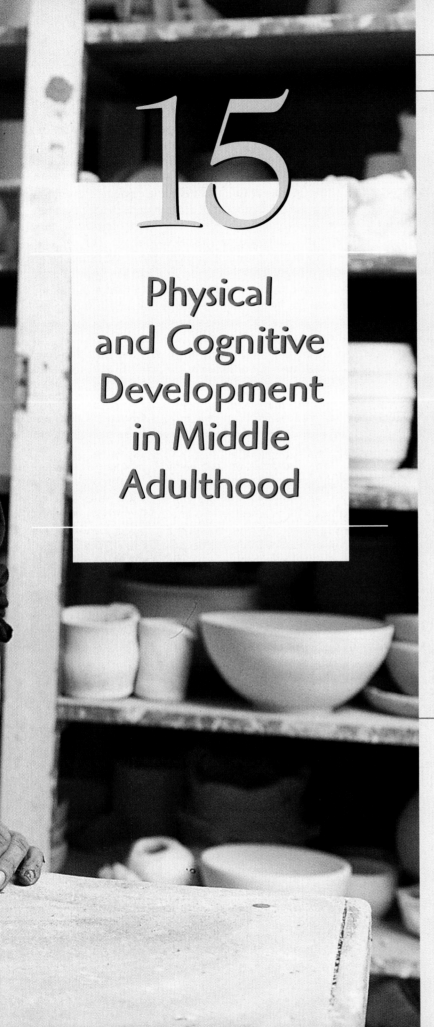

15

Physical and Cognitive Development in Middle Adulthood

■ *Middle adulthood is a time of narrowing life options, but it brings compensating gains. Expertise—a wealth of accumulated knowledge that supports a high level of performance in a vocational or leisure pursuit—reaches its height, as the artistic creations of this Mexican-American potter reveal. (Photo courtesy: Michael Newman/PhotoEdit)*

On a snowy December evening, Devin and Trisha sat down to read the holiday cards that were piled high on the kitchen counter. Devin's fifty-fifth birthday had just passed; Trisha would reach 48 within two months. During the past year, they had celebrated their twenty-fourth wedding anniversary. These milestones, along with greetings from friends who sent annual updates about their lives, brought the changes of midlife into bold relief.

Instead of new births, children starting school, or a first promotion at work, notations on the cards sounded new themes. Jewel's recap of the past year reflected a growing awareness of a finite lifespan, one in which time had become more precious. She wrote,

My mood has been lighter ever since my birthday. There was some burden I laid down by turning 49. My mother passed away when she was 48, so it all feels like a gift now. Blessed be!

George and Anya reported on their son's graduation from law school and their daughter Michelle's first year of university. The house empty of children, George wrote,

Anya is filling the gap created by the children's departure by returning to college for a nursing degree. After enrolling this fall, she was surprised to find herself in the same psychology class as Michelle. At first, Anya was worried about whether she'd be able to handle the academic work, but after a semester of success, she's feeling much more confident.

Tim's message reflected continuing robust health, acceptance of physical change, and a new burden: caring for aging parents—a certain reminder of the limits of the lifespan:

I used to be a good basketball player in college, but I've recently noticed that my 20-year-old nephew Brent can dribble and shoot circles around me. It must be my age! I ran our city marathon in September, coming in seventh in the over-50 division. Brent ran, too, but he opted out a few miles short of the finish line to get some pizza while I pressed on. That must be my age, too!

The saddest news this year is that my dad had a bad stroke. His mind is clear, but his body is partially paralyzed. It's really upsetting because he was getting to enjoy the computer I gave him, and it was so wonderfully upbeat to talk with him about it in the months before the stroke.

Middle age begins around age 40 and ends at about 60. This phase is marked by a narrowing of life options and sense of a shrinking future as children leave home and career paths become more determined. In other ways, middle adulthood is difficult to define, since wide variations in at-

titudes and behaviors exist. Some individuals seem physically and mentally young at age 60—active and optimistic, having attained a sense of serenity and stability. Others feel old at age 35 or 40—as if their lives had peaked and were on a downhill course.

Yet another reason that middle age escapes clear definition is that it is a product of modern times. Before the twentieth century, only a brief interval existed between the tasks of early adulthood and those of old age. For example, women often became widows by their mid-fifties, before their youngest child left home. And harsh living conditions led people to accept a ravaged body as a natural part of life. As average life expectancy—and with it, health and vigor—increased over this century, adults became more aware of their own aging and mortality.

Societal forces also affect whether a middle-aged person feels stagnant or in the prime of life. In a depressed job market, employers can tell 40-year-olds that they are "too old." Hearing this often enough, they come to believe what they are told. When people have highly valued skills and are financially well off, middle age can be an exciting and liberating time of life.

In this chapter, we trace physical and cognitive development during the fifth and sixth decades of the lifespan. In both domains, we will encounter not just progressive declines, but sustained performance and compensating gains. As in earlier chapters, we will be reminded that change occurs in manifold ways. Besides heredity and biological aging,

■ *Middle adulthood is difficult to define, since it encompasses wide variations in attitudes and behaviors. These middle-aged individuals seem physically and mentally young—active and optimistic. As volunteers for Habitat for Humanity, they build a house for a needy family. (Photo courtesy: Judy Gelles/Stock Boston)*

our personal approach to passing years combines with family, community, and cultural contexts to profoundly affect the way we age.

PHYSICAL DEVELOPMENT

Physical development in midlife is a continuation of the gradual changes already under way in early adulthood. Yet enough time has passed that a look in the mirror or at family photos prompts awareness of an older body, even in the most vigorous adults. Hair grays and thins, new lines appear on the face, and a less youthful, fuller body shape is evident. In addition to these obvious signs, it is during midlife that most individuals begin to experience life-threatening health episodes personally—if not in themselves, then in their partners and friends. And a change in time orientation, from "years since birth" to "years left to live," adds to consciousness of aging (Neugarten, 1968).

These factors lead to a revised physical self-image, which often emphasizes fewer hoped-for gains and more feared declines. Prominent concerns among 40- to 60-year-olds are getting a fatal disease, being too ill to maintain independence, and losing mental capacities. Yet notice that these outcomes are common stereotypes of aging. Unfortunately, many middle-aged adults fail to mention realistic alternatives as central life goals—becoming a more physically fit person and developing into a healthy, energetic older adult (Hooker & Kaus, 1994).

As we examine physical changes and health issues of middle adulthood, we will see that certain aspects of aging cannot be controlled. Yet many positive outcomes can be attained and feared outcomes avoided. There is much we can do to promote physical vigor and good health during midlife.

PHYSICAL CHANGES

As they dressed one morning before work, Trisha commented half-jokingly to Devin, "I just let the mirror get dusty; then I can't see the wrinkles and gray hairs very well." As she turned and took a closer look, her tone became more serious. "I'm certainly not happy about my weight. Look at this fat pad on my abdomen. It just doesn't want to go! I need to get back to some regular exercise—adjust my life to fit it in." Devin responded by glancing down soberly at his own enlarged midriff.

■ *Because the lens of the eye gradually loses its ability to adjust its focus to nearby objects, difficulty reading small print is a common experience by the forties. Corrective lenses for reading, which for nearsighted people take the form of bifocals, ease this problem. (Photo courtesy: G. S. Zimbel/Monkmeyer Press)*

At breakfast, Devin took his glasses on and off and squinted while trying to read the paper. "Trish—what's the eye doctor's phone number? I need to get these bifocals adjusted again." When conversing between the kitchen and adjoining den, Devin sometimes asked Trisha to repeat herself. And he turned the radio and TV volume up high enough so that Trisha frequently remarked, "Does it need to be so loud?" Devin, it seemed, couldn't hear quite as clearly as before.

Let's examine the major physical changes of middle adulthood—those especially salient to Devin and Trisha along with others occurring in the reproductive system and skeleton. As we do so, you may find it helpful to refer back to Table 13.2 on page 426, which provides a summary.

VISION

By the forties, difficulty reading small print is a common experience. It is due to growth in size of the lens of the eye combined with weakening of the muscle that enables it to adjust its focus (accommodate) to nearby objects. As new fibers appear on the surface of the lens, they compress older fibers toward the center, creating a thicker, denser, less pliable structure that eventually cannot be transformed at all. By age 50, the accommodative ability of the lens is one-sixth of what it was at age 20. Around age 60, the lens loses its capacity to adjust to objects at varying distances entirely, a condition called **presbyopia** (meaning, literally, "old eyes"). Corrective lenses for reading, which for nearsighted people take the form of bifocals, ease this problem. Because of the enlarging lens, the eye gradually becomes more farsighted between ages 30 and 60 (Whitbourne, 1996).

A second set of changes limits ability to see clearly in dim light. Throughout adulthood, the size of the pupil shrinks and the lens yellows. In addition, starting at age 40, the vitreous (transparent gelatinlike substance that fills the eye) develops opaque areas. Consequently, the amount of light reaching the retina is reduced. Changes in the lens

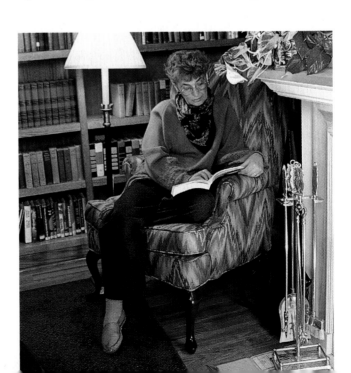

and vitreous also cause light to scatter within the eye, increasing sensitivity to glare. Devin, who as a college student had enjoyed driving at night, now found it more challenging to do so. He sometimes had trouble making out signs and moving objects. And his vision was more disrupted by bright light sources, such as the headlights of oncoming cars (Owsley et al., 1998).

Finally, yellowing of the lens and increasing density of the vitreous limit color discrimination, especially at the green-blue-violet end of the spectrum (Kraft & Werner, 1999; Weale, 1992). As a result, from time to time Devin had to ask whether his sport coat, tie, and socks matched. Besides structural changes in the eye, neural changes in the visual system occur. Gradual loss of light- and color-receptor cells in the retina (rods and cones) and of neurons in the optic nerve (the pathway between the retina and the cerebral cortex) contributes to declines in vision with age (Pardhan et al., 1996).

HEARING

An estimated 14 percent of American adults between 45 and 64 years of age have a hearing loss. Adult-onset hearing impairments account for many of these cases. Although some conditions run in families and may be hereditary, most are age-related. These are called **presbycusis** (meaning "old hearing") and are caused by several factors (Adams & Marano, 1995).

As we age, inner-ear structures that transform mechanical sound waves into neural impulses deteriorate due to natural cell death or reduced blood supply as a result of atherosclerosis. The first sign is a sharp hearing loss at high frequencies, around 50 years of age. Gradually, the impairment extends to all frequencies so that after age 60 human speech is more difficult to make out, although hearing loss remains greatest for high tones.

Men's hearing declines earlier and at a faster rate than women's, a difference thought to be due to exposure to environmental noise in male-dominated occupations (Wiley et al., 1998). Over 9 million American production workers are being or have been exposed to noise capable of doing damage—the most common cause of hearing loss in middle-aged adults (Brechtelsbauer, 1990).

Most middle-aged and elderly people with hearing difficulties benefit from sound amplification with hearing aids. Once perception of the human voice is affected, speaking to the person patiently, clearly, and with good eye contact aids understanding. Finally, many severe cases of adult hearing loss can be prevented—by avoiding intense noise or using ear plugs during noise exposure.

SKIN

Our skin consists of three layers: (1) the *epidermis*, or outer protective layer, where new skin cells are constantly produced; (2) the *dermis*, or middle supportive layer, which consists of connective tissue that stretches and bounces back, granting the skin flexibility; and (3) the *hypodermis*, an inner fatty layer that adds to the soft lines and shape of the skin. As we age, the epidermis becomes less firmly attached to the dermis, fibers in the dermis thin, and fat in the hypodermis diminishes.

These changes lead the skin to wrinkle and loosen. In the thirties, lines develop on the forehead as a result of smiling, furrowing the brow, and other facial expressions. In the forties, these become more pronounced, and "crow's-feet" appear around the eyes. Gradually, the skin loses elasticity and begins to sag, especially on the face, arms, and legs. After age 50, "age spots," collections of pigment under the skin, increase.

Because sun exposure hastens wrinkling and spotting, individuals who have spent much time outdoors without proper skin protection look older than their contemporaries. And partly because the dermis of women is not as thick as that of men, women's skin ages more quickly (Whitbourne, 1985, 1996).

MUSCLE–FAT MAKEUP

As Trisha and Devin make clear, weight gain—referred to as "middle-age spread"—is a concern to both men and women. A common pattern of change is an increase in body fat and loss of lean body mass (muscle and bone). The rise in fat largely affects the torso and occurs as fatty deposits within the body cavity; as noted earlier, fat beneath the skin on the limbs declines. On the average, size of the abdomen increases 6 to 16 percent in men, 25 to 35 percent in women from early through middle adulthood (Whitbourne, 1996). Sex differences in fat distribution also appear. Men accumulate more on the back and upper abdomen, women around the waist and upper arms.

Muscle mass declines very gradually in the forties and fifties, largely due to atrophy of fast-twitch fibers, responsible for speed and explosive strength. Yet as indicated in Chapter 13, large weight gain and loss of muscle power are not inevitable, since continued exercise offsets these changes. Within the same individual, strength varies between often-used and little-used muscles (Arking, 1991). And consider Devin's 57-year-old friend Tim, who has ridden his bike to and from work for years and jogged on weekends, averaging 1 hour of vigorous activity per day. Like many endurance athletes, he weighed the same and had the same muscular physique at age 57 as at 25 (Suominen et al., 1980).

SKELETON

As new cells accumulate on their outer layers, the bones broaden, but their mineral content declines, so they become more porous. This leads to a gradual loss in bone mass that begins in the late thirties and accelerates in the fifties, especially among women. Women's reserve of bone minerals is lower than men's to begin with. And following menopause, the favorable impact of estrogen on bone mineral absorption is lost. Reduction in bone density during adulthood is substantial—about 8 to 12 percent for men, 20 to 30 percent for women (Arking, 1991).

Loss of bone strength causes the disks in the spinal column to collapse. Consequently, height may drop by as much as 1 inch by age 60, a change that will hasten thereafter. In addition, the weakened bones cannot support as much load, fracture more easily, and heal more slowly. A healthy lifestyle, including exercise and adequate calcium intake, can slow bone loss—in postmenopausal women by as much as 30 to 50 percent (Reid, 1996). As we will see in the next section, hormone replacement therapy also helps preserve bone density and, consequently, prevents fractures.

When bone loss is very great, it leads to a debilitating disorder called *osteoporosis*. We will take up this condition shortly when we consider illness and disability.

REPRODUCTIVE SYSTEM

The midlife transition in which fertility declines is called the **climacteric**. It differs markedly between the two sexes, since it brings an end to reproductive capacity in women, whereas fertility in men diminishes but is retained.

■ REPRODUCTIVE CHANGES IN WOMEN. The changes involved in women's climacteric occur gradually over a 10-year period, during which the production of estrogen drops. As a result, the number of days in a woman's monthly cycle shortens, from about 28 in her twenties and thirties to perhaps 23 by her late forties. Her cycles also become more irregular. In some, ova are not released; when they are, more are defective (see Chapter 2, page 55). The climacteric concludes with **menopause**, the end of menstruation and reproductive capacity. This occurs, on the average, at age 51 among North American, European, and East Asian women, although the age range is large—from 42 to 58.

Following menopause, estrogen declines further. This causes the reproductive organs to shrink in size, the genitals to be less easily stimulated, and the vagina to lubricate more slowly during arousal. The drop in estrogen also contributes to other physical changes, including decreased elasticity of the skin and loss in bone mass. And estrogen's ability to slow accumulation of plaque on the walls of the arteries is lost.

Consequently, doctors often recommend **hormone replacement therapy** (HRT), involving daily doses of estrogen, for postmenopausal women. Its advantages are clear: protection against bone deterioration and cardiovascular disease and a reduction in certain discomforts of the climacteric, such as mood fluctuations and *hot flashes*—periodic sensations of warmth accompanied by a rise in body temperature; redness in the face, neck, and chest; followed by sweating. Hot flashes affect about 75 percent of women in Western industrialized nations and are a common cause of midlife sleeplessness and irritability. HRT may also improve memory and other aspects of cognition in postmenopausal women. And it may help maintain cognitive functioning in late adulthood (Hogervorst et al., 1998; Jacobs et al., 1998; Yaffe et al., 1998).

Nevertheless, HRT is controversial. Because long-term estrogen replacement is associated with an increase in cancer of the endometrium (lining of the uterus), doctors often prescribe a combination of estrogen and the female hormone progesterone, which lessens this risk. But HRT has also been linked to an increase in incidence of breast cancer, which may rise with the estrogen/progesterone combination (Persson et al., 1999; Schairer et al., 2000). Therefore, women and their doctors should make decisions about HRT carefully, and those with a family history of breast cancer are generally advised against it. Alternative medications that protect the bones and combat cardiovascular disease are available, but their long-term consequences are not yet clear.

According to some experts, the health benefits of HRT may be achieved more safely through lifestyle changes—a good diet, regular exercise, and avoidance of smoking (Willett, Colditz, & Stampfer, 2000). Compared with American and Canadian women, Asian women (Chinese, East Indian, Indonesian, and Japanese) report far fewer symptoms of menopause, including hot flashes (Avis, 1999; Haines et al., 1995). Asian diets—low in fat and high in soy-based foods, a rich source of plant estrogen—may be responsible.

■ WOMEN'S PSYCHOLOGICAL REACTIONS TO MENOPAUSE. How do women react to menopause—a clear-cut signal that their childbearing years are over? The answer lies in how they interpret the event in relation to their past and future lives.

For Jewel, who had wanted marriage and family but never attained these goals, menopause was traumatic. Her sense of physical competence was still bound up with the ability to have children. Discomfort from physical symptoms—hot flashes, headaches, and loss of sleep—can also turn menopause into a difficult time. And as the climacteric evokes concern about an aging body in a society that values a youthful appearance, some women respond with disappointment to a loss of sex appeal.

At the same time, many women find menopause to be little or no trouble at all. They do not want more children, and they are relieved to see their menstrual periods end and to no longer have to worry about birth control. More highly educated, career-oriented women with fulfilling lives outside the home usually have more positive attitudes than do women with less education (Theisen et al., 1995). And the little evidence we have suggests that African-American and

Mexican-American women have a generally favorable view, a trend that is stronger for Mexican-Americans who have not yet adopted the language (and perhaps certain beliefs) of the larger society (Bell, 1995; Holmes-Rovner et al., 1996).

The wide variation in physical symptoms and attitudes indicates that menopause is more than just a hormonal event; it is profoundly affected by societal beliefs and practices. For a cross-cultural look at menopause, turn to the Variations box on page 497.

■ REPRODUCTIVE CHANGES IN MEN. Men also experience a climacteric, but the change is limited to a decrease in quantity of semen and sperm after age 40 (Murray & Meacham, 1993). However, sperm continue to be produced throughout life, and men in their nineties have fathered children.

Testosterone production, along with its effects on male sex organs and sexual interest, remains stable throughout adulthood in healthy men who continue to engage in sexual activity (which stimulates cells that release testosterone). Consequently, no male counterpart to menopause exists.

Nevertheless, because of reduced blood flow to and changes in connective tissue in the penis, more stimulation is required for an erection, and it may be harder to maintain (Whitbourne, 1996). The inability to attain an erection when desired can occur at any age, but it becomes more common in midlife, affecting 20 percent of men by age 60. An episode or two of impotence is not serious, but frequent bouts can lead some men to fear that their sex life is over and undermine their self-image. Stress, alcohol abuse, and illness can contribute to the problem. But whatever the cause, the chances are excellent that with medical or psychological treatment, impotence can be cured (Larson, 1996).

ASK YOURSELF . . .

■ *When Stan was 42, his optician told him that he needed bifocals, and over the next 10 years, Stan required an adjustment to his corrective lenses almost every year. What physical changes account for Stan's repeated need for new eyewear?*

Nancy noticed that between ages 40 and 50, she gained 20 pounds, and her arm and leg muscles seemed weaker. She had trouble opening tightly closed jars, and her legs ached after she climbed a flight of stairs. Nancy thought to herself, "Exchanging muscle for fat must be an inevitable part of aging." Is Nancy correct? Why or why not?

■ *Cite cultural and gender-role influences on the experience of menopause.*

HEALTH AND FITNESS

In midlife, nearly 60 percent of people rate their health as either "excellent" or "good"—still a majority, but nevertheless far fewer than in early adulthood, when the figure is nearly 75 percent. Whereas younger people usually attribute health complaints to temporary infections, middle-aged adults more often point to chronic diseases. Visits to the doctor's office and hospital stays become more frequent. Middle-aged men are slightly more likely to consider their health as either "excellent" or "poor," whereas women more often place themselves in the middle categories of "good" and "fair." The reason, as we will see shortly, is that men are more likely to suffer from fatal illnesses, whereas women more often have nonfatal, limiting health problems (Markides, 1994).

Our discussion takes up sexuality as a positive indicator of health, in addition to typical negative indicators—major diseases and disabling conditions. Before we begin, it is important to note that our understanding of health in middle and late adulthood is limited by insufficient research on women and ethnic minorities. Most studies of illness risk factors, prevention, and treatment have been carried out on men. Fortunately, this situation is changing. For example, the Women's Health Initiative represents a 15-year commitment by the U.S. federal government to study the impact of prevention strategies—diet, exercise, hormone replacement, and stress reduction—on the health of over 164,000 postmenopausal women of all ethnic groups and SES levels (Women's Health Initiative Group, 1998).

SEXUALITY

Frequency of sexual activity among married couples tends to decline in middle adulthood, but the drop is only slight and unrelated to the woman's menopausal status (Avis et al., 1995; Dennerstein et al., 1997). Longitudinal research reveals that stability of sexual activity is far more typical than dramatic change. Couples having sex often in early adulthood continue to do so in midlife. And the best predictor of sexual frequency is marital happiness (Edwards & Booth, 1994). Apparently, sexual pleasure and emotional intimacy remain strongly linked for most people.

Having sex is also associated with psychological well-being in the middle years of marriage. In a study of 3,000 married men and women, people not having sex with reasonable frequency were usually dissatisfied with the entire relationship (Blumenstein & Schwartz, 1983). The sexual activity–well-being association is probably bidirectional. Sex is more likely to occur in the context of a good marriage, and couples having sex often probably view their relationship more positively.

MENOPAUSE AS A BIOCULTURAL EVENT

Biology and culture join forces to influence women's response to menopause, making it a *biocultural event.* In the United States and other industrialized nations, menopause is "medicalized"—assumed to be a syndrome requiring treatment. Many women experience physical and emotional symptoms, and the more symptoms they report, the more negative their attitude toward menopause tends to be (Theisen et al., 1995).

Yet change the circumstances in which menopause is evaluated, and attitudes toward it change as well. In one study, nearly 600 men and women between ages 19 and 85 described their view of menopause in one of three contexts—when discussing it as a medical problem, as a life transition, or as a symbol of aging. The medical context evoked many more negative statements than did the other contexts (Gannon & Ekstrom, 1993).

Research in non-Western cultures reveals that changes in women's roles also affect the experience of menopause. In tribal and village societies in which social power rests in the hands of men and non-childbearing women have low social status, women report the greatest distress during the climacteric. In cultures in which older women are respected and the mother-in-law and grandmother roles bring new privileges and responsibilities, complaints about menopausal symptoms are rare (Patterson & Lynch, 1988).

A comparison of rural Mayan women of the Yucatan with rural Greek women on the island of Evia reveals additional biocultural influences on the menopausal experience (Beyene, 1992). In both cultures, old age is a time of increased status, and menopause brings freedom from child rearing and more time to participate in leisure activities. Otherwise, the experiences of the Mayan and Greek women, before and during the climacteric, differ greatly.

Mayan women marry at age 13 or 14. By 35 to 40, they have had many children but few menstrual periods (due to repeated pregnancies and breast-feeding). Because they are eager for childbearing to end, they welcome menopause, describing it with such phrases as "being happy" and "free like a young girl again." None report hot flashes or any other symptoms of discomfort.

Like Americans, rural Greek women use birth control to limit family size. And most report hot flashes and cold sweats during the climacteric. But they regard these as temporary discomforts that will stop on their own, not as medical symptoms requiring treatment. "Pay no attention," "Go outside for fresh air," and "Throw off the covers at night," the Greek women reply when asked what they do when they have hot flashes.

Does frequency of childbearing affect menopausal symptoms, as this contrast between Mayan and Greek women suggests? Much more research is needed to find out for sure. At the same time, the difference between American and Greek women in attitudes toward and management of hot flashes is striking. This—along with other cross-cultural findings—highlights the impact of culture on the menopausal experience.

■ *For these rural Mayan women of the Yucatan, old age is a time of increased status, and menopause brings freedom. After decades of childbearing, Mayan women welcome menopause, describing it as "being happy" and "free like a young girl again." (Photo courtesy: Michael Gallagher/Liaison Agency)*

Nevertheless, *intensity* of sexual response declines somewhat in midlife, due to physical changes of the climacteric. Both men and women take longer to feel aroused and to reach orgasm (Edwards & Booth, 1994). If partners perceive each other as less attractive, this may contribute to a drop in sexual desire. Yet in the context of a positive outlook, sexual activity can become more satisfying. Devin and Trisha, for example, viewed each other's aging bodies with acceptance and affection—as a sign of their enduring and deepening relationship. And with greater freedom from the demands of work and family, their sex life became more spontaneous.

Finally, when surveys include both married and unmarried people, a striking difference between men and women in age-related sexual activity appears. The proportion of men with no sexual partners in the previous year increases only slightly, from 8 percent in the thirties to 11 percent in the late fifties. In contrast, the rise for women is dramatic, from 9 to 30 percent, a gender gap that will become even greater in late adulthood (Michael et al., 1994). Opportunity, not desire, is responsible. A higher male mortality rate and the value women place on affection and continuity in sexual relations make partners less available to them. When we look at the evidence as a whole, sexual activity in midlife, as in earlier periods, is the combined result of biological, psychological, and social forces.

ILLNESS AND DISABILITY

As Table 15.1 shows, cancer and cardiovascular disease are the leading causes of death in middle age, with cancer by far the leading killer of women. Despite a rise in vision problems, the unintentional injury rate due to motor vehicle collisions declines in midlife, perhaps because older people compensate with many years of driving experience or are more cautious. Not evident in the table is that certain injuries increase, especially bone fractures. Finally, although stroke is a leading cause of death in midlife, it is not yet very common (U.S. Bureau of the Census, 1999). Since it increases sharply from middle to late adulthood, we will consider it in Chapter 17.

Extending trends established in earlier decades, men continue to be more vulnerable than women to most health problems, and economic disadvantage remains a strong predictor of poor health and premature death (see Chapter 13, page 429). As we look closely at major causes of illness, disability, and death, we will encounter yet another familiar theme: the close connection between emotional and physical well-being. Personality traits that magnify stress—especially hostility and anger—are serious threats to health in midlife.

TABLE 15.1

Death Rates[a] by Leading Causes in the United States

	25–44 YEARS TOTAL	45–64 YEARS TOTAL	MALES	FEMALES
Cancer	26	245	270	222
Cardiovascular Disease	20	197	287	113
Stroke	4	29	33	25
Unintentional Injury	32	29	46	18
Motor Vehicle	17	14	19	9

[a] Number of deaths per 100,000 population.
Source: U.S. Bureau of the Census, 1999.

■ C A N C E R . The death rate due to cancer multiplies 10-fold from early to middle adulthood (see Table 15.1). In midlife, it is responsible for approximately 130,000 deaths in the United States each year—34 percent of all deaths. Although the incidence of many types of cancer is currently leveling off or declining, cancer mortality was on the rise for many decades, largely because of a dramatic increase in lung cancer due to cigarette smoking. In the last 10 years, lung cancer dropped in men, since 50 percent fewer smoke today than did in the 1950s. In contrast, lung cancer has increased in women, many of whom took up smoking after World War II (National Cancer Institute, 1998).

Cancer occurs when the genetic programming of a normal cell is disrupted, leading to uncontrolled growth and spread of abnormal cells that crowd out normal tissues and organs. Why does this happen? Recall from Chapter 13 that according to one theory, random error in duplication of body cells increases with age, either due to release of free radicals or breakdown of the immune system. External agents may also initiate or intensify this process. Recently, scientists discovered that damage to a gene called p53, which keeps cells with defective DNA from multiplying, is involved in 60 percent of cancers, including bladder, breast, cervix, liver, lung, prostate, and skin. New cancer therapies are beginning to target the p53 gene (Hager, 1996). Furthermore, an inherited proneness to certain cancers exists. For example, many patients with familial breast cancer who respond poorly to treatment lack a particular tumor-suppressing gene (either BRCA1 or BRCA2). Genetic screening for these mutations is available so prevention can begin as early as possible (Coughlin, Khoury, & Steinberg, 1999).

Overall, a complex interaction of heredity, biological aging, and environment contributes to cancer. Figure 15.1

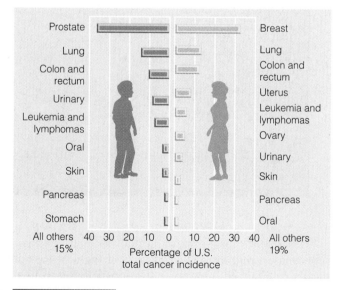

FIGURE 15.1

■ **Cancer incidence in the United States by site and sex.** (Adapted from National Cancer Institute, 1998.)

shows the most frequent types and the incidence of each. Illness and mortality rates are higher for certain groups of people than for others. For cancers that affect both sexes, men are generally more vulnerable than women. The difference may be due to genetic makeup, exposure to cancer-causing agents as a result of lifestyle or occupation, and a tendency to delay going to the doctor. In Chapter 13, we noted that heart disease occurs more often among African Americans than Caucasian Americans. The same is true for cancer (Flack et al., 1995). Researchers believe that unhealthy living conditions and behaviors linked to poverty, along with limited access to health care, are responsible.

Many people fear cancer because they believe it is incurable. Yet 40 percent of people with cancer are cured (free of the disease for 5 or more years). Breast cancer is the leading type for women, prostate cancer for men. Lung cancer—largely preventable through avoiding tobacco—ranks second for both sexes, followed closely by colon and rectal cancer. Scheduling annual medical checkups that screen for these and other forms and taking the additional steps listed in the Caregiving Concerns table below can reduce the incidence of and mortality from cancer considerably. Although the relationship of SES to cancer varies with site (for example, lung and stomach cancers are linked to lower SES, breast and prostate cancers to higher SES), cancer survival drops sharply as SES decreases (Balfour & Kaplan, 1998).

Poorer quality medical care and reduced ability to fight the disease, due to inadequate diet, high life stress, and lack of social support, underlie this trend.

Surviving cancer is a triumph, but it also brings emotional challenges. During cancer treatment, relationships focus on the illness. Afterward, they must refocus on health and full participation in daily life. Unfortunately, stigmas associated with cancer exist. Friends, family, and co-workers may need to be reminded that cancer is not contagious and that research shows cancer survivors to be just as productive on the job as other people (Kornblith, 1998).

■ CARDIOVASCULAR DISEASE. Despite a decline in heart disease during the last few decades (see Chapter 13), about one hundred thousand 45- to 64-year-old Americans die of it annually, accounting for nearly 27 percent of deaths in this age group (U.S. Bureau of the Census, 1999). We associate cardiovascular disease with heart attacks, but Devin (like many middle-aged and older adults) first discovered it during an annual checkup. The doctor detected high blood pressure, high blood cholesterol, and *atherosclerosis*—a buildup of plaque in his coronary arteries, which encircle the heart and provide its muscles with oxygen and nutrients. These signs of cardiovascular disease are known as "silent killers," since they often have no symptoms.

CAREGIVING CONCERNS

Reducing the Incidence of Cancer and Cancer Deaths

INTERVENTION	DESCRIPTION
Know the seven warning signs of cancer.	Change in bowel or bladder habits; sore that does not heal; unusual bleeding or discharge; thickening or lump in a breast or elsewhere in your body; indigestion or swallowing difficulty; obvious change in a wart or mole; nagging cough or hoarseness. If you have any of these signs, consult your doctor immediately.
Do self-examination.	Women should self-examine the breasts and men the testicles for lumps and other changes once a month. If detected early, breast and testicular cancers can usually be cured.
Schedule regular medical checkups and cancer-screening tests.	Regular medical checkups, mammograms every 1 to 2 years and Pap tests every year for women, and other screening tests for both sexes increase early detection and cure.
Avoid tobacco.	Cigarette smoking causes 90 percent of lung cancer deaths and 30 percent of all cancer deaths. Smokeless (chewing) tobacco increases risk of cancer of the mouth, larynx, throat, and esophagus.
Avoid sun exposure.	Sun exposure causes many cases of skin cancer. When in the sun for an extended time, use a sun blocker and cover exposed skin.
Avoid unnecessary X-ray exposure.	Excessive exposure to X-rays increases cancer risk. Most medical X-rays are adjusted to deliver the lowest possible dose but should not be used unnecessarily.
Avoid exposure to industrial chemicals and other pollutants.	Exposure to nickel, chromate, asbestos, vinyl chloride, and other industrial agents increases risk of various cancers.
Weigh the benefits versus risks of hormone replacement therapy (HRT)	Because estrogen replacement increases risk of uterine and breast cancer and estrogen/progesterone replacement may further elevate risk of breast cancer, carefully consider HRT with your doctor.
Maintain a healthy diet.	Avoid too much dietary fat and salt-cured, smoked, and nitrite-cured foods; eat vegetables and foods rich in fiber and vitamins A and C.

Source: Holland, 1998.

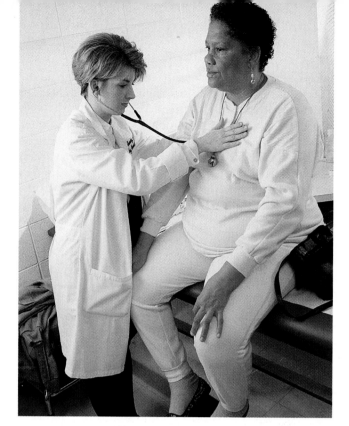

Accurate diagnosis of cardiovascular disease is of special concern in women. Because doctors often view a heart condition as a "male problem," they tend to overlook women's symptoms. African-American women, who are at increased risk for heart disease, are particularly likely to experience lack of appropriate follow-up tests. (Photo courtesy: Bob Schatz/Liaison Agency)

When symptoms are evident, they take different forms. The most extreme is a *heart attack*—blockage of normal blood supply to an area of the heart. It is usually brought on by a blood clot in one or more plaque-filled coronary arteries. Intense pain results as muscle in the affected region dies. A heart attack is a medical emergency; over 50 percent of victims die before reaching the hospital, another 15 percent during treatment, and an additional 7 to 10 percent over the next few years (Manson et al., 1992).

Among other less extreme symptoms of cardiovascular disease are *arrhythmia,* or irregular heartbeat. When it persists, it can prevent the heart from pumping enough blood and result in faintness. It can also allow clots to form within the heart's chambers, which may break loose and travel to the brain. In some individuals, indigestion-like or crushing chest pains, called *angina pectoris,* reveal an oxygen-deprived heart.

Today, cardiovascular disease can be treated in many ways—through coronary bypass surgery, medication, pacemakers to regulate heart rhythm, and more. To relieve arterial blockage, Devin had *angioplasty,* a procedure in which a surgeon threaded a needle-thin catheter into his arteries and inflated a balloon at its tip, which flattened fatty deposits to allow blood to flow more freely. At the same time,

his doctor warned that unless Devin took other measures to reduce his risk, the arteries would clog again within a year. As the Caregiving Concerns table on the following page indicates, there is much we can do to prevent heart disease or slow its progress.

Of course, some risks, such as heredity, advanced age, and being male, cannot be changed. But cardiovascular disease is so disabling and deadly that we must be alert for it even where it is least expected. A special concern is accurate diagnosis in women. Since men account for over 70 percent of cases in middle adulthood, doctors often view a heart condition as a "male problem." Consequently, they tend to overlook women's symptoms, which tend to be milder, more often taking the form of angina than a full-blown heart attack (Roger et al., 2000). In one study, researchers had male and female actors present identical symptoms of angina to a sample of over 700 doctors. The doctors were far less likely to suspect heart problems in women—especially African-American women, who are at greater risk for heart disease than are Caucasian-American women. This combined gender–racial bias greatly reduced the extent to which African-American women were referred for a standard follow-up test (Schulman et al., 1999).

■ OSTEOPOROSIS. When age-related bone loss (described earlier in this chapter) is severe, a condition called **osteoporosis** is present. About 1 in every 4 postmenopausal women and the majority of people of both sexes over age 70 are affected (Donatelle & Davis, 2000; Larson, 1996). We associate osteoporosis with a slumped-over posture, a shuffling gait, and a "dowager's hump" in the upper back, but this extreme is rare. Because the bones gradually become more porous over many years, osteoporosis may not be evident until fractures—typically in the spine, hips, and wrist—occur or are discovered through X-rays.

A major factor related to osteoporosis is the decline in estrogen associated with menopause. Women lose about 50 percent of their bone mass over their lifetime, about half of which is lost in the 10 years following menopause (Sowers & La Pietra, 1995). Other contributors are a calcium-deficient diet; lack of physical activity (which reduces muscle and bone); a thin, small-framed body (which usually signifies a low peak bone mass); a family history of the disorder (heredity); cigarette smoking; and alcohol and caffeine intake (how these substances exert their effects is unknown). Much remains to be learned about osteoporosis, since some people with few of these risks still develop the disorder. Because of their higher bone density, African Americans are less likely than Caucasian and Asian Americans to be affected (Donatelle & Davis, 2000).

In the United States, osteoporosis affects over 25 million people and causes more than 1.5 million fractures annually. When major breaks (such as the hip) occur, 12 to 20 percent of patients die within a year (Center et al., 1999). To

Reducing the Risk of Heart Attack

INTERVENTION	RISK REDUCTION
Quit smoking.	→ 70% 5 years after quitting, up to 70 percent lower risk compared to current smokers
Reduce blood cholesterol level.	→ 60% 2 to 3 percent decline in risk for each 1 percent reduction in blood cholesterol. Reductions in cholesterol average 10 percent with diet therapy and can exceed 20 percent with drug therapy.
Treat high blood pressure.	→ 60% Combined diet and drug therapy can lower blood pressure substantially, leading to as much as a 60 percent risk reduction.
Maintain ideal weight.	→ 55% Up to 55 percent lower risk for people who maintain ideal body weight compared to those who are obese
Exercise regularly.	→ 45% 45 percent lower risk for people who maintain an active rather than sedentary lifestyle
Drink an occasional glass of wine or beer.[a]	→ 45% Up to 45 percent lower risk for people who consume small-to-moderate amounts of alcohol; believed to promote high-density lipoproteins, a form of "good cholesterol" that reduces "bad cholesterol"
Begin hormone replacement therapy (HRT) after menopause.	→ 44% 44 percent lower risk in users compared with nonusers (should be carefully considered; HRT increases risk of breast cancer)
Take low-dose aspirin.	→ 33% Up to 33 percent lower risk for people who take 162 mg (½ tablet) daily or every other day; reduces the likelihood of blood clots (should be medically recommended; long-term use can have serious side effects)
Reduce hostility and other forms of psychological stress.	Extent of risk reduction not yet known.

Source: Harpaz et al., 1996; Larson, 1996; Manson et al., 1992; Rimm, 1996.
[a]Recall from Chapter 13 that heavy alcohol use increases the risk of cardiovascular disease.

treat the disorder, doctors recommend a diet enriched with calcium and vitamin D (which promotes calcium absorption), weight-bearing exercise (walking rather than swimming), and hormone replacement therapy (for women not at high risk for breast and uterine cancer). Each of these interventions helps the bones regain mineral content (Southern Medical Association, 1999). Prevention early in life is an even better course of action. Increasing calcium and vitamin D intake and engaging in regular exercise in childhood, adolescence, and early adulthood reduce lifelong risk by maximizing peak bone density (Allen, 1999).

HOSTILITY AND ANGER

Each time Trisha's sister Dottie called, she seemed like a powder keg ready to explode. Dottie was critical of her boss at work and dissatisfied with the way Trisha, a lawyer, had handled the family's affairs after their father died. All conversations ended the same way—with Dottie making de-

meaning, hurtful remarks as her anger rose to the surface. "Any lawyer knows that, Trisha; how could you be so stupid! I should have called a *real* lawyer." "You and Devin are so stuck in your privileged lives that you can't think of anyone else. You don't know what work *is*."

Trisha listened as long as she could bear. Then she warned, "Dottie, if you continue, I'm going to hang up.... Dottie, I'm ending this right now!"

Off the telephone, Dottie's life was full of health-related complaints and problems. At age 53, she had high blood pressure, difficulty sleeping, and back pain. During the past 5 years, she had been hospitalized five times—twice for treatment of digestive problems, twice for an irregular heartbeat, and once for a benign tumor on her thyroid gland. Trisha often wondered whether Dottie's personal style was partly responsible for her physical condition.

That hostility and anger might have negative effects on health is a centuries-old idea. Several decades ago, researchers first tested it by identifying 35- to 59-year-old men who

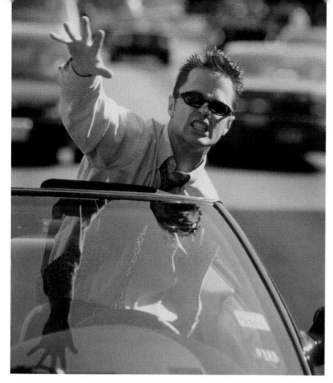

■ *Is this angry man headed for an early death? Recent evidence pinpoints hostility as the "toxic" ingredient in the Type A behavior pattern. Expressed hostility, especially in the form of frequent angry outbursts and rude, disagreeable behavior, leads to greater cardiovascular arousal, health complaints, and illness. (Photo courtesy: Bob Daemmrich)*

displayed the **Type A behavior pattern**—extreme competitiveness, ambition, impatience, hostility, angry outbursts, and a sense of time pressure. They found that within the next 8 years, Type A's were more than twice as likely as Type B's (people with a more relaxed disposition) to develop heart disease (Rosenman et al., 1975).

Later studies, however, often failed to confirm these results, perhaps because Type A is a mix of behaviors, only one or two of which affect health. Indeed, current evidence pinpoints hostility as the "toxic" ingredient of Type A, since isolating it from global Type A consistently predicts heart disease and other health problems as well (Adams, 1994; Dembroski et al., 1989; Helmers, Posluszny, & Krantz, 1994). And recent findings suggest that *expressed hostility* in particular—frequent angry outbursts; rude, disagreeable behavior; critical and condescending nonverbal cues during social interaction, including glares; expressions of contempt and disgust; and a hard, insistent voice—leads to greater cardiovascular arousal, health complaints, and illness (Chesney et al., 1997). Why is this so? As people get angry, heart rate, blood pressure, and stress hormones rise—physical reactions that escalate anger, until the body's response is extreme.

Of course, people who are repeatedly enraged are more likely to be dissatisfied with their lives and to engage in unhealthy behaviors. But hostility predicts health problems even when such factors as smoking, alcohol consumption,

overweight, general unhappiness, and negative life events are controlled. And since men score higher in hostility than do women (Dottie is an exception), emotional style may contribute to the sex differences in heart disease described earlier (Stoney & Engebretson, 1994).

To preserve her health, should Dottie bottle up her hostility instead of expressing it? Repeatedly suppressing anger—seething inside while looking calm on the outside—is also associated with an increase in heart disease, and it may pose other as yet unknown health risks (Denollet et al., 1996; Julkunen, 1996). As we will see shortly, a better alternative is to develop effective ways of handling stress and conflict.

ADAPTING TO THE PHYSICAL CHALLENGES OF MIDLIFE

Middle adulthood is often a productive period in which people attain their greatest accomplishments and life satisfactions. Nevertheless, it takes considerable stamina to cope with the full array of changes this phase can bring. Devin responded to his enlarged waistline and cardiovascular symptoms by leaving his desk twice a week to attend a low-impact aerobics class and reducing job-related stress through daily 10-minute meditation sessions. Aware of her sister Dottie's difficulties, Trisha resolved to handle her own hostile feelings more adaptively. And her generally optimistic outlook enabled her to cope successfully with the physical changes of midlife, the pressures of her legal career, and Devin's chronic illness.

STRESS MANAGEMENT

Turn back to Chapter 13, page 439, and review the negative consequences of psychological stress on the cardiovascular, immune, and gastrointestinal systems. As adults encounter problems at home and at work, daily hassles can add up to a serious stress load. Stress management is important at any age for a more satisfying life. In middle adulthood, it can limit the age-related rise in illness and, when disease strikes, reduce its severity.

The Caregiving Concerns table on the following page summarizes effective ways to reduce stress. Take a moment to list significant stressors in your life. Notice that many cannot be eliminated. But you can change the way you handle some and the way you view others. At work, Trisha focused on problems she could control—not her boss's irritability, but how to delegate routine tasks to her staff so she could spend more time on problems that required her knowledge and skills. When Dottie's phone calls came, Trisha learned to distinguish normal emotional reactions

Managing Stress

TECHNIQUE	DESCRIPTION
Reevaluate the situation.	Learn to tell the difference between normal reactions and those based on irrational beliefs.
Focus on events you can control.	Don't worry about things you cannot change or that may never happen; focus on strategies for handling events under your control.
View life as fluid.	Expect change and accept it as inevitable; then many unanticipated changes will have less emotional impact.
Consider alternatives.	Don't rush into action; think before you act.
Set reasonable goals for yourself.	Aim high, but be realistic in terms of your capacities, motivation, and the situation.
Exercise regularly.	A physically fit person can handle stress better, both physically and emotionally.
Master relaxation techniques.	Relaxation helps refocus energies and reduce the physical discomfort of stress. Classes and self-help books can teach these techniques.
Use constructive approaches to anger reduction.	In addition to the techniques listed above, seek a delay in responding ("Let me check into that and get back to you"); use mentally distracting behaviors (counting to 10 backward) and self-instruction (a covert "Stop!") to control anger arousal; then engage in calm, self-controlled problem solving ("I should call him rather than confront him personally").
Seek social support.	Friends, family members, co-workers, and organized support groups can offer information, assistance, and suggestions for how to handle stressful situations.

from unreasonable self-blame. She stopped interpreting Dottie's anger as a sign of her own incompetence and, instead, reminded herself of Dottie's difficult temperament and hard life. And greater life experience helped her accept change as inevitable. Consequently, she was better equipped to deal with the jolt of sudden change, such as Devin's hospitalization for treatment of heart disease.

As Trisha illustrates, people use two general strategies to cope with stress. In *problem-centered coping,* they appraise the situation as changeable, identify the difficulty, and decide what to do about it. If problem solving does not work, people engage in *emotion-centered coping,* which is internal, private, and aimed at controlling distress when there is little we can do about a situation (Lazarus & Lazarus, 1994). Adults who cope effectively use a mixture of problem- and emotion-centered techniques, depending on the situation. And their approach is deliberate, thoughtful, and respectful of both themselves and others. In contrast, ineffective coping is largely emotion centered and either impulsive or escapist (Lazarus, 1991, 1999).

Constructive approaches to anger reduction are a vital health intervention (refer again to the Caregiving Concerns table). In terms of problem-centered coping, teaching people to be assertive rather than hostile and to negotiate rather than explode interrupts the intense physical response

that intervenes between psychological stress and illness. If reasonable communication is not possible, it is best to delay responding by leaving a provocative situation, as Trisha did when she told Dottie that one more insult would cause her to hang up the phone (Deffenbacher, 1994).

Although communities often provide social supports aimed at helping people cope with the challenges of early adulthood and old age, they are less likely to do so for the middle adult years. Jewel had little knowledge of what to expect during the climacteric. "It would have helped to have a support group at church or the community center so I could have learned about menopause," she commented in a phone call to Trisha. Support services addressing other midlife concerns, such as adult learners returning to college and caregivers of elderly parents, would also reduce stress during this period.

EXERCISE

Regular exercise, as noted in Chapter 13, has a wide variety of physical and psychological benefits, one of which is equipping adults to handle stress more effectively. On the way to his first aerobics class, Devin wondered, "Can starting to exercise at age 50 counteract my many years of physical inactivity?" Devin's question is important, since 40 to

50 percent of adults are sedentary. Of those who begin an exercise program, 50 percent discontinue within the first 6 months. Among those who stay active, fewer than 20 percent exercise at levels that lead to health benefits (McAuley & Jacobson, 1991).

A person beginning to exercise in midlife must overcome initial barriers and obstacles along the way, such as lack of time and energy, inconvenience, and work conflicts. What helps people start exercising and stay with it? *Self-efficacy*—belief in one's ability to succeed—is just as vital in adopting, maintaining, and exerting oneself in an exercise regimen as it is in career progress (see Chapter 14). An important outcome of starting an exercise program is that it leads sedentary adults to gain in self-efficacy, which promotes physical activity all the more (McAuley, Bane, & Mihalko, 1995). Enhanced physical fitness, in turn, prompts middle-aged adults to feel better about their physical selves. Over time, their physical self-esteem—sense of body conditioning and attractiveness—rises (McAuley, Mihalko, & Bane, 1997).

The exercise format that works best varies with the beginning exerciser's characteristics. Normal-weight adults are more likely to stick with group classes than are overweight adults, who may strain to keep up with the pace of the class and feel embarrassed in front of others. Overweight people do better in a home-based program planned by a consultant, who individualizes the routine and to whom they report on a regular basis. In contrast, adults with highly stressful lives are more likely to persist in group classes than in a home-based program, which requires them to find time to exercise. Without a scheduled exercise period and the face-to-face support of others, stress can

■ *The exercise format most likely to lead to sustained physical activity in midlife varies with the beginning exerciser's characteristics. Normal-weight adults are more likely to stick with group exercise classes than are overweight adults. They find it easier to keep up with the pace of the class and are less likely to feel embarrassed about their physical condition. (Photo courtesy: Karen Halverson/Omni-Photo Communications)*

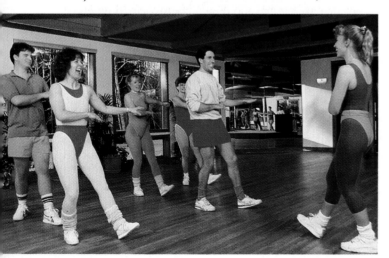

become a major barrier to behavior change (King et al., 1997). Yet when stressed people manage to sustain a home-based program, it substantially reduces stress, more so than the group format (King, Taylor, & Haskell, 1993). Perhaps succeeding on their own helps stressed adults gain better control over their lives.

■ AN OPTIMISTIC OUTLOOK

Our ability to handle the inevitable changes of life depends in part on personality strengths. What type of individual is likely to cope with stress adaptively, thereby reducing its impact on illness and mortality? Searching for answers to this question, researchers have studied a set of three personal qualities—control, commitment, and challenge—that, together, they call **hardiness** (Maddi & Kobasa, 1984; Maddi, 1999).

Trisha fit the pattern of a hardy individual. First, she regarded most experiences as *controllable*. "You can't stop all bad things from happening," she advised Jewel after hearing about her menopausal symptoms, "but you can try to do something about them." Second, Trisha displayed a *committed*, involved approach to daily activities, finding interest and meaning in almost all of them. Finally, she viewed change as a *challenge*—a normal part of life and a chance for personal growth.

Do these characteristics help people remain healthy in the face of stress? There is evidence that they do. Hardiness influences the extent to which people appraise stressful situations as manageable, interesting, and enjoyable. These positive appraisals, in turn, predict health-promoting behaviors, tendency to seek social support, and fewer physical symptoms (Florian, Mikulincer, & Taubman, 1995; Wiebe & Williams, 1992). Furthermore, high-hardy individuals are likely to use active, problem-centered coping strategies in situations they can control. In contrast, low-hardy people more often use emotion-centered and avoidant coping strategies—for example, saying, "I wish I could change how I feel," denying that the stressful event occurred, or eating and drinking to forget about it (Maddi & Hightower, 1999; Williams, Wiebe, & Smith, 1992).

In some studies, hardiness-related positive appraisals were associated with lower physiological arousal to stress—a major means by which hardiness is believed to protect against illness. The link between hardiness and reduced physiological reactivity does not always appear, perhaps because a hardy person's active coping sometimes leads to greater arousal. But over time, this increase may be offset by a calm that comes with effective stress management (Wiebe & Williams, 1992). In support of this idea, hardiness is associated with higher blood levels of cortisol, a hormone that regulates blood pressure and is involved in resistance to stress. And the optimistic component of hardiness predicts lower average blood pressure, measured over a three-day period (Räikkönen et al., 1999; Zorilla, DeRubeis, & Redei, 1995).

In this and previous chapters, we have seen that many factors act as stress-resistant resources—heredity, diet, exercise, social support, coping strategies, and more. Research on hardiness adds yet another ingredient: a generally optimistic outlook and zest for life.

GENDER AND AGING: A DOUBLE STANDARD

Earlier in this chapter, we mentioned that negative stereotypes of aging lead many middle-aged adults to fear what is happening to their bodies. These unfavorable stereotypes are more likely to be applied to women than to men. Despite the fact that many woman in midlife say they have "hit their stride"—feel assertive, confident, versatile, and capable of resolving life's problems—the broader cultural image of an older woman is one who is unattractive, incompetent, and passive (Sontag, 1979).

This double standard is evident when people are asked to evaluate older adults. Middle-aged women are rated as less attractive and as having more negative characteristics than are middle-aged men, a gender gap that widens with age. In some studies, aging men actually gain slightly in positive judgments of appearance, maturity, and power, whereas aging women show a sharp decline. Furthermore, women are often viewed as having reached middle and old age earlier (see Figure 15.2). And in some studies, the sex of the person doing the rating makes a difference: Compared with women, men judge an aging female much more harshly (Kogan & Mills, 1992).

These effects appear more often when people rate photos as opposed to verbal descriptions of men and women. Consequently, researchers believe that the ideal of a sexually attractive woman—smooth skin, good muscle tone, and lustrous hair—is at the heart of the double standard of aging. Recall from Chapter 14 that women prefer same-age or slightly older sexual partners, whereas men prefer younger partners. To explain why, ethological theory points to sex differences in reproductive capacity, whereas social learning theory emphasizes gender roles (see page 461). Does the end of a woman's ability to bear children contribute to negative judgments, especially by men? Some investigators think so (Kogan & Mills, 1992). Yet societal forces can exaggerate this view. For example, when media ads include middle-aged people, they are usually males—executives, fathers, and grandfathers who are images of competence and security. And the cosmetic industry offers many products designed to hide signs of aging for women, but far fewer for men (Harris, 1994).

At one time in our evolutionary history, a double standard of aging may have been adaptive. Today, as many couples limit childbearing and devote more time to career and leisure pursuits, it has become irrelevant. Role models of older women, whose lives are full of intimacy, hope, imagination, and accomplishment, can promote acceptance of

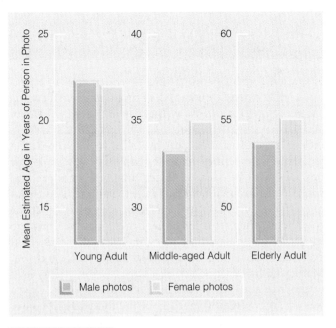

FIGURE 15.2

■ **Findings of a study in which adults were asked to classify photos as young, middle-aged, and elderly and estimate the age of the person in each.** In the middle-aged and elderly categories, age assignments were considerably younger for male than for female photos. Many people believe that middle and old age arrive earlier for women than for men. (From N. Kogan, 1979, "A Study of Categorization," *Journal of Gerontology, 34,* p. 363. Copyright 1979 by the Gerontological Society of America. Reprinted by permission.)

physical aging and a new vision of growing older—one that emphasizes gracefulness, fulfillment, and inner strength.

ASK YOURSELF . . .

■ *When Cara complained of chest pains to Dr. Furrow, he decided to "wait and see" before conducting additional tests. In contrast, Cara's husband, Bill, received a battery of tests aimed at detecting cardiovascular disease, even though he did not complain of symptoms. What might account for Dr. Furrow's different approach to Cara than to Bill?*

■ *Because his assistant misplaced some important files, Tom lost a client to a competitor. Tom felt his anger building to the breaking point. Explain why Tom's response is unhealthy, and suggest effective ways for dealing with it.*

■ *According to the lifespan perspective, development is multidimensional—affected by biological, psychological, and social forces. Explain how this is so for health at midlife, citing important influences.*

COGNITIVE DEVELOPMENT

In middle adulthood, the cognitive demands of every-day life extend to new and, at times, more challenging situations. Consider a typical day in the lives of Devin and Trisha. Recently appointed dean of faculty at a small college, Devin was at his desk by 7 A.M. In between strategic planning meetings, he reviewed files of applicants for new positions, worked on the coming year's budget, and spoke at an alumni luncheon. In the meantime, Trisha prepared for a civil trial, participated in jury selection at the courthouse, then returned to her firm to join the other top lawyers for a conference about management issues. That evening, Trisha and Devin advised their 20-year-old son, Mark, who had dropped by to discuss his uncertainty over whether to change his college major. By 7:30 P.M., Trisha was off to an evening meeting of the local school board. And Devin left for a biweekly gathering of an amateur quartet, in which he played the cello.

Recall from Chapter 13 that Schaie characterized middle adulthood as the *responsibility stage*—a time when expansion of responsibilities takes place on the job, in the community, and at home. To juggle diverse roles and perform effectively, Devin and Trisha called on a wide array of intellectual abilities, including accumulated knowledge, verbal fluency, memory, rapid analysis of information, reasoning, problem solving, and expertise in their areas of specialization. What changes in thinking take place in middle adulthood? How does vocational life—a major arena in which cognition is expressed—influence intellectual skills? And

what can we do to support the rising tide of adults who are returning to college in hopes of enhancing their knowledge and quality of life? Let's see what research has to say about these topics.

CHANGES IN MENTAL ABILITIES

At age 50, when he occasionally couldn't recall a name or had to pause in the midst of a lecture or speech to think about what to say next, Devin wondered to himself, "Are these the first signs of an aging mind?" Twenty years earlier, Devin took little notice of the very same mental events. His current questioning stems from a widely held stereotype—a view of the aging mind as on a path of inevitable decline. The majority of aging research has focused on deficits—because they are cause for concern—while neglecting cognitive stability and gains (Salthouse, 1991a).

In Chapter 13, we noted that some apparent decrements in cognitive aging result from weaknesses in the research itself. In cross-sectional studies, *cohort effects*, in which older participants are less educated and in poorer health, can create an inaccurate picture of both the timing and extent of decline. Also, the tests given may tap abilities less often used by older individuals, whose lives no longer require that they learn information for its own sake but, instead, build knowledge and skills that help them tackle current, real-world problems.

As we examine changes in thinking in middle adulthood, we will revisit the theme of diversity in development. Different aspects of cognitive functioning show different patterns of change. Although declines occur in some areas, most people display cognitive competence, especially in familiar contexts, and some attain outstanding accomplishment. Overall, the evidence supports an optimistic view of adult cognitive potential.

The changes we are about to consider bring into bold relief core assumptions of the lifespan perspective: development as *multidimensional*, or the combined result of biological, psychological, and social forces; development as *multidirectional*, or the joint expression of growth and decline, with the precise mix varying across abilities and individuals; and development as *plastic*, or open to change, depending on how a person's biological and environmental history combines with current life conditions. Before we begin, you may find it helpful to return to Chapter 1, pages 7–12, to review these important ideas.

■ *This police officer brings his 12-year-old daughter with him on "Take our daughters to work day." He exemplifies Schaie's responsibility stage—a time when responsibilities expand on the job, in the community, and at home. (Photo courtesy: Bob Daemmrich/The Image Works)*

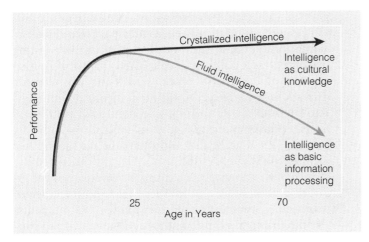

FIGURE 15.3

■ **Changes in crystallized and fluid intelligence over the lifespan.** Many cross-sectional studies reveal that crystallized intelligence increases into late adulthood, whereas fluid intelligence starts to decline in the late twenties or early thirties. Longitudinal research presents a somewhat more optimistic picture for fluid abilities. Nevertheless, it confirms that they decline earlier and more rapidly than crystallized abilities. (Adapted from Baltes, 1987.)

CRYSTALLIZED AND FLUID INTELLIGENCE

Many studies report consistent age-related trends in two broad-ranging mental abilities. Each includes a diverse array of specific intellectual factors tapped by intelligence tests.

The first of these broad abilities is called **crystallized intelligence**. It refers to skills that depend on accumulated knowledge and experience, good judgment, and mastery of social conventions. Together, these capacities represent abilities acquired because they are valued by the individual's culture. Devin made use of crystallized intelligence when he expressed himself articulately at the alumni luncheon and suggested effective ways to save money in budget planning. On intelligence tests, vocabulary, general information, verbal analogy, and logical reasoning items measure crystallized intelligence. (Turn back to Chapter 9, page 300, to see examples.)

In contrast, **fluid intelligence** depends more heavily on basic information-processing skills—the speed with which we can analyze information, the capacity of working memory, and the ability to detect relationships among stimuli. Fluid intelligence often works with crystallized intelligence to support effective reasoning, abstraction, and problem solving. But fluid intelligence is believed to be influenced more by conditions in the brain and learning unique to the individual, less by culture (Horn, 1982). Intelligence test items that reflect fluid abilities include number series, spatial visualization, figure matrices, and picture series. (Refer again to page 300 for examples.)

Research shows that crystallized intelligence increases steadily into late adulthood, whereas fluid intelligence starts to decline in the late twenties or early thirties (see Figure 15.3). These trends are found repeatedly in cross-sectional comparisons, even when education and health status of younger and older participants are equivalent (Horn & Donaldson, 1980; Horn, Donaldson, & Engstrom, 1981). The rise in crystallized abilities makes sense, since adults are constantly adding to their knowledge and skills at work, at

home, and in leisure activities. In addition, many crystallized skills are practiced almost daily. But perhaps you are questioning, as others have, the early decline in fluid intelligence on the basis of longitudinal evidence you read about in Chapter 13. Now let's take a closer look.

Recall the Seattle Longitudinal Study, which revealed modest gains in five mental abilities from early to middle adulthood that were sustained until the fifties and early sixties, after which performance gradually declined. Figure 15.4 shows these trends. The five abilities—verbal ability,

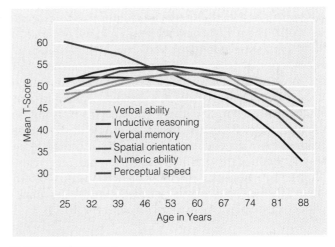

FIGURE 15.4

■ **Longitudinal trends in six mental abilities.** In five abilities, modest gains were sustained until the fifties and early sixties, followed by gradual declines. The sixth ability—perceptual speed—dropped steadily from the twenties to the late eighties. Late in life, fluid factors (spatial orientation, perceptual speed, and numeric ability) showed greater decrements than did crystallized factors (verbal ability, inductive reasoning, and verbal memory). (From K. W. Schaie, 1994, "The Course of Adult Intellectual Development," *American Psychologist, 49*, p. 308. Copyright © 1994 by the American Psychological Association. Reprinted by permission.)

inductive reasoning, verbal memory, spatial orientation, and numeric ability—tap both crystallized and fluid skills. Their paths of change show that midlife is the period of peak performance on some of the most complex mental abilities. Intellectually, middle-aged adults are "in their prime," not "over the hill" as aging stereotypes would have us believe (Willis & Schaie, 1999).

But a sixth ability is also shown in Figure 15.4: perceptual speed, a fluid skill in which participants must, for example, identify during a time limit which of five shapes is identical to a model or whether pairs of multidigit numbers are the same or different (Schaie, 1994, 1996, 1998). Perceptual speed dropped steadily from the twenties to the late eighties, a finding that fits with a wealth of research indicating that cognitive processing slows as people get older. And notice in Figure 15.4 how, late in life, the fluid factors (spatial orientation, numeric ability, and perceptual speed) show greater decrements than the crystallized factors (verbal ability, inductive reasoning, and verbal memory).

Some theorists believe that a general slowing of central nervous system functioning underlies nearly all age-related declines in cognitive performance (Salthouse, 1993, 1996). Many researchers have tested this idea and found at least partial support. They have also discovered other important changes in information processing, some of which may be triggered by the decline in speed (Kausler, 1994).

But before we turn to this evidence, let's clarify why longitudinal research reveals gains followed by stability in a variety of crystallized and fluid abilities during middle adulthood, despite declines in basic information-processing skills. There are several reasons. First, the decrease in basic processing is modest until late in life—not great enough to affect many well-practiced performances. For the most part, it shows up only on complex, unfamiliar tasks. Second, as we will see shortly, adults often find ways to compensate for cognitive weaknesses by drawing on their cognitive strengths. Finally, as people discover they are no longer as good as they once were at certain tasks, they accommodate, shifting to activities that depend less on cognitive efficiency and more on accumulated knowledge. The basketball player becomes a coach, the quick-witted salesperson a manager (Salthouse, 1991b).

INDIVIDUAL AND GROUP DIFFERENCES

Hidden beneath the age trends just described are large individual differences. Some people, because of disease or very unfavorable environments, begin to decline intellectually in their forties. A few maintain full functioning at a very advanced age (Schaie, 1989).

Using intellectual skills seems to affect the degree to which they are retained. In the Seattle Longitudinal Study, declines were delayed for people with above-average education, highly complex occupations, and stimulating leisure

pursuits that included reading, traveling, attending cultural events, and participating in clubs and professional organizations. People with flexible personalities, lasting marriages (especially to a cognitively high-functioning partner), and absence of cardiovascular and other chronic diseases were also likely to maintain mental abilities well into late adulthood. And being economically well off was linked to favorable cognitive development, undoubtedly because SES is associated with many of the factors just mentioned (Schaie, 1996).

Gender differences also emerged. Women showed an earlier decline in perceptual speed than did men, beginning in their twenties rather than thirties. But on mental abilities that increase into middle adulthood, women continued to gain over a longer period than did men, reaching peak performance in their early 60s rather than early 50s (Schaie, 1996). These findings mirror average health differences between the sexes. And they defy the double standard, discussed earlier in this chapter, that women are less competent and reach old age earlier than men.

Furthermore, cohort effects were evident. For example, when the baby boom generation, currently middle-aged, was compared with the previous generation at the same age, the baby boom cohort performed substantially better on verbal memory, inductive reasoning, and spatial orientation (Willis & Schaie, 1999). These generational gains reflect advances in education, technology, environmental stimulation, and health care. They are expected to continue in the twenty-first century, as today's children also attain higher mental test scores than did children of past generations (Flynn, 1996, 1999). Interestingly, numeric ability declined in later-born cohorts in the Seattle Longitudinal Study. The recent generation's reliance on calculators and computers seems to have compromised its calculation skills.

Finally, adults who maintained higher levels of perceptual speed tended to be advantaged on other mental abilities. As we turn now to information processing in midlife, we will see why a decrement in speed of processing affects other aspects of cognitive functioning.

INFORMATION PROCESSING

Information-processing researchers interested in adult development usually use the model of the mental system introduced in Chapter 5 (see page 156) to guide their exploration of different aspects of thinking. As processing speed slows, certain aspects of attention and memory decline. Yet midlife is also a time of great expansion in cognitive competence as adults apply their vast knowledge and life experience to problem solving in the everyday world.

SPEED OF PROCESSING

One day, Devin looked over the shoulder of his 20-year-old son, Mark, who was playing a computer game. Mark responded to multiple cues on the screen in rapid-fire fashion. "Let me try it," suggested Devin, who practiced over several days but remained well behind Mark in performance. And on a family holiday in Australia, Mark adjusted quickly to driving on the left side of the road. Trisha and Devin took longer. After several days, they still felt confused at intersections, where they had to respond rapidly to lights, cross traffic, and oncoming vehicles.

These real-life experiences fit with laboratory findings. On simple reaction time tasks (pushing a button in response to a light) and complex reaction time tasks (pushing a left-hand button to a blue light, a right-hand button to a yellow light), response time increases steadily from the early twenties into the nineties. Older adults are increasingly disadvantaged as situations requiring rapid responding become more complex. The decline is small, under 1 second in most studies, but it is nevertheless of practical significance. For unknown reasons, reaction time slows at a faster rate for women than for men (Fozard et al., 1994; Salthouse, 1985).

What causes this age-related slowing of cognitive processing? Although researchers agree that changes in the brain are probably responsible, they disagree on the precise explanation. According to the **neural network view**, as neurons in the brain die, breaks in neural networks occur. The brain adapts by forming bypasses—new synaptic connections that go around the breaks but are less efficient (Cerella, 1990). A second hypothesis, the **information-loss view**, suggests that older adults differ from younger adults in the rate at which information is lost as it moves through the system. Imagine making a photocopy and using it to make another copy. Each time we do this, the copy becomes less clear. Similarly, with each step of thinking, information degrades. The older the adult, the more exaggerated this effect. As a result, the whole system must slow down to inspect and interpret the information. Since complex tasks have more processing steps, they are more affected by information loss (Myerson et al., 1990).

Yet many older adults perform complex, familiar tasks with considerable efficiency. Devin, for example, played a Mozart quartet on his cello with great speed and dexterity, keeping up with three other players who were 10 years his junior. How did he manage? Compared with the other players, he more often looked ahead in the score. This compensatory approach permitted him to prepare a response in advance, thereby minimizing the importance of speed. In one study, researchers asked 19- to 72-year-olds to do transcription typing and also tested their reaction time. Although reaction time slowed with age, speed of typing did not change. Like Devin, older individuals looked further ahead in the transcription, anticipating their next keystrokes (Salthouse, 1984).

■ *How do older adults adapt to age-related slowing of cognitive processing? They make up for declines in processing speed through practice, experience, and a compensatory approach that permits them to prepare responses in advance. This older musician's many years of playing and familiarity with complex music help him perform swiftly and fluidly. He adapts readily to the tunes his granddaughter produces on the recorder. (Photo courtesy: George Shelley/The Stock Market)*

Practice and experience can also compensate for declines in processing speed. Devin's many years of playing the cello and his familiarity with the Mozart quartet undoubtedly supported his ability to play swiftly and fluidly.

ATTENTION

Studies of attention focus on how much information adults can take into their mental systems at once; the extent to which they can attend selectively, ignoring irrelevant information; and the ease with which they can adapt their attention, switching from one task to another as the situation demands. When Dottie telephoned, Trisha sometimes tried to prepare dinner or continue working on a legal brief while talking on the phone. With age, she found it harder to engage in two activities simultaneously. Consistent with Trisha's experience, laboratory research reveals that sustaining two complex tasks at once becomes more challenging with age (Kausler, 1991; Madden & Plude, 1993). An age-related decrement also occurs in the ability to attend to relevant information and to switch back and forth between mental operations, such as judging one of a pair of numbers as "odd or even" on some trials and as "more or less" on others (Hartley & McKenzie, 1991; Salthouse et al., 1998).

These declines in attention might be due to the slowdown in information processing described earlier, which limits the amount of information a person can attend to at once (Plude & Hoyer, 1985). Reduced speed of processing may also contribute to a related finding: a decrement with age in the ability to combine many pieces of visual information into a meaningful pattern. When the mind inspects stimuli slowly, they are more likely to remain disconnected. This problem, in turn, can intensify attentional difficulties (Plude & Doussard-Roosevelt, 1989). Without a coherent pattern to serve as a guide, *cognitive inhibition*—resisting interference from irrelevant information—is harder (Hasher, Zacks, & May, 1999). Consequently, at times older adults appear distractible, inappropriately captured by a thought or feature of the environment and unable to turn back to the task at hand.

But once again, adults can compensate for these changes. People highly experienced in attending to critical information and performing several tasks at once, such as air traffic controllers and pilots, know exactly what to look for. As a result, they show smaller age-related attentional declines (Morrow et al., 1994; Tsang & Shaner, 1998). Furthermore, practice can improve the ability to divide attention between two tasks, selectively focus on relevant information, and switch back and forth between mental operations. When older adults receive training in these skills, their performance improves as much as that of younger adults, although training does not close the gap between age groups (Kausler, 1994; Kramer, Hahn, & Gopher, 1998).

MEMORY

Memory is crucially important for all aspects of information processing—an important reason that we place great value on a good memory in middle and late adulthood. From the twenties into the sixties, the amount of information people can retain in working memory diminishes. Whether given lists of words or digits or meaningful prose passages to learn, middle-aged and older adults recall less than young adults, although memory for prose suffers less than memory for list items (Hultsch et al., 1998; Salthouse & Skovronek, 1992).

This change is largely due to a decline in use of memory strategies on these tasks. Older individuals rehearse less than do younger individuals—a difference believed to be due to a slower rate of thinking. Older people cannot repeat new information to themselves as quickly as younger people (Salthouse & Babcock, 1991).

Memory strategies of organization and elaboration are also applied less often and less effectively with age. (See Chapter 9, page 295, if you need to review these strategies.)

Both require people to link incoming information with already stored information. One reason older adults are less likely to use organization and elaboration is that they find it harder to retrieve information from long-term memory that would help them recall. For example, given a list of words containing *parrot* and *blue jay*, they don't immediately access the category "bird," even though they know it well (Hultsch et al., 1998). Why does this happen? Greater difficulty keeping attention on relevant as opposed to irrelevant information seems to be involved. As irrelevant stimuli take up space in working memory, less is available for the memory task at hand (Hartman & Hasher, 1991; Salthouse & Meinz, 1995).

But we must keep in mind that the memory tasks given by researchers require strategies that many adults seldom use and may not be motivated to use, since most are not in school (see Chapter 9, page 296). When a word list has a strong category-based structure, older adults organize as well as younger adults do (Small et al., 1999). And when instructed to organize or elaborate, middle-aged and older people willingly do so, and their performance improves. Furthermore, tasks can be designed to compensate for age-related declines in working memory. For example, we can slow the pace at which information is presented so adults have enough time to process it or cue the link between new and previously stored information ("To learn these words, try thinking of the category 'bird'") (Hay & Jacoby, 1999; Kausler, 1994).

Furthermore, when we consider the variety of memory skills we call on in daily life, the decrements just described are limited in scope. General *factual knowledge* (such as historical events), *procedural knowledge* (such as how to drive a car, ride a bike, or solve a math problem), and knowledge related to one's occupation either remain unchanged or increase into midlife (Baltes, Dittmann-Kohli, & Dixon, 1984). Middle-aged people who have trouble recalling something often draw on decades of accumulated *metacognitive knowledge* about how to maximize performance—reviewing major points before an important presentation, organizing notes and files so information can be found quickly, and parking the car in the same area of the parking lot each day.

In sum, age changes in memory vary widely across tasks and individuals as people use their cognitive capacities to meet the requirements of their everyday worlds. This may remind you of Sternberg's *triarchic theory of intelligence*, described in Chapter 9—in particular, his *contextual subtheory* (see page 301). It emphasizes that intelligent people adapt their information-processing skills to fit with their personal desires and the demands of their environments. To understand memory development (and other aspects of cognition) in adulthood, we must view it in context. As we turn to problem solving, expertise, and creativity, we will see this theme again.

PRACTICAL PROBLEM SOLVING AND EXPERTISE

One evening, as Devin and Trisha sat in the balcony of the Chicago Opera House awaiting curtain time, a small figure appeared on the stage to announce that 67-year-old Ardis Krainik, general director and "life force" of the opera company, had died. A hush fell over the theater. Soon, members of the audience turned to one another, wanting to know more about the woman who had made the opera company into one of the world's greatest.

Starting as a chorus singer and clerk typist, Ardis rose rapidly through the ranks, becoming assistant to the director and developing a reputation for tireless work and unmatched organizational skill. When the opera company fell deeply into debt, the board of directors turned to Ardis to save it from disaster. As newly appointed general director, she erased the deficit within a year and began to restore the company's sagging reputation. She charmed executives who knew nothing about opera into making big contributions, attracted world-class singers, and filled the house to 98 percent capacity. On her office wall hung a sign she received as a gift after 1 year as head of the company. It read, "Wonder Woman" (Rhein, 1997).

As Ardis's story illustrates, middle-aged adults have special opportunities to display continued cognitive growth in the realm of **practical problem solving,** which requires people to size up real-world situations and analyze how best to achieve goals that have a high degree of uncertainty.

■ *As its general director, Ardis Krainik (right) saved the Lyric Opera of Chicago from disaster, erasing the opera's deficit and restoring its sagging reputation. Her creative achievements depended on her ability to reconcile the company's subjective, artistic needs with its objective, financial needs. Drawing on her life experience, she dealt with a complex practical problem in a unique way. (She is shown here, during the 1980s, with Patricia Ryan of Lyric Opera's Executive Committee and world-renowned tenor Plácido Domingo.) (Photo courtesy: Lyric Opera of Chicago Archives)*

Gains in *expertise*—an extensive, highly organized, and integrated knowledge base that can be used to support a high level of performance—help us understand why practical problem solving takes a leap forward.

The development of expertise is under way in early adulthood. But it reaches its height in midlife, leading to highly efficient and effective approaches to solving problems that are organized around abstract principles and intuitive judgments. Saturated with experience, the expert intuitively feels when an approach to a problem will work and when it will not. This rapid, implicit application of knowledge is the result of years of learning and experience. It is unlikely to show up on laboratory tasks that assess basic processing but do not call on this knowledge (Smith & Baltes, 1992; Wagner & Sternberg, 1985).

Expertise is not just the province of the highly educated and those who rise to the top of administrative ladders. It can emerge in any field of endeavor. In a study of food service workers, researchers identified the diverse ingredients of expert performance in terms of physical skills (strength and dexterity), technical knowledge (of menu items, ordering, and food presentation); organizational skills (a sense of priority, anticipating customer needs); and social skills (confident presentation; pleasant, polished manner). Next, 20- to 60-year-olds with fewer than 2 to more than 10 years of experience were evaluated on these qualities. Although physical strength and dexterity declined with age, job knowledge and behavior increased. Among younger and older adults with similar years of experience, middle-aged employees performed more competently, serving customers in an especially adept, attentive way (Perlmutter, Kaplan, & Nyquist, 1990).

Age-related advantages in problem solving are also evident in leisure activities and everyday dilemmas. A study of middle-aged men who regularly attended harness races and were expert in predicting winners revealed that they used a highly complex reasoning process in which they integrated a large number of variables, such as a horse's speed, its lifetime earnings, the driver's ability, and track size. This permitted the men to compare eight or more horses at once. The ability to engage in high-level, integrative thinking in the harness-racing context was unrelated to IQ (Ceci, 1990).

Similarly, research on everyday problem solving reveals that it peaks between 40 and 59 years of age and may be sustained even longer (Denney, 1990; Denney & Pearce, 1989). Consider the following problem:

> What would you do if you had a landlord who refused to make some expensive repairs you want done because he or she thinks they are too costly?
>
> (a) Try to make the repairs yourself.
>
> (b) Try to understand your landlord's view and decide whether they are necessary repairs.

(c) Try to get someone to settle the dispute between you and your landlord.

(d) Accept the situation and don't dwell on it. (Cornelius & Caspi, 1987, p. 146)

On tasks like these, middle-aged and older adults select better strategies (as rated by independent judges) than do young adults. In the preceding example, the preferred choice is (b), a problem-centered approach that involves seeking information and using it to guide action (Cornelius & Caspi, 1987). As response (b) illustrates, from middle age on adults place greater emphasis on thinking through a practical problem—trying to understand it better, to solve it through logical analysis, and to reinterpret it from a different perspective. Perhaps for this reason, middle-aged and older adults are more likely to use a broader range of problem-solving strategies and to combine them to suit the situation (Blanchard-Fields, Chen, & Norris, 1997).

CREATIVITY

Like problem solving, creativity may change with advancing age. Some researchers believe it shifts from a focus on generating unusual products (divergent thinking) to an emphasis on integrating experience and knowledge into unique ways of thinking and acting (Abra, 1989; Sasser-Coen, 1993). A study of well-known visual artists age 60 and older revealed that they viewed the quality of their work as having improved steadily during their forties and fifties. The most common explanation they gave concerned new knowledge and skills: "I increased my involvement with art, so I became more skillful and knowledgeable." "I continued to study and learn—from life and nature." Other frequently mentioned reasons were more time to work after children had been reared and greater self-acceptance: "After many years of trying to do salable, 'relevant,' or so-called important work, I feel free to be myself and not concern myself about how others might judge me" (Lindauer, Orwoll, & Kelley, 1997, pp. 136–137).

Creativity in middle adulthood may also reflect a transition from a largely egocentric concern with self-expression to more altruistic goals. As the middle-aged person overcomes the illusion of youth that "life can last forever," the desire to contribute to humanity and enrich the lives of others increases (Dacey, 1989). This change may be partly responsible for the midlife decline in overall creative output described in Chapter 13. In reality, however, creativity in emerges in new forms.

INFORMATION PROCESSING IN CONTEXT

In sum, cognitive gains in midlife are especially likely in areas involving experience-based buildup and transforma-

tion of knowledge and skills. Consider the evidence we have just reviewed, and you will see that processing speed varies with the situation. When given a challenging real-world problem related to his or her expertise, the middle-aged adult is likely to win out not just in efficiency, but in quality and originality of thinking. And as the Lifespan Vista box on the following page illustrates, when researchers' laboratory tasks are relevant to the real-life endeavors of intelligent, cognitively active adults, older people respond as quickly and competently as their younger counterparts do!

By midlife, people's past and current experiences vary enormously—more so than in previous decades. Therefore, thinking in middle adulthood is characterized by an increase in specialization; it branches out in a multitude of directions. Yet for middle-aged adults to realize their cognitive potential, they must have opportunities for continued growth. Let's see how vocational and educational environments can support cognition in middle adulthood.

ASK YOURSELF . . .

In what aspects of cognition did Devin decline, and in what aspects did he gain? How do changes in Devin's thinking reflect assumptions of the lifespan perspective?

■ *Asked about hiring older adults as waiters, one restaurant manager replied, "I cannot hire enough older workers . . . they are my best employees. . . . I do not even know what you mean by slowness. They are the fastest ones on the floor" (Perlmutter, Kaplan, & Nyquist, 1990, p. 189). Why does this manager find older employees desirable, despite the age-related decline in speed of processing?*

VOCATIONAL LIFE AND COGNITIVE DEVELOPMENT

Vocational settings are vital contexts for encouraging people to maintain, restore, and apply old skills and to learn new ones. Yet they vary in the extent to which they are cognitively stimulating and promote autonomy. At times, work environments carry unfavorable stereotypes about age-related problem-solving and decision-making skills that may lead older employees to be assigned less challenging work or encouraged to retire before they would otherwise do so.

In Chapter 13, we indicated that intellectual and personality characteristics affect the occupations people select. Devin, for example, chose college teaching and administration because he enjoyed reading and writing, framing new ideas, and helping others learn. Once a person is immersed

A LIFESPAN VISTA

HOW GOOD IS YOUR PROFESSOR'S MEMORY? THE TASK MAKES A DIFFERENCE

Compare the performance of a typical-age college student and a professor on reaction time tasks and memory for unrelated information. Although the professor has many more years of education, the college student will probably do better. But when a task requires general or metacognitive knowledge used often in academic life, the professor is likely to display considerable competence, even at a mature age.

Research on professors' cognitive processing is especially revealing, since factors that ordinarily make age-related change difficult to interpret are controlled. For example, professors of different ages share similar cultural experiences, in that their years of education, work environments, and SES are alike. And as long as they are still employed, there is a good chance that all have been mentally active throughout their lives. These similarities reduce cohort effects.

In a recent study, three groups of university professors at the University of California, Berkeley—young (age 30 to 44), middle-aged (age 45 to 59), and senior (age 60 to 71)

—were administered a battery of speed-of-processing and memory tasks. All had 21 to 22 years of education and were actively engaged in academic work. Control groups of very young adults (college students age 18 to 23) and older adults (age 60 to 71) with 14 to 16 years of education were also tested (Shimamura et al., 1995).

How did the professors and the controls perform? When asked to push a button as rapidly as possible after a signal, both showed the typical age-related decline in speed of processing. Both groups also did less well with age on tasks requiring them to remember arbitrary associations. For example, in one task, they were given six pairs of faces, each consisting of a female and a male. Then they were shown each female face and asked to select its male partner from a display.

Older professors' performance on a task designed to tax the capacity of working memory, however, deviated from the researchers' expectations of age-related intellectual decrements. An array of 16 visual patterns was presented sixteen times on a computer screen, randomly arranged each time. On each trial, the adult had to point to a different pattern, monitoring previous responses so none would be repeated (see Figure 15.5). Then, a second block of six-

teen trials was presented, adding the challenge of considering responses not just within a block but also between blocks. In previous investigations and among controls in this study, older individuals typically did much worse on the second than on the first block of trials. The reason is believed to be their greater difficulty ignoring irrelevant information. Yet senior professors did not show this increasing error rate from one block of trials to the next!

Finally, when asked to recall meaningful prose passages, once again the professors showed no decline with age. In contrast, the recall of controls dropped off in a predictable pattern.

What are the implications of these results? The similar declines among professors and controls in cognitive speed and memory for unrelated information suggest that these trends are strongly affected by biological aging. But what about the two performances in which professors showed no age decrements? Both require metacognitive skills of planning, organization, and manipulating information in memory. And the prose recall task depends on integrating new knowledge with a large fund of existing knowledge. Perhaps years of applying these strategies in work life counteracted the effects of aging.

FIGURE 15.5

■ **Array of visual patterns in a task designed to tax the capacity of working memory.** On each trial, the adult had to point to a different pattern while monitoring previous responses so none would be repeated. The task was presented twice, yielding two blocks of sixteen trials. Senior professors did not show the expected age-related increase in errors from the first to the second block of trials, a pattern of change strongly evident in the performance of older controls. (From A. P. Shimamura, J. M. Berry, J. A. Mangels, C. L. Rusting, & P. J. Jurica, 1995, "Memory and Cognitive Abilities in University Professors: Evidence for Successful Aging." *Psychological Science, 6,* p. 272. Copyright © 1995 by the American Psychological Society. Reprinted by permission.)

in a job, it influences cognition. In a study of over 600 American men representing a wide range of occupations, researchers asked participants about the task complexity and self-direction of their jobs. During this interview, they also assessed cognitive flexibility, based on logical reasoning, seeing both sides of an issue, and making judgments independently. A decade later, the job and cognitive variables were remeasured, permitting a look at their effects on each other. As expected, findings indicated that cognitively flexible men sought work that offered challenge and autonomy. But complex work also led to gains in cognitive flexibility! In other words, the relation between vocational life and cognition was reciprocal (Kohn & Schooler, 1978).

These same findings emerged in large-scale studies carried out in Japan and Poland—cultures quite different from the United States (Kohn et al., 1990; Kohn & Slomczynski, 1990). In each nation, having a stimulating, nonroutine job helped explain the relationship between SES and flexible, abstract thinking. Furthermore, learning on the job generalizes to other realms of life. People who do intellectually demanding work seek out stimulating leisure pursuits (Miller & Kohn, 1983). And they come to value self-direction, both for themselves and for their children. Consequently, they are likely to pass their cognitive preferences to the next generation.

Is the impact of a challenging job on cognitive growth greater for young adults, who are in the early phase of vocational development? Research shows that it is not. People in their fifties and early sixties gain as much as do those in their twenties and thirties. The relationship also holds for people of different generations and, therefore, widely varying life experiences (Avolio & Sosik, 1999; Miller, Slomczynski, & Kohn, 1985). Once again, we are reminded of the plasticity of development. Cognitive flexibility is responsive to vocational experience well into middle adulthood, and perhaps beyond. This means that more jobs should be designed to promote intellectual stimulation and challenge—factors linked to higher cognitive functioning later in the lifespan.

ADULT LEARNERS: BECOMING A STUDENT IN MIDLIFE

Adults are returning to undergraduate and graduate study in large numbers. Over the past quarter century, students over age 25 (the definition of adult students) in American colleges and universities increased from 28 to 44 percent (U.S. Department of Education, 1999a). Their reasons for going back to school are diverse—a career change, a better income, self-enrichment,

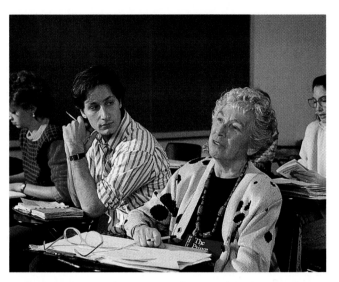

■ *This mature woman's return to college may have been sparked by a life transition, such as divorce, widowhood, or job layoff. At first, adult learners often question their ability to be successful at academic work. When family members, friends, and educational institutions are supportive, returning students reap great personal benefits and do well academically. (Yvonne Henesy/ Gamma Liaison)*

a sense of personal achievement, or simply a degree. Life transitions often trigger a return to formal education, as was the case for Devin and Trisha's friend Anya, who entered a nursing program after her last child left home. A divorce, widowhood, job layoff, or a youngest child going to school for the first time are other transitions that commonly precede reentry (Bradburn, Moen, & Dempster-McClain, 1995).

CHARACTERISTICS OF RETURNING STUDENTS

Women are the majority of adult learners—about 58 percent. A recent large rise in students over age 35 is due mostly to women, who make up nearly 65 percent of this age group. As Anya's fear of not being able to handle classwork suggests (see page 492), first-year reentry women report feeling more self-conscious, inadequate, and scared to talk in class than do either returning men or traditional-age students (under age 25). Their anxiety is partly due to not having practiced academic learning for many years. It is also promoted by stereotypes of aging, since returning women are often convinced that traditional-age students are smarter (Wilke & Thompson, 1993).

Role demands outside the educational setting—from spouses, children, other family members, friends, and employers—pull many returning women in several, often conflicting directions. Those reporting high psychological stress typically have career rather than enrichment goals, young children, limited financial resources, and nonsupportive husbands (Novak & Thacker, 1991; Padula & Miller, 1999). As a classmate told Anya one day, "I tried keeping the book open and reading, cooking, and talking to the kids. It didn't work. They felt I was ignoring them." Because of multiple demands on their time, mature-age women tend to take fewer credits, experience more interruptions in their academic programs, and progress at a slower rate than do mature-age men (Robertson, 1991).

SUPPORTING RETURNING STUDENTS

As these findings suggest, social supports for returning students can make the difference between continuing in school and dropping out. Adult students need family members and friends who encourage their efforts and help them find time for uninterrupted study. Anya's classmate explained, "My doubts subsided when my husband saw me with a book in one hand and a pile of dirty clothes in the other and volunteered, 'I can cook dinner and do the laundry. You take your books and do what you need to do.'" Institutional services for returning students are also essential. Personal relationships with faculty; peer networks enabling adults to get to know one another; conveniently scheduled evening, Saturday, and off-campus classes; and financial aid for part-time students (many of whom are returning adults) increase the chances of academic success (Novak & Thacker, 1991).

The Caregiving Concerns table below suggests a variety of ways to facilitate adult reentry to college. Low-income and ethnic minority students need special assistance. Without it, the gap between the educationally advantaged and disadvantaged can widen in adulthood. Some programs offer field trips to colleges, testing to identify academic strengths and weaknesses, and opportunities to speak with financial aid officers, academic advisers, and students before enrollment. After entry, academic tutoring and sessions in confidence building and assertiveness are provided (Safman, 1988).

Ethnic minority adults may need help adjusting to styles of learning that are at odds with their cultural background. One Chinese returning student noted that she found criticizing ideas and arguing with her professors very difficult, since Chinese students are taught to respect, not disagree with, their teachers.

Although nontraditional students rarely require assistance in settling on career goals, they report a strong desire for help in choosing the most appropriate courses and in exploring jobs related to their talents (Luzzo, 1999). Academic advising and professional internship opportunities responsive to their needs are vital for their vocational development.

BENEFITS OF RETURNING TO COLLEGE

When support systems are in place, most returning students reap great personal benefits and do well academically.

CAREGIVING CONCERNS

Facilitating Adult Reentry to College

SOURCE OF SUPPORT	DESCRIPTION
Partner and children	Value and encourage educational efforts. Assist with household tasks to permit time for uninterrupted study.
Extended family and friends	Value and encourage educational efforts.
Educational institution	Provide orientation programs and literature that inform adult students about services and social supports. Provide counseling and intervention addressing academic weaknesses, self-doubts about success, and matching courses to career goals. Facilitate peer networks through regular meetings or phone contact. Promote personal relationships with faculty. Encourage active engagement and discussion in classes and integration of course content with real-life experiences. Offer evening, Saturday, and off-campus classes. Provide financial aid for part-time students. Initiate campaigns to recruit returning students, including low-income and ethnic minority groups. Assist students with young children in finding child care arrangements, and provide on-campus child care.
Workplace	Value and encourage educational efforts. Accommodate work time to class schedules.

They especially value new personal relationships, sharing opinions and experiences, and relating subject matter to their own lives. An improved ability to integrate knowledge in midlife leads to a changed appreciation of classroom experiences and assignments, as these comments reveal:

> [As a traditional-age student,] I felt disaffiliated with most of my courses. Now courses are relevant. I'm taking them because I want to take them. I can see how everything relates. Before, they were disconnected.

> Most things used to be external to me.... It makes learning a lot more interesting and memorable when you can bring your experiences into it. It makes you want to learn and want to keep learning more and more. (Wilke & Thompson, 1993, p. 86)

 Another benefit of large numbers of adult students in college classes is intergenerational contact and communication. As young students see firsthand the capacities and talents of older individuals, unfavorable stereotypes of aging decline.

In previous chapters, we underscored the power of education to shape the life course. Returning to school continues to alter life paths in middle adulthood. For Anya, it led to a position as a parish nurse with creative opportunities to inform and counsel members of a large congregation about health concerns. Higher education granted Anya new options, paid labor force rewards, and a higher sense of self-esteem as she reevaluated her own competencies (Redding & Dowling, 1992). At times, revised values and greater self-reliance sparked by education prompt changes in other spheres of life, such as a divorce or a new intimate partnership (Esterberg, Moen, & Dempster-McClain, 1994). In this way, reentering school is both a result and a cause of life change, leading middle-aged adults to reshape the course of their development.

 ASK YOURSELF . . .

Consider the famous saying "You can't teach an old dog new tricks." Evaluate its accuracy in terms of evidence on the impact of vocational and educational experiences on cognitive development at midlife.

■ *Why do most high-level government and corporate positions go to middle-aged and older adults rather than to young adults? What cognitive capacities enable mature adults to perform well at these jobs?*

■ *Marcella completed only one year of college, in her twenties. Now, at age 42, she has returned to earn a degree. Plan a set of experiences for the month before Marcella enrolls and for her first semester that will increase her chances of success.*

SUMMARY

PHYSICAL DEVELOPMENT

PHYSICAL CHANGES

Describe the physical changes of middle adulthood, paying special attention to vision, hearing, the skin, muscle–fat makeup, and the skeleton.

■ The gradual physical changes begun in early adulthood continue in midlife, contributing to a revised physical self-image, which often emphasizes fewer hoped-for gains and more feared declines.

■ Vision is affected by **presbyopia,** or loss of the accommodative ability of the lens, a reduced ability to see in dim light, and diminished color discrimination. Middle-aged people experience hearing loss called **presbycusis,** which begins at high frequencies and spreads to other tones. Presbycusis begins earlier and is more rapid for men.

■ The skin wrinkles, loosens, and starts to develop age spots, especially in women and people exposed to the sun. Muscle mass declines and fat deposits increase, with men and women developing different patterns of fat distribution. Continued exercise can offset changes in strength and weight.

■ Bone density declines in both sexes, but to a greater extent in women, especially after menopause. Loss in height and bone fractures can result.

Describe reproductive changes in women during middle adulthood, and discuss women's psychological reactions to menopause.

■ The **climacteric** in women occurs gradually over a 10-year period as estrogen production drops and concludes with **menopause.** Doctors often recommend **hormone replacement therapy** (**HRT**) to protect postmenopausal women from bone deterioration, cardiovascular disease, skin changes, and discomforts such as hot flashes, sleeplessness, and irritability. HRT remains controversial because of an increased risk of certain cancers.

■ Menopause is a biocultural event—affected by hormonal changes as well as societal beliefs and practices. Physical symptoms and psychological reactions vary widely. Whether women find menopause to be traumatic or liberating depends on how they interpret it in relation to their past and future lives.

Describe reproductive changes in men during middle adulthood.

■ Although men also experience a climacteric, their reproductive capacity declines without ending. Therefore, no male counterpart to menopause exists. Occasional episodes of impotence are more common in midlife but can usually be treated successfully.

HEALTH AND FITNESS

Discuss sexuality in middle adulthood and its association with psychological well-being.

■ Frequency of sexual activity among married couples remains fairly stable in midlife, dropping only slightly, and is associated with psychological well-being. Intensity of sexual response declines more, due to physical changes of the climacteric. Many more women than men are without sexual partners, a trend that continues into later life.

Discuss cancer, cardiovascular disease, and osteoporosis, noting risk factors and interventions.

■ The death rate from cancer increases 10-fold from early to middle adulthood. Cancer is the leading killer of middle-aged women. A complex interaction of heredity, biological aging, and environment contributes to cancer. Today 40 percent of people with cancer are cured. Annual screenings and various preventive steps (such as not smoking) can reduce the incidence of cancer and cancer deaths.

■ Cardiovascular disease has declined in recent decades, but it remains a major cause of death in middle adulthood, especially among men. Symptoms include high blood pressure, high cholesterol, atherosclerosis, heart attack, arrhythmia, and angina pectoris. Diet, exercise, drug therapy, and stress reduction can reduce risks and aid in treatment. A special concern is accurate diagnosis in women.

■ **Osteoporosis** affects one in four postmenopausal women and the majority of people of both sexes over age 70. Weight-bearing exercise, calcium and vitamin D, and HRT (for women) can help prevent and treat osteoporosis.

Discuss the association of hostility and anger with heart disease and other health problems.

■ Hostility is the component of the **Type A behavior pattern** that predicts heart disease and other health problems, largely due to physiological arousal associated with anger. Since inhibiting the expression of emotion is also related to health problems, a better alternative is to develop effective ways of handling stress and conflict.

ADAPTING TO THE PHYSICAL CHALLENGES OF MIDLIFE

Discuss the benefits of stress management, exercise, and an optimistic outlook in dealing effectively with the physical challenges of midlife.

■ The changes and responsibilities of middle adulthood can cause psychological stress, with negative consequences for the cardiovascular, immune, and gastrointestinal systems. Effective stress management includes both problem-centered and emotion-centered coping, depending on the situation; constructive approaches to anger reduction; and social support.

■ Regular exercise confers many physical and psychological benefits, making it worthwhile for sedentary middle-aged people to begin exercising. Developing a sense of self-efficacy and choosing an exercise format that fits the individual's characteristics—home based for overweight adults, group based for highly stressed adults—increase the chances that a beginner will stick with an exercise regimen.

■ **Hardiness** is made up of three personal qualities: control, commitment, and challenge. By inducing a generally optimistic outlook on life, hardiness helps people cope with stress adaptively.

Explain the double standard of aging.

■ Negative stereotypes of aging discourage older adults of both sexes. Yet middle-aged women are more likely to be viewed unfavorably, especially by men. Although this double standard of aging may have been adaptive at an earlier time in our evolutionary history, it is irrelevant in an era of limited childbearing and greater involvement in career and leisure pursuits.

COGNITIVE DEVELOPMENT

CHANGES IN MENTAL ABILITIES

Describe changes in crystallized and fluid intelligence in middle adulthood, and discuss individual and group differences in intellectual development.

■ Longitudinal research reveals gains from early to middle adulthood in skills that tap both **crystallized intelligence** (which depends on accumulated knowledge and experience) and **fluid intelligence** (which depends more on information-processing skills). An exception is perceptual speed, a fluid skill that drops steadily from the twenties to the eighties.

■ Large individual differences among middle-aged adults remind us that intellectual development is multidimensional, multidirectional, and plastic. Some people decline intellectually in their forties due to disease or very unfavorable environments. Individuals who use their intellectual skills are likely to retain them. Stimulating occupations and leisure pursuits, good health, lasting marriages, flexible personalities, and economic advantage are linked to favorable cognitive development.

- Women show an earlier decline in perceptual speed but gain in other mental abilities over a longer period than do men. Generational gains in certain intellectual skills reflect advances in education, technology, environmental stimulation, and health care.

INFORMATION PROCESSING

How does information processing change in midlife?

- Speed of cognitive processing slows with age, a change that researchers explain with either the **neural network view** or the **information-loss view.** Slower processing speed makes it harder for middle-aged people to divide their attention, focus on relevant stimuli, and switch from one task to another as the situation demands. Cognitive inhibition becomes more difficult, at times prompting distractibility.

- Adults in midlife retain less information in working memory, largely due to a decline in use of memory strategies. Training, practice, improved design of tasks, and metacognitive knowledge enable middle-aged and older adults to compensate for decrements in processing speed, attention, and memory.

Discuss the development of practical problem solving, expertise, and creativity in middle adulthood.

- Middle-aged adults in all walks of life often become good at **practical problem solving,** largely due to development of expertise, which peaks in midlife. Creativity in middle adulthood shifts from generating unusual products and expressing oneself to integrating experience and knowledge in unique ways and fulfilling altruistic goals.

VOCATIONAL LIFE AND COGNITIVE DEVELOPMENT

Describe the relationship between vocational life and cognitive development.

- At all ages and in very different cultures, the relationship between vocational life and cognitive development is reciprocal. Stimulating, complex work and flexible, abstract, autonomous thinking support one another.

ADULT LEARNERS: BECOMING A COLLEGE STUDENT IN MIDLIFE

Discuss the challenges facing adults returning to college, ways to support returning students, and benefits of earning a degree in midlife.

- Often motivated to return to college by life transitions, women make up the majority of the growing number of adult students, especially those over age 35. Returning students must cope with a lack of recent practice at academic work, stereotypes of aging, and multiple role demands. Low-income and ethnic minority students need special assistance.

- Social support from family and friends and institutional services suited to their needs can help returning students succeed. Further education brings personal rewards, new relationships, intergenerational communication, and reshaped life paths.

IMPORTANT TERMS AND CONCEPTS

climacteric (p. 495)
crystallized intelligence (p. 507)
fluid intelligence (p. 507)
hardiness (p. 504)

hormone replacement therapy (HRT) (p. 495)
information-loss view (p. 509)
menopause (p. 495)
neural network view (p. 509)

osteoporosis (p. 500)
practical problem solving (p. 511)
presbycusis (p. 494)
presbyopia (p. 493)
Type A behavior pattern (p. 502)

Consult the companion website for this book, where you will find additional weblinks and associated learning activities: www.abacon.com/berk

MENOPAUSE

North American Menopause Society
www.menopause. org

Dedicated to enhancing women's understanding of menopause.

HEALTH AND FITNESS

Midlife Women's Network
www.users.aol.com/mdlfwoman/ info.htm

An organization that informs and empowers women who want to improve their health and quality of life during middle adulthood.

National Women's Health Resource Center
www.womenshealth.com

Disseminates information about women's health.

SEXUALITY

Sexuality Information and Education Council of the United States
www.siecus.org

Provides information about and advocacy of sexuality as a healthy part of life.

CANCER

American Cancer Society
www.cancer.org

Supports research and public education on cancer. Local chapters have lists of community resources, home care items for loan, transportation services, and public education programs.

Y-Me National Organization for Breast Cancer Information and Support
www.y-me.org

Offers presurgical counseling, support, and self-help meetings for women who have or suspect they have breast cancer, their families, and friends.

CARDIOVASCULAR DISEASE

(See page 453.)

OSTEOPOROSIS

National Osteoporosis Foundation
www.nof.org

Disseminates information about osteoporosis and supports research.

STRESS MANAGEMENT

American Institute of Stress
www.stress.org

Disseminates information on the personal and social consequences of stress and on stress management.

RETURNING STUDENTS

American Association of University Women Educational Foundations Program
www.aauw.org

Organization of graduates of community colleges, colleges, and universities that conducts research and advocates educational equity for women and girls.

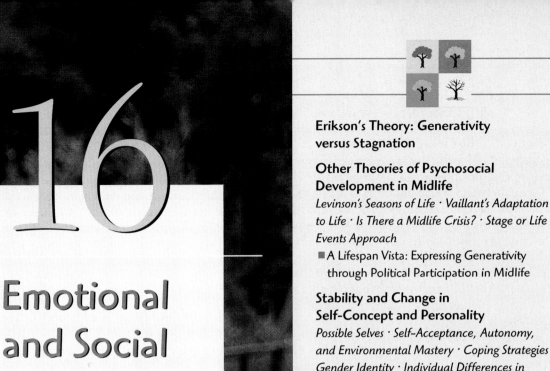

16

Emotional and Social Development in Middle Adulthood

■ *The sense of well-being that stems from generativity —giving to and guiding the next generation—is keenly apparent in the broad smile of this grandmother. For those who experience it, grandparenthood is a highly significant milestone of middle adulthood. (Photo courtesy: Bruce Plotkin/ Liaison Agency)*

On a Labor Day weekend in which Devin, Trisha, and their 24-year-old son, Mark, had traveled to Washington, D.C., for a brief vacation, the two middle-aged parents knocked on Mark's hotel room door early Monday morning. "Your dad and I are going off to see a crafts exhibit," Trisha explained. "No problem with your staying behind," she offered, recalling Mark's antipathy toward attending such events as an adolescent. "We'll be back around 12 for lunch. Relax and do whatever you like till then."

"The exhibit sounds great!" Mark replied. "I'll meet you in the hotel lobby. We've got so little time together as it is."

"At times I forget he's an adult!" exclaimed Trisha as she and Devin returned to their room to grab their coats. "It's been great to have Mark with us these few days, like spending time with a good friend."

During their forties and fifties, Trisha and Devin built on earlier strengths and intensified their commitment to values and concerns related to leaving a legacy for those who would come after them. As Mark graduated from college, took his first job, fell in love, and married, they felt a sense of pride at having escorted a member of the next generation into responsible adult roles. Family activities, which had declined during Mark's adolescent and college years, now increased as Trisha and Devin related to their son and daughter-in-law not just as kin but as enjoyable adult companions. Challenging work and more time for community involvement, leisure pursuits, and each other contributed to a richly diverse and gratifying time of life.

The years of midlife were not as smooth for two of Trisha and Devin's friends. Fearing that she might grow old alone, Jewel frantically pursued her quest for an intimate partner by attending singles events, registering with dating services, and traveling in hopes of meeting a like-minded companion. "I can't stand the thought of turning 50. I look like an old bag with big circles under my eyes," she lamented in a letter to Trisha. In other ways, Jewel's life had compensating satisfactions—friendships that had grown more meaningful, a warm relationship with a nephew and niece, and a successful consulting business.

Tim, Devin's best friend from graduate school, had been divorced for over 15 years. Recently, he had met Elena, for whom he cared deeply. But Elena was in the midst of major life changes. Besides her own divorce, she was dealing with a troubled daughter, a change in careers, and a move from the city that was a constant reminder of her unhappy past. Whereas Tim had reached the peak of his vocation and was ready to enjoy life, Elena wanted to recapture much of what she had missed in earlier decades—not just a satisfying close relationship, but opportunities to realize her talents. "I don't know where I fit into Elena's plans," Tim wondered aloud in a phone conversation with Trisha.

With the arrival of middle adulthood, half or more of the lifespan is over. Increasing awareness of limited time ahead prompts adults to reevaluate the meaning of their lives and reach out to future generations. As we will see, most middle-aged people make modest adjustments in their outlook and daily lives. A few experience profound inner turbulence and initiate major changes, often in an effort to make up for lost time. Besides advancing years, family and vocational transitions contribute greatly to emotional and social development.

ERIKSON'S THEORY: GENERATIVITY VERSUS STAGNATION

Erikson's critical psychological conflict of midlife is called **generativity versus stagnation.** Recall from Chapter 14 that generativity is under way in early adulthood, typically through childbearing and child rearing and establishing a niche in the occupational world. It expands greatly in midlife.

Generativity involves reaching out to others in ways that give to and guide the next generation. At this stage, commitment extends beyond oneself (identity) and one's life partner (intimacy) to a larger group—family, community, or society. The generative adult combines his or her need for self-expression with a need for communion, integrating personal goals with the welfare of the larger social environment (Wrightsman, 1994). The resulting strength

■ *Generativity expands greatly in midlife. It involves reaching out to others in ways that give to and guide the next generation. This middle-aged man volunteers regularly in an after-school reading program for elementary school children. (Photo courtesy: Charles Gupton/Stock Boston)*

is the capacity to care for others in a broader way than in previous stages.

Erikson (1950) selected the term *generativity* to encompass everything generated that can outlive the self and ensure society's continuity and improvement: children, ideas, products, and works of art. Although parenting is a major means of realizing generativity, some people, because of misfortune or special gifts, do not express it through their own children. Adults can be generative in other family relationships (as Jewel was with her nephew and niece), as mentors in the workplace, in volunteer endeavors, and through many forms of productivity and creativity.

Look closely at what we have said so far, and you will see that generativity brings together inner desires and cultural demands. Middle-aged adults feel a need to be needed; they want to attain symbolic immortality—that is, make a contribution that will survive their death (McAdams & de St. Aubin, 1992; McAdams, Hart, & Maruna, 1998). At the same time, society requires adults to take responsibility for the next generation in their roles as parents, teachers, mentors, leaders, organizers, and guardians of the culture. According to Erikson, a culture's "belief in the species"—the conviction that life is basically good and worthwhile, even in the face of human destructiveness and deprivation—is a major motivator of generative action (see Figure 16.1). Without this optimistic world view, people would not have

any hope of improving humanity. As the Lifespan Vista box on page 524 illustrates, cultural opportunities and injustices shape adults' generative activities.

The negative outcome of this stage is stagnation. Erikson recognized that once a person has attained certain life goals—marriage, children, and vocation—there is a temptation to become self-centered and self-indulgent. People with a sense of stagnation are unable to contribute to society's welfare because they place their own comfort and security above challenge and sacrifice. Their self-absorption is expressed in many ways—through lack of involvement with and concern for young people (including their own children); through a focus on what they can get from others rather than what they can give; and through little interest in being productive at work, developing their talents, or bettering the world in other ways (Hamachek, 1990).

To study generativity, some researchers assess personality traits, such as assertiveness, nurturance, responsibility, and breadth of interests (Ryff & Migdal, 1984). Others ask people to rate themselves on generative characteristics and activities—for example, serving as a leader or creating things that have had an impact on others (Ochse & Plug, 1986; Keyes & Ryff, 1998a). Still others look for generative themes in people's narrative descriptions of themselves. These indicate that generativity has become part of an expanding identity that gives purpose and meaning to life

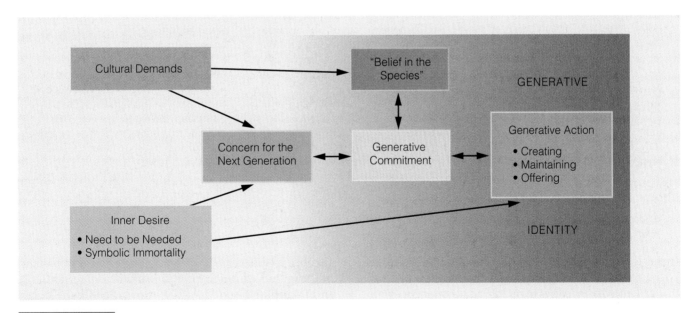

FIGURE 16.1

■ **Individual and cultural influences on generativity.** Inner desires combined with cultural demands—"belief in the species" and insistence that adults take responsibility for the next generation—lead to concern with and commitment to generative values and goals, which may produce generative action. Generative acts can involve creating, maintaining, or offering that which has been created or maintained to the community. The adult who behaves generatively observes his or her own efforts and their consequences and develops a generative identity. When generative individuals tell others their life stories, which are imbued with this identity, they ensure that generative values and goals are transferred to the next generation. (Adapted from McAdams, Hart, & Maruna, 1998.)

EXPRESSING GENERATIVITY THROUGH POLITICAL PARTICIPATION IN MIDLIFE

After age 40, adults show greater engagement with political issues that may affect future generations. Yet events in a person's life history can have a profound impact on midlife political consciousness. Specifically, politically relevant experiences in childhood, adolescence, and early adulthood are likely to mold identity development. Those occurring later have less opportunity to lead to a radical transformation of the self (Stewart & Healy, 1989).

Research on political activists of the 1960s and early 1970s reveals a strong link between early political convictions sparked by historical events and dedication to political causes in midlife. For example, follow-ups of male protesters in student movements of the 1960s showed that they became "ideal middle-aged citizens" who were more socially and politically involved than others of their generation (Fendrich, 1993). Similarly, women who as late adolescents and young adults were either concerned about or active participants in the civil rights and women's movements seemed empowered by their youthful experiences. When they reached their forties, they were highly involved in effecting political

change in their local communities (Cole & Stewart, 1996; Stewart & Healy, 1989).

Intensive case studies illustrate this connection between early identity and midlife political participation (Stewart & Gold-Steinberg, 1990). Consider Sarah, whose family and school upbringing instilled a profound sense of social responsibility. Her mother had devoted many hours to charitable causes; her father had often stressed the importance of good citizenship. As a young pupil, Sarah recalled a teacher saying, "[Y]ou are very privileged people and you absolutely have to make a difference in this world, you can't just sit back and enjoy it." Sarah frequently thought about her teacher's message, and her parents underscored it. During her college years, involvement in the civil rights, antiwar, and women's movements of the 1960s strengthened Sarah's political values. She became a socially committed college history teacher, an occupational identity that served her well after she married and had children.

In the 1980s, when her children were grown, Sarah experienced an intense desire to renew her political activism. Searching for a cause in which to invest her midlife con-

sciousness, she became involved in gender-equity issues on campus and in antinuclear education efforts in her community. Sarah recognized the link between her early experiences and her generative impulses in middle adulthood. She commented,

In my twenties, when we were trying to end the war in Vietnam, we simultaneously thought that we had all the power in the world and that we had no power at all. Neither was true. We did actually accomplish some things . . . but the 25-year-old consciousness . . . is not the 45-year-old consciousness. I now think that I have a much more accurate and, in some important ways, energizing and empowering sense of my own powers and limitations. (Stewart & Gold-Steinberg, 1990, p. 557)

Political awareness and student activism in the early decades of life seem to produce a sense of self-efficacy and commitment, which in turn promotes active political participation later in life. As the researchers comment, "In this light, student protesters may be seen not as society's malcontents but as tomorrow's exemplars of social responsibility" (Cole & Stewart, 1996, p. 138).

(refer again to Figure 16.1) (McAdams, de St. Aubin, & Logan, 1993; McAdams et al., 1997). Each approach reveals that generativity increases in middle adulthood. For example, a longitudinal study of highly educated women revealed that generativity desires increased over the early adulthood years and gradually transformed into generativity accomplishments in midlife. Participants reaching a high level of generativity accomplishment were especially well adjusted—low in anxiety and depression and high in life satisfaction (Stewart & Vandewater, 1998).

Just as Erikson's theory suggests, highly generative people tend to be psychologically fulfilled and healthy. They

are open to differing viewpoints, possess leadership qualities, want more from work than just financial rewards, use an authoritative style in child rearing, and care greatly about the welfare of their children, partner, and the wider society (Peterson & Klohnen, 1995; Peterson, Smirles, & Wentworth, 1997). Having children seems to foster men's generative development more than women's. In two studies, fathers scored higher in generativity than did childless men (McAdams & de St. Aubin, 1992; Snarey et al., 1987). Perhaps parenthood awakens in men a tender, caring attitude toward the next generation that women have opportunities to develop in many other ways.

OTHER THEORIES OF PSYCHOSOCIAL DEVELOPMENT IN MIDLIFE

Recall that Erikson's theory provides only a broad sketch of adult personality development. For a closer look at psychosocial change in midlife, let's revisit Levinson's and Vaillant's theories, to which you were introduced in Chapter 14.

LEVINSON'S SEASONS OF LIFE

Return to page 457 to review Levinson's eras (stages or seasons), and notice that like early adulthood, middle adulthood begins with a transitional period (age 40 to 45), followed by the building of an entry life structure (age 45 to 50). Then this structure is evaluated and revised (age 50 to 55), resulting in a culminating life structure (age 55 to 60). Among the men and women Levinson (1978, 1996) interviewed, the majority displayed the first two of these phases. Nevertheless, because of gender stereotypes and differences in opportunity, male and female experiences were somewhat different.

■ MIDLIFE TRANSITION. Around age 40, people evaluate their success in meeting early adulthood goals. Realizing that from now on, more time will lie behind than ahead, they regard the remaining years as increasingly precious. According to Levinson, virtually all people experience considerable confusion as they start to modify marriage/family and occupational components of the life structure. Some make drastic changes, divorcing, remarrying, shifting occupations and lifestyle, or displaying great progress in creativity. Others make smaller changes while staying in the same marriage, surroundings, occupation, and workplace.

Whether these years bring a gust of wind or a storm, most people turn inward for a time, focusing on personally meaningful living (Neugarten, 1968). Part of the reason is that for many middle-aged adults, only limited advancement and personal growth at work remain possible. Others are disappointed in not having fully realized their early adulthood dream and feel an inner pressure to find a more satisfying path before it is too late. They ask, Can I still achieve what I wanted? If not, can I accept what I have attained? What are my alternatives, and can I build a better life? Even people who have reached their goals ask, What good are these accomplishments to others, to society, and to myself?

According to Levinson, for middle-aged adults to reassess their relation to themselves and the external world, they must confront four developmental tasks, summarized in Table 16.1. Each requires the person to reconcile two opposing tendencies within the self. The midlife transition brings both an opportunity and a need to achieve a better balance than before. Let's see how this happens.

■ MODIFYING THE LIFE STRUCTURE: GENDER SIMILARITIES AND DIFFERENCES. At midlife, adults must give up certain youthful qualities, find age-appropriate ways to express others, and accept being older, thereby creating a youth–age balance more in tune with their time of life. Physical changes, personal encounters with illness, and aging parents intensify this task, and it often triggers reassessment of what is important. Due to the double standard of aging (see Chapter 15), women find it harder than men to accept being older. For Jewel, the stereotypical image of an older woman prompted a desperate fear of becoming unattractive and unlovable. She tried numerous remedies, from skin creams to a face lift, to maintain her youth. Indeed, women are more likely than men to perceive themselves as younger than their chronological age. And as Figure

TABLE 16.1

Levinson's Four Developmental Tasks of Middle Adulthood

TASK	DESCRIPTION
Young–Old	The middle-aged person must seek new ways of being both young and old. This means giving up certain youthful qualities, retaining and transforming others, and finding positive meaning in being older.
Destruction–Creation	With greater awareness of mortality, the middle-aged person focuses on ways he or she has acted destructively and others have done the same. Past hurtful acts toward parents, intimate partners, children, friends, and rivals are countered by a strong desire to become more creative—by making products of value to the self and others and participating in activities that advance human welfare.
Masculinity–Femininity	The middle-aged person must come to terms with masculine and feminine parts of the self, creating a better balance. For men, this means becoming more empathic and caring; for women, it often means becoming more autonomous, dominant, and assertive.
Engagement–Separateness	The middle-aged person must create a better balance between engagement with the external world and separateness. For men, this generally means pulling back from ambition and achievement and becoming more in touch with the self. Women who have devoted themselves to child rearing or who have unfulfilling jobs typically need to move in the other direction—toward greater involvement in the work world and wider community.

Sources: Levinson, 1978, 1996.

16.2 indicates, especially for women, the gap between subjective and objective age widens over time (Montepare & Lachman, 1989).

As middle-aged adults confront their own mortality and the actual or impending death of agemates, they become more aware of ways people can act destructively—to parents, intimate partners, children, friends, and co-workers. Countering this force is a desire to be creative through endeavors that advance human welfare. For example, Devin and Trisha became more involved in improving quality of life in their community, desiring to leave a legacy for future generations. The image of a legacy, which flourishes in midlife, can be satisfied in many ways—through charitable gifts, creating products valued by the self and others, volunteer service, or mentoring young people. According to Levinson, creativity in midlife is stimulated in part by recognition that destructiveness must be overcome by loving, life-affirming aspects of the self.

Middle age is also a time when people must reconcile masculine and feminine parts of the self. For men, this means being more accepting of "feminine" traits of nurturance and caring, which enhance love relationships and lead to a more compassionate exercise of authority in the work-

place. For women, it generally means being more open to "masculine" characteristics of autonomy, dominance, and assertiveness (Gilligan, 1982; Harris, Ellicott, & Holmes, 1986; Reinke, Holmes, & Harris, 1985). Recall from Chapter 8 that people who combine masculine and feminine traits have an androgynous gender identity. Later we will see that androgyny is associated with many favorable personality traits.

Finally, midlife requires a middle ground between engagement with the external world and separateness. Men generally need to reduce their concern with ambition and achievement and attend more fully to the self. A few women, who have had active, successful careers, may need to do so as well. But those who devoted their early adulthood to child rearing or an unfulfilling job, after a period of self-reflection, often feel compelled to move in the other direction (Levinson, 1996). At age 48, for example, Elena left her position as a reporter for a small-town newspaper, pursued an advanced degree in creative writing with passionate commitment, eventually accepted a college teaching position, and began work on two novels. As Tim looked inward, he recognized his overwhelming desire for a gratifying intimate partnership. He realized that by scaling back his own vocational pursuits, he could grant Elena the time and space she needed to build a rewarding career—and that doing so might deepen their attachment to one another.

■ THE LIFE STRUCTURE IN SOCIAL AND CULTURAL CONTEXT. Rebuilding the life structure depends on contexts that support people's reassessment of what they want to give to the world and to themselves. When poverty, unemployment, and lack of a respected place in society dominate the life course, energies are directed toward survival rather than pursuit of a satisfying life structure (Levinson, 1978).

Even adults whose jobs are secure and who live in pleasant neighborhoods may find that employment conditions place too much emphasis on productivity and profit and too little on the meaning of work, thereby restricting possibilities for growth. In her early forties, Trisha left a large law firm for a small practice because of constant pressures to bring in high-fee clients and little acknowledgment of the quality of her efforts by the managing partners.

Opportunities for advancement permit realization of the early adulthood dream, thereby easing the transition to middle adulthood. Yet they are far less available to women than to men. Individuals of both sexes in blue-collar jobs also have few possibilities for promotion. The industrial workers in Levinson's (1978) sample made whatever adjustments they could in middle age—becoming active union members, shop stewards, or mentors of younger workers. Many found compensating rewards in moving from the junior to senior generation in their families.

Education is crucial for personally enriching work, limiting family size so women can blend child rearing with vocational life, acquiring the abstract verbal skills needed

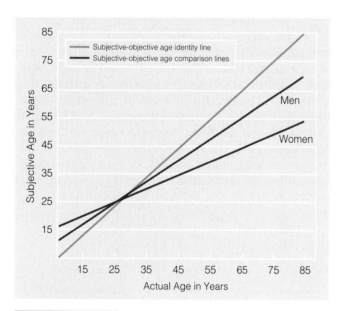

FIGURE 16.2

■ **Relationship between subjective and objective age across the lifespan.** After age 25, men and women report perceiving themselves as younger than they actually are. Especially for women, the gap between subjective and objective age widens over time. Due to the double standard of aging, women find it harder to accept being older. (Adapted from J. Montepare & M. Lachman, 1989, "You're Only as Old as You Feel: Self-Perceptions of Age, Fears of Aging, and Life Satisfaction from Adolescence to Old Age," *Psychology and Aging, 4,* p. 75. Copyright © 1989 by the American Psychological Association. Reprinted by permission.)

to reflect on the inner self, and attaining the economic security that grants time and energy for rebuilding the life structure. Yet on a worldwide basis, 26 percent of the adult population is illiterate—and nearly twice as many women as men can't read. Although great strides have been made in increasing literacy in developing nations, the majority of adult women in South Asia, Africa, and the Middle East remain illiterate. Many more adults have only limited schooling (United Nations, 1997). Without education, there is no dream to challenge in middle adulthood—and no hope of taking control of one's life.

VAILLANT'S ADAPTATION TO LIFE

Because the men and women interviewed by Levinson were between ages 35 and 45, they cannot tell us anything certain about psychosocial change in the fifties or beyond. In Vaillant's (1977) longitudinal study of men who attended a highly competitive liberal arts college, participants were followed past the half-century mark. Recall from Chapter 14 that they became "keepers of meaning," or guardians of their culture (see page 459). Adults in their late forties and fifties carry peak responsibility for the functioning of society. Vaillant reported that the most successful and best adjusted individuals entered a calmer, quieter time of life, an outcome verified for both men and women in other research (Whitbourne & Weinstock, 1979). "Passing the torch"—concern that the positive aspects of their culture survive—became a major preoccupation.

Older people in societies around the world are guardians of traditions, laws, and cultural values. This stabilizing force holds in check too rapid change sparked by the questioning and challenging of adolescents and young adults. As people move toward the end of middle age, they focus on longer-term, less personal goals, such as the state of human relations in their society. And they become more philosophical, accepting that not all problems can be solved in their lifetime.

IS THERE A MIDLIFE CRISIS?

Levinson (1978, 1996) reported that most men and women in his samples experienced substantial inner turmoil during the transition to middle adulthood. Yet Vaillant (1977) saw few examples of crisis. Instead, change was typically slow and steady. These contrasting findings raise the following questions: How much personal upheaval accompanies entry to midlife? Is self-doubt and stress especially great during the decade of the forties, and does it prompt major restructuring of the personality, as the term **midlife crisis** implies? Are men's and women's experiences similar or different?

Think about the reactions of Trisha, Devin, Jewel, Tim, and Elena to middle adulthood, and you will see that the picture is one of great diversity. Trisha and Devin moved easily into this period. In contrast, Jewel, Tim, and Elena displayed greater questioning of their situations and sought alternative life paths.

Similarly, research suggests wide individual differences in response to midlife. Overall, changes for men are more likely to occur in the early forties (in accord with Levinson's timetable). Those for women may be postponed to the late forties and fifties, until a reduction in parenting responsibilities grants time and freedom to confront personal issues (Harris, Ellicott, & Holmes, 1986; Mercer, Nichols, & Doyle, 1989). In addition, the direction of change for women is more variable than for men. It depends in part on whether they focused as young adults on a "feminine" social clock (marriage and motherhood), a "masculine" social clock (high-status career), or a combination of the two (Helson & Roberts, 1994; Stewart & Vandewater, 1992).

But sharp disruption and agitation are more the exception than the rule. For example, Elena had considered both a divorce and a new career long before she initiated these changes. In her thirties, she separated from her husband, later reconciled, and told him of her desire to return to school, which he firmly opposed. She put her own life on hold because of her daughter's academic and emotional difficulties and her husband's resistance. In an intensive study of ten people who changed careers between ages 35 and 55 (representing a minority of midlifers), only three were judged to be in a state of crisis. Like Elena, the remaining seven had planned the change for a long time. Although entry into the second career seemed sudden to outsiders, the career changers did not perceive it as a radical shift. Instead, the kind of work they did and enjoyed in

■ *These sisters responded to the midlife transition by opening a new restaurant and cooking school in a small Colorado town. Yet their career change was probably not the result of a crisis. Most middle-aged adults who decide to change careers plan carefully and choose a second career related to the kind of work they did and enjoyed in their first career. (Photo courtesy: Sean Cayton/The Image Works)*

their first careers was related to what they chose to do in their second (Lawrence, 1980).

Furthermore, midlife is sometimes experienced in a way that resembles relief rather than crisis. In Chapter 15, we noted that women often welcome menopause, as it liberates them from unwanted pregnancy and the need to use birth control. In a study of well-known contemporary novelists, many expressed "feeling safe at last in the middle years," free of anxieties about the adequacy of their performance. Midlife brought a sense of confidence and accomplishment and a more insightful view of difficulties—that even the bleakest event is an episode, that it too would pass (Gullette, 1988).

In sum, concern with mortality and life evaluation is common during middle age; only a minority of people drastically alter their life structure (Lachman & James, 1997). The few who are in crisis typically have had early adulthoods in which gender roles, family pressures, or low-income and poverty severely limited their ability to attain reasonable satisfaction of personal needs and goals, either at home or in the wider world (McAdams, 1988).

STAGE OR LIFE EVENTS APPROACH

If crisis and major restructuring are rare, is it appropriate to consider middle adulthood a stage of development, as Erikson, Levinson, and Vaillant's theories indicate? According to some researchers, the midadult transition is not stagelike; it does not lead to qualitatively different ways of thinking, feeling, and behaving. Instead, it is simply an adaptation to life events—external pressures that affect many people during the middle years, such as children growing up, reaching the crest of a career, and impending retirement (McCrae & Costa, 1990).

Yet recall from earlier chapters that life events are no longer as age graded as they were in the past. Their timing varies enough that they cannot be the single cause of midlife change. Furthermore, in several studies, people were asked to trace their thoughts, feelings, attitudes, and hopes during early and middle adulthood. Psychosocial change, in terms of personal disruption followed by reassessment, coincided with both family life cycle events and chronological age (Ellicott, 1985). For this reason, most experts regard adaptation during midlife as the combined result of growing older and social experiences (Schroots & Birren, 1990; Whitbourne et al., 1992). Return to our discussion of generativity and the midlife transition, and notice how both factors are involved.

Finally, in describing their lives, the large majority of middle-aged people report troubling moments that prompt new understandings and goals—a finding consistent with the stage approach. As we take a closer look at emotional and social development in middle adulthood, we will see that this period, like others, is characterized by *both continuity and stagewise change*. With this in mind, let's turn to the diverse inner concerns and outer experiences that contribute to psychological well-being and decision making during this phase of life.

ASK YOURSELF . . .

■ *Explain how Elena's decision to change careers is a joint product of inner needs and external pressures.*

🌳 *After years of experiencing little personal growth at work, 42-year-old Mel started to look for a new job. When he received an attractive offer in another city, he felt torn between leaving friendships built over many years and a long-awaited career opportunity. After several weeks of soul searching, he took the new job. Was Mel's dilemma a midlife crisis? Why or why not?*

STABILITY AND CHANGE IN SELF-CONCEPT AND PERSONALITY

Changes in self-concept and personality that accompany midlife reflect growing awareness of a finite lifespan, longer life experience, and generative concerns. At the same time, certain aspects of personality remain stable, revealing individual differences established during earlier phases that persist throughout adulthood.

POSSIBLE SELVES

On a business trip, Jewel found a spare afternoon to visit Trisha. The two women sat in a coffee shop, reminiscing about the past and thinking about the future. "It's been tough living on my own and building the business," Jewel commented. "What I hope for is to become better at my work, to be more community oriented, and to stay healthy and available to my friends. Of course, I don't want to grow old alone, but if I don't find that special person, I suppose I can take comfort in the fact that I'll never have to face divorce or widowhood."

Jewel is discussing **possible selves,** future-oriented representations of what she hopes to become and what she is afraid of becoming. Possible selves are the temporal dimension of self-concept—what the individual is striving for and attempting to avoid. Lifespan researchers regard these hopes and fears as just as vital for explaining behavior as people's views of their current characteristics. Indeed, possible selves may be an especially strong motivator of action in midlife, as more meaning becomes attached to time. Some researchers speculate that as we age, we rely less on social comparisons in judging our self-worth and more on temporal comparisons—how well we are doing in relation to what we had planned for ourselves (Suls & Mullen, 1982).

Throughout adulthood, the way people describe their current selves is quite stable. A 30-year-old who says he is cooperative, competent, outgoing, or successful is likely to report a similar picture at a later age. But possible selves show great change. Adults in their early twenties mention many possible selves, and they are lofty and idealistic—being "perfectly happy," "rich and famous," "healthy throughout life," and not being "down and out" or "a person who does nothing important." With age, possible selves become fewer in number and more modest and concrete. Most middle-aged people no longer desire to be the best and the most successful. Instead, they are largely concerned with performance of roles and responsibilities already begun—being "competent at work," "a good husband and father," "able to put my children through the colleges of their choice," and not being "in poor health" or "without enough money to meet my daily needs" (Cross & Markus, 1991; Ryff, 1991).

What explains these shifts in possible selves? As the future no longer holds limitless opportunities, adults adjust their hopes and fears so they can preserve mental health. They must maintain a sense of unachieved possibility to stay motivated, yet they must still manage to feel good about themselves and their lives in spite of disappointments (Whitbourne & Connolly, 1998). For example, Jewel no longer desired to be an executive in a large company, as she had in her twenties. Instead, she wanted to grow in her current occupation. And although she feared loneliness in old age, she reminded herself that marriage could also lead to equally negative outcomes, such as divorce and widowhood—possibilities that made not having attained an important interpersonal goal easier to bear.

Unlike current self-concept, which is constantly responsive to others' feedback, possible selves (although influenced by others) can be defined and redefined by the individual, as needed. Consequently, they permit affirmation of the self, even when things are not going well (Cross & Markus, 1991). Researchers believe that possible selves may be the key to continued well-being in adulthood, as people revise these future images to achieve a better match between desired and achieved goals. Many studies reveal that the self-esteem of middle-aged and older individuals equals or surpasses that of younger individuals, perhaps because of the protective role of possible selves (Bengston, Reedy, & Gordon, 1985).

SELF-ACCEPTANCE, AUTONOMY, AND ENVIRONMENTAL MASTERY

An evolving mix of competencies and experiences leads certain personality traits to change in middle adulthood. One of the most consistent findings is a rise in introspection as people contemplate the second half of life (Neugarten & Datan, 1973). Middle-aged adults tend to be in better touch with themselves than younger individuals, and many have reshaped contexts to suit their personal needs and values.

These developments undoubtedly contribute to other gains in personal functioning. In a study of well-educated Americans ranging in age from the late teens into the seventies, three traits increased from early to middle adulthood and then leveled off. The first was *self-acceptance.* More than young adults, middle-aged people acknowledged and accepted both their good and bad qualities and felt positively about themselves and life. Second, they saw themselves as more *autonomous*—less concerned about expectations and evaluations of others and more concerned with following self-chosen standards. Third, they regarded themselves as high in *environmental mastery*—capable of managing a complex array of tasks easily and effectively (Ryff, 1991).

In Chapter 15, we noted that midlife brings gains in expertise and practical problem solving. These cognitive changes may support the confidence, initiative, and decisiveness of this period. Overall, midlife is a time of increased comfort with the self, independence, and commitment to personal values—outcomes apparent not just in cross-sectional research, but in longitudinal studies as well (Block, 1982; Helson & Wink, 1992; Mitchell & Helson, 1990). Perhaps because of these personal attributes, people sometimes refer to middle age as "the prime of life." Although individual differences exist (see the Variations box on page 530), the middle-adulthood years are a time when many people report feeling especially happy and functioning at their best.

Notions of happiness, however, are not the same in all cultures. For example, a comparison of Korean and American adults in their fifties revealed that the Koreans reported lower levels of psychological well-being, largely because they were less willing to endorse individualistic traits, such as self-acceptance and autonomy, as characteristic of themselves (Keyes & Ryff, 1998b). Consistent with their collectivist orientation, Koreans' highest well-being scores were on positive relations with others. They conceived of personal fulfillment as being achieved through family, especially the success of children. American adults also regarded family relations as relevant to well-being. But they placed greater emphasis on their own traits and accomplishments than on their children's.

COPING STRATEGIES

In Chapter 15, we discussed the importance of stress management in the prevention of illness. It is also vital for psychological well-being. Longitudinal and cross-sectional research indicates that midlife brings an increase in effective coping strategies (Diehl, Coyle, & Labouvie-Vief, 1996; Helson & Wink, 1992; Vaillant, 1976). Middle-aged individuals are more likely to look for the "silver lining" or positive

WHAT FACTORS PROMOTE PSYCHOLOGICAL WELL-BEING IN MIDLIFE?

The midlife years brought contentment and high life satisfaction for Trisha and Devin. But for Jewel, Tim, and Elena, the road to happiness was rockier. What factors contribute to variations in psychological well-being at midlife? Consistent with the lifespan perspective, biological, psychological, and social forces are involved, and their effects are interwoven.

GOOD HEALTH AND EXERCISE.
Good health affects energy and zest for life. Adults of any age who rate their health as good to excellent are more likely to feel positively about their life circumstances. But during middle and late adulthood, taking steps to improve health and prevent disability becomes a better predictor of psychological well-being. In a study of over 3,000 20- to 64-year-olds, engaging in regular exercise—walking, dancing, jogging, or swimming—was more strongly associated with self-rated health and a positive outlook in older than in younger individuals (Ransford & Palisi, 1996). Middle-aged adults who maintain an exercise regimen are likely to perceive themselves as particularly active for their age and, therefore, to feel a special sense of accomplishment. And exercise may reduce feelings of vulnerability to illness that increase with age, conveying extra psychological benefits. Fear of disease and dis-

ability is one of the strongest contributors to poor psychological well-being at midlife (Barsky, Cleary, & Klerman, 1992).

SENSE OF CONTROL AND PERSONAL LIFE INVESTMENT.
Middle-aged adults who report a high sense of control over what is happening in various aspects of their lives—health, family, and work—report more favorable psychological well-being. A sense of control fosters self-efficacy, a belief in one's ability to surmount challenges. Consequently it helps sustain a positive outlook in the face of health, family, and work difficulties (Bandura, 1997; Seligman, 1991; Skinner, 1995).

But beyond feeling in control, personal life investment—firm commitment to goals and involvement in pursuit of those goals—adds to mental health and life satisfaction (Staudinger, Fleeson, & Baltes, 1999). According to Mihaly Csikszentmihalyi (1999), a vital wellspring of happiness is *flow*—the psychological state of being so engrossed in a demanding, meaningful activity that one loses a sense of time and self-awareness. People describe flow as the height of enjoyment, even as an ecstatic state. The more they experience it, the more they judge their lives to be gratifying. Although flow is common in creative endeavors, it is also reported by students who

love studying, by employees who like their jobs, by adults engaged in challenging leisure pursuits, and by parents and grandparents engaged in pleasurable learning activities with children. Flow depends on perseverance and skill at activities that are complex and that offer potential for growth. These qualities are well developed in middle adulthood.

POSITIVE SOCIAL RELATIONSHIPS.
Developing gratifying social ties is closely linked to midlife psychological well-being. In a longitudinal study of 90 men selected for good physical and mental health as college students and followed over 32 years, most maintained their physical health status. A good mentor relationship in early adulthood (which fosters high career achievement) and favorable peer ties were among the best predictors of well-being as the men reached their late forties and early fifties (Westermeyer, 1998). In a survey of college alumni, those who preferred occupational prestige and high income to close friends were twice as likely as other respondents to describe themselves as "fairly" or "very" unhappy (Perkins, 1991, as cited by Myers, 2000).

A GOOD MARRIAGE.
Although friendships and positive relationships with co-workers are important, a good marriage boosts psychological

side of a difficult situation, postpone action to permit evaluation of alternative courses of action, anticipate and plan ways to handle future discomforts, and use humor to express ideas and feelings without negative effects on others. Younger individuals more often engage in denial of troubling emotions, acting out (temper outbursts), avoidance (sleep, substance use), and blaming others. Notice how effective coping blends problem-centered and emotion-centered strategies, whereas ineffective coping is largely emotion centered (see Chapter 15, page 503).

Why might effective coping increase in middle adulthood? Other personality changes probably support it, such as greater self-acceptance and confidence at handling life's problems. Return to Chapter 11, page 358, to review evidence indicating that many individuals who were stress-ridden as adolescents developed into contented, well-adjusted adults. In contrast, teenagers who rarely faced troubling situations had more difficulty coping with later problems. Similarly, in a longitudinal study of well-educated women, taking initiative to overcome difficult times in early well-being even more. In the longitudinal study just described, the role of marriage as a marker of mental health increased with age, becoming powerfully associated with mental health by age 50 (Westermeyer, 1998). Although women's adjustment is more sensitive to the quality of the marital relationship than is men's (see Chapter 14), marriage brings considerable benefits for middle-aged men and women alike. Large-scale longitudinal studies that have tracked people as they moved in and out of intimate relationships suggest that marriage actually causes well-being.

For example, when interviews with over 13,000 Americans were repeated 5 years later, those who remained married reported higher levels of happiness than those who remained single. Those who separated or divorced became much less happy, reporting considerable depression. Men and women who married for the first time experienced a sharp increase in happiness, those who remarried a modest increase (Marks & Lambert, 1998).

What explains these findings? Marriage seems to change people's behavior in ways that make them better off. For example, married partners monitor each other's health. And they drink less alcohol and are less likely to use illegal drugs than are their unmarried counterparts. Married couples also earn and save more

money than do other people; higher income is modestly linked to psychological well-being (Myers, 2000; Waite, 1999). Furthermore, sexual satisfaction predicts mental health, and as our discussion in Chapter 14 revealed, married couples have more satisfying sex lives than do unmarried couples and singles. Of course, not everyone is better off married. But for many people, there is something protective about the long-term commitment that marriage entails.

MASTERY OF MULTIPLE ROLES.
Finally, success in handling multiple roles is linked to well-being. Women are generally happier today than they used to be because they reap satisfactions not just from family relationships but from vocational achievements. In a study of nearly 300 middle-aged women, researchers asked about feelings of competence and control in four roles: wife, mother, caregiver of an impaired parent, and employee. Participants experienced higher levels of mastery in their work roles than in any other. But competence and control in all four roles predicted life satisfaction and reduced depression (Christensen, Stephens, & Townsend, 1998). Women who occupied several roles—in work and family arenas—seemed to benefit from added opportunities to enhance their sense of mastery.

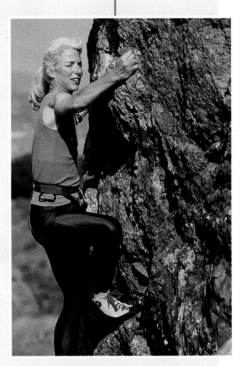

■ *Personal life investment adds to mental health and life satisfaction during middle adulthood. This middle-aged adult scaling the vertical surface of a mountain looks as if she is experiencing* flow—*the psychological state of being so engrossed in a demanding, meaningful activity that one loses a sense of time and self-awareness. The more people experience flow, the more they judge their lives to be gratifying. (Photo courtesy: Alan Kearney/FPG International)*

adulthood predicted advanced self-understanding, social and moral maturity, and high life satisfaction at age 43 (Helson & Roberts, 1994). These findings suggest that years of experience in overcoming stress may contribute to more sophisticated, flexible coping during middle age.

GENDER IDENTITY

In her forties and early fifties, Trisha appeared more assertive at work, speaking out more freely at meetings and

taking the lead in devising strategy when a team of lawyers worked on an especially complex case. She was also more dominant in family relationships, expressing her preferences and points of view to her husband and son more readily than she had 10 or 15 years earlier. In contrast, Devin's sense of empathy and caring became more apparent, and he was less assertive and more accommodating to Trisha's wishes than he had been in early adulthood.

Many studies report an increase in traditionally masculine traits in women and feminine traits in men across

■ *Gender identity becomes more androgynous in midlife—a mixture of both "masculine" and "feminine" characteristics. Like this father cooking for his children, men typically become more emotionally sensitive and nurturant. (Photo courtesy: Tony Freeman/PhotoEdit)*

middle age (Huyck, 1990; James et al., 1995). Women become more confident, self-sufficient, and forceful; men more emotionally sensitive, nurturant, considerate, and dependent. These trends appear in cross-sectional and longitudinal research, in people varying in SES, and in highly diverse cultures—not just Western industrialized nations, but small village societies such as the Mayans of Guatemala, the Navajo of the United States, and the Druze of the Middle East (Fry, 1985; Guttmann, 1977; Turner, 1982). They are evident in impressions of everyday behavior as well as in the personality traits people say are true of themselves. This indicates that gender identity becomes more androgynous in midlife—a mixture of both "masculine" and "feminine" characteristics. It also reveals a tendency for men and women to become more similar in gender-related self-descriptions as they age.

Although there is little argument that these changes occur, the reasons for them are controversial. According to a well-known ethological view called **parental imperative theory,** identification with traditional gender roles is maintained during the active parenting years to help ensure the survival of children. Men become more goal oriented, whereas women emphasize nurturance of husband and children. After children reach adulthood, parents are free to express the "other-gender" side of their personalities, which they had to restrain while rearing children (Gutmann & Huyck, 1994). A related explanation is that the decline in sex hormones associated with aging may contribute to androgyny in later life (Rossi, 1980).

These biological accounts have been criticized, and evidence for them is mixed. Think back to what you learned in earlier chapters, and you will see that both warmth and assertiveness (in the form of firmness and consistency) are necessary for parents to rear children effectively. Furthermore, although children's departure from the home is related to men's openness to the "feminine" side of their personalities, it is less clearly linked to a rise in "masculine" traits among women (Huyck, 1996, 1998). In longitudinal research, college-educated women in the labor force showed a rise in independence by their early forties, regardless of whether they had children; those who were homemakers did not. Women attaining high status at work gained most in dominance, assertiveness, and outspokenness by their early fifties (Helson & Picano, 1990; Wink & Helson, 1993). Finally, increased androgyny is not associated with menopause—a finding at odds with a hormonal explanation of gender-identity change (Helson & Wink, 1992).

Besides reduced parenting responsibilities, other demands and experiences of midlife may prompt a more androgynous orientation. For example, among men, a need to enrich a marital relationship after children have departed, along with reduced career advancement opportunities, may be involved in the awakening of emotionally sensitive traits. And men's greater number of health problems may prompt a rise in dependency and passivity. Compared with men, women are far more likely to face economic and social disadvantages. A greater number remain divorced, are widowed, and encounter discrimination in the workplace. Self-reliance and assertiveness are vital for coping with these circumstances.

In sum, androgyny in midlife is the product of a complex combination of social roles and life conditions. In Chapter 8, we noted that androgyny predicts high self-esteem. It is also associated with advanced moral reasoning and psychosocial maturity (Prager & Bailey, 1985; Waterman & Whitbourne, 1982). Indeed, men and women who do not integrate the masculine and feminine sides of their personalities tend to have mental health problems, perhaps because they are unable to adapt flexibly to the challenges of aging (Huyck, 1996; Turner, 1982).

INDIVIDUAL DIFFERENCES IN PERSONALITY TRAITS

Although Trisha and Jewel both became more self-assured and assertive in midlife, in other respects they differed. Trisha had always been more organized and hard-working, whereas Jewel was more gregarious and fun loving. Once the two women had traveled together. At the end of each day, Trisha was disappointed if she had not kept to a schedule and visited every tourist attraction. Jewel liked to "play it by ear"—wandering through streets and stopping to talk with shopkeepers and residents.

TABLE 16.2

The "Big Five" Personality Traits

TRAIT	DESCRIPTION
Neuroticism	Individuals who are high on this trait are worrying, temperamental, self-pitying, self-conscious, emotional, and vulnerable. Individuals who are low are calm, even-tempered, self-content, comfortable, unemotional, and hardy.
Extroversion	Individuals who are high on this trait are affectionate, talkative, active, fun loving, and passionate. Individuals who are low are reserved, quiet, passive, sober, and emotionally unreactive.
Openness to experience	Individuals who are high on this trait are imaginative, creative, original, curious, and liberal. Individuals who are low are down-to-earth, uncreative, conventional, uncurious, and conservative.
Agreeableness	Individuals who are high on this trait are soft-hearted, trusting, generous, acquiescent, lenient, and good-natured. Individuals who are low are ruthless, suspicious, stingy, antagonistic, critical, and irritable.
Conscientiousness	Individuals who are high on this trait are conscientious, hardworking, well organized, punctual, ambitious, and persevering. Individuals who are low are negligent, lazy, disorganized, late, aimless, and nonpersistent.

Source: McCrae & Costa, 1990.

In previous sections, we reviewed personality changes common to many middle-aged adults, but stable individual differences also exist. The hundreds of personality traits on which people differ have been organized into five basic factors, called the **"big five" personality traits:** neuroticism, extroversion, openness to experience, agreeableness, and conscientiousness. Table 16.2 provides a description of each. Notice that Trisha is high in conscientiousness, whereas Jewel is high in extroversion (Costa & McCrae, 1994; McCrae & Costa, 1990).

Cross-sectional studies of American men and women reveal that neuroticism, extroversion, and openness to experience show modest declines from the teenage years to the end of the twenties, whereas agreeableness and conscientiousness increase—changes reflect "settling down" and greater maturity. Similar trends extending into middle age have been identified in five countries—Croatia, Germany, Italy, Portugal, and South Korea (McCrae et al., 1999). The consistency of these cross-cultural findings has led some researchers to conclude that adult personality change is genetically influenced. As further support for a genetic view, individual differences in the "big five" traits are large and highly persistent. Longitudinal research shows that "big five" scores are strongly correlated from one age to the next, over intervals ranging from 3 to 30 years. A person who scores high or low at one age is likely to do the same at another (Costa & McCrae, 1994).

How can there be high stability on these characteristics, yet significant changes in aspects of personality discussed earlier, in which experience plays an important role? Studies of the "big five" traits include very large samples. Typically, they do not examine the impact of life events, the social clock, or cultural values, which shape aspirations, goals, and expectations for appropriate behavior. Look closely at the traits in Table 16.2, and you will see that they are very different from the attributes we considered in previous sections. They do not take into account motivations, preferred tasks, and coping styles. And they do not consider how certain aspects of personality, such as masculinity and femininity, are integrated (Block, 1995; Helson & Stewart, 1994).

Theorists concerned with change due to experience focus on life stories—the way personal needs and life events induce new strategies and goals. In contrast, theorists who emphasize stability and change due to heredity measure traits on which individuals can easily be compared and that are present at any time of life (McAdams, 1994; Rosenberg, Rosenberg, & Farrell, 1999). Perhaps we can resolve the apparent contradiction by thinking of people as changing in overall organization and integration of personality, but doing so on a foundation of basic, enduring dispositions.

ASK YOURSELF . . .

Around age 40, Luellen no longer thought about becoming a performing pianist. Instead, she decided to concentrate on accompanying other musicians in her community and expanding her studio of young pupils. How do Luellen's plans reflect changes in possible selves at midlife?

On his fifty-second birthday, Tom was asked how he felt now that another year had gone by. He replied, "I feel calmer and more content than at any time in my life." What personality changes might have contributed to Tom's response?

Jeff, age 46, suggested to his wife, Julia, that they set aside a special time each year to discuss their relationship—both positive aspects and ways to improve. Julia reacted to Jeff's suggestion with surprise, since he had never before seemed interested in working on the quality of their marriage. What developments at midlife probably fostered this new concern?

RELATIONSHIPS AT MIDLIFE

The emotional and social changes of midlife take place within a complex web of family relationships as well as friendships. Although a few middle-aged people (like Jewel and Tim) live alone, the vast majority (9 out of every 10 in the United States) live in families—most with a spouse (U.S. Bureau of the Census, 1999).

The middle adulthood phase of the family life cycle is often referred to as "launching children and moving on." At one time it was called the "empty nest," but this phrase implies a negative transition, especially for women. When adults devote themselves entirely to their children, the end of active parenting can trigger feelings of emptiness and regret. But for many people, middle adulthood is a liberating time, offering a sense of completion and an opportunity to strengthen existing ties and build new ones.

This phase is the newest and longest of the family life cycle. A century ago, most parents reared children for almost all of their active adulthood. Due to a declining birthrate and longer life expectancy, contemporary parents launch children about 20 years before retirement and then seek other rewarding activities. Because of the lengthening of this period, it is marked by the greatest number of exits and entries of family members (McGoldrick, Heiman, & Carter, 1993). As adult children leave home and marry, middle-aged people must adapt to new roles of parent-in-law and grandparent. At the same time, they must establish a different type of relationship with their aging parents, who may become ill or infirm and die. Let's see how ties within and beyond the family are modified during this time of life.

MARRIAGE AND DIVORCE

Although not all couples are financially comfortable, middle-aged households are well off economically compared to those in other age groups. Americans between 45 and 54 have the highest average annual income (U.S. Bureau of the Census, 1999). Partly for this reason and because the time between departure of the last child and retirement is so long, the contemporary social view of marriage in midlife has become one of expansion and new horizons.

These forces strengthen the need to review and adjust the marital relationship. For Devin and Trisha, this shift was gradual. By middle age, their marriage had permitted gratification of both family and individual needs, endured many changes, and culminated in a period in which more love was expressed than at any other time. Elena's marriage, in contrast, became more conflict ridden as her teenage daughter's problems introduced added strains and as departure of children made marital difficulties more obvious. Tim's failed marriage revealed yet another pattern. With passing years, both love expressed and number of problems declined. As less happened in the relationship, either good or bad, the couple had little to keep them together (McCullough & Rutenberg, 1989).

As the Variations box on pages 530–531 revealed, marital satisfaction is a strong predictor of midlife psychological well-being (Ishii-Kuntz, 1990). Middle-aged men who have focused only on career often realize the limited nature of their pursuits. At the same time, their wives may insist on a different and deeper relationship. In addition, children fully engaged in adult roles remind middle-aged parents that they are in the latter part of their lives. Consequently, many decide that the time for improving their marriages is now. Marital quality is on the rise for couples married over 25 years, in part because they strive to improve their relationships and in part because reduced parental responsibilities and greater economic security grant them time and resources to do so (Orbuch et al., 1996).

As in early adulthood, divorce is one way of resolving an unsatisfactory marriage in midlife. Although most divorces occur within 5 to 10 years of marriage, in the United States 11 percent take place after 20 years or more (U.S. Department of Health and Human Services, 1999g). Because the current midlife generation was married at a time when divorce rates were lower, marital breakup is often more difficult than it is for young adults. Middle-aged people are more likely to view it as a personal failure. And they typi-

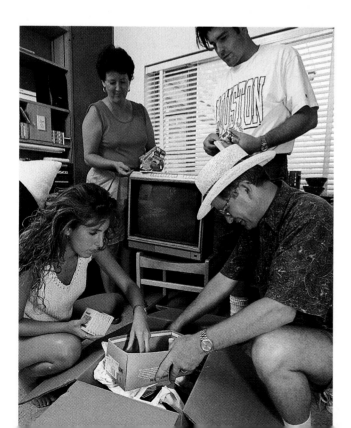

■ *These parents help their daughter unpack for her first year of college. Her older brother also assists, suggesting that the day marks a family milestone. For the parents, the middle-aged phase of the family life cycle—"launching children and moving on"— has arrived. Generally, this is a liberating time, bringing a sense of completion and a chance to strengthen existing ties and to invest in new, fulfilling relationships. (Photo courtesy: Bob Daemmrich/ The Image Works)*

■ *What does the future hold for this divorcing couple, who are trying to settle their financial and child-custody disputes with the help of divorce mediation? For the woman, divorce is likely to bring a sharp decline in standard of living. Yet if she weathers divorce successfully, she will probably experience personal growth, becoming more tolerant, comfortable with uncertainty, and nonconforming in personality. The man is likely to enter a new relationship within a short time. (Photo courtesy: Michael Newman/PhotoEdit)*

cally find less peer support because fewer divorces occur in their age group. Women in traditional marriages, who devoted themselves to caring for husband and children, have the hardest time adjusting to divorce.

A substantial number of midlife divorces occur to people who have had one or more previous unsuccessful marriages, since the divorce rate is more than twice as great among remarried couples as among couples in first marriages. Highly educated midlifers are more likely to divorce, probably because their more comfortable economic circumstances make it easier to leave an unhappy marriage (Wu & Penning, 1997). Nevertheless, for many women, the negative impact of marital breakup—especially when it is repeated—on standard of living is devastating. In a study of over five thousand 30- to 44-year-old women followed over 15 years, divorce led to a 39 percent drop in average income. Many African-American women opted for separation rather than divorce, probably because of the high cost of divorce proceedings. Women who separated had the highest poverty rate—before the marital transition (27 percent) and afterward (57 percent). Neither separated nor divorced women escaped economic disadvantage after adjusting to their new life circumstances. Even 7 or 8 years after their marriages ended, the high rate of poverty persisted (Morgan, 1991).

As these findings reveal, marital breakup, in midlife and earlier, is a strong contributor to the **feminization of poverty** —a trend in which women who support themselves or their families have become the majority of the adult poverty population, regardless of age and ethnic group. Because of weak public policies safeguarding families (see Chapter 2), the gender gap in poverty is much higher in the United States

than in other Western industrialized nations (Goldberg & Kremen, 1990; U.S. Bureau of the Census, 1999).

What do recently divorced middle-aged people say about why their marriages ended? In one study, women mentioned communication problems most often, followed by husband's substance abuse, husband's physical and verbal abuse, and their own desire for autonomy. Notice how these responses dwell on neutral circumstances (communication) and the husband's faults. When women attribute divorce to a cause that is more self-accusing ("my husband's lack of interest in me"), they show poorer adjustment (Davis & Aron, 1989).

Longitudinal evidence reveals that middle-aged women who weather divorce successfully tend to become more tolerant, comfortable with uncertainty, and nonconforming in personality—factors believed to be fostered by divorce-forced independence. As in earlier periods, divorce represents "both a time of trauma and a time of growth" (Rockwell, Elder, & Ross, 1979, p. 403). Unfortunately, little is known about divorce adjustment among middle-aged men, perhaps because most enter new relationships and remarry within a short time.

CHANGING PARENT–CHILD RELATIONSHIPS

Parents' positive relationships with their grown children are the result of a gradual process of "letting go," starting in childhood, gaining momentum in adolescence, and culminating in children's independent living. As mentioned earlier, most middle-aged parents adjust well to the launching phase of the family life cycle; only a minority have difficulty. Investment in nonparental relationships and roles, children's characteristics, parents' marital and economic circumstances, and cultural forces affect the extent to which this transition is expansive and rewarding or sad and distressing.

After moving their son Mark into his college dormitory at the start of his freshman year, Devin and Trisha felt a twinge of nostalgia. On the way home, they recalled his birth, first day of school, and high school graduation and commented on their suddenly tranquil household. Beyond this, they returned to rewarding careers and community participation and delighted in having more time for each other. Parents who have developed gratifying alternative activities typically welcome their children's adult status. A strong work orientation, especially, predicts gains in life satisfaction after children depart from the home (Seltzer & Ryff, 1994; Silverberg, 1996).

Regardless of whether they reside with parents, adolescent and young adult children who are "off time" in development—not showing expected signs of independence and accomplishment—can prompt parental strain (Aquilino, 1996; Ryff et al., 1994). Consider Elena, whose daughter was frequently truant from high school and in danger of not graduating. The need for greater parental oversight and guidance caused anxiety and unhappiness for Elena, who was ready to complete the active parenting phase and focus on her own personal and vocational development (Raup & Myers, 1989).

The end of parent–child coresidence is accompanied by a substantial decline in parental authority. Devin and Trisha no longer knew of Mark's daily comings and goings nor expected that he inform them. Nevertheless, Mark telephoned at regular intervals to report on events in his life and seek advice about major decisions. Although the parental role changes, its continuation is important to middle-aged adults. Departure of children is a relatively minor event when parent–child contact and affection are sustained. When it results in little or no communication, parents' life satisfaction declines (White, 1994). In a longitudinal study of several hundred German families, parents' relations with adult children were linked to child-rearing styles assessed 16 years before. The more loving and confident parents were early on, the greater their closeness to grown children, as rated by both parent and child (Schneewind & Ruppert, 1998).

Recall from Chapter 13 that many young people from low-income homes and with cultural traditions of extended family living do not leave home early. Consequently, the timing of the launching phase varies greatly with SES and ethnicity. In traditional families with strong investment of authority in the father, departure of an adult child can threaten parental status, undermining parent–child relations and well-being in midlife (Hartley, 1995).

Throughout middle adulthood, parents continue to give more assistance to children than they receive, especially while children are young adults and unmarried or when they face difficulties, such as marital breakup or unemployment (Rossi & Rossi, 1990). Providing emotional and financial support while children get their lives under way is related to midlife psychological well-being. Due to disrupted relationships and economic need, divorced and remarried parents are less likely than parents in first marriages to offer adult children support, and they are also less content (Marks, 1995). Children's psychological adjustment is more important for midlife parental well-being than is their educational and occupational success (Ryff, Schmutte, & Lee, 1996). When young adult children are relatively free of emotional and social problems, they relate more positively to their parents. Favorable adaptation to the launching phase depends on feeling successful as a parent and not being estranged from one's children.

When children marry, parents face additional challenges in enlarging the family network to include in-laws. Difficulties occur when parents do not approve of their child's partner or when the young couple adopts a way of life inconsistent with the values of the family of origin. When warm, supportive relationships endure, intimacy between parents and children increases over the adult years, with great benefits for parents' life satisfaction (Rossi & Rossi, 1990). Once young adults strike out on their own, members of the middle generation, especially mothers, usually take on the role of **kinkeeper,** gathering the family for celebrations and making sure everyone stays in touch.

As children become adults, parents expect a mature relationship with them, marked by tranquility and contentment. Yet many factors—on the child's and adult's side—affect whether that goal is achieved. The Caregiving Concerns table below suggests ways middle-aged parents can increase the chances that bonds with adult children will be loving and rewarding and serve as contexts for personal growth.

CAREGIVING CONCERNS

Ways Middle-Aged Parents Can Promote Positive Ties with Their Adult Children

SUGGESTION	DESCRIPTION
Emphasize positive communication.	Let adult children know of your respect, support, and interest. This not only communicates affection but permits conflict to be handled in a constructive context.
Avoid unnecessary comments that are a holdover from childhood.	Adult children, like younger children, appreciate an age-appropriate relationship. Comments that have to do with safety, eating, and cleanliness (for example, "Be careful on the freeway," "Don't eat those foods," and "Make sure you wear a sweater on a cold day") annoy adult children and can stifle communication.
Accept the possibility that some cultural values and practices and aspects of lifestyle will be modified in the next generation.	In constructing a personal identity, most adult children have gone through a process of evaluating the meaning of cultural values and practices for their own lives. Traditions and lifestyles cannot be imposed on adult children; parents' efforts to do so can be a source of great conflict and stress. Recognize that relationships with grown children can outlive each family member's beliefs and lifestyle preferences. Rather than focusing on conflicts, look for common ground.
When an adult child encounters difficulties, resist the urge to "fix" things.	Although you may have difficulty tolerating the situation, accept the fact that no meaningful change can take place without the willing cooperation of the adult child. Stepping in and taking over communicates a lack of confidence and respect. Find out whether the adult child wants your help, advice, and decision-making skills.
Be clear about your own needs and preferences.	When it is difficult to arrange for a visit, baby-sit, or provide other assistance, say so and negotiate a reasonable compromise rather than letting resentment build.

Source: Toder, 1994.

GRANDPARENTHOOD

Two years after Mark married, Devin and Trisha were thrilled to learn that a granddaughter was on the way. Although the stereotypical image of grandparents as very elderly persists, today the average age of grandparenthood in the United States is 46 for women, 49 for men. African Americans typically become grandparents 5 years earlier than Caucasian Americans, Hispanics 2 years earlier. A longer life expectancy means that adults will spend as much as one-third of their lifespan in the grandparent role (Szinovacz, 1998).

■ MEANINGS OF GRANDPARENTHOOD. Why did Trisha and Devin, like many people their age, greet the announcement of a grandchild with such enthusiasm? Grandparenthood is a highly significant milestone to most who experience it. When asked about its meaning, people generally mention one or more of the following gratifications:

- Valued elder—being perceived as a wise, helpful person

- Immortality through descendants—leaving behind not just one but two generations after death

- Reinvolvement with personal past—being able to pass family history and values to a new generation

- Indulgence—having fun with children without major child-rearing responsibilities (Kivnick, 1983; Miller & Cavanaugh, 1990)

■ GRANDPARENT–GRANDCHILD RELATIONSHIPS. Grandparents' styles of relating to grandchildren vary as widely as the meanings they derive from their new role. The grandparent and grandchild's age and sex make a difference. When their granddaughter was young, Trisha and Devin enjoyed an affectionate, playful relationship with her. As she got older, she looked to them for information and advice in addition to warmth and caring. By the time their granddaughter reached adolescence, Trisha and Devin had become role models, family historians, and conveyers of social, vocational, and religious values (Hurme, 1991; Kornhaber & Woodward, 1981). Typically, relationships are closer between grandparents and grandchildren of the same sex and, especially, between maternal grandmothers and granddaughters—a pattern found in many countries, including Canada, Finland, Poland, and the United States (Smith, 1991). Grandmothers also report higher satisfaction with the grandparent role than do grandfathers, perhaps because it is an important means through which middle-aged women satisfy their kinkeeping function (Somary & Stricker, 1998; Thomas, 1989).

Nearness of residence made Trisha and Devin's pleasurable interaction with their granddaughter possible. Grandparents who live far from grandchildren usually have more

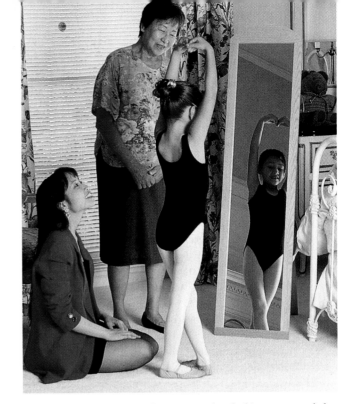

■ *In some subcultures, grandparents are absorbed into an extended family household and become actively involved in child rearing. When a Chinese-American, Japanese-American, or Mexican-American maternal grandmother is a homemaker, she is the preferred caregiver while parents of young children are at work. (Photo courtesy: David W. Hamilton/The Image Bank)*

distant relationships with them, appearing mainly on holidays, birthdays, and other formal occasions but otherwise having little contact. Despite high family mobility in Western industrialized nations, most grandparents live within 30 minutes of at least one grandchild, permitting regular visits (Werner, 1991). And even when grandparents reside far away, a strong desire to affect the development of grandchildren can motivate them to build a close bond and become active in grandchildren's lives (King & Elder, 1998).

SES and ethnicity are additional influences on grandparent–grandchild ties. In higher-income families, the grandparent role is not central to family maintenance and survival. For this reason, it is fairly unstructured and takes many forms. In contrast, grandparents perform essential activities in low-income families. For example, many single parents live with their families of origin, where grandparents' financial and caregiving assistance reduce the impact of poverty. Grandchildren in single-parent and stepparent families rate the quality and range of activities with their grandparents higher than do grandchildren in intact families (Kennedy & Kennedy, 1993). As children experience the stress of family transition, bonds with grandparents take on increasing importance.

In some subcultures, grandparents are absorbed into an extended family household and become actively involved in child rearing. When a Chinese-American, Korean-American, or Mexican-American maternal grandmother is a homemaker, she is the preferred caregiver while parents of young children are at work (Kamo, 1998; Williams & Torrez, 1998). Similarly, grandparent involvement in child care is high among Native Americans. In the absence of a biological grandparent, Native-American parents may adopt an unrelated elder into the family to serve as a mentor and disciplinarian for their children (Werner, 1991). (See Chapter 2, page 67, for a description of the grandmother's role in the African-American extended family.)

Increasingly, grandparents have stepped in as primary caregivers in the face of serious family problems. As the Social Issues box on the following page reveals, a rising number of American children live apart from their parents in grandparent-headed households. Despite their willingness to help and their competence at child rearing, grandparents taking full responsibility for young children experience considerable emotional and financial strain. They need much more assistance from community and government agencies than is currently available.

In most families, parents serve as gatekeepers of grandparents' contact with grandchildren. When grandparents and parents get along poorly, the grandparent–grandchild tie usually suffers. After marital breakup, for example, grandparents on the custodial parent's side have more frequent contact with grandchildren than do grandparents on the noncustodial side (Johnson, 1998). A growing concern among grandparents is maintaining contact with grandchildren after parental divorce. Currently, all 50 U.S. states permit grandparents to seek legal visitation judgments. Yet grandparent visitation rights can add to family difficulties. When parents are divorcing, the behavior of grandparents varies greatly, from constructive help to entanglement in parental battles (Stanton, 1998). Unfortunately, intense conflict usually lies behind the legal petitions of grandparents who fail to work out visitation informally. Consequently, the courts are wise to exercise restraint in awarding grandparents visitation privileges.

When family relationships are positive, grandparenthood provides an important means of fulfilling personal and societal needs in midlife and beyond. Typically, grandparents are a frequent source of pleasure, support, and knowledge for children, adolescents, and young adults. They also provide the young with firsthand experience in how older people think and function. In return, grandchildren become deeply attached to grandparents and keep them abreast of social change. Clearly, grandparenthood is a vital context for sharing between generations.

MIDDLE-AGED CHILDREN AND THEIR AGING PARENTS

Compared with earlier generations, today's adults spend more years not only as parents and grandparents, but also as children of aging parents. The percentage of middle-

aged people with living parents has risen dramatically— from 10 percent in 1900 to 50 percent in the 1990s (U.S. Bureau of the Census, 1999). A longer life expectancy means that adult children and their parents are increasingly likely to grow old together. What are middle-aged children's relationships with their aging parents like? And how does life change for adult children when an aging parent's health declines?

■ FREQUENCY AND QUALITY OF CONTACT. A widespread myth is that adults of past generations were more devoted to their aging parents than are adults of the present generation. Although adult children spend less time in close proximity to their parents, the reason is not neglect or isolation. Fewer aging adults live with younger generations now than in the past because of a desire to be independent, made possible by gains in health and financial security. Nevertheless, two-thirds of older adults in the United States live close to at least one of their children, and frequency of contact is high through both visits and telephone calls. Proximity increases with age. Elders who move usually do so in the direction of kin, and younger people tend to move in the direction of their aging parents. The majority of older people are satisfied with the amount of face-to-face contact they have with their children (Jerrome, 1990).

Middle age is a time when adults reassess relationships with their parents, just as they rethink other close ties (Helson & Moane, 1987). Many adult children become more appreciative of their parents' strengths and generosity. Trisha, for example, marveled at her parents' fortitude in rearing three college-educated children despite limited income. And she recalled her mother's sound advice just before her marriage to Devin nearly three decades earlier: "Build a life together but also forge your own life. You'll be happier." Trisha had called on that advice at several turning points, and it influenced her decisions.

In the non-Western world, older adults most often live with their married children. Chinese and Japanese elderly, for example, generally reside with the eldest son and his wife and children (Kamo, 1998). Regardless of whether coresidence and daily contact are typical, relationship quality varies widely. Usually, patterns established earlier persist; positive parent–child ties remain so, as do conflict-ridden interactions.

Help exchanged between adult children and their aging parents is responsive to past and current family circumstances. The closer family ties were when children were growing up, the more help given and received (Whitbeck, Hoyt, & Huck, 1994). Also, parents give more to single than to married children, and children give more to widowed parents and parents in poor health. At the same time, a shift in helping occurs over the adult years. Parent-to-child advice, household aid, gift giving, and financial assistance decline, whereas child-to-parent help of various kinds increases (Rossi & Rossi, 1991).

GRANDPARENTS REARING GRANDCHILDREN: THE SKIPPED-GENERATION FAMILY

Nearly 1.5 million American children and adolescents—2 percent of the child population—live with grandparents but apart from parents, in **skipped-generation families** (U.S. Bureau of the Census, 1999). The number of grandparents rearing grandchildren has increased over the past decade. The arrangement occurs in all ethnic groups, although more often among African-American and Hispanic children than among Caucasian-American children (Szinovacz, 1998).

The following grandmother's account illustrates the circumstances in which skipped-generation families form:

I think [the child's mother] is doing an awful lot of drugs. I don't know if it's serious drugs, but enough that she wasn't doing a good job. They were doing an awful lot of partying, and I just finally went to her one day and said, "Your life is messed up, let me take the baby for a while so you can get your life together." And it was just because we wanted her [the granddaughter] out of there. She had

become our main priority. (Jenrek, 1994, p. 209)

Usually, grandparents step in because emotional or substance abuse problems or physical illness prevent the child's parents, most often the mother, from engaging in competent child rearing (Hirshorn, 1998; Woodworth, 1996). At times, child welfare authorities, out of a preference for placing the child with relatives rather than in a foster home, approach the grandparent, who assumes temporary or permanent legal custody. In most instances, grandparents offer their assistance, sometimes with and sometimes without legal responsibility. Most say they took action to protect the child only when the parents' situation became intolerable.

Because the skipped-generation family structure is not freely chosen, many grandparents face a highly stressful child-rearing situation. Previous family experiences have left their mark, in the form of high rates of learning difficulties, depression, and antisocial behavior (Pinson-Millburn et al., 1996). These children are not only challenging to rear, but introduce financial burdens in-

to households, many of which are already low-income. Grandparents struggle daily with dilemmas—wanting to be grandparents, not parents; wanting the parent to be present in the child's life but fearing for the child's well-being if the parent returns and cannot provide good care. Daily child-rearing tasks mean that grandparents have less time for spouses, friends, and leisure when they had expected to have more time. Many report feeling tired, emotionally drained, and depressed (Goldberg-Glen et al., 1998; Minkler et al., 1997).

Skipped-generation families have a tremendous need for social and financial support. Despite the burdens, these grandparents seem to realize their widespread image as "silent saviors." A survey of a large representative sample of U.S. families revealed that compared with children in divorced, single-parent families or in blended families, children reared by grandparents were better behaved in school, less susceptible to physical illness, and doing just as well academically (Solomon & Marx, 1995). These outcomes foster compensating feelings of accomplishment and pride in grandparents, some of whom view the rearing of grandchildren as a "second chance" to "do it right," in contrast with earlier parenting experiences (Minkler & Roe, 1993).

■ *Vera Saunders, age 71, shown here with her 17-year-old grandson who still lives with her, is tired but proud. In middle age, she took custody of three grandchildren. For a time, she also cared for a great-grandchild. She takes special pleasure in the achievements of her 25-year-old granddaughter, who won a scholarship to Yale University and is now in medical school at Emory University. "I took her when she was only 3 days old," Vera recalls, "because her mother had a nervous breakdown." Grandparents in skipped-generation families face myriad problems, including shattered dreams of freedom and relaxation at this time in their lives and significant financial burdens. To Vera, the sacrifices were definitely worthwhile. (Photo courtesy: © 2000 Globe Newspaper Company, Inc.)*

■ CARING FOR AGING PARENTS. The burden of caring for aging parents can be great. In Chapter 2, we noted that the family structure has become more "top-heavy," with more generations alive, but fewer younger members as birthrates have declined. This means that more than one older family member is likely to need assistance, with fewer younger adults available to provide it. Today's middle-aged adults with ill or frail parents typically face competing demands of children (some of whom are under age 18 and still at home) and employment. They are called the **sandwich generation** because they are "sandwiched," or squeezed, between the needs of aging parents and financially dependent children. About 1 in every 10 middle-aged adults in the United States is involved in caring for a parent with a disability or chronic illness (Marks, 1996; Nichols & Junk, 1997).

When an aging parent's spouse cannot provide care, adult daughters are the next most likely relatives to do so. Even when the spouse is available, adult children—again, usually daughters—often pitch in as needed. Why are women more often elected as caregivers? Families turn to the person who seems most available—living nearby and with fewer commitments regarded as interfering with the ability to assist. These unstated rules, in addition to parents' preference for same-sex caregivers (aging mothers live longer), lead more women to fill the role. About 50 percent of women caregivers are employed; another 9 to 28 percent quit their jobs to provide care (Brody et al., 1987; Nichols & Junk, 1997).

Nevertheless, men make a substantial contribution to care of aging parents—one that should not be overlooked. Tim, for example, looked in on his father, a recent stroke victim, every evening, reading to him, running errands, making household repairs, and taking care of finances. His sister, however, provided more hands-on care in her own home—cooking, feeding, and bathing. The care sons and daughters provide tends to be divided along gender-role lines. However, no sex differences exist in sense of obligation or affection toward aging parents. About 10 percent of the time, sons become primary caregivers, generally when no other family member can do so (Harris, 1998; Kahana, Biegel, & Wykle, 1994).

As adults move from early to later middle age, the sex difference in parental caregiving declines (see Figure 16.3). Perhaps as men reduce their vocational commitments and feel less need to conform to a "masculine" gender role, they are more able and willing to provide basic care (Marks, 1996). At the same time, parental caregiving may contribute to men's greater openness to the "feminine" side of their personalities. A man who cared for his mother, severely impaired by Alzheimer's disease, commented on how the experience altered his outlook:

> Having to do personal care, becoming a male nurse, was a great adjustment. It was so difficult to do these tasks; things a man, a son, is not supposed to do. But, I had to alter, since charity must come before maintaining a selfish, conventional view. I have definitely modified my views on conventional expectations. (Hirsch, 1996, p. 112)

Although most adult children help willingly, caring for a chronically ill or disabled parent is highly stressful. Some people regard it as similar to caring for a young child, but it is very different. The need for parental care typically occurs suddenly, after a heart attack, fall, stroke, or diagnosis of cancer, leaving little time for preparation. Whereas children become increasingly independent, the parent usually gets worse and the caregiving task as well as its cost escalates. "One of the most difficult aspects is the emotional

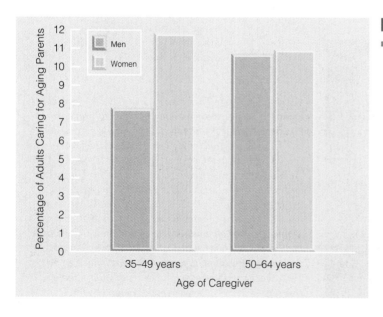

FIGURE 16.3

■ **Percentage of middle-aged men and women involved in caring for an aging parent in the United States, based on interviews with a nationally representative sample of over 13,000 adults.** Although women are usually the primary caregivers, men make substantial contributions to the care of ill and frail parents. With age, the sex difference in parental caregiving declines. (Adapted from Marks, 1996.)

strain of being such a close observer of my father's physical and mental decline," Tim explained to Devin and Trisha. Tim also felt a sense of grief over the loss of a cherished relationship, as his father no longer seemed to be his former self. Because duration of caregiving is uncertain, caregivers often feel as if they no longer have control over their lives (Gatz, Bengtson, & Blum, 1990).

Adults who share a household with ill parents—about 10 percent of caregivers—experience the most stress (Marks, 1996). In addition to the factors just mentioned, a parent and child who have lived separately for years usually dislike moving in together. Conflicts are likely to arise over routines and lifestyles. But the greatest source of stress is problem behavior, especially for caregivers of parents who have deteriorated mentally. Tim's sister reported that their father would wake during the night, ask repetitive questions, follow her around the house, and become agitated and combative (Gatz, Bengtson, & Blum, 1990). Parental caregiving often has emotional and physical health consequences. It leads to difficulties combining work and family, frequent job absenteeism, exhaustion, difficulty concentrating, and rates of depression as high as 30 to 50 percent (Merrill, 1997; Stephens, Franks, & Atienza, 1997).

Social support is highly effective in reducing caregiver stress. Tim's encouragement, assistance, and willingness to listen helped his sister cope with in-home care of their father. As a result, she found satisfactions and rewards in it. Despite more time to care for an ill parent, women who quit work generally fare poorly, probably because of social isolation and financial strain (Pohl et al., 1994). Positive experiences at work can actually reduce the stress of parental care as caregivers bring a favorable self-evaluation and a positive mood home with them (Stephens & Franks, 1999).

Surrogate in-home care (by a nonfamily member) is often not a solution because of its high cost and low availability outside large cities. And unless they must, few people want to place their parents in formal care, such as nursing homes, which are also expensive. At present, adult children have limited options in how to provide parental care. The Caregiving Concerns table below summarizes ways to relieve the stress of caring for an aging parent—at the individual, family, community, and societal levels.

SIBLINGS

As Tim's relationship with his sister reveals, siblings are ideally suited to provide social support. The majority of adult siblings report frequent contact, seeing or talking on the phone at least monthly. As in early adulthood, sister–sister relationships are closer than sister–brother and brother–brother ties, a trend apparent in many industrialized nations (Cicerelli, 1995; White & Riedmann, 1992).

Middle adulthood is often a time when sibling bonds strengthen in response to major life events. Parenting and employment pressures may have caused the sibling relationship to be set aside temporarily. Launching and mar-

CAREGIVING CONCERNS

Relieving the Stress of Caring for an Aging Parent

STRATEGY	DESCRIPTION
Use effective coping strategies.	Use problem-centered coping to manage the parent's behavior and caregiving tasks. Delegate responsibilities to other family members, seek assistance from friends and neighbors, and recognize the parent's limits while calling on capacities the parent does have. Use emotion-centered coping to reinterpret the situation in a positive way, such as emphasizing its opportunity for personal growth and for giving to parents in the last years of their lives. Avoid denial of anger, depression, and anxiety in response to the caregiver work burden, which heightens stress.
Seek social support.	Confide in family members and friends about the stress of caregiving, seeking their encouragement and help. So far as possible, avoid quitting work to care for an ill parent because it leads to social isolation and loss of financial resources.
Make use of community resources.	Contact your Area Agency on Aging (see Chapter 2, page 69), church, synagogue, and other community organizations to seek information and assistance, in the form of in-home respite help, home-delivered meals, transportation, and adult day care.
Press for workplace and public policies that relieve the emotional and financial burdens of caring for an aging parent.	Difficulties faced by caregivers are partly due to lack of workplace and societal supports. Encourage your employer to provide elder care benefits, such as flexible work hours and caregiver leave without pay. Communicate with lawmakers and other citizens about the need for additional government funding, in the form of tax relief and other reimbursements, to help pay for elder care. Emphasize the need for improved health insurance plans that reduce the financial strain of elder care on middle- and low-income families.

riage of children seem to prompt sisters and brothers to think more about each other. As Tim commented, "It helped our relationship when my sister's children were out of the house and married. I'm sure she cared about me. I think she just didn't have time!" Parental illness can have a profound impact on sibling closeness. Brothers and sisters who previously had little to do with one another find themselves in frequent contact as they cooperate to provide care. When parents die, adult children realize they have become the oldest generation in the family and must look to each other to sustain family ties (Gold, 1996; Moyer, 1992).

Although the trend is toward closer relationships, not all sibling bonds improve in midlife. Recall Trisha's negative encounters with her sister, Dottie (see Chapter 15, page 501). Yet Dottie's difficult temperament had made her hard to get along with since childhood. Her temper flared when their father died and problems arose over family finances. When siblings do not help with parental caregiving, powerful negative feelings can be unleashed in the child shouldering the burden (Merrill, 1997). As one expert expressed it, "As siblings grow older, good relationships [often] become better and rotten relationships get worse" (Moyer, 1992, p. 57). Clearly, sibling ties are affected by a combination of sibling personalities and events in siblings' lives.

In Western nations, adult siblings usually live independently, and the relationship is voluntary. Frequency of interaction depends on both psychological closeness and nearness of residence. Ethnic background also makes a difference. In one study, Italian-American siblings (especially sisters) had much greater contact and warmer relationships than did white Protestant siblings (Johnson, 1985). The researchers speculated that strong parental authority in Italian immigrant families led siblings to turn to one another for support early in life. These bonds persisted into adulthood.

Closer ties between sisters do not necessarily characterize nonindustrialized societies, where sibling relationships are basic to family functioning. For example, among Asian Pacific Islanders, brother–sister attachments are strong, and family social life is organized around them. A brother–sister pair is often treated as a special unit in exchange marriages with another family. After marriage, brothers are expected to protect sisters, and sisters serve as spiritual mentors for brothers. Families not only include a large number of biological siblings, but also grant other relatives, such as cousins, the status of brother or sister (Cicerelli, 1995). This leads to an unusually large network of sibling support throughout life.

In village and tribal societies, cultural norms prevent sibling conflict, which could threaten family cooperation (Weisner, 1993). In industrialized nations, promoting positive sibling interaction in childhood is vital for ensuring that siblings will support one another in later years. With each life event in middle adulthood, many siblings grow closer together, whereas others drift further apart.

FRIENDSHIPS

In his forties and fifties, Devin had more time to spend with friends than he did in the previous decade, when family responsibilities took away from friendship. Late Friday afternoons, he met several male friends at a coffee house, and they chatted for a couple of hours. However, the majority of Devin's friends were couple based—ones in which he and Trisha gathered with other husband–wife pairs. Compared with Devin, Trisha more often got together with friends on her own (Blieszner & Adams, 1992).

Characteristics of middle-age friendships are a continuation of trends discussed in Chapter 14. In a study of 18- to 75-year-olds, men were less expressive with friends than were women across all age groups. Whereas men tended to talk about sports, politics, and business, women focused on feelings and life problems. For this reason, when Trisha and Devin gathered with friends, men often congregated in one area, women in another (Fox, Gibbs, & Auerbach, 1985; Wellman, 1992). Women report a greater number of close friends and say they both receive and provide their friends with more emotional support. Not surprisingly, women are more satisfied with their friendships than are men (Antonucci, 1994).

Nevertheless, for both sexes, number of friends declines with age, probably because people become less willing to invest in nonfamily ties that are unimportant to them (Carbery & Buhrmester, 1998). As selectivity of friendship increases, middle-aged and older people express deeper and more complex ideas about friendship. They also try harder to reduce disagreements with friends than do young adults (Antonucci & Akiyama, 1995). Having chosen a friend, adults in midlife attach great value to the relationship and take extra steps to protect it.

By middle age, family relationships and friendships support different aspects of psychological well-being. Family ties protect the individual against serious threats and losses. Because such ties are based on obligation, they promote security within a long-term time frame. In contrast, friendships are voluntary ties that serve as current sources of pleasure and satisfaction (Antonucci & Akiyama, 1995). As middle-aged husbands and wives renew their sense of partnership and companionship, they may combine the best of family and friendship. Indeed, research indicates that viewing a spouse as a best friend contributes greatly to marital happiness (Bengtson, Rosenthal, & Burton, 1990).

RELATIONSHIPS ACROSS GENERATIONS

A widely recognized goal of families, communities, and society as a whole is that each generation of adults leaves the next better off. For more than two centuries, this aspiration has been met in the United States. For example, Trisha's high-school-educated parents did everything possible to support her desire to earn a professional degree. And Devin and Trisha reared their son under financially more comfortable circumstances than they had experienced as children.

Yet Trisha and Devin often wondered, as many Americans do, whether the current generation would ever be as well off as the previous one. And on the basis of high rates of marital breakup, single-parent families, youth crime rates, and geographical distance among extended family members, they questioned whether younger people would continue to respect their elders and look after their well-being. Trisha and Devin also worried that improved financial conditions among the elderly in comparison to the high poverty rate among families with young children (see Chapter 2, page 64) might fuel intergenerational anger and resentment.

Is solidarity between generations eroding in the United States? A survey of a nationally representative sample of 1,500 people between ages 18 and 90 addressed this question. Findings showed that despite the social changes just mentioned, supportive ties among younger and older citizens have endured (Bengtson & Harootyan, 1994).

At the family level, the large majority (90 percent) of adult children reported feeling close to an aging parent. In fact, adult children described closer ties to their aging parents than aging parents felt toward their adult children (although 80 percent of these ties were also strong). In line with the high rate of help giving noted earlier in this chapter, younger adults expressed a deep sense of obligation toward their parents—more than their parents expected from them! For example, only 19 percent of 18- to 34-year-olds and 28 percent of 35- to 44-year-olds agreed with the statement, "Grown children should not be expected to support their parents." In contrast, 51 percent of 45- to 64-year-olds and 55 percent of people age 65 and over agreed with this statement (Lawton, Silverstein, & Bengtson, 1994). Furthermore, adult children's willingness to grant time and assistance to aging parents is unaffected by parents' wealth (Wong, Kitayama, & Soldo, 1999).

Young, middle-aged, and older survey respondents reported a wide range of volunteer activities in their communities. Middle-aged adults frequently devoted time to children and adolescents—usually through church or synagogue activities and academic tutoring programs. Older adults, by contrast, more often provided volunteer assistance to the elderly. But they were more likely to do so if they had warm relationships with their adult children—a finding that reflects an important link between family relationships and giving to the community. More than 70 percent of the sample described some kind of informal assistance to relatives, friends, neighbors, and other community residents (Harootyan & Vorek, 1994).

Finally, most participants expressed no resentment about government benefits to other age groups. Instead, a *norm of equity* characterized their responses. When people believed the needs of one generation were unmet, they expressed dissatisfaction about government benefits to another age group. Only rarely did they say that their own age group was neediest and should get more (Schlesinger & Kronebusch, 1994). Very young adults (18- to 24-year-olds) are more likely than other age groups to view government programs serving the elderly as too costly. But having had frequent contact with grandparents increases their endorsement of these benefits (Silverstein & Parrott, 1997).

In sum, despite public concern over intergenerational conflicts, strong connections between age groups within the family and the community exist, and most people are not guided by self-interest in how they think government resources should be distributed. The values, opinions, and behaviors of ordinary citizens reveal "hidden bridges" among people of all ages. They suggest that intergenerational responsibility is likely to guide the activities of Americans for many years to come.

ASK YOURSELF . . .

Freda divorced her husband after 25 years of marriage. Compared with her daughter Salena, who got divorced at age 30, Freda had a harder time adjusting. Explain why adapting to divorce is more difficult for middle-aged than for young adults and is particularly stressful for women.

■ *Raylene and her brother Walter live in the same city as their aging mother, Elsie. When Elsie could no longer live independently, Raylene took primary responsibility for her care. What factors probably contributed to Raylene's involvement in caregiving and Walter's lesser role?*

As a young adult, Daniel maintained close friendship ties with six college classmates. At age 45, he continued to see only two of them. What explains Daniel's reduced circle of friends in midlife?

VOCATIONAL LIFE

We have already seen that the midlife transition typically involves vocational readjustments. For Devin, it resulted in a move up the career ladder to a demanding administrative post as college dean. Trisha reoriented her career from a large to a small law firm, where she could pursue cases that interested her and felt her efforts were appreciated. Recall from Chapter 15 that after her oldest child left home, Anya earned a college degree and entered the work force for the first time. Jewel strengthened her commitment to an already successful business, whereas

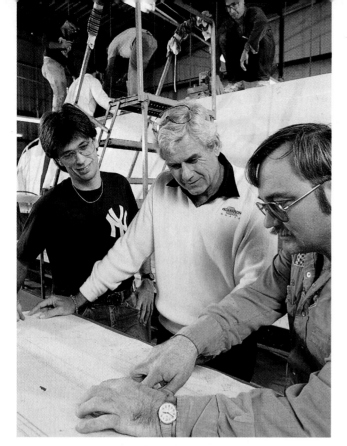

■ *These middle-aged boat designers share their thoughts with a younger co-worker as they look over new plans. Job satisfaction rises in midlife. Intrinsic satisfaction—contentment with the work itself—is largely responsible for the overall gain. (Photo courtesy: Bob Daemmrich/The Image Works)*

Elena changed careers. Finally, Tim reduced his vocational obligations as he prepared for retirement.

Work continues to be a salient aspect of identity and self-esteem in middle adulthood. More so than in earlier or later years, middle-aged workers attempt to increase the personal meaning and self-direction of their vocational lives (Levinson, 1978, 1996). At the same time, certain aspects of job performance improve. Older employees have lower rates of absenteeism, turnover, and accidents and show no change in work productivity (Warr, 1994). Consequently, the value of an older employee ought to be equal to, and possibly even greater than, that of a younger employee.

Understanding the midvocational years is especially important. The post–World War II baby boom, along with the elimination of mandatory retirement age in many industrialized nations, means that the number of older workers will rise dramatically over the next few decades (Salthouse & Maurer, 1996). Yet a favorable transition from adult worker to older worker is hindered by negative stereotypes of aging—incorrect beliefs about limited learning capacity, slower decision making, and resistance to change and supervision. Furthermore, gender discrimination continues to restrict the vocational attainments of many women. Let's take a close look at middle-aged work life.

JOB SATISFACTION

Job satisfaction has both psychological and economic significance. If people are dissatisfied at work, the consequences include strikes, grievances, absenteeism, and turnover, all of which are costly to employers.

Research shows that overall job satisfaction increases with age at all occupational levels, from executives to hourly workers. The relationship is weaker for women than for men, probably because of women's reduced chances for advancement, which result in a sense of unfairness. It is also weaker for blue-collar than for white-collar workers, perhaps because blue-collar workers have less control over their own work schedules and activities (Fotinatos-Ventouratos & Cooper, 1998; Avolio & Sosik, 1999). When different aspects of jobs are considered, intrinsic satisfaction—contentment with the work itself—shows a strong age-related gain. Extrinsic satisfaction—for example, with supervision, pay, and promotions—changes very little (Warr, 1994).

What explains the rise in job satisfaction over the adult years? A broader time perspective probably contributes. "I recall complaining about how much I had to do when I first started teaching," remarked Devin. "Since then, I've seen a lot of hard times. From my current vantage point, I can tell a big problem from a trivial one." Moving out of unrewarding work roles, as Trisha did, can also boost morale. Key characteristics that predict job well-being include involvement in decision making, reasonable workloads, and good physical working conditions. Older people may have greater access to jobs that are attractive in these ways. Finally, having fewer alternative positions into which they can move, older workers generally reduce their vocational aspirations. As the perceived gap between actual and possible achievements declines, work involvement and commitment increase (Warr, 1992).

Although emotional engagement with work is usually seen as psychologically healthy, it can also result in **burnout**—a condition in which long-term job stress leads to emotional exhaustion, a sense of loss of personal control, and feelings of reduced accomplishment (de Rijk et al., 1998; Lee & Ashforth, 1990). Burnout occurs more often in the helping professions, including health care, human services, and teaching. Managers with substantial responsibility for others are also susceptible. Although people in interpersonally demanding jobs are as psychologically healthy as other people, sometimes a worker's dedication exceeds his or her coping skills and the social supports available in the work setting. The combination of high intrinsic and low extrinsic job satisfaction is associated with the emotional exhaustion and loss of personal control aspects of burnout. A low intrinsic and low extrinsic job satisfaction combination is linked to feelings of reduced accomplishment (Zedeck et al., 1988).

Burnout is a serious occupational hazard, since it is linked to absenteeism, turnover, poor job performance, and impaired health (Wright & Bonett, 1997). It is more common today than several decades ago, perhaps because extraordinarily stressful conditions are more frequent in jobs involving work with people (Jenkins & Maslach, 1994). Employers can prevent burnout by making sure workloads are reasonable, providing opportunities for workers to take time out from stressful situations, and limiting hours of stressful work.

A widespread movement to increase worker participation in production planning and interaction through job teams is likely to boost job satisfaction at all ages. Other proposals include provisions for work at home, which would accommodate the desire of some people for less noise and time pressure and more opportunities to take breaks without disturbing others.

VOCATIONAL DEVELOPMENT

After several years as a parish nurse, Anya felt a need for additional training to find ways to do her job better. Trisha especially appreciated her current work setting because of its extensive support of workshop and course attendance, which helped her keep abreast of new legal developments. As college dean, Devin attended several seminars each year on management effectiveness and innovations in instructional technology. As Anya, Trisha, and Devin reveal, vocational development is vital during all phases of work life.

■ JOB TRAINING. Anya's 35-year-old supervisor, Roy, was surprised when she asked for time off to take several seminars to upgrade her skills. "You're in your fifties," he commented insensitively. "What're you going to do with so much new information at this point in your life?"

Although Roy's narrow-minded attitude is usually left unspoken, it is all too common among managers—even some who are older themselves! Research suggests that less training and on-the-job career counseling are available to older workers. And when vocational development activities are offered, older employees may be less likely to volunteer for them (Cleveland & Shore, 1992; Salthouse & Maurer, 1996). What influences willingness to engage in job training and updating? Characteristics of the person and the work environment make a difference.

On the person side, the degree to which an individual wants to change is important. With age, growth needs decline somewhat in favor of security needs. Consequently, learning and challenge may have less intrinsic value to many older workers. Perhaps for this reason, older employees depend more on co-worker and supervisor encouragement for vocational development. Yet we have just seen that they are less likely to have supportive supervisors. Furthermore, stereotypes of aging reduce older workers' self-efficacy, or confidence that they can renew and expand their skills—another reason they may not volunteer for training experiences (Maurer & Tarulli, 1994; Noe & Wilk, 1993).

Challenging tasks facilitate updating. An employee given work that requires new learning has to obtain that learning to complete the assignment. Unfortunately, older workers sometimes receive more routine tasks than do younger workers. Therefore, some of their reduced participation in vocational development may be due to the type of assignments they receive. Interaction among co-workers can also have a profound impact. Inside project teams, people similar in age communicate more often. Age-balanced work groups (with more than one person in each age range) foster on-the-job learning because communication is a source of support as well as a means of acquiring job-relevant information (Zenger & Lawrence, 1989).

Computer networks facilitate such team interaction and also enhance sharing of information between departments in large companies. In this way, they help employees at lower levels develop a broader perspective on their contribution to company goals and feel a part of the larger organization (Avolio & Sosik, 1999). Furthermore, expansion of computer technology compels older workers to upgrade their computer literacy. This, in turn, assists them in keeping pace with changing aspects of their jobs.

■ GENDER AND ETHNICITY: THE GLASS CEILING. In her thirties, Jewel became a company president by starting her own business. As a woman, she decided that her chances of rising to a top-flight executive position in a large corporation were so slim that she didn't even try. Recall from Chapter 14 that women and ethnic minorities rarely move into high-level management jobs. At major firms in the United States, only 10 percent of senior executives are women. Far fewer than 1 percent are Asian-American, African-American, or Hispanic (Barr, 1996; Morrison, 1992).

Women and ethnic minorities face a **glass ceiling,** or invisible barrier to advancement up the corporate ladder. Contrary to popular belief, their low numbers cannot be attributed to poor management skills. In a survey of employees at six large American firms, women managers were rated as more effective and satisfying to work for and more likely to generate extra effort from people than were men. Characteristics that distinguished them from their male counterparts were charisma, inspiration, and considerateness (Bass & Avolio, 1994). Modern businesses realize that the best managers must not only display "masculine" authority and decisiveness but build consensus through wider participation in decision making—an approach that requires "feminine" qualities of caring and collaboration.

Why is there a glass ceiling? Management is an art and skill that must be taught. Yet women and members of ethnic minorities have less access to mentors, role models, and informal networks that serve as training routes. Also, the majority of chief executives acknowledge that they spend less money on formal training programs for their female employees. Reasons given are stereotyped uncertainties about

■ *Women and ethnic minorities face a glass ceiling, or invisible barrier to advancement up the career ladder, in major corporate and government organizations. A few, such as Secretary of State Madeleine Albright, succeed in shattering the glass ceiling. Many others go around it by starting their own businesses. (Photo courtesy: Librado Romero/The New York Times)*

women's commitment to their jobs and their capacity to become strong managers. Furthermore, challenging, high-risk, high-visibility assignments that require leadership and open the door to advancement, such as startup ventures, international experience, and troubleshooting, are rarely granted to women and minorities (Barr, 1996; Lyness & Thompson, 1997). And when women do demonstrate qualities linked to leadership and advancement, such as assertiveness, confidence, forcefulness, and ambitiousness, they encounter prejudice because they deviate from traditional gender roles. They are evaluated more negatively than men with these traits (Carli & Eagly, 2000; Eagly, 1999).

Like Jewel, many women have shattered the glass ceiling by going around it. Nearly twice as many female as male middle managers quit their jobs in large corporations, largely because of lack of career opportunities (Stroh, Brett, & Reilly, 1996). Today, there are 4 million American women who, like Jewel, have started their own businesses—a number six times that of men (Mergenhagen, 1996).

When women and ethnic minorities leave the corporate world to further their careers, companies not only lose valuable talent but fail to address the leadership needs of an increasingly diversified work force. The Caregiving Concerns table below summarizes strategies for breaking the glass ceiling, enabling women and ethnic minorities to reach the top in major organizations.

CAREER CHANGE AT MIDLIFE

Although most people remain in the same vocation through middle age, career change does occur, as Elena's shift from journalism to teaching and creative writing illustrates. Recall that circumstances at home and at work motivated Elena's decision to pursue a new vocation. Like other career changers, she wanted a more satisfying life—a goal attained by ending an unhappy marriage and initiating a long-awaited vocational move at the same time.

As noted earlier, midlife career changes are usually not radical; they typically involve leaving one line of work for a related one. Elena sought a more stimulating, involving job. But other people move in the reverse direction—to careers that are more relaxing, free of painful decisions, and less demanding in terms of responsibility for others (Oleski & Subich, 1996). The decision to change is often difficult. The individual must weigh years invested in one set of skills, current income, and job security against present frustrations and hoped-for gains from a new vocation.

CAREGIVING CONCERNS

Strategies for Breaking the Glass Ceiling

STRATEGY	DESCRIPTION
Reduce gender and ethnic stereotypes among executives.	Workshops that teach executives about diversity through training in self-awareness, sensitivity to differences, effective mentoring, and leadership skills
Recruit women and ethnic minorities.	Procedures that seek out women and minorities as job candidates and that hold managers accountable for equal employment opportunities
Equalize access to management training.	The same variety of training experiences for men and women and ethnic majority and minority employees; should include access to mentoring, informal networking, and high-risk, high-visibility assignments
Establish equitable promotion and salary policies.	Policies assuring that everyone is judged by common criteria and that employees doing the same job are paid the same, regardless of gender and ethnicity

When an extreme career shift occurs, it usually signals a personal crisis (Young & Rodgers, 1997). In a study of professionals who abandoned their well-paid, prestigious positions for routine, poorly paid, semiskilled work, nonwork problems influenced the break with an established career. For example, an eminent 55-year-old TV producer became a school bus driver; a New York banker become a waiter in a ski resort. Each responded to feelings of personal meaninglessness by escaping from family conflict, difficult relationships with colleagues, and work that had become unsatisfying into a freer, more independent lifestyle (Sarason, 1977).

UNEMPLOYMENT

Devin and Trisha's friend George worked in a corporate retirement-planning office, counseling retirees on how to enjoy leisure time or find new work. When he lost his job at age 54, he had to apply his counseling skills to himself. George found unemployment to be a profound culture shock. For the first two weeks, he spent most of the day in bed, didn't shave, and drank heavily. Even after this initial phase, George was depressed and had frequent bouts of illness.

As companies downsize and jobs are eliminated, the majority of people affected are middle-aged and older. Although unemployment is difficult at any time, middle-aged workers show much greater psychological distress than do their younger counterparts. Older workers affected by layoffs remain without work for a longer time, suffering substantial income loss (Couch, 1998; Fallick, 1996). In addition, people over age 40 who must reestablish occupational security find themselves "off time" in terms of the social clock. Consequently, job loss can disrupt major tasks of midlife, including generativity and reappraisal of life goals and accomplishments. Finally, having become more involved in and committed to an occupation, the older employed worker has also lost something of greater value (Broomhall & Winefield, 1990).

After a despondent period, George began to follow the advice he had given his clients. He made a list of what he really liked to do, what he didn't want to do again, and the risks he could take given his current financial and life circumstances. He formed his own small business and continued to advise retirees, write articles, and give speeches on all aspects of retirement, working from home in a T-shirt instead of a business suit. Effective problem-centered coping strategies enabled George to adjust (Beck, 1992).

Social support is vital for reducing stress and reassuring middle-aged job seekers of their worth. However, not all forms of social support work equally well. Recognition of the person's abilities and communication with others who share interests and values help the most. Both are social experiences that occur often in relations with co-workers (Mallinckrodt & Fretz, 1988).

People who have lost their jobs in midlife usually do not duplicate the status and pay of their previous positions. As they search, they encounter age discrimination and find that they are overqualified for many openings. Counseling that focuses on financial planning, reducing unhappiness related to deprivation of the family provider role, and encouraging personal flexibility can help people find alternative, gratifying work roles.

PLANNING FOR RETIREMENT

One evening, Devin and Trisha met George and Anya for dinner. Halfway through the meal, Devin inquired, "George, you're an expert on the topic. Tell us what you and Anya are going to do about retirement. Are you planning to close down your business or work part-time? Do you think you'll stay here or move out of town?"

Three or four generations ago, the two couples would not have had this conversation. In 1900, 69 percent of men age 65 and over were in the labor force. By 1965, the figure had dropped to 30 percent. In 1997, it was 12 percent (U.S. Bureau of the Census, 1999). Retirement is no longer a privilege reserved for the wealthy. In 1935, the U.S. Social Security Act initiated government-sponsored retirement benefits based on employment history. Today, the federal government pays Social Security benefits to more than 82 percent of the aged. Others are covered by employer-based private pension plans (Meyer & Bellas, 1995).

Most American workers report looking forward to retirement, and an increasing number are leaving full-time work in midlife. The average age of retirement in the United States declined over the past two decades. Currently, it is age 62. One-third of all household heads retire before age 55, one-half before age 60 (Atchley, 1991; Turner, Bailey, & Scott, 1994). This means that increasing numbers of people spend up to one-fourth of their lives in retirement.

Retirement is a lengthy, complex process beginning as soon as the middle-aged person first thinks about it (Atchley, 1993). Planning is important, since retirement leads to a loss of two important work-related rewards—income and status—and to a change in many other aspects of life. Like other life transitions, retirement is often stressful.

"Retirement planning helps you evaluate your options, learn about the availability of resources, and prepare emotionally for the changes ahead," Devin and Trisha heard George explain when they attended one of his retirement seminars. Yet the majority of middle-aged people spend more time planning a two-week vacation than preparing for retirement. Research consistently shows that planning leads to better retirement adjustment and satisfaction (Atchley, 1991; Pery, 1995).

The Caregiving Concerns table on page 548 lists the variety of issues addressed in a typical retirement preparation program. Financial planning is vital, since income typically

CAREGIVING CONCERNS

Ingredients of Effective Retirement Planning

ISSUE	DESCRIPTION
Finances	Ideally, financial planning for retirement should start with the first paycheck; at a minimum, it should begin 10 to 15 years before retirement, since most people spend more than 20 years retired.
Fitness	Starting a fitness program in middle age is important, since good health is crucial for well-being in retirement.
Role adjustment	Retirement is harder for people accustomed to giving orders, delegating work, and being identified by their professions. Preparing for a radical role adjustment reduces stress.
Where to live	The pros and cons of moving should be considered carefully, since where one lives affects access to health care, friends, family, recreation, entertainment, and part-time employment.
Leisure activities	A retiree typically benefits from an additional 50 hours of time a week. Careful planning of what to do with that time has a major impact on psychological well-being.
Health insurance	Finding out about Medicare and Medicaid benefits and other health insurance options is important in ensuring quality of life after retirement.
Legal affairs	The preretirement period is an excellent time to finalize a will and begin estate planning.

Source: Pery, 1995.

drops by 50 percent. Although more people are involved in financial planning than other forms of preparation, even those who attend financial education programs often fail to look closely at their financial well-being and to make wise decisions (Hershey et al., 1998). Many could benefit from an expert's financial analysis and counsel.

Retirement leads to ways of spending time that are largely guided by what one wants to do, not by what one has to do. Individuals who have not thought carefully about how to fill this time may find their sense of purpose in life seriously threatened. Research in Canada and the United States reveals that planning for an active life has an even greater impact on happiness after retirement than does financial planning. Undoubtedly this is because participation in activities promotes many factors essential for psychological well-being, including a structured time schedule, social contact, and self-esteem (MacEwen et al., 1995; Ostling & Kelloway, 1992). Carefully considering whether or not to relocate at retirement is related to an active life, since it affects access to family, friends, recreation, entertainment, and part-time work.

Devin retired at age 62, George at age 66. Although several years younger, Trisha and Anya—like many married women—coordinated their retirements with those of their husbands (Ruhm, 1996). In good health but without an intimate partner to share her life, Jewel kept her consulting business going until age 75. Tim took early retirement and moved to be near Elena, where he devoted himself to public service—tutoring second graders in a public school, transporting inner-city children to museums, and coaching after-school and weekend youth sports. For Tim, like

many executives, retirement offered the first opportunity to pay attention to the world around him.

Unfortunately, people with lower lifetime earnings and less education are least likely to attend retirement preparation programs, yet they stand to benefit the most. Employers need to take extra steps to encourage their participation (Gibson & Burns, 1991). In addition, improving retirement among the economically disadvantaged depends on access to better health care, vocational training, and jobs at early ages. Clearly, a lifetime of opportunities and experiences affect the transition to retirement. In Chapter 18, we will consider the decision to retire and retirement adjustment in greater detail.

ASK YOURSELF . . .

Ira recalls complaining about his job far more in early than middle adulthood. At present, he finds his work interesting and gratifying. Describe factors that probably caused Ira's job satisfaction to increase with age.

Trevor assigned the older members of his work team routine tasks because he was certain they could no longer handle complex assignments. Cite evidence presented in this and the previous chapter that shows Trevor is wrong.

An executive asks you what his large corporation ought to do to promote advancement of women and ethnic minorities to upper management positions. What would you recommend?

SUMMARY

ERIKSON'S THEORY: GENERATIVITY VERSUS STAGNATION

According to Erikson, how does personality change in middle age?

■ Generativity begins in early adulthood but expands greatly as middle-aged adults face Erikson's psychological conflict of **generativity versus stagnation.** Highly generative people find fulfillment as they make contributions to society through parenthood, other family relationships, the workplace, volunteer activities, or intellectual and creative endeavors. Cultural demands and inner desires jointly shape adults' generative activities.

OTHER THEORIES OF PSYCHOSOCIAL DEVELOPMENT IN MIDLIFE

Describe Levinson's and Vaillant's views of psychosocial development in middle adulthood, and discuss similarities and differences between men and women.

■ According to Levinson, middle-aged adults reassess their relation to themselves and the external world. They must confront four developmental tasks, each of which requires them to reconcile two opposing tendencies within the self: young–old, destruction–creation, masculinity–femininity, and engagement–separateness.

■ Due to the double standard of aging, women have more trouble than men accepting being older. Men adopt "feminine" traits of nurturance and caring, whereas women take on "masculine" traits of autonomy, dominance, and assertiveness. Men and successful career-oriented women often reduce their focus on ambition and achievement. Women who

have devoted themselves to child rearing or an unfulfilling job typically increase their involvement in work and the community.

■ According to Vaillant, middle-aged adults become guardians of their culture. In their late forties and fifties, they carry peak responsibility for the functioning of society.

Does the term midlife crisis *fit most people's experience of middle adulthood?*

■ Wide individual differences exist in response to midlife. Only a minority of people experience a **midlife crisis** in which intense self-doubt and inner turmoil lead them to make drastic changes in their personal lives and careers.

Characterize middle adulthood using a life events approach and a stage approach.

■ Both continuity and stagewise change characterize emotional and social development in middle adulthood. Some changes are adaptations to external events (such as the family life cycle), but these events are less age graded than in the past. At the same time, the majority of middle-aged adults report stagelike development, involving troubling moments that prompt new understandings and goals.

STABILITY AND CHANGE IN SELF-CONCEPT AND PERSONALITY

Describe changes in self-concept and personality in middle adulthood.

■ **Possible selves** become fewer in number as well as more modest and concrete as middle-aged individuals adjust their hopes and fears to the circumstances of their lives. Revising possible selves enables adults to maintain self-esteem and stay motivated.

■ Adults become more introspective and in touch with themselves in midlife. Self-acceptance, autonomy, and environmental mastery increase, leading some people to consider middle age the "prime of life." In addition, coping strategies become more effective.

Describe changes in gender identity in midlife.

■ Both men and women become more androgynous in middle adulthood. Biological explanations, such as **parental imperative theory,** have been criticized, and evidence for them is mixed. A complex combination of social roles and life conditions is most likely responsible for midlife changes in gender identity.

Discuss stability and change in the "big five" personality traits in adulthood.

■ Among **"big five" personality traits,** neuroticism, extroversion, and openness to experience show modest declines during adulthood. At the same time individual differences in the "big five" traits are large and highly persistent over time. Although adults change in overall organization and integration of personality, they do so on a foundation of basic, enduring dispositions.

RELATIONSHIPS AT MIDLIFE

Describe the middle adulthood phase of the family life cycle, and discuss midlife relationships with a marriage partner, adult children, grandchildren, and aging parents.

■ "Launching children and moving on" is the newest and longest phase of the family life cycle. Middle-aged adults must adapt to many entries and exits of family members as their own children leave, marry, and produce grandchildren and as their own parents age and die.

- The changes of midlife prompt many adults to focus on improving their marriages. When divorce occurs, middle-aged adults typically have a harder time adjusting than do young adults. For women of all ages, marital breakup usually brings significant economic disadvantage, contributing to the **feminization of poverty** in the United States.

- Most middle-aged parents adjust well to the launching phase of the family life cycle, especially if they have a strong work orientation and parent–child contact and affection are sustained. As children marry and bring in-laws into the family network, middle-aged parents, especially mothers, often become **kinkeepers.**

- When family relationships are positive, grandparenthood is an important means of fulfilling personal and societal needs. In low-income families and in some subcultures, grandparents perform essential activities, including financial assistance and child care. Increasingly, grandparents have become primary caregivers when serious family problems exist, resulting in **skipped-generation families.**

- Middle-aged adults reassess their relationships with aging parents, often becoming more appreciative. Yet the earlier quality of the parent–child relationship— positive or conflict ridden— usually persists.

- Adults caught between the demands of ill or frail parents and financially dependent children are called the **sandwich generation.** The burden of caring for aging parents falls most heavily on adult daughters, but both men and women participate. As adults move from early to later middle age, the sex difference in parental caregiving declines. Social support is highly effective in relieving caregiver stress.

Describe midlife sibling relationships and friendships, and discuss relationships across generations in the United States.

- Bonds with siblings often strengthen in middle age, partly in response to major life events, such as launching and marriage of children and illness and death of parents. Sister–sister ties are typically closest in industrialized nations, where sibling relationships are voluntary. In nonindustrialized societies, where sibling relationships are basic to family functioning, other sibling attachments (such as brother–sister) may be unusually strong.

- In midlife, friendships are fewer, more selective, and more deeply valued. Men continue to be less expressive with their friends than are women, who have more close friendships and find them more satisfying. Viewing a spouse as a best friend can contribute greatly to marital happiness.

- Recent research reveals strong supportive ties across generations in American families and communities. Most people do not resent government benefits for other age groups.

VOCATIONAL LIFE

Discuss job satisfaction and vocational development in middle adulthood, paying special attention to sex differences and experiences of ethnic minorities.

- Vocational readjustments are common as middle-aged people seek to increase the personal meaning and self-direction of their work lives. Certain aspects of job performance improve. Overall job satisfaction increases at all occupational levels, though less so for women than for men.

- **Burnout** is a serious occupational hazard more common today than in the past, especially in jobs involving work with people. Greater worker participation in planning and decision making, job teams, and work at home are likely to reduce job stress and improve satisfaction at all ages.

- Vocational development is vital during all phases of work life. Job training is less available to older workers because of negative stereotypes of aging, lack of encouragement from supervisors, and routine work assignments.

- Women and ethnic minorities face a **glass ceiling,** or barrier to high-level executive positions, in corporations. Reduced access to formal and informal management training and prejudice against women who demonstrate qualities linked to leadership and advancement are responsible. Many women further their careers by leaving the corporate world, often to start their own businesses.

Discuss career change and unemployment in middle adulthood.

- Most middle-aged people remain in the same vocation. Those who change careers usually leave one line of work for a related one. Radical career change often signals a personal crisis.

- Unemployment is especially difficult for middle-aged adults, who make up the majority of workers affected by corporate downsizing and layoffs. Social support is vital for reducing stress. Counseling can help midlife job seekers find alternative, gratifying work roles, but these rarely duplicate the status and pay of their previous positions.

Discuss the importance of planning for retirement, noting various issues that middle-aged adults should address.

- An increasing number of American workers are retiring from full-time work in midlife. Planning for retirement is important because the changes it brings—loss of income and status and increase in free time—are often stressful. Besides financial planning, other important issues include where to live, leisure activities, health insurance, and legal affairs.

IMPORTANT TERMS AND CONCEPTS

"big five" personality traits (p. 533)

burnout (p. 544)

feminization of poverty (p. 535)

generativity versus stagnation (p. 522)

glass ceiling (p. 545)

kinkeeper (p. 536)

midlife crisis (p. 527)

parental imperative theory (p. 532)

possible selves (p. 528)

sandwich generation (p. 540)

skipped-generation family (p. 539)

FYI FOR FURTHER INFORMATION AND HELP

Consult the companion website for this book, where you will find additional weblinks and associated learning activities: www.abacon.com/berk

PSYCHOSOCIAL DEVELOPMENT

Midlife Research—MIDMAC
midmac.med.harvard.edu

An interdisciplinary research group that conducts research on development in midlife.

MARRIAGE IN MIDLIFE

Coalition for Marriage, Family, and Couples Education
www.smartmarriages.com

Aims to improve understanding of mar- riage as a relationship capable of encouraging personal growth and mutual fulfillment. Helps couples find marriage and family courses.

National Marriage Encounter
www.marriages.org

Offers weekend retreat programs aimed at encouraging communication between married partners and emphasizing personal and religious growth.

GRANDPARENTHOOD

Grandparents Resource Center
Grc4usa.org

Provides social support, legal assistance, and a unified voice for grandparents seeking to protect and care for their grandchildren. Works for the passage of legislation at state and national levels granting qualified grandparents legal custody rights.

CARING FOR AGING PARENTS

Children of Aging Parents
www.careguide.com/careguide.cgi/ caps/aboutcaps.htm!

A national information and referral service for caregivers of the elderly. Offers a speakers bureau for community organizations and conducts workshops, seminars, and conferences in the field of aging. Organizes and promotes caregivers' support groups.

OF DEVELOPMENT IN MIDDLE ADULTHOOD

AGE	PHYSICAL	COGNITIVE	EMOTIONAL/SOCIAL

40–50 years

PHYSICAL

- Accommodative ability of the lens of the eye and color discrimination decline; sensitivity to glare increases. (493)

- Sharp hearing loss at high frequency occurs. (494)

- Hair continues to gray and thin. (493)

- Lines on the face become more pronounced, and skin loses elasticity and begins to sag. (494)

- Weight gain continues, accompanied by a rise in fatty deposits in the torso, whereas fat beneath the skin declines. (494)

- Loss of lean body mass (muscle and bone) occurs. (494)

- In women, production of estrogen drops, leading to shortening of and irregularity in the menstrual cycle. (495)

- For men, quantity of semen and sperm declines. (496)

- Intensity of sexual response declines, but sexual activity drops only slightly; stability is more typical than dramatic change. (496–497)

- Proportion of women with no sexual partners increases dramatically. (498)

- Rates of cancer and cardiovascular disease increase, at a higher rate for men than women. (498)

COGNITIVE

- Consciousness of aging increases. (493)

- A variety of crystallized and fluid abilities assessed by intelligence tests stabilize. (507)

- The fluid ability of processing speed, assessed on reaction time tasks, declines; adults compensate by taking larger chunks of information into working memory and through practice and experience. (509)

- On complex tasks, ability to divide and control attention declines; adults compensate through practice and experience. (509)

- Amount of information that can be retained in working memory diminishes due to a decline in use of memory strategies. (509)

- Retrieving information from long-term memory becomes more difficult. (509)

- General factual knowledge, procedural knowledge, and knowledge related to one's occupation remain unchanged or increase. (510)

- Gains in practical problem solving and expertise occur. (511)

- Creativity shifts from a focus on generating unusual products to integrating experience and knowledge into unique ways of thinking and acting. (512)

- If in a vocation offering challenge and autonomy, shows gains in cognitive flexibility. (514)

EMOTIONAL/SOCIAL

- Desire to give to and guide the next generation intensifies. (522)

- Modifies components of the life structure, focusing on personally meaningful living. (525)

- Tries to reconcile four opposing tendencies within the self: young/old; destruction/creation; masculinity/femininity; engagement/separateness. (525)

- Possible selves become fewer in number and more modest and concrete. (529)

- Introspection increases as people contemplate the second half of life. (529)

- Self-acceptance, autonomy, and environmental mastery increase. (529)

- Coping strategies become more effective. (530)

- Gender identity becomes more androgynous: "masculine" traits increase in women; "feminine" traits increase in men. (532)

- May launch children. (534)

- May enlarge the family network to include in-laws. (536)

- May become a kinkeeper, especially if a mother. (536)

- May care for a parent with a disability or chronic illness. (540)

- Sibling bonds may strengthen. (541)

- Number of friends generally declines. (542)

- Job satisfaction increases. (544)

AGE	PHYSICAL	COGNITIVE	EMOTIONAL/SOCIAL
50–60 years	■ Lens of the eye loses its accommodative ability entirely. (493)	■ Changes in cognition described on the opposite page continue.	■ Emotional and social changes described on the opposite page continue.

AGE

50–60 years

PHYSICAL

■ Lens of the eye loses its accommodative ability entirely. (493)

■ Hearing loss extends to all frequencies but remains greatest for highest tones. (494)

■ Skin continues to wrinkle and sag, and "age spots" appear. (494)

■ Menopause occurs, usually between ages 50 and 55. (495)

■ Continued loss of bone mass, accelerating especially for women after menopause and leading to high rates of osteoporosis. (495)

■ Due to collapse of disks in the spinal column, height may drop by as much as 1 inch. (495)

COGNITIVE

■ Changes in cognition described on the opposite page continue.

EMOTIONAL/SOCIAL

■ Emotional and social changes described on the opposite page continue.

■ Re-evaluates life structure and tries to change components that are inadequate. (525)

■ Becomes concerned with "passing the torch"—that the positive aspects of the culture survive. (527)

■ May become a grandparent. (537)

■ Parent-to-child help-giving declines, and child-to-parent help-giving increases. (538)

■ Sex difference in parental care-giving declines. (540)

■ May retire. (547)

Note: Numbers in parentheses indicate the page on which each milestone is discussed.

17

Physical and Cognitive Development in Late Adulthood

PHYSICAL DEVELOPMENT

Longevity
- A Lifespan Vista: What Can We Learn About Aging from Centenarians?

Physical Changes
Nervous System · Sensory Systems · Cardiovascular and Respiratory Systems · Immune System · Sleep · Physical Appearance and Mobility · Adapting to Physical Changes of Late Adulthood
- Variations/Culture: Cultural Variations in the Experience of Aging

Health, Fitness, and Disability
Nutrition and Exercise · Sexuality · Physical Disabilities · Mental Disabilities · Health Care
- Social Issues: Squaring of the Population Pyramid and Intergenerational Inequity

COGNITIVE DEVELOPMENT

Memory
Deliberate versus Automatic Memory · Remote Memory · Prospective Memory

Language Processing

Problem Solving

Wisdom

Factors Related to Cognitive Change

Cognitive Interventions

Lifelong Learning
Types of Programs · Benefits of Continuing Education

- *Although elders do not see and hear as well or move and think as quickly as they did at younger ages, most are optimistic and strive to improve in the face of physical and cognitive challenges. These nature walkers, in their seventies and eighties, inspect the wild flowers awakening in a meadow at the arrival of spring. They find beauty and inspiration in the tiniest living creatures. (Photo courtesy: Jim Harrison/Stock Boston)*

At age 64, Walt gave up his photography business and looked forward to leisure years ahead with 60-year-old Ruth, who retired from her position as a social worker at the same time. This culminating phase of Walt's and Ruth's lives was filled with volunteer work, golfing three times a week, and joint summer vacations with Walt's older brother Dick and his wife, Goldie. Walt also took up activities he had always loved but had little time to pursue—writing poems and short stories, attending theater performances, enrolling in a class on world politics, and cultivating a garden that became the envy of the neighborhood. Ruth read voraciously, served on the board of directors of an adoption agency, and had more time to visit her sister Ida in a nearby city.

Over the next 20 years, Walt's and Ruth's energy and vitality were an inspiration to everyone who met them. Their warmth, concern for others, and generosity with their time led not just their own children and grandchildren, but former co-workers, nieces, nephews, and children of their friends to seek them out. On weekends, their home was alive with visitors.

Then, in their early eighties, the couple's lives changed profoundly. Walt had surgery to treat an enlarged, cancerous prostate gland and within 3 months was hospitalized again after a heart attack. He lingered for 6 weeks, with Ruth at his side, and then died. Ruth's grieving was interrupted by the need to care for Ida. Alert and spry at age 78, Ida deteriorated mentally in her seventy-ninth year, despite otherwise being in excellent physical health. In the meantime, Ruth's arthritis worsened and her vision and hearing weakened.

As Ruth turned 85, certain activities had become more difficult—but not impossible. It just takes a little adjustment!" Ruth exclaimed in her usual, upbeat manner. Reading was harder, so she checked out "talking books" from her local library. Her gait was slower and her eyesight less reliable, so she hesitated to go out alone. When her daughter and family took Ruth to dinner, the conversation moved so quickly in the noisy restaurant that Ruth felt overwhelmed and said little. But interacting with her on a one-to-one basis revealed that she was far from passive and withdrawn! In a calm environment, she showed the same intelligence, wit, and astute insights that she had displayed all her life.

Late adulthood stretches from age 60 to the end of the lifespan. Unfortunately, popular images of old age fail to capture the quality of these final decades. Instead, many myths prevail—that the elderly are feeble, senile, and sick; that they have little contact with their families, who set them aside in nursing homes; that they are no longer able to learn; and that they have entered a phase of deterioration and dependency. Young people who have little contact with older adults are often surprised that elders like Walt and Ruth even exist—active and involved in the world around them.

As we trace physical and cognitive development in old age, we will see that the balance of gains and declines does shift as death approaches. But the typical 60-year-old in industrialized nations can anticipate nearly two healthy, rewarding decades before this shift has meaning for everyday life. And as Ruth illustrates, even after members of the older generation become frail, they find ways of surmounting physical and cognitive challenges.

Late adulthood is best viewed as an extension of earlier periods, not a break with them. As long as social and cultural contexts grant the elderly support, respect, and purpose in life, these years are a time of continued potential.

PHYSICAL DEVELOPMENT

If you were to guess the ages of older people on the basis of their appearance, chances are that you would frequently be wrong. Indeed, we often remark that an older person "looks young" or "looks old" for his or her age—a statement acknowledging that chronological age is an imperfect indicator of **functional age,** or actual competence and performance. Because people age biologically at different rates, experts distinguish between the **young-old** elderly, who appear physically young for their advanced years, and the **old-old** elderly, who appear frail and show signs of decline.[1] According to this functional distinction, it is possible for an 80-year-old to be young-old and a 65-year-old to be old-old (Neugarten & Neugarten, 1987). Yet even these labels do not fully capture the wide variation in biological aging. Recall from Chapter 13 that within each person, change differs across parts of the body. For example, Ruth became infirm physically but remained active mentally, whereas Ida was physically fit for her age but found it hard to sustain a conversation, keep appointments, and complete familiar tasks.

So much variation exists between and within individuals that as yet, researchers have not been able to identify any biological measure that predicts the overall rate at which an elderly person will age (Hayflick, 1994). But we do have estimates of how much longer older adults can expect to live, and our knowledge of factors affecting longevity in late adulthood has increased rapidly.

[1]In the popular literature on aging, this distinction has been confused with chronological age: young-old referring to age 65 to 75, old-old to 75 to 85, and oldest-old to 85 to 99 (see, for example, Safire, 1997). In Western nations, persistence of the incorrect belief that age determines function is probably due to stereotypes of aging.

LONGEVITY

I wonder how many years I have left," Ruth asked herself each time a major life event, such as retirement and widowhood, occurred. In Chapter 13, we indicated that older adults are living longer than ever before. Recall that under the best of circumstances, the average human lives around 85 or 90 years and the very longest-lived about 120, our maximum lifespan.

Largely due to medical advances and improved life conditions, the number of people age 65 and older in the United States has risen dramatically, from 3 million in 1900 to 34 million in 1998. From the beginning to the end of the twentieth century, elderly Americans increased from 4 percent to 12.7 percent of the population—a figure expected to reach 23 percent by the middle of the twenty-first century. The fastest-growing segment of senior citizens is the 85-and-older group, who currently make up 1.7 percent of the population. By the year 2020, the proportion of people age 85 and older will double; by 2050 it will quadruple, reaching 5.1 percent (U.S. Department of Health and Human Services, 1999b).

Despite increasing numbers of senior citizens, the percentage of elderly in the United States is lower than in many other industrialized nations. The difference is largely due to high birthrates among America's poverty-stricken groups and less effective public policies ensuring health and well-being throughout the lifespan (see Chapter 2, page 68). In developing countries, high infant, childhood, and adult mortality rates mean that people age 65 and older typically make up no more than 3 to 5 percent of the population. In these nations, the elderly population has grown at a slower rate (Central Intelligence Agency, 1998).

Americans reaching age 65 in 2000 can look forward, on the average, to 18 additional years of life—7 years more than a 65-year-old could expect in 1900, when living to age 65 was unusual. As at earlier ages, life expectancy continues to be greater for women (19 years) than for men (16 years).

■ *How old are these two elders? How old do they look and feel? Because people age biologically at different rates, the 88-year-old woman on the right does not appear much older than her 65-year-old companion on the left. Yet their birthdays are nearly a quarter century apart. (Photo courtesy: Bob Daemmrich/The Image Works)*

Today, the 65- to 69-year age group consists of 123 women for every 100 men; for people age 85 and older, the ratio climbs to 259 to 100. Discrepancies like these occur in all developed countries. They are not always present in the developing world because of high death rates of women in childbirth (Hayflick, 1994).

Although women outnumber men by a greater margin with advancing age, differences in average life expectancy between the sexes decline. An American newborn girl can expect to live about 7 to 8 years longer than a newborn boy. At age 65, the difference narrows to about 3 ½ years; at age 85, to just over 1 year. Over age 100, the gender gap in life expectancy disappears. Similarly, differences in rates of chronic illness and in life expectancy between higher-SES whites and low-SES ethnic minorities (African Americans, Hispanics, and Native Americans) decline with age (House et al., 1990a). Around age 85, a **life expectancy crossover** occurs, in that surviving members of ethnic minority groups live longer than members of the white majority (see Table 17.1).

TABLE 17.1

Average Life Expectancy for White and Black Elderly in the United States, Illustrating the Life Expectancy Crossover

| AGE IN YEARS | WHITE MALE | AVERAGE LIFE EXPECTANCY IN YEARS | | |
		BLACK MALE	WHITE FEMALE	BLACK FEMALE
65	16.0	14.2	19.3	17.6
70	12.5	11.0	15.4	13.9
75	9.7	8.8	12.0	11.1
80	7.2	6.8	8.9	8.4
85 and over	5.4	5.7	6.6	6.7 ◄——————Life expectancy crossover

Note: Below age 85, life expectancy is greater for American whites than blacks. At age 85 and older, this trend reverses; average life expectancy is greater for blacks than whites. Notice, also, how the gender gap in life expectancy declines with age.
Source: U.S. Bureau of the Census, 1999.

Researchers speculate that only the sturdiest males and economically disadvantaged ethnic minorities survive into very old age. Many are at the extreme of human health and vigor (Barer, 1994).

Of course, average life expectancy does not tell us how enjoyable living to a ripe old age is likely to be. Perhaps the real question Ruth meant to ask was "How many years of active, healthy life lie ahead?" We can get some idea by looking at the percentage of noninstitutionalized elderly who require assistance with everyday activities. As Figure 17.1 shows, most Americans age 65 and older are capable of living independent, productive lives, although with age (and especially after age 80) need for care increases.

Think about factors we have considered in earlier chapters that contribute to a long and healthy life. Much research shows that heredity and environment are interconnected in the aging process (Jazwinski, 1996). Identical twins typically die within 3 years of each other, whereas fraternal twins of the same sex differ by more than 6 years. Furthermore, longevity runs in families. People with long-lived ancestors tend to survive longer and to be physically healthier in old age. And when both parents survive to age 70 or older, the chances that their children will live to 90 or 100 are double that of the general population (Hayflick, 1994; Sorensen et al., 1988). At the same time, evidence from studies of twins suggests that as we get older, the contribution of heredity to length of life decreases in favor of environmental factors (Vaillant, 1991).

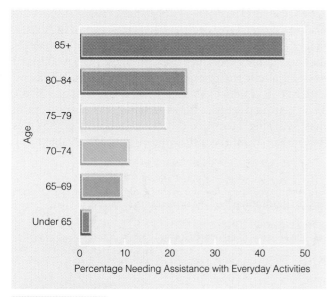

■ **Percentage of Americans by age needing assistance with everyday activities, such as shopping and meal preparation.** Although need for care increases with age, even at age 85 and beyond, over 50 percent of people lead fully independent lives. (From U.S. Department of Health and Human Services, 1999c.)

A wide array of environmental factors discussed in previous chapters, in combination with genetic makeup, predict longevity: higher socioeconomic status (SES); diet low in fat, high in essential nutrients; body weight, blood pressure, and blood cholesterol in normal range; regular exercise; abstinence from unhealthy tobacco, alcohol, and drug use; self-rated health; stable family life in childhood; lasting marriage; conscientious, dependable personality; hardiness (optimistic outlook); low hostility; low psychological stress; and social support.

The study of centenarians—people who cross the 100-year mark—offers special insights into how biological, psychological, and social influences work together to promote a long, satisfying life. Refer to the Lifespan Vista box on page 560 to find out more about the survival and successful adaptation of these longest-lived individuals.

PHYSICAL CHANGES

The programmed effects of specific genes and random cellular events believed to underlie aging (see Chapter 13) make physical declines more apparent in late adulthood. Compared with earlier phases, more organs and systems of the body are affected. Nevertheless, most structures are remarkably robust and can last into our eighties and beyond, if we take good care of them. For an overview of the physical changes we are about to discuss, return once again to Table 13.1 on page 426.

NERVOUS SYSTEM

On a routine office visit, 80-year-old Ruth responded to her doctor's query about how she was getting along by explaining, "During the last two days, I forgot the name of the family that just moved in next door, couldn't recall where I had put a pile of bills, and had trouble finding the right words to explain to a delivery service how to get to my house. Am I losing my mind?" Ruth asked anxiously.

"You're much too sharp for that," Dr. Wiley remarked. "Ruth, if you were losing your mind, you wouldn't be so concerned about forgetting." Ruth also wondered why extremes of hot and cold weather felt more uncomfortable than in earlier years. And she required more time to coordinate a series of movements and had become less sure of her balance.

Aging of the nervous system affects a wide range of complex thoughts and activities. Although brain weight declines throughout adulthood, the loss becomes greater after age 60 and may be as much as 5 to 10 percent by age 80, due to death of neurons and enlargement of ventricles (spaces) within the brain. Neuron loss occurs throughout the cerebral cortex but at different rates in different regions. In the visual, auditory, and motor areas, as many as 50 percent of neurons die. In contrast, parts of the cortex (such as the frontal lobes) responsible for integration of information, judgment, and reflective thought show far less change. Besides the cortex, the cerebellum (which controls balance and coordination) loses neurons—in all, about 25 percent. Glial cells, which myelinate neural fibers, decrease as well, contributing to diminished efficiency of the central nervous system (Drachman, 1997; Whitbourne, 1996, 1999).

But the brain can overcome some of these declines. In several studies, growth of neural fibers in the brains of older adults unaffected by illness took place at the same rate as in middle-aged people. Aging neurons established new synapses after other neurons had degenerated (Flood & Coleman, 1988). Furthermore, the aging cerebral cortex can, to some degree, generate new neurons (Gould et al., 1999). And exercise can increase blood circulation to the brain, which helps preserve brain structures and behavioral capacities (Baylor & Spirduso, 1988).

The autonomic nervous system, involved in many life support functions, also performs less well in old age. For example, Ruth's lower tolerance for hot weather was due to decreased sweating. And her body found it more difficult to raise its core temperature during cold exposure. For these reasons, the elderly are at risk during heat waves and cold spells. The autonomic nervous system also releases higher levels of stress hormones into the bloodstream than it did at younger ages, perhaps in an effort to arouse body tissues that have become less responsive to these hormones over the years (Whitbourne, 1996, 1999). Later we will see that this change may contribute to declines in immunity and to sleep problems among older adults.

SENSORY SYSTEMS

Changes in sensory functioning become increasingly noticeable in late life. Older adults see and hear less well, and taste, smell, and touch sensitivity may also decline. As Figure 17.2 shows, hearing impairments are far more common than visual impairments, and they extend trends we described for middle adulthood in that many more men than women are affected.

■ VISION. In Chapter 15 (see page 493), we noted that structural changes in the eye make it harder to focus on nearby objects, see in dim light, and perceive color. In late adulthood, vision diminishes further. For example, the cornea (clear covering of the eye) becomes more translucent and scatters light, which blurs images and increases sensitivity to glare. The lens continues to yellow, leading to further impairment in color discrimination. From middle to old age, cloudy areas in the lens called **cataracts** increase, resulting in foggy vision and (without surgery) eventual blindness. The number of individuals with cataracts increases tenfold from middle to late adulthood; 25 percent of people in their seventies and 50 percent of those in their eighties are affected (U.S. Bureau of the Census, 1999). Besides age, sun

(a) Visual Impairments

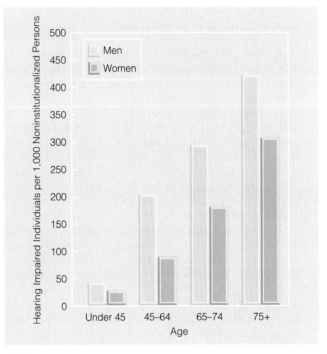

(b) Hearing Impairments

FIGURE 17.2

■ **Number of men and women with (a) visual impairments and (b) hearing impairments per 1,000 noninstitutionalized American adults of different ages.** Hearing impairments are far more common than visual impairments in aging individuals, and many more men than women are affected. Nevertheless, a visual impairment is more likely to interfere with self-care than is a hearing impairment. (Adapted from U.S. Bureau of the Census, 1999).

exposure and certain diseases, such as diabetes, increase the risk of cataracts. Fortunately, removal of the lens and replacement with an artificial lens implant or corrective eyewear are very successful in restoring vision (Larson, 1996).

Impaired eyesight in late adulthood largely results from a reduction in light reaching the retina (caused by yellowing of the lens, shrinking of the pupil, and clouding

WHAT CAN WE LEARN ABOUT AGING FROM CENTENARIANS?

Born in 1893 in Croatia, Dr. Bogdan Stojic continued to practice medicine until he became a centenarian. After retiring at age 101, he spent his days reading, writing, going for walks, and enjoying his many friends. During his long life, he surmounted many difficult times. In his youth, he fought in three wars—the Balkan War against Turkey, the Serbo-Bulgarian War, and World War I. As a middle-aged soldier during World War II, he was taken prisoner by the Nazis, served as a medic in a prisoner-of-war camp, and narrowly escaped a death sentence. After the war, he entered private practice. At age 68, he and his wife packed their belongings and traveled thousands of miles, settling in Australia to live close to their daughter. There Dr. Stojic continued to treat patients for another 33 years.

About living a long and healthy life, Dr. Stojic reflected, "My parents were 90, but I never thought about it—how old I'd live. It just happened. . . . don't smoke; don't drink too much. . . . My father and mother were very good. They spoke with us as if we were grown-up people when we

were 10 years of age . . . [and] my marriage has been very good." About his current trouble walking, he noted optimistically, "I'll be treated. Soon, I hope I will walk without the stick." He continues to have goals—among them, contributing to a cure for Alzheimer's disease (Deveson, 1994, pp. 218, 222–223).

Due to aging stereotypes and researchers' focus on the very old with the heaviest burden of illness and disability, popular images of the most senior members of the human species are ones of extreme frailty. Yet the past 40 years have seen a tenfold increase in centenarians in the industrialized world—a trend expected to accelerate in the twenty-first century. For example, the population of American centenarians, currently numbering about 72,000, will grow to nearly 1 million by 2050 (U.S. Department of Health and Human Services, 1999b). About one-third to one-half of centenarians lead active and independent lives; the rest have physical or mental impairments, ranging from mild to severe (Franceschi et al., 1995; Ritchie, 1998).

Robust centenarians are of special interest, since they represent the ulti-

mate potential of the human species. What are they like? Case studies reveal great diversity among them. Some have survived extreme illnesses in childhood and adulthood; others have rarely been sick throughout their lives. Growing up in an era when few were highly educated, most finished grade school. But some are illiterate, whereas others (like Dr. Stojik) hold advanced professional degrees. Although most describe themselves as middle income, a handful live in poverty or are millionaires (Beard, 1991).

At the same time, common threads characterize these centenarians' physical condition and life stories. Most have escaped age-related chronic illnesses, such as cardiovascular disease, cancer, diabetes, and dementia. Medical tests typically reveal a well-preserved and efficiently functioning immune system (Franceschi et al., 1995; Perls, 1995; Samuelsson et al., 1997). In a study in which robust centenarians donated their brains for after-death examination, physiological abnormalities were rare (Silver et al., 1998). As a group, they are of average or slender build and practice moderation in eating. Many have most or

---

of the vitreous) and from cell loss in the retina and optic nerve (refer again to Chapter 15). Dark adaptation—moving from a brightly lit to a dim environment—is harder, making entering a movie theater after the show has started a challenge. In addition, depth perception is less reliable, since binocular vision (the brain's ability to combine images received from both eyes) declines (Garzia & Trick, 1992). And visual acuity (fineness of discrimination) worsens, with a sharp drop after age 70 (Whitbourne, 1999).

When light-sensitive cells in the *macula,* or central region of the retina, break down, older adults may develop **macular degeneration,** in which central vision blurs and

gradually is lost. Macular degeneration is the leading cause of blindness among older adults. If diagnosed early, it can sometimes be treated with laser therapy (Mayo Clinic, 2000). Several large-scale studies suggest that a diet rich in green, leafy vegetables reduces the risk of macular degeneration and slows vision loss in those with the condition. These sources of vitamins A, C, E, and carotenoids (yellow and red plant pigments) are believed to exert their beneficial effects by protecting cells in the macula from free-radical damage. Vitamin supplements are helpful in reducing the incidence of both cataracts and macular degeneration (Jacques, 1999; Smith et al., 1999; Sperduto et al., 1993).

all of their own teeth—another sign of unusual physical health. Despite heavy tobacco use in their generation, the large majority report that they never smoked cigarettes. They also describe lifelong physical activity extending past age 100 (Beard, 1991; Kropf & Pugh, 1995).

In personality, these very senior citizens appear unusually forthright and genuine. They refuse to dwell on fears and tragedies but, instead, focus on a better tomorrow. The less anxious and fearful centenarians are, the more favorable their self-rated health and their psychological well-being (Quinn et al., 1999). Robust centenarians are also assertive—willing to express themselves in bold and unusual ways. When asked about their longevity, they often mention a long and happy marriage. And they have a history of community involvement, working for just causes that are central to their growth and happiness.

The activities of robust centenarians show that there is no age limit to stimulating work, leisure pursuits, and learning. Cooking; sewing; writing letters, poems, plays, and memoirs; making speeches; teaching music lessons and Sunday school; nursing the sick; chopping wood; selling merchandise, bonds, and insurance; painting; practicing medicine; and preaching sermons are among their varied involvements. In several cases, illiterate centenarians learned to read and write. One of the most impressive was a 105-year-old woman who enrolled in classes four nights a week. Within a short time, she could read road signs, newspaper headlines, and sections of the Bible. Although she found writing harder, she persisted, explaining, "I'm tired of having other people write letters for me" (Beard, 1991, p. 80).

Robust centenarians are often regarded as rare curiosities who do not represent the general population. As their numbers increase, they are likely to be viewed less as exceptions and more as people for whom normal development is at its best. These independent, mentally alert, fulfilled 100-year-olds illustrate how a healthy lifestyle, personal resourcefulness, and close ties to family and community can build on biological strengths, thereby pushing the limits of the active lifespan.

■ *Dr. Bogdan Stojic, centenarian, defies stereotypes of the very old as extremely frail. He practiced medicine until age 101. (Photo courtesy: Sidney Fay)*

Visual difficulties have a profound impact on older people's self-confidence and everyday behavior. Ruth gave up driving in her mid-seventies, and she worried greatly when Walt had trouble making decisions behind the wheel. He found it hard to shift focus between the road and the dashboard and strained to make out pedestrians at dusk and night (Owsley et al., 1998). On foot, older adults' problems with depth perception and dark adaptation increase their chances of stumbling.

When vision loss is extensive, it can affect leisure pursuits and be very isolating. Ruth could no longer enjoy museums, movies, playing bridge, and working crossword puzzles. Her poor vision also meant that she had to depend on others for help with housekeeping and shopping. Still, even among people age 85 and older, only 30 percent experience visual impairment severe enough to interfere with daily living (U.S. Department of Health and Human Services, 1999f). As in other aspects of aging, wide individual differences in visual capacity exist.

■ HEARING. At a Thanksgiving gathering with 12 family members present, 85-year-old Ruth had trouble hearing. "Mom, this is Leona, Joe's cousin. I'd like you to meet her," Ruth's daughter Sybil commented. In the clamor of boisterous children, banging dishes, television sounds, and nearby verbal exchanges, Ruth didn't catch Leona's name or her relationship to Sybil's husband, Joe.

"Tell me your name again," Ruth asked. "This is a mighty busy place right now, and it's hard for me to hear. Let's go into the next room so we can speak a bit."

Reduced blood supply and natural cell death in the inner ear, discussed in Chapter 15, in addition to stiffening of membranes (such as the eardrum) and degeneration of neural pathways lead hearing to decline in late adulthood. Decrements are greatest at high frequencies, although detection of soft sounds diminishes throughout the frequency range (see page 494). In addition, responsiveness to startling noises lessens, and discriminating complex tone patterns becomes harder (Fitzgibbons & Gordon-Salant, 1998; Ford et al., 1995; Stevens et al., 1998).

Although hearing loss has less impact on self-care than does vision, it affects safety and enjoyment of life. In the din of traffic on city streets, 80-year-old Ruth didn't always interpret warnings correctly—both spoken ("Watch it, don't step out yet") and nonspoken (the beep of a horn or a siren). And when she turned up the radio or television volume, she sometimes missed the ring of the telephone or a knock at the door.

Of all hearing difficulties, the age-related decline in speech perception has the greatest impact on life satisfaction. Ability to detect the content and emotionally expressive features of conversation declines after age 70, affecting the elder's capacity to respond appropriately (Villaume et al., 1997). Although Ruth used problem-centered coping to increase her chances of hearing conversation, she wasn't always successful. And sometimes people were inconsiderate. For example, on a dinner outing, Joe raised his voice impatiently when Ruth asked him to repeat himself. And he said to Sybil in Ruth's presence, "Be honest, Syb, Ruth's going deaf, isn't she?" This time, Ruth heard every word. At the family's Thanksgiving reunion, fewer relatives took time to talk with Ruth, and she felt some pangs of loneliness.

As with vision, most elders do not suffer from hearing loss great enough to disrupt their daily lives. Of those who do, compensating with a hearing aid and minimizing background noise are helpful. Furthermore, recall from Chapter 4 (page 142) that beginning at birth, our perception is *intermodal* (combines information from more than one sensory system). By attending to facial expressions, gestures, and lip movements, older adults can use vision to help interpret the spoken word. When interacting with the elderly, family members and others can seek a quiet environment. When they do, older people are far more likely to convey an image of alertness and competence than reduced sensitivity to the surrounding world.

■ TASTE AND SMELL. Walt's brother Dick was a heavy smoker. In his sixties, he poured salt and pepper over his food, stirred extra spoonfuls of sugar into his coffee, and satisfied his fondness for spicy foods by asking for "extra hot" in Mexican and Indian restaurants.

Dick's reduced sensitivity to the four basic tastes—sweet, salty, sour, and bitter—is evident in many adults after age 60. In addition, cross-sectional research reveals that older adults have greater difficulty recognizing familiar foods by taste alone (Stevens et al., 1995).

But the drop in taste sensitivity just described may be due to factors other than aging, since no change in the number or distribution of taste buds takes place late in life. Smoking, dentures, medications, and environmental pollutants can affect taste perception. When taste is harder to detect, food is less enjoyable, increasing the likelihood of deficiencies in the elderly person's diet. Flavor additives can help make food more attractive to older adults (Whitbourne, 1996).

Smell contributes to enjoyment of food and also has a self-protective function. An aging person who has difficulty detecting rancid food, gas fumes, or smoke may be in a life-threatening situation. A decrease in the number of smell receptors after age 60 undoubtedly contributes to declines in odor sensitivity. Older adults are less accurate at linking odors with such descriptors as *floral, musky, fruity,* or *sweet.* Researchers believe that odor perception becomes distorted in late adulthood, a change that may promote complaints that "food no longer smells and tastes right" (Russell et al., 1993). But other factors may lead this decline to appear greater than it actually is. For example, some older adults have difficulty recalling odor labels, making odor recognition tasks harder (Larsson & Bäckman, 1997, 1998). Furthermore, practicing odor discriminations affects their maintenance (Engen, 1982). Walt had been a wine enthusiast all his life. In his early eighties, he could still distinguish the aromas of fine wines.

■ TOUCH. Touch sensitivity is especially crucial for certain adults, such as the severely visually impaired who must read in Braille and people who make fine judgments about texture in their occupations or leisure pursuits (for example, in art and handicraft activities). To measure touch perception, researchers determine how close two stimuli on the skin must be before they are perceived as one. Findings indicate that aging brings a sharp decline on the hands, particularly the fingertips, and less of a drop on the arms and lips. It may be due to slowing of blood circulation, particularly in outlying body parts, such as fingers and toes. After age 70, nearly all elderly are affected (Stevens & Cruz, 1996).

Why does deterioration in touch sensitivity occur? Since it varies with area stimulated, researchers believe that loss of touch receptors in certain regions of the skin is responsible. More sluggish blood circulation to the extremities may also contribute.

If we consider the spacing among elements of Braille letters, 45 percent of middle-aged and 100 percent of elderly people should have difficulty interpreting them (Stevens, Foulke, & Patterson, 1996). Just as the sighted need new visual aids for reading as they age, so the visually impaired may need new tactile aids—an important consideration in responding to diversity in the aging population.

CARDIOVASCULAR AND RESPIRATORY SYSTEMS

Aging of the cardiovascular and respiratory systems proceeds gradually during early and middle adulthood, usually without notice. Signs of change are more likely to be apparent in late adulthood, and they prompt concern among aging individuals, who know these organ systems are vital for quality and length of life. In their sixties, Ruth and Walt noticed that they felt more physically stressed after running to catch a departing bus or to reach the far side of the street before the light changed.

As the years pass, the heart muscle becomes more rigid, and some of its cells die while others enlarge, leading the walls of the left ventricle (the largest heart chamber, from which blood is pumped to the body) to thicken. In addition, artery walls stiffen and accumulate some plaque (cholesterol and fats) due to normal aging (much more if the person has atherosclerosis). Finally, the heart muscle becomes less responsive to signals from pacemaker cells within the heart, which initiate each contraction (Arking, 1991; Whitbourne, 1996, 1999).

The combined result of these changes is that the heart pumps with less force, maximum heart rate decreases, and blood flow throughout the circulatory system slows. This

■ *Exercise is a powerful way of slowing the effects of aging on the cardiovascular system. By regularly doing Tai Chi, a Chinese system of exercise designed for meditation and self-defense, these elders protect their respiratory and immune systems, enhance flexibility and range of motion in their joints, and promote restful sleep. (Photo courtesy: A. Ramsey/Stock Boston)*

means that sufficient oxygen may not be delivered to body tissues during high physical activity (Schulman & Gerstenblith, 1989). (Recall from Chapter 13 that a healthy heart supports typical levels of exertion well into old age.)

Changes in the respiratory system compound the reduced oxygenation just described. In Chapter 13, we noted that between ages 20 and 80, vital capacity (amount of air that can be forced in and out of the lungs) is reduced by half. The reason is that lung tissue loses its elasticity. As a result, the lungs fill and empty less efficiently, causing the blood to absorb less oxygen and give off less carbon dioxide. This explains why older people increase their breathing rate more and feel more out of breath when exercising.

Cardiovascular and respiratory deficiencies are more extreme in people who have smoked cigarettes throughout their lives, failed to reduce dietary fat, or had many years of exposure to environmental pollutants. We have seen in previous chapters that exercise is one of the most powerful ways of slowing the effects of aging on the cardiovascular system. Exercise also facilitates respiratory functioning, as we will see when we discuss health and fitness in a later section.

IMMUNE SYSTEM

As the immune system ages, T cells, which attack antigens (foreign substances) directly, become less effective (see Chapter 13, page 428). In addition, the immune system is more likely to malfunction by turning against normal body tissues in an **autoimmune response.** A less competent immune system can increase the elderly person's risk for a variety of illnesses, including infectious diseases (such as the flu), cardiovascular disease, certain forms of cancer, and a variety of autoimmune disorders, such as rheumatoid arthritis and diabetes. But an age-related decline in immune functioning is not the cause of most illnesses among the elderly. It merely permits disease to progress when a stronger immune reaction would have rid the body of the disease agent (Pawelec et al., 1999b; Weksler, 1995).

We must keep in mind that immunity in old age varies tremendously. In longitudinal studies, a few elderly people continue to respond like young adults. But the responses of the majority range from partial to profound loss of function (Pawelec et al., 1999a). The strength of the aging person's immune system seems to be a sign of overall physical vigor. Certain immune indicators, such as high T cell activity, predict survival over the next 2 years in very old people (Ferguson et al., 1995; Miller, 1996).

In Chapter 13, we emphasized that although impaired immune functioning in late life seems to be genetic, other physical changes of aging can intensify it. Recall that stress hormones undermine immunity. With age, the autonomic nervous system releases higher levels of these into the bloodstream (refer back to page 559). New findings suggest that a healthy diet and moderate exercise help protect the immune response in old age, whereas obesity aggravates the age-related decline (Bogden & Louria, 1999; Moriguchi et al., 1995; Shephard & Shek, 1995).

SLEEP

When Walt climbed into bed at night, he usually lay awake for a half-hour to an hour before falling asleep, remaining in a drowsy state longer than when he was younger. During the night, he spent less time in the deepest phase of NREM sleep (see Chapter 4, page 108) and awoke multiple times. Again he sometimes lay awake for a half-hour or more before drifting back to sleep.

Older adults require about the same total sleep time as younger adults—around 7 hours per night. Yet as people age, they have more difficulty falling asleep, staying asleep, and sleeping deeply—a trend that begins after age 30 for men and after age 50 for women. The timing of sleep tends to change as well, toward earlier bedtime and morning awakenings (Hoch et al., 1997). Changes in brain structures controlling sleep and higher levels of stress hormones in the bloodstream, which have an alerting effect on the central nervous system, are believed to be responsible (Prinz et al., 1990; Whitbourne, 1996).

Until age 70 or 80, men experience more sleep disturbances than do women for several reasons. First, enlargement of the prostate gland, which occurs in almost all aging men, constricts the urethra (tube draining the bladder) and leads to a need to urinate more often, including during the night. Second, men are more prone to **sleep apnea,** a condition in which breathing ceases for 10 seconds or longer, resulting in many brief awakenings. The incidence of sleep apnea in elderly men is high; 30 to 50 percent have 20 or more episodes per night. Finally, periodic rapid movement of the legs sometimes accompanies sleep apnea but also occurs at other times of night. Called "restless legs," these movements may be due to muscle tension, reduced circulation, or age-related changes in motor areas of the brain. Although common among the elderly and not dangerous, they do disrupt sleep (Montplaisir & Godbout, 1989).

Older adults often express concern about sleep difficulties. From 25 to 35 percent report some degree of insomnia (Roberts, Shema, & Kaplan, 1999). Poor sleep can feed on itself, making matters worse. For example, Walt's nighttime wakings led to daytime fatigue and short naps, which made it harder to fall asleep the following evening (Whitney et al., 1998). As Walt expected to have trouble sleeping, he worried about it, which also interfered with sleep.

Fortunately, there are many ways to foster restful sleep, such as establishing a consistent bedtime and waking time, exercising regularly, and using the bedroom only for sleep (not for eating, reading, or watching TV). Explaining that even very healthy older adults have trouble sleeping is vital. It lets people know that age-related change in the sleep–waking pattern is normal. The elderly receive 66 percent more prescription sedatives for sleep complaints than do 40- to 60-year-olds. Used briefly, these drugs can help relieve temporary insomnia. But long-term medication can make things worse by increasing the frequency and severity of sleep apnea and by inducing rebound insomnia after the drug is discontinued (Englert & Linden, 1998). Finally, discomfort due to an enlarged prostate, including frequent urination at night, can be corrected with a new laser surgical procedure. It usually relieves all symptoms without complications (Gilling et al., 1999).

PHYSICAL APPEARANCE AND MOBILITY

The inner physical declines we have considered are accompanied by many outward signs of growing older—involving the skin, hair, facial structure, and body build. In earlier chapters, we saw that changes leading to an aged appearance are under way as early as the decades of the twenties and thirties. Because these occur gradually, people may not take notice until a point is reached where the arrival of old age is obvious. From year to year, Walt and Ruth observed that Dick's and Goldie's skin appeared more wrinkled. Their hair had turned from gray to white as all pigment was lost, and their bodies were rounder and arms and legs thinner. Each summer, Walt and Ruth returned from travels with Dick and Goldie more aware that they themselves were aging.

Creasing and sagging of the skin, described in Chapter 15, extends into old age. In addition, oil glands that lubricate the skin become less active, leading to dryness and roughness. "Age spots" increase; in some elderly individuals, the arms, backs of the hands, and face may be dotted with these pigmented marks. Moles and other small skin growths may also appear. Blood vessels can be seen beneath the more transparent skin, which has largely lost its layer of fatty support (Whitbourne, 1996, 1999). This loss further limits the older adult's ability to adapt to very hot and cold temperatures.

The face is especially likely to show these effects because it is frequently exposed to the sun, which accelerates aging. Other facial changes occur: The nose and ears broaden as new cells are deposited on the outer layer of the skeleton. Teeth may be yellowed, cracked, and chipped, and gums may recede; with better dental care, these outcomes are likely to be less pronounced in future generations. As hair follicles under the skin's surface die, hair on the head thins in both sexes, and the scalp may be visible. In men with hereditary pattern baldness, follicles do not die but, instead, begin to produce fine, downy hair (Whitbourne, 1996).

Body build changes as well. Height continues to decline, especially in women, as loss of bone mineral content leads to further collapse of the spinal column. Weight generally drops after age 60 due to additional loss in lean body mass (bone density and muscle), which is heavier than the fat deposits accumulating on the torso.

Several factors affect mobility. The first is muscle strength, which generally declines at a faster rate in late adulthood than it did in middle age. On the average, by 60 to 70 years of age, 10 to 20 percent of muscle power has been lost, a figure that climbs to 30 to 50 percent after ages 70 to 80 (Whitbourne, 1996). Second, bone strength deteriorates, as does flexibility and strength of the tendons and ligaments (which connect muscle to bone) and the joints. In her eighties, Ruth's reduced ability to flex her limbs and rotate her hips meant that walking at a steady, moderate pace, climbing stairs, and rising from a chair were difficult.

In Chapter 13, we noted that endurance athletes who continue training throughout adulthood retain their muscular physiques and much of their strength into their sixties and seventies. These especially active individuals lose fast-twitch muscle fibers like other aging individuals, but they compensate by strengthening remaining slow-twitch fibers so they work more efficiently.

Careful planning of an exercise program can also enhance joint flexibility and range of movement. When Ruth complained of joint stiffness and pain, her doctor pointed out that certain rhythmic and flexing exercises, including dance, could be helpful. "As a matter of fact, I'm taking a dance class myself," Dr. Wylie commented. "C'mon, Ruth, let me show you a few flamenco steps." As Dr. Wylie demonstrated, Ruth imitated. Outside the examining room, the nurses wondered what had sparked the sound of tapping shoes and peals of doctor–patient laughter.

ADAPTING TO PHYSICAL CHANGES OF LATE ADULTHOOD

Great diversity exists in older adults' adaptation to the physical changes of aging. Dick and Goldie took advantage of an enormous industry designed to stave off the appearance of old age, including cosmetics, wigs, and plastic surgery. In contrast, Ruth and Walt hardly gave a second thought to their thinning white hair and wrinkled skin. Their identities were not as bound up with their appearance as with the ability to remain actively engaged in their surroundings.

People vary in the aspects of physical aging that matter most to them. And because parts of the body age at different rates, older adults' sense of physical aging is multidimensional: they feel older in some domains than in others. Compared to Dick and Goldie, Ruth and Walt approached aging with a more positive outlook and greater peace of mind. They did not try to hang on to a youthful identity but, instead, attempted to intervene in those aspects of aging that could be changed and accept those that could not.

Indeed, research shows that the most obvious, outward signs of aging—graying hair, facial wrinkles, and baldness—bear no relationship to sensory, cognitive, and motor functioning and longevity (Schnohr et al., 1998). In con-

trast, neurological, sensory, cardiovascular, respiratory, immune-system, and skeletal and muscular health predict cognitive performance and both quality and length of later life (Korten et al., 1999; Stevens et al., 1998; van Boxtel et al., 1998). Furthermore, people can do more to prevent declines in the functioning of these internal body systems than they can do to prevent gray hair and baldness!

Think back to our discussion of problem-centered and emotion-centered coping in Chapter 15. It applies here as well. As Walt and Ruth prevented and compensated for age-related changes through diet, exercise, environmental adjustments, and an active, stimulating lifestyle, they felt a sense of personal control over their fates. This prompted additional positive coping and improved physical functioning. In contrast, older adults who avoid confronting age-related declines—who think they are inevitable and uncontrollable—tend to be passive when faced with them and to report more physical and psychological symptoms (Speake, 1987; Whitbourne & Primus, 1996).

In Western societies, where negative stereotypes of aging are widespread, adults of all ages regard signs of growing older negatively—a view that is strongest when men evaluate women. (See the section on the double standard of aging in Chapter 15, page 505.) Overall, the elderly respond less negatively than do younger people because they know that wrinkles, baldness, and a stockier body build describe themselves (Harris, 1994). The more older people endorse aging stereotypes, the less likely they are to cope adaptively with age-related change (Ryff, 1991). Also, the stereotype of a declining, incompetent elder encourages others to treat the elderly in condescending ways. This strengthens despondency in the face of aging.

In cultures where the elderly are treated with deference and respect, coping is much easier. An aging appearance may be a source of pride, signifying success in living to a ripe

■ *Adjusting to old age is easier in cultures in which the elderly are treated with deference and respect. Japanese-American grandchildren often plan a traditional ritual called* kanreki, *which recognizes grandparents' senior place in the family and society. The expressions on the faces of these Japanese elders as they pose with their six grandchildren reveal great pride and satisfaction. (Photo courtesy: David Young-Wolff/Stone)*

maturity, and elderly status is often cause for celebration. For example, a traditional Japanese ritual called *kanreki* recognizes the older person's release from the responsibilities of middle age, new freedoms and competencies, and senior place in the family and society. In Japanese-American families, grandchildren often plan the kanreki as a surprise sixtieth birthday party, incorporating elements of both the traditional ritual (such as dress) and the Western birthday (such as a special cake) (Doi, 1991; Gelfand, 1994). Cultural valuing of aging prompts a welcoming approach to late adulthood, including some of its physical transitions. (See, also, the Variations box on page 567.)

Although declines are inevitable, physical aging can be viewed with optimism or pessimism. As Walt commented, "You can think of your glass as half full or half empty." Today, a wealth of research supports the "half full" alternative. In the next section, we will see additional examples of the multiple ways that older people can control their own destiny.

■ ASK YOURSELF . . .

■ *Sixty-five-year-old Herman inspected his thinning hair and bare scalp in the mirror. "The best way to adjust to this is to learn to like it," he thought to himself. "I remember reading somewhere that bald older men are regarded as leaders." What type of coping is Herman using, and why is it an effective way to adapt to this aspect of physical aging?*

🌳 *Reread the story of Dr. Stojic, a robust centenarian, in the Lifespan Vista box on page 560. What aspects of his life history are consistent with research findings on factors that contribute to a long and healthy life?*

HEALTH, FITNESS, AND DISABILITY

At Walt and Ruth's fiftieth wedding anniversary, 77-year-old Walt thanked a roomful of well-wishers for joining in the celebration. Then he announced emotionally, "I'm so grateful Ruth and I are in good health and still able to give to our family, friends, and community."

As Walt's remarks affirm, health is central to psychological well-being in late life. When researchers ask the elderly about their possible selves (see Chapter 16, page 528), number of hoped-for physical selves declines with age and number of feared physical selves increases. Despite this realistic response to changes in physical capabilities, older adults are generally optimistic about their health. Because they judge themselves against same-age peers, they rate their health as favorably as do college students! And with respect to protecting their health, their sense of self-efficacy is as high as that of young adults and higher than that of middle-aged people (Hooker, 1992). When older adults describe their health as fair or poor, their risk of dying within 2 years rises sharply (Bernard et al., 1997).

A tendency to look on the bright side enables the elderly to keep striving in the face of physical difficulties instead of giving up and disengaging. The more optimistic elders are about their capacity to cope with physical challenges, the better they are at overcoming threats to health, which promotes further optimism and continued health-enhancing behaviors (Hooker & Kaus, 1992; Scheier & Carver, 1987; Schwarzer, 1999). Longitudinal research reveals that disability need not follow a path toward further disability and dependency. In several studies, 12 to 20 percent of elders with disabilities showed improvement 2 to 6 years later (Ostir et al., 1999). Furthermore, good health permits older adults to remain engaged in valued social roles, thereby preventing social isolation and fostering psychological well-being (Heidrich & Ryff, 1993). In this way, good physical and good mental health are intimately related in late life.

As mentioned earlier, SES and ethnic variations in health diminish in late adulthood. Nevertheless, before age 85, SES continues to predict physical functioning (Berkman & Gurland, 1998). African-American and Hispanic elderly (over one-third of whom live in poverty) remain at greater risk for certain health problems (see Table 17.2). Native-American older adults are even worse off. More than 80 percent are poor, and chronic health conditions are so widespread that the federal government grants Native Americans special health benefits. These begin as early as age 45, reflecting a much harder and shorter lifespan (Gelfand, 1994; Hopper, 1993). Unfortunately, low-income

TABLE 17.2

Poverty Rates and Health Problems Among Elderly Ethnic Minorities

ETHNIC MINORITY	POVERTY RATE AGE 65 AND OVER[a]	HEALTH PROBLEMS GREATER THAN IN THE GENERAL POPULATION OF 65- TO 84-YEAR-OLDS
African-American	25%	Cardiovascular disease, stroke, a variety of cancers, diabetes
Hispanic	24%	Cardiovascular disease, diabetes
Native-American	Over 80%	Diabetes, kidney disease, liver disease, tuberculosis, hearing and vision impairments

[a]The poverty rate for elderly Caucasian Americans is 9%; for all elderly people in the United States, it is 11%.
Sources: Gelfand, 1994; Hopper, 1993; U.S. Bureau of the Census, 1999.

CULTURAL VARIATIONS IN THE EXPERIENCE OF AGING

In a study of diverse communities around the world, a team of anthropologists found that older people fare best in contexts in which the positive social meaning of aging transcends chronological age and physical decline (Keith et al., 1994). They do well when they have status and opportunities for social participation, even when they are frail. When elders are excluded from important social roles and infirmity brings separation from the community, aging leads to diminished well-being.

Consider the Herero, a pastoral people of Botswana, Africa. Elders who are strong and active spend their days just as younger adults do, tending the cattle and performing other chores. When older people decline physically, they retain positions of seniority and are treated with respect. A status hierarchy makes the oldest man and his wife leaders of the village. They are responsible for pre-serving the sacred flame of the ancestors, who remain significant family members after death. Children are sent to live in the homes of frail elders to provide care—an assignment that is a source of great pride and prestige.

Old age is also a gratifying time of life in Momence, Illinois, a small, working-class farming and manufacturing town. Since the population is highly stable, elders are granted positions of authority due to their length of residence and intimate knowledge of the community. Town, church, and club leaders tend to be older, and past leaders are included in decision making. Frail elders remain part of community life in a less direct way. Because they are embedded in family, neighborhood, and church networks that have persisted for many years, other citizens often inquire about them and monitor their situations.

In Swarthmore, a middle-SES Philadelphia suburb with a less stable population, life for elders is less certain. Although 25 percent of residents are over age 60, most moved to the community after retirement, and their grown children live elsewhere. As a result, older people are granted no special status due to seniority, and they occupy few positions of importance. Unlike the Herero and the citizens of Momence, Swarthmore elders spend much time in age-segregated settings, such as bridge games and church groups for seniors. Townspeople tend to equate "being older" with chronological age—60 and beyond. In contrast, the Herero and the residents of Momence seldom refer to others in terms of their age. Rather, they mention knowledge and social position. When the elderly of Swarthmore become physically infirm, most have no network of support and must leave the community.

Among the Herero and in Momence, neither age nor physical decline threatens community ties. In Swarthmore, being old limits integration into community life, and frailty has profound, negative social consequences. It typically brings an end to community membership.

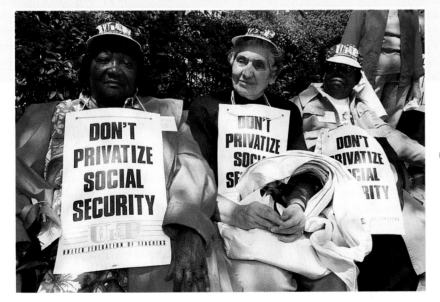

■ *These small-city elder residents belong to a highly active, retired teachers organization. Among their activities is political organizing in favor of causes that safeguard their own welfare and that of others. Here they demonstrate to protect Social Security benefits. Opportunities for community participation are vital for older adults' psychological well-being. (Photo courtesy: Fred Phillips/ Impact Visuals)*

elders are less likely than their higher-income counterparts to seek medical treatment. When they do, they often do not comply with the doctor's directions because they are less likely to believe they can control their health and that treatment will work (Hopper, 1993). A high sense of self-efficacy does not apply to these older adults, further impairing their physical condition.

The sex differences noted in Chapter 15, with men prone to fatal diseases and women to non-life-threatening disabling conditions, extend into late adulthood. By very old age (85 and beyond), women are more impaired than men because only the sturdiest men have survived (Arber & Cooper, 1999). In addition, with fewer physical limitations, older men are better able to remain independent and engage in exercise, hobbies, and involvement in the social world, all of which promote better health.

Widespread health-related optimism among the elderly means that substantial inroads into preventing disability can be made even in the last few decades of life. Yet the persistence of poverty and negative lifestyle factors means that as longevity increases, diseases of old age may rise as well, straining the nation's health care resources. Ideally, as life expectancy extends, we want the average period of diminished vigor before death to decrease. This public health goal is called the **compression of morbidity** (Fries, Green, & Levine, 1994). As we look closely at health, fitness, and disability in late adulthood, we will expand our discussion of health promotion in earlier chapters, taking up additional ways to reach this objective.

NUTRITION AND EXERCISE

The physical changes of late life lead to an increased need for certain nutrients—calcium and vitamin D to protect the bones; zinc and vitamins B_6, C, and E to protect the immune system; and vitamins A, C, and E to prevent free radicals (see Chapter 13, page 424). Yet declines in physical activity, in the senses of taste and smell, and in ease of chewing due to deteriorating teeth can reduce the quantity and quality of food eaten. Furthermore, the aging digestive system has greater difficulty absorbing certain nutrients, such as protein, calcium, and vitamin D (Blumberg, 1996). And older adults who live alone may have problems shopping or cooking and may feel less like eating when by themselves at mealtimes. Together, these physical and environmental conditions increase the risk of dietary deficiencies.

Older adults who take vitamin-mineral supplements show enhanced health and physical functioning. In one study, a daily vitamin-mineral tablet resulted in 48 percent fewer days of infectious illness (Chandra, 1992). In another study, elderly men in a weight-bearing exercise class who took a daily protein-energy supplement showed a larger increase in muscle mass than did exercising classmates who did not take the supplement (Meredith et al., 1992). And as discussed earlier, dietary supplements containing vitamins A, C, and E help prevent macular degeneration.

But their role in protecting against cardiovascular disease is still uncertain (Marchioli, 1999; Maxwell, 1999).

Besides nutrition, exercise continues to be a powerful health intervention. Sedentary healthy older adults up to age 80 who begin endurance training (walking, exercycling, aerobic dance) show gains in vital capacity that compare favorably with those of much younger individuals (Spina et al., 1993; Stratton et al., 1994). And weight-bearing exercise begun in late adulthood—even as late as age 90—promotes muscle size and strength, blood flow to muscles, and ability of muscles to extract oxygen from blood. This translates into improved walking speed, balance, posture, and ability to carry out everyday activities independently, such as opening a stubborn jar lid, carrying an armload of groceries, or lifting a 30-pound grandchild. However, it takes frequent, strenuous exercise to increase the heart's pumping capacity in old age; low-intensity exercise is no longer sufficient (Fiatarone et al., 1990; Goldberg, Dengel, & Hagberg, 1996; Pyka et al., 1994).

Although good nutrition and physical activity are most beneficial when they are lifelong, it is never too late to change. Beginning in his sixties until his death at age 94, Walt's Uncle Louie played 1 to 2 hours of tennis a day and did ballroom dancing three nights a week. Exercise led Louie to sustain a high sense of physical self-esteem. As a dancer, he dressed nattily and moved gracefully. He often commented on how dance and other sports could transform an older person's appearance from dowdy to elegant, expressing the beauty of the inner self.

Elders who come to value the intrinsic benefits of exercise—feeling stronger, healthier, and more energetic—are most likely to engage in it regularly (Caserta & Gillett, 1998). Yet expected discomforts from physical activity are a major barrier to getting older men and women to take up a fitness routine (Clark, 1999). This suggests that it is important to stress the health-enhancing rewards of exercise, especially those related to physical functioning and quality of life, in planning exercise programs for older adults.

SEXUALITY

When Walt turned 60, he asked his 90-year-old Uncle Louie at what age sexual desire and activity cease, if they do. Walt's question stemmed from a widely held myth that sex drive disappears among the elderly (Deacon, Minichiello, & Plummer, 1995). As Louie's response indicates, this stereotype has not been successful in stamping out sexuality in late adulthood—a tribute to the toughness of elders.

"It's especially important to be reasonably rested and patient during sex," Louie explained to Walt. "I can't do it as often, and it's a quieter experience than it was in my youth, but my sexual interest has never gone away. Rachella and I have led a happy intimate life, and it's still that way."

Compared with other parts of the body, such as the eyes, ears, bones, and cardiovascular system, age-related changes in the reproductive organs, described in Chapter

Most healthy older married couples report continued, regular sexual enjoyment. And even at the most advanced ages, there is more to sexuality than the sex act itself—feeling sensual, enjoying close companionship, and being loved and wanted. (Photo courtesy: Cleo/PhotoEdit)

15, are minimal. Although virtually all cross-sectional studies report a decline in sexual desire and frequency of sexual activity in older people, this trend may be exaggerated by cohort effects. A new generation of elders, accustomed to viewing sexuality positively, will probably be more sexually active. Furthermore, longitudinal evidence indicates that most healthy older married couples report continued, regular sexual enjoyment. The same generalization we discussed for midlife applies to late life: good sex in the past predicts good sex in the future. Among unmarried people over age 65, about 70 percent of men and 50 percent of women manage to have sex from time to time (Levy, 1994; Roughan, Kaiser, & Morley, 1993).

Too often, intercourse is used as the only measure of sexual activity—a circumstance that promotes a narrow view of pleasurable sex. Even at the most advanced ages, there is more to sexuality than the sex act itself—feeling sensual, enjoying close companionship, and being loved and wanted (Hodson & Skeen, 1994). Both older men and

older women report that the male partner is usually the one who ceases to interact sexually. In a culture that emphasizes an erection as necessary for being sexual, a man may withdraw from all erotic activity when he finds that erections are harder to achieve and more time must elapse between them (Pedersen, 1998).

Disabilities that disrupt blood flow to the penis—most often, disorders of the autonomic nervous system, cardiovascular disease, and diabetes—are responsible for dampening sexuality in older men. Cigarette smoking, excessive alcohol intake, and a variety of prescription medications also lead to diminished sexual performance (Schiavi, Mandeli, & Schreiner-Engel, 1994). Among women, poor health and absence of a partner are major factors that reduce sexual activity. As the sex ratio increasingly favors females, aging heterosexual women have fewer and fewer opportunities for sexual encounters (U.S. Bureau of the Census, 1999).

Older people who know little about normal age-related changes in sexual functioning may react with anxiety when faced with sexual difficulties. Educational programs that dispel myths and foster a view of sex as extending throughout adulthood promote positive sexual attitudes in late life (Hillman & Stricker, 1994). In nursing homes, education for caregivers is vital for ensuring older residents' rights to privacy and other living conditions that permit sexual expression (Levy, 1994).

PHYSICAL DISABILITIES

Illness and disability climb as the end of the lifespan approaches. If you compare Table 17.3 with Table 15.1 on page 498, you will see that cardiovascular disease and cancer—illnesses we discussed in Chapter 15—increase dramatically from mid- to late life and remain the leading causes of death. Notice how, with increasing years since menopause, the sex difference in deaths due to cardiovascular disease declines. The gender gap for another vascular condition, *stroke*, also diminishes with age. It is caused by hemorrhage or blockage of blood flow in the brain and is a

TABLE 17.3

Death Rates[a] Among the Elderly by Leading Causes in the United States

CAUSE	65+ YEARS TOTAL	65–74 YEARS MALES	65–74 YEARS FEMALES	75–84 YEARS MALES	75–84 YEARS FEMALES	85+ YEARS MALES	85+ YEARS FEMALES
Cardiovascular Disease	1,835	1,179	579	2,745	1,776	7,158	6,264
Cancer	1,137	1,111	687	1,883	1,026	2,803	1,394
Stroke	414	156	119	510	443	1,501	1,591
Emphysema	264	200	121	479	233	831	318
Pneumonia	222	74	41	310	176	1,310	911
Adult-onset diabetes	133	79	74	151	138	269	248
Unintentional injury	105	61	31	131	75	344	220

[a]Number of deaths per 100,000 population in specified group.
Source: U.S. Bureau of the Census, 1999.

major cause of disability in late adulthood and death after age 75. *Emphysema,* due to extreme loss of elasticity in lung tissue, results in serious breathing difficulty. Although a few cases of emphysema are inherited, most are caused by long-term cigarette smoking (Larson, 1996).

Notice in Table 17.3 that death due to pneumonia increases nearly eighteenfold during late adulthood. As the longest-lived people escape chronic diseases or weaken physically because of them, the immune system eventually encounters an infection it cannot fight. Consequently, many of the very old succumb to one of the more than 50 lung inflammations classified as pneumonia. Doctors recommend that people age 65 and older be vaccinated against the most common type.

Other diseases are less frequent killers, but they limit older adults' ability to live fully and independently. Osteoporosis, discussed in Chapter 15 (see page 500), continues to rise in late adulthood; recall that it affects the majority of men and women after age 70. Yet another bone disorder—*arthritis*—adds to the physical limitations of many elders. And as Table 17.3 reveals, *adult-onset diabetes* and *unintentional injuries* multiply in late adulthood. In the following sections, we take up these latter three conditions.

Finally, an important point must be kept in mind as we discuss physical and mental disabilities of late adulthood: None are considered a normal part of the aging process, even though they increase with advancing age. In other words, just because certain physical and mental disabilities are *related to age* does not mean that they are *caused by aging.* To clarify this distinction, some experts distinguish between **primary aging** (another term for *biological aging*), or genetically influenced declines that affect all members of our species and take place even in the context of overall good health, and **secondary aging,** declines due to hereditary defects and negative environmental influences, such as poor diet, lack of exercise, disease, substance abuse, environmental pollution, and psychological stress.

Throughout this and earlier chapters, we have seen that it is often difficult to distinguish primary from secondary aging. But if we do not try to do so, we are in danger of magnifying decrements and promoting a false, stereotyped view of aging as illness and disease (Lemme, 1999). All the disabilities we are about to discuss are extreme conditions that fall within *secondary aging.*

■ ARTHRITIS. Beginning in her fifties, Ruth felt a slight morning stiffness in her neck, back, hips, and knees. In her sixties, she developed bony lumps on the end joints of her fingers. As the years passed, she experienced periodic joint swelling and some loss of flexibility—changes that affected her ability to move quickly and easily.

Arthritis, a condition of inflamed, painful, stiff, and sometimes swollen joints and muscles, becomes more common in late adulthood. It comes in several forms. Ruth has

osteoarthritis, the most frequent type. Otherwise known as "wear-and-tear arthritis" or "degenerative joint disease," it is one of the few age-related disabilities in which years of use makes a difference. Although a genetic proneness seems to exist, the disease usually does not appear until the forties and fifties. In frequently used joints, cartilage on the ends of the bones, which reduces friction during movement, gradually deteriorates. Almost all older adults show some degree of osteoarthritis on X-rays, although wide individual differences in severity exist (Schwartz & Zimmerman, 1999; Strange, 1996).

Unlike osteoarthritis, which is limited to certain joints, **rheumatoid arthritis** involves the whole body. An autoimmune response leads to inflammation of connective tissue, particularly the membranes that line the joints. The result is overall stiffness, inflammation, and aching. Tissue in the cartilage tends to grow, damaging surrounding ligaments, muscles, and bones. The result is deformed joints and often serious loss of mobility. Sometimes other organs, such as the heart and lungs, are affected.

Disability due to arthritis affects about 45 percent of American men over age 65. Among women, the incidence is higher; 50 percent between ages 65 and 74 and 60 percent over age 75 are affected. The reason for the sex difference is not clear. Although rheumatoid arthritis can strike at any age, it tends to increase after menopause. But unlike osteoporosis, it does not respond to hormone replacement therapy (HRT), so something other than estrogen loss must be involved. It may be due to a late-appearing genetic defect in the immune system (Gomolka et al., 1995). Early treatment with new, powerful anti-inflammatory medications helps slow the course of the disease (Fleischmann, 1999).

Managing arthritis requires a balance of rest when the disease flares, pain relief (including, if necessary, certain drugs), and physical activity involving gentle stretching of all muscles to maintain mobility. Twice a week, 84-year-old Ruth attended a water-based exercise class. Within 2 months, her symptoms lessened, and she no longer needed a walker (Strange, 1996). Weight loss in obese people is helpful because it relieves the joints of added daily trauma from bearing an extra load (Eades, 1992).

Although osteoarthritis responds to treatment more easily than rheumatoid arthritis, the course of each varies greatly. With proper medication, joint protection, and lifestyle changes, many people with either form of the illness can lead long and productive lives. If hip or knee joints are badly damaged or deformed, they can be surgically rebuilt or replaced with plastic or metal devices.

■ ADULT-ONSET DIABETES. After we eat a meal, the body breaks down the food, releasing glucose (the primary energy source for cell activity) into the bloodstream. Insulin, produced by the pancreas, keeps the blood concentration of glucose within set limits by stimulating muscle and fat cells to absorb it. When this balance system fails, either because not enough insulin is produced or body cells become insensitive to it, *adult-onset diabetes* (otherwise known as *diabetes mellitus*) results. Over time, abnormally high blood glucose damages the blood vessels, increasing the risk of stroke, heart attack, circulatory problems in the legs, and injury to the eyes, kidneys, and nerves.

From middle to late adulthood, the incidence of adult-onset diabetes doubles, affecting 10 percent of the elderly in the United States and ranking as a leading cause of death (U.S. Bureau of the Census, 1999). Diabetes runs in families, suggesting that heredity is involved. But inactivity and abdominal fat deposits greatly increase the risk. Higher rates of adult-onset diabetes are found among African Americans, Mexican Americans, Puerto Ricans, and Native Americans for genetic as well as environmental reasons, including high-fat diets and obesity associated with poverty (Hopper, 1993; Markides, 1989).

Treating adult-onset diabetes requires lifestyle changes, including a carefully controlled diet, regular exercise, and weight loss. By promoting glucose absorption and reducing abdominal fat, physical activity lessens disease symptoms (Goldberg, Dengel, & Hagberg, 1996).

■ UNINTENTIONAL INJURIES. At age 65 and older, the death rate from unintentional injuries is at an all-time high—three times greater than in adolescence and young adulthood. Motor vehicle collisions and falls are largely responsible.

Motor Vehicle Accidents. Motor vehicle collisions account for only one-fourth of injury mortality in late life compared with one-half in middle adulthood. But a look at individual drivers tells a different story. Older adults have higher rates of traffic violations, accidents, and fatalities per mile driven of any age group, with the exception of drivers under age 25. The high rate of injury persists, even though many elders limit their driving after noticing that their ability to drive safely is slipping. Women are more likely to take these preventive steps. Deaths due to injuries—motor vehicle and otherwise—continue to be much higher for men than for women in late adulthood (Stewart et al., 1993).

Recall that visual declines led Walt to have difficulty seeing the dashboard and identifying pedestrians at night. Most information used in driving is visual. The greater elders' visual processing difficulties, the higher their rate of moving violations and crashes (Marottoli et al., 1994;

Owsley & McGwin, 1999). Compared with young drivers, the elderly are less likely to drive quickly and recklessly but more likely to fail to heed signs, give right-of-way, and turn appropriately. They often try to compensate for their difficulties by being more cautious. But slowed reaction time and indecisiveness can pose hazards as well (Garzia & Trick, 1992). Walt had several close calls when he took too long to change lanes, a maneuver that requires rapid, accurate judgment for safety.

The elderly are also at risk as pedestrians. Nearly 30 percent of deaths between ages 65 and 74 in the United States result from pedestrian accidents (U.S. Bureau of the Census, 1999). Confusing intersections and crossing signals that do not allow older people enough time to get to the other side of the street are often involved.

Falls. On one occasion, Ruth fell down the basement steps and lay there with a broken ankle until Walt arrived home an hour later. Ruth's tumble represents the leading type of accident among the elderly. About 30 percent of adults over age 65 and 40 percent over age 80 experienced a fall within the last year. Declines in balance due to neuronal loss in sensory and motor regions of the cerebral cortex contribute to increased risk of falling in late adulthood (Hobeika, 1999). Because of weakened bones and difficulty breaking a fall, about 10 percent of the time serious injury results. Among the most common is hip fracture. It increases twentyfold from age 65 to 85 and is associated with a 12 to 20 percent increase in mortality. Of those who survive, half never regain the ability to walk without assistance (Garzia & Trick, 1992; Simoneau & Leibowitz, 1996).

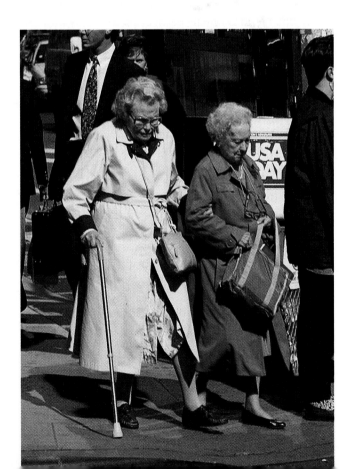

■ Declines in vision and reaction time and increased cautiousness and indecisiveness increase elders' risk of both motor vehicle collisions and pedestrian accidents. Confusing intersections with traffic lights that do not grant older adults enough time to cross the street also heighten the chances of a tragedy. (Photo courtesy: Robert Brennan/PhotoEdit)

Preventing Unintentional Injury in Late Adulthood

SUGGESTION	DESCRIPTION
MOTOR VEHICLE COLLISIONS AND PEDESTRIAN ACCIDENTS	
Modify driving behavior in accord with visual and other limitations.	Driving fewer miles; reducing or eliminating driving during rush hour, at night, or in bad weather
Modify pedestrian behavior in accord with visual and other limitations	Wearing light-colored clothing at night; allowing extra time to cross streets; walking with a companion
Attend training classes for older drivers; if not available, press for them in your community.	Practicing tracking vehicles and pedestrians in dim light, judging vehicle speed, and reading signs and dashboard displays; reviewing rules of the road
FALLS	
Schedule regular medical checkups.	Eye exams to ensure that corrective lenses are up to date; physical exams to identify health risks that increase the chances of falling; review of medications for effects on attention and coordination
Engage in regular exercise.	Strength and balance training to promote coordination and counteract fear of falling
Use walking aids when necessary.	Canes and walkers to compensate for poor balance and unsteady gait
Improve safety of the living environment.	Extra lighting in dim areas, such as entrances, hallways, and staircases; handrails in hallways and grab bars in bathrooms; loose rugs secured to floor or moved; furniture and other objects arranged so they are not obstacles
Be alert and plan ahead in risky situations.	Watching for slippery pavement; carrying a flashlight at night; allowing extra time to cross streets; becoming familiar with new settings before moving about freely

Sources: Kline et al., 1992; Simoneau & Leibowitz, 1996; Stewart et al., 1993.

Falling can also impair health indirectly—by promoting fear of falling. Almost half of older adults who have fallen admit that they purposefully avoid activities because they are afraid of falling again (Tinetti, Speechley, & Ginter, 1988). In this way, a fall can limit mobility and social contact, undermining both physical and psychological well-being. Although an active lifestyle may expose the elderly to more events and situations that can cause a fall, the health benefits of activity far outweigh the risk of serious injury due to falling (Tinetti, 1990).

Preventing Unintentional Injuries. Many steps can be taken to reduce unintentional injury in late adulthood. Designing motor vehicles and street signs to accommodate visual needs of the elderly is a goal for the future. In the meantime, training that enhances visual and cognitive skills essential for safe driving and that helps older adults avoid high-risk situations (such as busy intersections and rush hour) can save lives.

Similarly, efforts to prevent falls must address risks within the person and environment—through corrective eyewear, strength and balance training, and improved safety in homes and communities. The Caregiving Concerns table above summarizes ways to protect the elderly from injury.

MENTAL DISABILITIES

Normal age-related cell death in the brain, described earlier in this chapter, does not lead to loss of ability to engage in everyday activities. But when cell death and structural and chemical abnormalities are profound, serious deterioration of mental and motor functions occurs.

Dementia refers to a set of disorders occurring almost entirely in old age in which many aspects of thought and behavior are so impaired that everyday activities are disrupted (American Psychiatric Association, 1994). It rises sharply with age, striking adults of both sexes and different ethnic and SES groups about equally. Approximately 1 percent of people in their sixties are affected, a rate that doubles every 5 years until it stabilizes at 30 percent for people in their nineties (Andersen et al., 1999; Edland et al., 1999).

About a dozen types of dementia have been identified. Some are reversible with proper treatment, but most are

[2] In Parkinson's disease, neurons in the part of the brain that controls muscle movements deteriorate. Symptoms include tremors, shuffling gait, loss of facial expression, rigidity of limbs, difficulty maintaining balance, and stooped posture.

irreversible and incurable. A few forms, such as Parkinson's disease,[2] involve deterioration in subcortical brain regions (primitive structures below the cortex). But in the large majority of cases, progressive damage to the cerebral cortex—seat of human intelligence—occurs. *Cortical dementia* comes in two varieties: Alzheimer's disease and cerebrovascular dementia.

■ ALZHEIMER'S DISEASE. When Ruth took 79-year-old Ida to the ballet, an occasion that the two sisters looked forward to each year, Ida's behavior was different than before. Having forgotten the engagement, she reacted with anger at Ruth for arriving unannounced at her door. After Ida calmed down, she got lost driving in familiar parts of town on the way to the theater while insisting she knew her way perfectly well. Settled in the balcony, Ida talked loudly and dug noisily in her purse as the lights dimmed and the music began.

"Shhhhhh," responded a dozen voices from the surrounding seats.

"It's just the music!" Ida snapped at full volume. "You can talk all you want until the dancing starts." Ruth was astonished and embarrassed at the behavior of her once socially sensitive sister.

Six months later, Ida was diagnosed with **Alzheimer's disease,** the most common form of dementia, accounting for 50 to 60 percent of all cases. Approximately 5 to 7 percent of people over age 65 have the disorder. Of those over age 80, about 15 percent are affected (Gatz, Kasl-Godley, & Karel, 1996; Gurland et al., 1999). Each year in the United States, 100,000 people die of Alzheimer's, making it a leading cause of death in late adulthood (although on death certificates, more immediate causes, such as infection and respiratory failure, are usually listed).

Symptoms and Course of the Disease. Severe memory problems are often the earliest symptom—forgetting names, dates, appointments, familiar routes of travel, or the need to turn off the stove in the kitchen. At first, recent memory is most impaired, but as serious disorientation sets in, recall of distant events and such basic facts as time, date, and place evaporates. Faulty judgment puts the person in danger. For example, Ida insisted on driving after she was no longer capable of doing so. Personality changes occur—loss of spontaneity and sparkle, anxiety and angry outbursts due to uncertainties created by mental problems, reduced initiative, and social withdrawal. Depression, which often appears in the early phase of Alzheimer's and other forms of dementia, seems to be part of the disease process (Mulsant & Ganguli, 1999; Reifler, 1994). However, depression may worsen as the older adult reacts to disturbing mental changes.

As the disease progresses, skilled and purposeful movements disintegrate. When Ruth took Ida into her home, she had to help her dress, bathe, eat, brush her teeth, and (eventually) walk and use the bathroom. Ruth also found that Ida's sleep was disrupted by delusions and imaginary fears. She

often awoke in the night and banged on the wall, insisting that it was dinnertime. Sometimes she cried out that someone was choking her. Over time, Ida lost the ability to comprehend and produce speech. And when her brain ceased to process information, she could no longer recognize objects and familiar people. In the final months, Ida became increasingly vulnerable to infections, lapsed into a coma, and died.

The course of Alzheimer's varies greatly, from a few years to as many as 20 years. The average is about 8 to 10 years (National Institute on Aging, 1999).

Brain Deterioration. A diagnosis of Alzheimer's disease is made through exclusion—after other causes of dementia have been ruled out by a physical examination and psychological testing. Doctors can only know for sure that a person has Alzheimer's by inspecting the brain after death for a set of abnormalities that either cause or result from the disease (Gatz, Kasl-Godley, & Karel, 1996). However, new developments in functional brain-imaging techniques, which yield three-dimensional pictures of brain volume and activity, offer hope of accurately diagnosing Alzheimer's disease soon after symptoms appear. Shrinkage and reduced metabolism in memory areas appear as Alzheimer's develops (Bobinski et al., 1999; Jack et al., 1999; Reiman et al., 1996).

Two major structural changes in the brain occur. The greater their distribution in the cerebral cortex, the more severe the Alzheimer's dementia tends to be. Inside neurons, **neurofibrillary tangles** appear—bundles of twisted threads that are the product of collapsed neural structures. Outside neurons, *plaques,* or deposits of material surrounded by clumps of dead nerve cells, develop. They contain *amyloid,* a protein associated with many other diseases that is deposited in tissue with reduced immunity. These **amyloid plaques** may destroy surrounding neurons and their communication networks, perhaps by causing inflammation in the brain, by generating free radicals, or by reducing blood flow (Griffin et al., 1998; Knowles et al., 1999). Although some neurofibrillatory tangles and amyloid plaques are present in the brains of normal middle-aged and older people and increase with age, they are far more abundant and widely distributed in Alzheimer's victims (Price and Morris, 1999).

Accompanying structural changes in the brain are chemical changes—lowered levels of *neurotransmitters* necessary for communication between neurons. For example, a deficit of the neurotransmitter acetylcholine and destruction of its neural network, which transports messages between distant areas of the brain, disrupt perception, memory, reasoning, and judgment (Davis et al., 1999). A 50 to 75 percent drop in serotonin, a neurotransmitter that regulates arousal, may contribute to sleep disturbances and Alzheimer's-related depression (Cohen et al., 1993). As research continues, it is likely that other neurotransmitter imbalances will be discovered.

Risk and Protective Factors. Alzheimer's disease comes in two types: *familial,* which runs in families, and *sporadic,* which has no obvious family history. Familial Alzheimer's generally has an early onset (before age 65) and progresses more rapidly than the later-appearing, sporadic Alzheimer's. Researchers have identified genes on chromosomes 1, 14, and 21 that are linked to familial Alzheimer's. In each case, the abnormal gene is dominant; if it is present in only one of the pair of genes inherited from parents, the person will develop early-onset Alzheimer's (National Institute on Aging, 1999). Recall that chromosome 21 is involved in Down syndrome. Individuals with this chromosomal disorder who live past age 40 almost always have the brain abnormalities and symptoms of Alzheimer's.

Heredity may also play a role in sporadic Alzheimer's through spontaneous mutations. Many people with this form of the disease have an abnormal gene on chromosome 19, which results in excess levels of ApoE, a blood protein that carries cholesterol throughout the body. A high blood concentration of ApoE is linked to amyloid plaque formation in Alzheimer's victims (Holtzman et al., 1999). The abnormal ApoE gene is the most common known risk for this form of Alzheimer's; it is present in 50 percent of cases (Strittmatter et al., 1993).

Nevertheless, 50 percent of sporadic Alzheimer's victims show no currently known genetic marker (Kehoe et al., 1999; Plassman & Breitner, 1996). Besides heredity, the roles of toxic substances, viruses, defects in the blood–brain barrier (which protects the brain from harmful agents), and dietary deficiencies (especially folate) are being explored. Alzheimer's disease may result from several factors working together, and different combinations may lead to a somewhat different course of the disease. Although elevated levels of aluminum have been found in the brain tangles and plaques of Alzheimer's victims, the role of environmental exposure to aluminum remains uncertain (National Institute on Aging, 1999).

Finally, hormone replacement therapy (HRT) and anti-inflammatory drugs (such as aspirin, ibuprofen, and the steroid prednisone) seem to have protective effects. In recent longitudinal research, the incidence of Alzheimer's disease was substantially lower in women who had taken HRT as healthy middle-aged and older adults. Starting HRT after disease onset, however, did not improve cognitive functioning (Mulnard et al., 2000). Anti-inflammatory medication may slow the course of the Alzheimer's by reducing inflammation of brain tissue caused by amyloid and other abnormal proteins (McGeer, Schulzer, & McGeer, 1996). Yet another protective factor is education. Some researchers speculate that years of education lead to more synaptic connections. These act as a *cognitive reserve*, equipping the aging brain with greater tolerance for injury before it crosses the threshold into mental disability (Satz, 1993).

Interventions. As Ida's Alzheimer's worsened, the doctor prescribed a mild sedative and an antidepressant to help control her behavior. Drug treatments to correct neu-

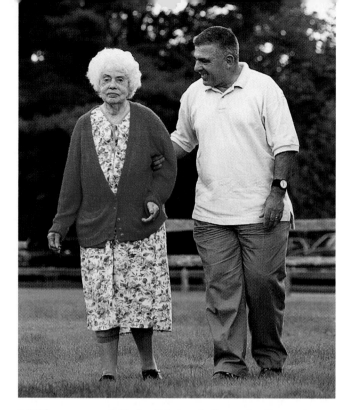

■ *With no cure available for Alzheimer's disease, family caregivers like this adult son need assistance, encouragement, social support, and education about the disease to ensure the best possible adjustment for all concerned. (Photo courtesy: Griffin/The Image Works)*

rotransmitter deficits have also been tried, but they are not effective, perhaps because Alzheimer's disease interferes with the ability of neurons to respond to them (Burns, Howard, & Pettit, 1995).

With no cure available, family interventions ensure the best adjustment possible for the Alzheimer's victim, his or her spouse, and other relatives. Compared with people caring for elders with physical disabilities, dementia caregivers spend substantially more time on caregiving tasks and experience more stress (Ory et al., 1999). They need assistance and encouragement from extended family members, friends, and community agencies. Education about the disease is vital. In combination with social support, it helps caregivers respond with patience and compassion to the victim's frequent, repetitive questions and stories and socially inappropriate behavior. Return to page 541 to review strategies for relieving the stress of caring for an aging parent. These techniques are just as helpful to spouses and siblings, who serve as caregivers about as often as do adult children (Marks, 1996).

Communicating with Alzheimer's victims is especially challenging. The Caregiving Concerns table on the following page lists some helpful suggestions. Avoiding dramatic changes in living conditions, such as moving to a new location, rearranging furniture, or modifying daily routines, is important for helping the patient, whose cognitive world is gradually disintegrating, feel as secure as possible.

Communicating Effectively with Alzheimer's Victims

PROBLEM BEHAVIOR	COMMUNICATION STRATEGY
Asking the same question over and over, telling ridiculous stories, or making socially inappropriate comments	Distract the person with other topics of discussion and activities; avoid arguing, responding with anger, or rebuking the person.
Failing to keep an appointment or complete a task	Use reminders and lists; make requests close to the time the task needs to be done; always ask for the desired behavior in the same setting (e.g., eating in the kitchen, dressing in the bedroom).
Denying memory problems, blaming others for mistakes	Do not force the person to face memory problems; respond with sympathy to the threat memory loss poses.
Reacting with anger to assistance from others	Avoid emphasizing the person's weaknesses; provide help in a kind manner; encourage and reinforce small successes and acceptance of help.
Restlessness, agitation, inability to sit still	Use a calm, reassuring approach; reduce noise and other distractions; involve the person in activities that relieve excess energy.
Failing to recognize familiar people, objects, and places	Agree that things look different, and calmly remind the person of people and objects in the situation.

Source: Gruetzner, 1992.

■ CEREBROVASCULAR DEMENTIA. In **cerebrovascular dementia,** a series of strokes leaves areas of dead brain cells, producing step-by-step degeneration of mental ability, with each step occurring abruptly after a stroke. About 5 to 10 percent of all cases of dementia are cerebrovascular, and about 10 percent are due to a combination of Alzheimer's and repeated strokes (Gatz, Kasl-Godley, & Karel, 1996; Leys, Pasquier, & Parnetti, 1998).

A hereditary tendency toward cerebrovascular dementia appears to be indirect, through high blood pressure, cardiovascular disease, and diabetes, each of which increases the risk of stroke. But many environmental influences, including cigarette smoking, heavy alcohol use, high salt intake, very low dietary protein, obesity, inactivity, and stress, also heighten stroke risk, so cerebrovascular dementia appears to be the combined result of genetic and environmental forces.

Because of their susceptibility to cardiovascular disease, more men than women have cerebrovascular dementia by their late sixties. Women are not at great risk until after age 75 (Leys, Pasquier, & Parnetti, 1998). The disease also varies among countries. For example, deaths due to stroke are high in Japan. Although a low-fat diet reduces Japanese adults' risk of cardiovascular disease, high intake of alcohol and salt and a diet very low in animal protein increase the risk of stroke. As Japanese consumption of alcohol and salt declined and intake of meat rose in recent decades, the rate of cerebrovascular dementia and stroke-caused deaths dropped, although they remain higher than in other developed nations (Goldman & Takahashi, 1996; Myers, 1996).

Although Japan presents a unique, contradictory picture (a culture where cardiovascular disease is low and stroke is high), in most cases cerebrovascular dementia is caused by atherosclerosis. Prevention is the only effective way to stop the disease. The incidence of cerebrovascular dementia has dropped in the last 2 decades, probably as a result of the decline in heart disease (see Chapter 13) and more effective stroke prevention methods (Elkind & Sacco, 1998). Signs that a stroke might be coming are weakness, tingling, or numbness in an arm, a leg, or the face; sudden vision loss or double vision; speech difficulty; and severe dizziness and imbalance. Doctors may prescribe drugs to reduce the tendency of the blood to clot. Once strokes occur, paralysis and loss of speech, vision, coordination, memory, and other mental abilities are common.

■ MISDIAGNOSED AND REVERSIBLE DEMENTIA. Careful diagnosis of dementia is crucial, since other disorders can be mistaken for it. And some forms of dementia can be treated and a few reversed.

Depression is the disorder most often misdiagnosed as dementia. The depressed (but not demented) older adult is likely to exaggerate his or her mental difficulties, whereas the demented person minimizes them and is not fully aware of cognitive declines. Fewer than 1 percent of people over age 65 are severely depressed and another 2 percent are moderately depressed—rates that are lower than for young and middle-aged adults (Reiger et al., 1988). Most older people have probably learned how to adjust what they expect from life, resulting in fewer feelings of worthlessness. However, as we will see in Chapter 18, depression rises with age. It is often related to physical illness and pain and can lead to cognitive deterioration (Magni & Frisoni, 1996; Nussbaum et al., 1995). As at younger ages, the support of family members and friends; antidepressant medication; and individual, family, and group therapy can help relieve depression. How-

Picture the population as a building, with the youngest at the bottom and the oldest at the top. Through most of the twentieth century, this structure resembled a pyramid, with fewer and fewer people at older ages. Aging of the "baby boom" generation, combined with declining birthrates and greater longevity, will cause a "senior boom" in the first half of the twenty-first century. By the year 2050, the number of young, middle-aged, and elderly people in the United States is expected to be about equal (see Figure 17.3). This **squaring of the population pyramid** has raised concerns about whether younger, employed citizens will be able to support the growing number of older, dependent seniors due to increasingly costly Social Security, Medicare, and Medicaid benefits.

In addition, some policymakers and citizens argue that population trends have led to **intergenerational inequity,** with the elderly receiving more than their fair share of public resources at the expense of the very young, who cannot vote and lobby for their needs (see Chapter 2). To create greater equity, a few people want to limit health care for aging individuals—a large part of the growing "public burden" of the elderly. They argue that after completion of a "natural life

span," somewhere in the late seventies or early eighties, medical treatment should be provided only to relieve suffering, not to save lives. Resources currently directed at expensive treatments for older adults with a small chance of success should, instead, be diverted into improving health at younger ages and, thereby, increasing the likelihood of better health in later life (Callahan, 1990, 1999).

Even if we set aside serious ethical issues, age-related rationing of health services would be difficult to implement. Because people age at widely varying rates, it would be impossible to reach consensus on what age signifies the completion of a "natural life span." In addition, savings would largely come from very expensive, acute health care interventions. Yet the popular belief that the elderly more often use the most aggressive, costly medical technologies is wrong. These procedures are applied fairly evenly across age groups (Binstock, 1992).

Public policies that pit one age group against another promote intergenerational conflict and age discrimination. Recall from Chapter 16 that younger and older citizens currently recognize their interdependence and support benefits to one another. Indeed, throughout this book, we have seen how enhancing both younger and

older citizens' well-being contributes to the welfare of all generations.

Other, more promising approaches to freeing up public resources so they are available for pressing social problems have been suggested:

- As the health and longevity of older Americans continues to increase, they are likely to remain in the work force for several additional years (U.S. Bureau of the Census, 1999). Responding to this trend, the age of initial eligibility for full Social Security benefits recently rose from age 65 to 67.

- For every dollar spent on medical care for Alzheimer's disease victims, less than two-tenths of one cent is spent on research aimed at finding a cure. Allocating additional resources to research on this and other major disabling diseases is the best way to prevent elderly health care costs from skyrocketing in the future (National Institute on Aging, 1999).

- Justice between the advantaged and disadvantaged at all ages is a far more promising principle of equity than justice between age groups, which trades off the value of one human life for another and diverts us from the larger goal of helping people of any age who are in need.

---

ever, the elderly in general and low-income, ethnic minorities in particular are unlikely to seek mental health services. This increases the chances that depression will deepen and be confused with dementia (Padgett et al., 1994).

The older we get, the more likely we are to be taking drugs that might have side effects resembling dementia. For example, some medications for coughs, diarrhea, and nausea inhibit the neurotransmitter acetylcholine, leading to Alzheimer's-like symptoms. Because tolerance for drugs decreases with age, these reactions are intensified in late adulthood. In addition, some diseases can cause temporary memory loss and mental symptoms, especially among the elderly, who often become confused and withdrawn when

ill. Treatment of the underlying illness relieves the problem. Finally, environmental changes and social isolation can trigger mental declines. When supportive ties are restored, cognitive functioning usually bounces back (Gruetzner, 1992).

HEALTH CARE

Health care professionals and lawmakers in industrialized nations worry about the economic consequences of rapid increase in the elderly population. Rising government-supported health care costs and demand for certain health care services, particularly long-term care, are of greatest concern.

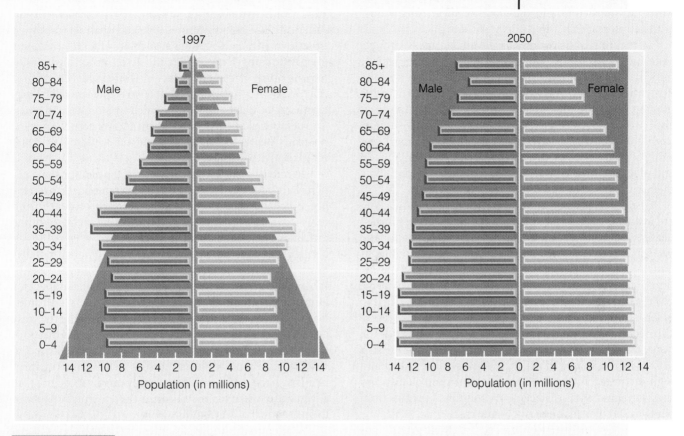

1997 2050

Population (in millions)

FIGURE 17.3

■ **Population pyramids for 1997 and 2050.** Notice the squaring of the population pyramid as the number of older adults rises and the number of young people shrinks. By 2050, the youngest and oldest generations are expected to be equally represented. (From U.S. Bureau of the Census, 1999.)

■ COST OF HEALTH CARE FOR THE ELDERLY. Americans age 65 and older, who make up 12.7 percent of the population, account for 30 percent of federal health care expenditures. According to current estimates, the cost of Medicare (government-sponsored health insurance for the elderly) is expected to double by the year 2020 and nearly triple by 2040 as the "baby boom" generation reaches late adulthood and average life expectancy extends further (Bodenheimer, 1999; Gramm, Rettenmaier, & Saving, 1998).

Medicare expenses rise steeply with age. People age 80 and older receive, on the average, 77 percent more benefits than do younger senior citizens. Most of this increase is due to

a need for long-term care—in hospitals and nursing homes—because of the age-related rise in disabling chronic diseases and acute illnesses.

Currently, the U.S. government pays about half of medical expenses for the aged. Some people argue that this degree of cost sharing must be drastically reduced. Otherwise, the elderly will become a burdensome responsibility, unfairly consuming national resources that ought to be given to other sectors of the population. Should society limit health care payments to older people as a way of achieving a more equitable distribution of resources to different age groups? To consider this controversial issue, read the Social Issues box above.

■ **LONG-TERM CARE.** When Ida moved into Ruth's home, Ruth promised that she'd never place Ida in an institution. But as Ida's condition worsened and Ruth faced health problems of her own, she couldn't keep her word. Ida needed round-the-clock medical care. Reluctantly, Ruth placed her in a nursing home.

As Figure 17.4 below reveals, advancing age is strongly associated with use of long-term care services, especially nursing homes. Among disorders of aging, hip fracture and dementia, especially Alzheimer's disease, most often lead to nursing home placement. Greater use of nursing homes is also prompted by loss of informal caregiving support through widowhood (which mostly affects women) and aging of adult children and other relatives. Of people age 85 and older in nursing homes, 69 percent have children who themselves are senior citizens (Doty, 1992).

Overall, only 5 percent of Americans age 65 and older are institutionalized, a rate about half that of other industrialized nations, such as Canada, the Netherlands, and Sweden. These countries provide more generous public financing of health services for the aged, including institutional care. In the United States, unless nursing home placement follows hospitalization for an acute illness, older adults must pay for it until their resources are exhausted. At that point, Medicaid (health insurance for the poor) takes over. Consequently, the largest users of nursing homes in the United States are people with very low and high incomes (Torrey, 1992). Middle-income elderly and their families are more likely to try to protect savings from being drained by high nursing home costs.

Nursing-home use also varies across ethnic groups. For example, among people age 75 and older, Caucasian Americans are one-and-a-half times more likely to be institutionalized than are African Americans. Large, closely knit extended families mean that over 70 percent of African-American elders do not live alone and over one-third reside with their adult children (Gibson & Jackson, 1992). Similarly, Asian Americans use nursing homes less often than do Caucasian Americans because of greater availability of family members to provide care—a factor that also accounts for low rates of nursing home placement in Japan (Doty, 1992; McCormick et al., 1996). Nevertheless, at least 60 to 80 percent of all long-term care for older adults is provided by family members in Australia, Canada, the United States, and Western Europe. As noted in Chapter 16, it is a myth that adult children, as well as other relatives, abandon the elderly.

To reduce institutionalized care of the elderly, some experts have advocated alternatives, such as publicly funded in-home help for family caregivers. However, evidence from other countries reveals that government financing of home care does not lower rates of nursing home placement much because the two types of care largely serve different populations. The elderly cared for at home are less impaired than those in nursing homes (Doty, 1992). Still, public support for home care is important for relieving the financial and emotional burdens on family caregivers and enhancing the well-being of the elderly. And dissemination of information about currently available community services, such as homemaker, visiting nurse, and adult day care, is vital. Many American ethnic minority elders and their family caregivers do not take advantage of these supports because they do not know about them (Moon, Lubben, & Villa, 1998).

When nursing home placement is the best choice, steps can be taken to improve the quality of services. For exam-

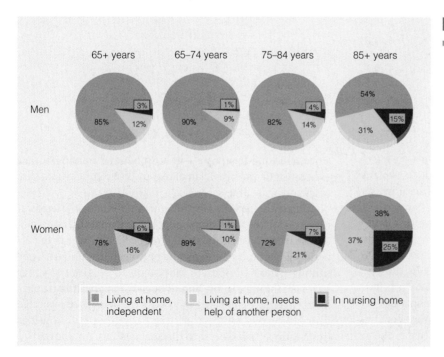

FIGURE 17.4

■ **Percentage of American elderly men and women by age who live at home independently; live at home but need the help of another person for tasks of daily living; and reside in a nursing home.** Although the majority of older adults of all ages live at home, need for long-term assistance and nursing home care rises sharply with age. (From U.S. Department of Health and Human Services, 1999f.)

■ *Health, a sense of personal control, and gratifying social relationships strongly predict life satisfaction for elderly people, even when they live in nursing homes. (Photo courtesy: Sondra Dawes/ The Image Works)*

ple, the Netherlands has established separate facilities for patients with mental and physical disabilities because each has distinctly different needs. And every elderly person, no matter how disabled, benefits from opportunities to maintain existing strengths and acquire new skills, which (as we will see in the next section) can compensate for declines. Among institutionalized elderly, health, sense of personal control, gratifying social relationships, and meaningful and enjoyable daily activities strongly predict life satisfaction (Logsdon, 2000). These aspects of living are vital for all older people, whether they are institutionalized or not.

ASK YOURSELF . . .

🌳 *Marissa complained to a counselor that at age 68, her husband, Wendell, stopped initiating sex and no longer touched, stroked, or cuddled her. Why might Wendell have ceased to interact sexually? What interventions—both medical and educational—could be helpful to Marissa and Wendell?*

■ *Explain how depression can combine with physical illness and disability to promote cognitive deterioration in the elderly. Should cognitive declines due to physical limitations and depression be called dementia? Why or why not?*

COGNITIVE DEVELOPMENT

When Ruth complained to her doctor about memory and verbal expression difficulties, she voiced common concerns about cognitive functioning in late life. Decline in speed of processing, under way throughout the adult years, is believed to affect many aspects of cognition in old age. In Chapter 15, we noted that reduced efficiency of thinking compromises attention, amount of information that can be held in working memory, use of memory strategies, and retrieval from long-term memory. These decrements continue in the final decades of life.

Recall that the more a mental ability depends on fluid intelligence (biologically based information-processing skills), the earlier it starts to decline. In contrast, mental abilities that rely on crystallized intelligence (culturally based knowledge) increase for a longer time. (Return to Figure 15.4 on page 507 to review these trends.) Gains in crystallized intelligence depend on continued opportunities to enhance cognitive skills. When these are available, crystallized abilities—general information and expertise in specific endeavors—can offset losses in fluid intelligence. Take a moment to list the various ways that adults compensate for intellectual declines, discussed in Chapter 15.

Look again at Figure 15.4 on page 507. In advanced old age, decrements in fluid intelligence eventually limit what people can accomplish with the help of cultural supports, including a rich background of experience, knowledge of how to remember and solve problems, and a stimulating daily life. Consequently, crystallized intelligence begins to decline as well (Baltes, 1997; Schaie, 1996b).

Overall, loss outweighs improvement and maintenance as people move closer to the end of life. But plasticity of development is still possible (Baltes & Carstensen, 1996). Research reveals large individual differences in cognitive functioning among the elderly—greater than at any other time of life (Hultsch & Dixon, 1990; Morse, 1993). Besides fuller expression of genetic and lifestyle influences, increased freedom to pursue self-chosen courses of action—some that enhance and others that undermine cognitive skills—may be responsible.

How can older adults make the most of their cognitive resources? According to one view, elders who sustain high levels of functioning engage in **selective optimization with compensation** (Baltes, 1997). That is, they narrow their goals, *selecting* personally valued activities as a way of *optimizing* (or maximizing) returns from their diminishing energy. They also come up with new ways of *compensating* for losses. One day, Ruth and Walt listened to a replay of an interview with 80-year-old concert pianist Arthur Rubinstein, who was asked how he managed to sustain such extraordinary piano playing, despite his advanced age. Rubinstein used each of the strategies just mentioned. He stated that he

■ *Concert pianist Arthur Rubinstein, performing before a sold-out audience in New York City at age 89, sustained his extraordinary piano playing through* selective optimization with compensation. *He was selective, playing fewer pieces so he could optimize his energy. He compensated for a decline in playing speed by playing extra slowly before a fast passage, so the fast section appeared to his audience to move more quickly. (Photo courtesy: Glenn A. Baker Archives/Redferns)*

was *selective;* he played fewer pieces. This enabled him to *optimize* his energy; he could practice each piece more. Finally, he developed new, *compensatory* techniques for a decline in playing speed. For example, before a fast passage, he played extra slowly, so the fast section appeared to his audience to move more quickly.

As we review major changes in memory, language processing, and problem solving, we will consider ways that older adults can optimize and compensate in the face of declines. We will also see that certain abilities that depend on extensive life experience, not processing efficiency, are sustained or increase in old age. Last, we take up programs that recognize the elderly as lifelong learners—empowered by new knowledge, just as they were at earlier periods of development.

MEMORY

As older adults take in information more slowly and find it harder to apply strategies and retrieve relevant knowledge from long-term memory, the chances of memory failure increase (Salthouse, 1991b). A reduced capacity to hold material in working memory while operating on it means that memory problems are especially evident on complex tasks.

DELIBERATE VERSUS AUTOMATIC MEMORY

"Ruth, you know that movie we saw—with the little 5-year-old boy who did such a wonderful acting job. I'd like to suggest it to Dick and Goldie. Do you recall the name of it?" asked Walt.

"I can't think of it, Walt. We've seen several movies lately, and that one just doesn't ring a bell. Which theater was it at, and who'd we go with? Tell me more about the little boy, and maybe I'll think of it."

Although all of us have had memory failures like this from time to time, difficulties with recall rise in old age. Decline in processing speed is a powerful predictor of them (Luszcz, Bryan, & Kent, 1997). When Ruth and Walt watched the movie, their slower cognitive processing meant that they retained fewer details. And because their working memories could hold less at once, they attended poorly to context—who they went with and where they saw the movie (Craik & Jacoby, 1996; Spencer & Raz, 1995). When we try to remember, contextual cues serve as important retrieval cues. Because older adults take in less about a stimulus and its context, they sometimes cannot distinguish an experienced event from one they imagined (Hashtroudi, Johnson, & Chrosniak, 1990). And they have difficulty inhibiting irrelevant information, both when processing an event and when trying to recall it (see Chapter 15).

A few days later, Ruth saw a clip from the movie on TV, and she recognized it immediately. Compared with recall, recognition memory suffers far less in late adulthood because a multitude of environmental supports for remembering are present (Craik & Jennings, 1992). Greater decrement in recall than in recognition suggests that providing more cues for remembering would enhance older adults' performance.

Age-related memory declines are largely limited to tasks that require deliberate processing. Because recognition is a fairly automatic type of memory that demands little mental effort, it does not change much in old age. Consider another automatic form of memory called **implicit memory,** or memory without conscious awareness. In a typical implicit memory task, you would be asked to fill in a word fragment (such as t _ _ k) after being shown a list of words. You would probably complete the sequence with a word you had just seen (*task*) rather than other words (*took* or *teak*). Notice that you engaged in recall without trying to do so.

Age differences in implicit memory are much smaller than in explicit, or deliberate, memory. When memory depends on familiarity rather than conscious use of strategies, it is spared from impairment in old age (Schugens et al., 1997; Titov & Knight, 1997). The memory problems elders report—for names; places they put important objects; directions for getting from one place to another; and (as we will see later) appointments and medication schedules—

all place substantial demands on their more limited working memories.

REMOTE MEMORY

Although older people often say that their **remote memory**, or very long-term recall, is clearer than their memory for recent events, research does not support this conclusion. In several studies, adults ranging in age from their twenties to their seventies were asked to recall names of grade school teachers and high school classmates and Spanish vocabulary from high school—information very well learned early in life. Memory declined rapidly for the first 3 to 6 years, then changed little for the next 20 years. After that, additional modest forgetting occurred (Bahrick, 1984; Bahrick, Bahrick, & Wittlinger, 1975).

How about *autobiographical memory*, or memory for personally meaningful events, such as what you did on your first date or how you celebrated your college graduation? To test for this type of memory, researchers typically give a series of words (such as *book, machine, sorry, surprised*) and ask adults to report a personal memory associated with each. People between 50 and 90 recall both remote and recent events more frequently than intermediate events, with recent events mentioned most often. Among remote events recalled, most happened between ages 10 and 30 (see Figure 17.5) (Jansari & Parkin, 1996; Rubin & Schulkind, 1997a, 1997b).

Why do older adults recall their adolescent and early adulthood experiences more readily than their mid-adulthood lives? Perhaps youthful events are remembered best because they occurred during a period of rapid life change. In times of rapid change, people are likely to have many more novel experiences—ones that stand out from the humdrum of daily life. Adolescence and early adulthood are also times of identity development, when many personally significant experiences occur. Recall from Chapter 5 that such events are likely to become part of the individual's life story and to be long-lasting. Even public events linked to this period—World Series winners, Academy Award winners, and current events—are especially salient to elders (Rubin, Rahhal, & Poon, 1998).

Nevertheless, older adults recall recent personal experiences more readily than remote ones. The likely reason is interference produced by years of additional experience (Kausler, 1994). As we accumulate more memories, some inevitably resemble others. As a result, certain early memories become less clear than they once were.

PROSPECTIVE MEMORY

Elderly people often complain that they have become more absentminded about daily events. Because Ruth and Walt knew they were more likely to forget an appointment, they often asked about it repeatedly. "Sybil, what time is

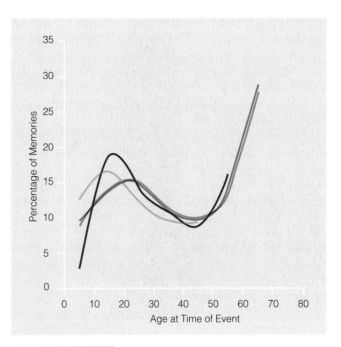

■ **Distribution of older adults' autobiographical memories by reported age at time of the event.** In the four studies of 50- to 90-year-olds represented here, later events were remembered better than early events. Among early events, most of those recalled occurred between ages 10 and 30. (Adapted from D. C. Rubin, T. A. Rahhal, & L. W. Poon, 1998, "Things learned in early adulthood are remembered best," *Memory & Cognition, 26*, p. 4. Copyright © 1998 by the Psychonomic Society, Inc. Reprinted by permission.)

our dinner engagement?" Walt said several times during the 2 days before the event. His questioning was not a sign of dementia. He simply wanted to be sure to remember an important date.

So far, we have considered various aspects of *retrospective memory* (or remembrance of things past). **Prospective memory** refers to remembering to engage in planned actions in the future. The amount of mental effort required determines whether older adults have trouble with prospective memory. Remembering the dinner date was challenging for Walt because he typically ate dinner with his daughter on Thursday evenings at 6 P.M., but this time, dinner was set for Tuesday at 7:15 P.M.

In the laboratory, older adults do better on *event-based* than on *time-based* prospective memory tasks. In an event-based task, an event (such as a certain word appearing on a computer screen) serves as a cue for remembering to do something (pressing a key) while the adult engages in another activity (memorizing word lists). Age decrements occur only when the event-based task is made complex (press a key when any one of four words appears) or the difficulty of the ongoing activity is increased (longer word lists to learn) (Einstein et al., 1997; Einstein et al., 1992). In time-based tasks, the adult must perform an action after a certain time interval has elapsed, without any obvious external cue (for example, press a key every 10 minutes). Time-based prospective memory takes more initiative, and declines in late adulthood are larger (Einstein et al., 1995; Park et al., 1997).

But prospective memory difficulties evident in the laboratory do not always appear in real life, since older adults are very good at setting up reminders for themselves, such as a buzzer ringing in the kitchen or a note tacked up in a prominent location. When trying to remember a future activity, younger adults rely more on strategies like rehearsal, older adults on external aids to memory (Loewen, Shaw, & Craik, 1990). In this way, the elderly compensate for their reduced-capacity working memories and the challenge of dividing attention between what they are doing now and what they must do in the future.

LANGUAGE PROCESSING

Language and memory skills are closely related. In language comprehension (understanding the meaning of spoken or written prose), we recollect what we have heard or read without conscious awareness. Like implicit memory, oral language comprehension changes very little in late life as long as conversational partners do not speak very quickly and elders are given enough time to process written text accurately (Brébion, Smith, & Ehrlich, 1997; Hultsch et al., 1998; Stine-Morrow & Miller, 1999). In one longitudinal study, 55- to 70-year-olds showed a slight increase over a 6-year period in their recall of written stories! And into their eighties and nineties, elders made good use of story organization to help them recall both main ideas and details (Small et al., 1999).

In contrast to language comprehension, two aspects of language production show age-related losses. The first is retrieving words from long-term memory. When conversing with others, Ruth and Walt sometimes had difficulty coming up with just the right word to convey their thoughts. Consequently, their speech contained a greater number of pronouns and other unclear references than it did at younger ages. They also spoke more slowly and paused more often, partly because they needed time to search their memories for certain words (MacKay & Abrams, 1996).

Second, planning what to say and how to say it is harder in late adulthood. As a result, Walt and Ruth displayed more hesitations, false starts, word repetitions, and sentence fragments as they aged. Their statements were also less well organized than before (Kemper, Kynette, & Norman, 1992).

What explains these changes? Once again, age-related limits on working memory seem to be responsible. Because less information can be held at once, the elderly have difficulty coordinating the multiple tasks required to produce speech. As a result, they sometimes have trouble remembering the nonverbal information they want to communicate, putting it into words, and conveying it in a coherent fashion.

As with memory, older adults develop compensatory techniques for their language production problems. For example, they simplify their grammatical structures so they can devote more effort to retrieving words and organizing their thoughts. In this way, they convey their message in more sentences, sacrificing efficiency for greater clarity (Kemper, Kynette, & Norman, 1992).

The elderly also compensate by representing information they want to communicate in terms of gist rather than details (Jepson & Labouvie-Vief, 1992). For example, when Walt told his granddaughter Marci fairy tales, he left out many concrete facts. Instead, he included personal inferences and a moral lesson—elements that appear less often in the storytelling of younger adults. Here is Walt's rendition of *Sleeping Beauty*: "An evil fairy condemns Sleeping Beauty to death. But a kind fairy changes the curse from death to sleep. Then a handsome prince awakens the girl with a kiss. So you see, Marci, both good and bad exist in the world. The bad things instill in us the need to think of and care for others."

Older adults often make the best of their limited working memories by extracting the essence of a message. Then they enrich it with symbolic interpretations, drawing on their extensive life experience.

■ *As storyteller Willard Lape, Jr., plays the part of Salty Sam for attentive elementary school students at the Erie Canal Museum in Syracuse, he is likely to enrich his tales with inferences and moral lessons grounded in extensive life experience. (Photo courtesy: The Image Works)*

PROBLEM SOLVING

Problem solving is yet another cognitive skill that illustrates how aging brings not only deterioration, but important adaptive changes. In late adulthood, traditional problem solving, which lacks a real-life context (as in playing Twenty Questions), shows declines. Older adults' memory limitations make it hard to keep all relevant facts in mind when dealing with a complex hypothetical problem (Sinnott, 1989).

Yet the problematic situations the elderly encounter in everyday life and care about differ from hypothetical problems devised by researchers. Elders' everyday problems also differ from those experienced at earlier ages. Being retired, most do not have to deal with problems in the workplace. Even the social problems they confront at home may be reduced. Their children are typically grown and living on their own, and their marriages have endured long enough to have fewer difficulties (Heidrich & Denney, 1994). Instead, major concerns involve managing activities of daily living, such as preparing nutritious meals, handling finances, and attending to health concerns. Surveys in Germany and the United States reveal that older adults spend a third to half of a typical day on these issues (Willis, 1996).

Everyday problems reported by older adults are evenly split between personal competence and social concerns. In contrast, those of middle-aged adults, whose daily lives involve relating to co-workers, dependent children, and aging parents, focus more on the social arena (Berg et al., 1998). How do the elderly solve problems of daily living? Their strategies extend the adaptive problem solving of midlife. As long as they perceive problems as under their control, elders are active and effective in solving them—an approach that characterizes their consumer and home management decisions. Perhaps because older adults often conclude that they cannot change other people, they are likely to avoid interpersonal conflicts (Blanchard-Fields, Chen, & Norris, 1997). But as we will see in Chapter 18, this strategy often makes sense for elders, who are highly motivated to conserve energy and limit stress.

The health arena, especially salient for elders, illustrates the adaptiveness of everyday problem solving in late adulthood (Sansone & Berg, 1993). Older adults make quicker decisions about whether they are ill and seek medical care sooner. In contrast, young and middle-aged adults are more likely to adopt a "wait and see" approach in favor of gathering more facts, even when the health problem is serious (Leventhal et al., 1993; Meyer, Russo, & Talbot, 1995). This swift response of the elderly is interesting in view of their slower cognitive processing. Perhaps years of experience in coping with illnesses enable them to draw on extensive personal knowledge and move ahead with greater certainty. Acting decisively when faced with health risks is sensible in old age.

WISDOM

We have seen that a wealth of life experience enhances the verbal messages and problem solving of the elderly. It also underlies another capacity believed to reach its height in old age: **wisdom.** When researchers ask people to describe wisdom, most mention breadth and depth of practical knowledge, ability to reflect on that knowledge in ways that make life more bearable and worthwhile, emotional maturity, and the integrative form of creativity we discussed in Chapter 15 (see page 512). The multiple cognitive and personality traits that make up wisdom can be summed up as expertise in the fundamental pragmatics of life (Baltes, Smith, & Staudinger, 1992; Staudinger et al., 1998).

During her college years, Ruth and Walt's granddaughter Marci telephoned with a pressing personal dilemma. Ruth's advice reflected the features of wisdom just mentioned. Unsure whether her love for her boyfriend Ken would endure, Marci began to date another student after Ken moved to another city to attend medical school. "I can't stand being pulled in two directions. I'm thinking of calling Ken and telling him about Steve," she exclaimed. "Do you think I should?"

"This is not a good time, Marci," Ruth advised. "You'll break Ken's heart before you've had a chance to size up your feelings for Steve. And you said Ken's taking some important exams in two weeks. If you tell him now and he's distraught, it could affect the rest of his life."

Cultures around the world assume that age and wisdom go together. In village and tribal societies, the most important social positions, such as chieftain and shaman (religious leader), are reserved for the old. Similarly, in industrialized nations, people over age 65 are chief executive officers of large corporations, high-level religious leaders, members of legislatures, and supreme court justices. What explains this widespread trend? According to an ethological view, the genetic program of our species grants health, fitness, and strength to the young. Culture tames this youthful advantage in physical power with the insights of the old, ensuring balance and interdependence between generations (Assmann, 1994; Csikszentmihalyi & Rathunde, 1990).

Only a few efforts have been made to investigate the development of wisdom. In one series of studies, participants' responses to uncertain real-life situations revealed that age was no guarantee of wisdom. The wisest choices were made by a very small number of adults—some young, some middle-aged, and some old. But type of life experience made a difference. People who had spent their careers in human services, where they received extensive training and practice in grappling with human problems, were well represented among the wise (Smith, Staudinger, & Baltes, 1994; Staudinger, Smith, & Baltes, 1992). Yet wisdom was not limited to people with formal training. Active elderly citizens who were highly regarded in their community and who came from many walks of life also excelled at wisdom tasks (Baltes et al., 1995).

In addition to general familiarity with human problems, having faced and overcome personal hardship appears to be an important contributor to late-life wisdom. In a longitudinal study of people who were young adults during the Great Depression of the 1930s, those who experienced economic hardship and surmounted it scored especially high in wisdom nearly 40 years later, as indicated by thoughtful interview responses to life events, insights into their own motives and behavior, and warmth and compassion (Ardelt, 1998). Stress-related growth may be one of several paths to the development of wisdom.

FACTORS RELATED TO COGNITIVE CHANGE

As we saw in Chapter 15, a mentally active life—above-average education, stimulating leisure pursuits, community participation, and a flexible personality—predicts maintenance of mental abilities into advanced old age. To illustrate, recall our discussion of age-related declines in prospective memory. In one study, well-educated elders high in verbal ability and involved in their communities performed as well as young adults on an event-based prospective memory task. In contrast, elders who had little more than a high school diploma and were low in verbal ability did very poorly (Cherry & LeCompte, 1999).

As noted earlier in this chapter, health status becomes an increasingly strong predictor of intellectual performance in late adulthood. A wide variety of chronic conditions, including vision and hearing impairments, cardiovascular disease, osteoporosis, and arthritis are associated with cognitive declines (Baltes & Lindenberger, 1997; Schaie 1996a). But we must be cautious in interpreting this link between physical and cognitive deterioration. The relationship may be exaggerated by the fact that brighter adults are more likely to engage in health-protective behaviors, which postpone the onset of serious disease.

Retirement also affects cognitive change, both positively and negatively. When people leave routine jobs for stimulating leisure activities, outcomes are favorable. In contrast, retiring from a highly complex job without developing challenging substitutes accelerates intellectual declines (Schaie, 1996).

After age 75, cognitive decrements are related to distance to death rather than chronological age (Small & Bäckman, 1999). In the year before Walt died, those close to him noticed that he had become less active and more withdrawn. In the company of friends, he talked and moved less. At home, he spent more time looking out the window instead of immersing himself in creative writing and gardening.

Terminal decline refers to a steady, marked decrease in cognitive functioning prior to death. Researchers are not certain if it is limited to a few aspects of intelligence or if it affects all aspects, signifying general deterioration. Furthermore, studies vary greatly in estimated length of terminal decline. Some report that it lasts only 1 to 3 years; others, that it extends for as much as 14 years. The average is about 5 years (Bosworth & Schaie, 1999; Maier & Smith, 1999; Small & Bäckman, 1997).

Perhaps the reason for these conflicting findings is that there are different kinds of terminal decline. One type might arise from disease processes. Another might be part of a general biological breakdown due to normal aging (Berg, 1996). At present, all we know for sure is that an extended, steep falloff in cognitive functioning is a sign of loss of vitality and impending death.

COGNITIVE INTERVENTIONS

For most of late adulthood, cognitive declines are gradual. Although aging of the brain contributes to them, recall from our earlier discussion that the brain can compensate by growing new neural fibers. Furthermore, some cognitive decrements may be due to disuse of particular skills rather than biological aging (Dixon & Hultsch, 1999). If plasticity of development is possible in old age, then interventions that train the elderly in cognitive strategies should at least partially reverse the age-related declines we have discussed.

The Adult Development and Enrichment Project (ADEPT) is the most extensive cognitive intervention program conducted to date. By using participants in the Seattle Longitudinal Study (see Chapter 13, page 443, and Chapter 15, page 507), researchers could do what no other investigation had yet done: assess the effects of cognitive training on long-term development (Schaie, 1996).

Intervention began with adults over age 64, some of whom had maintained their scores on two mental abilities (inductive reasoning and spatial orientation) over the previous 14 years and others of whom had shown declines. After just five 1-hour training sessions in relevant cognitive skills, two-thirds of the participants improved their performance. The gains for decliners were dramatic. Forty percent returned to the level at which they had been functioning 14 years earlier! A follow-up after 7 years revealed that although the scores of trained adults dropped somewhat, they were still doing better than untrained controls. Finally, "booster" training at this time led to further gains, although these were not as large as the earlier gains.

In other short-term studies, training resulted in improvements in memory and problem solving among the elderly (Kotler-Cope & Camp, 1990; Willis & Schaie, 1994). Clearly, a wide range of cognitive skills can be enhanced in old age. A vital goal is to transfer intervention from the laboratory to the community, weaving it into the daily experiences of elderly people. As we will see in the next section, a promising approach is to provide older adults with well-designed, highly interesting learning experiences in which cognitive training is an integral part.

LIFELONG LEARNING

Think about the competencies that older adults need to live in our complex, changing world. They are the same as those of younger people—communicating effectively through spoken and written systems; locating information, sorting through it, and selecting what is needed; using modern mathematical techniques, such as estimation; planning and organizing activities, including making good use of time and resources; mastering new technologies; and understanding past and current events and the relevance of each to their own lives. The elderly also need to develop new, problem-centered coping strategies—ways to sustain health and operate their households efficiently and safely—and self-employment skills for those who must continue their work lives.

Due to better health and earlier retirement, participation of the elderly in continuing education has increased substantially over the past few decades. Successful programs include a wide variety of offerings responsive to the diversity of senior citizens and teaching methods suited to their developmental needs (Knox, 1993).

TYPES OF PROGRAMS

One summer, Walt and Ruth attended an Elderhostel at a nearby university. After moving into a dormitory room, they joined 30 other senior citizens for 2 weeks of morning lectures on Shakespeare, afternoon visits to points of interest; and evening performances of plays at a nearby Shakespeare festival.

Elderhostel programs attract over a quarter million older Americans annually. Local educational institutions serve as hosts, combining stimulating 1- to 3-week courses taught by experts with recreational pursuits. Some programs make use of community resources through classes on local ecology or folk life. Others involve travel abroad. Still others focus on innovative topics and experiences—writing one's own life story, discussing contemporary films with screenwriters, whitewater rafting, and Chinese painting and calligraphy.

Similar educational programs have sprung up around the world. Originating in France, the University of the Third Age[3] offers community-sponsored courses for elders that

[3] The term *third age* refers to the period after the second age of midlife, when older people are freed of work and parenting responsibilities and have more time to invest in lifelong learning.

■ *Elderly participants in continuing education, like these women learning to explore the Internet at a local college, often come to see themselves differently. They abandon deeply ingrained stereotypes of aging as they realize that adults in their seventies and eighties can still engage in complex learning. (Photo courtesy: Wyman/ Monkmeyer Press)*

vary widely in content and style of presentation. These include open lectures, access to established university courses, workshops on special topics, excursions, and physical health programs. The model has spread to many countries. In Australia and Great Britain, elders often do the teaching, based on the idea that experts of all kinds retire (Swindell & Thompson, 1995). Some programs foster intergenerational relations and community involvement. In Austria, for example, training in modern math, foreign languages, and other subjects is offered to grandparents to enable them to help grandchildren, in whose education they are encouraged to participate.

Other routes to education among the elderly include returning to college. In the United States, nearly 80,000 adults age 65 and older take courses in institutions of higher education each fall (U.S. Department of Education, 1999a). Additional learning opportunities are available through libraries, museums, religious institutions, community agencies, and private businesses.

Participants in programs mentioned so far tend to be active, well educated, and financially well off who enroll primarily for intellectual stimulation and social interaction (Abraham, 1998). Much less is available for elders with little education and limited income. Community senior centers with inexpensive offerings related to everyday living attract more low-income people than do programs such as Elderhostel (Knox, 1993). Regardless of course content and which seniors attend, using the techniques summarized in the Caregiving Concerns table on page 586 increases the effectiveness of instruction for older adults.

Increasing the Effectiveness of Instruction for Older Adults

TECHNIQUE	DESCRIPTION
Providing a positive learning environment	Some elders have internalized negative stereotypes of their abilities and come to the learning environment with low self-esteem. A supportive group atmosphere, in which the instructor is viewed as a colleague, helps convince older adults that they can learn.
Allowing ample time to learn new information	Rate of learning varies widely among older adults, with some mastering new material at a fairly slow rate. Presenting information over several sessions or allowing for self-paced instruction aids mastery.
Presenting information in a well-organized fashion	Older adults do not organize information as effectively as younger adults. Material that is outlined, presented, and then summarized enhances memory and understanding. Introduction of irrelevant information and digressions make a presentation harder to comprehend.
Giving information related to elders' experiences	Relating new material to what has already been learned by drawing on elders' experiences and giving many vivid examples enhances recall.

Source: Thompson, 1992.

BENEFITS OF CONTINUING EDUCATION

Elderly participants in continuing education report a rich array of benefits. These include learning new facts, understanding new ideas in many disciplines, making new friends, and developing a broader perspective on the world (Long & Zoller-Hodges, 1995). Furthermore, seniors come to see themselves differently. Many arrive with deeply ingrained stereotypes of aging, which they abandon when they realize that adults in their seventies and eighties, including themselves, can still engage in complex learning. In Elderhostel courses, participants with the least education report learning the most, an argument for recruiting less economically privileged people into these programs (Brady, 1984).

The educational needs of senior citizens are likely to be given greater attention in coming decades, as their numbers grow and they assert their right to lifelong learning. Once this happens, false stereotypes, such as "the elderly are too old to learn" and "education is for the young," are likely to weaken and, perhaps, disappear.

ASK YOURSELF . . .

- *When Ruth couldn't recall which movie Walt was thinking about, she asked several questions: "Which theater was it at, and who'd we go with? Tell me more about the little boy [in the movie]." Which memory deficits of aging is Ruth trying to overcome?*

- *Ruth complained to her doctor that she had trouble finding the right words to explain to a delivery service how to get to her house. What cognitive changes account for Ruth's difficulty?*

- *Describe cognitive functions that are maintained and that improve in late adulthood. What aspects of aging contribute to them?*

SUMMARY

PHYSICAL DEVELOPMENT

LONGEVITY

Discuss aging and longevity among older adults.

- Vastly different rates of aging are apparent in late adulthood. In terms of **functional age,** older adults of any chronological age may be **young-old** or **old-old,** depending on their physical condition.

- In industrialized nations, the number of people aged 65 and older rose dramatically over the twentieth century, a trend expected to continue. With advancing age, women outnumber men by a greater margin, but sex differences in average life expectancy decline. Differences between higher-SES whites and low-SES ethnic minorities also diminish until around age 85, when a **life expectancy crossover** occurs.

- Longevity runs in families, but environmental factors become increasingly important with age.

PHYSICAL CHANGES

Describe changes in the nervous system and the senses in late adulthood.

■ Loss of neurons occurs throughout the cerebral cortex, with the visual, auditory, and motor areas most affected. However, the brain compensates by forming new synapses. The autonomic nervous system functions less well and releases more stress hormones.

■ Older adults tend to suffer impaired eyesight, including **cataracts** and **macular degeneration.** Visual deficits affect elders' self-confidence and everyday behavior and can be very isolating.

■ Hearing difficulties are more common than visual difficulties, especially in men. Impaired speech perception has the greatest impact on life satisfaction.

■ Taste and odor sensitivity decline, making food less appealing. Touch sensitivity also deteriorates, particularly on the fingertips.

Describe cardiovascular, respiratory, and immune system changes in late adulthood.

■ Reduced capacity of the cardio-vascular and respiratory systems becomes more apparent in late adulthood. As at earlier ages, not smoking, reducing dietary fat, avoiding environmental pollutants, and exercising can slow the effects of aging on these systems.

■ The immune system functions less effectively in late life, permitting diseases to progress and making **autoimmune responses** more likely.

Discuss sleep difficulties in late adulthood.

■ Older adults find it harder to fall asleep, stay asleep, and sleep deeply. Until age 70 or 80, men have more trouble sleeping than women, due to enlargement of the prostate leading to a need to urinate often, **sleep apnea,** and "restless legs."

Describe changes in physical appearance and mobility in late adulthood.

■ Outward signs of aging, such as white hair, wrinkled and sagging skin, age spots, and decreased height and weight, become more noticeable. Mobility diminishes due to declining muscle and bone strength and joint flexibility.

■ Widespread negative stereotypes of aging in Western society make coping with physical aging more difficult. Older people fare best when they have status and opportunities for social participation, even when they are frail.

HEALTH, FITNESS, AND DISABILITY

Discuss health and fitness in late life, paying special attention to nutrition, exercise, and sexuality.

■ Most elders are optimistic about their health and with respect to protecting it, have a high sense of self-efficacy. Low-income ethnic minority elders remain at greater risk for certain health problems and are less likely to believe they can control their health.

■ As in early adulthood, in late life men are more prone to fatal diseases and women to disabling conditions. By very old age, women are more impaired than surviving men.

■ Poverty and negative lifestyle factors make the public health goal of **compression of morbidity** hard to attain.

■ Because risk of dietary deficiencies increases, vitamin-mineral supplements are beneficial in late life. Exercise continues to be a powerful health intervention, even when begun in late adulthood.

■ Compared with other parts of the body, the reproductive organs undergo minimal change in late adulthood. Sexual desire and sexual activity decline but need not disappear.

Discuss common physical disabilities in late adulthood.

■ Illness and disability increase toward the end of life. Cardiovascular disease, cancer, stroke, and emphysema claim many lives. Because of declines in immune system functioning, vaccination against the most common type of pneumonia is advisable.

■ **Secondary aging,** rather than **primary aging,** is responsible for many disabilities in late adulthood. **Osteoarthritis** and **rheumatoid arthritis** strike at least half of older adults, especially women. Adult-onset diabetes increases.

■ Motor vehicle collisions per mile driven, pedestrian accidents, and falls increase in late adulthood. Changes in elders' lifestyles and environments can help prevent these causes of unintentional injury.

Discuss common mental disabilities in late adulthood.

■ **Alzheimer's disease** is the most common form of **dementia.** Often starting with severe memory problems, it brings personality changes, depression, loss of ability to comprehend and produce speech, disintegration of purposeful movements, and death. Underlying these changes are abundant **neurofibrillary tangles** and **amyloid plaques** and lowered neurotransmitter levels in the brain.

■ Familial Alzheimer's generally has an early onset, progresses rapidly, and is linked to a dominant gene on chromosomes 1, 14, or 21. Sporadic Alzheimer's may also be hereditary; people with this form often have an abnormal ApoE gene on chromosome 19. However, half of sporadic Alzheimer's victims show no currently known genetic marker.

■ Heredity contributes to **cerebrovascular dementia** indirectly, through high blood pressure, cardiovascular disease, and diabetes.

Many environmental influences also heighten stroke risk. Because of their greater susceptibility to cardiovascular disease, men are affected more than women.

- Treatable problems, such as depression, side effects of medication, and reactions to social isolation, can be mistaken for dementia. Therefore, careful diagnosis is essential.

Discuss health care issues that affect senior citizens.

- Recent **squaring of the population pyramid** has prompted concern about **intergenerational inequity**—elders receiving more than their fair share of public resources. More people fear that younger generations will not be able to support the rising cost of Social Security, Medicare, and Medicaid.

- Only 5 percent of American seniors are institutionalized, a rate about half that of other industrialized nations. Family members provide most long-term care, especially among ethnic minorities with closely knit extended families. Older adults cared for at home are generally less impaired than those in nursing homes.

COGNITIVE DEVELOPMENT

Describe overall changes in cognitive functioning in late adulthood.

- Individual differences in cognitive functioning are greater in late adulthood than at any other time of life. Although both fluid intelligence and crystallized intelligence decline in advanced old age, plasticity of development is still possible. Older adults can make the most of their cognitive resources through **selective optimization with compensation.**

MEMORY

How does memory change in late life?

- Age-related limitations on working memory make memory difficulties more apparent on tasks that are complex and require deliberate processing. Automatic forms of memory, such as recognition and **implicit memory,** are largely spared.

- Contrary to what older people sometimes report, **remote memory** is not clearer than recent memory. Autobiographical memory is best for recent experiences, followed by personally meaningful events that happened between ages 10 and 30, a period of rapid life change and identity development. Older adults do better on event-based than on time-based **prospective memory** tasks. They compensate for declines in prospective memory by using external memory aids.

LANGUAGE PROCESSING

Describe changes in language processing in late adulthood.

- Although language comprehension changes little in late life, two aspects of language production—finding the right words and planning what to say and how to say it—show age-related losses. Older adults compensate by simplifying their grammatical structures and communicating gist rather than details.

PROBLEM SOLVING

How does problem solving change in late life?

- Traditional problem solving declines in late adulthood. In everyday problem solving, older adults extend the adaptive strategies developed in midlife. Elders often respond more decisively than younger people in matters of health, perhaps because of greater experience in coping with illness.

WISDOM

Do age and wisdom go together, as cultures around the world assume?

- Although older adults occupy important positions in societies around the world, age does not guarantee **wisdom.** Adults of all ages with extensive experience in dealing with human problems, including elders highly regarded in their community, are most likely to be represented among the wise. Having faced and overcome hardship seems to foster wisdom in late adulthood.

FACTORS RELATED TO COGNITIVE CHANGE

List factors related to cognitive change in late adulthood.

- Mentally active people are likely to maintain their cognitive abilities into advanced old age. A wide array of chronic conditions are associated with cognitive decline. Retirement can bring about either positive or negative changes. As death approaches, **terminal decline** becomes evident.

COGNITIVE INTERVENTIONS

Can cognitive interventions help older adults sustain their mental abilities?

- The Adult Development and Enrichment Project (ADEPT) and various short-term studies show that training can enhance cognitive skills in older adults, including those who have suffered declines.

LIFELONG LEARNING

Discuss types of programs and benefits of continuing education in late life.

- Better health and earlier retirement permit increasing numbers of older people to continue their education through college courses, community offerings, and programs such as Elderhostel. Those who participate are enriched by new knowledge, new friends, a broader perspective on the world, and an image of themselves as more competent. Unfortunately, fewer continuing education opportunities are available to low-income, less educated seniors.

IMPORTANT TERMS AND CONCEPTS

Alzheimer's disease (p. 573)

amyloid plaques (p. 573)

autoimmune response (p. 563)

cataracts (p. 559)

cerebrovascular dementia (p. 575)

compression of morbidity (p. 568)

dementia (p. 572)

functional age (p. 556)

implicit memory (p. 580)

intergenerational inequity (p. 576)

life expectancy crossover (p. 557)

macular degeneration (p. 559)

neurofibrillary tangles (p. 573)

old-old (p. 556)

osteoarthritis (p. 570)

primary aging (p. 570)

prospective memory (p. 581)

remote memory (p. 581)

rheumatoid arthritis (p. 570)

secondary aging (p. 570)

selective optimization with compensation (p. 579)

sleep apnea (p. 564)

squaring of the population pyramid (p. 576)

terminal decline (p. 584)

wisdom (p. 583)

young-old (p. 556)

FYI FOR FURTHER INFORMATION AND HELP

Consult the companion website for this book, where you will find additional weblinks and associated learning activities: www.abacon.com/berk

HEALTH AND FITNESS

National Health Information Center
www.health-dev.health.org.8002/index.htm

Publishes materials on a variety of health topics, has about 100 hot lines on various subjects, and offers a database of over 1,100 health information resources. Operated by the U.S. Public Health Service.

National Institute on Aging
www.nih.gov/nia

Conducts research aimed at understanding the nature of aging and extending the healthy, active years of life. Disseminates information on a wide variety of health topics.

National Resource Center on Aging and Injury
www.olderadultinjury.org/index.cfm

Organization dedicated to preventing injuries among older adults.

Senior Health and Fitness
navigator.tufts.edu/focuson/

Created by Tufts University's School of Nutrition Science and Policy, provides information on nutrition and fitness for seniors.

United Seniors Health Cooperative
www.ushc-online.org

Assists the elderly with independent living and other health issues.

ARTHRITIS

Arthritis Foundation
www.arthritis.org

Publishes materials on arthritis and how to live with it. Provides prescription discount services for members. Local chapters offer water-based exercise classes.

National Institute of Arthritis, Musculoskeletal, and Skin Disease Information Clearinghouse
www.nih.gov/niams

Publishes materials on arthritis and provides information about federally funded research and treatment centers.

DIABETES

American Diabetes Association National Service Center
www.diabetes.org

Offers information on all aspects of diabetes, from research to self-care, including a wide variety of publications.

ALZHEIMER'S DISEASE

Alzheimer's Association
www.alz.org

Organization of family members of Alzheimer's disease victims. Promotes research, provides educational programs for the public, and works to develop family support systems for relatives of Alzheimer's sufferers. Has state and local chapters that sponsor support groups and provide lists of community resources.

LIFELONG LEARNING

Elderhostel
www.elderhostel.org

Sponsors short-term, intensive campus-based experiences for older adults in the United States and many other countries.

18

Emotional and Social Development in Late Adulthood

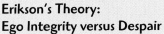

■ *This newly retired senior couple enjoys a relaxed approach to planning a vacation. When a marital relationship is positive, retirement can enrich it further by granting more time for companionship. (Photo courtesy: Fotopic)*

With Ruth at his side, Walt disclosed to guests on their fiftieth anniversary, "Even when there were hard times, it's the period of life I was in at the moment that I always liked the most. I adored playing baseball as a kid and learning the photography business when I was in my twenties. And I recall our wedding, the most memorable day of all," Walt continued, glancing affectionately at Ruth. "Then came the Depression, when professional picture taking was a luxury few people could afford. But we found ways to have fun without money, such as singing in the church choir and acting in community theater. A short time later, Sybil was born. It meant so much to me to be a father—and now a grandfather and a great-grandfather. Looking back at my parents and grandparents and forward at Sybil, Marci, and Marci's son, Jamel, I feel a sense of unity with past and future generations."

Walt and Ruth greeted old age with calm acceptance, grateful for the gift of long life and loved ones. Yet not all older adults find peace of mind in these final decades. Walt's brother Dick was contentious and critical, often over petty issues, at other times over major disappointments. "Goldie, why did you serve cheesecake? No one eats cheesecake on birthdays" and "You know the reason we've got these financial worries? Uncle Louie wouldn't lend me the money to keep the bakery going, so I *had* to retire."

A mix of gains and losses characterizes these twilight years, extending the multidirectionality of development begun early in life. On the one hand, old age is an Indian summer—a time of pleasure and tranquility. Children are grown, life's work is nearly done, and responsibilities are lightened. On the other hand, it brings concerns about declining physical functions, unwelcome loneliness, and the growing specter of imminent death.

In this chapter, we consider how older adults reconcile these opposing forces. Although some are weary and discontented, most elders traverse this phase with poise and calm composure. They attach deeper significance to life and reap great benefits from family and friendship bonds, leisure activities, and community involvements. We will see how personal attributes and life history combine with home, neighborhood, community, and societal conditions to mold emotional and social development in late life.

■ *Late adulthood is a time when individuals come to terms with their lives. Elders who arrive at a sense of integrity feel whole, complete, and satisfied with their achievements. Erik Erikson and his wife Joan provided ideal role models for Erikson's final stage: a couple who had grown old gracefully and who could often be seen walking hand in hand, deeply in love. (Photo courtesy: Palmer/Kane/Stone)*

ERIKSON'S THEORY: EGO INTEGRITY VERSUS DESPAIR

The final psychological conflict of Erikson's (1950) theory, **ego integrity versus despair,** involves coming to terms with one's life. Adults who arrive at a sense of integrity feel whole, complete, and satisfied with their achievements. They have adapted to the mix of triumphs and disappointments that are an inevitable part of love relationships, child rearing, work, friendships, and community involvement. They realize that the paths they followed, abandoned, and never selected were necessary for fashioning a meaningful life course.

The capacity to view one's life in the larger context of all humanity—as the chance combination of one person and one segment in history—contributes to the serenity and contentment that accompanies integrity. "These last few decades have been the happiest," Walt murmured as he clasped Ruth's hand, only weeks before the heart attack that would end his life. He was at peace with himself, his wife, and his children, having accepted his life course as something that had to be the way it was.

As he scanned the newspaper one day, Walt pondered, "I keep reading these percentages: 1 out of 5 people will get heart disease, 1 out of 3 will get cancer. But in truth, 1 out of 1 will die. We are all mortal and must accept this fate." The year before, Walt had given his granddaughter, Marci, his collection of prized photos, which had absorbed him for over a half century. With the realization that the integrity of one's own life is part of an extended chain of human existence, death loses its sting (Vaillant, 1994).

The negative outcome of this stage, despair, occurs when elders feel they have made many wrong decisions, yet time is too short to find an alternate route to integrity. Without another chance, the despairing person finds it hard to accept that death is near and is overwhelmed with bitterness, defeat, and hopelessness. According to Erikson, these attitudes are often expressed as anger and contempt for others, which disguise contempt for oneself. Dick's argumentative, fault-finding behavior, tendency to blame others for his personal failures, and regretful view of his own life reflect this deep sense of despair (Hamachek, 1990).

OTHER THEORIES OF PSYCHOSOCIAL DEVELOPMENT IN LATE ADULTHOOD

As with Erikson's stages of early and middle adulthood, other theorists have clarified and refined his vision of late adulthood, specifying the developmental tasks, thought processes, and activities that contribute to a sense of ego integrity. All agree that successful development in the later years involves greater integration and deepening of the personality.

PECK'S THEORY:
THREE TASKS OF EGO INTEGRITY

According to Robert Peck (1968), Erikson's conflict of ego integrity versus despair comprises three distinct tasks. Each must be resolved for integrity to develop:

- *Ego differentiation versus work-role preoccupation.* This task results from retirement. It requires aging people who have invested heavily in their vocations to find other ways of affirming their self-worth. The person striving for integrity must differentiate a set of family, friendship, and community roles that are equally as satisfying as his or her vocation.

- *Body transcendence versus body preoccupation.* As we saw in Chapter 17, old age brings changes in appearance and declines in physical capacities and resistance to disease. For people whose psychological well-being is heavily bound up with the state of their bodies, late adulthood can be a difficult time. Older adults need to *transcend* physical limitations by emphasizing cognitive and social powers, which can compensate and offer alternative rewards.

- *Ego transcendence versus ego preoccupation.* Whereas middle-aged people realize that life is finite, the elderly are reminded of the absolute certainty of death as siblings, friends, and peers in their community die. They must find a constructive way of facing this reality—through investing in a longer future than their own lifespan. Although the generative years of early and middle adulthood prepare people for a satisfying old age, attaining ego integrity requires a continuing effort to make life more secure, meaningful, and gratifying for those who will go on after one dies.

In Peck's theory, ego integrity requires that older adults move beyond their life's work, their bodies, and their separate identities. Drawing on their wisdom, they must reach out to others in ways that make the world better. Their success is apparent in their own inner state of contentment and their beneficial impact on others.

LABOUVIE-VIEF'S THEORY:
EMOTIONAL EXPERTISE

In Chapter 13, we discussed Gisella Labouvie-Vief's theory of cognitive change, noting how in early adulthood abstract thought becomes *pragmatic*—a tool for solving real-world problems. Labouvie-Vief has also explored the development of adults' reasoning about emotion. She believes that older and more psychologically mature individuals are more in touch with their feelings. They describe emotional reactions in more complex and personalized ways, perhaps as a result of reflecting on life experiences and using coping strategies that permit fuller acknowledgment of emotion.

In one study, participants from adolescence to old age were asked to relate personal experiences in which they were happy, angry, fearful, and sad and to indicate how they knew they felt the emotion. Younger people explained feelings technically, as if they were observing them from the outside. For example, they were likely to say, "My adrenaline was high," or, "My heart rate increased." They also emphasized how they *should* feel rather than how they did feel. In contrast, older adults gave vivid descriptions that viewed both mind and body as contributing to feeling states and that integrated subjective and objective aspects of emotion. Here is one:

You have sunshine in your heart. During the wedding the candles were glowing. And that's just how I felt.

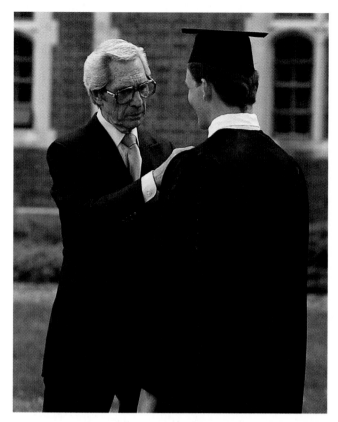

■ *How will this grandfather put this moment into words? Elders describe emotional reactions in more complex and personalized ways. (Photo courtesy: Palmer/Kane/Stone)*

I as glowing too. It was kind of dull outside. But that isn't how I felt. Everybody in the church felt like they were glowing. It was that kind of feeling. (Labouvie-Vief, DeVoe, & Bulka, 1989, p. 429)

Older adults' emotional perceptiveness assists them in separating emotional interpretations from objective aspects of situations more effectively than younger adults do. Consequently, their coping strategies often include making sure their own biases are fully understood before deciding on a course of action (Blanchard-Fields, 1997; Labouvie-Vief et al., 1995). Elders also acknowledge periods of intense rumination and are better able to interpret negative events in a positive light—factors that may contribute to the self-acceptance inherent in ego integrity. In sum, a significant late-life psychosocial attainment is becoming expert at processing emotional information and engaging in emotional self-regulation (Gross et al., 1997; Labouvie-Vief & Diehl, 1999).

REMINISCENCE AND LIFE REVIEW

When we think of the elderly, we often picture them engaged in **reminiscence**—telling stories about people and events from their past and reporting associated thoughts and feelings. Indeed, the image of a reminiscing elder is so widespread that it ranks among the negative stereotypes of aging. A common view is that older people live in the past to escape the realities of a shortened future and the nearness of death. Researchers do not yet have a full understanding of why older people reminisce more often than younger people do (Boden & Bielby, 1983; Lamme & Baars, 1993). But current theory and research indicate that reflecting on the past can be positive and adaptive.

Return to Walt's commentary about major events in his life at the beginning of this chapter. Walt engaged in a special form of reminiscence called **life review,** in which the person calls up, reflects on, and reconsiders past experiences, contemplating their meaning with the goal of achieving greater self-understanding. According to Robert Butler (1968), most older adults engage in life review as part of attaining ego integrity, preventing despair, and accepting the end of life. Butler's ideas have been so influential that many therapists encourage the elderly to engage in life-review reminiscence. In one study, homebound 61- to 99-year-olds who participated in a counselor-led life-review process showed gains in life satisfaction still apparent a year later. This did not occur for participants who simply enjoyed friendly visits or who received no treatment (Haight, 1992).

Although life review often prompts self-awareness and self-respect, many elders do not spend much time evaluating their pasts. When asked to do so, 30 percent of one sample claimed that the best part of life was "right now"! Middle age also received high marks, whereas childhood and adolescence ranked as less satisfying (Field, 1997). These findings clearly contradict the widespread belief that older adults wish to be young again. As the Lifespan Vista box on pages 596–597 illustrates, recollections of distant events are colored by many factors, including personality, subsequent life experiences, and the timing and nature of the events themselves. Despairing elders are especially likely to ruminate on negative content from the past, and some benefit from help in identifying worthwhile aspects of their lives (Sherman, 1993).

Besides life review, reminiscence in old age serves other functions. Elders may talk about their past because others, from social service professionals to curious grandchildren and great-grandchildren, expect them to! As they discuss life experiences, older adults may satisfy social needs, such as developing or reestablishing friendships and seeking confirmation from others. Finally, reminiscence—for young and old alike—often occurs during times of life transition (Parker, 1995). The older adult who has recently retired, been widowed, or moved to a new residence may turn to the past to sustain a sense of personal continuity. Indeed, elders who feel their current lives are adrift reminisce especially often to recapture feelings of meaning and purpose (Fry, 1991).

■ *Reflecting on the past can be positive and adaptive. Many older adults engage in reminiscence and life review as part of attaining ego integrity. And at times they talk about their past because others, such as curious grandchildren, expect them to! (Photo courtesy: R. Sidney/The Image Works)*

STABILITY AND CHANGE IN SELF-CONCEPT AND PERSONALITY

Longitudinal research reveals continuing stability of the "big five" personality traits from mid- to late life (see Chapter 16, page 533). Yet consider the ingredients of ego integrity: wholeness, contentment, and image of the self as part of a larger world order. These attributes are reflected in several significant late-life changes in both self-concept and personality.

SECURE AND MULTIFACETED SELF-CONCEPT

Older adults have accumulated a lifetime of self-knowledge, leading to more secure and complex conceptions of themselves than at earlier ages (Labouvie-Vief & Diehl, 1999). Ruth, for example, knew with certainty that she was good at counseling others, growing a flower garden, giving dinner parties, budgeting money, and figuring out who could be trusted and who couldn't. At the same time, she commented wistfully that she couldn't get around the city as easily as before.

The firmness and multifaceted nature of Ruth's self-concept permitted her to compensate for lack of skill in domains she had never tried, did not master, or could no longer perform as well as before. Consequently, it allowed for self-acceptance—a key feature of integrity. In a study of old (70 to 84 years) and very old (85 to 103 years) German elders asked to respond to the question "Who am I?", participants mentioned a broad spectrum of life domains, including hobbies, interests, social participation, family, health, and personality traits. Adults of both ages expressed more positive than negative self-evaluations, although a slight increase in negative comments occurred in the older group. Positive, multifaceted self-definitions predicted psychological well-being (Freund & Smith, 1999).

In Chapter 17, we noted that as the future shortens, hoped-for possible selves decline and feared selves increase in the realm of health. This shift also occurs in other domains. But most elders mention some hoped-for selves and are very active in pursuing them. These grant older adults goals in life and a sense of further development (Markus & Herzog, 1992). Even in advanced old age, when some capacities decline, the majority of older adults retain a coherent sense of self. They regard themselves as very much the same person they have always been (Troll & Skaff, 1997).

AGREEABLENESS, SOCIABILITY, AND ACCEPTANCE OF CHANGE

During late adulthood, shifts in three personality characteristics take place—changes that, once again, defy stereotypes of the elderly. Old age is not a time in which the personality inevitably becomes rigid and morale declines. Instead, a flexible, optimistic approach to life is common.

Rating open-ended interviews with elders in their sixties and, again, when they reached their eighties and nineties, researchers found that scores on adjectives that make up *agreeableness*—*generous, acquiescent,* and *good-natured*—were higher on the second occasion than the first for over one-third of the sample. These qualities seem to characterize people who have come to terms with life despite its imperfections. In addition, participants showed a slight dip in *sociability* as they aged (Field & Millsap, 1991). Perhaps this reflects a narrowing of social contacts as people become more selective about relationships and as family members and friends die—trends we will take up in a later section.

A third, related development is greater *acceptance of change*—an attribute the elderly frequently mention as important to psychological well-being (Ryff, 1989). That many older adults adjust well to change is evident in what they say when asked about dissatisfactions in their lives. They often respond that they are not unhappy about anything! A capacity to accept life's twists and turns, many of which are beyond one's control, is vital for positive functioning in late adulthood.

A LIFESPAN VISTA

WORLD WAR II REFUGEE AND EVACUEE CHILDREN
LOOK BACK FROM THE VANTAGE POINT OF OLD AGE

How do elders look back on a traumatic period occurring early in their lives? To find out, Glen Palmer (1997) interviewed people who had come to Australia just before or during World War II as Jewish refugees from Austria, Germany, and Poland or as evacuees from Great Britain. All had been under age 16 when their parents put them on boats, giving them up in anguish to protect them. Most parents of the Polish and German children were murdered by the Nazis. After kissing them good-bye, these children never saw their parents again. In contrast, the British evacuees were able to return to their homeland and families at the end of the war.

Looking back, these elders were largely supportive of their parents' decision to send them away. For the refugees, it meant that their lives had been spared (see Chapter 10, page 340). Beyond this, recollections of their experiences and assessments of its lifelong impact varied. Among factors that made a difference were the quality of care they received, their age at separation (child or adolescent), and their temperament.

Care situations included relatives, foster homes, group homes, and boarding schools. For children placed with families, being loved and wanted led to new attachments and pleasant memories, often at the expense of former bonds. As one interviewee noted, "If you send a child away in the formative years, you take the risk of losing the affection of that child." When relatives and foster families were unkind or outright rejecting, painful recollections of an "emotional limbo" emerged. Without new attachments, these children clung to fading images of their families, idealized their parents, and longed to return to them. Separation and inadequate care had a more profound, lasting impact on the memories of temperamentally withdrawn, anxious individuals than on those of outgoing individuals, who were better able to develop supportive social ties beyond the family.

Compared with interviewees who were children at the time of separation, those who were adolescents were less affected by the absence of affectional bonds with adults. "I knew in my mind that I had plenty of family support, even though they weren't around," one Polish refugee remarked. On the threshold of adulthood, these young people had little desire for substitute parents. Instead, they fared best in group homes and boarding schools that provided appropriate oversight, balancing security with independence. Often their warmest memories were of bonds established with one another. In contrast, when children were placed in group homes and denied family attachments, their sadness was often still apparent in old age: "There was a desolation because there was no love. . . . You need to be able to say to a child, 'You're my special one.'"

By the end of the war, the majority of interviewees had become young adults. Most of the British evacuees were reunited with their families, but rarely with "happily ever after" endings. Children and parents had changed during the intervening years. As one interviewee put it, "It was easier to go than to come back." Still, reunion was vital, since its absence usually brings a lifetime of unresolved grief.

For most Polish and German refugees, loss of immediate family was total. More than 50 years later, their searching and sorrow continues. One interviewee commented, "The Holocaust pursues us daily. It is like having a flea in your head." This suggests that rather than healing with the passage of time, the pain of childhood loss and trauma can intensify in later life. Reunions with other

SPIRITUALITY AND RELIGIOSITY

How are older adults able to accept change, feel whole and complete, and anticipate death with calm composure? One possibility is that they develop a more mature sense of spirituality. That is, they actively seek a higher meaning for life, knowing that it will end in the foreseeable future. Spirituality is not the same as religion. A transcendent sense of truth and beauty can be found in art, nature, and relationships with others. But religion provides many people with beliefs, symbols, and rituals that guide this quest for meaning.

Older adults attach great value to religious beliefs and behaviors. According to a national survey, 76 percent of Americans age 65 and older say that religion is very important in their lives, and 16 percent describe it as fairly important. Over half attend religious services weekly, nearly two-thirds watch religious TV programs, and about one-fourth pray at least three times a day (Princeton Religion Research Center, 1994).

Although declining health and transportation difficulties reduce organized religious participation in advanced old refugees helped soothe persisting wounds as elders shared experiences with those best able to understand their continued suffering.

Although many interviewees remained deeply affected by their childhood experiences, very few were maladjusted. To the contrary, most found turning points through their families, careers, or other interests and led productive, fulfilling lives. Some seemed to draw on inner strengths developed during early years of separation when late-life adversities arose. As one Holocaust survivor commented after her husband died, "[W]hen you've been through what I've been through, you can survive anything."

Nevertheless, these victims of genocide—and other similarly traumatized individuals around the world—probably cannot make a complete recovery. None of the refugees returned to live in Europe, although some had visited their countries of birth in recent years. Rarely were these journeys comfortable. Almost always, they brought heartaches to the surface—yet another reminder of the pervasive effects of ethnic and political violence throughout the lifespan.

■ *Above are the German Jewish children who boarded the* Orama *for Australia in June of 1939, just before the outbreak of World War II. Seven-year-old Laurie, shown on the left with his parents two days before his departure, kissed them goodbye and never saw them again. When the war ended, Laurie learned that his mother had been deported to a concentration camp and murdered by the Nazis. A tracing agency located a grave for Laurie's father, although Laurie never found out exactly how he died. (Photo courtesy: Glen Palmer, Griffith University, Queensland, Australia.)*

age, informal religious activities remain prominent in the lives of today's elders (Ainlay, Singleton, & Swigert, 1992). Does involvement in religion increase with age? Longitudinal research suggests that it is fairly stable throughout adulthood. Even so, the need for religious affiliation may rise among the elderly. In one study, over one-third of older people said they would devote more time to religion if they could (DeGenova, 1992).

Furthermore, spirituality and faith may advance to a higher level in late adulthood—away from prescribed beliefs to a more reflective approach that emphasizes links to others and is at ease with mystery and uncertainty (Birren, 1990). In his theory of faith development, James Fowler (1981) posits five stages, summarized in Table 18.1 on page 598, which have been confirmed in several studies. Stages 4 and 5 characterize mature adults. Notice how individuals become aware of their own belief system as one of many possible world views, contemplate the deeper significance of religious symbols and rituals, and open themselves to other religious perspectives as sources of inspiration (McFadden,

■ *After weeks of study, the 89-year-old on the left and the 86-year-old on the right prepare for the Jewish Bat Mitzvah ceremony, during which they will read in Hebrew from the Torah (the first five books of the Old Testament). As youths more than 70 years ago, they were denied this right of passage because they were girls. At long last, it is their turn to be called to the Torah. Older adults attach great value to religious beliefs and behaviors. (Photo courtesy: The Boston Globe)*

1996). For example, as a complement to his Catholicism, Walt became intensely interested in Buddhism, especially its focus on attaining perfect peace and happiness by mastering thoughts and feelings, never harming others, and resisting attachment to worldly objects.

Involvement in both organized and informal religious activities is especially high among low-income ethnic minority elders, including African-Americans, Hispanics, and Native Americans. In African-American communities, churches not only provide contexts for deriving meaning from life, but are centers for education, health, social welfare, and political activities aimed at improving life conditions. African-American elders look to religion as a powerful resource for social support beyond the family and for the inner strength to withstand daily stresses and physical impairments (Gelfand, 1994; Husaini, Blasi, & Miller, 1999). Asked about her philosophy of life, an African-American 65-year-old reveals how faith enabled her to do more than survive. As she tells it, she has much to be thankful for:

> We've had lots of misfortunes . . . but we always knowed that it could be worse. . . . I know somedays I get up I'd be stiff and my knees aching and my back is aching and my head is hurting and I can get up and go in the bathroom. I say, "Thank you Lord because I have the activities of my limbs. . . ." And then we get a meal on the table and we have . . . at least a portion of health and strength. . . . [I] thank the Lord for things being as well as they are. (Nye, 1993, p. 109)

Among elders of all backgrounds, religious involvement is linked to many positive outcomes. These include activi-

TABLE 18.1

Fowler's Stages of Faith Development

STAGE OF FAITH	PERIOD OF DEVELOPMENT	DESCRIPTION
1. Intuitive-projective	3–7 years	Children's fantasy and imitation lead them to be powerfully influenced by stories, moods, and behaviors demonstrating the faith of adults. They become aware of right and wrong actions.
2. Mythic-literal	7–11 years	Children begin to internalize the stories, beliefs, and observances of their religious community, which they take literally. For example, they often hold concrete images of God living on top of the world and watching over everybody.
3. Synthetic-conventional	Adolescence	Adolescents have a coherent set of deeply felt beliefs and values, which provides a basis for identity. They have not yet examined this ideology systematically.
4. Individuative-reflective	Adulthood	Adults who reach this stage critically reflect on their beliefs and values, recognizing that their world view is only one of many possible world views. They actively shape a personal ideology, forming and reforming it over time. About religious rituals and symbols, they ask, "What does this really mean?"
5. Conjunctive	Late Adulthood	The few people who attain this stage form an enlarged vision of an all-inclusive human community. They act to bring it about by standing up against persecution and injustice and by promoting a common good that serves the needs of diverse groups. Great religious leaders, such as Mahatma Gandhi and Martin Luther King, Jr., illustrate conjunctive faith.

Source: Fowler, 1981.

ties and social roles as diverse as exercising and feelings of closeness to family and friends as well as psychological well-being (Levin & Chatters, 1998). In one longitudinal study, religious participation was a strong predictor of better physical functioning over a 12-year period, beyond the effects of optimism, health practices, and social support (Idler & Kasl, 1997). In another study, the link between deteriorated neighborhoods and poor self-rated health was entirely offset for elders who often used religious coping strategies—praying and seeking strength and support from God during difficult times (Krause, 1998).

Sex differences in religious involvement are evident throughout adulthood. Women are more likely to be church or synagogue members and to engage in a variety of religious activities, from attending services to private prayer and Bible reading (Levin, Taylor, & Chatters, 1994). Women's greater experience of poverty and widowhood and participation in caregiving, including for chronically ill family members, expose them to higher levels of stress. As with ethnic minorities, they turn to religion for social support and for a larger vision of community that places life's challenges in perspective (Neill & Kahn, 1999).

INDIVIDUAL DIFFERENCES IN PSYCHOLOGICAL WELL-BEING

In this and the previous chapter, we have seen that most adults adapt constructively to old age. Yet a few feel dependent, incompetent, and worthless. Identifying personal and environmental influences on late-life psychological well-being is vital for designing interventions that foster positive adjustment.

CONTROL VERSUS DEPENDENCY

As Ruth's eyesight, hearing, and mobility declined in her eighties, Sybil visited daily to assist with self-care and household tasks. During the hours mother and daughter were together, Sybil interacted most often with Ruth when she asked for help with activities of daily living. When Ruth handled tasks on her own, Sybil usually withdrew.

Observations of older adults interacting with others in both private homes and institutions reveal a typical pattern in which dependency behaviors are attended to immedi-

ately, whereas independent behaviors are mostly ignored. Notice how these sequences, so predictable that they are called the **dependency–support script** and the **independence–ignore script,** reinforce dependent behavior at the expense of independent behavior, regardless of the older person's competencies. Even a self-reliant elder like Ruth did not always resist Sybil's unnecessary help, since it brought about social contact (Baltes, 1995, 1996).

Among elders who experience no difficulty with daily activities, opportunities to interact with others are associated with high satisfaction with everyday life. In contrast, among elders who have trouble performing daily activities, social contact is linked to a less positive everyday existence (Lang & Baltes, 1997). This suggests that social interaction while assisting elders with physical care, household chores, and errands is often not meaningful and rewarding but rather demeaning and unpleasant. Consider these typical reactions of care recipients to a spouse's help with daily activities: "felt dependent," "felt indebted," "felt like a weak, incapable person" (Newsom, 1999).

Longitudinal research shows that negative reactions to caregiving can foster persisting depression (Newsom & Schultz, 1998). But whether assistance from others undermines well-being is a function of many factors, including the quality of help, the caregiver–elder relationship, and the social and cultural context in which helping occurs. Why do family members and other caregivers often respond in ways that promote excessive dependency in old age? A stereotype of the elderly as passive and incompetent appears to be responsible. Older adults seem well aware of others' low

■ *Is this daughter encouraging her mother to be dependent by helping her dress? The answer lies in whether the mother assumes personal control over her dependency. Dependency can be adaptive if it permits older people to conserve their strength and invest it in highly valued activities. (Photo courtesy: Penny Tweedie/Stone)*

SOCIAL ISSUES

ELDER SUICIDE

When 65-year-old Abe's wife died, he withdrew from life. Living far from his two daughters, he spent his nonworking days alone, watching television and reading mystery novels. As grandchildren were born, Abe visited his daughters' homes from time to time. When he did, he carried his despondent behavior with him. "Look at my new pajamas, Grandpa!" Abe's 6-year-old grandson Tony exclaimed on one occasion. Abe didn't even acknowledge the little boy.

Abe retired after arthritis made walking difficult. With more empty days, his depression deepened. Gradually, Abe developed painful digestive difficulties, but he refused to go to the doctor. "Don't need to," he said abruptly when one of his daughters called and begged him to get medical attention. Answering her invitation to Tony's tenth birthday party, Abe wrote, "Maybe—if I'm still around next month. By the way, when I go, I want my body cremated." Two weeks later, Abe died from an intestinal blockage. His body was found in the living room chair where he habitually spent his days.

FACTORS RELATED TO ELDER SUICIDE. Return to Figure 12.3 on page 408, and notice that suicide peaks in late life. It climbs during the elder years, reaching its highest rate among people age 75 and older. Although the incidence of suicide varies among nations, older adults are at increased risk around the world (World Health Organization, 1999).

Recall from Chapter 12 that the suicide rate is much higher among adolescent males than females. This sex difference persists throughout the lifespan, increasing in old age. In addition, compared with the white majority, most American ethnic minority elders (including African Americans, Hispanics, and Native Americans) have very low suicide rates.

What explains these trends? Despite the lifelong pattern of higher rates of depression and more suicide attempts among females, elderly women's closer ties to family and friends, greater willingness to seek social support, and religiosity prevent many from taking their own lives. High levels of social support through extended families and church affiliations may also prevent suicide among ethnic minorities. And among certain minorities, such as Alaskan Native Americans, deep respect for and reliance on older adults to teach cultural traditions enhance social integration and self-esteem. This reduces elder suicide, making it nonexistent after age 80 (Kettl, 1998).

As in earlier years, the method favored by elder males (firearms) offers less chance of revival than that favored by elder females (poisoning or drug overdose). Nevertheless, failed suicides are much rarer in old age than in adolescence. The ratio of attempts to completions for the young is as high as 300 to 1; for the elderly, it is 4 to 1 or lower. When elders decide to die, they seem especially determined to succeed (Bille-Brahe, 1993).

Underreporting of suicides probably occurs at all ages, but it is more common in old age. Medical examiners are less likely to pursue suicide as a cause of death when a person is old. And many elders, like Abe, engage in indirect self-destructive acts rarely classified as suicide, such as deciding not to go to a doctor when ill and refusing to eat or take prescribed medications. Among institutionalized elders, these efforts to hasten death are widespread (Osgood, Brant, & Lipman, 1991). Consequently, elder suicide is an even larger problem than official statistics indicate.

Two types of events prompt suicide in late life. Losses—retirement from a highly valued occupation, wid-

---

expectations for them. They frequently attribute their dependency to overresponsive social partners (Wahl, 1991).

In Western societies, which place a high value on independence, many elders fear becoming dependent on others. They often say that when they can no longer care for themselves, it is time to die. Does this mean we should encourage elders to be as independent as possible? According to Mary Baltes (1996), this alternative is as counterproductive as promoting passivity and incompetence. Aging brings diminished energy at a time when people confront many challenging developmental tasks. Dependency can be adaptive if it permits older people to conserve their strength by investing it in highly valued activities, using a set of strategies we considered in Chapter 17: *selective optimization with compensation.*

HEALTH

As noted in Chapter 16, health is a powerful predictor of psychological well-being in late adulthood. Physical declines and chronic disease can be highly stressful, leading to a sense of loss of personal control—a major factor in adult mental health. Furthermore, physical illness resulting in disability is among the strongest risk factors for late-life depression (Ostir et al., 1999). Although fewer older than young and middle-aged adults are depressed (see Chapter owhood, and social isolation—place elders who have difficulty coping with change at risk. A second set of risks are chronic and terminal illnesses that cause severe physical pain. As comfort and quality of life diminish, feelings of hopelessness and helplessness deepen. Very old people, especially men, are particularly likely to take their own lives under these conditions. The chances are even greater when a sick elder is socially isolated—living alone or in a nursing home with high staff turnover and minimal caregiver support.

PREVENTION AND TREATMENT. Warning signs of suicide in late adulthood overlap with those at earlier ages. They include efforts to put personal affairs in order, statements about dying, despondency, and sleep and appetite changes. Family members, friends, and caregivers must also watch for indirect self-destructive acts, such as refusing food or medical treatment, which are unique to old age (Osgood, 1992).

When suicidal elders are depressed, the most effective treatment combines antidepressant medication with therapy. At-risk individuals need help in coping with role transitions, such as retirement, widowhood, and dependency brought about by illness.

Distorted ways of thinking, such as "I'm old, and nothing can be done about my problems," must be countered and revised. Meeting with the family to find ways to reduce loneliness and desperation can be helpful. And group approaches offer peer support and can lead to gratifying new relationships (Devons, 1996; McIntosh et al., 1994).

Although youth suicide has risen (see Chapter 12, page 408), elder suicide has declined during the past 50 years, due to increased economic security among older adults, improved medical care and social services, and more favorable cultural attitudes toward retirement. Communities are beginning to recognize the importance of additional preventive steps, such as telephone hot lines with trained volunteers who provide emotional support and agencies that arrange for regular home visitors or "buddy system" phone calls. In institutions, providing residents with privacy, autonomy, and space helps prevent self-destructive behavior (McIntosh et al., 1994; Osgood, 1992).

Finally, elder suicide raises a controversial ethical issue: Do people with incurable illnesses have the right to take their own lives? We will take up this topic in Chapter 19.

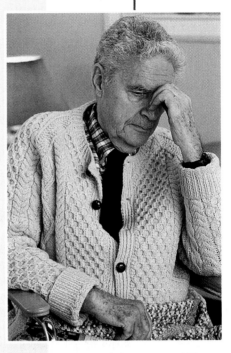

■ As comfort and quality of life diminish, feelings of hopelessness and helplessness deepen. Very old people, especially men, are particularly likely to take their own lives under these conditions. (Photo courtesy: Jon Feingersh/ The Stock Market)

17), profound feelings of hopelessness rise with age as physical disability and consequent social isolation increase (George, 1994; Roberts et al., 1997).

The relation between physical and mental health problems can become a vicious cycle, each intensifying the other. At times, the rapid decline of a sick elder is the work of despondency and "giving up" (Cohen, 1990). This downward spiral can be hastened by a move to a nursing home, requiring the older person to adjust to distance from family and friends and to a new self-definition as "a person who can survive only in an institution." In the month after admission, many residents deteriorate rapidly and become severely depressed. The stress of illness together with institutionalization is associated with heightened health problems and mortality (Tobin, 1989).

Depression in old age is often lethal. People age 65 and older have the highest suicide rate of any age group (see the Social Issues box above). What factors enable elders like Ruth to surmount the physical impairment–depression relationship, remaining optimistic and content? Personal characteristics we discussed in earlier chapters—effective coping and a sense of self-efficacy—are vitally important. But for frail elders to display these attributes, families and caregivers must grant them autonomy by avoiding the dependency– support script. When older adults remain in charge of personally important areas of their lives, they retain essential aspects of their identity in the face of change and report a more favorable outlook on their past and future (Brandtstädter & Rothermund, 1994).

NEGATIVE LIFE CHANGES

Ruth lost Walt to a heart attack, cared for Ida as her Alzheimer's symptoms worsened, and faced health problems of her own—all within a span of a few years. Elders are at risk for a variety of negative life changes—death of spouse, siblings, and friends; illness and physical disabilities; declining income; and greater dependency. Negative life changes are difficult for all people. But these events may actually evoke less stress and depression in older than in younger adults (Gatz, Kasl-Godley, & Karel, 1996). Many elders have learned to cope with hard times and come to accept loss as part of human existence.

Still, when negative changes pile up, they test the coping skills of older adults. In very old age, such changes are greater for women than for men. Women over age 75 are far less likely to be married, more often have lower incomes, and suffer from more illnesses—especially ones that restrict mobility. Furthermore, elderly women more often say that others depend on them for emotional support. This means that their social relations, even in very old age, are more often a source of stress. And because of failing health, older women may not be able to meet others' needs for caregiving, with negative consequences for their self-esteem. Not surprisingly, women of very advanced age report a lower sense of psychological well-being than do men (Smith & Baltes, 1998).

SOCIAL SUPPORT AND SOCIAL INTERACTION

In late adulthood, social support continues to play a powerful role in reducing stress, thereby promoting physical health and psychological well-being. Most of the time, elders receive informal assistance from family members—first from their spouse, but if none exists, from children and then siblings. If these individuals are not available, other relatives and friends may step in.

Nevertheless, many older adults place such high value on independence that they do not want a great deal of support from people close to them unless they can reciprocate. Perhaps for this reason, adult children express a deeper sense of obligation toward their aging parents than their parents expect from them (see Chapter 16, page 543). Formal support—a paid helper or agency-provided services—as a complement to informal assistance not only helps relieve caregiving burdens, but prevents elders from feeling overly dependent in their close relationships (Chappell & Guse, 1989; Krause, 1990).

Ethnic minority elders, however, do not readily accept formal agency services. But when social and medical interventions use culturally sensitive practices and are connected to a neighborhood organization such as the church, they are more willing to participate. Although African-American seniors say they rely on their families more than the church for

assistance, those with support and meaningful role involvement in both contexts score highest in mental health (Coke, 1992; Walls & Zarit, 1991).

Finally, having a sociable personality is related to high morale in old age (Adkins, Martin, & Poon, 1996). Extroverted elders are more likely to take advantage of opportunities to socialize. Interactions with others reduce loneliness and depression and foster self-esteem and life satisfaction. But as we will see in the next section, supportive communication in old age has little to do with quantity of contact. Instead, high-quality relationships, involving expressions of caring, encouragement, and respect, have the greatest impact on mental health in late life.

For dependency to foster well-being, elders need to assume personal control over it. For example, although she could handle the activities on her own, Ruth permitted Sybil to assist with dressing, financial matters, shopping, and food preparation so she would have more stamina for pleasurable reading. To optimize her energies, Ruth selected certain domains in which to become dependent. This permitted her to compensate for her poor eyesight by taking extra time to use a magnifying glass while reading or listening to a book on tape. Notice how Ruth chose dependency in some areas so she could maintain an important function in danger of decline. In many instances, dependency behaviors are not signs of helplessness. Instead, they grant elders autonomy—a means for managing their own aging.

When we intervene with older adults, we must ask ourselves, What kind of assistance are we providing? Help that is not wanted or needed or that exaggerates weaknesses can undermine mental health. It can also accelerate physical disability due to nonuse of existing skills. In contrast, help that frees up energy for pursuits that are personally satisfying and that lead to growth enhances elders' quality of life.

ASK YOURSELF . . .

■ *Compared to a few years earlier, 80-year-old Miriam took longer to get dressed in the morning. Joan, her paid home helper, said, "I'd like you to wait until I arrive before dressing. Then I can help you and it won't take so long." What impact is Joan's approach likely to have on Miriam's personality? What alternative approach to helping Miriam would you recommend to Joan?*

Many elders adapt effectively to negative life changes. List personal and environmental factors that facilitate this generally positive outcome.

Although involvement in religion is fairly stable throughout adulthood, it takes on greater meaning and is linked to many positive outcomes in old age. Explain why, drawing on late-life physical and psychosocial development.

A CHANGING SOCIAL WORLD

Walt and Ruth's outgoingness led many family members and friends to seek them out, and they often reciprocated. In contrast, Dick's stubborn nature meant that his and Goldie's network of social ties was far more restricted, as it had been for many years.

In late adulthood, extroverts (like Walt and Ruth) continue to interact with a wider range of people than do introverts and people (like Dick) with poor social skills. Nevertheless, both cross-sectional and longitudinal research reveals that size of social networks and therefore amount of social interaction decline for virtually everyone (Carstensen, 1992; Lang, Staudinger, & Carstensen, 1998). This finding presents a curious paradox. If social interaction and social support are necessary for mental health, how is it possible for elders to interact less yet be generally satisfied with life and less depressed than younger adults?

SOCIAL THEORIES OF AGING

Social theories of aging offer explanations of the decline in social relations just described. Two prominent perspectives—disengagement and activity theory—interpret it in opposite ways. Each of these theories has been criticized. A recent approach—selectivity theory—accounts for a wider range of findings on social contacts in old age.

■ DISENGAGEMENT THEORY. According to **disengagement theory,** mutual withdrawal between elders and society takes place in anticipation of death (Cumming & Henry, 1961). Older people decrease their activity levels and interact less frequently, becoming more preoccupied with their inner lives. At the same time, society frees elders from employment and family responsibilities. The result is viewed as beneficial for both sides. Elders are granted a life of tranquility. Once they disengage, their deaths are less disruptive to society.

Think back to our discussion of wisdom in Chapter 17. Because of their long life experience, older adults in many cultures move into new roles of prestige and power. Clearly, not everyone disengages! Even after retirement, some people sustain certain aspects of their work, and others develop new, rewarding social roles in the community and in leisure. In tribal and village societies, most elders continue to hold important positions in their families and communities (Luborsky & McMullen, 1999). Consequently, when old people disengage, it may not represent their personal preference. Instead, it may be due to a failure of the social world to provide opportunities for engagement. In a study of 60- to 80-year-olds, the more social opportunities elders said they had, the stronger their belief that they create worthwhile social experiences for themselves (Lang, Feath-

■ *Young people seek advice and learn about the land and history of their people from this Navajo elder. Because of his long life experience, he is granted increased prestige and power in his cultural community. The greater social responsibility of many older adults presents a major challenge to disengagement theory of aging. (Photo courtesy: Suzi Moore/Woodfin Camp & Associates)*

erman, & Nesselroade, 1997). (Return to the Variations box in Chapter 17, page 567, for some striking community variations in meaningful social roles available to elders.)

As we will see shortly, elders' retreat from interaction is considerably more complex than disengagement theory implies. Instead of disengaging from all social ties, they let go of unsatisfying contacts and maintain satisfying ones. And sometimes, they put up with less than satisfying relationships to remain engaged! For example, Ruth reluctantly agreed to travel with Dick and Goldie because she wanted to share the experience with Walt. But she often complained about Dick's insensitive behavior.

■ ACTIVITY THEORY. **Activity theory** tries to overcome the flaws of disengagement theory. It states that social barriers to engagement, not the desires of elders, cause declining rates of interaction. When elders lose certain roles (for example, through retirement or widowhood), they do their best to find others in an effort to stay active and busy. According to this view, arranging conditions that permit elders to remain engaged in roles and relationships is vital for life satisfaction (Havighurst & Albrecht, 1953; Maddox, 1963).

Although many people seek alternative sources of meaning and gratification in response to social losses, activity theory fails to acknowledge any psychological change in old age. Many studies show that merely offering opportunities for social contact does not lead to greater social activity on the part of elders. Indeed, the majority do not "take advantage" of such opportunities. In nursing homes, for example, social partners are abundant, but social interaction is very low even among the healthiest residents—a circumstance that we will examine when we discuss housing arrangements for the elderly. Finally, especially troubling for activity theory is the repeated finding that when health status is controlled, elders who have larger social networks are not necessarily happier (Lee & Markides, 1990). Instead, recall that quality, not quantity, of relationships predicts psychological well-being in old age.

■ SOCIOEMOTIONAL SELECTIVITY THEORY. A more recent approach asserts that our social networks become more selective as we age. In **socioemotional selectivity theory,** social interaction does not decline suddenly in late adulthood. Rather, it extends lifelong selection processes. In middle adulthood, marital relationships deepen, siblings become closer, and number of friendships declines. In old age, contacts with family and long-term friends are sustained until the eighties, when they diminish gradually in favor of a few very close relationships. In contrast, contacts with acquaintances and willingness to form new social ties fall off steeply from middle through late adulthood (see Figure 18.1) (Lang & Carstensen, 1994).

What explains these changes? According to socioemotional selectivity theory, physical and psychological aspects of aging lead to changes in the functions of social interac-

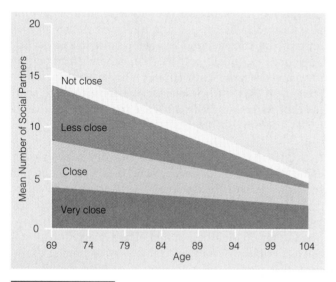

FIGURE 18.1

■ **Relationship of age to number of social partners varying in closeness.** In this cross-sectional study of elders between ages 69 and 104, the number of "not close" and "less close" partners fell off steeply with age, whereas the number of "close" and "very close" partners declined minimally and gradually. (Adapted from F. R. Lang, U. M. Staudinger, & L. L. Carstensen, 1998, "Perspectives on Socioemotional Selectivity in Late Life: How Personality and Social Context Do (and Do Not) Make a Difference," *Journal of Gerontology, 53B,* p. P24. Copyright © 1998 by the Gerontological Society of American. Reprinted by permission.)

tion most important to us. Consider the reasons you interact with members of your social network. At times, you approach them to get information. At other times, you seek affirmation of your uniqueness and worth as a person. And you also choose social partners to regulate emotion, approaching those who evoke positive feelings and avoiding those who make you feel sad, angry, or uncomfortable.

In old age, the information-gathering and self-affirmation functions of social interaction become less significant. Because older adults have gathered a lifetime of information, there are fewer people with knowledge that they desire. And elders realize it is risky to approach people they do not know for self-affirmation. Stereotypes of aging increase the odds of receiving a condescending, hostile, or indifferent response.

Instead, elders emphasize the emotion-regulating function of interaction. Physical fragility makes it more important to avoid stress and maintain emotional equilibrium (Carstensen & Turk, 1994). In one study, younger and older adults were asked to categorize their social partners. Younger people more often used information seeking and future contact as the basis for sorting. In contrast, older people stressed anticipated feelings (Frederickson & Carstensen, 1990). They appeared highly motivated to approach pleasant relationships and avoid unpleasant ones.

Interacting mostly with relatives and friends makes it more likely that elders' self-concepts and emotional equilibrium will be preserved. Although their social networks are smaller, more older adults than younger adults are happy with their current number of friends (Lansford, Sherman, & Antonucci, 1998). Indeed, as the Variations box on the following page reveals, people's perception of time is strongly linked to their social goals. When time is limited, adults of all ages place more emphasis on the emotional quality of their social experiences.

In sum, socioemotional selectivity theory views the reduction in social activity in old age as due to changing life conditions. As a result, elders much prefer partners with whom they have developed pleasurable, rewarding ties.

SOCIAL CONTEXTS OF AGING: COMMUNITIES, NEIGHBORHOODS, AND HOUSING

Elders live in contexts—both physical and social—that affect their social experiences and, consequently, their development and adjustment. Communities, neighborhoods, and housing arrangements vary in the extent to which they enable aging residents to satisfy their social needs.

■ COMMUNITIES AND NEIGHBORHOODS. About half of American ethnic minority older adults live in inner cities, whereas slightly fewer than one-third of Caucasian Americans do. The majority of senior citizens reside in suburbs, where they moved earlier in their lives and usually remain after retirement. Suburban elders have higher incomes,

TAKING TIME SERIOUSLY: TIME PERCEPTION AND SOCIAL GOALS

Who would you choose to spend time with if you knew you would be moving away from your community shortly? When young people are asked this question, they typically say they want to be with close friends and relatives, with whom they have enduring, positive relationships (Frederickson, 1995). Their response resembles that of older people. Increasingly aware that time is "running out," elders don't waste it on unlikely future payoffs. Instead, they opt for emotionally gratifying social experiences in the here and now.

Socioemotional selectivity theory underscores that our time perspective plays a crucial role in the social goals we select and pursue (Carstensen, Isaacowitz, & Charles, 1999). When time is limited, people search for meaningful social experiences. Yet tests of the theory documenting a rise with age in time spent with familiar, highly rewarding social partners do not permit us to separate the influence of age and time orientation on people's social goals. Is time perspective really at the heart of elders' focus on old friends and family members as desired social partners?

To find out, Laura Carstensen and her colleagues uncoupled age from time. In a study that held age constant but varied time left in life, the researchers compared three groups of men in their late thirties. The first group was HIV-negative, the second HIV-positive without AIDS symptoms, and the third HIV-positive and actively experiencing deadly symptoms of AIDS (Carstensen & Fredrickson, 1998). When asked to categorize a variety of potential social partners, each successive group increasingly emphasized the emotional rewards of the relationship. Men with AIDS symptoms—the group with the least time left— focused nearly exclusively on the emotional quality of social ties, just as very old people do.

In another investigation, the researchers permitted age to vary but attempted to hold time perspective constant by giving participants a hypothetical situation in which their future had expanded. People between ages 11 and 92 were asked to imagine that they had just received a telephone call from their doctor, who told them of a new medical breakthrough that would add 20 years to their life (Fung, Carstensen, & Lutz, 1999). Under these conditions, older people's strong bias for familiar, emotionally close social partners disappeared! Their social preferences were just as diverse as those of younger people.

In further research, this time in Hong Kong, the investigators capitalized on the country's impending return to the People's Republic of China in 1997 (Fung, Carstensen, & Lutz, 1999). This political transition produced a state of little time until a momentous ending in the entire population. Newspapers ran headlines, such as "Can Hong Kong Survive?", that emphasized the end of an era and possibly a way of life. In the months before the takeover, both younger and older adults preferred familiar over unfamiliar social relationships.

These findings underscore that the social preferences of old age are an active adaptation to changing life conditions. Elders revise their social goals just as all of us would do if the time we had left were limited. When our days are numbered, present-oriented goals—social connectedness, social support, and emotional depth in relationships—become high priorities.

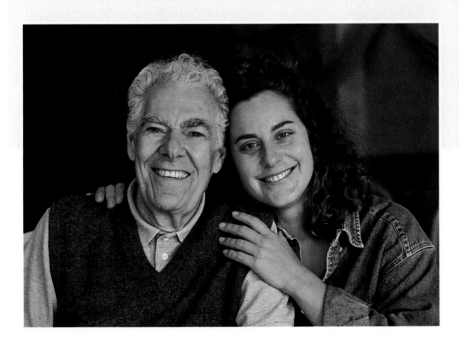

■ *This senior citizen delights in spending time with his adult granddaughter. When time is limited, people search for meaningful social experiences. Elders' focus on old friends and family members as desired social partners is no different from the preferences of individuals of any age who are confronted with a shortened time to live. (Photo courtesy: Bob Daemmrich/ The Image Works)*

report better health, and have easier access to social services than do inner-city elders. Inner-city elders, however, are better off in these ways than are the one-fourth of American senior citizens who live in small towns and rural areas. In addition, small-town and rural elderly are less likely to live near their children, who often leave the community in early adulthood (Coward, Lee, & Dwyer, 1993; U.S. Bureau of the Census, 1999).

Yet small-town and rural elderly compensate for distance from family members and social services by interacting more with neighbors and friends. Positive aspects of smaller communities—stability of residents and shared values and lifestyles—foster gratifying social relationships.

Both urban and rural older adults report greater life satisfaction when many senior citizens reside in their neighborhood and are available as like-minded companions. Presence of family is not as crucial, so long as neighbors and nearby friends provide social support (Lawton, Moss, & Moles, 1984; Lawton et al., 1999). This does not mean that neighbors replace family relationships. But elders are content as long as their children and other relatives arrange occasional visits (Hooyman & Kiyak, 1993).

Compared with older adults in urban areas, elders residing in quiet neighborhoods in small and mid-sized communities are more satisfied with life. The major reason is that smaller communities have lower crime rates (Scheidt & Windley, 1985). As we will see in the next section, fear of crime has profound, negative consequences for older adults' sense of security and comfort.

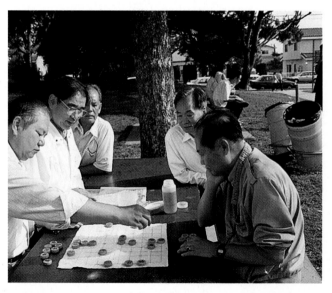

■ *These men gather regularly to play Chinese chess in Monterey Park, California. In both urban and rural areas, older adults report greater life satisfaction when many senior citizens reside in their neighborhood and are available as like-minded companions. (Photo courtesy: A. Ramsey/Woodfin Camp & Associates)*

■ VICTIMIZATION AND FEAR OF CRIME. Walt and Ruth's single-dwelling house stood in an urban neighborhood with a large Greek population, five blocks from the business district where Walt's photography shop had been prior to his retirement. When leaving home for more than a few hours, Walt and Ruth telephoned their next-door neighbor and asked her to keep an eye on the property. As the neighborhood aged, some homes fell into disrepair, and the population became more transient. Although shops were open Thursday and Friday evenings, Walt and Ruth saved their errands for bright daylight hours. Even then, they were circumspect. Although they had never been victimized, crime was on their minds and affected their behavior.

Media attention has led to a widely held belief that crime against the elderly is common. In reality, older adults are less often targets of crime, especially violent crime, than are other age groups. However, in urban areas, purse snatching and pickpocketing are more often committed against elders (especially women) than younger people, probably because perpetrators feel that they can easily overpower older and female victims (U.S. Department of Justice, 1999). A single incident can strike intense anxiety in the hearts of elders, given its financial consequences for those with low incomes and its potential for physical injury.

For older adults living alone and in inner-city areas, fear of crime is sometimes greater than worries about income, health, and housing. These elders feel especially vulnerable because they believe assistance will not be available should they need it. Their constant fear restricts their activities and seriously undermines their morale (Joseph, 1997; Thompson & Krause, 1998). Neighborhood Watch and other programs that encourage residents to get to know and look out for one another reduce fear and feelings of isolation from the community. Some cities have established special police units to investigate and prevent crimes against the elderly. They improve life satisfaction of elderly victims (Zevitz & Gurnack, 1991).

■ HOUSING ARRANGEMENTS. Overwhelmingly, older adults in Western industrialized nations want to stay in their own homes and neighborhoods where they spent their adult lives, and the large majority (88 percent) do so. In the United States, fewer than 5 percent relocate to other communities. These moves are usually motivated by a desire to live closer to children or, among more economically advantaged and healthy elders, a desire for a more temperate climate and a place to satisfy leisure interests.

Most elder relocations occur within the same town or city; are prompted by declining health, widowhood, or disability; and increase with age (U.S. Department of Health and Human Services, 1999c). As we look at housing arrangements for the elderly, we will see that the more a setting deviates from home life, the harder it is for elders to adjust.

Ordinary Homes. For the majority of elders, who are not physically impaired, staying in their own homes af-

More elders in Australia, Canada, the United States, and Western Europe live on their own today than ever before—a trend resulting from improved health and economic well-being. (Photo courtesy: Catherine Karnow/Woodfin Camp & Associates)

fords the greatest possible personal control—freedom to arrange space and schedule daily events as one chooses. More elders in Australia, Canada, the United States, and Western Europe live on their own today than ever before —a trend due to improved health and economic well-being (Glaser, 1997). But when health and mobility problems appear, independent living poses risks. Most homes are designed for younger people. They are seldom modified to suit the physical capacities of their elder residents (Parmelee & Lawton, 1990).

When Ruth reached her mid-eighties, Sybil begged her to move into her home. Like many adult children of Southern, Central, and Eastern European descent (Greek, Italian, Polish, and others), Sybil felt an especially strong obligation to care for her frail mother. Older adults of these cultural backgrounds, as well as African Americans, Asian Americans, Hispanics, and Native Americans, more often live in extended families (Angel et al., 1996; Clarke & Neidert, 1992; Kamo & Zhou, 1994; Worobey & Angel, 1990).

Yet increasing numbers of ethnic minority elders want to live on their own, but poverty often prevents them from doing so. For example, two decades ago, 75 percent of Korean-American older adults were living with their children, whereas today just over 50 percent are (Yoo & Sung, 1997). With sufficient income to keep her home, Ruth refused to move in with Sybil. Why do many elders react this way, even after health problems accumulate? Usually they are deeply attached to their homes as sites of memorable life events. They also value their independence, privacy, and network of nearby friends and neighbors (Fogel, 1992). Over the past half century, the number of unmarried, divorced, and widowed elders living alone has risen dramatically. Currently, one-third of older Americans live by themselves, a figure that rises to 47 percent for those age 85 and older. This trend is evident in all segments of the elderly population. However, it is not as pronounced for men, who are far more likely than women to be living with a spouse into advanced old age (U.S. Bureau of the Census, 1999).

Over 40 percent of American elders who live alone are poverty stricken—a rate five times greater than that of elderly couples. The large majority are widowed women. Although they draw on informal social supports as best they can, many have unmet needs. Some arrive at old age poor, whereas others become poor for the first time, often because they have outlived a spouse who suffered a lengthy, costly illness. With age, their financial status worsens as their assets shrink and their own health care costs rise. Under these conditions, isolation, loneliness, and depression can pile up.

As Figure 18.2 shows, elderly women living alone in other Western industrialized nations are spared these dire outcomes because of more generous government-sponsored income and health benefits (Hardy & Hazelrigg, 1993). In the United States, feminization of poverty deepens in old age.

FIGURE 18.2

Percentage of 65- to 74-year-old men and women living alone and earning less than 50 percent of the country's median income in six industrialized nations, based on the most recent available data. Although this criterion is actually above the U.S. poverty line, it marks a very low income and serves as an effective basis of comparison. Not only are the U.S. low-income rates much higher, but the U.S. gender gap is much larger. Because of less generous government-sponsored income and health benefits, elderly women living alone in the United States often suffer from poverty. (Adapted from Hardy & Hazelrigg, 1993.)

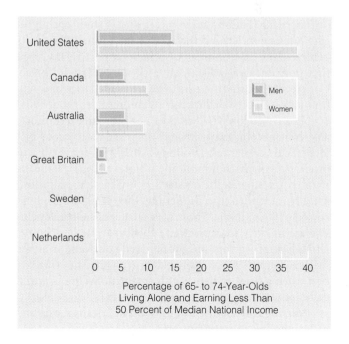

Percentage of 65- to 74-Year-Olds Living Alone and Earning Less Than 50 Percent of Median National Income

Residential Communities. About 8 percent of American senior citizens live in residential communities, which come in great variety (Pynoos & Golant, 1996). Housing developments for the aged, either single-dwelling or apartment complexes, differ from ordinary homes only in that they have been modified to suit elders' capacities (for example, single-level living space and grab bars in bathrooms). Some are federally subsidized units for the elderly poor, but most are privately developed retirement villages with adjoining recreational facilities. For elders who desire more assistance with daily living, **congregate housing** adds a variety of support services, including meals in a common dining room. Finally, **life care communities** offer a range of options, from independent or congregate housing to full nursing home care. For a large initial payment and additional monthly fees, life care guarantees that elders' needs will be met in one place as they age.

Unlike Ruth and Walt, who remained in their own home, Dick and Goldie entered congregate housing in their late sixties. For Dick, the move was a positive turn of events that permitted him to relate to peers on the basis of their current life together, setting aside past failures in the outside world. Dick found gratifying leisure pursuits—leading an exercise class, organizing a charity drive with Goldie, and using his skills as a baker to make cakes for birthday and anniversary celebrations.

Studies of diverse residential communities for the aged reveal that they can have positive effects on physical and mental health. A specially designed physical space helps elders overcome mobility limitations, thereby permitting greater social participation. And in societies in which old age leads to reduced status, age-segregated living is gratifying to most elders who choose it. It may open up useful roles and leadership opportunities, which result in a more vigorous social life (Holmes & Holmes, 1995). A study of congregate housing in Israel revealed that the more older adults perceived the environment as socially supportive, the more they provided assistance to other residents (Litwin, 1998). Congregate housing appears to be well suited to promoting mutually supportive relationships among elder residents.

Yet a collection of elders does not guarantee a comfortable, content community. Shared values and goals among residents with similar backgrounds, a small enough facility to promote frequent communication, and availability of meaningful roles enhance life satisfaction. When older adults feel socially integrated into the setting, they are more likely to consider it their home. Those who remain distant and reclusive are unlikely to characterize their apartment as home, citing lack of warmth and likeminded companions as the reason (Young, 1998). Finally, elders in planned housing fare best when a good fit between their functional abilities and environmental supports exists (Lawton, 1999).

Nursing Homes. The 5 percent of Americans age 65 and older who live in nursing homes experience the most extreme restriction of autonomy. As noted in Chapter 17, sense of personal control and social relationships are as vital for the mental health of nursing home residents as they are for community-dwelling elders.

Potential social partners are abundant in nursing homes, but interaction is low. To regulate emotion in social interaction (so important to elders), personal control over social experiences is vital. Yet nursing home residents have little opportunity to choose their social partners, and timing of contact is generally determined by the nursing-home staff rather than by elders' preferences. Social withdrawal is an adaptive response to these overcrowded, hospital-like settings (Carstensen, 1992). Interaction with people in the outside world predicts nursing home residents' life satisfaction; interaction within the institution does not (Baltes, Wahl, & Reichert, 1992).

Designing nursing homes to be more homelike could do much to increase residents' sense of security and control over their social experiences. Over the past decade, the number of nursing homes in the United States has decreased by nearly 13 percent, whereas the number of beds in these facilities has increased by 9 percent, largely because most are operated for profit. American nursing homes have become increasingly packed with residents and institutional in their operation (Strahan, 1997).

In contrast, European facilities are liberally supported by public funds. Residents live in private suites or small apartments furnished in part with their own belongings. Specially adapted parks and gardens draw residents away from passive activities, such as TV viewing, into outdoor communal spaces. When an elder's condition worsens, caregivers modify the existing space rather than move the individual to more medically oriented quarters (Horgas, Wilms, & Baltes, 1998; Schwarz, 1996). In this way, they preserve the person's identity, sense of place, and social relationships as best as possible. Because of high costs and stringent government regulations, efforts to modify American nursing homes in these ways have not met with much success.

ASK YOURSELF . . .

Sam lives by himself in the same home he has occupied for over 30 years. His adult children can't understand why he won't move across town to a modern apartment, which would be easier to care for than his old, dilapidated house. Cite as many possible reasons you can think of that Sam prefers to stay where he is.

Vera, a nursing home resident, speaks to her adult children and a close friend on the phone every day. In contrast, she seldom attends scheduled social events or interacts with the woman who shares her semiprivate room. Using socioemotional selectivity theory, explain Vera's behavior.

RELATIONSHIPS IN LATE ADULTHOOD

The **social convoy** is an influential model of changes in our social networks as we move through life. Picture yourself in the midst of a cluster of ships traveling together, granting one another safety and support. Ships in the inner circle represent people closest to you, such as a spouse, best friend, parent, or child. Those less close but still important travel on the outside. With age, ships exchange places in the convoy, and some drift off while others join the procession (Antonucci, 1990). But as long as the convoy continues to exist, you adapt positively.

In the following sections, we examine the ways elders with diverse lifestyles sustain social networks of family members and friends. We will see that as ties are lost, elders draw others closer and even add replacements, although not at the rate they did at younger ages. Tragically, for some older adults the social convoy breaks down. We will explore the circumstances in which elders experience abuse and neglect at the hands of those close to them.

MARRIAGE

Even with the high divorce rate, 1 in every 5 first marriages in the United States is expected to survive for at least 50 years. Walt's comment to Ruth that "the last few decades have been the happiest" characterizes the attitudes and behaviors of many elderly couples who have spent their adult lives together. Marital satisfaction rises from middle to late adulthood, when it is at its peak (Brubaker, 1985; Condie, 1989; Levenson, Carstensen, & Gottman, 1993). Several changes in life circumstance and couples' communication underlie this trend.

First, perceptions of fairness in the relationship increase as men participate more in household tasks after retirement. In today's elders, who experienced little social pressure for gender equality in their youth, division of labor in the home still reflects traditional roles. Men take on more home maintenance projects, whereas women's duties continue as before. Nevertheless, men's involvement in caring for the home results in a greater sense of equity in marriage than before (Condie, 1989; Vinick & Ekerdt, 1991).

Second, with extra time together, the majority of couples engage in more joint leisure activities. Ruth and Walt walked, worked in the garden, played golf, and took frequent day trips. In interviews with a diverse sample of retired couples, women often stated that more time with their husbands enhanced marital closeness (Vinick & Ekerdt, 1991).

Finally, greater emotional understanding and emphasis on regulating emotion in relationships lead to more positive interactions. Couples married for at least 35 years resolve conflicts in ways that are less negative and more affectionate than do middle-aged couples. Even in unhappy marriages,

elders are less likely to let disagreements escalate into expressions of anger and resentment (Carstensen, Gottman, & Levenson, 1995; Carstensen, Isaacowitz, & Charles, 1999). For example, when Dick complained about Goldie's cooking, Goldie tried to appease him: "All right, Dick, next birthday I won't make cheesecake." And when Goldie brought up Dick's bickering and criticism, Dick usually said, "I know, dear," and retreated to another room. As in other relationships, the elderly protect themselves from stress by molding marital ties to make them as pleasant as possible.

When marital dissatisfaction is present, it continues to take a greater toll on women than on men. Recall from Chapter 14 that women tend to confront marital problems and try to solve them. In old age, the energy expended is especially taxing on their physical and mental health. Husbands, in contrast, often protect themselves by withdrawing, as they did when they were in their twenties and thirties (Levensen, Carstensen, & Gottman, 1993).

DIVORCE AND REMARRIAGE

When Walt's uncle Louie was 61, he divorced his wife, Sandra, to whom he had been married for 17 years. Although she knew the marriage was far from perfect, Sandra had lived with Louie long enough that the divorce came as a shock. A year later, Louie married Rachella, a divorcée who shared his enthusiasm for sports and dance.

Couples who divorce in late adulthood constitute a very small proportion of all divorces in any given year—about 1 percent in the United States. But the divorce rate among people age 65 and older has increased as new generations of elders become more accepting of marital breakup and as the divorce risk rises for second and subsequent marriages (U. S. Bureau of the Census, 1999). When asked about the reasons for divorce, elderly men typically mention lack of shared interests and activities, whereas women frequently refer to their partner's refusal to communicate and emotional distance. "We never talked. I felt isolated," Sandra said (Weingarten, 1988).

Recall from Chapter 16 that the stress of divorce increases in midlife, a trend that continues into old age. The long-time married have given their adult lives to the relationship. Consequently, they find it harder to separate their identity from that of their former spouse, and they suffer more from a sense of personal failure. Relationships with family and friends shift at a time when close bonds are crucial for psychological well-being. Finally, women suffer most from late-life divorce because they are more likely than men to spend their remaining years living alone. The financial consequences are severe—greater than for widowhood because many accumulated assets are lost in property settlements (Miller, Hemesath, & Nelson, 1997).

In younger individuals, divorce often leads to greater awareness of and resolve to change negative patterns of behavior. In contrast, self-criticism in divorced elders heightens guilt and depression because their self-worth depends more on past than on future accomplishments. Louie and Sandra blamed each other. "I was always miserable with Sandra," Louie claimed, even though the couple's earlier days had been reasonably happy. Blaming the partner and believing oneself to have acted in the only way possible may distort the marital history, but it is a frequent coping strategy that enables older adults to preserve integrity and self-esteem (Weingarten, 1989).

Remarriage rates are low in late adulthood and decline with age, although they are considerably higher among divorced than widowed elders. Older men's opportunities for remarriage are far greater than women's. Nevertheless, the gender gap in elder remarriage is much smaller after divorce than after widowhood (see Figure 18.3). Perhaps divorcées find it easier than widows to enter a new relationship because their previous one was disappointing. Also, compared with widows, divorced older women may be highly motivated to remarry because of their more extreme economic circumstances. Finally, some divorced elders (like Louie and Rachella) leave their marriages only after a new bond is under way (Huyck, 1995).

Compared with their younger counterparts, remarried elders enter more stable relationships, as their divorce rate is much lower. In Louie and Rachella's case, the second marriage lasted for 32 years! Perhaps late-life marriages are more successful because they involve a better balance of romantic with practical concerns. Older couples who remarry are very satisfied with their new relationships, although men continue to be more content than women (Brubaker, 1985). With fewer potential mates, perhaps women who remarry in late life must settle for less desirable partners.

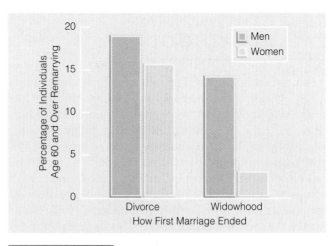

FIGURE 18.3

■ **Rates of remarriage after divorce and widowhood among men and women age 65 and older in the United States.** More divorced than widowed elders remarry. In addition, the gender gap in remarriage is much smaller after divorce than after widowhood. (U.S. Bureau of the Census, 1999.)

WIDOWHOOD

Walt died shortly after Ruth turned 80. Like over 70 percent of widowed elders, Ruth described the loss of her spouse as the most stressful event of her life (Lund, Caserta, & Dimond, 1993). She felt lonely, anxious, and depressed for several months after the funeral.

Widows make up 33 percent of the elderly population in the United States. Because women live longer than men and are less likely to remarry, nearly 50 percent of women age 65 and older are widowed, whereas only 15 percent of men are. African Americans, Hispanics, and other ethnic minorities with higher rates of poverty and chronic disease are more likely to be widowed (U.S. Bureau of the Census, 1999).

Earlier we mentioned that most widows and widowers live alone rather than in extended families, a trend that is stronger for whites than ethnic minorities. Although they are less well off financially than married elders, most want to retain control over their time and living space and avoid disagreements with their adult children. When widowed elders relocate because they cannot make mortgage payments or keep up their homes, they usually move closer to family rather than into the same residence (Lopata, 1996; O'Bryant & Hansson, 1995).

Although loss of a spouse is felt very deeply, wide variation in adaptation exists. Age, social support, and personality make a difference. Elders have fewer lasting problems than do younger individuals, probably because death in later life is expected and viewed as less unfair (Stroebe & Stroebe,

■ *Remarriage rates are low in late adulthood and decline with age, although they are considerably higher among divorced than widowed elders. Older men's opportunities to remarry are considerably greater than women's. (Photo courtesy: Joel Gordon)*

1993). In-laws and former couple friends often withdraw from the widowed person's support system. After Walt died, Ruth saw less of Dick and Goldie. But adult children usually step in, as Sybil did for Ruth. Widowed elders with daughters tend to receive more social support than do those with sons (Horowitz, 1985; O'Bryant, 1988a). Although loneliness is a problem, most widowed elders are not socially isolated. Many, especially those with outgoing, assertive personalities, compensate by increasing contacts with friends and neighbors. And some relish their solitude!

Widowed individuals must reorganize their lives, reconstructing an identity that is separate from the deceased spouse. The task is harder for wives whose roles depended on their husbands' than for those who developed rewarding roles of their own. But overall, men find it more difficult to adjust to widowhood (Lee, Willetts, & Seccombe, 1998). Most relied on their wives for social connectedness and essential household tasks. They mention these areas as major sources of strain and depression. Women point to financial worries as their greatest ongoing concern (Umberson, Wortman, & Kessler, 1992).

Sex differences in the experience of widowhood contribute to men's higher remarriage rate. Women's kinkeeper role (see Chapter 16, page 536) and ability to form close friendships may lead them to feel less need to remarry. In addition, because many elderly women share the widowed state, they probably offer one another helpful advice and sympathy. In contrast, men often lack skills for maintaining family relationships, forming emotionally satisfying ties outside marriage, and handling the chores of their deceased wives.

■ *These elderly women share the experience of widowhood and offer one another companionship, social support, helpful advice, and sympathy. In contrast, men often lack skills for maintaining family relationships and forming emotionally satisfying ties outside marriage. (Photo courtesy: Elizabeth Holmes/Omni-Photo Communications)*

Although widowhood affects lifestyle, in the long run most widowed elders in Western nations fare well. When followed up after several years, they do not differ from their married counterparts in psychological well-being or mortality (McCrae & Costa, 1988; Morycz, 1992). Once again, the elderly display a remarkable ability to cope with traumatic life events. The Caregiving Concerns table below suggests a variety of ways to foster adaptation to loss of a spouse in old age.

CAREGIVING CONCERNS

Fostering Adaptation to Widowhood in Late Adulthood

SUGGESTION	DESCRIPTION
FAMILY AND FRIENDS	
Social support and interaction	Social support and interaction need to extend beyond the grieving period to ongoing assistance and caring relationships. Family members and friends can be of most help by making support available while encouraging the widowed elder to develop skills to cope independently.
COMMUNITY	
Senior centers	About 5,000 senior centers in communities around the United States offer communal meals and other social activities, enabling widowed and other elders to connect with people in similar circumstances and to access other community resources, such as listings of part-time employment and available housing.
Support groups	Special support groups can be found in senior citizens centers, churches, and other agencies. Besides new relationships, they offer an accepting atmosphere for coming to terms with loss, effective role modeling, and assistance with developing skills for daily living.
Religious activities	Involvement in church, synagogue, or mosque can help relieve the loneliness associated with loss of a spouse and offer social support, new relationships, and meaningful roles.
Volunteer activities	One of the best ways widowed elders can find meaningful roles is through volunteer activities. Some are sponsored by formal service organizations, such as the American Red Cross or the Retired and Senior Volunteer Program. Other volunteer programs exist in hospitals, senior centers, schools, and charitable organizations.

Sources: Lopata, 1996; O'Bryant & Hansson, 1995.

NEVER-MARRIED, CHILDLESS OLDER ADULTS

Shortly after Ruth and Walt's marriage in their twenties, Ruth's father died. Her sister Ida continued to live with and care for their mother, who was in ill health until she died 16 years later. When, at age 25, Ida received a marriage proposal, she responded, "I can't marry anybody while my mother lives. I'm expected to look after her." Ida's decision was not unusual for a daughter of her day. She never married or had children.

About 5 percent of older Americans remain unmarried and childless throughout their lives. Almost all are conscious of being different from the norm, but most have developed alternative meaningful relationships. Ida, for example, formed a strong bond with a neighbor's son. In his childhood, she provided emotional support and financial assistance, which helped him overcome a stressful home life. He included Ida in all significant family events and visited her regularly until she died. Other nonmarried elders also speak of the centrality of younger people—often nieces and nephews—in their social networks and of influencing them in enduring ways (Rubinstein et al., 1991). In addition, same-sex friendships are key in never-married elderly women's lives. These tend to be unusually close and often involve joint travel, periods of co-residence, and associations with one another's extended families.

Never-married elderly women report a level of life satisfaction equivalent to that of married elders and greater than that of divorcées and recently widowed elders. Only when they agree with the widespread belief that "life is empty without a partner" or cannot maintain personal contacts due to declining health do they report feeling lonely (Dykstra, 1995; Rubinstein, 1987). These single women often state that they avoided many problems associated with being a wife and mother, and they view their enhanced friendships as an advantage of not marrying. At the same time, they realize that friendships are not the same as blood ties when it comes to caregiving in old age.

Still, most unmarried childless elders say that support is available from both friends and family members (Choi, 1996; Wu & Pollard, 1998). Never-married elders are also more likely than other elders to have siblings, other relatives, and nonrelatives living in their households (Stull & Scarisbrick-Hauser, 1989). Although little is known about never-married men, reaching old age without having married is clearly not the same as being alone and forsaken!

SIBLINGS

Nearly 80 percent of Americans over age 60 have at least one living sibling. Most elder siblings live within 100 miles of each other, communicate regularly, and visit each other at least several times a year. In one study, 77 percent of a sample of Canadian elders considered at least one sibling to be a close friend (Connidis, 1989). Both men and women perceive bonds with sisters to be closer than bonds with brothers. Perhaps because of women's greater emotional expressiveness and nurturance, the closer the tie to a sister, the higher elders' psychological well-being (Cicerelli, 1989; O'Bryant, 1988b).

Elderly siblings in industrialized nations are more likely to socialize than provide each other with direct assistance, as most older adults turn to their spouse and children before they turn to their siblings. Nevertheless, siblings seem to be an important "insurance policy" in late adulthood. Most elders say they would turn to a sibling for help in a crisis, less often in other situations (Connidis, 1994). Widowed and never-married elders have more contacts with siblings, perhaps due to stronger feelings of obligation, since they have fewer competing family relationships. They are also more likely to receive sibling support during illness (Connidis & Campbell, 1995). For example, when Ida's Alzheimer's symptoms worsened, Ruth came to her aid. Although Ida had many friends, Ruth was her only living biological relative.

Because siblings share a long and unique history, joint reminiscing about earlier times increases in late adulthood (Cicerelli, 1995). Walt and Dick often talked about their boyhood days, evoking the warmth of early family life. These discussions helped them appreciate the lifelong significance of the sibling bond and contributed to a sense of family harmony—important aspects of ego integrity.

FRIENDSHIPS

As family responsibilities and vocational pressures lessen in late adulthood, friendships take on increasing importance. Having friends is an especially strong predictor of mental health among the elderly (Blieszner & Adams, 1992; Nussbaum, 1994). In one study, retired adults were paged at random intervals and asked to write down what they were doing, whom they were with, and how they felt (much like the adolescents described on page 356 of Chapter 11). They reported more favorable experiences with friends than with family members, a difference partly due to the many pleasurable leisure activities shared with friends. But unique qualities of friendship interaction—openness, spontaneity, mutual caring, and common interests—seemed especially influential (Larson, Mannell, & Zuzanek, 1986).

■ FUNCTIONS OF ELDER FRIENDSHIPS. The diverse functions of friendship in late adulthood clarify its profound significance:

■ *Intimacy and companionship are basic to meaningful elder friendships.* As Ida and her best friend Rosie took walks, went shopping, or just visited each other, the two women disclosed their deepest sources of happiness and worry. They also engaged in pleasurable conversation, laughed, and had fun (Crohan & Antonucci, 1989). When elders are asked to describe qualities of their close friendships, their responses reveal that mutual interests, feelings of belongingness, and opportunities to express feelings and confide in another sustain these bonds over time (Field, 1999).

■ *Elderly women mention acceptance as a primary aspect of close friendship.* Late-life friends shield one another from others' negative judgments about their capabilities and worth as a person, which frequently stem from stereotypes of aging (Adams, 1985–1986). "Where's your cane, Rosie?" Ida asked when the two women were about to leave for a restaurant. "Come on, don't be self-conscious. When y'get one of those 'you're finished' looks from someone, just remember: In the Greek village where my mother grew up, there was no separation between generations, so the young ones got used to wrinkled skin and weak knees and recognized older women as the wise ones. Why, they were midwives, matchmakers, experts in herbal medicine; they knew about everything!" (Deveson, 1994).

■ *Friendships link elderly people to the larger community.* For elders who cannot go out as often, interactions between friends can keep them abreast of events in the wider world (Peterson, 1989). "Rosie," Ida reported,

■ *Friendships link elderly people to the larger community. When elders cannot go out as often, interactions between friends can keep them abreast of events in the wider world. (Photo courtesy: Bob Daemmrich/The Image Works)*

"did you know that the Thompson girl was named high school valedictorian. . . and the business community is putting its support behind Jesse for mayor." Friends can also open up new experiences that older adults might not take part in alone. Often a first trip to a senior citizens' center takes place within the context of friendship (Nussbaum, 1994).

■ *Friendships can help protect elders from the psychological consequences of loss.* Older adults in declining health who remain in contact with friends through phone calls and visits show improved psychological well-being. Similarly, when close relatives die, friends offer compensating social supports (Newsom & Schulz, 1996; Nussbaum, 1994).

■ CHARACTERISTICS OF ELDER FRIENDSHIPS. Although older adults prefer familiar, established relationships over new ones, friendship formation continues throughout life. Ties to old and dear friends who live far away are maintained, but practical restrictions promote more frequent interaction with friends in the immediate environment. With age, elders report that the friends they feel closest to are fewer in number and live in the same community. Nevertheless, close elder friendships are not affected by patterns of daily life, such as participation in social groups or volunteerism (Dugan & Kivett, 1998). Many elders find ways to sustain links with friends, even after declining health restricts their mobility.

As in earlier years, elders tend to choose friends whose age, sex, race, ethnicity, and values are like their own. However, as age peers die, the very old report more intergenerational friendships (Johnson & Troll, 1994). In her eighties, Ruth spent time with Margaret, a 55-year-old widow she met while serving on the board of directors of an adoption agency. Two or three times a month, Margaret came to Ruth's home for tea and several hours of lively conversation.

Sex differences in friendship, discussed in previous chapters, extend into late adulthood. Women are more likely to have intimate friends; men depend on their wives and, to a lesser extent, their sisters for warm, open communication. Also, older women have more **secondary friends**—people who are not intimates but with whom they spend time occasionally, such as a group that meets for lunch, bridge, or museum tours. Through these associates, elders meet new people, remain socially involved, and gain in psychological well-being (Gupta & Korte, 1994).

In elder friendships, affection and emotional support are both given and received to maintain a healthy balance in the relationship (Ikkink & Van Tilburg, 1998). Although friends call on each other for help with tasks of daily living, they generally do so only in emergencies or for occasional, limited assistance. As elders avoid excessive dependency on friends, they register their own autonomy.

RELATIONSHIPS WITH ADULT CHILDREN

About 80 percent of ever-married older adults in the United States are parents of living children, most of whom are middle aged. In Chapter 16, we noted that exchanges of help vary with the closeness of the parent–child bond and the parent and adult child's needs. Recall, also, that over time, parent-to-child help declines, whereas child-to-parent assistance increases. Elders and their adult children are often in touch, even when they live far from each other. Nevertheless, as with other ties, quality rather than quantity of these interactions affects older adults' life satisfaction. As people grow older, children usually continue to provide rich rewards, including love, companionship, and stimulation. These warm bonds reduce the negative impact of physical impairments and other losses (such as death of a spouse) on psychological well-being. Alternatively, conflict or unhappiness with adult children contributes to poor physical and mental health (Peterson, 1989; Silverstein & Bengtson, 1991).

Although aging parents and adult children in the United States provide each other with various forms of help, the level of assistance is typically modest. In interviews with a nationally representative sample, elders reported that exchanges of advice were most common. Fewer than one-fifth said their children had assisted with household tasks and transportation within the past month. To avoid dependency, older parents expect more emotional support than practical assistance and usually do not seek help from children in the absence of pressing need (Eggebeen, 1992). Moderate support, with opportunities to reciprocate, is psychologically beneficial to elders. Extensive support that cannot be returned is linked to poor psychological well-being (Davey & Eggebeen, 1998; Silverstein, Chen, & Heller, 1996).

Sex differences in older parent–adult child interaction are evident. As kinkeepers, adult daughters are primary agents of their aging parents' family contacts, telephoning, writing letters, and arranging visits more often than do sons. Mother–daughter ties are particularly warm (Choi, 1995; Suitor et al., 1995). In a study of African-American elders, men (especially those living alone) experienced substantially fewer phone calls and visits from their adult children than did women (Spitze & Miner, 1992). Perhaps the high rate of African-American father-absent homes weakens fathers' relationships with their adult children many years later. People of diverse ages indicate that closeness of the parent–child tie affects their sense of obligation to assist an aging parent who had not resided with them for much of their childhood (Ganong & Coleman, 1998). As large numbers of divorced, noncustodial fathers reach late adulthood in the next few decades, the number of elderly men with limited family contact may increase (Cooney & Uhlenberg, 1990).

As social networks shrink in size, relationships with adult children become more important sources of family involvement. Elders 85 years and older with children have substantially more contacts with relatives than do those without children (Johnson & Troll, 1992). Why is this so? Consider Ruth, whose daughter, Sybil, linked her to grandchildren, great-grandchildren, and relatives by marriage. When childless elders reach their eighties, siblings, other same-age relatives, and close friends may have become frail or died and no longer be available as companions.

RELATIONSHIPS WITH ADULT GRANDCHILDREN AND GREAT-GRANDCHILDREN

Older adults with adult grandchildren and great-grandchildren benefit from a wider potential network of support. Ruth and Walt saw their granddaughter, Marci, and great-grandson, Jamel, at family gatherings. At other times, Marci telephoned, visited, and sent greeting cards, expressing deep affection for her aging grandparents.

In developed nations, slightly more than half of elders over age 65 have a grandchild who is at least 18 years old (Farkas & Hogan, 1994). In the few studies available on grandparent–adult grandchild relationships, the overwhelming majority of grandchildren felt obligated to assist grandparents in need. Grandparents expected affection (but not practical help) from grandchildren, and in most cases they received it. They regarded the adult grandchild tie as very gratifying and as a vital link between themselves and the future (Langer, 1990).

Still, grandparent–adult grandchild relationships vary greatly. Often the tie with one grandchild is "special,"

■ *Grandparents' affection for their adult grandchildren strengthens with age, even though contact declines as grandchildren establish distant homes and become immersed in work and family roles. Grandchildren seem to become increasingly important sources of emotional meaning for elders in the last decade or two of life. (Photo courtesy: Ron Chapple)*

characterized by more frequent contact, mutual expressions of affection, and enjoyable times together—factors that enhance elders' psychological well-being (Fingerman, 1998). However, longitudinal research reveals that as grandparents and grandchildren move through life, contact declines. Many grandchildren establish distant homes and become immersed in work and family roles that compete for time with extended-family members. But despite less contact, grandparents' affection for their adult grandchildren strengthens with age (Silverstein & Long, 1998). Even in ethnic minority families in which young adults have given up traditional beliefs and practices, grandparents typically say their relations with their grandchildren are close (Silverstein & Chen, 1999). Grandchildren seem to become increasingly important sources of emotional meaning for elders in the last decade or two of life.

About 40 percent of older adults have great-grandchildren. Most describe their new role as limited and a sign of advancing age. Nevertheless, they welcome it with enthusiasm, commenting that it reaffirms the continuance of their families. Parents mediate great-grandchild contact, just as they did contact with young grandchildren (see Chapter 16). Relationships are often closer on the maternal side, especially through daughters and granddaughters (Doka & Mertz, 1988).

ELDER MALTREATMENT

Although the majority of older adults enjoy positive relationships with family members, friends, and professional caregivers, some suffer maltreatment at the hands of these individuals. Recent media attention has led elder maltreatment to become a serious public concern in Western nations.

Estimates indicate that about 1.5 million American adults age 65 and older are mistreated by people closest to them each year (Baron & Welty, 1996). Reports from Australia, Canada, Finland, Great Britain, the Netherlands, and the United States reveal surprisingly similar rates of maltreatment—about 3 to 7 percent of all elders (Comijs et al., 1998; Kingston & Reay, 1996). Elder maltreatment crosses ethnic lines, although it is lower in Asian-, Hispanic-, and Native-American groups with strong traditions of respect for and obligation to the aged (Rittman, Kuzmeskus, & Flum, 2000). Yet all figures underestimate the actual incidence, since most acts take place in private and victims are often unable or unwilling to complain.

Elder maltreatment takes the following forms:

- *Physical abuse*—intentional infliction of pain, discomfort, or injury, through hitting, cutting, burning, physical force, restraint, sexual assault, and other acts.

- *Physical neglect*—intentional or unintentional failure to fulfill caregiving obligations, which results in lack of food, medication, or health services or in the elderly person being left alone or isolated.

- *Psychological abuse*—verbal assaults (such as name calling), humiliation (being treated as a child), and intimidation (threats of isolation or placement in a nursing home).

- *Financial abuse*—illegal or improper exploitation of the elder's property or financial resources, through theft or use without the elder's consent.

Although these four types are widely recognized, a common definition of elder maltreatment does not exist. Like child maltreatment (see Chapter 8, page 270), an agreed-on definition is vital for finding out why elder maltreatment occurs and preventing it. A person with multiple bruises and head injuries has surely been abused, but maltreatment is harder to detect in other circumstances. For example, when a frail elder is left alone, how much time must elapse to constitute neglect? And when a relative demands that an elder give back a treasured gift received years earlier and the elder complies in fear of an angry outburst, has financial abuse occurred?

Reported cases suggest that financial abuse is the most common form, followed by psychological abuse and neglect. Often several types occur in combination (Neale et al., 1996; Peake, Oelschlager, & Kearns, 2000). The perpetrator is usually a person the older adult loves, trusts, and depends on for care and assistance. Most are spouses (usually men), followed by children of both sexes, then other relatives, friends, neighbors, and paid caregivers (Hornick, McDonald, & Robertson, 1992; Pillemer & Finkelhor, 1988).

■ RISK FACTORS. Characteristics of the victim, the abuser, their relationship, and its social context are related to the incidence and severity of elder maltreatment. The more of the following risk factors that are present, the greater the likelihood that abuse and neglect will occur.

Dependency of the Victim. Very old, frail, and mentally and physically impaired elders are more vulnerable to maltreatment. This does not mean that physical declines cause abuse, since most older adults with disabilities do not experience it. Rather, when other conditions are ripe for maltreatment, elders with severe disabilities are least able to protect themselves (Lachs et al., 1997). Those with physical or cognitive impairments may also have personality traits that make them vulnerable to abuse—a tendency to lash out when angry or frustrated, a passive or avoidant approach to handling problems, and a low sense of self-efficacy (Comijs et al., 1999).

Dependency of the Perpetrator. Many abusers are dependent, emotionally or financially, on their victims. This dependency, experienced as powerlessness, can lead to aggressive, exploitative behavior. Often the perpetrator–victim relationship is one of mutual dependency. The abuser needs the older person for money or housing, and the older person needs the abuser for assistance with everyday tasks or to relieve loneliness (Kingston & Reay, 1996).

Psychological Disturbance and Stress of the Perpetrator.
Abusers are more likely than other caregivers to have psychological problems and to be dependent on alcohol or other drugs. Often they are socially isolated, have difficulties at work, or are unemployed, with resulting financial worries. These factors increase the likelihood that they will lash out when caregiving is highly demanding or the behavior of an elder with dementia is irritating or hard to manage.

History of Family Violence. Elder abuse is often part of a long history of family violence. In Chapter 8, we showed how aggressive cycles between family members can easily become self-sustaining, leading to the development of individuals who cope with anger through hostility toward others (Buttell, 1999). In many instances, elder abuse may simply be an extension of many years of spouse abuse (see Chapter 14, page 470).

Institutional Conditions. Elder maltreatment is more likely to occur in nursing homes that are run down and overcrowded and that have staff shortages, minimal staff supervision, high staff turnover, and few visitors (Glendenning, 1993). When highly stressful work conditions combine with minimal oversight of caregiving quality, the stage is set for abuse and neglect.

■ PREVENTING ELDER MALTREATMENT. Preventing elder maltreatment by family members is especially challenging. Once abuse or neglect is discovered, intervention must be negotiated with the perpetrator and the victim, neither of whom may desire help. Each must be convinced that assistance can improve their situation—treatment and social support aimed at reducing stress for the caregiver and protection and provision of unmet needs for the elder.

Prevention programs offer counseling and education for caregivers and respite (relief) services, such as elder day care and in-home help. Sometimes trained volunteer "buddies" make visits to the home to combat social isolation and assist elders with problem solving to avoid further harm. Support groups help seniors identify abusive acts, practice appropriate responses, and form new relationships. And agencies that provide informal financial services to older adults unable to manage on their own, such as writing and cashing checks and holding valuables in a safe, reduce financial abuse (Peake, Oelschlager, & Kearns, 2000; Reis & Nahmiash, 1995).

When elder abuse is extreme, legal action is the best way to shield elders from abusers, yet it seldom happens. Many victims are reluctant to initiate court procedures or, because of mental impairments, cannot do so (Griffiths, Roberts, & Williams, 1993). In these instances, social service professionals need to help caregivers rethink their role, even if it means the aging person might be institutionalized. In nursing homes, abuse and neglect can be prevented by improving staff selection, training, and working conditions.

Combating elder maltreatment also requires efforts at the level of the larger society. Public education to encourage reporting of suspected cases and improved understanding of the needs of older people is vital (Baron & Welty, 1996). Finally, countering negative stereotypes of aging reduces maltreatment, since recognition of elders' dignity, individuality, and autonomy is incompatible with acts of physical and psychological harm.

■ ASK YOURSELF . . .

Seventy-year-old Sean says his 40-year marriage to Caitlin is the happiest it's ever been. Caitlin agrees that she's more content than before, but she isn't quite as positive as Sean. What might account for Sean and Caitlin's high marital satisfaction and Sean's especially favorable response?

■ *Lottie, a never-married elder, lives by herself. Curt, a college student who just moved in next door, is certain Lottie must be very lonely. Why is Curt's assumption probably wrong?*

■ *Mae, who lost her job at age 51 and couldn't afford her own apartment, moved in with her 78-year-old widowed mother, Beryl, who was glad to have Mae's companionship. Mae grew depressed and spent her days watching TV and drinking heavily. Although Beryl tried to be patient, she complained about Mae's failure to look for work. Mae became belligerent, pushed her mother against the wall, and slapped her. Explain why this mother–daughter relationship led to elder abuse.*

RETIREMENT AND LEISURE

In Chapter 16, we noted that the period of retirement has lengthened due to increased life expectancy and a steady decline in average age of retirement—trends occurring in all Western industrialized nations. These changes have also led to a blurring of the distinction between work and retirement. Because mandatory retirement no longer exists for most workers in Western countries, older adults have more choices about when to retire and how they spend their time. The retirement process may include a planning period that may last for years, the decision itself, diverse acts of retiring, and continuous adjustment and readjustment of one's activities for the rest of the life course (Atchley, 1988; Mutchler et al., 1997).

Some older adults retire gradually by cutting down their hours and responsibilities, taking part-time *bridge jobs* that serve as transitions between full-time career and retirement (Quinn & Kozy, 1996). Others give up their jobs but later return to full-time work both to support themselves because of limited financial resources and to introduce interest and challenge into the retirement years. Recent evidence indicates that almost one-third of American retirees re-enter the labor force, most within 1 year of initial retirement, although the likelihood of return declines with age (Hayward, Hardy, & Liu, 1994).

In the following sections, we examine factors that affect the decision to retire, happiness during the retirement years, and leisure pursuits. We will see that the process of retirement and retired life reflect an increasingly diverse retired population.

THE DECISION TO RETIRE

When Walt and Ruth retired, both had worked for enough years to be eligible for comfortable income-replacement benefits—Walt's through the government-sponsored Social Security program, Ruth's through a private pension plan. In addition, Walt and Ruth had planned for retirement (see Chapter 16, page 547) and decided when they would leave the work force. They wanted to retire early enough to pursue leisure activities while they were both in good health and could enjoy them together. In contrast, Walt's brother Dick was forced to retire as the operating costs of his bakery rose and his clientele dropped off. His wife Goldie kept her part-time job as a bookkeeper to help cover their living expenses.

Affordability of retirement is usually the first consideration in the decision to retire. Yet even in the face of some economic concerns, many preretirees favor letting go of a steady work life for alternative, personally meaningful work or leisure activities. As one retired automobile worker said, "I was working since I was 10 years old. I thought of all the years I've been working, and I wanted a rest." Exceptions to this favorable outlook are people like Dick—forced into retirement or anticipating serious financial difficulties (Bossé, Spiro, & Kressin, 1996).

Figure 18.4 summarizes personal and workplace factors in addition to income that influence the decision to retire. People in good health, for whom vocational life is central to self-esteem, and whose work environments are pleasant and stimulating are likely to keep on working. For these reasons, individuals in professional occupations usually retire later than those in blue-collar or clerical jobs (Moen, 1996). Self-employed elders also stay with their jobs longer, probably because they can flexibly adapt their working hours to changing needs. In contrast, people in declining health; who are engaged in routine, boring work; and who have compelling leisure interests often opt for retirement.

Societal factors also affect retirement decisions. When many younger, less costly workers are available to replace older workers, industries are likely to offer added incentives for people to retire, such as increments to pension plans and earlier benefits—a trend that has contributed to a rising number of retirements before age 62 in Western nations (Sterns & Gray, 1999). When concern increases about the burden on younger generations of a rising population of retirees, eligibility for retirement benefits may be postponed to a later age.

Retirement decisions vary with gender and ethnicity. On the average, women tend to retire earlier than men, largely because family events—husband's retirement or the need to care for an ill spouse or parent—play larger roles in their decisions (Quadagno & Hardy, 1996; Smith & Moen, 1998). However, women in or near poverty are an exception. Many find themselves without the financial resources to retire and must continue working into old age. This trend is especially pronounced among African-American women, who are more likely to have minimal retirement benefits and to be caring for other family members (Choi, 1994; Perkins, 1993).

In other Western nations, higher minimum pension benefits make retirement feasible for the economically dis-

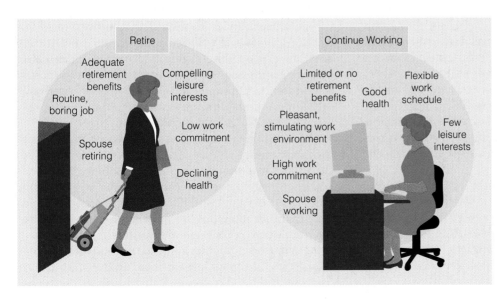

FIGURE 18.4

■ **Personal and workplace factors that influence the decision to retire.**

advantaged. In addition, some countries have retirement policies sensitive to women's more interrupted work lives. In Canada, France, and Germany, for example, time devoted to child rearing is given some credit when figuring retirement benefits (O'Grady-LeShane & Williamson, 1992).

In sum, individual preferences shape retirement decisions. At the same time, older adults' opportunities and limitations greatly affect their choices.

ADJUSTMENT TO RETIREMENT

Because retirement involves giving up roles that are a vital part of identity and self-esteem, it is often thought of as a stressful process that contributes to declines in physical and mental health. Yet consider Dick, who reacted to the closing of his bakery with anxiety and depression. His adjustment difficulties were not very different from those of younger people experiencing job loss (see Chapter 16, page 547). Also, recall that Dick had a cranky, disagreeable personality. In this respect, his psychological well-being after retirement was similar to what it had been before!

We must be careful not to assume a cause-and-effect relationship each time retirement and an unfavorable reaction are paired. For example, a wealth of evidence confirms that physical health problems lead elders to retire, rather than the reverse. And for most people, mental health is fairly stable from the pre- to postretirement years, with little change prompted by retirement itself (Bossé, Spiro, & Kressin, 1996).

The widely held belief that retirement inevitably leads to adjustment problems is contradicted by countless research findings indicating that most older adults adapt well. They describe themselves as active and socially involved—major determinants of retirement satisfaction. But the opposite view—that retirement never produces ill effects—is also wrong. When elders are asked about the stresses of retirement, about 30 percent mention some adjustment difficulties (Bossé et al., 1990).

Workplace factors—especially, having to give up one's job and financial worries—predict stress following retirement. In addition, pressures at work make a difference. Moving out of a high-stress job is associated with positive adaptation to retirement, whereas leaving a pleasant, low-stress job or a highly satisfying job is linked to slightly greater difficulties (Gray & Citera, 1996; Wheaton, 1990). And especially for women, a continuous worklife leading to consistency between career expectations and actual achievements enhances retirement quality (Quick & Moen, 1998).

Among psychological factors, people who find it hard to give up the predictable schedule and social contacts of the work setting often react negatively to their less structured way of life (Fletcher & Hansson, 1991). Also, control over the retirement decision—having engaged in substantial planning and retired for internally motivated reasons (to do

other things)—is linked to retirement satisfaction (Quick & Moen, 1998).

Social support reduces stress associated with retirement, just as it helps relieve the stress of other major life events. Although size of the social network typically shrinks as relationships with co-workers decline, quality of social support (number of people elders "can count on") remains fairly stable. In Dick's case, entering congregate housing eased a difficult postretirement period. It led to new friends and rewarding leisure pursuits, some of which he shared with Goldie. Besides friends, spouses are a vital source of support in fostering retirement adjustment. The number of leisure activities couples enjoy together predicts retirement satisfaction (Dorfman et al., 1988; Reeves & Darville, 1994).

Finally, earlier in this chapter we noted that marital happiness tends to rise after retirement. When a couple's relationship is generally positive, retirement can increase satisfaction by granting husband and wife more time for companionship (Myers & Booth, 1996). Consequently, a good marriage not only promotes adjustment to retirement, but benefits from the greater freedom of the retirement years. Return to Chapter 16, page 548, for ways adults can plan ahead to increase the chances of a favorable transition to retirement.

LEISURE ACTIVITIES

With retirement, most older adults have more time for leisure pursuits than ever before. After a "honeymoon period" of trying out new activities, many find that leisure interests and skills do not develop suddenly. Instead meaningful leisure pursuits are usually formed earlier and sustained or expanded during retirement (Cutler & Hendricks, 1990). For example, Walt's fondness for writing, theater, and gardening dated back to his youth. And Ruth's strong focus on her vocation of social work led her to become an avid community volunteer. The stability of leisure activities over the lifespan suggests that the best preparation for leisure in late life is to develop rewarding interests at a young age.

Involvement in leisure activities is positively related to elders' psychological well-being. But simply participating does not explain this relationship. Instead, elders select leisure pursuits because they permit self-expression, new achievements, the rewards of helping others, or pleasurable social interaction. These factors account for gains in well-being (Cutler & Hendricks, 1990; Guinn, 1999).

With age, frequency and variety of leisure pursuits decline, with travel, outdoor recreation, and exercise especially likely to drop off. After age 75, mobility limitations lead leisure activities to become more sedentary and home based (Kelly & Ross, 1989). Elders in residential communities participate more than do those in ordinary homes because activities are conveniently available. But regardless of living arrangements, older adults do not spend much time in programs designed just for them. Rather, they choose activities on the basis of whether they are personally gratifying. Partly for this reason, organized activities in community senior centers attract only about 15 percent of elders who live nearby (Krout, Cutler, & Coward, 1990). Nevertheless, these structured opportunities are important for elders with limited incomes and for those who lack daily companionship.

Older adults make a vital contribution to society through volunteer work—in hospitals, senior centers, schools, charitable organizations, and other community settings. Younger, better educated, and financially secure elders with social interests are more likely to volunteer, and women do so more often than men. Volunteering also varies with ethnicity. African Americans are more likely to assist others informally, often through their church. In Native American communities, providing food and lodging to older people is common (Hooyman & Kiyak, 1993). However, volunteer work is seldom begun in late adulthood. Like other leisure pursuits, it originates earlier, usually during the individual's working years. Nevertheless, nonvolunteers are especially receptive to volunteer activities in the first 2 years after retiring—a prime time to recruit them into these personally rewarding and socially useful pursuits (Caro & Bass, 1997).

Finally, when Walt and Ruth got together with Dick and Goldie, the two couples could often be heard discussing politics. Older adults report greater awareness of and interest in public affairs and vote at a higher rate than any age group. And their political knowledge shows no sign of decline, even in late old age. Why is this so? After retiring, elders have more time to read and watch TV, through which they keep abreast of current events. They also have a major stake in politics as debate, sparked by intergenerational inequity, continues over policies central to their welfare (see Chapter 17, page 576). But elders' political concerns are far broader than those that serve their own age group, and their voting behavior is not driven by self-interest (Binstock & Day, 1996). Instead, their political involvement may stem from a deep desire for a safer, more secure world for future generations.

SUCCESSFUL AGING

Walt, Ruth, Dick, Goldie, and Ida, and the findings of research they illustrate, reveal great diversity in development during the final decades of life. Experts would undoubtedly apply the term **successful aging** to Walt and Ruth. They were reasonably healthy until an advanced age, were happily married, and had daily lives filled with gratifying activities and relationships. And Ruth, especially, displayed a remarkable capacity to adapt to negative life changes. Ida, too, was a successful ager until the onset of Alzheimer's symptoms overwhelmed her ability to manage life's challenges. As a single adult, she built a rich

social network that sustained her into old age, despite the hardship of having spent many years caring for her ailing mother. In contrast, Dick and Goldie reacted with despondency to physical aging and other losses (such as Dick's forced retirement). And Dick's angry outbursts restricted their social contacts, although the couple's move to congregate housing eventually led to an improved social life.

Successful agers are people for whom growth, vitality, and striving limit and, at times, overcome physical, cognitive, and social declines. Researchers want to know more about their characteristics and development so they can help more seniors age successfully. Yet theorists disagree on the precise ingredients of successful aging. Some focus on easily measurable outcomes, such as excellent cardiovascular functioning, absence of disability, superior cognitive performance, and creative accomplishments. Yet this view has been heavily criticized (Baltes & Carstensen, 1996). Not everyone can become an outstanding athlete, a Nobel laureate, or an acclaimed artist. Each of us is limited by our genetic potential as it combines with environments we encounter and select for ourselves. Furthermore, outcomes valued in one culture may not be valued in others.

Recent definitions of successful aging have turned away from specific achievements toward processes people use to reach personally valued goals (Freund & Baltes, 1998; Schultz & Heckhausen, 1996). This perspective avoids identifying one set of standards as "successful." Instead, it focuses on how people minimize losses while maximizing gains. Take a moment to list the many ways, considered in this and the previous chapter, that older adults realize their goals. Here are the most important ones, with page references so you can review:

- Effective coping with physical changes and negative life events (page 565)

- Optimism and sense of self-efficacy in improving health and physical functioning (page 566)

- Selective optimization with compensation to make the most of limited physical energies and cognitive resources (pages 579 and 602)

- Strengthening of self-concept, which promotes self-acceptance and pursuit of hoped-for possible selves (page 595)

- Enhanced emotional understanding and emotional self-regulation, which supports meaningful, rewarding social ties (pages 593–594)

- Acceptance of change, which fosters life satisfaction (page 595)

- A mature sense of spirituality and faith, permitting anticipation of death with calmness and composure (page 596–599)

- Personal control over domains of dependency and independence (pages 599–600, 602)

- High-quality relationships, which offer social support and pleasurable companionship (pages 604–606)

Successful aging is facilitated by societal contexts that permit elders to manage life changes effectively. Older adults need adequate health care, safe housing, and social services. In the United States, the federal government guarantees all citizens age 60 and older access to a wide variety of services tailored to their needs. (See the description of the Area Agencies on Aging in Chapter 2, page 69.) Nevertheless, inadequate funding and difficulties reaching rural communities mean that many older adults are not served. And isolated elders with little education often do not know how to seek available assistance. Furthermore, we have seen that America's system of sharing health care costs strains the financial resources of many senior citizens. And housing that adjusts to changes in elders' capacities, permitting them to age in place without disruptive and disorienting moves, is available only to the economically well-off in the United States.

Besides improving policies that meet older adults' basic needs, new future-oriented approaches must prepare for increased aging of the population. More emphasis on life-long learning for workers of all ages would help people maintain as well as increase skills and productivity as they grow older. Otherwise, society has little to gain from keeping more elders in the work force by raising the age of eligibility for full Social Security benefits (Hicks, 1997). Finally, reforms that prepare for expected growth in the number of frail elders are vital, including affordable adapted housing, help for family caregivers, and sensitive nursing home care.

All these changes involve recognizing, improving, and supporting the contributions senior citizens make to society—both the elders of today and those now aging to be the future elderly. A nation that takes care of its senior citizens and grants them a multitude of opportunities for personal growth maximizes the chances that each of us, when our time comes to be old, will age successfully.

ASK YOURSELF . . .

Nate, happily married to Gladys, adjusted well to retirement. He also found that after he retired, his marriage became even happier. How can a good marriage ease the transition to retirement? How can retirement enhance marital satisfaction?

SUMMARY

ERIKSON'S THEORY: EGO INTEGRITY VERSUS DESPAIR

According to Erikson, how does personality change in late adulthood?

- The final psychological conflict of Erikson's theory, **ego integrity versus despair,** involves coming to terms with one's life. Adults who arrive at a sense of integrity feel whole and satisfied with their achievements. Despair occurs when elders feel they have made many wrong decisions, yet time is too short for change.

OTHER THEORIES OF PSYCHOSOCIAL DEVELOPMENT IN LATE ADULTHOOD

Describe Peck's and Labouvie-Vief's views of development in late adulthood, and discuss the functions of reminiscence and life review in older adults' lives.

- According to Robert Peck, the conflict of ego integrity versus despair comprises three distinct tasks: (1) ego differentiation versus work-role preoccupation; (2) body transcendence versus body preoccupation; and (3) ego transcendence versus ego preoccupation.

- Gisella Labouvie-Vief addresses the development of adults' reasoning about emotion, pointing out that older, more psychologically mature individuals are more in touch with their feelings. They become expert at processing emotional information and engaging in emotional self-regulation.

- Researchers do not yet fully understand why older people engage in **reminiscence** more often than do younger people. In a special form of reminiscence called **life review,** elders call up, reflect on, and reconsider past experiences with the goal of achieving greater self-understanding. Reminiscence may also serve social needs and help elders cope with life transitions.

STABILITY AND CHANGE IN SELF-CONCEPT AND PERSONALITY

Cite stable and changing aspects of self-concept and personality in late adulthood.

- The "big five" personality traits show continuing stability from mid- to late life. Elders have accumulated a lifetime of self-knowledge, leading to more secure and complex self-concepts than at earlier ages.

- During late adulthood, shifts in three personality traits take place.

Agreeableness and acceptance of change tend to rise, whereas sociability dips slightly.

Discuss spirituality and religiosity in late adulthood, and trace the development of faith.

- Although organized religious participation declines, informal religious activities remain common in late adulthood. Religious involvement is especially high among low-income ethnic minority elders and women and is linked to many positive outcomes, including physical functioning and psychological well-being.

- Faith and spirituality may advance to a higher level in late adulthood, away from prescribed beliefs to a more reflective approach that is at ease with uncertainty.

INDIVIDUAL DIFFERENCES IN PSYCHOLOGICAL WELL-BEING

Discuss individual differences in psychological well-being as older adults respond to increased dependency, declining health, and negative life changes.

- Friends, family members, and caregivers often promote excessive dependency in elders. In sequences of behavior called the **dependency–support script** and **independence–ignore script,** older adults' dependency behaviors are attended to immediately and their independent behaviors are ignored. For dependency to foster well-being, elders need to assume personal control over it.

- Health is a powerful predictor of psychological well-being in late adulthood. The relation between physical and mental health problems can become a vicious cycle, each intensifying the other.

- Although elders are at risk for a variety of negative life changes, these events may evoke less stress and depression than they do in younger adults. Many seniors have learned to cope with hard times.

Describe the role of social support and social interaction in promoting physical health and psychological well-being in late adulthood.

- In late adulthood, social support from family, friends, and paid helpers reduces stress, thereby promoting physical health and psychological well-being. At the same time, older adults do not want a great deal of support from people close to them unless they can reciprocate.

A CHANGING SOCIAL WORLD

Describe social theories of aging, including disengagement theory, activity theory, and socioemotional selectivity theory.

- **Disengagement theory** holds that social interaction declines due to mutual withdrawal between elders and society in anticipation of death. However, not everyone disengages, and elders' retreat from interaction is more complex than this theory implies.

- According to **activity theory,** social barriers to engagement, not the desires of elders, cause declining rates of interaction. Yet offering older adults opportunities for social contact does not guarantee greater social activity.

- **Socioemotional selectivity theory** states that social networks become more selective as we age. As older adults emphasize the emotion-regulating function of interaction, they tend to limit their contacts to familiar partners with whom they have developed pleasurable, rewarding relationships.

How do communities, neighborhoods, and housing arrangements affect elders' social lives and adjustment?

- Elders residing in suburbs are better off in terms of income, health, and access to social services than are those in inner cities. Those in small towns and rural areas are least well

off in these ways. Older adults with many senior citizens in their neighborhood and who live in small and mid-sized communities report greater life satisfaction.

- For elders living alone and in inner-city areas, fear of crime is sometimes greater than worries about income, health, and housing. It restricts their activities and seriously undermines their morale.

- The housing arrangement offering seniors the greatest personal control is their own home. Nevertheless, many older adults who live alone, especially widowed women, are poverty stricken and have unmet needs.

- Most residential communities for senior citizens are privately developed retirement villages with adjoining recreational facilities. **Congregate housing** offers a variety of support services, including meals in a common dining room. **Life care communities** provide a range of options, from independent or congregate housing to full nursing home care. A sense of community in planned housing enhances life satisfaction.

- Only 5 percent of Americans age 65 and older live in nursing homes. Typically, social interaction among residents is low. Designing homelike nursing homes could enhance elders' sense of control over their social experiences.

RELATIONSHIPS IN LATE ADULTHOOD

Describe changes in social relationships in late adulthood, including marriage, divorce, remarriage, and widowhood, and discuss never-married, childless older adults.

- As we move through life, a **social convoy,** or cluster of family members and friends, provides safety and support. With age, some bonds become closer, others more distant, while still others are added or drift away.

- Marital satisfaction rises from middle to late adulthood as perceptions of fairness in the relationship increase, couples engage in joint leisure activities, and communication becomes more positive.

- When divorce occurs, stress is higher for older than younger adults. Although remarriage rates are low in late adulthood, those who do remarry enter into more stable relationships.

- Wide variation in adaptations to widowhood exists. Elders fare better than younger individuals. Women—especially those who developed rewarding roles outside the marital relationship—adjust more easily than men.

- Most older adults who remain unmarried and childless throughout their lives develop alternative meaningful relationships. At the same time, they often worry about how care will be provided in old age if it is needed.

How do sibling relationships and friendships change in late life?

- Because siblings share a long and unique history, joint reminiscing increases in late adulthood. Elder siblings continue to serve as vital sources of social support. Bonds with sisters are closer than bonds with brothers.

- Among the functions of friendship in late adulthood are intimacy and companionship, acceptance, a link to the larger community, and pro-

tection from the psychological consequences of loss. Women are more likely than men to have both intimate friends and **secondary friends** —people with whom they spend time occasionally.

Describe older adults' relationships with adult children, adult grandchildren, and great-grandchildren.

- Elders and their adult children are often in touch, typically exchanging advice rather than direct assistance. Adult daughters are primary agents of elderly parents' family contacts.

- Seniors with adult grandchildren and great-grandchildren benefit from a wider network of support. Most often, grandparents expect and receive affection rather than practical help from their grandchildren. Over time grandparent–grandchild contact declines, but grandparents' affection for their adult grandchildren remains high.

Discuss elder maltreatment, including risk factors and strategies for prevention.

- Some elders suffer maltreatment at the hands of family members, friends, and professional caregivers. Risk factors include a mutually dependent perpetrator–victim relationship; perpetrator psychological disturbance and stress; a history of family violence; and overcrowded nursing homes with staff shortages and turnover.

- Prevention of elder maltreatment requires both perpetrator and victim to recognize that help can improve their situation. Societal efforts, including public education to encourage reporting suspected cases and

improved understanding of the needs of older people, are also vital.

RETIREMENT AND LEISURE

Discuss the decision to retire, adjustment to retirement, and involvement in leisure activities.

- The decision to retire depends on affordability, health status, opportunities to pursue meaningful activities, societal factors such as early retirement benefits, gender, and ethnicity.

- Such factors as control over the retirement decision, involvement in and enjoyment of work, prior retirement planning, social support, and marital happiness affect adjustment to retirement.

- Engaging in meaningful and pleasurable leisure activities is positively related to elders' psychological well-being. The best preparation for leisure experiences in late life is to develop rewarding interests at a young age.

SUCCESSFUL AGING

Discuss the meaning of successful aging.

- Elders who experience **successful aging** have developed many effective ways to minimize losses and maximize gains. Social contexts that permit elders to manage life changes effectively foster successful aging. These include adequate health care, safe housing that adjusts to changes in elders' capacities, social services, and opportunities for lifelong learning.

IMPORTANT TERMS AND CONCEPTS

activity theory (p. 603)

congregate housing (p. 608)

dependency–support script (p. 599)

disengagement theory (p. 603)

ego integrity versus despair (p. 592)

independence-ignore script (p. 599)

life care communities (p. 608)

life review (p. 594)

reminiscence (p. 594)

secondary friends (p. 613)

social convoy (p. 609)

socioemotional selectivity theory (p. 604)

successful aging (p. 619)

FYI · FOR FURTHER INFORMATION AND HELP

Consult the companion website for this book, where you will find additional weblinks and associated learning activities: www.abacon.com/berk

HOUSING ARRANGEMENTS

American Association of Homes and Services for the Aged
www.aahsa.org

Organization of not-for-profit nursing homes, housing, retirement communities, and health-related facilities and services for the elderly. Provides a coordinated means of protecting and advancing the interests of residents.

National Institute of Senior Housing
www.ncoa.org

Works to promote a national response to the growing need for affordable, decent housing and living arrangements for older adults.

WIDOWHOOD

Widowed Persons Service
c/o American Association of Retired Persons
www.aarp.org

A national outreach group of volunteers, widowed for at least 18 months, who listen to and support people adjusting to widowhood.

ELDER MALTREATMENT

National Committee for the Prevention of Elder Abuse
www.preventelderabuse.org

Promotes understanding of elder maltreatment and development of services to protect older adults from abuse and neglect.

RETIREMENT

American Association of Retired Persons
www.aarp.org

An active advocacy organization for older people, with 32 million members 50 years of age or older, working or retired. Aims to enhance quality of life, independence, and dignity of the elderly.

VOLUNTEERISM

National Senior Service Corps
www.cns.gov/senior/index.html

Brings retired people more fully into community life through volunteer services that vary according to preference and community needs. Projects are organized and operated at the local level in schools, courts, and health care, day care, youth, and other community centers.

AGE	PHYSICAL	COGNITIVE	EMOTIONAL/SOCIAL
60–80 years	■ Neurons die at a faster rate, but the brain compensates through growth of new synapses. (559) ■ Autonomic nervous system performs less well, impairing adaptation to hot and cold weather. (559) ■ Declines in vision continue, in terms of increased sensitivity to glare and impaired color discrimination, dark adaptation, depth perception, and visual acuity. (559) ■ Declines in hearing continue throughout the frequency range. (562) ■ Taste and odor sensitivity may decline. (562) ■ Touch sensitivity declines on the hands, particularly the fingertips, less so on the arms. (562) ■ Declines in cardiovascular and respiratory functioning lead to greater physical stress during exercise. (563) ■ Aging of the immune system increases risk for a variety of illnesses. (563) ■ Sleep difficulties increase, especially for men. (564)	■ Processing speed continues to decline; crystallized abilities are largely sustained. (567) ■ Amount of information that can be retained in working memory diminishes further; memory problems are greatest on complex tasks requiring deliberate processing. (580) ■ Modest forgetting of remote memories occurs. (581) ■ Use of external aids for prospective memory increases. (582) ■ Retrieving words from long-term memory and planning what to say and how to say it become more difficult. (582) ■ Information is more likely to be remembered in terms of gist than details. (582) ■ Traditional problem solving declines; everyday problem solving remains adaptive. (583) ■ May hold one of the most important positions in society, such as chief executive officer, religious leader, or Supreme Court justice. (583)	■ Comes to terms with life, developing ego integrity. (592) ■ Describes emotional reactions in more complex and personalized ways; improves in emotional self-regulation. (593–594) ■ May engage in reminiscence and life review. (594) ■ Self-concept strengthens, becoming more secure and complex. (595) ■ Agreeableness and acceptance of change increase. (595) ■ Faith and spirituality may advance to a higher level. (597–598) ■ Size of social network and amount of social interaction decline. (603) ■ Selects social partners on the basis of emotion, approaching pleasant and avoiding unpleasant relationships. (604) ■ Marital satisfaction increases. (609) ■ May be widowed. (610) ■ Sibling bonds may strengthen further. (612) ■ Number of friends generally declines. (613)

AGE	PHYSICAL	COGNITIVE	EMOTIONAL/SOCIAL
60–80 years (continued)	■ Graying and thinning of the hair continue; the skin wrinkles further and becomes more transparent as it loses its fatty layer of support (564) ■ Height and weight (due to loss of lean body mass) decline. (564–565) ■ Loss of bone mass continues, leading to rising rates of osteoporosis. (564, 570) ■ Intensity of sexual response and sexual activity decline, although most healthy married couples report regular sexual enjoyment. (569)	■ May excel at wisdom. (583–584) ■ Can improve a wide range of cognitive skills through training. (584) 	■ May become a great-grandparent. (615) ■ May retire. (616–617) ■ More likely to vote and be knowledgeable about politics. (619)
80 years and older	■ Physical changes described above continue. ■ Mobility diminishes, due to loss of muscle and bone strength and joint flexibility. (565) 	■ Cognitive changes described above continue. ■ Fluid abilities decline further; crystallized abilities begin to drop as well. (567) 	■ Emotional and social changes described above continue. ■ As relatives and friends die, may develop friendships with younger individuals. (613) ■ Relationships with adult children become more important. (614) ■ Frequency and variety of leisure activities decline. (618)

Note: Numbers in parentheses indicate the page on which each milestone is discussed.

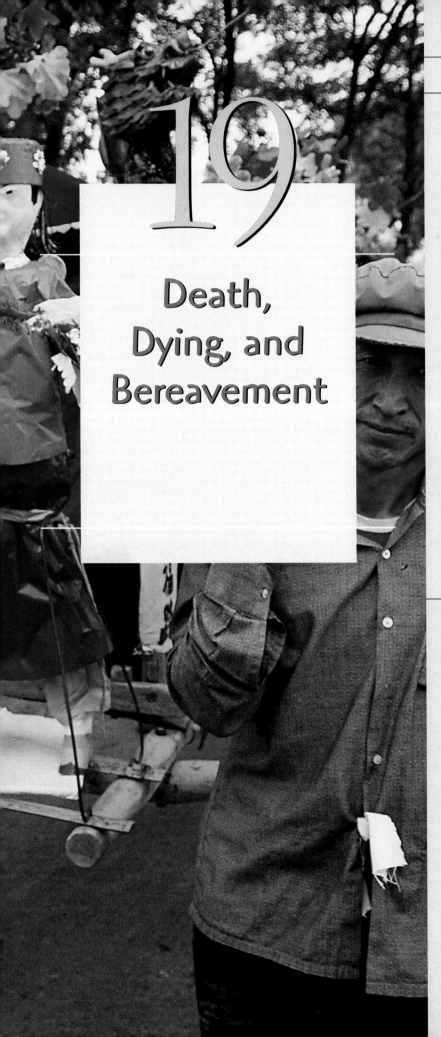

19

Death, Dying, and Bereavement

■ *All cultures have special rituals for celebrating the end of life and helping the bereaved cope with profound loss. Here residents of a small city in the People's Republic of China march in a funeral procession, bearing the remains of a respected local-government official. (Photo courtesy: © 1994 Dennis Cox/ChinaStock)*

As every life is unique, so each death is unique. The final forces of the human spirit separate themselves from the body in manifold ways.

My mother Sofie's death was the culmination of a five-year battle against cancer. In her last months, the disease invaded organs throughout her body, attacking the lungs in its final fury. She withered slowly, having been granted the mixed blessing of time to prepare against certain knowledge that death was just around the corner. My father, Philip, lived another 18 years. At age 80, he was outwardly healthy, active, and about to depart on a long-awaited vacation when a heart attack snuffed out his life suddenly, without time for last words or deathbed reconciliations.

As I set to work on this chapter, my 65-year-old neighbor Nicholas gambled for a higher quality of life. To be eligible for a kidney transplant, he elected bypass surgery to strengthen his heart. Doctors warned that his body might not withstand the operation. But Nicholas knew that without taking a chance, he would live only a few years, in debilitated condition. Shortly after the surgery, infection set in, traveling throughout his system and so weakening him that only extreme measures—a respirator to sustain breathing and powerful drugs to elevate his fading blood pressure—could keep him alive.

"Come on, Dad, you can do it," encouraged Nicholas's daughter Sasha, standing by his bedside and stroking his hand. But Nicholas could not. After two months in intensive care, he experienced brain seizures and slipped into a coma. Three doctors met with his wife, Giselle, to tell her there was no hope. She asked them to disconnect the respirator, and within a half hour Nicholas drifted away.

Death is essential for the survival of our species. We die so that our own children and the children of others may live. When it comes to this fate, nature treats humankind, with all its unique capabilities, just as it treats every other living creature (Nuland, 1993). As hard as it is to accept the reality that we too will die, our greatest solace lies in the knowledge that death is part of ongoing life.

In this chapter, we address the culmination of lifespan development. Over the past century, technology has provided us with so much to keep death at bay that many people regard it as a forbidden topic. But pressing social and economic dilemmas that are an outgrowth of the dramatic increase in life expectancy are forcing us to attend to life's end—its quality, its timing, and ways to help people adjust to their own and others' final leavetaking.

Our discussion addresses the physical changes of dying; understanding of and attitudes toward death in childhood, adolescence, and adulthood; the thoughts and feelings of people as they stand face to face with death; hopelessly ill patients' right to die; and coping with the death of a loved one. The experiences of Sofie, Philip, Nicholas, their fami-

lies, and others illustrate how each person's life history joins with social and cultural contexts to shape death and dying, lending great diversity to this universal experience.

HOW WE DIE

Our vast literature on death is largely aimed at helping people cope with the emotional trauma of dying and its aftermath. Few people are aware of the physical aspects of death, since opportunities to witness them are less available than in previous generations. Today, the large majority of people in industrialized nations die in hospitals, where doctors and nurses, not loved ones, typically attend their last moments. Nevertheless, many people want to know how we die, either to anticipate their own end or grasp what is happening to a dying loved one.

PHYSICAL CHANGES

My father's fatal heart attack came suddenly during the night. On being told the news, I longed for reassurance that his death had been swift and without suffering.

When asked how they would like to die, most people say they want "death with dignity"—either a quick, agony-free end during sleep or a clear-minded final few moments in which they can say farewell and review their lives. In reality, death is the culmination of a straightforward biological process. In about 20 percent of people, it is gentle—especially when narcotic drugs ease pain and mask the destructive events taking place (Nuland, 1993). But most of the time it is not.

Recall that unintentional injuries are the leading cause of death in childhood and adolescence, cardiovascular disease and cancer in adulthood. Of the one-quarter of people in industrialized nations who die suddenly, within a few hours of symptoms, 80 to 90 percent are victims of heart attacks (Nuland, 1993). My yearning for a painless death for my father was probably not fulfilled. Undoubtedly he felt the sharp, crushing sensation of a heart deprived of oxygen. As his heart twitched uncontrollably (called *fibrillation*) or stopped entirely, blood circulation slowed and ceased, and he was thrust into unconsciousness. A brain starved of oxygen for more than 2 to 4 minutes is irreversibly damaged—an outcome indicated by the pupils of the eye becoming unresponsive to light and widening into large, black circles. Other oxygen-deprived organs stop functioning as well.

Death is long and drawn out for three-fourths of people—many more than in times past, due to life-saving medical technology (Benoliel & Degner, 1995). They succumb in many different ways. Of those with heart disease, most have congestive heart failure, the cause of Nicholas's death. His scarred heart could no longer contract with the force needed to deliver enough oxygen to his tissues. As it tried harder, its muscle weakened further. Without sufficient blood pressure, fluid backed up in Nicholas's lungs. This hampered his breathing and created ideal conditions for inhaled bacteria to multiply, enter the bloodstream, and run rampant in his system, leading multiple organs to fail.

Cancer, as well, chooses diverse paths to wreak its damage. When it *metastasizes*, bits of tumor travel through the bloodstream and implant and grow in vital organs—perhaps the liver, the kidneys, the intestinal tract, the lungs, or the brain—disrupting their functioning. Medication made my mother's final days as comfortable as possible, granting a relatively easy death. But the preceding weeks involved physical suffering, including impaired breathing and digestion and turning and twisting to find a comfortable position in bed.

In general, dying takes place in three phases:

1. The **agonal phase:** The Greek word *agon* means "struggle." Here *agonal* refers to gasps and muscle spasms during the first moments in which the body cannot sustain life anymore.

2. **Clinical death:** A short interval follows in which heartbeat, circulation, breathing, and brain functioning stop, but resuscitation is still possible.

3. **Mortality:** The individual passes into permanent death. Within a few hours, the newly lifeless being appears shrunken, not at all like the person he or she was when alive.

DEFINING DEATH

Think about what we have said so far, and you will see that death is not an event that happens at a single point in time. Rather, it is a process in which organs stop functioning in a sequence that varies from person to person. Because the dividing line between life and death is fuzzy, societies need a definition of death to help doctors decide when life-saving measures should be terminated, to signal survivors that they must begin to grieve their loss and reorganize their lives, and to establish when donated organs can be removed.

Several decades ago, loss of heartbeat and respiration signified death. But these criteria are no longer adequate, since resuscitation techniques frequently permit vital signs to be restored. Today, **brain death,** defined as irreversible cessation of all activity in the brain and the brain stem (which controls reflexes), is used in most industrialized nations.

It is important to note that not all countries accept this standard. In Japan, for example, no legal definition of death exists. Instead, doctors rely on traditional criteria (absence of heartbeat and respiration) that fit with Japanese laypeople's views. This approach stands in the way of a na-

■ *Japanese elders visit a Buddhist shrine to pray for a happy death. Buddhist, Confucian, and Shinto beliefs about death, which stress ancestor worship, may be partly responsible for Japanese people's discomfort with organ donation. (Photo courtesy: Fujifotos/The Image Works)*

tional organ transplant program, since few organs can be salvaged from bodies without artificially maintaining vital signs. Buddhist, Confucian, and Shinto beliefs about death, which stress ancestor worship and time for the spirit to leave the corpse, may be partly responsible for Japan's discomfort with brain death and organ donation (Yeung, 1996). Marring the body to harvest organs violates respect for the deceased. Although public attitudes are changing, there is less consensus on defining death in Japan than in other developed countries (Brannigan, 1998).

Furthermore, in a great many cases the brain death standard does not solve the dilemma of when to halt treatment. Consider Nicholas, whose brain stem, but not cortex, registered electrical activity. Although not brain dead, he had entered a **persistent vegetative state.** Doctors were sure they could not restore consciousness or body movement. Medical intervention could do no more than postpone the natural process of dying. Because approximately 10,000 Americans are in a persistent vegetative state, with health care costs totaling $1.2 billion annually, many experts believe that absence of activity in the cortex should be sufficient to declare a person dead (Maier & Newman, 1995). In other instances, a fully conscious but very sick, suffering person refuses life-saving measures—an issue we will consider later when we take up the right to die.

DEATH WITH DIGNITY

Our brief look at the process of dying indicates that nature rarely delivers the idealized, easy end most people want, and medical science cannot guarantee it. Therefore, the greatest dignity in death can be found in the integrity of the life that precedes it—an integrity we can foster by the way we communicate with and care for the dying person.

First, we can assure the majority of dying people, who succumb gradually, that we will support them through their physical and psychological distress. We can do everything possible to provide the utmost in humane and compassionate care.

Second, we can be candid about death's certainty. Unless people are aware that they are dying and understand (so far as possible) the likely circumstances of their death, they cannot share the sentiments that bring closure to relationships they hold most dear. Because Sofie knew how and when her death would probably take place, she chose a time when she, Philip, and her children could express what their lives had meant to one another. Among those precious bedside exchanges was Sofie's memorable last wish that Philip remarry after her death so he would not live out his final years alone. Openness about impending death granted Sofie a final generative act, helped her let go of the person closest to her, and offered comfort as she faced death.

Finally, doctors and nurses can help dying people learn enough about their condition to make reasoned choices about whether to fight on or say no to further treatment. An understanding of how the normal body works simplifies comprehension of how disease affects it—education that can begin as early as the childhood years.

In sum, although the conditions of illness often do not permit a graceful, serene death, we can ensure the most dignified exit possible by offering the dying person care, affection, and companionship; the truth about his or her diagnosis; and the maximum personal control over this final phase of life.

■ *We can best ensure death with dignity by offering the dying person care, affection, companionship, and the maximum personal control over this final phase of life. This teenager, diagnosed with lymphoblastic leukemia, a highly aggressive cancer of the lymph system, poses with Kona, one of the dolphins she played with in Hawaii, thanks to the Make-a-Wish Foundation. It makes special dreams come true for children and adolescents with life-threatening illnesses. (Photo courtesy: AP/Wide World Photos)*

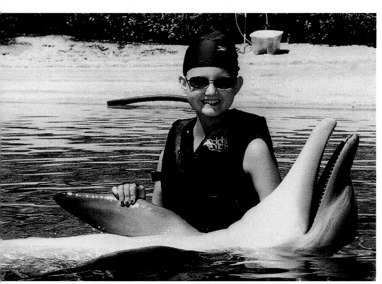

These are essential ingredients of a "good death," and we will revisit them throughout this chapter.

UNDERSTANDING OF AND ATTITUDES TOWARD DEATH

A century ago, deaths most often occurred at home. People of all ages, including children, helped with care of the dying family member and were present at the moment of death. They saw their loved one buried on family property or in the local cemetery, where the grave could be visited regularly. Since infant and childhood mortality rates were high, all people were likely to know someone the same age as or younger than themselves who had died. And it was common for children to experience the death of a parent.

Compared with earlier generations, today's children and adolescents in developed nations are insulated from death. Residents of inner-city ghettos, where violence is part of everyday existence, are exceptions. But overall, more young people reach adulthood without having experienced the death of someone they know well. When they do, professionals in hospitals and funeral homes take care of most tasks that involve confronting death directly (Wass, 1995).

This distance from death undoubtedly contributes to a sense of uneasiness about it. Despite constant images of death in television shows, movies, and news reports of accidents, murders, and natural disasters, ours is a death-denying society. Adults are often reluctant to talk about death with children and adolescents. And a variety of substitute expressions, such as "passing away," "going out," and "departing," permit us to avoid acknowledging it candidly. In the following sections, we examine the development of conceptions of and attitudes toward death, along with ways to foster increased understanding and acceptance.

CHILDHOOD

Five-year-old Miriam arrived at our university laboratory preschool the day after her dog Pepper died. Leslie, her teacher, noticed that instead of joining the other children as she usually did, Miriam stood by herself, looking anxious and unhappy. "What's wrong, Miriam?" Leslie asked.

"Daddy said Pepper had a sick tummy. He fell asleep and died." For a moment, Miriam looked hopeful. "When I get home, Pepper might be up."

Leslie answered directly, "No, Pepper won't get up again. He's not asleep. He's dead, and that means he can't sleep, eat, run, or play anymore."

Miriam wandered off. Later, she returned and confessed to Leslie, "I chased Pepper too hard," tears streaming from her eyes.

Leslie put her arm around Miriam. "Pepper didn't die because you chased him. He was very old and very sick," she explained.

Over the next few days, Miriam asked many questions: "When I go to sleep, will I die?" "Can a tummy ache make you die?" "Will Mommy and Daddy die?" "Can Pepper see me?" "Does Pepper feel better now?" (Corr, 1997).

■ DEVELOPMENT OF THE DEATH CONCEPT. A realistic understanding of death is based on three ideas:

1. **Permanence:** Once a living thing dies, it cannot be brought back to life.

2. **Universality:** All living things eventually die.

3. **Nonfunctionality:** All living functions, including thought, feeling, movement, and body processes, cease at death.

Without clear explanations, preschoolers rely on egocentric and magical thinking to make sense of death. They may believe, as Miriam did, that they are responsible for a relative or pet's death. And they can easily arrive at incorrect conclusions—in Miriam's case, that sleeping or a stomachache can cause someone to die.

Preschoolers grasp the three components of the death concept in the order just given, with most mastering them by age 7. *Permanence* is the first and most easily understood idea. When Leslie explained that Pepper would not get up again, Miriam accepted this fact quickly, perhaps because she had seen it in other less emotionally charged situations, such as the dead butterflies and beetles that she picked up and inspected while playing outside (Furman, 1990). Appreciation of *universality* comes slightly later. At first, children think that certain people do not die, especially those with whom they have close emotional ties or who are like themselves—

other children. Finally, *nonfunctionality* is the most difficult component for children to grasp. Many preschoolers view dead things as retaining living capacities. When they first comprehend nonfunctionality, they do so in terms of its most visible aspects, such as heartbeat and breathing. Only later do they understand that thinking, feeling, and dreaming cease (Lazar & Torney-Purta, 1991; Speece & Brent, 1996).

■ INDIVIDUAL AND CULTURAL VARIATIONS. Although children usually have an accurate conception of death by middle childhood, there are wide individual differences. Experiences with death make a difference (Speece & Brent, 1996). For example, terminally ill children under age 6 often have a well-developed concept of death. If parents and health professionals have not been forthright with them, children find out that they are deathly ill in other ways—through nonverbal communication, eavesdropping, and talking with other child patients (O'Halloran & Altmaier, 1996). Children growing up on Israeli kibbutzim (agricultural settlements) who have experienced terrorist attacks, their father's departure on army tours to high-tension areas, and parental anxiety about safety express an accurate understanding of death by 5 to 6 years of age (Mahon, Goldberg, & Washington, 1999).

Ethnic variations suggest that religious teachings also affect children's understanding. A comparison of four ethnic groups in Israel revealed that Druze and Moslem children's death concepts lagged behind those of Christian and Jewish children (Florian & Kravetz, 1985). The Druze emphasis on reincarnation and the greater religiosity of both the Druze and Moslem groups may underlie these findings. Religious teachings seem to have an especially strong impact on children's grasp of the permanence of death. For example, children of Southern Baptist families, who believe in an afterlife, are less likely to endorse permanence than are children of northern Unitarian families, who focus on the here and now—peace and justice in today's world (Candy-Gibbs, Sharp, & Petrun, 1985).

■ ENHANCING CHILDREN'S UNDERSTANDING. Parents often worry that discussing death candidly with children will fuel their fears, but this is not so. Instead, children with a good grasp of the facts of death have an easier time accepting it (Essa & Murray, 1994). Direct explanations, like Leslie's, that fit the child's cognitive maturity, work best.

When adults use clichés or make misleading statements, children may take these literally and react with confusion. For example, after a parent said to her 5-year-old daughter,

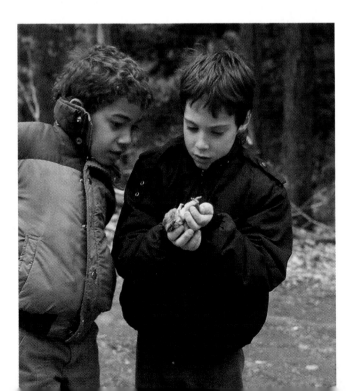

■ *Examining this dead mouse will help these children understand the permanence of death. Appreciation of two additional components of the death concept—*universality *and* nonfunctionality—*will come later. (Photo courtesy: A. Carey/The Image Works)*

"Grandpa went on a long trip," the child wondered, "Why didn't he take me?" In another instance, a father whose wife died of cancer said to his 9-year-old son that his mother "was sick," explaining nothing else about the illness. The father was surprised when, 10 months later, the boy caught the flu and became terribly afraid of dying (Wolfelt, 1997). Sometimes children ask very difficult questions, such as "Will I die? Will you die?" Parents can be truthful as well as comforting by taking advantage of children's sense of time. They can say something like "Not for many, many years. First I'm going to enjoy you as a grown-up and become a grandparent."

Discussions with children should also be culturally sensitive. Rather than presenting scientific evidence as counteracting religious beliefs, parents and teachers can assist children in blending the two sources of knowledge. As children get older, they often combine an accurate conception of death with spiritual and philosophical views, which offer solace during times of bereavement (Cuddy-Casey & Orvaschel, 1997). As we will see later, open, honest discussions with children not only contribute to a realistic understanding of death, but facilitate grieving after a child has experienced a loss.

A DOLESCENCE

Adolescents can easily voice the permanence, universality, and nonfunctionality of death, but their understanding is largely limited to the realm of possibility. Recall that teenagers have difficulty integrating logical insights with the realities of everyday life (Corr, 1995). Consequently, their understanding of death is not yet fully mature.

■ THE GAP BETWEEN LOGIC AND REALITY. Teenagers' difficulty applying what they know about death is evident in both their reasoning and their behavior. Although they can explain the permanence and nonfunctionality of death, they are attracted to alternatives. Consequently, the dividing line between life and death actually becomes less sharp in adolescence than it was in childhood. For example, teenagers often describe death as an enduring abstract state, such as "darkness," "eternal light," "transition," or "nothingness" (Brent et al., 1996). They also formulate personal theories about life after death. Besides images of heaven and hell influenced by religious background, they speculate about reincarnation, transmigration of souls, and spiritual survival on earth or at another level (Noppe & Noppe, 1997).

Although mortality in adolescence is low compared with infancy and adulthood, teenage deaths are typically sudden and human-induced; unintentional injuries, homicide, and suicide are leading causes. Adolescents are clearly aware that death happens to everyone and can occur at any time. But this does not make them more safety conscious. Rather, their high-risk activities suggest that they do not take death personally. When asked to comment on death, teenagers often make statements like these: "Why

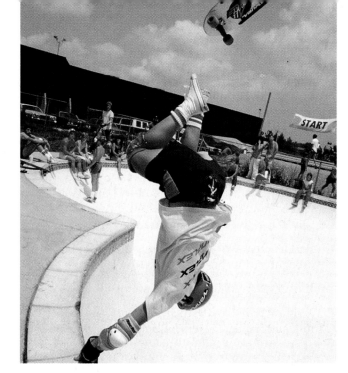

■ *This adolescent knows that death happens to everyone and can occur at any time, but his risk taking suggests otherwise. Teenagers' difficulty integrating logic with reality extends to their understanding of death. (Photo courtesy: D. & I. MacDonald/ Index Stock)*

dwell on it? There is nothing I can do about it." (Wass, 1991, p. 27). In one study, the lower adolescent boys' consciousness of personal mortality, the more they engaged in risky behavior (Word, 1996).

What explains teenagers' difficulty integrating logic with reality in the domain of death? First, adolescence is a period of rapid growth in size and strength and onset of reproductive capacity—attainments that are the opposite of death! Second, recall the adolescent personal fable, which leads teenagers to be so wrapped up in their own uniqueness that they can conclude they are beyond the reach of death. Finally, as teenagers construct a personal identity and experience their first freely chosen love relationships, they may be strongly attracted to romantic notions of death, which challenge logic (Noppe & Noppe, 1991, 1996). Not until early adulthood are they capable of the relativistic thinking needed to handle these conflicting ideas (see Chapter 13, page 440).

■ ENHANCING ADOLESCENTS' UNDERSTANDING. By encouraging adolescents to discuss concerns about death, adults can help them build a bridge between death as a logical concept and their personal experiences. In Chapter 12, we noted that teenagers with authoritative parents are more likely to turn to adults for guidance on important issues. In one study of 12- to 15-year-olds, most wanted to talk with parents rather than peers about the "meaning of life and death" and "what happens when you die." But 60 percent thought that their parents would not be genuinely interested, and the majority of parents felt inadequately prepared for the task (McNeil, 1986).

Taking up adolescents' thoughts and feelings about death can be part of everyday conversation, sparked by a news report or the death of an acquaintance. Parents can capitalize on these moments to express their own views, listen closely, accept teenagers' feelings, and correct misconceptions. Such mutual sharing deepens bonds of love and provides the basis for further exploration when the need arises. The Caregiving Concerns table below suggests ways to discuss concerns about death with children and adolescents.

ADULTHOOD

In early adulthood, many people brush aside thoughts of death (Gresser, Wong, & Reker, 1987). This avoidance may be prompted by death anxiety, which we will consider in the next section. Alternatively, it may be due to relative disinterest in death-related issues, as young adults typically do not know very many people who have died and (like adolescents) think of their own death as a long way off.

In Chapters 15 and 16, we described midlife as a time of stock taking in which people begin to view the lifespan in terms of time left to live, focusing on tasks to be completed. Middle-aged people no longer have a vague conception of their own death. They know that in the not-too-distant future it will be their turn to grow old and die.

In late adulthood, adults think and talk more about death, as it is much closer. Increasing evidence of mortality comes from physical changes, higher rates of illness and disability, and loss of relatives and friends (see Chapter 17). Compared with middle-aged people, older adults spend more time pondering the process and circumstances of dying than the state of death. Nearness to death seems to lead to a practical concern with how and when it might happen (de Vries, Bluck, & Birren, 1993; Kastenbaum, 1999a).

Finally, although we have traced age-related changes, we must keep in mind that large individual differences exist. Some people focus on life and death issues early on, whereas others are less reflective, moving into advanced old age having given these matters little attention.

DEATH ANXIETY

As you read the following statements, do you find yourself agreeing, disagreeing, or reacting neutrally?

"Never feeling anything again after I die upsets me."

"I hate the idea that I will be helpless after I die."

"The total isolation of death is frightening to me."

"The feeling that I will be missing out on so much after I die disturbs me." (Thorson & Powell, 1994, pp. 38–39)

Items like these appear on questionnaires used to measure **death anxiety**—fear and apprehension of death. Even people who are very accepting of the reality of death may be afraid of it (Firestone, 1994).

What predicts whether thoughts of our own demise trigger intense distress, relative calm, or something in between? To answer this question, researchers measure both general

CAREGIVING CONCERNS

Discussing Concerns About Death with Children and Adolescents

SUGGESTION	DESCRIPTION
Take the lead.	Be alert to the child's or adolescent's nonverbal behaviors, bringing up the subject sympathetically, especially after a death-related situation has occurred.
Listen perceptively.	Grant full attention to the child or adolescent and the feelings underlying his or her words. When adults pretend to listen while thinking about other things, young people quickly pick up this sign of indifference and withdraw their confidence.
Acknowledge feelings.	Accept the child's or adolescent's emotions as real and important; avoid being judgmental. For example, paraphrase sentiments you detect, such as "I see you're very puzzled about that. Let's talk more about it."
Provide factual information in a candid, culturally sensitive fashion.	For children who do not yet have a realistic understanding of the permanence, universality, and nonfunctionality of death, provide simple, direct, and accurate explanations. Avoid misleading statements, such as "Grandpa went away on a long trip." Do not contradict the young person's religious beliefs. Rather, assist him or her in blending scientific with religious sources of knowledge.
Engage in joint problem solving.	When questions do not have easy answers, such as "Where does your soul go when you die?", convey your belief in the young person's worth by indicating that you do not want to impose a point of view but rather to help him or her come to personally satisfying conclusions. To questions you cannot answer, say, "I don't know." Such honesty shows a willingness to generate and evaluate solutions jointly.

death anxiety and a variety of specific factors—fear of no longer existing, loss of control, a painful death, the body decaying, being separated from loved ones, the unknown, and others (Neimeyer, 1994). Findings reveal large individual and cultural variations in fear-arousing aspects of death. For example, in a study of devout Islamic Saudi Arabians, certain factors that appear repeatedly in the responses of Westerners, such as fear of the body decaying and the unknown, were entirely absent (Long, 1985).

Among Westerners, spirituality—a sense of life's meaning—seems to be more important than religious commitment in limiting death anxiety (Rasmussen & Johnson, 1994). Having a well-developed personal philosophy of death also reduces fear. In one study, both devout Christians and devout atheists viewed death as less threatening than did people with ambivalent religious views (Moore, 1992). Death anxiety is especially low among adults with deep faith in some form of higher force or being—one that may or may not be religiously influenced (Rasmussen & Johnson, 1994; Thorson & Powell, 1991).

From what you have learned about adult psychosocial development, how do you think death anxiety might change with age? If you predicted it would decline, reaching its lowest level in late adulthood, you are correct. This age-related drop has been found in many cultures and ethnic groups. Recall from Chapter 18 that the attainment of ego integrity and a more mature sense of spirituality reduce fear of death. Older adults have also had more time to develop certain modes of *symbolic immortality*—the sense that one will continue to live on through one's children or through one's work or personal influence. In a study of Israeli adults, these modes of symbolic immortality predicted reduced fear of death, especially among adults with secure attachments. Gratifying, close interpersonal ties seem to help people de-

velop a sense of symbolic immortality and, thereby, transcend death anxiety (Florian & Mikulincer, 1998).

Regardless of age, women appear more anxious about death than men do—a difference apparent in both Eastern and Western cultures (Cicerelli, 1998; Neimeyer & Van Brunt, 1995). Researchers are not sure why this is so. Perhaps women are more likely to admit and men more likely to avoid troubled feelings about mortality—an explanation consistent with females' greater emotional expressiveness throughout the lifespan.

Experiencing some anxiety about death is normal. But like other fears, when it is very intense, it can undermine effective adjustment. Although physical health in adulthood is not related to death anxiety, mental health clearly is. People who are depressed or generally anxious are likely to have more severe death concerns (Neimeyer & Van Brunt, 1995). A large gap between their actual and ideal self-concepts leaves these individuals with a sense of incompleteness when they contemplate death. In contrast, self-confident individuals with a clear sense of purpose in life express little fear of death.

Death anxiety is largely limited to adolescence and adulthood. Children rarely display it unless they live in dangerous neighborhoods or war-torn areas where they are in constant danger (see Chapter 10, page 340). Terminally ill children are also at risk for high death anxiety. Compared with other same-age patients, children with cancer express more destructive thoughts and negative feelings about death (Malone, 1982). For those whose parents make the mistake of not telling them they are going to die, loneliness and death anxiety can be extreme (O'Halloran & Altmaier, 1996).

■ ━━ **ASK YOURSELF...**

■ *When 4-year-old Chloe's aunt died, Chloe asked, "Where's Aunt Susie?" Her mother explained, "Aunt Susie is taking a long, peaceful sleep." For the next 2 weeks, Chloe refused to go to bed, and when finally coaxed into her room, she lay awake for hours. Explain the likely reason for Chloe's behavior, and suggest a better way of answering Chloe's question.*

🌳 *Explain why older adults think and talk more about death than do younger people but nevertheless feel less anxious about it.*

THINKING AND EMOTIONS OF DYING PEOPLE

In the year before her death, Sofie did everything possible to surmount her illness. In between treatments to control the cancer, she tested her strength. She continued to teach high school, traveled to visit her children, cul-

■ *What do people fear about death? Findings reveal large individual and culture variations. For example, in a study of devout Islamic Saudi Arabians, fear of the decaying body and the unknown—common among Westerners—was entirely absent. Islam teaches that life on earth is a period of testing and preparation for life to come. Here, a devout Saudi Arabian Muslim pauses to face in the direction of Mecca and recite sacred prayers. (Photo courtesy: Fulvio Roiter/Corbis)*

tivated a garden, and took weekend excursions with Philip. Hope pervaded Sofie's approach to her deadly condition, and she spoke often about the disease—so much so that her friends wondered how she could confront it so directly.

As Sofie deteriorated physically, she moved in and out of a range of mental and emotional states. She was frustrated, and at times angry and depressed, about her inability to keep on fighting. I recall her lamenting anxiously on a day when she was in pain, "I'm sick, so very sick! I'm trying so hard, but I can't keep on." Once she asked when my husband and I, who were newly married, would have children. "If only I could live long enough to hold them in my arms!" she cried. In the last week, she appeared tired but free of struggle. Occasionally, she spoke of her love for us and commented on the beauty of the hills outside her window. But mostly, she looked and listened rather than actively participated in conversation. One afternoon, she fell permanently unconscious.

DO STAGES OF DYING EXIST?

As dying people move closer to death, are their reactions predictable? Do they go through a series of changes that are the same for everyone, or are their thoughts and feelings unique?

■ KÜBLER-ROSS'S THEORY. Although her theory has been heavily criticized, Elisabeth Kübler-Ross (1969) is credited with awakening society's sensitivity to the psychological needs of dying patients. From interviews with over 200 terminally ill people, she devised a stage theory of typical responses to the prospect of death and the ordeal of dying. Progress can be arrested at any stage, and some people move back and forth between stages. But overall, five

■ *What is this woman—a young wife and mother—thinking and feeling during her final weeks? Dying people move in and out of a range of mental and emotional states affected by many personal and situational variables. (Photo courtesy: Jerry Koontz/Index Stock)*

reactions characterize dying people. According to Kübler-Ross, when family members and health professionals understand these, they are in a better position to provide compassionate support.

1. **Denial.** On learning of the terminal illness, the person denies its seriousness to escape from the prospect of death. While the patient still feels reasonably well, denial is self-protective, allowing the individual to invest in rewarding activities and deal with the illness at his or her own pace. In reality, most people move in and out of denial, making great plans one day and acknowledging that death is near the next (Smith, 1993b).

   Kübler-Ross recommends accepting the dying patient's denial as a coping strategy he or she may need initially. But family members and health professionals should not act in ways that prolong denial by distorting the truth about the person's condition. In doing so, they can hinder planning for what should and should not be done medically once the person is near death.

2. **Anger.** As the illness worsens, it is harder to maintain denial. The realization that time is short promotes anger at having to die without being given a chance to do all one wants to do. Family members and health professionals are often targets of the patient's rage, resentment, and envy of those who will go on living. Still, they must tolerate rather than lash out at the patient's behavior, recognizing that the underlying cause is the unfairness of death.

3. **Bargaining.** Realizing the inevitability of death, the terminally ill person attempts to forestall it by bargaining for extra time—a deal he or she may try to strike with family members, friends, doctors, nurses, or God. Listening sympathetically is the best response to these efforts to sustain hope, as one doctor did to the pleas of a young AIDS-stricken father to live long enough to dance with his 8-year-old daughter at her wedding (Selwyn, 1996). At times, bargains are altruistic acts. Witness the following request from Tony, a 15-year-old leukemia patient, expressed to his mother:

   > I don't want to die yet. Gerry [youngest brother] is only 3 and not old enough to understand. If I could live just one more year, I could explain it to him myself and he will understand. Three is just too young. (Komp, 1996, pp. 69–70)

   Although many dying patients' bargains are unrealistic and impossible to fulfill, Tony lived for exactly one year—a gift to those who survived him.

4. **Depression.** When denial, anger, and bargaining fail to postpone the course of illness, the person becomes depressed about the loss of his or her life. Kübler-Ross regards depression as necessary

preparation for the last stage, acceptance. Unfortunately, many experiences associated with dying, including physical and mental deterioration, pain, lack of control, and being hooked to machines, promote despondency (Maier & Newman, 1995). Health care that responds humanely to the patient's wishes can limit hopelessness and despair.

5. **Acceptance.** Most people who reach acceptance, a state of peace and quiet about upcoming death, do so only in the last weeks or days. The weakened patient yields to death with its release from pain and anxiety. Disengagement from all but a few family members, friends, and caregivers occurs. Some dying people, in an attempt to pull away from all they have loved, withdraw into themselves for long periods of time. "I'm getting my mental and emotional house in order," one patient explained (Samarel, 1995, p. 101).

As in the other stages, people who have reached acceptance usually maintain some hope of living, if only a flicker. When hope is entirely gone, Kübler-Ross observed, death follows quickly.

■ EVALUATION OF KÜBLER-ROSS'S THEORY. Kübler-Ross cautioned that her five stages should not be viewed as a fixed sequence and that not all people display each of them—warnings that might have been better heeded had she not called them stages! Too often her theory has been interpreted simplistically, as a series of steps a "normal" dying person follows. Some health professionals, unaware of diversity in dying experiences, have insensitively tried to push patients through Kübler-Ross's sequence. And caregivers, through callousness or ignorance, can too easily dismiss a dying patient's legitimate complaints about treatment as "just what you would expect in Stage 2" (Corr, 1993; Kastenbaum, 1999b).

Research confirms, in line with Kübler-Ross's observations, that dying people are more likely to display denial after learning of their condition and acceptance shortly before death (Kalish, 1985). But rather than stages, the five reactions Kübler-Ross observed are best viewed as coping strategies that anyone may call on in the face of threat. Furthermore, her list is much too limited. Dying people react in many additional ways—for example, through efforts to conquer the illness, as Sofie displayed; through an overwhelming need to control what happens to their bodies during the dying process; and through acts of generosity and caring, as Tony's concern for his 3-year-old brother, Gerry, illustrates.

As these examples suggest, the most serious drawback to Kübler-Ross's theory is that dying patients' thoughts and feelings are removed from the contexts that grant them meaning. As we will see next, people's adaptations to impending death can be understood only in relation to the multidimensional influences that have contributed to their life course and that also shape this final phase.

CONTEXTUAL INFLUENCES ON ADAPTATIONS TO DYING

From the moment of her diagnosis, Sofie spent little time denying the deadliness of her disease. Instead, she met it head on, just as she had dealt with other challenges of life. Her impassioned plea to hold her grandchildren in her arms was less a bargain with fate than an expression of profound defeat that on the threshold of late adulthood, she would not live to enjoy its rewards. At the end, her quiet, withdrawn demeanor was probably resignation, not acceptance. She had been a person with a fighting spirit all her life, unwilling to give in to challenge.

According to recent theorists, a single strategy, such as acceptance, is not best for every dying patient. Instead, an **appropriate death** is one that makes sense in terms of the individual's pattern of living and values and, at the same time, preserves or restores significant relationships and is as free of suffering as possible (Pattison, 1978; Samarel, 1995; Weisman, 1984). New evidence reveals that biological, psychological, and social and cultural forces combine to affect the way people cope with their own dying—reactions that are as diverse as the life paths considered in previous chapters.

■ NATURE OF THE DISEASE. The course of the illness and its symptoms affect the dying person's reactions. For example, the extended nature of Sofie's illness and her physician's initial optimism about achieving a remission undoubtedly contributed to her efforts to try to conquer the disease. During the final month, when cancer had spread to Sofie's lungs and she could not catch her breath, she was agitated and fearful until oxygen and medication relieved her uncertainty about being able to breathe. In contrast, Nicholas's weakened heart and failing kidneys so depleted his strength that he responded only with passivity.

■ PERSONALITY AND COPING STYLE. Understanding the way individuals view stressful life events and have coped with them in the past helps us appreciate the way they manage the dying process. In one study, terminally ill patients were asked to describe their image of dying. Each regarded it differently—for example, as a responsibility, an insurmountable obstacle, a punishment, or an act of courage. These meanings helped explain their responses to their worsening illness (Paige, 1980, as reported by Samarel, 1995). Poorly adjusted individuals—those with conflict-ridden relationships and many disappointments in life—are usually more distressed (Kastenbaum, 1999).

■ FAMILY MEMBERS' AND HEALTH PROFESSIONALS' BEHAVIOR. Earlier we noted that a candid approach, in which everyone close to and caring for the dying person acknowledges the terminal illness, is best. Yet this also introduces the burden of participating in the work of dying with

■ *The individual's personality and coping style affect his or her adaptation to dying. Chuck Snook, a 59-year-old high school principal stricken with terminal prostate cancer and pictured here with his three grown children, approached death as he approached life. He loved his job and family and always did his best to greet challenges optimistically. "I have learned that attitude is everything," he wrote in his journal shortly after learning he had cancer. "I hope that I have prepared myself for my greatest adventure —the knowledge that my life is coming to an end." (Photo courtesy: The Pantagraph, Bloomington, IL)*

the patient—bringing relationships to closure, reflecting on life, and dealing with fears and regrets.

Because some people find it hard to engage in these tasks, they pretend that the disease is not as bad as it is. In patients inclined toward denial, a game of mutual pretense can be set in motion, in which all participants know the patient is dying but act as if it were not so. The game softens psychological pain for the moment but makes dying much more difficult (Samarel, 1995). At other times, the patient comes to suspect what he or she has not been told. In one instance, a terminally ill child flew into a rage because his doctor and a nurse spoke to him in ways that denied the fact that he would not grow up. Trying to get the child to cooperate with a medical procedure, the doctor said,

> "I thought you would understand, Sandy. You told me once you wanted to be a doctor."
>
> He screamed back, "I'm not going to be anything!" and threw an empty syringe at her.
>
> The nurse standing nearby asked, "What are you going to be?"
>
> "A ghost," said Sandy, and turned away from them. (Bluebond-Langner, 1977, p. 59)

The behavior of health professionals impeded Sandy's efforts to form a realistic time perspective and intensified his anger at the injustice of his premature death.

Care of the terminally ill is demanding and stressful. In one study, nurses trained to respond to the psychological

needs of dying patients and their families consistently provided empathetic and supportive care. Keys to their success were staff meetings aimed at strengthening interpersonal skills; day-to-day mutual support among staff; and development of a personal philosophy of living and dying, which ensured that each nurse did not feel especially threatened by his or her own death (Samarel, 1991). Research indicates that highly death-anxious health professionals are more likely to delay informing terminal patients of their diagnoses and to prolong life-saving treatment when death is near (Eggerman & Dustin, 1985; Schulz & Aderman, 1979).

Social support from family members also affects adaptation to dying. Dying people who feel they have much unfinished business to attend to are more anxious about impending death. But family contact reduces their sense of urgency to prolong life, perhaps because it permits at least some incomplete tasks to be worked through (Mutran et al., 1997).

Effective communication with the dying person is open and honest, fostering a trusting relationship. At the same time, it is oriented toward maintaining hope. Dying patients often move through a hope trajectory—at first, hope for a cure; later, hope for prolonging life; and finally, hope for a peaceful death with as few burdens as possible (Fanslow, 1981). Once patients near death stop expressing hope, those close to them need to accept. Family members who find letting go very difficult may benefit from the sensitive guidance of health professionals and counselors. The Caregiving Concerns table on page 638 offers suggestions for communicating with the dying.

■ SPIRITUALITY, RELIGION, AND CULTURE. Earlier we noted that a strong sense of spirituality reduces fear of death. Informal reports from health professionals suggest that this is as true for dying patients as for people in general. One experienced nurse commented,

> At the end, those [patients] with a faith—it doesn't really matter in what, but a faith in something—find it easier. Not always, but as a rule. I've seen people with faith panic and I've seen those without faith accept it [death]. But, as a rule, it's much easier for those with faith. (Samarel, 1991, pp. 64–65)

Vastly different cultural attitudes, guided by religious beliefs, also shape peoples' dying experiences. Buddhism, widely practiced in China, India, and Southeast Asia, fosters acceptance of death. By reading sutras (teachings of Buddha) to the dying person to calm the mind and emphasizing that dying leads to rebirth, Buddhists believe it is possible to reach Nirvana, a state beyond the world of suffering (Yeung, 1996). In many Native American societies, death is met with stoic self-control, an approach taught at an early age through stories that emphasize a circular, rather than linear, relationship between life and death and the impor-

Communicating with Dying People

SUGGESTION	DESCRIPTION
Be truthful about the diagnosis and course of the disease.	Be honest about what the future is likely to hold, thereby permitting the dying person to bring closure to his or her life by expressing sentiments and wishes and participating in decisions about treatment.
Listen perceptively and acknowledge feelings.	Be truly present, focusing full attention on what the dying person has to say and accepting the patient's feelings. Patients who sense another's presence and concern are more likely to relax physically and emotionally and express themselves.
Maintain realistic hope.	Assist the dying person in maintaining hope by encouraging him or her to focus on a realistic goal that might yet be achieved—for example, resolution of a troubled relationship or special moments with a loved one. Knowing the dying person's hope, family members and health professionals can often help fulfill it.
Assist in the final transition.	Assure the dying person that he or she is not alone, offering a sympathetic touch, a caring thought, or just a calm presence. Some patients who struggle may benefit from being granted *permission to die*—the message that giving up and letting go is all right.

Sources: Benoliel & Degner, 1995; Samarel, 1995.

tance of making way for others (Lewis, 1990). Among African Americans, a dying loved one signals a crisis that unites family members in caregiving. The terminally ill person remains an active and vital force within the family until he or she no longer can carry out this role—an attitude of respect that undoubtedly eases the dying process (Sullivan, 1995).

In sum, dying prompts a multitude of thoughts and emotions. Which ones are selected and emphasized depends on a wide array of contextual influences and differs greatly across individuals. Does this remind you of vital aspects of the lifespan perspective—that development is multidimensional and multidirectional? These assumptions are just as relevant to this final phase as they are to each earlier period.

A PLACE TO DIE

Unlike times past, when most deaths occurred at home, today about 80 percent take place in hospitals (Nuland, 1996). In the large, impersonal hospital environment, meeting the human needs of dying patients and their families is secondary, not because professionals lack concern, but because the work to be done focuses on saving lives. A dying patient represents a failure.

In the 1960s, a death awareness movement arose as a reaction to the death-avoiding practices of hospitals—complicated machinery hooked to patients with no chance of survival and lack of communication with dying patients. It led to medical care suited to the needs of dying people and to hospice programs, which have spread throughout the world. Let's visit each of these settings for dying.

HOME

Had Sofie and Nicholas been asked where they wanted to die, undoubtedly each would have responded, "At home" —the preference of 9 out of 10 Americans (Grande, Addington-Hall, & Todd, 1998; National Hospice Organization, 1999a). The reason is clear; the home offers an atmosphere of intimacy and loving care in which the terminally ill person is unlikely to feel abandoned or humiliated by physical decline or dependence on others.

Nevertheless, it is important not to romanticize home death. Because of dramatic improvements in medicine, dying people are sicker or much older than they used to be. Consequently, their bodies may be extremely frail, making ordinary activities—eating, sleeping, taking a pill, toileting, and bathing—major ordeals (Sankar, 1993). Health problems of elderly spouses; work and other responsibilities of family members; and the physical, psychological, and financial strain of providing home care can make it difficult to honor a terminally ill person's wish to die at home.

For many people, the chance to be with the dying person until the very end is a rewarding trade-off for the high stress of caregiving—a view reflected in the dramatic decline in AIDS deaths in hospitals. Currently, nearly half of AIDS victims die at home (Kelly, Chu, & Buehler, 1993). But the advantages and disadvantages of home death should be carefully weighed before undertaking it. Adequate support for the caregiver is essential. A home health aide is often necessary—a service (as we will see shortly) that hospice programs have made more accessible. When family relationships are conflict ridden, a dying patient introduces additional strains, negating the benefits of home death. Finally, even with professional help, most homes are poorly equipped to handle the medical and comfort care needs of the dying.

HOSPITAL

Hospital dying takes many forms. Each pattern is affected by the physical state of the dying person, the hospital unit in which it takes place, and the goal and quality of care.

Sudden deaths, due to injury or critical illness, typically occur in emergency rooms. Doctors and nurses must evaluate the problem and take action quickly. Little time is available for contact with family members. When staff break the news of death in a sympathetic manner and provide explanations, family members are grateful. Otherwise, feelings of anger, frustration, and confusion can add to their grief (Benoliel & Degner, 1995). Crisis intervention services are needed to help survivors cope with sudden death, and some hospitals are doing a better job of providing them.

Nicholas died on an intensive care ward, organized to prevent death in patients whose condition can worsen quickly. Privacy and communicating with the family were secondary to monitoring his condition. To prevent disruption of nurses' activities, Giselle and Sasha could be at Nicholas's side only at scheduled times. Dying in intensive care is an experience unique to technologically sophisticated societies. It is especially depersonalizing for patients like Nicholas, who linger between life and death while hooked to machines for months.

Cancer patients, who account for most cases of prolonged dying, typically die in general or specialized cancer care hospital units. When hospitalized for a long time, they reach out for help with physical and emotional needs, usually with mixed success. In these hospital settings, as in intensive care, a conflict of values is apparent (Hanson, Danis, & Garrett, 1997). The tasks associated with dying must be performed efficiently, so all patients can be served and health professionals are not drained emotionally by repeated attachments and separations. But we have seen that dying is a transition with profound personal, social, and cultural meanings. The hospice approach has done much to resolve this caregiving contradiction.

THE HOSPICE APPROACH

In medieval times, a **hospice** was a place where travelers could find rest and shelter. In the nineteenth and twentieth centuries, the word referred to homes for dying patients. Today, a hospice is not a place, but a comprehensive program of support services for terminally ill people and their families. It aims to provide a caring community sensitive to the dying person's needs so patients and family members can prepare for death in ways that are satisfying to them. Quality of life is central to the hospice approach. Here are its main features:

- The patient and family as a unit of care

- Emphasis on meeting the patient's physical, emotional, social, and spiritual needs, including controlling pain, retaining dignity and self-worth, and feeling cared for and loved

- Care provided by an interdisciplinary team, including the patient's doctor; a nurse or nurse's aid; a chaplain, counselor, or social worker; and a pharmacist

- The patient kept at home or in an inpatient setting with a homelike atmosphere where coordination of care is possible

- Focus on improving the quality of remaining life with **palliative,** or **comfort, care** that relieves pain and other symptoms (such as nausea, breathing difficulties, insomnia, and depression), aimed at protecting the patient's quality of life rather than prolonging life

- In addition to regularly scheduled home care visits, on-call services available 24 hours a day, 7 days a week

- Follow-up bereavement services offered to families in the year after a death

Because hospice care is a philosophy, not a facility, it can be applied in diverse ways. In Great Britain, care in a special inpatient unit, sometimes associated with a hospital, is typical. Home care has been emphasized in the United States. But hospice programs everywhere have expanded to include a continuum of care, from home to inpatient options. Central to the hospice approach is that the dying person and his or her family should be offered choices that guarantee an appropriate death. Some programs offer hospice day care, which permits caregivers to continue working or be relieved of the stresses of long-term care (Mahoney, 1998). Contact with others facing terminal illness is a supportive by-product of many hospice arrangements.

Currently, the United States has over 3,000 hospices, serving over 540,000 terminally ill patients annually. About 50 percent of patients dying of cancer and over 30 percent dying of AIDS choose hospice. Programs also admit patients suffering from a variety of other terminal illnesses (National Hospice Organization, 1999a, 1999b). Because the federal government recognizes that hospice care is a cost-effective alternative to expensive life-saving treatments, Medicare and Medicaid benefits are available, making it affordable for most dying patients and their families. Hospices also serve dying children—a tragedy so devastating that social support and bereavement intervention are vital (Wolfe, 1997).

As a long-range goal, hospice organizations are striving for broader acceptance of their patient and family-centered approach. At present, the majority of Americans are unfamiliar with the philosophy, although three out of four say they are very interested when it is described to them (National Hospice Organization, 1999a). The highly personalized attention hospices give to terminally ill patients and their families could be adapted for chronically ill patients and people faced with bereavement for any type of death—prolonged or sudden, expected or unexpected.

ASK YOURSELF . . .

Reread the description of Sofie's mental and emotional reactions to dying on pages 634–635. Then review the story of Sofie's life on page 4. To what extent did Sofie follow Kübler-Ross's stages? How were Sofie's responses consistent with her personality and lifelong style of coping with adversity?

■ *When 5-year-old Timmy's kidney failure was diagnosed as terminal, his parents could not accept the tragic news. Their hospital visits became shorter, and they evaded his anxious questions. Timmy tried to figure out what he had done to drive his parents away. Eventually, he blamed himself. He died with little physical pain but very much alone, and his parents suffered prolonged guilt after his death. Explain how hospice care could have helped Timmy and his family.*

THE RIGHT TO DIE

In 1976, the parents of Karen Ann Quinlan, a young woman who took drugs at a party and fell into an irreversible coma, sued to have her respirator turned off. The New Jersey Supreme Court, calling on Karen's right to privacy and the power of her parents as guardians, complied with this request. Although Karen was expected to die quickly, she breathed independently, continued to be fed intravenously, and lived another 10 years in a persistent vegetative state.

In 1983, 25-year-old Nancy Cruzan fell asleep at the wheel and was thrown from her car. After resuscitation, her heart and lungs worked but her brain was badly damaged. Like Karen, Nancy lay in a persistent vegetative state. Her parents wanted to end her meaningless existence by halting artificial feeding—a preference consistent with Nancy's statement to a friend a year earlier. But the Missouri courts refused, claiming that no written evidence of Nancy's

wishes existed. The U.S. Supreme Court upheld this ruling, but it encouraged the state of Missouri to reconsider. Eventually, Nancy's doctor agreed that it was in her best interests to terminate treatment, and a county judge honored this request. She died a week later, nearly 8 years after losing consciousness.

Before the 1950s, medical science could do little to extend the lives of terminal patients, so the right to die was of little concern. Today, medical advances mean that the same procedures that preserve life can prolong inevitable death, diminishing both quality of life and personal dignity.

The Quinlan and Cruzan cases brought right-to-die issues to the forefront of public attention, sparking over 40 states to pass legislation honoring patients' desires concerning withdrawal of treatment in case of terminal illness and, in a few instances, a persistent vegetative state. But the Supreme Court accepts variation among the states in standards of proof of a patient's intentions. In the United States, no uniform right-to-die policy exists, and controversy persists over how to handle the diverse circumstances in which patients and families make requests (Filene, 1998).

Euthanasia refers to the practice of ending the life of a person suffering from an incurable condition. Its forms, depicted in Figure 19.1, vary along a continuum from least active to most active. As we will see when we discuss the most common types in the following sections, public acceptance declines as euthanasia moves from permitting a natural death to deliberately killing a suffering person.

PASSIVE EUTHANASIA

In **passive euthanasia,** life-sustaining treatment is withheld or withdrawn, permitting a patient to die naturally. Should Nancy Cruzan have been allowed to die sooner? Was it right for Nicholas's doctors to have turned off his respirator at Giselle's request? Consider an Alzheimer's victim, whose disease has progressed to the point where he has lost all awareness and body functions. Should life support be withheld?

Recent polls reveal that the majority of people answer yes to these questions. When there is no hope of recovery, 85 percent of Americans support the patient's right to end treatment and 80 percent support family members' right to do so (Woodman, 1998). In 1986, the American Medical Association endorsed withdrawing all forms of treatment from

FIGURE 19.1

■ **Forms of euthanasia, from least active and highest public acceptance to most active and lowest public acceptance.**

the terminally ill when death is imminent and from those in a permanent vegetative state. Consequently, passive euthanasia is widely practiced as part of ordinary medical procedure, in which doctors exercise professional judgment.

Still, a minority of citizens do not endorse passive euthanasia. Religious denomination has surprisingly little effect on people's opinions. For example, most Catholics hold favorable views, despite slow official church acceptance due to fears that passive euthanasia might be a first step toward government-approved mercy killing. And because of controversial court cases, some doctors and health care institutions are unwilling to end treatment without legal protection.

In the absence of a national consensus on passive euthanasia, people can best ensure that their wishes will be followed by preparing an **advance medical directive**—a written statement of desired medical treatment should they

become incurably ill. Two types of advance directives are recognized in most states.

The first is a **living will,** which specifies the treatments a person does or does not want in case of a terminal illness, coma, or other near-death situation (see Figure 19.2). For example, a person might state that without reasonable expectation of recovery, he or she should not be kept alive through medical intervention of any kind. In addition, living wills sometimes specify that pain-relieving medication be given, even though this may shorten life. In Sofie's case, her doctor administered a powerful narcotic to relieve labored breathing and quiet her fear of suffocation. The narcotic suppressed respiration, leading death to occur hours or days earlier than if the medication had not been prescribed, but without distress. Such palliative care is accepted as appropriate and ethical medical practice.

Living Will

THIS DECLARATION is made this _____ day of _____ , 20 _____ .

I, _____ , being of sound mind, willfully and voluntarily make known my desires that my moment of death shall not be artificially postponed. If at any time I should have an incurable and irreversible injury, disease, or illness judged to be a terminal condition by my attending physician who has personally examined me and has determined that my death is imminent except for death delaying procedures. I direct that such procedures which would only prolong the dying process be withheld or withdrawn, and that I be permitted to die naturally with only the administration of medication, sustenance, or the performance of any medical procedure deemed necessary by my attending physician to provide me with comfort care.

In the absence of my ability to give directions regarding the use of such death delaying procedures, it is my intention that this declaration shall be honored by my family and physician as the final expression of my legal right to refuse medical or surgical treatment and accept the consequences from such refusal.

Signed: _____

City, County and State of Residence: _____

_____

_____

The declarant is personally known to me and I believe him or her to be of sound mind. I saw the declarant sign the declaration in my presence (or the declarant acknowledged in my presence that he or she had signed the declaration) and I signed the declaration as a witness in the presence of the declarant. At the date of this instrument, I am not entitled to any portion of the estate of the declarant according to the laws of intestate succession or, to the best of my knowledge and belief, under any will of declarant or other instrument taking effect at declarant's death, or directly financially responsible for declarant's medical care.

Witness: _____

Witness: _____

FIGURE 19.2

■ **Example of a living will.** This document is legal in the State of Illinois. Each person completing a living will should use a form specific to the state in which he or she resides, since state laws vary widely. (Courtesy of Office of the Attorney General, State of Illinois.)

Although living wills help ensure personal control, they do not guarantee it. Recognition of living wills is usually limited to patients who are terminally ill or otherwise expected to die shortly. Only a few states cover people in a persistent vegetative state due to injury or elders who linger with many chronic problems, including Alzheimer's disease—none of which are classified as terminal.

Because state laws vary widely and living wills cannot anticipate all future medical conditions and treatment options, a second form of advance directive—the **durable power of attorney for health care**—has become more common. It authorizes appointment of another person (usually, although not always, a family member) to make health care decisions on one's behalf and requires only a short signed and witnessed statement like this:

> I hereby appoint [name] to act for me and in my name (in any way I could act in person) to make any and all decisions for me concerning my personal care, medical treatment, hospitalization, and health care and to require, withhold, or withdraw any type of medical treatment or procedure, even though my death may ensue. (Courtesy of Office of the Attorney General, State of Illinois.)

The durable power of attorney for medical care is more flexible than the living will, since it permits a trusted spokesperson to confer with the doctor as medical circumstances arise. Because authority to speak for the patient is not limited to terminal illnesses, more latitude exists for dealing with unexpected situations. The majority of states have been receptive to this option, since it is a simple extension of existing durable powers of attorney, such as those that cover disposition of property when people cannot act for themselves (Jasper, 1996). In gay and lesbian and other close relationships not sanctioned by law, the durable power of attorney can ensure the partner's role.

Whether or not a person advocates passive euthanasia, it is important to have a living will, durable power of attorney, or both, since most deaths occur in hospitals. Surprisingly, fewer than 20 percent of Americans have executed such documents, perhaps because of widespread uneasiness about bringing up the topic of death, especially with relatives (Humphrey & Clement, 1998). To encourage people to make decisions about potential treatment while they are able, federal law now requires all medical facilities receiving federal funds to provide information at admission about state laws and institutional policies on patients' rights and advance directives.

Health care professionals, unclear about a patient's intent and fearing liability, will probably decide to continue treatment regardless of cost and a person's prior oral statements. Perhaps for this reason, a few states permit appointment of a *health care proxy*, or substitute decision maker, if a patient failed to provide an advance medical directive

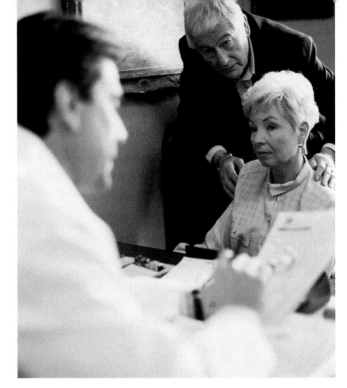

■ *This elderly man and woman talk with their doctor about an advance medical directive, a written statement that ensures their wishes about medical treatment will be followed should they become incurably ill. Appointing, through a durable power of attorney, a trusted spokesperson to confer with the doctor as medical circumstances arise is the most flexible approach, since it grants more latitude for dealing with unexpected situations. This couple will probably appoint each other. (Photo courtesy: Mike Malyszko/FPG International)*

while competent (Jasper, 1996). Proxies are an important means for covering children and adolescents, who cannot legally execute advance medical directives.

VOLUNTARY ACTIVE EUTHANASIA

In recent years, the right-to-die debate has shifted from withdrawal of treatment for the hopelessly ill to more active alternatives. In **voluntary active euthanasia,** doctors or others act directly, at a patient's request, to end suffering before a natural end to life. The practice is a form of mercy killing and is a criminal offense in most countries. Nevertheless, support for it is growing. In recent polls, about 90 percent of Dutch, 70 percent of American, and 65 percent of Canadian citizens approved of it, although more disagreement exists about the conditions in which it is warranted (Caddell & Newton, 1995; Genuis, Genuis, & Chang, 1994; van der Maas, Pijnenborg, & van Delden, 1995). When voluntary active euthanasia occurs in the United States, judges are usually lenient, granting suspended sentences or probation. These trends reflect rising public interest in self-determination in death as in life.

Nevertheless, attempts to legalize voluntary active euthanasia have prompted heated controversy. Supporters believe that it represents the most compassionate option for terminally ill people in severe pain. Opponents stress the moral difference between "letting die" and "killing" and point out that at times, even very sick patients recover. They also argue that involving doctors in taking the lives of suffering patients may impair people's trust in health professionals. Finally, a fear exists that legalizing this practice—even when strictly monitored to make sure it does not arise out of depression, loneliness, coercion, or a desire to diminish the burden of illness on others—could lead to a broadening of euthanasia. Initially limited to the terminally ill, it might be applied involuntarily to the frail, demented, or disabled—outcomes that most people find unacceptable and immoral (Kerridge & Mitchell, 1996).

Will legalizing voluntary active euthanasia lead us down a "slippery slope" to the killing of vulnerable people who did not ask to die? The Social Issues box on page 644 presents lessons from the Australian state of the Northern Territory, where a law allowing voluntary active euthanasia was passed in 1996, and from the Netherlands, where doctors can practice it without fear of prosecution.

ASSISTED SUICIDE

After checking Diane's blood count, Dr. Timothy Quill gently broke the news: leukemia. If she were to have any hope of survival, a strenuous course of treatment with only a 25 percent success rate would have to begin immediately. Convinced that she would suffer unspeakably from side effects and lack of control over her body, Diane chose not to undergo chemotherapy and a bone marrow transplant.

Dr. Quill made sure that Diane understood her options. As he adjusted to her decision, she opened another issue: Diane wanted no part of a lingering death. She calmly insisted that when the time came, she desired to take her own life in the least painful way possible—a choice she had discussed with her husband and son, who respected it. Realizing that Diane could get the most out of the time she had left only if her fears of prolonged pain were allayed, Dr. Quill granted her request for sleeping pills, making sure she knew the amounts needed for both sleep and suicide.

Diane's next few months were busy and fulfilling. Her son took leave from college to be with her, and her husband worked at home as much as possible. Gradually, bone pain, fatigue, and fever set in. Saying good-bye to her family and friends, Diane asked to be alone for an hour, took a lethal dose of medication, and died at home (Quill, 1991).

Assisting a suicide is illegal in many, but not all, U.S. states. Oregon is unique in having passed a law, called the Death with Dignity Act, that explicitly allows physicians to prescribe drugs so terminally ill patients can end their lives. Consistent with its policy of leaving assisted suicide in the hands of the states, the Supreme Court refused to review a challenge to the Oregon statute but also upheld the right of other states to ban assisted suicide (Mariner, 1997). In a 1997 ballot, Oregon residents voted to retain their assisted-suicide law.

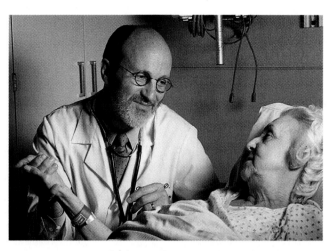

■ *In a prestigious medical journal, Dr. Timothy Quill explained how and why he assisted a terminally ill patient in taking her own life. With over half the public in favor of it, assisted suicide may become a more widespread, unofficial practice in the United States. Yet grave dilemmas surround it. (Photo courtesy: Bob Mahoney)*

Less public consensus exists for assisted suicide than for passive and voluntary active euthanasia. About 60 percent of Americans approve of the practice (Miller et al., 1994). But in a study in which nearly four hundred 60- to 100-year-olds were asked what they themselves would do if they were terminally ill with a low quality of life, only one-tenth said they would opt to end their lives. One-third favored yielding the decision to someone else, such as a family member, close friend, or doctor—a finding that, once again, underscores the importance of signing a durable power of attorney for health care. Those who stated they would choose assisted suicide tended to be higher-SES and were more often Caucasian- than African-American (Cicerelli, 1997).

Interest in assisted suicide has been sparked by Dr. Jack Kevorkian's "suicide machines," which permit terminally ill patients, after brief counseling, to self-administer lethal drugs and carbon monoxide. By 1999, Dr. Kevorkian had participated in over 50 such deaths. Less publicity surrounded Dr. Quill's decision to assist Diane—a patient he knew well after serving as her doctor for many years—in taking her own life. After he told her story in a prestigious medical journal, letters to the editor were mixed: "Dr. Quill provided . . . deep concern for the patient's well-being and respect for her choices," wrote one respondent. "It is never the role of a physician to perform such an act . . . [but rather] to apply his or her knowledge, skill, and caring to save lives," stated another (Cardo, 1991; Freer, 1991, p. 658).

With over half of the public in favor of it, assisted suicide may become a more widespread, unofficial practice in the United States, as it was in Diane's case and is in the Netherlands. Yet grave dilemmas, like those we discussed for voluntary active euthanasia, surround it. Analyzing the

SOCIAL ISSUES

VOLUNTARY ACTIVE EUTHANASIA: LESSONS FROM AUSTRALIA AND THE NETHERLANDS

In 1996, Australia's Northern Territory passed legislation allowing a terminally ill patient of sound mind and suffering from pain or other distress to ask a doctor to end his or her life. Two other doctors had to agree that the patient could not be cured, and a psychiatrist had to confirm that he or she was not suffering from treatable depression.

In the months after its passage, four deaths occurred under the Northern Territory euthanasia statute, and it was heavily criticized. The Aborigines, valuing harmony and balance with nature, regarded it as culturally inappropriate. Their leaders claimed the law would discourage Aboriginal elders, many of whom have experienced a lifetime of persecution at the hands of European settlers, from seeking medical care (Kerridge & Mitchell, 1996). Others considered the law to be a national issue, since patients traveled from other states to make use of it.

In 1997, the Northern Territory legislation was overturned by the Australian Parliament, which claimed that assemblies do not have the right to legislate intentional killing. But the episode placed Australia at the center of the euthanasia debate, and the issue continues to spark high passions across the country. Opponents have questioned the mental condition of patients seeking euthanasia. Supporters, such as June Burns, a 59-year-old woman with bladder cancer participating in TV ads that document the course of her illness, respond, "If I were a dog, they would have put me down by now. I feel life is very precious and . . . I wish I could go on, but I can't and I'd like to die with dignity." Some doctors who favor legalizing euthanasia claim to be building an underground network

of euthanasia clinics (British Broadcasting Corporation, 1999).

In the Netherlands, voluntary active euthanasia is a criminal offense. However, doctors who engage in it are exempt from punishment as long as they follow certain rules. They must make sure that the patient's physical or mental suffering is severe, with no prospect of relief; that no doubt exists about the patient's desire to die; that the patient's decision is free, well informed, and stable over time; that all other options for care have been exhausted or refused; and that another doctor has been consulted.

Over 50 percent of Dutch doctors say they practice euthanasia, with cancer patients being the majority of their cases. Despite safeguards, research reveals that both voluntary and involuntary euthanasia have occurred. In over 1,500 cases in a single year, doctors admitted actively causing death when a patient did not ask for it. Justifications varied; they included the impossibility of treating pain, a low quality of life, and terminal patients not dying after withdrawal of treatment. Although doctors judged most of these patients to be incompetent to decide for themselves, 21 percent were competent. When asked the reason for not discussing the decision with competent patients, doctors usually said they had done so previously; they did not voice a need to check how the patient felt currently (Hendin, Rutenfrans, & Zylicz, 1997). The elderly may be at special risk, since recent evidence suggests that a sharp decline in Dutch elder suicide has been compensated for by a rise in active euthanasia (Hendin, 1999).

The Northern Territory and Dutch examples reveal that legalizing voluntary active euthanasia can spark both

■ *Australian Aborigines' valuing of harmony with nature is evident in the natural images that permeate their artwork. They regarded the Northern Territory's legislation permitting voluntary active euthanasia as unnatural and culturally inappropriate. Their leaders also worried that the law would discourage Aboriginal elders from seeking medical care. It was eventually overturned by the Australian Parliament, which opposed legislation of intentional killing. The issue continues to spark heated debate across Australia. (Photo courtesy: Penny Tweedie/Corbis)*

the fear and the reality of death without consent. Nevertheless, terminally ill individuals in severe pain continue to plead for such laws. Recently, Canada and England established committees to investigate reforming laws on euthanasia. Each recommended against both active euthanasia and assisted suicide (Coatney, 1997; Scherer & Simon, 1999). Probably all would agree that when doctors feel compelled by respect for self-determination and relief of suffering to assist a patient in dying, they should be subject to the closest possible professional and legal oversight.

practice, one group of medical experts concluded that it is warranted only when the following conditions are met:

- The patient requests assisted suicide repeatedly and freely and is suffering intolerably, with no satisfactory options.

- The doctor thoroughly explores comfort-care alternatives with the patient.

- The practice is consistent with the doctor's fundamental values. (If not, the doctor should recommend transfer of care.)

- Even when the doctor and patient agree that there is no other acceptable choice, independent monitoring is crucial for preventing abuse. (Stevens, 1997)

Juries have seldom returned guilty verdicts in cases involving doctor-assisted suicide. Yet in April 1999, Kevorkian—the most vigorous American proponent of assisted suicide—was sentenced to 10 to 25 years in prison for second-degree murder and delivery of a controlled substance. Seven months earlier, he had given a terminally ill man a lethal injection, videotaped the death, and permitted the event to be broadcast on the CBS TV program *60 Minutes.* Then he dared prosecutors to charge him. The murder indictment prevented Kevorkian from introducing evidence indicating that the man wanted to kill himself. Such evidence would have been permissible had the charge been assisted suicide or voluntary active euthanasia.

Previously we noted that public opinion favors voluntary active euthanasia over assisted suicide. Yet in assisted suicide, the final act is solely the patient's, reducing the possibility of coercion. For this reason, some experts believe that legalizing assisted suicide is preferable to legalizing voluntary active euthanasia. However, in an atmosphere of intense pressure to contain health care costs and of high family caregiving burdens (see Chapter 17), legalizing either practice can be dangerous (Woodman, 1998). Although currently the U.S. Supreme Court does not recognize the right of terminally ill patients to a doctor's help in ending their lives, the majority of justices have indicated that they might change their minds in the future, after they have more evidence on the practical impact of such a right (Dworkin, 1997). Helping incurable, suffering patients who yearn for death is a profound moral and legal problem.

ASK YOURSELF . . .

Noreen knows that the majority of people die gradually. Thinking ahead to the day she dies, she imagines a peaceful scene in which she says good-bye to loved ones. What social and medical practices are likely to increase Noreen's chances of dying in the manner she desires?

- *If he should ever fall terminally ill, Ramon is certain that he wants doctors to halt life-saving treatment. To best ensure that his wish will be granted, what should Ramon do? Why is it impossible to guarantee that Ramon's desires will be honored in the United States at this time?*

BEREAVEMENT: COPING WITH THE DEATH OF A LOVED ONE

Loss is an inevitable part of existence throughout the lifespan. Even when change takes place for the better, we let go of some aspects of experience so we can embrace others. Consequently, our development prepares us for profound loss.

Bereavement is the experience of losing a loved one by death. The root of this word means "to be robbed," suggesting unjust and injurious stealing of something valuable. Consistent with this image, we respond to loss with **grief**—intense physical and psychological distress. When we say someone is grief-stricken, we imply that his or her total way of being is affected.

Because grief can be overwhelming, cultures have devised ways of helping their members move beyond it to deal with the life changes demanded by death of a loved one. **Mourning** is the culturally specified expression of the bereaved person's thoughts and feelings. Customs—such as gathering with family and friends, dressing in black, attending the funeral, and observing a prescribed mourning period with special rituals—vary greatly among societies and ethnic groups. But all have in common the goal of helping people work through their grief and learn to live in a world that does not include the deceased.

Clearly, grief and mourning are closely linked. In fact, we often use the two words interchangeably in everyday language. Let's look closely at how people respond to the death of a loved one.

PHASES OF GRIEVING

Many theorists studying a wide range of types of loss and bereaved individuals—both children and adults—have concluded that grieving usually takes place in three phases, each characterized by a different set of responses (Bowlby, 1980; Parkes & Weiss, 1983; Pollock, 1987; Rando, 1995):

1. **Avoidance.** On hearing the news, the survivor experiences shock followed by disbelief, which may last from hours to weeks. A numbed feeling serves as "emotional anesthesia" while the bereaved person begins to experience painful awareness of the loss. The loved one has been a part of daily life for so long that his or her death is too much to comprehend immediately.

2. **Confrontation.** In this phase, the mourner begins to confront the reality of the loss. Consequently, grief is experienced most intensely. The bereaved person may display a range of emotional reactions, including anxiety, sadness, protest, anger, helplessness, frustration, abandonment, and yearning for the loved one. In addition, the person may be absentminded, unable to concentrate, and preoccupied with thoughts of the deceased. At times, self-destructive behaviors, such as taking drugs or driving too fast, occur. Loss of sleep and appetite are common. Most of these responses are symptoms of depression—an invariable component of grieving (Karam, 1994).

Although the confrontation phase is the most difficult, each pang of grief that results from an unmet wish to be reunited with the deceased brings the mourner closer to the realization that the loved one is gone. After hundreds, perhaps thousands, of these painful moments, the bereaved person comprehends that a cherished relationship will have to be given up.

3. **Accommodation.** As grief subsides, attention starts to shift to the surrounding world. The survivor must transform the relationship with the deceased from physical presence to an inner representation. Although the loved one is not forgotten, emotional energies are freed for meeting everyday responsibilities, investing in new activities and goals, and seeking the companionship and love of others. On certain days, such as family celebrations or the anniversary of death, grief reactions may resurface and require attention, but they do not interfere with a healthy, positive approach to life.

How long does grieving last? No single answer can be given. Confrontation, the period of acute grief, may continue for several months to over a year. An occasional upsurge of grief, typical during the accommodation phase, may persist for a lifetime and is a normal response to losing a much-loved spouse, partner, child, or friend (Shuchter & Zisook, 1995).

PERSONAL AND SITUATIONAL VARIATIONS

Like dying, grieving is affected by many factors that make the duration of each phase and the reactions within it unique. Once again, personality, coping style, and religious and cultural background are influential. Sex differences are also evident, with women better prepared to deal with grief because they express feelings and seek social support more readily (Rando, 1995). Furthermore, the quality of the mourner's relationship with the deceased is important. For example, an end to a loving, fulfilling bond may lead to anguished grieving, but it is unlikely to leave the residue of guilt and regret that often follows a conflict-ridden, ambivalent tie.

Circumstances surrounding the death—whether it is sudden and unanticipated or follows a prolonged illness—also shape mourners' responses. And the nature of the lost relationship in addition to when the death occurs in the life course makes a difference as well.

■ SUDDEN, UNANTICIPATED VERSUS PROLONGED, EXPECTED DEATHS. Sudden, unexpected deaths are usually the result of murder, suicide, war, accident, or natural disaster (Kastenbaum, 1999a). In these instances, the phase of avoidance may be especially pronounced and confrontation highly traumatic because shock and disbelief are extreme. In a survey of a representative sample of 18- to 45-year-old adults in a large American city, the trauma most often reported as prompting an intense, debilitating stress reaction was the sudden, unanticipated death of a loved one, an event experienced by 60 percent of the participants (Breslau et al., 1998). In contrast, during prolonged dying, the bereaved person has had time to engage in **anticipatory grieving**—acknowledging that the loss is inevitable and preparing emotionally for it.

Adjusting to a death is made easier when the survivor understands the reasons for it. Without explanations that make sense, mourners often remain anxious and confused. This barrier to confronting loss is tragically apparent in cases of sudden infant death syndrome (SIDS), in which doctors cannot tell parents exactly why their apparently healthy baby has died (see Chapter 4, page 123). That death seems "senseless" also complicates grieving after suicides; terrorist attacks; school and drive-by shootings; and hurricanes, earthquakes, and other natural disasters. In Western societies, people tend to believe that momentous events should be comprehensible and nonrandom. When a death is sudden and unexpected, it can threaten basic assumptions about a just, benevolent, and controllable world (Gluhoski & Wortman, 1996).

Suicide, particularly that of a young person, is especially hard to bear. Compared with survivors of other sudden deaths, people grieving a suicidal loss are more likely to blame themselves for what happened, concluding that they contributed to or could have prevented it. In one study, college students who had survived a suicide scored higher than those who had experienced any other type of loss in feelings of shame, a sense of rejection by the deceased, and self-destructive behavior, perhaps because of persisting feelings of responsibility for what had happened (Silverman, Range, & Overholser, 1994). Typically, recovery from grief after a suicide is quite prolonged (Thompson & Range, 1992).

■ PARENTS GRIEVING THE LOSS OF A CHILD. The death of a child, whether unexpected or foreseen, is the most difficult loss an adult can face (Stillion, 1995). It brings special grieving problems because children are extensions of parents' feelings about themselves—the focus of hopes and dreams, including parents' sense of immortality. Also, since children depend on, admire, and appreciate their parents in a deeply gratifying way, they are an unmatched source of love. Finally, the unnaturalness of a child's death complicates it. Children are not supposed to die before their parents.

Parents who have lost a child often report considerable distress many years later, along with frequent thoughts of the deceased (Finkbeiner, 1996). The guilt triggered by outliving their child frequently becomes a tremendous burden, even when parents "know" better. For example, a psychologist who understood that his daughter's cancer was not

■ *Sudden, unanticipated deaths often prompt an intense, debilitating stress reaction. Here teenagers express their feelings for a peer victim of an automobile accident by constructing a shrine at the site of the crash. Shock and disbelief make confronting the reality of this avoidable, premature death especially traumatic. (Photo courtesy: Conklin/Monkmeyer Press)*

hereditary nevertheless said to a therapist, "Her genes allowed her to develop cancer. I gave her her genes. Therefore, I killed my daughter" (Rando, 1991b, p. 239).

Although a child's death sometimes leads to marital breakup, this is likely to happen only when the relationship was unsatisfactory before. If parents can reorganize the family system and reestablish a sense of life's meaning by investing in other children and activities, then the result can be firmer family commitments and personal growth.

■ CHILDREN AND ADOLESCENTS GRIEVING THE LOSS OF A PARENT. The loss of an attachment figure has long-standing consequences for children. When a parent dies, children's basic sense of security and being cared for is threatened. Death of a sibling not only deprives children of a close emotional tie, but informs them, often for the first time, of their own vulnerability.

In several longitudinal studies, children grieving a family loss described frequent crying, trouble concentrating in school, sleep difficulties, headaches, and other physical symptoms several months to years after a death (Davies, 1987; Silverman & Worden, 1992). At the same time, many children said they actively maintained mental contact with their dead parent or sibling, dreaming about and speaking to them regularly. In a follow-up 7 to 9 years after sibling loss, thinking about the deceased brother or sister at least once a day was common (Martinson, Davies, & McClowry, 1987; Silverman & Nickman, 1996). These images seem to facilitate coping with loss and are sometimes reported by bereaved adults as well.

Cognitive development contributes to the ability to grieve. For example, children with an immature understanding of death may believe the dead parent left voluntarily, perhaps in anger, and that the other parent may also disappear. For these reasons, young children need careful, repeated explanations assuring them that the parent did not want to die and was not angry at them (Furman, 1984). Keeping the truth from children isolates them and often leads to profound regrets. One 8-year-old who learned only a half-hour in advance that his sick brother was dying reflected, "If only I'd known, I could have said good-bye."

Regardless of children's level of understanding, honesty, affection, and reassurance help them tolerate painful feelings of loss. Grief-stricken school-age children are usually more willing to confide in parents than are adolescents. To appear normal, teenagers tend to keep their grieving from both adults and peers. Consequently, they are more likely than children to become depressed or to escape from grief through acting-out behavior (Corr & Balk, 1996).

■ ADULTS GRIEVING THE LOSS OF AN INTIMATE PARTNER. Recall from Chapter 18 that after the death of a spouse, adaptation to widowhood varies greatly, with age, social support, and personality making a difference.

After a period of intense grieving, most widowed elders in Western nations fare well (see pages 610–611 to review). Younger individuals display more negative outcomes (Stroebe & Stroebe, 1993). Loss of a spouse or partner in early or middle adulthood is a nonnormative event that profoundly disrupts life plans. Finding a positive new direction as a single person is harder than it is for widowed elders. Older widows and widowers have many more contemporaries in similar circumstances. And most have already attained important life goals or adjusted to the fact that they will not be attained.

In addition to dealing with feelings of loss, young and middle-aged widows and widowers often must assume a greater role in comforting others, especially children. They also face the stresses of single parenthood and a rapid shrinking of the social network established during their lives as couples (Lopata, 1996). Younger widows frequently report that the most valuable support they received came from their mothers, many of whom were also widowed, and from other widows (Bankoff, 1983).

The death of an intimate partner in a gay or lesbian relationship presents unique challenges. Death due to AIDS is stigmatized—feared greatly by the surrounding culture. Consequently, the dying person and his or her partner are vulnerable to avoidance and criticism from heterosexual family members. When relatives limit or bar the partner from participating in funeral services, they profoundly disrupt the process of grieving (Housel, 1995). Fortunately, gay and lesbian communities provide helpful alternative support, in the form of memorial services and other rituals, such as the international AIDS Quilt, in which survivors contribute panels memorializing those they have lost to AIDS.

■ BEREAVEMENT OVERLOAD. When a person experiences several deaths in succession, *bereavement overload* can occur. Multiple losses deplete the coping resources of even well-adjusted people, leaving them emotionally overwhelmed and unable to resolve their grief. For many young adults, especially members of the gay community who have lost partners and friends, AIDS presents this challenge. In a study of over 700 homosexual men, those experiencing two or more losses in close succession reported more distress and substance use than did those with only a single loss (Martin & Dean, 1993).

Since old age often brings the death of spouse, siblings, and friends in close succession, elders are also at risk for bereavement overload. But recall from Chapter 18 that compared with young people, older adults are often better equipped to handle these losses. They know that decline and death are expected in late adulthood, and they have had a lifetime of experience through which to develop effective coping strategies.

Finally, the recent rash of random murders in American schools has led more children and adolescents to wit-

■ *In the Columbine High School shooting aftermath, these students wear ribbons in memory of slain victims and are overcome as they stand before a memorial in a city park. Because of the recent rash of random murders in American schools, more children and adolescents have witnessed the unexpected, violent deaths of teachers and classmates. They are at risk for bereavement overload—prolonged, overwhelming grief that is difficult to resolve. (Photo courtesy: Jeff Mitchell/Reuters/Archive Photos)*

ness the unexpected, violent deaths of teachers and classmates. These young survivors suffer profoundly—from intense shock, prolonged grief, frequent mental replays of the vicious attack and gruesome outcomes, and fear of the settings in which those events occurred (Nader, 1997). The greater the exposure to the catastrophic death scene, the more severe these reactions—an effect further magnified if the young person knows one or more people who died (Nader et al., 1990).

Funerals and other bereavement rituals, illustrated in the Variations box on pages 650–651, assist mourners of all ages in resolving grief with the help of family and friends. Bereaved individuals who remain preoccupied with loss and who have difficulty resuming interest in everyday activities benefit from special interventions designed to help them adjust.

BEREAVEMENT INTERVENTIONS

Social support is crucial during the aftermath of death. Yet it is often difficult to provide. Parents, caught up in their own grief, may not be available to their children. And relatives and friends trying to be helpful may not always succeed. When bereaved people were asked to describe contacts that were supportive, they mentioned freedom to express feelings in a receptive, nonjudgmental atmosphere. They regarded giving advice and encouraging recovery negatively. Nongrieving individuals were aware of what they should and should not say to the bereaved. Nevertheless, mourners often reported that they did not get as much help as they needed, perhaps because of others' inexperience or fear of doing the wrong thing (Lehman, Ellard, & Wortman, 1986).

Experts agree that sympathy and understanding are sufficient for most people to undertake the tasks necessary to recover from grief (see the Caregiving Concerns table below). But relatives and friends could clearly benefit from training in how to respond to the bereaved. Often mourners are too overcome to acknowledge well-meaning interactions, causing others to withdraw (Stylianos & Vachon, 1993). Listening patiently and "just being there" are among the best ways to help.

Bereavement interventions typically assist people in drawing on their existing social network and provide extra social support. Many self-help groups exist, bringing together mourners who have experienced the same type of loss for regular sessions over several months. Research supports their effectiveness in reducing stress and, in the case of a child's death, assisting couples in reworking a damaged relationship (Lieberman, 1993). Groups for bereaved children and adolescents provide valuable peer support that teenagers, especially, are unwilling to seek on their own (Bacon, 1996; Corr & Balk, 1996). Interventions following multiple violent deaths in schools or neighborhoods must protect young people from unnecessary reexposure, assist parents and teachers with their own distress so they can effectively offer comfort, and be culturally sensitive. After shootings on the grounds of one school, administrators arranged for a ceremony that removed angry dead souls. Only then would the large number of Vietnamese Buddhist pupils return to their classrooms (Nader, Dubrow, & Stamm, 1999).

At times, mourning does not proceed smoothly. Sudden, violent, and unexplainable deaths; the loss of a child; a death that the mourner feels he or she could have prevented; or an ambivalent or dependent relationship with the deceased make it harder for bereaved people to overcome their loss (Murphy et al., 1999; Raphael et al., 1993). In these instances, *grief therapy*, or individual counseling with a specially trained professional, is often necessary. One potentially helpful approach for adults is to assist the person in finding some value in the grieving experience—for example, gaining insight into the meaning of relationships and into their own capacity to cope with adversity. In a study tracking middle-aged adults' adjustment after a family member's death, the ability to see benefits for one's own life was strongly related to well-being 13 and 18 months later (Davis, Nolen-Hoeksema, & Larson, 1998).

DEATH EDUCATION

Preparatory steps can be taken to help people of all ages cope with death more effectively. The death awareness movement that sparked increased sensitivity to the needs of dying patients has also led to the rise of death education. Courses in death, dying, and bereavement are now a familiar part of offerings in colleges and universities. Instruction has been integrated into the professional

CAREGIVING CONCERNS

Suggestions for Resolving Grief After a Loved One Dies

SUGGESTION	DESCRIPTION
Give yourself permission to feel the loss.	Clarify the reasons for the death and permit yourself to confront all thoughts and emotions associated with it. Make a conscious decision to overcome your grief, recognizing that this will take time.
Accept social support.	In the early part of grief, let others reach out to you by making meals, running errands, and keeping you company. Be assertive; ask for what you need so people who would like to help know what to do.
Be realistic about the course of grieving.	Expect to have some negative and intense reactions, such as feeling anguished, sad, and angry, that last from weeks to months and may occasionally resurface years after the death. Since there is no one way to grieve, find the best way for you.
Remember the deceased.	Review your relationship to and experiences with the deceased, permitting yourself to see that you can no longer be with him or her as before. Form a new relationship based on memories, keeping it alive through photographs, commemorative donations, prayers, and other symbols and actions.
At the appropriate time, invest in new activities and relationships.	Determine which roles you must give up and assume as a consequence of the death and take deliberate steps to incorporate these into your life. Set small goals at first, such as a night at the movies, a dinner date with a friend, or a week's vacation.

Source: Rando, 1991a.

CULTURAL VARIATIONS IN MOURNING BEHAVIOR

The ceremonies that commemorated Sofie's and Nicholas's deaths—the first Jewish, the second Quaker —were strikingly different. Yet they served common goals: providing a setting in which loss could be shared and mobilizing the community in support of the bereaved.

At the funeral home, Sofie's body was washed and shrouded, a Jewish ritual signifying return to a state of purity. Then it was placed in a plain wooden (not metal) coffin, so as not to impede the natural process of decomposition. To underscore the finality of death, Jewish tradition does not permit viewing of the body; it remains in a closed coffin. Traditionally, the coffin is not left alone until burial; the community maintains a day-and-night vigil (Getzel, 1995).

To return the body quickly to the life-giving earth from which it sprang, Sofie's funeral was scheduled 3 days after death, as soon as relatives could gather. As the service began, Sofie's husband and children symbolized their anguish by cutting a black ribbon and pinning it to their clothing. The rabbi recited psalms of comfort, followed by a eulogy in which he

related memories of Sofie that family members had shared with him. The service continued at the graveside. Once the coffin had been lowered into the ground, relatives and friends took turns shoveling earth on it, each participating in the irrevocable act of burial. The service concluded with the "homecoming" prayer called *Kaddish*, which affirms life while accepting death.

The family returned home to light a memorial candle, which burned throughout *shiva*, the 7-day period of mourning. A meal of consolation prepared by others followed, creating a warm feeling of community. Jewish custom prescribes that after 30 days, life should gradually return to normal. When a parent dies, the mourning period is extended to 12 months.

In the tradition of Quaker simplicity, Nicholas's death did not require elaborate preparation of the body, a casket, or a hearse to carry him to a cemetery. He was cremated promptly. During the next week, relatives and close friends gathered with Giselle and Sasha at their home. Together, they planned a memorial service uniquely suited to celebrating Nicholas's life.

On the appointed day, people who had known Nicholas sat in chairs arranged in concentric circles. Standing at the center, a clerk of the Friends (Quaker) Meeting extended a welcome and explained to newcomers the custom of worshipping silently, with those who feel moved to speak rising and sharing thoughts and feelings at any time. Over the next hour, many people offered personal statements about Nicholas or read poems and selections from Scripture. Giselle and Sasha provided concluding comments. Then everyone joined hands to close the service, and a reception for the family followed.

Religious and cultural variations in mourning behavior are vast—both within and across societies. For most Jews and Christians, extensive ritual accompanies a funeral and burial. In contrast, the Quaker memorial service is among the least ritualized. In some groups, grief is expressed freely. For example, venting deep emotion is often part of African-American funerals, particularly in the southern United States. Christians and Jews of European descent are usually restrained in their display of sorrow (Cytron, 1993; Sullivan, 1995). And in some

---

training of doctors, nurses, psychologists, social workers, and other helping professionals. It can also be found in adult education programs in many communities. And it has filtered down to a few elementary and secondary schools.

Death education at all levels has the following goals:

■ Increasing students' understanding of the physical and psychological changes that accompany dying

■ Helping students learn how to cope with the death of a loved one

■ Preparing students to be informed consumers of medical and funeral services

■ Promoting understanding of social and ethical issues involving death

Courses vary widely in format. Some focus on conveying information, whereas others are experiential and include many activities—role-playing, discussions with the terminally ill, visits to mortuaries and cemeteries, and personal awareness exercises. Research reveals that using a lecture style leads to gains in knowledge, but it often leaves students more uncomfortable about death than when they entered. In contrast, experiential programs that help people confront their own mortality are less likely to heighten death anxiety and sometimes reduce it (Durlak & Riesenberg, 1991; Maglio & Robinson, 1994). These findings suggest that to reach students cognitively and emotionally, death educators need to be more than well informed. They must be sensitive and responsive, skilled at communication, and able to help people deal with distress.

societies, letting any feeling show is actively discouraged. The Balinese of Indonesia must remain calm in the face of death if the gods are to hear their prayers. With the help of supporters who joke, tease, and distract, mourners work hard to keep their composure, al- though the Balinese acknowledge the existence of underlying grief (Rosenblatt, 1993).

Religions also render accounts of the aftermath of death—teachings that console both dying and bereaved individuals. Jewish tradition affirms personal survival, although its form is not clearly specified. Greater emphasis is placed on the survival of a people— living on by granting life and care to others. Unlike other Christian faiths, Quakers focus almost exclusively on the here and now—"salvation by character" through working for peace, justice, and a loving community. Little attention is given to fear of hell or hope of heaven. The religions of tribal and village cultures typically include elaborate beliefs about ancestor spirits and the afterlife and customs designed to ease the journey of the deceased to the spiritual world.

By announcing that a death has occurred, ensuring social support,

memorializing the deceased, and conveying a philosophy of life after death, funerals and memorial services are of great assistance to the bereaved. Yet some evidence indicates that these customs may be on the decline in the United States (Fulton, 1995). In large cities, more deaths are being followed by disposal of the body, without a public or religious observance of any kind. The trend is worrisome, since it deprives grief-stricken people of community assurance of love and concern. And in a death-denying society, it robs new generations of a crucial opportunity to learn about life's most basic fact: the inevitability of human mortality.

 Venting deep emotion is often part of African-American funerals, particularly in the southern United States. In this Baptist funeral in a small North Carolina town, the coffin of a beloved community member is escorted out the church door for its journey to the cemetery. Family members and friends express their feelings openly. (Photo courtesy: Bruce Dale/National Geographic Society)

Whether acquired in the classroom or in our daily lives, our ideas and feelings about death are forged through interactions with others. Becoming more aware of how we die and our own mortality, we encounter our greatest loss, but we also gain. Dying people have at times confided in those close to them that awareness of the limits of their lifespan permitted them to dispense with superficial distractions and wasted energies and focus on what is truly important in their lives. As one AIDS patient summed up, "[It's] kind of like life, just speeded up"—an accelerated process in which over a period of weeks to months one grapples with issues that normally would have taken years to decades (Selwyn, 1996, p. 36). Applying this lesson to ourselves, we learn that by being in touch with death and dying, we can live ever more fully.

ASK YOURSELF . . .

■ *Compare the phases of grieving with terminally ill patients' thoughts and feelings as they move closer to death, described on pages 635–637. Can a dying person's reactions be viewed as a form of grieving? Explain.*

Cite examples of age-graded, history-graded, and nonnormative influences on the grieving process, referring to research findings on pages 645–649. If you need to review these contexts for lifespan development, return to Chapter 1, pages 11–12.

■ *Explain how death education can help people cope with death more effectively.*

HOW WE DIE

Describe the physical changes of dying, along with their implications for defining death and the meaning of death with dignity.

■ Of the one-quarter of people in industrialized nations who die suddenly, the overwhelming majority are victims of heart attacks. Death is long and drawn out for three-fourths of people—many more than in times past, due to life-saving medical technology.

■ In general, dying takes place in three phases: the **agonal phase**, during which the body first cannot sustain life any more; **clinical death**, a short interval in which resuscitation is still possible; and **mortality**, or permanent death.

■ In most industrialized nations, **brain death** is accepted as the definition of death. However, the thousands of patients who remain in a **persistent vegetative state** reveal that the brain death standard does not always solve the dilemma of when to halt treatment of the incurably ill.

■ Most people will not experience an easy death. Therefore, we can best ensure death with dignity by supporting dying patients through their physical and psychological distress, being candid about death's certainty, and helping them learn enough about their condition to make reasoned choices about treatment.

UNDERSTANDING OF AND ATTITUDES TOWARD DEATH

Discuss age-related changes in conceptions of and attitudes toward death, and cite factors that influence death anxiety.

■ Ours is a death-denying society. Compared with earlier generations, more young people reach adulthood having had little contact with death, and adults are often reluctant to bring up the topic.

■ By age 7, children typically grasp the three components of the death concept—**permanence, universality,** and **nonfunctionality**—in the order just given. Experiences with death and religious teachings affect children's understandings. When parents talk about death candidly, children usually have a good grasp of the facts of death and an easier time accepting it.

■ Adolescents often fail to apply their understanding of death to everyday life. Aware that death happens to everyone and can occur at any time, teenagers are nevertheless high risk takers and do not take death personally. By discussing concerns about death with adolescents, adults can help them build a bridge between death as a logical concept and their personal experiences.

■ As people pass from early to middle adulthood, they become more conscious of the finiteness of their lives. Compared with middle-aged adults, elders focus more on practical matters of how and when death might happen.

■ Large individual and cultural variations in **death anxiety** exist. Overall, fear of death declines with age, reaching its lowest level in late adulthood and in adults with deep faith in some form of higher being. People with mental health problems generally express more severe death concerns.

THINKING AND EMOTIONS OF DYING PEOPLE

Describe and evaluate Kübler-Ross's stage theory, citing factors that influence the responses of dying patients.

■ According to Elisabeth Kübler-Ross's stage theory, five responses are typical as dying patients move closer to death: **denial, anger, bargaining, depression,** and **acceptance.** However, these reactions do not necessarily occur, and dying people often display other coping strategies.

■ An **appropriate death** is one that makes sense in terms of the individual's pattern of living and values. A host of contextual variables—nature of the disease; personality and coping style; family members' and health professionals' truthfulness and sensitivity; and spirituality, religion, and cultural background—combine to affect the way people respond to their own dying.

A PLACE TO DIE

Evaluate the extent to which homes, hospitals, and the hospice approach meet the needs of dying people and their families.

■ Although the overwhelming majority of people want to die at home, caring for a dying patient is highly stressful. Even with professional help, most homes are poorly equipped to handle the medical and comfort-care needs of the dying.

■ In hospitals, sudden deaths typically occur in emergency rooms. Sympathetic explanations from staff can reduce family members' anger, frustration, and confusion. Intensive care is especially depersonalizing for patients who are hooked to machines for months. Even in general or specialized cancer care units, emphasis on efficiency usually interferes with a dignified death.

■ Whether a person dies at home or in a hospital, the **hospice** approach strives to meet the dying person's physical, emotional, social, and spiritual needs and emphasizes quality of life over life-prolonging measures through **palliative,** or **comfort, care.** In the year after death, bereavement services are offered to families.

THE RIGHT TO DIE

Discuss controversies surrounding euthanasia and assisted suicide.

■ The same medical procedures that preserve life can prolong inevitable death, diminishing quality of life and personal dignity. Forms of **euthanasia** vary along a continuum from least active to most active.

■ **Passive euthanasia,** withholding or withdrawing life-sustaining treatment from a hopelessly ill patient, is widely accepted and practiced. Because U.S. state laws vary widely, people can best ensure that their wishes will be followed by preparing an **advance medical directive**—either a **living will** that contains directions for treatment or a **durable power of attorney for health care.** When no advance medical directive exists, a few U.S. states permit appointment of a health care proxy.

■ Public support for **voluntary active euthanasia,** in which doctors or others comply with a suffering patient's request to die before a natural end to life, is growing. Nevertheless, the practice has sparked heated controversy, fueled by fears that it will undermine trust in health professionals and lead us down a "slippery slope" to killing of vulnerable people who did not ask to die.

■ Less public consensus exists for assisted suicide. Like voluntary active euthanasia, it is surrounded by grave ethical dilemmas.

BEREAVEMENT: COPING WITH THE DEATH OF A LOVED ONE

Describe the phases of grieving, factors that underlie individual variations, and bereavement interventions.

■ **Bereavement** refers to the experience of losing a loved one by death, **grief** to the intense physical and psychological distress that accompanies loss. **Mourning** customs are culturally prescribed expressions of thoughts and feelings designed to help people work through their grief.

■ Grieving usually takes place in three phases: **avoidance,** involving shock and disbelief; **confrontation,** in which the mourner confronts the reality of the loss and experiences grief most intensely; and **accommodation,** or shifting attention to the surrounding world as grief subsides.

■ Like dying, grieving is affected by many personal and situational factors that make the duration of each phase and reactions within it unique. After a sudden, unanticipated death, avoidance may be especially pronounced and confrontation highly traumatic because shock and disbelief are extreme. In contrast, a prolonged, expected death grants the bereaved person time to engage in **anticipatory grieving.**

■ When a parent loses a child or a child loses a parent or sibling, grieving is generally very intense and prolonged. Loss of a spouse or partner in early or middle adulthood profoundly disrupts life plans. Younger widowed individuals usually display more negative outcomes than do widowed elders. Adjusting to the death of a gay or lesbian partner may be complicated by stigma associated with AIDS and by avoidance and criticism from heterosexual family members. Young adult members of the gay community and the elderly are at risk for bereavement overload.

■ Sympathy and understanding are usually sufficient for people to recover from grief. Self-help groups can provide extra social support. When a bereaved individual finds it very hard to overcome loss, grief therapy may be necessary.

DEATH EDUCATION

Explain how death education can help people cope with death more effectively.

■ Today, instruction in death, dying, and bereavement can be found in colleges and universities; training programs for doctors, nurses, and helping professionals; adult education programs; and some elementary and secondary schools. When courses include an experiential component, they are more likely to reach students cognitively and emotionally.

FYI — FOR FURTHER INFORMATION AND HELP

Consult the companion website for this book, where you will find additional weblinks and associated learning activities: www.abacon.com/berk

HOSPICE CARE

Children's Hospice International
www.chionline.org/twl.htm

Organization of professionals, volunteers, and students who work with, or are interested in extending the hospice approach to, terminally ill children and their families.

National Hospice Organization
www.nho.org

An organization of hospices and individuals interested in the promotion of the hospice philosophy and program of care.

EUTHANASIA

Choice in Dying—The National Council for the Right to Die
www.choices.org

An organization that engages in legal research, produces educational publications and videos, and sponsors professional conferences on choices in dying.

On request, distributes one free set of state-specific advance medical directives.

Hemlock Society
www.hemlock.org/hemlock

A nonprofit educational organization that advocates carefully safeguarded laws that would permit terminally ill, mentally competent adults to receive help in dying from a doctor.

DeathNET
www.rights.org/deathnet/open.html

An archive specializing in all aspects of death and dying. Includes up-to-date information on Australian, Canadian, and U.S. euthanasia legislation and the Kevorkian File, containing patient case histories, interviews, court transcripts, and opposing viewpoints related to Kevorkian's doctor-assisted suicides.

LIVING WILL

U.S. Living Will Registry
www.uslivingwillregistry.com

Provides registration materials for individuals interested in an electronically stored living will, which can be accessed by any hospital.

BEREAVEMENT

The Compassionate Friends
www.needsyou.org/comp.html

A self-help organization that supports parents and siblings in resolving grief on the death of their child or brother/sister.

Journey of Hearts
www.journeyofhearts.org

Offers a variety of resources for those grieving the loss of a loved one.

DEATH EDUCATION

Association for Death Education and Counseling
www.adec.org

Association of individuals and institutions committed to effective death education and counseling. Aims to upgrade the quality of death education, patient care, and counseling in the areas of death, dying, and bereavement.

academic preschools Preschools in which teachers structure the program, training children in academic skills through repetition and drill. Distinguished from *child-centered preschools.* (p. 236)

acceptance Kübler-Ross's stage of dying in which the person, in the last weeks or days, enters a state of peace and quiet about upcoming death. (p. 636)

accommodation In Piaget's theory, that part of adaptation in which new schemes are created and old ones adjusted to produce a better fit with the environment. Distinguished from *assimilation.* Also, the third phase of grieving, in which grief subsides and emotional energies are freed for meeting everyday responsibilities, investing in new activities and goals, and seeking the companionship and love of others. (p. 148; p. 646)

achieving stage Schaie's stage of early adulthood in which people adapt their cognitive skills to situations that have profound implications for achieving long-term goals. Consequently, they focus less on acquiring knowledge and more on applying it to everyday life. (p. 440)

acquisitive stage Schaie's stage of childhood and adolescence in which the goal of mental activity is knowledge acquisition. (p. 440)

active lifespan The number of years of vigorous, healthy life. Distinguished from *average life expectancy* and *maximum lifespan.* (p. 423)

activity theory A social theory of aging that states that the decline in social interaction in late adulthood is due to failure of the social environment to offer opportunities for social contact, not the desires of elders. Distinguished from *disengagement theory* and *socioemotional selectivity theory.* (p. 603)

adaptation In Piaget's theory, the process of building schemes through direct interaction with the environment. Made up of two complementary processes: *assimilation* and *accommodation.* (p. 148)

adolescence The period of development in which the individual crosses the dividing line between childhood and adulthood. Begins with puberty and involves accepting one's full-grown body, acquiring adult ways of thinking, attaining emotional and economic independence, developing more mature ways of relating to peers of both sexes, and constructing an identity. (p. 350)

advance medical directive A written statement of desired medical treatment should a person become incurably ill. (p. 641)

age of viability The age at which the fetus can first survive if born early. Occurs sometime between 22 and 26 weeks. (p. 84)

age-graded influences Influences on lifespan development that are strongly related to age and therefore fairly predictable in when they occur and how long they last. (p. 11)

agonal phase The phase of dying in which gasps and muscle spasms occur during the first moments in which the body cannot sustain life anymore. Distinguished from *clinical death* and *mortality.* (p. 629)

Alzheimer's disease The most common form of dementia, in which structural and chemical deterioration in the brain is associated with gradual loss of many aspects of thought and behavior, including memory, skilled and purposeful movements, and comprehension and production of speech. (p. 573)

amnion The inner membrane that forms a protective covering around the prenatal organism. (p. 82)

amyloid plaques A structural change in the brain associated with Alzheimer's disease in which deposits of the protein amyloid are surrounded by clumps of dead nerve cells, which amyloid appears to destroy. (p. 573)

androgyny A type of gender identity in which the person scores high on both masculine and feminine personality characteristics. (p. 266)

anger Kübler-Ross's stage of dying in which the person expresses anger at having to die without being given a chance to do all he or she wants to do. (p. 635)

animistic thinking The belief that inanimate objects have lifelike qualities, such as thoughts, wishes, feelings, and intentions. (p. 223)

anorexia nervosa An eating disorder in which individuals (usually females) starve themselves because of a compulsive fear of getting fat. (p. 359)

anoxia Inadequate oxygen supply. (p. 100)

anticipatory grieving Before a prolonged, expected death, acknowledging that the loss is inevitable and preparing emotionally for it. (p. 646)

Apgar Scale A rating used to assess the newborn baby's physical condition immediately after birth. (p. 98)

applied behavior analysis A set of practical procedures that combine conditioning and modeling to eliminate undesirable behaviors and increase socially acceptable responses. (p. 19)

appropriate death A death that makes sense in terms of the individual's pattern of living and values and, at the same time, preserves or restores significant relationships and is as free of suffering as possible. (p. 636)

assimilation In Piaget's theory, that part of adaptation in which the external world is interpreted in terms of current schemes. Distinguished from *accommodation*. (p. 148)

associative play A form of true social participation in which children are engaged in separate activities, but they interact by exchanging toys and comment on one another's behavior. Distinguished from *nonsocial activity, parallel play,* and *cooperative play.* (p. 253)

attachment The strong, affectional tie that humans feel toward special people in their lives. (p. 190)

attention-deficit hyperactivity disorder (ADHD) A childhood disorder involving inattentiveness, impulsivity, and excessive motor activity. Often leads to academic failure and social problems. (p. 294)

authoritarian style A child-rearing style that is demanding but low in responsiveness to children's rights and needs. Conformity and obedience are valued over open communication with the child. Distinguished from *authoritative* and *permissive styles.* (p. 269)

authoritative style A child-rearing style that is demanding and responsive. A rational, democratic approach in which parents' and children's rights are respected. Distinguished from *authoritarian* and *permissive styles.* (p. 269)

autobiographical memory Representations of special, one-time events that are long lasting because they are imbued with personal meaning. (p. 159)

autoimmune response An abnormal response of the immune system in which it turns against normal body tissues. (p. 563)

autonomous morality Piaget's second stage of moral development, in which children view rules as flexible, socially agreed-on principles that can be revised when there is a need to do so. Begins around age 10. (p. 396)

autonomy At adolescence, a sense of oneself as a separate, self-governing individual. Involves relying more on oneself and less on parents for direction and guidance and engaging in careful, well-reasoned decision making. (p. 401)

autonomy versus shame and doubt In Erikson's theory, the psychological conflict of toddlerhood, which is resolved positively if parents provide young children with suitable guidance and appropriate choices. (p. 179)

autosomes The 22 matching chromosome pairs in each human cell. (p. 48)

average life expectancy The number of years an individual born in a particular year can expect to live. Distinguished from *maximum lifespan* and *active lifespan.* (p. 421)

avoidance The first phase of grieving, in which the survivor experiences shock followed by disbelief. Distinguished from *confrontation* and *accommodation.* (p. 645)

avoidant attachment The quality of insecure attachment characterizing infants who are usually not distressed by parental separation and who avoid the parent when she returns. Distinguished from *secure, resistant,* and *disorganized/disoriented attachment.* (p. 192)

babbling Repetition of consonant–vowel combinations in long strings, beginning around 4 months of age. (p. 168)

bargaining Kübler-Ross's stage of dying in which the person attempts to forestall death by bargaining for extra time—a deal he or she may try to strike with family members, friends, caregivers, or God. (p. 635)

basal metabolic rate (BMR) The amount of energy the body uses at complete rest. (p. 430)

basic emotions Emotions that can be directly inferred from facial expressions, such as happiness, interest, surprise, fear, anger, sadness, and disgust. (p. 180)

basic trust versus mistrust In Erikson's theory, the psychological conflict of infancy, which is resolved positively if caregiving, especially during feeding, is sympathetic and loving. (p. 178)

basic-skills approach An approach to beginning reading instruction that emphasizes training in phonics—the basic rules for translating written symbols into sounds—and simplified reading materials. Distinguished from *whole-language approach.* (p. 298)

behaviorism An approach that views directly observable events—stimuli and responses—as the appropriate focus of study and the development of behavior as taking place through classical and operant conditioning. (p. 18)

bereavement The experience of losing a loved one by death. (p. 645)

bicultural identity The identity constructed by adolescents who explore and adopt values from both their subculture and the dominant culture. (p. 395)

"big five" personality traits Five basic factors, into which hundreds of personality traits have been organized: neuroticism, extroversion, openness to experience, agreeableness, and conscientiousness. (p. 533)

biological aging, or senescence Genetically influenced, age-related declines in the functioning of organs and systems that are universal in all members of our species. Sometimes called *primary aging.* (p. 420)

body image Conception of and attitude toward one's physical appearance. (p. 357)

brain death Irreversible cessation of all activity in the brain and the brain stem. The definition of death accepted in most industrialized nations. (p. 629)

brain plasticity The ability of other parts of the brain to take over functions of damaged regions. (p. 122)

breech position A position of the baby in the uterus that would cause the buttocks or feet to be delivered first. (p. 101)

bulimia An eating disorder in which individuals (mainly females) go on eating binges followed by deliberate vomiting, other purging techniques such as heavy doses of laxatives, and strict dieting. (p. 360)

burnout A condition in which long-term job stress leads to emotional exhaustion, a sense of loss of personal control, and feelings of reduced accomplishment. (p. 544)

canalization The tendency of heredity to restrict the development of some characteristics to just one or a few outcomes. (p. 74)

cardinality The mathematical principle that the last number in a counting sequence indicates the quantity of items in the set. (p. 234)

carrier A heterozygous individual who can pass a recessive gene to his or her children. (p. 49)

cataracts Cloudy areas in the lens of the eye that increase from middle to old age, resulting in foggy vision and (without surgery) eventual blindness. (p. 559)

centration The tendency to focus on one aspect of a situation and neglect other important features. Distinguished from *decentration*. (p. 224)

cephalocaudal trend An organized pattern of physical growth and motor control that proceeds from head to tail. Distinguished from *proximodistal trend*. (p. 120)

cerebellum A brain structure that aids in balance and control of body movements. (p. 211)

cerebral cortex The largest structure of the human brain, which accounts for the highly developed intelligence of the human species. (p. 121)

cerebrovascular dementia A form of dementia in which a series of strokes leaves dead brain cells, producing step-by-step degeneration of mental ability, with each step occurring abruptly after a stroke. (p. 575)

cesarean delivery A surgical delivery in which the doctor makes an incision in the mother's abdomen and lifts the baby out of the uterus. (p. 101)

child-centered preschools Preschools in which teachers provide a wide variety of activities from which children select, and most of the day is devoted to free play. Distinguished from *academic preschools*. (p. 236)

child-directed speech A form of language used by adults to speak to infants and toddlers that consists of short sentences with high-pitched, exaggerated expression and very clear pronunciation. (p. 171)

chorion The outer membrane that forms a protective covering around the prenatal organism. It sends out tiny fingerlike villi, from which the placenta begins to emerge. (p. 82)

chromosomes Rodlike structures in the cell nucleus that store and transmit genetic information. (p. 46)

chronosystem In ecological systems theory, temporal changes in environments, which produce new conditions that affect development. These changes can be imposed externally or arise from within the organism, since people select, modify, and create many of their own settings and experiences. (p. 25)

circular reaction In Piaget's theory, a means of building schemes in which infants try to repeat a chance event caused by their own motor activity. (p. 149)

classical conditioning A form of learning that involves associating a neutral stimulus with a stimulus that leads to a reflexive response. (p. 129)

climacteric Midlife transition in which fertility declines. Brings an end to reproductive capacity in women and diminished fertility in men. (p. 495)

clinical death The phase of dying in which heartbeat, circulation, breathing, and brain functioning stop, but resuscitation is still possible. Distinguished from *agonal phase* and *mortality*. (p. 629)

clinical interview A method that uses a flexible, conversational style to probe for the participant's point of view. (p. 29)

clinical, or case study, method A method in which the researcher tries to understand the unique person by combining interview data, observations, and sometimes test scores. (p. 30)

clique A small group of about five to seven members who are good friends and, therefore, resemble one another in family background, attitudes, and values. (p. 404)

codominance A pattern of inheritance in which both genes, in a heterozygous combination, are expressed. (p. 50)

cognitive inhibition The ability to control internal and external distracting stimuli, preventing them from capturing attention and cluttering working memory with irrelevant information. (p. 293)

cognitive self-regulation The process of continuously monitoring progress toward a goal, checking outcomes, and redirecting unsuccessful efforts. (p. 297)

cognitive-developmental theory An approach introduced by Piaget that views children as actively building psychological structures as they explore and manipulate their world and cognitive development as taking place in stages. (p. 20)

cohabitation The lifestyle of unmarried couples who have an intimate, sexual relationship and share a residence. (p. 476)

cohort effects The effects of history-graded influences on research findings: People born in one period of time are influenced by particular historical and cultural conditions. (p. 37)

collectivist societies Societies in which people define themselves as part of a group and stress group over individual goals. Distinguished from *individualistic societies*. (p. 68)

companionate love Love based on warm, trusting affection and caregiving. Distinguished from *passionate love*. (p. 461)

compliance Voluntary obedience to requests and commands. (p. 200)

compression of morbidity The public health goal of reducing the average period of diminished vigor before death as life expectancy extends. So far, persistence of poverty and negative lifestyle factors have interfered with progress toward this goal. (p. 568)

concordance rate The percentage of instances in which both twins show a trait when it is present in one twin. Used to study the role of heredity in emotional and behavior disorders, which can be judged as either present or absent. (p. 72)

concrete operational stage Piaget's third stage, during which thought is logical, flexible, and organized in its application to concrete information. However, the capacity for abstract thinking is not yet present. Spans the years from 7 to 11. (p. 291)

conditioned response (CR) In classical conditioning, an originally reflexive response that is produced by a conditioned stimulus (CS). (p. 130)

conditioned stimulus (CS) In classical conditioning, a neutral stimulus that through pairing with an unconditioned stimulus (UCS) leads to a new response (CR). (p. 130)

confrontation The second phase of grieving, in which the mourner begins to confront the reality of the loss and grief is experienced most intensely. Distinguished from *avoidance* and *accommodation*. (p. 646)

congregate housing Housing for the elderly that adds a variety of support services, including meals in a common dining room. (p. 608)

conservation The understanding that certain physical characteristics of objects remain the same, even when their outward appearance changes. (p. 223)

contexts Unique combinations of personal and environmental circumstances that can result in markedly different paths of development. (p. 7)

continuous development A view that regards development as a cumulative process of adding on more of the same types of skills that were there to begin with. Distinguished from *discontinuous development*. (p. 6)

contrast sensitivity A general principle accounting for early pattern preferences, which states that if babies can detect a difference in contrast between two patterns, they will prefer the one with more contrast. (p. 140)

controversial children Children who get a large number of positive and negative votes on sociometric measures of peer acceptance. Distinguished from *popular, neglected,* and *rejected* children. (p. 329)

conventional level Kohlberg's second level of moral development, in which moral understanding is based on conforming to social rules to ensure positive human relationships and societal order. (p. 397)

convergent thinking The generation of a single correct answer to a problem. The type of cognition emphasized on intelligence tests. Distinguished from *divergent thinking*. (p. 310)

cooing Pleasant vowel-like noises made by infants beginning around 2 months of age. (p. 168)

cooperative play A form of true social participation in which children's actions are directed toward a common goal. Distinguished from *nonsocial activity, parallel play,* and *associative play*. (p. 254)

coregulation A transitional form of supervision in which parents exercise general oversight, while permitting children to be in charge of moment-by-moment decision making. (p. 333)

corpus callosum A large bundle of fibers that connects the two hemispheres of the brain. (p. 212)

correlation coefficient A number, ranging from +1.00 to –1.00, that describes the strength and direction of the relationship between two variables. The size of the number shows the strength of the relationship. The sign of the number (+ or -) refers to the direction of the relationship. (p. 32)

correlational design A research design that gathers information without altering participants' experiences and examines relationships between variables. Cannot determine cause and effect. (p. 31)

cross-linkage theory A theory of biological aging asserting that the formation of bonds, or links, between normally separate protein fibers causes the body's connective tissue to become less elastic over time, leading to many negative physical consequences. (p. 424)

cross-sectional design A research design in which groups of participants of different ages are studied at the same point in time. Distinguished from *longitudinal design*. (p. 38)

crowd A large, loosely organized group consisting of several cliques with similar normative characteristics. (p. 404)

crystallized intelligence Intellectual skills that depend on accumulated knowledge and experience, good judgment, and mastery of social conventions. Together, these capacities represent abilities acquired because they are valued by the individual's culture. Distinguished from *fluid intelligence*. (p. 507)

death anxiety Fear and apprehension of death. (p. 633)

decentration The ability to focus on several aspects of a problem at once and relate them. Distinguished from *centration*. (p. 291)

deferred imitation The ability to remember and copy the behavior of models who are not immediately present. (p. 152)

dementia A set of disorders occurring almost entirely in old age in which many aspects of thought and behavior are so impaired that everyday activities are disrupted. (p. 572)

denial Kübler-Ross's stage of dying in which the person denies the seriousness of his or her terminal condition to escape from the prospect of death. (p. 635)

deoxyribonucleic acid (DNA) Long, double-stranded molecules that make up chromosomes. (p. 47)

dependency-support script A typical pattern of interaction in which elders' dependency behaviors are attended to immediately, thereby reinforcing those behaviors. Distinguished from *independence-ignore script*. (p. 599)

dependent variable The variable the researcher expects to be influenced by the independent variable in an experiment. Distinguished from *independent* variable. (p. 34)

depression Kübler-Ross's stage of dying in which the person becomes depressed, grieving the ultimate loss of his or her life. (p. 635)

deprivation dwarfism A growth disorder observed between 2 and 15 years of age. Characterized by very short stature, light weight in proportion to height, immature skeletal age, and decreased GH secretion. Caused by emotional deprivation. (p. 214)

developmental quotient, or DQ A score on an infant intelligence test, based primarily on perceptual and motor responses. Computed in the same manner as an IQ. (p. 163)

developmentally appropriate practice A set of standards devised by the National Association for the Education of Young Children that specify program characteristics that meet the developmental and individual needs of young children of varying ages, based on current research and the consensus of experts. (p. 164)

differentiation theory The view that perceptual development involves the detection of increasingly fine-grained, invariant features in the environment. (p. 142)

difficult child A child whose temperament is such that he or she is irregular in daily routines, is slow to accept new experiences, and tends to react negatively and intensely. Distinguished from *easy child* and *slow-to-warm-up child*. (p. 185)

discontinuous development A view in which new and different ways of interpreting and responding to the world emerge at particular time periods. Distinguished from *continuous development*. (p. 6)

disengagement theory A social theory of aging that states that the decline in social interaction in late adulthood is due to mutual withdrawal between elders and society in anticipation of death. Distinguished from *activity theory* and *socioemotional selectivity theory*. (p. 603)

dishabituation Increase in responsiveness after stimulation changes. (p. 131)

disorganized/disoriented attachment The quality of insecure attachment characterizing infants who respond in a confused, contradictory fashion when reunited with the parent. Distinguished from *secure, avoidant,* and *resistant attachment.* (p. 192)

distributive justice Beliefs about how to divide resources fairly. (p. 326)

divergent thinking The generation of multiple and unusual possibilities when faced with a task or problem. Associated with creativity. Distinguished from *convergent thinking.* (p. 310)

divorce mediation A series of meetings between divorcing adults and a trained professional, who tries to help them settle disputes. Aimed at reducing family conflict during the period surrounding divorce. (p. 336)

dominant cerebral hemisphere The hemisphere of the brain responsible for skilled motor action. The left hemisphere is dominant in right-handed individuals. In left-handed individuals, the right hemisphere may be dominant, or motor and language skills may be shared between the hemispheres. (p. 211)

dominant–recessive inheritance A pattern of inheritance in which, under heterozygous conditions, the influence of only one gene is apparent. (p. 49)

dual-earner marriage A family form in which both husband and wife are employed. (p. 482)

dualistic thinking In Perry's theory, the cognitive approach of younger college students, who search for absolute truth and therefore divide information, values, and authority into right and wrong, good and bad, we and they. Distinguished from *relativistic thinking.* (p. 440)

durable power of attorney for health care A written statement that authorizes appointment of another person (usually, although not always, a family member) to make health care decisions on one's behalf in case of incompetence. (p. 642)

dynamic systems of action In motor development, combinations of previously acquired abilities that lead to more advanced ways of exploring and controlling the environment. Each new skill is a joint product of central nervous system development, movement possibilities of the body, environmental supports for the skill, and the goal the child has in mind. (p. 134)

easy child A child whose temperament is such that he or she quickly establishes regular routines in infancy, is generally cheerful, and adapts easily to new experiences. Distinguished from *difficult child* and *slow-to-warm-up child.* (p. 185)

ecological systems theory Bronfenbrenner's approach, which views the person as developing within a complex system of relationships affected by multiple levels of the environment, from immediate settings of family and school to broad cultural values and programs. (p. 25)

educational self-fulfilling prophecy The idea that children may adopt teachers' positive or negative attitudes toward them and start to live up to these views. (p. 309)

egalitarian marriage A form of marriage in which husband and wife share power and authority. Both try to balance the time and energy they devote to the workplace, the children, and their relationship. Distinguished from *traditional marriage.* (p. 468)

ego integrity versus despair In Erikson's theory, the psychological conflict of late adulthood, which is resolved positively when elders feel whole, complete, and satisfied with their achievements, having accepted their life course as something that had to be the way it was. (p. 592)

egocentrism The inability to distinguish the symbolic viewpoints of others from one's own. (p. 223)

elaboration The memory strategy of creating a relation between two or more items that are not members of the same category. (p. 295)

embryo The prenatal organism from 2 to 8 weeks after conception, during which time the foundations of all body structures and internal organs are laid down. (p. 83)

emotional self-regulation Strategies for adjusting our emotional state to a comfortable level of intensity so we can accomplish our goals. (p. 184)

empathy The ability to understand another's emotional state and feel with that person, or respond emotionally in a similar way. (p. 199)

ethnography A method by which the researcher attempts to understand the unique values and social processes of a culture or a distinct social group by living with its members and taking field notes for a period of months or years. (p. 30)

ethological theory of attachment A theory formulated by Bowlby, which views the infant's emotional tie to the mother as an evolved response that promotes survival. (p. 190)

ethology An approach concerned with the adaptive, or survival, value of behavior and its evolutionary history. (p. 23)

euthanasia The practice of ending the life of a person suffering from an incurable condition. (p. 640)

executive stage In Schaie's theory, a more advanced form of the responsibility stage that characterizes people at the helm of large organizations, whose responsibilities have become highly complex. (p. 441)

exosystem In ecological systems theory, settings that do not contain children but that affect their experiences in immediate settings. (p. 26)

expansions Adult responses that elaborate on children's speech, increasing its complexity. (p. 241)

experimental design A research design in which the investigator randomly assigns participants to two or more treatment conditions. Permits inferences about cause and effect. (p. 34)

expertise Acquisition of extensive knowledge in a field or endeavor, supported by the specialization that begins with selecting a college major or an occupation in early adulthood. (p. 442)

expressive style A style of early language learning in which toddlers use language mainly to talk about the feelings and needs of themselves and other people. Distinguished from *referential style.* (p. 170)

extended family household A household in which three or more generations live together. (p. 66)

family life cycle A sequence of phases that characterizes the development of most families around the world. In early adulthood, people typically live on their own, marry, and bear and rear children. During middle age, their parenting responsibilities diminish. Late adulthood brings retirement, growing old, and (mostly for women) death of one's spouse. (p. 466)

fantasy period Period of vocational development in which young children fantasize about career options through make-believe play. Distinguished from *tentative period* and *realistic period.* (p. 445)

fast-mapping Connecting a new word with an underlying concept after only a brief encounter. (p. 239)

feminization of poverty A trend in which women who support themselves or their families have become the majority of the adult poverty population, regardless of age and ethnic group. (p. 535)

fetal alcohol effects (FAE) The condition of children who display some but not all of the defects of fetal alcohol syndrome. Usually their mothers drank alcohol in smaller quantities during pregnancy than did mothers of children with fetal alcohol syndrome (FAS). (p. 91)

fetal alcohol syndrome (FAS) A set of defects that results when women consume large amounts of alcohol during most or all of pregnancy. Includes mental retardation; impaired motor coordination, attention, memory, and language; overactivity; slow physical growth, and facial abnormalities. (p. 91)

fetal monitors Electronic instruments that track the baby's heart rate during labor. (p. 101)

fetus The prenatal organism from the beginning of the third month to the end of pregnancy, during which time completion of body structures and dramatic growth in size takes place. (p. 83)

fluid intelligence Intellectual skills that largely depend on basic information-processing skills—the speed with which we can analyze information, the capacity of working memory, and the ability to detect relationships among stimuli. Distinguished from *crystallized intelligence.* (p. 507)

formal operational stage Piaget's final stage, in which adolescents develop the capacity for abstract, scientific thinking. Begins around 11 years of age. (p. 370)

fraternal, or dizygotic, twins Twins resulting from the release and fertilization of two ova. They are genetically no more alike than ordinary siblings. Distinguished from *identical,* or *monozygotic, twins.* (p. 48)

free radicals Naturally occurring, highly reactive chemicals that form in the presence of oxygen and destroy cellular material, including DNA, proteins, and fats essential for cell functioning. (p. 424)

full inclusion Placement of pupils with learning difficulties in regular classrooms for the entire school day. (p. 309)

functional age Actual competence and performance of an older adult (as distinguished from chronological age). (p. 556)

gametes Human sperm and ova, which contain half as many chromosomes as a regular body cell. (p. 47)

gender constancy The understanding that sex remains the same even if clothing, hairstyle, and play activities change. (p. 266)

gender identity An image of oneself as relatively masculine or feminine in characteristics. (p. 265)

gender intensification Increased gender stereotyping of attitudes and behavior. Occurs in early adolescence. (p. 401)

gender schema theory An information-processing approach to gender typing that combines social learning and cognitive-developmental features to explain how environmental pressures and children's cognitions work together to shape gender-role development. (p. 266)

gender typing The process of developing gender roles, or gender-linked preferences and behaviors valued by the larger society. (p. 262)

gene A segment of a DNA molecule that contains instructions for production of various proteins that contribute to growth and functioning of the body. (p. 47)

general growth curve A curve that represents overall changes in body size—rapid growth during infancy, slower gains in early and middle childhood, and rapid growth once more during adolescence. (p. 209)

generativity versus stagnation In Erikson's theory, the psychological conflict of midlife, which is resolved positively if the adult can integrate personal goals with the welfare of the larger social environment. The resulting strength is the capacity to give to and guide the next generation. (p. 522)

genetic counseling A communication process designed to help couples assess their chances of giving birth to a baby with a hereditary disorder. (p. 55)

genetic imprinting A pattern of inheritance in which genes are imprinted, or chemically marked, in such a way that one pair member is activated, regardless of its makeup. (p. 52)

genetic–environmental correlation The idea that heredity influences the environments to which people are exposed. (p. 74)

genotype The genetic makeup of the individual. Distinguished from *phenotype.* (p. 46)

giftedness Exceptional intellectual ability. Includes high IQ, high creativity, and specialized talent. (p. 310)

glass ceiling Invisible barrier, faced by women and ethnic minorities, to advancement up the corporate ladder. (p. 545)

glial cells Cells serving the function of myelinization. (p. 121)

goodness of fit An effective match between child-rearing practices and a child's temperament, leading to favorable adjustment. (p. 189)

grief Intense physical and psychological distress following a loss. (p. 645)

growth hormone (GH) A pituitary hormone that affects the development of almost all body tissues. (p. 212)

growth spurt Rapid gain in height and weight during adolescence. (p. 352)

habituation A gradual reduction in the strength of a response as the result of repetitive stimulation. (p. 131)

hardiness A set of three personal qualities—control, commitment, and challenge—that help people cope with stress adaptively, thereby reducing its impact on illness and mortality. (p. 504)

heritability estimate A statistic that measures the extent to which individual differences in complex traits, such as intelligence or personality, in a specific population are due to genetic factors. (p. 71)

heteronomous morality Piaget's first stage of moral development, in which children view moral rules as permanent features of the external world that are handed down by authorities and cannot be changed. Extends from about 5 to 10 years of age. (p. 396)

heterozygous Having two different genes at the same place on a pair of chromosomes. Distinguished from *homozygous*. (p. 49)

hierarchical classification The organization of objects into classes and subclasses on the basis of similarities and differences between the groups. (p. 224)

history-graded influences Influences on lifespan development that are unique to a particular historical era and explain why people born around the same time (called a *cohort*) tend to be alike in ways that set them apart from people born at other times. (p. 12)

Home Observation for Measurement of the Environment (HOME) A checklist for gathering information about the quality of children's home lives through observation and parental interview. (p. 163)

homozygous Having two identical genes at the same place on a pair of chromosomes. Distinguished from *heterozygous*. (p. 49)

horizontal décalage Development within a Piagetian stage. Gradual mastery of logical concepts during the concrete operational stage is an example. (p. 292)

hormone replacement therapy (HRT) Treatment in which a woman takes daily doses of estrogen, sometimes combined with progesterone, during the climacteric and after menopause. Relieves menopausal symptoms (hot flashes and vaginal dryness) and prevents cardiovascular disease and loss of bone mass. (p. 495)

hospice A comprehensive program of support services that focuses on meeting terminally ill patients' physical, emotional, social, and spiritual needs and that offers follow-up bereavement services to families. (p. 639)

hostile aggression Aggression intended to harm another individual. Distinguished from *instrumental aggression*. (p. 260)

human development A field of study devoted to understanding constancy and change throughout the lifespan. (p. 5)

hypothetico-deductive reasoning A formal operational problem-solving strategy in which adolescents begin with a general theory of all possible factors that could affect an outcome in a problem and deduce specific hypotheses, which they test systematically. (p. 371)

I-self A sense of self as subject, or agent, who is separate from but attends to and acts on objects and other people. Distinguished from *me-self*. (p. 199)

identical, or monozygotic, twins Twins that result when a zygote, during the early stages of cell duplication, divides in two. They have the same genetic makeup. Distinguished from *fraternal*, or *dizygotic, twins*. (p. 48)

identification In Freud's theory, the process leading to formation of the superego in which children take the same-sex parent's characteristics into their personality. (p. 249)

identity A well-organized conception of the self, made up of values, beliefs, and goals to which the individual is solidly committed. (p. 390)

identity achievement The identity status of individuals who have explored and committed themselves to self-chosen values and occupational goals. Distinguished from *moratorium, identity foreclosure*, and *identity diffusion*. (p. 392)

identity diffusion The identity status of individuals who do not have firm commitments to values and goals and are not actively trying to reach them. Distinguished from *identity achievement, moratorium*, and *identity foreclosure*. (p. 392)

identity foreclosure The identity status of individuals who have accepted ready-made values and goals that authority figures have chosen for them. Distinguished from *identity achievement, moratorium*, and *identity diffusion*. (p. 392)

identity versus identity confusion In Erikson's theory, the psychological conflict of adolescence, which is resolved positively when adolescents attain an identity after a period of exploration and inner soul-searching. (p. 390)

imaginary audience Adolescents' belief that they are the focus of everyone else's attention and concern. (p. 375)

imitation Learning by copying the behavior of another person. Also called *modeling* or *observational learning*. (p. 132)

implantation Attachment of the blastocyst to the uterine lining 7 to 9 days after fertilization. (p. 82)

implicit memory Memory without conscious awareness. (p. 580)

independence-ignore script A typical pattern of interaction in which elders' independent behaviors are mostly ignored, thereby leading them to occur less often. Distinguished from *dependency-support script*. (p. 599)

independent variable The variable manipulated by the researcher in an experiment by randomly assigning participants to treatment conditions. Distinguished from *dependent variable*. (p. 34)

individualistic societies Societies in which people think of themselves as separate entities and are largely concerned with their own personal needs. Distinguished from *collectivist societies*. (p. 68)

induction A type of discipline in which the effects of the child's misbehavior on others are communicated to the child. (p. 256)

industry versus inferiority In Erikson's theory, the psychological conflict of middle childhood, which is resolved positively when experiences lead children to develop a sense of competence at useful skills and tasks. (p. 320)

infant mortality rate The number of deaths in the first year of life per 1,000 live births. (p. 104)

information processing An approach that views the human mind as a symbol-manipulating system through which information flows, that often uses flowcharts to map the precise series of steps individuals use to solve problems and complete tasks, and that regards cognitive development as a continuous process. (p. 22)

information-loss view A view that attributes age-related slowing of cognitive processing to greater loss of information as it moves through the system. As a result, the whole system must slow down to inspect and interpret the information. Distinguished from *neural network* view. (p. 509)

inhibited, or shy, child A child whose temperament is such that he or she reacts negatively to and withdraws from novel stimuli. Distinguished from *uninhibited*, or *sociable, child*. (p. 187)

initiative versus guilt In Erikson's theory, the psychological conflict of early childhood, which is resolved positively through play experiences that foster a healthy sense of initiative and through development of a superego, or conscience, that is not overly strict and guilt-ridden. (p. 248)

instrumental aggression Aggression aimed at obtaining an object, privilege, or space with no deliberate intent to harm another person. Distinguished from *hostile aggression.* (p. 260)

intelligence quotient, or IQ A score that permits an individual's performance on an intelligence test to be compared to the performances of other individuals of the same age. (p. 163)

intentional, or goal-directed, behavior A sequence of actions in which schemes are deliberately combined to solve a problem. (p. 151)

interactional synchrony A sensitively tuned "emotional dance," in which the caregiver responds to infant signals in a well-timed, appropriate fashion and both partners match emotional states, especially the positive ones. (p. 193)

intergenerational inequity A state in which the elderly receive more than their fair share of public resources at the expense of the very young. (p. 576)

intermodal perception Perception that combines information from more than one modality, or sensory system. (p. 142)

internal working model A set of expectations derived from early caregiving experiences concerning the availability of attachment figures and their likelihood of providing support during times of stress. Becomes a model, or guide, for all future close relationships. (p. 191)

intimacy versus isolation In Erikson's theory, the psychological conflict of young adulthood, which is resolved positively when young adults give up some of their newfound independence and make a permanent commitment to an intimate partner. (p. 456)

invariant features Features that remain stable in a constantly changing perceptual world. (p. 142)

irreversibility The inability to mentally go through a series of steps in a problem and then reverse direction, returning to the starting point. Distinguished from *reversibility.* (p. 224)

joint custody A child custody arrangement following divorce in which the court grants each parent equal say in important decisions about the child's upbringing. (p. 336)

kinkeeper Role assumed by members of the middle generation, especially mothers, who take responsibility for gathering the family for celebrations and making sure everyone stays in touch. (p. 536)

kinship studies Studies comparing the characteristics of family members to determine the importance of heredity in complex human characteristics. (p. 71)

kwashiorkor A disease usually appearing between 1 and 3 years of age that is caused by a diet low in protein. Symptoms include an enlarged belly, swollen feet, hair loss, skin rash, and irritable, listless behavior. (p. 128)

language acquisition device (LAD) In Chomsky's theory, a biologically based innate system that permits children, no matter which language they hear, to understand and speak in a rule-oriented fashion as soon as they have picked up enough words. (p. 167)

lanugo A white, downy hair that covers the entire body of the fetus, helping the vernix stick to the skin. (p. 84)

lateralization Specialization of functions of the two hemispheres of the cerebral cortex. (p. 122)

learned helplessness Attributions that credit success to external factors, such as luck, and failure to low ability. Leads to anxious loss of control in the face of challenging tasks. Distinguished from *mastery-oriented attributions.* (p. 323)

learning disabilities Specific learning disorders that lead children to achieve poorly in school, despite an average or above-average IQ. Believed to be due to faulty brain functioning. (p. 309)

life care communities Housing for the elderly that offers a range of options, from independent or congregate housing to full nursing home care. For a large initial payment and monthly fees, guarantees that elders' needs will be met in one place as they age. (p. 608)

life expectancy crossover An age-related reversal in life expectancy of sectors of the population. For example, members of ethnic minorities who survive to age 85 live longer than members of the white majority. (p. 557)

life review The process of calling up, reflecting on, and reconsidering past experiences, contemplating their meaning with the goal of achieving greater self-understanding. (p. 594)

life structure In Levinson's theory, the underlying pattern or design of a person's life at a given time. Consists of relationships with significant others (the most important of which have to do with marriage/family and occupation) that are reorganized during each period of adult development. (p. 457)

lifespan perspective A balanced perspective that assumes development is lifelong, multidimensional and multidirectional, highly plastic, and embedded in multiple contexts. (p. 8)

living will A written statement that specifies the treatments a person does or does not want in case of a terminal illness, coma, or other near-death situation. (p. 641)

loneliness Feelings of unhappiness that result from a gap between actual and desired social relationships. (p. 465)

longitudinal design A research design in which in which one group of participants is studied repeatedly at different ages. Distinguished from *cross-sectional design.* (p. 35)

longitudinal-sequential design A research design with both longitudinal and cross-sectional components in which groups of participants born in different years are followed over time. (p. 38)

long-term memory In information processing, the part of the mental system that contains our permanent knowledge base. (p. 157)

macrosystem In ecological systems theory, the values, laws, customs, and resources of a culture that influence experiences and interactions at inner levels of the environment. (p. 26)

macular degeneration Blurring and eventual loss of central vision due to a break-down of light-senstivie cells in the macula, or central region of the retina. (p. 560)

mainstreaming The integration of pupils with learning difficulties into regular classrooms for part of the school day. (p. 309)

make-believe play A type of play in which children pretend, acting out everyday and imaginary activities. (p. 152)

marasmus A disease usually appearing in the first year of life that is caused by a diet low in all essential nutrients. Leads to a wasted condition of the body. (p. 128)

mastery-oriented attributions Attributions that credit success to high ability and failure to insufficient effort. Leads to high self-esteem and a willingness to approach challenging tasks. Distinguished from *learned helplessness.* (p. 323)

maturation A genetically determined, naturally unfolding course of growth. (p. 14)

maximum lifespan The genetic limit to length of life for a person free of external risk factors. Distinguished from *average life expectancy* and *active lifespan.* (p. 421)

me-self A reflective observer who treats the self as an object of knowledge and evaluation. Distinguished from *I-self.* (p. 199)

meiosis The process of cell division through which gametes are formed and in which the number of chromosomes in each cell is halved. (p. 47)

memory strategies Deliberate mental activities that improve the likelihood of remembering. (p. 230)

menarche First menstruation. (p. 354)

menopause The end of menstruation and, therefore, reproductive capacity in women. Occurs, on the average, at age 51 among North American women, although the age range is large—from 42 to 58. (p. 495)

mental representation An internal image of an absent object or a past event. (p. 152)

mental strategies In information processing, procedures that operate on and transform information, increasing the efficiency of thinking as well as the chances that information will be retained. (p. 156)

mesosystem In ecological systems theory, connections between children's immediate settings. (p. 26)

metacognition Thinking about thought; awareness of mental activities. (p. 231)

microsystem In ecological systems theory, the activities and interaction patterns in the person's immediate surroundings. (p. 26)

midlife crisis Inner turmoil, self-doubt, and major restructuring of the personality during the transition to middle adulthood. Characterizes the experiences of only a minority of adults. (p. 527)

mild mental retardation Substantially below-average intellectual functioning, resulting in an IQ between 55 and 70 and problems in adaptive behavior, or skills of everyday living. (p. 309)

mitosis The process of cell duplication, in which each new cell receives an exact copy of the original chromosomes. (p. 47)

moratorium The identity status of individuals who are exploring alternatives in an effort to find values and goals to guide their life. Distinguished from *identity achievement, identity foreclosure,* and *identity diffusion.* (p. 392)

mortality The phase of dying in which the individual passes into permanent death. Distinguished from *agonal phase* and *clinical death.* (p. 629)

mourning The culturally specified expression of the bereaved person's thoughts and feelings through funerals and other rituals. (p. 645)

mutation A sudden but permanent change in a segment of DNA. (p. 53)

myelinization A process in which neural fibers are coated with an insulating fatty sheath called *myelin* that improves the efficiency of message transfer. (p. 121)

natural, or prepared, childbirth An approach designed to reduce pain and medical intervention and to make childbirth a rewarding experience for parents. (p. 99)

naturalistic observation A method in which the researcher goes into the natural environment to observe the behavior of interest. Distinguished from *structured observation.* (p. 28)

nature–nurture controversy Disagreement among theorists about whether genetic or environmental factors are the most important determinants of development and behavior. (p. 7)

neglected children Children who are seldom chosen, either positively or negatively, on sociometric measures of peer acceptance. Distinguished from *popular, rejected,* and *controversial children.* (p. 329)

Neonatal Behavioral Assessment Scale (NBAS) A test developed to assess the behavior of the infant during the newborn period. (p. 111)

neural network view A view that attributes age-related slowing of cognitive processing to breaks in neural networks as neurons die. The brain forms bypasses—new synaptic connections that go around the breaks but are less efficient. Distinguished from *information-loss view.* (p. 509)

neural tube The primitive spinal cord that develops from the ectoderm, the top of which swells to form the brain. (p. 83)

neurofibrillary tangles A structural change in the brain associated with Alzheimer's disease in which abnormal bundles of threads run through the body of the neuron and into fibers establishing synaptic connections with other neurons. (p. 573)

neurons Nerve cells that store and transmit information. (p. 120)

niche-picking A type of genetic–environmental correlation in which individuals actively choose environments that complement their heredity. (p. 75)

noble savage Rousseau's view of the child as naturally endowed with an innate plan for orderly, healthy growth. (p. 14)

nocturnal enuresis Repeated bedwetting during the night. (p. 285)

nonfunctionality The component of the death concept specifying that all living functions, including thought, feeling, movement, and body processes, cease at death. (p. 631)

nonnormative influences Influences on lifespan development that are irregular, in that they happen to just one or a few individuals and do not follow a predictable timetable. (p. 12)

nonorganic failure to thrive A growth disorder usually present by 18 months of age that is caused by lack of affection and stimulation. (p. 129)

non-rapid-eye-movement (NREM) sleep A "regular" sleep state in which the body is quiet and heart rate, breathing, and brain wave activity are slow and regular. Distinguished from *rapid-eye-movement (REM) sleep.* (p. 108)

nonsocial activity Unoccupied, onlooker behavior and solitary play. Distinguished from *parallel, associative,* and *cooperative play.* (p. 253)

normative approach An approach in which measures of behavior are taken on large numbers of individuals and age related averages are computed to represent typical development. (p. 15)

obesity A greater-than-20-percent increase over average body weight, based on the individual's age, sex, and physical build. (p. 282)

object permanence The understanding that objects continue to exist when they are out of sight. (p. 151)

old-old Showing signs of physical decline in old age. Distinguished from *young-old*. (p. 556)

open classroom An elementary school classroom based on the educational philosophy that children are active agents in their own development and learn at different rates. Teachers share decision making with pupils. Pupils are evaluated in relation to their own prior development. Distinguished from *traditional classroom.* (p. 307)

operant conditioning A form of learning in which a spontaneous behavior is followed by a stimulus that changes the probability that the behavior will occur again. (p. 131)

oral rehydration therapy (ORT) A treatment for diarrhea, in which sick children are given a glucose, salt, and water solution that quickly replaces fluids the body loses. (p. 215)

ordinality A principle specifying order relationships between quantities, such as three is more than two and two is more than one. (p. 234)

organization In Piaget's theory, the internal rearrangement and linking together of schemes so that they form a strongly interconnected cognitive system. In information processing, the memory strategy of grouping together related items. (p. 149; p. 295)

osteoarthritis A form of arthritis characterized by deteriorating cartilage on the ends of bones of frequently used joints. Leads to swelling, stiffness, and loss of flexibility. Otherwise known as "wear-and-tear" arthritis. Distinguished from *rheumatoid arthritis*. (p. 570)

osteoporosis A severe version of age-related bone loss. Porous bones are easily fractured and when very extreme, lead to a slumped-over posture, a shuffling gait, and a "dowager's hump" in the upper back. (p. 500)

overextension An early vocabulary error in which a word is applied too broadly, to a wider collection of objects and events than is appropriate. Distinguished from *underextension*. (p. 169)

overregularization Application of regular grammatical rules to words that are exceptions. (p. 240)

overt aggression A form of hostile aggression that harms others through physical injury or the threat of such injury—for example, hitting, kicking, or threatening to beat up a peer. (p. 260)

palliative, or comfort, care Care for terminally ill, suffering patients that relieves pain and other symptoms (such as breathing difficulties, insomnia, and depression), aimed at protecting the patient's quality of life rather than prolonging life. (p. 639)

parallel play A form of limited social participation in which the child plays near other children with similar materials but does not interact with them. Distinguished from *nonsocial, associative,* and *cooperative play.* (p. 253)

parental imperative theory A theory that claims that traditional gender roles are maintained during the active parenting years to help ensure the survival of children. After children reach adulthood, parents are free to express the "other-gender" side of their personalities. (p. 532)

passionate love Love based on intense sexual attraction. Distinguished from *companionate love.* (p. 461)

passive euthanasia The practice of withholding or withdrawing life-sustaining treatment, permitting a patient to die naturally. Distinguished from *voluntary active euthanasia.* (p. 640)

peer group Peers who form a social unit by generating unique values and standards of behavior and a social structure of leaders and followers. (p. 327)

peer victimization A destructive form of peer interaction in which certain children become frequent targets of verbal and physical attacks or other forms of abuse. (p. 330)

perception-bound Being easily distracted by the concrete, perceptual appearance of objects. (p. 224)

permanence The component of the death concept specifying that once a living thing dies, it cannot be brought back to life. (p. 631)

permissive style A child-rearing style that is responsive but undemanding. An overly tolerant approach to child rearing. Distinguished from *authoritative* and *authoritarian styles.* (p. 269)

persistent vegetative state A state produced by absence of brain wave activity in the cortex, in which the person is unconscious, displays no voluntary movements, and has no hope of recovery. (p. 629)

personal fable Adolescents' belief that they are special and unique. Leads them to conclude that others cannot possibly understand their thoughts and feelings and may promote a sense of invulnerability to danger. (p. 375)

perspective taking The capacity to imagine what other people may be thinking and feeling. (p. 325)

phenotype The individual's physical and behavioral characteristics, which are determined by both genetic and environmental factors. Distinguished from *genotype.* (p. 46)

physical causality The causal action one object exerts on another through contact. (p. 151)

pituitary gland A gland located near the base of the brain that releases hormones affecting physical growth. (p. 212)

placenta The organ that separates the mother's bloodstream from the embryo or fetal bloodstream but permits exchange of nutrients and waste products. (p. 82)

polygenic inheritance A pattern of inheritance in which many genes determine a characteristic. (p. 53)

popular children Children who get many positive votes on sociometric measures of peer acceptance. Distinguished from *rejected, controversial,* and *neglected children.* (p. 329)

possible selves Future-oriented representations of what one hopes to become and is afraid of becoming. The temporal dimension of self-concept. (p. 528)

postconventional level Kohlberg's highest level of moral development, in which individuals define morality in terms of abstract principles and values that apply to all situations and societies. (p. 398)

postformal thought Cognitive development beyond Piaget's formal operational stage. (p. 440)

practical problem solving Problem solving that requires people to size up real-world situations and analyze how best to achieve goals that have a high degree of uncertainty. (p. 511)

pragmatic thought In Labouvie-Vief's theory, adult thought in which logic becomes a tool to solve real-world problems and inconsistencies and imperfections are accepted. (p. 441)

pragmatics The practical, social side of language that is concerned with how to engage in effective and appropriate communication with others. (p. 240)

preconventional level Kohlberg's first level of moral development, in which moral understanding is based on rewards, punishments, and the power of authority figures. (p. 397)

preformationism Medieval view of the child as a miniature adult. (p. 13)

premenstrual syndrome (PMS) An array of physical and psychological symptoms that usually appear 6 to 10 days prior to menstruation. The most common are abdominal cramps, fluid retention, diarrhea, tender breasts, backache, headache, fatigue, tension, irritability, and depression. (p. 438)

prenatal diagnostic methods Medical procedures that permit detection of developmental problems before birth. (p. 55)

preoperational stage Piaget's second stage, in which rapid growth in representation takes place. However, thought is not yet logical. Spans the years from 2 to 7. (p. 221)

presbycusis Age-related hearing impairments that involve a sharp loss at high frequencies around age 50, which gradually extends to all frequencies. (p. 494)

presbyopia Condition of aging in which, around age 60, the lens of the eye loses its capacity to accommodate entirely to nearby objects. (p. 493)

preterm Infants born several weeks or more before their due date. (p. 102)

primary aging Genetically influenced age-related declines in the functioning of organs and systems that affect all members of our species and take place even in the context of overall good health. Also called *biological aging*. Distinguished from *secondary aging*. (p. 570)

primary sexual characteristics Physical features that involve the reproductive organs directly (ovaries, uterus, and vagina in females; penis, scrotum, and testes in males). Distinguished from *secondary sexual characteristics*. (p. 354)

principle of mutual exclusivity The assumption by children in the early stages of vocabulary growth that words mark entirely separate (nonoverlapping) categories. (p. 239)

private speech Self-directed speech that children use to plan and guide their own behavior. (p. 228)

Project Head Start A federal program that provides low-income children with a year or two of preschool education before school entry and that encourages parent involvement in children's development. (p. 236)

propositional thought A type of formal operational reasoning in which adolescents evaluate the logic of verbal statements without referring to real-world circumstances. (p. 371)

prosocial, or altruistic, behavior Actions that benefit another person without any expected reward for the self. (p. 252)

prospective memory Recall that involves remembering to engage in planned actions at an appropriate time in the future. (p. 581)

proximodistal trend An organized pattern of physical growth and motor control that proceeds from the center of the body outward. Distinguished from *cephalocaudal trend*. (p. 120)

psychoanalytic perspective An approach to personality development introduced by Freud that assumes children move through a series of stages in which they confront conflicts between biological drives and social expectations. The way these conflicts are resolved determines psychological adjustment. (p. 16)

psychosexual theory Freud's theory, which emphasizes that how parents manage children's sexual and aggressive drives during the first few years is crucial for healthy personality development. (p. 16)

psychosocial theory Erikson's theory, which emphasizes that the demands of society at each Freudian stage not only promote the development of a unique personality, but also ensure that individuals acquire attitudes and skills that help them become active, contributing members of their society. (p. 17)

puberty Biological changes at adolescence that lead to an adult-sized body and sexual maturity. (p. 350)

public policies Laws and government programs designed to improve current conditions. (p. 68)

punishment In operant conditioning, removing a desirable stimulus or presenting an unpleasant one to decrease the occurrence of a response. (p. 131)

random assignment An evenhanded procedure for assigning participants to treatment groups, such as drawing numbers out of a hat or flipping a coin. Increases the chances that participants' characteristics will be equally distributed across treatment conditions in an experiment. (p. 34)

range of reaction Each person's unique, genetically determined response to a range of environmental conditions. (p. 73)

rapid-eye-movement (REM) sleep An "irregular" sleep state in which brain wave activity is similar to that of the waking state; eyes dart beneath the lids, heart rate, blood pressure, and breathing are uneven, and slight body movements occur. Distinguished from *non-rapid-eye-movement (NREM) sleep*. (p. 107)

realistic period Period of vocational development in which older adolescents and young adults focus on a general career category and, slightly later, settle on a single occupation. Distinguished from *fantasy period* and *tentative period*. (p. 445)

recall A type of memory that involves remembering a stimulus that is not present. (p. 157)

recasts Adult responses that restructure children's incorrect speech into a more mature form. (p. 241)

recognition A type of memory that involves noticing whether a stimulus is identical or similar to one previously experienced. (p. 157)

referential style A style of early language learning in which toddlers use language mainly to label objects. Distinguished from *expressive style*. (p. 170)

reflex An inborn, automatic response to a particular form of stimulation. (p. 106)

rehearsal The memory strategy of repeating information. (p. 295)

reinforcer In operant conditioning, a stimulus that increases the occurrence of a response. (p. 131)

reintegrative stage Schaie's stage of late adulthood, in which people reexamine and reintegrate their interests, attitudes, and values, using them as a guide for what knowledge to acquire and apply. (p. 441)

rejected children Children who are actively disliked and get many negative votes on sociometric measures of peer acceptance. Distinguished from *popular, controversial,* and *neglected children.* (p. 329)

rejected-aggressive children A subgroup of rejected children who engage in high rates of conflict, hostility, and hyperactive, inattentive, and impulsive behavior. Distinguished from *rejected-withdrawn children.* (p. 329)

rejected-withdrawn children A subgroup of rejected children who are passive and socially awkward. Distinguished from *rejected-aggressive children.* (p. 329)

relational aggression A form of hostile aggression that damages another's peer relationships, as in social exclusion or rumor spreading. (p. 260)

relativistic thinking In Perry's theory, the cognitive approach of older college students, who favor multiple truths, each relative to its context of evaluation. Distinguished from *dualistic thinking.* (p. 440)

reminiscence The process of telling stories about people and events from the past and reporting associated thoughts and feelings. (p. 594)

remote memory Recall of events that happened long ago. (p. 581)

resiliency The ability to adapt effectively in the face of adverse life circumstances. (p. 10)

resistant attachment The quality of insecure attachment characterizing infants who remain close to the parent before departure and display angry, resistive behavior when she returns. Distinguished from *secure, avoidant,* and *disorganized/disoriented attachment.* (p. 192)

respiratory distress syndrome A disorder of preterm infants in which the lungs are so immature that the air sacs collapse, causing serious breathing difficulties. (p. 103)

responsibility stage Schaie's stage of middle adulthood in which people adapt their cognitive skills to the expansion of responsibilities to others that takes place on the job, in the community, and at home. (p. 441)

reticular formation A brain structure that maintains alertness and consciousness. (p. 211)

reversibility The ability to think through a series of steps in a problem and then mentally reverse direction, returning to the starting point. Distinguished from *irreversibility.* (p. 291)

Rh factor A protein that, when present in the fetus's blood but not in the mother's, can cause the mother to build up antibodies. If these return to the fetus's system, they destroy red blood cells, reducing the oxygen supply to organs and tissues. (p. 94)

rheumatoid arthritis A form of arthritis in which the immune system attacks the body, resulting in inflammation of connective tissue, particularly the membranes that line the joints. The result is stiffness, inflammation, aching, deformed joints, and serious loss of mobility. Distinguished from *osteoarthritis.* (p. 570)

sandwich generation Today's middle-aged adults, who are "sandwiched," or squeezed, between the needs of ill or frail parents and financially dependent children. (p. 540)

scheme In Piaget's theory, a specific structure, or organized way of making sense of experience, that changes with age. (p. 148)

school phobia Severe apprehension about attending school, often accompanied by physical complaints that disappear once the child is allowed to remain home. (p. 339)

scripts General descriptions of what occurs and when it occurs in a particular situation. A basic means through which children organize and interpret their everyday experiences. (p. 231)

secondary aging Declines due to hereditary defects and environmental influences, such as poor diet, lack of exercise, substance abuse, environmental pollution, and psychological stress. Distinguished from *primary aging.* (p. 570)

secondary friends People who are not intimates but with whom the individual spends time occasionally, such as a group that meets for lunch, bridge, or museum tours. (p. 613)

secondary sexual characteristics Features visible on the outside of the body that serve as signs of sexual maturity but do not involve the reproductive organs (for example, breast development in females, appearance of underarm and pubic hair in both sexes). Distinguished from *primary sexual characteristics.* (p. 354)

secular trend in physical growth Change in body size and rate of growth from one generation to the next. For example, in industrialized nations, age of menarche declined from 1860 to 1970, signifying faster physical maturation in modern young people. (p. 355)

secure attachment The quality of attachment characterizing infants who are distressed by parental separation and easily comforted by the parent when she returns. Distinguished from *avoidant, resistant,* and *disorganized/disoriented attachment.* (p. 191)

secure base The use of the familiar caregiver as a base from which the infant confidently explores the environment and returns for emotional support. (p. 191)

selective optimization with compensation A set of strategies that permits the elderly to sustain high levels of functioning. They *select* personally valued activities as a way of *optimizing* returns from their diminishing energies and come up with new ways of *compensating* for losses. (p. 579)

self-care children Children who look after themselves while their parents are at work. (p. 338)

self-concept The sum total of attributes, abilities, attitudes, and values that an individual believes defines who he or she is. (p. 249)

self-conscious emotions Emotions that involve injury to or enhancement of the sense of self. Examples are shame, embarrassment, guilt, envy, and pride. (p. 183)

self-control The capacity to resist an impulse to engage in socially disapproved behavior. (p. 200)

self-esteem An aspect of self-concept that involves judgments about one's own worth and the feelings associated with those judgments. (p. 249)

sensitive period A time span that is optimal for certain capacities to emerge and in which the individual is especially responsive to environmental influences. (p. 23)

sensorimotor stage Piaget's first stage, during which infants and toddlers "think" with their eyes, ears, hands, and other sensorimotor equipment. Spans the first 2 years of life. (p. 148)

sensory register In information processing, that part of the mental system in which sights and sounds are held briefly before they decay or are transferred to working, or short-term, memory. (p. 156)

separation anxiety An infant's distressed reaction to the departure of the familiar caregiver. (p. 191)

seriation The ability to order items along a quantitative dimension, such as length or weight. (p. 291)

sex chromosomes The twenty-third pair of chromosomes, which determines the sex of the individual. In females, called *XX*; in males, called *XY*. (p. 48)

skipped-generation family A family structure in which children live with grandparents but apart from parents. (p. 539)

sleep apnea A condition during sleep in which breathing ceases for 10 seconds or longer, resulting in many brief awakenings. (p. 564)

slow-to-warm-up child A child whose temperament is such that he or she is inactive, shows mild, low-key reactions to environmental stimuli, is negative in mood, and adjusts slowly when faced with new experiences. Distinguished from *easy child* and *difficult child*. (p. 185)

small for date Infants whose birth weight is below their expected weight when length of pregnancy is taken into account. Some are full term; others are preterm infants who are especially underweight. (p. 102)

social clock Age-graded expectations for life events, such as beginning a first job, getting married, birth of the first child, buying a home, and retiring. (p. 459)

social comparisons Judgments of one's own abilities, behavior, appearance, and other characteristics in relation to those of others. (p. 321)

social convoy A model of age-related changes in social networks, which views the individual within a cluster of relationships moving through life. Close ties are in the inner circle, less close ties on the outside. With age, people change places in the convoy, new ties are added, and some are lost entirely. (p. 609)

social learning theory An approach that emphasizes the role of modeling, or observational learning, in the development of behavior. (p. 19)

social referencing Relying on a trusted person's emotional reaction to decide how to respond in an uncertain situation. (p. 183)

social smile The smile evoked by the stimulus of the human face. First appears between 6 and 10 weeks. (p. 182)

sociocultural theory Vygotsky's theory, in which children acquire the ways of thinking and behaving that make up a community's culture through cooperative dialogues with more knowledgeable members of society. (p. 24)

sociodramatic play The make-believe play with others that first appears around age 2½ and increases rapidly until 4 to 5 years. (p. 222)

socioeconomic status (SES) A measure of a family's social position and economic well-being that combines three interrelated, but not completely overlapping, variables: (1) years of education and (2) the prestige of and skill required by one's job, both of which measure social status; and (3) income, which measures economic status. (p. 63)

socioemotional selectivity theory A social theory of aging that states that the decline in social interaction in late adulthood is due to physical and psychological changes, which lead elders to emphasize the emotion-regulating function of interaction. Consequently, they prefer familiar partners with whom they have developed pleasurable relationships. Distinguished from *disengagement theory* and *activity theory*. (p. 604)

spermarche First ejaculation of seminal fluid. (p. 354)

squaring of the population pyramid The current trend toward equalization of the number of young, middle-aged, and elderly people in the United States, due to declining birth rates, aging of the "baby boom" generation, and greater longevity. (p. 576)

stability versus change Disagreement among theorists about whether there are stable individual differences throughout the lifespan that are largely influenced by heredity and early experiences, or whether change is possible and likely if new experiences support it. (p. 7)

stage A qualitative change in thinking, feeling, and behaving that characterizes a particular time period of development. (p. 6)

states of arousal Different degrees of sleep and wakefulness. (p. 107)

states rather than transformations The tendency to treat the initial and final states in a problem as completely unrelated. (p. 224)

Strange Situation A procedure involving short separations from and reunions with the parent that assesses the quality of the attachment bond. (p. 191)

stranger anxiety The infant's expression of fear in response to unfamiliar adults. Appears in many babies after 6 months of age. (p. 182)

structured interview An interview method in which each participant is asked the same questions in the same way. (p. 29)

structured observation A method in which the investigator sets up a cue for the behavior of interest and observes it in a laboratory. Distinguished from *naturalistic observation*. (p. 29)

subculture A group of people with beliefs and customs that differ from those of the larger culture. (p. 66)

successful aging Aging in which gains are maximized and losses minimized. (p. 619)

sudden infant death syndrome (SIDS) The unexpected death, usually during the night, of an infant under 1 year of age that remains unexplained after thorough investigation. (p. 123)

sympathy Feelings of concern or sorrow for another's plight. (p. 252)

synapses The gaps between neurons, across which chemical messages are sent. (p. 120)

synaptic pruning Loss of connective fibers by seldom-stimulated neurons, thereby returning them to an uncommitted state so they can support the development of future skills. (p. 120)

tabula rasa Locke's view of the child as a blank slate whose character is shaped by experience. (p. 13)

telegraphic speech Toddlers' two-word utterances that, like a telegram, leave out smaller and less important words. (p. 170)

temperament Stable individual differences in quality and intensity of emotional reaction. (p. 185)

tentative period Period of vocational development in which adolescents weigh vocational options against their interests, abilities, and values. Distinguished from *fantasy period* and *realistic period*. (p. 445)

teratogen Any environmental agent that causes damage during the prenatal period. (p. 86)

terminal decline A steady, marked decrease in cognitive functioning prior to death. (p. 584)

theory An orderly, integrated set of statements that describes, explains, and predicts behavior. (p. 5)

theory of multiple intelligences Gardner's theory, which identifies eight independent intelligences on the basis of distinct sets of processing operations that permit individuals to engage in a wide range of culturally valued activities. (p. 301)

thyroid-stimulating hormone (TSH) A pituitary hormone that stimulates the thyroid gland to release thyroxine, which is necessary for normal brain development and body growth. (p. 212)

time out A form of mild punishment in which children are removed from the immediate setting until they are ready to act appropriately. (p. 258)

traditional classroom An elementary school classroom based on the educational philosophy that children are passive learners who acquire information presented by teachers. Pupils are evaluated in terms of how well they keep up with a uniform set of standards for all children in their grade. Distinguished from *open classroom*. (p. 307)

traditional marriage A form of marriage involving clear division of husband's and wife's roles. The man is the head of household and economic provider. The woman devotes herself to caring for her husband and children and creating a nurturant, comfortable home. Distinguished from *egalitarian marriage*. (p. 468)

transition Climax of the first stage of labor, in which the frequency and strength of contractions are at their peak and the cervix opens completely. (p. 97)

transitive inference The ability to seriate—or order items along a quantitative dimension—mentally. (p. 291)

triarchic theory of intelligence Sternberg's theory, which states that information-processing skills, prior experience with tasks, and contextual (or cultural) factors interact to determine intelligent behavior. (p. 300)

trimesters Three equal time periods in the prenatal period, each of which lasts three months. (p. 83)

Type A behavior pattern A behavior pattern consisting of extreme competitiveness, ambition, impatience, hostility, angry outbursts, and a sense of time pressure. (p. 502)

umbilical cord The long cord connecting the prenatal organism to the placenta that delivers nutrients and removes waste products. (p. 82)

unconditioned response (UCR) In classical conditioning, a reflexive response that is produced by an unconditioned stimulus (UCS). (p. 130)

unconditioned stimulus (UCS) In classical conditioning, a stimulus that leads to a reflexive response. (p. 130)

underextension An early vocabulary error in which a word is applied too narrowly, to a smaller number of objects and events than is appropriate. Distinguished from *overextension*. (p. 169)

uninhibited, or sociable, child A child whose temperament is such that he or she displays positive emotion to and approaches novel stimuli. Distinguished from *inhibited, or shy, child*. (p. 187)

universality The component of the death concept specifying that all living things eventually die. (p. 631)

vernix A white, cheeselike substance covering the fetus and preventing the skin from chapping due to constant exposure to the amniotic fluid. (p. 84)

visual acuity Fineness of visual discrimination. (p. 111)

voluntary active euthanasia The practice of ending a patient's suffering, at the patient's request, before a natural end to life. A form of mercy killing. Distinguished from *passive euthanasia*. (p. 642)

whole-language approach An approach to beginning reading instruction that parallels children's natural language learning and keeps reading materials whole and meaningful. Distinguished from *basic-skills approach*. (p. 297)

wisdom A form of cognition that combines breadth and depth of practical knowledge, ability to reflect on that knowledge in ways that make life more bearable and worthwhile, emotional maturity, and creative integration of experience and knowledge into new ways of thinking and acting. (p. 583)

working, or short-term, memory In information processing, the conscious part of the mental system, where we actively "work" on a limited amount of information to ensure that it will be retained. (p. 156)

X-linked inheritance A pattern of inheritance in which a recessive gene is carried on the X chromosome. Males are more likely to be affected. (p. 51)

young-old Appearing physically young for one's advanced years. Distinguished from *old-old*. (p. 556)

zone of proximal development In Vygotsky's theory, a range of tasks that the child cannot yet handle alone but can do with the help of more skilled partners. (p. 160)

zygote The newly fertilized cell formed by the union of sperm and ovum at conception. (p. 47)

Abbott, S. (1992). Holding on and pushing away: Comparative perspectives on an eastern Kentucky child-rearing practice. *Ethos, 20,* 33–65.

Abbotts, B., & Osborn, L. M. (1993). Immunization status and reasons for immunization delay among children using public health immunization clinics. *American Journal of Diseases of Children, 147,* 965–968.

Abood, D. A., & Chandler, S. B. (1997). Race and the role of weight, weight change, and body dissatisfaction in eating disorders. *American Journal of Health Behavior, 21,* 21–25.

Abra, J. (1989). Changes in creativity with age: Data, explanations, and further predictions. *International Journal of Aging and Human Development, 28,* 105–126.

Abraham, S. (1998). Satisfaction of participants in university-administered elderhostel programs. *Educational Gerontology, 24,* 529–536.

Abramovitch, R., Freedman, J. L., Henry, K., & Van Brunschot, M. (1995). Children's capacity to agree to psychological research: Knowledge of risks and benefits and voluntariness. *Ethics and Behavior, 5,* 25–48.

Abramovitch, R., Freedman, J. L., Thoden, K., & Nikolich, C. (1991). Children's capacity to consent to participation in psychological research: Some empirical findings. *Child Development, 62,* 1100–1109.

Abrass, I. B. (1990). The biology and physiology of aging. *West Journal of Medicine, 153,* 641–645.

Achenbach, T. M., Phares, V., Howell, C. T., Rauh, V. A., & Nurcombe, B. (1990). Seven-year outcome of the Vermont program for low-birthweight infants. *Child Development, 61,* 1672–1681.

Acker, M. M., & O'Leary, S. G. (1996). Inconsistency of mothers' feedback and toddlers' misbehavior and negative affect. *Journal of Abnormal Child Psychology, 24,* 703–714.

Ackerman, B. P. (1978). Children's understanding of speech acts in unconventional frames. *Child Development, 49,* 311–318.

Adams, P. F., & Marano, M. A. (1995). Current estimates from the National Health Interview Survey, 1994. National Center for Health Statistics. *Vital Health Statistics, 10*(193), 83–84.

Adams, R. G. (1985–1986). Emotional closeness and physical distance between friends: Implications for elderly women living in age-segregated and age-integrated settings. *International Journal of Aging and Human Development, 22,* 55–76.

Adams, R. J. (1987). An evaluation of color preference in early infancy. *Infant Behavior and Development, 10,* 143–150.

Adams, R. J., Courage, M. L., & Mercer, M. E. (1994). Systematic measurement of human neonatal color vision. *Vision Research, 34,* 1691–1701.

Adams, S. H. (1994). Role of hostility in women's health during midlife: A longitudinal study. *Health Psychology, 13,* 488–495.

Adelman, C. (1991). *Women at thirtysomething: Paradoxes of attainment.* Washington, DC: U.S. Government Printing Office.

Adkins, G., Martin, P., & Poon, L. W. (1996). Personality traits and states as predictors of subjective well-being in centenarians, octogenarians, and sexagenarians. *Psychology and Aging, 11,* 408–416.

Adler, N. E., Boyce, T., Chesney, M. A., Cohen, S., Folkman, S., Kahn, R. L., & Syme, L. (1994). Socioeconomic status and health. *American Psychologist, 49,* 15–24.

Adolph, K. E. (1997). Learning in the development of infant locomotion. *Monographs of the Society for Research in Child Development, 62*(3, Serial No. 251).

Adolph, K. E. A., Vereijken, B., & Denny, M. A. (1998). Learning to crawl. *Child Development, 69,* 1299–1312.

Ahaja, K. K., Emerson, G., Seaton, A., Mamiso, J., & Simons, E. G. (1997). Widow's attempt to use her dead husband's sperm. *British Medical Journal, 314,* 143.

Ahlsten, G., Cnattingius, S., & Lindmark, G. (1993). Cessation of smoking during pregnancy improves fetal growth and reduces infant morbidity in the neonatal period: A population-based prospective study. *Acta Paediatrica, 82,* 177–181.

Ainlay, S. C., Singleton, R., & Swigert, V. L. (1992). Aging and religious participation: Reconsidering the effects of health. *Journal for the Scientific Study of Religion, 31,* 175–188.

Ainsworth, M. D. S., Blehar, M. C., Waters, E., & Wall, S. (1978). *Patterns of attachment.* Hillsdale, NJ: Erlbaum.

Alan Guttmacher Institute. (1994). *Sex and America's teenagers.* New York: Author.

Alan Guttmacher Institute. (1998). *Facts in brief—Teen sex and pregnancy.* New York: Author.

Albanes, D., Blair, A., & Taylor, P. R. (1989). Physical activity and risk of cancer in the NHANES I population. *American Journal of Public Health, 79,* 744–750.

Albert, R. S. (1994). The achievement of eminence: A longitudinal study of exceptionally gifted boys and their families. In R. F. Sobotnik & K. D. Arnold (Eds.), *Beyond Terman: Contemporary studies of giftedness and talent* (pp. 282–315). Norwood, NJ: Ablex.

Aldwin, C. (1994). *Stress, coping, and development.* New York: Guilford.

Ales, K. L., Druzin, M. L., & Santini, D. L. (1990). Impact of advanced maternal age on the outcome of pregnancy. *Surgery, Gynecology and Obstetrics, 171,* 209–216.

Alessandri, S. M., Bendersky, M., & Lewis, M. (1998). Cognitive functioning in 8- to 18-month-old drug-exposed infants. *Developmental Psychology, 34,* 565–573.

Alessandri, S. M., & Wozniak, R. H. (1987). The child's awareness of parental beliefs concerning the child: A developmental study. *Child Development, 58,* 316–323.

Alessio, H. M., & Blasi, E. R. (1997). Physical activity as a natural antioxidant booster and its effect on a healthy life span. *Research Quarterly in Exercise and Sport, 68,* 292–302.

Alexander, J. M., Lucas, M. J., Ramin, S. M., McIntire, D. D., & Leveno, K. J. (1998). The course of labor with and without epidural analgesia. *American Journal of Obstetrics and Gynecology, 178,* 516–520.

Allan, K., & Coltrane, S. (1996). Gender displaying television commercials: A comparative study of television commercials in the 1950s and 1980s. *Sex Roles, 35,* 185–203.

Allen, J. P., Hauser, S. T., Bell, K. L., & O'Connor, T. G. (1994). Longitudinal assessment of autonomy and relatedness in adolescent–family interactions as predictors of adolescent ego development and self-esteem. *Child Development, 65,* 179–194.

Allen, J. P., Philliber, S., Herrling, S., & Kuperminc, G. P. (1997). Preventing teen pregnancy and academic failure: Experimental evaluation of a developmentally based approach. *Child Development, 64,* 729–742.

Allen, K., Calsyn, D. A., Fehrenbach, P. A., & Benton, G. (1989). A study of the interpersonal behaviors of male batterers. *Journal of Interpersonal Violence, 4,* 79–89.

Allen, S. H. (1999). *Osteoporosis: Genetics, prevention and treatment.* Norwell, MA: Kluwer.

Allen, W. A., Piccone, N. L., & D'Amanda, C. (1993). *How drugs can affect your life.* Springfield, IL: Charles C Thomas.

Allison, D. B., Fontaine, K. R., Manson, J. E., Stevens, J., & Vanitallie, T. B. (1999). Annual deaths attributable to obesity in the United States. *Journal of the American Medical Association, 282,* 1530–1538.

Allison, D. B., & Pi-Sunyer, X. (1994, May–June). Fleshing out obesity. *The Sciences, 34*(3), 38–43.

Allison, J. A., & Wrightsman, L. S. (1993). *Rape: The misunderstood crime.* Newbury Park, CA: Sage.

Alpert-Gillis, L. J., & Connell, J. P. (1989). Gender and sex-role influences on children's self-esteem. *Journal of Personality, 57,* 97–114.

Alsaker, F. D. (1995). Timing of puberty and reactions to pubertal changes. In M. Rutter (Ed.), *Psychosocial disturbances in young people* (pp. 37–82). New York: Cambridge University Press.

Amaro, H. (1995). Love, sex and power: Considering women's realities in HIV prevention. *American Psychologist, 50,* 437–447.

Amato, P. R. (1996). Explaining the intergenerational transmission of divorce. *Journal of Marriage and the Family, 58,* 628–640.

Amato, P. R., & Booth, A. (1996). A prospective study of divorce and parent–child relationships. *Journal of Marriage and the Family, 58,* 356–365.

Amato, P. R., & Gilbreth, J. (1999). Nonresident fathers and children's well-being: A meta-analysis. *Journal of Marriage and the Family, 61,* 557–573.

Amato, P. R., Loomis, L. S., & Booth, A. (1995). Parental divorce, marital conflict, and offspring well-being during early adulthood. *Social Forces, 73,* 895–915.

Amato, P. R., & Rogers, S. J. (1997). A longitudinal study of marital problems and subsequent divorce. *Journal of Marriage and the Family, 59,* 612–624.

Ambry, M. (1992). Childless chances. *American Demographics, 14,* 55.

American Academy of Family Physicians. (1997). Decline in SIDS rates. *American Family Physician, 55,* 358–359.

American College of Sports Medicine. (1998). *ASCM's resource manual for guidelines for exercise testing and prescription.* Baltimore: Lippincott, Williams and Wilkins.

American Psychiatric Association. (1994). *Diagnostic and statistical manual of mental disorders* (4th ed.). Washington, DC: Author.

American Psychological Association. (1994). *Publication manual of the American Psychological Association.* Washington, DC: Author.

Ames, C. (1992). Classrooms: Goals, structures, and student motivation. *Journal of Educational Psychology, 84,* 261–271.

Andersen, K., Nielsen, H., Lolk, A., Andersen, J., Becker, I., & Kragh-Sorensen, P. (1999). Incidence of very mild to severe dementia and Alzheimer's disease in Denmark: The Odense Study. *Neurology, 52,* 85–90.

Anderson, D. A. (1994). Lesbian and gay adolescents: Social and developmental considerations. *High School Journal, 77,* 13–19.

Anderson, D. N., Huston, A. C., Wright, J. C., & Collins, P. A. (1998). *Sesame Street* and educational television for children. In R. G. Noll & M. E. Price (Eds.), *A communications cornucopia: Markle Foundation essays on information policy* (pp. 279–296). Washington, DC: Brookings Institute.

Anderson, E. S. (1984). The acquisition of sociolinguistic knowledge: Some evidence from children's verbal role play. *Western Journal of Speech Communication, 48,* 125–144.

Anderson, P. J., & Graham, S. M. (1994). Issues in second-language phonological acquisition among children and adults. *Topics in Language Disorders, 14,* 84–100.

Anderson, S. A., Russell, C. S., & Schumm, W. R. (1983). Perceived marital quality and family life-cycle categories: A further analysis. *Journal of Marriage and the Family, 45,* 127–139.

Andersson, B.-E. (1989). Effects of public day care—A longitudinal study. *Child Development, 60,* 857–866.

Andersson, B.-E. (1992). Effects of day care on cognitive and socioemotional competence of thirteen-year-old Swedish schoolchildren. *Child Development, 63,* 20–36.

Angel, J. L., Angel, R. J., McClellan, J. L., & Markides, K. S. (1996). Nativity, declining health, and preferences in living arrangements among elderly Mexican Americans: Implications for long-term care. *Gerontologist, 36,* 464–473.

Angle, J., & Wissmann, D. A. (1980). The epidemiology of myopia. *American Journal of Epidemiology, 111,* 220–228.

Anglin, J. M. (1993). Vocabulary development: A morphological analysis. *Monographs of the Society for Research in Child Development, 58*(10, Serial No. 238).

Anthenelli, R. M., & Schuckit, M. A. (1992). Genetics. In J. H. Lowinson, P. Ruiz, & R. B. Millman (Eds.), *Substance abuse* (2nd ed., pp. 39–50). Baltimore: Williams & Wilkins.

Antonucci, T. (1990). Social supports and social relationships. In R. Binstock & L. K. George (Eds.), *Handbook of aging and the social sciences* (3rd ed., pp. 205–227). New York: Academic Press.

Antonucci, T., & Akiyama, H. (1997). Concern with others at midlife: Care, comfort, or compromise? In M. E. Lachman & J. B. James (Eds.), *Multiple paths of midlife development* (pp. 145–169). Chicago: University of Chicago Press.

Antonucci, T. C. (1994). A life-span view of women's social relations. In B. F. Turner & L. E. Troll (Eds.), *Women growing older* (pp. 239–269). Thousand Oaks, CA: Sage.

Antonucci, T. C., & Akiyama, H. (1995). Convoys of social relations: Family and friendships within a life span context. In R. Blieszner & V. H. Bedford (Eds.), *Handbook of aging and the family* (pp. 355–371). Westport, CT: Greenwood Press.

Apgar, V. (1953). A proposal for a new method of evaluation in the newborn infant. *Current Research in Anesthesia and Analgesia, 32,* 260–267.

Aquilino, W. S. (1996). The returning adult child and parental experience at midlife. In C. D. Ryff & M. M. Seltzer (Eds.), *The parental experience in midlife* (pp. 423–458). Chicago: University of Chicago Press.

Arata, C. M. (1999). Coping with rape: The roles of prior sexual abuse and attributions of blame. *Journal of Interpersonal Violence, 14,* 62–78.

Arber, S., & Cooper, H. (1999). Gender differences in health in later life: The new paradox? *Social Science and Medicine, 48,* 61–76.

Archer, S. L. (1982). The lower age boundaries of identity development. *Child Development, 53,* 1551–1556.

Archer, S. L. (1989). The status of identity: Reflections on the need for intervention. *Journal of Adolescence, 12,* 345–359.

Archer, S. L., & Waterman, A. S. (1990). Varieties of identity diffusions and foreclosures: An exploration of subcategories of the identity statuses. *Journal of Adolescent Research, 5,* 96–111.

Archer, S. L., & Waterman, A. S. (1994). Adolescent identity development: Contextual perspectives. In C. B. Fisher & R. M. Lerner (Eds.), *Applied developmental psychology* (pp. 76–100). New York: McGraw-Hill.

Arcus, D., & Kagan, J. (1995). Temperament and craniofacial variation in the first two years. *Child Development, 66,* 1529–1540.

Ardelt, M. (1998). Social crisis and individual growth: The long-term effects of the Great Depression. *Journal of Aging Studies, 12,* 291–314.

Arendt, R., Singer, L., Angelopoulos, J., Bass-Busdiecker, O., & Mascia, J. (1998). Sensorimotor development in cocaine-exposed infants. *Infant Behavior and Development, 21,* 627–640.

Arias, I. (1999). Women's responses to physical and psychological abuse. In X. B. Arriaga & S. Oskamp (Eds.), *Violence in intimate relationships* (pp. 139–161). Thousand Oaks, CA: Sage.

Ariès, P. (1962). *Centuries of childhood.* New York: Random House.

Arking, R. (1991). *Biology of aging.* Englewood Cliffs, NJ: Prentice Hall.

Arlin, P. K. (1984). Adolescent and adult thought: A structural interpretation. In M. Commons, F. Richards, & C. Armom (Eds.), *Beyond formal operations: Late adolescent and adult cognitive development* (pp. 258–271). New York: Praeger.

Arlin, P. K. (1989). Problem solving and problem finding in young artists and young scientists. In M. L. Commons, J. D. Sinnott, F. A. Richards, & C. Armon (Eds.), *Adult development: Vol 1. Comparisons and applications of developmental models* (pp. 197–216). New York: Praeger.

Arnold, K. (1994). The Illinois Valedictorian Project: Early adult careers of academically talented male and female high school students. In R. F. Subotnik & K. D. Arnold (Eds.), *Beyond Terman: Contemporary longitudinal studies of giftedness and talent* (pp. 24–51). Norwood, NJ: Ablex.

Aronson, M., Hagberg, B., & Gillberg, C. (1997). Attention deficits and autistic spectrum problems in children exposed to alcohol during gestation: A follow-up study. *Developmental Medicine and Child Neurology, 39,* 583–587.

Arsenio, W., & Fleiss, K. (1996). Typical and behaviourally disruptive children's understanding of the emotional consequences of socio-moral events. *British Journal of Developmental Psychology, 14,* 173–186.

Artman, L., & Cahan, S. (1993). Schooling and the development of transitive inference. *Developmental Psychology, 29,* 753–759.

Asher, S. R., & Rose, A. J. (1997). Promoting children's social-emotional adjustment with peers. In P. Salovey & D. J. Sluyter (Eds.), *Emotional development and emotional intelligence* (pp. 193–195). New York: Basic Books.

Ashmead, D. H., McCarty, M. E., Lucas, L. S., & Belvedere, M. C. (1993). Visual guidance in infants' reaching toward suddenly displaced targets. *Child Development, 64,* 1111–1127.

Ashmead, D. H., & Perlmutter, M. (1980). Infant memory in everyday life. In M. Perlmutter (Ed.), *New directions for child development* (Vol. 10, pp. 1–16). San Francisco: Jossey-Bass.

Aslin, R. N. (1993). Perception of visual direction in human infants. In C. E. Granrud (Ed.), *Visual perception and cognition in infancy* (pp. 91–119). Hillsdale, NJ: Erlbaum.

Assmann, A. (1994). Wholesome knowledge: Concepts of wisdom in a historical and cross-cultural perspective. In D. L. Featherman, R. M. Lerner, & M. Perlmutter (Eds.), *Lifespan development and behavior* (pp. 187–224). Hillsdale, NJ: Erlbaum.

Astley, S. J., Clarren, S. K., Little, R. E., Sampson, P. D., & Daling, J. R. (1992). Analysis of facial shape in children gestationally exposed to marijuana, alcohol, and/or cocaine. *Pediatrics, 89,* 67–77.

Aström, L. (1986). *I kvinnoled [In womenline].* Lund: Liber Förlag.

Atchley, R. (1988). *Social forces and aging: An introduction to social gerontology.* Belmont, CA: Wadsworth.

Atchley, R. C. (1991). *Social forces and aging* (6th ed.). Belmont, CA: Wadsworth.

Atchley, R. C. (1993). Critical perspectives on retirement. In T. R. Cole & W. A. Achenbaum (Eds.), *Voices and visions of aging* (pp. 3–19). New York: Springer.

Atkinson, R. C., & Shiffrin, R. M. (1968). Human memory: A proposed system and its control processes. In K. W. Spence & J. T. Spence (Eds.), *Advances in the psychology of learning and motivation* (Vol. 2, pp. 90–195). New York: Academic Press.

Attie, I., & Brooks-Gunn, J. (1996). The development of eating regulation across the life span. In D. Cicchetti & D. J. Cohen (Eds.), *Developmental psychology: Vol. 2. Risk, disorder, and adaptation* (pp. 332–368). New York: Wiley.

Au, K. H. (1997). A sociocultural model of reading instruction: The Kamehameha Elementary Education Program. In S. A. Stahl & D. A. Hayes (Eds.), *Instructional models in reading* (pp. 181–202). Mahwah, NJ: Erlbaum.

Au, T. K., Sidle, A. L., & Rollins, K. B. (1993). Developing an intuitive understanding of conservation and contamination: Invisible particles as a plausible mechanism. *Developmental Psychology, 29,* 286–299.

August, D., & Garcia, E. E. (1988). *Language minority education in the United States.* Springfield, IL: Thomas.

Avis, N. E. (1999). Women's health at midlife. In S. Willis & J. D. Reid (Eds.), *Life in the middle* (pp. 105–146). San Diego: Academic Press.

Avis, N. E., Stellato, R., Crawford, S., & Johannes, C. (1995). How does menopause impact sexual activity? *Menopause, 2,* 245.

Avolio, B. J., & Sosik, J. J. (1999). A lifespan framework for assessing the impact of work on white-collar workers. In S. L. Willis & J. D. Reid (Eds.), *Life in the middle* (pp. 249–274). San Diego, CA: Academic Press.

Axia, G., & Baroni, R. (1985). Linguistic politeness at different age levels. *Child Development, 56,* 918–927.

Azmitia, M. (1988). Peer interaction and problem solving: When are two heads better than one? *Child Development, 59,* 87–96.

Bacon, J. B. (1996). Support groups for bereaved children. In C. A. Corr & D. M. Corr (Eds.), *Handbook of childhood death and bereavement* (pp. 285–304). New York: Springer-Verlag.

Baenninger, M., & Newcombe, N. (1995). Environmental input to the development of sex-related differences in spatial and mathematical ability. *Learning and Individual Differences, 7,* 363–379.

Bagwell, C. L., Newcomb, A. F., & Bukowski, W. M. (1998). Preadolescent friendship and peer rejection as predictors of adult adjustment. *Child Development, 69,* 140–153.

Bahrick, H. P. (1984). Semantic memory content in permastore: Fifty years of memory for Spanish learned in school. *Journal of Experimental Psychology: General, 113,* 1–29.

Bahrick, H. P., Bahrick, P. O., & Wittlinger, R. P. (1975). Fifty years of memory for names and faces: A cross-sectional approach. *Journal of Experimental Psychology: General, 104,* 54–75.

Bahrick, L. E. (1992). Infants' perceptual differentiation of amodal and modality-specific audio-visual relations. *Journal of Experimental Child Psychology, 53,* 180–199.

Bahrick, L. E., Moss, L., & Fadil, C. (1996). Development of visual self-recognition in infancy. *Ecological Psychology, 8,* 189–208.

Bahrick, L. E., Netto, D., & Hernandez-Reif, M. (1998). Intermodal perception of adult and child faces and voices by infants. *Child Development, 69,* 1263–1275.

Bai, D. L., & Bertenthal, B. L. (1992). Locomotor status and the development of spatial search skills. *Child Development, 63,* 215–226.

Bailey, D. A., & Rasmussen, R. L. (1996). Sport and the child: Physiological and skeletal issues. In F. L. Smoll & R. E. Smith (Eds.), *Children and youth in sport: A biopsychological perspective* (pp. 187–199). Dubuque, IA: Brown & Benchmark.

Bailey, J. M., Bobrow, D., Wolfe, M., & Mikach, S. (1995). Sexual orientation of adult sons of gay fathers. *Developmental Psychology, 31,* 124–129.

Bailey, J. M., & Pillard, R. C. (1991). A genetic study of male sexual orientation. *Archives of General Psychology, 43,* 808–812.

Bailey, J. M., Pillard, R. C., Neale, M. C., & Agyei, Y. (1993). Heritable factors influence sexual orientation in women. *Archives of General Psychiatry, 50,* 217–223.

Bailey, T. (1993). Can youth apprenticeship thrive in the United States? *Educational Researcher, 22*(3), 4–10.

Baillargeon, R. (1987). Object permanence in 3½- and 4½-month-old infants. *Developmental Psychology, 23,* 655–664.

Baillargeon, R. (1994a). How do infants learn about the physical world? *Current Directions in Psychological Science, 3,* 133–140.

Baillargeon, R. (1994b). Physical reasoning in infancy. In M. S. Gazzaniga (Ed.), *The cognitive neurosciences* (pp. 181–204). Cambridge, MA: MIT Press.

Baillargeon, R. (1995). A model of physical reasoning in infancy. In C. Rovee-Collier & L. P. Lipsitt (Eds.), *Advances in infancy research* (Vol. 9, pp. 305–371). Norwood, NJ: Ablex.

Baillargeon, R. (1998). Infants' understanding of the physical world. In M. Sabourin, F. I. M. Craik, & M. Robert (Eds.), *Advances in psychological science: Vol. 1. Cognitive and biological aspects,* pp. 503–529. London: Psychology Press.

Baillargeon, R., & DeVos, J. (1991). Object permanence in young infants: Further evidence. *Child Development, 62,* 1227–1246.

Baillargeon, R., Graber, M., DeVos, J., & Black, J. (1990). Why do young infants fail to search for hidden objects? *Cognition, 36,* 255–284.

Baker-Ward, L., Gordon, B. N., Ornstein, P. A., Larus, D. M., & Clubb, P. A. (1993). Young children's long-term retention of a pediatric examination. *Child Development, 64,* 1519–1533.

Balfour, J. L., & Kaplan, G. A. (1998). Social class/socioeconomic factors. In J. C. Holland (Ed.), *Psycho-oncology* (pp. 78–90). New York: Oxford University Press.

Ballard, B. D., Gipson, M. T. Guttenberg, W., & Ramsey, K. (1980). Palatability of food as a factor influencing obese and normal-weight children's eating habits. *Behavior Research and Therapy, 18,* 598–600.

Baltes, M. M. (1995, February). Dependency in old age: Gains and losses. *Psychological Science, 4*(1), 14–19.

Baltes, M. M. (1996). *The many faces of dependency in old age.* New York: Cambridge University Press.

Baltes, M. M. (1998). The psychology of the oldest-old: The fourth age. *Current Opinion in Psychiatry, 11,* 411–418.

Baltes, M. M., & Carstensen, L. L. (1996). The process of successful ageing. *Ageing and Society, 16,* 397–422.

Baltes, M. M., Wahl, H.-W., & Reichert, M. (1992). Successful aging in long-term care institutions. In K. W. Schaie & M. P. Lawton (Eds.), *Annual review of gerontology and geriatrics* (pp. 311–337). New York: Springer.

Baltes, P. B. (1987). Theoretical propositions of life-span developmental psychology: On the dynamics between growth and decline. *Developmental Psychology, 23,* 611–626.

Baltes, P. B. (1997). On the incomplete architecture of human ontogeny: Selection, optimization, and compensation as foundation of developmental theory. *American Psychologist, 52,* 366–380.

Baltes, P. B., Dittmann-Kohli, F., & Dixon, R. A. (1984). New perspectives on the development of intelligence in adulthood: Toward a dual-process conception and a model of selective optimization with compensation. In P. B. Baltes & O. G. Brim, Jr. (Eds.), *Life-span development and behavior* (Vol. 6, pp. 33–76). San Diego, CA: Academic Press.

Baltes, P. B., Lindenberger, U., & Staudinger, U. M. (1997). Life-span theory in developmental psychology. In R. M. Lerner (Ed.), *Handbook of child psychology: Vol. 1. Theoretical models of human development* (5th ed., pp. 1029–1143). New York: Wiley.

Baltes, P. B., Smith, J., & Staudinger, U. M. (1992). Wisdom and successful aging. In T. Sonderegger (Ed.), *Nebraska Symposia on Motivation* (Vol. 39, pp. 123–167). Lincoln, NE: University of Nebraska Press.

Baltes, P. B., Staudinger, U. M., Maercker, A., & Smith, J. (1995). People nominated as wise: A comparative study of wisdom-related knowledge. *Psychology and Aging, 10,* 155–166.

Bandura, A. (1977). *Social learning theory.* Englewood Cliffs, NJ: Prentice Hall.

Bandura, A. (1989). Social cognitive theory. In R. Vasta (Ed.), *Annals of child development* (Vol. 6, pp. 1–60). Greenwich, CT: JAI Press.

Bandura, A. (1992). Perceived self-efficacy in cognitive development and functioning. *Educational Psychologist, 28,* 117–118.

Bandura, A. (1997). *Self-efficacy: The exercise of control.* New York: Freeman.

Banish, M. T. (1998). Integration of information between the cerebral hemispheres. *Current Directions in Psychological Science, 7,* 32–37.

Banish, M. T., & Heller, W. (1998). Evolving perspectives on lateralization of function. *Current Directions in Psychological Science, 7,* 1–2.

Bankoff, E. A. (1983). Aged parents and their widowed daughters: A support relationship. *Journal of Gerontology, 38,* 226–230.

Banks, M. S. (1980). The development of visual accommodation during early infancy. *Child Development, 51,* 646–666.

Banks, M. S., & Bennett, P. J. (1988). Optical and photoreceptor immaturities limit the spacial and chromatic vision of human neonates. *Journal of the Optical Society of America, 5,* 2059–2097.

Banks, M. S., & Ginsburg, A. P. (1985). Early visual preferences: A review and new theoretical treatment. In H. W. Reese (Ed.), *Advances in child development and behavior* (Vol. 19, pp. 207–246). New York: Academic Press.

Banks, M. S., & Salapatek, P. (1983). Infant visual perception. In M. M. Haith & J. J. Campos (Eds.), *Handbook of child psychology: Vol. 2. Infancy and developmental psychobiology* (4th ed., pp. 435–571). New York: Wiley.

Barer, B. M. (1994). Men and women aging differently. *International Journal of Aging and Human Development, 38,* 29–40.

Barinaga, M. (1991). How long is the human life span? *Science, 254,* 936–938.

Barker, D. J. (1999). Fetal origins of cardiovascular disease. *Annals of Medicine, 31*(Suppl. 1), 3–6.

Barker, D. J. P. (1994). *Mothers, babies, and disease in later life.* London: British Medical Journal Publishing.

Barker, D. J. P., Gluckman, P. D., Godfrey, K. M., Harding, J. E., Owens, J. A., & Robinson, J. S. (1993). Fetal nutrition and cardiovascular disease in adult life. *Lancet, 341,* 938–941.

Barker, R. G. (1955). *Midwest and its children.* Stanford, CA: Stanford University Press.

Barkley, R. A. (1997a). *ADHD and the nature of self-control.* New York: Guilford.

Barkley, R. A. (1997b). Behavioral inhibition, sustained attention, and executive functions: Constructing a unifying theory of ADHD. *Psychological Bulletin, 121,* 65–94.

Barling, J., Rogers, K., & Kelloway, K. (1995). Some effects of teenagers' part-time employment: The quantity and quality of work make the differences. *Journal of Organizational Behavior, 16,* 143–154.

Barnas, M. V., & Cummings, E. M. (1994). Caregiver stability and toddlers' attachment-related behavior toward caregivers in day care. *Infant Behavior and Development, 17,* 141–147.

Barnett, D., Manly, J., & Cicchetti, D. (1993). Defining child maltreatment: The interface between policy and research. In D. Cicchetti & S. Toth (Eds.), *Child abuse, child development, and social policy* (pp. 7–73). Norwood, NJ: Ablex.

Barnett, R. C., & Rivers, C. (1996). *She works/he works.* San Francisco: Harper.

Barnett, W. S. (1995). Long-term effects of early childhood programs on cognitive and school outcomes. *Future Child, 5,* 25–50.

Baron, S., & Welty, A. (1996). Elder abuse. *Journal of Gerontological Social Work, 25,* 33–57.

Baron-Cohen, S. (1993). From attention–goal psychology to belief–desire psychology: The development of a theory of mind and its dysfunction. In S. Baron-Cohen, H. Tager-Flusberg, & D. Cohen (Eds.), *Understanding other minds: Perspectives from autism* (pp. 59–82). Oxford: Oxford University Press.

Baron-Cohen, S., Baldwin, D. A., & Crowson, M. (1997). Do children with autism use the speaker's direction of gaze strategy to crack the code of language? *Child Development, 68,* 48–57.

Barr, H. M., Streissguth, A. P., Darby, B. L., & Sampson, P. D. (1990). Prenatal exposure to alcohol, caffeine, tobacco, and aspirin: Effects on fine and gross motor performance in 4-year-old children. *Developmental Psychology, 26,* 339–348.

Barr, R., Dowden, A., & Hayne, H. (1996). Developmental changes in deferred imitation by 6- to 24-month-old infants. *Infant Behavior and Development, 19,* 159–170.

Barr, S. (1996, September). Up against the glass. *Management Review, 85*(9), 12–17.

Barratt, M. S., Roach, M. A., & Leavitt, L. A. (1996). The impact of low-risk prematurity on maternal behaviour and toddler outcomes. *International Journal of Behavioral Development, 19,* 581–602.

Barringer, F. (1993, April 1). Viral sexual diseases are found in 1 of 5 in the U.S. *The New York Times,* pp. A1, B9.

Barsky, A. J., Cleary, P. D., & Klerman, G. L. (1992). Determinants of perceived health status of medical outpatients. *Social Science and Medicine, 34,* 1147–1154.

Bartholomew, K., & Horowitz, L. M. (1991). Attachment styles among young adults: A test of a four-category model. *Journal of Personality and Social Psychology, 61,* 226–244.

Bastian, H. (1993). Personal beliefs and alternative childbirth choices: A survey of 552 women who planned to give birth at home. *Birth, 20,* 186–192.

Bates, E. (1995). *Modularity, domain specificity, and the development of language.* Unpublished manuscript, University of California, San Diego.

Bates, E., Marchman, V., Thal, D., Fenson, L., Dale, P., Reznick, J. S., Reilly, J., & Hartung, J. (1994). Developmental and stylistic variation in the composition of early vocabulary. *Journal of Child Language, 21,* 85–123.

Bates, J. E., Wachs, T. D., & Emde, R. N. (1994). Toward practical uses for biological concepts. In J. E. Bates & T. D. Wachs (Eds.), *Temperament: Individual differences at the interface of biology and behavior* (pp. 275–306). Washington, DC: American Psychological Association.

Bauer, P. J. (1996). What do infants recall of their lives? Memory for specific events by one- to two-year-olds. *American Psychologist, 51,* 29–41.

Baumrind, D. (1967). Child care practices anteceding three patterns of preschool behavior. *Genetic Psychology Monographs, 75,* 43–88.

Baumrind, D. (1971). Current patterns of parental authority. *Developmental Psychology Monograph, 4*(No. 1, Pt. 2).

Baumrind, D., & Black, A. E. (1967). Socialization practices associated with dimension of competence in preschool boys and girls. *Child Development, 38,* 291–327.

Baumwell, L., Tamis-LeMonda, C. S., & Bornstein, M. H. (1997). Maternal verbal sensitivity and child language comprehension. *Infant Behavior and Development, 20,* 247–258.

Bayley, N. (1969). *Bayley Scales of Infant Development.* New York: Psychological Corporation.

Bayley, N. (1993). *Bayley Scales of Infant Development* (2nd ed.). San Antonio, TX: Psychological Corporation.

Baylor, A. M., & Spirduso, W. W. (1988). Systematic aerobic exercise and components of reaction time in older women. *Journal of Gerontology, 43,* P121–P126.

Beard, B. B. (1991). *Centenarians: The new generation.* New York: Greenwood Press.

Bearison, D. J. (1998). Pediatric psychology and children's medical problems. In I. G. Sigel & K. A. Renninger (Eds.), *Handbook of child psychology: Vol. 4. Child psychology in practice* (5th ed., pp. 635–711). New York: Wiley.

Beatty, W. W. (1992). Gonadal hormones and sex differences in nonreproductive behaviors. In A. A. Gerall, H. Moltz, & I. L. Ward (Eds.), *Handbook of behavioral neurobiology: Vol. 11. Sexual differentiation* (pp. 85–128). New York: Plenum.

Beauchamp, G. K., Cowart, B. J., Mennella, J. A., & Marsh, R. R. (1994). Infant salt taste: Developmental, methodological, and contextual factors. *Developmental Psychobiology, 27,* 353–365.

Beautrais, A. L., Fergusson, D. M., & Shannon, F. T. (1982). Life events and childhood morbidity: A prospective study. *Pediatrics, 70,* 935–940.

Beck, M. (1992, March 16). Finding work after 50. *Newsweek,* pp. 58–60.

Beck, M. (1994, January 17). How far should we push mother nature? *Newsweek,* pp. 54–57.

Beckwith, L., Cohen, S. E., & Hamilton, C. E. (1999). Maternal sensitivity during infancy and subsequent life events relate to attachment representation at early adulthood. *Developmental Psychology, 35,* 693–700.

Beckwith, L., & Sigman, M. D. (1995). Preventive interventions in infancy. *Child and Adolescent Psychiatric Clinics of North America, 4,* 683–700.

Begley, S. (1995, February 13). Three is not enough. *Newsweek,* pp. 67–69.

Behrend, D. A. (1988). Overextensions in early language comprehension: Evidence from a signal detection approach. *Journal of Child Language, 15,* 63–75.

Behrend, D. A., Rosengren, K. S., & Perlmutter, M. (1992). The relation between private speech and parental interactive style. In R. M. Diaz & L. E. Berk (Eds.), *Private speech: From social interaction to self-regulation* (pp. 85–100). Hillsdale, NJ: Erlbaum.

Behrman, R. D., Kliegman, R. M., & Arvin, A. M. (Eds.). (1996). *Nelson textbook of pediatrics* (15th ed.). Philadelphia: Saunders.

Beidel, D. (1991). Social phobia and overanxious disorder in school-age children. *Journal of the American Academy of Child and Adolescent Psychiatry, 30,* 545–552.

Beilin, H. (1992). Piaget's enduring contribution to developmental psychology. *Developmental Psychology, 28,* 191–204.

Bell, K. L., Allen, J. P., Hauser, S. T., & O'Connor, T. G. (1996). Family factors and young adult transitions: Educational attainment and occupational prestige. In J. A. Graber, J. Brooks-Gunn, & A. C. Petersen (Eds.), *Transitions through adolescence: Interpersonal domains and context* (pp. 345–366). Mahwah, NJ: Erlbaum.

Bell, M. A., & Fox, N. A. (1992). The relations between frontal brain electrical activity and cognitive development during infancy. *Child Development, 63,* 1142–1163.

Bell, M. A., & Fox, N. A. (1994). Brain development over the first year of life: Relations between EEG frequency and coherence and cognitive and affective behaviors. In G. Dawson & K. W. Fischer (Eds.), *Human behavior and the developing brain* (pp. 314–345). New York: Guilford.

Bell, M. A., & Fox, N. A. (1996). Crawling experience is related to changes in cortical organization during infancy: Evidence from EEG coherence. *Developmental Psychobiology, 29,* 551–561.

Bell, M. L. (1995). Attitudes toward menopause among Mexican American women. *Health Care for Women International, 16,* 425–435.

Bell, R. J., Palma, S. M., & Lumley, J. M. (1995). The effect of vigorous exercise during pregnancy on birth-weight. *Australian and New Zealand Journal of Obstetrics and Gynaecology, 35,* 46–51.

Bellamy, C. (1998). *The state of the world's children 1998*. New York: Oxford University Press (in cooperation with UNICEF).

Bellamy, C. (1999). *The state of the world's children 1999*. New York: Oxford University Press (in cooperation with UNICEF).

Bellinger, D., Leviton, A., Waternaux, C., Needleman, H., & Rabinowitz, M. (1987). Longitudinal analysis of prenatal and postnatal lead exposure and early cognitive development. *New England Journal of Medicine, 316,* 1037–1043.

Belsky, J. (1989). Infant–parent attachment and day care: In defense of the Strange Situation. In J. Lande, S. Scarr, & N. Gunzenhauser (Eds.), *Caring for children: Challenge to America* (pp. 23–48). Hillsdale, NJ: Erlbaum.

Belsky, J. (1992). Consequences of child care for children's development: A deconstructionist view. In A. Booth (Ed.), *Child care in the 1990s: Trends and consequences* (pp. 83–85). Hillsdale, NJ: Erlbaum.

Belsky, J. (1993). Etiology of child maltreatment: A developmental–ecological analysis. *Psychological Bulletin, 114,* 413–434.

Belsky, J. (1996). Parent, infant, and social-contextual antecedents of father–son attachment security. *Developmental Psychology, 32,* 905–913.

Belsky, J., Campbell, S. B., Cohn, J. F., & Moore, G. (1996). Instability of infant–parent attachment security. *Developmental Psychology, 32,* 921–924.

Belsky, J., & Cassidy, J. (1994). Attachment theory and evidence. In M. Rutter & D. Hay (Eds.), *Development through life* (pp. 373–402). Oxford, England: Oxford University Press.

Bem, S. L. (1974). The measurement of psychological androgyny. *Journal of Consulting and Clinical Psychology, 42,* 155–162.

Bem, S. L. (1989). Genital knowledge and gender constancy in preschool children. *Child Development, 60,* 649–662.

Bem, S. L. (1998). *An unconventional family.* New Haven, CT: Yale University Press.

Benbow, C. P., & Arjmand, O. (1990). Predictors of high academic achievement in mathematics and science by mathematically talented students: A longitudinal study. *Journal of Educational Psychology, 82,* 430–441.

Benbow, C. P., & Stanley, J. C. (1983). Sex differences in mathematical reasoning: More facts. *Science, 222,* 1029–1031.

Bench, R. J., Collyer, Y., Mentz, L., & Wilson, I. (1976). Studies in infant behavioural audiometry: I. Neonates. *Audiology, 15,* 85–105.

Bender, S. L., Word, C. O., DiClemente, R. J., Crittenden, M. R., Persaud, N. A., &
Ponton, L. (1995). The developmental implications of prenatal and/or postnatal crack cocaine exposure in preschool children: A preliminary report. *Developmental and Behavioral Pediatrics, 16,* 418–424.

Bender, W. N. (1996). Learning disabilities. In P. J. McLaughlin & P. Wehman (Eds.), *Mental retardation and developmental disabilities* (2nd ed., pp. 259–279). Austin, TX: PRO-ED.

Benedict, R. (1934). Anthropology and the abnormal. *Journal of Genetic Psychology, 10,* 59–82.

Benediktsson, R., Calder, A. A., Edwards, C. R., & Seckl, J. R. (1997). Placental 11 beta-hydroxysteroid dehydrogenase: A key regulator of fetal glucocorticoid exposure. *Clinical Endocrinology, 46,* 161–166.

Benenson, J. F., Apostoleris, N. H., & Parnass, J. (1997). Age and sex differences in dyadic and group interaction. *Developmental Psychology, 33,* 538–543.

Bengtson, V. L., & Harootyan, R. A. (1994). *Intergenerational linkages: Hidden connections in American society.* New York: Springer.

Bengston, V. L., Reedy, M. N., & Gordon, C. (1985). Aging and self-conceptions: Personality processes and social contexts. In J. E. Birren & K. W. Schaie (Eds.), *Handbook of the psychology of aging* (pp. 544–593). New York: Van Nostrand Reinhold.

Bengtson, V. L., Rosenthal, C. L., & Burton, L. (1990). Families and aging: Diversity and heterogeneity. In R. H. Binstock & L. K. George (Eds.), *Handbook of aging and the social sciences* (3rd ed., pp. 263–287). San Diego: Academic Press.

Bennetto, L., Pennington, B. F., & Rogers, S. J. (1996). Intact and impaired memory functions in autism. *Child Development, 67,* 1816–1835.

Benoliel, J. Q., & Degner, L. F. (1995). Institutional dying: A convergence of cultural values, technology, and social organization. In H. Wass & R. A. Neimeyer (Eds.), *Dying: Facing the facts* (pp. 117–162). Washington, DC: Taylor and Francis.

Bercu, B. B. (1996). Use of growth hormone for non–growth hormone deficient children [letter]. *Journal of the American Medical Association, 276,* 1878.

Berg, C. A., Strough, J., Calderone, K. S., Sansone, C., & Weir, C. (1998). The role of problem definitions in understanding age and context effects on strategies for solving everyday problems. *Psychology and Aging, 13,* 29–44.

Berg, S. (1996). Aging, behavior, and terminal decline. In J. E. Birren & K. W. Schaie (Eds.), *Handbook of the psychology of aging* (4th ed., pp. 323–337). San Diego: Academic Press.
Bergeman, C. S. (1997). *Aging: Genetic and environmental influences.* Thousand Oaks, CA: Sage.

Berk, L. E. (1985). Relationship of caregiver education to child-oriented attitudes, job satisfaction, and behaviors toward children. *Child Care Quarterly, 14,* 103–129.

Berk, L. E. (1992a). Children's private speech: An overview of theory and the status of research. In R. M. Diaz & L. E. Berk (Eds.), *Private speech: From social interaction to self-regulation* (pp. 17–53). Hillsdale, NJ: Erlbaum.

Berk, L. E. (1992b). The extracurriculum. In P. W. Jackson (Ed.), *Handbook of research on curriculum* (pp. 1002–1043). New York: Macmillan.

Berk, L. E. (1994). Vygotsky's theory: The importance of make-believe play. *Young Children, 50,* 30–39.

Berk, L. E. (2000). Development. In J. Halonen & S. Davis (Eds.), *The many faces of psychological research in the twenty-first century.* Washington, DC: American Psychological Association.

Berk, L. E., & Landau, S. (1993). Private speech of learning disabled and normally achieving children in classroom academic and laboratory contexts. *Child Development, 64,* 556–571.

Berk, L. E., & Spuhl, S. (1995). Maternal interaction, private speech, and task performance in preschool children. *Early Childhood Research Quarterly, 10,* 145–169.

Berkman, C. S., & Gurland, B. J. (1998). The relationship between ethnoracial group and functional level in older persons. *Ethnicity and Health, 3,* 175–188.

Berkowitz, M. W., & Gibbs, J. C. (1983). Measuring the developmental features of moral discussion. *Merrill-Palmer Quarterly, 29,* 399–410.

Berman, P. W. (1980). Are women more responsive than men to the young? A review of developmental and situational variables. *Psychological Bulletin, 88,* 668–695.

Berman, P. W., & Pedersen, F. A. (Eds.). (1987). *Men's transition to parenthood: Longitudinal studies and early family experience.* Hillsdale, NJ: Erlbaum.

Bermejo, V. (1996). Cardinality development and counting. *Developmental Psychology, 32,* 263–268.

Bernard, S., Kincade, J. E., Konrad, T. R., Arcury, T. A., Rabiner, D. J., Woomert, A., DeFriese, G. H., & Ory, M. G. (1997). Predicting mortality from community surveys of older adults: The importances of self-rated functional ability. *Journal of Gerontology, 52B,* S155–S163.

Berndt, T. J., Cheung, P. C., Lau, S., Hau, K.-T., & Lew, W. J. F. (1993). Perceptions of parenting in mainland China, Taiwan, and Hong Kong: Sex differences and societal differences. *Developmental Psychology, 29,* 156–164.

Berndt, T. J., & Keefe, K. (1995). Friends' influence on adolescents' adjustment to school. *Child Development, 66,* 1312–1329.

Berndt, T. J., & Perry, T. B. (1990). Distinctive features and effects of early adolescent friendships. In R. Montemayor, G. R. Adams, & T. P. Gullotta (Eds.), *From childhood to adolescence: A transitional period?* (pp. 269–287). Newbury Park, CA: Sage.

Berne, P. H., & Savary, L. M. (1993). *Building self-esteem in children.* New York: Continuum.

Bernier, J. C., & Siegel, D. H. (1994). Attention-deficit hyperactivity disorder: A family ecological systems perspective. *Families in Society, 75,* 142–150.

Bernston, G. G., Malarkey, W. B., Kiecolt-Glaser, J. K., Sheridan, J. F., & Poehlmann, K. M. (1998). Autonomic, neuroendocrine, and immune responses to psychological stress: the reactivity hypothesis. *Annals of the New York Academy of Sciences, 840,* 664–673.

Bersoff, D. M., & Miller, J. G. (1993). Culture, context, and the development of moral accountability judgments. *Developmental Psychology, 29,* 664–676.

Bertenthal, B. I. (1993). Infants' perception of biomechanical motions: Instrinsic image and knowledge-based constraints. In C. Granrud (Ed.), *Visual perception and cognition in infancy* (pp. 175–214). Hillsdale, NJ: Erlbaum.

Bertenthal, B. I., & Campos, J. J. (1987). New directions in the study of early experience. *Child Development, 58,* 560–567.

Bertenthal, B. I., Campos, J. J., & Barrett, K. (1984). Self-produced locomotion: An organizer of emotional, cognitive, and social development in infancy. In R. Emde & R. Harmon (Eds.), *Continuities and discontinuities in development* (pp. 174–210). New York: Plenum.

Best, D. L., Williams, J. E., Cloud, J. M., Davis, S. W., Robertson, L. S., Edwards, J. R., Giles, H., & Fowles, J. (1977). Development of sex-trait stereotypes among young children in the United States, England, and Ireland. *Child Development, 48,* 1375–1384.

Betz, C. (1994, March). Beyond time-out: Tips from a teacher. *Young Children, 49*(3), 10–14.

Betz, N. E. (1993). Women's career development. In F. L. Denmark & M. A. Paludi (Eds.), *Psychology of women* (pp. 627–684). Westport, CT: Greenwood Press.

Betz, N. E., & Fitzgerald, L. F. (1987). *The career psychology of women.* New York: Academic Press.

Beunen, G., & Malina, R. M. (1996). Growth and biological maturation: Relevance to athletic performance. In O. Bar-Or (Ed.), *The child and adolescent athlete* (pp. 2–24). Oxford, England: Blackwell Science.

Beyene, Y. (1992). Menopause: A biocultural event. In A. J. Dan & L. L. Lewis (Eds.), *Menstrual health in women's lives* (pp. 169–177). Urbana, IL: University of Illinois Press.

Beyth-Marom, R., & Fischhoff, B. (1997). Adolescents' decisions about risks: A cognitive perspective. In J. Schulenberg, J. L. Maggs, & K. Hurrelmann (Eds.), *Health risks and developmental transitions during adolescence* (pp. 110–135). New York: Cambridge University Press.

Bhatt, R. S., Rovee-Collier, C., & Weiner, S. (1994). Developmental changes in the interface between perception and memory retrieval. *Developmental Psychology, 30,* 151–162.

Bialystok, E. (1997). Effects of bilingualism and biliteracy on children's emerging concepts of print. *Developmental Psychology, 33,* 429–440.

Bialystok, E. (1999). Cognitive complexity and attentional control in the bilingual mind. *Child Development, 70,* 636–644.

Bielinski, J., & Davison, M. L. (1998). Gender differences by item difficulty interactions in multiple-choice mathematics items. *American Educational Research Journal, 35,* 455–476.

Biernat, M. (1991). Gender stereotypes and the relationship between masculinity and femininity: A developmental analysis. *Journal of Personality and Social Psychology, 61,* 351–365.

Bigelow, A. (1992). Locomotion and search behavior in blind infants. *Infant Behavior and Development, 15,* 179–189.

Bigler, R. S. (1995). The role of classification skill in moderating environmental influences on children's gender stereotyping: A study of the functional use of gender in the classroom. *Child Development, 66,* 1072–1087.

Bigler, R. S., & Liben, L. S. (1992). Cognitive mechanisms in children's gender stereotyping: Theoretical and educational implications of a cognitive-based intervention. *Child Development, 63,* 1351–1363.

Bigner, J. J., & Jacobsen, R. B. (1989). Parenting behaviors of homosexual and heterosexual fathers. *Journal of Homosexuality, 18,* 173–186.

Bijeljac-Babic, R., Bertoncini, J., & Mehler, J. (1993). How do 4-day-old infants categorize multisyllabic utterances? *Developmental Psychology, 29,* 711–721.

Bille-Brahe, U. (1993). The role of sex and age in suicidal behavior. *Acta Psychiatrica Scandinavica, 87*(Suppl. 371), 21–27.

Billson, J. M., & Terry, M. B. (1987). A student retention model for higher education. *College and University, 62,* 290–305.

Billy, J. O. G., Tanfer, K., Grady, W. R., & Klepinger, D. H. (1993). The sexual behavior of men in the United States. *Family Planning Perspectives, 25,* 52–60.

Binstock, R. H. (1992). The oldest old and "intergenerational inequity." In R. M. Suzman, D. P. Willis, & K. G. Manton (Eds.), *The oldest old* (pp. 394–417). New York: Oxford University Press.

Binstock, R. H., & Day, C. L. (1996). Aging and politics. In R. H. Binstock & L. K. George (Eds.), *Handbook of aging and the social sciences* (pp. 362–387). San Diego: Academic Press.

Birch, E. E. (1993). Stereopsis in infants and its developmental relation to visual acuity. In K. Simons (Ed.), *Early visual development: Normal and abnormal* (pp. 224–236). New York: Oxford University Press.

Birch, L. L., & Fisher, J. A. (1995). Appetite and eating behavior in children. *Pediatric Clinics of North America, 42,* 931–953.

Birch, L. L., Johnson, S. L., & Fisher, J. A. (1995, January). Children's eating: The development of food acceptance patterns. *Young Children, 50*(2), 71–78.

Bird, C. E. (1999). Gender, household labor, and psychological distress: The impact of the amount and division of housework. *Journal of Health and Social Behavior, 40,* 32–45.

Biringen, Z., Emde, R. N., Campos, J. J., & Appelbaum, M. I. (1995). Affective reorganization in the infant, the mother, and the dyad: The role of upright locomotion and its timing. *Child Development, 66,* 499–514.

Birmaher, B., Ryan, N., Williamson, D., Brent, D., & Kaufman, J. (1996). Childhood and adolescent depression: A review of the past 10 years. Part II. *Journal of the American Academy of Child and Adolescent Psychiatry, 35,* 1575–1583.

Birren, J. E. (1990). Spiritual maturity in psychological development. In J. J. Seeber (Ed.), *Spiritual maturity in later years* (pp. 41–53). New York: Haworth.

Bischof-Köhler, D. (1991). The development of empathy in infants. In M. E. Lamb & H. Keller (Eds.), *Infant development: Perspectives from German-speaking countries* (pp. 1–33). Hillsdale, NJ: Erlbaum.

Bivens, J. A., & Berk, L. E. (1990). A longitudinal study of the development of elementary school children's private speech. *Merrill-Palmer Quarterly, 36,* 443–463.

Bjorklund, D. F. (1997). In search of a metatheory for cognitive development (or, Piaget is dead and I don't feel so good myself). *Child Development, 68,* 144–148.

Bjorklund, D. F., & Coyle, T. R. (1995). Utilization deficiencies in the development of memory strategies. In F. E. Weinert & W. Schneider (Eds.), *Research on memory development: State of the art and future directions* (pp. 161–180). Hillsdale, NJ: Erlbaum.

Bjorklund, D. F., & Muir, J. E. (1988). Children's development of free recall memory: Remembering on their own. In R. Vasta (Ed.), *Annals of child development* (Vol. 5, pp. 79–123). Greenwich, CT: JAI Press.

Bjorklund, D. F., Schneider, W., Cassel, W. S., & Ashley, E. (1994). Training and extension of a memory strategy: Evidence for utilization deficiencies in high- and low-IQ children. *Child Development, 65,* 951–965.

Bjorklund, D. F., & Shackelford, T. K. (1999). Differences in parental investment contribute to important differences between men and women. *Current Directions in Psychological Science, 8,* 86–89.

Black, M. M., Hutcheson, J. J., Dubowitz, H., & Berenson-Howard, J. (1994). Parenting style and developmental status among children with nonorganic failure to thrive. *Journal of Pediatric Psychology, 19,* 689–707.

Blagg, N., & Yule, W. (1996). School phobia. In T. H. Ollendick, N. J. King, & W. Yule (Eds.), *International handbook of phobic and anxiety disorders in children and adolescents* (pp. 169–186). New York: Plenum.

Blair, S. N., Kohl, H. W., III, Paffenbarger, R. S., Jr., Clark, D. G., Cooper, K. H., & Gibbons, L. W. (1989). Physical fitness and all-cause mortality: A prospective study of healthy men and women. *Journal of the American Medical Association, 262,* 2395–2401.

Blake, I. K. (1994). Language development and socialization in young African-American children. In P. M. Greenfield & R. R. Cocking (Eds.), *Cross-cultural roots of minority child development* (pp. 167–195). Hillsdale, NJ: Erlbaum.

Blanchard, R., & Bogaert, A. F. (1996). Homosexuality in men and number of older brothers. *American Journal of Psychiatry, 153,* 27–31.

Blanchard, R., Zucker, K. J., Bradley, S. J., & Hume, C. S. (1995). Birth order and sibling sex ratio in homosexual male adolescents and probably prehomosexual feminine boys. *Developmental Psychology, 31,* 22–30.

Blanchard-Fields, F. (1997). The role of emotion in social cognition across the adult life span. In K. W. Schaie & M. P. Lawton (Eds.), *Annual review of gerontology and geriatrics* (Vol. 17, pp. 325–352). New York: Springer.

Blanchard-Fields, F., Chen, Y., & Norris, L. (1997). Everyday problem solving across the adult life span: Influence of domain specificity and cognitive appraisal. *Psychology and Aging, 12,* 684–693.

Blanco, J., Gabau, E., Gómez, D., Baena, N., Guitart, M., Egozcue, J., & Vidal, F. (1998). Chromosome 21 disomy in spermatozoa of the fathers of children with trisomy 21, in a population with a high prevalence of Down syndrome: Increased incidence in cases of paternal origin. *American Journal of Human Genetics, 63,* 1067–1072.

Blasi, A. (1990). Kohlberg's theory and moral motivation. In D. Schrader (Ed.), *New directions for child development* (No. 47, pp. 51–57). San Francisco: Jossey-Bass.

Blass, E. M., Ganchrow, J. R., & Steiner, J. E. (1984). Classical conditioning in newborn humans 2–48 hours of age. *Infant Behavior and Development, 7,* 223–235.

Blatchford, P., & Mortimore, P. (1994). The issue of class size for young children in schools: What can we learn from research? *Oxford Review of Education, 20,* 411–428.

Blieszner, R., & Adams, R. G. (1992). *Adult friendship.* Newbury Park, CA: Sage.

Block, J. (1971). *Lives through time.* Berkeley, CA: Bancroft.

Block, J. (1982). Assimilation, accommodation, and the dynamics of personality development. *Child Development, 53,* 281–295.

Block, J. (1995). A contrarian view of the five-factor approach to personality description. *Psychological Bulletin, 117,* 187–215.

Block, J., Block, J. H., & Gjerde, P. F. (1988). Parental functioning and home environment in families of divorce: Prospective and concurrent analyses. *Journal of the American Academy of Child and Adolescent Psychiatry, 27,* 207–213.

Block, J., & Robins, R. W. (1994). A longitudinal study of consistency and change in self-esteem from early adolescence to early adulthood. *Child Development, 64,* 909–923.

Bloom, L. (1993). *The transition from infancy to language: Acquiring the power of expression.* Cambridge, UK: Cambridge University Press.

Bloom, L. (1998). Language acquisition in its developmental context. In D. Kuhn & R. S. Siegler (Eds.), *Handbook of child psychology: Vol. 2. Cognition, perception, and language* (5th ed., pp. 309–370). New York: Wiley.

Bloom, M. V. (1987). Leaving home: A family transition. In J. Bloom-Feshbach & S. Bloom-Feshbach (Eds.), *The psychology of separation and loss* (pp. 232–266). San Francisco: Jossey-Bass.

Bluebond-Langner, M. (1977). Meanings of death to children. In H. Feifel (Ed.), *New meanings of death* (pp. 47–66). New York: McGraw-Hill.

Blum, N. J., & Carey, W. B. (1996). Sleep problems among infants and young children. *Pediatrics in Review, 17,* 87–93.

Blumberg, J. B. (1996). Status and functional impact of nutrition in older adults. In E. L. Schneider & J. W. Rowe (Eds.), *Handbook of the biology of aging* (4th ed., pp. 393–414). San Diego: Academic Press.

Blumberg, M. S., & Lucas, D. E. (1996). A developmental and component analysis of active sleep. *Developmental Psychobiology, 29,* 1–22.

Blumenstein, P., & Schwartz, P. (1983). *American couples.* New York: Morrow.

Blyth, D. A., Simmons, R. G., & Zakin, D. F. (1985). Satisfaction with body image for early adolescent females: The impact of pubertal timing within different school environments. *Journal of Youth and Adolescence, 14,* 207–225.

Bobinski, M., de Leon, M. J., Convit, A., De Santi, S., Wegiel, J., Tarshish, C. Y., Saint Louis, L. A., & Wisniewski, H. M. (1999). MRI of entorhinal cortex in mild Alzheimer's disease. *Lancet, 353,* 38–40.

Boden, D., & Bielby, D. D. V. (1983). The past as resource: A conversational analysis of elderly talk. *Human Development, 26,* 308–319.

Bodenheimer, T. (1999). Questions and answers about Medicare. *International Journal of Health Services, 29,* 519–523.

Bogden, J. D., & Louria, D. B. (1999). Aging and the immune system: The role of micronutrient nutrition. *Nutrition, 15,* 593–595.

Bohannon, J. N., III, & Bonvillian, J. D. (1997). Theoretical approaches to language acquisition. In J. B. Gleason (Ed.), *The development of language* (4th ed., pp. 259–316). Boston: Allyn and Bacon.

Bohannon, J. N., III, & Stanowicz, L. (1988). The issue of negative evidence: Adult responses to children's language errors. *Developmental Psychology, 24,* 684–689.

Bohman, M., & Sigvardsson, S. (1990). Outcome in adoption: Lessons from longitudinal studies. In D. M. Brodzinsky & M. D. Schechter (Eds.), *The psychology of adoption* (pp. 93–106). New York: Oxford University Press.

Bohr, L., Pascarella, E., Nora, A., Zusman, B., Jacobs, M., Desler, M., & Bulakowski, C. (1994). Cognitive effects of two-year and four-year institutions: A preliminary study. *Community College Review, 22,* 4–11.

Boivin, M., & Hymel, S. (1997). Peer experiences and social self-perceptions: A sequential model. *Developmental Psychology, 33,* 135–145.

Bokovoy, J. L., & Blair, S. N. (1994). Aging and exercise. *Journal of Aging and Physical Activity, 2,* 243–260.

Boldizar, J. P. (1991). Assessing sex typing and androgyny in children: The children's sex role inventory. *Developmental Psychology, 27,* 505–515.

Borke, H. (1975). Piaget's mountains revisited: Changes in the egocentric landscape. *Developmental Psychology, 11,* 240–243.

Borkowski, J. G., & Muthukrisna, N. (1995). Learning environments and skill generalization: How contexts facilitate regulatory processes and efficacy beliefs. In F. Weinert & W. Schneider (Eds.), *Memory performances and competence: Issues in growth and development* (pp. 283–300). Hillsdale, NJ: Erlbaum.

Bornholt, L. J., Goodnow, J. J., & Cooney, G. H. (1994). Influences of gender stereotypes on adolescents' perceptions of their own achievement. *American Educational Research Journal, 31,* 675–692.

Bornstein, M. H. (1989). Sensitive periods in development: Structural characteristics and causal interpretations. *Psychological Bulletin, 105,* 179–197.

Bornstein, M. H. (1999). Perception across the life span. In M. H. Bornstein & M. E. Lamb (Eds.), *Developmental psychology: An advanced textbook* (pp. 155–209). Mahwah, NJ: Erlbaum.

Bornstein, M. H., Haynes, O. M., Pascual, L., Painter, K. M., & Galperin, C. (1999a). Play in two societies: Pervasiveness of process, specificity of structure. *Child Development, 70,* 317–331.

Bornstein, M. H., & Lamb, M. E. (1992). *Development in infancy: An introduction* (3rd ed.). New York: McGraw-Hill.

Bornstein, M. H., Selmi, A. M., Haynes, O. M., Painter, K. M., & Marx, E. S. (1999b). Representational abilities and the hearing status of child/mother dyads. *Child Development, 70,* 833–852.

Bornstein, M. H., Vibbert, M., Tal, J., & O'Donnell, K. (1992). Toddler language and play in the second year: Stability, covariation, and influences of parenting. *First Language, 12,* 323–338.

Borst, C. G. (1995). *Catching babies: The professionalization of childbirth, 1870–1920.* Cambridge, MA: Harvard University Press.

Borstelmann, L. J. (1983). Children before psychology: Ideas about children from antiquity to the late 1800s. In W. Kessen (Ed.), *Handbook of child psychology: Vol. 1. History, theory, and methods* (pp. 1–40). New York: Wiley.

Bossé, R., Aldwin, C. M., Levenson, M. R., Workman-Daniels, K., & Ekerdt, D. J. (1990). Differences in social support among retirees and workers: Findings from the Normative Aging Study. *Psychology and Aging, 5,* 41–47.

Bossé, R., Spiro, A., III, & Kressin, N. R. (1996). The psychology of retirement. In R. T. Woods (Ed.), *Handbook of the clinical psychology of aging* (pp. 141–157). Chicester, England: Wiley.

Boston Women's Health Book Collective. (1992). *The new Our Bodies, Ourselves: A book by and for women* (2nd ed.). New York: Simon & Schuster.

Bosworth, H. B., & Schaie, K. W. (1999). Survival effects in cognitive function, cognitive style, and sociodemographic variables. *Experimental Aging Research, 25,* 121–140.

Bouchard, C. (1994). *The genetics of obesity.* Boca Raton, FL: CRC Press.

Bouchard, T. J., Jr. (1994). Genes, environment, and personality. *Science, 264,* 1700–1701.

Bouchard, T. J., Jr., Lykken, D. T., McGue, M., Segal, N. L., & Tellegen, A. (1990). Sources of human psychological differences: The Minnesota Study of Twins Reared Apart. *Science, 250,* 223–228.

Boukydis, C. F. Z., & Burgess, R. L. (1982). Adult physiological response to infant cries: Effects of temperament of infant, parental status and gender. *Child Development, 53,* 1291–1298.

Boulton, M. J. (1999). Concurrent and longitudinal relations between children's playground behavior and social preference, victimization, and bullying. *Child Development, 70,* 944–954.

Boulton, M. J., & Smith, P. K. (1994). Bully/victim problems in middle-school children: Stability, self-perceived competence, peer perceptions and peer acceptance. *British Journal of Developmental Psychology, 12,* 315–329.

Boulton, M. J., & Underwood, K. (1992). Bully/victim problems among middle school children. *British Journal of Educational Psychology, 62,* 73–87.

Bowlby, J. (1969). *Attachment and loss: Vol. 1. Attachment.* New York: Basic Books.

Bowlby, J. (1979). *The making and breaking of affectional bonds.* London: Tavistock.

Bowlby, J. (1980). *Attachment and loss: Vol. 3. Loss: Sadness and depression.* New York: Basic Books.

Bowman, M. C., & Saunders, D. M. (1994). Community attitudes to maternal age and pregnancy after assisted reproductive technology: Too old at 50 years? *Human Reproduction, 9,* 167–171.

Boyer, K., & Diamond, A. (1992). Development of memory for temporal order in infants and young children. In A. Diamond (Ed.), *Development and neural bases of higher cognitive function* (pp. 267–317). New York: New York Academy of Sciences.

Boyes, M. C., & Allen, S. G. (1993). Styles of parent–child interaction and moral reasoning in adolescence. *Merrill-Palmer Quarterly, 39,* 551–570.

Boyes, M. C., & Chandler, M. (1992). Cognitive development, epistemic doubt, and identity formation in adolescence. *Journal of Youth and Adolescence, 21,* 277–304.

Brackbill, Y., McManus, K., & Woodward, L. (1985). *Medication in maternity: Infant exposure and maternal information.* Ann Arbor: University of Michigan Press.

Bradburn, E. M., Moen, P., & Dempster-McClain, D. (1995). Women's return to school following the transition to motherhood. *Social Forces, 73,* 1517–1551.

Bradley, R. H., & Caldwell, B. M. (1979). Home Observation for Measurement of the Environment: A revision of the preschool scale. *American Journal of Mental Deficiency, 84,* 235–244.

Bradley, R. H., & Caldwell, B. M. (1981). The HOME Inventory: A validation of the preschool scale for black children. *Child Development, 52,* 708–710.

Bradley, R. H., & Caldwell, B. M. (1982). The consistency of the home environment and its relation to child development. *International Journal of Behavioral Development, 5,* 445–465.

Bradley, R. H., Caldwell, B. M., Rock, S. L., Ramey, C. T., Barnard, D. E., Gray, C., Hammond, M. A., Mitchell, S., Gottfried, A., Siegel, L., & Johnson, D. L. (1989). Home environment and cognitive development in the first 3 years of life: A collaborative study involving six sites and three ethnic groups in North America. *Developmental Psychology, 25,* 217–235.

Bradley, R. H., Whiteside, L., Mundfrom, D. J., Casey, P. H., Kelleher, K. J., & Pope, S. K. (1994). Early indications of resilience and their relation to experiences in the home environments of low birthweight, premature children living in poverty. *Child Development, 65,* 346–360.

Brady, E. M. (1984). Demographic and educational correlates of self-reported learning among older students. *Educational Gerontology, 10,* 27–38.

Braet, C., & Mervielde, I. (1997). Psychological aspects of childhood obesity: A controlled study in a clinical and nonclinical sample. *Journal of Pediatric Psychology, 22,* 59–71.

Braine, L. G., Pomerantz, E., Lorber, D., & Krantz, D. H. (1991). Conflicts with authority: Children's feelings, actions, and justifications. *Developmental Psychology, 27,* 829–840.

Braine, L. G., Schauble, L., Kugelmass, S., & Winter, A. (1993). Representation of depth by children: Spatial strategies and lateral biases. *Developmental Psychology, 29,* 466–479.

Brandtstädter, J., & Rothermund, K. (1994). Self-percepts of control in middle and later adulthood: Buffering losses by rescaling goals. *Psychology and Aging, 9,* 265–273.

Brannigan, M. (1998). On asking the right questions: Personal death vs. brain death in Japan. *Death Studies, 22,* 157–169.

Braverman, P. K., & Strasburger, V. C. (1993). Adolescent sexual activity. *Clinical Pediatrics, 32,* 658–668.

Bray, J. (1992). Family relationships and children's adjustment in clinical and nonclinical stepfather families. *Journal of Family Psychology, 6,* 60–68.

Bray, J. H. (1999). From marriage to remarriage and beyond: Findings from the Developmental Issues in Stepfamilies Research Project. In E. M. Hetherington (Ed.), *Coping with divorce, single parenting, and remarriage: A risk and resiliency perspective* (pp. 295–319). Mahwah, NJ: Erlbaum.

Bray, J. H., & Berger, S. H. (1993). Developmental issues in Stepfamilies Research Project: Family relationships and parent–child interactions. *Journal of Family Psychology, 7,* 7–17.

Brazelton, T. B., Koslowski, B., & Tronick, E. (1976). Neonatal behavior among urban Zambians and Americans. *Journal of the American Academy of Child Psychiatry, 15,* 97–107.

Brazelton, T. B., & Nugent, J. K. (1995). *Neonatal Behavioral Assessment Scale.* London, Mac Keith Press.

Brazelton, T. B., Nugent, J. K., & Lester, B. M. (1987). Neonatal Behavioral Assessment Scale. In J. D. Osofsky (Ed.), *Handbook of infant development* (2nd ed., pp. 780–817). New York: Wiley.

Brébion, G., Smith, M. J., & Ehrlich, M.-F. (1997). Working memory and aging: Deficit or strategy differences? *Aging, Neuropsychology, and Cognition, 4,* 58–73.

Brechtelsbauer, D. A. (1990). Adult hearing loss. *Disorders of the Ears, Nose, and Throat, 17,* 249–266.

Bredekamp, S., & Copple, C. (Eds.). (1997). *Developmentally appropriate practice in early childhood programs* (rev. ed.). Washington, DC: National Association for the Education of Young Children.

Brehm, S. S. (1992). *Intimate relationships* (2nd ed.). New York: McGraw-Hill.

Brennan, K. A., & Shaver, P. R. (1995). Dimensions of adult attachment, affect regulation, and romantic relationship functioning. *Personality and Social Psychology Bulletin, 21,* 267–283.

Brennan, W. M., Ames, E. W., & Moore, R. W. (1966). Age differences in infants' attention to patterns of different complexities. *Science, 151,* 354–356.

Brenner, D., & Hinsdale, G. (1978). Body build stereotypes and self-identification in three age groups of females. *Adolescence, 13,* 551–562.

Brent, S. B., Speece, M. W., Lin, C., Dong, Q., & Yang, C. (1996). The development of the concept of death among Chinese and U.S. children 3–17 years of age: From binary to "fuzzy" concepts? *Omega, 33,* 67–83.

Breslau, N. (1993). Daily cigarette consumption in early adulthood: Age of smoking initiation and duration of smoking. *Drug and Alcohol Dependence, 33,* 287–291.

Breslau, N., Kessler, R. C., Chilcoat, H. D., Schultz, L. R., Davis, G. C., & Andreski, P. (1998). Trauma and posttraumatic stress disorder in the community: The 1996 Detroit Area Survey of Trauma. *Archives of General Psychiatry, 55,* 626–632.

Bretherton, I. (1992). The origins of attachment theory: John Bowlby and Mary Ainsworth. *Developmental Psychology, 28,* 759–775.

Bretherton, I., Fritz, J., Zahn-Waxler, C., & Ridgeway, D. (1986). Learning to talk about emotions: A functionalist perspective. *Child Development, 57,* 529–548.

Brewaeys, A., Ponjaert, I., Van Hall, E. V., & Golombok, S. (1997). Donor insemination: Child development and family functioning in lesbian mother families. *Human Reproduction, 12,* 1349–1359.

Brien, M. J., & Willis, R. J. (1997). Costs and consequences for the fathers. In R. A. Maynard (Ed.), *Kids having kids* (pp. 95–144). Washington, DC: Urban Institute.

Briggs, F., & Hawkins, R. (1996). *Keeping ourselves safe: Who benefits?* Wellington, NZ: New Zealand Council for Educational Research.

Briggs, F., & Hawkins, R. (1999). The importance of parent involvement in child protection curricula. In L. E. Berk (Ed.), *Landscapes of development* (pp. 321–335). Belmont, CA: Wadsworth.

Brigham, J. (1998). *Dying to quit: Why we smoke and how we stop.* Washington, DC: National Academy Press.

British Broadcasting Corporation. (1999, May 11). *Euthanasia special report: Lessons from down under.* London: Author.

Broberg, A. G., Wessels, H., Lamb, M. E., & Hwang, C. P. (1997). Effects of day care on the development of cognitive abilities in 8-year-olds: A longitudinal study. *Developmental Psychology, 33,* 62–69.

Brody, E. M., Kleban, M. H., Johnsen, P. T., Hoffman, C., & Schoonover, C. B. (1987). Patterns of parent-care when adult daughters work and when they do not. *Gerontologist, 26,* 372–381.

Brody, G. H., & Flor, D. L. (1998). Maternal resources, parenting practices, and child competence in rural, single-parent African American families. *Child Development, 69,* 803–816.

Brody, G. H., Stoneman, Z., & McCoy, J. K. (1994). Forecasting sibling relationships in early adolescence from child temperaments and family processes in middle childhood. *Child Development, 65,* 771–784.

Brody, J. E. (1992, November 11). PMS is a worldwide phenomenon. *The New York Times,* p. C14.

Brody, L. R., & Hall, J. A. (1993). Gender and emotion. In M. Lewis & J. M. Haviland (Eds.), *Handbook of emotions* (pp. 447–460). New York: Guilford.

Brody, N. (1992). *Intelligence* (2nd ed.). San Diego: Academic Press.

Brody, N. (1994). Heritability of traits. *Psychological Inquiry, 5,* 117–119.

Brody, N. (1997). Intelligence, schooling, and society. *American Psychologist, 52,* 1046–1050.

Bronfenbrenner, U. (1979). *The ecology of human development: Experiments by nature and design.* Cambridge, MA: Harvard University Press.

Bronfenbrenner, U. (1989). Ecological systems theory. In R. Vasta (Ed.), *Annals of child development* (Vol. 6, pp. 187–251). Greenwich, CT: JAI Press.

Bronfenbrenner, U. (1993). The ecology of cognitive development: Research models and fugitive findings. In R. H. Wozniak & K. W. Fischer (Eds.), *Development in context* (pp. 3–44). Hillsdale, NJ: Erlbaum.

Bronfenbrenner, U. (1995). The bioecological model from a life course perspective: Reflections of a participant observer. In P. Moen, G. H. Elder, Jr., & K. Lüscher (Eds.), *Examining lives in context* (pp. 599–618). Washington, DC: American Psychological Association.

Bronfenbrenner, U. (1997). The ecology of developmental processes. In R. M. Lerner (Ed.), *Handbook of child psychology: Vol. 1. Theoretical models of human development.* New York: Wiley.

Bronfenbrenner, U., & Ceci, S. J. (1994). Nature–nurture reconceptualized in developmental perspective: A bioecological model. *Psychological Review, 101,* 568–586.

Bronfenbrenner, U., & Morris, P. A. (1998). The ecology of developmental processes. In R. M. Lerner (Ed.), *Handbook of child psychology: Vol. 1. Theoretical models of human development* (5th ed., pp. 535–584). New York: Wiley.

Bronson, G. W. (1991). Infant differences in rate of visual encoding. *Child Development, 62,* 44–54.

Brooks-Gunn, J. (1986). The relationship of maternal beliefs about sex typing to maternal and young children's behavior. *Sex Roles, 14,* 21–35.

Brooks-Gunn, J. (1988a). Antecedents and consequences of variations in girls' maturational timing. *Journal of Adolescent Health Care, 9,* 365–373.

Brooks-Gunn, J. (1988b). The impact of puberty and sexual activity upon the health and education of adolescent girls and boys. *Peabody Journal of Education, 64,* 88–113.

Brooks-Gunn, J., & Chase-Lansdale, P. L. (1995). Adolescent parenthood. In M. H. Bornstein (Ed.), *Handbook of parenting: Vol. 3. Status and social conditions of parenting* (pp. 113–149). Mahwah, NJ: Erlbaum.

Brooks-Gunn, J., McCarton, C. M., Casey, P. H., McCormick, M. C., Bauer, C. R., Bernbaum, J. C., Tyson, J., Swanson, M., Bennett, F. C., Scott, D. T., Tonascia, J., & Meinert, C. L. (1994). Early intervention in low-birth-weight premature infants. *Journal of the*

American Medical Association, 272, 1257–1262.

Brooks-Gunn, J., & Ruble, D. N. (1980). Menarche: The interaction of physiology, cultural, and social factors. In A. J. Dan, E. A. Graham, & C. P. Beecher (Eds.), *The menstrual cycle: A synthesis of interdisciplinary research* (pp. 141– 159). New York: Springer-Verlag.

Brooks-Gunn, J., & Ruble, D. N. (1983). The experience of menarche from a developmental perspective. In J. Brooks-Gunn & A. C. Petersen (Eds.), *Girls at puberty* (pp. 155–177). New York: Plenum.

Brooks-Gunn, J., Warren, M. P., Samelson, M., & Fox, R. (1986). Physical similarity of and disclosure of menarcheal status to friends: Effects of grade and pubertal status. *Journal of Early Adolescence, 6,* 3–14.

Broomhall, H. S., & Winefield, A. H. (1990). A comparison of the affective well-being of young and middle-aged unemployed men matched for length of employment. *British Journal of Medical Psychology, 63,* 43–52.

Brown, A. M. (1990). Development of visual sensitivity to light and color vision in human infants: A critical review. *Vision Research, 30,* 1159–1188.

Brown, B. B., Clasen, D., & Eicher, S. (1986). Perceptions of peer pressure, peer conformity dispositions, and self-reported behavior among adolescents. *Developmental Psychology, 22,* 521–530.

Brown, B. B., Lohr, M. J., & McClenahan, E. L. (1986). Early adolescents' perceptions of peer pressure. *Journal of Early Adolescence, 6,* 139–154.

Brown, R. W. (1973). *A first language: The early stages.* Cambridge, MA: Harvard University Press.

Browne, A. (1993). Violence against women by male partners: Prevalence, outcomes and policy implications. *American Psychologist, 48,* 1077–1087.

Brownell, C. A., & Carriger, M. S. (1990). Changes in cooperation and self-other differentiation during the second year. *Child Development, 61,* 1164–1174.

Brubaker, T. (1985). *Later life families.* Beverly Hills, CA: Sage.

Bruce, B., & Wilfley, D. (1996). Binge eating among the overweight population: A serious and prevalent problem. *Journal of the American Dietetic Association, 96,* 58–61.

Bruch, M. A., Gorsky, J. M., Collins, T. M., & Berger, P. A. (1989). Shyness and sociability examined: A multicomponent analysis. *Journal of Personality and Social Psychology, 57,* 904–915.

Bruck, M., Ceci, S. J., & Hembrooke, H. (1998). Reliability and credibility of young children's reports. *American Psychologist, 53,* 136–151.

Bruer, J. T. (1999). *The myth of the first three years.* New York: Free Press.

Bruerd, B., & Jones, C. (1996). Preventing baby bottle tooth decay: Eight-year results. *Public Health Reports, 111,* 63–65.

Bryant, B. K. (1985). The neighborhood walk: Sources of support in middle childhood. *Monographs for the Society for Research in Child Development, 50*(3, Serial No. 210).

Buchanan, A. (1996). *Cycles of child maltreatment.* Chichester, UK: Wiley.

Buchanan, C. M., Eccles, J. S., & Becker, J. B. (1992). Are adolescents the victims of raging hormones? Evidence for activational effects of hormones on moods and behavior at adolescence. *Psychological Bulletin, 111,* 62–107.

Buchanan, C. M., Maccoby, E. E., & Dornbusch, S. M. (1996). *Adolescents after divorce.* Cambridge, MA: Harvard University Press.

Buck, G. M., Cookfair, D. L., Michalek, A. M., Nasca, P. C., Standfast, S. J., Sever, L. E., & Kramer, A. A. (1989). Intrauterine growth retardation and risk of sudden infant death syndrome (SIDS). *American Journal of Epidemiology, 129,* 874–884.

Buekens, P., Kotelchuck, M., Blondel, B., Kristensen, F. B., Chen, J.-H., & Masuy-Stroobant, G. (1993). A comparison of prenatal care use in the United States and Europe. *American Journal of Public Health, 83,* 31–36.

Bugental, D. B., Blue, J., & Cruzcosa, M. (1989). Perceived control over caregiving outcomes: Implications for child abuse. *Developmental Psychology, 25,* 532–539.

Buhrmester, D. (1996). Need fulfillment, interpersonal competence, and the developmental contexts of early adolescent friendship. In W. M. Bukowski, A. F. Newcomb, & W. W. Hartup (Eds.), *The company they keep: Friendship during childhood and adolescence* (pp. 158–185). New York: Cambridge University Press.

Buhrmester, D., & Furman, W. (1987). The development of companionship and intimacy. *Child Development, 58,* 1101–1115.

Buhrmester, D., & Furman, W. (1990). Perceptions of sibling relationships during middle childhood and adolescence. *Child Development, 61,* 1387–1398.

Buhrmester, D., & Prager, K. (1995). Patterns and functions of self-disclosure during childhood and adolescence. In K. J. Rotenberg (Ed.), *Disclosure processes in children and adolescents* (pp. 10–56). New York: Cambridge University Press.

Burchinal, M. R., Roberts, J. E., Nabors, L. A., & Bryant, D. M. (1996). Quality of center child care and infant cognitive and language development. *Child Development, 67,* 606–620.

Burhans, K. K., & Dweck, C. S. (1995). Helplessness in early childhood: The role of contingent worth. *Child Development, 66,* 1719–1738.

Burkett, G., Yasin, S. Y., Palow, D., La Voie, L., & Martinez, M. (1994). Patterns of cocaine binging: Effect on pregnancy. *American Journal of Obstetrics and Gynecology, 171,* 372–379.

Burkhardt, S. A., & Rotatori, A. F. (1995). *Treatment and prevention of child hood sexual abuse.* Washington, DC: Taylor & Francis.

Burns, S. M., & Brainerd, C. J. (1979). Effects of constructive and dramatic play on perspective taking in very young children. *Developmental Psychology, 15,* 512–521.

Burr, D. C., Morrone, C., & Fiorentini, A. (1996). Spatial and temporal properties of infant colour vision. In F. Vital-Durand, J. Atkinson, & O. J. Braddick (Eds.), *Infant vision* (pp. 63–77). Oxford, England: Oxford University Press.

Burts, D. C., Hart, C. H., Charlesworth, R., Fleege, P. O., Mosley, J., & Thomasson, R. H. (1992). Observed activities and stress behaviors of children in developmentally appropriate and inappropriate kindergarten classrooms. *Early Childhood Research Quarterly, 7,* 297–318.

Bushnell, E. W. (1985). The decline of visually guided reaching during infancy. *Infant Behavior and Development, 8,* 139–155.

Bushnell, E. W., & Boudreau, J. P. (1993). Motor development and the mind: The potential role of motor abilities as a determinant of aspects of perceptual development. *Child Development, 64,* 1005–1021.

Buss, D. M. (1999). *Evolutionary psychology: The new science of the mind.* Boston: Allyn and Bacon.

Butler, R. (1998). Age trends in the use of social and temporal comparison for self-evaluation: Examination of a novel developmental hypothesis. *Child Development, 69,* 1054–1073.

Butler, R. N. (1968). The life review: An interpretation of reminiscence in the aged. In B. Neugarten (Ed.), *Middle age and aging* (pp. 486–496). Chicago: University of Chicago Press.

Buttell, F. P. (1999). The relationship between spouse abuse and the maltreatment of dementia sufferers by their caregivers. *American Journal of Alzheimer's Disease, 14,* 230–232.

Buunk, B. P., & van Driel, B. (1989). *Variant lifestyles and relationships.* Newbury Park, CA: Sage.

Buysse, U., & Bailey, D. B. (1993). Behavioral and developmental outcomes in young children with disabilities in integrated and segregated settings: A review of comparative studies. *Journal of Special Education, 26,* 434–461.

Byars, A. M., & Hackett, G. (1998). Applications of social cognitive theory to the career development of women of color. *Applied and Preventive Psychology, 7,* 255–267.

Byrnes, J. P. (1993). Analyzing perspectives on rationality and critical thinking: A commentary on the *Merrill-Palmer Quarterly* invitational issue. *Merrill-Palmer Quarterly, 39,* 159–171.

Byrnes, J. P., & Takahira, S. (1993). Explaining gender differences on SAT-math items. *Developmental Psychology, 29,* 805–810.

Caddell, D. P., & Newton, R. R. (1995). Euthanasia: American attitudes toward the physician's role. *Social Science and Medicine, 40,* 1671–1681.

Cadoff, J. (1995, March). Can we prevent SIDS? *Parents, 70*(3), 30–31, 35.

Cain, K. M., & Dweck, C. S. (1995). The relation between motivational patterns and achievement cognitions through the elementary school years. *Merrill-Palmer Quarterly, 41,* 25–52.

Caine, N. (1986). Behavior during puberty and adolescence. In G. Mitchell & J. Erwin (Eds.), *Comparative primate biology: Vol. 2A. Behavior, conservation, and ecology* (pp. 327–361). New York: Liss.

Cairns, E. (1996). *Children and political violence.* Cambridge: Blackwell.

Cairns, R. B. (1998). The making of developmental psychology. In R. M. Lerner (Ed.), *Handbook of child psychology: Vol. 1. Theoretical models of human development* (5th ed., pp. 25–105). New York: Wiley.

Cairns, R. B., Leung, M.-C., Buchanan, L., & Cairns, B. D. (1995). Friendships and social networks in childhood and adolescence: Fluidity, reliability, and interrelations. *Child Development, 66,* 1330–1345.

Caldwell, B. M., & Bradley, R. H. (1994). Environmental issues in developmental follow-up research. In S. L. Friedman & H. C. Haywood (Eds.), *Developmental follow-up* (pp. 235–256). San Diego: Academic Press.

Caldwell, C. H., & Antonucci, T. C. (1997). Childbearing during adolescence: Mental health risks and opportunities. In J. Schulenberg, J. L. Maggs, & K. Hurrelmann (Eds.), *Health risks and developmental transitions during adolescence* (pp. 220–245). New York: Cambridge University Press.

Calhoun, D. A. (1992). Hypertension in blacks: Socioeconomic stress and sympathetic nervous system activity. *American Journal of the Medical Sciences, 304,* 306–311.

Caliso, J., & Milner, J. (1992). Childhood history of abuse and child abuse screening. *Child Abuse and Neglect, 16,* 647–659.

Calkins, S. D., Fox, N. A., & Marshall, T. R. (1996). Behavioral and physiological antecedents of inhibited and uninhibited behavior. *Child Development, 67,* 523–540.

Callahan, D. (1990). *What kind of life: The limits of medical progress.* New York: Simon & Schuster.

Callahan, D. (1999). Aging, death, and population health. *Journal of the American Medical Association, 282,* 2077–2078.

Camara, K. A., & Resnick, G. (1988). Interparental conflict and cooperation: Factors moderating children's post-divorce adjustment. In E. M. Hetherington & J. D. Arasteh (Eds.), *Impact of divorce, single parenting, and stepparenting on children* (pp. 169–195). Hillsdale, NJ: Erlbaum.

Cameron, C. A., & Lee, K. (1997). The development of children's telephone communication. *Journal of Applied Developmental Psychology, 18,* 55–70.

Campbell, F. A., & Ramey, C. T. (1991). *The Carolina Abecedarian Project.* Paper presented at the biennial meeting of the Society for Research in Child Development, Seattle, WA.

Campbell, F. A., & Ramey, C. T. (1994). Effects of early intervention on intellectual and academic achievement: A follow-up study of children from low-income families. *Child Development, 65,* 684–698.

Campbell, F. A., & Ramey, C. T. (1995). Cognitive and school outcomes for high-risk African-American students at middle adolescence: Positive effects of early intervention. *American Educational Research Journal, 32,* 743–772.

Campbell, J. R., Voelkl, K. E., & Donahue, P. L. (1997). *NAEP 1996 trends in academic progress.* Washington, DC: U.S. Government Printing Office.

Campbell, R., & Sais, E. (1995). Accelerated metalinguistic phonological awareness in bilingual children. *British Journal of Developmental Psychology, 13,* 61–68.

Campbell, S. B., Cohn, J. F., & Meyers, T. (1995). Depression in first-time mothers: Mother–infant interaction and depression chronicity. *Developmental Psychology, 31,* 349–357.

Campos, J., & Bertenthal, B. (1989). Locomotion and psychological development. In F. Morrison, K. Lord, & D. Keating (Eds.), *Applied developmental psychology* (Vol. 3, pp. 229–258). New York: Academic Press.

Campos, J. J., Kermoian, R., & Zumbahlen, M. R. (1992). Socioemotional transformation in the family system following infant crawling onset. In N. Eisenberg & R. A. Fabes (Eds.), *New directions for child development* (No. 55, pp. 25–40). San Francisco: Jossey-Bass.

Campos, R. G. (1989). Soothing pain-elicited distress in infants with swaddling and pacifiers. *Child Development, 60,* 781–792.

Camras, L. A., Oster, H., Campos, J., Campos, R., Ujie, T., Miyake, K., Wang, L., & Meng, Z. (1998). Production of emotional and facial expressions in European American, Japanese, and Chinese infants. *Developmental Psychology, 34,* 616–628.

Camras, L. A., Oster, H., Campos, J. J., Miyake, K., & Bradshaw, D. (1992). Japanese and American infants' responses to arm restraint. *Developmental Psychology, 28,* 578–583.

Candy-Gibbs, S., Sharp, K., & Petrun, C. (1985). The effects of age, object, and cultural/religious background on children's concepts of death. *Omega, 154,* 329–345.

Cangemi, J. P. (1983). Interpersonal relations on the college campus and declining enrollment: Any relationship? In C. J. Kowalski & J. P. Cangemi (Eds.), *Perspectives in higher education* (pp. 81–85). New York: Philosophical Library.

Canick, J. A., & Saller, D. N., Jr. (1993). Maternal serum screening for aneuploidy and open fetal defects. *Obstetrics and Gynecology Clinics of North America, 20,* 443–454.

Cannella, G. S. (1993). Learning through social interaction: Shared cognitive experience, negotiation strategies, and joint concept construction for young children. *Early Childhood Research Quarterly, 8,* 427–444.

Canobi, K. H., Reeve, R. A., & Pattison, P. E. (1998). The role of conceptual understanding in children's addition problem solving. *Developmental Psychology, 34,* 882–891.

Cantor, J., & Harrison, K. (1996). Ratings and advisories for television programming: University of Wisconsin, Madison study. In Mediascope (Ed.), *National Television Violence Study: Scientific Papers 1994–1995.* Studio City, CA: Author.

Capaldi, D. M., & Clark, S. (1998). Prospective family predictors of aggression toward female partners for at-risk young men. *Developmental Psychology, 34,* 1175–1188.

Caplan, M., Vespo, J., Pedersen, J., & Hay, D. F. (1991). Conflict and its resolution in small groups of one- and two-year-olds. *Child Development, 62,* 1513–1524.

Carbery, J., & Buhrmester, D. (1998). Friendship and need fulfillment during three phases of young adulthood. *Journal of Social and Personal Relationships, 15,* 393–409.

Carden, A. D. (1994). Wife abuse and the wife abuser: Review and recommendations. *Counseling Psychologist, 22,* 539–582.

Cardo, L. M. (1991). Death and dignity: The case of Diane [Letter to the Editor]. *New England Journal of Medicine, 325,* 658.

Carli, L. L., & Eagly, A. H. (2000). Gender effects on influence and emergent leadership. In G. N. Powell (Ed.), *Handbook of gender in organizations* (pp. 203–222). Newbury Park, CA: Sage.

Carlson, E. A. (1998). A prospective longitudinal study of attachment disorganization/disorientation. *Child Development, 69,* 1107–1128.

Carlson, K. J., Eisenstat, S. A., & Ziporyn, T. (1996). *The Harvard guide to women's health.* Cambridge, MA: Harvard University Press.

Caro, F. G., & Bass, S. A. (1997). Receptivity to volunteering in the immediate post-retirement period. *Journal of Applied Gerontology, 16,* 427–441.

Carpendale, J. I., & Chandler, M. J. (1996). On the distinction between false belief understanding and subscribing to an interpretive theory of mind. *Child Development, 67,* 1686–1706.

Carpenter, C. J. (1983). Activity structure and play: Implications for socialization. In M. Liss (Eds.), *Social and cognitive skills: Sex roles and children's play* (pp. 117–145). New York: Academic Press.

Carpenter, M., Nagell, K., & Tomasello, M. (1998). Social cognition, joint attention, and communicative competence. *Monographs of the Society for Research in Child Development, 63*(4, Serial No. 255).

Carrado, M., George, M. J., Loxam, E., Jones, L., & Templar, D. (1996). Aggression in British heterosexual relationships: A descriptive analysis. *Aggressive Behavior, 22,* 401–415.

Carskadon, M. A., Viera, C., & Acebo, C. (1993). Association between puberty and delayed phase preference. *Sleep, 16,* 258–262.

Carstensen, L. L. (1992). Selectivity theory: Social activity in life-span context. In K. W. Schaie & M. P. Lawton (Eds.), *Annual review of gerontology and geriatrics* (pp. 195–217). New York: Springer.

Carstensen, L. L., & Fredrickson, B. F. (1998). Socioemotional selectivity in healthy older people and younger people living with the human immunodeficiency virus: The centrality of emotion when the future is constrained. *Health Psychology, 17,* 1–10.

Carstensen, L. L., Gottman, J. M., & Levenson, R. W. (1995). Emotional behavior in long-term marriages. *Psychology and Aging, 10,* 140–149.

Carstensen, L. L., Isaacowitz, D. M., & Charles, S. T. (1999). Taking time seriously: A theory of socioemotional selectivity. *American Psychologist, 54,* 165–181.

Carstensen, L. L., & Turk, C. S. (1994). The salience of emotion across the adult life span. *Psychology and Aging, 9,* 315–324.

Carus, F. A. (1808). *Psychologie. Zweiter Teil: Specialpsychologie.* Leipzig: Barth & Kummer.

Casaer, P. (1993). Old and new facts about perinatal brain development. *Journal of Child Psychology and Psychiatry, 34,* 101–109.

Case, R. (1991). Stages in the development of the young child's first sense of self. *Developmental Review, 11,* 210–230.

Case, R. (1992). *The mind's staircase: Exploring the conceptual underpinnings of children's thought and knowledge.* Hillsdale, NJ: Erlbaum.

Case, R. (1996). Introduction: Reconceptualizing the nature of children's conceptual structures and their development in middle childhood. In R. Case & Y. Okamoto (Eds.), The role of central conceptual structures in the development of children's thought. *Monographs of the Society for Research in Child Development, 246*(61, Serial No. 246), pp. 1–26.

Case, R. (1998). The development of central conceptual structures. In D. Kuhn & R. Siegler (Eds.), *Handbook of child psychology: Vol. 2. Cognition, perception, and language* (5th ed., pp. 745–800). New York: Wiley.

Case, R., & Okamoto, Y. (1996). (Eds.). The role of central conceptual structures in the development of children's thought. *Monographs of the Society for Research in Child Development, 61*(1–2, Serial No. 246).

Caserta, M. S., & Gillett, P. A. (1998). Older women's feelings about exercise and their adherence to an aerobic regimen over time. *Gerontologist, 38,* 602–609.

Casey, M. B. (1986). Individual differences in selective attention among prereaders: A key to mirror-image confusions. *Developmental Psychology, 22,* 824–831.

Casey, M. B., Nuttall, R. L., & Pezaris, E. (1997). Mediators of gender differences in mathematics college entrance test scores: A comparison of spatial skills with internalized beliefs and anxieties. *Developmental Psychology, 33,* 669–680.

Casey, M. B., Nuttall, R., Pezaris, E., & Benbow, C. P. (1995). The influence of spatial ability on gender differences in mathematics collect entrance test scores across diverse samples. *Developmental Psychology, 31,* 697–705.

Caspi, A. (1998). Personality development across the life course. In N. Eisenberg (Ed.), *Handbook of child psychology: Vol. 3. Social, emotional, and personality development* (5th ed., pp. 311–388). New York: Wiley.

Caspi, A., Elder, G. H., Jr., & Bem, D. J. (1987). Moving against the world: Life-course patterns of explosive children. *Developmental Psychology, 23,* 308–313.

Caspi, A., Elder, G. H., Jr., & Bem, D. J. (1988). Moving away from the world: Life-course patterns of shy children. *Developmental Psychology, 24,* 824–831.

Caspi, A., & Herbener, E. (1990). Continuity and change: Assortative marriage and the consistency of personality in adulthood. *Journal of Personality and Social Psychology, 58,* 250–258.

Caspi, A., Lynam, D., Moffitt, T. E., & Silva, P. A. (1993). Unraveling girls' delinquency: Biological, dispositional, and contextual contributions to adolescent misbehavior. *Developmental Psychology, 29,* 19–30.

Caspi, A., & Silva, P. A. (1995). Temperamental qualities at age three predict personality traits in young adulthood: Longitudinal evidence from a birth cohort. *Child Development, 66,* 486–498.

Cassel, C. K. (1987). Informed consent for research in geriatrics: History and concepts. *Journal of the American Geriatrics Society, 35,* 542–544.

Cassel, C. K. (1988). Ethical issues in the conduct of research in long-term care. *Gerontologist, 28*(Suppl.), 90–96.

Cassidy, J., & Berlin, L. J. (1994). The insecure/ambivalent pattern of attachment: Theory and research. *Child Development, 65,* 971–991.

Catsambis, S. (1994). The path to math: Gender and racial-ethnic differences in mathematics participation from middle school to high school. *Sociology of Education, 67,* 199–215.

Ceci, S. J. (1990). *On intelligence . . . More or less.* Englewood Cliffs, NJ: Prentice-Hall.

Ceci, S. J. (1991). How much does schooling influence general intelligence and its cognitive components? A reassessment of the evidence. *Developmental Psychology, 27,* 703–722.

Ceci, S. J., & Bruck, M. (1993). Suggestibility of the child witness: A historical review and synthesis. *Psychological Bulletin, 113,* 403–439.

Ceci, S. J., & Bruck, M. (1998). Children's testimony: Applied and basic issues. In I. Sigel & K. A. Renninger (Eds.), *Handbook of child psychology: Vol. 4. Child psychology in practice* (5th ed., pp. 713–774). New York: Wiley.

Ceci, S. J., Leichtman, M. D., & Bruck, M. (1994). The suggestibility of children's eyewitness reports: Methodological issues. In F. Weinert & W. Schneider (Eds.), *Memory development: State of the art and future directions* (pp. 323–347). Englewood Cliffs, NJ: Erlbaum.

Ceci, S. J., & Roazzi, A. (1994). The effects of context on cognition: Postcards from Brazil. In R. J. Sternberg (Ed.), *Mind in context* (pp. 74–101). New York: Cambridge University Press.

Ceci, S. J., & Williams, W. M. (1997). Schooling, intelligence, and income. *American Psychologist, 52,* 1051–1058.

Center for Communication and Social Policy. (Ed.). (1998). *National Television Violence Study* (Vol. 2). Newbury Park, CA: Sage.

Center, J. R., Nguyen, T. V., Schneider, D., Sambrook, P. N., & Eisman, J. A. (1999). Mortality after all major types of osteoporotic fracture in men and women: An observational study. *Lancet, 353,* 878–882.

Central Intelligence Agency. (1998). *The world factbook.* Washington, DC: U.S. Government Printing Office.

Central Intelligence Agency. (1999). *The world factbook.* Washington, DC: U.S. Government Printing Office.

Cerella, J. (1990). Aging and information processing rate. In J. E. Birren & K. W. Schaie (Eds.), *Handbook of the psychology of aging* (3rd ed.), pp. 201–221). San Diego: Academic Press.

Cernoch, J. M., & Porter, R. H. (1985). Recognition of maternal axillary odors by infants. *Child Development 56,* 1593–1598.

Cervantes, C. A., & Callanan, M. A. (1998). Labels and explanations in mother–child emotion talk: Age and gender differentiation. *Developmental Psychology, 34,* 88–98.

Chadwick, S. (1996). The impact of asthma in an inner city general practice. *Child: Care, Health, and Development, 22,* 175–186.

Chalmers, J. B., & Townsend, M. A. R. (1990). The effects of training in social perspective taking on socially maladjusted girls. *Child Development, 61,* 178–190.

Chan, R. W., Raboy, B., & Patterson, C. J. (1998). Psychosocial adjustment among children conceived via donor insemination by lesbian and heterosexual mothers. *Child Development, 69,* 443–457.

Chandler, M. (1994). Adolescent suicide and the loss of personal continuity. In D. Cicchetti & S. L. Toth (Eds.), *Rochester Symposium on Developmental Psychopathology: Vol. 5. Disorders and dysfunctions of the self* (pp. 371–390). Rochester, NY: University of Rochester Press.

Chandler, M. J. (1973). Egocentrism and antisocial behavior: The assessment and training of social perspective-taking skills. *Developmental Psychology, 9,* 326–332.

Chandler, M. J., & Carpendale, J. I. (1998). Inching toward a mature theory of mind. In M. Ferrari & R. J. Sternberg (Eds.), *Self-awareness: Its nature and development* (pp. 148–190). New York: Guilford.

Chandra, R. K. (1991). Interactions between early nutrition and the immune system. In *Ciba Foundation Symposium No. 156* (pp. 77–92). Chichester, England: Wiley.

Chandra, R. K. (1992). Effect of vitamin and trace-element supplementation on immune responses and infection in elderly subjects. *Lancet, 340,* 1124–1127.

Chao, R. K. (1994). Beyond parental control and authoritarian parenting style: Understanding Chinese parenting through the cultural notion of training. *Child Development, 65,* 1111–1119.

Chapman, M., & Lindenberger, U. (1988). Functions, operations, and décalage in the development of transitivity. *Developmental Psychology, 24,* 542–551.

Chappell, N. L., & Guse, L. W. (1989). Linkages between informal and formal support. In K. S. Markides & C. L. Cooper (Eds.), *Aging, stress and health* (pp. 219–237). Chichester, England: Wiley.

Charman, T., Swettenham, J., Baron-Cohen, S., Cox, A., Baird, G., & Drew, A. (1997). Infants with autism: An investigation of empathy, pretend play, joint attention, and imitation. *Developmental Psychology, 33,* 781–789.

Chase-Lansdale, P. L., Brooks-Gunn, J., & Zamsky, E. S. (1994). Young African-American multigenerational families in poverty: Quality of mothering and grandmothering. *Child Development, 65,* 373–393.

Chase-Lansdale, P. L., Cherlin, A. J., & Kiernan, K. E. (1995). The long-term effects of parental divorce on the mental health of young children. *Child Development, 66,* 1614–1634.

Chase-Lansdale, P. L., & Vinovskis, M. A. (1995). *Escape from poverty: What makes a difference for children?* New York: Cambridge University Press.

Chasnoff, I. J., Anson, A., Hatcher, R., Stenson, H., Iaukea, K., & Randolph, L. A. (1998). Prenatal exposure to cocaine and other drugs: Outcome at four to six years. In J. A. Harvey & B. E. Kosofsky (Eds.), *Annals of the New York Academy of Sciences* (Vol. 846, pp. 314–328). New York: New York Academy of Sciences.

Chassin, L., Curran, P. J., Hussong, A. M., & Colder, C. R. (1996). The relation of parent alcoholism to adolescent substance use: A longitudinal follow-up study. *Journal of Abnormal Psychology, 105,* 70–80.

Chassin, L., Presson, C. C., Todd, M., Rose, J. S., & Sherman, S. J. (1998). Maternal socialization of adolescent smoking: The intergenerational transmission of parenting and smoking. *Developmental Psychology, 34,* 1189–1201.

Chasteen, A. L. (1994). "The world around me": The environment and single women. *Sex Roles, 31,* 309–328.

Chatterjee, S., Handcock, M. S., & Simonoff, J. S. (1995). *A casebook for a first course in statistics and data analysis.* New York: Wiley.

Cheek, J. M., & Busch, C. M. (1981). The influence of shyness on loneliness in a new situation. *Personality and Social Psychology Bulletin, 7,* 572–577.

Chen, X., Hastings, P. D., Rubin, K. H., Chen, H., Cen, G., & Stewart, S. L. (1998). Child-rearing attitudes and behavioral inhibition in Chinese and Canadian toddlers: A cross-cultural study. *Developmental Psychology, 34,* 677–686.

Chen, X., Rubin, K. H., & Li, B. (1994). Only children and sibling children in urban China: A re-examination. *International Journal of Behavioral Development, 17,* 413–421.

Chen, X., Rubin, K. H., & Li, Z. (1995). Social functioning and adjustment in Chinese children: A longitudinal study. *Developmental Psychology, 31,* 531–539.

Chen, Y.-C., Yu, M.-L., Rogan, W., Gladen, B., & Hsu, C.-C. (1994). A 6-year follow-up of behavior and activity disorders in the Taiwan Yu-cheng children. *American Journal of Public Health, 84,* 415–421.

Chen, Y.-J., & Hsu, C.-C. (1994). Effects of prenatal exposure to PCBs on the neurological function of children: A neuropsychological and neurophysiological study. *Developmental Medicine and Child Neurology, 36,* 312–320.

Chen, Z., Sanchez, R. P., & Campbell, T. (1997). From beyond to within their grasp: The rudiments of analogical problem solving in 10- to 13-month-olds. *Developmental Psychology, 33,* 790–801.

Cheng, M., & Hannah, M. (1993). Breech delivery at term: A critical review of the literature. *Obstetrics and Gynecology, 82,* 605–618.

Cherlin, A. J. (1992). *Marriage, divorce, remarriage* (rev. ed.). Cambridge, MA: Harvard University Press.

Cherlin, A. J., Furstenberg, F. F., Jr., Chase-Lansdale, P. L., Kiernan, K. E., Robins, P. K., Morrison, D. R., & Teitler, J. O. (1991). Longitudinal studies of effects of divorce on children in Great Britain and the United States. *Science, 252,* 1386–1389.

Cherlin, A. J., Kiernan, K. E., & Chase-Lansdale, P. L. (1995). Parental divorce in childhood and demographic outcomes in young adulthood. *Demography, 32,* 299–318.

Cherney, S. S. (1994). Home environmental influences on general cognitive ability. In J. C. DeFries, R. Plomin, & D. W. Fulker (Eds.), *Nature and nurture during middle childhood* (pp. 262–280). Cambridge, MA: Blackwell.

Cherry, K. E., & LeCompte, D. C. (1999). Age and individual differences influence prospective memory. *Psychology and Aging, 14,* 60–76.

Chesney, M. A., Ekman, P., Friesen, W. V., Black, G. W., & Hecker, M. H. L. (1997). Type A behavior pattern: Facial behavior and speech components. In P. Ekman & E. L. Rosenberg (Eds.*), What the face reveals* (pp. 453–468). New York: Oxford University Press.

Chess, S., & Thomas, A. (1984). *Origins and evolution of behavior disorders.* New York: Brunner/Mazel.

Chez, B. F. (1997). Electronic fetal monitoring then and now. *Journal of Perinatal and Neonatal Nursing, 10,* 1–4.

Chi, M. T. H. (1978). Knowledge structures and memory development. In R. S. Siegler (Ed.), *Children's thinking: What develops?* (pp. 73–96). Hillsdale, NJ: Erlbaum.

Chi, M. T. H., Glaser, R., & Farr, M. J. (Eds.). (1988). *The nature of expertise.* Hillsdale, NJ: Erlbaum.

Child, A. H. (1997). Marfan syndrome—current medical and genetic knowledge: How to treat and when. *Journal of Cardiac Surgery, 12*(2, Suppl.), 131–135.

Children's Defense Fund (1999). *The state of America's children: Yearbook 1999.* Washington, DC: Author.

Childs, C. P., & Greenfield, P. M. (1982). Informal modes of learning and teaching: The case of Zinacanteco weaving. In N. Warren (Ed.), *Advances in cross-cultural psychology* (Vol. 2, pp. 269–316). London: Academic Press.

Chisholm, J. S. (1989). Biology, culture, and the development of temperament: A Navajo example. In J. K. Nugent, B. M. Lester, & T. B. Brazelton (Eds.), *Biology, culture, and development* (Vol. 1, pp. 341–364). Norwood, NJ: Ablex.

Chiu, L.-H. (1992–1993). Self-esteem in American and Chinese (Taiwanese) children. *Current Psychology: Research and Reviews, 11,* 309–313.

Chodorow, N. (1978). *The reproduction of mothering.* Berkeley: University of California Press.

Choi, N. G. (1994). Racial differences in timing and factors associated with retirement. *Journal of Sociology and Social Welfare, 21,* 31–52.

Choi, N. G. (1995). Racial differences in the determinants of the coresidence of and contacts between elderly parents and their children. *Journal of Gerontological Social Work, 24,* 77–95.

Choi, N. G. (1996). The never-married and divorced elderly: Comparison of economic and health status, social support, and living arrangement. *Journal of Gerontological Social Work, 26,* 3–25.

Choi, S., & Gopnik, A. (1995). Early acquisition of verbs in Korean: A cross-linguistic study. *Journal of Child Language, 22,* 497–529.

Chollar, S. (1995, June). The psychological benefits of exercise. *American Health, 14*(5), 72–75.

Chomsky, C. (1969). *The acquisition of syntax in children from five to ten.* Cambridge, MA: MIT Press.

Chomsky, N. (1957). *Syntactic structures.* The Hague: Mouton.

Christensen, K. A., Stephens, M. A. P., & Townsend, A. L. (1998). Mastery in women's multiple roles and well-being: Adult daughters providing care to impaired parents. *Health Psychology, 17,* 163–171.

Christophersen, E. R., & Edwards, K. J. (1992). Treatment of elimination disorders: State of the art 1991. *Applied and Preventive Psychology, 1,* 15–22.

Chu, G. C. (1985). The changing concept of self in contemporary China. In A. J. Marsella, G. DeVos, & F. L. K. Hsu (Eds.), *Culture and self: Asian and Western perspectives* (pp. 252–277). London: Tavistock.

Chugani, H. T. (1994). Development of regional brain glucose metabolism in relation to behavior and platicity. In G. Dawson & K. W. Fischer (Eds.), *Human behavior and the developing brain* (pp. 153–175). New York: Guilford.

Cicchetti, D., & Aber, J. L. (1986). Early precursors of later depression: An organizational perspective. In L. P. Lipsitt & C. Rovee-Collier (Eds.), *Advances in infancy research* (Vol. 4, pp. 87–137). Norwood, NJ: Ablex.

Cicchetti, D., & Garmezy, N. (1993). Prospects and promises in the study of resilience. *Development and Psychopathology, 5,* 497–502.

Cicchetti, D., & Toth, S. L. (1998a). Perspectives on research and practice in developmental psychology. In I. E. Sigel & K. A. Renninger (Eds.), *Handbook of child psychology: Vol. 4. Child psychology in practice* (5th ed., pp. 479–582). New York: Wiley.

Cicchetti, D., & Toth, S. L. (1998b). The development of depression in children and adolescents. *American Psychologist, 53,* 221–241.

Cicerelli, V. G. (1989). Feelings of attachment to siblings and well-being in later life. *Psychology and Aging, 4,* 211–216.

Cicerelli, V. G. (1995). *Sibling relationships across the life span.* New York: Plenum.

Cicerelli, V. G. (1997). Relationship of psychosocial and background variables to older adults' end-of-life decisions. *Psychology and Aging, 12,* 72–83.

Cicerelli, V. G. (1998). Personal meanings of death in relation to fear of death. *Death Studies, 22,* 713–733.

Clark, D. C., & Mokros, H. R. (1993). Depression and suicidal behavior. In P. H. Tolan & B. J. Cohler (Eds.), *Handbook of clinical research and practice with adolescents* (pp. 333–358). New York: Wiley.

Clark, D. O. (1999). Identifying psychological, physiological, and environmental barriers and facilitators to exercise among older low income adults. *Journal of Clinical Geropsychology, 5,* 51–62.

Clark, E. V. (1983). Meanings and concepts. In J. H. Flavell & E. M. Markman (Eds.), *Handbook of child psychology: Vol. 3. Cognitive development* (pp. 787–840). New York: Wiley.

Clark, E. V. (1995). The lexicon and syntax. In J. L. Miller & P. D. Eimas (Eds.), *Speech, language, and communication* (pp. 303–337). San Diego: Academic Press.

Clark, R., Hyde, J. S., Essex, M. J., & Klein, M. H. (1997). Length of maternity leave and quality of mother–infant interaction. *Child Development, 68,* 364–383.

Clarke, C. J., & Neidert, L. J. (1992). Living arrangements of the elderly: An examination of differences according to ancestry and generation. *Gerontologist, 32,* 796–804.

Clarke-Stewart, K. A. (1992). Consequences of child care for children's development. In A. Booth (Ed.), *Child care in the 1990s: Trends and consequences* (pp. 63–83). Hillsdale, NJ: Erlbaum.

Clarke-Stewart, K. A., & Hayward, C. (1996). Advantages of father custody and contact for the psychological well-being of school-age children. *Journal of Applied Developmental Psychology, 17,* 239–270.

Clausen, J. A. (1975). The social meaning of differential physical and sexual maturation. In S. E. Dragastin & G. H. Elder (Eds.), *Adolescence in the life cycle: Psychological change and the social context* (pp. 25–47). New York: Halsted.

Cleveland, J., & Shore, L. (1992). Self- and supervisory perspectives on age and work attitudes and performance. *Journal of Applied Psychology, 77,* 469–484.

Clifford, C., & Kramer, B. (1993). Diet as risk and therapy for cancer. *Medical Clinics of North America, 77,* 725–744.

Clifton, R. K., Muir, D. W., Ashmead, D. H., & Clarkson, M. G. (1993). Is visually guided reaching in early infancy a myth? *Child Development, 64,* 1099–1110.

Clifton, R. K., Perris, E., & Bullinger, A. (1991). Infants' perception of auditory space. *Developmental Psychology, 27,* 161–171.

Clifton, R. K., Rochat, P., Robin, D. J., & Berthier, N. E. (1994). Multimodal perception in the control of infant reaching. *Journal of Experimental Psychology: Human Perception and Performance, 20,* 876–886.

Coakley, J. (1990). *Sport and society: Issues and controversies* (4th ed.). St. Louis: Mosby.

Coatney, C. (1997, January 8). Australia diver's world's first dose of legal euthanasia. *The Christian Science Monitor,* pp. 1, 18.

Cohen, D., Eisdorfer, C., Gorelick, P., Pavesa, G., Luchins, D. J., Freels, S., Ashford, J. W., Semla, T., Levy, P., & Hirschman, R. (1993). Psychopathology associated with Alzheimer's disease and related disorders. *Journal of Gerontology, 48,* M255–M260.

Cohen, G. D. (1990). Psychopathology and mental health in the mature and elderly adult. In J. E. Birren & K. W. Schaie (Eds.), *Handbook of the psychology of aging* (3rd ed., pp. 359–371). San Diego: Academic Press.

Cohen, K. M., & Savin-Williams, R. C. (1996). Developmental perspectives on coming out to self and others. *The lives of lesbians, gays, and bisexuals: Children to adults* (pp. 113–151). Ft. Worth, TX: Harcourt Brace.

Cohen, S., & Herbert, T. B. (1996). Health psychology: Psychological factors and physical disease from the perspective of human psychoneuroimmunology. *Annual Review of Psychology, 47,* 113–142.

Cohen, S., & Williamson, G. M. (1991). Stress and infectious disease in humans. *Psychological Bulletin, 109,* 5–24.

Coie, J. D., & Dodge, K. A. (1998). *Aggression and antisocial behavior.* In N. Eisenberg (Ed.), *Handbook of child psychology: Vol. 3. Social, emotional, and personality development* (5th ed., pp. 779–862). New York: Wiley.

Coie, J. D., Dodge, K. A., & Coppotelli, H. (1982). Dimensions and types of social status: A cross-age perspective. *Developmental Psychology, 18,* 557–570.

Coie, J. D., & Kreihbel, G. (1984). Effects of academic tutoring on the social status of low-achieving, socially rejected children. *Child Development, 55,* 1465–1478.

Coke, M. M. (1992). Correlates of life satisfaction among elderly African Americans. *Journal of Gerontology, 47,* P316–P320.

Colby, A., Kohlberg, L., Gibbs, J., & Lieberman, M. (1983). A longitudinal study of moral judgment. *Monographs of the Society for Research in Child Development, 48*(1–2, Serial No. 200).

Cole, D. A., Martin, J. M., Peeke, L. A., Seroczynski, A. D., & Fier, J. (1999). Children's over- and underestimation of academic competence: A longitudinal study of gender differences, depression, and anxiety. *Child Development, 70,* 459–473.

Cole, E. R., & Stewart, A. J. (1996). Meanings of political participation among black and white women: Political identity and social responsibility. *Journal of Personality and Social Psychology, 71,* 130–140.

Cole, M. (1990). Cognitive development and formal schooling: The evidence from cross-cultural research. In L. C. Moll (Ed.), *Vygotsky and education* (pp. 89–110). New York: Cambridge University Press.

Coley, R. L. (1998). Children's socialization experiences and functioning in single-mother households: The importance of fathers and other men. *Child Development, 69,* 219–230.

Coley, R. L., & Chase-Lansdale, P. L. (1998). Adolescent pregnancy and parenthood: Recent evidence and future directions. *American Psychologist, 53,* 152–166.

Collaer, M. L., & Hines, M. (1995). Human behavioral sex differences: A role for gonadal hormones during early development? *Psychological Bulletin, 118,* 55–107.

Collins, J. A. (1994). Reproductive technology—the price of progress. *New England Journal of Medicine, 331,* 270–271.

Collins, N. L., & Read, S. J. (1990). Adult attachment, working models, and relationship quality in dating couples. *Journal of Personality and Social Psychology, 58,* 644–663.

Collins, W. A., Harris, M. L., & Susman, A. (1996). Parenting during middle childhood. In M. H. Bornstein (Ed.), *Handbook of parenting: Vol. 1. Children and parenting* (pp. 65–90). Mahwah, NJ: Erlbaum.

Collins, W. A., Laursen, B., Mortensen, N., Luebker, C., & Ferreira, M. (1997). Conflict processes and transitions in parent and peer relationships: Implications for autonomy and regulation. *Journal of Adolescent Research, 12,* 178–198.

Collins, W. A., Wellman, H., Keniston, A. H., & Westby, S. D. (1978). Age-related aspects of comprehension and inference from a televised dramatic narrative. *Child Development, 49,* 389–399.

Colman, L. L., & Colman, A. D. (1991). *Pregnancy: The psychological experience.* New York: Noonday Press.

Colombo, J. (1995). On the neural mechanism underlying developmental and individual differences in visual fixation in infancy. *Developmental Review, 15,* 97–135.

Colonia-Willner, R. (1998). Practical intelligence at work: Relationship between aging and cognitive efficiency among managers in a bank environment. *Psychology and Aging, 13,* 45–57.

Coltrane, S. (1990). Birth timing and the division of labor in dual-earner families. *Journal of Family Issues, 11,* 157–181.

Coltrane, S. (1996). *Family man.* New York: Oxford University Press.

Comijs, H. C., Jonker, C., van Tilburg, W., & Smit, J. H. (1999). Hostility and coping capacity as risk factors of elder mistreatment. *Social Psychiatry and Psychiatric Epidemiology, 34,* 48–52.

Comijs, H. C., Pot, A. M., Smit, J. H., Bouter, R. M., & Jonker, C. (1998). Elder abuse in the community: Prevalence and consequences. *Journal of the American Geriatrics Society, 46,* 885–888.

Compas, B., Phares, V., & Ledoux, N. (1989). Stress and coping: Preventive interventions for children and adolescents. In L. Bond & B. Compas (Eds.), *Primary prevention in the schools* (pp. 319–340). London: Sage.

Comstock, G. A. (1993). The medium and society: The role of television in American life. In G. L. Berry & J. K. Asamen (Eds.), *Children and television* (pp. 117–131). Newbury Park, CA: Sage.

Condie, S. J. (1989). Older married couples. In S. J. Bahr & E. T. Peterson (Eds.), *Aging and the family* (pp. 143–158). Lexington, MA: Lexington Books.

Condry, J., & Ross, D. F. (1985). Sex and aggression: The influence of gender label on the perceptions of aggression in children. *Child Development, 56,* 225–233.

Conel, J. L. (1959). *The postnatal development of the human cerebral cortex.* Cambridge, MA: Harvard University Press.

Conger, K. J., Conger, R. D., & Scaramella, L. V. (1997). Parents, siblings, psychological control, and adolescent adjustment. *Journal of Adolescent Research, 12,* 113–138.

Conger, R. D., Conger, K. J., Elder, G. H., Jr., Lorenz, F. O., Simons, R. L., & Whitbeck, L. B. (1992). A family process model of economic hardship and adjustment of early adolescent boys. *Child Development, 63,* 527–541.

Conger, R. D., Patterson, G. R., & Ge, X. (1995). It takes two to replicate: A mediational model for the impact of parents' stress on adolescent adjustment. *Child Development, 66,* 80–97.

Connell, J. P., Spencer, M. B., & Aber, J. L. (1994). Educational risk and resilience in African-American youth: Context, self, action, and outcomes in school. *Child Development, 65,* 493–503.

Conner, D. B., Knight, D. K., & Cross, D. R. (1997). Mothers' and fathers' scaffolding of their 2-year-olds during problem-solving and literacy interactions. *British Journal of Developmental Psychology, 15,* 323–338.

Connidis, I. A. (1989). Siblings as friends in later life. *American Behavioral Scientist, 33,* 81–93.

Connidis, I. A. (1994). Sibling support in older age. *Journal of Gerontology, 49,* S309–S317.

Connidis, I. A., & Campbell, L. D. (1995). Closeness, confiding, and contact among siblings in middle and late adulthood. *Journal of Family Issues, 16,* 722–745.

Connidis, I. A., & McMullin, J. A. (1993). To have or have not: Parent status and the subjective well-being of older men and women. *The Gerontologist, 33,* 630–636.

Connolly, J. A., & Doyle, A. B. (1984). Relations of social fantasy play to social competence in preschoolers. *Developmental Psychology, 20,* 797–806.

Connors, L. J., & Epstein, J. L. (1996). Parent and school partnerships. In M. H. Bornstein (Ed.), *Handbook of parenting: Vol. 4. Applied and practical parenting* (pp. 437–458). Mahwah, NJ: Erlbaum.

Cook, P. W. (1997). *Abused men: the hidden side of domestic violence.* Westport, CT: Praeger.

Cook, R., Golombok, S., Bish, A., & Murray, C. (1995). Disclosure of donor insemination: Parental attitudes. *American Journal of Orthopsychiatry, 65,* 549–559.

Cooke, R. A. (1982). The ethics and regulation of research involving children. In B. B. Wolman (Ed.), *Handbook of developmental psychology* (pp. 149–172). Englewood Cliffs, NJ: Prentice-Hall.

Cooney, T. M., & Uhlenberg, P. (1990). The role of divorce in men's relations with their adult children after mid-life. *Journal of Marriage and the Family, 52,* 677–688.

Cooper, C. R. (1998). *The weaving of maturity: Cultural perspectives on adolescent development.* New York: Oxford University Press.

Cooper, M. L., & Orcutt, H. K. (1997). Drinking and sexual experience on first dates among adolescents. *Journal of Abnormal Psychology, 106,* 191–202.

Cooper, P., & Murray, L. (1997). Prediction, detection, and treatment of postnatal depression. *Archives of Diseases of Children, 77,* 97–99.

Cooper, R. P., & Aslin, R. N. (1994). Developmental differences in infant attention to the spectral properties of infant-directed speech. *Child Development, 65,* 1663–1677.

Copper, R. L., Goldenberg, R. L., Creasy, R. K., DuBard, M. B., Davis, R. O., Entman, S. S., Iams, J. D., & Cliver, S. P. (1993). A multi-center study of preterm birthweight and gestational age-specific neonatal mortality. *American Journal of Obstetrics and Gynecology, 168,* 78–84.

Cornelius, M. D., Day, N. L., Richardson, G. A., & Taylor, P. M. (1999). Epidemiology of substance abuse during pregnancy. In P. J. Ott & R. E. Tarter (Eds.), *Sourcebook on substance abuse: Etiology, epidemiology, assessment, and treatment* (pp. 1–13). Boston: Allyn and Bacon.

Cornelius, S. W., & Caspi, A. (1987). Everyday problem solving in adulthood and old age. *Psychology and Aging, 2,* 144–153.

Corr, C. A. (1993). Coping with dying: Lessons that we should and should not learn from the work of Elisabeth Kübler-Ross. *Death Studies, 17,* 69–83.

Corr, C. A. (1995). Entering into adolescent understandings of death. In E. A. Grollman (Eds.), *Bereaved children and teens* (pp. 21–35). Boston: Beacon Press.

Corr, C. A. (1997). Children and questions about death. In S. Strack (Ed.), *Death and the quest for meaning* (pp. 217–238). Northvale, NJ: Jason Aronson.

Corr, C. A., & Balk, D. E. (1996). *Handbook of adolescent death and bereavement.* New York: Springer.

Corrigan, R. (1987). A developmental sequence of actor–object pretend play in young children. *Merrill-Palmer Quarterly, 33,* 87–106.

Corwin, M. J., Lester, B. M., Sepkoski, C., Peucker, M., Kayne, H., & Golub, H. L. (1995). Newborn acoustic cry characteristics of infants subsequently dying of sudden infant death syndrome. *Pediatrics, 96,* 73–77.

Cosden, M., Peerson, S., & Elliott, K. (1997). Effects of prenatal drug exposure on birth outcomes and early child development. *Journal of Drug Issues, 27,* 525–539.

Cost, Quality, and Outcomes Study Team. (1995). Cost, quality, and child outcomes in child care centers: Key findings and recommendations. *Young Children, 50*(4), 40–44.

Costa, P. T., Jr., & McCrae, R. R. (1994). Set like plaster? Evidence for the stability of adult personality. In T. F. Heatherton & J. L. Weinberger (Eds.), *Can personality change?* (pp. 21–40). Washington, DC: American Psychological Association.

Costello, E. J., & Angold, A. (1995). Developmental epidemiology. In D. Cicchetti & D. Cohen (Eds.), *Developmental psychopathology: Vol. 1. Theory and method* (pp. 23–56). New York: Wiley.

Cotton, P. (1990). Sudden infant death syndrome: Another hypothesis offered but doubts remain. *Journal of the American Medical Association, 263,* 2865, 2869.

Cotton, P. (1994). Smoking cigarettes may do developing fetus more harm than ingesting cocaine, some experts say. *Journal of the American Medical Association, 271,* 576–577.

Couch, K. A. (1998). Late life job displacement. *Gerontologist, 38,* 7–17.

Coughlin, S. S., Khoury, M. J., & Steinberg, K. K. (1999). BRCA1 and BRCA2 gene mutations and risk of breast cancer: Public health perspectives. *American Journal of Preventive Medicine, 16,* 91–98.

Coulton, C. J., Korbin, J. E., Su, M., & Chow, J. (1995). Community level factors and child maltreatment rates. *Child Development, 66,* 1262–1276.

Courage, M. L., & Adams, R. J. (1990). Visual acuity assessment from birth to three years using the acuity card procedures: Cross-sectional and longitudinal samples. *Optometry and Vision Science, 67,* 713–718.

Cowan, C. P., & Cowan, P. A. (1992). *When partners become parents.* New York: Basic Books.

Cowan, C. P., & Cowan, P. A. (1995). Interventions to ease the transition to parenthood: Why they are needed and what they can do. *Family Relations, 44,* 412–423.

Cowan, C. P., & Cowan, P. A. (1997). Working with couples during stressful transitions. In S. Dreman (Ed.), *The family on the threshold of the 21st century* (pp. 17–47). Mahwah, NJ: Erlbaum.

Coward, R. T., Lee, G. R., & Dwyer, J. W. (1993). The family relations of rural elders. In C. N. Bull (Ed.), *Aging in rural America* (pp. 216–231). Newbury Park, CA: Sage.

Cox, K., & Schwartz, J. D. (1990). *The well-informed patient's guide to caesarean births.* New York: Dell.

Cox, M. (1993). *Children's drawings of the human figure.* Hillsdale, NJ: Erlbaum.

Cox, M. J., Owen, M. T., Henderson, V. K., & Margand, N. A. (1992). Prediction of infant–father and infant–mother attachment. *Developmental Psychology, 28,* 474–483.

Coyle, T. R., & Bjorklund, D. F. (1997). Age differences in, and consequences of, multiple- and variable-strategy use on a multitrial sort-recall task. *Developmental Psychology, 33,* 372–380.

Craik, F. I. M., & Jacoby, L. L. (1996). Aging and memory: Implications for skilled performance. In W. A. Rogers, A. D. Fisk, & N. Walker (Eds.), *Aging and skilled performance* (pp. 113–137). Mahwah, NJ: Erlbaum.

Craik, F. I. M., & Jennings, J. M. (1992). Human memory. In F. I. M. Craik & T. A. Salthouse (Eds.), *Handbook of aging and cognition* (pp. 51–110). Hillsdale, NJ: Erlbaum.

Cramond, B. (1994). The Torrance Tests of Creative Thinking: From design through establishment of predictive validity. In R. F. Subotnik & K. D. Arnold (Eds.), *Beyond Terman: Contemporary longitudinal studies of giftedness and talent* (pp. 229–254). Norwood, NJ: Ablex.

Cratty, B. J. (1986). *Perceptual and motor development in infants and children* (3rd ed.), Englewood Cliffs, NJ: Prentice-Hall.

Crawford, J. (1995). *Bilingual education: History, politics, theory, and practice.* Los Angeles: Bilingual Education Services.

Crawford, J. (1997). *Best evidence: Research foundations of the bilingual education act.* Washington, DC: National Clearinghouse for Bilingual Education.

Creasey, G. L., Jarvis, P. A., & Berk, L. E. (1998). Play and social competence. In O. N. Saracho & B. Spodek (Eds.), *Multiple perspectives on play in early childhood education* (pp. 116–143). Albany: State University of New York Press.

Creatsas, G. K., Vekemans, M., Horejsi, J., Uzel, R., Lauritzen, C., & Osler, M. (1995). Adolescent sexuality in Europe a multicentric study. *Adolescent and Pediatric Gynecology, 8,* 59–63.

Creer, T. L., & Bender, B. G. (1995). Pediatric asthma. In M. C. Roberts (Ed.), *Handbook of pediatric psychology* (2nd ed., pp. 219–240). New York: Guilford.

Crick, N. R., Casas, J. F., & Ku, H.-C. (1999). Relational and physical forms of peer victimization in preschool. *Developmental Psychology, 35,* 376–385.

Crick, N. R., Casas, J. F., & Mosher, M. (1997). Relational and overt aggression in preschool. *Developmental Psychology, 33,* 579–588.

Crick, N. R., & Grotpeter, J. K. (1995). Relational aggression, gender, and social-psychological adjustment. *Child Development, 66,* 710–722.

Crick, N. R., & Grotpeter, J. K. (1996). Children's treatment by peers: Victims of relational and overt aggression. *Development and Psychopathology, 8,* 367–380.

Crick, N. R., & Ladd, G. W. (1993). Children's perceptions of their peer experiences: Attributions, loneliness, social anxiety, and social avoidance. *Developmental Psychology, 29,* 244–254.

Cristofalo, V. J., Tresini, M., Francis, M. K., & Volker, C. (1999). Biological theories of senescence. In V. L. Bengtson & K. W. Schaie (Eds.), *Handbook of theories of aging* (pp. 98–112). New York: Springer.

Crockett, L. J. (1990). Sex role and sex-typing in adolescence. In R. M. Lerner, A. C. Petersen, & J. Brooks-Gunn (Eds.), *The encyclopedia of adolescence* (Vol. 2, pp. 1007–1017). New York: Garland.

Crohan, S. E., & Antonucci, T. C. (1989). Friends as a source of social support in old age. In R. G. Adams & R. Blieszner (Eds.), *Older adult friendship* (pp. 129–146). Newbury Park, CA: Sage.

Crook, C. K., & Lipsitt, L. P. (1976). Neonatal nutritive sucking: Effects of taste stimulation upon sucking rhythm and heart rate. *Child Development, 47,* 518–522.

Crosby, F. J. (1998). The developing literature on developmental relationships. In A. J. Murrell, F. J. Crosby, & R. J. Ely (Eds.), *Mentoring dilemmas* (pp. 3–20). Mahwah, NJ: Erlbaum.

Cross, S., & Markus, H. (1991). Possible selves across the life span. *Human Development, 34,* 230–255.

Crouter, A. C., Manke, B. A., & McHale, S. M. (1995). The family context of gender intensification in early adolescence. *Child Development, 66,* 317–329.

Crystal, D. S., Chen, C., Fuligni, A. J., Stevenson, H. W., Hsu, C-C., Ko, H-J., Kitamura, S., & Kimura, S. (1994). Psychological maladjustment and academic achievement: A cross-cultural study of Japanese, Chinese, and American high school students. *Child Development, 65,* 738–753.

Csikszentmihalyi, M. (1999). If we are so rich, why aren't we happy? *American Psychologist, 54,* 821–827.

Csikszentmihalyi, M., & Larson, R. (1984). *Being adolescent: Conflict and growth in the teenage years.* New York: Basic Books.

Csikszentmihalyi, M., & Rathunde, K. (1990). The psychology of wisdom: An evolutionary interpretation. In R. J. Sternberg (Ed.), *Wisdom: Its nature, origins, and development* (pp. 25–51). New York: Cambridge University Press.

Cuddy-Casey, M., & Orvaschel, H. (1997). Children's understanding of death in relation to child suicidality and homicidality. *Clinical Psychology Review, 17,* 33–45.

Culbertson, F. M. (1997). Depression and gender: An international review. *American Psychologist, 52,* 25–51.

Cummings, E. M., & Cicchetti, D. (1990). Toward a transactional model of relations between attachment and depression. In M. Greenberg, D. Cicchetti, & E. M. Cummings (Eds.), *Attachment in the preschool years: Theory, research, and intervention* (pp. 339–372). Chicago: University of Chicago Press.

Cummings, E. M., & Davies, P. (1994a). *Children and marital conflict.* New York: Guilford.

Cummings, E. M., & Davies, P. T. (1994b). Maternal depression and child development. *Journal of Child Psychology and Psychiatry, 35,* 73–112.

Cummings, E. M., Iannotti, R. J., & Zahn-Waxler, C. (1985). Influence of conflict between adults on the emotions and aggression of young children. *Developmental Psychology, 21,* 495–507.

Cummings, E. M., & Zahn-Waxler, C. (1992). Emotions and the socialization of aggression: Adults' angry behavior and children's arousal and aggression. In A. Fraczek & H. Zumkley (Eds.), *Socialization and aggression* (pp. 61–84). New York: Springer-Verlag.

Cunningham, J. D., & Antill, J. K. (1994). Cohabitation and marriage: Retrospective and predictive comparisons. *Journal of Social and Personal Relationships, 11,* 77–93.

Currie, D. H. (1999). Violent men or violent women? Whose definition counts? In R. K. Bergen (Ed.), *Issues in intimate violence* (pp. 97–111). Thousand Oaks, CA: Sage.

Currie, J., & Thomas, D. (1997, Spring). Can Head Start lead to long-term gains in cognition after all? *SRCD Newsletter, 40*(2), 3–5.

Cutler, S. J., & Hendricks, J. (1990). Leisure and time use across the life course. In R. Binstock & L. George (Eds.), *Aging and the social sciences* (3rd ed., pp. 169–185). New York: Academic Press.

Cuttler, L., Silvers, J. B., Singh, J., Marrero, U., Finkelstein, B., Tannin, G., & Neuhauser, D. (1996). Short stature and growth hormone therapy. *Journal of the American Medical Association, 276,* 531–537.

Cytron, B. D. (1993). To honor the dead and comfort the mourners: Traditions in Judaism. In D. P. Irish, K. F. Lundquist, & V. J. Nelson (Eds.), *Ethnic variations in dying, death, and grief* (pp. 113–124). Washington, DC: Taylor & Francis.

Dacey, J. S. (1989). Peak periods of creative growth across the life span. *Journal of Creative Behavior, 23,* 224–248.

Dahl, R.E., Scher, M. S., Williamson, D. E., Robles, N., & Day, N. (1995). A longitudinal study of prenatal marijuana use: Effects on sleep and arousal at age 3 years. *Archives of Pediatric and Adolescent Medicine, 149,* 145-150.

Dalton, S. T. (1992). Lived experience of never-married women. *Issues in Mental Health Nursing, 13,* 69–80.

Damon, W. (1977). *The social world of the child.* San Francisco: Jossey-Bass.

Damon, W. (1988). *The moral child.* New York: Free Press.

Damon, W. (1990). Self-concept, adolescent. In R. M. Lerner, A. C. Petersen, & J. Brooks-Gunn (Eds.), *The encyclopedia of adolescence* (Vol. 2, pp. 87–91). New York: Garland.

Damon, W., & Hart, D. (1988). *Self-understanding in childhood and adolescence.* New York: Cambridge University Press.

Danforth, J. S., Barkley, R. A., & Stokes, T. F. (1990). Observations of parent–child interactions with hyperactive children: Research and clinical applications. *Clinical Psychology Review, 11,* 703–727.

Daniels, K., & Lewis, G. M. (1996). Openness of information in the use of donor gametes: Developments in New Zealand. *Journal of Reproductive and Infant Psychology, 14,* 57–68.

Dannemiller, J. L., & Stephens, B. R. (1988). A critical test of infant pattern preference models. *Child Development, 59,* 210–216.

Darwin, C. (1936). *On the origin of species by means of natural selection.* New York: Modern Library. (Original work published 1859)

Dattel, B. J. (1997). Antiretroviral therapy during pregnancy. Beyond AZT (ZDV). *Obstetrics and Gynecology Clinics of North America, 24,* 645–657.

Daugirdas, J. T. (1992). *Sexually transmitted diseases.* Hinsdale, IL: Medtext.

Davenport, E. C., Jr., Davison, M. L., Kuang, H., Ding, S., Kim, S., & Kwak, N. (1998). High school mathematics course-taking by gender and ethnicity. *American Educational Research Journal, 35,* 497–514.

Davey, A., & Eggebeen, D. J. (1998). Patterns of intergenerational exchange and mental health. *Journal of Gerontology, 53B,* P86–P95.

Davidson, R. J. (1994). Asymmetric brain function, affective style, and psychopathology: The role of early experience and plasticity. *Development and Psychopathology, 6,* 741–758.

Davies, E. B. (1987). After a sibling dies. In M. A. Morgan (Ed.), *Bereavement: Helping the survivors. Proceedings of the 1987 King's College Conference.* London, Ontario: King's College.

Davis, B., & Aron, A. (1989). Perceived causes of divorce and postdivorce adjustment among recently divorced midlife women. *Journal of Divorce, 12,* 41–55.

Davis, C. G., Nolen-Hoeksema, S., & Larson, J. (1998). Making sense of loss and benefiting from the experience: Two construals of meaning. *Journal of Personality and Social Psychology, 75, 561–574.

Davis, D. L., Gottlieb, M. B., & Stampnitzky, J. R. (1998). Reduced ratio of male to female births in several industrial countries. Journal of the American Medical Association, 279, 1018–1023.

Davis, K. L., Mohs, R. C., Marin, D., Purohit, D. P., Perl, D. P., Lantz, M., Austin, G., & Haroutunian, V. (1999). Cholinergic markers in elderly patients with early signs of Alzheimer's disease. Journal of the American Medical Association, 281, 1401–1406.

Day, S. (1993, May). Why genes have a gender. New Scientist, 138 (1874), 34–38.

Deacon, S., Minichiello, V., & Plummer, D. (1995). Sexuality and older people: Revisiting the assumptions. Educational Gerontology, 21, 497–513.

Deák, G. O., & Maratsos, M. (1998). On having complex representations of things: Preschoolers use multiple words for objects and people. Developmental Psychology, 34, 224–240.

Dean, R. S., & Anderson, J. L. (1997). Lateralization of cerebral function. In A. M. Horton, Jr., D. Wedding, & J. Webster (Eds.), The neuropsychology handbook: Vol. 1. Foundations and assessment (2nd ed., pp. 139–168). New York: Springer.

Deary, I. J. (1995). Auditory inspection time and intelligence: What is the direction of causation? Developmental Psychology, 31, 237–250.

Deater-Deckard, K., & Dodge, K. A. (1997). Externalizing behavior problems and discipline revisited: Nonlinear effects and variation by culture, context, and gender. Psychological Inquiry, 8, 161–175.

Deater-Deckard, K., Dodge, K. A., Bates, J. E., & Petit, G. S. (1996). Physical discipline among African American and European American mothers: Links to children's externalizing behaviors. Developmental Psychology, 32, 1065–1072.

DeCasper, A. J., & Spence, M. J. (1986). Prenatal maternal speech influences newborns' perception of speech sounds. Infant Behavior and Development, 9, 133–150.

Declercq, E. R. (1992). The transformation of American midwifery: 1975 to 1988. American Journal of Public Health, 82, 680–684.

Deffenbacher, J. L. (1994). Anger reduction: Issues, assessment, and intervention strategies. In A. W. Siegman & T. W. Smith (Eds.), Anger, hostility, and the heart (pp. 239–269). Hillsdale, NJ: Erlbaum.

DeGarmo, D. S., & Forgatch, M. S. (1997). Determinants of observed confidant support for divorced mothers. Journal of Personality and Social Psychology, 72, 336–345.

DeGarmo, D. S., & Forgatch, M. S. (1999). Contexts as predictors of changing maternal parenting practices in diverse family structures: A social interactional perspective of risk and resilience. In E. M. Hetherington (Ed.), Coping with divorce, single parenting, and remarriage: A risk and resiliency perspective (pp. 227–252). Mahwah, NJ: Erlbaum.

DeGenova, M. K. (1992). If you had your life to live over again: What would you do differently? International Journal of Aging and Human Development, 34, 135–143.

Dejin-Karlsson, E., Hanson, B. S., Estergren, P.-O., Sjoeberg, N.-O., & Marsal, K. (1998). Does passive smoking in early pregnancy increase the risk of small-for-gestational-age infants? American Journal of Public Health, 88, 1523–1527.

Deković, M., & Gerris, J. R. M. (1994). Developmental analysis of social cognitive and behavioral differences between popular and rejected children. Journal of Applied Developmental Psychology, 15, 367–386.

Deković, M., & Meeus, W. (1997). Peer relations in adolescence: Effects of parenting and adolescents' self-concept. Journal of Adolescence, 20, 163–176.

Deković, M., Noom, M. J., & Meeus, W. (1997). Expectations regarding development during adolescence: Parent and adolescent perceptions. Journal of Youth and Adolescence, 26, 253–271.

De Lisi, R., & Gallagher, A. M. (1991). Understanding gender stability and constancy in Argentinean children. Merrill-Palmer Quarterly, 37, 483–502.

DeLoache, J. S., & Todd, C. M. (1988). Young children's use of spatial categorization as a mnemonic strategy. Journal of Experimental Child Psychology, 46, 1–20.

DeMarie-Dreblow, D. (1991). Relation between knowledge and memory: A reminder that correlation does not imply causality. Child Development, 62, 484–498.

Dembroski, T. M., MacDougall, J. M., Costa, P. T., & Grandits, G. A. (1989). Components of hostility as predictors of sudden death and myocardial infarction in the Multiple Risk Factor Intervention Trial. Psychosomatic Medicine, 51, 514–522.

Demetriou, A., Efklides, A., Papadaki, M., Papantoniou, G., & Economou, A. (1993). Structure and development of causal–experimental thought: From early adolescence to youth. Developmental Psychology, 29, 480–497.

Demetriou, A., Efklides, A., & Platsidou, M. (1993). The architecture and dynamics of developing mind. Monographs of the Society for Research in Child Development, 58(No. 5–6, Serial No. 234).

Demetriou, A., Pachaury, A., Metallidou, Y., & Kazi, S. (1996). Universals and specificities in the structure and development of quantitative-relational throught: A cross-cultural study in Greece and India. International Journal of Behavioral Development, 19, 255–290.

Dempster, F. N. (1993). Resistance to interference: Developmental changes in a basic processing mechanism. In M. L. Howe & R. Pasnak (Eds.), Emerging themes in cognitive development: Vol. 1 (pp. 3–27). New York: Springer-Verlag.

Dempster, F. N. (1995). Interference and inhibition in cognition: An historical perspective. In F. N. Dempster & C. J. Brainerd (Eds.), Interference and inhibition in cognition (pp. 3–26). San Diego: Academic Press.

Denckla, M. B. (1996). Biological correlates of learning and attention: What is relevant to learning disability and attention-deficit hyperactivity disorder? Developmental and Behavioral Pediatrics, 17, 114–119.

Denner, J., Cooper, C. R., Lopez, E. M., & Dunbar, N. (1999). Beyond "giving science away": How university–community partnerships inform youth programs, research, and policy. Social Policy Report of the Society for Research in Child Development, 13(1).

Dennerstein, L., Dudley, E., Hopper, J., & Burger, H. (1997). Sexuality, hormones and the menopausal transition. Maturitas, 26, 83–93.

Denney, N. W. (1990). Adult age differences in traditional and practical problem solving. Advances in Psychology, 72, 329–349.

Denney, N. W., & Pearce, K A. (1989). A developmental study of practical problem solving in adults. Psychology and Aging, 4, 438–442.

Dennis, W. (1960). Causes of retardation among institutionalized children: Iran. Journal of Genetic Psychology, 96, 47–59.

Dennison, E., Fall, C., Cooper, C., & Barker, D. (1997). Prenatal factors influencing long-term outcome. Hormone Research, 48(Suppl. 1), 25–29.

Denollet, J., Sys, S. U., Stroobant, N., Rombouts, H., Gillebert, T. C., & Brutsaert, D. L. (1996). Personality as independent predictor of long-term mortality in patients with coronary heart disease. Lancet, 347, 417–421.

de Rijk, A. E., Le Blance, P. M., Schaufeli, W. B., & de Jonge, J. (1998). Active coping and need for control as moderators of the job demand–control model: Effects on burnout. Journal of Occupational and Organizational Psychology, 7, 1–18.

Derom, C., Thiery, E., Vlietinck, R., Loos, R., & Derom, R. (1996). Handedness in twins according to zygosity and chorion type: A preliminary report. Behavior Genetics, 26, 407–408.

Deutsch, F. M., Ruble, D. N., Fleming, A., Brooks-Gunn, J., & Stangor, C. (1988).

Information-seeking and maternal self-definition during the transition to motherhood. *Journal of Personality and Social Psychology, 55,* 420–431.

Deutsch, W., & Pechmann, T. (1982). Social interaction and the development of definite descriptions. *Cognition, 11,* 159–184.

Deveson, A. (1994). *Coming of age: Twenty-one interviews about growing older.* Newham, Australia: Scribe.

de Villiers, J. G., & de Villiers, P. A. (1973). A cross-sectional study of the acquisition of grammatical morphemes in child speech. *Journal of Psycholinguistic Research, 2,* 267–278.

Devons, C. A. J. (1996). Suicide in the elderly: How to identify and treat patients at risk. *Geriatrics, 51*(3), 67–72.

de Vries, B., Bluck, S., & Birren, J. E. (1993). The understanding of death and dying in a life-span perspective. *Gerontologist, 33,* 366–372.

de Winter, M., Balleduz, M., & de Mare, J. (1997). A critical evaluation of Dutch preventive child health care. *Child: Care, Health and Development, 23,* 437–446.

De Wolff, M. S., & van IJzendoorn, M. H. (1997). Sensitivity and attachment: A meta-analysis on parental antecedents of infant attachment. *Child Development, 68,* 571–591.

Dewsbury, D. A. (1992). Comparative psychology and ethology: A reassessment. *American Psychologist, 47,* 208–215.

Diamond, A., Cruttenden, L., & Neiderman, D. (1994). AB with multiple wells: 1. Why are multiple wells sometimes easier than two wells? 2. Memory or memory + inhibition. *Developmental Psychology, 30,* 192–205.

Diamond, A., Prevor, M. B., Callender, G., & Druin, D. P. (1997). Prefrontal cortex cognitive deficits in children treated early and continuously for PKU. *Monographs of the Society for Research in Child Development, 62*(4, Serial No. 252).

Diamond, L. M. (1998). Development of sexual orientation among adolescent and young adult women. *Developmental Psychology, 34,* 1085–1095.

Diamond, M., & Hopson, J. (1999). *Magic trees of the mind.* New York: Plume.

Dickinson, D. K. (1984). First impressions: Children's knowledge of words gained from a single exposure. *Applied Psycholinguistics, 5,* 359–373.

Dick-Read, G. (1959). *Childbirth without fear.* New York: Harper & Row.

DiClemente, R. J. (1993). Preventing HIV/AIDS among adolescents. *Journal of the American Medical Association, 270,* 760–762.

Diehl, M., Coyle, N., & Labouvie-Vief, G. (1996). Age and sex differences in strategies of coping and defense across the life span. *Psychology and Aging, 11,* 127–139.

Diekstra, R. F. W., Kienhorst, C. W. M., & de Wilde, E. J. (1995). Suicide and suicidal behaviour among adolescents. In M. Rutter & D. J. Smith (Eds.), *Psychosocial disorders in young people* (pp. 686–761). Chichester: Wiley.

DiLalla, L. F., Kagan, J., & Reznick, J. S. (1994). Genetic etiology of behavioral inhibition among 2-year-old children. *Infant Behavior and Development, 17,* 405–412.

Dildy, G. A., Jackson, G. M., Fowers, G. K., Oshiro, B. T., Varner, M. W., & Clark, S. L. (1996). Very advanced maternal age. Pregnancy after age 45. *American Journal of Obstetrics and Gynecology, 175,* 668–674.

Diller, L. (1996). Use of growth hormone for non–growth hormone deficient children [letter]. *Journal of the American Medical Association, 276,* 1877–1878.

Dillon, P. A., & Emery, R. E. (1996). Divorce mediation and resolution of child custody disputes: Long-term effects. *American Journal of Orthopsychiatry, 66,* 131–140.

DiMatteo, M. R., & Kahn, K. L. (1997). Psychosocial aspects of childbirth. In S. J. Gallant, G. P. Keita, & R. Royak-Schaler (Eds.), *Health care for women: Psychological, social, and behavioral influences* (pp. 175–186). Washington, DC: American Psychological Association.

DiNitto, D. M. (1999). *Social welfare: Politics and public policy* (2nd ed.). Boston: Allyn and Bacon.

Dion, K. L., & Dion, K. K. (1993). Gender and ethnocultural comparisons in styles of love. *Journal of Social Issues, 49,* 53–69.

DiPietro, J. A., Hodgson, D. M., Costigan, K. A., & Hilton, S. C. (1996a). Fetal neurobehavioral development. *Child Development, 67,* 2553–2567.

DiPietro, J. A., Hodgson, D. M., Costigan, K. A., & Johnson, T. R. B. (1996b). Fetal antecedents of infant temperament. *Child Development, 67,* 2568–2583.

Diplock, A. T. (1997). Will the "good fairies" please prove to us that vitamin E lessens human degenerative disease? *Free Radical Research, 27,* 511–532.

Dirks, J. (1982). The effect of a commercial game on children's Block Design scores on the WISC–R test. *Intelligence, 6,* 109–123.

Dishion, T. J., Andrews, D. W., & Crosby, L. (1995). Antisocial boys and their friends in early adolescence: Relationship characteristics, quality, and interactional processes. *Child Development, 66,* 139–151.

Dixon, J. A., & Moore, C. F. (1990). The development of perspective taking: Understanding differences in information and weighting. *Child Development, 61,* 1502–1513.

Dixon, R. A., & Hultsch, D. F. (1999). Intelligence and cognitive potential in late life.

In J. C. Cavanaugh & S. K. Whitbourne (Eds.), *Gerontology: An interdisciplinary perspective* (pp. 213–237). New York: Oxford University Press.

Dixon, R. A., & Lerner, R. M. (1999). History and systems in developmental psychology. In M. H. Bornstein & M. E. Lamb (Eds.), *Developmental psychology: An advanced textbook* (4th ed., pp. 3–46). Mahwah, NJ: Erlbaum.

Dlugosz, L., & Bracken, M. B. (1992). Reproductive effects of caffeine: A review and theoretical analysis. *Epidemiological Review, 14,* 83–100.

Dodge, K. A., Pettit, G. S., & Bates, J. E. (1994). Socialization mediators of the relation between socioeconomic status and child conduct problems. *Child Development, 65,* 649–655.

Dodge, K. A., & Somberg, D. R. (1987). Hostile attributional biases among aggressive boys are exacerbated under conditions of threats to the self. *Child Development, 58,* 213–224.

Dodwell, P. C., Humphrey, G. K., & Muir, D. W. (1987). Shape and pattern perception. In P. Salapatek & L. Cohen (Eds.), *Handbook of infant perception* (Vol. 2, pp. 1–77). Orlando, FL: Academic Press.

Doi, M. (1991). A transformation of ritual: The Nisei 60th birthday. *Journal of Cross-Cultural Gerontology, 6,* 153–161.

Doka, K. J., & Mertz, M. E. (1988). The meaning and significance of great-grandparenthood. *Gerontologist, 28,* 192–197.

Donatelle, R. J., & Davis, L. G. (2000). *Health: The basics* (4th ed.). Boston: Allyn and Bacon.

Dondi, M., Simion, F., & Caltran, G. (1999). Can newborns discriminate between their own cry and the cry of another newborn infant? *Developmental Psychology, 35,* 418–426.

Donnerstein, E., & Linz, D. (1998). Mass media, sexual violence, and male viewers. In M. E. Odem & J. Clay-Warner (Eds.), *Confronting rape and sexual assault* (pp.181–198). Wilmington, DE: Scholarly Resources.

Donnerstein, E., Slaby, R. G., & Eron, L. D. (1994). The mass media and youth aggression. In L. D. Eron, J. H. Gentry, & P. Schlegel (Eds.), *Reason to hope: A psychosocial perspective on violence and youth* (pp. 219–250). Washington, DC: American Psychological Association.

Dorfman, L. T., Heckert, D. A., Hill, E. A., & Kohout, F. J. (1988). Retirement satisfaction in rural husbands and wives. *Rural Sociology, 53,* 25–39.

Dornbusch, S. M., Glasgow, K. L., & Lin, I.-C. (1996). The social structure of schooling. *Annual Review of Psychology, 47,* 401–429.

Dornbusch, S. M., Ritter, P. L., Liederman, P. H., Roberts, D. F., & Fraleigh, M. J.

(1987). The relation of parenting style to adolescent school performance. *Child Development, 58,* 1244–1257.

Dornbusch, S. M., Ritter, P. L., Mont-Reynaud, R., & Chen, Z. (1990). Family decision making and academic performance in a diverse high school population. *Journal of Adolescent Research, 5,* 143–160.

Dorris, M. (1989). *The broken cord.* New York: Harper & Row.

Doty, P. J. (1992). The oldest old and the use of institutional long-term care from an international perspective. In R. M. Suzman, D. P. Willis, & K. G. Manton (Eds.), *The oldest old* (pp. 251–267). New York: Oxford University Press.

Downey, D. B. (1995). When bigger is not better: Family size, parental resources, and children's educational performance. *American Sociological Review, 60,* 746–761.

Downs, A. C., & Fuller, M. J. (1991). Recollections of spermarche: An exploratory investigation. *Current Psychology: Research and Reviews, 10,* 93–102.

Doyle, C. (1994). *Child sexual abuse.* London: Chapman & Hall.

Drabman, R. S., Cordua, G. D., Hammer, D., Jarvie, G. J., & Horton, W. (1979). Developmental trends in eating rates of normal and overweight preschool children. *Child Development, 50,* 211–216.

Drachman, D. A. (1997). Aging and the brain: A new frontier. *Annals of Neurology, 42,* 819–828.

Drotar, D., Pallotta, J., & Eckerle, D. (1994). A prospective study of family environments of children hospitalized for non-organic failure-to-thrive. *Developmental and Behavioral Pediatrics, 15,* 78–85.

DuBois, D. L., & Hirsch, B. J. (1990). School and neighborhood friendship patterns of blacks and whites in early adolescence. *Child Development, 61,* 524–536.

Dubow, E. F., & Miller, L. S. (1996). Television violence viewing and aggressive behavior. In T. M. MacBeth (Ed.), *Tuning into young viewers* (pp. 117–147). Thousand Oaks, CA: Sage.

Duck, S. (1994). *Meaningful relationships.* Thousand Oaks, CA: Sage.

Dugan, E., & Kivett, V. R. (1998). Implementing the Adams and Blieszner conceptual model: Predicting interactive friendship processes of older adults. *Journal of Social and Personal Relationships, 15,* 607–622.

Duncan, G. J., Brooks-Gunn, J., & Klebanov, P. K. (1994). Economic deprivation and early childhood development. *Child Development, 65,* 296–318.

Dunham, P. J., & Dunham, F. (1996). The semantically reciprocating robot: Adult influences on children's early conversational skills. *Social Development, 5,* 261–274.

Dunham, P. J., Dunham, F., & Curwin, A. (1993). Joint-attentional states and lexical acquisition at 18 months. *Developmental Psychology, 29,* 827–831.

Duniz, M., Scheer, P. J., Trojovsky, A., Kaschnitz, W., Kvas, E., & Macari, S. (1996). *European Child and Adolescent Psychiatry, 5,* 93–100.

Dunn, J. (1989). Siblings and the development of social understanding in early childhood. In P. G. Zukow (Ed.), *Sibling interaction across cultures* (pp. 106–116). New York: Springer-Verlag.

Dunn, J. (1992). Sisters and brothers: Current issues in developmental research. In F. Boer & J. Dunn (Eds.), *Children's sibling relationships* (pp. 1–17). Hillsdale, NJ: Erlbaum.

Dunn, J. (1994). Temperament, siblings, and the development of relationships. In W. B. Carey & S. C. McDevitt (Eds.), *Prevention and early intervention* (pp. 50–58). New York: Brunner/Mazel.

Dunn, J. (1996). Sibling relationships and perceived self-competence: Patterns of stability between childhood and early adolescence. In A. J. Sameroff & M. M. Haith (Eds.), *The five to seven year shift* (pp. 253–270). Chicago: University of Chicago Press.

Dunn, J., Slomkowski, C., & Beardsall, L. (1994). Sibling relationships from the preschool period through middle childhood and early adolescence. *Developmental Psychology, 30,* 315–324.

Durbin, D. L., Darling, N., Steinberg, L., & Brown, B. B. (1993). Parenting style and peer group membership among European-American adolescents. *Journal of Research on Adolescence, 3,* 87–100.

Durlak, J. A., & Riesenberg, L. A. (1991). The impact of death education. *Death Studies, 15,* 39–58.

Dusek, J. B. (1987). Sex roles and adjustment. In D. B. Carter (Ed.), *Current conceptions of sex roles and sex typing* (pp. 211–222). New York: Praeger.

Duvall, E. M. (1977). *Marriage and family development* (5th ed.). New York: Harper & Row.

Duxbury, L., & Higgins, C. (1994). Interference between work and family: A status report on dual-career and dual-earner mothers and fathers. *Employee Assistance Quarterly, 9,* 55–80.

Dworkin, R. (1997, September 25). Assisted suicide: What the court really said. *New York Review of Books,* pp. 40–44.

Dwyer, T., Ponsonby, A. L., & Couper, D. (1999). Tobacco smoke exposure at one month of age and subsequent risk of SIDS: A prospective study. *American Journal of Epidemiology, 149,* 593–602.

Dybing, E., & Sanner, T. (1999). Passive smoking, sudden infant death syndrome (SIDS), and childhood infections. *Human Experimental Toxicology, 18,* 202–205.

Dye-White, E. (1986). Environmental hazards in the work setting: Their effect on women of child-bearing age. *American Association of Occupational Health and Nursing Journal, 34,* 76–78.

Dykstra, P. A. (1995). Loneliness among the never and formerly married: The importance of supportive friendships and a desire for independence. *Journal of Gerontology, 50B,* S321–S329.

Eades, M. D. (1992). *Arthritis: Reducing your risk.* New York: Bantam.

Eagly, A. H. (1999, May). *Few women at the top: Is prejudice a cause?* Paper presented at the annual meeting of the Midwest Psychological Association, Chicago.

Eagly, A. H., & Wood, W. (1999). The origins of sex differences in human behavior: Evolved dispositions versus social roles. *American Psychologist, 54,* 408–423.

East, P. L., & Felice, M. E. (1996). *Adolescent pregnancy and parenting: Findings from a racially diverse sample.* Mahwah, NJ: Erlbaum.

Ebeling, K. S., & Gelman, S. A. (1994). Children's use of context in interpreting "big" and "little." *Child Development, 65,* 1178–1192.

Eberhart-Phillips, J. E., Frederick, P. D., & Baron, R. C. (1993). Measles in pregnancy: A descriptive study of 58 cases. *Obstetrics and Gynecology, 82,* 797–801.

Eccles, J. S. (1994). Understanding women's educational and occupational choices: Applying the Eccles et al. model of achievement-related choices. *Psychology of Women Quarterly, 18,* 585–609.

Eccles, J. S., Early, D., Frasier, K., Belansky, E., & McCarthy, K. (1997). The relation of connection, regulation, and support for autonomy to adolescents' functioning. *Journal of Adolescent Research, 12,* 263–286.

Eccles, J. S., & Harold, R. D. (1991). Gender differences in sport involvement: Applying the Eccles' expectancy-value model. *Journal of Applied Sport Psychology, 3,* 7–35.

Eccles, J. S., & Harold, R. D. (1993). Parent–school involvement during the early adolescent years. *Teachers College Record, 94,* 568–587.

Eccles, J. S., & Harold, R. D. (1996). Family involvement in children's and adolescents' schooling. In A. Booth & J. F. Dunn (Eds.), *Family–school links: How do they affect educational outcomes?* (pp. 3–34). Mahwah, NJ: Erlbaum.

Eccles, J. S., Jacobs, J. E., & Harold, R. D. (1990). Gender-role stereotypes, expectancy effects, and parents' role in the socialization of gender differences in self-perceptions and skill acquisition. *Journal of Social Issues, 46,* 183–201.

Eccles, J. S., Lord, S., & Buchanan, C. M. (1996). School transitions in early adolescence: What are we doing to our young people? In J. A. Graber, J. Brooks-Gunn, & A. C. Petersen (Eds.), *Transitions through adolescence* (pp. 251–284). Mahwah, NJ: Erlbaum.

Eccles, J. S., Midgley, C., Wigfield, A., Buchanan, C. M., Reuman, D., Flanagan, C., & MacIver, D. (1993a). Development during adolescence: The impact of stage–environment fit on young adolescents' experiences in schools and in families. *American Psychologist, 48,* 90–101.

Eccles, J. S., Wigfield, A., Harold, R., & Blumenfeld, P. B. (1993c). Age and gender differences in children's self- and task perceptions during elementary school. *Child Development, 64,* 830–847.

Eccles, J. S., Wigfield, A., Midgley, C., Reuman, D., MacIver, D., & Feldlaufer, H. (1993b). Negative effects of traditional middle schools on students' motivation. *Elementary School Journal, 93,* 553–574.

Eccles, J. S., Wigfield, A., & Schiefele, U. (1998). Motivation to succeed. In N. Eisenberg (Ed.), *Handbook of child psychology: Vol. 3. Social, emotional, and personality development* (5th ed., pp. 1017–1095). New York: Wiley.

Eckenrode, J., Laird, M., & Doris, J. (1993). School performance and disciplinary problems among abused and neglected children. *Developmental Psychology, 29,* 53–62.

Edelstein, B. L., & Douglass, C. W. (1995). Dispelling the myth that 50 percent of U.S. schoolchildren have never had a cavity. *Public Health Reports, 110,* 522–530.

Eder, R. A. (1989). The emergent personologist: The structure and content of 3½, 5½, and 7½-year-olds' concepts of themselves and other persons. *Child Development, 60,* 1218–1228.

Edland, S. D., Graves, A. B., McCormick, W. C., & Larson, E. B. (1999). Estimation and sample design in prevalence surveys of dementia. *Journal of Clinical Epidemiology, 52,* 399–403.

Edwards, J. N., & Booth, A. (1994). Sexuality, marriage, and well-being: The middle years. In A. S. Rossi (Ed.), *Sexuality across the life course* (pp. 233–259). Chicago: University of Chicago Press.

Edwards, M., Cangemi, J. P., & Kowalski, C. J. (1990). The college dropout and institutional responsibility. *Education, 111,* 107–116.

Edwards, W. J. (1996). A sociological analysis of an invisible minority group: Male adolescent homosexuals. *Youth and Society, 27,* 334–353.

Egeland, B., & Hiester, M. (1995). The long-term consequences of infant day-care and mother–infant attachment. *Child Development, 66,* 474–485.

Egeland, B., Jacobvitz, D., & Sroufe, L. A. (1988). Breaking the cycle of abuse. *Child Development, 59,* 1080–1088.

Eggebeen, D. J. (1992). Parent–child support in aging American families. *Generations, 16*(3), 45–49.

Eggerman, S., & Dustin, D. (1985). Death orientation and communication with the terminally ill. *Omega, 16,* 255–265.

Eiben, B., Hammans, W., Hansen, S., Trawicki, W., Osthelder, B., Stelzer, A., Jaspers, K.-D., & Goebel, R. (1997). On the complication risk of early amniocentesis versus standard amniocentesis. *Fetal Diagnosis and Therapy, 12,* 140–144.

Eiden, R. D., & Reifman, A. (1996). Effects of Brazelton demonstrations on later parenting: A meta-analysis. *Journal of Pediatric Psychology, 21,* 857–868.

Eilers, R. E., & Oller, D. K. (1994). Infant vocalizations and the early diagnosis of severe hearing impairment. *Journal of Pediatrics, 124,* 199–203.

Einstein, G. O., Holland, L. J., McDaniel, M. A., & Guynn, M. J. (1992). Age-related deficits in prospective memory: The influence of task complexity. *Psychology and Aging, 7,* 471–478.

Einstein, G. O., McDaniel, M. A., Richardson, S. L., & Guynn, M. J. (1995). Aging and prospective memory: Examining the influences of self-initiated retrieval processes. *Journal of Experimental Psychology: Learning, Memory, and Cognition, 21,* 996–1007.

Einstein, G. O., Smith, R. E., McDaniel, M. A., & Shaw, P. (1997). Aging and prospective memory: The influence of increased task demands at encoding and retrieval. *Psychology and Aging, 12,* 479–488.

Eisenberg, N. (1998). Introduction. In N. Eisenberg (Ed.), *Handbook of child psychology: Vol. 3. Social, emotional, and personality development* (5th ed., pp. 1–24). New York: Wiley.

Eisenberg, N., & Fabes, R. A. (1998). Prosocial development. In N. Eisenberg (Ed.), *Handbook of child psychology: Vol. 3. Social, emotional, and personality development* (5th ed., pp. 701–778). New York: Wiley.

Eisenberg, N., Fabes, R. A., Carlo, G., & Karbon, M. (1992). Emotional responsivity to others: Behavioral correlates and socialization antecedents. In N. Eisenberg & R. A. Fabes (Eds.), *New directions in child development* (No. 55, pp. 57–73). San Francisco: Jossey-Bass.

Eisenberg, N., Fabes, R. A., Carlo, G., Speer, A. L., Switzer, G., Karbon, M., & Troyer, D. (1993). The relations of empathy-related emotions and maternal practices to children's comforting behavior. *Journal of Experimental Child Psychology, 55,* 131–150.

Eisenberg, N., Fabes, R. A., & Losoya, S. (1997). Emotional responding: Regulation, social correlates, and socialization. In P. Alovey & D. J. Sluyter (Eds.),

Emotional development and emotional intelligence (pp. 129–162). New York: Basic Books.

Eisenberg, N., Fabes, R. A., Murphy, B., Karbon, M., Smith, M., & Maszk, P. (1996). The relations of children's dispositional empathy-related responding to their emotionality, regulation, and social functioning. *Developmental Psychology, 32,* 195–209.

Eisenberg, N., Fabes, R. A., Murphy, B., Maszk, P., Smith, M., & Karbon, M. (1995). The role of emotionality and regulation in children's social functioning: A longitudinal study. *Child Development, 66,* 1360–1384.

Eisenberg, N., Fabes, R. A., Shepard, S. A., Murphy, B. C., Guthrie, I. K., Jones, S., Friedman, J., Poulin, R., & Maszk, P. (1997a). Contemporaneous and longitudinal prediction of children's social functioning from regulation and emotionality. *Child Development, 68,* 642–664.

Eisenberg, N., Fabes, R. A., Shepard, S. A., Murphy, B. C., Jones, S., & Guthrie, I. K. (1998). Contemporaneous and longitudinal prediction of children's sympathy from dispositional regulation and emotionality. *Developmental Psychology, 34,* 910–924.

Eisenberg, N., Guthrie, I. K., Fabes, R. A., Reiser, M., Murphy, B. C., Holgren, R., Maszk, R., & Losoya, S. (1997b). The relations of regulation and emotionality to resiliency and competent social functioning in elementary school children. *Child Development, 68,* 295–311.

Eisenberg, N., & McNally, S. (1993). Socialization and mothers' and adolescents' empathy-related characteristics. *Journal of Research on Adolescence, 3,* 171–191.

Ekman, P., & Friesen, W. (1972). Constants across culture in the face of emotion. *Journal of Personality and Social Psychology, 17,* 124–129.

Elardo, R., & Bradley, R. H. (1981). The Home Observation for Measurement of the Environment (HOME) Scale: A review of research. *Developmental Review, 1,* 113–145.

Elder, G., Jr. (1998). The life course and human development. In R. M. Lerner (Ed.), *Handbook of child psychology: Vol. 1. Theoretical models of human development* (5th ed., pp. 939–991). New York: Wiley.

Elder, G. H., Jr. (1974). *Children of the Great Depression.* Chicago: University of Chicago Press.

Elder, G. H., Jr., & Hareven, T. K. (1993). Rising above life's disadvantage: From the Great Depression to war. In G. H. Elder, Jr., J. Modell, & R. D. Parke (Eds.), *Children in time and place* (pp. 47–72). Cambridge, UK: Cambridge University Press.

Elder, G. H., Jr., Liker, J. K., & Cross, C. E. (1984). Parent–child behavior in the

Great Depression: Life course and intergenerational influences. In P. B. Baltes & O. G. Brim (Eds.), *Life-span development and behavior* (Vol. 6, pp. 109–158). New York: Academic Press.

Elder, G. H., Jr., Van Nguyen, T., & Caspi, A. (1985). Linking family hardship to children's lives. *Child Development, 56,* 361–375.

Elicker, J., Englund, M., & Sroufe, L. A. (1992). Predicting peer competence and peer relationships in childhood from early parent–child relationships. In R. D. Parke & G. W. Ladd (Eds.), *Family– peer relationships: Modes of linkage* (pp. 77–106). Hillsdale, NJ: Erlbaum.

Elkind, D. (1994). *A sympathetic understanding of the child: Birth to sixteen* (3rd ed.). Boston: Allyn & Bacon.

Elkind, D., & Bowen, R. (1979). Imaginary audience behavior in children and adolescents. *Developmental Psychology, 15,* 33–44.

Elkind, M. S., & Sacco, R. L. (1998). Stroke risk factors and stroke prevention. *Seminars in Neurology, 18,* 429–440.

Ellicott, A. M. (1985). Psychosocial changes as a function of family-cycle phase. *Human Development, 28,* 270–274.

Elliott, D. S. (1994). Serious violent offenders: Onset, developmental course, and termination. *Criminology, 32,* 1–21.

Elliott, D. S., Wilson, W. J., Huizinga, D., Sampson, R. J., Elliott, A., & Rankin, B. (1996). The effects of neighborhood disadvantage on adolescent development. *Journal of Research in Crime and Delinquency, 33,* 389–426.

Elliott, E. S., & Dweck, C. S. (1988). Goals: An approach to motivation and achievement. *Journal of Personality and Social Psychology, 54,* 5–12.

Ellis, A. L., & Vasseur, R. B. (1993). Prior interpersonal contact with and attitudes toward gays and lesbians in an interviewing context. *Journal of Homosexuality, 25,* 31–45.

Elman, J. L., Bates, E. A., Johnson, M. H., Karmiloff-Smith, A., Parisi, D., & Plunkett, K. (1996). *Rethinking innateness: A connectionist perspective on development.* Cambridge, MA: MIT Press.

Else, L., Wonderlich, S. A., Beatty, W. W., Christie, D. W., & Staton, R. D. (1993). Personality characteristics of men who physically abuse women. *Hospital and Community Psychiatry, 44,* 54–58.

Emde, R. N. (1992). Individual meaning and increasing complexity: Contributions of Sigmund Freud and René Spitz to developmental psychology. *Developmental Psychology, 28,* 347–359.

Emde, R. N., Plomin, R., Robinson, J., Corley, R., DeFries, J., Fulker, D. W., Reznick, J. S., Campos, J., Kagan, J., & Zahn-Waxler, C. (1992). Temperament, emotion, and cognition at fourteen months: The MacArthur Longitudinal Twin Study. *Child Development, 63,* 1437–1455.

Emery, R. E., & Laumann-Billings, L. (1998). An overview of the nature, causes, and consequences of abusive family relationships: Toward differentiating maltreatment and violence. *American Psychologist, 53,* 121–135.

Emory, E. K., Schlackman, L. J., & Fiano, K. (1996). Drug–hormone interactions on neurobehavioral responses in human neonates. *Infant Behavior and Development, 19,* 213–220.

Emory, E. K., & Toomey, K. A. (1988). Environmental stimulation and human fetal responsibility in late pregnancy. In W. P. Smotherman & S. R. Robinson (Eds.), *Behavior of the fetus* (pp. 141–161). Caldwell, NJ: Telford.

Engen, T. (1982). *The perception of odors.* New York: Academic Press.

Englert, M. D., & Linden, M. D. (1998). Differences in self-reported sleep complaints in elderly persons living in the community who do or do not take sleep medication. *Journal of Clinical Psychiatry, 59,* 137–144.

Enright, R. D., Gassin, E. A., & Wu, C. (1992). Forgiveness: A developmental view. *Journal of Moral Education, 21,* 99–114.

Enright, R. D., Lapsley, D. K., & Shukla, D. (1979). Adolescent egocentrism in early and late adolescence. *Adolescence, 14,* 687–695.

Epstein, L. H., McCurley, J., Wing, R. R., & Valoski, A. (1990). Five-year follow-up of family-based treatments for childhood obesity. *Journal of Consulting and Clinical Psychology, 58,* 661–664.

Epstein, L. H., McKenzie, S. J., Valoski, A., Klein, K. R., & Wing, R. R. (1994). Effects of mastery criteria and contingent reinforcement for family-based child weight control. *Addictive Behaviors, 19,* 135–145.

Epstein, L. H., Saelens, B. E., Myers, M. D., & Vito, D. (1997). Effects of decreasing sedentary behaviors on activity choice in obese children. *Health Psychology, 16,* 107–113.

Epstein, L. H., Saelens, B. E., & O'Brien, J. G. (1995). Effects of reinforcing increases in active versus decreases in sedentary behavior for obese children. *International Journal of Behavioral Medicine, 2,* 41–50.

Erel, O., & Burman, B. (1995). Interrelatedness of marital relation and parent–child relations: A meta-analytic review. *Psychological Bulletin, 118,* 108–132.

Ericsson, K. A. (1990). Peak performance and age: An examination of peak performance in sports. In P. B. Baltes & M. M. Baltes (Eds.), *Successful aging* (pp. 164–196). Cambridge: Cambridge University Press.

Erikson, E. H. (1950). *Childhood and society.* New York: Norton.

Erikson, E. H. (1964). *Insight and responsibility.* New York: Norton.

Erikson, E. H. (1968). *Identity, youth, and crisis.* New York: Norton.

Eskenazi, B. (1993). Caffeine during pregnancy: Grounds for concern? *Journal of the American Medical Association, 270,* 2973–2974.

Espy, K. A., Kaufmann, P. M., & Glisky, M. L. (1999). Neuropsychological function in toddlers exposed to cocaine in utero: A preliminary study. *Developmental Neurospsychology, 15,* 447–460.

Essa, E. L., & Murray, C. I. (1994). Young children's understanding and experience with death. *Young Children, 49*(4), 74–81.

Esterberg, K. G., Moen, P., & Dempster-McClain, D. (1994). Transition to divorce: A life-course approach to women's marital duration and dissolution. *Sociological Quarterly, 35,* 289–307.

Evans, G. W., Maxwell, L. E., & Hart, B. (1999). Parental language and verbal responsiveness to children in crowded homes. *Developmental Psychology, 35,* 1020–1023.

Eveleth, P. B., & Tanner, J. M. (1976). *Worldwide variation in human growth.* Cambridge, England: Cambridge University Press.

Fabes, R. A., Eisenberg, N., McCormick, S. E., & Wilson, M. S. (1988). Preschoolers' attributions of the situational determinants of others' naturally occurring emotions. *Developmental Psychology, 24,* 376–385.

Fabsitz, R. R., Sholinsky, P., & Carmelli, D. (1994). Genetic influences on adult weight gain and maximum body mass index in male twins. *American Journal of Epidemiology, 140,* 711–720.

Fagan, J. F., III. (1973). Infants' delayed recognition memory and forgetting. *Journal of Experimental Child Psychology, 16,* 424–450.

Fagan, J. F., III, & Singer, L. T. (1979). The role of simple feature differences in infants' recognition of faces. *Infant Behavior and Development, 2,* 39–45.

Fagard, J., & Pezé, A. (1997). Age changes in interlimb coupling and the development of bimanual coordination. *Journal of Motor Behavior, 29,* 199–208.

Fagot, B. I. (1984). The child's expectations of differences in adult male and female interactions. *Sex Roles, 11,* 593–600.

Fagot, B. I., & Hagan, R. I. (1991). Observations of parent reactions to sex-stereotyped behaviors: Age and sex effects. *Child Development, 62,* 617–628.

Fagot, B. I., & Leinbach, M. D. (1989). The young child's gender schema: Environmental input, internal organization. *Child Development, 60,* 663–672.

Fagot, B. I., Leinbach, M. D., & O'Boyle, C. (1992). Gender labeling, gender stereotyping, and parenting behaviors. *Developmental Psychology, 28,* 225–230.

Fagot, B. I., Pears, K. C., Apaldi, D. M., Crosby, L., & Lee, C. S. (1998). Becoming an adolescent father: Precursors and parenting. *Developmental Psychology, 34,* 1209–1219.

Fahrmeier, E. D. (1978). The development of concrete operations among the Hausa. *Journal of Cross-Cultural Psychology, 9,* 23–44.

Fairburn, C. G., & Belgin, S. J. (1990). Studies of the epidemiology of bulimia nervosa. *American Journal of Psychiatry, 147,* 401–408.

Fairburn, C. G., Doll, H. A., Welch, S. L., Hay, P. J., Davies, B. A., & O'Connor, M. E. (1998). Risk factors for binge eating disorder. *Archives of General Psychiatry, 55,* 425–432.

Falbo, T. (1992). Social norms and the one-child family: Clinical and policy implications. In F. Boer & J. Dunn (Eds.), *Children's sibling relationships* (pp. 71–82). Hillsdale, NJ: Erlbaum.

Falbo, T., & Polit, D. (1986). A quantitative review of the only-child literature: Research evidence and theory development. *Psychological Bulletin, 100,* 176–189.

Falbo, T., & Poston, D. L., Jr. (1993). The academic, personality, and physical outcomes of only children in China. *Child Development, 64,* 18–35.

Falbo, T., Poston, D. L., Jr., Triscari, R. S., & Zhang, X. (1997). Self-enhancing illusions among Chinese schoolchildren. *Journal of Cross-Cultural Psychology, 28,* 172–191.

Fall, C. H., Stein, C. E., Kumaran, K., Cox, V., Osmond, C., Barker, D. J., & Hales, C. N. (1998). Size at birth, maternal weight, and type 2 diabetes in South India. *Diabetic Medicine, 15,* 220–227.

Faller, K. C. (1990). *Understanding child sexual maltreatment.* Newbury Park, CA: Sage.

Fallick, B. C. (1996). A review of the recent literature on displaced workers. *Industrial and Labor Relations Review, 50,* 5–16.

Fanslow, C. A. (1981). Death: A natural facet of the life continuum. In D. Krieger (Ed.), *Foundations for holistic health nursing practices: The renaissance nurse* (pp. 249–272). Philadelphia: Lippincott.

Fantz, R. L. (1961, May). The origin of form perception. *Scientific American, 204* (5), 66–72.

Farkas, J., & Hogan, D. (1994). The demography of changing intergenerational relationships. In V. L. Bengtson, K. W. Schaie, & L. M. Burton (Eds.), *Adult intergenerational relations: Effects of societal change* (pp. 1–19). New York: Springer.

Farmer, H. S. (1997). Future directions for research on women's career development. In H. S. Farmer (Ed.), *Diversity and women's career development*

(pp. 293–306). Thousand Oaks, CA: Sage.

Farrington, D. P. (1987). Epidemiology. In H. C. Quay (Ed.), *Handbook of juvenile delinquency* (pp. 33–61). New York: Wiley.

Farver, J. M. (1993). Cultural differences in scaffolding pretend play: A comparison of American and Mexican mother–child and sibling–child pairs. In K. MacDonald (Ed.), *Parent–child play* (pp. 349–366). Albany, NY: SUNY Press.

Farver, J. M., & Branstetter, W. H. (1994). Preschoolers' prosocial responses to their peers' distress. *Developmental Psychology, 30,* 334–341.

Farver, J. M., Kim, Y. K., & Lee, Y. (1995). Cultural differences in Korean- and Anglo-American preschoolers' social interaction and play behaviors. *Child Development, 66,* 1088–1099.

Farver, J., & Wimbarti, S. (1995). Indonesian toddlers' social play with their mothers and older siblings. *Child Development, 66,* 1493–1503.

Featherman, D. (1980). Schooling and occupational careers: Constancy and change in worldly success. In O. Brim, Jr., & J. Kagan (Eds.), *Constancy and change in human development* (pp. 675–738). Cambridge, MA: Harvard University Press.

Feeney, J. A. (1994). Attachment style, communication patterns, and satisfaction across the life cycle of marriage. *Personal Relationships, 1,* 333–348.

Feeney, J. A. (1998). Adult attachment and relationship-centered anxiety: Responses to physical and emotional distancing. In J. A. Simpson & W. S. Rholes (Eds.), *Attachment theory and close relationships* (pp. 189–218). New York: Guilford.

Feeney, J. A. (1999). Adult romantic attachment and couple relationships. In J. Cassidy & P. R. Shaver (Eds.), *Handbook of attachment* (pp. 355–377). New York: Guilford.

Fehr, B. (1994). Prototype based assessment of laypeoples' views of love. *Personal Relationships, 1,* 309–331.

Fein, G. G., Gariboldi, A., & Boni, R. (1993). The adjustment of infants and toddlers to group care: The first six months. *Early Childhood Research Quarterly, 8,* 1–14.

Feingold, A. (1992). Gender differences in mate selection preferences: A test of the parental investment model. *Psychological Bulletin, 112,* 125–139.

Feingold, A. (1994). Gender differences in personality: A meta-analysis. *Psychological Bulletin, 116,* 429–456.

Feinleib, J. A., & Michael, R. T. (1998). Reported changes in sexual behavior in response to AIDS in the United States. *Preventive Medicine, 27,* 400–411.

Feiring, C., & Taska, L. S. (1996). Family self-concept: Ideas on its meaning. In B. Bracken (Ed.), *Handbook of*

self-concept (pp. 317–373). New York: Wiley.

Feldman, D. H. (1991). *Nature's gambit.* New York: Teachers College Press.

Feldman, D. H., & Goldsmith, L. T. (1991). *Nature's gambit.* New York: Teachers College Press.

Feldman, S. S., & Weinberger, D. A. (1994). Self-restraint as a mediator of family influences on boys' delinquent behavior: A longitudinal study. *Child Development, 65,* 195–211.

Felner, R. D., & Adan, A. M. (1988). The School Transitional Environment Project: An ecological intervention and evaluation. In R. H. Price, E. L. Cowan, R. P. Lorion, & J. Ramos-McKay (Eds.), *14 ounces of prevention: A casebook for practitioners* (pp. 111–122). Washington, DC: American Psychological Association.

Fendrich, J. M. (1993). *Ideal citizens: The legacy of the civil rights movement.* Albany: State University of New York Press.

Fenson, L., Dale, P. S., Reznick, J. S., Bates, E., Thal, D. J., & Pethick, S. J. (1994). Variability in early communicative development. *Monographs of the Society for Research in Child Development, 59*(5, Serial No. 242).

Fergus, M. A. (1995, March 19). 99 years and . . . a joy to be around. *The Pantagraph,* pp. C1–C2.

Ferguson, F. G., Wikby, A., Maxson, P., Olsson, J., & Johansson, B. (1995). Immune parameters in a longitudinal study of a very old population of Swedish people: A comparison between survivors and nonsurvivors. *Journal of Gerontology, 50,* B378–B382.

Ferguson, T. J., Stegge, H., & Damhuis, I. (1991). Children's understanding of guilt and shame. *Child Development, 62,* 827–839.

Ferguson, T. J., Stegge, H., Miller, E. R., & Olsen, M. E. (1999). Guilt, shame, and symptoms in children. *Developmental Psychology, 35,* 347–357.

Fergusson, D. M., Horwood, L. J., & Lynskey, M. T. (1993). Maternal smoking before and after pregnancy: Effects on behavioral outcomes in middle childhood. *Pediatrics, 92,* 815–822.

Fergusson, D. M., & Woodward, L. J. (1999). Breast-feeding and later psychosocial adjustment. *Paediatric and Perinatal Epidemiology, 13,* 144–157.

Fernald, A., & Morikawa, H. (1993). Common themes and cultural variations in Japanese and American mothers' speech to infants. *Child Development, 64,* 637–656.

Fernald, A., Taeschner, T., Dunn, J., Papousek, M., Boyssen-Bardies, B., & Fukui, I. (1989). A cross-language study of prosodic modifications in mothers' and fathers' speech to preverbal infants. *Journal of Child Language, 16,* 477–502.

Feshbach, N. D., & Feshbach, S. (1982). Empathy training and the regulation of aggression: Potentialities and limitations. *Academic Psychology Bulletin, 4,* 399–413.

Fiatarone, M. A., Marks, E. C., Meredith, C. N., Lipsitz, L. A., & Evans, W. J. (1990). High intensity strength training in nonagenarians: Effects on skeletal muscle. *Journal of the American Medical Association, 263,* 3029–3034.

Fichter, M. M., & Quadflieg, N. (1996). Course and two-year outcome in anorexic and bulimic adolescents. *Journal of Youth and Adolescence, 25,* 545–562.

Field, D. (1997). "Looking back, what period of your life brought you the most satisfaction?" *International Journal of Aging and Human Development, 45,* 169–194.

Field, D. (1999). Stability of older women's friendships: A commentary on Roberto. *International Journal of Aging and Human Development, 48,* 81–83.

Field, D., & Millsap, R. E. (1991). Personality in advanced old age: Continuity or change? *Journal of Gerontology, 46,* 299–308.

Field, D., & Minkler, M. (1988). Continuity and change in social support between young–old, old–old, and very-old adults. *Journal of Gerontology, 43,* P100–P106.

Field, T. M. (1994). The effects of mother's physical and emotional unavailability on emotion regulation. In N. A. Fox (Ed.), The development of emotion regulation: Biological and behavioral considerations. *Monographs of the Society for Research in Child Development, 59*(2–3, Serial No. 240).

Field, T. M. (1998). Massage therapy effects. *American Psychologist, 53,* 1270–1281.

Field, T. M., Schanberg, S. M., Scafidi, F., Bauer, C. R., Vega-Lahr, N., Garcia, R. Nystrom, J., & Kuhn, C. M. (1986). Effects of tactile/kinesthetic stimulation on preterm neonates. *Pediatrics, 77,* 654–658.

Field, T. M., Woodson, R., Greenberg, R., & Cohen, D. (1982). Discrimination and imitation of facial expressions by neonates. *Science, 218,* 179–181.

Fiese, B. (1990). Playful relationships: A contextual analysis of mother-toddler interaction and symbolic play. *Child Development, 61,* 1648–1656.

Filene, P. G. (1998). *In the arms of others: A cultural history of the right-to-die in America.* New York: Ivan R. Dee.

Filipovic, Z. (1994). *Zlata's diary: A child's life in Sarajevo.* New York: Penguin.

Fine, G. A. (1980). The natural history of preadolescent male friendship groups. In H. C. Foot, A. J. Chapman, & J. R. Smith (Eds.), *Friendship and social relations in children* (pp. 293–320). Chichester, England: Wiley.

Finegan, J. K., Niccols, G. A., & Sitarenios, G. (1992). Relations between prenatal testosterone levels and cognitive abilities at 4 years. *Developmental Psychology, 28,* 1075–1089.

Fingerman, K. L. (1998). The good, the bad, and the worrisome: Emotional complexities in grandparents' experiences with individual grandchildren. *Family Relations, 47,* 403–414.

Finkbeiner, A. K. (1996). *After the death of a child: Living with loss through the years.* New York: Free Press.

Firestone, R. W. (1994). Psychological defenses against death anxiety. In R. A. Neimeyer (Ed.), *Death anxiety handbook* (pp. 217–241). Washington, DC: Taylor & Francis.

Fisch, S. M., Truglio, R. T., & Cole, C. F. (1999). The impact of *Sesame Street* on preschool children: A review and synthesis of 30 years' research. *Media Psychology, 1,* 165–190.

Fischer, C. S., & Phillips, S. L. (1982). Who is alone? Social characteristics of people with small networks. In L. A. Peplau & D. Perlman (Eds.), *Loneliness: A sourcebook of current theory, research, and therapy* (pp. 21–39). New York: Wiley.

Fischer, J. L., & Narus, L. R. (1981). Sex roles and intimacy in same sex and other sex relationships. *Psychology of Women Quarterly, 5,* 444–455.

Fischer, K. M. (1996). Genes for Praeder-Willi syndrome/Angelman syndrome and fragile X syndrome are homologous, with genetic imprinting and unstable trinucleotide repeats causing mental retardation, autism, and aggression. *Medical Hypotheses, 47,* 289–298.

Fischer, K. W., & Bidell, T. R. (1998). Dynamic development of psychological structures in action and thought. In R. M. Lerner (Ed.), *Handbook of child psychology: Vol. 1. Theoretical models of human development* (5th ed., pp. 467–562). New York: Wiley.

Fischer, K. W., & Farrar, M. J. (1987). Generalizations about generalizations: How a theory of skill development explains both generality and specificity. *International Journal of Psychology, 22,* 643–677.

Fischer, K. W., & Pipp, S. L. (1984). Processes of cognitive development: Optimal level and skill acquisition. In R. J. Sternberg (Ed.), *Mechanisms of cognitive development* (pp. 45–80). New York: Freeman.

Fischer, K. W., & Rose, S. P. (1995, Fall). Concurrent cycles in the dynamic development of brain and behavior. *SRCD Newsletter,* pp. 3–4, 15–16.

Fisher, C. B. (1993, Winter). Integrating science and ethics in research with high-risk children and youth. *Social Policy Report of the Society for Research in Child Development, 4*(4).

Fisher, E. A., Van Horn, L., & McGill, H. C., Jr. (1997). Nutrition and children: A statement for healthcare professionals from the Nutrition Committee, American Heart Association. *Circulation, 95,* 2332–2333.

Fitzgibbons, P. J., & Gordon-Salant, S. (1998). Auditory temporal order perception in younger and older adults. *Journal of Speech, Language, and Hearing Research, 41,* 1052–1060.

Fivush, R., Kuebli, J., & Clubb, P. A. (1992). The structure of events and event representations: A developmental analysis. *Child Development, 63,* 188–201.

Flack, J. M., Amaro, H., Jenkins, W., Kunitz, S., Levy, J., Mixon, M., & Yu, E. (1995). Panel I: Epidemiology of minority health. *Health Psychology, 14,* 592–600.

Flake, A., Roncarolo, M., Puck, J. M., Almeidaporada, G., Evins, M. I., Johnson, M. P., Abella, E. M., Harrison, D. D., & Zanjani, E. D. (1996). Treatment of X-linked severe combined immunodeficiency by in utero transplantation of paternal bone marrow. *New England Journal of Medicine, 335,* 1806–1810.

Flamm, B. L., & Quilligan, E. J. (Eds.). (1995). *Cesarean section: Guidelines for appropriate utilization.* New York: Springer-Verlang.

Flannery, K. A., & Liederman, J. (1995). Is there really a syndrome involving the co-occurrence of neurodevelopmental disorder, talent, non–right handedness and immune disorder among children? *Cortex, 31,* 503–515.

Flavell, J. H. (1993). The development of children's understanding of false belief and the appearance–reality distinction. *International Journal of Psychology, 28,* 595–604.

Flavell, J. H., Green, F. L., & Flavell, E. R. (1987). Development of knowledge about the appearance–reality distinction. *Monographs of the Society for Research in Child Development, 51*(1, Serial No. 212).

Flavell, J. H., Green, F. L., & Flavell, E. R. (1995). Young children's knowledge about thinking. *Monographs of the Society for Research in Child Development, 60*(1, Serial No. 243).

Flavell, J. H., Green, F. L., Flavell, E. R., & Grossman, J. B. (1997). The development of children's knowledge about inner speech. *Child Development, 68,* 39–47.

Flavell, J. H., & Miller, P. H. (1998). Social cognition. In D. Kuhn & S. R. Siegler (Eds.), *Handbook of child psychology: Vol. 2. Cognition, perception, and language* (5th ed., pp. 851–898). New York: Wiley.

Fleischmann, R. M. (1999). Early diagnosis and treatment of rheumatoid arthritis for improved outcomes: Focus on Etanercept, a new biologic response modifier. *Clinical Therapy, 21,* 1429–1442.

Fletcher, A. C., Darling, N. E., Steinberg, L., & Dornbusch, S. M. (1995). The company they keep: Relation of adolescents' adjustment and behavior to their friends' perceptions of authoritative parenting in the social network. *Developmental Psychology, 31*, 300–310.

Fletcher, J. M., Landry, S. H., Bohan, T. P., Davidson, K. C., Brookshire, B. L., Lachar, D., Dramer, L. A., & Francis, D. J. (1997). Effects of intraventricular hemorrhage and hydrocephalus on the long-term neurobehavioral development of preterm very-low-birthweight infants. *Developmental Medicine and Child Neurology, 39*, 596–606.

Fletcher, W. L., & Hansson, R. O. (1991). Assessing the social components of retirement anxiety. *Psychology and Aging, 6*, 76–85.

Floccia, C., Christophe, A., & Bertoncini, J. (1997). High-amplitude sucking and newborns: The quest for underlying mechanisms. *Journal of Experimental Child Psychology, 64*, 175–198.

Flood, D. G., & Coleman, P. D. (1988). Cell type heterogeneity of changes in dendritic extent in the hippocampal region of the human brain in normal aging and in Alzheimer's disease. In T. L. Petit & G. O. Ivy (Ed.), *Neural plasticity: A lifespan approach* (pp. 265–281). New York: Alan R. Liss.

Florian, V., & Kravetz, S. (1985). Children's concepts of death: A cross-cultural comparison among Muslims, Druze, Christians, and Jews in Israel. *Journal of Cross-Cultural Psychology, 16*, 174–179.

Florian, V., & Mikulincer, M. (1998). Symbolic immortality and the management of the terror of death: The moderating role of attachment style. *Journal of Personality and Social Psychology, 74*, 725–734.

Florian, V., Mikulincer, M., & Taubman, O. (1995). Does hardiness contribute to mental health during a stressful real-life situation? The roles of appraisal and coping. *Journal of Personality and Social Psychology, 68*, 687–695.

Florsheim, P., Tolan, P., & Gorman-Smith, D. (1998). Family relationships, parenting practices, the availability of male family members, and the behavior of inner-city boys in single-mother and two-parent families. *Child Development, 69*, 1437–1447.

Florsheim, P., Tolan, P. H., & Gorman-Smith, D. (1996). Family processes and risk for externalizing behavior problems among African American and Hispanic boys. *Journal of Consulting and Clinical Psychology, 64*, 1222–1230.

Floyd, F. J., Gilliom, L. A., & Costigan, C. L. (1998). Marriage and the parenting alliance: Longitudinal prediction of change in parenting perceptions and behaviors. *Child Development, 69*, 1461–1479.

Flynn, J. R. (1996). What environmental factors affect intelligence: The relevance of IQ gains over time. In D. K. Detter-man (Ed.), *The environment: Current topics in human intelligence* (Vol. 5, pp. 17–29). Norwood, NJ: Ablex.

Flynn, J. R. (1999). Searching for justice: The discovery of IQ gains over time. *American Psychologist, 54*, 5–20.

Fogel, A. (1993). *Developing through relationships: Origins of communication, self and culture.* New York: Harvester Wheatsheaf.

Fogel, A., Toda, S., & Kawai, M. (1988). Mother–infant face-to-face interaction in Japan and the United States: A laboratory comparison using 3-month-old infants. *Developmental Psychology, 24*, 398–406.

Fogel, B. S. (1992). Psychological aspects of staying at home. *Generations, 16*, 15–19.

Foltz, C., Overton, W. F., & Ricco, R. B. (1995). Proof construction: Adolescent development from inductive to deductive problem-solving strategies. *Journal of Experimental Child Psychology, 59*, 179–195.

Ford, J. M., Roth, W. T., Isaacks, B. G., White, P. M., Hood, S. H., & Pfefferbaum, A. (1995). *Biological Psychology, 39*, 57–80.

Forehand, R., Wierson, M., Thomas, A. M., Fauber, R., Armistead, L., Kempton, T., & Long, N. (1991). A short-term longitudinal examination of young adolescent functioning following divorce: The role of family factors. *Journal of Abnormal Child Psychology, 19*, 97–111.

Forgatch, M. S., Patterson, G. R., & Ray, J. A. (1996). Divorce and boys' adjustment problems: Two paths with a single model. In E. M. Hetherington (Ed.), *Stress, coping, and resiliency in children and the family* (pp. 67–105). Hillsdale, NJ: Erlbaum.

Forman, E. A., Minick, N., & Stone, C. A. (1993). *Contexts for learning.* New York: Oxford University Press.

Fotinatos-Ventouratos, R., & Cooper, C. L. (1998). Social class differences and occupational stress. *International Journal of Stress Management, 5*, 211–222.

Fowler, J. W. (1981). *Stages of faith.* San Francisco: Harper & Row.

Fox, M., Gibbs, M., & Auerbach, D. (1985). Age and gender dimensions of friendship. *Psychology of Women Quarterly, 9*, 489–501.

Fox, N. A. (1995). Of the way we were: Adult memories about attachment experiences and their role in determining infant–parent relationships: A commentary on van IJzendoorn. *Psychological Bulletin, 117*, 404–410.

Fox, N. A., Calkins, S. D., & Bell, M. A. (1994). Neural plasticity and development in the first two years of life: Evidence from cognitive and socioemotional domains of research. *Development and Psychopathology, 6*, 677–696.

Fox, N. A., & Davidson, R. J. (1986). Taste-elicited changes in facial signs of emo-tion and the asymmetry of brain electrical activity in newborn infants. *Neuropsychologia, 24*, 417–422.

Fozard, J. L., Vercruyssen, M., Reynolds, S. L., Hancocke, P. A., & Quilter, R. E. (1994). Age differences and changes in reaction time: The Baltimore Longitudinal Study of Aging. *Journal of Gerontology, 49*, P179–P189.

Fraiberg, S. (1977). *Insights from the blind: Comparative studies of blind and sighted infants.* New York: Basic Books.

Framo, J. L. (1994). The family life cycle: Impressions. *Contemporary Family Therapy, 16*, 87–117.

Franceschi, C., Monti, D., Sansoni, P., & Cossarizza, A. (1995). The immunology of exceptional individuals: The lesson of centenarians. *Immunology Today, 16*(1), 12–16.

Franklin, M. (1995). The effects of differential college environments on academic learning and student perceptions of cognitive development. *Research in Higher Education, 36*, 127–153.

Frazier, J. A., & Morrison, F. J. (1998). The influence of extended-year schooling on growth of achievement and perceived competence in early elementary school. *Child Development, 69*, 495–517.

Frederickson, B. L. (1995). Socioemotional behavior at the end of college life. *Journal of Social and Personal Relationships, 12*, 261–276.

Frederickson, B. L., & Carstensen, L. L. (1990). Relationship classification using grade of membership analysis: A typology of sibling relationships in later life. *Journal of Gerontology, 45*, S43–S51.

Freeman, D. (1983). *Margaret Mead and Samoa: The making and unmaking of an anthropological myth.* Cambridge, MA: Harvard University Press.

Freeman, E. W., & Halbreich, U. (1998). Premenstrual syndromes. *Psychopharmacological Bulletin, 34*, 291–295.

Freer, J. P. (1991). Death and dignity: The case of Diane [Letter to the Editor]. *New England Journal of Medicine, 325*, 658.

Freud, S. (1973). *An outline of psychoanalysis.* London: Hogarth. (Original work published 1938)

Freud, S. (1974). *The ego and the id.* London: Hogarth. (Original work published 1923)

Freund, A. M., & Baltes, P. B. (1998). Selection, optimization, and compensation as strategies of life management: Correlations with subjective indicators of successful aging. *Psychology and Aging, 13*, 531–543.

Freund, A. M., & Smith, J. (1999). Content and function of the self-definition in old and very old age. *Journal of Gerontology, 54B*, P55–P67.

Fried, P. A. (1993). Prenatal exposure to tobacco and marijuana: Effects during pregnancy, infancy, and early childhood.

Clinical Obstetrics and Gynecology, 36, 319–337.

Fried, P. A., & Makin, J. E. (1987). Neonatal behavioral correlates of prenatal exposure to marijuana, cigarettes, and alcohol in a low risk population. *Neurobehavioral Toxicology and Teratology, 9,* 1–7.

Fried, P. A., Watkinson, B., & Gray, R. (1998). Differential effects on cognitive functioning in 9- to 12-year-olds prenatally exposed to cigarettes and marihuana. *Neurotoxicology and Teratology, 20,* 293–306.

Friedman, H. S., Tucker, J. S., Schwartz, J. E., Tomlinson-Keasey, C., Martin, L. R., Wingard, D. L., & Criqui, M. H. (1995). Psychosocial and behavioral predictors of longevity: The aging and death of the "Termites." *American Psychologist, 50,* 69–78.

Friedman, J. M. (1996). *The effects of drugs on the fetus and nursing infant: A handbook for health care professionals.* Baltimore: Johns Hopkins University Press.

Friedman, S. L., & Scholnick, E. K. (1997). An evolving "blueprint" for planning: Psychological requirements, task characteristics, and social–cultural influences. In S. L. Friedman & E. K. Scholnick (Eds.), *The developmental psychology of planning: Why, how, and when do we plan?* (pp. 3–22). Mahwah, NJ: Erlbaum.

Fries, J. F., Green, L. W., & Levine, S. (1994). Health promotion and the compression of morbidity. In A. Steptoe & J. Wardle (Eds.), *Psychosocial processes and health* (pp. 308–315). Cambridge: Cambridge University Press.

Frodi, A. (1985). When empathy fails: Aversive infant crying and child abuse. In B. M. Lester & C. F. Z. Boukydis (Eds.), *Infant crying: Theoretical and research perspectives* (pp. 263–277). New York: Plenum.

Frost, J. J., & Forrest, J. D. (1995). Understanding the impact of effective teenage pregnancy prevention programs. *Family Planning Perspectives, 27,* 188–195.

Fry, C. L. (1985). Culture, behavior, and aging in the comparative perspective. In J. E. Birren & K. W. Schaie (Eds.), *Handbook of the psychology of aging* (2nd ed., pp. 216–244). New York: Van Nostrand Reinhold.

Fry, P. S. (1991). Individual differences in reminiscence among older adults: Predictors of frequency and pleasantness ratings of reminiscence activity. *International Journal of Aging and Human Development, 33,* 311–326.

Fuchs, I., Eisenberg, N., Hertz-Lazarowitz, R., & Sharabany, R. (1986). Kibbutz, Israeli city, and American children's moral reasoning about prosocial moral conflicts. *Merrill-Palmer Quarterly, 32,* 37–50.

Fuligni, A. J. (1997). The academic achievement of adolescents from immigrant families: The roles of family background, attitudes, and behavior. *Child Development, 68,* 261–273.

Fuligni, A. J. (1998). The adjustment of children from immigrant families. *Current Directions in Psychological Science, 7,* 99–103.

Fuligni, A. J., Burton, L., Marshall, S., Perez-Febles, A., Yarrington, J., Kirsh, L.B., & Merriwether-DeVries, C. (1999). Attitudes toward family obligations among American adolescents with Asian, Latin American, and European backgrounds. *Child Development, 70,* 1030–1044.

Fuligni, A. J., & Stevenson, H. W. (1995). Time use and mathematics achievement among American, Chinese, and Japanese high school students. *Child Development, 66,* 830–842.

Fulton, R. (1995). The contemporary funeral: Functional or dysfunctional? In H. Wass & R. A. Neimeyer (Eds.), *Dying: Facing the facts* (3rd ed., pp. 185–209). Washington, DC: Taylor and Francis.

Fung, H. H., Carstensen, L. L., & Lutz, A. (1999). The influence of time on social preferences: Implications for life-span development. *Psychology and Aging, 14,* 595–604.

Furman, E. (1984). Children's patterns in mourning the death of a loved one. In H. Wass & C. A. Corr (Eds.), *Childhood and death* (pp. 185–203). Washington, DC: Hemisphere.

Furman, E. (1990, November). Plant a potato—learn about life (and death). *Young Children, 46*(1), 15–20.

Furman, W., & Buhrmester, D. (1992). Age and sex differences in perceptions of networks of personal relationships. *Child Development, 63,* 103–115.

Furman, W., & Wehner, E. A. (1994). Romantic views: Toward a theory of adolescent romantic relationships. In R. Montemayor, G. R. Adams, & T. P. Gullotta (Eds.), *Advances in adolescent development: Vol. 3. Relationships in adolescence* (pp. 168–195). Beverly Hills, CA: Sage.

Furstenberg, F. F., Jr., Brooks-Gunn, J., & Morgan, S. P. (1987). *Adolescent mothers and their children in later life.* Cambridge, England: Cambridge University Press.

Furstenberg, F. F., Jr., & Harris, K. M. (1993). When and why fathers matter: Impact of father involvement on children of adolescent mothers. In R. I. Lerman & T. J. Ooms (Eds.), *Young unwed fathers* (pp. 117–138). Philadelphia: Temple University Press.

Furstenberg, F. F., Jr., Hughes, M. E., & Brooks-Gunn, J. (1992). The next generation: Children of teenage mothers grow up. In M. K. Rosenheim & M. F. Testa (Eds.), *Early parenthood* (pp. 113–135). New Brunswick, NJ: Rutgers University Press.

Furuno, S., O'Reilly, K., Inatsuka, T., Hosaka, C., Allman, T., & Zeisloft-Falbey, B. (1987). *Hawaii Early Learning Profile.* Palo Alto, CA: VORT Corporation.

Fuson, K. C. (1988). *Children's counting and concepts of number.* New York: Springer-Verlag.

Fuson, K. C. (1992). Research on learning and teaching addition and subtraction of whole numbers. In G. Leinhardt, R. T. Putnam, & R. A. Hattrup (Eds.), *The analysis of arithmetic for mathematics teaching* (pp. 53–187). Hillsdale, NJ: Erlbaum.

Gaddis, A., & Brooks-Gunn, J. (1985). The male experience of pubertal change. *Journal of Youth and Adolescence, 14,* 61–69.

Galambos, N. L., Almeida, D. M., & Petersen, A. C. (1990). Masculinity, femininity, and sex role attitudes in early adolescence: Exploring gender intensification. *Child Development, 61,* 1905–1914.

Galambos, N. L., & Maggs, J. L. (1991). Children in self-care: Figures, facts, and fiction. In J. V. Lerner & N. L. Galambos (Eds.), *Employed mothers and their children* (pp. 131–157). New York: Garland.

Galinsky, E., Howes, C., Kontos, S., & Shinn, M. (1994). *The study of children in family child care and relative care: Highlights of findings, selected initiatives to improve the quality of family child care.* New York: Families and Work Institute.

Galler, J. R., Ramsey, C. F., Morley, D. S., Archer, E., & Salt, P. (1990). The long-term effects of early kwashiorkor compared with marasmus. IV. Performance on the National High School Entrance Examination. *Pediatric Research, 28,* 235–239.

Galler, J. R., Ramsey, F., & Solimano, G. (1985a). A follow-up study of the effects of early malnutrition on subsequent development: I. Physical growth and sexual maturation during adolescence. *Pediatric Research, 19,* 518–523.

Galler, J. R., Ramsey, F., & Solimano, G. (1985b). A follow-up study of the effects of early malnutrition on subsequent development: II. Fine motor skills in adolescence. *Pediatric Research, 19,* 524–527.

Galler, J. R., Ramsey, F., Solimano, G., Kucharski, L. T., & Harrison, R. (1984). The influence of early malnutrition on subsequent behavioral development: IV. Soft neurological signs. *Pediatric Research, 18,* 826–832.

Galotti, K. M., Kozberg, S. F., & Farmer, M. C. (1991). Gender and developmental differences in adolescents' conceptions of moral reasoning. *Journal of Youth and Adolescence, 20,* 13–30.

Galuska, D. A., Will, J. C., Serdula, M. K., & Ford, E. S. (1999). Are health care professionals advising obese patients to lose weight? *Journal of the American Medical Association, 282,* 1576–1578.

Gannon, L., & Ekstrom, B. (1993). Attitudes toward menopause: The influence of sociocultural paradigms. *Psychology of Women Quarterly, 17,* 275–288.

Gannon, S., & Korn, S. J. (1983). Temperament, cultural variation, and behavior disorder in preschool children. *Child Psychiatry and Human Development, 13,* 203–212.

Ganong, L. H., & Coleman, M. (1992). Gender differences in expectations of self and future partner. *Journal of Family Issues, 13,* 55–64.

Ganong, L. H., & Coleman, M. (1994). *Remarried family relationships.* Thousand Oaks, CA: Sage.

Ganong, L. H., & Coleman, M. (1998). Attitudes regarding filial responsibilities to help elderly divorced parents and stepparents. *Journal of Aging Studies, 12,* 271–290.

Ganong, L. H., Coleman, M., & Fine, M. (1995). Remarriage and stepfamilies. In W. Burr & R. Day (Eds.), *Advanced family science.* Provo, UT: Brigham Young University Press.

Garbarino, J. (1997). The role of economic deprivation in the social context of child maltreatment. In M. E. Helfer, R. S. Kempe, & R. D. Krugman (Eds.), *The battered child* (5th ed., pp. 49–60). Chicago: University of Chicago Press.

Garbarino, J. (1999). *Lost boys: Why our sons turn violent and how we can save them.* New York: Free Press.

Garbarino, J., & Kostelny, K. (1993). Neighborhood and community influences on parenting. In T. Luster & L. Okagaki (Eds.), *Parenting: An ecological perspective* (pp. 203–226). Hillsdale, NJ: Erlbaum.

Garber, J., Braafladt, N., & Weiss, B. (1995). Affect regulation in depressed and nondepressed children and young adolescents. *Development and Psychopathology, 7,* 93–115.

Garber, J., Quiggle, N., Panak, W., & Dodge, K. (1991). Aggression and depression in children: Comorbidity, specificity, and social cognitive processing. In D. Cicchetti & S. L. Toth (Eds.), *Rochester Symposium on Developmental Psychopathology: Vol. 2. Internalizing and externalizing expressions of dysfunction* (pp. 225–264). Hillsdale, NJ: Erlbaum.

García Coll, C., & Magnuson, K. (1997). The psychological experience of immigration: A developmental perspective. In A. Booth, A. C. Crouter, & N. Landale (Eds.), *Immigration and the family* (pp. 91–131). Mahwah, NJ: Erlbaum.

Gardner, H. (1980). *Artful scribbles: The significance of children's drawings.* New York: Basic Books.

Gardner, H. (1983). *Frames of mind: The theory of multiple intelligences.* New York: Basic Books.

Gardner, H. (1993). *Multiple intelligences: The theory in practice.* New York: Basic Books.

Gardner, H. E. (1998a). Are there additional intelligences? The case of the naturalist, spiritual, and existential intelligences. In J. Kane (Ed.), *Educational information and transformation.* Upper Saddle River, NJ: Prentice-Hall.

Gardner, H. E. (1998b). Extraordinary cognitive achievements (ECA): A symbol systems approach. In R. M. Lerner (Ed.), *Handbook of child psychology: Vol. 1. Theoretical models of human development* (5th ed., pp. 415–466). New York: Wiley.

Gardner, H. E. (2000). *Intelligence reframed: Multiple intelligences for the twenty-first century.* New York: Basic Books.

Gardner, M. J., Snee, M. P., Hall, A. J., Powell, C. A., Downes, S., & Terrell, J. D. (1990). Leukemia cases linked to fathers' radiation dose. *Nature, 343,* 423–429.

Garfinkel, I., & McLanaham, S. (1995). The effects of child support reform on child well-being. In P. L. Chase-Lansdale & J. Brooks-Gunn (Eds.), *Escape from poverty: What makes a difference for children?* (pp. 211–238). New York: Cambridge University Press.

Garland, A. F., & Zigler, E. (1993). Adolescent suicide prevention: Current research and social policy implications. *American Psychologist, 48,* 169–182.

Garmezy, N. (1993). Children in poverty: Resilience despite risk. *Psychiatry, 56,* 127–136.

Garmon, L. C., Basinger, K. S., Gregg, V. R., & Gibbs, J. C. (1996). Gender differences in stage and expression of moral judgment. *Merrill-Palmer Quarterly, 42,* 418–437.

Garnier, H. E., Stein, J. A., & Jacobs, J. K. (1997). The process of dropping out of high school: A 19-year perspective. *American Educational Research Journal, 34,* 395–410.

Garrett, P., Ng'andu, N., & Ferron, J. (1994). Poverty experiences of young children and the quality of their home environments. *Child Development, 65,* 331–345.

Garvey, C. (1975). Requests and responses in children's speech. *Journal of Child Language, 2,* 41–63.

Garvey, C. (1990). *Play.* Cambridge, MA: Harvard University Press.

Garwood, S. G., Phillips, D., Hartman, A., & Zigler, E. F. (1989). As the pendulum swings: Federal agency programs for children. *American Psychologist, 44,* 434–440.

Garzia, R. P., & Trick, L. R. (1992). Vision in the 90's: The aging eye. *Journal of Optometric Vision Development, 23,* 4–41.

Gathercole, S. E., Adams, A.-M., & Hitch, G. (1994). Do young children rehearse? An individual-differences analysis. *Memory and Cognition, 22,* 201–207.

Gatz, M., Bengtson, V. L., & Blum, M. J. (1990). Caregiving families. In J. E. Birren & K. W. Schaie (Eds.), *Handbook of the psychology of aging* (3rd ed., pp. 404–426). San Diego, CA: Academic Press.

Gatz, M., Kasl-Godley, J. E., & Karel, M. J. (1996). Aging and mental disorders. In J. E. Birren & K. W. Schaie (Eds.), *Handbook of the psychology of aging* (pp. 365–382). Sand Diego: Academic Press.

Gaub, M., & Carlson, C. L. (1997). Gender differences in ADHD: A meta-analysis and critical review. *Journal of the American Academy of Child and Adolescent Psychiatry, 36,* 1036–1045.

Gauvain, M. (1999). Cognitive development in social and cultural context. *Current Directions in Psychological Science, 7,* 188–192.

Gauvain, M., & Rogoff, B. (1989). Ways of speaking about space: The development of children's skill in communicating spatial knowledge. *Cognitive Development, 4,* 295–307.

Ge, X., Conger, R. D., & Elder, G. H., Jr. (1996). Coming of age too early: Pubertal influences on girls' vulnerability to psychological distress. *Child Development, 67,* 3386–3400.

Geary, D. C. (1994). *Children's mathematical development.* Washington, DC: American Psychological Association.

Geary, D. C. (1995). *Children's mathematical development: Research and practical applications.* Washington, DC: American Psychological Association.

Geary, D. C. (1996). International differences in mathematics achievement: The nature, causes, and consequences. *Current Directions in Psychological Science, 5,* 133–137.

Geary, D. C., Bow-Thomas, C. C., Liu, F., & Siegler, R. S. (1996). Development of arithmetical competencies in Chinese and American children: Influence of age, language, and schooling. *Child Development, 67,* 2022–2044.

Gellatly, A. R. H. (1987). Acquisition of a concept of logical necessity. *Human Development, 30,* 32–47.

Gelman, R. (1972). Logical capacity of very young children: Number invariance rules. *Child Development, 43,* 75–90.

Gelman, R., & Shatz, M. (1978). Appropriate speech adjustments: The operation of conversational constraints on talk to two-year-olds. In M. Lewis & L. A. Rosenblum (Eds.), *Interaction, conversation, and the development of language* (pp. 27–61). New York: Wiley.

Gelman, S. A., Coley, J. D., Rosengren, K. S., Hartman, E., & Pappas, A. (1998). Beyond labeling: The role of maternal input in the acquisition of richly structured categories. *Monographs of the Society for Research in Child Development, 63*(1, Serial No. 253).

Gentry, J. R. (1981, January). Learning to spell developmentally. *The Reading Teacher, 35*(2), 378–381.

Genuis, S. J., Genuis, S. K., & Chang, W. C. (1994). Public attitudes toward the right to die. *Canadian Medical Association Journal, 150,* 701–708.

George, C., Kaplan, N., & Main, M. (1985). *The Adult Attachment Interview.* Unpublished manuscript, University of California at Berkeley.

George, L. K. (1994). Social factors and depression in late life. In L. S. Schneider, C. F. Reynolds, III, B. D. Lebowitz, & A. J. Friedhoff (Eds.), *Diagnosis and treatment of depression in late life* (pp. 131–153). Washington, DC: American Psychiatric Press.

Gervai, J., Turner, P. J., & Hinde, R. A. (1995). Gender-related behaviour, attitudes, and personality in parents of young children in England and Hungary. *International Journal of Behavioral Development, 18,* 105–126.

Gesell, A. (1933). Maturation and patterning of behavior. In C. Murchison (Ed.), *A handbook of child psychology.* Worcester, MA: Clark University Press.

Gesell, A., & Ilg, F. L. (1949a). The child from five to ten. In A. Gesell & F. Ilg (Eds.), *Child development* (pp. 394–454). New York: Harper & Row. (Original work published 1946)

Gesell, A., & Ilg, F. L. (1949b). The infant and child in the culture of today. In A. Gesell & F. Ilg (Eds.), *Child development* (pp. 1–393). New York: Harper & Row. (Original work published 1943)

Getzel, G. S. (1995). Judaism and death: Practice implications. In J. K. Parry & A. S. Ryan (Eds.), *A cross-cultural look at death, dying, and religion* (pp. 18–31). Chicago: Nelson-Hall.

Ghim, H. R. (1990). Evidence for perceptual organization in infants: Perception of subjective contours by young infants. *Infant Behavior and Development, 13,* 221–248.

Gibbs, J. C. (1991). Toward an integration of Kohlberg's and Hoffman's theories of morality. In W. M. Kurtines & J. L. Gewirtz (Eds.), *Handbook of moral behavior and development* (Vol. 1, pp. 183–222). Hillsdale, NJ: Erlbaum.

Gibbs, J. C. (1995). The cognitive developmental perspective. In W. M. Kurtines & J. L. Gewirtz (Eds.), *Moral development: An introduction* (pp. 27–48). Boston: Allyn and Bacon.

Gibson, E. J. (1970). The development of perception as an adaptive process. *American Scientist, 58,* 98–107.

Gibson, E. J. (1988). Exploratory behavior in the development of perceiving, acting, and the acquiring of knowledge. *Annual Review of Psychology, 39,* 1–41.

Gibson, E. J., & Walk, R. D. (1960). The "visual cliff." *Scientific American, 202,* 64–71.

Gibson, J. J. (1979). *The ecological approach to visual perception.* Boston: Houghton Mifflin.

Gibson, R. C., & Burns, C. J. (1991, Winter). The health, labor force, and retirement experiences of aging minorities. *Generations, 15*(4), 31–35.

Gibson, R. C., & Jackson, J. S. (1992). The black oldest old: Health, functioning, and informal support. In R. M. Suzman, D. P. Willis, & K. G. Manton (Eds.), *The oldest old* (pp. 321–340). New York: Oxford University Press.

Gilbert, L. A., & Brownson, C. (1998). Current perspectives on women's multiple roles. *Journal of Career Assessment, 6,* 433–448.

Gilchrest, B. A., & Bohr, V. A. (1997). Aging processes, DNA damage, and repair. *FASEB Journal, 11,* 322–330.

Gilfillan, M. C., Curtis, L., Liston, W. A., Pullen, I., Whyte, D. A., & Brock, J. J. H. (1992). Prenatal screening for cystic fibrosis. *Lancet, 340,* 214–216.

Gilligan, C. F. (1982). *In a different voice.* Cambridge, MA: Harvard University Press.

Gilling, P. J., Mackey, M., Cresswell, M., Kennett, K., Kabalin, J. N., & Fraundorfer, M. R. (1999). Holmium laser versus transurethral resection of the prostate: A randomized prospective trial with 1-year followup. *Journal of Urology, 162,* 1640–1644.

Gillmore, M. R., Hawkins, J. D., Day, L. E., & Catalano, R. F. (1997). Friendship and deviance: New evidence on an old controversy. *Journal of Early Adolescence, 16.*

Ginsburg, H. P. (1997). *Entering the child's mind: The clinical interview in psychological research and practice.* New York: Cambridge University Press.

Ginzberg, E. (1972). Toward a theory of occupational choice: A restatement. *Vocational Guidance Quarterly, 20,* 169–176.

Ginzberg, E. (1988). Toward a theory of occupational choice. *Career Development Quarterly, 36,* 358–363.

Giusti, R. M., Iwamoto, K., & Hatch, E. E. (1995). Diethylstilbestrol revisited: A review of the long-term health effects. *Annals of Internal Medicine, 122,* 778–788.

Gjerde, P. F. (1995). Alternative pathways to chronic depressive symptoms in young adults: Gender differences in developmental trajectories. *Child Development, 66,* 1277–1300.

Gladwell, M. (1998, February 2). The Pima paradox. *The New Yorker,* pp. 44–57.

Glaser, K. (1997). The living arrangements of elderly people. *Reviews in Clinical Gerontology, 7,* 63–72.

Glasgow, K. L., Dornbusch, S. M., Troyer, L., Steinberg, L., & Ritter, P. L. (1997). Parenting styles, adolescents' attributions, and educational outcomes in nine heterogeneous high schools. *Child Development, 68,* 507–523.

Glassman, B. S. (Ed.). (1996). *The new view almanac.* Woodbridge, CT: Blackbirch Press.

Gleitman, L. R., & Newport, E. (1996). *The invention of language by children.* Cambridge, MA: MIT Press.

Glendenning, F. (1993). What is elder abuse and neglect? In P. Decalmer & F. Glendenning (Eds.), *The mistreatment of elderly people* (pp. 1–34). London: Sage.

Glick, P. C. (1997). Demographic pictures of African American families. In H. P. McAdoo (Ed.), *Black families* (3rd ed., pp. 118–138). Thousand Oaks, CA: Sage.

Glidden, L. M., & Pursley, J. T. (1989). Longitudinal comparisons of families who have adopted children with mental retardation. *American Journal on Mental Retardation, 94,* 272–277.

Glosten, B. (1998). Controversies in obstetric anesthesia. *Anesthesia and Analgesia, 428*(Suppl. 32–8), 32–38.

Gluhoski, V. L., & Wortman, C. B. (1996). The impact of trauma on world views. *Journal of Social and Clinical Psychology, 15,* 417–429.

Gnepp, J. (1983). Children's social sensitivity: Inferring emotions from conflicting cues. *Developmental Psychology, 19,* 805–814.

Gold, D. T. (1996). Continuities and discontinuities in sibling relationships across the life span. In V. L. Bengtson (Ed.), *Adulthood and aging: Research on continuities and discontinuities* (pp. 228–243). New York: Springer.

Goldberg, A. P., Dengel, D. R., & Hagberg, J. M. (1996). Exercise physiology and aging. In E. L. Schneider & J. W. Rowe (Eds.), *Handbook of the biology of aging* (pp. 331–354). San Diego: Academic Press.

Goldberg, G. S., & Kremen, E. (1990). *The feminization of poverty: Only in America?* New York: Praeger.

Goldberg-Glen, R., Sands, R. G., Cole, R. D., & Cristofalo, C. (1998). Multigenerational patterns and internal structures in families in which grandparents raise grandchildren. *Families in Society, 79,* 477–489.

Goldman, N., & Takahashi, S. (1996). Old-age mortality in Japan: Demographic and epidemiological perspectives. In G. Caselli & A. D. Lopez (Eds.), *Health and mortality among elderly populations* (pp. 157–181). New York: Oxford University Press.

Goldscheider, F. K., & Goldscheider, C. (1993). *Leaving home before marriage: Ethnicity, familism, and generational relationships.* Madison: University of Wisconsin Press.

Goldsmith, H. H., Buss, K. A., & Lemery, K. S. (1997). Toddler and childhood temperament: Expanded content, stronger genetic evidence, new evidence for the importance of the environment. *Developmental Psychology, 33,* 891–905.

Goldstein, E. (1979). Effect of same-sex and cross-sex role models on the subsequent academic productivity of scholars. *American Psychologist, 34,* 407–410.

Golomb, C. (1992). *The child's creation of a pictorial world.* Berkeley: University of California Press.

Golomb, C., & Galasso, L. (1995). Make believe and reality: Explorations of the imaginary realm. *Developmental Psychology, 31,* 800–810.

Golombok, S., Cook, R., Bish, A., & Murray, C. (1995). Families created by the new reproductive technologies: Quality of parenting and social and emotional development of the children. *Child Development, 66,* 285–298.

Golombok, S., & Tasker, F. L. (1996). Do parents influence the sexual orientation of their children? Findings from a longitudinal study of lesbian families. *Developmental Psychology, 32,* 3–11.

Golub, M. S. (1996). Labor analgesia and infant brain development. *Pharmacology, Biochemistry and Behavior, 55,* 619–628.

Gomez-Schwartz, B., Horowitz, J. M., & Cardarelli, A. P. (1990). *Child sexual abuse: Initial effects.* Newbury Park, CA: Sage.

Gomolka, M., Menninger, H., Saal, J. E., Lemmel, E.-M., Albert, E. D., Niwa, O., Epplen, J. T., & Epplen, C. (1995). Immunoprinting: Various genes are associated with increased risk to develop rheumatoid arthritis in different groups of adult patients. *Journal of Molecular Medicine, 73,* 19–29.

Göncü, A. (1993). Development of intersubjectivity in the dyadic play of preschoolers. *Early Childhood Research Quarterly, 8,* 99–116.

Good, T. L., & Brophy, J. E. (1996). *Looking in classrooms* (7th ed.). New York: Addison-Wesley.

Goodman, G. S., Hirschman, J. E., Hepps, D., & Rudy, L. (1991). Children's memory for stressful events. *Merrill-Palmer Quarterly, 37,* 109–158.

Goodman, K. S. (1986). *What's whole in whole language?* Portsmouth, NH: Heinemann.

Goodman, L. A., Koss, M. P., & Russo, N. F. (1993). Violence against women: Physical and mental health effects. *Applied and Preventive Psychology, 2,* 79–89.

Goodman, S. H., Brogan, D., Lynch, M. E., & Fielding, B. (1993). Social and emotional competence in children of depressed mothers. *Child Development, 64,* 516–531.

Goodman, S. H., Gravitt, G. W., Jr., & Kaslow, N. J. (1995). Social problem solving: A moderator of the relation between negative life stress and depressive symptoms in children. *Journal of Abnormal Child Psychology, 23,* 473–485.

Goodwin, D. W. (1997). Alcohol: Clinical aspects. In J. H. Lowinson, P. Ruiz, & R. B. Millman (Eds.), *Substance abuse* (3rd ed.). Baltimore: Lippincott, Williams & Wilkins.

Goodyear-Smith, F. A., & Laidlaw, T. M. (1999). Aggressive acts and assaults in intimate relationships: Towards an understanding of the literature. *Behavioral Sciences and the Law, 17,* 285–304.

Gopnik, A., & Meltzoff, A. N. (1986). Relations between semantic and cognitive development in the one-word stage: The specificity hypothesis. *Child Development, 57,* 1040–1053.

Gopnik, A., & Meltzoff, A. N. (1987). The development of categorization in the second year and its relation to other cognitive and linguistic developments. *Child Development, 58,* 1523–1531.

Gortmaker, S. L., Dietz, W. H., Jr., & Cheung, L. W. Y. (1990). Inactivity, diet, and the fattening of America. *Journal of the American Dietetic Association, 90,* 1247–1252.

Gortmaker, S. L., Must, A., Perrin, J. M., Sobol, A. M., & Dietz, W. H. (1993). Social and economic consequences of overweight in adolescence and young adulthood. *New England Journal of Medicine, 329,* 1008–1012.

Goswami, U. (1996). Analogical reasoning and cognitive development. In H. Reese (Ed.), *Advances in child development and behavior* (Vol. 26, pp. 91–138). New York: Academic Press.

Gottesman, I. I. (1963). Genetic aspects of intelligent behavior. In N. Ellis (Ed.), *Handbook of mental deficiency* (pp. 253–296). New York: McGraw-Hill.

Gottesman, I. I. (1991). *Schizophrenia genetics: The origins of madness.* New York: Freeman.

Gottfredson, L. S. (1996). Godfredson's theory of circumscription and compromise. In D. Brown & L. Brooks (Eds.), *Career choice and development* (3rd ed.). San Francisco: Jossey-Bass.

Gottlieb, G. (1991). Experiential canalization of behavioral development: Theory. *Developmental Psychology, 27,* 4–13.

Gottman, J., Coan, J., Carrere, S., & Swanson, C. (1998). Predicting marital happiness and stability from newlywed interactions. *Journal of Marriage and the Family, 60,* 5–22.

Goubet, N., & Clifton, R. K. (1998). Object and event representation in 6½-month-old infants. *Developmental Psychology, 34,* 63–76.

Gould, E., Reeves, A. J., Graziano, M. S. A., & Gross, C. G. (1999). Neurogenesis in the neocortex of adult primates. *Science, 286,* 548–552.

Gould, J. L., & Keeton, W. T. (1996). *Biological science* (6th ed.). New York: Norton.

Gould, S. J. (1996). *The mismeasure of man.* New York: Norton.

Goya, R. G., & Bolognani, F. (1999). Homeostatis, thymic hormones, and aging. *Gerontology, 45,* 174–178.

Graber, J. A., & Brooks-Gunn, J. (1996). Expectations for and precursors to leaving home in young women. In J. A. Graber & J. S. Dubas (Eds.), *New directions for child development* (No. 71, pp. 21–38). San Francisco: Jossey-Bass.

Graber, J. A., Brooks-Gunn, J., Paikoff, R. L., & Warren, M. P. (1994). Prediction of eating problems: An 8-year study of adolescent girls. *Developmental Psychology, 30,* 823–834.

Graber, J. A., Petersen, A. C., & Brooks-Gunn, J. (1996). Pubertal processes: Methods, measures, and models. In J. A. Graber, J. Brooks-Gunn, & A. C. Petersen (Eds.), *Transitions through adolescence* (pp. 23–53). Mahwah, NJ: Erlbaum.

Graham, S., Doubleday, C., & Guarino, P. A. (1984). The development of relations between perceived controllability and the emotions of pity, anger, and guilt. *Child Development, 55,* 561–565.

Gralinski, J. H., & Kopp, C. B. (1993). Everyday rules for behavior: Mothers' requests to young children. *Developmental Psychology, 29,* 573–584.

Gramm, P., Rettenmaier, A. J., & Saving, T. R. (1998). Medicare policy for future generations: A search for a permanent solution. *New England Journal of Medicine, 338,* 1307–1310.

Grande, G. E., Addington-Hall, J. M., & Todd, C. J. (1998). Place of death and access to home care services: Are certain patient groups at a disadvantage? *Social Science and Medicine, 47,* 565–57779.

Granot, M., Spitzer, A., Aroian, K. J., Ravid, C., Tamir, B., & Noam, R. (1996). Pregnancy and delivery practices and beliefs of Ethiopian immigrant women in Israel. *Western Journal of Nursing Research, 18,* 299–313.

Grant, J. P. (1995). *The state of the world's children 1995.* New York: Oxford University Press (in cooperation with UNICEF).

Grantham-McGregor, S., Powell, C., Walker, S., Chang, S., & Fletcher, P. (1994). The long-term follow-up of severely malnourished children who participated in an intervention program. *Child Development, 65,* 428–439.

Grantham-McGregor, S., Schofield, W., & Powell, C. (1987). Development of severely malnourished children who received psychosocial stimulation: Six-year follow-up. *Pediatrics, 79,* 247–254.

Graves, S. B. (1993). Television, the portrayal of African Americans, and the development of children's attitudes. In G. L. Berry & J. K. Asamen (Eds.), *Children and television* (pp. 179–190). Newbury Park, CA: Sage.

Gray, J. H., & Citera, M. (1996). *A meta-analytical review of the relation between work attitudes and retirement attitudes.* Paper presented at the annual meeting of the Society for Industrial and Organizational Psychology, San Diego, CA.

Green, G. D., & Bozett, F. W. (1991). Lesbian mothers and gay fathers. In J. C. Gonsiorek & J. D. Weinrich (Eds.), *Homosexuality: Research implications for public policy* (pp. 197–214). Newbury Park, CA: Sage.

Greenberger, E., & Goldberg, W. A. (1989). Work, parenting, and the socialization of children. *Developmental Psychology, 25,* 22–35.

Greenberger, E., O'Neil, R., & Nagel, S.K. (1994). Linking workplace and home-place: Relations between the nature of adults' work and their parenting behavior. *Developmental Psychology, 30,* 990–1002.

Greendorfer, S. L., Lewko, J. H., & Rosengren, K. S. (1996). Family and gender-based socialization of children and adolescents. In F. L. Smoll & R. E. Smith (Eds.), *Children and youth in sport: A biopsychological perspective* (pp. 89–111). Dubuque, IA: Brown & Benchmark.

Greenfield, P. (1992, June). *Notes and references for developmental psychology.* Conference on Making Basic Texts in Psychology More Culture-Inclusive and Culture-Sensitive, Western Washington University, Bellingham, WA.

Greenfield, P. M. (1994). Independence and interdependence as developmental scripts: Implications for theory, research, and practice. In P. M. Greenfield & R. R. Cocking (Eds.), *Cross-cultural roots of minority child development* (pp. 1–37). Hillsdale, NJ: Erlbaum.

Greenfield, P. M., & Suzuki, L. (1998). Culture and human development: Implications for parenting education, pediatrics, and mental health. In I. E. Sigel & K. A. Renninger (Eds.), *Handbook of child psychology: Vol. 4. Child psychology in practice* (5th ed., pp. 1059–1109). New York: Wiley.

Greeno, J. G. (1989). A perspective on thinking. *American Psychologist, 44,* 134–141.

Greenough, W. T., & Black, J. E. (1992). Induction of brain structure by experience: Substrates for cognitive development. In M. R. Gunnar & C. A. Nelson (Eds.), *Minnesota Symposia on Child Psychology* (pp. 155–200). Hillsdale, NJ: Erlbaum.

Greenough, W. T., Wallace, C. S., Alcantara, A. A., Anderson, B. J., Hawrylak, N., Sirevaag, A. M., Weiler, I. J., & Withers, G. S. (1993). Experience affects the structure of neurons, glia, and blood vessels. In N. J. Anastasiow & S. Harel (Eds.), *At-risk infants: Interventions, family, and research* (pp. 175–185). Baltimore: Paul H. Brookes.

Greenstein, D., Carlson, J., & Howell, C. W. (1993). Counseling with interfaith couples. *Individual Psychology, 49,* 428–437.

Gresham, F. M., & MacMillan, D. L. (1997). Social competence and affective characteristics of students with mild disabilities. *Review of Educational Research, 67,* 377–415.

Gresser, G., Wong, P., & Reker, G. (1987). Death attitudes across the life-span: The development and validation of the Death Attitude Profile (DAP). *Omega, 18,* 113–128.

Griffin, W. S., Sheng, J. G., Royston, M. C., Gentleman, S. M., McKenzie, J. E., Graham, D. I., Roberts, G. W., & Mrak, R. E. (1998). Glial-neuronal interactions in Alzheimer's disease: The potential role of a "cytokine cycle" in disease progression. *Brain Pathology, 8,* 65–72.

Griffiths, A., Roberts, G., & Williams, J. (1993). Elder abuse and the law. In P. Decalmer & F. Glendenning (Eds.), *The mistreatment of elderly people* (pp. 62–75). London: Sage.

Grigorenko, E. L., & Sternberg, R. J. (1998). Dynamic testing. *Psychological Bulletin, 124,* 75–111.

Groff, J. Y., Mullen, P. D., Mongoven, M., & Burau, K. (1997). Prenatal weight gain patterns and infant birthweight associated with maternal smoking. *Birth, 24,* 234–239.

Grolnick, W. S., Bridges, L. J., & Connell, J. P. (1996). Emotion regulation in two-year-olds: Strategies and emotional expression in four contexts. *Child Development, 67,* 928–941.

Grolnick, W. S., & Slowiaczek, M. L. (1994). Parents' involvement in children's schooling: A multidimensional conceptualization and motivational model. *Child Development, 65,* 237–252.

Groome, L. J., Swiber, M. J., Atterbury, J. L., Bentz, L. S., & Holland, S. B. (1997). Similarities and differences in behavioral state organization during sleep periods in the perinatal infant before and after birth. *Child Development, 68,* 1–11.

Gross, J. J., Carstensen, L. L., Pasupathi, M., Tsai, J., Skorpen, C. G., & Hsu, A. Y. C. (1997). Emotion and aging: Experience, expression, and control. *Psychology and Aging, 12,* 590–599.

Grossmann, K., Grossmann, K. E., Spangler, G., Suess, G., & Unzner, L. (1985). Maternal sensitivity and newborns' orientation responses as related to quality of attachment in Northern Germany. In I. Bretherton & E. Waters (Eds.), Growing points of attachment theory and research. *Monographs of the Society for Research in Child Development, 50*(1–2, Serial No. 209).

Grotevant, H. D. (1998). Adolescent development in family contexts. In N. Eisenberg (Ed.), *Handbook of child psychology: Vol. 3. Social, emotional, and personality development* (5th ed., pp. 1097–1149). New York: Wiley.

Grotevant, H. D., & Cooper, C. R. (1985). Patterns of interaction in family relationships and the development of identity exploration in adolescence. *Child Development, 56,* 415–428.

Grotevant, H. D., & Cooper, C. R. (1998). Individuality and connectedness in adolescent development: Review and prospects for research on identity, relationships, and context. In E. Skoe & A. von der Lippe (Eds.), *Personality development in adolescence* (pp. 3–37). London: Routledge & Kegan Paul.

Grotpeter, J. K., & Crick, N. R. (1996). Relational aggression, overt aggression, and friendship. *Child Development, 67,* 2328–2338.

Gruetzner, H. (1992). *Alzheimer's.* New York: Wiley.

Grusec, J. E. (1988). *Social development: History, theory, and research.* New York: Springer.

Grusec, J. E., & Goodnow, J. J. (1994). Impact of parental discipline methods on the child's internalization of values: A reconceptualization of current points of view. *Developmental Psychology, 30,* 4–19.

Grych, J. H., & Clark, R. (1999). Maternal employment and development of the father–infant relationship in the first year. *Developmental Psychology, 35,* 893–903.

Grych, J. H., & Fincham, F. D. (1997). Children's adaptation to divorce: from description to explanation. In S. A. Wolchik & I. N. Sandler (Eds.), *Handbook of children's coping: Linking theory to intervention* (pp. 159–193). New York: Plenum.

Guerra, N. B., Attar, B., & Weissberg, R. P. (1997). Prevention of aggression and violence among inner-city youths. In D. M. Stoff, J. Breiling, & J. D. Maser (Eds.), *Handbook of antisocial behavior* (pp. 375–383). New York: Wiley.

Guerri, C. (1998). Neuroanatomical and neurophysiological mechanisms involved in central nervous system dysfunctions induced by prenatal alcohol exposure. *Alcoholism: Clinical and Experimental Research, 22,* 304–312.

Guidubaldi, J., & Cleminshaw, H. K. (1985). Divorce, family health and child adjustment. *Family Relations, 34,* 35–41.

Guilford, J. P. (1985). The structure-of-intellect model. In B. B. Wolman (Ed.), *Handbook of intelligence* (pp. 225–266). New York: Wiley.

Guinn, B. (1999). Leisure behavior motivation and the life satisfaction of retired persons. *Activities, Adaptation, and Aging, 23,* 13–20.

Gullette, M. M. (1988). *Safe at last in the middle years.* Berkeley: University of California Press.

Gullone, E., & King, N. J. (1997). Three-year follow-up of normal fear in children and adolescents aged 7 to 18 years. *British Journal of Developmental Psychology, 15,* 97–111.

Gunnar, M. R. (1998). Quality of early care and buffering of neuroendocrine stress reactions: Potential effects on the developing human brain. *Preventive Medicine, 27,* 208–211.

Gunnar, M. R., & Nelson, C. A. (1994). Event-related potentials in year-old infants: Relations with emotionality and cortisol. *Child Development, 65,* 80–94.

Gupta, V., & Korte, C. (1994). The effects of a confidant and a peer group on the well-being of single elders. *International Journal of Aging and Human Development, 39,* 293–302.

Gurland, B. J., Wilder, D. E., Lantigua, R., Stern, Y., Chen, J., Killeffer, E. H., & Mayeux, R. (1999). Rates of dementia in three ethnoracial groups. *International Journal of Geriatric Psychiatry, 14,* 481–493.

Gustafson, G. E., Green, J. A., & Cleland, J. W. (1994). Robustness of individual identity in the cries of human infants. *Developmental Psychobiology, 27,* 1–9.

Gustafson, G. E., & Harris, K. L. (1990). Women's responses to young infants' cries. *Developmental Psychology, 26,* 144–152.

Gutmann, D. (1977). The cross-cultural perspective: Notes toward a comparative psychology of aging. In J. E. Birren & K. W. Schaie (Eds.), *Handbook of the psychology of aging* (pp. 302–326). New York: Van Nostrand Reinhold.

Gutmann, D. L., & Huyck, M. H. (1994). Development and pathology in post-parental men: A community study. In E. Thompson, Jr. (Ed.), *Older men's lives* (pp. 65–84). Thousand Oaks, CA: Sage.

Haan, N., Aerts, E., & Cooper, B. (1985). *On moral grounds: The search for practical morality.* New York: New York University Press.

Hack, M., Wright, L. L., Shankaran, S., & Tyson, J. E. (1995). Very low birth weight outcomes of the National Institute of Child Health and Human Development Neonatal Network, November 1989 to October 1990. *American Journal of Obstetrics and Gynecology, 172,* 457–464.

Hack, M. B., Taylor, H. G., Klein, N., Eiben, R., Schatschneider, C., & Mercuri-Minich, N. (1994). School-age outcomes in children with birth weights under 750 g. *New England Journal of Medicine, 331,* 753–759.

Hackel, L. S., & Ruble, D. N. (1992). Changes in the marital relationship after the first baby is born: Predicting the impact of expectancy disconfirmation. *Journal of Personality and Social Psychology, 62,* 944–957.

Haden, C. A., Haine, R. A., & Fivush, R. (1997). Developing narrative structure in parent–child reminiscing across the preschool years. *Developmental Psychology, 33,* 295–307.

Hagberg, J. M. (1987). Effects of training on the decline of VO$_{2max}$ with aging. *Federation Proceedings, 46,* 1830–1833.

Hagberg, J. M., Allen, W. K., Seals, D. R., Hurley, B. F., Ehsani, A. A., & Holloszy, J. O. (1985). A hemodynamic comparison of young and older endurance athletes during exercise. *Journal of Applied Physiology, 58,* 2041–2046.

Hagekull, B., Bohlin, G., & Rydell, A. (1997). Maternal sensitivity, infant temperament, and the development of early feeding problems. *Infant Mental Health Journal, 18,* 92–106.

Hager, M. (1996, December 23). The cancer killer. *Newsweek,* pp. 42–47.

Haight, B. K. (1992). Long-term effects of a structured life review process. *Journal of Gerontology, 47,* P312–P315.

Haight, W. L., & Miller, P. J. (1993). *Pretending at home: Early development in a sociocultural context.* Albany, NY: State University of New York Press.

Haines, C. J., Rong, L., Chung, T. K. H., & Leung, D. H. Y. (1995). The perception of the menopause and the climacteric among women in Hong Kong and Southern China. *Preventive Medicine, 24,* 245–248.

Hainline, L. (1993). Conjugate eye movements of infants. In K. Simons (Ed.), *Early visual development: Normal and abnormal* (pp. 47–55). New York: Oxford University Press.

Haith, M. M., & Benson, J. B. (1998). Infant cognition. In D. Kuhn & R. S. Siegler (Eds.), *Handbook of child psychology: Vol. 2. Cognition, perception, and language* (5th ed., pp. 199–254). New York: Wiley.

Hakuta, K., Ferdman, B. M., & Diaz, R. M. (1987). Bilingualism and cognitive development: Three perspectives. In S. Rosenberg (Ed.), *Advances in applied psycholinguistics: Vol. 2. Reading, writing, and language learning* (pp. 284–319). New York: Cambridge University Press.

Halford, G. S. (1992). *Children's understanding: The development of mental models.* Hillsdale, NJ: Erlbaum.

Hall, D. G. (1996). Preschoolers' default assumptions about word meaning: Proper names designate unique individuals. *Developmental Psychology, 32,* 177–186.

Hall, D. G., & Graham, S. A. (1999). Lexical form class information guides word-to-object mapping in preschoolers. *Child Development, 70,* 78–91.

Hall, G. S. (1904). *Adolescence.* New York: Appleton.

Hall, S. S. (1996, January/February). Short life me. *Health,* pp. 98–106.

Halliday, J. L., Watson, L. F., Lumley, J., Danks, D. M., & Sheffield, L. S. (1995). New estimates of Down syndrome risks of chorionic villus sampling, amniocentesis, and live birth in women of advanced maternal age from a uniquely defined population. *Prenatal Diagnosis, 15,* 455–465.

Halmi, K. A. (1987). Anorexia nervosa and bulimia. In V. B. Van Hasselt & M. Hersen (Eds.), *Handbook of adolescent psychology* (pp. 265–287). New York: Pergamon.

Halpern, C. T., Udry, J. R., Campbell, B., & Schindran, C. (1999). Effects of body fat on weight concerns, dating, and sexual activity: A longitudinal analysis of black and white adolescent girls. *Developmental Psychology, 35,* 721–736.

Halpern, C. T., Udry, J. R., & Suchindran, C. (1997). Testosterone predicts initiation of coitus in adolescent females. *Psychosomatic Medicine, 59,* 161–171.

Halpern, D. F. (1992). *Sex differences in cognitive abilities* (2nd ed.). Hillsdale, NJ: Erlbaum.

Halpern, D. F. (1997). Sex differences in intelligence. *American Psychologist, 52,* 1091–1102.

Halpern, L. F., MacLean, W. E., & Baumeister, A. A. (1995). Infant sleep–wake characteristics: Relation to neurological status and the prediction of developmental outcome. *Developmental Review, 15,* 255–291.

Hamachek, D. (1990). Evaluating self-concept and ego status in Erikson's last three psychosocial stages. *Journal of Counseling and Development, 68,* 677–683.

Hamberger, L. K., Lohr, J. M., Bonge, D., & Tolin, D. (1997). An empirical classification of motivations for domestic violence. *Violence Against Women, 3,* 401–423.

Hamberger, L. K., Saunders, D. G., & Hovey, M. (1992). The prevalence of domestic violence in community practice and rate of physician inquiry. *Family Medicine, 24,* 283–287.

Hamelin, K., & Ramachandran, C. (1993, June). Kangaroo care. *Canadian Nurse, 89*(6), 15–17.

Hamer, D. H., Hu, S., Magnuson, V. L., Hu, N., & Pattatucci, A. M. L. (1993). A linkage between DNA markers on the X chromosome and male sexual orientation. *Science, 261,* 321–327.

Hamilton, S. F. (1990). *Apprenticeship for adulthood: Preparing youth for the future.* New York: Free Press.

Hamilton, S. F. (1993). Prospects for an American-style youth apprenticeship system. *Educational Researcher, 22*(3), 11–16.

Hamilton, S. F. (1994). Social roles for youths: Interventions in unemployment. In A. C. Petersen & J. T. Mortimer (Eds.), *Youth employment and society* (pp. 248–269). New York: Cambridge University Press.

Hammersley, M. (1992). *What's wrong with ethnography?* New York: Routledge.

Han, J. J., Leichtman, M. D., & Wang, Q. (1998). Autobiographical memory in Korean, Chinese, and American children. *Developmental Psychology, 34,* 701–713.

Hanna, E., & Meltzoff, A. N. (1993). Peer imitation by toddlers in laboratory, home, and day-care contexts: Implications for social learning and memory. *Developmental Psychology, 29,* 701–710.

Hanson, L. C., Danis, M., & Garrett, J. (1995). What is wrong with end-of-life care? Opinions of bereaved family members. *Journal of the American Geriatric Society, 45,* 1339–1344.

Happé, F. G. E. (1995). The role of age and verbal ability in the theory of mind task performance of subjects with autism. *Child Development, 66,* 843–855.

Hardy, J. B., Astone, N. M., Brooks-Gunn, J., Shapiro, S., & Miller, T. L. (1998). Like mother, like child: Intergenerational patterns of age at first birth and associations with childhood and adolescent characteristics and adult outcomes in the second generation. *Developmental Psychology, 34,* 1220–1232.

Hardy, M. A., & Hazelrigg, L. E. (1993). The gender of poverty in an aging population. *Research on Aging, 15,* 243–278.

Hare, J. (1994). Concerns and issues faced by families headed by a lesbian couple. *Families in Society, 43,* 27–35.

Hare, J., & Richards, L. (1993). Children raised by lesbian couples: Does context of birth affect father and partner involvement? *Family Relations, 42,* 249–255.

Harley, K., & Reese, E. (1999). Origins of autobiographical memory. *Developmental Psychology, 35,* 1338–1348.

Harlow, H. F., & Zimmerman, R. (1959). Affectional responses in the infant monkey. *Science, 130,* 421–432.

Harold, G. T., & Conger, R. D. (1997). Marital conflict and adolescent distress: The role of adolescent awareness. *Child Development, 68,* 333–350.

Harootyan, R. A., & Vorek, R. E. (1994). Volunteering, helping and gift giving in families and communities. In V. L. Bengtson & R. A. Harootyan (Eds.), *Intergenerational linkages: Hidden connections in American society* (pp. 77–111). New York: Springer.

Harpaz, D., Benderly, M., Goldbourt, U., Kishan, Y., & Behar, S. (1996). Effect of aspirin on mortality in women with symptomatic or silent myocardial ischemia. *American Journal of Cardiology, 78,* 1215–1219.

Harrington, R., Rutter, M., & Fombonne, E. (1996). Developmental pathways in depression: Multiple meanings, antecedents, and endpoints. *Development and Psychopathology, 8,* 601–616.

Harris, G. (1997). Development of taste perception and appetite regulation. In G. Bremner, A. Slater, & G. Butterworth (Eds.), *Infant development: Recent advances* (pp. 9–30). East Sussex, England: Erlbaum.

Harris, I. B. (1996). *Children in jeopardy.* New Haven, CT: Yale University Press.

Harris, K. M. (2000). The health status and risk behavior of adolescents in immigrant families. In D. J. Hernandez (Ed.), *Children of immigrants: Health, adjustment, and public assistance.* Washington, DC: National Academy Press.

Harris, M. B. (1994). Growing old gracefully: Age concealment and gender. *Journal of Gerontology, 49,* P149–P158.

Harris, P. B. (1998). Listening to caregiving sons: Misunderstood realities. *Gerontologist, 38,* 342–352.

Harris, R. I. (1978). Impulse control in deaf children: Research and clinical issues. In L. S. Liben (Ed.), *Deaf children: Developmental perspectives* (pp. 137–156). New York: Academic Press.

Harris, R. L., Ellicott, A. M., & Holmes, D. S. (1986). The timing of psychosocial transitions and changes in women's lives: An examination of women aged 45 to 60. *Journal of Personality and Social Psychology, 51,* 409–416.

Harris, S., Mussen, P. H., & Rutherford, E. (1976). Some cognitive, behavioral, and personality correlates of maturity of moral judgment. *Journal of Genetic Psychology, 128,* 123–135.

Harrison, A. O., Wilson, M. N., Pine, C. J., Chan, S. Q., & Buriel, R. (1994). Family ecologies of ethnic minority children. In G. Handel & G. G. Whitchurch (Eds.), *The psychosocial interior of the family* (pp. 187–210). New York: Aldine de Gruyter.

Harrist, A. W., Zaia, A. F., Bates, J. E., Dodge, K. A., & Pettit, G. S. (1997). Subtypes of social withdrawal in early childhood: Sociometric status and social–cognitive differences across four years. *Child Development, 68,* 278–294.

Hart, B. (1991). Input frequency and children's first words. *First Language, 11,* 289–300.

Hart, B., & Risley, T. R. (1995). *Meaningful differences in the everyday experience of young American children.* Baltimore: Paul H. Brookes.

Hart, C. H., Burts, D. C., Durland, M. A., Charlesworth, R., DeWolf, M., & Fleege, P. O. (1998). Stress behaviors and activity type participation of preschoolers in more and less developmentally appropriate classrooms: SES and sex differences. *Journal of Research in Childhood Education, 13,* 176–196.

Harter, S. (1982). The perceived competence scale for children. *Child Development, 53,* 87–97.

Harter, S. (1990). Issues in the assessment of the self-concept of children and adolescents. In A. LaGreca (Ed.), *Through the eyes of a child* (pp. 292–325). Boston: Allyn & Bacon.

Harter, S. (1996). Developmental changes in self-understanding across the 5 to 7 shift. In A. J. Sameroff & M. M. Haith (Eds.), *The five to seven year shift* (pp. 207–236). Chicago: University of Chicago Press.

Harter, S. (1998). The development of self-representations. In N. Eisenberg (Ed.), *Handbook of child psychology: Vol. 3. Social, emotional, and personality development* (5th ed., pp. 553–618). New York: Wiley.

Harter, S., Marold, D. B., Whitesell, N. R., & Cobbs, G. (1996). A model of the effects of parent and peer support on adolescent false self-behavior. *Child Development, 67,* 360–374.

Harter, S., & Whitesell, N. (1989). Developmental changes in children's understanding of simple, multiple, and blended emotion concepts. In C. Saarni & P. Harris (Eds.), *Children's understanding of emotion* (pp. 81–116). Cambridge, England: Cambridge University Press.

Harter, S., Wright, K., & Bresnick, S. (1987). *A developmental sequence of the emergence of self affects.* Paper presented at the biennial meeting of the Society for Research in Child Development, Baltimore.

Hartley, A. A., & McKenzie, C. R. M. (1991). Attentional and perceptual contributions to the identification of extrafoveal stimuli: Adult age comparisons. *Journal of Gerontology, 46,* P202–P206.

Hartley, R. (1995). *Families and cultural diversity in Australia.* Sydney: Allen & Unwin.

Hartman, M., & Hasher, L. (1991). Aging and suppression: Memory for previously relevant information. *Psychology and Aging, 6,* 587–594.

Hartup, W., & Stevens, N. (1999). Friendships and adaptation across the lifespan. *New Directions in Psychological Science, 8,* 76–76.

Hartup, W. W. (1996). The company they keep: Friendships and their developmental significance. *Child Development, 67,* 1–13.

Harvey, J. H., & Omarzu, J. (1997). Minding the close relationship. *Personality and Social Psychology Review, 1,* 224–240.

Harvey, J. H., & Pauwels, B. G. (1999). Recent developments in close-relationships theory. *Current Directions in Psychological Science, 8,* 93–99.

Harway, M., & Hansen, M. (1994). *Spouse abuse.* Sarasota, FL: Professional Resource Press.

Hasher, L., Zacks, R. T., & May, C. P. (1999). Inhibitory control, circadian arousal, and age. In D. Gopher & A. Koriat (Eds.), *Attention and performance* (Vol. 17, pp. 653–675). Cambridge, MA: MIT Press.

Hashimoto, K., Noguchi, M., & Nakatsuji, N. (1992). Mouse offspring derived from fetal ovaries or reaggregates which were cultured and transplanted into adult females. *Development: Growth and Differentiation, 34,* 233–238.

Hashtroudi, S., Johnson, M. K., & Chrosniak, L. D. (1990). Aging and qualitative characteristics of memories for perceived and imagined complex events. *Psychology and Aging, 5,* 119–126.

Hatch, M. C., Shu, X.-O., McLean, D. E., Levin, B., Begg, M., Reuss, L., & Susser, M. (1993). Maternal exercise during pregnancy, physical fitness, and fetal growth. *American Journal of Epidemiology, 137,* 1105–1114.

Hatcher, P. J., Hulme, C., & Ellis, A. W. (1994). Ameliorating early reading failure by integrating the teaching of reading and phonological skills: The phonological linkage hypothesis. *Child Development, 65,* 41–57.

Hatfield, E. (1988). Passionate and companionate love. In R. J. Sternberg & M. L. Barnes (Eds.), *The psychology of love* (pp. 191–217). New Haven, CT: Yale University Press.

Hatfield, E. (1993). *Love, sex, and intimacy: Their psychology, biology, and history.* New York: HarperCollins.

Hatton, D. D., Bailey, D. B., Jr., Burchinal, M. R., & Ferrell, K. A. (1997). Developmental growth curves of preschool children with vision impairments. *Child Development, 68,* 788–806.

Hausfather, A., Toharia, A., LaRoche, C., & Engelsmann, F. (1997). Effects of age of entry, day-care quality, and family characteristics on preschool behavior. *Journal of Child Psychology and Psychiatry, 38,* 441–448.

Hauth, J. C., Goldenberg, R. L., Parker, C. R., Cutter, G. R., & Cliver, S. P. (1995). Low-dose aspirin—Lack of association with an increase in abruptio placentae or perinatal mortality. *Obstetrics and Gynecology, 85,* 1055–1058.

Havighurst, R., & Albrecht, R. (1953). *Older people.* New York: Longmans, Green.

Hawkins, A. J., Christiansen, S. L., Sargent, K. P., & Hill, E. J. (1993). Rethinking fathers' involvement in child care: A developmental perspective. *Journal of Family Issues, 14,* 531–549.

Hawkins, J. D., Catalano, R. F., & Miller, J. Y. (1992). Risk and protective factors for alcohol and other drug problems in ado-lescence and early adulthood: Implications for substance abuse prevention. *Psychological Bulletin, 112,* 64–105.

Hawkins, J. D., & Lam, T. (1987). Teacher practices, social development, and delinquency. In J. D. Burchard & S. N. Burchard (Eds.), *Prevention of delinquent behavior* (pp. 241–274). Newbury Park, CA: Sage.

Hawkins, J. N. (1994). Issues of motivation in Asian education. In H. F. O'Neil, Jr., & M. Drillings (Eds.), *Motivation: Theory and research* (pp. 101–115). Hillsdale, NJ: Erlbaum.

Haworth, K., & Strosnider, K. (1997, March 14). Controversy grows over cloning research as scientists report new breakthoughs. *Chronicle of Higher Education,* p. A14.

Hay, J. F., & Jacoby, L. L. (1999). Separating habit and recollection in young and older adults: Effects of elaborative processing and distinctiveness. *Psychology and Aging, 14,* 122–134.

Hayflick, L. (1994). *How and why we age.* New York: Ballantine.

Hayne, H., Rovee-Collier, C., & Perris, E. E. (1987). Categorization and memory retrieval by three-month-olds. *Child Development, 58,* 750–767.

Hayslip, B., Jr. (1994). Stability of intelligence. In R. J. Sternberg (Ed.), *Encyclopedia of human intelligence* (Vol. 2, pp. 1019–1026). New York: Macmillan.

Hayward, M. D., Hardy, M. A., & Liu, M. (1994). Work after retirement: The experiences of older men in the U.S. *Social Science Research, 23,* 82–107.

Hazan, C., & Shaver, P. R. (1987). Romantic love conceptualized as an attachment process. *Journal of Personality and Social Psychology, 52,* 511–524.

Heath, S. B. (1982). Questioning at home and at school: A comparative study. In G. Spindler (Ed.), *Doing the ethnography of schooling: Educational anthropology in action* (pp. 102–127). New York: Holt.

Heath, S. B. (1989). Oral and literate traditions among black Americans living in poverty. *American Psychologist, 44,* 367–373.

Heath, S. B. (1990). The children of Trackton's children: Spoken and written in social change. In J. Stigler, G. Herdt, & R. A. Shweder (Eds.), *Cultural psychology: Essays on comparative human development* (pp. 496–519). New York: Cambridge University Press.

Hecht, M., Marston, P. J., & Larkey, L. K. (1994). Love ways and relationship quality. *Journal of Social and Personal Relationships, 11,* 25–43.

Hedges, L. V., & Nowell, A. (1995). Sex differences in mental scores, variability, and numbers of high-scoring individuals. *Science, 269,* 41–45.

Heffner, R. W., & Kelley, M. L. (1994). Nonorganic failure to thrive: Develop-mental outcomes and psychosocial assessment and intervention issues. *Research in Developmental Disabilities, 15,* 247–268.

Heidrich, S. M., & Denney, N. W. (1994). Does social problem solving differ from other types of problem solving during the adult years? *Experimental Aging Research, 20,* 105–126.

Heidrich, S. M., & Ryff, C. D. (1993). Physical and mental health in later life: The self-system as mediator. *Psychology and Aging, 8,* 327–338.

Heine, S. J., & Lehman, D. R. (1995). Cultural variation in unrealistic optimism: Does the West feel more invulnerable than the East? *Journal of Personality and Social Psychology, 68,* 595–607.

Heinl, T. (1983). *The baby massage book.* London: Coventure.

Heinonen, O. P., Slone, D., & Shapiro, S. (1977). *Birth defects and drugs in pregnancy.* Littleton, MA: PSG Publishing Company.

Helburn, S. W. (Ed.). (1995). *Cost, quality and child outcomes in child care centers.* Denver: University of Colorado.

Helmers, K. F., Posluszny, D. M., & Krantz, D. S. (1994). Associations of hostility and coronary artery disease: A review of studies. In A. W. Siegman & T. W. Smith (Eds.), *Anger, hostility, and the heart* (pp. 67–96). Hillsdale, NJ: Erlbaum.

Helson, R. (1992). Women's difficult times and the rewriting of the life story. *Psychology of Women Quarterly, 16,* 331–347.

Helson, R. (1997). The self in middle age. In M. E. Lachman & J. B. James (Eds.), *Multiple paths of midlife development* (pp. 21–43). Chicago: University of Chicago Press.

Helson, R., Mitchell, V., & Moane, G. (1984). Personality and patterns of adherence and nonadherence to the social clock. *Journal of Personality and Social Psychology, 46,* 1079–1096.

Helson, R., & Moane, G. (1987). Personality change in women from college to midlife. *Journal of Personality and Social Psychology, 53,* 176–186.

Helson, R., & Picano, J. (1990). Is the traditional role bad for women? *Journal of Personality and Social Psychology, 59,* 311–320.

Helson, R., & Roberts, B. W. (1994). Ego development and personality change in adulthood. *Journal of Personality and Social Psychology, 66,* 911–920.

Helson, R., & Stewart, A. (1994). Personality change in adulthood. In T. F. Heatherton & J. L. Weinberger (Eds.), *Can personality change?* (pp. 201–225). Washington, DC: American Psychological Association.

Helson, R., & Wink, P. (1992). Personality change in women from the early 40s to the early 50s. *Psychology and Aging, 7,* 46–55.

Hendin, H. (1999). Suicide, assisted suicide, and euthanasia. In D. G. Jacobs (Ed.), *The Harvard Medical School guide to suicide assessment and intervention* (pp. 540–560). San Francisco: Jossey-Bass.

Hendin, H., Rutenfrans, C., & Zylicz, Z. (1997). Physician-assisted suicide and euthanasia in the Netherlands: Lessons from the Dutch. *Journal of the American Medical Association, 277,* 1720–1722.

Hendrick, S. S., & Hendrick, C. (1992). *Romantic love.* Newbury Park, CA: Sage.

Hendrick, S. S., & Hendrick, C. (1993). Lovers as friends. *Journal of Social and Personal Relationships, 10,* 459–466.

Herdt, G., & Boxer, A. M. (1993). *Children of horizons: How gay and lesbian teens are leading a new way out of the closet.* Boston: Beacon Press.

Herman, M. R., Dornbusch, S. M., Herron, M. C., & Herting, J. R. (1997). The influence of family regulation, connection, and psychological autonomy on six measures of adolescent functioning. *Journal of Adolescent Research, 12,* 34–67.

Herrnstein, R. J., & Murray, C. (1994). *The bell curve.* New York: Free Press.

Hershey, D. A., Walsh, D. A., Brougham, R., & Carter, S. (1998). Challenges of training pre-retirees to make sound financial planning decisions. *Educational Gerontology, 24,* 447–470.

Hetherington, E. M. (1989). Coping with family transitions: Winners, losers, and survivors. *Child Development, 60,* 1–14.

Hetherington, E. M. (1991). The role of individual differences and family relationships in children's coping with divorce and remarriage. In P. A. Cowan & E. M. Hetherington (Eds.), *Family transitions* (pp. 165–194). Hillsdale, NJ: Erlbaum.

Hetherington, E. M. (1993). An overview of the Virginia Longitudinal Study of Divorce and Remarriage: A focus on early adolescence. *Journal of Family Psychology, 7,* 39–56.

Hetherington, E. M. (1995, March). *The changing American family and the well-being of children.* Master lecture presented at the biennial meeting of the Society for Research in Child Development, Indianapolis.

Hetherington, E. M. (1997). Teenaged childbearing and divorce. In S. Luthar, J. A. Burack, D. Cicchetti, & J. Weisz (Eds.), *Developmental psychopathology: Perspectives on adjustment, risk, and disorders* (pp. 350–373). Cambridge, UK: Cambridge University Press.

Hetherington, E. M. (1999). Social capital and the development of youth from nondivorced, divorced, and remarried families. In A. Collins (Ed.), *Minnesota Symposia on Child Psychology* (Vol. 29). Hillsdale, NJ: Erlbaum.

Hetherington, E. M., Bridges, M., & Insabella, G. M. (1998). What matters? What does not? Five perspectives on the association between marital transitions and children's adjustment. *American Psychologist, 53,* 167–184.

Hetherington, E. M., & Clingempeel, W. G. (1992). Coping with marital transitions: A family systems perspective. *Monographs of the Society for Research in Child Development, 57*(2–3, Serial No. 227).

Hetherington, E. M., Cox, M., & Cox, R. (1985). Long-term effects of divorce and remarriage on the adjustment of children. *Journal of the American Academy of Child Psychiatry, 24,* 518–530.

Hetherington, E. M., & Henderson, S. H. (1997). Fathers in stepfamilies. In M. E. Lamb (Ed.), *The role of the father in child development* (pp. 212–226). New York: Wiley.

Hetherington, E. M., & Jodl, K. M. (1994). Stepfamilies as settings for child development. In A. Booth & J. Dunn (Eds.), *Stepfamilies: Who benefits? Who does not?* (pp. 55–79). Hillsdale, NJ: Erlbaum.

Hetherington, E. M., Law, T. C., & O'Connor, T. G. (1994). Divorce: Challenges, changes, and new chances. In F. Walsh (Ed.), *Normal family processes* (2nd ed., pp. 208–234). New York: Guilford.

Hetherington, E. M., & Stanley-Hagan, M. M. (1997). The effects of divorce on fathers and their children. In M. E. Lamb (Ed.), *The role of the father in child development* (pp. 191–211). New York: Wiley.

Hetherington, S. E. (1990). A controlled study of the effect of prepared childbirth classes on obstetric outcomes. *Birth, 17,* 86–90.

Hewlett, B. S. (1992). Husband–wife reciprocity and the father–infant relationship among Aka pygmies. In B. S. Hewlett (Ed.), *Father–child relations: Cultural and biosocial contexts* (pp. 153–176). New York: Aldine de Gruyter.

Heyman, G. D., & Dweck, C. S. (1998). Children's thinking about traits: Implications for judgments of the self and others. *Child Development, 69,* 391–403.

Heyman, G. D., Dweck, C. S., & Cain, K. M. (1992). Young children's vulnerability to self-blame and helplessness: Relationship to beliefs about goodness. *Child Development, 63,* 401–415.

Heyman, G. D., & Gelman, S. A. (1999). The use of trait labels in making psychological inferences. *Child Development, 70,* 604–619.

Hicks, P. (1997, January). The impact of aging on public policy. *OECD Observer,* No. 203, 19–21.

Hier, D. B., & Crowley, W. F. (1982). Spatial ability in androgen-deficient men. *New England Journal of Medicine, 302,* 1202–1205.

Hill, E. M., Young, J. P., & Nord, J. L. (1994). Childhood adversity, attachment security, and adult relationships: A preliminary study. *Ethology and Sociobiology, 15,* 323–338.

Hill, J. P., & Holmbeck, G. (1986). Attachment and autonomy during adolescence. In G. Whitehurst (Ed.), *Annals of child development* (Vol. 3, pp. 145–189). Greenwich, CT: JAI Press.

Hill, R. B. (1997). Social welfare policies and African American families. In H. P. McAdoo (Ed.), *Black families* (3rd ed., pp. 349–364). Thousand Oaks, CA: Sage.

Hillman, J. L., & Stricker, G. (1994). A linkage of knowledge and attitudes toward elderly sexuality: Not necessarily a uniform relationship. *Gerontologist, 34,* 256–260.

Hills-Banczyk, S. G., Avery, M. D., Savik, K., Potter, S., & Duckett, L. J. (1993). Women's experiences with combining breast-feeding and employment. *Journal of Nurse-Midwifery, 38,* 257–266.

Himes, J. H., Story, M., Czaplinski, K., & Dahlberg-Luby, E. (1992). Indications of early obesity in low-income Hmong children. *American Journal of Diseases of Children, 146,* 67–69.

Hinde, R. A. (1989). Ethological and relationships approaches. In R. Vasta (Ed.), *Annals of child development* (Vol. 6, pp. 251–285). Greenwich, CT: JAI Press.

Hirsch, C. (1996). Understanding the influence of gender role identity on the assumption of family caregiving roles by men. *International Journal of Aging and Human Development, 42,* 103–121.

Hirschfeld, L. A. (1995). Do children have a theory of race? *Cognition, 54,* 209–252.

Hirshorn, B. A. (1998). Grandparents as caregivers. In M. E. Szinovacs (Ed.), *Handbook on grandparenthood* (pp. 200–214). Westport, CT: Greenwood Press.

Hirsh-Pasek, K., Kemler Nelson, D. G., Jusczyk, P. W., Cassidy, K. W., Druss, B., & Kennedy, L. (1987). Clauses are perceptual units for young infants. *Cognition, 26,* 269–286.

Hobart, C., & Brown, D. (1988). Effects of prior marriage children on adjustment in remarriages: A Canadian study. *Journal of Comparative Family Studies, 19,* 381–396.

Hobeika, C. P. (1999). Equilibrium and balance in the elderly. *Ear, Nose, and Throat Journal, 78,* 558–562.

Hobson, R. P. (1993). *Autism and the development of mind.* London: Erlbaum.

Hoch, C. C., Dew, M. A., Reynolds, C. F., III, Buysse, D. J., Nowell, P. D., Monk, T. H., Mazumdar, S., Borland, M. D., Miewald, J., & Kupfer, D. J. (1997). Longitudinal changes in diary- and laboratory-based sleep measures in healthy "old old" and "young old" subjects: A three-year follow-up. *Sleep, 20,* 192–202.

Hocutt, A. M. (1996). Effectiveness of special education: Is placement the critical factor? *Future of Children, 6,* 77–102.

Hodapp, R. M. (1996). Down syndrome: Developmental, psychiatric, and management issues. *Child and Adolescent Psychiatric Clinics of North America, 5,* 881–894.

Hodges, E. V. E., Boivin, M., Vitaro, F., & Bukowski, W. M. (1999). The power of friendship: Protection against an escalating cycle of peer victimization. *Developmental Psychology, 35,* 94–101.

Hodges, J., & Tizard, B. (1989). Social and family relationships of ex-institutional adolescents. *Journal of Child Psychology and Psychiatry, 30,* 77–97.

Hodges, R. M., & French, L. A. (1988). The effect of class and collection labels on cardinality, class-inclusion, and number conservation tasks. *Child Development, 59,* 1387–1396.

Hodson, D. S., & Skeen, P. (1994). Sexuality and aging: The hammerlock of myths. *Journal of Applied Gerontology, 13,* 219–235.

Hoff-Ginsburg, E. (1986). Function and structure in maternal speech: Their relation to the child's development of syntax. *Developmental Psychology, 22,* 155–163.

Hoff-Ginsberg, E., & Tardiff, T. (1995). Socioeconomic status and parenting. In M. Bornstein (Ed.), *Handbook of parenting* (Vol. 2, pp. 161–188). Hillsdale, NJ: Erlbaum.

Hoffman, L. W. (1989). Effects of maternal employment in the two-parent family. *American Psychologist, 44,* 283–292.

Hoffman, M. L. (1988). Moral development. In M. H. Bornstein & M. E. Lamb (Eds.), *Developmental psychology: An advanced textbook* (2nd ed., pp. 497–548). Hillsdale, NJ: Erlbaum.

Hoffman, M. L. (1991). Empathy, cognition, and social action. In W. M. Kurtines & J. L. Gewirtz (Eds.), *Handbook of moral behavior and development* (Vol. 1, pp. 275–303). Hillsdale, NJ: Erlbaum.

Hoffman, S., & Hatch, M. C. (1996). Stress, social support and pregnancy outcome: A reassessment based on research. *Paediatric and Perinatal Epidemiology, 10,* 380–405.

Hoffner, C., & Badzinski, D. M. (1989). Children's integration of facial and situational cues to emotion. *Child Development, 60,* 411–422.

Hofstede, G. (1980). *Culture's consequences: International differences in work-related values.* London: Sage.

Hogervorst, E., Boshuisen, M., Riedel, W., Willeken, C., & Jolles, J. (1998). The effect of hormone replacement therapy on cognitive function in elderly women. *Psychoneuroendocrinology, 24,* 43–68.

Hokoda, A., & Fincham, F. D. (1995). Origins of children's helpless and mastery achievement patterns in the family. *Journal of Educational Psychology, 87,* 375–385.

Holahan, C. K. (1984). Marital attitudes over 40 years: A longitudinal cohort analysis. *Journal of Gerontology, 39,* 49–57.

Holden, G. W., Coleman, S. M., & Schmidt, K. L. (1995). Why 3-year-old children get spanked: Determinants as reported by college-educated mothers. *Merrill-Palmer Quarterly, 41,* 431–452.

Holden, G. W., Geffner, R., & Jouriles, E. N. (Eds.). (1998). *Children exposed to marital violence.* Washington, DC: American Psychological Association.

Holden, G. W., & West, M. J. (1989). Proximate regulation by mothers: A demonstration of how differing styles affect young children's behavior. *Child Development, 60,* 64–69.

Holland, J. C. (Ed.). (1998). *Psycho-oncology.* New York: Oxford University Press.

Holland, J. L. (1966). *The psychology of vocational choice.* Waltham, MA: Blaisdell.

Holland, J. L. (1985). *Making vocational choices: A theory of vocational personalities and work environments.* Englewood Cliffs, NJ: Prentice Hall.

Holmbeck, G. N. (1996). A model of family relational transformations during the transition to adolescence: Parent–adolescent conflict and adaptation. In J. A. Graber, J. Brooks-Gunn, & A. C. Petersen (Eds.), *Transitions through adolescence* (pp. 167–199). Mahwah, NJ: Erlbaum.

Holmbeck, G. N., & Hill, J. P. (1991). Conflictive engagement, positive affect, and menarche in families with seventh-grade girls. *Child Development, 62,* 1030–1048.

Holmbeck, G. N., & Wandrei, M. L. (1993). Individual and relational predictors of adjustment in first-year college students. *Journal of Counseling Psychology, 40,* 73–78.

Holmbeck, G. N., Waters, K. A., & Brookman, R. R. (1990). Psychosocial correlates of sexually transmitted diseases and sexual activity in black adolescent females. *Journal of Adolescent Research, 5,* 431–448.

Holmes, E. R., & Holmes, L. D. (1995). *Other cultures, elder years* (2nd ed.). Thousand Oaks, CA: Sage.

Holmes, W. C., & Slap, G. B. (1998). Sexual abuse of boys: Definition, prevalence, correlates, sequelae, and management. *Journal of the American Medical Association, 280,* 1855–1862.

Holmes-Rovner, M., Rovner, D. R., Padonu, G., Talarczyk, G., Kroll, J., Rothert, M., & Breer, L. (1996). African-American women's attitudes and expectations of menopause. *American Journal of Preventive Medicine, 12,* 420–423.

Holtzman, D. M., Bales, K. R., Wu, S., Bhat, P., Parsadanian, M., Fagan, A. M., Chang, L. K., Sun, Y., & Paul, S. M. (1999). Expression of human apolipoprotein E reduces amyloid-beta deposition in a mouse model of Alzheimer's disease. *Journal of Clinical Investigation, 103*(6), R15–R21.

Hooker, K. (1992). Possible selves and perceived health in older adults and college students. *Journal of Gerontology, 47,* P85–P89.

Hooker, K., & Kaus, C. R. (1992). Possible selves and health behaviors in later life. *Journal of Aging and Health, 4,* 390–411.

Hooker, K., & Kaus, C. R. (1994). Health-related possible selves in young and middle adulthood. *Psychology and Aging, 9,* 126–133.

Hooyman, N. R., & Kiyak, H. A. (1998). *Social gerontology: A multidisciplinary perspective* (3rd ed.). Boston: Allyn and Bacon.

Hopkins, B., & Butterworth, G. (1997). Dynamical systems approaches to the development of action. In G. Bremner, A. Slater, & G. Butterworth (Eds.), *Infant development: Recent advances* (pp. 75–100). East Sussex, England: Psychology Press.

Hopkins, B., & Westra, T. (1988). Maternal handling and motor development: An intracultural study. *Genetic, Social and General Psychology Monographs, 14,* 377–420.

Hopper, S. V. (1993). The influence of ethnicity on the health of older women. *Clinics in Geriatric Medicine, 9,* 231–259.

Horgan, D. (1978). The development of the full passive. *Journal of Child Language, 5,* 65–80.

Horgas, A. L., Wilms, H., & Baltes, M. M. (1998). Daily life in very old age: Everyday activities as expression of successful living. *Gerontologist, 38,* 556–568.

Horn, J. L. (1982). The aging of human abilities. In B. B. Wolman (Ed.), *Handbook of developmental psychology* (pp. 847–870). Englewood Cliffs, NJ: Prentice-Hall.

Horn, J. L., & Donaldson, G. (1980). Cognitive development in adulthood. In O. G. Brim, Jr., & J. Kagan (Eds.), *Constancy and change in human development* (pp. 445–529). Cambridge, MA: Harvard University Press.

Horn, J. L., Donaldson, G., & Engstrom, R. (1981). Apprehension, memory, and fluid intelligence decline through the "vital years" of adulthood. *Research on Aging, 3,* 33–84.

Horn, J. M. (1983). The Texas Adoption Project: Adopted children and their intellectual resemblance to biological and adoptive parents. *Child Development, 54,* 268–275.

Horner, T. M. (1980). Two methods of studying stranger reactivity in infants: A review. *Journal of Child Psychology and Psychiatry, 21,* 203–219.

Hornick, J. P., McDonald, L., & Robertson, G. B. (1992). Elder abuse in Canada and the United States: Prevalence, legal, and service issues. In R. D. Peters, R. J. McMahon, & V. L. Quinsey (Eds.), *Aggression and violence throughout the life span* (pp. 301–335). Newbury Park, CA: Sage.

Horowitz, A. (1985). Sons and daughters as caregivers to older parents: Differences in role performance and consequences. *Gerontologist, 25,* 612–617.

Horowitz, A. V., McLaughlin, J., & White, H. R. (1997). How the negative and positive aspects of partner relationships affect the mental health of young married people. *Journal of Health and Social Behavior, 39,* 124–136.

Horowitz, A. V., White, H. R., & Howell-White, S. (1996). Becoming married and mental health: A longitudinal study of a cohort of young adults. *Journal of Marriage and the Family, 58,* 895–907.

Horowitz, F. D. (1992). John B. Watson's legacy: Learning and environment. *Developmental Psychology, 28,* 360–367.

Hotz, V. J., McElroy, S. W., & Sanders, S. G. (1997). The costs and consequences of teenage childbearing for mothers. In R. A. Maynard (Ed.), *Kids having kids* (pp. 55–94). Washington, DC: Urban Institute.

House, J. S., Kessler, R. C., Herzog, A. R., Mero, R. P., Kinney, A. M., & Breslow, M. J. (1990a). Age, socioeconomic status, and health. *Milbank Quarterly, 68,* 383–411.

House, J. S., Kessler, R. C., Herzog, A. R., Mero, R. P., Kinney, A. M., & Breslow, M. J. (1990b). *The social stratification of aging and health.* Ann Arbor, MI: Institute for Social Research.

Houseknecht, S. K. (1987). Voluntary childlessness. In M. B. Sussman & S. K. Steinmetz (Eds.), *Handbook of marriage and the family* (pp. 369–392). New York: Plenum.

Housel, D. A. (1995). Spirituality and death and dying from a gay perspective. In J. K. Parry & A. S. Ryan (Eds.), *A cross-cultural look at death, dying, and religion* (pp. 117–130). Chicago: Nelson-Hall.

Houts, A. C. (1991). Nocturnal enuresis as a biobehavioral problem. *Behavior Therapy, 22,* 133–151.

Houts, A. C., Berman, J. S., & Abramson, H. (1994). Effectiveness of psychological and pharmacological treatments for noctural enuresis. *Journal of Consulting and Clinical Psychology, 62,* 737–745.

Howard, A., & Bray, D. W. (1988). *Managerial lives in transition: Advancing age and changing times.* New York: Guilford Press.

Howe, M. L., & Courage, M. L. (1997). The emergence and early development of autobiographical memory. *Psychological Review, 104,* 499–523.

Howe, N., & Ross, H. S. (1990). Socialization, perspective-taking, and the sibling relationship. *Developmental Psychology, 26,* 160–165.

Howes, C. (1988). Relations between early child care and schooling. *Developmental Psychology, 24,* 53–57.

Howes, C. (1990). Can the age of entry into child care and the quality of child care predict adjustment in kindergarten? *Developmental Psychology, 26,* 292–303.

Howes, C. (1992). *The collaborative construction of pretend.* Albany, NY: SUNY Press.

Howes, C., & Matheson, C. C. (1992). Sequences in the development of competent play with peers: Social and social pretend play. *Developmental Psychology, 28,* 961–974.

Howes, C., Phillips, D. A., & Whitebook, M. (1992). Thresholds of quality: Implications for the social development of children in center-based child care. *Child Development, 63,* 449–460.

Hsu, F. L. K. (1981). *Americans and Chinese: Passage to difference* (3rd ed.). Honolulu: University of Hawaii Press.

Hudson, J. A., Fivush, R., & Kuebli, J. (1992). Scripts and episodes: The development of event memory. *Applied Cognitive Psychology, 6,* 483–505.

Huesmann, L. R. (1986). Psychological processes promoting the relation between exposure to media violence and aggressive behavior by the viewer. *Journal of Social Issues, 42,* 125–139.

Hughes, C. (1998). Finding your marbles: Does preschoolers' strategic behavior predict later understanding of mind? *Developmental Psychology, 34,* 1326–1339.

Hughes, C., & Dunn, J. (1998). Understanding mind and emotion: Longitudinal associations with mental-state talk between young friends. *Developmental Psychology, 34,* 1026–1037.

Hughes, F. P. (1998). Play in special populations. In O. N. Saracho & B. Spodek (Eds.), *Multiple perspectives on play in early childhood education* (pp. 171–193). Albany: State University of New York Press.

Hultsch, D. F., & Dixon, R. A. (1990). Learning and memory in aging. In J. E. Birren & K. W. Schaie (Eds.), *Handbook of the psychology of aging* (3rd ed., pp. 258–274). San Diego: Academic Press.

Hultsch, D. F., Hertzog, C., Dixon, R. A., & Small, B. J. (1998). *Memory change in the aged.* New York: Cambridge University Press.

Human Genome Program. (2000). *Count of mapped genes by chromosome.* Washington, DC: U.S. Department of Energy, Office of Biological and Environmental Research.

Humphrey, D., & Clement, M. (1998). *Freedom to die: People, politics, and the right-to-die movement.* New York: St. Martin's Press.

Humphrey, T. (1978). Function of the nervous system during prenatal life. In U. Stave (Ed.), *Perinatal physiology* (pp. 651–683). New York: Plenum.

Hunt, E., Streissguth, A. P., Kerr, B., & Olson, H. C. (1995). Mothers' alcohol consumption during pregnancy: Effects on spatial-visual reasoning in 14-year-old children. *Psychological Science, 6,* 339–342.

Huntington, L., Hans, S. L., & Zeskind, P. S. (1990). The relations among cry characteristics, demographic variables, and developmental test scores in infants prenatally exposed to methadone. *Infant Behavior and Development, 13,* 533–538.

Huntsinger, C. S., Jose, P. E., & Larson, S. L. (1998). Do parent practices to encourage academic competence influence the social adjustment of young European American and Chinese American Children? *Developmental Psychology, 34,* 747–756.

Hurme, H. (1991). Dimensions of the grandparent role in Finland. In P. K. Smith (Ed.), *The psychology of grandparenthood: An international perspective* (pp. 19–31). London: Routledge.

Husaini, B. A., Blasi, A. J., & Miller, O. (1999). Does public and private religiosity have a moderating effect on depression? A bi-racial study of elders in the American south. *International Journal of Aging and Human Development, 48,* 63–72.

Huston, A. C. (1983). Sex-typing. In E. M. Hetherington (Ed.), *Handbook of child psychology: Vol. 4. Socialization, personality, and social development* (4th ed., pp. 387–467). New York: Wiley.

Huston, A. C. (1994, Summer). *Children in poverty: Child development and public policy.* Cambridge, England: Cambridge University Press.

Huston, A. C., & Alvarez, M. M. (1990). The socialization context of gender role development in early adolescence. In R. Montemayor, G. R. Adams, & T. P. Gullotta (Eds.), *From childhood to adolescence: A transitional period?* (pp. 156–179). Newbury Park, CA: Sage.

Huston, A. C., Donnerstein, E., Fairchild, H., Feshbach, N. D., Katz, P. A., Murray, J. P., Rubinstein, E. A., Wilcox, B. L., & Zuckerman, D. (1992). *Big world, small screen: The role of television in American society.* Lincoln: University of Nebraska Press.

Huston, P., McHale, S., & Crouter, A. (1986). When the honeymoon's over: Changes in the marriage relationship over the first year. In R. Gilmour & S. Duck (Eds.), *The emerging field of personal relationships* (pp. 109–132). Hillsdale, NJ: Erlbaum.

Huston, T. L., & Vangelisti, A. L. (1995). How parenthood affects marriage. In M. A. Fitzpatrick & A. L. Vangelisti (Eds.), *Explaining family interactions* (pp. 147–176). Thousand Oaks, CA: Sage.

Huttenlocher, P. R. (1994). Synaptogenesis in the human cerebral cortex. In

G. Dawson & K. W. Fischer (Eds.), *Human behavior and the developing brain* (pp. 137– 152). New York: Guilford.

Huyck, M. H. (1990). Gender differences in aging. In J. E. Birren & K. W. Schaie (Eds.), *Handbook of the psychology of aging* (3rd ed., pp. 124–134). New York: Academic Press.

Huyck, M. H. (1995). Marriage and close relationships of the marital kind. In R. Blieszner & V. H. Bedford (Eds.), *Handbook of aging and the family* (pp. 181– 200). Westport, CT: Greenwood Press.

Huyck, M. H. (1996). Continuities and discontinuities in gender identity. In V. L. Bengtson (Ed.), *Adulthood and aging* (pp. 98– 121). New York: Springer-Verlag.

Huyck, M. H. (1998). Gender roles and gender identity in midlife. In S. L. Willis & J. D. Reid (Eds.), *Life in the middle* (pp. 209–232). San Diego: Academic Press.

Hyde, J. S. (1995). Women and maternity leave: Empirical data and public policy. *Psychology of Women Quarterly, 19,* 299–313.

Hyde, J. S., Klein, M. H., Essex, M. J., & Clark, R. (1995). Maternity leave and women's mental health. *Psychology of Women Quarterly, 19, 257–285.*

Hyde, J. S., & Linn, M. C. (1988). Gender differences in verbal ability: A meta-analysis. *Psychological Bulletin, 104,* 53–69.

Ianni, F. A. J., & Orr, M. T. (1996). Dropping out. In J. A. Graber, J. Brooks-Gunn, & A. C. Petersen (Eds.), *Transitions through adolescence: Interpersonal domains and context* (pp. 285–322). Mahwah, NJ: Erlbaum

Idler, E. L., & Kasl, S. V. (1997). Religion among disabled and nondisabled persons I: Cross-sectional patterns in health practices, social activities, and well-being. *Journal of Gerontology, 52B,* S294–S305.

Ihinger-Tallman, M., & Pasley, K. (1997). Stepfamilies in 1984 and today—A scholarly perspective. *Marriage and Family Review, 26,* 19–40.

Ikkink, K. K., & van Tilburg, T. (1998). Do older adults' network members continue to provide instrumental support in unbalanced relationships? *Journal of Social and Personal Relationships, 15,* 59–75.

Inhelder, B., & Piaget, J. (1958). *The growth of logical thinking from childhood to adolescence: An essay on the construction of formal operational structures.* New York: Basic Books. (Original work published 1955)

Innis, S. M., Nelson, C. M., Lwanga, D., Rioux, F. M., & Waslen, P. (1996). Feeding formula without arachidonic acid and docosahexaenoic acid has no effect on preferential looking acuity or recognition memory in healthy full-term infants at 9 months of age. *American Journal of Clinical Nutrition, 64,* 40–46.

Intons-Peterson, M. J. (1988). *Gender concepts of Swedish and American youth.* Hillsdale, NJ: Erlbaum.

Irvine, J. J. (1986). Teacher–student interactions: Effects of student race, sex, and grade level. *Journal of Educational Psychology, 78,* 14–21.

Isabella, R. (1993). Origins of attachment: Maternal interactive behavior across the first year. *Child Development, 64,* 605–621.

Isabella, R., & Belsky, J. (1991). Interactional synchrony and the origins of infant–mother attachment: A replication study. *Child Development, 62,* 373–384.

Ishii-Kuntz, M. (1990). Social interaction and psychological well-being: Comparison across stages of adulthood. *International Journal of Aging and Human Development, 30,* 15–36.

Isley, S. L., O'Neil, R., Clatfelter, D., & Parke, R. D. (1999). Parent and child expressed affect and children's social competence: Modeling direct and indirect pathways. *Developmental Psychology, 35,* 547–560.

Iverson, J. M., Capirci, O., & Caselli, M. C. (1994). From communication to language in two modalities. *Cognitive Development, 9,* 23–43.

Izard, C. E. (1991). *The psychology of emotions.* New York: Plenum.

Izard, C. E., Fantauzzo, C. A., Castle, J. M., Haynes, O. M., Rayias, M. F., & Putnam, P. H. (1995). The ontogeny and significance of infants' facial expressions in the first 9 months of life. *Developmental Psychology, 31,* 997–1013.

Jack, C. R., Petersen R. C., Xu, Y. C., O'Brien, P. C., Smith, G. E., Ivnik, R. J., Boeve, B. F., Waring, S. C., Tangalos, E. G., & Kokmen, E. (1999). Prediction of AD with MRI-based hippocampal volume in mild cognitive impairment. *Neurology, 52,* 1397–1403.

Jacobs, D. M., Tang, M. X., Stern, Y., Sano, M., Marder, K., & Bell, K. L. (1998). Cognitive function in nondemented older women who took estrogen after menopause. *Neurology, 50,* 368–373.

Jacobs, J. E., & Weisz, V. (1994). Gender stereotypes: Implications for gifted education. *Roeper Review, 16,* 152–155.

Jacobson, C. K., & Heaton, T. B. (1989). Voluntary childlessness among American men and women in the late 1980s. *Social Biology, 38,* 79–93.

Jacobson, J. L., Jacobson, S. W., Fein, G., Schwartz, P. M., & Dowler, J. (1984). Prenatal exposure to an environmental toxin: A test of the multiple effects model. *Developmental Psychology, 20,* 523–532.

Jacobson, J. L., Jacobson, S. W., Padgett, R. J., Brumitt, G. A., & Billings, R. L. (1992). Effects of prenatal PCB exposure on cognitive processing efficiency and sustained attention. *Developmental Psychology, 28,* 297–306.

Jacobson, S. W. (1998). Specificity of neurobehavioral outcomes associated with prenatal alcohol exposure. *Alcoholism: Clinical and Experimental Research, 22,* 313–320.

Jacobson, S. W., Jacobson, J. L., Sokol, R. J., Martier, S. S., & Ager, J. W. (1993). Prenatal alcohol exposure and infant information processing ability. *Child Development, 64,* 1706–1721.

Jacques, P. F. (1999). The potential preventive effects of vitamins for cataract and age-related macular degeneration. *International Journal of Vitamin Nutrition Research, 69,* 198–205.

Jadack, R. A., Hyde, J. S., Moore, C. F., & Keller, M. L. (1995). Moral reasoning about sexually transmitted diseases. *Child Development, 66,* 167–177.

Jamieson, J. R. (1994). Teaching as transaction: Vygotskian perspectives on deafness and mother–child interaction. *Exceptional Children, 60,* 434–449.

Jamieson, J. R. (1995a). Interactions between mothers and children who are deaf. *Journal of Early Intervention, 19,* 108–117.

Jamieson, J. R. (1995b). Visible thought: Deaf children's use of signed and spoken private speech. *Sign Language Studies, 86,* 63–80.

Jansari, A., & Parkin, A. J. (1996). Things that go bump in your life: Explaining the reminiscence bump in autobiographical memory. *Psychology and Aging, 11,* 85–91.

Janssens, J. M. A. M., & Deković, M. (1997). Child rearing, prosocial moral reasoning, and prosocial behaviour. *International Journal of Behavioral Development, 20,* 509–527.

Jasper, M. (1996). *The right to die .* Dobbs Ferry, NY: Oceana Publications.

Jazwinski, S. M. (1996). Longevity, genes, and aging. *Science, 273,* 54–59.

Jenkins, J. M., & Astington, J. W. (1996). Cognitive factors and family structure associated with theory of mind development in young children. *Developmental Psychology, 32,* 70–78.

Jenkins, S. R., & Maslach, C. (1994). Psychological health and involvement in interpersonally demanding occupations: A longitudinal perspective. *Journal of Organizational Behavior, 15,* 101–127.

Jenrek, M. P. (1994). Grandparents who parent their grandchildren: Circumstances and decisions. *Gerontologist, 34,* 206–216.

Jensen, A. R. (1969). How much can we boost IQ and scholastic achievement? *Harvard Educational Review, 39,* 1–123.

Jensen, A. R. (1980). *Bias in mental testing.* New York: Free Press.

Jensen, A. R. (1985). The nature of the black–white difference on various psychometric tests: Spearman's hypothesis. *Behavioral and Brain Sciences, 8,* 193–219.

Jensen, A. R. (1998). *The g factor: The science of mental ability.* New York: Praeger.

Jepson, K. L., & Labouvie-Vief, G. (1992). Symbolic processing of youth and elders. In R. L. West and J. D. Sinnott (Eds.), *Everyday memory and aging* (pp. 124–137). New York: Springer.

Jerrome, D. (1990). Intimate relationships. In J. Bond & P. Coleman (Eds.), *Aging in society* (pp. 181–208). London: Sage.

Jessor, R. (1996). Ethnographic methods in contemporary perspective. In R. Jessor, A. Colby, & R. A. Shweder (Eds.), *Ethnography and human development* (pp. 3–14). Chicago: University of Chicago Press.

Jiao, S., Ji, G., & Jing, Q. (1996). Cognitive development of Chinese urban only children and children with siblings. *Child Development, 67,* 387–395.

Johnson, C., & Connors, M. E. (1987). *The etiology and treatment of bulimia nervosa: A biopsychosocial perspective.* New York: Basic Books.

Johnson, C. L. (1985). *Growing up and growing old in Italian-American families.* New Brunswick, NJ: Rutgers University Press.

Johnson, C. L. (1998). Effects of adult children's divorce on grandparenthood. In M. E. Szinovacz (Ed.), *Handbook on grandparenthood* (pp. 87–96). Westport, CT: Greenwood Press.

Johnson, C. L., & Troll, L. (1992). Family functioning in late life. *Journal of Gerontology, 47,* S66–S72.

Johnson, C. L., & Troll, L. E. (1994). Constraints and facilitators to friendships in late life. *Gerontologist, 34,* 79–87.

Johnson, J. E., & Hooper, F. E. (1982). Piagetian structuralism and learning: Two decades of educational application. *Contemporary Educational Psychology, 7,* 217–237.

Johnson, K. E., Scott, P., & Mervis, C. B. (1997). Development of children's understanding of basic–subordinate inclusion relations. *Developmental Psychology, 33,* 745–763.

Johnson, M. H. (1998). The neural basis of cognitive development. In D. Kuhn & R. S. Siegler (Ed.), *Handbook of child psychology: Vol. 2. Cognition, perception, and language* (5th ed., pp. 1–49). New York: Wiley.

Johnson, S. L., & Birch, L. L. (1994). Parents' and children's adiposity and eating style. *Pediatrics, 94,* 653–661.

Jones, G. P., & Dembo, M. H. (1989). Age and sex role differences in intimate friendships during childhood and adolescence. *Merrill-Palmer Quarterly, 35,* 445–462.

Jones, M. C. (1965). Psychological correlates of somatic development. *Child Development, 36,* 899–911.

Jones, M. C., & Bayley, N. (1950). Physical maturing among boys as related to behavior. *Journal of Educational Psychology, 41,* 129–148.

Jones, M. C., & Mussen, P. H. (1958). Self-conceptions, motivations, and interpersonal attitudes of early- and late-maturing girls. *Child Development, 29,* 491–501.

Jones, S. S., & Raag, T. (1989). Smile production in older infants: The importance of a social recipient for the facial signal. *Child Development, 60,* 811–818.

Jones, W. H. (1990). Loneliness and social exclusion. *Journal of Social and Clinical Psychology, 9,* 214–220.

Jonsen, A., & Stryker, J. (Eds.). (1992). *The social impact of AIDS in the United States.* Washington, DC: National Academy Press.

Jordan, B. (1993). *Birth in four cultures.* Prospect Heights, IL: Waveland.

Jordan, P. (1990). Laboring for relevance: The male experience of expectant and new parenthood. *Nursing Research, 39,* 15–19.

Jorgensen, M., & Keiding, K. (1991). Estimation of spermarche from longitudinal spermaturia data. *Biometrics, 47,* 177–193.

Joseph, J. (1997). Fear of crime among black elderly. *Journal of Black Studies, 27,* 698–717.

Josselson, R. (1994). The theory of identity development and the question of intervention. In S. L. Archer (Ed.), *Interventions for adolescent identity development* (pp. 12–25). Thousand Oaks, CA: Sage.

Jovanovic, J., & King, S. S. (1998). Boys and girls in the performance-based science classroom: Who's doing the performing? *American Educational Research Journal, 35,* 477–496.

Joyner, M. H., & Kurtz-Costes, B. (1997). Metamemory development. In W. Schneider & F. E. Weinert (Eds.), *Memory performance and competencies: Issues in growth and development* (pp. 275–300). Hillsdale, NJ: Erlbaum.

Julkunen, J. (1996). Suppressing your anger: Good manners, bad health? In C. D. Spielberger & I. G. Sarason (Eds.), *Stress and emotion: Anxiety, anger, and curiosity* (Vol. 16, pp. 227–240). Washington, DC: Taylor & Francis.

Jusczyk, P. (1995). Language acquisition: Speech sounds and phonological development. In J. L. Miller & P. D. Eimas (Eds.), *Handbook of perception and cognition: Vol. 2. Speech, language, and communication* (pp. 263–301). Orlando, FL: Academic Press.

Jusczyk, P. W. (1997). Finding and remembering words: Some beginnings by English-learning infants. *Current Directions in Psychological Science, 6,* 170–174.

Jusczyk, P. W., & Hohne, E. A. (1997). Infants' memory for spoken words. *Science, 277,* 1984–1986.

Justice, E. M., Baker-Ward, L., Gupta, S., & Jannings, L. R. (1997). Means to the goal of remembering: Developmental changes in awareness of strategy use–performance relations. *Journal of Experimental Child Psychology, 65,* 293–314.

Kagan, J. (1989). *Unstable ideas: Temperament, cognition, and self.* Cambridge, MA: Harvard University Press.

Kagan, J. (1994). *Galen's prophecy.* New York: Basic Books.

Kagan, J. (1998). Biology and the child. In N. Eisenberg (Ed.), *Handbook of child psychology: Vol. 3. Social, emotional, and personality development* (5th ed., pp. 177–236). New York: Wiley.

Kagan, J., Arcus, D., Snidman, N., Feng, W. Y. Hendler, J., & Greene, S. (1994). Reactivity in infants: A cross-national comparison. *Developmental Psychology, 30,* 342–345.

Kagan, J., Kearsley, R. B., & Zelazo, P. R. (1978). *Infancy: Its place in human development.* Cambridge, MA: Harvard University Press.

Kagan, J., & Snidman, N. (1991). Temperamental factors in human development. *American Psychologist, 46,* 856–862.

Kagan, J., Snidman, N., & Arcus, D. (1998). Childhood derivatives of high and low reactivity in infancy. *Child Development, 69,* 1483–1493.

Kahana, E., Biegel, D., & Wykle, M. (1994). *Family caregiving across the lifespan.* Thousand Oaks, CA: Sage.

Kahn, P. H., Jr. (1992). Children's obligatory and discretionary moral judgments. *Child Development, 63,* 416–430.

Kail, R. (1991). Processing time declines exponentially during childhood and adolescence. *Developmental Psychology, 27,* 259–266.

Kail, R., & Park, Y. (1992). Global developmental change in processing time. *Merrill-Palmer Quarterly, 38,* 525–541.

Kail, R., & Park, Y. (1994). Processing time, articulation time, and memory span. *Journal of Experimental Child Psychology, 57,* 281–291.

Kalb, C. (1997, May 5). How old is too old? *Newsweek,* p. 64.

Kaler, S. B., & Kopp, C. B. (1990). Compliance and comprehension in very young toddlers. *Child Development, 61,* 1997–2003.

Kalish, R. A. (1985). The social context of death and dying. In R. H. Binstock & E. Shanas (Eds.), *Handbook of aging and the social sciences* (2nd ed., pp. 149–170). New York: Van Nostrand Reinhold.

Kallós, D., & Broman, I. T. (1997). Swedish child care and early childhood education in transition. *Early Education and Development, 8,* 265–284.

Kamerman, S. B. (1993). International perspectives on child care policies and programs. *Pediatrics, 91,* 248–252.

Kamo, Y. (1998). Asian grandparents. In M. E. Szinovacz (Ed.), *Handbook on grandparenthood* (pp. 97–112). Westport, CT: Greenwood Press.

Kamo, Y., & Zhou, M. (1994). Living arrangements of elderly Chinese and Japanese in the United States. *Journal of Marriage and the Family, 56,* 544–558.

Kandall, S. R., & Gaines, J. (1991). Maternal substance use and subsequent sudden infant death syndrome (SIDS) in offspring. *Neurotoxicology and Teratology, 13,* 235–240.

Kanner, A. D., Feldman, S. S., Weinberger, D. A., & Ford, M. E. (1987). Uplifts, hassles, and adaptational outcomes in early adolescents. *Journal of Early Adolescence, 7,* 371–394.

Kao, G. (2000). Psychological well-being and educational achievement among immigrant youth. In D. J. Hernandez (Ed.), *Children of immigrants: Health, adjustment, and public assistance.* Washington, DC: National Academy Press.

Kao, G., & Tienda, M. (1995). Optimism and achievement: The educational performance of immigrant youth. *Social Science Quarterly, 76,* 1–19.

Kaplan, D. L., & Keys, C. B. (1997). Sex and relationship variables as predictors of sexual attraction in cross-sex platonic friendships between young heterosexual adults. *Journal of Social and Personal Relationships, 14,* 191–206.

Kaplowitz, P. B. (1995). Effect of growth hormone therapy on final versus predicted height in short twelve- to sixteen-year-old boys without growth hormone deficiency. *Journal of Pediatrics, 126,* 478–480.

Karadsheh, R. (1991, April). *This room is a junkyard!: Children's comprehension of metaphorical language.* Paper presented at the biennial meeting of the Society for Research in Child Development, Seattle, WA.

Karam, E. G. (1994). The nosological status of bereavement-related despressions. *British Journal of Psychiatry, 165*(7), 48–52.

Karney, B. R., & Bradbury, T. N. (1997). Neuroticism, marital interaction, and the trajectory of marital satisfaction. *Journal of Personality and Social Psychology, 72,* 1075–1092.

Kaslow, F. W., Hansson, K., & Lundblad, A. (1994). Long-term marriages in Sweden: And some comparisons with similar couples in the United States. *Contemporary Family Therapy, 16,* 521–537.

Kastenbaum, R. J. (1999a). *Death, society, and human experience* (6th ed.). Boston: Allyn and Bacon.

Kastenbaum, R. J. (1999b). *The psychology of death* (3rd ed.). New York: Springer.

Katchadourian, H. (1990). Sexuality. In S. S. Feldman & G. R. Elliott (Eds.), *At the threshold: The developing adolescent* (pp. 330–351). Cambridge, MA: Harvard University Press.

Kausler, D. H. (1991). *Experimental psychology, cognition, and human aging.* New York: Springer.

Kausler, D. H. (1994). *Learning and memory in normal aging.* San Diego: Academic Press.

Kavanaugh, R. D., & Engel, S. (1998). The development of pretense and narrative in early childhood. In O. N. Saracho & B. Spodek (Eds.), *Multiple perspectives on play in early childhood education* (pp. 80–99). Albany: State University of New York Press.

Kavanaugh, R. D., & Harris, P. L. (1994). Imagining the outcome of pretend transformations: Assessing the competence of normal children and children with autism. *Developmental Psychology, 30,* 847–854.

Kawasaki, C., Nugent, J. K., Miyashita, H., Miyahara, H., & Brazelton, T. B. (1994). The cultural organization of infants' sleep. *Children's Environments, 11,* 135–141.

Kay, J., Mortimer, M. J., & Jaron, A. G. (1995). Do both paternal and maternal smoking influence the prevalence of childhood asthma? A study into the prevalence of asthma in children and the effects of parental smoking. *Journal of Asthma, 32,* 47–55.

Kaye, K., Elkind, L., Goldberg, D., & Tytun, A. (1989). Birth outcomes for infants of drug abusing mothers. *New York State Journal of Medicine, 89,* 256–261.

Kaye, K., & Marcus, J. (1981). Infant imitation: The sensory-motor agenda. *Developmental Psychology, 17,* 258–265.

Kayman, S., Bruvold, W., & Stern, J. S. (1990). Maintenance and relapse after weight loss in women: Behavioral aspects. *American Journal of Clinical Nutrition, 52,* 800–807.

Kearins, J. M. (1981). Visual spatial memory in Australian aboriginal children of desert regions. *Cognitive Psychology, 13,* 434–460.

Keasey, C. B. (1971). Social participation as a factor in the moral development of preadolescents. *Developmental Psychology, 5,* 216–220.

Keating, D. (1979). Adolescent thinking. In J. Adelson (Ed.), *Handbook of adolescent psychology* (pp. 211–246). New York: Wiley.

Kehoe, P., Wavrant-De Vrieze, F., Crook, R., Wu, W. S., Holmans, P., Fenton, I., Spurlock, G., & Norton, N. (1999). A full genome scan for late onset Alzheimer's disease. *Human Molecular Genetics, 8*(2), 237–245.

Keil, F. C. (1986). Conceptual domains and the acquisition of metaphor. *Cognitive Development, 1,* 73–96.

Keith, J., Fry, C. L., Glascock, A. P., Ikels, C., Dickerson-Putman, J., Harpending, H. C., & Draper, P. (1994). *The aging experience: Diversity and commonality across cultures.* Thousand Oaks, CA: Sage.

Keith, P. M., & Schafer, R. B. (1991). *Relationships and well-being over the life stages.* New York: Praeger.

Kelley, M. L., Power, T. G., & Wimbush, D. D. (1992). Determinants of disciplinary practices in low-income black mothers. *Child Development, 63,* 573–582.

Kelly, J. J., Chu, S. Y., & Buehler, J. W. (1993). AIDS deaths shift from hospital to home. *American Journal of Public Health, 83,* 1433–1437.

Kelly, J. R., & Ross, J.-E. (1989). Later-life leisure: Beginning a new agenda. *Leisure Sciences, 11,* 47–59.

Kempe, C. H., Silverman, B. F., Steele, B. W., Droegemueller, P. W., & Silver, H. K. (1962). The battered-child syndrome. *Journal of the American Medical Association, 181,* 17–24.

Kemper, S., Kynette, D., & Norman, S. (1992). Age differences in spoken language. In R. L. West & J. D. Sinnott (Eds.), *Everyday memory and aging* (pp. 138–152). New York: Springer-Verlag.

Kendall-Tackett, K. A., Williams, L. M., & Finkelhor, D. (1993). Impact of sexual abuse on children: A review and synthesis of recent empirical studies. *Psychological Bulletin, 113,* 164–180.

Kendrick, A. S., Kaufmann, R., & Messenger, K. P. (1991). *Healthy young children: A manual for programs.* Washington, DC: National Association for the Education of Young Children.

Kennedy, G. E., & Kennedy, C. E. (1993). Grandparents: A special resource for children in stepfamilies. *Journal of Divorce and Remarriage, 19,* 45–68.

Kennell, J., Klaus, M., McGrath, S., Robertson, S., & Hinkley, C. (1991). Continuous emotional support during labor in a U.S. hospital. *Journal of the American Medical Association, 265,* 2197–2201.

Kenrick, D. T., & Keefe, R. C. (1992). Age preferences in mates reflect sex differences in human reproductive strategies. *Behavioral and Brain Sciences, 15,* 75–133.

Kerckhoff, A. C., & Macrae, J. (1992). Leaving the parental home in Great Britain: A comparative perspective. *Sociological Quarterly, 33,* 281–301.

Kerns, K. A., & Berenbaum, S. A. (1991). Sex differences in spatial ability in children. *Behavior Genetics, 21,* 383–396.

Kerr, M., Lambert, W. W., Stattin, H., & Klackenberg-Larsson, I. (1994). Stability of inhibition in a Swedish longitudinal sample. *Child Development, 65,* 138–146.

Kerridge, I. H., & Mitchell, K. R. (1996). The legislation of active voluntary euthanasia in Australia: Will the slippery slope prove fatal? *Journal of Medical Ethics, 22,* 273–278.

Kessler, R., McGonagle, K., Zhao, S., Nelson, C., Hughes, M., Eshleman, S., Wittchen, H., & Kendler, K. (1994). Lifetime and 12-month prevalence of DSM-III-R psychiatric disorders in the United States: Results from the national comorbidity survey. *Archives of General Psychiatry, 51,* 8–19.

Kettl, P. (1998). Alaska Native suicide: Lessons for elder suicide. *International Psychogeriatrics, 10,* 205–211.

Keyes, C. L. M., & Ryff, C. D. (1998a). Generativity in adult lives: Social structural contours and quality of life consequences. In D. P. McAdams & E. de St. Aubin (Eds.), *Generativity and adult development* (pp. 227–257). Washington, DC: American Psychological Association.

Keyes, C. L. M., & Ryff, C. D. (1998b). Psychological well-being in midlife. In S. L. Willis & J. D. Reid (Eds.), *Life in the middle* (pp. 161–180). San Diego: Academic Press.

Killen, M., & Nucci, L. P. (1995). Morality, autonomy, and social conflict. In M. Killen & D. Hart (Eds.), *Morality in everyday life: Developmental perspectives* (pp. 52–86). Cambridge, U.K.: Cambridge University Press.

Kim, K., & Spelke, E. S. (1992). Infants' sensitivity to effects of gravity on visible object motion. *Journal of Experimental Psychology: Human Perception and Performance, 18,* 385–393.

Kimmel, D. C., & Moody, H. R. (1990). Ethical issues in gerontological research and services. In J. E. Birren & K. W. Schaie (Eds.), *Handbook of the psychology of aging* (3rd ed., pp. 489–501). San Diego, CA: Academic Press.

King, A. C., Kiernan, M., Oman, R. F., Kraemer, H., Hull, M., & Ahn, D. (1997). Can we identify who will adhere to long-term physical activity? Signal detection methodology as a potential aid to clinical decision making. *Health Psychology, 16,* 380–389.

King, A. C., Taylor, C. B., & Haskell, W. L. (1993). Effects of differing intensities and formats of 12 months of exercise training on psychological outcomes in older adults. *Health Psychology, 12,* 292–300.

King, C. A. (1997). Suicidal behavior in adolescence. In R. W. Maris, M. M. Silverman, & S. S. Canetto (Eds.), *Review of suicidology, 1997* (pp. 61–95). New York: Guilford.

King, V., & Elder, G. H., Jr. (1998). Perceived self-efficacy and grandparenting. *Journal of Gerontology, 53B,* S249–S257.

Kingston, P., & Reay, A. (1996). Elder abuse and neglect. In R. T. Woods (Ed.), *Handbook of the clinical psychology of ageing* (pp. 423–438). Chichester, England: Wiley.

Kinzie, J. D., Sack, W., Angell, R., Clarke, G., & Ben, R. (1989). A three-year follow-up of Cambodian young people traumatized as children. *Journal of the American Academy of Child and Adolescent Psychiatry, 28,* 501–504.

Kirk, W. G. (1993). *Adolescent suicide.* Champaign, IL: Research Press.

Kirkby, R. J., & Lindner, H. (1998). Exercise is linked to reductions in anxiety but not premenstrual syndrome in women with prospectively-assessed symptoms. *Psychology, Health and Medicine, 3,* 211–222.

Kirkpatrick, L. A., & Davis, K. E. (1994). Attachment style, gender, and relationship stability: A longitudinal analysis. *Journal of Personality and Social Psychology, 66,* 502–512.

Kisilevsky, B. S., & Low, J. A. (1998). Human fetal behvior: 100 years of study. *Developmental Review, 18,* 1–29.

Kitchener, K. S., Lynch, C. L., Fischer, K. W., & Wood, P. K. (1993). Developmental range of reflective judgment: The effect of contextual support and practice on developmental stage. *Developmental Psychology, 29,* 893–906.

Kite, M. E., & Whitley, B. E., Jr. (1998). Do heterosexual women and men differ in their attitudes toward homosexuality? In G. M. Herek (Ed.), *Stigma and sexual orientation* (pp. 39–61). Thousand Oaks, CA: Sage.

Kivnick, H. Q. (1983). Dimensions of grandparenthood meaning: Deductive conceptualization and empirical derivation. *Journal of Personality and Social Psychology, 44,* 1056–1068.

Klahr, D., & MacWhinney, B. (1998). Information processing. In D. Kuhn & R. S. Siegler (Eds.), *Handbook of child psychology: Vol. 2. Cognition, perception, and language* (5th ed., pp. 631–678). New York: Wiley.

Klebanov, P. K., Brooks-Gunn, J., McCarton, C., & McCormick, M. C. (1998). The contribution of neighborhood and family income to developmental test scores over the first three years of life. *Child Development, 69,* 1420–1436.

Kleeman, W. J., Schlaud, M., Fieguth, A., Hiller, A. S., Rothamel, T., & Troger, H. D. (1999). Body and head position, covering of the head by bedding and risk of sudden infant death (SID). *International Journal of Legal Medicine, 112,* 22–26.

Kliewer, W. (1997). Children's coping with chronic illness. In S. A. Wolchik & I. N. Sandler (Eds.), *Handbook of children's coping* (pp. 275–300). New York: Plenum.

Kliewer, W., Fearnow, M. D., & Miller, P. A. (1996). Coping socialization in middle childhood: Tests of maternal and paternal influences. *Child Development, 67,* 2339–2357.

Klimes-Dougan, B., & Kistner, J. (1990). Physically abused preschoolers' responses to peers' distress. *Developmental Psychology, 26,* 599–602.

Kline, D. W., Kline, T. J. B., Fozard, J. L., Kosnik, W., Schieber, F., & Sekuler, R. (1992). Vision, aging, and driving: The problems of older drivers. *Journal of Gerontology, 47,* P27–P34.

Knapp, M. L., & Taylor, E. H. (1994). Commitment and its communication in romantic relationships. In A. L. Weber & J. H. Harvey (Eds.), *Perspectives on close relationships* (pp. 153–175). Boston: Allyn and Bacon.

Knobloch, H., & Pasamanick, B. (Eds.), (1974). *Gesell and Amatruda's Developmental Diagnosis.* Hagerstown, MD: Harper & Row.

Knoers, N., van den Ouweland, A., Dreesen, J., Verdijk, M., Monnens, L. S., & van Oost, B. A. (1993). Nephrogenic diabetes insipidus: Identification of the genetic defect. *Pediatric Nephrology, 7,* 685–688.

Knowles, R. B., Wyart, C., Buldyrev, S. V., Cruz, L., Urbanc, B., Hasselmo, M. E., Stanley, H. E., & Hyman, B. T. (1999). Plaque-induced neurite abnormalities: Implications of disruption of neuronal networks in Alzheimer's disease. *Proceedings of the National Academy of Sciences, 96,* 5274–5279.

Knox, A. B. (1993). *Strengthening adult and continuing education.* San Francisco: Jossey-Bass.

Kobak, R. R., & Sceery, A. (1988). The transition to college: Working models of attachment, affect regulation, and perceptions of self and others. *Child Development, 88,* 135–146.

Kochanska, G. (1991). Socialization and temperament in the development of guilt and conscience. *Child Development, 62,* 1379–1392.

Kochanska, G. (1992). Children's interpersonal influence with mothers and peers. *Developmental Psychology, 28,* 491–499.

Kochanska, G. (1993). Toward a synthesis of parental socialization and child temperament in early development of conscience. *Child Development, 64,* 325–347.

Kochanska, G. (1995). Children's temperament, mothers' discipline, and security of attachment: Multiple pathways to emerging internalization. *Child Development, 66,* 597–615.

Kochanska, G. (1997a). Multiple pathways to conscience for children with different temperaments: From toddlerhood to age 5. *Developmental Psychology, 33,* 228–240.

Kochanska, G. (1997b). Mutually responsive orientation between mothers and their young children: Implications for early socialization. *Child Development, 68,* 94–112.

Kochanska, G. (1998). Mother–child relationship, child fearfulness, and emerging attachment: A short-term longitudinal study. *Developmental Psychology, 34,* 480–490.

Kochanska, G., Casey, R. J., & Fukumoto, A. (1995). Toddlers' sensitivity to standard violations. *Child Development, 66,* 643–656.

Kochanska, G., & Radke-Yarrow, M. (1992). Inhibition in toddlerhood and the dynamics of the child's interaction with an unfamiliar peer at age five. *Child Development, 63,* 325–335.

Kochanska, G., Tjebkes, T. L., & Forman, D. R. (1998). Children's emerging regulation of conduct: Restraint, compliance, and internalization from infancy to the second year. *Child Development, 69,* 1378–1389.

Koestner, R., Franz, C., & Weinberger, J. (1990). The family origins of empathic concern: A 26-year longitudinal study. *Journal of Personality and Social Psychology, 58,* 709–717.

Koff, T. H., & Park, R. W. (1999). *Aging public policy: Bonding the generations* (2nd ed.). Amityville, NY: Baywood.

Kogan, N. (1979). A study of categorization. *Journal of Gerontology, 34,* 358–367.

Kogan, N., & Mills, M. (1992). Gender influences on age cognitions and preferences: Sociocultural or sociobiological? *Psychology and Aging, 7,* 98–106.

Kohlberg, L. (1966). A cognitive-developmental analysis of children's sex-role concepts and attitudes. In E. E. Maccoby (Ed.), *The development of sex differences* (pp. 82–173). Stanford, CA: Stanford University Press.

Kohlberg, L. (1969). Stage and sequence: The cognitive-developmental approach to socialization. In D. A. Goslin (Ed.), *Handbook of socialization theory and research* (pp. 347–480). Chicago: Rand McNally.

Kohlberg, L., Levine, C., & Hewer, A. (1983). *Moral stages: A current formulation and a response to critics.* Basel, Switzerland: Karger.

Kohn, M. L., Naoi, A., Schoenbach, C., Schooler, C., & Slomczynski, K. M. (1990). Position in the class structure and psychological functioning in the United States, Japan, and Poland. *American Journal of Sociology, 95,* 964–1008.

Kohn, M. L., & Schooler, C. (1978). The reciprocal effects of the substantive complexity of work and intellectual flexibility: A longitudinal assessment. *American Journal of Sociology, 84,* 24–52.

Kohn, M. L., & Slomczynski, D. M. (1990). *Social structure and self-direction: A comparative analysis of the United States and Poland.* Cambridge: Blackwell.

Kojima, H. (1986). Childrearing concepts as a belief–value system of the society and the individual. In H. Stevenson, H. Azuma, & K. Hakuta (Eds.), *Child development and education in Japan* (pp. 39–54). New York: Freeman.

Kolata, G. (1992, April 26). A parents' guide to kids' sports. *New York Times Magazine,* pp. 12–15, 40, 44, 46.

Kolominsky, Y., Igumnov, S., & Drozdovitch, V. (1999). The psychological development of children from Belarus exposed in the prenatal period to radiation from the Chernobyl atomic power plant. *Journal of Child Psychology and Psychiatry, 40,* 299–305.

Kolvin, I., & Trowell, J. (1996). Child sexual abuse. In I. Rosen (Ed.), *Sexual deviation* (3rd ed., pp. 337–360). Oxford: Oxford University Press.

Komp, D. M. (1996). The changing face of death in children. In H. M. Spiro, M. G. M. Curnen, & L. P. Wandel (Eds.), *Facing death: Where culture, religion, and medicine meet* (pp. 66–76). New Haven: Yale University Press.

Koplan, J. P., & Dietz, W. H. (1999). Caloric imbalance and public health policy. *Journal of the American Medical Association, 282,* 1579–1580.

Kopp, C. B. (1987). The growth of self-regulation: Caregivers and children. In N. Eisenberg (Ed.), *Contemporary topics in developmental psychology* (pp. 34–55). New York: Wiley.

Kopp, C. B. (1994). Infant assessment. In C. B. Fisher & R. M. Lerner (Eds.), *Applied developmental psychology* (pp. 265–293). New York: McGraw-Hill.

Kornblith, A. B. (1998). Psychosocial adaptation of cancer survivors. In J. C. Holland (Ed.), *Psycho-oncology* (pp. 78–90). New York: Oxford University Press.

Kornhaber, A., & Woodward, K. L. (1981). *Grandparent/grandchildren: The vital connection.* Garden City, NJ: Anchor.

Korte, D. (1997). *The VBAC companion: The expectant mother's guide to vaginal birth after cesarean.* Cambridge, MA: Harvard Common Press.

Korten, A. E., Jorm, A. F., Jiao, Z., Letenneur, L., Jacomb, P. A., Henderson, A. S., Christensen, H., & Rodgers, B. (1999). Health, cognitive, and psychosocial factors as predictors of mortality in an elderly community sample. *Journal of Epidemiology and Community Health, 53,* 83–88.

Koss, M. P. (1993). Rape: Scope, impact, interventions, and public policy responses. *American Psychologist, 48,* 1062–1069.

Koss, M. P. (1998). Hidden rape: Sexual aggression and victimization in a national sample of students in higher education. In M. E. Odem & J. Clay-Warner (Eds.), *Confronting rape and sexual assault* (pp. 51–69). Wilmington, DE: Scholarly Resources.

Koss, M. P., & Harvey, M. (1991). *The rape victim: Clinical and community interventions.* Newbury Park, CA: Sage.

Koss, M. P., Koss, P., & Woodruff, W. J. (1991). Deleterious effects of criminal victimization on women's health and medical utilization. *Archives of Internal Medicine, 151,* 342–357.

Kotler-Cope, S., & Camp, C. J. (1990). Memory interventions in aging populations. In E. A. Lovelace (Ed.), *Aging and cognition* (pp. 231–261). Amsterdam: North-Holland.

Kotovsky, L., & Baillargeon, R. (1998). The development of calibration-based reasoning about collision events in young infants. *Cognition, 57,* 311–351.

Kovacs, M., Akiskal, H., Gatsonis, C., & Parrone, P. (1994). Childhood-onset dysthymic disorder: Clinical features and prospective naturalistic outcome. *Archives of General Psychiatry, 51,* 365–374.

Kowalski, N., & Allen, R. (1995). School sleep lag is less but persists with a very late starting high school. *Sleep Research, 24,* 124.

Kraft, J. M., & Werner, J. S. (1999). Aging and the saturation of colors. 2. Scaling of color appearance. *Journal of the Optical Society of America, 16,* 231–235.

Kramer, A. F., Hahn, S., & Gopher, D. (1998). Task coordination and aging: Explorations of executive control processes in the task switching paradigm. *Acta Psychologica, 101,* 339–378.

Kranzler, J. H., & Jensen, A. R. (1989). Inspection time and intelligence: A meta-analysis. *Intelligence, 13,* 329–347.

Krascum, R. M., & Andrews, S. (1998). The effects of theories on children's acquisition of family-resemblance categories. *Child Development, 69,* 333–346.

Krause, N. (1990). Perceived health problems, formal/informal support, and life satisfaction among older adults. *Journal of Gerontology, 45,* S193–S205.

Krause, N. (1998). Neighborhood deterioration, religious coping, and changes in health during late life. *Gerontologist, 38,* 653–664.

Krevans, J., & Gibbs, J. C. (1996). Parents' use of inductive discipline: Relations to children's empathy and prosocial behavior. *Child Development, 67,* 3263–3277.

Krishnan, V. (1998). Premarital cohabitation and marital disruption. *Journal of Divorce and Remarriage, 28,* 157–170.

Kriska, A. M., Blair, S. N., & Pereira, M. A. (1994). The potential role of physical activity in the prevention of non-insulin-dependent diabetes mellitus: The epidemiological evidence. *Exercise and Sport Sciences Reviews, 22,* 121–143.

Kroger, J. (1995). The differentiation of "firm" and "developmental" foreclosure identity statuses: A longitudinal study. *Journal of Adolescent Research, 10,* 317–337.

Kronenfeld, J. J., & Glik, D. C. (1995). Unintentional injury: A major health problem for young children and youth. *Journal of Family and Economic Issues, 16,* 365–393.

Kropf, N. P., & Pugh, K. L. (1995). Beyond life expectancy: Social work with centenarians. *Journal of Gerontological Social Work, 23,* 121–137.

Krout, J., Cutler, S. J., & Coward, R. T. (1990). Correlates of senior center participation: A national analysis. *Gerontologist, 30,* 72–79.

Kübler-Ross, E. (1969). *On death and dying.* New York: Macmillan.

Kuchner, J. (1989, April). *Chinese-American and European-American mothers and infants: Cultural influences in the first three months of life.* Paper presented at the biennial meeting of the Society for Research in Child Development, Kansas City, MO.

Kuczynski, L. (1984). Socialization goals and mother–child interaction: Strategies for long-term and short-term compliance. *Developmental Psychology, 20,* 1061–1073.

Kuczynski, L., & Kochanska, G. (1995). Function and content of maternal demands: Developmental significance of early demands for competent action. *Child Development, 66,* 616–628.

Kuebli, J., & Fivush, R. (1992). Gender differences in parent–child conversations about past emotions. *Sex Roles, 27,* 683–698.

Kuhl, P. K., Williams, K. A., Lacerda, F., Stevens, K. N., & Lindblom, B. (1992). Linguistic experience alters phonetic perception in infants by 6 months of age. *Science, 255,* 606–608.

Kuhn, D. (1989). Children and adults as intuitive scientists. *Psychological Review, 96,* 674–689.

Kuhn, D. (1992). Cognitive development. In M. H. Bornstein & M. E. Lamb (Eds.), *Developmental psychology: An advanced textbook* (3rd ed., pp. 211–272). Hillsdale, NJ: Erlbaum.

Kuhn, D. (1993). Connecting scientific and informal reasoning. *Merrill-Palmer Quarterly, 39,* 74–103.

Kuhn, D., Amsel, E., & O'Loughlin, M. (1988). *The development of scientific thinking skills.* Orlando, FL: Academic Press.

Kuhn, D., Garcia-Mila, M., Zohar, A., & Andersen, C. (1995). Strategies of knowledge acquisition. *Monographs of the Society for Research in Child Development, 60*(245, Serial No. 4).

Kuhn, L., & Stein, Z. (1997). Infant survival, HIV infection, and feeding alternatives in less-developed countries. *American Journal of Public Health, 87,* 926–931.

Kunzinger, E. L., III. (1985). A short-term longitudinal study of memorial development during early grade school. *Developmental Psychology, 21,* 642–646.

Kurdek, L. A. (1998). Relationship outcomes and their predictors: Longitudinal evidence from heterosexual married, gay cohabiting, and lesbian cohabiting couples. *Journal of Marriage and the Family, 60,* 553–568.

Kutner, L. (1993, June). Getting physical. *Parents,* pp. 96–98.

Labouvie-Vief, G. (1980). Beyond formal operations: Uses and limits of pure logic in life-span development. *Human Development, 23,* 141–160.

Labouvie-Vief, G. (1985). Logic and self-regulation from youth to maturity: A model. In M. Commons, F. Richards, & C. Armon (Eds.), *Beyond formal operations: Late adolescent and adult cognitive development* (pp. 158–180). New York: Praeger.

Labouvie-Vief, G., Chiodo, L. M., Goguen, L. A., Diehl, M., & Orwoll, L. (1995). Representations of self across the life span. *Psychology and Aging, 10,* 404–415.

Labouvie-Vief, G., DeVoe, M., & Bulka, D. (1989). Speaking about feelings: Conceptions of emotion across the life span. *Psychology and Aging, 4,* 425–437.

Labouvie-Vief, G., & Diehl, M. (1999). Self and personality development. In J. C. Kavanaugh & S. K. Whitbourne (Eds.), *Gerontology: An interdisciplinary perspective* (pp. 238–268). New York: Oxford University Press.

Lachman, M. E., & James, J. B. (1997). Charting the course of midlife development: An overview. In M. E. Lachman & J. B. James (Eds.), *Multiple paths of midlife development* (pp. 1–17). Chicago: University of Chicago Press.

Lachs, M. S., Williams, C., O'Brien, S., Hurst, L., & Horwitz, R. (1997). Risk factors for reported elder abuse and neglect: A nine-year observational cohort study. *Gerontologist, 37,* 469–474.

Ladd, G. W., & Burgess, K. B. (1999). Charting the relationship trajectories of aggressive, withdrawn, and aggressive/withdrawn children during early grade school. *Child Development, 70,* 910–929.

Ladd, G. W., & Cairns, E. (1996). Children: Ethnic and political violence. *Child Development, 67,* 14–18.

Ladd, G. W., Kochenderfer, B. J., & Coleman, C. C. (1997). Classroom peer acceptance, friendship, and victimization: Distinct relational systems that contribute uniquely to children's school adjustment? *Child Development, 68,* 1181–1197.

Ladd, G. W., & Ladd, B. K. (1998). Parenting behaviors and parent–child relationships: Correlates of peer victimization in kindergarten? *Developmental Psychology, 34,* 1450–1458.

Ladd, G. W., LeSieur, K., & Profilet, S. M. (1993). Direct parental influences on young children's peer relations. In S. Duck

(Ed.), *Learning about relationships* (Vol. 2, pp. 152–183). London: Sage.

Ladd, G. W., & Price, J. M. (1987). Predicting children's social and school adjustment following the transition from preschool to kindergarten. *Child Development, 58,* 1168–1189.

Lagattuta, K. H., Wellman, H. M., & Flavell, J. H. (1997). Preschoolers' understanding of the link between thinking and feeling: Cognitive cuing and emotional change. *Child Development, 68,* 1081–1104.

Lagercrantz, H., & Slotkin, T. A. (1986). The "stress" of being born. *Scientific American, 254,* 100–107.

Lahey, B. B., & Loeber, R. (1997). Attention-deficit/hyperactivity disorder, oppositional defiant disorder, conduct disorder, and adult antisocial behavior: A life span perspective. In D. M. Stoff, J. Breiling, & J. D. Maser (Eds.), *Handbook of antisocial behavior* (pp. 51–59). New York: Wiley.

Lamaze, F. (1958). *Painless childbirth.* London: Burke.

Lamb, M. E. (1987). *The father's role: Cross-cultural perspectives.* Hillsdale, NJ: Erlbaum.

Lamb, M. E. (1997). The development of father–infant relationships. In M. E. Lamb (Ed.), *The role of the father in child development* (3rd ed., pp. 104–120). New York: Wiley.

Lamb, M. E. (1998). Nonparental child care: Context, quality, correlates, and consequences. In I. E. Sigel & K. A. Renninger (Eds.), *Handbook of child psychology: Vol. 4. Child psychology in practice* (5th ed., pp. 73–133). New York: Wiley.

Lamb, M. E., & Oppenheim, D. (1989). Fatherhood and father–child relationships: Five years of research. In S. H. Cath, A. Gurwitt, & L. Gunsberg (Eds.), *Fathers and their families* (pp. 11–26). Hillsdale, NJ: Erlbaum.

Lamb, M. E., Sternberg, K. J., & Prodromidis, M. (1992). Nonmaternal care and the security of infant–mother attachment: A reanalysis of the data. *Infant Behavior and Development, 15,* 71–83.

Lamb, M. E., Thompson, R. A., Gardner, W., Charnov, E. L., & Connell, J. P. (1985). Infant–mother attachment: The origins and developmental significance of individual differences in the Strange Situation: Its study and biological interpretation. *Behavioral and Brain Sciences, 7,* 127–147.

Lamme, S., & Baars, J. (1993). Including social factors in the analysis of reminiscence in elderly individuals. *International Journal of Aging and Human Development 37,* 297–311.

Lampit, M., Lorber, A., Vilkos, D. L., Nave, T., & Hochberg, Z. (1998). GH dependence and GH withdrawal syndrome in GH treatment of short normal children: Evidence from growth and cardiac output. *European Journal of Endocrinology, 138,* 401–407.

Lampl, M. (1993). Evidence of saltatory growth in infancy. *American Journal of Human Biology, 5,* 641–652.

Lampl, M., Veldhuis, J. D., & Johnson, M. L. (1992). Saltation and stasis: A model of human growth. *Science, 258,* 801–803.

Lander, E. S. (1996). The new genomics: Global views of biology. *Science, 274,* 536–539.

Lander, J., Brady-Fryer, B., Metcalfe, J. B., Nazarali, S., & Muttitt, S. (1997). Comparison of ring block, dorsal penile nerve block, and topical anesthesia for neonatal circumcision. *Journal of the American Medical Association, 279,* 1170–1171.

Landesman, S., & Ramey, C. (1989). Developmental psychology and mental retardation: Integrating scientific principles with treatment practices. *American Psychologist, 44,* 409–415.

Landry, S. H., & Whitney, J. A. (1996). The impact of prenatal cocaine exposure: Studies of the developing infant. *Seminars in Perinatology, 20,* 99–106.

Lang, F. R., & Baltes, M. M. (1997). Being with people and being alone in later life: Costs and benefits for everyday functioning. *International Journal of Behavioral Development, 21,* 729–749.

Lang, F. R., & Carstensen, L. L. (1994). Close emotional relationships in late life: Further support for proactive aging in the social domain, *Psychology and Aging, 9,* 315–324.

Lang, F. R., Featherman, D. L., & Nesselroade, J. R. (1997). Social self-efficacy and short-term variability in social relationships: The MacArthur Successful Aging Studies. *Psychology and Aging, 12,* 657–666.

Lang, F. R., Staudinger, U. M., & Carstensen, L. L. (1998). Perspectives on socioemotional selectivity in late life: How personality and social context do (and do not) make a difference. *Journal of Gerontology, 53B,* P21–P30.

Langer, N. (1990). Grandparents and adult grandchildren: What do they do for one another? *International Journal of Aging and Human Development, 31,* 101–110.

Langlois, J. H., & Downs, A. C. (1980). Mothers, fathers, and peers as socialization agents of sex-typed play behaviors in young children. *Child Development, 51,* 1237–1247.

Langreth, R. (1993, November). Can we live to 150? *Popular Science,* pp. 77–82.

Lansford, J. E., Sherman, A. M., & Antonucci, T. C. (1998). Satisfaction with social networks: An examination of socioemotional selectivity theory across cohorts. *Psychology and Aging, 13,* 544–552.

Lantz, P. M., House, J. S., Lepkowski, J. M., Williams, D. R., Mero, R. P., & Chen, J. (1998). Socioeconomic factors, health behaviors, and mortality. *Journal of the American Medical Association, 279,* 1703–1708.

Lapointe, A. E., Askew, J. M., & Mead, N. A. (1992). *Learning mathematics.* Princeton, NJ: Educational Testing Service.

Lapointe, A. E., Mead, N. A., & Askew, J. M. (1992). *Learning science.* Princeton NJ: Educational Testing Service.

Lapsley, D. K. (1993). Toward an integrated theory of adolescent ego development: The "new look" at adolescent egocentrism. *American Journal of Orthopsychiatry, 63,* 562–571.

Lapsley, D. K., Jackson, S., Rice, K., & Shadid, G. (1988). Self-monitoring and the "new look" at the imaginary audience and personal fable: An ego-developmental analysis. *Journal of Adolescent Research, 3,* 17–31.

Lapsley, D. K., Rice, K. G., & FitzGerald, D. P. (1990). Adolescent attachment, identity, and adjustment to college: Implications for the continuity of adaptation hypothesis. *Journal of Counseling and Development, 68,* 561–565.

Larson, D. E. (1996). *Mayo Clinic family health book.* New York: Morrow.

Larson, J. H. (1988). The marriage quiz: College students' beliefs in selected myths about marriage. *Family Relations, 37,* 3–11.

Larson, R., & Ham, M. (1993). Stress and "storm and stress" in early adolescence: The relationship of negative events with dysphoric affect. *Developmental Psychology, 29,* 130–140.

Larson, R., & Lampman-Petraitis, C. (1989). Daily emotional states as reported by children and adolescents. *Child Development, 60,* 1250–1260.

Larson, R., Mannell, R., & Zuzanek, J. (1986). Daily well-being of older adults with friends and family. *Psychology and Aging, 1,* 117–126.

Larson, R., & Richards, M. H. (1991). Daily companionship in late childhood and early adolescence: Changing developmental contexts. *Child Development, 62,* 284–300.

Larson, R. W., Richards, M. H., Moneta, G., Holmbeck, G., & Duckett, E. (1996). Changes in adolescents' daily interactions with their families from ages 10 to 18: Disengagement and transformation. *Developmental Psychology, 32,* 744–754.

Larsson, M., & Bäckman, L. (1997). Age-related differences in episodic odour recognition: The role of access to specific odour names. *Memory, 5,* 361–378.

Larsson, M., & Bäckman, L. (1998). Modality memory across the adult life span: Evidence for selective age-related olfactory deficits. *Experimental Aging Research, 24,* 63–82.

Larzelere, R. E., Schneider, W. N., Larson, D. B., & Pike, P. L. (1996). The effects of discipline responses in delaying toddler misbehavior recurrences. *Child and Family Behavior Therapy, 18,* 35–57.

Laucht, M., Esser, G., & Schmidt, M. H. (1997). Developmental outcome of infants born with biological and psychosocial risks. *Journal of Child Psychology and Psychiatry, 38,* 843–853.

Laumann, E. O., Gagnon, J. H., Michael, R. T., & Michaels, S. (1994). *The social organization of sexuality.* Chicago: University of Chicago Press.

Laumann, E. O., Paik, A., & Rosen, R. C. (1999). Sexual dysfunction in the United States: Prevalence and predictors. *Journal of the American Medical Association, 281,* 537–544.

Laursen, B., Hartup, W. W., & Koplas, A. L. (1996). Toward understanding peer conflict. *Merrill-Palmer Quarterly, 42,* 76–102.

Law, C. M., Gordon, G. S., Shiell, A. W., Barker, D. J., & Hales, C. N. (1995). Thinness at birth and glucose tolerance in seven-year-old children. *Diabetic Medicine, 12,* 330–336.

Lawrence, B. S. (1980, Summer). The myth of the midlife crisis. *Sloan Management Review, 21*(4), 35–49.

Lawton, L., Silverstein, M., & Bengtson, V. L. (1994). Solidarity between generations in families. In V. L. Bengtson & R. A. Harootyan (Eds.), *Intergenerational linkages: Hidden connections in American society* (pp. 19–42). New York: Springer-Verlag.

Lawton, M. P. (1980). Environment and aging. Monterey, CA: Brooks/Cole.

Lawton, M. P. (1999). Environmental design features and the well-being of older persons. In M. Duffy (Ed.), *Handbook of counseling and psychotherapy with older adults* (pp. 350–363). New York: Wiley.

Lawton, M. P., Moss, M., & Moles, E. (1984). The supra-personal neighborhood context of older people: Age heterogeneity and well-being. *Environment and Behavior, 16,* 89–109.

Lawton, M. P., Winter, L., Kleban, M. H., & Ruckdeschel, K. (1999). Affect and quality of life. *Journal of Aging and Health, 11,* 169–198.

Lazar, A., & Torney-Purta, J. (1991). The development of the subconcepts of death in young children: A short-term longitudinal study. *Child Development, 62,* 1321–1333.

Lazar, I., & Darlington, R. (1982). Lasting effects of early education: A report from the Consortium for Longitudinal Studies. *Monographs of the Society for Research in Child Development, 47*(2–3, Serial No. 195).

Lazarus, R. (1985). The trivialization of distress. In J. Rosen & L. Solomon (Eds.), *Preventing health risk behaviors and promoting coping with illness* (Vol. 8, pp. 279–298). Hanover, NH: University Press of New England.

Lazarus, R. (1991). *Emotion and adaptation.* New York: Oxford University Press.

Lazarus, R. S. (1999). *Stress and emotion: A new synthesis.* New York: Springer.

Lazarus, R. S., & Lazarus, B. N. (1994). *Passion and reason.* New York: Oxford University Press.

Leaper, C. (1994). Exploring the correlates and consequences of gender segregation: Social relationships in childhood, adolescence, and adulthood. In C. Leaper (Ed.), *New directions for child development* (No. 65, pp. 67–86). San Francisco: Jossey-Bass.

Leaper, C., Anderson, K. J., & Sanders, P. (1998). Moderators of gender effects on parents' talk to their children: A meta-analysis. *Developmental Psychology, 34,* 3–27.

Leaper, C., Leve, L., Strasser, T., & Schwartz, R. (1995). Mother–child communication sequences: Play activity, child gender, and marital status effects. *Merrill-Palmer Quarterly, 41,* 307–327.

Leaper, C., Tenenbaum, H. R., & Shaffer, T. G. (1999). Communication patterns of African-American girls and boys from low-income, urban backgrounds. *Child Development, 70,* 1489–1503.

Lee, A. M. (1980). Child-rearing practices and motor performance of Black and White children. *Research Quarterly for Exercise and Sport, 51,* 494–500.

Lee, C. L., & Bates, J. E. (1985). Mother–child interaction at age two years and perceived difficult temperament. *Child Development, 56,* 1314–1325.

Lee, D. J., & Markides, K. S. (1990). Activity and morality among aged persons over an eight-year period. *Journal of Gerontology, 45,* S39–S42.

Lee, G. R., Willetts, M. C., & Seccombe, K. (1998). Widowhood and depression. *Research on Aging, 20,* 611–630.

Lee, R. T., & Ashforth, B. E. (1990). On the meaning of Maslach's three dimensions of burnout. *Journal of Applied Psychology, 75,* 743–747.

Lee, S. H., Ewert, D. P., Frederick, P. D., & Mascola, L. (1992). Resurgence of congenital rubella syndrome in the 1990s. *Journal of the American Medical Association, 267,* 2616–2620.

Lee, V. E., Brooks-Gunn, J., & Schnur, E. (1988). Does Head Start work? A 1-year follow-up of disadvantaged children attending Head Start, no preschool. *Developmental Psychology, 24,* 210–222.

Lee, V. E., Brooks-Gunn, J., Schnur, E., & Liaw, F. (1990). Are Head Start effects sustained? A longitudinal follow-up comparison of disadvantaged children attending Head Start, no preschool, and other preschool programs. *Child Development, 61,* 495–507.

Lehman, D., Ellard, J., & Wortman, C. (1986). Social support for the bereaved: Recipients' and providers' perspectives on what is helpful. *Journal of Consulting and Clinical Psychology, 54,* 438–446.

Lehman, D. R., & Nisbett, R. E. (1990). A longitudinal study of the effects of undergraduate training on reasoning. *Developmental Psychology, 26,* 952–960.

Lehnert, K. L., Overholser, J. C., & Spirito, A. (1994). Internalized and externalized anger in adolescent suicide attempters. *Journal of Adolescent Research, 9,* 105–119.

Leichtman, M. D., & Ceci, S. J. (1995). The effect of stereotypes and suggestions on preschoolers' reports. *Developmental Psychology, 31,* 568–578.

Lemery, K. S., Goldsmith, H. H., Klinnert, M. D., & Mrazek, D. A. (1999). Developmental models of infant and childhood temperament. *Developmental Psychology, 35,* 189–204.

Lemme, B. H. (1999). *Development in adulthood* (2nd ed.). Boston: Allyn and Bacon.

Lempert, H. (1989). Animacy constraints on preschoolers' acquisition of syntax. *Child Development, 60,* 237–245.

Leonard, K. E. (1999). Alcohol use and husband marital aggression among newly-wed couples. In X. B. Arriaga & S. Oskamp (Eds.), *Violence in intimate relationships* (pp. 113–135). Thousand Oaks, CA: Sage.

Leonard, K. E., & Roberts, L. J. (1998). Marital aggression, quality, and stability in the first year of marriage: Findings from the Buffalo Newlywed Study. In T. N. Bradbury (Ed.), *The developmental course of marital dysfunction* (pp. 44–73). New York: Cambridge University Press.

Leonard, M. F., Rhymes, J. P., & Solnit, A. J. (1986). Failure to thrive in infants: A family problem. *American Journal of Diseases of Children, 111,* 600–612.

Lerman, R. I. (1993). A national profile of young unwed fathers. In R. I. Lerman & T. J. Ooms (Eds.), *Young unwed fathers* (pp. 27–51). Philadelphia: Temple University Press.

Lerner, J. V., & Abrams, A. (1994). Developmental correlates of maternal employment influences on children. In C. B. Fisher & R. M. Lerner (Eds.), *Applied developmental psychology* (pp. 174–206). New York: McGraw-Hill.

Lerner, J. W. (1989). Educational interventions in learning disabilities. *Journal of the American Academy of Child and Adolescent Psychiatry, 28,* 326–331.

Lerner, R. M., & Schroeder, C. (1971). Physique identification, preference, and aversion in kindergarten children. *Developmental Psychology, 5,* 538.

Lester, B. M. (1985). Introduction: There's more to crying than meets the ear. In B. M. Lester & C. F. Z. Boukydis (Eds.), *Infant crying* (pp. 1–27). New York: Plenum.

Leung, M.-C. (1996). Social networks and self-enhancement in Chinese children: A comparison of self reports and peer reports of group membership. *Social Development, 5,* 146–157.

LeVay, S. (1993). *The sexual brain.* Cambridge, MA: MIT Press.

Levenson, R. W., Carstensen, L. L., & Gottman, J. M. (1993). Long-term marriage: Age, gender, and satisfaction. *Psychology and Aging, 8,* 301–313.

Leventhal, E. A., Leventhal, H., Schaefer, P. M., & Easterling, D. (1993). Conservation of energy, uncertainty reduction, and swift utilization of medical care among the elderly. *Journal of Gerontology, 48,* P78–P86.

Levin, J. S., & Chatters, L. M. (1998). Religion, health, and psychological well-being in older adults. *Journal of Aging and Health, 10,* 504–531.

Levin, J. S., Taylor, R. J., & Chatters, L. M. (1994). Race and gender differences in religiosity among older adults: Findings from four national surveys. *Journal of Gerontology, 49,* S137–S145.

Levine, L. E. (1983). Mine: Self-definition in 2-year-old boys. *Developmental Psychology, 19,* 544–549.

Levine, L. J. (1995). Young children's understanding of the causes of anger and sadness. *Child Development, 66,* 697–709.

LeVine, R. A., Dixon, S., LeVine, S., Richman, A., Leiderman, P. H., Keefer, C. H., & Brazelton, T. B. (1994). *Child care and culture: Lessons from Africa.* New York: Cambridge University Press.

Levinson, D. J. (1978). *The seasons of a man's life.* New York: Knopf.

Levinson, D. J. (1986). A conception of adult development. *American Psychologist, 41,* 3–13.

Levinson, D. J. (1996). *The seasons of a woman's life.* New York: Knopf.

Levitt, A. G., & Utmann, J. G. A. (1992). From babbling towards the sound systems of English and French: A longitudinal two-case study. *Journal of Child Language, 19,* 19–40.

Levy, G. D., Taylor, M. G., & Gelman, S. A. (1995). Traditional and evaluative aspects of flexibility in gender roles, social conventions, moral rules, and physical laws. *Child Development, 66,* 515–531.

Levy, J. A. (1994). Sex and sexuality in later life stages. In A. S. Rossi (Ed.), *Sexuality across the life course* (pp. 287–309). Chicago: University of Chicago Press.

Levy-Shiff, R. (1994). Individual and contextual correlates of marital change across the transition to parenthood. *Developmental Psychology, 30,* 591–601.

Levy-Shiff, R., & Israelashvili, R. (1988). Antecedents of fathering: Some further exploration. *Developmental Psychology, 24,* 434–440.

Lewis, C., Freeman, N. H., Kyriadidou, C., Maridakikassotaki, K., & Berridge, D. M. (1996). Social influences on false belief access—specific sibling influences or general apprenticeship? *Child Development, 67,* 2930–2947.

Lewis, L. L. (1992). PMS and progesterone: The ongoing controversy. In A. J. Dan & L. L. Lewis (Eds.), *Menstrual health in women's lives* (pp. 61–74). Urbana: University of Illinois Press.

Lewis, M. (1992). *Shame: The exposed self.* New York: Free Press.

Lewis, M. (1994). Myself and me. In S. T. Parker, R. W. Mitchell, & M. L. Boccia (Eds.), *Self-awareness in animals and humans: Developmental perspectives* (pp. 20–34). New York: Cambridge University Press.

Lewis, M. (1995). Embarrassment: The emotion of self-exposure and evaluation. In J. P. Tangney & K. W. Fischer (Eds.), *Self-conscious emotions* (pp. 198–218). New York: Guilford Press.

Lewis, M. (1997). *Altering fate: Why the past does not predict the future.* New York: Guilford.

Lewis, M., & Brooks-Gunn, J. (1979). *Social cognition and the acquisition of self.* New York: Plenum.

Lewis, M., Ramsay, D. S., & Kawakami, K. (1993). Differences between Japanese infants and Caucasian American infants in behavioral and cortisol response to inoculation. *Child Development, 64,* 1722–1731.

Lewis, M., Sullivan, M. W., Stanger, C., & Weiss, M. (1989). Self development and self-conscious emotions. *Child Development, 60,* 146–156.

Lewis, R. (1990). Death and dying among the American Indians. In J. K. Parry (Ed.), *Social work practice with the terminally ill: A transcultural perspective* (pp. 23–32). Springfield, IL: Charles C Thomas.

Leys, D., Pasquier, F., & Parnetti, L. (1998). Epidemiology of vascular dementia. *Haemostatis, 28,* 134–150.

Liaw, F., & Brooks-Gunn, J. (1993). Patterns of low-birth-weight children's cognitive development. *Developmental Psychology, 29,* 1024–1035.

Liben, L. S., & Signorella, M. L. (1993). Gender-schematic processing in children: The role of initial interpretations of stimuli. *Developmental Psychology, 29,* 141–149.

Lidz, C. S. (1997). Dynamic assessment: Psychoeducational assessment with cultural sensitivity. *Journal of Social Distress and the Homeless, 6,* 95–111.

Lieberman, M. A. (1993). Bereavement self-help groups: A review of conceptual and methodological issues. In M. S. Stroebe, W. Stroebe, & R. O. Hansson (Eds.), *Handbook of bereavement* (pp. 427–453). New York: Cambridge University Press.

Liefbroer, A. C., & de Jong-Gierveld, J. (1990). Age differences in loneliness among young adults with and without a partner relationship. In P. J. D. Drenth, J. A. Sergeant, & R. J. Takens (Eds.), *European perspectives in psychology* (Vol. 3, pp. 265–278). Chicester: Wiley.

Lifschitz, M., Berman, D., Galili, A., & Gilad, D. (1977). Bereaved children: The effects of mother's perception and social system organization on their short range adjustment. *Journal of Child Psychiatry, 16,* 272–284.

Light, P., & Perret-Clermont, A.-N. (1989). Social context effects in learning and testing. In A. Gellatly, D. Rogers, & J. Sloboda (Eds.), *Cognition and social worlds* (pp. 99–112). Oxford: Clarendon Press.

Lillard, A. S. (1998). Playing with a theory of mind. In O. N. Saracho & B. Spodek (Eds.), *Multiple perspectives on play in early childhood education* (pp. 11–33). Albany: State University of New York Press.

Lindauer, M. S., Orwoll, L., & Kelley, M. C. (1997). Aging artists on the creativity of their old age. *Creativity Research Journal, 10,* 133–152.

Lindsay-Hartz, J., de Rivera, J., & Mascolo, M. F. (1995). Differentiating guilt and shame and their effects on motivation. In J. P. Tangney & K. W. Fischer (Eds.), *Self-conscious emotions* (pp. 274–300). New York: Guilford.

Link, S. C., & Ancoli-Israel, S. (1995). Sleep and the teenager. *Sleep Research, 24a,* 184.

Linn, M. C., & Petersen, A. C. (1985). Emergence and characterization of sex differences in spatial ability: A meta-analysis. *Child Development, 56,* 1479–1498.

Lipsitt, L. P. (1990). Learning and memory in infants. *Merrill-Palmer Quarterly, 36,* 53–66.

Lissens, W., & Sermon, K. (1997). Preimplantation genetic diagnosis—current status and new developments. *Human Reproduction, 12,* 1756–1761.

Litovsky, R. Y., & Ashmead, D. H. (1997). Development of binaural and spatial hearing in infants and children. In R. H. Gilkey & T. R. Anderson (Eds.), *Binaural and spatial hearing in real and virtual environments* (pp. 571–592). Mahwah, NJ: Erlbaum.

Litwin, H. (1998). The provision of informal support by elderly people residing in assisted living facilities. *Gerontologist, 38,* 239–246.

Livesley, W. J., & Bromley, D. B. (1973). *Person perception in childhood and adolescence.* London: Wiley.

Livson, N., & Peshkin, H. (1980). Perspectives on adolescence from longitudinal research. In J. Adelson (Ed.), *Handbook of adolescent psychology* (pp. 47–98). New York: Wiley.

Lloyd, L. (1999). Multi-age classes and high ability students. *Review of Educational Research, 69,* 187–212.

Loche, S., Cambiaso, P., Carta, D., Marini, R., Borelli, P., & Capps, M. (1994). Final height after growth hormone therapy in non-growth-hormone-deficient children with short stature. *Journal of Pediatrics, 125,* 196–200.

Locke, J. (1892). Some thoughts concerning education. In R. H. Quick (Ed.), *Locke on education* (pp. 1–236). Cambridge, England: Cambridge University Press. (Original work published 1690)

Lockhart, R. S., & Craik, F. I. M. (1990). Levels of processing: A retrospective commentary on a framework for memory research. *Canadian Journal of Psychology, 44,* 87–112.

Loeber, R., & Stouthamer-Loeber, M. (1998). Development of juvenile aggression and violence: Some common misconceptions and controversies. *American Psychologist, 53,* 242–259.

Loehlin, J. C., Horn, J. M., & Willerman, L. (1997). Heredity, environment, and IQ in the Texas Adoption Project. In R. J. Sternberg & E. L. Grigorenko (Eds.), *Intelligence, heredity, and environment* (pp. 105–125). New York: Cambridge University Press.

Loehlin, J. C., Willerman, L., & Horn, J. M. (1988). Human behavior genetics. *Annual Review of Psychology, 38,* 101–133.

Loewen, E. R., Shaw, R. J., & Craik, F. I. M. (1990). Age differences in components of metamemory. *Experimental Aging Research, 16,* 43–48.

Logsdon, R. G. (2000). *Enhancing quality of life in long term care: A comprehensive guide.* New York: Hatherleigh Press.

Lombardo, J. P., & Lavine, L. O. (1981). Sex-role stereotyping and patterns of self-disclosure. *Sex Roles, 7,* 403–411.

Long, D. D. (1985). A cross-cultural examination of fears of death among Saudi Arabians. *Omega, 16,* 43–50.

Long, H. B., & Zoller-Hodges, D. (1995). Outcomes of Elderhostel participation. *Educational Gerontology, 21,* 113–127.

Looney, M. A., & Plowman, S. A. (1990). Passing rates of American children and youth on the FITNESSGRAM criterion-referenced physical fitness standards. *Research Quarterly of Exercise and Sport, 61,* 215–223.

Lopata, H. Z. (1996). *Current widowhood: Myths and realities.* Thousand Oaks, CA: Sage.

Lopez, F. G. (1989). Current family dynamics, trait anxiety, and academic adjustment: Test of a family-based model of vocational identity. *Journal of Vocational Behavior, 35,* 76–87.

Lorenz, K. (1952). *King Solomon's ring.* New York: Crowell.

Lorenz, K. Z. (1943). Die angeborenen Formen möglicher Erfahrung. *Zeitschrift für Tierpsychologie, 5,* 235–409.

Losey, K. M. (1995). Mexican-American students and classroom interaction: An overview and critique. *Review of Educational Research, 65,* 283–318.

Lowinson, J. H., Ruiz, P. & Millman, R. B. (Eds.). (1992). *Substance abuse.* Baltimore: Williams & Wilkins.

Lozoff, B., Askew, G. L., & Wolf, A. W. (1996). Cosleeping and early childhood sleep problems: Effects of ethnicity and socioeconomic status. *Developmental and Behavioral Pediatrics, 17,* 9–15.

Lozoff, B., Jordan, B., & Malone, S. (1988). Childbirth in cross-cultural perspective. *Marriage and Family Review, 13,* 35–60.

Lozoff, B., Wolf, A., Latz, S., & Paludetto, R. (1995, March). *Cosleeping in Japan, Italy, and the U.S.: Autonomy versus interpersonal relatedness.* Paper presented at the biennial meeting of the Society for Research in Child Development, Indianapolis.

Lubinski, D., & Benbow, C. P. (1994). The study of mathematically precocious youth: The first three decades of a planned 50-year study of intellectual talent. In R. F. Subotnik & K. D. Arnold (Eds.), *Beyond Terman: Contemporary longitudinal studies of giftedness and talent* (pp. 255–281). Norwood, NJ: Ablex.

Luborsky, M. R., & McMullen, K. (1999). Culture and aging. In J. C. Kavanaugh & S. K. Whitbourne (Eds.), *Gerontology: An interdisciplinary perspective* (pp. 65–90). New York: Oxford University Press.

Ludemann, P. M. (1991). Generalized discrimination of positive facial expressions by seven- and ten-month-old infants. *Child Development, 62,* 55–67.

Luker, K. (1996). *Dubious conceptions: The politics of teenage pregnancy.* Cambridge, MA: Harvard University Press.

Lund, D. A., Caserta, M. S., & Dimond, M. F. (1993). The course of spousal bereavement in later life. In M. S. Stroebe, W. Stroebe, & R. O. Hansson (Eds.), *Handbook of bereavement* (pp. 240–245). New York: Cambridge University Press.

Luster, T., & Dubow, E. (1992). Home environment and maternal intelligence: A comparison of preschool and school-age children. *Merrill-Palmer Quarterly, 38,* 151–175.

Luster, T., & McAdoo, H. (1996). Family and child influences on educational attainment: A secondary analysis of the High/Scope Perry Preschool data. *Developmental Psychology, 32,* 26–39.

Luszcz, M. A., Bryan, J., & Kent, P. (1997). Predicting episodic memory performance of very old men and women: Contributions from age, depression, activity, cognitive ability, and speed. *Psychology and Aging, 12,* 565–573.

Luthar, S. S., & Cushing, G. (1997). Substance use and personal adjustment among disadvantaged teenagers: A six-month prospective study. *Journal of Youth and Adolescence, 26,* 353–372.

Luthar, S. S., Cushing, T. J., & McMahon, T. J. (1997). Interdisciplinary interface: Developmental principles brought to substance abuse research. In S. S. Luthar, J. A. Burack, D. Cicchetti, & J. R. Weisz (Eds.), *Developmental psychopathology* (pp. 437–456). Cambridge, England: Cambridge University Press.

Lutz, D. J., & Sternberg, R. J. (1999). Cognitive development. In M. H. Bornstein & M. E. Lamb (Eds.), *Developmental psychology: An advanced textbook* (4th ed., pp. 275–311). Mahwah, NJ: Erlbaum.

Luzzo, D. A. (1999). Identifying the career decision-making needs of nontraditional college students. *Journal of Counseling and Development, 77,* 135–140.

Lyness, K., & Thompson, D. (1997). Above the glass ceiling? A comparison of matched samples of female and male executives. *Journal of Applied Psychology, 82,* 359–375.

Lyon, T. D., & Flavell, J. H. (1994). Young children's understanding of "remember" and "forget." *Child Development, 65,* 1357–1371.

Lyons-Ruth, K., & Block, D. (1996). The disturbed caregiving system: Relations among childhood trauma, maternal caregiving, and infant affect and attachment. *Infant Mental Health Journal, 17,* 257–275.

Lyons-Ruth, K., Connell, D. B., Grunebaum, H. U., & Botein, S. (1990). Infants at social risk: Maternal depression and family support services as mediators of infant development and security of attachment. *Child Development, 61,* 85–98.

Lyoo, K., Noam, G. G., Lee, C. K., Lee, H. K., Kennedy, B. P., & Renshaw, P. F. (1996). The corpus callosum and lateral ventricles in children with attention-deficit hyperactivity disorder: A brain magnetic resonance imaging study. *Biological Psychiatry, 40,* 1060–1063.

Lytton, H., & Romney, D. M. (1991). Parents' sex-related differential socialization of boys and girls: A meta-analysis. *Psychological Bulletin, 109,* 267–296.

Maccoby, E. E. (1984). Socialization and developmental change. *Child Development, 55,* 317–328.

Maccoby, E. E. (1990). Gender and relationships. *American Psychologist, 45,* 513–520.

Maccoby, E. E., & Jacklin, C. N. (1987). Gender segregation in childhood. In E. H. Reese (Ed.), *Advances in child development and behavior* (Vol. 20, pp. 239–287). New York: Academic Press.

Maccoby, E. E., & Martin, J. A. (1983). Socialization in the context of the family: Parent–child interaction. In E. M. Hetherington (Ed.), *Handbook of child psychology: Vol. 4. Socialization, personality, and social development* (4th ed., pp. 1–101). New York: Wiley.

MacDonald, W. L., & DeMaris, A. (1996). The effects of stepparent's gender and new biological children. *Journal of Family Issues, 17,* 5–25.

MacEwen, K. E., Barling, J., Kelloway, E. K., & Higginbottom, S. F. (1995). Predicting retirement anxiety: The roles of parental socialization and personal planning. *Journal of Social Psychology, 135,* 203–213.

Macfarlane, J. (1971). From infancy to adulthood. In M. C. Jones, N. Bayley, J. W. Macfarlane, & M. P. Honzik (Eds.), *The course of human development* (pp. 406–410). Waltham, MA: Xerox College Publishing.

MacKay, D. G., & Abrams, L. (1996). Language, memory, and aging: Distributed deficits and the structure of new-versus-old connections. In J. E. Birren & K. W. Schaie (Eds.), *Handbook of the psychology of aging* (pp. 251–265). San Diego: Academic Press.

Mackey, M. C. (1995). Women's evaluation of their childbirth performance. *Maternal–Child Nursing Journal, 23,* 57–72.

MacKinnon, C. E. (1989). An observational investigation of sibling interactions in married and divorced families. *Developmental Psychology, 25,* 36–44.

Mackinnon, L. T. (1992). *Exercise and immunology.* Champaign, IL: Human Kinetics.

MacKinnon-Lewis, C., Starnes, R., Volling, B., & Johnson, S. (1997). Perceptions of parenting as predictors of boys' sibling and peer relations. *Developmental Psychology, 33,* 1024–1031.

MacMillan, D. L., Keogh, B. K., & Jones, R. L. (1986). Special educational research on mildly handicapped learners. In M. C. Wittrock (Ed.), *Handbook of research on teaching* (3rd ed., pp. 686–724). New York: Macmillan.

MacWhinney, B. (1996). Lexical connectionism. In P. Broeder & J. M. J. Murre (Eds.), *Models of language acquisition: Inductive and deductive approaches.* Cambridge, MA: MIT Press.

Madden, D. J., & Plude, D. J. (1993). Selective preservation of selective attention. In J. Cerella & J. M. Rybash (Eds.), *Adult information processing: Limits on loss* (pp. 273–300). San Diego: Academic Press.

Maddi, S. R. (1999). The personality construct of hardiness: I. Effects on experiencing, coping, and strain. *Consulting Psychology Journal: Practice and Research, 51,* 83–94.

Maddi, S. R., & Hightower, M. (1999). Hardiness and optimism as expressed in coping patterns. *Consulting Psychology Journal: Practice and Research, 51,* 95–105.

Maddi, S. R., & Kobasa, S. C. (1984). *The hardy executive: Health under stress.* Homewood, IL: Dow Jones–Irwin.

Maddox, G. L. (1963). Activity and morale: A longitudinal study of selected elderly subjects. *Social Forces, 42,* 195–204.

Madon, S., Jussim, L., & Eccles, J. (1997). In search of the powerful self-fulfilling prophecy. *Journal of Personality and Social Psychology, 72,* 791–809.

Magdol, L., Moffitt, T. E., Caspi, A., & Silva, P. A. (1998). Developmental antecedents of partner abuse: A prospective-longitudinal study. *Journal of Abnormal Psychology, 107,* 375–389.

Maglio, C. J., & Robinson, S. E. (1994). The effects of death education on death anxiety: A meta-analysis. *Omega, 29,* 319–335.

Magni, E., & Frisoni, G. B. (1996). Depression and somatic symptoms in the elderly: The role of cognitive function. *International Journal of Geriatric Psychiatry, 11,* 517–522.

Magnusson, D., & Stattin, H. (1998). Person-context interaction theories. In R. M. Lerner (Ed.), *Handbook of child psychology: Vol. 1. Theoretical models of human development* (5th ed., pp. 685–759). New York: Wiley.

Magura, S., & Laudet, A. B. (1996). Parental substance abuse and child maltreatment: Review and implications for intervention. *Children and Youth Services Review, 18,* 193–220.

Mahon, M. M., Goldberg, E. Z., & Washington, S. K. (1999). Concept of death in a sample of Israeli kibbutz children. *Death Studies, 23,* 43–59.

Mahoney, J. (1998). An update on efforts by the hospice community and the National Hospice Organization to improve access to quality hospice care. *Hospital Journal, 13,* 139–144.

Mahoney, J. L., & Cairns, R. B. (1997). Do extracurricular activities protect against early school dropout? *Developmental Psychology, 33,* 241–253.

Maier, D. M., & Newman, M. J. (1995). Legal and psychological considerations in the development of a euthanasia statute for adults in the United States. *Behavioral Sciences and the Law, 13,* 3–25.

Maier, H., & Smith, J. (1999). Psychological predictors of mortality in old age. *Journal of Gerontology, 54B,* P44–P54.

Maier, S. F., Watkins, L. R., & Fleshner, M. (1994). Psychoneuroimmunology: The interface between behavior, brain, and immunity. *American Psychologist, 49,* 1004–1017.

Main, M., & Solomon, J. (1990). Procedures for identifying infants as disorganized/disoriented during the Ainsworth Strange Situation. In M. Greenberg, D. Cicchetti, & M. Cummings (Eds.), *Attachment in the preschool years: Theory, research, and intervention* (pp. 121–160). Chicago: University of Chicago Press.

Makin, J., Fried, P. A., & Watkinson, B. (1991). A comparison of active and passive smoking during pregnancy: Long-term effects. *Neurotoxicology and Teratology, 13,* 5–12.

Malatesta, C. Z., Grigoryev, P., Lamb, C., Albin, M., & Culver, C. (1986). Emotion socialization and expressive development in preterm and full-term infants. *Child Development, 57,* 316–330.

Malatesta-Magai, C. Z., Izard, C. E., & Camras, L. (1991). Conceptualizing early infant affect: Emotions as fact, fiction or artifact? In K. Strongman (Ed.), *International review of studies on emotion* (pp. 1–36). New York: Wiley.

Malina, R. M. (1975). *Growth and development: The first twenty years in man.* Minneapolis: Burgess.

Malina, R. M. (1990). Physical growth and performance during the transitional years (9–16). In R. Montemayor, G. R. Adams, & T. P. Gullotta (Eds.), *From childhood to adolescence: A transitional period?* (pp. 41–62). Newbury Park, CA: Sage.

Malina, R. M., & Bouchard, C. (1991). *Growth, maturation, and physical activity.* Champaign, IL: Human Kinetics.

Mallinckrodt, B., & Fretz, B. R. (1988). Social support and the impact of job loss on older professionals. *Journal of Counseling Psychology, 35,* 281–286.

Malloy, M. H., & Berendes, H. (1998). Does breast-feeding influence intelligence quotients at 9 and 10 years of age? *Early Human Development, 50,* 209-217.

Malloy, M. H., & Hoffman, H. J. (1995). Prematurity, sudden infant death syndrome, and age of death. *Pediatrics, 96,* 464–471.

Malone, M. M. (1982). Consciousness of dying and projective fantasy of young children with malignant disease. *Developmental and Behavioral Pediatrics, 3,* 55–60.

Maloney, M., & Kranz, R. (1991). *Straight talk about eating disorders.* New York: Facts on File.

Mandler, J. M. (1998). Representation. In D. Kuhn & R. S. Siegler (Eds.), *Handbook of child psychology: Vol. 2. Cognition, perception, and language* (5th ed., pp. 255–308). New York: Wiley.

Mandler, J. M., & McDonough, L. (1993). Concept formation in infancy. *Cognitive Development, 8,* 291–318.

Mandler, J. M., & McDonough, L. (1996). Drinking and driving don't mix: Inductive generalization in infancy. *Cognition, 59,* 307–335.

Mandler, J. M., & McDonough, L. (1998). On developing a knowledge base in infancy. *Developmental Psychology, 34,* 1274–1288.

Mange, E. J., & Mange, A. P. (1998). *Basic human genetics* (2nd ed.). Sunderland, MA: Sinauer Associates.

Mangelsdorf, S., Gunnar, M., Kestenbaum, R., Lang, S., & Andreas, D. (1990). Infant proneness-to-distress temperament, maternal personality, and mother–infant attachment: Associations and goodness of fit. *Child Development, 61,* 820–831.

Manson, J. E., Hosteson, H., Satterfield, S., Hebert, P., O'Connor, G. T., Buring, J. F., & Hennekens, C. H. (1992). The primary prevention of myocardial infarction. *New England Journal of Medicine, 326,* 1406–1416.

Manson, J. E., Willett, W. C., Stampfer, M. J., Colditz, G. A., Hunter, D. J., Hankinson, S. E., Hennekens, C. H., & Speizer, F. E. (1995). Body weight and mortality among women. *New England Journal of Medicine, 333,* 678–685.

Maratsos, M. (1998). The acquisition of grammar. In D. Kuhn & R. S. Siegler (Eds.), *Handbook of child psychology: Vol. 2. Cognition, perception, and language* (5th ed., pp. 421–466). New York: Wiley.

March of Dimes. (1999). *International comparisons of infant mortality rates.* White Plains, NY: March of Dimes Birth Defects Foundation.

Marchioli, R. (1999). Antioxidant vitamins and prevention of cardiovascular disease: Laboratory, epidemiological and clinical trial data. *Pharmacological Research, 40,* 227–238.

Marcia, J. E. (1980). Identity in adolescence. In J. Adelson (Ed.), *Handbook of adolescent psychology* (pp. 159–187). New York: Wiley.

Marcia, J. E., Waterman, A. S., Matteson, D. R., Archer, S. L., & Orlofsky, J. L. (1993). *Ego identity: A handbook for psychosocial research.* New York: Springer-Verlag.

Marcon, R. A. (1999). Differential impact of preschool models on development and early learning of inner-city children: A three-cohort study. *Developmental Psychology, 35,* 358–375.

Marcus, G. F. (1993). Negative evidence in language acquisition. *Cognition, 46,* 53–85.

Marcus, G. F. (1995). Children's over-regularization of English plurals: A quantitative analysis. *Journal of Child Language, 22,* 447–459.

Marcus, G. F., Pinker, S., Ullman, M., Hollander, M., Rosen, T. J., & Xu, F. (1992). Overregularization in language acquisition. *Monographs of the Society for Research in Child Development, 57*(4, Serial No. 228).

Margolin, B. H., Morrison, H. I., & Hulka, B. S. (1994). Cigarette smoking and sperm density: A meta-analysis. *Fertility and Sterility, 61,* 35–43.

Mariner, W. K. (1997). Physician assisted suicide and the Supreme Court: Putting the constitutional claim to rest. *American Journal of Public Health, 87,* 2058–2062.

Markides, K. S. (1989). Aging, gender, race/ethnicity, class, and health: A conceptual overview. In K. S. Markides (Ed.), *Aging and health* (pp. 9–21). Newbury Park, CA: Sage.

Markides, K. S. (1994). Gender and ethnic diversity in aging. In R. J. Manheimer (Ed.), *Older Americans almanac* (pp. 49–69). Detroit: Gale Research, Inc.

Markides, K. S., & Cooper, C. L. (1989). Aging, stress, social support and health: An overview. In K. S. Markides & C. L. Cooper (Eds.), *Aging, stress and health* (pp. 1–10). Chicester: Wiley.

Markman, E. M. (1989). *Categorization and naming in children.* Cambridge, MA: MIT Press.

Markman, E. M. (1992). Constraints on word learning: Speculations about their nature, origins, and domain specificity. In M. R. Gunnar & M. P. Maratsos (Eds.), *Minnesota Symposia on Child Psychology* (Vol. 25, pp. 59–101). Hillsdale, NJ: Erlbaum.

Markman, H., Stanley, S., & Blumberg, S. (1994). *Fighting for your marriage.* San Francisco: Jossey-Bass.

Markovits, H., & Vachon, R. (1989). Reasoning with contrary-to-fact propositions. *Journal of Experimental Child Psychology, 47,* 398–412.

Markovits, H., & Vachon, R. (1990). Conditional reasoning, representation, and level of abstraction. *Developmental Psychology, 26,* 942–951.

Marks, N. (1995). Midlife marital status differences in social support relationships with adult children and psychological well-being. *Journal of Family Issues, 16,* 5–28.

Marks, N. F. (1996). Caregiving across the lifespan: National prevalence and predictors. *Family Relations, 45,* 27–36.

Marks, N. F., & Lambert, J. D. (1998). Marital status continuity and change among young and midlife adults. *Journal of Family Issues, 19,* 652–686.

Markstrom-Adams, C., & Adams, G. R. (1995). Gender, ethnic group, and grade differences in psychosocial functioning during middle adolescence. *Journal of Youth and Adolescence, 24,* 397–417.

Markus, H. R., & Herzog, A. R. (1992). The role of self-concept in aging. In K. W. Schaie & M. P. Lawton (Eds.), *Annual review of gerontology and geriatrics* (pp. 110–143). New York: Springer.

Marlier, L., & Schaal, B. (1997). La perception de la familiarité olfactive chez le nouveau-né: Influence différentielle du mode d'alimentation? [The perception of olfactory familiarity in the neonate: Differential influence of the mode of feeding?] *Enfance, 1,* 47–61.

Marlier, L., Schaal, B., & Soussignan, R. (1998). Neonatal responsiveness to the odor of amniotic and lacteal fluids: A test of perinatal chemosensory continuity. *Child Development, 69,* 611–623.

Marottoli, R. A., Cooney, L. M., Wagner, D. R., Doucette, J., & Tinetti, M. E. (1994). Predictors of automobile crashes and moving violations among elderly drivers. *Annals of Internal Medicine, 121,* 842–846.

Marsh, H. W. (1990). The structure of academic self-concept: The Marsh/Shavelson model. *Journal of Educational Psychology, 82,* 623–636.

Marsh, H. W., Smith, I. D., & Barnes, J. (1985). Multidimensional self-concepts: Relations with sex and academic achievement. *Journal of Educational Psychology, 77,* 581–596.

Marshall, E. (1996). The genome program's conscience. *Science, 274,* 488–491.

Marshall, N. L. (1997). Combining work and family. In S. J. Gallant, G. P. Keita, & R. Royak-Schaler (Eds.), *Health care for women* (pp. 163–174). Washington, DC: American Psychological Association.

Marshall, R. (1997). School-to-work processes in the United States. In R. Takanishi & D. A. Hamburg (Eds.), *Preparing adolescents for the twenty-first century: Challenges facing Europe and the United States* (pp. 195–226). New York: Cambridge University Press.

Martin, C. L. (1989). Children's use of gender-related information in making social judgments. *Developmental Psychology, 25,* 80–88.

Martin, C. L. (1993). New directions for investigating children's gender knowledge. *Developmental Review, 13,* 184–204.

Martin, C. L., & Halverson, C. F. (1981). A schematic processing model of sex typing and stereotyping in children. *Child Development, 52,* 1119–1134.

Martin, C. L., & Halverson, C. F. (1987). The role of cognition in sex role acquisition. In D. B. Carter (Ed.), *Current conceptions of sex roles and sex typing: Theory and research* (pp. 123–137). New York: Praeger.

Martin, C. L., & Little, J. K. (1990). The relation of gender understanding to children's sex-typed preferences and gender stereotypes. *Child Development, 61,* 1427–1439.

Martin, J. A. (1981). A longitudinal study of the consequences of early mother–infant interaction: A microanalytic approach. *Monographs of the Society for Research in Child Development, 46*(3, Serial No. 190).

Martin, J. E., & Dean, L. (1993). Bereavement following death from AIDS: Unique problems, reactions, and special needs. In M. S. Stroebe, W. Stroebe, & R. O. Hansson (Eds.), *Handbook of bereavement* (pp. 317–330). Cambridge, England: Cambridge University Press.

Martin, R. M. (1975). Effects of familiar and complex stimuli on infant attention. *Developmental Psychology, 11,* 178–185.

Martinson, I. M., Davies, E., & McClowry, S. G. (1987). The long-term effect of sibling death on self-concept. *Journal of Pediatric Nursing, 2,* 227–235.

Martlew, M., & Connolly, K. J. (1996). Human figure drawings by schooled and unschooled children in Papua New Guinea. *Child Development, 67,* 2743–2762.

Martyn, C. N., Barker, D. J. P., & Osmond, C. (1996). Mothers' pelvic size, fetal growth, and death from stroke and coronary heart disease in men in the UK. *Lancet, 348,* 1264–1268.

Masataka, N. (1996). Perception of motherese in a signed language by 6-month-old deaf infants. *Developmental Psychology, 32,* 874–879.

Mascolo, M. F., & Fischer, K. W. (1995). Developmental transformations in appraisals for pride, shame, and guilt. In J. P. Tangney & K. W. Fischer (Eds.), *Self-conscious emotions* (pp. 114-139). New York: Guilford.

Mason, C. A., Cauce, A. M., Gonzales, N., & Hiraga, Y. (1996). Neither too sweet nor too sour: Problem peers, maternal control, and problem behavior in African American adolescents. *Child Development, 67,* 2115–2130.

Mason, M. G., & Gibbs, J. C. (1993). Social perspective taking and moral judgment among college students. *Journal of Adolescent Research, 8,* 109–123.

Massad, C. M. (1981). Sex role identity and adjustment during adolescence. *Child Development, 52,* 1290–1298.

Massey, C. M., & Gelman, R. (1988). Preschoolers' ability to decide whether a photographed unfamiliar object can move itself. *Developmental Psychology, 24,* 307–317.

Masten, A. S., & Coatsworth, J. D. (1998). The development of competence in favorable and unfavorable environments: Lessons from research on successful children. *American Psychologist, 53,* 205–220.

Masten, A. S., Hubbard, J. J., Gest, S. D., Tellegen, A., Garmezy, N., & Ramirez, M. (1999). Adaptation in the context of adversity: Pathways to resilience and maladaptation from childhood to late adolescence. *Development and Psychopathology, 11,* 143–169.

Masur, E. F., McIntyre, C. W., & Flavell, J. H. (1973). Developmental changes in apportionment of study time among items in a multi-trial free recall task. *Journal of Experimental Child Psychology, 15,* 237–246.

Matas, L., Arend, R., & Sroufe, L. A. (1978). Continuity of adaptation in the second year: The relationship between quality of attachment and later competence. *Child Development, 49,* 547–556.

Matheny, A. P., Jr. (1991). Children's unintentional injuries and gender: Differentiation and psychosocial aspects. *Children's Environment Quarterly, 8,* 51–61.

Mattson, S. N., Riley, E. P., Delis, D. C., & Jones, K. L. (1998). Neuropsychological comparison of alcohol-exposed children with or without physical features of fetal alcohol syndrome. *Neuropsychology, 12,* 146–153.

Matute-Bianchi, M. E. (1986). Ethnic identities and patterns of school success and failure among Mexican-descent and Japanese-American students in a California high school: An ethnographic analysis. *American Journal of Education, 95,* 233–255.

Maurer, T., & Tarulli, B. (1994). Perceived environment, perceived outcome, and person variables in relationship to voluntary development activity by employees. *Journal of Applied Psychology, 79,* 3–14.

Maxwell, S. R. (1999). Antioxidant vitamin supplements: Update of their potential benefits and possible risks. *Drug Safety, 21,* 253–266.

Mayberry, R. I. (1994). The importance of childhood to language acquisition: Evidence from American Sign Language. In J. C. Goodman & H. C. Nusbaum (Eds.), *The development of speech perception: The transition from speech sounds to spoken words* (pp. 57–90). Cambridge, MA: MIT Press.

Mayes, L. C. (1999). Reconsidering the concept of vulnerability in children using the model of prenatal cocaine exposure. In T. B. Cohen & E. M. Hossein (Eds.), *The vulnerable child* (Vol. 3, pp. 35–54). Madison, CT: International Universities Press.

Mayes, L. C., & Bornstein, M. H. (1997). Attention regulation in infants born at risk: Prematurity and prenatal cocaine exposure. In J. A. Burack & J. T. Enns (Eds.), *Attention, development, and psychopathology* (pp. 97–122). New York: Guilford.

Mayes, L. C., & Zigler, E. (1992). An observational study of the affective concomitants of mastery in infants. *Journal of Child Psychology and Psychiatry, 33,* 659–667.

Maylor, E., & Valentine, T. (1992). Linear and nonlinear effects of aging on categorizing and naming faces. *Psychology and Aging, 7,* 317–323.

Mayo Clinic. (2000, March). Age-related macular degeneration: Who gets it and what you can do about it. *Women's Healthsource, 4*(3), 1–2.

Mays, V. M., Bullock, M., Rosenzweig, M. R., & Wessells, M. (1998). Ethnic conflict: Global challenges and psychological conflict. *American Psychologist, 53,* 737–742.

Mazur, E. (1993). Developmental differences in children's understanding of marriage, divorce, and remarriage. *Journal of Applied Developmental Psychology, 14,* 191–212.

McAdams, D. P. (1988). *Power, intimacy, and the life story.* New York: Guilford.

McAdams, D. P. (1993). *The stories we live by: Personal myths and the making of the self.* New York: Morrow.

McAdams, D. P. (1994). Can personality change? Levels of stability and growth in personality across the life span. In T. F. Heatherton & J. L. Weinberger (Eds.), *Can personality change?* (pp. 299–313). Washington, DC: American Psychological Association.

McAdams, D. P., & de St. Aubin, E. (1992). A theory of generativity and its assessment through self-report, behavioral acts, and narrative themes in autobiography. *Journal of Personality and Social Psychology, 62,* 1003–1015.

McAdams, D. P., de St. Aubin, E., & Logan, R. L. (1993). Generativity among young, midlife, and older adults. *Psychology and Aging, 8,* 221–230.

McAdams, D. P., Diamond, A., de St. Aubin, E., & Mansfield, E. (1997). Stories of commitment: The psychosocial construction of generative lives. *Journal of Personality and Social Psychology, 72,* 678–694.

McAdams, D. P., Hart, H. M., & Maruna, S. (1998). The anatomy of generativity. In D. P. McAdams & E. de St. Aubin (Eds.), *Generativity and adult development* (pp. 7–43). Washington, DC: American Psychological Association.

McAdoo, H. P. (1993). Ethnic families: Strengths that are found in diversity. In H. P. McAdoo (Ed.), *Family ethnicity* (pp. 3–14). Newbury Park, CA: Sage.

McAnarney, E. R., Kreipe, R. E., Orr, D. P., & Comerci, G. D. (1992). *Textbook of adolescent development.* Philadelphia: Saunders.

McAuley, E., Bane, S. M., & Mihalko, S. L. (1995). Exercise in middle-aged adults: Self-efficacy and self-presentational outcomes. *Preventive Medicine, 24,* 319–328.

McAuley, E., & Jacobson, L. (1991). Self-efficacy and exercise participation in sedentary adult females. *American Journal of Health Promotion, 5,* 185–191, 207.

McAuley, E., Mihalko, S. L., & Bane, S. M. (1997). Exercise and self-esteem in middle-aged adults: Multidimensional relationships and physical fitness and self-efficacy influences. *Journal of Behavioral Medicine, 20,* 67–83.

McBride, B. A., & Rane, T. R. (1998). Parenting alliance as a predictor of father involvement: An exploratory study. *Family Relations, 47,* 229–236.

McBride, J. (1997). Foods to be fortified with folic acid. *Agricultural Research, 45,* 16–17.

McCabe, A. E., & Peterson, C. (1988). A comparison of adults' versus children's spontaneous use of *because* and *so. Journal of Genetic Psychology, 149,* 257–268.

McCall, R. B. (1993). Developmental functions for general mental performance.

In D. K. Detterman (Ed.), *Current topics in human intelligence* (Vol. 3, pp. 3–29). Norwood, NJ: Ablex.

McCall, R. B., & Carriger, M. S. (1993). A meta-analysis of infant habituation and recognition memory performance as predictors of later IQ. *Child Development, 64,* 57–79.

McCarton, C. M., Brooks-Gunn, J., Wallace, I. F., Bauer, C. R., Bennett, F. C., Bernbaum, J. C., Broyles, R. S., Casey, P. H., McCormick, M. C., Scott, D. T., Tyson, J., Tonascia, J., and Meinert, C. L. (1997). Results at age 8 years of early intervention for low-birth-weight premature infants: The infant health and development program. *Journal of the American Medical Association, 277,* 126–132.

McConaghy, M. J. (1979). Gender permanence and the genital basis of gender: Stages in the development of constancy of gender identity. *Child Development, 50,* 1223–1226.

McCormick, W. C., Uomoto, J., Young, H., Graves, A. B., Vitaliano, P., Mortimer, J. A., Edland, S. D., & Larson, E. B. (1996). Attitudes toward use of nursing homes and home care in older Japanese-Americans. *Journal of the American Gerontological Society, 44,* 769–777.

McCrae, R. R., & Costa, P. T., Jr. (1988). Psychological resilience among widowed men and women: A 10-year follow-up of a national sample. *Journal of Social Issues, 44,* 129–142.

McCrae, R. R., & Costa, P. T., Jr. (1990). *Personality in adulthood.* New York: Guilford.

McCrae, R. R., Costa, P. T., Jr., de Lima, M. P., Simoes, A., Ostendorf, F., Angleitner, A., Marusic, I., Bratko, D., Caprara, G. V., Barbaranelli, C., Chae, J.-H., & Piedmont, R. L. (1999). Age differences in personality across the adult life span: Parallels in five cultures. *Developmental Psychology, 35,* 466–477.

McCullough, P., & Rutenberg, S. (1989). Launching children and moving on. In B. Carter & M. McGoldrick (Eds.), *The changing family life cycle* (pp. 285–309). Boston: Allyn and Bacon.

McCune, L. (1993). The development of play as the development of consciousness. In M. H. Bornstein & A. O'Reilly (Eds.), *New directions for child development* (No. 59, pp. 67–79). San Francisco: Jossey-Bass.

McFadden, S. H. (1996). Religion, spirituality, and aging. In J. E. Birren & K. W. Schaie (Eds.), *Handbook of the psychology of aging* (pp. 162–177). San Diego: Academic Press.

McGee, G. (1997). Legislating gestation. *Human Reproduction, 12,* 407–408.

McGee, L. M., & Richgels, D. J. (1996). *Literacy's beginnings* (2nd ed.) Boston: Allyn and Bacon.

McGee, L. M., & Richgels, D. J. (2000). *Literacy's beginnings* (3rd ed.). Boston: Allyn and Bacon.

McGeer, P. L., Schulzer, M., & McGeer, E. G. (1996). Arthritis and anti-inflammatory agents as possible protective factors for Alzheimer's disease: A review of 17 epidemiologic studies. *Neurology, 47,* 425–432.

McGillicuddy-De Lisi, A. V., Watkins, C., & Vinchur, A. J. (1994). The effect of relationship on children's distributive justice reasoning. *Child Development, 65,* 1694–1700.

McGinnis, J. M., & Lee, P. R. (1995). Healthy People 2000 at mid decade. *Journal of the American Medical Association, 273,* 1123–1129.

McGoldrick, M., Heiman, M., & Carter, B. (1993). The changing family life cycle: A perspective on normalcy. In F. Walsh (Ed.), *Normal family processes* (pp. 405–443). New York: Guilford.

McGroarty, M. (1992, March). The societal context of bilingual education. *Educational Researcher, 21*(2), 7–9.

McGue, M., Bouchard, T. J., Jr., Iacono, W. G., & Lykken, D. T. (1993). Behavioral genetics of cognitive ability: A life-span perspective. In R. Plomin & G. E. McClearn (Eds.), *Nature, nurture, and psychology* (pp. 59–76). Washington, DC: American Psychological Association.

McGue, M., Vaupel, J. W., Holm, W., & Harvald, L. S. (1993). Longevity is moderately heritable in a sample of Danish twins born 1870–1880. *Journal of Gerontology, 48,* B224–B237.

McGuffin, P., & Sargeant, M. P. (1991). Major affective disorder. In P. McGuffin & R. Murray (Eds.), *The new genetics of mental illness* (pp. 165–181). London: Butterworth-Heinemann.

McHale, S. M., Bartko, W. T., Crouter, A. C., & Perry-Jenkins, M. (1990). Children's housework and psychosocial functioning: The mediating effects of parents' sex-role behaviors and attitudes. *Child Development, 61,* 1413–1426.

McHale, S. M., Crouter, A. C., McGuire, S. A., & Updegraff, K. A. (1995). Congruence between mothers' and fathers' differential treatment of siblings: Links with family relations and children's well-being. *Child Development, 66,* 116–128.

McIntosh, J. L., Santos, J. F., Hubbard, R. W., & Overholser, J. C. (1994). *Elder suicide: Research, theory, and treatment.* Washington, DC: American Psychological Association.

McKusick, V. A. (1998). *Mendelian inheritance in man: A catalog of human genes and genetic disorders.* Baltimore: Johns Hopkins University Press.

McLean, D. F., Timajchy, K. H., Wingo, P. A., & Floyd, R. L. (1993). Psychosocial measurement: Implications of the study of preterm delivery in black women. *American Journal of Preventive Medicine, 9,* 39–81.

McLeod, J. D., & Shanahan, M. J. (1996). Trajectories of poverty and children's mental health. *Journal of Health and Social Behavior, 37,* 207–220.

McLoyd, V. (1998). Socioeconomic disadvantage and child development. *American Psychologist, 53,* 185–204.

McLoyd, V. C. (1998). Children in poverty: Development, public policy, and practice. In I. Sigel & A. Renninger (Eds.), *Handbook of child psychology: Vol. 4. Child psychology in practice* (5th ed., pp. 135–208). New York: Wiley.

McLoyd, V. C., Jayaratne, T. E., Ceballo, R., & Borquez, J. (1994). Unemployment and work interruption among African-American single mothers: Effects on parenting and adolescent socioemotional functioning. *Child Development, 65,* 562–589.

McManus, I. C., Sik, G., Cole, D. R., Mellon, A. F., Wong, J., & Kloss, J. (1988). The development of handedness in children. *British Journal of Developmental Psychology, 6,* 257–273.

McNamee, S., & Peterson, J. (1986). Young children's distributive justice reasoning, behavior, and role taking: Their consistency and relationship. *Journal of Genetic Psychology, 146,* 399–404.

McNeil, J. N. (1986). Talking about death: Adolescents, parents, and peers. In C. A. Corr & J. N. McNeil (Eds.), *Adolescence and death* (pp. 185–201). New York: Springer.

MCR Vitamin Study Research Group. (1991). Prevention of neural tube defects: Results of the Medical Research Council Vitamin Study. *Lancet, 338,* 131–137.

Mead, G. H. (1934). *Mind, self, and society.* Chicago: University of Chicago Press.

Mead, M. (1928). *Coming of age in Samoa.* Ann Arbor, MI: Morrow.

Mead, M., & Newton, N. (1967). Cultural patterning of perinatal behavior. In S. Richardson & A. Guttmacher (Eds.), *Childbearing: Its social and psychological aspects* (pp. 142–244). Baltimore: Williams & Wilkins.

Meadow-Orlans, K. P., & Steinberg, A. G. (1993). Effects of infant hearing loss and maternal support on mother–infant interactions at 18 months. *Journal of Applied Developmental Psychology, 14,* 407–426.

Mecham, M. J. (1996). *Cerebral palsy.* Austin, TX: PRO-ED.

Mehlmadrona, L., & Madrona, M. M. (1997). Physician- and midwife-attended home births—effects of breech, twin, and post-dates outcome data on mortality rates. *Journal of Nurse-Midwifery, 42,* 91–98.

Meilman, P. W. (1979). Cross-sectional age changes in ego identity status during adolescence. *Developmental Psychology, 15,* 230–231.

Melby, J. N., & Conger, R. D. (1996). Parental behaviors and adolescent academic performance: A longitudinal analysis. *Journal of Research on Adolescence, 6,* 113–137.

Melnikow, J., & Alemagno, S. (1993). Adequacy of prenatal care among inner-city women. *Journal of Family Practice, 37,* 575–582.

Meltzoff, A. N. (1990). Towards a developmental cognitive science. *Annals of the New York Academy of Sciences, 608,* 1–37.

Meltzoff, A. N. (1994). What infant memory tells us about infantile amnesia: Long-term recall and deferred imitation. *Journal of Experimental Child Psychology, 59,* 497–515.

Meltzoff, A. N. (1995). Understanding the intentions of others: Re-enactment of intended acts by 18-month-old children. *Developmental Psychology, 31,* 838–850.

Meltzoff, A. N., & Borton, R. W. (1979). Intermodal matching by human neonates. *Nature, 282,* 403–404.

Meltzoff, A. N., & Kuhl, P. K. (1994). Faces and speech: Intermodal processing of biologically relevant signals in infants and adults. In D. J. Lewkowicz & R. Lickliter (Eds.), *The development of intersensory perception* (pp. 335–369). Hillsdale, NJ: Erlbaum.

Meltzoff, A. N., & Moore, M. K. (1977). Imitation of facial and manual gestures by human neonates. *Science, 198,* 75–78.

Meltzoff, A. N., & Moore, M. K. (1992). Early imitation within a functional framework: The importance of person identity, movement, and development. *Infant Behavior and Development, 15,* 479–505.

Meltzoff, A. N., & Moore, M. K. (1994). Imitation, memory, and the representation of persons. *Infant Behavior and Development, 17,* 83–99.

Mendelson, B. K., White, D. R., & Mendelson, M. J. (1996). Self-esteem and body esteem: Effects of gender, age, and weight. *Journal of Applied Developmental Psychology, 17,* 321–346.

Menyuk, P., Liebergott, J. W., & Schultz, M. C. (1995). *Early language development in full-term and premature infants.* Hillsdale, NJ: Erlbaum.

Mercer, R. T., Nichols, E. G., & Doyle, G. C. (1989). *Transitions in a woman's life: Major life events in developmental context.* New York: Springer-Verlag.

Meredith, C. N., Frontera, W. R., O'Reilly, K. P., & Evans, W. J. (1992). Body composition in elderly men: Effect of dietary modification during strength training. *Journal of the American Geriatrics Society, 40,* 155–162.

Mergenhagen, P. (1996). Her own boss. *American Demographics, 18,* 36–41.

Merrill, D. M. (1997). *Caring for elderly parents.* Westport, CT: Auburn House.

Meyer, B. J. F., Russo, C., & Talbot, A. (1995). Discourse comprehension and problem solving: Decisions about the treatment of breast cancer by women across the life-span. *Psychology and Aging, 10,* 84–103.

Meyer, M. H., & Bellas, M. L. (1995). U.S. old-age policy and the family. In R. Blieszner & V. H. Bedford (Eds.), *Handbook of aging and the family* (pp. 263–283). Westport, CT: Greenwood Press.

Meyer-Bahlburg, H. F. L. (1990). Short stature: Psychological issues. In F. Lifshitz (Ed.), *Pediatric endocrinology: A critical guide* (2nd ed., pp. 173–196). New York: Marcel Dekker.

Meyer-Bahlburg, H. F. L., Ehrhardt, A. A., Rosen, L. R., Gruen, R. S., Veridiano, N. P., Vann, F. H., & Neuwalder, H. F. (1995). Prenatal estrogens and the development of homosexual orientation. *Developmental Psychology, 31,* 12–21.

Meyers, C., Adam, R., Dungan, J., & Prenger, V. (1997). Aneuploidy in twin gestations: When is maternal age advanced? *Obstetrics and Gynecology, 89,* 248–251.

Michael, R. T., Gagnon, J. H., Laumann, E. O., & Kolata, G. (1994). *Sex in America.* Boston: Little, Brown.

Michaels, G. Y. (1988). Motivational factors in the decision and timing of pregnancy. In G. Y. Michaels & W. A. Goldberg (Eds.), *The transition to parenthood: Current theory and research* (pp. 23–61). New York: Cambridge University Press.

Michaels, S. (1996). The prevalence of homosexuality in the United States. In R. P. Cabaj & T. S. Stein (Eds.), *Textbook of homosexuality and mental health* (pp. 43–63). Washington, DC: American Psychiatric Press.

Michel, C. (1989). Radiation embryology. *Experientia, 45,* 69–77.

Michels, K. B., Trichopoulos, D., Robins, J. M., Rosner, B. A., Manson, J. E., Hunter, D. J., Colditz, G. A., Hankinson, S. E., Speizer, F. E., & Willett, W. C. (1996). Birthweight as a risk factor for breast cancer. *Lancet, 348,* 1542–1546.

Mikulincer, M., & Erev, I. (1991). Attachment style and the structure of romantic love. *British Journal of Social Psychology, 30,* 273–291.

Milberger, S., Biederman, J., Faraone, S. V., Guite, J., & Tsuang, M. T. (1997). Pregnancy, delivery and infancy complications and attention deficit hyperactivity disorder: Issues of gene–environment interaction. *Biological Psychiatry, 41,* 65–75.

Milgram, N. A., & Palti, G. (1993). Psychosocial characteristics of resilient children. *Journal of Research in Personality, 27,* 207–221.

Millberger, S., Biederman, J., Faraone, S. V., & Jones, J. (1998). Further evidence of an association between maternal smoking during pregnancy and attention-deficit hyperactivity disorder: Findings from a

high-risk sample of siblings. *Journal of Clinical Child Psychology, 27,* 352–358.

Miller, F. G., Quill, T. E., Brody, H., Fletcher, J. C., Gostin, L. O., & Meier, D. E. (1994). Regulating physician-assisted death. *New England Journal of Medicine, 118,* 119–123.

Miller, G. A. (1991). *The science of words.* New York: Scientific American Library.

Miller, J., Slomczynski, K. M., & Kohn, M. L. (1985). Continuity of learning-generalization: The effect of job on men's intellective process in the United States and Poland. *American Journal of Sociology, 91,* 593–615.

Miller, J. G. (1997). Culture and self: Uncovering the cultural grounding of psychological theory. In J. G. Snodgrass & R. L. Thompson (Eds.), *Annals of the New York Academy of Sciences* (Vol. 18, pp. 217–231). New York: New York Academy of Sciences.

Miller, J. M., Boudreaux, M. C., & Regan, F. A. (1995). A case-control study of cocaine use in pregnancy. *American Journal of Obstetrics and Gynecology, 172,* 180–185.

Miller, K. A., & Kohn, M. L. (1983). The reciprocal effects of job conditions and the intellectuality of leisure-time activities. In M. L. Kohn & C. Schooler (Eds.), *Work and personality: An inquiry into the impact of social stratification* (pp. 217–241). Norwood, NJ: Ablex.

Miller, K. F., Smith, C. M., Zhu, J., & Zhang, H. (1995). Preschool origins of cross-national differences in mathematical competence: The role of number-naming systems. *Psychological Science, 6,* 56–60.

Miller, L. T., & Vernon, P. A. (1992). The general factor in short-term memory, intelligence, and reaction time. *Intelligence, 16,* 5–29.

Miller, L. T., & Vernon, P. A. (1997). Developmental changes in speed of information processing in young children. *Developmental Psychology, 33,* 549–554.

Miller, N., & Maruyama, G. (1976). Ordinal position and peer popularity. *Journal of Personality and Social Psychology, 33,* 123–131.

Miller, N. B., Cowan, P. A., Cowan, C. P., Hetherington, E. M., & Clingempeel, W. G. (1993). Externalizing in pre-schoolers and early adolescents: A cross-study replication of a family model. *Developmental Psychology, 29,* 3–16.

Miller, P. H. (1993). *Theories of developmental psychology* (3rd ed.). New York: Freeman.

Miller, P. H., & Bigi, L. (1979). The development of children's understanding of attention. *Merrill-Palmer Quarterly, 25,* 235–250.

Miller, P. H., & Seier, W. L. (1994). Strategy utilization deficiencies in children: When, where, and why. In H. W. Reese (Ed.), *Advances in child development and*

behavior (Vol. 24, pp. 107–156). New York: Academic Press.

Miller, R. A. (1996). The aging immune system: Primer and prospectus. *Science, 273,* 70–74.

Miller, R. B., Hemesath, K., & Nelson, B. (1997). Marriage in middle and later life. In T. D. Hargrave & S. M. Hanna (Eds.), *The aging family* (pp. 178–198). New York: Brunner/Mazel.

Miller, S. S., & Cavanaugh, J. C. (1990). The meaning of grandparenthood and its relationship to demographic, relationship, and social participation variables. *Journal of Gerontology, 45,* P244–P246.

Mills, D. L., Coffey-Corina, S. A., & Neville, H. J. (1993). Language acquisition and cerebral specialization in 20-month-old infants. *Journal of Cognitive Neuroscience, 5,* 317–334.

Mills, D. L., Coffey-Corina, S. A., & Neville, H. J. (1994). Variability in cerebral organization during primary language acquisition. In G. Dawson & K. W. Fischer (Eds.), *Human behavior and the developing brain* (pp. 427–455). New York: Guilford.

Mills, R., Coffey-Corina, S., & Neville, H. J. (1997). Language comprehension and cerebral specialization from 13 to 20 months. *Developmental Neuropsychology, 13,* 397–445.

Mills, R., & Grusec, J. (1989). Cognitive, affective, and behavioral consequences of praising altruism. *Merrill-Palmer Quarterly, 35,* 299–326.

Millstein, S. G., & Litt, I. F. (1990). Adolescent health. In S. S. Feldman & G. R. Elliott (Eds.), *At the threshold: The developing adolescent* (pp. 431–456). Cambridge, MA: Harvard University Press.

Minkler, M., Fuller-Thomson, E., Miller, D., & Drive, D. (1997). Depression in grandparents raising grandchildren: Results of a national longitudinal study. *Archives of Family Medicine, 6,* 445–452.

Minkler, M., & Roe, K. M. (1993). *Grandmothers as caregivers: Raising children of the crack cocaine epidemic.* Newbury Park, CA: Sage.

Mischel, W., & Liebert, R. M. (1966). Effects of discrepancies between observed and imposed reward criteria on their acquisition and transmission. *Journal of Personality and Social Psychology, 3,* 45–53.

Mitchell, V., & Helson, R. (1990). Women's prime of life. *Psychology of Women Quarterly, 14,* 451–470.

Mize, J., & Pettit, G. S. (1997). Mothers' social coaching, mother–child relationship style, and children's peer competence: Is the medium the message? *Child Development, 68,* 312–332.

Moen, P. (1996). Gender, age, and the life course. In R. H. Binstock & L. K. George (Eds.), *Handbook of aging and the social sciences* (pp. 171–187). San Diego: Academic Press.

Moffitt, T. E. (1990). Juvenile delinquency and attention deficit disorder: Boys' developmental trajectories from age 3 to age 15. *Child Development, 61,* 893–910.

Moffitt, T. E., Caspi, A., Dickson, N., Silva, P., & Stanton, W. (1996). Childhood-onset versus adolescent-onset antisocial conduct problems in males: Natural history from ages 3 to 18 years. *Development and Psychopathology, 8,* 399–424.

Moffitt, T. E., Lynam, D. R., & Silva, P. A. (1994). Neuropsychological tests predicting persistent male delinquency. *Criminology, 32,* 277–300.

Mohanty, A. K., & Perregaux, C. (1997). Language acquisition and bilingualism. In J. W. Berry, P. R. Dasen, & T. S. Saraswathi (Eds.), *Handbook of cross-cultural psychology: Vol. 2. Basic processes and human development* (2nd ed., pp. 217–254). Boston: Allyn and Bacon.

Moilanen, I. (1989). The growth, development, and education of Finnish twins: A longitudinal follow-up study in a birth cohort from pregnancy to nineteen years of age. *Growth, Development and Aging, 18,* 302–306.

Mokdad, A. H., Serdula, M. K., Dietz, W. H., Bowman, B. A., Marks, J. S., & Koplan, J. P. (1999). The spread of the obesity epidemic in the United States, 1991–1998. *Journal of the American Medical Association, 282,* 1519–1522.

Mondimore, F. M. (1996). *A natural history of homosexuality.* Baltimore: Johns Hopkins University Press.

Money, J. (1993). Specific neurocognitional impairments associated with Turner (45,X) and Klinefelter (47,XXY) syndromes: A review. *Social Biology, 40,* 147–151.

Monroe, S., Goldman, P., & Smith, V. E. (1988). *Brothers: Black and poor—A true story of courage and survival.* New York: Morrow.

Monsour, M., Harris, B., Kurzweil, N., & Beard, C. (1994). Challenges confronting cross-gender friendships: "Much ado about nothing?" *Sex Roles, 31,* 55–77.

Montemayor, R., & Eisen, M. (1977). The development of self-conceptions from childhood to adolescence. *Developmental Psychology, 13,* 314–319.

Montepare, J., & Lachman, M. (1989). "You're only as old as you feel": Self-perceptions of age, fears of aging, and life satisfaction from adolescence to old age. *Psychology and Aging, 4,* 73–78.

Montplaisir, J., & Godbout, R. (1989). Restless legs syndrome and periodic movements during sleep. In M. H. Kryger, T. Roth, & W. C. Dement (Eds.), *Principles and practice of sleep medicine* (pp. 402– 409). Philadelphia: Saunders.

Moon, A., Lubben, J. E., & Villa, V. (1998). Awareness and utilization of community long-term care services by elderly Korean and non-Hispanic white Americans. *Gerontologist, 38,* 309–316.

Moon, C., Cooper, R. P., & Fifer, W. P. (1993). Two-day-old infants prefer their native language. *Infant Behavior and Development, 16,* 495–500.

Moon, S. M., & Feldhusen, J. F. (1994). The Program for Academic and Creative Enrichment (PACE): A follow-up study ten years later. In R. F. Subotnik & K. D. Arnold (Eds.), *Beyond Terman: Contemporary longitudinal studies of giftedness and talent* (pp. 375–400). Norwood, NJ: Ablex.

Moore, E. G. J. (1986). Family socialization and the IQ test performance of traditionally and transracially adopted black children. *Developmental Psychology, 22,* 317–326.

Moore, G. A., Cohn, J. F., & Campbell, S. B. (1997). Mothers' affective behavior with infant siblings: Stability and change. *Developmental Psychology, 33,* 856–860.

Moore, K. A., Miller, B. C., Sugland, B. W., Morrison, D. R., Glei, D. A., & Blumenthal, C. (1998). *Beginning too soon: Adolescent sexual behavior, pregnancy and parenthood.* Washington, DC: U.S. Government Printing Office.

Moore, K. A., Morrison, D. R., & Green, A. D. (1997). Effects on the children born to adolescent mothers. In R. A. Maynard (Ed.), *Kids having kids* (pp. 145–180). Washington, DC: Urban Institute.

Moore, K. A., Myers, D. E., Morrison, D. R., Nord, C. W., Brown, B., & Edmonston, B. (1993). Age at first childbirth and later poverty. *Journal of Research on Adolescence, 3,* 393–422.

Moore, K. L., & Persaud, T. V. N. (1998). *Before we are born* (5th ed.). Philadelphia: Saunders.

Moore, M. K. (1992). An empirical investigation of the relationship between religiosity and death concern. *Dissertation Abstracts International, 53*(2–A), 527.

Moorehouse, M. J. (1991). Linking maternal employment patterns to mother–child activities and children's school competence. *Developmental Psychology, 27,* 295–303.

Moran, G. F., & Vinovskis, M. A. (1986). The great care of godly parents: Early childhood in Puritan New England. *Monographs of the Society for Research in Child Development, 50*(4–5, Serial No. 211).

Morell, C. M. (1994). *Unwomanly conduct: The challenges of intentional childlessness.* New York: Routledge.

Morelli, G., Rogoff, B., Oppenheim, D., & Goldsmith, D. (1992). Cultural variation in infants' sleeping arrangements: Questions of independence. *Developmental Psychology, 28,* 604–613.

Morgan, J. L., & Saffran, J. R. (1995). Emerging integration of sequential and suprasegmental information in preverbal speech segmentation. *Child Development, 66,* 911–936.

Morgan, L. A. (1991). *After marriage ends: Economic consequences for midlife women.* Newbury Park, CA: Sage.

Morgane, P. J., Austin-LaFrance, R., Bronzino, J., Tonkiss, J., Diaz-Cintra, S., Cintra, L., Kemper, T., & Galler, J. R. (1993). Prenatal malnutrition and development of the brain. *Neuroscience and Biobehavioral Reviews, 17,* 91–128.

Mori, L., & Peterson, L. (1995). Knowledge of safety of high and low active–impulsive boys: Implications for child injury prevention. *Journal of Clinical Child Psychology, 24,* 370–376.

Moriguchi, S., Oonishi, K., Kato, M., & Kishino, Y. (1995). Obesity is a risk factor for deteriorating cellular immune functions decreased with aging. *Nutrition Research, 15,* 151–160.

Morrison, A. M. (1992). Women and minorities in management. *American Psychologist, 45,* 200–208.

Morrongiello, B. A. (1986). Infants' perception of multiple-group auditory patterns. *Infant Behavior and Development, 9,* 307–319.

Morrow, D., Leirer, V., Altieri, P., & Fitzsimmons, C. (1994). When expertise reduces age differences in performance. *Psychology and Aging, 9,* 134–148.

Morse, C. K. (1993). Does variability increase with age? An archival study of cognitive measures. *Psychology and Aging, 8,* 156–164.

Mortimer, J. T., & Borman, K. M. (Eds.). (1988). *Work experience and psychological development through the lifespan.* Boulder, CO: Westview.

Morton, J. (1993). Mechanisms in infant face processing. In B. de Boysson-Bardies, S. de Schonen, P. Jusczyk, P. McNeilage, & J. Morton (Eds.), *Developmental neurocognition: Speech and face processing in the first year of life* (pp. 93–102). London: Kluwer.

Morycz, R. K. (1992). Widowhood and bereavement in late life. In V. B. Van Hasselt & M. Hersen (Eds.), *Handbook of social development* (pp. 545–582). New York: Plenum.

Moshman, D. (1998). Identity as a theory of oneself. *Genetic Epistemologist, 26*(3), 1–9.

Moshman, D. (1999). *Adolescent psychological development: Rationality, morality, and identity.* Mahwah, NJ: Erlbaum.

Moshman, D., & Franks, B. A. (1986). Development of the concept of inferential validity. *Child Development, 57,* 153–165.

Mosteller, F. (1995, Fall). The Tennessee Study of Class Size in the Early School Grades. *Future of Children, 5*(2), 113–127.

Mott, S. R., James, S. R., & Sperhac, A. M. (1990). *Nursing care of children and families.* Redwood City, CA: Addison-Wesley.

Mounts, N. S., & Steinberg, L. (1995). An ecological analysis of peer influence on adolescent grade point average and drug use. *Developmental Psychology, 31,* 915–922.

Moyer, M. S. (1992). Sibling relationships among older adults. *Generations, 16*(3), 55–58.

Mullen, M. K. (1994). Earliest recollections of childhood: A demographic analysis. *Cognition, 52,* 55–79.

Mullis, I. V. S., Dossey, J. A., Campbell, J. R., Gentile, C. A., O'Sullivan, C., & Latham, A. S. (1994). *NAEP 1992 trends in academic progress.* Washington, DC: U.S. Government Printing Office.

Mulnard, R. A., Cotman, C. W., Kawas, C., van Dyck, C. H., Sano, M., Doody, R., Koss, E., Pfeiffer, E., Jin, S., Gamst, A., Grundman, M., Thomas, R., & Thal, L. J. (2000). Estrogen replacement therapy for treatment of mild to moderate Alzheimer's disease: A randomized control trial. *Journal of the American Medical Association, 283,* 1007–1015.

Mulsant, B. H., & Ganguli, M. (1999). Epidemiology and diagnosis of depression in late life. *Journal of Clinical Psychiatry, 60*(Suppl. 20), 9–15.

Mumme, D. L., Fernald, A., & Herrera, C. (1996). Infants' responses to facial and vocal emotional signals in a social referencing paradigm. *Child Development, 67,* 3219–3237.

Munro, G., & Adams, G. R. (1977). Ego identity formation in college students and working youth. *Developmental Psychology, 13,* 523–524.

Muret-Wagstaff, S., & Moore, S. G. (1989). The Hmong in America: Infant behavior and rearing practices. In J. K. Nugent, B. M. Lester, & T. B. Brazelton (Eds.), *Biology, culture, and development* (Vol. 1, pp. 319–339). Norwood, NJ: Ablex.

Murphy, C. M., & O'Farrell, T. J. (1996). Marital violence among alcoholics. *Current Directions in Psychological Science, 5,* 183–186.

Murphy, S. A., Gupta, A. D., Cain, K. C., Johnson, L. C., Lohan, J., Wu, L., & Mekwa, J. (1999). Changes in parents' mental distress after the violent death of an adolescent or young adult child: A longitudinal prospective analysis. *Death Studies, 23,* 129–159.

Murray, A. D. (1985). Aversiveness is in the mind of the beholder. In B. M. Lester & C. F. Z. Boukydis (Eds.), *Infant crying* (pp. 217–239). New York: Plenum.

Murray, A. D., Johnson, J., & Peters, J. (1990). Fine-tuning of utterance length to preverbal infants: Effects on later language development. *Journal of Child Language, 17,* 511–525.

Murray, L., & Cooper, P. J. (1997). Postpartum depression and child development. *Psychological Medicine, 27,* 253–260.

Murray, M. J., & Meacham, R. B. (1993). The effect of age on male reproductive function. *World Journal of Urology, 11,* 137–140.

Mussen, P., & Eisenberg-Berg, N. (1977). *Roots of caring, sharing, and helping.* San Francisco: Freeman.

Must, A., Spadano, J., Coakley, E. H., Field, A. E., Colditz, G., & Dietz, W. H. (1999). The disease burden associated with overweight and obesity. *Journal of the American Medical Association, 282,* 1523–1529.

Mutchler, J. E., Burr, J. A., Pienta, A. M., & Massagli, M. P. (1997). Pathways to labor force exit: Work transitions and instability. *Journal of Gerontology, 52B,* S4–S12.

Mutran, E. J., Danis, M., Bratton, K. A., Sudha, S., & Hanson, L. (1997). Attitudes of the critically ill toward prolonging life: The role of social support. *Gerontologist, 37,* 192–199.

Myers, D. G. (2000). The funds, friends, and faith of happy people. *American Psychologist, 55,* 56–67.

Myers, G. C. (1996). Comparative mortality trends among older persons in developed countries. In G. Caselli & A. D. Lopez (Eds.), *Health and mortality among elderly populations* (pp. 87–111). Oxford, England: Clarendon Press.

Myers, S. M., & Booth, A. (1996). Men's retirement and marital quality. *Journal of Family Issues, 17,* 336–357.

Myerson, J., Hale, S., Wagstaff, D., Poon, L. W., & Smith, G. A. (1990). The information-loss model: A mathematical theory of age-related cognitive slowing. *Psychological Review, 97,* 475–487.

Nachtigall, R. D. (1993). Secrecy: An unresolved issue in the practice of donor insemination. *American Journal of Obstetrics and Gynecology, 168,* 1846–1851.

Nachtigall, R. D., Pitcher, L., Tschann, J. M., Becker, G., & Quiroga, S. S. (1997). Stigma, disclosure, and family functioning among parents of children conceived through donor insemination. *Fertility and Sterility, 68,* 83–89.

Nader, K., Dubrow, N., & Stamm, B. H. (1999). *Honoring differences: Cultural issues in the treatment of trauma and loss.* Washington, DC: Taylor & Francis.

Nader, K. O. (1997). Treating traumatic grief in systems. In C. R. Figley, B. E. Bride, & N. Mazza (Eds.), *Death and trauma: The traumatology of grieving* (pp. 159–192). Washington, DC: Taylor & Francis.

Nader, K. O., Pynoos, R., Rairbanks, L., & Frederick, C. (1990). Childen's PTSD reactions one year after a sniper attack at their school. *American Journal of Psychiatry, 147,* 1526–1530.

Naigles, L. G., & Gelman, S. A. (1995). Overextensions in comprehension and production revisited: Preferential-looking in a study of dog, cat, and cow. *Journal of Child Language, 22,* 19–46.

Nakamura, S., Wind, M., & Danello, M.A. (1999). Review of hazards associated with children in adult beds. *Archives of Pediatric and Adolescent Medicine, 153,* 1019–1023.

Namy, L. L., & Waxman, S. R. (1998). Words and gestures: Infants' interpretations of different forms of symbolic reference. *Child Development, 69,* 295–308.

Nánez, J., Sr., & Yonas, A. (1994). Effects of luminance and texture motion on infant defensive reactions to optical collision. *Infant Behavior and Development, 17,* 165–174.

National Association for the Education of Young Children. (1998). *Accreditation criteria and procedures of the National Academy of Early Childhood Programs* (2nd ed.). Washington, DC: Author.

National Cancer Institute. (1998). *SEER cancer statistics review: 1973–1994.* Washington, DC: U.S. Government Printing Office.

National Federation of State High School Associations. (1999). *High school athletic participation survey.* Kansas City, MO: Author.

National Hospice Organization. (1999a). *Fact sheet.* Arlington, VA: Author.

National Hospice Organization. (1999b). *1992 provider census data.* Arlington, VA: Author.

National Institute for Child Health and Development (NICHD), Early Child Care Research Network. (1996). Characteristics of infant care: Factors contributing to positive caregiving. *Early Childhood Research Quarterly, 11,* 269–306.

National Institute for Child Health and Development (NICHD), Early Child Care Research Network. (1997). The effects of infant child care on infant–mother attachment security: Results of the NICHD Study of Early Child Care. *Child Development, 68,* 860–879.

National Institute for Child Health and Development (NICHD), Early Child Care Research Network. (1998). Early child care and self-control, compliance, and problem behavior at twenty-four and thirty-six months. *Child Development, 69,* 1145–1170.

National Institute on Aging, National Institutes of Health. (1999). *Progress report on Alzheimer's disease.* Washington, DC: U.S. Government Printing Office.

Neale, A. V., Hwalek, M. A., Goodrich, C. S., & Quinn, K. M. (1996). The Illinois Elder Abuse System: Program description and administrative findings. *Gerontologist, 36,* 502–511.

Neill, C. M., & Kahn, A. S. (1999). The role of personal spirituality and religious social activity on the life satisfaction of older widowed women. *Sex Roles, 40,* 319–329.

Neimeyer, R. A. (Ed.). (1994). *Death anxiety handbook.* Washington, DC: Taylor & Francis.

Neimeyer, R. A., & Van Brunt, D. (1995). Death anxiety. In H. Waas & R. A. Neimeyer (Eds.), *Dying: Facing the facts* (3rd ed., pp. 49–88). Washington, DC: Taylor & Francis.

Nelson, C. A. (1995). The ontogeny of human memory: A cognitive neuroscience perspective. *Developmental Psychology, 31,* 723–738.

Nelson, K. (1973). Structure and strategy in learning to talk. *Monographs of the Society for Research in Child Development, 38*(1–2, Serial No. 149).

Nelson, K. (1993). The psychological and social origins of autobiographical memory. *Psychological Science, 1,* 1–8.

Netley, C. T. (1986). Summary overview of behavioral development in individuals with neonatally identified X and Y aneuploidy. *Birth Defects, 22,* 293–306.

Neugarten, B., & Neugarten, D. (1987, May). The changing meanings of age. *Psychology Today, 21*(5), 29–33.

Neugarten, B. L. (1968a). Adult personality: Toward a psychology of the life cycle. In B. Neugarten (Ed.), *Middle age and aging* (pp. 137–147). Chicago: University of Chicago Press.

Neugarten, B. L. (1968b). The awareness of middle aging. In B. L. Neugarten (Ed.), *Middle age and aging* (pp. 93–98). Chicago: University of Chicago Press.

Neugarten, B. L. (1979). Time, age, and the life cycle. *American Journal of Psychiatry, 136,* 887–894.

Neugarten, B. L., & Datan, N. (1973). Sociological perspectives on the life course. In P. B. Baltes & K. W. Schaie (Eds.), *Lifespan developmental psychology: Personality and socialization* (pp. 53–69). San Diego, CA: Academic Press.

Neuman, S. B., Copple, C., & Bredekamp, S. (2000). *Learning to read and write: Developmentally appropriate practices for young children.* Washington, DC: National Association for the Education of Young Children.

Neumärker, K. (1997). Mortality and sudden death in anorexia nervosa. *International Journal of Eating Disorders, 21,* 205–212.

Newborg, J., Stock, J. R., & Wnek, L. (1984). *Batelle Developmental Inventory.* Allen, TX: LINC Associates.

Newcomb, A. F., Bukowski, W. M., & Pattee, L. (1993). Children's peer relations: A meta-analytic review of popular, rejected, neglected, controversial, and average sociometric status. *Psychological Bulletin, 113,* 99–128.

Newcombe, N., & Fox, N. A. (1994). Infantile amnesia: Through a glass darkly. *Child Development, 65,* 31–40.

Newcombe, N., & Huttenlocher, J. (1992). Children's early ability to solve perspective-taking problems. *Developmental Psychology, 28,* 635–643.

Newcombe, P. A., & Boyle, G. J. (1995). High school students' sports personalities: Variations across participation level, gender, type of sport, and success. *International Journal of Sports Psychology, 26,* 277–294.

Newman, B. S., & Muzzonigro, P. G. (1993). The effects of traditional family values on the coming out process of gay male adolescents. *Adolescence, 28,* 213–226.

Newnham, J. P., Evans, S. F., Michael, C. A., Stanley, F. J., & Landau, L. I. (1993). Effects of frequent ultrasound during pregnancy: A randomized control trial. *Lancet, 342,* 887–890.

Newport, E. L. (1991). Contrasting conceptions of the critical period for language. In S. Cary & R. Gelman (Eds.), *The epigenesis of mind: Essays on biology and cognition* (pp. 111–130). Hillsdale, NJ: Erlbaum.

Newsom, J. T. (1999). Another side to caregiving: Negative reactions to being helped. *Current Directions in Psychological Science, 8,* 183–187.

Newsom, J. T., & Schulz, R. (1996). Social support as a mediator in the relation between functional status and quality of life in older adults. *Psychology and Aging, 11,* 34–44.

Newsom, J. T., & Schulz, R. (1998). Caregiving from the recipient's perspective: Negative reactions to being helped. *Health Psychology, 17,* 172–181.

Nichols, L. S., & Junk, V. W. (1997). The sandwich generation: Dependency, proximity, and task assistance needs of parents. *Journal of Family and Economic Issues, 18,* 299–326.

Nicolopoulou, A. (1993). Play, cognitive development, and the social world: Piaget, Vygotsky, and beyond. *Human Development, 36,* 1–23.

Nidorf, J. F. (1985). Mental health and refugee youths: A model for diagnostic training. In T. C. Owen (Ed.), *Southeast Asian mental health: Treatment, prevention, services, training, and research* (pp. 391–427). Washington, DC: National Institute of Mental Health.

Nieman, D. (1994). Exercise: Immunity from respiratory infections. *Swimming Technique, 31*(2), 38–43.

Niikawa, N. (1997). Genomic imprinting relevant to genetic diseases. *Southeast Asian Journal of Tropical Medicine and Public Health, 28*(Suppl. 3), 46–57.

Nilsson, L., & Hamberger, L. (1990). *A child is born.* New York: Delacorte.

Nix, R. L., Pinderhughes, E. E., Dodge, K. A., Bates, J. E., Pettit, G. S., & McFadyen-Ketchum, S. A. (1999). The relation between mothers' hostile attribution tendencies and children's externalizing behavior problems: The mediating role of mothers' harsh discipline practices. *Child Development, 70,* 896–909.

Noe, R., & Wilk, S. (1993). Investigation of factors that influence employees' participation in development activities. *Journal of Applied Psychology, 78,* 291–302.

Nolen-Hoeksema, S., & Girgus, J. S. (1994). The emergence of gender differences in depression in adolescence. *Psychological Bulletin, 115,* 424–443.

Noppe, I. C., & Noppe, L. D. (1997). Evolving meanings of death during early, middle, and later adolescence. *Death Studies, 21,* 253–275.

Noppe, L. D., & Noppe, I. C. (1991). Dialectical themes in adolescent conceptions of death. *Journal of Adolescent Research, 6,* 28–42.

Noppe, L. D., & Noppe, I. C. (1996). Ambiguity in adolescent understanding of death. In C. A. Corr & D. E. Balk (Eds.), *Handbook of adolescent death and bereavement* (pp. 25–41). New York: Springer.

Nottelmann, E. D. (1987). Competence and self-esteem during transition from childhood to adolescence. *Developmental Psychology, 23,* 441–450.

Nourse, C. B., & Butler, K. M. (1998). Perinatal transmission of HIV and diagnosis of HIV infection in infants: A review. *Irish Journal of Medical Science, 167,* 28–32.

Novak, G. P., Solanto, M., & Abikoff, H. (1995). Spatial orienting and focused attention in attention deficit hyperactivity disorder. *Journal of Psychophysiology, 32,* 546-559.

Novy, M. J., McGregor, J. A., & Iams, J. D. (1995). New perspectives on the prevention of extreme prematurity. *Clinical Obstetrics and Gynecology, 38,* 790–808.

Nucci, L. P. (1996). Morality and the personal sphere of action. In E. Reed, E. Turiel, & T. Brown (Eds.), *Values and knowledge* (pp. 41–60). Hillsdale, NJ: Erlbaum.

Nucci, L. P., Camino, C., & Sapiro, C. M. (1996). Social class effects on Northeastern Brazilian children's conceptions of areas of personal choice and social regulation. *Child Development, 67,* 1223–1242.

Nucci, L. P., & Weber, E. (1995). Social interactions in the home and the development of young children's conceptions of the personal. *Child Development, 66,* 1438–1452.

Nuckolls, K. B., Cassel, J., & Kaplan, B. H. (1972). Psychosocial assets, life crisis, and the prognosis of pregnancy. *American Journal of Epidemiology, 95,* 431–441.

Nuland, S. B. (1993). *How we die.* New York: Random House.

Nuland, S. B. (1996). The doctor's role in death. In H. M. Spiro, M. G. M. Curnen, & L. P. Wandel (Eds.), *Facing death: Where culture, religion, and medicine meet* (pp. 38–43). New Haven, CT: Yale University Press.

Nussbaum, J. F. (1994). Friendship in older adulthood. In M. L. Hummer, J. M. Wiemann, & J. F. Nussbaum (Eds.), *Interpersonal communication in older adulthood* (pp. 209–225). Thousand Oaks, CA: Sage.

Nussbaum, P. D., Kaszniak, A. W., Allender, J., & Rapcsak, S. (1995). Depression and cognitive decline in the elderly: A follow-up study. *Clinical Neurologist, 9,* 101–111.

Nye, W. P. (1993). Amazing grace: Religion and identity among elderly black individuals. *International Journal of Aging and Human Development, 36,* 103–114.

Oakes, J., Gamoran, A., & Page, R. N. (1992). Curriculum differentiation: Opportunities, outcomes, and meanings. In P. W. Jackson (Ed.), *Handbook of research on curriculum* (pp. 570–608). New York: Macmillan.

Oakes, L. M., Coppage, D. J., & Dingel, A. (1997). By land or by sea: The role of perceptual similarity in infants' categorization of animals. *Developmental Psychology, 33,* 396–407.

Oates, R. K., Peacock, A., & Forrest, D. (1985). Long-term effects of nonorganic failure to thrive. *Pediatrics, 75,* 36–40.

Oberg, C. N., Bryant, N., & Bach, M. L. (1995). A portrait of America's children: The impact of poverty and a call to action. *Journal of Social Distress and the Homeless, 4,* 43–57.

O'Bryant, S. L. (1988a). Sex-differentiated assistance in older widows' support networks. *Sex Roles, 19,* 91–106.

O'Bryant, S. L. (1988b). Sibling support and older widows' well-being. *Journal of Marriage and the Family, 50,* 173–183.

O'Bryant, S. L., & Hansson, R. O. (1995). Widowhood. In R. Blieszner & V. H. Bedford (Eds.), *Handbook of aging and the family* (pp. 440–458). Westport, CT: Greenwood Press.

O'Callaghan, M. J., Burn, Y. R., Mohay, H. A., Rogers, Y., & Tudehope, D. I. (1993). The prevalence and origins of left hand preference in high risk infants, and its implications for intellectual, motor, and behavioral performance at four and six years. *Cortex, 29,* 617–627.

Ochse, R., & Plug, C. (1986). Cross-cultural investigation of the validity of Erikson's theory of personality development. *Journal of Personality and Social Psychology, 50,* 1240–1252.

O'Connor, B. P. (1995). Identity development and perceived parental behavior as sources of adolescent egocentrism. *Journal of Youth and Adolescence, 24,* 205–227.

O'Connor, C. (1997). Dispositions toward (collective) struggle and educational resilience in the inner city: A case analysis of six African-American high school students. *American Educational Research Journal, 34,* 593–629.

O'Connor, P. (1992). *Friendships between women.* New York: Guilford.

Oden, M. H., & Terman, L. M. (1968). The fulfillment of promise—40-year follow-up of the Terman gifted group. *Genetic Psychology Monographs, 77,* 3–93.

Office of Educational Research and Improvement. (1999). *Youth indicators 1999: Trends in the well-being of American youth.* Washington, DC: U.S. Government Printing Office.

Ogbu, J. U. (1997). Understanding the school performance of urban blacks: Some essential background knowledge. In H. J. Walberg, O. Reyes, & R. P. Weissberg (Ed.), *Children and youth: Interdisciplinary perspectives* (pp. 190–222). Thousand Oaks, CA: Sage.

O'Grady-LeShane, R., & Williamson, J. B. (1992). Family provisions in old-age pensions. In M. E. Szinovacz, D. J. Ekerdt, & B. H. Vinick (Eds.), *Families and retirement* (pp. 64–77). Newbury Park, CA: Sage.

O'Halloran, C. M., & Altmaier, E. M. (1996). Awareness of death among children: Does a life-threatening illness alter the process of discovery? *Journal of Counseling and Development, 74,* 259–262.

Okagaki, L., Diamond, K. E., Kontos, S. J., & Hestenes, L. L. (1998). Correlates of young children's interactions with classmates with disabilities. *Early Childhood Research Quarterly, 13,* 67–86.

Okagaki, L., & Frensch, P. A. (1996). Effects of video game playing on measures of spatial performance: Gender effects in late adolescence. In P. M. Greenfield & R. R. Cocking (Eds.), *Interacting with video* (pp. 115–140). Norwood, NJ: Ablex.

Okagaki, L., & Sternberg, R. J. (1993). Parental beliefs and children's school performance. *Child Development, 64,* 36–56.

Oleski, D., & Subich, L. M. (1996). Congruence and career change in employed adults. *Journal of Vocational Behavior, 49,* 221–229.

Oliker, S. J. (1989). *Best friends and marriage: Exchange among women.* Berkeley: University of California Press.

Oliver, M. B., & Hyde, J. S. (1993). Gender differences in sexuality: A meta-analysis. *Psychological Bulletin, 114,* 29–51.

Olsen, O. (1997). Meta-analysis of the safety of home birth. *Birth: Issues in Perinatal Care, 24,* 4–13.

Olweus, D. (1993). *Bullying at school.* Oxford: Blackwell.

Olweus, D. (1995). Bullying or peer abuse at school: Facts and intervention. *Current Directions in Psychological Science, 4,* 196–200.

Omer, H., & Everly, G. S. (1988). Psychological factors in preterm labor: Critical review and theoretical synthesis. *American Journal of Psychiatry, 145,* 1507–1513.

O'Neill, R., Welsh, M., Parke, R. D., Wang, S., & Strand, C. (1997). A longitudinal assessment of the academic correlates of early peer acceptance and rejection. *Journal of Clinical Child Psychology, 26,* 290–303.

O'Neill, R. M., Horton, S., & Crosby, F. J. (1999). *Mentoring dilemmas* (pp. 63–80). Mahwah, NJ: Erlbaum.

Oosterwegel, A., & Openheimer, L. (1993). *The self-system: Developmental changes between and within self-concepts.* Hillsdale, NJ: Erlbaum.

Orbuch, T. L., House, J. S., Mero, R. P., & Webster, P. S. (1996). Marital quality over the life course. *Social Psychology Quarterly, 59,* 162–171.

O'Reilly, A. W. (1995). Using representations: Comprehension and production of actions with imagined objects. *Child Development, 66,* 999–1010.

O'Reilly, A. W., & Bornstein, M. H. (1993). Caregiver–child interaction in play. In M. H. Bornstein & A. W. O'Reilly (Eds.), *New directions for child development* (No. 59, pp. 55–66). San Francisco: Jossey-Bass.

Ornstein, P. A., Shapiro, L. R., Clubb, P. A., & Follmer, A. (1997). The influence of prior knowledge on children's memory for salient medical experiences. In N. Stein, P. A. Ornstein, C. J. Brainerd, & B. Tversky (Eds.), *Memory for everyday and emotional events* (pp. 83–112). Hillsdale, NJ: Erlbaum.

Ornstein, S., & Isabella, L. (1990). Age vs. stage models of career attitudes of women: A partial replication and extension. *Journal of Vocational Behavior, 36,* 1–19.

Ory, M. G., Hoffman, R. R., Yee, J. L., Tennstedt, S., & Schulz, R. (1999). Prevalence and impact of caregiving: A detailed comparison between dementia and nondementia caregivers. *Gerontologist, 39,* 177–185.

Osgood, N. J. (1992). *Suicide in later life: Recognizing the warning signs.* New York: Lexington Books.

Osgood, N. J., Brant, B. A., & Lipman, A. (1991). *Suicide among the elderly in long-term care facilities.* New York: Greenwood Press.

Osherson, D. N., & Markman, E. M. (1975). Language and the ability to evaluate contradictions and tautologies. *Cognition, 2,* 213–226.

Ostir, G. V., Carlson, J. E., Black, S. A., Rudkin, L., Goodwin, J. S., & Markides, K. S. (1999). Disability in older adults 1: Prevalence, causes, and consequences. *Behavioral Medicine, 24,* 147–156.

Ostling, I., & Kelloway, E. K. (1992, June). *Predictors of life satisfaction in retirement: A mediational model.* Paper presented at the annual conference of the Canadian Psychological Association, Quebec City.

Ostrea, E. M., Jr., Ostrea, A. R., & Simpson, P. M. (1997). Mortality within the first 2 years in infants exposed to cocaine, opiate, or cannabinoid during gestation. *Pediatrics, 100,* 79–83.

Owen, M. T., & Cox, M. J. (1997). Marital conflict and the development of infant–parent attachment relationships. *Journal of Family Psychology, 11,* 152–164.

Owen, M. T., Easterbrooks, M. A., Chase-Lansdale, L., & Goldberg, W. A. (1984). The relation between maternal employment status and the stability of attachments to mother and father. *Child Development, 55,* 1894–1901.

Owens, T. (1982). Experience-based career education: Summary and implications of research and evaluation findings. *Child and Youth Services Journal, 4,* 77–91.

Owsley, C., Ball, K., McGwin, G., Jr., Sloane, M. E., Roenker, D. L., White, M. F., & Overley, E. T. (1998). Visual processing impairment and risk of motor vehicle crash among older adults. *Journal of the American Medical Association, 279,* 1083–1088.

Owsley, C., & McGwin, G., Jr. (1999). Vision impairment and driving. *Survey of Ophthalmology, 43,* 535–550.

Padgett, D. K., Patrick, C., Bruns, B. J., & Schlesinger, H. J. (1994). Women and outpatient mental health services: Use by black, Hispanic, and white women in a national insured population. *Journal of Mental Health Administration, 2,* 347–360.

Padgham, J. J., & Blyth, D. A. (1990). Dating during adolescence. In R. M. Lerner, A. C. Petersen, & J. Brooks-Gunn (Eds.), *The encyclopedia of adolescence* (Vol. 1, pp. 196–198). New York: Garland.

Padilla, M. L., & Landreth, G. L. (1989). Latchkey children: A review of the literature. *Child Welfare, 68,* 445–454.

Padula, M. A., & Miller, D. L. (1999). Understanding graduate women's reentry experiences. *Psychology of Women Quarterly, 23,* 327–343.

Paffenbarger, R. S., Jr., Hyde, R. T., Wing, A. L., Lee, I.-M., Jung, D. L., & Kampert, J. B. (1993). The association of changes in physical-activity level and other lifestyle characteristics with mortality among men. *New England Journal of Medicine, 329,* 538–545.

Paikoff, R. L., & Brooks-Gunn, J. (1991). Do parent–child relationships change during puberty? *Psychological Bulletin, 110,* 47–66.

Palmer, G. (1997). *Reluctant refugee.* Sydney: Kangaroo Press.

Palmlund, I. (1996). Exposure to a xenoestrogen before birth: The diethylstilbestrol experience. *Journal of Psychosomatic Obstetrics and Gynaecology, 17,* 71–84.

Pan, H. W. (1994). Children's play in Taiwan. In J. L. Roopnarine, J. E. Johnson, & F. H. Hooper (Eds.), *Children's play in diverse cultures* (pp. 31–50). Albany, NY: SUNY Press.

Papernow, P. (1993). *Becoming a stepfamily: Patterns of development in remarried families.* New York: Gardner.

Papini, D. R. (1994). Family interventions. In S. L. Archer (Ed.), *Interventions for adolescent identity development* (pp. 47–61). Thousand Oaks, CA: Sage.

Pardhan, S., Gilchrist, J., Elliott, D. B., & Beh, G. K. (1996). A comparison of sampling efficiency and internal noise level in young and old subjects. *Vision Research, 36,* 1641–1648.

Park, D. C., Hertzog, C., Kidder, D. P., Morrell, R. W., & Mayhorn, C. B. (1997). Effect of age on event-based and time-based prospective memory. *Psychology and Aging, 12,* 314–327.

Parke, R. D., & Buriel, R. (1998). Socialization in the family: Ethnic and ecological perspectives. In N. Eisenberg (Ed.), *Handbook of child psychology: Vol. 3. Social, emotional, and personality development* (pp. 463–552). New York: Wiley.

Parker, J. G., Rubin, K. H., Price, J., & DeRosier, M. E. (1995). Peer relationships, child development, and adjustment: A developmental psychopathology perspective. In D. Cicchetti & D. Cohen (Eds.), *Developmental psychopathology: Vol. 2. Risk, disorder, and adaptation* (pp. 96–161). New York: Wiley.

Parker, R. G. (1995). Reminiscence: A continuity theory framework. *Gerontologist, 35,* 515–525.

Parkes, C. M., & Weiss, R. S. (1983). *Recovery from bereavement.* New York: Basic Books.

Parks, W. (1996). Human immunodeficiency virus. In R. D. Behrman, R. M. Kliegman, & A. M. Arvin (Eds.), *Nelson textbook of pediatrics* (15th ed., pp. 916–919). Philadelphia: Saunders.

Parmelee, P. A., & Lawton, M. P. (1990). The design of special environments for the aged. In J. E. Birren & K. W. Schaie (Eds.), *Handbook of the psychology of aging* (3rd ed., pp. 464–488). San Diego, CA: Academic Press.

Parsons, J. E., Adler, T. F., & Kaczala, C. M. (1982). Socialization of achievement attitudes and beliefs: Parental influences. *Child Development, 53,* 310–321.

Parten, M. (1932). Social participation among preschool children. *Journal of Abnormal and Social Psychology, 27,* 243–269.

Pascarella, E., Bohr, L., Nora, A., Zusman, B., Inman, P., & Desler, M. (1993). Cognitive impacts of living on campus versus commuting to college. *Journal of College Student Development, 34,* 216–220.

Pascarella, E. T., & Terenzini, P. T. (1991). *How college affects students.* San Francisco: Jossey-Bass.

Pascarella, E. T., Whitt, E. J., Edison, M. I., Nora, A., Hagecdorn, L. S., Yeager, P. M., & Terenzini, P. T. (1997). Women's perceptions of a "chilly climate" and their cognitive outcomes during the first year of college. *Journal of College Student Development, 38,* 109–124.

Passman, R. H. (1987). Attachment to inanimate objects: Are children who have security blankets insecure? *Journal of Consulting and Clinical Psychology, 55,* 825–830.

Patterson, C. J. (1995). Sexual orientation and human development: An overview. *Developmental Psychology, 31,* 3–11.

Patterson, C. J. (1996). Lesbian and gay parenthood. In M. H. Bornstein (Ed.), *Handbook of parenting* (Vol. 3, pp. 255–274). Mahwah, NJ: Erlbaum.

Patterson, G. R. (1982). *Coercive family processes.* Eugene, OR: Castilia Press.

Patterson, G. R. (1995). Coercion—A basis for early age of onset for arrest. In J. McCord (Ed.), *Coercion and punishment in long-term perspective* (pp. 81–105). New York: Cambridge University Press.

Patterson, G. R. (1997). Performance models for parenting: A social interactional perspective. In J. E. Grusec & L. Kuczynski (Eds.), *Parenting and children's internalization of values* (pp. 193–226). New York: Wiley.

Patterson, G. R., DeBaryshe, B. D., & Ramsey, E. (1989). A developmental perspective on antisocial behavior. *American Psychologist, 44,* 329–335.

Patterson, G. R., Reid, J. B., & Dishion, T. J. (1992). *Antisocial boys.* Eugene, OR: Castalia.

Patterson, M. M., & Lynch, A. Q. (1988). Menopause: Salient issues for counselors. *Journal of Counseling and Development, 67,* 185–188.

Pattison, E. M. (1978). The living–dying process. In C. A. Garfield (Ed.), *Psychological care of the dying patient* (pp. 133–168). New York: McGraw-Hill.

Pawelec, G., Effros, R. B., Caruso, C., Remarque, E., Barnett, Y., & Solana, R. (1999a). T cells and aging. *Frontiers of Bioscience, 4,* D216–D269.

Pawelec, G., Wagner, W., Adibzadeh, M., & Engel, A. (1999b). T cell immunosenescence in vitro and in vivo. *Experimental Gerontology, 34,* 419–429.

Peake, T. H., Oelschlager, J. R., & Kearns, D. F. (2000). Elder abuse: Families, systems, causes, and interventions. In F. W. Kaslow (Ed.), *Handbook of couple and family forensics* (pp. 400–425). New York: Wiley.

Pearson, J. D., Morell, C. H., Gordon-Salant, S., Brant, L. J., Metter, E. J., Klein, L. L., & Fozard, J. L. (1995). Gender differences in a longitudinal study of age-associated hearing loss. *Journal of the Acoustical Society of America, 97,* 1196–1205.

Pearson, J. L., Hunter, A. G. Ensminger, M. E., & Kellam, S. G. (1990). Black grand-mothers in multigenerational house-holds: Diversity in family structure and parenting involvement in the Woodlawn community. *Child Development, 61,* 434–442.

Peck, R. C. (1968). Psychological developments in the second half of life. In B. L. Neugarten (Ed.), *Middle age and aging* (pp. 88–92). Chicago: University of Chicago Press.

Peckham, C. S., & Logan, S. (1993). Screening for toxoplasmosis during pregnancy. *Archives of Disease in Childhood, 68,* 3–5.

Pedersen, J. B. (1998). Sexuality and aging. In I. H. Nordhus, G. R. VandenBos, S. Berg, & P. Fromholt (Eds.), *Clinical geropsychology* (pp. 141–145). Washington, DC: American Psychological Association.

Pederson, D. R., Gleason, K. E., Moran, G., & Bento, S. (1998). Maternal attachment representations, maternal sensitivity, and the infant–mother attachment relationship. *Developmental Psychology, 34,* 925–933.

Pederson, D. R., & Moran, G. (1995). A categorical description of infant–mother relationships in the home and its relation to Q-sort measures of infant–mother interaction. In E. Waters, B. E.Vaughn, G. Posada, & K. Kondo-Ikemura (Eds.). (1995). Caregiving, cultural, and cognitive perspectives on secure-base behavior and working models: New growing points of attachment theory and research. *Monographs of the Society for Research in Child Development, 60*(2–3, Serial No. 244).

Pederson, D. R., & Moran, G. (1996). Expressions of the attachment relationship outside of the Strange Situation. *Child Development, 67,* 915–927.

Pedlow, R., Sanson, A., Prior, M., & Oberklaid, F. (1993). Stability of maternally reported temperament from infancy to 8 years. *Developmental Psychology, 29,* 998–1007.

Pelham, W. E., Jr., & Hoza, B. (1996). Intensive treatment: A summer treatment program for children with ADHD. In E. D. Hibbs & P. S. Jensen (Eds.), *Psychosocial treatments for child and adolescent disorders: Empirically based strategies for clinical practice* (pp. 311–340). Washington, DC: American Psychological Association.

Pellegrini, A. D., & Smith, P. K. (1998). Physical activity play: The nature and function of a neglected aspect of play. *Child Development, 69,* 557–598.

Peplau, L. A. (1991). Lesbian and gay relationships. In J. C. Gonsiorek & J. D. Weinrich (Eds.), *Homosexuality* (pp. 177–196). Newbury Park, CA: Sage.

Perfetti, C. A. (1988). Verbal efficiency in reading ability. In M. Daneman, G. E. MacKinnon, & T. G. Waller (Eds.), *Reading research: Advances in theory and practice* (Vol. 6, pp. 109–143). San Diego, CA: Academic Press.

Perkins, H. W. (1991). Religious commitment, yuppie values, and well-being in post-collegiate life. *Review of Religious Research, 32,* 244–251.

Perkins, K. (1993). Working-class women and retirement. *Journal of Gerontological Social Work, 20,* 129–146.

Perleth, C., & Heller, K. A. (1994). The Munich Longitudinal Study of Giftedness. In R. F. Subotnik & K. D. Arnold (Eds.), *Beyond Terman: Contemporary studies of giftedness and talent* (pp. 77–114). Norwood, NJ: Ablex.

Perlmutter, M. (1984). Continuities and discontinuities in early human memory: Paradigms, processes, and performances. In R. V. Kail, Jr., & N. R. Spear (Eds.), *Comparative perspectives on the development of memory* (pp. 253–287). Hillsdale, NJ: Erlbaum.

Perlmutter, M., Kaplan, M., & Nyquist, L. (1990). Development of adaptive competence in adulthood. *Human Development, 33,* 185–197.

Perls, T. T. (1995, January). The oldest old. *Scientific American, 272*(1), 70–75.

Perry, D. G., Perry, L. C., & Weiss, R. J. (1989). Sex differences in the consequences that children anticipate for aggression. *Developmental Psychology, 25,* 312–319.

Perry, D. G., Williard, J. C., & Perry, L. C. (1990). Peers' perceptions of the consequences that victimized children provide aggressors. *Child Development, 61,* 1310–1325.

Perry, W. G., Jr. (1970). *Forms of intellectual and ethical development in the college years.* New York: Holt, Rinehart & Winston.

Perry, W. G., Jr. (1981). Cognitive and ethical growth. In A. Chickering (Ed.), *The modern American college* (pp. 76–116). San Francisco: Jossey-Bass.

Persson, I., Weiderpass, E., Bergkvist, L., Bergstrom, R., & Schairer, C. (1999). Risks of breast and endometrial cancer after estrogen and progestin replacement therapy. *Cancer Causes and Control, 10,* 253–260.

Pery, F. (1995, November–December). Careers: Retirement planning essentials. *Healthcare Executive, 10*(6), 42–43.

Peshkin, A. (1978). *Growing up American: Schooling and the survival of the community.* Chicago: University of Chicago Press.

Peshkin, A. (1997). *Places of memory: Whiteman's schools and native American communities.* Mahwah, NJ: Erlbaum.

Peterson, B. E., & Klohnen, E. C. (1995). Realization of generativity in two samples of women at midlife. *Psychology and Aging, 10,* 20–29.

Peterson, B. E., Smirles, K. A., & Wentworth, P. A. (1997). Generativity and authoritarianism: Implications for personality, political involvement, and parenting. *Journal of Personality and Social Psychology, 72,* 1202–1216.

Peterson, C. C. (1996). The ticking of the social clock: Adults' beliefs about the timing of transition events. *International Journal of Aging and Human Development, 42,* 189–203.

Peterson, L. (1989). Latchkey children's preparation for self-care: Overestimated, underrehearsed, and unsafe. *Journal of Clinical Child Psychology, 18,* 36–43.

Peterson, L., & Brown, D. (1994). Integrating child injury and abuse–neglect research: Common histories, etiologies, and solutions. *Psychological Bulletin, 116,* 293–315.

Pettit, G. S., Bates, J. E., & Dodge, K. A. (1998). Supportive parenting, ecological context, and children's adjustment: A seven-year longitudinal study. *Child Development, 68,* 908–923.

Pettit, G. S., Bates, J. E., Dodge, K. A., & Meece, D. W. (1999). The impact of after-school peer contact on early adolescent externalizing problems is moderated by parental monitoring, perceived neighborhood safety, and prior adjustment. *Child Development, 70,* 768–778.

Phelps, K. E., & Woolley, J. D. (1994). The form and function of young children's magical beliefs. *Developmental Psychology, 30,* 385–394.

Phillips, D. A., Voran, M., Kisker, E., Howes, C., & Whitebook, M. (1994). Child care for children in poverty: Opportunity or inequity? *Child Development, 65,* 472–492.

Phillips, D. A., & Zimmerman, M. (1990). The developmental course of perceived competence and incompetence among competent children. In R. Sternberg & J. Kolligian (Eds.), *Competence considered* (pp. 41–66). New Haven, CT: Yale University Press.

Phillips, M. (1997). What makes schools effective? A comparison of the relationships of communitarian climate and academic climate to mathematics achievement and attendance during middle school. *American Educational Research Journal, 34,* 633–662.

Phillips, O. P., & Elias, S. (1993). Prenatal genetic counseling issues in women of advanced reproductive age. *Journal of Women's Health, 2,* 1–5.

Phillips, S. D., & Imhoff, A. R. (1997). Women and career development: A decade of research. *Annual Review of Psychology, 48,* 31–59.

Phinney, J. S. (1989). Stages of ethnic identity development in minority group adolescents. *Journal of Early Adolescence, 9,* 34–49.

Phinney, J. S. (1993). Multiple group identities: Differentiation, conflict, and integration. In J. Kroger (Ed.), *Discussions on ego identity* (pp. 47–73). Hillsdale, NJ: Erlbaum.

Phinney, J. S., & Kohatsu, E. L. (1997). Ethnic and racial identity development and mental health. In J. Schulenberg, J. L. Maggs, & K. Hurrelmann (Eds.), *Health risks and developmental transitions during adolescence* (pp. 420–443). Cambridge, U.K.: Cambridge University Press.

Piaget, J. (1926). *The language and thought of the child.* New York: Harcourt, Brace & World. (Original work published 1923)

Piaget, J. (1930). *The child's conception of the world.* New York: Harcourt, Brace, & World. (Original work published 1926)

Piaget, J. (1950). *The psychology of intelligence.* New York: International Universities Press.

Piaget, J. (1951). *Play, dreams, and imitation in childhood.* New York: Norton. (Original work published 1945)

Piaget, J. (1952). *The origins of intelligence in children.* New York: International Universities Press. (Original work published 1936)

Piaget, J. (1965). *The moral judgment of the child.* New York: Free Press. (Original work published 1932)

Piaget, J. (1967). *Six psychological studies.* New York: Vintage.

Piaget, J. (1971). *Biology and knowledge.* Chicago: University of Chicago Press.

Piaget, J. (1985). *The equilibration of cognitive structures: The central problem of intellectual development.* Chicago: University of Chicago Press.

Pianta, R., Egeland, B., & Erickson, M. F. (1989). The antecedents of maltreatment: Results of the Mother–Child Interaction Research Project. In D. Cicchetti & V. Carlson (Eds.), *Child maltreatment* (pp. 203– 253). New York: Cambridge University Press.

Piatt, B. (1993). *Only English? Law and language policy in the United States.* Albuquerque: University of New Mexico Press.

Pickering, L. K., Granoff, D. M., Erickson, J. R., Mason, M. L., & Cordle, C. T. (1998). Modulation of the immune system by human milk and infant formula containing nucleotides. *Pediatrics, 101,* 242–249.

Pierce, K. M., Hamm, J. V., & Vandell, D. L. (1999). Experiences in after-school programs and children's adjustment in first-grade classrooms. *Child Development, 70,* 756–767.

Pierce, W. D., & Epling, W. F. (1995). *Behavior analysis and learning.* Englewood Cliffs, NJ: Prentice Hall.

Pietz, J., Dunckelmann, R., Rupp, A., Rating, D., Meinck, H. M., Schmidt, H., & Bremer, H. J. (1998). Neurological outcome in adult patients with early-treated phenylketonuria. *European Journal of Pediatrics, 157,* 824–830.

Pilkington, C. L., & Piersel, W. C. (1991). School phobia: A critical analysis of the separation anxiety theory and an alternative conceptualization. *Psychology in the Schools, 28,* 290–303.

Pillemer, K. A., & Finkelhor, D. (1988). The prevalence of elder abuse: A random sample survey. *Gerontologist, 28,* 51–57.

Pillow, B. H. (1995). Two trends in the development of conceptual perspective taking. An elaboration of the passive–active hypothesis. *International Journal of Behavioral Development, 18,* 649–676.

Pines, A. M. (1998). A prospective study of personality and gender differences in romantic attraction. *Personality and Individual Differences, 25,* 147–157.

Pinker, S., Lebeaux, D. S., & Frost, L. A. (1987). Productivity and constraints in the acquisition of the passive. *Cognition, 26,* 195–267.

Pinson-Milburn, N. M., Fabian, E. S., Schlossberg, N. K., & Pyle, M. (1996). Grandparents raising grandchildren. *Journal of Counseling and Development, 74,* 548–554.

Pipes, P. L. (1996). *Nutrition in infancy and childhood* (6th ed.). St. Louis: Mosby.

Pipp, S., Easterbrooks, M. A., & Brown, S. R. (1993). Attachment status and complexity of infants' self- and other-knowledge when tested with mother and father. *Social Development, 2,* 1–14.

Plassman, B. L., & Breitner, C. S. (1996). Recent advances in the genetics of Alzheimer's disease and vascular dementia with an emphasis on gene–environment interactions. *Journal of the American Genetics Society, 44,* 1242–1250.

Plomin, R. (1994a). The Emanuel Miller Memorial Lecture 1993: Genetic research and identification of environmental influences. *Journal of Child Psychology and Psychiatry, 35,* 817–834.

Plomin, R. (1994b). *Genetics and experience: The interplay between nature and nurture.* Thousand Oaks, CA: Sage.

Plomin, R. (1994c). Nature, nurture, and social development. *Social Development, 3,* 37–53.

Plomin, R., Reiss, D., Hetherington, E. M., & Howe, G. W. (1994). Nature and nurture: Genetic contributions to measures of the family environment. *Developmental Psychology, 30,* 32–43.

Plucker, J. A., Callahan, C. M., & Tomchin, E. M. (1996). Wherefore art thou, multiple intelligences? Alternative assessments for identifying talent in ethnically diverse and low income students. *Gifted Child Quarterly, 40,* 81–92.

Plude, D. J., & Doussard-Roosevelt, J. A. (1989). Aging, selective attention, and feature integration. *Psychology and Aging, 4,* 98–105.

Plude, D. J., & Hoyer, W. J. (1985). Attention and performance: Identifying and localizing age deficits. In N. Charness (Ed.), *Aging and human performance* (pp. 47–99). Chichester, England: Wiley.

Plumert, J. M., Pick, H. L., Jr., Marks, R. A., Kintsch, A. S., & Wegesin, D. (1994). Locating objects and communicating about locations: Organizational differences in children's searching and direction-giving. *Developmental Psychology, 30,* 443–453.

Podrouzek, W., & Furrow, D. (1988). Preschoolers' use of eye contact while speaking: The influence of sex, age, and conversational partner. *Journal of Psycholinguistic Research, 17,* 89–93.

Pohl, J. M., Given, C. W., Collins, C. E., & Given, B. A. (1994). Social vulnerability and reactions to caregiving in daughters and daughters-in-law caring for disabled aging parents. *Health Care for Women International, 15,* 385–395.

Polansky, N. A., Gaudin, J. M., Ammons, P. W., & Davis, K. B. (1985). The psychological ecology of the neglectful mother. *Child Abuse and Neglect, 9,* 265–275.

Polka, L., & Werker, J. F. (1994). Developmental changes in perception of non-native vowel contrasts. *Journal of Experimental Psychology: Human Perception and Performance, 20,* 421–435.

Pollitt, E. (1996). A reconceptualization of the effects of undernutrition on children's biological, psychosocial, and behavioral development. *Social Policy Report of the Society for Research in Child Development, 10*(5).

Pollock, G. H. (1987). The mourning–liberation process in health and disease. *Psychiatric Clinics of North America, 10,* 345–354.

Pollock, L. (1987). *A lasting relationship: Parents and children over three centuries.* Hanover, NH: University Press of New England.

Polloway, E. A., Patton, J. R., Smith, T. E. C., & Buck, G. H. (1997). Mental retardation and learning disabilities: Conceptual and applied issues. *Journal of Learning Disabilities, 30,* 297–308.

Pomerantz, E. M., & Ruble, D. N. (1998). The multidimensional nature of control: Implications for the development of sex differences in self-evaluation. In J. Heckhausen & C. S. Dweck (Eds.), *Motivation and self-regulation across the lifespan* (pp. 159–184). New York: Cambridge University Press.

Popkin, B. M. (1994). The nutrition transition in low-income countries: An emerging crisis. *Nutrition Review, 52,* 285–298.

Popkin, B. M., & Doak, C. M. (1998). The obesity epidemic is a worldwide phenomenon. *Nutrition Reviews, 56,* 106–114.

Popkin, B. M., Richards, M. K., & Montiero, C. A. (1996). Stunting is associated with overweight in children of four nations that are undergoing the nutrition transition. *Journal of Nutrition, 126,* 3009–3016.

Porter, R. H., Makin, J. W., Davis, L. B., & Christensen, K. M. (1992). An assessment of the salient olfactory environment of formula-fed infants. *Physiology and Behavior, 50,* 907–911.

Portman, P. A. (1995). Who is having fun in physical education classes? Experiences of sixth-grade students in elementary and middle schools. *Journal of Teaching in Physical Education, 14,* 445–453.

Posner, J. K., & Vandell, D. L. (1994). Low-income children's after-school care: Are there beneficial effects of after-school programs? *Child Development, 58,* 568–595.

Posner, J. K., & Vandell, D. L. (1999). After-school activities and the development of low-income urban children: A longitudinal study. *Developmental Psychology, 35,* 868–879.

Poulin-Dubois, D., & Héroux, G. (1994). Movement and children's attributions of life properties. *International Journal of Behavioral Development, 17,* 329–347.

Poulin-Dubois, D., Serbin, L. A., Kenyon, B., & Derbyshire, A. (1994). Infants' intermodal knowledge about gender. *Developmental Psychology, 30,* 436–442.

Powell, B., & Steelman, L. C. (1993). The educational benefits of being spaced out: Sibship density and educational progress. *American Sociological Review, 58,* 367–381.

Powell, D. R. (1986, March). Parent education and support programs. *Young Children, 41*(3), 47–53.

Powers, S. I., Hauser, S. T., & Kilner, L. A. (1989). Adolescent mental health. *American Psychologist, 44,* 200–208.

Powls, A., Botting, N., Cooke, R. W. I., & Marlow, N. (1996). Handedness in very-low-birthweight (VLBW) children at 12 years of age: Relation to perinatal and outcome variables. *Developmental Medicine and Child Neurology, 38,* 594–602.

Prado, L. M., & Markman, H. J. (1998). Unearthing the seeds of marital distress: What we have learned from married and remarried couples. In M. J. Cox & J. Brooks-Gunn (Eds.), *Conflict and cohesion in families* (pp. 51–85). Mahwah, NJ: Erlbaum.

Prager, K. J., & Bailey, J. M. (1985). Androgyny, ego development, and psychological crisis resolution. *Sex Roles, 13,* 525–535.

Prechtl, H. F. R., & Beintema, D. (1965). *The neurological examination of the full-term newborn infant.* London: Heinemann Medical Books.

Preisler, G. M. (1991). Early patterns of interaction between blind infants and their sighted mothers. *Child: Care, Health and Development, 17,* 65–90.

Preisler, G. M. (1993). A descriptive study of blind children in nurseries with sighted children. *Child: Care, Health and Development, 19,* 295–315.

Pressley, M. (1995). More about the development of self-regulation: Complex, long-term, and thoroughly social. *Educational Psychologist, 30,* 207–212.

Previc, F. H. (1991). A general theory concerning the prenatal origins of cerebral lateralization. *Psychological Review, 98,* 299–334.

Price, J. L., & Morris, J. C. (1999). Tangles and plaques in nondemented aging and "preclinical" Alzheimer's disease. *Annals of Neurology, 45,* 358–368.

Princeton Religion Research Center. (1994). *Religion in America.* Princeton, NJ: Gallup Poll.

Prinz, P. N., Vitiello, M. V., Raskind, M. A., & Thorpy, M. J. (1990). Geriatrics: Sleep disorders and aging. *New England Journal of Medicine, 323,* 520–526.

Prochaska, J. O., DiClemente, C. C., & Norcross, J. C. (1992). In search of how people change: Applications to addictive behaviors. *American Psychologist, 47,* 1102–1114.

Provins, K. A. (1997). Handedness and speech: A critical reappraisal of the role of genetic and environmental factors in the cerebral lateralization of function. *Psychological Review, 104,* 554–571.

Purcell, D. W., & Hicks, D. W. (1996). Lesbian sexuality. In R. P. Cabaj & T. S. Stein (Eds.), *Textbook of homosexuality and mental health* (pp. 763–782). Washington, DC: American Psychiatric Press.

Purcell-Gates, V. (1996). Stories, coupons, and the TV Guide: Relationships between home literacy experiences and emergent literacy knowledge. *Reading Research Quarterly, 31,* 406–428.

Pyeritz, R. E. (1998). Sex: What we make of it. *Journal of the American Medical Association, 279,* 269.

Pyka, G., Lindenberger, E., Charette, S., & Marcus, R. (1994). Muscle strength and fiber adaptations to a year-long resistance training program in elderly men and women. *Journal of Gerontology, 49,* M22–M27.

Pynoos, J., & Golant, S. (1996). Housing and living arrangements for the elderly. In R. H. Binstock & L. K. George (Eds.), *Handbook of aging and the social sciences* (pp. 303–324). San Diego: Academic Press.

Quadagno, J., & Hardy, M. (1996). Work and retirement. In R. H. Binstock & L. K. George (Eds.), *Handbook of aging and the social sciences* (pp. 325–345). San Diego: Academic Press.

Quick, H. E., & Moen, P. (1998). Gender, employment, and retirement quality: A life course approach to the differential experiences of men and women. *Journal of Occupational Health Psychology, 3,* 44–64.

Quill, T. E. (1991). Death and dignity: A case of individualized decision making. *New England Journal of Medicine, 324,* 691–694.

Quinn, J. F., & Kozy, M. (1996). The role of bridge jobs in the retirement transition: Gender, race, and ethnicity. *Gerontologist, 36,* 363–372.

Quinn, M. E., Johnson, M. A., Poon, L. W., & Martin, P. (1999). Psychosocial correlates of subjective health in sexagenarians, octogenarians, and centenarians. *Issues in Mental Health Nursing, 20,* 151–171.

Quinn, T. M., & Adzick, N. S. (1997). Fetal surgery. *Obstetrics and Gynecology Clinics of North America, 24,* 143–157.

Quint, J. C., Box, J. M., & Polit, D. F. (1997). *New Chance: Final report on a comprehensive program for disadvantaged young mothers and their children.* New York: Manpower Demonstration Research Corporation.

Quintero, R. A., Puder, K. S., & Cotton, D. B. (1993). Embryoscopy and fetoscopy. *Obstetrics and Gynecology Clinics of North America, 20,* 563–581.

Radin, N. (1994). Primary caregiving fathers in intact families. In A. E. Gottfried & A. W. Gottfried (Eds.), *Redefining families: Implications for children's development* (pp. 11–54). New York: Plenum.

Radziszewska, B., & Rogoff, B. (1988). Influence of adult and peer collaboration on the development of children's planning skills. *Developmental Psychology, 24,* 840–848.

Rafferty, Y. (1995). The legal rights and educational problems of homeless children and youth. *Educational Evaluation and Policy Analysis, 17,* 39–61.

Räihä, N. C. R., & Axelsson, I. E. (1995). Protein nutrition in infancy. *Pediatric Clinics of North America, 42,* 745–763.

Räikkönen, K., Matthews, K. A., Flory, J. D., Owens, J. F., & Gump, B. B. (1999). Effects of optimism, pessimism, and trait anxiety on ambulatory blood pressure and mood during everyday life. *Journal of Personality and Social Psychology, 76,* 104–113.

Rakison, D. H., & Butterworth, G. E. (1998). Infants' use of object parts in early categorization. *Developmental Psychology, 34,* 49–62.

Raley, R. K. (1996). A shortage of marriageable men? A note on the role of cohabitation in black–white differences in marriage rates. *American Sociological Review, 61,* 973–983.

Ramey, C. T., & Ramey, S. L. (1998). Early intervention and early experience. *American Psychologist, 53,* 109–120.

Ramirez, J. D., Yuen, S. D., Ramey, D. R., & Pasta, D. (1991). *Longitudinal study of structured English immersion strategy, early exit and late-exit transitional bilingual education programs for language minority: Final report* (Vols. 1 & 2). San Mateo, CA: Aguirre International.

Ramsøy, N. R. (1994). Non-marital cohabitation and change in norms: The case of Norway. *Acta Sociologica, 37,* 23–37.

Rando, T. A. (1991a). *How to go on living when someone you love dies.* New York: Bantam.

Rando, T. A. (1991b). Parental adjustment to the loss of a child. In D. Papadatou & C. Papadatos (Eds.), *Children and death* (pp. 233–253). New York: Hemisphere.

Rando, T. A. (1995). Grief and mourning: Accommodating to loss. In H. Wass & R. A. Neimeyer (Eds.), *Dying: Facing the facts* (3rd ed., pp. 211–241). Washington, DC: Taylor & Francis.

Ransford, H. E., & Palisi, B. J. (1996). Aerobic exercise, subjective health and psychological well-being within age and gender subgroups. *Social Science and Medicine, 42,* 1555–1559.

Raphael, B., Middleton, W., Martinek, N., & Misso, V. (1993). Counseling and therapy of the bereaved. In M. S. Stroebe, W. Stroebe, & R. O. Hansson (Eds.), *Handbook of bereavement* (pp. 427–453). New York: Cambridge University Press.

Rappaport, L. (1993). The treatment of nocturnal enuresis—Where are we now? *Pediatrics, 92,* 465–466.

Rasmussen, C. H., & Johnson, M. E. (1994). Spirituality and religiosity: Relative relationships to death anxiety. *Omega, 29,* 313–318.

Rast, M., & Meltzoff, A. N. (1995). Memory and representation in young children with Down syndrome: Exploring deferred imitation and object permanence. *Development and Psychopathology, 7,* 393–407.

Ratner, N., & Bruner, J. S. (1978). Social exchange and the acquisition of language. *Journal of Child Language, 5,* 391–402.

Raup, J. L., & Myers, J. E. (1989). The empty nest syndrome: Myth or reality? *Journal of Counseling and Human Development, 68,* 180–183.

Ravussin, E., Valencia, M. E., Esparza, J., Bennett, P. H., & Schulz, L. O. (1994). Effects of a traditional lifestyle on obesity in Pima Indians. *Diabetes Care, 17,* 1067–1074.

Rayner, K., & Pollatsek, A. (1989). *The psychology of reading.* Englewood Cliffs, NJ: Prentice Hall.

Read, C. R. (1991). Achievement and career choices: Comparisons of males and females. *Roeper Review, 13,* 188–193.

Receputo, G., Di Stefano, S., Fornaro, D., Malaguarnera, M., & Motta, L. (1994). Comparison of tactile sensitivity in a group of elderly and young adults and children using a new instrument called a "Tangoceptometer." *Archives of Gerontology and Geriatrics, 18,* 207–214.

Redding, N. P., & Dowling, W. D. (1992). Rites of passage among women reentering higher education. *Adult Education Quarterly, 42,* 221–236.

Redl, F. (1966). *When we deal with children.* New York: The Free Press.

Rees, M. (1993). Menarche when and why? *Lancet, 342,* 1375–1376.

Reese, E., Haden, C. A., & Fivush, R. (1996). Mothers, fathers, daughters, sons: Gender differences in autobiographical reminiscing. *Research on Language and Social Interaction, 29,* 27–56.

Reeves, J. B., & Darville, R. L. (1994). Social contact patterns and satisfaction with retirement of women in dual-career/earner families. *International Journal of Aging and Human Development, 39,* 163–175.

Reid, H. M., & Fine, A. (1992). Self-disclosure in men's friendships: Variations associated with intimate relations. In P. M. Nardi (Ed.), *Men's friendships* (pp. 153–171). Newbury Park, CA: Sage.

Reid, I. R. (1996). Therapy of osteoporosis — calcium, vitamin D and exercise. *American Journal of the Medical Sciences, 312,* 278–286.

Reifler, B. V. (1994). Depression: Diagnosis and comorbidity. In L. S. Schneider, C. F. Reynolds, III, B. D. Lebowitz, & A. J. Friedhoff (Eds.), *Diagnosis and treatment of depression in late life* (pp. 55–59). Washington, DC: American Psychiatric Press.

Reiger, D. A., Boyd, J. H., Burke, J. D., Rae, D. S., Myers, J. K., Dramer, M., Robins, L. N., George, L. K., Karno, M., & Locke, B. Z. (1988). One-month prevalence of mental disorders in the United States. *Archives of General Psychiatry, 45,* 977–986.

Reiman, E. M., Caselli, R. J., Yun, L. S., Chen, K., Bandy, D., Minoshima, S., Thibodeau, S. N., & Osborne, D. (1996). Preclinical evidence of Alzheimer's disease in persons homozygous for the epsilon 4 allele for apolipoprotein E. *New England Journal of Medicine, 334,* 752–758.

Reinke, B. J., Holmes, D. S., & Harris, R. L. (1985). The timing of psychosocial changes in women's lives: The years 25 to 45. *Journal of Personality and Social Psychology, 48,* 1353-1364.

Reis, M., & Nahmiash, D. (1995). When seniors are abused: An intervention model. *Gerontologist, 35,* 666–671.

Reiser, J., Yonas, A., & Wikner, K. (1976). Radial localization of odors by human neonates. *Child Development, 47,* 856–859.

Reisman, J. E. (1987). Touch, motion, and proprioception. In P. Salapatek & L. Cohen (Eds.), Handbook of infant perception: Vol. 1. *From sensation to perception* (pp. 265–303). Orlando, FL: Academic Press.

Renninger, K. A. (1998). Developmental psychology and instruction: Issues from and for practice. In I. Sigel & K. A. Renninger (Eds.), *Handbook of child psychology: Vol. 4. Child psychology and practice* (pp. 211–274). New York: Wiley.

Repacholi, B. M., & Gopnik, A. (1997). Early reasoning about desires: Evidence from 14- and 18-month-olds. *Developmental Psychology, 33,* 12–21.

Resnick, H. S., & Newton, T. (1992). Assessment and treatment of post-traumatic stress disorder in adult survivors of sexual assault. In D. Fox (Ed.), *Treating PTSD: Procedures for combat veterans, battered women, adult and child sexual assaults* (pp. 99–126). New York: Guilford.

Rest, J. R. (1979). *Development in judging moral issues.* Minneapolis: University of Minnesota Press.

Rest, J. R., & Narvaez, D. (1991). The college experience and moral development. In W. M. Kurtines & J. L. Gewirtz (Eds.), *Handbook of moral behavior and development* (Vol. 2, pp. 229–245). Hillsdale, NJ: Erlbaum.

Reynolds, A. J., & Temple, J. A. (1998). Extended early childhood intervention and school achievement: Age thirteen findings from the Chicago Longitudinal Study. *Child Development, 69,* 231–246.

Reynolds, C. R., & Kaiser, S. M. (1990). Test bias in psychological assessment. In T. B. Gutkin & C. R. Reynolds (Eds.), *The handbook of school psychology* (pp. 487–525). New York: Wiley.

Reznick, J. S., & Goldfield, B. A. (1992). Rapid change in lexical development in comprehension and production. *Developmental Psychology, 28,* 406–413.

Rhein, J. von (1997, January 19). Ardis Krainik, Lyric Opera's life force, dies. *Chicago Tribune,* pp. 1, 16.

Ricard, M., & Kamberk-Kilicci, M. (1995). Children's empathic responses to emotional complexity. *International Journal of Behavioral Development, 18,* 211–225.

Ricciardelli, L. A. (1992). Bilingualism and cognitive development: Relation to threshold theory. *Journal of Psycholinguistic Research, 21,* 301–316.

Riccio, C. A., Hynd, G. W., Cohen, M. J., & Gonzalez, J. J. (1993). Neurological basis of attention deficit hyperactivity disorder. *Exceptional Children, 60,* 118–124.

Rice, F. P. (1999). *The adolescent: Development, relationships, and culture* (8th ed.). Boston: Allyn and Bacon.

Rice, J. K. (1994). Reconsidering research on divorce, family life cycle, and the meaning of family. *Psychology of Women Quarterly, 18,* 559–584.

Richards, M. H., & Duckett, E. (1994). The relationship of maternal employment to early adolescent daily experience with and without parents. *Child Development, 65,* 225–236.

Richards-Colocino, N., McKenzie, P., & Newton, R. R. (1996). Project Success: Comprehensive intervention services for middle school high-risk youth. *Journal of Adolescent Research, 11,* 130–163.

Richardson, G. A. (1998). Prenatal cocaine exposure: A longitudinal study of development. In J. A. Harvey & B. E. Kosofsky (Eds.), *Annals of the New York Academy of Sciences* (Vol. 846, pp. 144–152). New York: New York Academy of Sciences.

Richardson, G. A., Hamel, S. C., Gold-schmidt, L., & Day, N. L. (1996). The effects of prenatal cocaine use on neonatal neurobehavioral status. *Neurotoxicology and Teratology, 18,* 519–528.

Richardson, S. A., Koller, H., & Katz, M. (1986). Factors leading to differences in the school performance of boys and girls. *Developmental and Behavioral Pediatrics, 7,* 49–55.

Rich-Edwards, J. W., Colditz, G. A., Stampfer, M. J., Willett, W. C., Gillman, M. W., Hennekens, C. H., Speizer, F. E., & Manson, J. E. (1999). Birthweight and the risk for type 2 diabetes mellitus in adult women. *Annals of Internal Medicine, 130,* 278–284.

Rich-Edwards, J. W., Stampfer, M. J., Manson, J. E., Rosner, B., Hankinson, S. E., Colditz, G. A., Willett, W. C., & Hennekens, C. H. (1997). Birth weight and risk of cardiovascular disease in a cohort of women followed up since 1976. *British Medical Journal, 315,* 396–400.

Richgels, D. J., McGee, L. M, & Slaton, E. A. (1989). Teaching expository text structure in reading and writing. In K. D. Muth (Ed.), *Children's comprehension of text* (pp. 167–184). Newark, DE: International Reading Association.

Richie, B. S., Fassinger, R. E., Linn, S. G., Johnson, J., Prosser, J., & Robinson, S. (1997). Persistence, connection, and passion: A qualitative study of the career development of highly achieving African American–black and white women. *Journal of Counseling Psychology, 44,* 133–148.

Rickel, A. U., & Becker, E. (1997). *Keeping children from harm's way.* Washington, DC: American Psychological Association.

Rigler, S. K. (1999). Preventing falls in older adults. *Hospital Practice, 34,* 117–120.

Rimm, E. B. (1996). Alcohol consumption and coronary heart disease: Good habits may be more important than just good

wine. *American Journal of Epidemiology, 143,* 1094–1098.

Ritchie, K. (1998). Mental health of the oldest old: The relevance of centenarian studies to psychogeriatric research. *International Psychogeriatrics, 10,* 7–9.

Rittman, M., Kuzmeskus, L. B., & Flum, M. A. (2000). A synthesis of current knowledge on minority elder abuse. In T. Tatara (Ed.), *Understanding elder abuse in minority populations* (pp. 221–238). Philadelphia: Brunner/Mazel.

Rivara, F. P. (1995). Developmental and behavioral issues in childhood injury prevention. *Developmental and Behavioral Pediatrics, 16,* 362–370.

Roazzi, A., & Bryant, P. (1997). Explicitness and conservation: Social class differences. *International Journal of Behavioral Development, 21,* 51–70.

Roberto, K. A., & Kimboko, P. J. (1989). Friendships in later life: Definitions and maintenance patterns. *International Journal of Aging and Human Development, 28,* 9–19.

Roberton, M. A. (1984). Changing motor patterns during childhood. In J. R. Thomas (Ed.), *Motor development during childhood and adolescence* (pp. 48–90). Minneapolis: Burgess.

Roberts, M. C., Alexander, K., & Knapp, L. G. (1990). Motivating children to use safety belts: A program combining rewards and "flash for life." *Journal of Community Psychology, 18,* 110–119.

Roberts, P., & Newton, P. M. (1987). Levinsonian studies of women's adult development. *Psychology and Aging, 2,* 154–163.

Roberts, R. E., Kaplan, G. A., Shema, S. J., & Strawbridge, W. J. (1997). Prevalence and correlates of depression in an aging cohort: The Alameda County Study. *Journal of Gerontology, 52B,* S252–S258.

Roberts, R. E., Shema, S. J., & Kaplan, G. A. (1999). Prospective data on sleep complaints and associated risk factors in an older cohort. *Psychosomatic Medicine, 61,* 188–196.

Roberts, R. J., Jr., & Aman, C. J. (1993). Developmental differences in giving directions: Spatial frames of reference and mental rotation. *Child Development, 64,* 1258–1270.

Roberts, W., & Strayer, J. (1996). Empathy, emotional expressiveness, and prosocial behavior. *Child Development, 67,* 449–470.

Robertson, D. L. (1991). Gender differences in the academic progress of adult undergraduates: Patterns and policy implications. *Journal of College Student Development, 32,* 490–496.

Robin, D. J., Berthier, N. E., & Clifton, R. K. (1996). Infants' predictive reaching for moving objects in the dark. *Developmental Psychology, 32,* 824–835.

Robinson, E. J., & Mitchell, P. (1994). Young children's false-belief reasoning: Interpretation of messages is not easier than the classic task. *Developmental Psychology, 30,* 67–72.

Robinson, J., & Godbey, G. (1997). *Time for life.* College Park: Pennsylvania State University.

Robinson, T. N. (1999). Reducing children's television viewing to prevent obesity. *Journal of the American Medical Association, 282,* 1561–1567.

Robinson, T. N., Killen, J. D., Litt, I. F., Hammer, L. D., Wilson, D. M., Haydel, K. F., Hayward, C., & Taylor, C. B. (1996). Ethnicity and body dissatisfaction: Are Hispanic and Asian girls at increased risk for eating disorders? *Journal of Adolescent Health, 19,* 384–393.

Robison, J. I., Hoerr, S. L., Strandmark, J., & Mavis, B. (1993). Obesity, weight loss, and health. *Journal of the American Dietetic Association, 93,* 445–449.

Rochat, P., & Goubet, N. (1995). Development of sitting and reaching in 5- to 6-month-old infants. *Infant Behavior and Development, 18,* 53–68.

Roche, A. F. (1979). Secular trends in stature, weight, and maturation. In A. F. Roche (Ed.), Secular trends in human growth, maturation, and development. *Monographs of the Society for Research in Child Development, 44*(3–4, Serial No. 179).

Rockwell, R. C., Elder, G. H., & Ross, D. J. (1979). Psychological patterns in marital timing and divorce. *Social Psychology Quarterly, 42,* 399–404.

Roebuck, T. M., Mattson, S. N., & Riley, E. P. (1999). Prenatal exposure to alcohol: Effects on brain structure and neuropsychological functioning. In J. H. Hannigan & L. P. Spear (Eds.), *Alcohol and alcoholism: Effects on brain and development* (pp. 1–16). Mahwah, NJ: Erlbaum.

Roffwarg, H. P., Muzio, J. N., & Dement, W. C. (1966). Ontogenetic development of the human sleep–dream cycle. *Science, 152,* 604–619.

Roger, V. L., Farkouh, M. E., Weston, S. A., Reeder, G. S., Jacobsen, S. J., Zinsmeister, A. R., Yawn, B. P., Kopecky, S. L., & Gabriel, S. E. (2000). Sex differences in evaluation and outcome of unstable angina. *Journal of the American Medical Association, 283,* 646–652.

Rogers, L., Resnick, M. D., Mitchell, J. E., & Blum, R. W. (1997). The relationship between socioeconomic status and eating disordered behaviors in a community sample of adolescent girls. *International Journal of Eating Disorders, 22,* 15–23.

Rogers, S. J., & White, L. K. (1998). Satisfaction with parenting: The role of marital happiness, family structure, and parents' gender. *Journal of Marriage and the Family, 60,* 293–308.

Roggman, L. A., Langlois, J. H., Hubbs-Tait, L., & Rieser-Danner, L. A. (1994). Infant day-care, attachment, and the "file drawer problem." *Child Development, 65,* 1429–1443.

Rogoff, B. (1986). The development of strategic use of context in spatial memory. In M. Perlmutter (Ed.), *Perspectives on intellectual development* (pp. 107–123). Hillsdale, NJ: Erlbaum.

Rogoff, B. (1996). Developmental transitions in children's participation in socio-cultural activities. In A. J. Sameroff & M. M. Haith (Eds.), *The five to seven year shift: The age of reason and responsibility* (pp. 273–294). Chicago: University of Chicago Press.

Rogoff, B. (1998). Cognition as a collaborative process. In D. Kuhn & R. S. Siegler (Eds.), *Handbook of child psychology: Vol. 2. Cognition, perception, and language* (5th ed., pp. 679–744). New York: Wiley.

Rogoff, B., & Chavajay, P. (1995). What's become of research on the cultural basis of cognitive development? *American Psychologist, 50,* 859–877.

Rogoff, B., Malkin, C., & Gilbride, K. (1984). Interaction with babies as guidance in development. In B. Rogoff & J. V. Wertsch (Eds.), *New directions for child development* (No. 23, pp. 31–44). San Francisco: Jossey-Bass.

Rogoff, B., Mosier, C., Mistry, J., & Göncü, A. (1993). Toddlers' guided participation with their caregivers in cultural activity. In E. A. Forman, N. Minick, & C. A. Stone (Eds.), *Contexts for learning* (pp. 230–253). New York: Oxford University Press.

Rogow, S. (1988). *Helping the visually impaired child with developmental problems: Effective practice in home, school, and community.* New York: Teachers College Press.

Romans, S. M., Roeltgen, D. P., Kushner, H., & Ross, J. L. (1997). Executive function in girls with Turner's syndrome. *Developmental Neuropsychology, 13,* 23–40.

Rook, K. S., Catalano, R., & Dooley, D. (1989). The timing of major life events: Effects of departing from the social clock. *American Journal of Community Psychology, 17,* 233–258.

Roopnarine, J. L., Hossain, Z., Gill, P., & Brophy, H. (1994). Play in the East Indian context. In J. L. Roopnarine, J. E. Johnson, & F. H. Hooper (Eds.), *Children's play in diverse cultures* (pp. 9–30). Albany: State University of New York Press.

Roopnarine, J. L., Lasker, J., Sacks, M., & Stores, M. (1998). The cultural contexts of children's play. In O. N. Saracho & B. Spodek (Eds.), *Multiple perspectives on play in early childhood education* (pp. 194–219). Albany: State University of New York Press.

Roopnarine, J. L., Talukder, E., Jain, D., Joshi, P., & Srivastav, P. (1990). Characteristics of holding, patterns of play, and social behaviors between parents and infants in New Delhi, India. *Developmental Psychology, 26,* 667–673.

Roscoe, B., Diana, M. S., & Brooks, R. H. (1987). Early, middle, and late adolescents' views on dating and factors influencing partner selection. *Adolescence, 22,* 59–68.

Rose, A. J., & Asher, S. R. (1999). Children's goals and strategies in response to conflicts within a friendship. *Developmental Psychology, 35,* 69–79.

Rose, R. J. (1995) Genes and human behavior. *Annual Review of Psychology, 46,* 625–654.

Rose, S. A., & Feldman, J. F. (1997). Memory and speed: Their role in the relation of infant information processing to later IQ. *Child Development, 68,* 610–620.

Rose, S. A., Jankowski, J. J., & Senior, G. J. (1997). Infants' recognition of contour-deleted figures. *Journal of Experimental Psychology: Human Perception and Performance, 23,* 1206–1216.

Rosen, A. B., & Rozin, P. (1993). Now you see it, now you don't: The preschool child's conception of invisible particles in the context of dissolving. *Developmental Psychology, 29,* 300–311.

Rosen, W. D., Adamson, L. B., & Bakeman, R. (1992). An experimental investigation of infant social referencing: Mothers' messages and gender differences. *Developmental Psychology, 28,* 1172–1178.

Rosenberg, S. (1988). Self and others: Studies in social personality and autobiography. In L. Berkowitz (Ed.), *Advances in experimental social psychology* (Vol. 21, pp. 56–96). New York: Academic Press.

Rosenberg, S. D., Rosenberg, H. J., & Farrell, M. P. (1999). The midlife crisis revisited. In S. L. Willis & J. D. Reid (Eds.), *Life in the middle* (pp. 47–73). San Diego: Academic Press.

Rosenblatt, P. C. (1993). Cross-cultural variation in the experience, expression, and understanding of grief. In D. P. Irish, K. F. Lundquist, & V. J. Nelsen (Eds.), *Ethnic variations in dying, death, and grief* (pp. 13–19). Washington, DC: Taylor & Francis.

Rosenman, R. H., Brand, R. J., Jenkins, C. D., Friedman, M., Strauss, R., & Wurm, M. (1975). Coronary heart disease in the Western Collaborative Group Study: Final follow-up experience of 8½ years. *Journal of the American Medical Association, 223,* 872–877.

Rosenthal, J. A. (1992). *Special-needs adoption: A study of intact families.* New York: Praeger.

Roskos, K., & Neuman, S. B. (1998). Play as an opportunity for literacy. In O. N. Saracho & B. Spodek (Eds.), *Multiple perspec-* *tives on play in early childhood education* (pp. 100–115). Albany: State University of New York Press.

Rossi, A. S. (1980). Life-span theories and women's lives. *Signs: Journal of Women in Culture and Society, 6,* 4–32.

Rossi, A. S., & Rossi, P. H. (1990). *Of human bonding: Parent–child relations across the life course.* New York: Aldine de Gruyter.

Rothbart, M. K., & Bates, J. E. (1998). Temperament. In N. Eisenberg (Ed.), *Handbook of child psychology: Vol. 3. Social, emotional, and personality development* (5th ed., pp. 105–176). New York: Wiley.

Rothbart, M. K., Derryberry, D., & Posner, M. I. (1994). A psychobiological approach to the development of temperament. In J. E. Bates & T. D. Wachs (Eds.), *Temperament: Individual differences at the interface of biology and behavior* (pp. 83–116). Washington, DC: American Psychological Association.

Rothbart, M. K., & Mauro, J. A. (1990). Questionnaire approaches to the study of infant temperament. In J. W. Fagen & J. Colombo (Eds.), *Individual differences in infancy: Reliability, stability and prediction* (pp. 411–429). Hillsdale, NJ: Erlbaum.

Roughan, P. A., Kaiser, F. E., & Morley, J. E. (1993). Sexuality and the older woman. *Clinics in Geriatric Medicine, 9,* 87–106.

Rousseau, J. J. (1955). *Emile.* New York: Dutton. (Original work published 1762)

Rovee-Collier, C. (1996). Shifting the focus from what to why. *Infant Behavior and Development, 19,* 385–400.

Rovee-Collier, C. (1999). The development of infant memory. *Current Directions in Psychological Science, 8,* 80–85.

Rovee-Collier, C. K. (1987). Learning and memory. In J. D. Osofsky (Ed.), *Handbook of infant development* (2nd ed., pp. 98–148). New York: Wiley.

Rovee-Collier, C. K., & Bhatt, R. S. (1993). Evidence of long-term memory in infancy. *Annals of Child Development, 9,* 1–45.

Royal College of Obstetricians and Gynecologists. (1997, October). *Report of the panel to review fetal pain.* London: Author.

Rubenstein, C. M., & Shaver, P. (1982). *In search of intimacy.* New York: Delacorte Press.

Rubin, D. C., Rahhal, T. A., & Poon, L. W. (1998). Things learned in early adulthood are remembered best. *Memory and Cognition, 26,* 3–19.

Rubin, D. C., & Schulkind, M. D. (1997a). Distribution of important and word-cued autobiographical memories in 20-, 35-, and 70-year-old adults. *Psychology and Aging, 12,* 524–535.

Rubin, D. C., & Schulkind, M. D. (1997b). The distribution of autobiographical memories across the lifespan. *Memory and Cognition, 25,* 859–866.

Rubin, K., Bukowski, W., & Parker, J. G. (1998). Peer interactions, relationships, and groups. In N. Eisenberg (Ed.), *Handbook of child psychology: Vol. 3. Social, emotional, and personality development* (5th ed., pp. 619–700). New York: Wiley.

Rubin, K. H., & Coplan, R. J. (1998). Social and nonsocial play in childhood: An individual differences perspective. In O. N. Saracho & B. Spodek (Eds.), *Multiple perspectives on play in early childhood education* (pp. 144–170). Albany: State University of New York Press.

Rubin, K. H., Coplan, R. J., Fox, N. A., & Calkins, S. (1995). Emotionality, emotion regulation, and preschoolers' social adaptation. *Development and Psychopathology, 7,* 49–62.

Rubin, K. H., Fein, G. G., & Vandenberg, B. (1983). Play. In E. M. Hetherington (Ed.), *Handbook of child psychology: Vol. 4. Socialization, personality, and social development* (4th ed., pp. 693–744). New York: Wiley.

Rubin, K. H., Hastings, P. D., Stewart, S. L., Henderson, H. A., & Chen, X. (1997). The consistency and concomitants of inhibition: Some of the children, all of the time. *Child Development, 68,* 467–483.

Rubin, K. H., Watson, K. S., & Jambor, T. W. (1978). Free-play behaviors in preschool and kindergarten children. *Child Development, 49,* 539–536.

Rubinstein, R. L. (1987). Never married elderly as a social type: Re-evaluating some images. *Gerontologist, 27,* 108–113.

Rubinstein, R. L., Alexander, B. B., Goodman, M., & Luborsky, M. (1991). Key relationships of never married, childless older women: A cultural analysis. *Journal of Gerontology, 46,* S270–S277.

Ruble, D. N., & Frey, K. S. (1991). Changing patterns of comparative behavior as skills are acquired: A functional model of self-evaluation. In J. Suls & T. A. Wills (Eds.), *Social comparison: Contemporary theory and research* (pp. 70–112). Hillsdale, NJ: Erlbaum.

Ruble, D. N., & Martin, C. L. (1998). Gender development. In N. Eisenberg (Ed.), *Handbook of child psychology: Vol. 3. Social, emotional, and personality development* (5th ed., pp. 933–1016). New York: Wiley.

Rudolph, K. D., & Hammen, C. (1999). Age and gender as determinants of stress exposure, genderation, and reactions in youngsters: A transactional perspective. *Child Development, 70,* 660–677.

Ruff, H. A., & Lawson, K. R. (1990). Development of sustained, focused attention in young children during free play. *Developmental Psychology, 26,* 85–93.

Ruff, H. A., Lawson, K. R., Parrinello, R., & Weissberg, R. (1990). Long-term stability of individual differences in sustained attention in the early years. *Child Development, 61,* 60–75.

Ruff, H. A., & Rothbart, M. K. (1996). *Attention in early development.* New York: Oxford University Press.

Ruffman, T. (1999). Children's understanding of logical inconsistency. *Child Development, 70,* 887–895.

Ruffman, T., Perner, J., Naito, M., Parkin, L., & Clements, W. A. (1998). Older (but not younger) siblings facilitate false belief understanding. *Developmental Psychology, 34,* 161–174.

Ruffman, T., Perner, J., Olson, D. R., & Doherty, M. (1993). Reflecting on scientific thinking: Children's understanding of the hypothesis–evidence relation. *Child Development, 64,* 1617–1636.

Ruhm, C. J. (1996). Gender differences in employment behavior during late middle age. *Journal of Gerontology, 51B,* S11–S17.

Rumbaut, R. G. (1997). Ties that bind: Immigration and immigrant families in the United States. In A. Booth, A. C. Crouter, & N. Landale (Eds.), *Immigration and the family: Research and policy on U.S. immigrants* (pp. 3–46). Mahwah, NJ: Erlbaum.

Rumberger, R. W. (1990). Second chance for high school dropouts: Dropout recovery programs in the United States. In D. Inbar (Ed.), *Second chance in education: An interdisciplinary and international perspective* (pp. 227–250). Philadelphia: Falmer.

Runco, M. A. (1992). Children's divergent thinking and creative ideation. *Developmental Review, 12,* 233–264.

Russell, J. A. (1990). The preschooler's understanding of the causes and consequences of emotion. *Child Development, 61,* 1872–1881.

Russell, M. J., Cummings, B. J., Proffitt, B. F., Wysocki, C. J., Gilbert, A. N., & Cotman, C. W. (1993). Life span changes in the verbal categorization of odors. *Journal of Gerontology, 48,* P49–P53.

Russell, R. J. H., & Wells, P. A. (1994). Predictors of happiness in married couples. *Personality and Individual Differences, 17,* 313–321.

Rutter, M. (1987). Psychosocial resilience and protective mechanisms. *American Journal of Orthopsychiatry, 57,* 316–331.

Rutter, M. (1996). Maternal deprivation. In M. H. Bornstein (Ed.), *Handbook of parenting: Vol. 4. Applied and practical parenting* (pp. 3–31). Mahwah, NJ: Erlbaum.

Rutter, M., & the English and Romanian Adoptees Study Team. (1998). Developmental catch-up, and deficit, following adoption after severe global early privation. *Journal of Child Psychology and Psychiatry, 39,* 465–476.

Ryff, C. D. (1989). In the eye of the beholder: Views of psychological well-being among middle-aged and older adults. *Psychology and Aging, 4,* 195–210.

Ryff, C. D. (1991). Possible selves in adulthood and old age: A tale of shifting horizons. *Psychology and Aging, 6,* 286–295.

Ryff, C. D., Lee, Y. H., Essex, M. J., & Schmutte, P. S. (1994). My children and me: Midlife evaluations of grown children and of self. *Psychology and Aging, 9,* 195–205.

Ryff, C. D., & Migdal, S. (1984). Intimacy and generativity: Self-perceived transitions. *Signs: Journal of Women in Culture and Society, 9,* 470–481.

Ryff, C. D., Schmutte, P. S., & Lee, Y. H. (1996). How children turn out: Implications for parental self-evaluation. In C. D. Ryff & M. M. Seltzer (Eds.), *The parental experience in midlife* (pp. 383–422). Chicago: University of Chicago Press.

Ryynänen, M., Kirkinen, P., Mannermaa, A., & Saarikoski, S. (1995). Carrier diagnosis of the fragile X syndrome—A challenge in antenatal clinics. *American Journal of Obstetrics and Gynecology, 172,* 1236–1239.

Saarni, C. (1993). Socialization of emotion. In M. Lewis & J. M. Haviland (Eds.), *Handbook of emotions* (pp. 435–446). New York: Guilford.

Saarni, C., Mumme, D. L., & Campos, J. J. (1998). Emotional development: Action, communication, and understanding. In N. Eisenberg (Ed.), *Handbook of child psychology: Vol. 3. Social, emotional, and personality development* (5th ed., pp. 237–309). New York: Wiley.

Sacks, C. H., & Mergendoller, J. R. (1997). The relationship between teachers' theoretical orientation toward reading and student outcomes in kindergarten children with different initial reading abilities. *American Educational Research Journal, 34,* 721–739.

Sadeh, A. (1997). Sleep and melatonin in infants: A preliminary study. *Sleep, 20,* 185–191.

Sadler, T. W. (1995). *Langman's medical embryology* (7th ed.). Baltimore: Williams & Wilkins.

Safire, W. (1997, March 9). The young old. *New York Times Magazine,* p. 14.

Safman, P. C. (1988). Women from special populations: The challenge of reentry. In L. H. Lewis (Ed.), *Addressing the needs of returning women* (pp. 79–94). San Francisco: Jossey-Bass.

Safyer, A. W., Leahy, B. H., & Colan, N. B. (1995). The impact of work on adolescent development. *Families in Society, 76,* 38–45.

Sahni, R., Schulze, K. F., Stefanski, M., Myers, M. M., & Fifer, W. P. (1995). Methodological issues in coding sleep states in immature infants. *Developmental Psychobiology, 28,* 85–101.

Salapatek, P. (1975). Pattern perception in early infancy. In L. B. Cohen & P. Salapatek (Eds.), *Infant perception: From sensation to cognition* (pp. 133–248). New York: Academic Press.

Salthouse, T. A. (1984). Effects of age and skill in typing. *Journal of Experimental Psychology: General, 113,* 345–371.

Salthouse, T. A. (1985). Speed of behavior and its implications for cognition. In J. E. Birren & K. W. Schaie (Eds.), *Handbook of the psychology of aging* (2nd ed., pp. 400–426). New York: Van Nostrand Reinhold.

Salthouse, T. A. (1991a). Cognitive facets of aging well. *Generations, 51*(1), 35–38.

Salthouse, T. A. (1991b). *Theoretical perspectives in cognitive aging.* Hillsdale, NJ: Erlbaum.

Salthouse, T. A. (1993). Speed mediation of adult age differences in cognition. *Developmental Psychology, 29,* 722–738.

Salthouse, T. A. (1996). Constraints on theories of cognitive aging. *Psychonomic Bulletin and Review, 3,* 287–299.

Salthouse, T. A., & Babcock, R. L. (1991). Decomposing adult age differences in working memory. *Developmental Psychology, 27,* 763–776.

Salthouse, T. A., Fristoe, N., McGuthry, K. E., & Hambrick, D. Z. (1998). Relation of task switching to speed, age, and fluid intelligence. *Psychology and Aging, 13,* 445–461.

Salthouse, T. A., & Maurer, T. J. (1996). Aging, job performance, and career development. In J. E. Birren & K. W. Schaie (Eds.), *Handbook of the psychology of aging* (pp. 353–364). San Diego, CA: Academic Press.

Salthouse, T. A., & Meinz, E. J. (1995). Aging, inhibition, working memory, and speed. *Journal of Gerontology, 50,* P297–P306.

Salthouse, T. A., & Skovronek, E. (1992). Within-context assessment of working memory. *Journal of Gerontology, 47,* P110–P129.

Samarel, N. (1991). *Caring for life and death.* Washington, DC: Hemisphere.

Samarel, N. (1995). The dying process. In H. Wass & R. A. Neimeyer (Eds.), *Dying: Facing the facts* (3rd ed., pp. 89–116). Washington, DC: Taylor & Francis.

Sameroff, A. J., Seifer, R., Baldwin, A., & Baldwin, C. (1993). Stability of intelligence from preschool to adolescence: The influence of social and family risk factors. *Child Development, 64,* 80–97.

Sampson, R. J., & Laub, J. H. (1993). *Crime in the making: Pathways and turning points through life.* Cambridge, MA: Harvard University Press.

Samuels, N., & Samuels, M. (1996). *The new well pregnancy book.* New York: Summitt.

Samuelsson, S. M., Alfredson, B. B., Hagberg, B., Anonymous, Nordbeck, B., Brun, A., Gustafson, L., & Risberg, J. (1997). The Swedish Centenarian Study: A multidisciplinary study of five consecutive cohorts at the age of 100. *International Journal of Aging and Human Development, 45,* 223–253.

Sandberg, D. E., Brook, A. E., & Campos, S. P. (1994). Short stature: A psychosocial burden requiring growth hormone therapy? *Pediatrics, 94,* 832–840.

Sanderson, J. A., & Siegal, M. (1988). Conceptions of moral and social rules in rejected and nonrejected preschoolers. *Journal of Clinical Child Psychology, 17,* 66–72.

Sandman, C. A., Wadhwa, P., Hetrick, W., Porto, M., & Peeke, H. V. S. (1997). Human fetal heart rate dishabituation between thirty and thirty-two weeks gestation. *Child Development, 68,* 1031–1040.

Sandqvist, K. (1992). Sweden's sex-role scheme and commitment to gender equality. In S. Lewis, D. N. Izraeli, & H. Hottsmans (Eds.), *Dual-earner families: International perspective.* London: Sage.

Sanford, J. P. (1985). *Comprehension-level tasks in secondary classrooms.* Austin: Research and Development Center for Teacher Education, University of Texas at Austin.

Sankar, A. (1993). Images of home death and the elderly patient: Romantic versus real. *Generations, 27*(2), 59–63.

Sankaranarayanan, K. (1998). Ionizing radiation and genetic risks IX. Estimates of the frequencies of Mendelian diseases and spontaneous mutation rates in human populations: A 1998 perspective. *Mutation Research, 411,* 129–178.

Sansavini, A., Bertoncini, J., & Giovanelli, G. (1997). Newborns discriminate the rhythm of multisyllabic stressed words. *Developmental Psychology, 33,* 3–11.

Sanson, A. V., Pedlow, R., Cann, W., Prior, M., & Oberklaid, F. (1996). Shyness ratings: Stability and correlates in early childhood. *International Journal of Behavioural Development, 19,* 705–724.

Sansone, C., & Berg, C. A. (1993). Adapting to the environment across the life span: Different process or different inputs? *International Journal of Behavioral Development, 16,* 215–241.

Sarason, S. B. (1977). *Work, aging, and social change.* New York: Free Press.

Sasser-Coen, J. A. (1993). Qualitative changes in creativity in the second half of life: A life-span developmental perspective. *Journal of Creative Behavior, 27,* 18–27.

Satz, P. (1993). Brain reserve capacity on symptom onset after brain injury: A formulation and review of evidence for threshold theory. *Neuropsychology, 7,* 273–295.

Savin-Williams, R. C. (1996). Dating and romantic relationships among gay, lesbian, and bisexual youths. In R. C. Savin-Williams & K. M. Cohen (Eds.), *The lives of lesbians, gays, and bisexuals* (pp. 166–180). Fort Worth: Harcourt Brace.

Savin-Williams, R. C. (1998). *. . . . And then I became gay: Young men's stories.* New York: Routledge.

Saxe, G. B. (1988, August–September). Candy selling and math learning. *Educational Researcher, 17*(6), 14–21.

Scaramella, L. V., Conger, R. D., Simons, R. L., & Whitbeck, L. B. (1998). Predicting risk for pregnancy by late adolescence: A social contextual perspective. *Developmental Psychology, 34,* 1233–1245.

Scarr, S. (1985). Constructing psychology: Making facts and fables for our times. *American Psychologist, 40,* 499–512.

Scarr, S. (1996). Individuality and community: The contrasting role of the state in family life in the United States and Sweden. *Scandinavian Journal of Psychology, 37,* 93–102.

Scarr, S. (1997). Behavior-genetic and socialization theories of intelligence: Truce and reconciliation. In R. J. Sternberg & E. L. Grigorenko (Eds.), *Intelligence, heredity, and environment* (pp. 3–41). New York: Cambridge University Press.

Scarr, S. (1998). American child care today. *American Psychologist, 53,* 95–108.

Scarr, S., & McCartney, K. (1983). How people make their own environments: A theory of genotype environment effects. *Child Development, 54,* 424–435.

Scarr, S., Phillips, D. A., & McCartney, K. (1990). Facts, fantasies, and the future of child care in America. *Psychological Science, 1,* 26–35.

Scarr, S., & Weinberg, R. A. (1983). The Minnesota Adoption Studies: Genetic differences and malleability. *Child Development, 54,* 260–267.

Schachter, F. F., & Stone, R. K. (1985). Difficult sibling–easy sibling: Temperament and the within-family environment. *Child Development, 56,* 1335–1344.

Schaffer, J., & Kral, R. (1988). Adoptive families. In C. S. Chilman, E. W. Nunnally, & F. M. Cox (Eds.), *Variant family forms* (pp. 165–184). Newbury Park, CA: Sage.

Schaie, K. W. (1977/1978). Toward a stage theory of adult cognitive development. *Aging and Human Development, 8,* 129–138.

Schaie, K. W. (1988). Ageism in psychological research. *American Psychologist, 43,* 179–183.

Schaie, K. W. (1989). Individual differences in rate of cognitive change in adulthood. In V. L. Bengtson & K. W. Schaie (Eds.), *The course of later life: Research and reflections* (pp. 68–83). New York: Springer.

Schaie, K. W. (1994). The course of adult intellectual development. *American Psychologist, 49,* 304–313.

Schaie, K. W. (1996). *Intellectual development in adulthood: The Seattle Longitudinal Study.* New York: Cambridge University Press.

Schaie, K. W. (1998). The Seattle Longitudinal Studies of Adult Intelligence. In M. P. Lawton & T. A. Salthouse (Eds.), *Essential papers on the psychology of aging* (pp. 263–271). New York: New York University Press.

Schaie, K. W., & Willis, S. L. (1992). *Adult development and aging* (3rd ed.). New York: HarperCollins.

Schaie, K. W., & Willis, S. L. (1996). *Adult development and aging* (4th ed.). Boston: Addison-Wesley.

Schairer, C., Lubin, J., Troisi, R., Sturgeon, S., Brinton, L., & Hoover, R. (2000). Menopausal estrogen and estrogen-progestin replacement therapy and breast cancer risk. *Journal of the American Medical Association, 283,* 485–491.

Schauble, L. (1996). The development of scientific reasoning in knowledge-rich contexts. *Developmental Psychology, 32,* 102–119.

Scheidt, R. J., & Windley, P. G. (1985). The ecology of aging. In J. E. Birren & K. W. Schaie (Eds.), *Handbook of the psychology of aging* (pp. 245–258). New York: Van Nostrand Reinhold.

Scheier, M. F., & Carver, C. S. (1987). Dispositional optimism and physical well-being: The influence of generalized outcome expectancies on health. *Journal of Personality, 55,* 169–210.

Scherer, J. M., & Simon, R. J. (1999). *Euthanasia and the right to die: A comparative view.* Lanham, MD: Rowman & Littlefield.

Schiavi, R. C., Mandeli, J., & Schreiner-Engel, P. (1994). Sexual satisfaction in healthy aging men. *Journal of Sex and Marital Therapy, 20,* 3–13.

Schlaud, M., Eberhard, C., Trumann, B., Kleemann, W. J., Poets, C. F., Tietze, K. W., & Schwartz, F. W. (1999). Prevalence and determinants of prone sleeping position in infants: Results for two cross-sectional studies on risk factors for SIDS in Germany. *American Journal of Epidemiology, 150,* 51–57.

Schlegel, A., & Barry, H., III (1991). *Adolescence: An anthropological inquiry.* New York: Free Press.

Schlesinger, M., & Kronebusch, K. (1994). The sources of intergenerational burdens and tensions. In V. L. Bengtson & R. A. Harootyan (Eds.), *Intergenerational linkages: Hidden connections in American society* (pp. 185–209). New York: Springer.

Schneewind, K. A., & Ruppert, S. (1998). *Personality and family development: An intergenerational longitudinal comparison.* Mahwah, NJ: Erlbaum.

Schneider, B., & Stevenson, D. (1999). *The ambitious generation: America's teenagers, motivated but directionless.* New Haven, CT: Yale University Press.

Schneider, E. L. (1992). Biological theories of aging. *Generations, 16*(4), 7–10.

Schneider, W. (1993). Domain-specific knowledge and memory performance in children. *Educational Psychology Review, 5,* 257–274.

Schneider, W., & Bjorklund, D. F. (1998). Memory. In D. Kuhn & R. S. Siegler (Eds.), *Handbook of child psychology: Vol. 2. Cognition, perception, and language* (5th ed., pp. 467–521). New York: Wiley.

Schneider, W., & Pressley, M. (1997). *Memory development between two and twenty* (2nd ed.). Mahwah, NJ: Erlbaum.

Schnohr, P., Nyboe, J., Lange, P., & Jensen, G. (1998). Longevity and gray hair, baldness, facial wrinkles, and arcus senilis in 13,000 men and women: The Copenhagen City Heart Study. *Journal of Gerontology, 53,* M347–350.

Scholl, T. O., Heidiger, M. L., & Belsky, D. H. (1996). Prenatal care and maternal health during adolescent pregnancy: A review and meta-analysis. *Journal of Adolescent Health, 15,* 444–456.

Scholnick, E. K. (1995, Fall). Knowing and constructing plans. *SRCD Newsletter,* pp. 1–2, 17.

Schothorst, P. F., & van Engeland, H. (1996). Long-term behavioral sequelae of prematurity. *Journal of the American Academy of Child and Adolescent Psychiatry, 35,* 175–183.

Schroeder, K. A., Blood, L. L., & Maluso, D. (1993). Gender differences and similarities between male and female undergraduate students regarding expectations for career and family roles. *College Student Journal, 27,* 237–249.

Schroots, J., & Birren, J. (1990). Concept of time and aging in science. In J. E. Birren & K. W. Schaie (Eds.), *Handbook of the psychology of aging* (3rd ed., pp. 45–64). San Diego: Academic Press.

Schugens, M. M., Daum, I., Spindler, M., & Birbaumer, N. (1997). Differential effects of aging on explicit and implicit memory. *Aging, Neuropsychology, and Cognition, 4,* 33–44.

Schulman, K. A., Berlin, J. A., Harless, W., Kerner, J. F., Sistrunk, S., & Gersh, B. J. (1999). The effect of race and sex on physicians' recommendations for cardiac catheterization. *New England Journal of Medicine, 340,* 618–626.

Schulman, S. P., & Gerstenblith, G. (1989). Cardiovascular changes with aging: The response to exercise. *Journal of Cardiopulmonary Rehabilitation, 9,* 12–16.

Schulz, R., & Heckhausen, J. (1996). A life span model of successful aging. *American Psychologist, 51,* 702–714.

Schulz, R., & Aderman, D. (1979). Physicians' death anxiety and patient outcomes. *Omega, 9,* 327–332.

Schulz, R., & Curnow, C. (1988). Peak performance and age among superathletes: Track and field, swimming, baseball, tennis, and golf. *Journal of Gerontology, 43,* P113–P120.

Schunk, D. H., & Zimmerman, B. J. (Eds.). (1994). *Self-regulation of learning and performance.* Englewood Cliffs, NJ: Erlbaum.

Schwartz, J. E., Friedman, H. S., Tucker, J. S., Tomlinson-Keasey, C., Wingard, D. L., & Criqui, M. H. (1995). Childhood sociodemographic and psychosocial factors as predictors of longevity across the lifespan. *American Journal of Public Health, 85,* 1237–1245.

Schwartz, S. T., & Zimmermann, B. (1999). Update on osteoarthritis. *Medical and Health Research and Intervention, 82,* 321–324.

Schwarz, B. (1996). *Nursing home design: Consequences of employing the medical model.* New York: Garland.

Schwarzer, R. (1999). Self-regulatory processes in the adoption and maintenance of health behaviors. *Journal of Health Psychology, 4,* 115–127.

Schwebel, M., Maher, C. A., & Fagley, N. S. (1990). Introduction: The social role in promoting cognitive growth over the life span. In M. Schwebel, C. A. Maher, & N. S. Fagley (Eds.), *Promoting cognitive growth over the life span* (pp. 1–20). Hillsdale, NJ: Erlbaum.

Schweinhart, L. J., Barnes, H. V., & Weikart, D. P. (1993). Significant benefits: The High/Scope Perry Preschool Study through age 27. *Monographs of the High/Scope Educational Research Foundation* (No. 10). Ypsilanti, MI: High/Scope Press.

Scully, D., & Marolla, J. (1998). "Riding the bull at Gilley's": Convicted rapists describe the rewards of rape. In M. E. Odem & J. Clay-Warner (Eds.), *Confronting rape and sexual assault* (pp. 181–198). Wilmington, DE: Scholarly Resources.

Seal, D. W., & Ehrhardt, A. A. (1999). Heterosexual men's attitudes toward the female condom. *AIDS Education and Prevention, 11,* 93–106.

Sears, J. T. (1991). *Growing up gay in the South: Race, gender, and journeys of the spirit.* New York: Harrington Park Press.

Sears, P. S., & Barbie, A. H. (1977). Career and life satisfaction among Terman's gifted women. In J. C. Stanley, W. George, & C. Solano (Eds.), *The gifted and creative: Fifty year perspective* (pp. 154–172). Baltimore: Johns Hopkins University Press.

Sears, R. R., Maccoby, E. E., & Levin, H. (1957). *Patterns of child rearing.* New York: Harper & Row.

Sebald, H. (1986). Adolescents' shifting orientation toward parents and peers: A curvilinear trend over recent decades. *Journal of Marriage and the Family, 48,* 5–13.

Seefeldt, V. (1996). The concept of readiness applied to the acquisition of motor skills. In F. L. Smoll & R. E. Smith (Eds.), *Children and youth in sport: A biopsychological perspective* (pp. 49–56). Dubuque, IA: Brown & Benchmark.

Segal, B. M., & Stewart, J. C. (1996). Substance use and abuse in adolescence: An overview. *Child Psychiatry and Human Development, 26,* 193–210.

Seidman, E., Allen, L., Aber, J. L., Mitchell, C., & Feinman, J. (1994). The impact of school transitions in early adolescence on the self-system and perceived social context of poor urban youth. *Child Development, 65,* 507–522.

Seidman, E., & French, S. E. (1997). Normative school transitions among urban adolescents: When, where, and how to intervene. In H. J. Walberg, O. Reyes, & R. P. Weissberg (Eds.), *Children and youth: Interdisciplinary perspectives* (pp. 166–189). Thousand Oaks, CA: Sage.

Seifer, R., & Schiller, M. (1995). The role of parenting sensitivity, infant temperament, and dyadic interaction in attachment theory and assessment. In E. Waters, B. E. Vaughn, G. Posada, & K. Kondo-Ikemura (Eds.), *Caregiving, cultural, and cognitive perspectives on secure-base behavior and working models: New growing points of attachment theory and research. Monographs of the Society for Research in Child Development, 60*(2–3, Serial No. 244).

Seifer, R., Schiller, M., Sameroff, A. J., Resnick, S., & Riordan, K. (1996). Attachment, maternal sensitivity, and infant temperament during the first year of life. *Developmental Psychology, 32,* 12–25.

Seippel, L., & Backstrom, T. (1998). Luteal-phase estradiol relates to symptom severity in patients with premenstrual syndrome. *Journal of Clinical Endocrinology and Metabolism, 83,* 1988–1992.

Seitz, V., & Apfel, N. H. (1993). Adolescent mothers and repeated childbearing: Effects of a school-based intervention program. *American Journal of Orthopsychiatry, 63,* 572–581.

Seitz, V., & Apfel, N. H. (1994). Effects of a school for pregnant students on the incidence of low-birthweight deliveries. *Child Development, 65,* 666–676.

Seligman, L. (1994). *Developmental career counseling and assessment* (2nd ed.). Thousand Oaks, CA: Sage.

Seligman, M. E. P. (1975). *Helplessness: On depression, development, and death.* San Francisco: Freeman.

Seligman, M. E. P. (1991). *Learned optimism.* New York: Knopf.

Selikowitz, M. (1997). *Down syndrome: The facts* (2nd ed.). Oxford, UK: Oxford University Press.

Selman, R. L. (1976). Social-cognitive understanding: A guide to educational and clinical practice. In T. Lickona (Ed.), *Moral development and behavior: Theory, research, and social issues* (pp. 299–316). New York: Holt, Rinehart and Winston.

Selman, R. L. (1980). *The growth of interpersonal understanding.* New York: Academic Press.

Selman, R. L., & Byrne, D. F. (1974). A structural-developmental analysis of levels of role taking in middle childhood. *Child Development, 45,* 803–806.

Seltzer, M. M., & Ryff, C. D. (1994). Parenting across the life span: The normative and nonnormative cases. In D. L. Featherman, R. M. Lerner, & M. Perlmutter (Eds.), *Lifespan development and behavior* (pp. 1–40). Hillsdale, NJ: Erlbaum.

Selwyn, P. A. (1996). Before their time: A clinician's reflections on death and AIDS. In H. M. Spiro, M. G. M. Curnen, & L. P. Wandel (Eds.), *Facing death: Where culture, religion, and medicine meet* (pp. 33–37). New Haven, CT: Yale University Press.

Serbin, L. A., Powlishta, K. K., & Gulko, J. (1993). The development of sex typing in middle childhood. *Monographs of the Society for Research in Child Development, 58*(2, Serial No. 232).

Serdula, M., Ivery, D., Coates, R. J., Freedman, D. S., Williamson, D. F., & Byers, T. (1993). Do obese children become obese adults? A review of the literature. *Preventive Medicine, 22,* 167–177.

Shagle, S. C., & Barber, B. K. (1993). Effects of family, marital, and parent–child conflict on adolescent self-derogation and suicidal ideation. *Journal of Marriage and the Family, 55,* 964–974.

Shainess, N. (1961). A re-evaluation of some aspects of femininity through a study of menstruation: A preliminary report. *Comparative Psychiatry, 2,* 20–26.

Shantz, C. U. (1987). Conflicts between children. *Child Development, 58,* 283–305.

Shapiro, L. R., Crawford, P. B., Clark, M. J., Pearson, D. L., Raz, J., & Huenemann, R. (1984). Obesity prognosis: A longitudinal study of children from the age of 6 months to 9 years. *American Journal of Public Health, 74,* 968–972.

Shaver, P., Furman, W., & Buhrmester, D. (1985). Transition to college: Network changes, social skills, and loneliness. In S. Duck & D. Perlman (Eds.), *Understanding personal relationships: An interdisciplinary approach* (pp. 193–219). London: Sage.

Shaver, P. R., & Brennan, K. A. (1992). Attachment styles and the "big five" personality traits: Their connections with each other and with romantic relationship outcomes. *Personality and Social Psychology Bulletin, 18,* 536–545.

Shedler, J., & Block, J. (1990). Adolescent drug use and psychological health: A longitudinal inquiry. *American Psychologist, 45,* 612–630.

Shephard, R. J., & Shek, P. N. (1995). Exercise, aging and immune function. *International Journal of Sports Medicine, 16,* 1–6.

Sherman, D. K., Iacono, W. G., & McGue, M. K. (1997). Attention-deficit hyperactivity disorder dimensions: A twin study of inattention and impulsivity–hyperactivity. *Journal of the American Academy of Child and Adolescent Psychiatry, 36,* 745–753.

Sherman, E. (1993). Mental health and successful adaptation in later life. *Generations, 17*(1), 43–46.

Sheth, S. S., & Malpani, A. N. (1997). Inappropriate use of new technology—impact on women's health. *International Journal of Gynecology and Obstetrics, 58,* 159–165.

Shields, P. J., & Rovee-Collier, C. K. (1992). Long-term memory for context-specific category information at six months. *Child Development, 63,* 245–259.

Shiloh, S. (1996). Genetic counseling: A developing area of interest for psychologists. *Professional Psychology: Research and Practice, 27,* 475–486.

Shimamura, A. P., Berry, J. M., Mangels, J. A., Rusting, C. L., & Jurica, P. J. (1995). Memory and cognitive abilities in university professors: Evidence for sucessful aging. *Psychological Science, 6,* 271–277.

Shock, N. W. (1977). Biological theories of aging. In J. E. Birren & K. W. Schaie (Eds.), *Handbook of the psychology of aging* (pp. 103–115). New York: Van Nostrand Reinhold.

Shostak, A. B. (1987). Singlehood. In M. B. Sussmann & S. K. Steinmetz (Eds.), *Handbook of marriage and the family* (pp. 355–367). New York: Plenum.

Shuchter, S. R., & Zisook, S. (1995). The course of normal grief. In M. S. Stroebe, W. Stroebe, & R. O. Hansson (Eds.), *Handbook of bereavement* (pp. 44–61). Cambridge: Cambridge University Press.

Shulman, S., Elicker, J., & Sroufe, A. (1994). Stages of friendship growth in preadolescence as related to attachment history. *Journal of Social and Personal Relationships, 11,* 341–361.

Shumow, L. (1998). Contributions of parent education to adult development. In C. M. Smith & T. Pourchot (Eds.), *Adult learning and development: Perspectives from educational psychology* (pp. 239–255). Mahwah, NJ: Erlbaum.

Shure, M. B. (1997). Interpersonal cognitive problem solving: Primary prevention of early high-risk behaviors in the preschool and primary years. In G. W. Albee & T. P. Gullotta (Eds.), *Primary prevention works* (pp. 167–188). Thousand Oaks, CA: Sage.

Shurtleff, D. B., & Lemire, R. J. (1995). Epidemiology, etiologic factors, and prenatal diagnosis of open spinal dysraphism. *Neurosurgery Clinics of North America, 6,* 183–193.

Shweder, R. A. (1996). True ethnography: The lore, the law, and the lure. In R. Jessor, A. Colby, & R. A. Shweder (Eds.), *Ethnography and human development* (pp. 15–52). Chicago: University of Chicago Press.

Shweder, R. A., Goodnow, J., Hatano, G., LeVine, R. A., Markus, H., & Miller, P. (1998). The cultural psychology of development: One mind, many mentalities. In R. M. Lerner (Ed.), *Handbook of child psychology: Vol. 1. Theoretical models of human development* (5th ed., pp. 865–937). New York: Wiley.

Shweder, R. A., Mahapatra, M., & Miller, J. G. (1990). Culture and moral development. In J. Stigler, R. A. Shweder, & G. Herdt (Eds.), *Cultural psychology: Essays on comparative human development* (pp. 130–204). New York: Cambridge University Press.

Siegel, B. (1996, Spring). Is the emperor wearing clothes? Social policy and the empirical support for full inclusion of children with disabilities in the preschool and early elementary school grades. *Social Policy Report of the Society for Research in Child Development, 10*(2–3), 2–17.

Siegler, R. S. (1995). How does change occur: A microgenetic study of number conservation. *Cognitive Psychology, 28,* 225–273.

Siegler, R. S. (1996). *Emerging minds: The process of change in children's thinking.* New York: Oxford University Press.

Siegler, R. S. (1998). *Children's thinking* (3rd ed.). Upper Saddle River, NJ: Prentice-Hall.

Sierra, J., & Kaminski, R. (1995). *Children's traditional games.* Phoenix, AZ: Oryx.

Sigman, M. (1995). Nutrition and child development: More food for thought. *Current Directions in Psychological Science, 4,* 52–55.

Sigman, M., Cohen, S. E., & Beckwith, L. (1997). Why does infant attention predict adolescent intelligence? *Infant Behavior and Development, 20,* 133–140.

Sigman, M. D., Kasari, C., Kwon, J. H., & Yirmiya, N. (1992). Responses to the negative emotions of others by autistic, mentally retarded, and normal children. *Child Development, 63,* 786–807.

Signorella, M., & Liben, L. S. (1984). Recall and reconstruction of gender-related pictures: Effects of attitude, task difficulty, and age. *Child Development, 55,* 393–405.

Silver, M., Newell, K., Hyman, B., Growdon, J., Hedley-White, E. T., & Perls, T. (1998). Unraveling the mystery of cognitive changes in old age: Correlation of neuropsychological evaluation with neuropathological findings in the extreme old. *International Psychogeriatrics, 10,* 25–41.

Silverberg, S. B. (1996). Parents' well-being at their children's transition to adolescence. In C. D. Ryff & M. M. Seltzer (Eds.), *The parental experience in midlife* (pp. 215–254). Chicago: University of Chicago Press.

Silverman, E., Range, L., & Overholser, J. (1994). Bereavement from suicide as compared to other forms of bereavement. *Omega, 30,* 41–51.

Silverman, P. R., & Nickman, S. L. (1996). Children's construction of their dead parents. In D. Klass, P. R. Silverman, & S. L. Nickman (Ed.), *Continuing bonds: New understandings of grief* (pp. 73–86). Washington, DC: Taylor & Francis.

Silverman, P. R., & Worden, J. M. (1992). Children's reactions in the early months after the death of a parent. *American Journal of Orthopsychiatry, 62,* 93–104.

Silverman, W. K., La Greca, A. M., & Wasserstein, S. (1995). What do children worry about? Worries and their relation to anxiety. *Child Development, 66,* 671–686.

Silverstein, M., & Bengtson, V. L. (1991). Do close parent–child relations reduce the mortality risk of older parents? *Journal of Health and Social Behavior, 32,* 382–395.

Silverstein, M., & Chen, X. (1999). The impact of acculturation in Mexican American families on the quality of adult grandchild–grandparent relationships. *Journal of Marriage and the Family, 61,* 188–198.

Silverstein, M., Chen, X., & Heller, K. (1996). Too much of a good thing? Intergenerational social support and the psychological well-being of older parents. *Journal of Marriage and the Family, 58,* 970–982.

Silverstein, M., & Long, J. D. (1998). Trajectories of grandparents' perceived solidarity with adult grandchildren: A growth curve analysis over 23 years. *Journal of Marriage and the Family, 60,* 912–923.

Silverstein, M., & Parrott, T. M. (1997). Attitudes toward public support of the elderly: Does early involvement with grandparents moderate generational tensions? *Research on Aging, 19,* 108–132.

Simmons, R. G., Black, A., & Zhou, Y. (1991). African-American versus white children and the transition to junior high school. *American Journal of Education, 99,* 481–520.

Simmons, R. G., & Blyth, D. A. (1987). *Moving into adolescence.* New York: Aldine de Gruyter.

Simon, R., Alstein, H., & Melli, M. S. (1994). *The case for transracial adoption.* Washington, DC: American University Press.

Simoneau, G. G., & Leibowitz, H. W. (1996). Posture, gait, and falls. In J. Birren & K. W. Schaie (Eds.), *Handbook of the psychology of aging* (4th ed., pp. 204–217). San Diego: Academic Press.

Simons, R. L., & Chao, W. (1996). Conduct problems. In R. L. Simons & Associates (Eds.), *Understanding differences between divorced and intact families* (pp. 125–143). Thousand Oaks, CA: Sage.

Simons, R. L., & Johnson, C. (1996). Mother's parenting. In R. L. Simons & Associates (Eds.), *Understanding differences between divorced and intact families* (pp. 45–63). Thousand Oaks, CA: Sage.

Simons, R. L., Lorenz, F. O., Conger, R. D., & Wu, C.-I. (1992). Support from spouse as a mediator and moderator of the disruptive influence of economic strain on parenting. *Child Development, 63,* 1282–1301.

Simons, R. L., Lorenz, F. O., Wu, C.-I., & Conger, R. D. (1993). Social network and marital support as mediators and moderators of the impact of stress and depression on parental behavior. *Developmental Psychology, 29,* 368–381.

Simons, R. L., Whitbeck, L. B., Conger, R. D., & Wu, C.-I. (1991). Intergenerational transmission of harsh parenting. *Developmental Psychology, 27,* 159–171.

Simons, R. L., Wu, C., Conger, R. D., & Lorenz, F. O. (1994). Two routes to delinquency: Differences between early and late starters in the impact of parenting and deviant peers. *Criminology, 32,* 247–274.

Simonton, D. K. (1988). Age and creative productivity: What do we know after a century of research? *Psychological Bulletin, 104,* 251–267.

Simonton, D. K. (1991). Creative productivity through the adult years. *Generations, 15*(2), 13–16.

Simpson, J. A., Rholes, W. S., & Nelligan, J. S. (1992). Support-seeking and support-giving within couple members in an anxiety-provoking situation: The role of attachment styles. *Journal of Personality and Social Psychology, 62,* 434–446.

Simpson, S. A., & Harding. A. E. (1993). Predictive testing for Huntington's disease after the gene. *Journal of Medical Genetics, 30,* 1036–1038.

Singer, D. G., & Singer, J. L. (1990). *The house of make-believe.* Cambridge, MA: Harvard University Press.

Singer, J. L., & Singer, D. G. (1998). "Barney and Friends" as entertainment and education: Evaluating the quality and effectiveness of a television series for preschool children. In J. K. Asamen & G. L. Berry (Eds.), *Research paradigms, television, and social behavior* (pp. 305–367). Thousand Oaks, CA: Sage.

Sinnott, J. D. (1989). A model for solution of ill-structured problems: Implications for everyday and abstract problem solving. In J. D. Sinnott (Ed.), *Everyday problem solving: Theory and applications* (pp. 72–99). New York: Praeger.

Sinnott, J. D. (1998). *The development of logic in adulthood: Postformal thought and its applications.* New York: Plenum.

Sivard, R. L. (1996). *World military and social expenditures* (16th ed.). Leesburg, VA: WMSE.

Skinner, B. F. (1983). Intellectual self-management in old age. *American Psychologist, 38,* 239–244.

Skinner, E. A. (1995). *Perceived control, motivation, and coping.* Thousand Oaks, CA: Sage.

Skinner, E. A., & Belmont, M. J. (1993). Motivation in the classroom: Reciprocal effects of teacher behavior and student engagement across the school year. *Journal of Educational Psychology, 85,* 571–581.

Skinner, E. A., Zimmer-Gembeck, M. J., & Connell, J. P. (1998). Individual differences and the development of perceived control. *Monographs of the Society for Research in Child Development, 63*(2–3, Serial No. 254).

Slaby, R. G., & Frey, K. S. (1975). Development of gender constancy and selective attention to same-sex models. *Child Development, 46,* 849–856.

Slade, A., Belsky, J., Aber, J. L., & Phelps, J. L. (1999). Mothers' representations of their relationships with their toddlers: Links to adult attachment and observed mothering. *Developmental Psychology, 35,* 611–619.

Slater, A., Brown, E., Mattock, A., & Bornstein, M. H. (1996). Continuity and change in habituation in the first 4 months from birth. *Journal of Reproductive and Infant Psychology, 14,* 187–194.

Slobin, D. I. (1985). Crosslinguistic evidence for language-making capacity. In D. I. Slobin (Ed.), *The crosslinguistic study of language acquisition: Vol. 2. Theoretical issues* (pp. 1157–1256). Hillsdale, NJ: Erlbaum.

Small, B. J., & Bäckman, L. (1997). Cognitive correlates of mortality: Evidence from a population-based sample of very old adults. *Psychology and Aging, 12,* 309–313.

Small, B. J., & Bäckman, L. (1999). Time to death and cognitive performance. *Current Directions in Psychological Science, 8,* 168–172.

Small, B. J., Dixon, R. A., Hultsch, D. F., & Hertzog, C. (1999). Longitudinal changes in quantitative and qualitative indicators of word and story recall in young–old and old–old adults. *Journal of Gerontology, 54B,* P107–P115.

Smetana, J. G., & Asquith, P. (1994). Adolescents' and parents' conceptions of parental authority and personal autonomy. *Child Development, 65,* 1147–1162.

Smetana, J. G., & Braeges, J. L. (1990). The development of toddlers' moral and conventional judgments. *Merrill-Palmer Quarterly, 36,* 329–346.

Smiley, P. A., & Dweck, C. S. (1994). Individual differences in achievement goals among young children. *Child Development, 65,* 1723–1743.

Smith, B. A., & Blass, E. M. (1996). Taste-mediated calming in premature, preterm, and full-term human infants. *Developmental Psychology, 32,* 1084–1089.

Smith, D. (1993a). *Human longevity.* New York: Oxford University Press.

Smith, D. B., & Moen, P. (1998). Spousal influence on retirement: His, her, and their perceptions. *Journal of Marriage and the Family, 60,* 734–744.

Smith, D. C. (1993b). The terminally ill patient's right to be in denial. *Omega, 27,* 115–121.

Smith, J., & Baltes, M. M. (1998). The role of gender in very old age: Profiles of functioning and everyday life patterns. *Psychology and Aging, 13,* 676–695.

Smith, J., & Baltes, P. B. (1992). A life-span perspective on thinking and problem-solving. In M. Schwebel, C. A. Maher, & N. S. Fagley (Eds.), *Promoting cognitive growth over the life span* (pp. 47–69). Hillsdale, NJ: Erlbaum.

Smith, J., & Baltes, P. B. (1999). Life-span perspectives on development. In M. H. Bornstein & M. E. Lamb (Eds.), *Developmental psychology: An advanced textbook* (4th ed., pp. 275–311). Mahwah, NJ: Erlbaum.

Smith, J., & Prior, M. (1995). Temperament and stress resilience in school-age children: A within-families study. *Journal of the American Academy of Child and Adolescent Psychiatry, 34,* 168–179.

Smith, J., Staudinger, U. M., & Baltes, P. B. (1994). Occupational settings facilitating wisdom-related knowledge: The sample case of clinical psychologists. *Journal of Consulting and Clinical Psychology, 66,* 989–999.

Smith, K. E., Landry, S. H., Swank, P. R., Baldwin, C. D., Denson, S. E., & Wildin, S. (1996). The relation of medical risk and maternal stimulation with preterm infants' development of cognitive, language and daily living skills. *Journal of Child Psychology and Psychiatry, 37,* 855–864.

Smith, P. (1991). Introduction: The study of grandparenthood. In P. K. Smith (Ed.), *The psychology of grandparenthood:*

An international perspective (pp. 1–16). London: Routledge.

Smith, R. E., & Smoll, F. L. (1997). Coaching the coaches: Youth sports as a scientific and applied behavior setting. *Current Directions in Psychological Science, 6,* 16–21.

Smith, S. (Ed.). (1995). Two-generation programs for families in poverty: A new intervention strategy. *Advances in applied developmental psychology* (Vol. 9). Norwood, NJ: Ablex.

Smith, W., Mitchell, P., Webb, K., & Leeder, S. R. (1999). Dietary antioxidants and age-related maculopathy: The Blue Mountains Eye Study. *Ophthalmology, 106,* 761–767.

Smoll, F. L., & Smith, R. E. (Eds.). (1996). *Children and youth in sport: A biopsychological perspective.* Dubuque, IA: Brown & Benchmark.

Smolucha, L., & Smolucha, F. (1998). The social origins of mind: Post-Piagetian perspectives on pretend play. In O. N. Saracho & B. Spodek (Eds.), *Multiple perspectives on play in early childhood education* (pp. 34–58). Albany: State University of New York Press.

Snarey, J. (1995). In a communitarian voice: The sociological expansion of Kohlbergian theory, research, and practice. In W. M. Kurtines & J. L. Gewirtz (Eds.), *Moral development: An introduction* (pp. 109–134). Boston: Allyn and Bacon.

Snarey, J., Son, L., Kuehne, V. S., Hauser, S., & Vaillant, G. (1987). The role of parenting in men's psychosocial development: A longitudinal study of early adulthood infertility and midlife generativity. *Developmental Psychology, 23,* 593–603.

Snarey, J. R., Reimer, J., & Kohlberg, L. (1985). The development of social– moral reasoning among kibbutz adolescents: A longitudinal cross-cultural study. *Developmental Psychology, 21,* 3–17.

Snidman, N., Kagan, J., Riordan, L., & Shannon, D. C. (1995). Cardiac function and behavioral reactivity. *Psychophysiology, 32,* 199–207.

Society for Research in Child Development (1993). Ethical standards for research with children. In *Directory of Members* (pp. 337–339). Ann Arbor, MI: Author.

Sodian, B., Taylor, C., Harris, P. L., & Perner, J. (1991). Early deception and the child's theory of mind: False trails and genuine markers. *Child Development, 62,* 468–483.

Sohal, R. S., & Weindruch, R. (1996). Oxidative stress, caloric restriction, and aging. *Science, 273,* 59–63.

Soken, H. H., & Pick, A. D. (1992). Intermodal perception of happy and angry expressive behaviors by seven-month-old infants. *Child Development, 63,* 787–795.

Solomon, J. C., & Marx, J. (1995). "To grandmother's house we go": Health and school adjustment of children raised solely by grandparents. *Gerontologist, 35,* 386–394.

Somary, K., & Stricker, G. (1998). Becoming a grandparent: A longitudinal study of expectations and early experiences as a function of sex and lineage. *Gerontologist, 38,* 53–61.

Sonenstein, F. L., Pleck, J. H., & Ku, L. C. (1991). Levels of sexual activity among adolescent males in the United States. *Family Planning Perspectives, 23,* 162–167.

Sonnenschein, S. (1986). Development of referential communication skills: How familiarity with a listener affects a speaker's production of redundant messages. *Developmental Psychology, 22,* 549–552.

Sontag, S. (1979). The double standard of aging. In J. Williams (Ed.), *Psychology of women* (pp. 462–478). San Diego, CA: Academic Press.

Sorce, J., Emde, R., Campos, J., & Klinnert, M. (1985). Maternal emotional signaling: Its effect on the visual cliff behavior of 1-year-olds. *Developmental Psychology, 21,* 195–200.

Sorensen, T. I. A., Nielsen, G. G., Andersen, P. K., & Teasdale, T. W. (1988). Genetic and environmental influences on premature death in adult adoptees. *New England Journal of Medicine, 318,* 727–732.

Sosa, R., Kennell, J., Klaus, M., Robertson, S., & Urrutia, J. (1980). The effect of a supportive companion on perinatal problems, length of labor, and mother-infant interaction. *New England Journal of Medicine, 303,* 597–600.

Southard, B. (1985). Interlimb movement control and coordination in children. In J. E. Clark & J. E. Humphrey (Eds.), *Motor development* (Vol. 1, pp. 55–66). Princeton, NJ: Princeton Books.

Southern Medical Association. (1999). Proceedings, SMA's Second Conference on Osteoporosis: Diagnosis, management, and prevention. *Southern Medical Journal, 92,* 1116–1133.

Sowers, M. R., & La Pietra, M. T. (1995). Menopause: Its epidemiology and potential association with chronic diseases. *Epidemiologic Reviews, 17,* 287–302.

Speake, D. L. (1987). Health promotion activities and the well elderly. *Health Values, 11,* 25–30.

Speece, M. W., & Brent, S. B. (1996). The development of children's understanding of death. In C. A. Corr & D. M. Corr (Eds.), *Handbook of childhood death and bereavement* (pp. 29–50). New York: Springer.

Speicher, B. (1994). Family patterns of moral judgment during adolescence and early adulthood. *Developmental Psychology, 30,* 624–632.

Spelke, E. S. (1987). The development of intermodal perception. In P. Salapatek & L. Cohen (Eds.), *Handbook of infant perception: Vol. 2. From perception to cognition* (pp. 233–273). Orlando, FL: Academic Press.

Spelke, E. S., Breinlinger, K., Macomber, J., & Jacobson, K. (1992). Origins of knowledge. *Psychological Review, 99,* 605–632.

Spelke, E. S., & Newport, E. L. (1998). Nativism, empiricism, and the development of knowledge. In R. M. Lerner (Ed.), *Handbook of child psychology: Vol. 1. Theoretical models of human development* (5th ed., pp. 199–254). New York: Wiley.

Spence, M. J., & DeCasper, A. J. (1987). Prenatal experience with low-frequency maternal voice sounds influences neonatal perception of maternal voice samples. *Infant Behavior and Development, 10,* 133–142.

Spencer, P. E., Bodner-Johnson, B. A., & Gutfreund, M. K. (1992). Interacting with infants with a hearing loss: What can we learn from mothers who are deaf? *Journal of Early Intervention, 16,* 64–78.

Spencer, P. E., & Lederberg, A. (1997). Different modes, different models: Communication and language of young deaf children and their mothers. In L. B. Adamson & M. Romski (Eds.), *Communication and language acquisition: Discoveries from atypical development* (pp. 203–230). Baltimore, MD: Paul H. Brookes.

Spencer, P. E., & Meadow-Orlans, K. P. (1996). Play, language, and maternal responsiveness: A longitudinal study of deaf and hearing infants. *Child Development, 67,* 3176–3191.

Spencer, W. D., & Raz, N. (1995). Differential effects of aging on memory for context and context: A meta-analysis. *Psychology and Aging, 10,* 527–539.

Sperduto, R. D., Hiller, R., Podgor, M. J., Freidlin, V., Milton, R. C., Wolf, P. A., Myers, R. H., Dagostine, R. B., Roseman, M. J., Stockman, M. E., & Wilson, P. W. (1996). Familial aggregation and prevalence of myopia in the Framingham Offspring Eye Study. *Archives of Ophthalmology, 114,* 326–33.

Sperduto, R. D., Hu, T. S., Milton, R. C., Zhao, J. L., Everett, D. F., Cheng, Q. F., Blot, W. J., Bing, L., Taylor, P. R., & Li, J. Y. (1993). The Linxian cataract studies: Two nutrition intervention trials. *Archives of Opthalmology, 111,* 1246–1253.

Spina, R. J., Ogawa, T., Miller, T. R., Hohrt, W. M., & Ehsani, A. A. (1993). Effect of exercise training on left ventricular performance in older women free of cardiopulmonary disease. *American Journal of Cardiology, 71,* 99–104.

Spinetta, J., & Rigler, D. (1972). The child-abusing parent: A psychological review. *Psychological Bulletin, 77,* 296–304.

Spira, A. (1992). *Les comportements sexuels en France.* Paris: La documentation Française.

Spitz, R. A. (1945). Hospitalism: An inquiry into the genesis of psychiatric conditions in early childhood. *Psychoanalytic Study of the Child, 1,* 113–117.

Spitz, R. A. (1946). Anaclitic depression. *Psychoanalytic Study of the Child, 2,* 313–342.

Spitze, G., & Miner, S. (1992). Gender differences in adult–child contact among black elderly parents. *Gerontologist, 32,* 213–218.

Spock, B., & Parker, S. J. (1998). *Dr. Spock's baby and child care* (7th ed.). New York: Pocket Books.

Sprecher, S. (1999). "I love you more today than yesterday": Romantic partners' perceptions of changes in love and related affect over time. *Journal of Personality and Social Psychology, 76,* 46–53.

Sroufe, L. A. (1979). Socioemotional development. In J. D. Osofsky (Ed.), *Handbook of infant development* (pp. 462–516). New York: Wiley.

Sroufe, L. A. (1988). A developmental perspective on day care. *Early Childhood Research Quarterly, 3,* 283–292.

Sroufe, L. A., Egeland, B., & Kreutzer, T. (1990). The fate of early experience following developmental change: Longitudinal approaches to individual adaptation. *Child Development, 61,* 1363–1373.

Sroufe, L. A., & Waters, E. (1976). The ontogenesis of smiling and laughter: A perspective on the organization of development in infancy. *Psychological Review, 83,* 173–189.

Sroufe, L. A., & Wunsch, J. P. (1972). The development of laughter in the first year of life. *Child Development, 43,* 1324–1344.

Stahl, S. A. (1992). Saying the "P" word: Nine guidelines for effective phonics instruction. *The Reading Teacher, 45,* 618–625.

Stahl, S. A. (1999). Why innovations come and go (and mostly go): The case of whole language. *Educational Research, 28*(6), 13–22.

Stahl, S. A., McKenna, M. C., & Pagnucco, J. R. (1994). The effects of whole-language instruction: An update and a reappraisal. *Educational Psychologist, 29,* 175–185.

Stamler, J., Stamler, R., Neaton, J. D., Wentworth, D., Daviglus, M. L., Garside, D., Dyer, A. R., Liu, K. A., & Greenland, P. (1999). Low risk-factor profile and long-term cardiovascular and noncardiovascular mortality and life expectancy: Findings for five large cohorts of young adult and middle-aged men and women. *Journal of the American Medical Association, 282,* 2012–2018.

Stanley, B., & Seiber, J. E. (Eds.). (1992). *Social research on children and adolescents: Ethical issues.* Newbury Park, CA: Sage.

Stanton, A. M. (1998). Grandparents' visitation rights and custody. *Child Custody, 7,* 409–422.

Starrels, M. E. (1994). Husbands' involvement in female gender-typed household chores. *Sex Roles, 31,* 473–491.

Stattin, H., & Magnusson, C. (1996). Leaving home at an early age among females. In J. A. Graber & J. S. Dubas (Eds.), *New directions for child development* (No. 71, pp. 53–69). San Francisco: Jossey-Bass.

Stattin, H., & Magnusson, D. (1990). *Pubertal maturation in female development.* Hillsdale, NJ: Erlbaum.

Staub, E. (1996). Cultural–societal roots of violence. *American Psychologist, 51,* 117–132.

Staudinger, U. M., Fleeson, W., & Baltes, P. B. (1999). Predictors of subjective physical health and global well-being: Similarities and differences between the United States and Germany. *Journal of Personality and Social Psychology, 76,* 305–319.

Staudinger, U. M., Maciel, A. G., Smith, J., & Baltes, P. B. (1998). What predicts wisdom-related performance? A first look at personality, intelligence, and facilitative experiential contexts. *European Journal of Personality, 12,* 1–17.

Staudinger, U. M., Smith, J., & Baltes, P. B. (1992). Wisdom-related knowledge in a life-review task: Age differences and the role of professional specialization. *Psychology and Aging, 7,* 271–281.

Steele, C. D., Wapner, R. J., Smith, J. B., Haynes, M. K., & Jackson, L. G. (1996). Prenatal diagnosis using fetal cells isolated from maternal blood: A review. *Clinical Obstetrics and Gynecology, 39,* 801–813.

Steinberg, L. (1984). The varieties and effects of work during adolescence. In M. Lamb, A. Brown, & B. Rogoff (Eds.), *Advances in developmental psychology* (pp. 1–37). Hillsdale, NJ: Erlbaum.

Steinberg, L., Darling, N. E., & Fletcher, A. C. (1995). Authoritative parenting and adolescent development: An ecological journey. In P. Moen, G. H. Elder, Jr., & K. Luscher (Eds.), *Examining lives in context* (pp. 423–466). Washington, DC: American Psychological Association.

Steinberg, L., Fletcher, A., & Darling, N. (1994). Parental monitoring and peer influences on adolescent substance use. *Pediatrics, 93,* 1060–1064.

Steinberg, L., Lamborn, S. D., Darling, N., Mounts, N. S., & Dornbusch, S. M. (1994). Over-time changes in adjustment and competence among adolescents from authoritative, authoritarian, indulgent, and neglectful families. *Child Development, 65,* 754–770.

Steinberg, L., & Silverberg, S. (1986). The vicissitudes of autonomy in early adolescence. *Child Development, 57,* 841–851.

Steinberg, L. D. (1987). The impact of puberty on family relations: Effects of pubertal status and pubertal timing. *Developmental Psychology, 23,* 451–460.

Steinberg, L. D. (1990). Interdependence in the family: Autonomy, conflict, and harmony in the parent–adolescent relationship. In S. S. Feldman & G. R. Elliott (Eds.), *At the threshold: The developing adolescent* (pp. 255–276). Cambridge, MA: Harvard University Press.

Steinberg, L. D., Fegley, S., & Dornbusch, S. (1993). Negative impact of part-time work on adolescent adjustment: Evidence from a longitudinal study. *Developmental Psychology, 29,* 171–180.

Steiner, J. E. (1979). Human facial expression in response to taste and smell stimulation. In H. W. Reese & L. P. Lipsitt (Eds.), *Advances in child development and behavior* (Vol. 13, pp. 257–295). New York: Academic Press.

Steinhardt, M. A. (1992). Physical education. In P. W. Jackson (Ed.), *Handbook of research on curriculum* (pp. 964–1001). New York: Macmillan.

Stenberg, C., & Campos, J. (1990). The development of anger expressions in infancy. In N. Stein, B. Leventhal, & T. Trabasso (Eds.), *Psychological and biological approaches to emotion* (pp. 247–282). Hillsdale, NJ: Erlbaum.

Stephens, M. A. P., & Franks, M. M. (1999). Parent care in the context of women's multiple roles. *Current Directions in Psychological Science, 8,* 149–152.

Stephens, M. A. P., Franks, M. M., & Atienza, A. A. (1997). Where two roles intersect: Spillover between parent care and employment. *Psychology and Aging, 12,* 30–37.

Stern, M., & Karraker, K. H. (1989). Sex stereotyping of infants: A review of gender labeling studies. *Sex Roles, 20,* 501–522.

Sternberg, K. J., Lamb, M. E., Greenbaum, C., Cicchetti, D., Dawaud, S., Cortes, R. M., Krispin, O., & Lorey, F. (1993). Effects of domestic violence on children's behavior problems and depression. *Developmental Psychology, 29,* 44–52.

Sternberg, R. J. (1985). *Beyond IQ: A triarchic theory of human intelligence.* New York: Cambridge University Press.

Sternberg, R. J. (1987). Liking versus loving: A comparative evaluation of theories. *Psychological Bulletin, 102,* 331–345.

Sternberg, R. J. (1988). Triangulating love. In R. J. Sternberg & M. L. Barnes (Eds.), *The psychology of love* (pp. 119–138). New Haven, CT: Yale University Press.

Sternberg, R. J. (1997). *Successful intelligence.* New York: Plume.

Sternberg, R. J., & Grigorenko, E. L. (Eds.). (1997). *Intelligence, heredity, and environ-*

ment. New York: Cambridge University Press.

Sternberg, R. J., & Lubart, T. I. (1991). Creating creative minds. *Phi Delta Kappan, 72*(8), 608–614.

Sternberg, R. J., & Lubart, T. I. (1995). *Defying the crowd.* New York: Basic Books.

Sterns, H. L., & Gray, J. H. (1999). Work, leisure, and retirement. In J. C. Cavanaugh & S. K. Whitbourne (Eds.), *Gerontology: An interdisciplinary perspective* (pp. 355–390). New York: Oxford University Press.

Stets, J. E., & Straus, M. A. (1990). Gender differences in reporting of marital violence and its medical and psychological consequences. In M. A. Straus & R. J. Gelles (Eds.), *Physical violence in American families: Risk factors and adaptations to violence in 8,145 families* (pp. 151–165). New Brunswick, NJ: Transaction.

Stevens, J. C., & Cruz, L. A. (1996). Spatial acuity of touch: Ubiquitous decline with aging revealed by repeated threshold testing. *Somatosensory and Motor Research, 13,* 1–10.

Stevens, J. C., Cruz, L. A., Hoffman, J. M., & Patterson, M. Q. (1995). Taste sensitivity and aging: High incidence of decline revealed by repeated threshold measures. *Chemical Senses, 20,* 451–459.

Stevens, J. C., Cruz, L. A., Marks, L. E., & Lakatos, S. (1998). A multimodal assessment of sensory thresholds in aging. *Journal of Gerontology, 53B,* P263–P272.

Stevens, J. C., Foulke, E., & Patterson, M. Q. (1996). Tactile acuity, aging, and Braille reading in long-term blind adults. *Journal of Experimental Psychology: Applied, 2,* 91–106.

Stevens, M. L. T. (1997, March–April). What Quinlan can tell Kevorkian about the right to die. *The Humanist, 57*(2), 10–14.

Stevenson, H. W. (1992, December). Learning from Asian schools. *Scientific American, 267*(6), 32–38.

Stevenson, H. W., Chen, C., & Lee, S.-Y. (1993). Mathematics achievement of Chinese, Japanese, and American children: Ten years later. *Science, 259,* 53–58.

Stevenson, H. W., & Lee, S.-Y. (1990). Contexts of achievement: A study of American, Chinese, and Japanese children. *Monographs of the Society for Research in Child Development, 55*(1–2, Serial No. 221).

Stevenson, M. R., & Black, K. N. (1995). *How divorce affects offspring: A research approach.* Dubuque, IA: Brown & Benchmark.

Stevenson, R., & Pollitt, C. (1987). The acquisition of temporal terms. *Journal of Child Language, 14,* 533–545.

Stewart, A. J., & Gold-Steinberg, S. (1990). Case studies of psychosocial development and political commitment. *Psychology of Women Quarterly, 14,* 543–566.

Stewart, A. J., & Healy, J. M. (1989). Linking individual development and social changes. *American Psychologist, 44,* 30–42.

Stewart, A. J., & Vandewater, E. A. (1992, August). *Combining tough and tender methods to study women's lives.* Paper presented at the annual meeting of the American Psychological Association, Washington, DC.

Stewart, A. J., & Vandewater, E. A. (1998). The course of generativity. In D. P. McAdams & E. de St. Aubin (Eds.), *Generativity and adult development* (pp. 75–100). Washington, DC: American Psychological Association.

Stewart, D. A. (1982). *Children with sex chromosome aneuploidy: Follow-up studies.* New York: Liss.

Stewart, R. B. (1983). Sibling attachment relationships: Child–infant interactions in the Strange Situation. *Developmental Psychology, 19,* 192–199.

Stewart, R. B., Moore, M. T., Marks, R. G., May, F. E., & Hale, W. E. (1993). *Driving cessation and accidents in the elderly: An analysis of symptoms, diseases, cognitive dysfunction and medications.* Washington, DC: AAA Foundation for Traffic Safety.

Stifter, C. A., Coulehan, C. M., & Fish, M. (1993). Linking employment to attachment: The mediating effects of maternal separation anxiety and interactive behavior. *Child Development, 64,* 1451–1460.

Stiles, J. (1998). The effects of early focal brain injury on lateralization of cognitive function. *Current Directions in Psychological Science, 7,* 21–26.

Stiles, J., Bates, E. A., Thai, D., Trauner, D., & Reilly, J. (2000). Linguistic, cognitive, and affective development in children with pre- and perinatal focal brain injury: A ten-year overview from the San Diego Longitudinal Project. In C. Rovee-Collier (Ed.), *Advances in infancy research: Vol. 13.* Norwood, NJ: Ablex.

Stillion, J. M. (1995). Death in the lives of adults: Responding to the tolling of the bell. In H. Wass & R. A. Neimeyer (Eds.), *Dying: Facing the facts* (pp. 303–322). New York: Taylor & Francis.

Stine-Morrow, E. A. L., & Miller, L. M. S. (1999). Basic cognitive processes. In J. C. Cavanaugh & S. K. Whitbourne (Eds.), *Gerontology: An interdisciplinary perspective* (pp.186–212). New York: Oxford University Press.

Stipek, D. (1995). The development of pride and shame in toddlers. In J. P. Tangney & K. W. Fischer (Eds.), *Self-conscious emotions* (pp. 237–252). New York: Guilford.

Stipek, D., & MacIver, D. (1989). Developmental change in children's assessment of intellectual competence. *Child Development, 60,* 531–538.

Stipek, D., Recchia, S., & McClintic, S. (1992). Self-evaluation in young children. *Monographs of the Society for Research in Child Development, 57* (1, Serial No. 226).

Stipek, D. J., & Byler, P. (1997). Early childhood education teachers: Do they practice what they preach? *Early Childhood Research Quarterly, 12,* 305–326.

Stipek, D. J., Feiler, R., Daniels, D., & Milburn, S. (1995). Effects of different instructional approaches on young children's achievement and motivation. *Child Development, 66,* 209–223.

Stipek, D. J., Gralinski, J. H., & Kopp, C. B. (1990). Self-concept development in the toddler years. *Developmental Psychology, 26,* 972–977.

Stith, S. M., & Farley, S. C. (1993). A predictive model of male spousal violence. *Journal of Family Violence, 8,* 183–201.

Stoch, M. B., Smythe, P. M., Moodie, A. D., & Bradshaw, D. (1982). Psychosocial outcome and CT findings after growth undernourishment during infancy: A 20-year developmental study. *Developmental Medicine and Child Neurology, 24,* 419–436.

Stocker, C., & Dunn, J. (1994). Sibling relationships in childhood and adolescence. In J. C. DeFries, R. Plomin, & D. W. Fulker (Eds.), *Nature and nurture in middle childhood* (pp. 214–232). Cambridge, MA: Blackwell.

Stodolsky, S. S. (1988). *The subject matters.* Chicago: University of Chicago Press.

Stoel-Gammon, C., & Otomo, K. (1986). Babbling development of hearing-impaired and normal hearing subjects. *Journal of Speech and Hearing Disorders, 51,* 33–41.

Stoneman, Z., Brody, G. H., & MacKinnon, C. E. (1986). Same-sex and cross-sex siblings: Activity choices, roles, behavior, and gender stereotypes. *Sex Roles, 15,* 495–511.

Stoney, C. M., & Engebretson, T. O. (1994). Anger and hostility: Potential mediators of the gender difference in coronary artery disease. In A. W. Siegman & T. W. Smith (Eds.), *Anger, hostility, and the heart* (pp. 215–238). Hillsdale, NJ: Erlbaum.

Strahan, G. W. (1997). An overview of nursing homes and their current residents: Data from the 1995 National Nursing Home Survey. *Advance Data* No. 280. Atlanta. GA: U.S. Centers for Disease Control and Prevention.

Strand, D. A. (1998). Civil liberties, civil rights, and stigma. In G. M. Herek (Ed.), *Sigma and sexual orientation* (pp. 108–137). Thousand Oaks, CA: Sage.

Strange, C. J. (1996). *Coping with arthritis in its many forms.* Washington, DC: U.S. Government Printing Office. (Reprint from *FDA Consumer Magazine.*)

Strassberg, Z., Dodge, K., Pettit, G. S., & Bates, J. E. (1994). Spanking in the home and children's subsequent aggression toward kindergarten peers. *Development and Psychopathology, 6,* 445–461.

Stratton, J. R., Levy, W. C., Cereueira, M. D., Schwartz, R. S., & Abrass, I. B. (1994). Cardiovascular responses to exercise: Effects of aging and exercise training in healthy men. *Circulation, 89,* 1648–1655.

Straus, M. A. (1999). The controversy over domestic violence by women: A methodological, theoretical, and sociology of science analysis. In X. B. Arriaga & S. Oskamp (Eds.), *Violence in intimate relationships* (pp.17–44). Thousand Oaks, CA: Sage.

Strayer, J. (1993). Children's concordant emotions and cognitions in response to observed emotions. *Child Development, 64,* 188–201.

Streissguth, A. (1997). *Fetal alcohol syndrome.* Baltimore: Paul H. Brookes.

Streissguth, A., Bookstein, F. L., & Barr, H. M. (1996). A dose-response study of the enduring effects of prenatal alcohol exposure: Birth to 14 years. In H.-L. Spohr & H.-C. Steinhausen (Eds.), *Alcohol, pregnancy and the developing child* (pp. 141–168). New York: Cambridge University Press.

Streissguth, A. P., Barr, H. M., Sampson, P. D., Darby, B. L., & Martin, D. C. (1989). IQ at age 4 in relation to maternal alcohol use and smoking during pregnancy. *Developmental Psychology, 25,* 3–11.

Streissguth, A. P., Treder, R., Barr, H. M., Shepard, T., Bleyer, W. A., Sampson, P. D., & Martin, D. G. (1987). Aspirin and acetaminophen use by pregnant women and subsequent child IQ and attention decrements. *Teratology, 35,* 211–219.

Streitmatter, J. L., & Pate, G. S. (1989). Identity status development and cognitive prejudice in early adolescents. *Journal of Early Adolescence, 9,* 142–152.

Strickland, C. J. (1997). Suicide among American Indian, Alaskan Native, and Canadian Aboriginal youth: Advancing the research agenda. *International Journal of Mental Health, 25,* 11–32.

Strittmatter, W. J., Saunders, A. M., Schmechel, D., Pericak-Vance, M., Enghild, J., Salvesen, G. S., & Roses, A. D. (1993). Apolipoprotein E: High-avidity binding to beta-amyloid and increased frequency of type 4 allele in late-onset familial Alzheimer disease. *Proceedings of the National Academy of Sciences, 90,* 1977–1981.

Strober, M., McCracken, J., & Hanna, G. (1990). Affective disorders. In R. M. Lerner, A. C. Petersen, & J. Brooks-Gunn (Eds.), *The encyclopedia of adolescence* (Vol. 1, pp. 18–25). New York: Garland.

Stroebe, W., Stroebe, M., Abakoumkin, G., & Schut, H. (1996). The role of loneliness and social support in adjustment to loss: A test of attachment versus stress theory. *Journal of Personality and Social Psychology, 70,* 1241–1249.

Stroebe, W., & Stroebe, M. S. (1993). Determinants of adjustment to bereavement in younger widows and widowers. In M. S. Stroebe, W. Stroebe, & R. O. Hansson (Eds.), *Handbook of bereavement* (pp. 208–226). New York: Cambridge University Press.

Stroh, L. K., Brett, J. M., & Reilly, A. H. (1996). Family structure, glass ceiling, and traditional explanations for the differential rate of turnover of female and male managers. *Journal of Vocational Behavior, 49,* 99–118.

Stryker, J., Coates, T. J., DeCarlo, P., Haynes-Sanstad, K., Shriver, M., & Makadon, H. J. (1995). Prevention of HIV infection: Looking back, looking ahead. *Journal of the American Medical Association, 273,* 1143–1148.

Stull, D., & Scarisbrick-Hauser, A. (1989). Never-married elderly. *Research on Aging, 11,* 124–139.

Stunkard, A. J., & Sørensen, T. I. A. (1993). Obesity and socioeconomic status—a complex relation. *New England Journal of Medicine, 329,* 1036–1037.

Stunkard, A. J., Sørenson, T. I. A., Hanis, C., Teasdale, T. W., Chakraborty, R., Schull, W. J., & Schulsinger, F. (1986). An adoption study of human obesity. *New England Journal of Medicine, 314,* 193–198.

Stylianos, S. K., & Vachon, M. L. S. (1993). The role of social support in bereavement. In M. S. Stroebe, W. Stroebe, & R. O. Hansson (Eds.), *Handbook of bereavement* (pp. 397–410). New York: Cambridge University Press.

Suarez-Orozco, C., & Suarez-Orozco, M. M. (1995). *Transformation: Immigration, family life, and achievement motivation among Latino adolescents.* Stanford, CA: Stanford University Press.

Subbotsky, E. V. (1994). Early rationality and magical thinking in preschoolers: Space and time. *British Journal of Developmental Psychology, 12,* 97–108.

Subrahmanyam, K., & Greenfield, P. M. (1996). Effect of video game practice on spatial skills in girls and boys. In P. M. Greenfield & R. R. Cocking (Eds.), *Interacting with video* (pp. 95–114). Norwood, NJ: Ablex.

Suitor, J. J., Pillemer, K., Keeton, S., & Robison, J. (1995). Aging parents and aging children: Determinants of relationships quality. In R. Blieszner & V. H. Bedford (Eds.), *Handbook of aging and the family* (pp. 223–242). Westport, CT: Greenwood Press.

Sullivan, M. A. (1995). May the circle be unbroken: The African-American experience of death, dying, and spirituality. In J. K. Parry & A. S. Ryan (Eds.), *A cross-cultural look at death, dying, and religion* (pp. 160–171). Chicago: Nelson-Hall.

Sullivan, M. L. (1993). Culture and class as determinants of out-of-wedlock childbearing and poverty during late adolescence. *Journal of Research on Adolescence, 3,* 295–316.

Sullivan, S. A., & Birch, L. L. (1990). Pass the sugar, pass the salt: Experience dictates preference. *Developmental Psychology, 26,* 546–551.

Sullivan, S. A., & Birch, L. L. (1994). Infant dietary experience and acceptance of solid foods. *Pediatrics, 93,* 271–277.

Suls, J., & Mullen, B. (1982). From the cradle to the grave: Comparison and self-evaluation across the life span. In J. Suls (Ed.), *Psychological perspectives on the self* (Vol. 1, pp. 97–128). Hillsdale, NJ: Erlbaum.

Sulzby, E. (1985). Children's emergent reading of favorite books: A developmental study. *Reading Research Quarterly, 20,* 458–481.

Suominen, H., Heikkinen, E., Parkatti, T., Forsberg, S., & Kiiskinen, A. (1980). Effect of lifelong physical training on functional aging in men. *Scandinavian Journal of the Society of Medicine, 14*(Suppl.), 225–240.

Super, C. M. (1981). Behavioral development in infancy. In R. H. Monroe, R. L. Monroe, & B. B. Whiting (Eds.), *Handbook of cross-cultural human development* (pp. 181–270). New York: Garland.

Super, C. M., & Harkness, S. (1982). The infant's niche in rural Kenya and metropolitan America. In L. L. Adler (Ed.), *Cross-cultural research at issue* (pp. 247–255). New York: Academic Press.

Super, D. (1980). A life-span, life-space approach to career development. *Journal of Vocational Behavior, 16,* 282–298.

Super, D. (1984). Career and life development. In D. Brown & L. Brooks (Eds.), *Career choice and development* (pp. 192–234). San Francisco: Jossey-Bass.

Sureau, C. (1997). Trials and tribulations of surrogacy: From surrogacy to parenthood. *Human Reproduction, 12,* 410–411.

Suzuki, L. A., & Valencia, R. R. (1997). Race–ethnicity and measured intelligence: Educational implications. *American Psychologist, 52,* 1103–1114.

Swain, S. O. (1992). Men's friendships with women: Intimacy, sexual boundaries, and the informant role. In P. M. Nardi (Eds.), *Men's friendships* (pp. 153–171). Newbury Park, CA: Sage.

Swanson, N. G., Piotrkowski, C. S., Keita, G. P., & Becker, A. B. (1997). Occupational stress and women's health. In S. J. Gallant, G. P. Keita, & R. Royak-Schaler (Eds.), *Health care for women* (pp. 147–159).

Washington, DC: American Psychological Association.

Swindell, R., & Thompson, J. (1995). An international perspective on the University of the Third Age. *Educational Gerontology, 21,* 429–447.

Szepkouski, G. M., Gauvain, M., & Carberry, M. (1994). The development of planning skills in children with and without mental retardation. *Journal of Applied Developmental Psychology, 15,* 187–206.

Szinovacz, M. (1998). Grandparents today: A demographic profile. *Gerontologist, 38,* 37–52.

Taddio, A., Katz, J., Ilersich, A. L., & Koren, G. (1997). Effect of neonatal circumcision on pain response during subsequent routine vaccination. *Lancet, 349,* 599–603.

Tager-Flusberg, H. (1997). Putting words together: Morphology and syntax in the preschool years. In J. B. Gleason (Ed.), *The development of language* (pp. 159–209). Boston: Allyn and Bacon.

Tager-Flusberg, H., & Sullivan, K. (1994). Predicting and explaining behavior: A comparison of autistic, mentally retarded, and normal children. *Journal of Child Psychology and Psychiatry, 35,* 1059–1079.

Takahashi, K. (1990). Are the key assumptions of the "Strange Situation" procedure universal? A view from Japanese research. *Human Development, 33,* 23–30.

Tamis-LeMonda, C. S., & Bornstein, M. H. (1989). Habituation and maternal encouragement of attention in infancy as predictors of toddler language, play, and representational competence. *Child Development, 60,* 738–751.

Tamis-LeMonda, C. S., & Bornstein, M. H. (1994). Specificity in mother–toddler language–play relations across the second year. *Developmental Psychology, 30,* 283–292.

Tamis-LeMonda, C. S., & Cabrera, N. (1999). Perspectives on father involvement: Research and policy. *Social Policy Report of the Society for Research in Child Development, 13*(2).

Tanner, J. M. (1990). *Foetus into man* (2nd ed.). Cambridge, MA: Harvard University Press.

Tardif, T., Gelman, S. A., & Xu, F. (1999). Putting the "noun bias" in context: A comparison of English and Mandarin. *Child Development, 70,* 620–635.

Tasker, F. L., & Richards, M. P. M. (1994). Adolescents' attitudes toward marriage and marital prospects after parental divorce: A review. *Journal of Adolescent Research, 9,* 340–362.

Taylor, M., & Carlson, S. M. (1997). The relation between individual differences in fantasy and theory of mind. *Child Development, 68,* 436–455.

Taylor, M. C., & Hall, J. A. (1982). Psychological androgyny: Theories, methods, and conclusions. *Psychological Bulletin, 92,* 347–366.

Taylor, R. D., & Roberts, D. (1995). Kinship support and maternal and adolescent well-being in economically disadvantaged African-American families. *Child Development, 66,* 1585–1597.

Tebbutt, J., Swanston, H., Oates, R. K., & O'Toole, B. I. (1997). Five years after child sexual abuse: Persisting dysfunction and problems of prediction. *Journal of the American Academy of Child and Adolescent Psychiatry, 36,* 330–339.

Tedder, J. L. (1991). Using the Brazelton neonatal assessment scale to facilitate the parent–infant relationship in a primary care setting. *Nurse Practitioner, 16,* 27–36.

Temple, C. M., & Carney, R. A. (1995). Patterns of spatial functioning in Turner's syndrome. *Cortex, 31,* 109–118.

Terestchenko, N. Y., Lyaginskaya, A. M., & Burtzeva, L. I. (1991). Stochastic, non-stochastic effects and some population-genetic characteristics in children of the critical group in period of basic organogenesis. In *The scientific and practical aspects of preservation of health of the people exposed to radiation influence as a result of the accident at the Chernobyl atomic power station* (in Russian) (pp. 73–74). Minsk: Publishing House of Belarussian Committee "Chernobyl Children."

Tertinger, D. A., Greene, B. F., & Lutzker, J. R. (1984). Home safety: Development and validation of one component of an eco-behavioral treatment program for abused and neglected children. *Journal of Applied Behavior Analysis, 17,* 159–174.

Tetens, J. N. (1777). *Philosophische Versuche über die menschliche Natur und ihre Entwicklung.* Leipzig: Weidmanns Erben & Reich.

Teti, D. M., Gelfand, D. M., Messinger, D. S., & Isabella, R. (1995). Maternal depression and the quality of early attachment: An examination of infants, preschoolers, and their mothers. *Developmental Psychology, 31,* 364–376.

Teti, D. M., Saken, J. W., Kucera, E., & Corns, K. M. (1996). And baby makes four: Predictors of attachment security among preschool-age firstborns during the transition to siblinghood. *Child Development, 67,* 579–596.

Teyber, E. (1992). *Helping children cope with divorce.* New York: Lexington Books.

Thackwray, D. E., Smith, M. C., Bodfish, J. W., & Meyers, A. W. (1993). A comparison of behavioral and cognitive-behavioral interventions for bulimia nervosa. *Journal of Consulting and Clinical Psychology, 61,* 639–645.

Tharp, R. G. (1993). Institutional and social context of educational practice and reform. In E. A. Forman, N. Minick, &

C. A. Stone (Eds.), *Contexts for learning* (pp. 269–282). New York: Oxford University Press.

Tharp, R. G. (1994). Intergroup differences among Native Americans in socialization and child cognition: An ethnogenetic analysis. In P. M. Greenfield & R. Cocking (Eds.), *Cross-cultural roots of minority child development* (pp. 87–105). Hillsdale, NJ: Erlbaum.

Thatcher, R. W., Lyon, G. R., Rumsey, J., & Krasnegor, J. (1996). *Developmental neuroimaging.* San Diego, CA: Academic Press.

Thatcher, R. W., Walker, R. A., & Giudice, S. (1987). Human cerebral hemispheres develop at different rates and ages. *Science, 236,* 1110–1113.

Theisen, S. C., Mansfield, P. K., Seery, B. L., & Voda, A. (1995). Predictors of midlife women's attitudes toward menopause. *Health Values, 19,* 22–31.

Thelen, E. (1989). The (re)discovery of motor development: Learning new things from an old field. *Developmental Psychology, 25,* 946–949.

Thelen, E., Fisher, D. M., & Ridley-Johnson, R. (1984). The relationship between physical growth and a newborn reflex. *Infant Behavior and Development, 7,* 479–493.

Thelen, E., & Smith, L. B. (1998). Dynamic systems theories. In R. M. Lerner (Ed.), *Handbook of child psychology: Vol. 1. Theoretical models of human development* (5th ed., pp. 563–634). New York: Wiley.

Thomas, A., & Chess, S. (1977). *Temperament and development.* New York: Brunner/Mazel.

Thomas, A., Chess, S., & Birch, H. G. (1968). *Temperament and behavior disorders in children.* New York: New York University Press.

Thomas, J. L. (1989). Gender and perceptions of grandparenthood. *International Journal of Aging and Human Development, 29,* 269–282.

Thompson, D. N. (1992). Applications of psychological research for the instruction of elderly adults. In R. L. West & J. D. Sinnott (Eds.), *Everyday memory and aging* (pp. 173–181). New York: Springer-Verlag.

Thompson, E. E., & Krause, N. (1998). Living alone and neighborhood characteristics as predictors of social support in late life. *Journal of Gerontology, 53,* S354–S364.

Thompson, K., & Range, L. (1992). Bereavement following suicide and other deaths: Why support attempts fail. *Omega, 26,* 61–70.

Thompson, R. A. (1990a). On emotion and self-regulation. In R. A. Thompson (Ed.), *Nebraska Symposia on Motivation* (Vol. 36, pp. 383–483). Lincoln: University of Nebraska Press.

Thompson, R. A. (1990b). Vulnerability in research: A developmental perspective on research risk. *Child Development, 61,* 1–16.

Thompson, R. A. (1994). Emotion regulation: A theme in search of a definition. In N. A. Fox (Ed.), The development of emotion regulation: Biological and behavioral considerations. *Monographs of the Society for Research in Child Development, 59*(2–3, Serial No. 240), pp. 25–52.

Thompson, R. A. (1998). Early sociopersonality development. In N. Eisenberg (Ed.), *Handbook of child psychology: Vol. 3. Social, emotional, and personality development* (5th ed., pp. 25–104). New York: Wiley.

Thompson, R. A., Lamb, M., & Estes, D. (1982). Stability of infant–mother attachment and its relationship to changing life circumstances in an unselected middle-class sample. *Child Development, 53,* 144–148.

Thompson, R. A., & Leger, D. W. (1998). From squalls to calls: The cry as a developing socioemotional signal. In B. Lester, J. Newman, & F. Pedersen (Eds.), *Biological and social aspects of infant crying.* New York: Plenum.

Thompson, R. A., & Limber, S. (1991). "Social anxiety" in infancy: Stranger wariness and separation distress. In H. Leitenberg (Ed.), *Handbook of social and evaluation anxiety* (pp. 85–137). New York: Plenum.

Thompson, R. J., Gustafson, K. E., Oehler, J. M., Catlett, A. T., Brazy, J. E., & Goldstein, R. F. (1997). Developmental outcome of very low birth weight infants at four years of age as a function of biological risk and psychosocial risk. *Developmental and Behavioral Pediatrics, 18,* 91–96.

Thornbury, J. M., & Mistretta, C. M. (1981). Tactile sensitivity as a function of age. *Journal of Gerontology, 36,* 34–39.

Thorndike, R. L., Hagen, E. P., & Sattler, J. M. (1986). *The Stanford-Binet Intelligence Scale: Guide for administering and scoring* (4th ed.). Chicago: Riverside Publishing.

Thornton, A. (1991). Influence of the marital history of parents on the marital and cohabitational experiences of children. *American Journal of Sociology, 96,* 868–894.

Thornton, A., Axinn, W. G., & Hill, D. H. (1992). Reciprocal effects of religiosity, cohabitation, and marriage. *American Journal of Sociology, 98,* 628–651.

Thorson, J. A., & Powell, F. C. (1991). Constructions of death among those high in intrinsic religious motivation: A factor analytic study. *Death Studies, 15,* 131–138.

Thorson, J. A., & Powell, F. C. (1994). A Revised Death Anxiety Scale. In R. A. Neimeyer (Ed.), *Death anxiety handbook* (pp. 31–43). Washington, DC: Taylor & Francis.

Tinetti, M. E. (1990). Falls. In C. K. Cassel, D. E. Risenberg, L. B. Sorensen, & J. R. Walsh (Eds.), *Geriatric medicine* (2nd ed., pp. 528–534). New York: Springer-Verlag.

Tinetti, M. E., Speechley, M., & Ginter, S. F. (1988). Risk factors for falls among elderly persons living in the community. *New England Journal of Medicine, 319,* 1701–1707.

Tisak, M. S. (1995). Domains of social reasoning and beyond. In R. Vasta (Ed.), *Annals of child development* (Vol. 11, pp. 95–130). London: Jessica Kingsley.

Tishman, S., Perkins, D. N., & Jay, E. (1995). *The thinking classroom.* Boston: Allyn and Bacon.

Titov, N., & Knight, R. G. (1997). Adult age differences in controlled and automatic memory processing. *Psychology and Aging, 12,* 565–573.

Tizard, B., & Hodges, J. (1978). The effect of early institutional rearing on the development of eight-year-old children. *Journal of Child Psychology and Psychiatry, 19,* 99–118.

Tizard, B., & Rees, J. (1975). The effect of early institutional rearing on the behaviour problems and affectional relationships of four-year-old children. *Journal of Child Psychology and Psychiatry, 16,* 61–73.

Tobin, J. J., Wu, D. Y. H., & Davidson, D. H. (1989). *Preschool in three cultures.* New Haven, CT: Yale University Press.

Toder, F. A. (1994). *Your kids are grown: Moving on with and without them.* New York: Plenum.

Todres, R., & Bunston, T. (1993). Parent education program evaluation: A review of the literature. *Canadian Journal of Community Mental Health, 12,* 225–257.

Tolson, T. F. J., & Wilson, M. N. (1990). The impact of two- and three-generational black family structure on perceived family climate. *Child Development, 61,* 416–428.

Tomasello, M. (1995). Language is not an instinct. *Cognitive Development, 10,* 131–156.

Tomasello, M. (1999). Having intentions, understanding intentions, and understanding communicative intentions. In P. D. Zelazo, J. W. Astington, & J. Wilde (Eds.), *Developing theories of intention: Social understanding and self-control* (pp. 63–75). Mahwah, NJ: Erlbaum.

Tomasello, M., & Akhtar, N. (1995). Two-year-olds use pragmatic cues to differentiate reference to objects and actions. *Cognitive Development, 10,* 201–224.

Tomasello, M., Akhtar, N., Dodson, K., & Rekau, L. (1997). Differential productivity in young children's use of nouns and verbs. *Journal of Child Language, 24,* 373–387.

Tomasello, M., & Barton, M. (1994). Learning words in nonostensive contexts. *Developmental Psychology, 30,* 639–650.

Tomasello, M., & Brooks, P. (1999). Early syntactic development: A construction grammar approach. In M. Barrett (Ed.), *The development of language* (pp. 161–190). Philadelphia: Psychology Press.

Toner, M. A., & Munro, D. (1996). Peer-social attributions and self-efficacy of peer-rejected preadolescents. *Merrill-Palmer Quarterly, 42,* 339–357.

Tong, S., Caddy, D., & Short, R. V. (1997). Use of dizygotic to monozygotic twinning ratio as a measure of fertility. *Lancet, 349,* 843–845.

Torrance, E. P. (1988). The nature of creativity as manifest in its testing. In R. J. Sternberg (Ed.), *The nature of creativity: Contemporary psychological perspectives* (pp. 43–75). New York: Cambridge University Press.

Torrey, B. B. (1992). Sharing increasing costs on declining income: The visible dilemma of the invisible aged. In R. M. Suzman, D. P. Willis, & K. G. Manton (Eds.), *The oldest old* (pp. 381–393). New York: Oxford University Press.

Touwen, B. C. L. (1984). Primitive reflexes—Conceptual or semantic problem? In H. F. R. Prechtl (Ed.), *Continuity of neural functions from prenatal to postnatal life* (Clinics in Developmental Medicine No. 94, pp. 115–125). Philadelphia: Lippincott.

Tower, R. B., Singer, D. G., Singer, J. L., & Biggs, A. (1979). Differential effects of television programming on preschoolers' cognition, imagination, and social play. *American Journal of Orthopsychiatry, 49,* 265–281.

Trent, K., & Harlan, S. L. (1994). Teenage mothers in nuclear and extended households. *Journal of Family Issues, 15,* 309–337.

Triandis, H. C. (1995). *Individualism and collectivism.* Boulder, CO: Westview Press.

Triandis, H. C. (1998, May). *Cross-cultural versus cultural psychology: A synthesis?* Colloquium presented at Illinois Wesleyan University, Bloomington, IL.

Trickett, P. K., Aber, J. L., Carlson, V., & Cicchetti, D. (1991). Relationship of socioeconomic status to the etiology and developmental sequelae of physical child abuse. *Developmental Psychology, 27,* 148–158.

Troiana, R. P., & Flegal, K. M. (1998). Overweight children and adolescents: Description, epidemiology, and demographics. *Pediatrics, 101,* 497–504.

Troll, L. E., & Skaff, M. M. (1997). Perceived continuity of self in very old age. *Psychology and Aging, 12,* 162–169.

Tronick, E., Morelli, G., & Ivey, P. (1992). The Efe forager infant and toddler's pattern of social relationships: Multiple and simultaneous. *Developmental Psychology, 28,* 568–577.

Tronick, E. Z. (1989). Emotions and emotional communication in infants. *American Psychologist, 44,* 112–119.

Tröster, H., & Brambring, M. (1992). Early social-emotional development in blind infants. *Child: Care, Health and Development, 18,* 207–227.

Tröster, H., & Brambring, M. (1993). Early motor development in blind infants. *Journal of Applied Developmental Psychology, 14,* 83–106.

Trovato, F., & Lalu, N. M. (1998). Narrowing sex differentials in life expectancy in the industrialized world: Early 1970's to early 1990's. *Life Expectancy, 43,* 20–37.

Truglio, R. (2000, April). *Research guides "Sesame Street."* Public lecture presented as part of the Consider the Children program, Illinois State University, Normal, IL.

Tsang, P. S., & Shaner, T. L. (1998). Age, attention, expertise, and time-sharing performance. *Psychology and Aging, 13,* 323–347.

Tuchfarber, B. S., Zins, J. E., & Jason, L. A. (1997). Prevention and control of injuries. In R. Weissberg, T. P. Gullotta, R. L. Hampton, B. A. Ryan, & G. R. Adams (Eds.), *Enhancing children's wellness* (pp. 250–277). Thousand Oaks, CA: Sage.

Tucker, J. S., Friedman, H. S., Schwartz, J. E., Criqui, M. H., Tomlinson-Keasey, C., & Wingard, D. (1997). Parental divorce: Effects on individual behavior and longevity. *Journal of Personality and Social Psychology, 73,* 381–391.

Tudge, J. R. H. (1992). Processes and consequences of peer collaboration: A Vygotskian analysis. *Child Development, 63,* 1364–1397.

Tur, E., Yosipovitch, F., & Oren-Vulfs, S. (1992). Chronic and acute effects of cigarette smoking on skin blood flow. *Angiology, 43,* 328–335.

Turiel, E. (1998). The development of morality. In N. Eisenberg (Ed.), *Handbook of child psychology: Vol. 3. Social, emotional, and personality development* (5th ed., pp. 863–932). New York: Wiley.

Turiel, E., Smetana, J. G., & Killen, M. (1991). Social contexts in social cognitive development. In W. M. Kurtines & J. L. Gewirtz (Eds.), *Handbook of moral behavior and development* (Vol. 2, pp. 307–332). Hillsdale, NJ: Erlbaum.

Turkheimer, E., & Gottesman, I. I. (1991). Individual differences and the canalization of human behavior. *Developmental Psychology, 27,* 18–22.

Turner, B. F. (1982). Sex-related differences in aging. In B. B. Wolman (Ed.), *Handbook of developmental psychology* (pp. 912–936). Englewood Cliffs, NJ: Prentice Hall.

Turner, M. (1998, February 2). Suicidal tendencies. *Time Australia*, p. 66.

Turner, M. J., Bailey, W. C., & Scott, J. P. (1994). Factors influencing attitude toward retirement and retirement planning among midlife university employees. *Journal of Applied Gerontology, 13*, 143–156.

Turner, P. J., & Gervai, J. (1995). A multidimensional study of gender typing in preschool children and their parents: Personality, attitudes, preferences, behavior, and cultural differences. *British Journal of Developmental Psychology, 11*, 323–342.

Tuszynski, M. H., & Kordower, J. H. (Eds.) (1999). *CNS regeneration: Basic science and clinical advances*. San Diego, CA: Academic Press.

Udry, J. R. (1990). Hormonal and social determinants of adolescent sexual initiation. In J. Bancroft & J. M. Reinisch (Eds.), *Adolescence and puberty* (pp. 70–87). New York: Oxford University Press.

Ugarriza, D. N., Klingner, S., & O'Brien, S. (1998, September). Premenstrual syndrome: diagnosis and intervention. *Nurse Practitioner, 23*(9), 40–52.

Ullman, S. E. (1996). Social reactions, coping strategies, and self-blame attributions in adjustment to sexual assault. *Psychology of Women Quarterly, 20*, 505–526.

Ulrich, B. D., & Ulrich, D. A. (1985). The role of balancing in performance of fundamental motor skills in 3-, 4-, and 5-year-old children. In J. E. Clark & J. H. Humphrey (Eds.), *Motor development* (Vol. 1, pp. 87–98). Princeton, NJ: Princeton Books.

Umberson, D., Wortman, C. B., & Kessler, R. C. (1992). Widowhood and depression: Explaining long-term gender differences in vulnerability. *Journal of Health and Social Behavior, 33*, 10–24.

United Nations. (1996). *World social situation in the 1990s*. New York: Author.

United Nations. (1997). *Human development report. 1997*. New York: Oxford University Press.

U.S. Bureau of the Census. (1960). *Statistical abstract of the United States* (81st ed.). Washington, DC: U.S. Government Printing Office.

U.S. Bureau of the Census. (1997). *Who's minding our preschoolers?* (Current Population Reports, P70-62). Washington, DC: U.S. Government Printing Office.

U.S. Bureau of the Census. (1999). *Statistical abstract of the United States* (119th ed.). Washington, DC: U.S. Government Printing Office.

U.S. Centers for Disease Control. (1999). *Sexually transmitted disease surveillance, 1998*. Atlanta: Author.

U.S. Department of Education. (1998). *Pursuing excellence: A study of U.S. twelfth-grade mathematics and science achievement in international context*. Washington, DC: U.S. Government Printing Office.

U.S. Department of Education, National Center for Education Statistics. (1999a). *Digest of education statistics 1998*. Washington, DC: U.S. Government Printing Office.

U.S. Department of Education. (1999b). *Dropout rates in the United States: 1997*. Washington, DC: U.S. Government Printing Office.

U.S. Department of Health and Human Services. (1994). *National survey of families and households, 1992–1993*. Washington, DC: U.S. Government Printing Office.

U.S. Department of Health and Human Services, National Center for Health Statistics. (1999a). *Advance report of final natality statistics* (Vol. 47). Washington, DC: U.S. Government Printing Office.

U.S. Department of Health and Human Services. (1999b). *Centenarians in the United States*. Washington, DC: U.S. Government Printing Office.

U.S. Department of Health and Human Services. (1999c). *Health United States 1998–1999 and injury chartbook*. Washington, DC: U.S. Bureau of the Census.

U.S. Department of Health and Human Services. (1999d). *Impaired fecundity by age and selected characteristics*. Washington, DC: U.S. Government Printing Office.

U.S. Department of Health and Human Services. (1999e). *National survey results on drug use from the Monitoring the Future Study, 1975–1998: Vol. 1. Secondary school students*. Washington, DC: U.S. Government Printing Office.

U.S. Department of Health and Human Services. (1999f). *Profile of older Americans: 1999*. Washington, DC: U.S. Government Printing Office.

U.S. Department of Health and Human Services. (1999g). *Vital statistics of the United States, 1997*. Washington, DC: U.S. Government Printing Office.

U.S. Department of Health and Human Services. (1999h). Youth risk behavior surveillance—U.S., 1998. *MMWR, 48*(No. SS–3).

U.S. Department of Health and Human Services. (2000). *Healthy People 2000*. Washington, DC: U.S. Bureau of the Census.

U.S. Department of Justice. (1999). *Crime in the United States*. Washington, DC: U.S. Government Printing Office.

U.S. Department of Labor, Bureau of Labor Statistics. (1999). *Usual weekly earnings of wage and salary workers: First quarter 1999*. Washington, DC: U.S. Government Printing Office.

U.S. Department of Labor, Bureau of Labor Statistics. (2000, February). Consumer price index. *Monthly Labor Review, 121*(2).

Updegraff, K. A., McHale, S. M., & Crouter, A. C. (1996). Gender roles in marriage: What do they mean for girls' and boys' school achievement? *Journal of Youth and Adolescence, 25*, 73–88.

Urberg, K. A., Degirmencioglue, S. M., Tolson, J. M., & Halliday-Scher, K. (1995). The structure of adolescent peer networks. *Developmental Psychology, 31*, 540–547.

Uribe, F. M. T., LeVine, R. A., & LeVine, S. E. (1994). Maternal behavior in a Mexican community: The changing environments of children. In P. M. Greenfield & R. R. Cocking (Eds.), *Cross-cultural roots of minority child development* (pp. 41–54). Hillsdale, NJ: Erlbaum.

Usmiani, S., & Daniluk, J. (1997). Mothers and their adolescent daughters: Relationship between self-esteem, gender role identity, and body image. *Journal of Youth and Adolescence, 26*, 45–60.

Vaillant, G. E. (1976). Natural history of male psychological health: V. Relation of choice of ego mechanisms of defense to adult adjustment. *Archives of General Psychiatry, 33*, 535–545.

Vaillant, G. E. (1977). *Adaptation to life*. Boston: Little, Brown.

Vaillant, G. E. (1991). The association of ancestral longevity with successful aging. *Journal of Gerontology, 46*, P292–P298.

Vaillant, G. E. (1993). *The wisdom of the ego*. Cambridge, MA: Harvard University Press.

Vaillant, G. E. (1994). "Successful aging" and psychosocial well-being. In E. H. Thompson, Jr. (Ed.), *Older men's lives* (pp. 22–41). Thousand Oaks, CA: Sage.

Vaillant, G. E., & Koury, S. H. (1994). Late midlife development. In G. H. Pollock & S. I. Greenspan (Eds.), *The course of life* (pp. 1–22). Madison, CT: International Universities Press.

Vaillant, G. E., & Vaillant, C. O. (1990). Determinants and consequences of creativity in a cohort of gifted women. *Psychology of Women Quarterly, 14*, 607–616.

Valarino, E. (1997). *On the other side of life: Exploring the phenomenon of near-death experiences*. New York: Plenum.

Valdés, G. (1998). The world outside and inside schools: Language and immigrant children. *Educational Researcher, 27*(6), 4–18.

Valdez, R., Athens, M. A., Thompson, G. H., Bradshaw, G. H., & Stern, M. P. (1994). Birthweight and adult health outcomes in a biethnic population in the U.S.A. *Diabetologia, 37*, 624.

Valian, V. V. (1996). *Parental replies: Linguistic status and didactic roles*. Cambridge, MA: MIT Press.

van Balen, F. (1996). Child rearing following in vitro fertilization. *Journal of Child Psychology and Psychiatry, 37*, 687–693.

van Boxtel, M. P., Buntinx, F., Houx, P. J., Metsemakers, J. F., Knottnerus, A., & Jolles, J. (1998). The relation between morbidity and cognitive performance in a normal aging population. *Journal of Gerontology, 53*, M147–M154.

van Boxtel, M. P. J., Paas, F. G. W. C., Houz, P. J., Adam, J. J., Teeken, J. C., & Jolles, J. (1997). Aerobic capacity and cognitive performance in a cross-sectional aging study. *Medicine and Science in Sports and Exercise, 29*, 1357–1365.

Vance, M. D. (1994, April). *Short stature and psychosocial risks in a nonclinical sample.* Proceedings of the Fourth North Coast Conference of the Society for Pediatric Psychology, Amherst, NY.

Vandell, D. L., & Posner, J. K. (1999). Conceptualization and measurement of children's after-school environments. In S. L. Friedman & T. D. Wachs (Eds.), *Measuring environment across the life span* (pp. 167–196). Washington, DC: American Psychological Association.

van den Boom, D. C. (1995). Do first-year intervention effects endure? Follow-up during toddlerhood of a sample of Dutch irritable infants. *Child Development, 66*, 1798–1816.

van den Boom, D. C., & Hoeksma, J. B. (1994). The effect of infant irritability on mother–infant interaction: A growth-curve analysis. *Developmental Psychology, 30*, 581–590.

van der Maas, P. J., Pijnenborg, L., & van Delden, J. J. M. (1995). Changes in Dutch opinions on active euthanasia, 1966 through 1991. *Journal of the American Medical Association, 273*, 1411–1414.

Vandewater, E. A., & Stewart, A. J. (1997). Women's career commitment patterns and personality development. In M. E. Lachman & J. B. James (Eds.), *Multiple paths of midlife development* (pp. 375–410). Chicago: University of Chicago Press.

Vanfossen, B., Jones, J., & Spade, J. (1987). Curriculum tracking and status maintenance. *Sociology of Education, 60*, 104–122.

van IJzendoorn, M. H. (1995a). Adult attachment representations, parental responsiveness, and infant attachment: A meta-analysis on the predictive validity of the Adult Attachment Interview. *Psychological Bulletin, 117*, 387–403.

van IJzendoorn, M. H. (1995b). Of the way we are: On temperament, attachment, and the transmission gap: A rejoinder to Fox (1995). *Psychological Bulletin, 117*, 411–415.

van IJzendoorn, M. H., & De Wolff, M. S. (1997). In search of the absent father—meta-analyses of infant–father attach-ment: A rejoinder to our discussants. *Child Development, 68*, 604–609.

van IJzendoorn, M. H., & Kroonenberg, P. M. (1988). Cross-cultural patterns of attach-ment: A meta-analysis of the Strange Sit-uation. *Child Development, 59*, 147–156.

Vartanian, L. R. (1997). Separation--individuation, social support, and adolescent egocentrism: An exploratory study. *Journal of Early Adolescence, 17*, 245–270.

Vartanian, L. R., & Powlishta, K. K. (1996). A longitudinal examination of the social-cognitive foundations of adolescent ego-centrism. *Journal of Early Adolescence, 16*, 157–178.

Vaselle-Augenstein, R., & Ehrlich, A. (1992). The male batterer. In E. C. Viano (Eds.), *Intimate violence: Interdisciplinary per-spectives* (pp. 139–154). Washington, DC: Hemisphere.

Vasudev, J., & Hummel, R. C. (1987). Moral stage sequence and principled reasoning in an Indian sample. *Human Develop-ment, 30*, 103–118.

Vaughn, B. E., Kopp, C. B., & Krakow, J. B. (1984). The emergence and consoli-dation of self-control from eighteen to thirty months of age: Normative trends and individual differences. *Child Development, 55*, 990–1004.

Vaughn, B. E., Stevenson-Hinde, J., Waters, E., Kotsaftis, A., Lefever, G. B., Shouldice, A., Trudel, M., & Belsky, J. (1992). Attach-ment security and temperament in infancy and early childhood: Some conceptual clarifications. *Developmental Psychology, 28*, 463–473.

Vaughn, S., Elbaum, B. E., & Schumm, J. S. (1996). The effects of inclusion on the social functioning of students with learning disabilities. *Journal of Learning Disabilities, 29*, 598–608.

Vaziri, H., & Benchimol, S. (1998). Reconsti-tution of telomerase activity in normal human cells leads to elongation of telomeres and extended replicative life span. *Current Biology, 8*, 279–282.

Veldhuis, J. D., Iranmanesh, A., & Weltman, A. (1997). Elements in the pathophysi-ology of diminished growth hormone (GH) secretion in aging humans. *Endocrine, 7*, 41–48.

Veniegas, R., & Peplau, L. A. (1997). Power and the quality of same-sex friendships. *Psychology of Women Quarterly, 21*, 279–297.

Ventura, S. J. (1989). Trends and variations in first births to older women in the United States, 1970–1986. *Vital and Health Statistics* (Series 21). Hyattsville, MD: U.S. Department of Health and Human Services.

Ventura, S. J., Martin, J. A., Curtin, S. C., & Mathews, T. J. (1997). Report of final natality statistics, 1995. *Monthly Vital Statistics Report, 45*(11, Suppl. 2).

Hyattsville, MD: National Center for Health Statistics.

Verhulst, F. C., & Versluis-Den Bieman, H. J. M. (1995). Developmental course of problem behaviors in adolescent adoptees. *Journal of the American Academy of Child and Adolescent Psychiatry, 34*, 151–159.

Vernon, P. A. (1993). Intelligence and neural efficiency. In D. K. Detterman (Ed.), *Current topics in human intelligence* (Vol. 3, pp. 171–187). Norwood, NJ: Ablex.

Villaume, W. A., Brown, M. H., Darling, R., Richardson, D., Hawk, R., Henry, D. M., & Reid, T. (1997). Presbycusis and con-versation: Elderly interactants adjusting to multiple hearing losses. *Research on Language and Social Interaction, 30*, 235–262.

Vinden, P. G. (1996). Junín Quechua chil-dren's understanding of mind. *Child Development, 67*, 1707–1716.

Vinick, B. H., & Ekerdt, D. J. (1991). Retire-ment: What happens to husband–wife relationships? *Journal of Geriatric Psychiatry, 24*, 23–40.

Vogel, D. A., Lake, M. A., Evans, S., & Kar-raker, H. (1991). Children's and adults' sex-stereotyped perceptions of infants. *Sex Roles, 24*, 605–616.

Vohr, B. R., & Garcia-Coll, C. T. (1988). Follow-up studies of high-risk low-birth-weight infants: Changing trends. In H. E. Fitzgerald, B. M. Lester, & M. W. Yogman (Eds.), *Theory and research in behavioral pediatrics* (pp. 1–65). New York: Plenum.

Volling, B. L., & Belsky, J. (1992). Contribu-tion of mother–child and father– child relationships to the quality of sibling interaction: A longitudinal study. *Child Development, 63*, 1209–1222.

Volling, B. L., & Elins, J. L. (1998). Family relationships and children's emotional adjustment as correlates of maternal and paternal differential treatment: A repli-cation with toddlers and preschool sib-lings. *Child Development, 69*, 1640–1656.

Vorhees, C. V., & Mollnow, E. (1987). Behavioral teratogenesis: Long-term influences on behavior from early expo-sure to environmental agents. In J. D. Osofsky (Ed.), *Handbook of infant development* (2nd ed., pp. 913–971). New York: Wiley.

Vostanis, P., Grattan, E., & Cumella, S. (1997). Psychosocial functioning of homeless children. *Journal of the Ameri-can Academy of Child and Adolescent Psy-chiatry, 36*, 881–889.

Voyer, D., Voyer, S., & Bryden, M. P. (1995). Magnitude of sex differences in spatial abilities: A meta-analysis and considera-tion of critical variables. *Psychological Bulletin, 117*, 250–270

Vygotsky, L. S. (1978). *Mind in society: The development of higher mental processes.* Cambridge, MA: Harvard University

Press. (Original works published 1930, 1933, and 1935)

Vygotsky, L. S. (1987). Thinking and speech. In R. W. Rieber, & A. S. Carton (Eds.), & N. Minick (Trans.), *The collected works of L. S. Vygotsky: Vol. 1. Problems of general psychology* (pp. 37–285). New York: Plenum. (Original work published 1934)

Wachs, T. D. (1975). Relation of infants' performance on Piagetian scales between twelve and twenty-four months and their Stanford-Binet performance at thirty-one months. *Child Development, 46,* 929–935.

Wachs, T. D. (1995). Relation of mild-to-moderate malnutrition to human development: Correlational studies. *Journal of Nutrition Supplement, 125,* 22455–22545.

Wachs, T. D., Bishry, Z., Moussa, W., Yunis, F., McCabe, G., Harrison, G., Swefi, I., Kirksey, A., Galal, O., Jerome, N., & Shaheen, F. (1995). Nutritional intake and context as predictors of cognition and adaptive behavior of Egyptian school-age children. *International Journal of Behavioral Development, 18,* 425–450.

Waddington, C. H. (1957). *The strategy of the genes.* London: Allen & Unwin.

Wagner, R. K., & Sternberg, R. J. (1985). Practical intelligence in real-world pursuits: The role of tacit knowledge. *Journal of Personality and Social Psychology, 49,* 436–458.

Wahl, H.-W. (1991). Dependence in the elderly from an interactional point of view: Verbal and observational data. *Psychology and Aging, 6,* 238–246.

Wahlsten, D. (1994). The intelligence of heritability. *Canadian Psychology, 35,* 244–259.

Waite, L. J. (1999, July). *Debunking the marriage myth: It works for women, too.* Paper presented at the annual Smart Marriages Conference, Washington, DC.

Wakat, D. K. (1978). Physiological factors of race and sex in sport. In L. K. Bunker & R. J. Rotella (Eds.), *Sport psychology: From theory to practice* (pp. 194–209). Charlotte, VA: University of Virginia. (Proceedings of the 1978 Sport Psychology Institute)

Walberg, H. J. (1986). Synthesis of research on teaching. In M. C. Wittrock (Ed.), *Handbook of research on teaching* (3rd ed., pp. 214–229). New York: Macmillan.

Walco, G. A. (1997). Growing pains. *Developmental and Behavioral Pediatrics, 18,* 107–108.

Walker, D., Greenwood, C., Hart, B., & Carta, J. (1994). Prediction of school outcomes based on early language production and socioeconomic factors. *Child Development, 65,* 606–621.

Walker, L. (1995). Sexism in Kohlberg's moral psychology? In W. M. Kurtines & J. L. Gewirtz (Eds.), *Moral development:*

An introduction (pp. 83–107). Boston: Allyn and Bacon.

Walker, L. E. (1979). *The battered woman.* New York: Harper & Row.

Walker, L. J. (1989). A longitudinal study of moral reasoning. *Child Development, 60,* 157–166.

Walker, L. J., & Hennig, K. H. (1997). Moral development in the broader context of personality. In S. Hala (Ed.), *The development of social cognition* (pp. 297–327). Hove, UK: Psychology Press.

Walker, L. J., Pitts, R. C., Hennig, K. H., & Matsuba, M. K. (1995). Reasoning about morality and real-life moral problems. In M. Killen & D. Hart (Eds.), *Morality in everyday life* (pp. 371–407). New York: Cambridge University Press.

Walker, L. J., & Taylor, J. H. (1991a). Family interactions and the development of moral reasoning. *Child Development, 62,* 264–283.

Walker, L. J., & Taylor, J. H. (1991b). Stage transitions in moral reasoning: A longitudinal study of developmental processes. *Developmental Psychology, 27,* 330–337.

Walker-Andrews, A. S. (1997). Infants' perception of expressive behaviors: Differentiation of multimodal information. *Psychological Bulletin, 121,* 437–456.

Wallerstein, J. S., & Blakeslee, S. (1995). *The good marriage.* Boston: Houghton Mifflin.

Wallerstein, J. S., & Kelly, J. B. (1980). *Surviving the break-up: How children and parents cope with divorce.* New York: Basic Books.

Walls, C. T., & Zarit, S. H. (1991). Informal support from black churches and the well-being of elderly blacks. *Gerontologist, 31,* 490–495.

Wangby, M., Bergman, L. R., & Magnesson, D. (1999). Development of adjustment problems in girls: What syndromes emerge? *Child Development, 70,* 678–699.

Wannamethee, G., Shaper, A. G., & Macfarlane, P. W. (1993). Heart rate, physical activity, and mortality from cancer and other noncardiovascular diseases. *American Journal of Epidemiology, 137,* 735–748.

Wapner, R. J. (1997). Chorionic villus sampling. *Obstetrics and Gynecology Clinics of North America, 24,* 83–110.

Ward, L. M. (1995). Talking about sex: Common themes about sexuality in the prime-time television programs children and adolescents view most. *Journal of Youth and Adolescence, 24,* 595–616.

Wark, G. R., & Krebs, D. L. (1996). Gender and dilemma differences in real-life moral judgment. *Developmental Psychology, 32,* 220–230.

Warr, P. B. (1992). Age and occupational well-being. *Psychology and Aging, 7,* 37–45.

Warr, P. B. (1994). Age and employment. In M. D. Dunnette, L. Hough, & H. Triandis (Eds.), *Handbook of industrial and organizational psychology* (pp. 485–550). Palo Alto, CA: Consulting Psychologists Press.

Warren, A. R., & Tate, C. S. (1992). Egocentrism in children's telephone conversations. In R. M. Diaz & L. E. Berk (Eds.), *Private speech: From social interaction to self-regulation* (pp. 245–264). Hillsdale, NJ: Erlbaum.

Warren, D. H. (1994). *Blindness and children: An individual difference approach.* New York: Cambridge University Press.

Wartner, U. G., Grossmann, K., Fremmer-Bombik, E., & Suess, G. (1994). Attachment patterns at age six in south Germany: Predictability from infancy and implications for preschool behavior. *Child Development, 65,* 1014–1027.

Wass, H. (1991). Helping children cope with death. In D. Papadatou & C. Papadatos (Eds.), *Children and death* (pp. 11–32). New York: Hemisphere.

Wass, H. (1995). Death in the lives of children and adolescents. In H. Wass & R. A. Neimeyer (Eds.), *Dying: Facing the facts* (3rd ed., pp. 269–301). Washington, DC: Taylor & Francis.

Waterman, A. S. (1985). Identity in context of adolescent psychology. In A. S. Waterman (Ed.), *New directions for child development* (No. 30, pp. 5–24). San Francisco: Jossey-Bass.

Waterman, A. S. (1989). Curricula interventions for identity change: Substantive and ethical considerations. *Journal of Adolescence, 12,* 389–400.

Waterman, A. S., & Whitbourne, S. K. (1982). Androgyny and psychosocial development among college students and adults. *Journal of Personality, 50,* 121–133.

Watkins, W. E., & Pollitt, E. (1998). Iron deficiency and cognition among school-age children. In S. G. McGregor (Ed.), *Recent advances in research on the effects of health and nutrition on children's development and school achievement in the Third World.* Washington, DC: Pan American Health Organization.

Watson, A. C., Nixon, C. L., Wilson, A., & Capage, L. (1999). Social interaction skills and theory of mind in young children. *Developmental Psychology, 35,* 386–391.

Watson, D. J. (1989). Defining and describing whole language. *Elementary School Journal, 90,* 129–141.

Watson, J. B., & Raynor, R. (1920). Conditioned emotional reactions. *Journal of Experimental Psychology, 3,* 1–14.

Watson, M. (1990). Aspects of self development as reflected in children's role playing. In D. Cicchetti & M. Beeghly (Eds.), *The self in transition: Infancy to childhood* (pp. 281–307). Chicago: University of Chicago Press.

Waxman, S. R., & Hatch, T. (1992). Beyond the basics: Preschool children label objects flexibly at multiple hierarchical levels. *Journal of Child Language, 19,* 153–166.

Waxman, S. R., & Markow, D. B. (1998). Object properties and object kind: Twenty-one-month-old infants' extension of novel adjectives. *Child Development, 69,* 1313–1329.

Waxman, S. R., & Senghas, A. (1992). Relations among word meanings in early lexical development. *Developmental Psychology, 28,* 862–873.

Weale, R. A. (1992). *The senescence of human vision.* New York: Oxford University Press.

Wechsler, D. (1991). *Manual for the Wechsler Intelligence Test for Children–III.* New York: Psychological Corporation.

Wechsler, H., Rigotti, N. A., Gledhill-Hoyt, J., & Lee, H. (1998). Increased levels of cigarette use among college students. *Journal of the American Medical Association, 280,* 1673–1678.

Wehren, A., De Lisi, R., & Arnold, M. (1981). The development of noun definition. *Journal of Child Language, 8,* 165–175.

Wei, Y. H. (1998). Mitochondrial DNA mutations and oxidative damage in aging and diseases: An emerging paradigm of gerontology and medicine. *Proceedings of the National Science Council of the Republic of China, 22,* 55–67.

Weiland, S. (1993). Erik Erikson: Ages, stages, and stories. *Generations, 17*(2), 17–22.

Weinberg, M. K., & Tronick, E. Z. (1994). Beyond the face: An empirical study of infant affective configurations of facial, vocal, gestural, and regulatory behaviors. *Child Development, 65,* 1503–1515.

Weinberg, M. K., & Tronick, E. Z. (1996). Infant affective reactions to the resumption of maternal interaction after the still face. *Child Development, 67,* 905–914.

Weinberg, M. K., Tronick, E. Z., Cohn, J. F., & Olson, K. L. (1999). Gender differences in emotional expressivity and self-regulation during early infancy. *Developmental Psychology, 35,* 175–188.

Weinberg, R. A., Scarr, S., & Waldman, I. D. (1992). The Minnesota transracial adoption study: A follow-up of IQ test performance at adolescence. *Intelligence, 16,* 117–135.

Weingarten, H. R. (1988). Late life divorce and the life review. *Journal of Gerontological Social Work, 12*(3–4), 83–97.

Weingarten, H. R. (1989). The impact of late life divorce: A conceptual and empirical study. *Journal of Divorce, 12,* 21–38.

Weinstein, R. S., Marshall, H. H., Sharp, L., & Botkin, M. (1987). Pygmalion and the student: Age and classroom differences in children's awareness of teacher expectations. *Child Development, 58,* 1079–1093.

Weisman, A. D. (1984). *The coping capacity: On the nature of being mortal.* New York: Sciences Press.

Weisner, T. S. (1993). Ethnographic and ecocultural perspectives on sibling relationships. In Z. Stoneman & P. W. Berman (Eds.), *The effects of mental retardation, disability, and illness on sibling relationships* (pp. 51–83). Baltimore: Paul H. Brookes.

Weisner, T. S. (1996). The 5 to 7 year transition as an ecocultural project. In A. J. Sameroff & M. M. Haith (Eds.), *The five to seven year shift* (pp. 295–326). Chicago: University of Chicago Press.

Weisner, T. S., & Wilson-Mitchell, J. E. (1990). Nonconventional family lifestyles and sex typing in six-year-olds. *Child Development, 61,* 1915–1933.

Weiss, G., & Hechtman, L. T. (1993). *Hyperactive children grown up* (2nd ed.). New York: Guilford.

Weksler, M. E. (1995). Immune senescence: Deficiency or dysregulation. *Nutrition Reviews, 53,* S3–S7.

Wellings, K., Field, J., Johnson, A., & Wadsworth, J. (1994). *Sexual behavior in Britain: The National Survey of Sexual Attitudes and Lifestyles.* New York: Penguin.

Wellman, B. (1992). Men in networks: Private communities, domestic friendships. In P. Nardi (Ed.), *Men's friendships* (pp. 74–114). Newbury Park, CA: Sage.

Wellman, H. M. (1990). *The child's theory of mind.* Cambridge, MA: MIT Press.

Wellman, H. M., & Hickling, A. K. (1994). The mind's "I": Children's conception of the mind as an active agent. *Child Development, 65,* 1564–1580.

Wellman, H. M., Somerville, S. C., & Haake, R. J. (1979). Development of search procedures in real-life spatial environments. *Developmental Psychology, 15,* 530–542.

Werner, E. E. (1989, April). Children of the garden island. *Scientific American, 260*(4), 106–111.

Werner, E. E. (1991). Grandparent–grandchild relationships amongst U.S. ethnic groups. In P. K. Smith (Ed.), *The psychology of grandparenthood: An international perspective* (pp. 68–82). London: Routledge.

Werner, E. E. (1993). Risk, resilience, and recovery: Perspectives from the Kauai Longitudinal Study. *Development and Psychopathology, 5,* 503–515.

Werner, E. E., & Smith, R. S. (1982). *Vulnerable but invincible.* New York: McGraw-Hill.

Werner, E. E., & Smith, R. S. (1992). *Overcoming the odds: High-risk children from birth to adulthood.* Ithaca, NY: Cornell University Press.

Wertsch, J. V., & Tulviste, P. (1992). L. S. Vygotsky and contemporary developmental psychology. *Developmental Psychology, 28,* 548–557.

Westermeyer, J. F. (1998). Predictors and characteristics of mental health among men at midlife: A 32-year longitudinal study. *American Journal of Orthopsychiatry, 68,* 265–273.

Wheaton, B. (1990). Life transitions, role, histories, and mental health. *American Sociological Review, 55,* 209–223.

Wheeler, M. D. (1991). Physical changes of puberty. *Endocrinology and Metabolism Clinics of North America, 20,* 1–14.

Wheeler, T., Barker, D. J. P., & O'Brien, P. M. S. (1999). *Fetal programming: Influences on development and disease in later life.* London: RCOG Press.

Whitbeck, L., Hoyt, D. R., & Huck, S. M. (1994). Early family relationships, intergenerational solidarity, and support provided to parents by their adult children. *Journal of Gerontology, 49,* 585–594.

Whitbourne, S. K. (1985). *The aging body.* New York: Springer.

Whitbourne, S. K. (1996). *The aging individual: Physical and psychological perspectives.* New York: Springer.

Whitbourne, S. K. (1999). Physical changes. In J. C. Kavanaugh & S. K. Whitbourne (Eds.), *Gerontology: An interdisciplinary perspective* (pp. 33–64). New York: Oxford University Press.

Whitbourne, S. K., & Connolly, L. A. (1998). The developing self in midlife. In S. L. Willis & J. D. Reid (Eds.), *Life in the middle* (pp. 25–45). San Diego: Academic Press.

Whitbourne, S. K., & Primus, L. (1996). Identity, physical. In J. E. Birren (Ed.), *Encyclopedia of aging* (pp. 733–742). San Diego: Academic Press.

Whitbourne, S. K., & Weinstock, C. S. (1979). *Adult development: The differentiation of experience.* New York: Holt, Rinehart & Winston.

Whitbourne, S. K., Zuschlag, M. K., Elliot, L. B., & Waterman, A. S. (1992). Psychosocial development in adulthood: A 22-year sequential study. *Journal of Personality and Social Psychology, 63,* 260–271.

White, B. (1990). *The first three years of life.* New York: Prentice-Hall.

White, B., & Held, R. (1966). Plasticity of sensorimotor development in the human infant. In J. F. Rosenblith & W. Allinsmith (Eds.), *The causes of behavior* (pp. 60–70). Boston: Allyn and Bacon.

White, J. L., Moffitt, T. E., Caspi, A., Bartusch, D. J., Needles, D. J., & Stouthamer-Loeber, M. (1996). Measuring impulsivity and examining its relationship to delinquency. *Journal of Abnormal Psychology, 103,* 192–205.

White, L. K. (1994). Coresidence and leaving home: Young adults and their parents. *Annual Review of Sociology, 20,* 81–102.

White, L. K., & Kim, H. (1987). The family-building process: Childbearing choices by parity. *Journal of Marriage and the Family, 49,* 271–279.

White, L. K., & Riedmann, A. (1992). Ties among adult siblings. *Social Forces, 71,* 85–102.

White, S. H. (1992). G. Stanley Hall: From philosophy to developmental psychology. *Developmental Psychology, 28,* 25–34.

Whitehead, J. R., & Corbin, C. B. (1997). Self-esteem in children and youth: The role of sport and physical education. In K. R. Fox (Ed.), *The physical self: From motivation to well-being* (pp. 175–204). Champaign, IL: Human Kinetics.

Whitehurst, G., & Vasta, R. (1975). Is language acquired through imitation? *Journal of Psycholinguistic Research, 4,* 37–59.

Whitehurst, G. J., & Lonigan, C. J. (1998). Child development and emergent literacy. *Child Development, 69,* 848–872.

Whiting, B., & Edwards, C. P. (1988a). *Children in different worlds.* Cambridge, MA: Harvard University Press.

Whiting, B., & Edwards, C. P. (1988b). A cross-cultural analysis of sex differences in the behavior of children aged 3 through 11. In G. Handel (Ed.), *Childhood socialization* (pp. 281–297). New York: Aldine de Gruyter.

Whitney, C. W., Enright, P. L., Newman, A. B., Bonekat, W., Foley, D., & Quan, S. F. (1998). Correlates of daytime sleepiness in 4578 elderly persons: The cardiovascular health study. *Sleep, 21,* 27–36.

Whitney, M. P., & Thoman, E. B. (1994). Sleep in premature and full-term infants from 24-hour home recordings. *Infant Behavior and Development, 17,* 223–234.

Wichstrøm, L. (1999). The emergence of gender difference in depressed mood: The role of intensified gender socialization. *Developmental Psychology, 35,* 232–245.

Wiebe, D. J., & Williams, P. G. (1992). Hardiness and health: A social psychophysiological perspective on stress and adaptation. *Journal of Social and Clinical Psychology, 11,* 238–262.

Wilcox, A. J., Weinberg, C. R., & Baird, D. D. (1995). Timing of sexual intercourse in relation to ovulation: Effects on the probability of conception, survival of the pregnancy, and sex of the baby. *New England Journal of Medicine, 333,* 1517–1519.

Wiley, T. L., Cruickshanks, K. J., Nondahl, D. M., Tweed, T. S., Klein, R., & Klein, B. E. K. (1998). Aging and high-frequency hearing sensitivity. *Journal of Speech, Language, and Hearing Research, 41,* 1061–1072.

Wilke, C. J., & Thompson, C. A. (1993). First-year reentry women's perceptions of their classroom experiences. *Journal of the Freshman Year Experience, 5,* 69–90.

Wilkie, J. R., Ferree, M. M., & Ratcliff, K. S. (1998). Gender and fairness: Marital satisfaction and two-earner couples. *Journal of Marriage and the Family, 60,* 577–594.

Wille, D. E. (1991). Relation of preterm birth with quality of infant–mother attachment at one year. *Infant Behavior and Development, 14,* 227–240.

Willett, W. C., Colditz, G., & Stampfer, M. (2000). Postmenopausal estrogens opposed, unopposed, or none of the above. *Journal of the American Medical Association, 283,* 485–491.

Williams, B. C., & Kotch, J. B. (1990). Excess injury mortality among children in the United States: Comparison of recent international statistics. *Pediatrics, 86*(6, Pt. 2), 1067–1073.

Williams, E., & Radin, N. (1993). Paternal involvement, maternal employment, and adolescents' academic achievement: An 11-year follow-up. *American Journal of Orthopsychiatry, 63,* 306–312.

Williams, N., & Torrez, D. J. (1998). Grandparenthood among Hispanics. In M. E. Szinovacz (Ed.), *Handbook on grandparenthood* (pp. 87–96). Westport, CT: Greenwood Press.

Williams, P. G., Wiebe, D. J., & Smith, T. W. (1992). Coping processes as mediators of the relationship between hardiness and health. *Journal of Behavioral Medicine, 20,* 138–148.

Willis, S. (1996). Everyday problem solving. In J. E. Birren & K. W. Schaie (Eds.), *Handbook of the psychology of aging* (4th ed., pp. 287–307). San Diego: Academic Press.

Willis, S. L., & Schaie, K. W. (1994). Cognitive training in the normal elderly. In F. Forette, Y. Christen, & F. Boller (Eds.), *Plasticité cérébrale et stimulation cognitive* [Cerebral plasticity and cognitive stimulation] (pp. 91–113). Paris: Fondation Nationale de Gérontologie.

Willis, S. L., & Schaie, K. W. (1999). Intellectual functioning in midlife. In S. L. Willis & J. D. Reid (Eds.), *Life in the middle* (pp. 105–146). San Diego: Academic Press.

Wills, T. A., McNamara, G., Vaccaro, D., & Hirky, A. E. (1996). Escalated substance use: A longitudinal grouping analysis from early to middle adolescence. *Journal of Abnormal Psychology, 105,* 166–180.

Wilson, M. N., Greene-Bates, C., McKim, L., Simmons, T. A., Curry-El, J., & Hinton, I. D. (1995). African American family life: The dynamics of interactions, relationships, and roles. In M. N. Wilson (Ed.), *African American family life: Its structural and ecological aspects* (pp. 5–21). San Francisco: Jossey-Bass.

Windle, M. A. (1994). A study of friendship characteristics and problem behaviors among middle adolescents. *Child Development, 65,* 1764–1777.

Wink, P., & Helson, R. (1993). Personality change in women and their partners. *Journal of Personality and Social Psychology, 65,* 597–605.

Winn, S., Roker, D., & Coleman, J. (1995). Knowledge about puberty and sexual development in 11–16 year olds: Implications for health and sex education in schools. *Educational Studies, 21,* 187–201.

Winner, E. (1986, August). Where pelicans kiss seals. *Psychology Today, 20*(8), 25–35.

Winner, E. (1988). *The point of words: Children's understanding of metaphor and irony.* Cambridge, MA: Harvard University Press.

Winner, E. (1996). *Gifted children: Myths and realities.* New York: Basic Books.

Wintre, M. G., & Vallance, D. D. (1994). A developmental sequence in the comprehension of emotions: Intensity, multiple emotions, and valence. *Developmental Psychology, 30,* 509–514.

Wolfe, J. J. (1997). Hospice support for families facing multiple deaths of children. *American Journal of Hospital Palliative Care, 14,* 224–227.

Wolfelt, A. D. (1997). Death and grief in the school setting. In T. N. Fairchild (Ed.), *Crisis intervention strategies for school-based helpers* (pp. 199–244). Springfield, IL: Charles C Thomas.

Wolff, P. H. (1966). The causes, controls and organization of behavior in the neonate. *Psychological Issues, 5*(1, Serial No. 17).

Wolfson, A. R., & Carskadon, M. A. (1998). Sleep schedules and daytime functioning in adolescents. *Child Development, 69,* 875–887.

Wolpe, J., & Plaud, J. J. (1997). Pavlov's contributions to behavior therapy: The obvious and not so obvious. *American Psychologist, 52,* 966–972.

Women's Health Initiative Group. (1998). Design of the Women's Health Initiative Clinical Trial and Observational Study. *Controlled Clinical Trials, 19,* 61–109.

Wong, R., Kitayama, K. E., & Soldo, B. J. (1999). Ethnic differences in time transfers from adult children to elderly parents: Unobserved heterogeneity across families? *Research on Aging, 21,* 144–175.

Wood, D. J. (1989). Social interaction as tutoring. In M. H. Bornstein & J. S. Bruner (Eds.), *Interaction in human development* (pp. 59–80). Hillsdale, NJ: Erlbaum.

Woodman, S. (1998). *Last rights: The struggle over the right to die.* New York: Plenum.

Woodworth, R. S. (1996). You're not alone.... You're one in a million. *Child Welfare, 65,* 619–635.

Woolley, J. D. (1997). Thinking about fantasy: Are children fundamentally different thinkers and believers from adults? *Child Development, 68,* 991–1011.

Woolley, J. D., Phelps, K. E., Davis, D. L., & Mandell, D. J. (1999). Where theories of mind meet magic: The development of children's beliefs about wishing. *Child Development, 70,* 571–587.

Word, S. (1996). Mortality awareness and risk-taking in late adolescence. *Death Studies, 20,* 133–148.

World Health Organization. (1999). *World health statistics annual 1998.* Geneva: Author.

Worobey, J. L., & Angel, R. J. (1990). Functional capacity and living arrangements of unmarried elderly persons. *Journal of Gerontology, 45,* S95–S101.

Wright, J. C., Huston, A. C., Reitz, A. L., & Piemyat, S. (1994). Young children's perceptions of television reality: Determinants and developmental differences. *Developmental Psychology, 30,* 229–239.

Wright, J. W. (Ed.). (1999). *The universal almanac 1999.* Kansas City: Andrews and McMeel.

Wright, T. A., & Bonett, D. G. (1997). The contribution of burnout to work performance. *Journal of Organizational Behavior, 18,* 491–499.

Wrightsman, L. S. (1994). *Adult personality development: Vol. 1. Theories and concepts.* Thousand Oaks, CA: Sage.

Wu, Z., & Penning, M. J. (1997). Marital instability after midlife. *Journal of Family Issues, 18,* 459–478.

Wu, Z., & Pollard, M. S. (1998). Social support among unmarried childless elderly persons. *Journal of Gerontology, 53B,* S324–S335.

Wurtele, S. K. (1996). Health promotion. In M. C. Roberts (Ed.), *Handbook of pediatric psychology* (2nd ed., pp. 200–216). New York: Guilford.

Wyman, P. A., Cowen, E. L., Work, W. C., Hoyt-Meyers, L., Magnus, K. B., & Fagen, D. B. (1999). Caregiving and developmental factors differentiating young at-risk urban children showing resilient versus stress-affected outcomes: A replication and extension. *Child Development, 70,* 645–659.

Yaffe, K., Sawaya, G., Lieberburg, I., & Grady, D. (1998). Estrogen therapy in postmenopausal women. *Journal of the American Medical Association, 279,* 688–695.

Yale, M. E., Messinger, D. S., Cobo-Lewis, A. B., Oller, D. K., & Eilers, R. E. (1999). An event-based analysis of the coordination of early infant vocalizations and facial actions. *Developmental Psychology, 35,* 505–513.

Yarrow, M. R., Scott, P. M., & Waxler, C. Z. (1973). Learning concern for others. *Developmental Psychology, 8,* 240–260.

Yazigi, R. A., Odem, R. R., & Polakoski, K. L. (1991). Demonstration of specific binding of cocaine to human spermatozoa. *Journal of the American Medical Association, 266,* 1956–1959.

Yeung, W. (1996). Buddhism, death, and dying. In J. K. Parry & A. S. Ryan (Eds.), *A cross-cultural look at death, dying, and religion* (pp. 74–83). Chicago: Nelson-Hall.

Yip, R., Scanlon, K., & Trowbridge, F. (1993). Trends and patterns in height and weight status of low-income U.S. children. *Critical Reviews in Food Science and Nutrition, 33,* 409–421.

Yirmiya, N., & Shulman, C. (1996). Seriation, conservation, and theory of mind abilities in individuals with autism, individuals with mental retardation, and normally developing children. *Child Development, 67,* 2045–2059.

Yirmiya, N., Solomonica-Levi, D., & Shulman, C. (1996). The ability to manipulate behavior and to understand manipulation of beliefs: A comparion of individuals with autism, mental retardation, and normal development. *Developmental Psychology, 32,* 62–69.

Yogman, M. W. (1981). Development of the father–infant relationship. In H. Fitzgerald, B. Lester, & M. W. Yogman (Eds.), *Theory and research in behavioral pediatrics* (Vol. 1, pp. 221–279). New York: Plenum.

Yonas, A., Granrud, E. C., Arterberry, M. E., & Hanson, B. L. (1986). Infants' distance perception from linear perspective and texture gradients. *Infant Behavior and Development, 9,* 247–256.

Yonas, A., & Hartman, B. (1993). Perceiving the affordance of contact in four- and five-month-old infants. *Child Development, 64,* 298–308.

Yoo, S. H., & Sung, K.-T. (1997). Elderly Koreans' tendency to live independently from their adult children: Adaptation to cultural differences in America. *Journal of Cross-Cultural Gerontology, 12,* 225–244.

Young, H. M. (1998). Moving to congregate housing: The last chosen home. *Journal of Aging Studies, 12,* 149–165.

Young, J. B., & Rodgers, R. F. (1997). A model of radical career change in the context of psychosocial development. *Journal of Career Assessment, 5,* 167–172.

Young, P. (1991). Families with adolescents. In F. H. Brown (Ed.), *Reweaving the family tapestry* (pp. 131–168). New York: Norton.

Youniss, J. (1980). *Parents and peers in social development: A Piagetian-Sullivan perspective.* Chicago: University of Chicago Press.

Yuill, N., & Perner, J. (1988). Intentionality and knowledge in children's judgments of actor's responsibility and recipient's emotional reaction. *Developmental Psychology, 24,* 358–365.

Zabin, L. S., & Hayward, S. C. (1993). *Adolescent sexual behavior and childbearing.* Newbury Park, CA: Sage.

Zahn-Waxler, C., Kochanska, G., Krupnick, J., & McKnew, D. (1990). Patterns of guilt in children of depressed and well mothers. *Developmental Psychology, 26,* 51–59.

Zahn-Waxler, C., Radke-Yarrow, M., & King, R. M. (1979). Child-rearing and children's prosocial initiations toward victims of distress. *Child Development, 50,* 319–330.

Zahn-Waxler, C., Radke-Yarrow, M., Wagner, E., & Chapman, M. (1992). Development of concern for others. *Developmental Psychology, 28,* 126–136.

Zahn-Waxler, C., & Robinson, J. (1995). Empathy and guilt: Early origins of feelings of responsibility. In J. P. Tangney & K. W. Fischer (Eds.), *Self-conscious emotions* (pp. 143–173). New York: Guilford.

Zajonc, R. B., & Mullally, P. R. (1997). Birth order: Reconciling conflicting effects. *American Psychologist, 52,* 685–699.

Zani, B. (1993). Dating and interpersonal relationships in adolescence. In S. Jackson & H. Rodriguez-Tomé (Eds.), *Adolescence and its social worlds* (pp. 95–119). Hillsdale, NJ: Erlbaum.

Zedeck, S., Maslach, C., Mosier, K., & Skitka, L. (1988). Affective response to work and quality of family life: Employee and spouse perspectives. *Journal of Social Behavior and Personality, 3,* 135–157.

Zelazo, N. A., Zelazo, P. R., Cohen, K. M., & Zelazo, P. D. (1993). Specificity of practice effects on elementary neuromotor patterns. *Developmental Psychology, 29,* 686–691.

Zelazo, P. R. (1983). The development of walking: New findings on old assumptions. *Journal of Motor Behavior, 2,* 99–137.

Zenger, T., & Lawrence, B. (1989). Organizational demography: The differential effects of age and tenure distributions on technical communication. *Academy of Management Journal, 32,* 353–376.

Zevitz, R. G., & Gurnack, A. M. (1991). Factors related to elderly crime victims' satisfaction with police service: The impact of Milwaukee's Gray Squad. *Gerontologist, 31,* 92–101.

Zhou, M., & Bankston, C. L. (1998). *Growing up American: How Vietnamese children adapt to life in the United States.* New York: Russell Sage Foundation.

Ziegler, C. B., Dusek, J. B., & Carter, D. B. (1984). Self-concept and sex-role orientation: An investigation of multidimensional aspects of personality development in adolescence. *Journal of Early Adolescence, 4,* 25–39.

Zigler, E., & Hall, N. W. (1989). Physical child abuse in America: Past, present, and future. In D. Cicchetti & V. Carlson (Eds.), *Child maltreatment* (pp. 203–253). New York: Cambridge University Press.

Zigler, E., & Styfco, S. J. (1994a). Head Start: Criticisms in a constructive context.

American Psychologist, 49, 127–132.

Zigler, E., & Styfco, S. J. (1994b). Is the Perry Preschool better than Head Start? Yes and no. *Early Childhood Research Quarterly, 9,* 269–287.

Zigler, E. F., & Finn-Stevenson, M. (1999). Applied developmental psychology. In M. H. Bornstein & M. E. Lamb (Eds.), *Developmental psychology: An advanced textbook* (4th ed., pp. 555–598). Mahwah, NJ: Erlbaum.

Zill, N., Davies, E., & Daly, M. (1994). *Viewing of Sesame Street by preschool children in the United States and its relationship to school readiness.* Rockville, MD: Westat.

Zillman, D., Bryant, J., & Huston, A. C. (1994). *Media, family, and children.* Hillsdale, NJ: Erlbaum.

Zimmerman, B. J., & Risemberg, R. (1997). Self-regulatory dimensions of academic learning and motivation. In G. D. Phye (Ed.), *Handbook of academic learning: Construction of knowledge* (pp. 105–125). San Diego: Academic Press.

Zimmerman, M. A., & Arunkumar, R. (1994). Resiliency research: Implications for schools and policy. *Social Policy Report of the Society for Research in Child Development, 8*(4).

Zimmerman, M. A., Copeland, L. A., Shope, J. T., & Dielman, T. E. (1997). A longitudinal study of self-esteem: Implications for adolescent development. *Journal of Youth and Adolescence, 26,* 117–141.

Zins, J. E., Garcia, V. F., Tuchfarber, B. S., Clark, K. M., & Laurence, S. C. (1994). Preventing injury in children and adolescents. In R. J. Simeonsson (Ed.), *Risk, resilience, and prevention: Promoting the well-being of all children* (pp. 183–202). Baltimore: Paul H. Brookes.

Zlotnick, C., Kohn, R., Peterson, J., & Pearlstein, T. (1998). Partner physical victimization in a national sample of American families: Relationship to psychological functioning, psychosocial factors, and gender. *Journal of Interpersonal Violence, 13,* 156–166.

Zorilla, E. P., DeRubeis, R. J., & Redei, E. (1995). High self-esteem, hardiness and affective stability are associated with higher basal pituitary–adrenal hormone levels. *Psychoneuroendocrinology, 20,* 591–601.

pattern perception, 140-141, 142
presbyopia, 493
sensitive periods in development of, 124
strabismus, 124
subjective boundaries in visual patterns, 141
Visitation rights of grandparents, 538
Visual acuity, 111
infancy and toddlerhood, 137
late adulthood, 560
newborns, 111
strabismus and, 124
Visual cliff, 137, 182
Visual cortex, 121
Visual impairments, 559-561
development of infants with severe, 138-139
Vital capacity
endurance training and, 568
in late adulthood, 563, 568
maximum, 427, 428
Vitamins and minerals. *See also* Nutrition
diet deficient in, 214-215
folic acid, prenatal supplementation of, 93
free-radical damage prevention and, **424**
late adulthood, supplements in, 568
osteoporosis and, 500, 501
premenstrual syndrome and, 439
vision in late adulthood and, 560
Vitreous
changes with aging in, 493-494, 560
REM sleep and circulation of, 108
Vocabulary. *See also* Language development
categorization and, 226
development of, 166, 170
early childhood, 239-240
first words, 169-170
middle childhood, 304-305
parental speech and, 170
understanding emotion and, 251
Vocational choice, 512
decision to have children and, 472
early adulthood, 445-449
factors influencing, 445-448
information resources on, 453

preparation of non-college-bound young adults, 448
selection of vocation, 445
women, 446-447
Vocational development. *See also* Employment; Maternal employment; Unemployment
career change in middle adulthood, 527-528, 546-547
cognitive development and, 512-514
combining work and family, 482-484
early adulthood, 480-484
establishing vocation, 481
mentors and, 458
middle adulthood, 512-514, 527-528, 543-548
returning students in middle adulthood and, 515
women and ethnic minorities, 481-483
Vocational training, 382, 383, 448
Voice change in adolescence, 354
Voluntary active euthanasia, 642-643, 644, 645
Voluntary reaching, 135-136
Volunteerism
generativity through, 523
information resources on, 623
intergenerational relationships and, 543
late adulthood, 619

W

Walking. *See* Motor development
War, children of, 340
War on Poverty, 236
Water, fluoridated, 209
"Wear-and-tear" theory of biological aging, 424
Wechsler Intelligence Scale for Children (WISC-III), 299
Weight. *See also* Birth weight; Obesity; Overweight
adolescence, 352
aging and, 426
anorexia nervosa and, 359
deprivation dwarfism, 214
early childhood, 208, 209
infancy and toddlerhood, 118
late adulthood, 564-565
middle adulthood, 493, 494
middle childhood, 280, 281

Weight-bearing exercise, 501, 568
Weight-loss programs, 430-431
arthritis and, 570
middle childhood, 284-285
Well-being. *See* Emotional well-being; Psychological well-being
Western Europe. *See also specific countries*
cohabitation, attitude toward, 476
independent living in late adulthood, 607
national examinations, 381
social security systems, 70
Western nations, experience of love in, 463
West Indians of Jamaica motor development among, 134, 135
White blood cells, 428
Whole-language approach, 297-298
WHO (World Health Organization), 145
Widowed Persons Service c/o American Association of Retired Persons, 623
Widowhood
adaptation to, 610-611, 647-648
information resources on, 623
in late adulthood, 610-611, 623
remarriage after, 610
Wisdom, 10, 583-584
Withdrawal of privileges, 258
Withdrawal reflex, 106
Wives. *See* Marital *entries*; Marriage
Women. *See also* African-American women; Maternal employment; Sex differences
age 30 transition in, 458
battered, 471
caring for aging parents, 540
creativity and, 442
divorce's impact on, 478, 535
in dual-earner marriages, 482-484
earnings gap and, 481
feminization of poverty and, 535, 607
glass ceiling faced by, 545-546
heart problems in, 500
identity after divorce, 478
illiterate, in developing countries, 527
instability during thirties of, 459

in labor force, rise in independence in, 532
living alone in old age, 607
menstrual cycle. *See* Menstrual cycle
as mentors, 481-482
negative life changes for older, 607
never-married elderly, 612
never-married mothers, 479-480
post-menopausal, in vitro fertilization of, 56-57
poverty and, 64
reproductive changes in middle adulthood, 495
research on health of, 496
as returning students in middle adulthood, 514-515
sexual coercion of, 437-438
vocational choices, nontraditional, 446-447
vocational development, 446-447, 481-483
voluntarily childless, 477
widowhood and, 610
Women's Health Initiative, 496
Women's movement, political involvement in middle adulthood and, 524
Words, first, 169-170. *See also* Language development; Speech
Work. *See* Employment; Job *entries*; Vocational *entries*
Work environment, decision to retire and, 617
Work-family role conflict, 447, 483, 484
strategies to reduce, 484
Work groups, age-balanced, 545
Working mothers. *See* Maternal employment
Working (short-term) memory, 156-157
age-related declines in, 510
late adulthood, 580, 582
middle-aged professors, 513
middle childhood, 293, 296
Work overload, dual-earner marriage and, 483
Work-role preoccupation, ego differentiation versus, 593
Work-study programs, 382
apprenticeships in Germany, 448, 449
World Health Organization (WHO), 145

World Hypertension League, 453
World views, generation gap and, 375-376
World War II
impact on life course, 37
refugee and evacuee children in, 596-597
Writing
cursive, 288
early childhood, 219, 220, 232-234
early printing, 220
fine motor coordination and, 287

X

X chromosome, 46, 48
fragile X syndrome, 53
missing or extra, abnormalities of, 54
sexual orientation linkage to, 363
X-linked diseases, 51
X-linked inheritance, 51-52
XO syndrome, 54
XX chromosome, 48
XXX syndrome, 54
XXY syndrome, 54
XYY syndrome, 54

Y

Y chromosome, 46, 48
Y-Me National Organization for Breast Cancer Information and Support, 519
Yolk sac, 82, 84
Young adults. *See* Early adulthood
Young-old elderly, 556
Youth. *See* Adolescence
Yurok Indians, child-rearing practices of, 17

Z

Zero to Three, 145
Zidovudine (ZDV), 93
Zinacanteco Indians
motor development in, 134
social transmission of knowledge in, 25
Zone of proximal development, 160, 173
in early childhood, 228-229
teaching adapted to each child's, 307
Zuni Indians, self-conscious emotions among, 184
Zygote, 47
Zygote, period of, 81, 82, 87
teratogen impact on, 87